DIO CHRYSOSTOM

V

385

DIO CHRYSOSTOM

WITH AN ENGLISH TRANSLATION BY

H. LAMAR CROSBY

PROFESSOR OF GREEK, UNIVERSITY OF PENNSYLVANIA

IN FIVE VOLUMES

V

CAMBRIDGE, MASSACHUSETTS
HARVARD UNIVERSITY PRESS

LONDON
WILLIAM HEINEMANN LTD
MCMLXXXV

American ISBN 0-674-99424-8
British ISBN 0 434 99385 9

First printed 1951
Reprinted 1964, 1985

Printed in Great Britain

CONTENTS

	PAGE
THE SIXTY-FIRST DISCOURSE : CHRYSEÏS . .	1
THE SIXTY-SECOND DISCOURSE : ON KINGSHIP AND TYRANNY	23
THE SIXTY-THIRD DISCOURSE : ON FORTUNE (I) .	33
THE SIXTY-FOURTH DISCOURSE : ON FORTUNE (II)	34
THE SIXTY-FIFTH DISCOURSE : ON FORTUNE (III)	73
THE SIXTY-SIXTH DISCOURSE : ON REPUTATION .	86
THE SIXTY-SEVENTH DISCOURSE : ON POPULAR OPINION	117
THE SIXTY-EIGHTH DISCOURSE : ON OPINION .	127
THE SIXTY-NINTH DISCOURSE : ON VIRTUE . .	137
THE SEVENTIETH DISCOURSE : ON PHILOSOPHY .	149
THE SEVENTY-FIRST DISCOURSE : ON THE PHILOSOPHER	161
THE SEVENTY-SECOND DISCOURSE : ON PERSONAL APPEARANCE	174
THE SEVENTY-THIRD DISCOURSE : ON TRUST .	193
THE SEVENTY-FOURTH DISCOURSE : ON DISTRUST	207
THE SEVENTY-FIFTH DISCOURSE : ON LAW . .	239

DIO CHRYSOSTOM

	PAGE
THE SEVENTY-SIXTH DISCOURSE : ON CUSTOM	251
THE SEVENTY-SEVENTH/EIGHTH DISCOURSE : ON ENVY	258
THE SEVENTY-NINTH DISCOURSE : ON WEALTH	303
THE EIGHTIETH DISCOURSE : ON FREEDOM	313
ENCOMIUM ON HAIR	331
FRAGMENTS	345
LETTERS	353
TESTIMONY REGARDING DIO'S LIFE AND WRITINGS	361
INDEX	425

DIO CHRYSOSTOM

THE SIXTY-FIRST DISCOURSE: CHRYSEÏS

In this little dialogue it would seem that Dio had chosen for discussion the most unpromising of topics. Little as is known about Briseïs, Homer at least tells us that when Agamemnon's messengers came to fetch her she followed them unwillingly, but Chryseïs, the involuntary cause of the quarrel out of which grew the *Iliad*, is restored to the arms of her father without giving the slightest clue to her emotions or desires. Apart from the epithet " fair-cheeked " which she shares with Briseïs, our only testimony regarding her personality is the tribute paid her by Agamemnon when he compares her with Clytemnestra to the disadvantage of the latter, a tribute, it may be, inspired as much by arrogant pride as by passion.

So far as is known, none of the Greek playwrights found in her story material suitable for dramatic treatment; yet Dio here undertakes the task of endowing this lay figure with life. His partner in the discussion is not a colourless individual, as is often the case, merely providing the cues for further argumentation and meekly assenting to the conclusions reached, but a woman with a mind of her own, repeatedly raising logical objections and asking pertinent questions. Her final utterance shows that, despite the dexterity of Dio, she has some lingering doubts about the true character of Chryseïs. It is of course peculiarly fitting that in treating such a topic as Chryseïs the interlocutor should be a woman, but that Dio should have cast a woman for such a rôle is of itself noteworthy, and there is such an atmosphere of verisimilitude surrounding the dialogue as to suggest that it may actually have taken place.

ΔΙΩΝ ΧΡΥΣΟΣΤΟΜΟΣ

61. ΧΡΥΣΗΙΣ

1 Δ. Ἐπεὶ τυγχάνεις οὐ φαύλως ἐπαινοῦσα Ὅμηρον
οὐδέ, ὥσπερ οἱ πολλοί, πιστεύουσα τῇ δόξῃ προσ-
ποιῇ θαυμάζειν, ὃ δὲ δεινότατός ἐστιν ᾔσθησαι
τοῦ ποιητοῦ, τὴν περὶ τὰ πάθη τῶν ἀνθρώπων
ἐμπειρίαν, τἄλλα μὲν ἐάσωμεν, εἰ ἐθέλεις, τὰ νῦν,
τὰ τῶν βασιλέων καὶ στρατηγῶν, περὶ δὲ μιᾶς
γυναικὸς σκεψώμεθα τῶν αἰχμαλώτων, ὁποίαν τινὰ
πεποίηκε τὴν θυγατέρα τοῦ ἱερέως, ἧς εὐθὺς ἐμνή-
σθη κατ᾽ ἀρχὰς τῆς ποιήσεως. ὁ μὲν γὰρ Ἀγαμέμνων οὐ μόνον τὸ εἶδος, ἀλλὰ καὶ τὸν τρόπον
ἐπαινεῖν ἔοικε τῆς παιδίσκης, λέγει γὰρ ὡς οὐδὲν
εἴη τὰς φρένας χείρων τῆς αὑτοῦ γυναικός· δῆλον
δὲ ὡς ἐκείνην οἰόμενος νοῦν ἔχειν.

2 Τί δέ;[1] οὐκ ἄλλως τοῦτο εἴρηκε διὰ τὸν ἔρωτα
ἀπατώμενος;

Δ. Ἰδεῖν ἄξιον· καίτοι χαλεπώτατον πείθειν τοὺς
ἐρῶντας. καὶ γὰρ ὑπονοοῦσιν οἱ πολλοὶ καὶ ὀργίζονται ῥᾳδίως, καὶ οὐδέποτέ φασιν ἀγαπᾶσθαι κατ᾽

---

[1] Τί δέ; Wilamowitz : εἰ δέ.

---

[1] Cf. *Iliad* 1. 113-115, spoken in praise of Chryseïs.

DIO CHRYSOSTOM

THE SIXTY-FIRST DISCOURSE:
CHRYSEÏS

Dio. Since, as it happens, you praise Homer in no ordinary manner and you do not, like most persons, merely pretend to admire him, trusting to his reputation, but instead have discerned that quality in the poet in which he is most effective, his acquaintance with the passions of mankind, let us, if you please, pass by all else for the moment, the fortunes of kings and generals, and turn our attention to just one woman among the captives, aiming to discover how the poet has depicted the daughter of the priest whom he has mentioned at the very beginning of his poem. For Agamemnon seems to praise not only the beauty but also the character of the young woman, for he says that she is in no wise inferior in mind to his own wife [1]—clearly believing that Clytemnestra has intelligence.

Interlocutor. What of it ? Has he not said this thoughtlessly, beguiled by his infatuation ?

Dio. That is worth looking into ; and yet it is very difficult to convince men who are in love, for most of them are suspicious and easily angered, and they never admit that they are loved as they deserve by

ἀξίαν ὑπὸ τῶν ἐρωμένων, ἄλλως τε ὅταν ὦσι κρείττους τοσοῦτον καὶ συνόντες μετ' ἐξουσίας.

Ταῦτα δέ φημι συμβαίνειν τοῖς φαύλοις ἐρασταῖς.

Δ. Εἴτε οὖν σπουδαῖος ἦν ὁ Ἀγαμέμνων, ὀρθῶς ἐγίγνωσκε περὶ αὐτῆς, εἴτε τοῖς πολλοῖς ὅμοιος, οὐ ῥᾴδιον φαύλην οὖσαν ἀρέσαι τὸν τοιοῦτον, ὥστε ἀγαθὴν ὑπολαβεῖν. φέρε δὴ καὶ τἆλλα ἴδωμεν.

3 Καὶ τίνα ἄλλην ἀπόδειξιν ἔχεις παρά γε Ὁμήρῳ τοῦ τρόπου τῆς γυναικός; οὐδὲν γοῦν πεποίηκεν αὐτὴν πράττουσαν ἢ λέγουσαν, ἀλλὰ σιγῇ τῷ πατρὶ διδομένην.

Δ. Τί γάρ; ἐκ τῶν γενομένων περὶ αὐτὴν οὐκ ἄν τις συμβάλοι τὴν διάνοιαν μὴ πάνυ ἁπλῶς μηδὲ εὐήθως σκοπῶν;

Ἴσως.

Δ. Πότερον οὖν[1] οἰώμεθα[2] τὸν Χρύσην ἀκούσης τῆς θυγατρὸς εἰς τὸ στρατόπεδον ἐλθεῖν μετὰ λύτρων ἅμα τὰ στέμματα κομίζοντα τοῦ θεοῦ καὶ τὸ πλῆθος ἱκετεύειν καὶ τοὺς βασιλέας ἀφιέναι αὐτήν, ἢ τοὐναντίον ἐκείνης δεομένης τοῦ πατρός,
4 εἴ τι δύναιτο, βοηθεῖν; εἰ γὰρ ἔστεργε τοῖς παροῦσιν ἡ Χρυσηὶς καὶ τῷ Ἀγαμέμνονι συνεῖναι ἠβούλετο, οὐδέποτ' ἂν εἵλετο Χρύσης ἅμα τὴν θυγατέρα λυπῶν τῷ βασιλεῖ ἀπεχθάνεσθαι, οὐκ ἀγνοῶν ὅπως εἶχε πρὸς αὐτήν. τὸ γὰρ συνεῖναι τῷ βασιλεῖ τὴν Χρυσηίδα στεργομένην οὐχ ἧττον τῷ Χρύσῃ συνέφερεν. καὶ γὰρ ἡ χώρα καὶ τὸ ἱερὸν καὶ αὐτὸς

---

[1] Πότερον οὖν Selden : ποτὲ.
[2] οἰώμεθα Reiske : οἰόμεθα.

---

[1] Cf. *Iliad* 1. 12-16.

their beloved, especially when they are so superior in station to the objects of their passion and associate with them by virtue of authority.

Int. That kind of thing, in my opinion, happens with lovers of the low sort.

Dio. Well then, if Agamemnon was of the superior kind, he was right in his appraisal of the girl; but if he was no better than most men, it is not easy for a woman of low degree to please a man like him to the point of taking her to be noble. Well now, let us examine also the other points.

Int. Why, what additional proof have you in Homer of the character of the woman? At any rate he has not depicted her as doing or saying anything, but rather as being silently handed over to her father.

Dio. What! Could one not deduce her faculties of mind from what took place in connexion with her, provided one were to consider the matter in a manner not wholly superficial and foolish?

Int. Perhaps.

Dio. Are we, then, to suppose that against the wishes of his daughter Chryses came into the camp, bearing the fillets of the god along with the ransom, and besought the assembly and the kings to release her,[1] or, on the contrary, was it because she kept begging her father to aid her if he could? For if Chryseïs was content with her situation and wished to live with Agamemnon, Chryses would never have chosen at one and the same time to grieve his daughter and to incur the malice of the king, not being unaware of the king's feelings toward her. For it was no less to the interest of Chryses that Chryseïs should live with the king, so long as he was fond of her, since the priest's country, his sanctuary, and he himself had

ὑπὸ τοῖς Ἀχαιοῖς ἐγεγόνει, κἀκεῖνος ἦν αὐτῶν
5 κύριος. ἔτι δὲ πῶς παραχρῆμα μὲν ἁλούσης οὔτε
ἦλθεν οὔτε ἐμέμνητο περὶ λύτρων, ὅτε εἰκὸς ἦν
χαλεπώτερον φέρειν, χρόνῳ δὲ ὕστερον τῆς μὲν
λύπης ἐλάττονος γεγενημένης, συνηθείας δὲ πρὸς
τὸν Ἀγαμέμνονα πλείονος; δεκάτῳ γὰρ ἔτει τῆς
πολιορκίας ταῦτα συμβῆναί φησιν ὁ ποιητής, τὰ
περὶ τὴν ἄφιξιν τοῦ ἱερέως καὶ τὴν κομιδὴν τῶν
λύτρων. τὰς δὲ περιοίκους πόλεις καὶ τὰς ἐλάτ-
τονας εἰκὸς ἦν εὐθὺς ἁλῶναι κατ' ἀρχὰς τοῦ πολέμου, ὧν ὑπῆρχεν ἡ Χρῦσα καὶ τὸ ἱερόν.

Οὐκοῦν ὁ λόγος οὗτος πολλὴν ἀτοπίαν ἐπιδείκνυσι τῆς Χρυσηίδος, τὸ πρότερον μὲν αἰχμάλωτον
οὖσαν ἀνέχεσθαι, προσφάτως στερομένην τοῦ πατρὸς καὶ τῆς πατρίδος, διελθόντων δὲ δέκα[1] ἐτῶν
χαλεπῶς φέρειν.

6 Δ. Εἴ γε καὶ τὰ ἄλλα ἀκούσειας· οὐδὲ γὰρ τὸν
τυχόντα ἐραστὴν ἅπαξ γενόμενον ἡδὺ ἀπολιπεῖν
ταῖς ἐλευθέραις, μή τί γε τὸν ἐνδοξότατον καὶ
πλουσιώτατον, βασιλέα μὲν τῶν Ἑλλήνων ξυμπάν-
των, μεγίστην δὲ ἔχοντα δύναμιν ἐν τοῖς τότε
ἀνθρώποις, κύριον δὲ οὐ μόνον ἐκείνης, ἀλλὰ καὶ
τοῦ πατρὸς καὶ τῆς πατρίδος, ἐλπίζοντα δὲ κρατή-
σειν ὀλίγου χρόνου καὶ τῆς Ἀσίας· τὸ γὰρ Ἴλιον
φαύλως εἶχεν ἐκ πολλοῦ, καὶ μόλις διεφύλαττον
αὐτὴν τὴν πόλιν, ἐπεξῄει δὲ οὐδεὶς εἰς μάχην· καὶ
ταῦτα οὐ παρέργως ἔχοντος πρὸς[2] αὐτὴν τοῦ βασι-

---

[1] δέκα added by Reiske.
[2] πρός added by Reiske.

---

[1] Strabo places Chrysa at the head of the Adramyttic
Gulf, close to Cilla with which it is associated in *Iliad* 1. 37-38.
[2] Dio accepts the term " singular " as a compliment to

come under the sway of the Achaeans, and Agamemnon was their sovereign. And, besides, how is it that immediately after her capture, at a time when she might be expected to be in greater distress, Chryses neither came nor made any mention of ransom, but rather some time later, at a time when her grief had diminished and her intimacy with Agamemnon had increased? For the poet says these things took place in the tenth year of the siege —I mean the coming of the priest and the bringing of the ransom—while it is reasonable to suppose that the cities in the neighbourhood of Troy, and especially the smaller ones, would have been taken in the very beginning of the war, and it is to this group that Chrysa and its sanctuary belonged.[1]

Int. Then this reasoning of yours attributes to Chryseïs very singular conduct, in that formerly she endured her lot as a captive, though newly robbed of her father and her country, but after ten years had passed she took it hard.

Dio. Yes, at least if you listen to what else I have to say[2]; for it is not pleasant for free women to abandon even an ordinary man, once he has become their lover, to say nothing of the most illustrious and wealthy man, king of all the Greeks, a man who held the greatest power of all among the men of that day, who had authority over not merely Chryseïs but her father and her country too, and who expected in a short time to become lord of Asia as well—for Ilium had long been in a bad way and its people were having difficulty in defending the city itself and no one went out for battle. And observe also that the

Chryseïs, but the interlocutor does not catch his meaning at once.

λέως, ἀλλὰ καὶ φανερῶς ὁμολογοῦντος προτιμᾶν
τῆς αὐτοῦ γυναικός. τοσαῦτα ἀποπτύουσαν καὶ
τηλικαῦτα ἀγαθά, καὶ τὸ μέγιστον ἐραστὴν οὐ
μόνον βασιλέα μέγαν καὶ ἀνδρεῖον ἐν ὀλίγοις, ἀλλὰ
καὶ νέον καὶ καλόν, ὥς φησιν Ὅμηρος τῷ Διὶ
προσεικάζων αὐτόν, ἔπειτα εἰς ἑαλωκυῖαν ἀφικέ-
σθαι τὴν πατρίδα καὶ συνοικεῖν ἑνὶ τῶν δούλων
τῶν Ἀγαμέμνονος, εἴ γε ἔμελλε γαμεῖσθαι τῶν
7 ἐγχωρίων τινί, πῶς οὐκ ἄτοπον; τὸ γὰρ αἰχμάλωτον εἶναι καὶ διὰ τοῦτο μὴ στέργειν τὸν λαβόντα
οὐχ ἱκανόν. ἡ γοῦν Βρισηὶς ἀγαπᾶν ἔοικε τὸν
Ἀχιλλέα, καὶ ταῦτα ὅν φησιν ἀποκτεῖναι τὸν ἄνδρα
αὐτῆς καὶ τοὺς ἀδελφούς. τῷ δὲ Ἀγαμέμνονι
τοιοῦτον οὐδὲν ἐπέπρακτο περὶ τὴν Χρυσηίδα.

Καλῶς. οὐκοῦν ἐκ τῶν λόγων τούτων οὐκ ἐβου-
λήθη Χρυσηὶς ἀποπεμφθῆναι παρὰ τοῦ Ἀγαμέμνονος, ἀλλὰ Χρύσης ταῦτα ἔπραττε καθ' αὑτόν· ἢ
εἴπερ ἐβούλετο, ἀφρονεστέρα ἂν εἴη, καὶ τὸν λόγον
ἐναντίον εἶπας ἢ ὑπέσχου.

8   Δ. Ἀλλ' οὖν μηδὲ δίκην δικάσῃς, φασί, πρὶν
ἀμφοτέρων ἀκοῦσαι. λέγεις δὴ σοφὸν ὄντα τὸν
Ὅμηρον;

Ἴσως.

Δ. Οὐκοῦν τὰ μὲν αὐτὸν λέγειν οἷον, τὰ δὲ τοῖς
ἐντυγχάνουσι καταλιπεῖν αἰσθάνεσθαι. τοῦτο δὲ οὐ
τῶν¹ πάνυ ἀδήλων ἐστίν. ἡ γὰρ Χρυσηὶς κατ'

---

¹ τῶν Pflugk : λόγων.

---

¹ *Iliad* 1. 113-115.   ² *Ibid.* 2. 477-478.
³ *Ibid.* 19. 282-300.
⁴ He only promised to deduce her character from Homer's
words. The speaker may be thinking of the appraisal of
Chryseïs in § 1.

8

king had no casual regard for her, but even openly admitted that he preferred her to his own wife.[1] That she should spurn such numerous and exceptional advantages, and in particular a lover who was not only a great king and had few who vied with him in valour, but was also young and handsome, as Homer says in comparing him to Zeus,[2] and that she should then go to her native land, now a prize of war, and live as the wife of one of Agamemnon's slaves—that is, assuming that she would wed one of the men of the district—is not that singular ? For that she was a prisoner of war and for that reason did not care for the man who got her is not enough to explain her conduct. At any rate Briseïs apparently loved Achilles, and that although, as she declares, it was he who slew her husband and her brothers.[3] But as for Agamemnon, nothing like that had been done regarding Chryseïs.

Int. Very good. Then from this line of reasoning it follows that Chryseïs did not wish to be parted from Agamemnon, but that Chryses was conducting these negotiations independently ; or else, if indeed she did wish it, she would be rather foolish and the case you have made out is contrary to what you promised.[4]

Dio. Well now, as the saying goes, do not judge a case before you hear both sides.[5] Of course you speak of Homer as being a man of wisdom ?

Int. Possibly.

Dio. Then you should assume that he tells some things but leaves others to the perception of his readers. But this is not one of the very obscure instances. For Chryseïs at the outset apparently

---

[5] A familiar maxim supposed to obtain in Athenian law-courts.

ἀρχὰς μέν, ὡς ἔοικεν, ἠγάπα μένειν παρὰ τῷ
Ἀγαμέμνονι δι' ἃς εἶπον αἰτίας καὶ τοῖς θεοῖς ᾔδει
χάριν ὅτι μηδενὶ δοθείη τῶν ἀδοξοτέρων, ἀλλὰ τῷ
πάντων βασιλεῖ, κἀκεῖνος οὐκ ἀμελῶς ἔχοι πρὸς
9 αὐτήν· ὥστε οὐκ ἔπραττε περὶ λύτρων. ἐπεὶ δὲ
ἤκουε τὰ περὶ τὴν οἰκίαν τὴν τοῦ Ἀγαμέμνονος
ὁποῖα ἦν, ὡς χαλεπά, καὶ τὴν ὠμότητα τῆς Κλυταιμνήστρας καὶ τὸ θράσος, ἐνταῦθα ἐφοβεῖτο τὴν
εἰς τὸ Ἄργος ἄφιξιν. καὶ τὸν μὲν ἄλλον χρόνον
παρέμενε στέργουσα ἴσως τὸν Ἀγαμέμνονα· ὅτε δὲ
ἦν πρὸς τέλει ὁ πόλεμος καὶ διέρρει λόγος ὡς οὐκέτι δυνήσονται πλείω χρόνον ἀντέχειν οἱ Τρῶες,
οὐ περιέμεινε τοῦ Ἰλίου τὴν ἅλωσιν. ᾔδει γὰρ ὡς
τὸ πολὺ τοὺς νικῶντας ὑπερηφάνους γιγνομένους[1]
καὶ τὴν δεισιδαιμονίαν τότε μᾶλλον ἰσχύουσαν τὴν
περὶ τῶν θεῶν,[2] ὅταν πολεμῶσιν οἱ ἄνθρωποι.

10 Διὰ ταῦτα ἐκάλει τότε τὸν πατέρα καὶ δεῖσθαι
τῶν Ἀχαιῶν ἐκέλευεν· ἐπυνθάνετο γάρ, ὡς ἔοικεν,
ὅτι ἐγυναικοκρατοῦντο οἱ Ἀτρεῖδαι καὶ μεῖζον
ἐφρόνουν τῶν ἀνδρῶν τούτων αἱ γυναῖκες, οὐκ ἐπὶ
κάλλει μόνον, ἀλλὰ καὶ τὴν ἀρχὴν αὐταῖς νομί-
ζουσαι προσήκειν μᾶλλον. τοὺς μὲν γὰρ Πελο-
πίδας τε εἶναι καὶ ἐπήλυδας τῆς Ἑλλάδος, αὐταὶ
δὲ Ἀχαιίδες, Τυνδάρεω θυγατέρες καὶ Λήδας. ὁ
δὲ Τυνδάρεως ἔνδοξος ἦν καὶ βασιλεὺς τῆς Σπάρ-
της, ὥστε καὶ τὴν Ἑλένην διὰ τοῦτο ἐμνήστευσαν

---

[1] γιγνομένους Dindorf : γενομένους.

was content to remain with Agamemnon for the reasons I have named, and she was grateful to the gods that she had not been given to any of the less illustrious persons, but rather to the king of all, and also that he was not indifferent toward her; and so she made no move regarding ransom. But when she heard what conditions were like in the house of Agamemnon, how disagreeable they were, and when she heard also about the cruelty of Clytemnestra and about her boldness, then she looked with dread to her arrival in Argos. Moreover, although she had hitherto remained with Agamemnon, possibly for love of him, still when the war was near its close and a report was current that the Trojans no longer would be able to hold out, she did not wait for the capture of Ilium. For she knew that in general men who are victorious grow arrogant, and that the time when religious scruples are more potent is when men are at war.

For these reasons at that juncture she summoned her father and bade him entreat the Achaeans; for she learned, it would appear, that the Atreidae were dominated by their wives and that the wives felt themselves superior to these men, not alone because of their beauty, but also because they believed that the right to rule belonged rather to themselves. For the Atreidae were descendants of Pelops and new-comers in Greece,[1] whereas they themselves were women of Achaia, daughters of Tyndareüs and Leda. Now Tyndareüs had been illustrious and king of Sparta, and so not only had Helen on this account been courted by the noblest among the Greeks, but

[1] Tradition made Pelops a native of Phrygia in Asia Minor.

[2] τῶν θεῶν Pflugk : τὸν θεόν.

οἱ ἄριστοι τῶν Ἑλλήνων καὶ βοηθήσειν ὤμοσαν.
11 πρὸς δὲ τούτοις ἀδελφαὶ Κάστορος καὶ Πολυδεύ-
κους ἦσαν, οἳ Διὸς παῖδες ἐνομίσθησαν καὶ θεοὶ
μέχρι νῦν πᾶσι δοκοῦσι διὰ τὴν δύναμιν ἣν τότε
ἔσχον. τῶν μὲν γὰρ ἐν Πελοποννήσῳ προεῖχον·
τῶν δὲ ἔξω Πελοποννήσου μεγίστη δύναμις ἦν ἡ
περὶ τὰς Ἀθήνας, καὶ ταύτην καθεῖλον ἐπιστρα-
τεύσαντες Θησέως βασιλεύοντος. ἔτι δὲ ἀνεψιὸς
ἐγεγόνει αὐτοῖς Μελέαγρος ὁ τῶν Ἑλλήνων
ἄριστος.

Ταῦτα μὲν οὖν οὐκ ἠπίστατο ἡ Χρυσηίς, τὸ δὲ
φρόνημα ἤκουε τῶν γυναικῶν καὶ τὴν Ἑλένην
ἐπεγίγνωσκεν ὅσον ὑπερεῖχε¹ τοῦ ἀνδρός· ὥστε
ἐπειδὴ τὰ περὶ τὴν Ἀσίαν μεγάλα ἤκουε διά τε
χώρας ἀρετὴν καὶ πλῆθος ἀνθρώπων καὶ χρημάτων, κατεφρόνησεν οὐ τοῦ Μενελάου μόνον, ἀλλὰ
τοῦ τε Ἀγαμέμνονος καὶ ξυμπάσης τῆς Ἑλλάδος,
12 καὶ ταῦτα εἵλετο ἀντ᾽ ἐκείνων. ὁ μὲν οὖν Μενέλαος
καὶ πρότερον ὑπεῖκε περὶ πάντων τῇ Ἑλένῃ καὶ
ὕστερον εἰληφὼς αἰχμάλωτον ὅμως ἐθεράπευεν· ὁ
δὲ Ἀγαμέμνων διὰ τὴν ἀρχὴν ἐπαιρόμενος τὴν
Κλυταιμνήστραν ἠτίμασεν,² ὥστε δῆλον ἦν ὅτι οὐκ
ἀνέξοιντο ἀλλήλων, ἀλλ᾽ ἔσοιτο τοιαῦτα σχεδὸν

---

¹ ὑπερεῖχε] ὑπερεῖδε Arnim.
² ἠτίμασεν] ἠτίμαζεν Arnim.

---

¹ Apollodorus, *Bibliotheca* 3. 10. 8-9, lists thirty-two
suitors, adding that, on the advice of Odysseus, Tyndareüs
exacted an oath that they stand by whoever might be chosen
to wed Helen, in case any one should wrong him in his marriage rights.
² According to tradition Leda bore Castor and Clytemnestra to Tyndareüs, Polydeuces and Helen to Zeus.
³ Helen had been carried off by Theseus and Peirithoüs.

they had sworn to render aid in case of need.[1] Besides, these women were sisters of Castor and Polydeuces, who had come to be regarded as sons of Zeus,[2] and who to this day are deemed gods by all men because of the power they acquired at that time. For not only were they pre-eminent among the dwellers in the Peloponnese, but among those outside the Peloponnese the greatest power was that of Athens, and Castor and Polydeuces had overwhelmed that city in a campaign which they made in the reign of Theseus.[3] Furthermore, Meleager, the noblest among the Greeks, had been a cousin of theirs.[4]

Now though Chryseïs did not know these things, she did hear of the proud spirit of the women, and she learned how far above her husband Helen stood— so far that, when Helen heard of the great advantages of Asia, due alike to excellence of soil and size of population and abundance of riches, she came to scorn, not only Menelaüs, but Agamemnon too and Greece as a whole and she chose the one in preference to the other. Now Menelaüs had been accustomed to yield to Helen in everything before her elopement, and also, when later on he took her captive, he was kind to her in spite of all[5] ; but Agamemnon, puffed up because of his position as commander, had disparaged Clytemnestra, and so it was clear that they were not going to get along well together, but that instead there would be just about such actions as

[4] Meleager's mother was Leda's sister. The Calydonian boarhunt, of which he was the hero, was popular with both poet and artist.

[5] Aristophanes, *Lysistrata* 155-156, says that when Troy was taken Menelaüs was so moved by Helen's beauty that he let fall the sword with which he meant to slay her. He treats her with marked courtesy in the *Odyssey*.

ὁποῖα συνέπεσεν. οὐδὲ γὰρ ἐκεῖνα ἤδετο λέγοντος
τοῦ Ἀγαμέμνονος ἡ Χρυσηίς, καὶ ταῦτα φανερῶς
ἐν ἐκκλησίᾳ τῶν Ἀχαιῶν, ὅτι προτιμᾷ τῆς γυναικὸς αὐτὴν καὶ οὐδὲν ἡγοῖτο χείρονα· φθόνον γὰρ
13 καὶ ζηλοτυπίαν ᾔδει φέροντα. καὶ νὴ Δία τὸν
τρόπον ἑώρα τοῦ Ἀγαμέμνονος ὅτι οὐ βέβαιος
ἀλλὰ ὑπερήφανος εἴη καὶ ὑβριστής, καὶ τί ποιήσει
πρὸς αὐτὴν αἰχμάλωτον οὖσαν ἐλογίζετο παυσάμε-
νος τῆς ἐπιθυμίας, ὅπου γε τῆς ἑαυτοῦ γυναικός,
βασιλίδος τε οὔσης καὶ παῖδας ἐξ αὐτῆς πεποιημένος, οὕτως ὀλιγώρως ἐμνημόνευεν. αἱ μὲν γὰρ
ἀνόητοι χαίρουσιν ἐπὶ τοῖς ἐρασταῖς, ὅταν φαίνων-
ται τὰς ἄλλας ἀτιμάζοντες· αἱ δὲ νοῦν ἔχουσαι τὴν
φύσιν ὁρῶσι[1] τοῦ ταῦτα ποιοῦντος ἢ λέγοντος.
14 Ἅμα δὲ καὶ πρὸς αὐτὴν[2] ᾐσθάνετο αὐτὸν ὑβρι-
στικῶς ἔχειν,[3] καὶ ταῦτα ὅτε μάλιστα ἤρα. τὸ γὰρ
οὕτως ἀπελάσαι τὸν[4] πατέρα τῆς ἐρωμένης καὶ μὴ
φείσασθαι δι’ αὐτὴν καὶ οὐχ ὅπως παραμυθήσασθαι
τὸν πρεσβύτην εἰπόντα ὡς οὐδὲν αὐτοῦ τῇ θυγατρὶ
δεινὸν εἴη, τοὐναντίον δὲ μὴ μόνον ἐκείνῳ ἀπειλεῖν,
ἀλλὰ καὶ τὴν Χρυσηίδα ἀτιμάζειν λέγοντα,

τὴν δ’ ἐγὼ οὐ λύσω πρίν μιν καὶ γῆρας ἔπεισιν
ἡμετέρῳ ἐνὶ οἴκῳ ἐν Ἄργεϊ, τηλόθι πάτρης,
ἱστὸν ἐποιχομένην καὶ ἐμὸν λέχος ἀντιόωσαν

πόσης τινὸς ὑπερηφανίας; τί γὰρ ἂν ὕστερον
ἐποίησεν, ὅτε ἐρῶν οὕτως ὑπὲρ αὐτῆς διαλέγεται;

---

[1] ὁρῶσι] ὑφορῶσι Geel.   [2] αὐτὴν Emperius : αὑτὴν.
[3] ἔχειν] ἔχοντα Arnim.
[4] After τὸν Arnim deletes Χρύσην.

---

[1] A reference to Clytemnestra's slaughter of Agamemnon
and Cassandra ; cf. § 15 and Aeschylus' *Agamemnon*.

came to pass.[1] Nor was Chryseïs pleased when Agamemnon said what he did, moreover publicly in the assembly of the Achaeans, namely, that he prized her more than his own wife and thought her not inferior to her, for Chryseïs knew that such talk breeds envy and jealousy. Then too, she observed Agamemnon's character and saw that he was not stable but arrogant and overbearing, and she calculated what he would do to her, a captive, when he ceased to desire her, seeing that he referred to his wife, queen though she was and the mother of his children, in such disparaging terms. For though foolish women delight in their lovers when they are seen to disparage all other women, those who are sensible discern the true nature of the man who acts or talks that way.

And at the same time Chryseïs was aware that he was insolent too in his treatment of herself, and that too at a time when he was most in love with her. For example, that he should so roughly have driven off the father of his beloved, instead of sparing him on her account, to say nothing of his not having soothed the old man by saying that his daughter had nothing to fear from him, but, on the contrary, not only threatening him but also speaking slightingly of Chryseïs by saying,

> But I'll not free her ere old age o'ertakes
> Her far from home, at Argos, in our house,
> Plying the loom and visiting my couch.[2]

What overweening insolence ! Why, what would he have done later on, seeing that while still in love he talks of her in such a fashion ? Therefore, to

[2] *Iliad* 1. 29-31.

ταῦτα οὖν φυλάξασθαι καὶ προϊδεῖν οὐδαμῶς φαύλης
15 γυναικός. ἐδήλωσε δέ, οἶμαι, τὰ περὶ τὴν Κασ-
σάνδραν γενόμενα ἐν τῷ Ἄργει καὶ τὸν Ἀγαμέμνονα αὐτόν, ὅτι νοῦν εἶχεν ἡ Χρυσηὶς ῥυσαμένη τῶν
κακῶν τούτων ἑαυτήν. οὐκοῦν τὸ μήτε ἔρωτι μήτε
βασιλείᾳ μήτε τοῖς δοκοῦσιν ἐνδόξοις καὶ ἀγαθοῖς
νέαν οὖσαν ἐπαίρεσθαι[1] μηδ' εἰς πράγματα σφαλερὰ
καὶ τεταραγμένην οἰκίαν καὶ εἰς φθόνον καὶ ζηλοτυπίαν αὐτὴν προέσθαι γυναικὸς σώφρονος καὶ τῷ
ὄντι ἀξίας ἱερέως εἶναι θυγατρός, παρὰ θεῷ τεθραμ-
μένης.

Τί οὖν; ἐκ τούτων σὺ φῂς νοῦν ἔχειν αὐτὴν
ἡγήσασθαι τὸν Ἀγαμέμνονα;

16 Δ. Οὐδαμῶς· οὐδὲ γὰρ εἰκὸς ἦν λέγειν αὐτὴν
τοιοῦτον οὐδὲν πρὸς ἐκεῖνον· ἀλλ' ἀπὸ τῶν ἄλλων
συνεῖναι.

Πῶς οὖν οὔ φησι χαίρουσαν αὐτὴν ὁ ποιητὴς
ἀπιέναι, καθάπερ τὴν Βρισηίδα λυπουμένην;

Δ. Ὅτι καὶ τοῦτο σωφρονοῦσα ἔπραττεν, ὅπως
μὴ παροξύναι τὸν Ἀγαμέμονα μηδὲ εἰς φιλονικίαν
ἀγάγοι. δηλοῖ δὲ ὅμως, ὅπου φησὶν αὐτὴν ὑπὸ
τοῦ Ὀδυσσέως τῷ πατρὶ δοθῆναι παρὰ τὸν βωμόν·

ὣς εἰπὼν ἐν χερσὶ τίθει, ὁ δ' ἐδέξατο χαίρων
παῖδα φίλην.

οὐ γὰρ ἄν,[2] οἶμαι, λυπουμένην αὐτὴν ὁ πατὴρ ἐδέ-

---

[1] ἐπαίρεσθαι added by Reiske.
[2] ἄν added by Jacobs.

---

[1] Cf. § 12 and note.   [2] *Iliad* 1. 348.

guard against these things and to forecast them is the mark of a woman by no means ordinary. However, to my way of thinking, what happened in Argos both to Cassandra and to Agamemnon himself [1] revealed that Chryseïs was a sensible woman to have saved herself from these disasters. Accordingly, that neither passion nor kingly station nor those things which are deemed glorious and good turned her head, young though she was, and that she did not plunge into perilous ventures and a disordered house and envy and jealousy—these are the marks of a prudent woman, one truly worthy of being daughter of a priest, nurtured in the house of a god.

Int. How so ? Do you mean that these are the reasons why Agamemnon thought her wise ?

Dio. By no means, for it is not likely that she said any such thing to him ; rather that he formed his judgement on the basis of her conduct in general.

Int. Why, then, does not the poet say that she departed in gladness, just as he says that Briseïs departed in sorrow ? [2]

Dio. Because in this too she was showing her prudence, her aim being not to exasperate Agamemnon or drive him to contentiousness. However, the poet makes the situation plain in the passage in which he says she was restored by Odysseus to her father beside the altar :

> Thus having said, he placed her in his arms,
> And he rejoicing took his darling child. [3]

For, methinks, if she were sorrowing, her father would not be receiving her " rejoicing " ; nor, per-

---

[3] *Ibid.* 1. 446-447.

χετο χαίρων· οὐδ' ἂν φίλην εἶπε τυχόν, εἰ μὴ σφόδρα ἠγάπα τοῖς γεγονόσι τὸν πατέρα.[1]

17 Εἶεν· ἀλλὰ τί[2] μᾶλλον ἢ Χρυσηὶς ταῦτα ἐλογίζετο ἃ σὺ λέγεις ἢ[3] Χρύσης καθ' αὑτόν;

Δ. Ὅτι τὰ περὶ τὴν Κλυταιμνήστραν εἰκὸς ἦν[4] μᾶλλον ἐκείνην πολυπραγμονεῖν· εἰ δὲ[5] καὶ λογιζομένου τοῦ πατρὸς ταῦτα συνεχώρει καὶ ἐπείθετο, οὐδὲ τοῦτο φαῦλον. αἱ γοῦν πολλαὶ καὶ ἀνόητοι τοὺς ἐραστὰς μᾶλλον ἀγαπῶσιν ἢ τοὺς γονέας.

Διὰ τί οὖν, εἴπερ ἦν φρόνιμος, οὐκ ἐκώλυε τὸν Χρύσην ἐν τῷ φανερῷ δεῖσθαι τοῦ Ἀγαμέμνονος, ἵνα ἧττον ἐχαλέπαινεν;

18 Δ. Ὅτι ᾔδει τοὺς ἐρῶντας ἰδίᾳ μὲν πάντα βουλομένους χαρίζεσθαι τῷ ἔρωτι, τὸν δὲ ὄχλον αἰδουμένους ἐνίοτε, καὶ τὰ τοῦ θεοῦ στέμματα ἔχειν[6] τινὰ ἡγεῖτο πρὸς τὸ πλῆθος δύναμιν, ὥσπερ[7] ἐγένετο.

Ἀλλὰ ἐκεῖνο ἐνθυμοῦμαι· πῶς συνέτυχε τὸν Ἀγαμέμνονα καὶ τότε τῆς τοῦ ἱερέως θυγατρὸς καὶ ὕστερον ἐρασθῆναι τῆς Κασσάνδρας, θεοφορήτου καὶ ἱερᾶς κόρης;

Δ. Ὅτι καὶ τοῦτο σημεῖον ὑπερηφανίας καὶ τρυφῆς, τὸ μᾶλλον ἐπιθυμεῖν τῶν παρανόμων καὶ σπανίων ἢ τῶν ἑτοίμων.

---

[1] τὸν πατέρα deleted by Wendland.
[2] ἀλλὰ τί Emperius, ἀλλ' οἴει Pflugk : ἀλλ' εἰ UBM (εἰ in ras. M).
[3] After ἢ Wilamowitz adds ὁ.
[4] ἦν Pflugk : εἶναι.
[5] εἰ δὲ added by Wilamowitz.

chance, would the poet have called her " darling "
unless she loved her father dearly for what had taken
place.

Int. Very well ; yet why did Chryseïs reason thus
rather than Chryses on his own account ?

Dio. Because it was to be expected that what
concerned Clytemnestra would hold greater interest
for Chryseïs ; but even if it was her father who
reasoned thus and she agreed with him and followed
his advice, that was no trifling feat either. At any
rate most women in their folly are more devoted to
their lovers than to their parents.

Int. Why, then, if she really was sensible, did she
not try to prevent Chryses from appealing to Agamemnon publicly, in order that he might be less
angry ?

Dio. Because she knew that, though in private
lovers desire in every matter to gratify their passion, they are sometimes embarrassed in the presence
of the crowd, and she believed that the fillets of the
god had a certain power with the people, as proved
to be the case.[1]

Int. Still here is something that troubles me How
did it happen that Agamemnon not only fell in love
with the priest's daughter at the time in question,
but afterwards with Cassandra too, a divinely inspired
and holy maid ?[2]

Dio. Because this too is a sign of pride and wantonness—to desire the forbidden and rare rather than
the easily obtainable.

---

[1] Cf. *Iliad* 1. 22-23.
[2] Loved by Apollo, Cassandra received from him the gift
of prophecy.

---

[6] ἔχειν] ἔξειν Arnim.   [7] After ὥσπερ Emperius adds καί.

Οὐκ ἀντιλέγω τὸ μὴ οὐ φρόνιμον εἶναι τὴν Χρυσηίδα, εἰ ταῦτα οὕτω γέγονε.

Δ. Σὺ δὲ πότερον ἀκούειν θέλοις ἂν ὡς γέγονε πάντως[1] ἢ ὅπως καλῶς εἶχε γενέσθαι;

[1] γέγονε πάντως] γέγονεν ὄντως Emperius.

THE SIXTY-FIRST DISCOURSE

Int. I do not gainsay that Chryseïs was prudent, if these things took place as you claim.

Dio. Would you rather hear how they assuredly did take place, or how it would be well for them to have taken place ?

THE SIXTY-SECOND DISCOURSE:
ON KINGSHIP AND TYRANNY

THE complimentary address contained in §§ 1 and 3 of our Discourse could hardly have been intended for any one but Trajan. Yet the document is so abrupt in both beginning and ending and so brief when compared with the four treatises on kingship supposed to have been addressed to Trajan (Or. 1-4) that it is difficult to imagine that it ever was delivered as a distinct entity in the form in which we have it. It is of course conceivable that we are dealing with a fragment of a fifth speech on kingship addressed to the much-enduring Trajan, but it is more likely that we have before us a variant version of a portion of one of the addresses just mentioned. Dio himself makes it plain (Or. 57. 10-12) that on occasion he took the liberty of repeating to other hearers speeches previously delivered before " the Emperor." On such an occasion he doubtless felt free to modify the original wording, and such a procedure would explain the existence of certain doublets in his text. We may conjecture that his editor, finding the substance of Or. 62 imbedded in such a variant version of one of the four speeches to which we have referred and not wishing to discard it, gave it independent existence here. Finally, it may be noted that, though the second element in the title, tyranny, is not specifically mentioned in our document, it is dealt with in Or. 3, and also that there is a notable similarity between Or. 3. 10 and Or. 62. 3.

62. ΠΕΡΙ ΒΑΣΙΛΕΙΑΣ ΚΑΙ ΤΥΡΑΝΝΙΔΟΣ

1 Καὶ μὴν εἴ τις ἑνὸς ἀνδρὸς οὐχ οἷός τε ἄρχειν
ἐστί, καὶ τούτου σφόδρα ἐγγὺς ὄντος, ᾧ δὴ¹ ξύν-
εστιν, οὐδὲ αὖ μίαν ψυχὴν κατευθύνειν τὴν αὑτοῦ,
πῶς ἂν δύναιτο βασιλεύειν μυριάδων ἀναριθμήτων
πανταχοῦ διεσπαρμένων, ὥσπερ σύ,² καὶ πολλῶν
γε οἰκούντων ἐπὶ πέρασι γῆς, ὧν οὐδὲ ἑώρακε τοὺς
πλείστους οὐδ᾽ ἂν ἴδοι ποτὲ οὐδὲ τῆς φωνῆς ξυνή-
σει; ὅμοιον γὰρ ὥσπερ εἴ τις λέγοι τὸν οὕτως
ἀδύνατον τὴν ὄψιν ὡς μηδὲ τὰ ἐν ποσὶν ὁρᾶν, ἀλλὰ
προσδεόμενον χειραγωγοῦ, τοῦτον ἐφικνεῖσθαι βλέ-
ποντα μέχρι τῶν πλεῖστον ἀπεχόντων, ὥσπερ οἱ
πόρρωθεν ὁρῶντες ἐκ τοῦ πελάγους τά τε ὄρη καὶ
τὰς νήσους, ἢ τὸν οὐ δυνάμενον φθέγγεσθαι τοῖς
παρεστῶσιν ἱκανὸν ὅλοις δήμοις καὶ στρατοπέδοις
2 εἰς ἐπήκοον φθέγγεσθαι. καὶ γὰρ οὖν ἔχει τι
παραπλήσιον ὁ νοῦς τῇ ὄψει· ὡς ἐκείνη διεφθαρμένη
μὲν οὐδὲν οὐδὲ τῶν πλησιαίτατα ὁρᾷ, ὑγιὴς δὲ
οὖσα μέχρις οὐρανοῦ τε καὶ ἀστέρων ἐξικνεῖται·
ταὐτὸ δὴ τοῦτο ἡ μὲν τοῦ φρονίμου διάνοια καὶ
πάντας ἀνθρώπους ἱκανὴ γίγνεται διοικεῖν, ἡ δὲ
τοῦ ἄφρονος οὐδὲ ἓν σῶμα τὸ ἐκείνου δύναται
φυλάττειν οὐδὲ ἕνα οἶκον.

¹ After δὴ Arnim adds ἀεὶ.
² After σύ Emperius deletes λέγεις.

---

¹ I.e., the man himself.

THE SIXTY-SECOND DISCOURSE : ON KINGSHIP AND TYRANNY

And indeed, if a person is not competent to govern a single man, and that too a man who is very close to him, in fact his constant companion,[1] and if, again, he cannot guide a single soul, and that his own, how could he be king, as you are,[2] over unnumbered thousands scattered everywhere, many even dwelling at the ends of the earth, most of whom he has not even seen and never could see, and whose speech he will not understand ?   Why, it is as if one were to say of the man with vision so impaired that he cannot see even what lies at his feet but needs some one to lead him by the hand, that he can reach with his eyes the most distant objects, like those who at sea behold from afar both the mountains and the islands ; or as if one were to say of the man who cannot make himself heard even by those who stand beside him, that he is able to speak so as to be heard by whole communities and armies.   In fact, the intellect has something comparable to vision—as vision, when it is ruined, can see nothing even of what is very near, although when in health it can reach sky and stars, just so the mind of the prudent man shows itself competent to direct all men whatsoever, whereas the mind of the fool cannot protect a single body, his own, or a single household.

[2] Presumably Trajan ; cf. § 3 and Introduction.

Οἱ μὲν γὰρ πολλοὶ τῶν ἐν ταῖς δυναστείαις, ὅτι μὲν ἔξεστιν αὐτοῖς πάντα λαμβάνειν, πάντων ἐπιθυμοῦσιν· ὅτι δὲ ἐπ' αὐτοῖς ἐστι τὸ δίκαιον, διὰ τοῦτό εἰσιν ἄδικοι· ὅτι δὲ οὐ φοβοῦνται τοὺς νόμους, οὐδὲ εἶναι νομίζουσιν· ὅτι δὲ οὐκ ἀναγκάζονται πονεῖν, οὐδέποτε παύονται τρυφῶντες· ὅτι δὲ οὐδεὶς ἀμύνεται κακῶς πάσχων, οὐδέποτε παύονται ποιοῦντες· ὅτι δὲ οὐδεμιᾶς σπανίζουσιν ἡδονῆς, οὐδέποτε ἐμπίμπλανται ἡδόμενοι· ὅτι δὲ οὐδεὶς ψέγει ἐκ τοῦ φανεροῦ, οὐδὲν ἀπολείπουσι τῶν οὐ δικαίως[1] λεγομένων· ὅτι δὲ οὐδεὶς αὐτοὺς βούλεται λυπεῖν, διὰ τοῦτο πᾶσι χαλεπαίνουσιν· ὅτι δὲ ὀργισθεῖσιν ἔξεστι πάντα ποιεῖν, διὰ τοῦτο συνεχῶς 3 ὀργίζονται. ὁ δὲ ἀγαθὸς ἄρχων, ὥσπερ σύ, τἀναντία ἐπιτηδεύει· οὐδενὸς μὲν ἐπιθυμεῖ διὰ τὰ πάντα οἴεσθαι ἔχειν, φείδεται δὲ τῶν ἡδονῶν διὰ τὸ μηδεμιᾶς ἂν ἀπορῆσαι ὀρεχθείς, δικαιότερος δὲ τῶν ἄλλων ἐστίν, ἅτε πᾶσι παρέχων τὴν δικαιοσύνην, ἥδεται δὲ τοῖς πόνοις, ὅτι ἑκὼν πονεῖ, ἀγαπᾷ δὲ τοὺς νόμους, ὅτι οὐ δέδοικε.

Καὶ ταῦτα ὀρθῶς ὑπολαμβάνει. τίνι μὲν γὰρ φρονήσεως δεῖ πλείονος ἢ τῷ περὶ τοσούτων βουλευομένῳ; τίνι δὲ ἀκριβεστέρας δικαιοσύνης ἢ τῷ μείζονι τῶν νόμων; τίνι δὲ σωφροσύνης ἐγκρα- 4 τεστέρας ἢ ᾧ πάντα ἔξεστι; τίνι δὲ ἀνδρείας μείζονος ἢ τῷ πάντα σῴζοντι; καὶ τοίνυν τῷ μὲν ἄλλων ἄρχοντι πολλῶν τοῦτο μὲν δαπάνης δε παμπόλλης, τοῦτο δὲ στρατοπέδων καὶ πεζικῶν

Take, for example, most men who hold unbridled power—because they have the power to obtain everything, they crave everything ; because justice is lodged in their hands, for this reason they are unjust ; because they do not fear the laws, they do not even believe in their existence ; because they are not compelled to labour, they never cease their luxurious living ; because no one defends himself when mal-treated, they never cease maltreating ; because they lack no pleasure, they never get their fill of it ; because no one censures them openly, they miss no occasion for unjust criticism ; because no one wishes to hurt their feelings, for this reason they display ill-temper toward everyone ; because they have it in their power to do anything when enraged, for this reason they are continually in a rage. On the other hand, the good ruler, such as you are, practises the opposite conduct—he covets nothing for the reason that he feels he has everything ; he is sparing in his pleasures for the reason that he would lack for no pleasure he might crave ; he is more just than any other man inasmuch as he provides justice for all ; he delights in labour because he labours of his own accord ; he cherishes the laws because he does not fear them.

Moreover, he is right in reasoning so. For who needs ampler wisdom than he who deliberates on so many matters ? Who needs stricter justice than he who is superior to the laws ? Who needs more stead-fast self-control than he to whom anything is per-missible ? Who needs greater courage than he who is the preserver of all ? Furthermore, he who is to govern many others needs, not only very great outlay of wealth, but also armies, both infantry and cavalry,

καὶ ἱππικῶν, ἔτι δὲ τειχῶν καὶ νεῶν καὶ μηχανη-
μάτων, εἰ μέλλει καθέξειν μὲν τοὺς ὑπηκόους,
ἀμυνεῖσθαι δὲ τοὺς πολεμίους, ἐὰν δέ τις ἀφιστῆται
τῆς ἀρχῆς, καταστρέψεσθαι.¹ τὸ δὲ αὐτοῦ κρατεῖν
πάντων ἀδαπανώτατον καὶ ἀπραγμονέστατόν ἐστι
καὶ ἀκινδυνότατον· οὔτε γὰρ πολυδάπανος οὔτε
ἐργώδης οὔτε ἐπισφαλὴς ὁ τοῦ ἐγκρατοῦς ἀνθρώπου βίος· ἀλλ᾽ ὅμως τοιοῦτον ὂν πάντων χαλεπώτατον πέφυκεν.

5 Ἐπεὶ Σαρδανάπαλλος ἐκεῖνος ὁ θρυλούμενος εἶχε
μὲν Νίνον, εἶχε δὲ Βαβυλῶνα, τὰς μεγίστας τῶν
πρότερον γεγενημένων πόλεων, ὑπήκουε δὲ αὐτῷ
πάντα τὰ ἔθνη τὰ νεμόμενα τὴν ἑτέραν ἤπειρον
μέχρι τῶν ἀοικήτων τῆς γῆς λεγομένων· βασιλείας
δὲ οὐδὲν ἦν αὐτῷ προσῆκον, οὐ μᾶλλον ἢ τῶν
σηπομένων τινὶ νεκρῶν. βουλεύεσθαι μὲν γὰρ ἢ
δικάζειν ἢ στρατηγεῖν οὔτε ἐβούλετο οὔτε ἐδύνατο.
6 ἐν δὲ τοῖς βασιλείοις ἀποδιδράσκων εἰς τὴν γυναι-
κωνῖτιν καθῆστο ἐπὶ χρυσηλάτου κλίνης ἀναβάδην
ὑπὸ ἁλουργέσι παστοῖς, ὥσπερ ὁ θρηνούμενος ὑπὸ
τῶν γυναικῶν Ἄδωνις, ὀξύτερον φθεγγόμενος εὐνούχων, τὸν μὲν τράχηλον ἀποκλίνων, ὑπὸ δὲ
ἀργίας καὶ σκιᾶς λευκὸς καὶ τρέμων, τὸ σῶμα
πελιδνός,² τοὺς δὲ ὀφθαλμοὺς ἀναστρέφων, ὥσπερ
ἐξ ἀγχόνης· ὃν οὐκ ἦν διαγνῶναι τῶν παλλακῶν.
καίτοι χρόνον τινὰ κατέσχεν, ὡς ἐδόκει, τὴν ἀρχὴν

¹ καταστρέψεσθαι Emperius : καταστρέφεσθαι.
² λευκὸς . . . πελιδνός] λευκὸς τὸ σῶμα καὶ τρέμων, τὸ χρῶμα
πελιδνός Emperius.

¹ Assurbanipal, last of the great Assyrian rulers, 668–625
B.C. Herodotus (2. 150) speaks only of his wealth ; Dio's
account of his effeminacy and indolence may have been
drawn from Ctesias. See Diodorus Siculus 2. 23–28.

and in addition fortifications, ships, and engines of war, if he is to control his subjects, defend himself against the foe, and, should some one try to revolt from his authority, reduce him to subjection. However, to control one's self is of all things least costly, least difficult, least dangerous; for neither costly nor laborious nor precarious is the life of the man of self-control; yet for all that, though so desirable, it is naturally the most difficult thing of all.

For instance, the famous Sardanapallus,[1] whose name is a by-word, held Nineveh and Babylon as well, the greatest cities that had yet existed, and all the nations which occupy the second continent,[2] as far as what are called the uninhabited parts of the earth, were subject to him; but to kingship he could lay no claim, no more than could some rotting corpse. For the fact is, he neither would nor could take counsel or give judgement or lead troops. On the contrary, it was his custom to slip away into the women's quarters in his palace and there sit with legs drawn up on a golden couch, sheltered by purple bed-hangings, just like the Adonis who is lamented by the women,[3] his voice shriller than that of eunuchs, his neck lolling to one side, his face pale and twitching from indolence and living in the shade, his body livid, his eyes upturned as if he were being throttled—in short, one whom it would be impossible to distinguish from his concubines. And yet for a time, as it seemed,

[2] Asia.

[3] As early as the fifth century Athenian women honoured him with a two-day festival in which the lament was prominent; cf. Aristophanes, *Lysistrata* 389. A celebration in Alexandria forms the background of Theocritus' fifteenth idyl; cf. also Bion's *Lament* in Edmonds, *Greek Bucolic Poets* (L.C.L.), pp. 386-395.

29

εἰκῇ φερομένην, ὥσπερ ναῦν δίχα κυβερνήτου πολλάκις ἀλωμένην μηδενὸς κατέχοντος ἐν τῷ πελάγει
κατὰ τύχην, εὐδίας ἐπεχούσης· ἔπειτα ὀλίγος κλύ-
7 δων ἐπαρθεὶς καὶ ῥᾳδίως ἓν κῦμα ἐπέκλυσεν. καὶ
δὴ καὶ ἅρμα ἰδεῖν ἔστιν οὐδενὸς ἡνιοχοῦντος ἐν
ἀγῶνι ῥεμβόμενον, ὃ νίκης μὲν οὐκ ἄν ποτε τύχοι,
ταράττει δὲ καὶ ἀπόλλυσι τὸν ἐγγὺς ὄχλον τῶν
θεατῶν.

Οὔτε γὰρ ἄφρων βασιλεὺς ἔσται ποτέ, οὐ μᾶλλον
ἢ τυφλὸς ἡγεμὼν ὁδοῦ γένοιτ' ἄν, οὔτε ἄδικος, οὐ
μᾶλλον ἢ κανὼν σκολιὸς καὶ ἄνισος ἄλλου προσδεόμενος κανόνος, οὔτε δειλός, οὐ μᾶλλον ἢ λέων
ἐλάφου λαβὼν ψυχὴν ἢ σίδηρος κηροῦ καὶ μολίβδου
μαλακώτερος. τίνι δ' ἰσχυροτέρας ἐγκρατείας
προσῆκον[1] ἢ τῷ πλείστων μὲν ἡδονῶν ἐν μέσῳ
ζῶντι, πλεῖστα δὲ πράγματα διοικοῦντι, ἐλαχίστην
δὲ σχολὴν ἄγοντι, ὑπὲρ μεγίστων δὲ καὶ πλείστων
φροντίζοντι;

[1] προσῆκον Emperius : προσῆκεν.

---

[1] Nineveh fell in 612 b.c., some years after the death of
Assurbanipal. The story of Sardanapallus, as told by Ctesias,
however, is not that of the historical ruler. In the Greek
account Sardanapallus was the last king of the Assyrians,

he maintained his empire,[1] though it was drifting aimlessly, just as, for instance, a ship without a helmsman, roving on the sea, with no one in control, as fate directs, so long as fair weather holds ; then, should a little sea arise, even a single wave easily swamps it. Yes, and one may also see a chariot, with no one holding the reins, wobbling crazily in a race, a chariot which, while it could never win a victory, nevertheless throws into confusion and even works destruction in the mob of spectators near the course.

Nay, there will never be a foolish king any more than there could be a blind guide for a traveller ; nor an unjust king any more than a crooked, uneven measuring-rod needing a second rod to set it straight ; nor a timid king any more than a lion with the spirit of a deer, or than iron softer than wax or lead. On the contrary, to whom appropriately belongs a sterner self-control than to him who lives surrounded by the greatest number of pleasures, who administers the greatest number of affairs, who has the least leisure, and who is concerned over the greatest and most numerous problems ?

who burned himself together with his treasures and concubines when he foresaw the capture of Nineveh.

THE SIXTY-THIRD DISCOURSE :
ON FORTUNE (I)

THE authenticity of this encomium on Fortune was denied long ago by Emperius, and his judgement has been reaffirmed by Arnim. The criteria are stylistic : there is a notable disregard of hiatus, a phenomenon not to be expected of an able sophist in a composition such as this—Arnim cites the particularly objectionable passage in § 5 : πολλὰ δὲ αὕτη ἔχουσα χρώματα ἐοικότα ἀφρῷ ἠμαγμένῳ ἐφήρμοσε τῇ γραφῇ— and the subject matter is treated in a dull and uninspired fashion. The one redeeming feature of the document is the anecdote, elsewhere recorded only by Sextus Empiricus, of Apelles and his sponge.

Although Tychê appears in Hesiod's *Theogony* among the progeny of Tethys and Oceanus and is occasionally named by poets of later date, notably Pindar, the personification seems not to have taken firm hold upon Greek imagination. With the Romans, however, the case was different, and Tychê in her Latinized form, Fortuna, received ample honours as a deity in many parts of the Empire, being intimately associated with the ruling house.

63. ΠΕΡΙ ΤΥΧΗΣ ΠΡΩΤΟΣ ΛΟΓΟΣ

1 Οἱ ἄνθρωποι ἐοίκασι πρὸς τὴν τύχην διακεῖσθαι ὃν τρόπον οἱ πλέοντες πρὸς τοὺς ἀνέμους τοὺς φορούς[1]· ἄσμενοι γὰρ προσκαρτεροῦσι τῷ δρόμῳ, καὶ[2] οἷς ἂν ὁ ἄνεμος παρῇ, ἐκεῖνοι[3] ἦλθον ὅπου ἤθελον, οἱ δὲ ἀπολειφθέντες ἐν πελάγει μέσῳ μάτην ὀδύρονται· οὕτως οὖν καὶ τῆς τύχης παρούσης μὲν χαίρειν καὶ ἥδεσθαι τοὺς ἀνθρώπους, μὴ παρούσης δὲ λύπην ἔχειν καὶ ἀπορίαν. πάντα γὰρ ἐκ τῆς δαίμονος ταύτης· καὶ γὰρ τὸ ἄπορον εὔπορον φαίνεται[4] καὶ τὸ ἀσθενὲς ἰσχυρὸν καὶ τὸ αἰσχρὸν καλὸν καὶ ἡ πενία γίγνεται πλοῦτος.

2 Τύχης γοῦν ἐν θαλάττῃ γενομένης εὐπλοεῖ ναῦς καὶ ἐν ἀέρι φανείσης εὐτυχεῖ γεωργός. καὶ ψυχὴ γέγηθεν ὑπὸ τῆς τύχης αἰωρουμένη[5]· εἰ δὲ ἀπολίποι τύχη, περίεισιν[6] ὡς ἐν τάφῳ τῷ σώματι. οὔτε γὰρ εἰ λέγοι τις, εὐδοκιμεῖ,[7] οὔτε εἰ πράττοι τις, ἐπιτυγχάνει, οὐδὲ ὄφελός τι εὐφυῆ γενέσθαι ἀπολιπούσης τύχης. ταύτης γὰρ μὴ παρούσης οὐκ ἦλθε[8] παιδεία οὐδὲ ἄλλο τι ἀγαθόν. ἀλλὰ μὴν καὶ ἀρετὴ τότε ἔργων ἕνεκεν θαυμάζεται, ὅταν παρῇ τύχη· εἰ

---

[1] φορούς Reiske : σφοδρούς.
[2] καί deleted by Arnim.
[3] ἐκεῖνοι] ἐκεῖ τε Arnim.
[4] φαίνεται deleted by Arnim.
[5] αἰωρουμένη Emperius : γεωργουμένη.
[6] περίεισιν with UBM : περιΐησιν PH, περίεστιν Emperius.

THE SIXTY-THIRD DISCOURSE:
ON FORTUNE (I)

MANKIND seems to feel toward Fortune as sailors do toward the winds that waft them on their way ; for sailors gladly and with vigour apply themselves to their course, and those who have the breeze reach the port for which they aimed, while those who are abandoned by it in the midst of the open sea lament to no avail ; so too when men have Fortune with them they rejoice and are glad, but when she is absent they are grieved and distressed. Yes, everything is the work of this goddess, for indeed when she is present the difficult appears easy, the weak strong, the ugly beautiful, and poverty turns to wealth.

For instance, when Fortune comes at sea a ship has fair sailing, and when she shows herself in the atmosphere a farmer prospers. Moreover, a man's spirit rejoices when uplifted by Fortune, yet should Fortune fail, it goes about in its body as in a tomb. For neither does a man win approval if he speaks, nor does he succeed if he acts, nor is it any advantage to have been born a man of genius when Fortune fails. For when she is not present learning is not forthcoming, nor any other good thing. Why, even valour gains recognition for its achievements only when Fortune

---

⁷ εὐδοκιμεῖ PH : ἐπαινεῖν δοκεῖ UBM, εὐπορεῖ Sonny.
⁸ οὐκ ἦλθε] οὐ προῆλθε Gasda.

δὲ ἀφεθείη μόνη, λόγος ἐστὶ καλοῦ πράγματος
ἄπρακτος. αὕτη πολεμούντων μέν ἐστι νίκη καὶ
εἰρήνην ἀγόντων ὁμόνοια καὶ γαμούντων εὔνοια καὶ
ἐρώντων ἡδονὴ καὶ ὅλως ἡ ἐπὶ παντί τῳ¹ γιγνο-
μένῳ εὐπραγία.

3 Γῆν ὅταν καταλίπῃ τύχη, τότε καὶ σείεται καὶ
τρέμει καὶ τὰ ἐπ' αὐτῆς καλὰ διαρριπτεῖ· καὶ² τοῦτο
γῆς νόσημα, μὴ παρούσης τύχης.³ ὡς γὰρ⁴ ναῦς
εἰκῇ φέρεται καὶ ταχὺ βυθίζεται, κυβερνήτου στερο-
μένη, καὶ ὡς τείχη κατέπεσε θεμελίων πονησάντων,
οὕτω πόλις εἰς φθορὰν ὅλη χωρεῖ σπάνει τύχης.
Ἀθῆναί ποτε εἰς ῥήτορας ἠδικήθησαν⁵ καὶ ἤγετο
Δημοσθένης, οὐκέτι τῆς τύχης ἐπισκοπούσης τὰς
Ἀθήνας. ἐμοὶ δὲ δοκεῖ καὶ οὐρανὸς τύχην ἔχειν,
ὁπόταν⁶ αἰθρίαν ἔχῃ, μὴ σκότος.

4 Ὁρᾶν δὲ χρὴ καὶ τὸ εὐμήχανον αὐτῆς. ἤδη γοῦν
τις ἐκπεσὼν νεὼς ἐν πελάγει εὐπόρησε τοῦ ζῆν,
ἐλθούσης τύχης. ἄξιον δὲ εἰπεῖν καὶ τὸ συμβὰν
ἀπὸ τῆς τύχης Ἀπελλῇ τῷ ζωγράφῳ. ὡς γὰρ
λόγος, ἵππον οὐχὶ ἐξ ἐργασίας ἀλλὰ ἐκ πολέμου
ἐποίει· ὑψηλὸς ἦν τῷ αὐχένι καὶ ἐπανεστὼς καὶ τὰ
ὦτα ὄρθιος καὶ δριμὺς τὰς ὄψεις, ὡς ἐκ πολέμου
παρών, τὸν ἐκ τοῦ δρόμου θυμὸν ἐν ταῖς ὄψεσιν
ἔχων, οἱ δὲ πόδες ὑπεφέροντο⁷ ἐν τῷ ἀέρι, μικρὰ

¹ τῳ Bally : τῷ. ² διαρριπτεῖ· καὶ] διαρριπτεῖται· Reiske.
³ τοῦτο γῆς . . . τύχης deleted by van Herwerden.
⁴ ὡς γὰρ Budé, ὡς δὲ Wilamowitz : ὥσπερ.
⁵ τοῖς ῥήτορσιν ἠδικήθησαν, εἰς ῥήτορας ἠδίκησαν Emperius : εἰς ῥήτορας ἠδικήθησαν.
⁶ ὁπόταν Dindorf : ὁπότε ἄν.
⁷ ὑπεφέροντο Arnim : ἐπεφέροντο or ἀνεφέροντο.

¹ Though the text is corrupt, the allusion seems to refer
to the Harpalus affair. Several Athenian politicians were

is present; on the other hand, if valour should be left to itself it is just a word, productive of no noble action. In time of war Fortune means victory; in time of peace, concord; at a marriage, goodwill; with lovers, enjoyment—in short, success in each and every undertaking.

When Fortune deserts a land, then that land is shaken and trembles and tosses the lovely things upon it in all directions—this too a disease of the earth, Fortune not being present. Again, as a ship moves aimlessly and founders quickly when deprived of a pilot, or as fortifications crumble when foundations are damaged, so a city goes to utter ruin for lack of Fortune. Athens once suffered wrong to its orators and Demosthenes was haled to prison,[1] all because Fortune no longer was watching over Athens. But, methinks, even the sky has Fortune, when it has clear weather instead of darkness.

But one should consider also the resourcefulness of the goddess. For example, there have been times when a man who had fallen overboard from a ship at sea was able to save his life because Fortune came to his aid. Moreover, what happened to Apelles the painter because of Fortune deserves recounting.[2] For, as the story goes, he was painting a horse—not a work-horse but a war-horse. Its neck was high and arched, its ears erect, its eyes fierce, like one come not from work but from war, with the spirit of the charge in their glance, and its feet were rising in the

suspected of embezzlement and Demosthenes was even lodged in prison.

[2] Apelles flourished in the time of Philip and Alexander. His fame as a painter was such that many stories gathered about his name; this particular story is recorded also by Sextus Empiricus, *Outlines of Pyrrhonism* 1. 28.

ψαύοντες ἀνὰ μέρος τῆς γῆς. καὶ ὁ ἡνίοχος ἐκράτει
τοῦ χαλινοῦ, τὸ πολεμικὸν σάλευμα τοῦ ἵππου ἀπὸ
5 ῥυτῆρος ἄγχων. ἅπαντα δὲ ἐχούσης τῆς εἰκόνος
ἐοικότα ἔλειπεν ἀφροῦ χρῶμα, οἷον ἂν γένοιτο
μιγέντος αἵματος καὶ ὑγροῦ κατὰ συνεχῆ μῖξιν,
διώκοντος μὲν τοῦ ἄσθματος τὸ ὑγρὸν τῶν στο-
μάτων, ἀφρίζοντος δὲ τῇ κοπῇ τοῦ πνεύματος, αἷμα
δὲ ἐπιρραινούσης τῷ ἀφρῷ τῆς ἐκ τοῦ χαλινοῦ
ὕβρεως. οὐ δὴ εὐπόρει γράφειν ἵππου ἀφρὸν
κεκμηκότος ἐν ἀγῶνι. ἀπορῶν δὲ ἐπὶ πλέον, τέλος
ἀπαλγήσας ἐνέσεισε περὶ τοὺς χαλινοὺς τῇ γραφῇ
τὴν σπογγιάν. πολλὰ δὲ αὕτη ἔχουσα χρώματα
ἐοικότα ἀφρῷ ἡμαγμένῳ ἐφήρμοσε τῇ γραφῇ[1] τὸ
χρῶμα. Ἀπελλῆς δὲ ἰδὼν ἐχάρη τῷ ἐν ἀπογνώσει
τύχης ἔργῳ καὶ ἐτέλεσεν οὐ διὰ τῆς τέχνης, ἀλλὰ
διὰ τῆς τύχης τὴν γραφήν.

6   Τί δὲ ἄλλο Ἡρακλέα μέγιστον ἐποίησεν; ἀλλὰ
γὰρ καὶ λέοντα ἄγξας ἔπνιξε καὶ πτηνὰ ζῷα ἐδίωξε
τοῦ ἀέρος, καὶ τοῦ ἕλους τὴν ὕδραν ἀφείλετο,
συντρίψας αὐτῆς τὰς κεφαλάς, καὶ οὐκ ἐφόβησεν
αὐτὸν ὁ περὶ τὸν Ἐρύμανθον κάπρος, ἀλλὰ καὶ ἐπὶ
τὴν ἑσπέραν ἦλθε καὶ τοῦ ἐκεῖ φυτοῦ τὸν καρπὸν
ἐκόμισε. Γηρυόνου δὲ τὰς βόας ἀφείλετο καλὰς
οὔσας, καὶ Διομήδη τὸν Θρᾷκα ἐνουθέτησεν ἵπποις
σῖτον διδόναι, μὴ ἀνθρώπους, ἐσθίειν, τάς τε Ἀμα-
ζόνας, ὅτι εἶεν γυναῖκες, ἤλεγξεν. ἅπαντα δὲ
ταῦτα ἔπραττεν ἑπομένης αὐτῷ τύχης.

---

[1] τῇ γραφῇ Reiske : τῆς γραφῆς.

---

[1] Our author has here listed eight of the famous " labours "
of Heracles. The remaining four were the capture of the
Cerynean hind, the cleaning of the Augean stables, the van-
quishing of the Cretan bull, and the theft of Cerberus.

air, touching the ground lightly one after the other. Moreover, the driver had a firm grip on the reins, throttling the martial gallop of the horse in mid-career. But though the picture had everything true to life, there was lacking a colour wherewith to depict froth such as there would be when blood and saliva have mixed in constant intermingling, the panting breath driving before it the moisture of the lips and forming froth because of laboured breathing, while the cruel bit spattered blood upon the froth. So, then, Apelles knew not how to represent froth of a horse wearied in action. But as he was more and more perplexed, finally in a fit of desperation he hurled his sponge at the painting, striking it near the bit. But the sponge, containing as it did many colours, which when taken together resembled bloody froth, fitted its colour to the painting. And at the sight Apelles was delighted by what Fortune had accomplished in his moment of despair and finished his painting, not through his art, but through the aid of Fortune.

Again, what else was it that made Heracles most mighty? Why, he not only throttled and choked to death a lion, pursued winged creatures of the air, ejected the Hydra from the swamp, crushing its heads, and refused to be frightened by the boar which haunted Erymanthus; he even journeyed to the West and bore away the fruit of the tree which grew there. Moreover, he carried off the cattle of Geryones, fine animals that they were, admonished Diomedes the Thracian to give his horses grain, not men, to eat, and proved the Amazons to be mere women.[1] But all these exploits he was able to accomplish because Fortune attended him.

7 Ἔχει δ' οὐ κακῶς οὐδὲ τὰ τῶν παλαιῶν αἰνίγ-
ματα περὶ αὐτήν. οἱ μὲν γὰρ ἐπὶ ξυροῦ ἔστησαν
αὐτήν, οἱ δὲ ἐπὶ σφαίρας, οἱ δὲ πηδάλιον ἔδωκαν
κρατεῖν· οἱ δὲ τὰ κρείττω γράφοντες τὸ τῆς Ἀμαλθείας ἔδοσαν κέρας πλῆρες καὶ βρύον ταῖς ὥραις,
ὃ ἐν μάχῃ Ἡρακλῆς Ἀχελῴου ἀπέρρηξεν. τὸ μὲν
οὖν ξυρὸν τὸ ἀπότομον τῆς εὐτυχίας μηνύει· ἡ δὲ
σφαῖρα ὅτι εὔκολος ἡ μεταβολὴ αὐτῆς ἐστιν· ἐν
κινήσει γὰρ τυγχάνει πάντοτε ὂν τὸ θεῖον. τὸ δὲ
πηδάλιον δηλοῖ ὅτι κυβερνᾷ τὸν τῶν ἀνθρώπων βίον
ἡ τύχη. τὸ δὲ τῆς Ἀμαλθείας κέρας μηνύει τὴν
τῶν ἀγαθῶν δόσιν τε καὶ εὐδαιμονίαν. μὴ ὀνομά-
ζωμεν οὖν κακήν τινα τύχην· οὐδὲ γὰρ τὴν ἀρετὴν
λέγει τις εἶναι κακὴν οὐδὲ τὸ ἀγαθὸν κακόν.

---

[1] The Greeks used the word *aenigmata* to denote that
which was not plainly stated but rather hinted.

[2] The " razor's edge " to denote fine balance is a figure
as old as Homer ; cf. *Iliad* 10. 173.

[3] According to Apollodorus, *Bibliotheca* 2. 7. 5, Heracles
fought with the river-god Acheloüs for the hand of Deïaneira.
Having broken off one of the horns of Acheloüs, who took

THE SIXTY-THIRD DISCOURSE

Moreover, the riddles [1] of the ancients in their representations of Fortune are not without merit. For instance, some have placed her on a razor's edge,[2] others on a sphere, others have given her a rudder to wield, while those who depict her most effectively have given her the horn of Amaltheia, full to overflowing with the fruits of the seasons, the horn which Heracles in battle broke off from Acheloüs.[3]   Now the razor's edge betokens the abruptness with which good fortune changes ; the sphere, that change of fortune is easy, for the divine power is, in fact, ever in motion ; the rudder indicates that Fortune directs the life of men ; and the horn of Amaltheia calls attention to the giving of good things and prosperity. Let us not, then, call any fortune evil ; for one does not say that virtue is evil, or that goodness is evil.

the form of a bull, Heracles restored it to him in exchange for the horn of Amaltheia, daughter of Haemonius, which had the power of bestowing abundant food and drink in answer to the prayer of him who possessed it.   Sophocles describes briefly but vividly the encounter with Acheloüs in his *Trachiniae* (504-530).

THE SIXTY-FOURTH DISCOURSE :
ON FORTUNE (II)

THIS laudation of the goddess Fortune, though longer than the foregoing, is hardly on a higher level. Arnim was doubtless correct in denying it a place among the genuine works of Dio. There is a monotony in its phrasing which one would be reluctant to associate with him, and also a certain indifference toward hiatus. But more objectionable still is a tedious parade of erudition, ranging all the way from the commonplaces of myth and history to points so obscure that one is tempted to ascribe them to the fertile imagination of the author. Was it his purpose to overawe with his learning a less erudite company ?

Where was his address delivered ? In §§ 12-17 he traces the ancestry of his hearers to Athens *via* Euboea. His account sounds a bit fanciful and the twofold migration from Athens is not found elsewhere in Greek tradition, so that it is impossible to identify with certainty the people to whom he is speaking. However, Strabo (5. 246) reports that, after the original settlement of Naples by citizens of Cumae, additional settlers later came from Athens. Furthermore, a Neapolitan coin of about the middle of the fifth century B.C. depicts Pallas wearing an olive crown, and at some time or other the name Phaleron came to be associated with Naples. Finally, the complimentary remarks regarding the city in which the address was being delivered seem to fit Naples better than any other likely possibility. It might seem surprising, however, that the Naples of the first century of our era should still cherish the memory of Athenian contributions to its parent stock. Possibly our Discourse was addressed to a select group of Neapolitans, who, however unintelligently, strove to keep alive traditions of ancient days.

46. ΠΕΡΙ ΤΥΧΗΣ ΔΕΥΤΕΡΟΣ

1 Τὰ γιγνόμενα παρὰ τῶν ἀνθρώπων εἰς τὴν τύχην
ἐγκλήματα μέγιστα ἂν ἔγωγε θείην ὑπὲρ αὐτῆς
ἐγκώμια. τὰς γοῦν ἀδήλους τῶν πραγμάτων μεταβολὰς εἰς ταύτην ἀναφέρουσι, καὶ οἷς ἀπὸ γνώμης
ἐπιχειρήσαντες διήμαρτον, τούτων ἀφῃρῆσθαι νομίζουσιν ὑπὸ[1] τῆς τύχης, ὡς πάντα περιποιεῖν, εἰ
θελήσαι, δυναμένης. ἀκούσαις δ' ἂν αἰτιωμένων
αὐτὴν καὶ γεωργῶν καὶ ἐμπόρων καὶ πλουσίων ἐπὶ
τοῖς χρήμασι καὶ καλῶν ἐπὶ τοῖς σώμασι καὶ
Πανθείας ἐπὶ τῷ ἀνδρὶ καὶ Κροίσου ἐπὶ τῷ παιδὶ
καὶ Ἀστυάγους ἡττηθέντος καὶ Πολυκράτους ἑα-
λωκότος. καὶ Πέρσαι δὲ ἐμέμφοντο τὴν τύχην
μετὰ τὴν Κύρου σφαγὴν καὶ Μακεδόνες μετὰ τὴν
Ἀλεξάνδρου τελευτήν.

2 Ἤδη δέ τινα καὶ τῶν ἰδίων παθῶν τῇ τύχῃ
προφέρουσιν, ἡ Μήδεια τὸν ἔρωτα, ὁ Μίδας τὴν

---

[1] ὑπὸ Reiske : ἀπό.

---

[1] Pantheia, wife of Abradatas, king of Susa, was taken
captive by Cyrus. Through her efforts Abradatas accepted
service with Cyrus and was slain fighting for him. Pantheia
committed suicide at his grave. Xenophon devotes much
space to the tale in his *Cyropaedeia* but he fails to note anywhere that Pantheia blamed Fortune.

[2] Warned in a dream, Croesus vainly tries to save his son
Atys ; cf. Herodotus 1. 34-35.

THE SIXTY-FOURTH DISCOURSE:
ON FORTUNE (II)

THE charges which men lay to the account of Fortune I would consider to be highest encomia in her favour. For example, the inscrutable vicissitudes in their affairs they ascribe to her, and whenever they unwisely set their hands to certain projects and meet with failure they imagine they have been robbed of their purposes by her, since, in their opinion, she could do any and every thing if she only would. Again, you may hear farmers, shippers, and men of wealth blaming her for their loss of money, dandies for their persons, Pantheia for her husband,[1] Croesus for his son,[2] Astyages for his defeat,[3] and Polycrates for his capture.[4] Moreover, the Persians blamed Fortune after the slaying of Cyrus,[5] as did the Macedonians after Alexander's death.

Furthermore, men even reproach Fortune for some of their own emotional weaknesses—Medea for her

[3] Learning that his daughter is fated to bear a son who will bring ruin on her father, Astyages tries to thwart fate, but to no avail, and he is dethroned by that son (Cyrus); cf. Herodotus 1. 107-130.

[4] Though warned by soothsayers, Polycrates, tyrant of Samos, is taken captive and crucified by the Persian Oroetes; cf. Herodotus 3. 120-125.

[5] Though warned in a dream, Cyrus is slain by Tomyris, the nomad queen; cf. Herodotus 1. 205-213.

εὐχήν, ἡ Φαίδρα τὴν διαβολήν, ὁ Ἀλκμαίων ὅτι
ἐπλανᾶτο, ὁ Ὀρέστης ὅτι ἐμαίνετο. ἐρῶ δὲ ὑμῖν
τινα καὶ Κύπριον λόγον, εἰ βούλεσθε. ἤνεγκεν ὁ
παλαιὸς βίος καὶ ἐνδόξους γυναῖκας, Ῥοδογούνην
πολεμικήν, Σεμίραμιν βασιλικήν, Σαπφὼ μουσικήν,
Τιμάνδραν καλήν· οὕτω καὶ ἐν Κύπρῳ Δημώνασσα
ἐγένετο, πολιτική τε ὁμοῦ γυνὴ καὶ νομοθετική.
3 τρεῖς ἔθηκεν αὐτὴ τοῖς Κυπρίοις νόμους· τὴν μοι-
χευθεῖσαν κειραμένην πορνεύεσθαι· θυγάτηρ αὐτῆς
ἐμοιχεύθη καὶ τὴν κόμην ἀπεκείρατο κατὰ τὸν
νόμον καὶ ἐπορνεύετο. τὸν αὐτὸν ἀποκτείναντα
ἄταφον ῥίπτεσθαι· δεύτερος οὗτος Δημονάσσης
νόμος· τρίτος ὥστε μὴ ἀποκτεῖναι βοῦν ἀρότριον.
δυοῖν δὲ αὐτῇ παίδων ἀρρένων ὄντων, ὁ μὲν ἐπὶ
τῷ βοῦν ἀποκτεῖναι ἀπέθανε· τὸν δὲ αὐτὸν ἀπο-
4 κτείναντα οὐκ ἔθαψεν. ἡ δὲ τέως μὲν ἐκαρτέρει
καὶ ἄπαις οὖσα καὶ νομοθετοῦσα, ἰδοῦσα δὲ βοῦν
ἐπὶ μόσχῳ ἀπολλυμένῳ μυκωμένην καὶ τὴν ἑαυτῆς
ἐν ἄλλῳ συμφορὰν γνωρίσασα, τήξασα χαλκὸν εἰς
αὐτὸν ἥλατο. καὶ ἦν ἐκεῖ πύργος ἀρχαῖος ἀνδριάντα χάλκεον ἔχων, χαλκῷ ἐντετηκότα καὶ πρὸς
ἀσφάλειαν τοῦ ἱδρύματος καὶ πρὸς μίμημα τοῦ

---

[1] Medea, in his tragedy of that name, is depicted by
Euripides as resentful for the evil results of her passion for
Jason but without remorse for her own misdeeds.

[2] Midas owed his ruin to his prayer that all that he might
touch should turn to gold.

[3] Instead of feeling shame because of her passion for her
stepson Hippolytus, Phaedra at her death leaves a false
accusation that causes his death too ; cf. Euripides' *Hippolytus.*

[4] Both Alcmaeon and Orestes were pursued by the Furies
for matricide. In Euripides' *Iphigeneia among the Taurians*
Orestes blames Apollo as the author of his crime.

passion,[1] Midas for his prayer,[2] Phaedra for her false accusation,[3] Alcmaeon for his wandering,[4] Orestes for his madness. But I will tell you also a certain Cyprian tale if you wish. The days of old produced women of distinction as well as men—Rhodogunê the warrior,[5] Semiramis the queen,[6] Sappho the poetess, Timandra the beauty [7] ; just so Cyprus too had its Demonassa,[8] a woman gifted in both statesmanship and law-giving. She gave the people of Cyprus the following three laws : a woman guilty of adultery shall have her hair cut off and be a harlot—her daughter became an adulteress, had her hair cut off according to the law, and practised harlotry ; whoever commits suicide shall be cast out without burial —this was the second law of Demonassa ; third, a law forbidding the slaughter of a plough-ox. Of the two sons which she had, the one met his death for having slain an ox, while the other, who slew himself, she refrained from burying. Now for a time she not only bore with fortitude the loss of her children but also persevered in her regulations ; but having observed a cow lowing in sorrow over a calf which was dying, and having recognized her own misfortune in the case of another, Demonassa melted bronze and leaped into the molten mass. And there used to be at that place an ancient tower holding a bronze image, an image embedded in bronze, both in order to insure the stability of the statue and also as a

[5] Daughter of Mithradates I and wife of Demetrius Nicator ; cf. Or. 21. 7.

[6] Semi-mythical queen of Assyria, frequently named as builder of the walls of Nineveh or Babylon.

[7] Probably the mistress of Alcibiades ; cf. Plutarch, *Alcibiades* 39.

[8] Nothing is known of Demonassa of Cyprus.

διηγήματος· ἐπιγραφὴ δὲ ἐπί τινος στήλης πλησίον,
σοφὴ μὲν ἤμην, ἀλλὰ πάντ' οὐκ εὐτυχής.

5 Φέρε οὖν μὴ ἐρήμην ἡ τύχη ἁλισκέσθω μηδὲ
φοβώμεθα τὸν τῶν κατηγορούντων θόρυβον. ἴσως
γὰρ ἄν τι ἡμῖν πρὸς τὸ εἰπεῖν εὖ καὶ αὐτὴ συλλάβοι.[1]
δοκοῦσιν οἱ τεχνῖται πρῶτον[2] τῷ τρόπῳ τῆς κατα-
σκευῆς τὴν δύναμιν αὐτῆς δεδηλωκέναι. πρῶτον
μὲν γὰρ ἕστηκεν ἑτοίμη πρὸς τὰ ἔργα, εἶτα τῇ μὲν
δεξιᾷ χειρὶ πηδάλιον κατέχει, καί, ὡς ἂν[3] εἴποι τις,
ναυτίλλεται. τί δὲ ἄρα τοῦτο ἦν; πότερον ὡς
μάλιστα τῶν πλεόντων τῆς τύχης δεομένων, ἢ διότι
τὸν βίον ἡμῶν ὥς τινα μεγάλην ναῦν κυβερνᾷ καὶ
πάντας σῴζει τοὺς ἐμπλέοντας; Ἀσσυρίους μέχρι
τῆς Σαρδαναπάλου τρυφῆς, Μήδους μέχρι τῆς
Κύρου τροφῆς,[4] Πέρσας μέχρι τῆς διαβάσεως,
Ἀθηναίους μέχρι τῆς ἁλώσεως, Κροῖσον μέχρι
Σόλωνος;

6   ἦν Οἰδίπους τὸ πρῶτον εὐτυχὴς ἀνήρ.

ἡ τύχη γὰρ αὐτῷ τὸ μηδὲν παθεῖν περιποιουμένη[5]
τὸ ἀγνοεῖν ἔδωκεν, ὅπερ ὅμοιον ἦν τῷ μὴ παθεῖν.
εἶτα ἅμα τῆς εὐτυχίας ἐπαύσατο καὶ τοῦ γιγνώσκειν ἤρξατο. ἐγὼ δὲ[6] καὶ τὴν ἐκείνου πήρωσιν
εὐτυχίαν καλῶ. Τέλλος[7] μὲν γὰρ βλεπέτω τοὺς

---

[1] After συλλάβοι Arnim suspects a lacuna.
[2] πρῶτον deleted by Emperius.
[3] ἂν added by Emperius.
[4] τροφῆς] ἀρχῆς Dindorf.
[5] περιποιουμένη PH : περιποιησαμένη UBM.
[6] δὲ added by Arnim.
[7] Τέλλος Casaubon : τέλος or πέλλος.

---

[1] Nauck, *T.G.F.*, adesp. 124.
[2] Cf. Or. 63. 7.   [3] Cf. Or. 62. 5-6.

representation of the story ; and near-by on a tablet there was an inscription :

Wise was I, yet in everything ill-starred.[1]

Well then, let not Fortune be condemned unheard, and let us not fear the clamour of those who accuse her. For perhaps even she herself might aid us somewhat in speaking well of her. In the first place, the artists are believed to have revealed her power by the way they have equipped her. For, to begin with, she stands ready for her tasks ; secondly, in her right hand she holds a rudder and, as one might say, she is sailing a ship. But why, then, was this ? Was it in the belief that sailors more than others need Fortune, or was it because she steers our lives like some great ship [2] and preserves all on board—the Assyrians until the wanton luxury of Sardanapalus [3] ; the Medes until the rearing of Cyrus ; the Persians until they crossed the sea [4] ; the Athenians until their capture [5] ; Croesus until the visit of Solon ? [6]

At first a fortunate man was Oedipus.[7]

Yes, for Fortune, trying to provide freedom from suffering, granted him ignorance, which was tantamount to freedom from suffering. Then at one and the same time he reached the end of his good fortune and began to understand. For my part I call even his blindness good fortune.[8] For let Tellus behold

---

[4] To invade Greece.

[5] At the close of the Peloponnesian War.

[6] One of the most famous tales in Herodotus (1. 29-33).

[7] Nauck, *T.G.F.*, Euripides, frag. 157.

[8] In the *Oedipus Rex* of Sophocles, at first self-confident and happy, on learning that he has slain his father and married his mother, Oedipus puts out his eyes ; cf. especially verses 1369-1383.

παῖδας καὶ Κυδίππη καὶ Αἴολος καὶ εἴ τις ἄλλος ἦν
πατὴρ εὐτυχής· Οἰδίπους δὲ ἐκ τῆς πηρώσεως
αἰσχρὰ κερδανεῖ θεάματα.

7 Τῇ δὲ ἑτέρᾳ τῶν χειρῶν ἡ θεὸς καρποὺς ἑτοί-
μους κατέχει συνειλεγμένους, μηνύουσα τὸ πλῆθος
τῶν ἀγαθῶν ἅπερ αὐτὴ δίδωσιν. τοῦτο ἦν ἄρα καὶ
χρυσοῦν γένος καὶ νῆσοι μακάρων τινές, αὐτομάτας
ἔχουσαι τροφάς, καὶ Ἡρακλέους κέρας καὶ Κυ-
κλώπων βίος, ὅτι τοῖς πονήσασι τὸν βίον[1] αὐτο-
μάτη λοιπὸν ἡ τῶν ἀγαθῶν ἀφθονία παραγίγνεται.
Τάνταλος δὲ ἄρα ἐπὶ γήρως ἀργὸς ἦν[2]· διὰ τοῦτο
ἄρα μέχρι τῶν χειλῶν ηὐδαιμόνει καὶ τοῖς ὀφθαλ-
μοῖς μόνον ηὐτύχει· τὰ πάντα δὲ ἐκεῖνα ἁρπασθέντα
οἴχεται καὶ λίμνη καὶ καρποὶ καὶ τροφὴ καὶ ποτὸν
ὑπὸ τῆς τύχης, οὕτω γ' ὡς ὑπὸ πνεύματος.

8 Ὠνόμασται δὲ ἡ τύχη καὶ πολλοῖς τισιν ἐν ἀνθρώποις ὀνόμασι, τὸ μὲν ἴσον αὐτῆς νέμεσις, τὸ δὲ
ἄδηλον ἐλπίς, τὸ δὲ ἀναγκαῖον μοῖρα, τὸ δὲ δίκαιον
θέμις, πολυώνυμός τις ὡς ἀληθῶς θεὸς καὶ πολύ-
τροπος. ταύτῃ ἐπέθεσαν καὶ γεωργοὶ Δήμητρος
ὄνομα καὶ ποιμένες Πανὸς καὶ ναῦται Λευκοθέας
καὶ κυβερνῆται Διοσκόρων.

---

[1] After βίον Arnim deletes ἐπὶ τῆς δεξιᾶς χειρὸς δεδήλωκεν,
ὡς.
[2] Τάνταλος . . . ἦν suspected by Arnim.

---

[1] See Herodotus 1. 30.
[2] Argive priestess whose sons, Cleobis and Biton, were
rewarded for their piety by the gift of painless death ; cf.
Herodotus 1. 31. Their archaic statues may be seen at
Delphi.
[3] Aeolus had six sons and six daughters, each of whom
enjoyed a happy wedded life ; cf. *Odyssey* 10. 2-12.

his children,[1] and Cydippê,[2] and Aeolus,[3] and whoever else may have been fortunate as a parent ; yet by his blindness Oedipus

Will gain escape from shameful sights.[4]

And, to resume, in her other hand the goddess holds fruits plucked and ready for use, indicating the multitude of good things she herself provides—this, you see, would be both Golden Age and Isles of the Blest, as it were, with foods for the taking, and Horn of Heracles,[5] and life of the Cyclopes [6] all in one, since to those who have toiled for their living an abundance of good things comes thereafter spontaneously. But Tantalus, you know, was idle in old age ; on that account, therefore, he was prosperous only as far as his lips, fortunate only with his eyes, while all those things he longed for—lake, fruits, food, and drink—vanished, snatched away by Fortune as by a blast of wind.[7]

Again, Fortune has been given many names among men. Her impartiality has been named Nemesis or Retributive Justice ; her obscurity, Elpis or Hope ; her inevitability, Moira or Fate ; her righteousness, Themis or Law—truly a deity of many names and many ways. Farmers have given her the name Demeter ; shepherds Pan ; sailors Leucothea ; pilots Dioscuri.[8]

---

[4] Nauck, *T.G.F.*, adesp. 125.

[5] Called the Horn of Amaltheia in Or. 63. 7.

[6] For the carefree life of the Cyclopes see *Odyssey* 9. 106-111.

[7] According to Apollodorus (epitome 2. 1), Tantalus, mythical king of Phrygia, was punished for presumption, not for idleness.

[8] Tutelary deities of these respective callings.

ῥεῖα δ' ἀρίζηλον μινύθει καὶ ἄδηλον ἀέξει,
ῥεῖα δέ τ' ἰθύνει σκολιὸν καὶ ἀγήνορα κάρφει.

9 τοῦτο ἄρα ἦν ὁ Ζεύς,[1] κατέχων μὲν ἐπὶ τῆς δεξιᾶς
τὸ ὅπλον, ἐπὶ δὲ τῆς ἀριστερᾶς τὸ σκῆπτρον, ὅτι
τοῖς πολεμικοῖς τῶν ἀνθρώπων καὶ βασιλείαν δίδωσιν.

Εἶτα Εὐριπίδης τὸν ναύτην μέμφεται

ἀωρὶ πόντου κύματ' εὐρέος περῶντα·

καὶ διὰ τῶν ἑξῆς ἐπιτιμᾷ λέγων ὅτι

σμικραῖς ἐπιτρέπουσιν αὑτοὺς ἐλπίσιν.

10 ὦ παῖ Μνησαρχίδον, ποιητὴς μὲν[2] ἦσθα, σοφὸς δὲ
οὐδαμῶς. οὔτε γὰρ πίττῃ[3] τὴν ψυχὴν οὔτε σχοι-
νίοις ἐπιτρέπουσιν οὐδὲ[4] τριδάκτυλον αὐτοὺς σῴζει
ξύλον πεύκινον, ἀλλ' ἐπέτρεψαν βεβαίῳ καὶ μεγάλῳ
πράγματι, τῇ τύχῃ. ἀσθενὲς μὲν πλοῦτος, ἂν τύχη
μὴ παρῇ, ἀβέβαιον δὲ φιλία μὴ συλλαμβανούσης
τύχης. αὕτη σῴζει καὶ τὸν νοσοῦντα ἐν τῷ τέλει[5]
καὶ τὸν νηχόμενον ἐν τῇ θαλάσσῃ καὶ τὸν Ἀγαμέμνονα ἐπὶ τῶν χιλίων νεῶν καὶ τὸν Ὀδυσσέα ἐπὶ
11 τῆς σχεδίας φερόμενον. τί δέδοικας, ὦ δειλέ; τὸ
μῆκος τῆς θαλάσσης φοβῇ; ὄψεται μέν σε ὁ
Ποσειδῶν καὶ παρακαλέσει τοὺς ἀνέμους καὶ τὴν
τρίαιναν λήψεται καὶ πάσας ὀροθυνεῖ τὰς ἀέλλας,
οὐκ ἀποκτενεῖ δὲ σέ· ἡ τύχη γὰρ οὐ βούλεται.

---

[1] After Ζεύς Arnim deletes ἡ τύχη.
[2] μὲν Valckenaer : μὲν μόνον or μόνον.
[3] οὔτε γὰρ πίττῃ Emperius: οὐδὲ γὰρ πίττῃ UB, οὐδ' ἐπίστη
PH, οὐδ' ἐπιστήμων M.

THE SIXTY-FOURTH DISCOURSE

With ease the eminent he curbs, the meek
Exalts, makes straight the crooked, blasts the
    proud.[1]

This refers, of course, to Zeus, holding in his right
hand his weapon[2] and in his left his sceptre, for the
reason that to martial men he gives kingship too.

    Furthermore, Euripides censures the sailor

Untimely seeking to cross the broad sea's waves[3];

he also utters reproof in the following, when he says

    To slender hopes do they entrust themselves.

O son of Mnesarchides,[4] you were a poet, to be sure,
yet not at all wise! For they entrust their lives
to neither pitch nor ropes, nor is it a two-inch plank
of pine that keeps them safe; nay, they entrust
them to a sure and mighty thing, Fortune. A weak
thing is wealth unless accompanied by Fortune; an
uncertain thing is friendship unless Fortune bears a
hand. She preserves alike the sick man in his extremity, the swimmer amidst the waves, Agamemnon
sailing with his thousand ships, and Odysseus drifting
on his raft. What dost thou fear, thou craven?
Dost fear the vastness of the sea? Poseidon, indeed,
will spy thee, summon his winds, seize his trident,
and stir up all the blasts; yet he will not slay thee,
for Fortune wills it not.

---

[1] Hesiod, *Works and Days* 6-7.
[2] The thunderbolt. Zeus is here viewed as a form of
Fortune.
[3] For this and the following verse see Nauck, *T.G.F.*,
Euripides, frag. 921.
[4] The reference is to Euripides.

---

    [4] οὐδὲ Crosby : οὔτε.
    [5] τέλει] λέχει Casaubon.

οὕτως νῦν κακὰ πολλὰ παθὼν ἀλόω κατὰ πόντον,
εἰσόκεν ἀνθρώποισι διοτρεφέεσσι μιγείης.

θεοῦ λόγος ὑπὸ τύχης νενικημένου.

12 Αὕτη καὶ τὸ[1] τῶν ὑμετέρων προγόνων[2] ἀρχαῖον
γένος, τῶν αὐτοχθόνων καὶ πρώτων Ἀθηναίων,
μητέρα μὲν τὴν γῆν αὐχοῦντας,[3] τροφὸν δὲ τὴν
Δήμητραν, ἐπώνυμον δὲ καὶ σύμμαχον τὴν Ἀθηνᾶν, τὸ μὲν[4] πρῶτον τῶν Ἀθηνῶν εἰς Εὔβοιαν
ἐξήγαγεν· ὡς δ'[5] ἐκεῖ μένοντας αὐτοὺς οὔτε ἡ
θάλασσα τέρπειν οὔτε ἡ γῆ τρέφειν ἐδύνατο, καὶ
οὐδὲ τὸ αἰσχρὸν ἔφερον τοῦ πράγματος, ἀντ' ἠπει-
ρωτῶν νησιῶται γενόμενοι, δεύτερον ἡ τύχη κρεῖσ-
13 σον ἐβουλεύσατο. σεμνὴ μὲν γὰρ Εὔβοια ὡς
ἀληθῶς· ἀλλὰ τίς ὑμῶν[6] φέρειν ἠδύνατο γῆν[7] τρα-
χεῖαν κατοικῶν ἢ θαλάσσῃ στενῇ παροικῶν καὶ
πολλὰς ἀνεχόμενος τῶν πραγμάτων μεταβολάς,
τῶν ἐν τῷ ῥεύματι γιγνομένων πλείονας; νῦν
Βοιωτοὺς ἔδει φέρειν καὶ τὴν Θηβαίων ἀναισθησίαν,
εἶτα Ἀθηναίους, οὐκέτι ὡς παισὶν ὑμῖν, ἀλλ' ὡς
δούλοις χρωμένους. διὰ τοῦτο ἀγαγοῦσα ἐνθάδε
ἵδρυσε, τῇ ἑτέρᾳ μὲν[8] τῶν χειρῶν μηχανωμένη τε
τὸν πλοῦν καὶ κατιθύνουσα, τῇ[9] δὲ τοὺς καρποὺς
ἀφθόνως διδοῦσά τε καὶ δωρουμένη.

---

[1] Αὕτη καὶ τὸ Emperius: αὐτηι· τούτων καὶ UB, αὕτη τούτων
καὶ MP, αὐτῇ τούτων καὶ H.
[2] After προγόνων Emperius deletes ἦν.
[3] αὐχοῦντας] αὐχοῦν or αὐχούντων Reiske.
[4] After μὲν Emperius deletes γάρ.   [5] ὡς δ' Selden : ὥστ'.
[6] ὑμῶν Emperius : ἡμῶν.   [7] γῆν Reiske : τήν.
[8] ἵδρυσε, τῇ ἑτέρᾳ μὲν Jacobs : ἵδρυσε τεταμένων.
[9] τῇ Valesius : τῆς.

---

[1] *Odyssey* 5. 377-378; spoken by Poseidon to Odysseus
after the loss of his raft.

THE SIXTY-FOURTH DISCOURSE

Thus do thou wander now upon the deep,
With many an evil mischance, till the day
When thou dost meet with men beloved of Zeus.[1]

An utterance of a god vanquished by Fortune !

What is more, the ancient stock of your ancestors, those autochthonous and earliest Athenians who boasted the soil as mother, Demeter as nurse, and Athena as namesake and ally, Fortune first led forth from Athens to Euboea ; but since if they remained there the sea could not please them nor the land support, and since also they could not endure the disgrace of what had happened, their having turned islanders instead of occupants of the mainland, Fortune made a second and a better plan. For though Euboea is truly a venerable island, still who among you ever was able to endure dwelling in a rugged land,[2] or being neighbour to narrow waters and subjected to many shifts of condition, more numerous than the shifts of current in the strait ?[3] At one moment you must needs endure the Boeotians and the stupidity of the Thebans,[4] and the next it was the Athenians, who treated you no longer as sons, but rather as slaves. So it came to pass that the goddess took and established you here,[5] with one of her hands contriving and directing the voyage, and with the other abundantly providing and bestowing her fruits.

[2] Euboea is conspicuous for its lofty mountains, yet it afforded good pasturage for Athenian cattle.

[3] The Euripus, which separates Euboea from the mainland, is so narrow that it was bridged even in antiquity. Its current is very swift and changes direction frequently.

[4] Theban stupidity was a byword with Attic writers. Chalcis, which led in the founding of Cumae, the forerunner of Naples, faced Boeotia across the Euripus.

[5] Presumably Naples ; cf. Introduction.

Τὴν μὲν οὖν τῶν λοιπῶν γνώμην εἰκάσαι χαλεπόν
14 ἐστιν. ἐγὼ δέ, ὦ τύχη· πρὸς σὲ γὰρ δικαίως ἂν
ἴσως ῥηθείη ὁ λόγος· εἴ μέ τις ὑψηλὸν ἄρας ἄγοι[1]
μετέωρον ἐπί τινων ἢ Πηγάσου νώτων ἢ Πέλοπος
πτηνῶν[2] ἁρμάτων ὑποτείνων[3] τὴν γῆν ἅπασαν καὶ
τὰς πόλεις, οὐκ ἂν τὴν Λυδῶν ἑλοίμην τρυφὴν οὔτ'
εὐτέλειαν τὴν Ἀττικὴν οὔτε πενίαν τὴν[4] Λακωνι-
κὴν οὔτε Κρότωνα[5] οὔτε Σύβαριν, ὅτι οὐ πονοῦσιν,
οὔτε Σκύθας, ὅτι οὐ γεωργοῦσιν, οὔτε Αἰγυπτίους,
ὅτι ἄλλοις γεωργοῦσιν·

15 καὶ Λιβύην, ὅθι τ' ἄρνες ἄφαρ κεραοὶ τελέθουσιν·
εὐτυχία ποιμένων. οὐ Θήβας Αἰγυπτίας,
  αἵθ' ἑκατόμπυλοί εἰσι, διηκόσιοι δ' ἀν' ἑκάστην
  ἀνέρες ἐξοιχνεῦσι σὺν ἵπποισιν καὶ ὄχεσφιν·
ἱπποκόμων βίος καὶ πυλωρῶν.

Δήλῳ δή ποτε τοῖον Ἀπόλλωνος παρὰ βωμῷ·
οὐκ ἀρκεῖ μοι βωμὸς θύειν οὐκ ἔχοντι, οὐκ ἀρκεῖ
μοι φυτὰ τρέφειν με μὴ δυνάμενα.

  τρηχεῖ', ἀλλ' ἀγαθὴ κουροτρόφος·
οὔτε τραχεῖα αὕτη καὶ κουροτρόφος·

---

[1] ἄγοι Arnim : ἄνω. [2] πτηνῶν deleted by Jacobs.
[3] ὑποτείνων Emperius, ὑποκλίνων Jacobs : ὑποκινῶν.
[4] τὴν added by Dindorf.
[5] After Κρότωνα Dindorf deletes πένονται γάρ.

---

[1] The horses were winged. Pelops' horses were so depicted on the Chest of Cypselus ; cf. Pausanias 5. 17. 7.
[2] Pericles boasted φιλοκαλοῦμέν τε γὰρ μετ' εὐτελείας (Thucydides 2. 40).
[3] Croton and Sybaris typify ancient wealth. Croton
decayed after the Second Punic War and Sybaris was wiped
out in 510 B.C. [4] They were nomads.

Now the idea in what yet remains to say it is difficult to portray. But as for me, O Mistress Fortune —for to thee, no doubt, my words would justly be addressed—if some one should raise me aloft and transport me through the sky, either, as it were, on the back of some Pegasus or in some winged car of Pelops,[1] offering me the whole earth and its cities, neither would I choose the luxury of Lydia or the thrift of Attica [2] or the meagre living of Laconia, nor would I choose Croton or Sybaris,[3] because they do not toil, or the Scythians, because they do not farm,[4] or the Egyptians, because they farm for others,[5]

And Libya, where the lambs have horns at birth [6]—

a shepherd's heaven! No, I would not choose Egyptian Thebes,

> Which hath a hundred gates, and at each one
> Two hundred men go forth with chariots and
> steeds [7]—

a life for grooms and gate-keepers!

> In Delos such a tree I once did see
> Beside Apollo's altar [8]—

an altar does not satisfy my wants, since I have naught to sacrifice thereon ; no more do trees, if they afford no food.

> 'Tis rugged, yet a goodly nurse of youth [9]—

this land [10] not only is not rugged but a nurse of youth besides.

[5] Egypt was the granary of the Mediterranean world.
[6] *Odyssey* 4. 85.   [7] *Iliad* 9. 383-384.
[8] *Odyssey* 6. 162. Odysseus is about to speak of the palm tree sacred to Apollo. Dates do not ripen so far north.
[9] *Ibid.* 9. 27 ; Odysseus' tribute to his native Ithaca.
[10] Naples ; see Introduction.

16   δέσποιν' ἁπασῶν¹ πότνι' 'Αθηναίων πόλι·

μὴ λέγε, ἄνθρωπε. οὐκέτ' εἰσὶν ἐκεῖνοι δεσπόται.

ὡς καὶ καλόν σου φαίνεται τὸ νεώριον.

ἀλλὰ μεθ' Ἑλλήσποντον καὶ Λύσανδρον αἰσχρόν.

—καλὸς δ'² ὁ Πειραιεύς·

ἔτι γὰρ μετὰ τῶν τειχῶν αὐτὸν βλέπεις.

    ἄλση δὲ τίς πω τοιάδ' ἔσχ' ἄλλη πόλις ;³

εἶχε μέν, δῃωθεῖσα⁴ δὲ ὡς ἐπὶ συμφοραῖς γυνὴ⁵
ἀπεκείρατο.

    καὶ τοὐρανοῦ γ', ὥς⁶ φασιν, ἐστὶν ἐν καλῷ.

καὶ πῶς, οἵ γε λοιμώττουσι⁷ καὶ νοσοῦσι καὶ⁸ πλέον
αὐτῶν ἀπόλλυται μέρος ὑπὸ τῶν ἀέρων ἢ τῶν
πολεμίων;

17 Καὶ μή τις ἀχθέσθω διότι οὕτως τῶν πατέρων
ἐμνημόνευσα. τῶν μὲν γὰρ πρωτείων οὐκ ἂν⁹
ἄλλως τύχοιμεν μὴ τοῖς πρώτοις ἁμιλλώμενοι.
ἀλλὰ καὶ παλαιός τις στρατιώτης ὡς γεγονὼς τοῦ
πατρὸς κρείσσων ἐσεμνύνετο, καὶ οὐδὲ 'Αθηναίοις
αἰσχρὸν πατράσιν οὖσιν ὑπὸ τῶν παίδων ἡττω-
μένοις. τῆς γὰρ ὑμετέρας μεθέξουσιν ἀρετῆς κατὰ
τὴν αὐτῶν ἐλαττούμενοι. πῶς οὖν οὐκ ἂν εἰδείητε

---

¹ δέσποιν' ἁπασῶν Meineke : δέσποινα δ' ἁπασῶν or δέσποινα
δ' ἁπασῶν ποι or δέσποινα δ' ἁπασῶν πόλεων.
² δ' Valckenaer : δὲ.   ³ πόλις Porson : γυνή.
⁴ δῃωθεῖσα Valckenaer : δὴ σωθεῖσα.
⁵ γυνὴ added by Dindorf.
⁶ γ', ὥς Reiske : πῶς or πως.
⁷ λοιμώττουσι Dindorf : λιμώττουσι.
⁸ After καὶ Arnim deletes τό.   ⁹ ἂν added by Emperius.

---

¹ Kock, *C.A.F.*, adesp. 340. It has been suggested that
this and the next four verses are from the *Demes* of Eupolis.

THE SIXTY-FOURTH DISCOURSE

O Athens, august mistress of them all ! [1]

Say not so, fellow : those Athenians no more are masters.

How beauteous too thy shipyard is to view.

Nay, rather say ugly, after the Hellespont and Lysander.[2]

Peiraeus is a lovely sight.[3]

Yes, for your mind's eye still sees it with its walls.[4]

What other city yet obtained such groves ! [5]

It did have, yes, but it was ravaged and, like a woman in her mourning, it had its tresses shorn.

For climate, so they say, 'tis nobly set.

Indeed ! how so, since they are subject to plague and sickness, and more of them are slain by their climate than by the foe ? [6]

Now let no one be vexed that I speak thus of his forebears. For we could not attain first rank in any other way than by competing with those who are first. Why, not only did a certain warrior of old take pride in having proved superior to his sire,[7] but even for the Athenians it is no disgrace, ancestors of ours though they be, to be outstript by their sons. For they will share your merit while being surpassed in their own. How, then, could you help being grate-

---

[2] Spartan Lysander destroyed the Athenian navy at Aegospotami.
[3] The first part of the verse read ὡς καλὸς ὁ Παρθενών, *How beautiful the Parthenon.*
[4] The walls were torn down after the Peloponnesian War.
[5] Kock, *ad loc. cit.*, refers this specially to the Academy.
[6] Possibly an allusion to the plague of 430 B.C. ; cf. Thucydides 2. 47-52.
[7] Sthenelus son of Capaneus ; cf. *Iliad* 4. 405-410.

τούτων ἁπάντων τῇ τύχῃ τὴν χάριν καὶ τοῦ γένους, ὅτι Ἕλληνες,[1] καὶ τῆς μεταβολῆς, ὅτι ἐκ
πενήτων εὐδαίμονες;[2] Σωκράτης γοῦν ἐπὶ πολλοῖς αὐτὸν ἐμακάριζε, καὶ ὅτι ζῷον λογικὸν καὶ
18 ὅτι Ἀθηναῖος.[3] Διογένης δὲ ὁ κύων ἀγροίκως καὶ
τέλεον οὐ πολιτικῶς ηὔχει κατὰ[4] τῆς τύχης, ὡς[5]
πολλὰ μὲν βέλη ἐφιείσης αὐτῷ ὡς σκοπῷ, τυχεῖν
δὲ μὴ δυναμένης. οὐ φέρω θρασυνόμενον οὕτω
φιλόσοφον. μὴ καταψεύδου τῆς τύχης· οὐ τοξεύει
γάρ σε, ὅτι οὐ βούλεται· θελούσῃ δὲ τῇ τύχῃ πανταχοῦ ῥᾴδιον. καὶ τὰ μὲν σύντομα ἐκεῖνα οὐ λέγω
τὰ Λακωνικά, τοὺς δουλεύοντας Πέρσαις καὶ τὸν ἐν
Κορίνθῳ Διονύσιον καὶ τὴν Σωκράτους καταδίκην
καὶ τὴν Ξενοφῶντος φυγὴν καὶ τὸν Φερεκύδους
θάνατον καὶ τὴν εὐδαιμονίαν[6] τὴν Ἀναξάρχου·[7]
ἀλλ' αὐτοῦ τούτου τοῦ χαλεποῦ σκοποῦ πόσοις
ἔτυχε τοξεύμασιν; φυγάδα σε ἐποίησεν, εἰς Ἀθήνας ἤγαγεν, Ἀντισθένει προυξένησεν, εἰς Κρήτην
ἐπώλησεν. εἰ δέ σοι τὸν τῦφον[8] βακτηρία καὶ
πήρα περιτίθησι καὶ λεπτὸς καὶ ἀφελὴς βίος, ἴσθι

---

[1] τοῦ γένους, ὅτι Ἕλληνες Casaubon : τοῦ γένους ὁ πελληνεύς
(or παλληνεύς).
[2] εὐδαίμονες Emperius : εὐδαιμόνησε.
[3] After Ἀθηναῖος Arnim suspects a lacuna.
[4] ηὔχει κατὰ Dindorf, εὔχετο κατὰ Emperius : εὐτύχει καίτοι.
[5] ὡς added by Emperius.
[6] εὐδαιμονίαν] δυσδαιμονίαν Reiske.
[7] Ἀναξάρχου Reiske : Ἀναξάνδρου.
[8] εἰ δέ σοι τὸν τῦφον Emperius : εἰ δὲ οἷον τυφλὸν UBP, εἰ
δέοι τὸν τυφλὸν M, εἰ δὲ οἷον τὸν τυφλὸν H.

---

[1] These phrases were doubtless hackneyed illustrations
of Fortune's unfairness. On " Dionysius at Corinth " cf.

ful to Fortune for all this—both for parentage, in
that you are Greek, and for your changed condition,
in that, though once poor, you now are prosperous?
Socrates, at any rate, counted himself fortunate for
many reasons—not only because he was a rational
being, but also because he was an Athenian. Diogenes the Cynic, on the other hand, with boorishness and downright discourtesy was wont to rail
at Fortune, claiming that, though she shot many
shafts with him as her target, she could not hit
him. I cannot endure a philosopher's behaving so
brazenly. Do not lie about Fortune, Diogenes, for
the reason why she does not shoot you is that she
has no wish to do so; on the contrary, if Fortune
did wish it, she could easily hit you wherever you
might be. While I do not use those " pithy laconic
expressions "—slaves to the Persians, Dionysius at
Corinth, Socrates' condemnation, Xenophon's exile,
Pherecydes' death, luck of Anaxarchus [1]—still, let
me ask you, with how many shafts has she hit this
difficult mark itself? [2] She made you an exile;
she brought you to Athens; she introduced you to
Antisthenes [3]; she sold you into Crete. But if staff
and wallet and a meagre, simple mode of living serve
you as a cloak of affectation, you have Fortune

Or. 37. 19. Xenophon was exiled for his association with
Cyrus, who had favoured Sparta in the Peloponnesian War;
cf. *Anabasis* 3. 1. 5. Plutarch (*Pelopidas* 21) says of this
Pherecydes that he was slain by the Spartans in accordance
with an oracle and thereafter his skin was carefully guarded
by the Spartan kings. Anaxarchus of Abdera, a Democri-
tean philosopher, favoured by Alexander the great, won the
sobriquet εὐδαιμονικός, but later he suffered the tragic end
referred to in Or. 37. 45.

[2] Diogenes.
[3] Pupil of Socrates and founder of the Cynic School.

καὶ τούτων τῇ τύχῃ τὴν χάριν· κατὰ τύχην γὰρ
φιλοσοφεῖς.

19 Ἦν δὲ καὶ Τιμόθεος Ἀθηναίων στρατηγός, ὃς
πάντα εὐτύχει καὶ σκωπτόμενος οὐκ ἠνείχετο, καί
ποτέ τι καὶ κατὰ τῆς τύχης ἐθρασύνετο καὶ πάλιν
δυστυχεῖν ἤρξατο. τίς ἄν ποτε ἤλπισεν Ἰνδῶν
ἄρξειν κουρέα,[1] Λυδῶν βασιλεύσειν ποιμένα, τῆς
Ἀσίας ἡγεμονεύσειν γυναῖκα; ὅτι τὸν Ἡρακλέα
ἀποκτενεῖ χιτὼν καὶ γυνή, ὅτι τὸν Ἀλέξανδρον
δοῦλος[2] καὶ κύλιξ; ἔχει γὰρ ἐν αὐτῇ πλεῖστον ἀεὶ
τὸ βασιλικόν,[3] καὶ τοὺς παρὰ φύσιν δ᾿ ἐπαιρομένους
καθαιρεῖ. πολλὰ γοῦν Ἀλέξανδρος τολμηρὰ ἔπρασ-
20 σεν—οὐκ ἔφερεν υἱὸς Φιλίππου λεγόμενος, τοῦ
Διὸς κατεψεύδετο, τῶν Διοσκόρων κατεφρόνει, τὸν
Διόνυσον ἐλοιδόρει, καίτοι γε ἀφθόνως οὕτως αὐτοῦ τοῖς δώροις χρώμενος. ἀπέκτεινε δὲ καὶ
Κλεῖτον τὸν σωτῆρα[4] καὶ Φιλώταν τὸν καλὸν καὶ
τὸν γέροντα[5] Παρμενίωνα καὶ τὸν διδάσκαλον
Καλλισθένην καὶ Ἀριστοτέλην ἐμέλλησε καὶ Ἀν-
τίπατρον ἐβουλεύσατο. τοιγαροῦν ζῶντα αὐτὸν

---

[1] κουρέα Valesius : οὐρέα or ὀρέα.
[2] δοῦλος] Ἰόλας Casaubon.
[3] πλεῖστον ἀεὶ τὸ βασιλικόν] πλεῖον κῦρος ἀεὶ τοῦ βασιλικοῦ
Arnim.
[4] σωτῆρα Capps : σοφὸν.
[5] γέροντα Valesius : γείτονα.

---

[1] Famous Athenian of the fourth century B.C. Maligned
by a colleague, he fled to Euboea, where he died shortly after.
[2] Angrammes. Quintus Curtius (9. 2. 6-7) calls him son
of a barber.
[3] Gyges ; cf. Plato, *Republic* 359 c—360 B.
[4] Semiramis.
[5] The story is told by Sophocles in his *Trachiniae* ; cf.
Or. 60.

to thank even for these things, for it is by grace of Fortune that you practise philosophy.

Again, there was once an Athenian general, Timotheüs,[1] who was fortunate in everything and could not stand being made the butt of jokes ; and one day he committed some act of effrontery against Fortune, and in turn he began to be unfortunate. Who would ever have expected that a barber would become ruler of the Indians[2] ; that a shepherd would become king of the Lydians[3] ; that a woman would become leader of Asia[4] ; that a tunic and a woman would cause the death of Heracles[5] ; that a slave and a goblet would cause the death of Alexander ?[6] The explanation is that Fortune has within herself the essence of royalty ever in fullest measure, and she destroys those who exalt themselves unduly. For instance, Alexander did many daring things— he could not stand being called the son of Philip ; he lied about Zeus[7] ; he scorned the Dioscuri ; he abused Dionysus, though indulging so lavishly in that god's gifts. Moreover, he slew his saviour Cleitus, the handsome Philotas, the aged Parmenion, his teacher Callisthenes ; he aimed to slay Aristotle and had planned the death of Antipater.[8] Therefore

---

[6] Plutarch (*Alexander* 76-77) says he died of a fever, not of poison.

[7] Olympias is said to have told him that Zeus was his father, and the priest of Ammon hailed him as *paidios*, either " son of Zeus," παῖ Διός, or an Egyptian blunder for *paidion*, " son." On at least one occasion he is said to have resented doubts as to Philip's fatherhood.

[8] Cleitus, Philotas, and Parmenion were his generals. Plutarch reports their murder and that of Callisthenes, but he is less clear as to Alexander's plans concerning Aristotle and Antipater, the aged Macedonian whom he had left in charge of European affairs.

21 ὁμολογεῖν ἠνάγκασεν ὅτι ἄνθρωπος ἦν. τρωθεὶς
γοῦν πρὸς τοὺς φίλους, Ἀλλὰ τοῦτό γε οὐκ ἰχώρ
ἐστιν, ἔφη, τὸ ῥέον, ἀλλὰ αἷμα ἀληθινόν. ἀπο-
θνῄσκων δὲ καὶ πάνυ ὡμολόγησε μεγάλην τινὰ
οὖσαν καὶ ἀνίκητον ὡς ἀληθῶς τὴν τύχην. ἐκεῖνος
γοῦν¹ ἐκφυγὼν καὶ τὸ Θηβαίων ὁπλιτικὸν καὶ τὸ
Θεσσαλῶν ἱππικὸν καὶ τοὺς ἀκοντιστὰς Αἰτωλοὺς
καὶ τοὺς μαχαιροφόρους Θρᾷκας καὶ τοὺς μαχίμους
Πέρσας καὶ τὸ τῶν ἀμάχων Μήδων γένος καὶ ὄρη
μεγάλα καὶ ποταμοὺς ἀδιαβάτους² καὶ κρημνοὺς
ἀνυπερβάτους καὶ Δαρεῖον καὶ Πῶρον καὶ πολλὰ
ἄλλα ἐθνῶν καὶ βασιλέων ὀνόματα, ἐν Βαβυλῶνι
ἄνευ μάχης καὶ τραυμάτων ὁ στρατιώτης ἔθνῃσκε.

22 Τί δὲ δεῖ λέγειν τοὺς διαδεξαμένους τὴν βασιλείαν ἢ τοὺς ἐπ᾽ ἐκείνοις γενομένους καὶ τὰ ἀλα-
ζονικὰ αὐτῶν ὀνόματα, κεραυνοὺς καὶ πολιορκητὰς
καὶ ἀετοὺς καὶ θεούς· ὧν τὸν μὲν ὁ θάνατος
ἤλεγξεν· ὁ δὲ ὑψηλοτέραν εὗρε τὴν τύχην, καίτοι
πεζῇν³ δοκῶν· ὁ δὲ πολιορκητὴς Δημήτριος αἰχ-
μάλωτος γενόμενος ἐξ οἴνου καὶ μέθης ἀτίμως
ἀπέθανεν, ὑπὸ τῆς τύχης πολιορκούμενος. τί οὖν
οἱ τύραννοι μέγα φρονοῦσιν ἐπὶ τοῖς τείχεσι; τί
δὲ Ἀμφίων ᾄδει; τί δὲ Δηιόκης πονεῖ; τί δὲ
Σεμίραμις οἰκοδομεῖ; τί δὲ ὁ Ἀπόλλων μισθαρ-
νεῖ; τί δὲ μετὰ τοῦ λέοντος Μήλης τὸ τεῖχος

---

¹ After γοῦν Arnim adds ὁ.
² ἀδιαβάτους deleted by Arnim.
³ πεζῇν Emperius : παίζειν.

---

¹ Cf. Plutarch, *Alexander* 28.
² An Indian prince subdued by Alexander.
³ The first of these " braggart titles " would refer to either
the elder son of Ptolemy Soter or Seleucus III ; the remaining three refer respectively to Demetrius, Pyrrhus, and

Fortune made him while yet alive admit that he was a human being. At any rate when he had been wounded he said to his friends, " Why, this fluid which I behold is not ichor but real blood ! "[1] But by his dying he admitted fully that Fortune is a mighty being and truly invincible. At any rate after escaping from the Theban hoplites, the Thessalian cavalry, the Aetolian javelin-throwers, the Thracians with their daggers, the martial Persians, the tribe of irresistible Medes, from lofty mountains, impassable rivers, unscalable cliffs, from Darius, Porus,[2] and many other tribes and kings I might name, yet in Babylon, remote from battle and from wounds, our warrior died !

But what should one say of those who took over his empire, or of those who followed after them, with their braggart titles [3]—Thunderbolts, Takers-of-cities, Eagles, Gods ? One of the lot death proved mistaken ; another found Fortune to be a loftier being than himself, though he had considered her pedestrian ; our Taker-of-cities, Demetrius, was taken captive and died a shameful death from wine and drunkenness, beleaguered as he was by Fortune ! Why, then, are tyrants proud of their ramparts ? Why does Amphion sing,[4] Deïoces toil,[5] Semiramis build,[6] Apollo work for hire,[7] Meles encompass the

Antiochus II. Their fortunes are sketched, in reverse order, in the following sentence.

[4] At his music the stones for the walls of Thebes moved into place.

[5] Founder of the Median empire ; cf. Herodotus 1. 96-100.

[6] Cf. § 2 and note.

[7] Apollo served more than one mortal, but the reference to Troy points to his serving Laomedon in building the walls of that city.

DIO CHRYSOSTOM

περιέρχεται; κρατήσει γὰρ Μήδων Κῦρος καὶ
Βαβυλωνίων Ζώπυρος καὶ Σάρδεων Μάρδος[1] καὶ
Τροίας ὁ ἵππος.

23 Μεγάλη γὰρ ῥοπή, μᾶλλον δὲ τὸ[2] ὅλον, εἰπέ τις,
ἡ τύχη. αὕτη καὶ Πίνδαρον εὗρεν ἐκκείμενον ἐν
Βοιωτίᾳ καὶ Τήλεφον ἐν Ἀρκαδίᾳ καὶ τοὺς βασιλεῖς Ῥωμαίων ἐν Ἰταλίᾳ· καὶ τῷ μὲν ἔπεμψε
μελίττας, τοῖς δὲ ποιμένας, Τηλέφῳ δὲ ἔλαφον,
Κύρῳ δὲ ἢ κύνα ἢ γυναῖκα. Εὐμένης ἦν ἁμαξέως
υἱός, ἀλλ᾽ ὅμως βασιλεὺς ἐγένετο, Ἡρακλῆς
Ἀλεξάνδρου παῖς, ἀλλ᾽ οὐκ ἐβασίλευσεν· ἄταφος
γοῦν Ὀλυμπιάδι ἐκομίσθη, καὶ πενθήσασα αὐτὸν
24 καὶ αὐτὴ ἐτελεύτησεν ἡ μήτηρ τοῦ θεοῦ. Δαρείου
δὲ ἡ μήτηρ καὶ Ἀλέξανδρον προσεκύνησε καί, τὸ
ἀτιμότερον, Ἡφαιστίωνα. τί δὲ ὁ Λιβύων βασι-
λεύς; οὐ πεντακοσίας μὲν πόλεις Ῥωμαίων ἐπόρ-
θησεν; ἐπάρας δὲ τὸν χιτῶνα τὸν[3] αὑτοῦ τοῖς
πολίταις ἔδειξε Ῥωμαϊκῶν σφραγίδων ἀνάπλεων,
ὧν ἑκάστην εἶχεν ἀπὸ πολεμίων σκῦλον ὑπ᾽ αὐτοῦ
πεφονευμένων; ταῦτα δὲ πάντα δράσας ἀτίμως

---

[1] Μάρδος Valesius : μαρδόνιος or μαρδώνιος.
[2] τὸ added by Emperius.
[3] τὸν added by Dindorf.

---

[1] Meles, king of Sardis, had a concubine who bore him a
lion. An oracle said that Sardis would be safe if he carried
the lion around the citadel, but he neglected a spot where
the rock was sheer, and so the Mardian Hyroeades took the
city ; cf. Herodotus 1. 84.
[2] Zopyrus took Babylon for Darius ; cf. Herodotus 3.
151-158.
[3] A quotation from Demosthenes, *Olynthiac* 2. 22.
[4] Photius says a bee dropped honey on Pindar's lips as

wall with his lion ? [1] For Cyrus will master the Medes,
Zopyrus the Babylonians,[2] a Mardian Sardis, and the
horse Troy !

Yes, as some one has put it, Fortune is a great
weight in the scales, or rather the whole thing.[3] She
found the infant Pindar lying exposed in Boeotia,
Telephus in Arcadia, the kings of Rome in Italy ;
and to Pindar she sent honey-bees,[4] to the kings of
Rome shepherds,[5] to Telephus a deer,[6] and to Cyrus
either a dog or a woman.[7] Eumenes was a wagoner's
son, but for all that he became king [8] ; Heracles was
Alexander's son, yet he did not become king [9] ; in
fact, his body, denied the rites of burial, was brought
to Olympias, and after mourning for him she too
died, a god's mother, forsooth ! Moreover, the
mother of Darius made obeisance, not merely to
Alexander, but, what is more disgraceful, to Hephaestion.[10] What about the king of the Libyans ?
Did he not sack five hundred cities of the Romans ?
Did he not lift up his tunic and display it to his fellow
townsmen filled with Roman finger rings, each of
which he had as loot from foes he had slaughtered ?
Yet after he had done all this he met an ignominious

he lay asleep on Helicon. Similar tales were told of other
Greeks.   [5] The familiar tale of Romulus and Remus.
   [6] Telephus, son of Heracles, was exposed on Mt. Par-
thenium.
   [7] Herodotus (1. 110-113) says the wife of his rescuer was
named Spako, which meant Dog.
   [8] He became governor, not king, of Cappadocia and
Paphlagonia after Alexander's death ; cf. Plutarch, *Eumenes* 1.
   [9] Son of Alexander by Barsinê, he was murdered by
Polyperchon ; cf. Diodorus 20. 28.
   [10] One of Alexander's generals. Mistaken for Alexander
according to Curtius, *Hist. Alex.* iii. 12. 16 f.

ἀπέθανε, μάτην πολλὰ φιλονεικήσας πρὸς τὴν τύχην.

25 Διόπερ μοι δοκοῦσιν οἱ ἄνθρωποι τὰ μεγάλα[1] πάντα τῶν πραγμάτων ἐπιτρέπειν τῇ τύχῃ, κληρωτὰς τὰς[2] ἀρχὰς καὶ στρατηγίας ποιούμενοι· καὶ ἀδελφοὶ κτῆσιν αὐτῶν οὕτως διανέμονται. ἔδει δὲ ἄρα καὶ τὸν Πολυνείκην, εἴπερ καλῶς ἐβουλεύετο, κλήρῳ πρὸς τὸν ἀδελφὸν περὶ τῆς βασιλείας λαχεῖν· νυνὶ δὲ αὐτός τε ἀπέθανε καὶ τὸν ἀδελφὸν προσαπώλεσεν, ἡλικίᾳ τὸ πρᾶγμα ἐπιτρέψας, οὐ τύχῃ.

26 κλήρῳ νῦν πεπάλαχθε διαμπερές, ὅς κε λάχῃσιν.

οὗτος γὰρ δὴ ὀνήσει ἐϋκνήμιδας Ἀχαιούς·

καὶ ὤνησε λαχών· ὁ δὲ Ἕκτωρ ἡττήθη γνώμῃ πιστεύσας, οὐ[3] τύχῃ.

δοιοὶ γάρ τε πίθοι κατακείαται ἐν Διὸς οὔδει.

θησαυροὶ μὲν εἰς ἀνθρώπους οὗτοι παρὰ θεοῖς· ταμιεύει δὲ αὐτῶν πρὸς τὸ ἐπιβάλλον ἡ τύχη καὶ ῥήτορι καὶ στρατηγῷ καὶ πένητι καὶ πλουσίῳ καὶ 27 πρεσβύτῃ καὶ νέῳ. Κροίσῳ δίδωσι χρυσόν, Καν-

---

[1] μεγάλα Selden : μὲν ἄλλα.   [2] τὰς added by Dindorf.
[3] οὐ Emperius : ἦ.

---

[1] Our author must have Hannibal in mind. However, his data do not square completely with common tradition. Appian says Hannibal sacked 400 cities ; and it was his brother Mago, according to Livy (23. 12), who after the battle of Cannae dumped the signet rings at the entrance to the senate house in Carthage. Hannibal committed suicide when Prusias, king of Bithynia, was about to surrender him to the Romans.

death, having contended much with Fortune all in vain.[1]

This, it seems to me, is why men entrust all their important matters to Fortune, making their public offices and generalships subject to allotment[2]; brothers also divide their patrimony in that way. And so Polyneices too, if indeed he had been well advised, ought to have drawn lots with his brother for the throne; but as it was, not only was he himself slain, he destroyed his brother as well, all because he referred the matter to priority of birth and not to Fortune.[3]

> Now shake the lot in turn and see who draws;
> For the well-greaved Achaeans he will aid[4]—

and, having drawn, aid he did; however, Hector was defeated because he trusted to judgement and not to Fortune.

> For on his threshold Zeus has set two jars.[5]

These are storage jars for mankind in the keeping of the gods; however, it is Fortune who administers them with regard to what is allotted—to orator or to general, to rich or poor, to old or young. To Croesus she gives gold, to Candaules a wife,[6] to

---

[2] Most Athenian offices were filled by lot, but not that of general.

[3] Polyneices and Eteocles were sons of Oedipus, king of Thebes. Aeschylus tells the tale in his *Seven against Thebes.*

[4] *Iliad* 7. 171-172; spoken by Nestor as the Greeks were choosing a champion to oppose Hector. The lot fell to Ajax.

[5] *Ibid.* 24. 527.

[6] Herodotus (1. 7-12) tells of the infatuation of Candaules for his wife that caused his death and the transfer of the throne to Gyges.

δαύλη γυναῖκα, Πηλεῖ ξίφος, Νέστορι ἀσπίδα, Πτερέλᾳ[1] κόμην χρυσῆν, Νίσῳ πλόκαμον πορφυροῦν, Ἀλκιβιάδῃ κάλλος, Σωκράτει[2] φρόνησιν, Ἀριστείδῃ δικαιοσύνην, Λακεδαιμονίοις γῆν, Ἀθηναίοις[3] θάλατταν. εἶτα ἐν μέρει τούτων μὲν ἀφείλετο, ἄλλοις δὲ ἔδωκεν. καὶ οὐδέν μοι δοκεῖ ὁ βίος τῶν ἀνθρώπων πομπῆς διαφέρειν ἐν ταῖς ἡμερησίαις[4] μεταβολαῖς.

[1] Πτερέλᾳ Valesius : πτερίλα or πτερίλᾳ.
[2] After Σωκράτει Emperius deletes δὲ.
[3] γῆν, Ἀθηναίοις Dindorf : τὴν Ἀθηναίων.
[4] ἡμερησίαις Emperius : ἡμετέραις.

[1] When Peleus was a fugitive on Pelium, Hephaestus brought him a sword with which to ward off wild beasts.
[2] Nestor's shield is shrouded in mystery. It is referred to only once in classical literature (*Iliad* 8. 192-193).

Peleus a sword,[1] to Nestor a shield,[2] to Pterelas golden locks,[3] to Nisus a purple tress,[4] to Alcibiades beauty, to Socrates wisdom, to Aristeides uprightness, to Spartans land, to Athenians a sea. Then in turn she takes from these and gives to others. And it seems to me that the life of man in its daily vicissitudes is in no wise different from a procession.[5]

[3] According to Apollodorus, *Bibliotheca* 2. 4. 5, a grandson of Poseidon named Pterelaüs (*sic*) was made immortal by the gift of a strand of golden hair.

[4] Nisus, king of Megara, had a purple hair on which his life depended. His daughter Scylla plucked it out for love of his enemy, Minos of Crete; cf. Apollodorus, *op. cit.* 3. 15. 8.

[5] The simile of the procession perhaps has reference to the temporary dignity with which some of the participants were clothed. That the speech ends thus abruptly, without elaboration of the simile, suggests that we have it in an unfinished state.

THE SIXTY-FIFTH DISCOURSE:
ON FORTUNE (III)

THIS essay deals with the injustice of human behaviour with respect to Fortune. Unlike the two essays on Fortune which precede it, there seems to be no good reason to doubt its authenticity; yet there are signs which suggest that its present form is not that in which it was composed. The author seems to repeat himself to an extent not to be expected in so brief a composition. Besides, one misses from time to time those particles and formulas commonly employed by Dio and other Greek writers to indicate transition and to knit together the argument, *e.g.*, at the beginning of the new paragraph in § 7 and at the beginning of §§ 8, 10, and 13. On the other hand, the γὰρ which is found in the beginning of the new paragraph in § 4 seems so unwarranted in that setting that Wilamowitz proposed to strike it out. In view of these phenomena it is not unlikely that we have before us, not one unified composition, but rather a collection of passages drawn from various contexts and here put together because of their common theme. It is possible that Dio's editor desired thus to preserve passages in writings now lost to us which he deemed noteworthy; though Dio himself may for his own convenience have grouped together paragraphs on related topics. It is worth noting that the passages that have been cited as marked by asyndeton have the earmarks of prooemia. For a fuller discussion of the general problem see von Arnim, *Dio von Prusa* 268-271.

65. ΠΕΡΙ ΤΥΧΗΣ ΤΡΙΤΟΣ

1 Οἱ σφόδρα τῇ τύχῃ πεπιστευκότες καὶ τῇ παρ-
ουσίᾳ ταύτης ἐπαιρόμενοι δοκοῦσί μοι κάλλιστα
συνηγορεῖν αὐτῇ καὶ παρασκευάζειν ὅπως, ἐπειδὰν
μεταπέσῃ, μηδεὶς αὐτῇ μέμφηται. τοὐναντίον γὰρ
ἅπαντες τῇ βαρύτητι τῶν εὐτυχούντων δυσχεραί-
νοντες καὶ τὴν ὕβριν αὐτῶν μεμισηκότες, ὅταν
καταλίπῃ τινὰ αὐτῶν, ἐπαινοῦσι καί φασι δικαίαν
αὐτοῖς γεγονέναι τὴν μεταβολήν. δεῖ δὲ τοὺς νοῦν
ἔχοντας οὕτως χρῆσθαι τοῖς αὐτομάτοις ἀγαθοῖς
ὥστε ὑπαρχόντων μὲν αὐτῶν μηδένα ἐγκαλεῖν,
2 ἐὰν δὲ παύσηταί ποτε, μηδένα ἐφήδεσθαι. τῷ
παντὶ γὰρ κρεῖττόν ἐστιν ἐνδεῶς πράττοντα
ἀγαπᾶσθαι καὶ δοκεῖν πᾶσι παρὰ τὴν ἀξίαν ἀπαλλάττειν ἢ τοὐναντίον εὐτυχοῦντα μισεῖσθαι καὶ
προσέτι καὶ τῇ τύχῃ γίγνεσθαι βλασφημίας αἴτιον
ὡς τοὺς πονηροὺς ἀντὶ τῶν χρηστῶν εὐεργετεῖν
προαιρουμένη. οἱ μὲν οὖν πολλοὶ τῶν ἀνθρώπων
τοὺς βαρέως χρωμένους τοῖς ἐκ τῆς τύχης ὑπ-
άρχουσι πονηροὺς μὲν εἶναί φασι καὶ τῶν ἀγαθῶν
ἀναξίους, οὐ μὴν ἀτυχεῖς γε εἰώθασι λέγειν· ἐμοὶ
δὲ τοὐναντίον οὗτοι δοκοῦσι πάντων ἀτυχέστατοι
3 καθεστηκέναι. τὸ γὰρ ἐκ τῶν νομιζομένων

74

THE SIXTY-FIFTH DISCOURSE:
ON FORTUNE (III)

Those who have relied greatly on Fortune and are elated by her presence are, it seems to me, her most effective advocates and insure that, whenever she does shift, no one shall blame her for it. For, on the contrary, all men, being disgusted at the offensiveness of those who enjoy good fortune and having come to hate their insolence, as soon as Fortune abandons any of these, applaud and declare that the change of fortune they have experienced is deserved. Nay, men of intelligence should so employ the blessings which come to them unearned that, while they last, no one may censure them and, if some day they come to an end, no one may rejoice thereat. For it is altogether better that one should be in straitened circumstances but well liked, and that he should be thought by all to be getting less than his deserts, than, on the contrary, that he should be prosperous but hated, and, besides, become the occasion for blasphemous railing at Fortune as preferring to benefit the wicked rather than the good. Now though most men say that those who are obnoxious in their use of the gifts of Fortune are wicked and unworthy of their blessings, they assuredly do not as a rule call them unfortunate; yet to me, on the contrary, such persons seem to have become the most unfortunate of all. For when from what commonly are deemed

ἀγαθῶν μηδενὸς χρηστοῦ, βλασφημίας δὲ καὶ
μίσους ἀπολαύειν πρὸς τῷ τὴν αὑτοῦ κακίαν
γνωριμωτέραν πᾶσι ποιεῖν, πῶς οὐχὶ μεγάλη καὶ
φανερὰ δυστυχία; διόπερ, οἶμαι, τοῖς ἀνοήτοις
λυσιτελεῖ τῷ παντὶ μᾶλλον ἐνδεῶς πράττειν καὶ
μήτε ἐξουσίας μήτε πλούτου μήτε τῶν τοιούτων
μηδενὸς τυγχάνειν. ταπεινοὶ μὲν γὰρ ὄντες
λανθάνειν τοὺς πολλοὺς ἔμελλον ὁποῖοι κατὰ
τρόπον[1] ὑπάρχουσιν, ἀρθέντες δὲ ὑπὸ τῆς τύχης
4 ἐπίσημον τὴν πονηρίαν ἔσχον. ὥσπερ οὖν τοῖς
τὸ σῶμα φαύλως διακειμένοις βέλτιον καθ’ αὑτοὺς
ἀποδύεσθαι καὶ μηδέποτε εἰς τὸ κοινόν, ὅπως
μηδένα ἔχωσι τῆς περὶ τοῦτο αἰσχύνης μάρτυρα·
τὸν αὐτόν, οἶμαι, τρόπον, οἷς συμβέβηκε τὴν
ψυχὴν ἀγεννῆ καὶ μοχθηρὰν ὑπάρχειν λυσιτελὲς
ἂν εἴη δήπου ἐν[2] ἀγνοίᾳ τοῦ βίου καὶ σκότει τῆς
τύχης διατελεῖν.

Ἀδίκως γάρ[3] μοι δοκοῦσιν οἱ πολλοὶ τῶν ἀνθρώπων τῆς τύχης κατηγορεῖν ὡς οὐδὲν ἐχούσης
βέβαιον οὐδὲ πιστόν, ἀλλὰ ταχὺ δὴ μάλα, οἷς ἂν
παρῇ, τούτους καταλειπούσης καὶ[4] μεθισταμένης
5 πρὸς ἑτέρους. εἰ μὲν γὰρ καλῶς ἦν ἰδεῖν χρωμένους ὡς τὸ πολὺ τοῖς παρ’ αὐτῆς ἀγαθοῖς τοὺς
λαμβάνοντας καὶ μὴ τοὐναντίον εὐθὺς ὕβρεως καὶ
μισανθρωπίας καὶ θρασύτητος ἐμπιπλαμένους,
οὐκ ἂν ὀρθῶς ἐποίει μὴ τοῖς αὐτοῖς παρα-
μένουσα· νῦν δέ, οἶμαι, προαιρεῖται μὲν εὐεργετεῖν
ἕκαστον ὡς χρηστὸν καὶ τῶν παρ’ αὐτῆς δωρεῶν
ἄξιον, ἐπειδὰν δὲ φαῦλον αἴσθηται καὶ ταπεινόν,

---

[1] κατὰ τρόπον] τὸν τρόπον Reiske, κατὰ τὸν τρόπον Emperius,
καὶ τὸν τρόπον Post.
[2] δήπου ἐν Emperius : δήπουθεν.

blessings one reaps nothing that is good, but rather vilification and hatred, besides making his own wickedness more notorious for all the world, how can that be anything but a great and conspicuous misfortune? And so, in my opinion, for those who lack intelligence it is in every way more profitable to be in needy circumstances and to acquire neither power nor riches nor any such thing at all. For as long as they were in lowly station most persons would fail to perceive their true character, whereas if they are exalted by Fortune their villainy is made conspicuous. Accordingly, just as with those whose bodies are in bad condition it is better that they undress in private and never in public, in order that they may have no witness of their shame in that respect, in the same way, I fancy, those whose misfortune it has been to possess a soul which is ignoble and corrupt would surely find it to their interest to remain inconspicuous as to their lives and obscure as to their fortunes.

It seems to me unfair that most men arraign Fortune on the ground that she has no stability or trustworthiness but all too speedily deserts those whom she visits and shifts to others. For if we could observe that the recipients of her blessings were for the most part making an honourable use of them and not, on the contrary, becoming filled immediately with arrogance and malevolence and effrontery, Fortune would not be acting right if she did not remain with the same people; but as it is, I imagine, she chooses in each instance to benefit a person because she supposes him to be a good man and worthy of her gifts, but when she finds him to be

---

[3] γάρ deleted by Wilamowitz.   [4] καὶ Geel : ἤ.

καταισχύνοντα τὴν εὔνοιαν τὴν παρ' αὐτῆς, εἰκότως
ἀφίαται στκαὶ ζητεῖ πάλιν ἄλλον, ἐὰν ἄρα ἐπιει-
6 κέστερον εὑρεῖν δύνηται. πονηρῶν δὲ τῶν πλείστων ὑπαρχόντων καὶ τῆς ἀνθρωπίνης φύσεως
σπανίως τινὰ φερούσης ἐπιτήδειον εὖ πράττειν,
ἐξ ἀνάγκης συνεχεῖς ποιεῖται τὰς μεταβολάς, πολὺ
δὲ μᾶλλον διὰ τὴν ἡμετέραν ἢ τὴν αὐτῆς φύσιν.
ἔστι δὲ ἄτοπον εἴ τις αὐτὸς μὲν[1] οὐ δύναται φέρειν
ἐνίους τῶν εὐτυχούντων, ἀλλὰ μικρὸν χρόνον
ὁμιλήσας ἀφίσταται, καὶ μᾶλλον αἱρεῖται τὴν
αὐτοῦ πενίαν ὅπως ἂν ἐνδέχηται φέρειν ἢ φορτικῶν
καὶ ἀνοήτων ἀνέχεσθαι τρόπων· τὴν δὲ τύχην,
θεὸν οὖσαν, ἀξιοῖ τοῖς αὐτοῖς τούτοις συζῆν ἄχρι
παντὸς καὶ πολλάκις ὑβριζομένην ὕβρεις δεινὰς
7 παραμένειν ἀνδραπόδῳ μηδενὸς ἀξίῳ. παρὰ γὰρ
τῶν πλουσίων εἰς μὲν τοὺς συμβιοῦντας ἀνθρώπους
ἡ ὕβρις ἐστὶ λοιδορία, προπηλακισμός, κατάγελως,
τὸ πληγῆναι πολλάκις, εἰς δὲ τὴν τύχην αὐτὴν
ὑπερηφανία, βαρύτης, μικρολογία.

Ἀδικώτατά μοι δοκοῦσιν ἐγκαλεῖν οἱ πολλοὶ τῇ
τύχῃ. νῦν μὲν γὰρ αὐτὴν αἰτιῶνται, φάσκοντες
ἄπιστον εἶναι καὶ μηδὲν ἔχειν βέβαιον. εἰ δ' ἀεὶ
τοῖς αὐτοῖς παρέμενεν, οὐκ ἔστιν ὅπως οὐχὶ τῷ
παντὶ μείζονος καὶ δικαιοτέρας ἐτύγχανεν ἂν[2]
κατηγορίας. ὅπου γὰρ νῦν ὁρᾶτε τοὺς εὖ πράττοντας οὕτως ὄντας πονηροὺς καὶ βαρεῖς, καὶ
ταῦτα τοῦ μέλλοντος ὑπάρχοντος ἀδήλου, πόσης
ἂν οἴεσθε αὐτοὺς ὑπερηφανίας καὶ σκαιότητος
εἶναι μεστούς, εἰ καθόλου μὴ τὴν ἐλπίδα τῆς
μεταβολῆς ὑφεωρῶντο;

---

[1] After μὲν Arnim deletes ἕκαστος. Cobet reads εἰ εἷς μὲν
ἕκαστος.

mean and base, bringing shame upon her benevolence, with good reason she leaves him and seeks somebody else in turn, hoping to find some one who is more honourable. But since most men are evil and human nature rarely produces anybody fitted to enjoy prosperity, Fortune must needs shift continually, and much rather because of our nature than because of her own. Yet it is strange that one who cannot himself endure some who enjoy the favours of Fortune, but who after a brief association leaves them and prefers to bear his own poverty as best he can rather than put up with cheap and senseless manners, nevertheless expects Fortune, goddess though she be, to live with these same persons for ever and, though frequently subjected to outrageous insults, to remain with an utterly worthless slave ! For the fact is that the insolence shown by the rich toward the human beings with whom they live consists of abusive language, contumely, ridicule, and often a blow, but toward Fortune herself it is arrogance, harshness, captiousness.

Most unfair, it seems to me, are the charges most men bring against Fortune. For as it is they find fault with her as being untrustworthy and having no constancy at all. Yet if she always stayed with the same persons she would inevitably incur an altogether more serious and justifiable accusation. For when you now see that the prosperous are so base and disagreeable, even though what is in store for them is uncertain, with what arrogance and boorishness do you suppose they would be filled if they were not at all apprehensive of a change ?

---

² ἐτύγχανεν ἄν Capps : ἐτύγχανε.

8 Φασὶ πολλοὶ τὴν τύχην ἄκριτον εἶναι καὶ πονηροῖς ἀνθρώποις προσμένειν τῶν χρηστῶν δὲ
ἀμελεῖν, ὅταν ὁρῶσι τοὺς ἠξιωμένους τῶν παρ'
ἐκείνης ἀγαθῶν βαρεῖς ὄντας καὶ δυσχρήστους
καὶ ἀγεννεῖς. δοκεῖ δέ μοι ἡ τύχη πρὸς αὐτοὺς
δίκαια¹ ἂν εἰπεῖν ὅτι φύσει φιλάνθρωπος οὖσα
ἀεί τισι πάρεστιν ἡμῶν οὐχ αἱρουμένη τοὺς ἀξίους
οὐδὲ τοὺς πονηρούς, ἀεὶ δὲ οἷος ἂν αὐτοῖς παρα-
γένηται, τοιούτους αὐτοὺς ὄντας ἐξελέγχεσθαι·
δεῖν οὖν τὴν αὐτῶν αἰτιᾶσθαι φύσιν, μὴ τὴν
9 ἐκείνης, ὅτι τοιοῦτοι καθεστήκασιν· ὥστε ὁ μὲν
ἐνδεῶς τι² πράττων εὐθὺς³ ἄξιος εἶναι δοκεῖ
βέλτιον ἀπαλλάττειν, ὅτῳ δ' ἂν ὑπάρξῃ τὰ παρ'
αὐτῆς ἀγαθά, μοχθηρὸς πέφηνεν. ἔστι γὰρ ὅμοιον
ὥσπερ εἴ τις, ἀγγείων πολλῶν ὄντων, καὶ μηδενὸς⁴
ὑγιοῦς, τὸν εἰς αὐτὰ ἐγχέοντα ψέγοι⁵ βλέπων ῥέον
τὸ ἀεὶ⁶ πληρούμενον. εἴποι γὰρ ἄν, Ἀλλ' ἔστι
πάντα τοιαῦτα· ἕως δ' ἂν ᾖ κενά, λανθάνει.
10 Θαυμάζω πῶς ποτε οἱ πολλοὶ τὴν τύχην φασὶν
ἐπικίνδυνον εἶναι καὶ μηδὲν τῶν παρ' αὐτῆς
ὑπάρχειν βέβαιον. ἐκείνη γὰρ ἐπειδάν τινι δῷ
τὰ παρ' αὐτῆς ἀγαθά—ταῦτα δ' ἐστὶ χρήματα,
ἰσχύς, δόξα, τιμαί—τούτοις οὐδένα κωλύει χρῆσθαι
κατὰ τρόπον καὶ νὴ Δία γε εἰς τἀσφαλὲς αὐτοῖς
κατατίθεσθαι, λέγω δὲ οὐκ εἰς τὴν οἰκίαν ἔνδον
οὐδ' εἰς τὸ ταμιεῖον οὐδὲ κλεῖς ἐφιστάντας καὶ
μοχλούς· οὐ φυλάττεται γὰρ ὑπὸ τούτων οὐδὲν
τῶν παρ' αὐτῆς· ἀλλ' εἰς εὔνοιαν ἀνθρώπων,
11 πατρίδος εὐεργεσίαν, φίλων βοήθειαν. οὐκοῦν

---

¹ δίκαια] δικαίως Pflugk.　　² τι] ἔτι Reiske.
³ εὐθὺς transferred by Emperius to second line below, to
follow ἀγαθά.　　⁴ καὶ μηδενὸς] μηδενὸς δὲ Emperius.

THE SIXTY-FIFTH DISCOURSE

Many charge that Fortune lacks discrimination and stays with bad persons but neglects the good, when they observe that those who have been deemed worthy of her favours are disagreeable and hard to deal with and ignoble. But it seems to me that Fortune might justly say to them that, being naturally benevolent, she is always helping some among us, without selecting the deserving or the base either, but that invariably the character they have when she comes to them is that which they show when the moral test is applied ; and that therefore they should blame their own nature, not hers, as being so constituted that he who is faring somewhat badly immediately seems worthy of better fortune, while he who receives her favours turns out to be a knave. Aye, it is very much as if, given a number of vessels and not one of them sound, one were to find fault with the person pouring liquid into them, on seeing that whatever vessel was being filled leaked. For the man might say, " Why, they all are like that : however, so long as they are empty it is unnoticed."

I wonder why in the world most persons say that Fortune is precarious and that none of her gifts is to be relied upon. For whenever she gives any one her good things—wealth, power, fame, honours— she never prevents him from using these in a proper way or, by Heaven, from storing them away in safety for himself ; and I do not mean indoors in the house, or in the storehouse, or putting them under lock and key—for none of her gifts is protected by these things —but rather storing them away in goodwill toward mankind, in service to one's country, in aid to friends.

---

[5] ψέγοι added by Pflugk, ἐλέγχοι by Duemmler.
[6] τὸ ἀεὶ Crosby, ἀεὶ τὸ Reiske : ἀεὶ.

οὐδέποτε¹ οὐδὲν ἀφείλετο ἡ τύχη τοὺς ἅπαξ
κτησαμένους τῶν οὕτως ἀποκειμένων. οὗτοι γὰρ
εἰσι θησαυροὶ βέβαιοι καὶ πᾶσι φανεροὶ τῶν
αὐτομάτως περιγιγνομένων. ἐὰν δέ τις λαβὼν
ῥίψῃ ἢ καὶ νὴ Δία κακῶς θῇ, θύραις καὶ σφραγῖσι
καὶ κλεισὶ² πιστεύων, οὐκέτ', οἶμαι, δι' ἐκείνην
ἀπόλλυνται.

12 Σφόδρα δὲ καὶ τοῦτο ἄτοπον· πρὸς γὰρ τῷ
πολλὰ βλασφημεῖν διὰ λόγων κατὰ τῆς τύχης ἔτι
καὶ πλάσται καὶ γραφεῖς αὐτὴν λοιδοροῦσιν, οἱ
μὲν ὡς μαινομένην καὶ διαρρίπτουσαν γράφοντες,
οἱ δὲ ἐπὶ σφαίρας βεβηκυῖαν, ὡς οὐκ ἀσφαλῶς
οὐδὲ ἀκινδύνως ἐρηρεισμένην, δέον ἡμᾶς αὐτοὺς
τοιούτους πλάττειν καὶ γράφειν τοὺς ἐμπλήκτως
καὶ κακῶς πᾶσι χρωμένους καὶ μὰ Δία γε οὐκ
ἐπὶ σφαίρας, ἀλλ' ἐπ' ἀνοίας ἑστηκότας, καὶ μὴ
μάτην τῇ τύχῃ μέμφεσθαι.

13 Περὶ πάντων μέν, ὡς εἰπεῖν, οἱ πολλοὶ τῶν
ἀνθρώπων οὐκ ὀρθῶς ὑπολαμβάνουσι, μάλιστα
δὲ τὴν ὑπὲρ τῆς τύχης δόξαν ψευδῆ καὶ πεπλανη-
μένην ἔχουσιν. φασὶ γὰρ αὐτὴν διδόναι μὲν τοῖς
ἀνθρώποις τἀγαθά,³ ῥᾳδίως δὲ ἀφαιρεῖσθαι· καὶ
διὰ τοῦτο ὡς ἄπιστον βλασφημοῦσι καὶ φθονεράν.
ἐγὼ δὲ οὐ διδόναι φημὶ τὴν τύχην τούτων οὐδέν,
14 ὡς⁴ οἱ πολλοὶ νομίζουσιν. ᾧ γὰρ κύριος ἕκαστος
γίγνεται τῶν ὑπαρχόντων καὶ δι' οὗ μόνου κεκτῆσθαι τἀγαθὰ ἀσφαλῶς ἔστιν, οὐ δίδωσιν αὐτοῖς
μετὰ τῶν χρημάτων καὶ τῆς δόξης καὶ τῆς δυνά-

¹ After οὐδέποτε Arnim deletes αὐτούς, Geel conjectures
αὖθις.
² θύραις καὶ σφραγῖσι καὶ κλεισὶ Post with B, θύραις καὶ κλεισὶ
Arnim : θύραις σφραγῖσι καὶ κλεισὶ U, θύραις καὶ σφόδρα κλείσει
M, ἢ θύραις καὶ κλεισὶ σφόδρα κλείσῃ PH.

Assuredly, Fortune never takes away from those who have once acquired them any of the things thus stored away. For these are dependable repositories and visible to all wherein to store the windfalls of Fortune. However, if after having got them a man squanders them or even, by Heaven, puts them in the wrong place, trusting to doors and seals and locks, no longer, I fancy, is their loss ascribable to her.

And here is something else which is very strange : besides the many verbal blasphemies against Fortune, sculptors and painters alike also traduce her, some representing her as mad and tossing her gifts recklessly about, some as standing on a sphere, as if to say that she has no safe or secure support, whereas it is ourselves that we ought to mould or paint like that, since we treat everything in a mad and evil fashion—and not, by Heaven, standing on a sphere but rather on folly—in place of idly finding fault with Fortune.

While on virtually every topic most men make incorrect assumptions, the opinion they hold regarding Fortune is particularly false and erroneous. For they say that, though she gives mankind their good things, she lightly takes them away again ; and for that reason they malign her as being untrustworthy and jealous. But I claim that Fortune does not really give any of those things, as most men think she does. For that which gives each man control over his possessions and through which alone it is possible to have secure possession of one's goods she does not bestow upon them along with their wealth and fame

---

[3] τἀγαθά Dindorf : ἀγαθά.
[4] ὡς] ὧν Arnim.

μεως. τοῦτο δέ ἐστιν οὗ χωρὶς οὐκ ἔστιν οὐδὲ
τῶν ἄλλων ἔχειν οὐδέν, οἴεσθαι μέντοι καὶ ἀπα-
τᾶσθαι. καθάπερ οὖν οὐδὲ ἡμεῖς, ὅταν εἰς τὴν
οἰκίαν τινὰ εἰσαγάγωμεν ἢ τὸ χωρίον ἢ σκεύη
τινὰ παράσχωμεν, εὐθὺς κύριον ἐκείνων τοῦτον
ἀπεδείξαμεν, ἂν μὴ προσῇ τὸ μετὰ ἀσφαλείας
τινὸς καὶ γράμματος, οὕτω καὶ ἡ τύχη κύριον
οὐδένα ποιεῖ τῶν ὑφ' αὑτῆς διδομένων, ἐὰν μὴ
προσῇ τὸ μετὰ νοῦ καὶ φρονήσεως τινὰ λαμβάνειν.
15 Οἱ μὲν δὴ πολλοὶ τῶν ἀνθρώπων εἰώθασιν
εὐδαιμονίζειν εὐθὺς οἷς ἂν ὁρῶσι τὰ παρὰ τῆς
τύχης ὑπάρχοντα, ὥσπερ τοῖς πλέουσι συνήδονται
πνεῦμα ὁρῶντες ἐπέχον, οὐκ εἰδότες οὔτ' εἰ φορὸν
αὐτοῖς τοῦτό ἐστιν οὔτ' εἰ κυβερνήτην ἔχουσιν
ἔμπειρον. ἐγὼ δ' οἶμαι τότε δεῖν μακαρίους
κρίνειν τοὺς ἐν ἀφθόνοις ὄντας τοῖς παρὰ τῆς
τύχης, ὅταν αὐτοῖς καὶ τὸ φρονεῖν παρῇ. καθ'
αὑτὰ γὰρ ταῦτα δηλονότι,[1] εἰ τοῖς ἀνοήτοις γένοιτο,
κινδύνου καὶ δυστυχίας αἴτια.

---

[1] δηλονότι Wilamowitz : δῆλον.

and power. No, that thing it is without which it is not possible to possess any of the other things but only to imagine that one does and to be the victim of delusion. For example, just as when we bring some one into our house or our farm or when we provide certain equipment, we ourselves do not forthwith appoint him master over those things, unless there is included in the transaction some written guarantee, so also Fortune does not make any one master of the things offered by her, unless there is attached to the grant the stipulation that they are accepted with intelligence and good judgement.

Most men, of course, are wont immediately to congratulate those whom they see supplied with the gifts of Fortune, just as people rejoice with men at sea when they observe that they have a breeze, although they know neither whether this breeze is favourable to them nor whether they have a helmsman with experience. But as for myself, I believe the time to judge fortunate those who are surrounded in abundance with the gifts of Fortune is when they have prudence too. For manifestly these gifts of themselves, should they become the property of fools, might be a source of danger and disaster.

THE SIXTY-SIXTH DISCOURSE :
ON REPUTATION

THE theme of this Discourse is the fickleness of the crowd
and the folly of those who seek to win and hold its favour.
Dio regards those who yield to that ambition as victims of
delusion. The public honours for which they strive have no
real utility and are purchased at too high a price, sometimes
reducing to beggary those who aim to reach them. What is
more, the aspirant for popular acclaim sacrifices his independence. He is forced to order his life to suit the whims
of those whose favour he is courting—in itself an impossible
task—and he cringes before the hostile criticism of citizen
and alien alike. No matter what scheme of life a man
adopts, he is sure to be misjudged. The sane policy is,
therefore, to steel oneself against criticism, in other words,
to adopt the attitude of the philosopher.

Arnim argues that the Discourse originally ended in the
midst of § 26, and that what follows has been appended by
Dio's editor, who, coming upon three passages of similar
purport, chose to preserve them through inclusion in our
Discourse. He is led to this belief by the presence in the
section referred to of the sentence beginning τί δεῖ δόξης
ἐπιθυμεῖν, which is thought to form a logical close. He
might have found additional support for his belief in the
fact that the beginning of each of the succeeding passages
is marked by asyndeton. All three resemble introductory
paragraphs of exordia. The extant work of Dio reveals other
instances of the existence of variant versions of a common
theme, apparently testifying to his practice of delivering
a given speech on more than one occasion.

Peculiar interest attaches to the present Discourse because
of an allusion in § 6 : ἔτι δὲ ἰδεῖν ἔστιν οἰκίαν συντριβεῖσαν
πλουσιωτέραν ἐκείνης διὰ γλῶτταν καὶ νὴ Δία ἑτέραν κινδυ-

νεύουσαν. The two " houses " there referred to are thought by Arnim to have been respectively that of Nero, whose pretensions as a singer (διὰ γλῶτταν) are being credited with his downfall, and that of Domitian, whose assassination is here predicted. Arnim observes that toward the close of Domitian's career such predictions were current, even being known by the emperor himself, and he points out that Apollonius of Tyana was able to announce in Ephesus the murder of Domitian at the very moment when it was taking place in Rome ! If Arnim's reasoning is correct, our Discourse can with confidence be dated shortly before Domitian's death, while Dio was still in exile.

66. ΠΕΡΙ ΔΟΞΗΣ ΠΡΩΤΟΣ

1 Εἰσί τινες, οἳ τοὺς μὲν φιλαργύρους ἢ φιλόψους
ἢ οἰνόφλυγας ἢ περὶ γυναῖκας ἢ παῖδας ἐπτοημένους
ἀσώτους ἀποκαλοῦσι καὶ δυστυχεῖς, καὶ τούτων
ἕκαστον ἡγοῦνται τὸ μέγιστον ὄνειδος, τοὺς δὲ
φιλοτίμους καὶ φιλοδόξους τοὐναντίον ἐπαινοῦσιν,
ὡς λαμπρούς· ὥστε καὶ αὐτὸς ἕκαστος ὀψοφαγῶν
μὲν ἢ πίνων ἢ ἐρῶν τινος αἰσχύνεται καὶ περι-
στέλλει τὴν ἀκρασίαν, δοξοκοπῶν δὲ καὶ φιλοτιμούμενος οὐδένα ἀνθρώπων βούλεται λανθάνειν,
ἀλλὰ ἐν τῷ μέσῳ ταῦτα ποιεῖ.

2 Τῶν γὰρ πολλῶν ἕκαστος εὐφημεῖ τὴν τοιαύτην
νόσον, λυσιτελεῖν ἡγούμενος αὑτῷ. καὶ δημοσίᾳ
σχεδὸν αἱ πόλεις ἅπασαι δελέατα ἐξευρήκασι
παντοῖα τοῖς ἀνοήτοις, στεφάνους καὶ προεδρίας
καὶ κηρύγματα. τοιγαροῦν ἤδη τινὰς τούτων
ἐπιθυμοῦντας ἀθλίους καὶ πένητας ἀπέδειξαν,
οὐδὲν ὀρέγοντες μέγα οὐδὲ θαυμαστόν, ἀλλ᾽ ἐνίους
ἀπὸ θαλλοῦ περιάγοντες, ὥσπερ τὰ πρόβατα, ἢ
στέφανόν τινα ἢ ταινίαν ἐπιβάλλοντες. οὐκοῦν

---

[1] Cf. Plato, *Phaedrus* 230 D.

[2] On the subject of crowns cf. Athenaeus 15. 669 c–686 c.
Crowns were favourite prizes in the athletic games. Best
known is the crown of wild olive, awarded at Olympia. The
Diadumenos of Polycleitus portrays an athlete binding his
brow with a ribbon. Crowns were awarded also for public
service, as in the famous case of Demosthenes. In either
sports or politics the crown might prove costly.

THE SIXTY-SIXTH DISCOURSE :
ON REPUTATION

THERE are some who brand as dissolute and ill-starred such men as have a craving for money or for dainties or for wine or who are inflamed with lust for women or boys, and they regard each of these vices as the greatest disgrace, yet those who crave distinction and reputation, on the contrary, they applaud, thinking them illustrious ; and therefore, while each one of his own accord, if a gourmet or a tippler or a lover of somebody, feels ashamed and tries to cloak his incontinence, yet when seeking reputation and distinction he does not want to escape the eye of any man on earth, but rather he carries on his quest in the open.

And no wonder, for among men in general each speaks well of this type of malady, deeming it advantageous for himself. Furthermore, by official act virtually all the states have devised lures of every kind for the simpletons—crowns and front seats and public proclamations. Accordingly, in some instances men who craved these things have actually been made wretched and reduced to beggary, although the states held before them nothing great or wonderful at all, but in some cases led their victims about with a sprig of green, as men lead cattle,[1] or clapped upon their heads a crown or a ribbon.[2] Therefore, while

ὁ τοιοῦτος, ἐξὸν αὐτῷ μυρίους, εἰ ἐθέλοι, στεφάνους προῖκα ἔχειν οὐ μόνον ἐλαίας ἢ δρυός, ἀλλὰ
καὶ κιττοῦ καὶ μυρρίνης, πολλάκις τὴν οἰκίαν
ἀπέδοτο καὶ τὰ χωρία, καὶ μετὰ ταῦτα περιέρχεται
πεινῶν καὶ φαῦλον τριβώνιον ἔχων. ἀλλὰ κηρύττεται, φησίν, ὑπὸ τῶν πολιτῶν, ὥσπερ ἀπολωλὸς
3 ἀνδράποδον. οὐκοῦν εἰκότως χρῶνται πρὸς τὰς
χειροτονίας τῷ τῆς ἐλαίας θαλλῷ διὰ τὸ φύσει
πικρὸν ὑπάρχειν. τοὺς γὰρ[1] δοξοκόπους ἐκβάλ-
λουσιν ἐκ τῶν ἀγρῶν[2] οἱ δῆμοι κραυγῇ καὶ ψόφῳ,
καθάπερ,[3] οἶμαι, τοὺς ψᾶρας οἱ γεωργοί. κἀκεῖνοι
μὲν μεθίστανται πρὸς ὀλίγον· τοῖς δὲ οὐκ ἔστιν
εἰς οὐδὲν ἔτι τῶν ἰδίων ἐπάνοδος, ἀλλὰ περίασι
μικρὸν ὕστερον πτωχοί, καὶ οὐδεὶς ἂν προσαγο-
ρεύσειεν ἰδὼν ἔτι τῶν πρότερον διαρρηγνυμένων.[4]
4 Τοσαύτη δ' ἐστὶν ἡ τοῦ τύφου δύναμις ὥστε
παρὰ μὲν τῶν βαφέων[5] ἀγοράσεις δυοῖν μνῶν ἢ
τριῶν καλὴν πορφύραν· δημοσίᾳ δ' εἰ ἐθέλοις
πολλῶν πάνυ ταλάντων ὤνιος. καὶ τὰς μὲν ἐκ
τῆς ἀγορᾶς ταινίας ὀλίγων δραχμῶν, τὰς δὲ ἐκ
τῆς ἐκκλησίας πολλάκις ἁπάσης τῆς οὐσίας. καὶ
τοὺς μὲν ἐπὶ τῆς ἀγορᾶς κηρυττομένους ἀθλίους

---

[1] τοὺς γὰρ U : τοὺς BM.

[2] ἀγρῶν] ἀγορῶν H, marginal correction adopted by Arnim and Budé.

[3] καθάπερ Pflugk : καθώσπερ.

[4] τοὺς γὰρ δοξοκόπους . . . διαρρηγνυμένων deleted by Emperius.

[5] βαφέων Emperius : βαρβάρων.

---

[1] Crowns of ivy or myrtle were sometimes worn to ward off drunkenness ; cf. Athenaeus 15. 675 d–e.

a fool like that, if he so desired, might have for the asking any number of crowns, not merely of olive or of oak, but even of ivy or of myrtle,[1] often he sells his house and his lands and thereafter goes about hungry and clad in a shabby little cloak. Ah but, says he, his name is publicly proclaimed by his fellow citizens—just as is that of a runaway slave ! With good reason, therefore, men use in connexion with the votes passed in Assembly the branch of the olive,[2] because of its native bitterness ! For the notoriety-seekers are driven out of their fields by the democracies with shouting and clamour,[3] just as, methinks, the starlings are driven out by the farmers. Moreover, though the starlings withdraw for a little while, the notoriety-seekers can never again return to anything that once was theirs, nay, a short while later they go about as beggars and no longer would any one of all who formerly were fain to burst their lungs with shouting greet them if he saw them.

However, such is the spell of this infatuation that, though you will buy from the dyers for two or three minas a handsome purple mantle, should you wish one by public award it would cost you very many talents.[4] Again, though you will buy the ribbons of the market-place for a few drachmas, those of the Assembly will often cost you all your fortune. Furthermore, while persons who are cried for sale in the market-place [5] all deem wretched, those cried

[2] Perhaps an allusion to the wreaths carved on certain stones containing official records.

[3] To gain the shouts of the mob they are driven to sacrifice their property.

[4] The intrinsic value of the mina was one sixtieth part of the talent, but one hundred times that of the drachma.

[5] The slaves ; cf. § 2.

πάντες[1] νομίζουσι, τοὺς δ' ἐν τῷ θεάτρῳ μακαρίους·
καὶ τούτους μὲν κηρύττεσθαί φασιν, ἐκείνους δὲ
ἀποκηρύττεσθαι, δῆλον ὅτι παρὰ μίαν συλλαβὴν
γιγνομένης τῆς διαφορᾶς.

5   Οὕτω δὲ πάνυ τῶν ἀνθρώπων κατεφρόνησαν οἱ
πρότερον καὶ τὴν εὐήθειαν αὐτῶν συνεῖδον ὥστε
ὑπὲρ τῶν μεγίστων πόνων καὶ πληγῶν[2] φύλλα
προύθεσαν. ἀλλ' ὅμως εἰσὶν οἱ χάριν τούτων
ἀποθνήσκειν αἱρούμενοι. τῶν δὲ αἰγῶν οὐκ ἂν
οὐδεμία κατακρημνίσειεν αὑτὴν κοτίνου χάριν,
καὶ ταῦτα παρούσης ἑτέρας νομῆς. καίτοι ταῖς
μὲν αἰξὶν οὐκ ἀηδὴς ὁ κότινος, ἄνθρωπος δὲ οὐκ
ἂν φάγοι. καὶ τὴν μὲν ἐξ Ἰσθμοῦ πίτυν, οὐδὲν
οὖσαν τῶν ἄλλων χλωροτέραν, μετὰ πολλοῦ πόνου
καὶ κακῶν ἀναιροῦνται, πολλάκις ἀργύριον πολὺ
διδόντες· καὶ ταῦτα τοῦ φυτοῦ μηδεμίαν ὠφέλειαν
ἔχοντος· οὔτε γὰρ σκιὰν ποιεῖν οὔτε καρπὸν φέρειν
δύναται τό τε φύλλον δριμὺ καὶ καπνῶδες· τῆς δ'
ἐκ Μεγάρων πίτυος οὐδεὶς ἐπιστρέφεται. κἂν μὲν
ἕτερός τις μὴ κατεαγὼς τὴν κεφαλὴν δήσηται,[3]
καταγελᾶται· τοῖς δὲ βασιλεῦσι πρέπειν δοκεῖ καὶ
πολλαὶ μυριάδες τεθνήκασιν ὑπὲρ τούτου τοῦ
ῥάκους.

6   Ὅτι μὲν γὰρ διὰ χρυσοῦν πρόβατον ἀνάστατον
συνέβη γενέσθαι τηλικαύτην οἰκίαν τὴν Πέλοπος

---

[1] πάντες P : πάντας UBH, ἅπαντας M.
[2] πληγῶν] δαπανῶν Arnim.   [3] δήσηται] διαδήσηται Cobet.

in the theatre [1] they deem fortunate ; besides, they claim that the latter are cried, the former decried, a single syllable evidently constituting the sole difference !

Yes, so completely did the men of old despise mankind, and so clearly did they see their fatuity, that as a reward for the greatest hardships and buffetings they offered leaves ! [2] Yet there are some who to gain those leaves elect to die. But no nanny-goat would hurl herself over a cliff for the sake of a sprig of wild olive, especially when other pasturage is handy. And yet, though goats do not find the wild olive distasteful, a human being could not eat it. Again, take the Isthmian pine [3] ; while it is no greener than the other varieties, with much toil and hardship men strive to gain it, often paying much money for it—and that too, although the tree has no utility at all, for it can neither provide shade nor bear fruit, and, besides, the leaf is acrid and smoky ; on the other hand, no one turns his head to look at the pine from Megara. [4] Moreover, if any one else has his head bound—unless he has suffered a fracture—he is the object of ridicule ; yet for kings the headband is thought becoming and untold thousands have given their lives for the sake of this scrap of cloth.

Why, because of a golden lamb it came to pass that a mighty house like that of Pelops was over-

[1] Honours voted in Assembly often were conferred in the theatre.

[2] An allusion to the wreaths awarded the athletic victor.

[3] The " Isthmian pine " was awarded the victor in the Isthmian Games held at the Isthmus of Corinth in honour of Poseidon.

[4] There seems to have been no great botanical difference, but Megara had no national games of its own.

οἱ τραγῳδοί φασιν. καὶ κατεκόπη μὲν τὰ τοῦ
Θυέστου τέκνα, τῇ Πελοπίᾳ δὲ ὁ πατὴρ ἐμίχθη
καὶ τὸν Αἴγισθον ἔσπειρεν. οὗτος δ' ἀπέκτεινε
μὲν μετὰ τῆς Κλυταιμνήστρας τὸν Ἀγαμέμνονα
τὸν ποιμένα τῶν Ἀχαιῶν, κἀκείνην Ὀρέστης ὁ
υἱός, καὶ τοῦτο ποιήσας εὐθὺς ἐμαίνετο. τούτοις
δὲ οὐκ ἄξιον ἀπιστεῖν, ἃ γέγραπται μὲν οὐχ ὑπὸ
τῶν τυχόντων ἀνδρῶν, Εὐριπίδου καὶ Σοφοκλέους,
λέγεται δὲ ἐν μέσοις τοῖς θεάτροις· ἔτι δὲ ἰδεῖν
ἔστιν ἑτέραν οἰκίαν συντριβεῖσαν πλουσιωτέραν
ἐκείνης διὰ γλῶτταν[1] καὶ νὴ Δία ἑτέραν κιν-
δυνεύουσαν.

7   Τοιούτων δὲ τῶν κατὰ τὴν δόξαν ὄντων καὶ
μυρίων ἄλλων ἀτοπωτέρων, πῶς οὐχὶ τῷ παντὶ
δυσχερέστερος[2] ὁ πρὸς ταύτην κεχηνὼς τοῦ πρὸς
ἄλλ' ὁτιοῦν ἐπτοημένου; τὸν φίλοψον εἷς ἰχθὺς
ἀποπίμπλησι καὶ οὐδεὶς ἂν[3] αὐτὸν κωλύσειεν
ἥδεσθαι τῶν ἐχθρῶν· ὁμοίως ὁ πρὸς παῖδας
ἀθλίως ἔχων, ἐὰν εἰς ὡραῖον[4] ἐμπέσῃ, τοῦτον ἕνα
ὄντα θεραπεύει, καὶ πολλάκις μικροῦ κατειργάσατο.
τὸν οἰνόφλυγα ἐν Θάσιον κατέπλησε,[5] καὶ πιὼν
Ἐνδυμίωνος ἥδιον καθεύδει· τῷ δοξοκόπῳ δὲ

---

[1] γλῶτταν] δόξαν Herwerden.
[2] δυσχερέστερος] δυστυχέστερος UH.
[3] ἂν added by Emperius.
[4] εἰς ὡραῖον Casaubon : εἰς ῥωμαῖον BPH, εἰς ῥωμαίων
M, εἰς ῥωμαίων U.
[5] κατέπλησε] κατέπιε M, ὃ κατέπιεν UB.

---

[1] The fortunes of the house of Pelops were a favourite
theme with the tragic poets. One of Sophocles' extant
dramas (Electra) and at least three now lost testify to his
interest in the story. Four of the extant plays of Euripides
(Electra, Iphigeneia at Aulis, Iphigeneia among the Taurians,

turned, as we learn from the tragic poets.[1] And
not only were the children of Thyestes cut in pieces,
but Pelopia's father [2] lay with her and begot Aegisthus ; and Aegisthus with Clytemnestra's aid slew
Agamemnon, " the shepherd of the Achaeans "[3];
and then Clytemnestra's son Orestes slew her, and,
having done so, he straightway went mad. One
should not disbelieve these things, for they have
been recorded by no ordinary men—Euripides and
Sophocles—and also are recited in the midst of the
theatres. Furthermore, one may behold another
house, more affluent than that of Pelops, which has
been ruined because of a tongue, and, in sooth,
another house which is now in jeopardy.[4]

But such being the accompaniments of notoriety,
yes, and countless others even more absurd, why is
not he who gapes hungrily in that direction altogether
more disgusting than the person who is distraught
with passion for anything else at all ? The gourmet
is satisfied with a single fish and none of his enemies
would interfere with his enjoyment of it ; similarly
he who is a pitiable victim of lust for boys, if he comes
upon a handsome lad, devotes himself to this one
only and often prevails upon him at a small cost. A
single jar of Thasian wine is all the drunkard can hold,
and when he has swallowed it he sleeps more sweetly
than Endymion ; yet your notoriety-seeker would not

and *Orestes*) deal with the same theme. Dio should have
known the famous trilogy of Aeschylus, the *Oresteia*, but
for some reason he overlooks it.

[2] Thyestes was father of Pelopia ; cf. Apollodorus, *Bibliotheca*, epitome 2. 14.

[3] A familiar Homeric tag.

[4] The houses of Nero and Domitian respectively ; cf.
Introduction.

οὐκ ἂν εἷς[1] ἐπαινῶν ἐξαρκέσειεν, ἀλλ᾽ οὐδὲ χίλιοι πολλάκις.

8 Ὅτι μὲν γὰρ ῥᾷον ἐστι μεταχειρίσασθαι τὸ χαλεπώτατον μειράκιον τοῦ μετριωτάτου δήμου τίς οὐκ ἂν φήσειεν; ὅσῳ μέντοι προχωρεῖ τὸ τῆς δόξης ἐπὶ πλέον, τοσούτῳ μᾶλλον οὐκ ἔστιν ὕπνου λαχεῖν· ἀλλ᾽ ὥσπερ οἱ φρενιτίζοντες, ἀεὶ μετέωρος οὗτος καὶ νύκτωρ καὶ μεθ᾽ ἡμέραν. νὴ Δί᾽, ἀλλ᾽ ἐκείνους ἰδεῖν ἔστιν περὶ τὸν οἶνον καὶ τὰς ἑταίρας καὶ τὰ ὀπτανεῖα. τῷ τοιούτῳ δὲ οὐκ ἀνάγκη πολὺ μὲν ὄψον ἀγοράζειν, πολὺν δὲ οἶνον; αὐλητὰς δὲ καὶ μίμους καὶ κιθαριστὰς καὶ θαυματοποιοὺς συνακτέον, ἔτι δὲ πύκτας καὶ παγκρατιαστὰς καὶ παλαιστὰς καὶ δρομεῖς καὶ τὸ τοιοῦτον ἔθνος, εἴ γε μὴ μέλλει φαύλως μηδὲ ἀγεννῶς ἑστιάσειν τὸ πλῆθος.

9 Τοιοῦτος μὲν γὰρ οὐδεὶς πώποτε τῶν ὀψοφάγων γέγονεν ὅστις ἐπεθύμησε λέοντος ἀγρίου ἢ ταύρων ἑκατόν· οἱ δὲ τοῖς πολλοῖς ἀρέσκειν ἐθέλοντες οὐ μόνον τούτων ἐπιθυμοῦσιν, ἀλλ᾽ ὅσων οὐδὲ εἰπεῖν ἔστιν. οὐ γὰρ ὀλίγοις λίνοις, φασίν, ἢ δυσὶν ἢ τρισὶν ἑταίραις οὐδὲ δέκα Λεσβίαις[2] θηρεύεται δόξα καὶ δῆμος ὅλος εἰς πειθὼ καὶ φιλίαν ἄγεται, μυρίων ἀντιπραττόντων· ἀλλὰ ἀνάγκη πόλεως ἀκολασίαν ἔχειν καὶ φιλῳδὸν καὶ φιλοχορευτὴν καὶ φιλοπότην καὶ ὀψοφάγον εἶναι καὶ πάντα δὴ τὰ τοιαῦτα μὴ ὡς ἕνα ἄνδρα, ἀλλὰ μυρίους ἢ δὶς

---

[1] εἷς Reiske : οὐδείς.
[2] Λεσβίαις UB : λεσβίοις MPH.

---

[1] The term mime, frequently used to designate a low form of comedy popular in Sicily and southern Italy, is here used of the performers in such productions.

be satisfied with the praise of just one person, nay, not even with that of a thousand in many instances.

Who would not agree that it is easier to handle the most difficult youth than the most moderate community ? And yet the farther the craze for notoriety progresses, so much the more impossible it is to get any sleep ; instead, like the victims of delirium, your seeker after fame is always up in the air both night and day. " Right, by Heaven," somebody may say, " but you can see those other chaps busy with their wine and their mistresses and their kitchens." Yes, but does not the seeker after fame find it necessary to buy a lot of food and wine ? And he must collect flute-players and mimes [1] and harpists and jugglers and, more than that, pugilists and pancratiasts [2] and wrestlers and runners and all that tribe—at least unless he intends to entertain the mob in a cheap and beggarly manner.

For though there has never been a gourmet so voracious as to crave a savage lion or a hundred bulls, those who wish to please the masses crave not merely the things just listed but things too numerous to mention. For " not with a few nets," as the saying goes, or with two or three harlots, or even with ten Lesbian girls, is popularity hunted and a whole community rendered obedient and friendly, since thousands are competing for it ; nay, he who courts popular favour must have a whole city's licentiousness and be a devotee of singing, of dancing, of drinking, of eating, and, indeed, of all such things, not as one single individual, but rather as ten thousand or twenty thousand or a hundred thousand, in keeping

[2] The pancratiast used a combination of wrestling and boxing.

μυρίους ἢ δεκάκις, ἡλίκης ἄν¹ ποτε ἐραστὴς ᾖ²
10 πόλεως. ἀεὶ δ' ἂν παρὰ τῷ τοιούτῳ καταλάβοις
αὐλῶν συρίγγων τ' ἐνοπὴν ὅμαδόν τ' ἀνθρώπων.

παρὰ δὲ πλήθουσι τράπεζαι σίτου καὶ κρειῶν,
μέθυ δ' ἐκ κρητήρων οἰνοχόοι φορέουσι.

κνισῆεν δέ τε δῶμα περιστεναχίζεται αὐλῇ
ἤματα, νύκτας δ' αὖτε παρ' αἰδοίῃς ἀλόχοισιν

οὐδέποθ' εὕδουσιν, οὐδ' ἂν πάνυ πολλοὺς ὑπο-
στορέσωνται τάπητας.

11 Ὥστε τούς γε φιλόπαιδας καὶ σφόδρα, οἶμαι,
μακαρίζειν αὐτοὺς τοῖς φιλοδόξοις παραβάλλοντας,
ὅταν αὐτοὶ μὲν ὄρτυγας ζητῶσιν ἢ ἀλεκτρυόνα ἢ
ἀηδόνιον, τοῖς δὲ ὁρῶσιν³ ἀνάγκην οὖσαν Ἀμοιβέα
ἢ Πῶλον⁴ ζητεῖν ἢ τῶν Ὀλυμπίασι νενικηκότων
τινὰ πέντε μισθοῦσθαι ταλάντων. καὶ αὐτοὶ μὲν ἢ⁵
τὸν παιδαγωγὸν ἢ τὸν ἀκόλουθον ἐγάστρισαν· οἱ
δὲ ἂν μὴ τοὐλάχιστον ἑκατὸν τῆς ἡμέρας πολυτελῶς ἑστιάσωσιν οὐδὲν αὐτοῖς ὄφελος.

Τοῖς μὲν οὖν κάμνουσιν ἡσυχίας προνοοῦσιν οἱ
θεραπεύοντες ὅπως καθεύδωσι· τοῖς δὲ δοξοκόποις,
ὅταν ἡσυχίας τυγχάνωσι, τότε μάλιστα ὕπνος οὐκ
12 ἔπεισιν. οἱ μὲν οὖν χρημάτων ἢ γένους ἐπιτυ-

---

¹ ἡλίκης ἄν Selden: ἤδίκης ἄν U, ἠδίκεις ἄν B, ἢ δίκησάν
MH, εἰδήκεις ἄν P.
² ᾖ added by Selden.
³ ὁρῶσιν Emperius: ἐρῶσιν UBM, δόξης ἐρῶσιν PH.
⁴ Ἀμοιβέα ἢ Πῶλον Wilamowitz: ἀμοιβαίαν πῶλον.
⁵ ᾖ] ᾖτε B, εἴς τε M, ἕνα Arnim.

---

¹ Iliad 10. 13.
² A paraphrase of Odyssey 9. 8-10, descriptive of palace
life at the court of Alcinoüs in Phaeacia.

with the size of the city whose favour he is courting. At such a person's house you will always find

> The shrill of flutes and pipes, the din of men.[1]

And at his house tables are laden with bread and meat, and from mixing-bowls cupbearers bear drink.[2]

> By day the hall with fatty savour reeks
> And makes the court to echo with its din,
> While in the night, beside their wives revered [3]—

they never sleep, not though they spread beneath them very many rugs.

Thus the boy-lovers, I fancy, count themselves extremely fortunate as they compare themselves with the popularity-seekers, seeing that they themselves seek only quails or a cock or a tiny nightingale,[4] while those others, they observe, must needs seek some Amoebeus [5] or Polus [6] or hire some Olympic victor for a fee of five talents. Moreover, while they themselves have filled the belly of one man, the tutor or the attendant of the lad, the others, unless they provide a sumptuous banquet for at least a hundred daily, derive no advantage at all.

Again, when men are ill, their attendants provide quiet for them so that they may sleep ; but with the popularity-seekers, whenever they do obtain a bit of quiet, that is the time above all when sleep will not come. Now those who have been blessed with

---

[3] *Odyssey* 10. 10-11, spoken by Odysseus about the palace of Aeolus.

[4] As gifts for their beloved.

[5] Famous singer of the third century ; cf. Athenaeus 14. 623 d.

[6] Famous tragic actor ; cf. Lucian, *Necyomanteia* 16, and J. B. O'Connor, *Chapters in History of Actors and Acting in Ancient Greece*, pp. 128 ff.

χόντες ἤ τινος τῶν τοιούτων ἢ σώματος ἢ διανοίας[1]
ἢ λαλιὰν γοῦν περιποιησάμενοι, καθάπερ ἐπτερω-
μένοι μόνον οὐ κατ' ἄστρων φέρονται, δημαγωγοί
τε καὶ ξεναγοὶ καὶ σοφισταὶ λεγόμενοι, δήμους
καὶ σατράπας καὶ μαθητὰς θηρεύοντες· τῶν δὲ
ἄλλων ἕκαστος τῶν μηδεμίαν χορηγίαν ἐχόντων
ὑπὸ δὲ τῆς αὐτῆς νόσου κρατουμένων, περιέρχεται
πρὸς ἕτερον ζῶν[2] καὶ τί περὶ αὑτοῦ λέγει τις
φροντίζων, κἂν μὲν εὐφημήσῃ τις, ὡς οἴεται,
μακάριος καὶ φαιδρός, εἰ δὲ μή, ταπεινός τε καὶ
κατηφὴς καὶ τοιοῦτον αὑτὸν εἶναι νομίζων ὁποῖον
ἂν εἴπῃ τις. καὶ δίαιταν μὲν ἢ δίκην ἂν ἔχῃ πρός
τινα, οὐκ ἀξιοῖ τὸν διαιτητὴν ἢ τὸν δικαστὴν τοῖς
τυχοῦσι προσέχειν μάρτυσιν, αὐτὸς δ' ὑπὲρ ἑαυτοῦ
πάντας ἀξιόχρεως ἡγεῖται.

13 Τί δὴ κακοδαιμονέστερον ἀνθρώπων ἐπ' ἄλλοις
κειμένων καὶ τὸν ἀπαντῶντα κύριον ἐχόντων, πρὸς
ὃν ἀεὶ βλέπειν ἀνάγκη καὶ σκοπεῖν τὸ πρόσωπον
ἑκάστου, καθάπερ τοῖς οἰκέταις τὸ τῶν δεσποτῶν;
πᾶσα μὲν οὖν ἐστι δουλεία χαλεπή· τοὺς δὲ ἀπὸ
τύχης ἐν οἰκίᾳ τοιαύτῃ[3] δουλεύοντας ἐν ᾗ δύο ἢ
τρεῖς δεσπόται, καὶ ταῦτα ταῖς τε ἡλικίαις καὶ
ταῖς φύσεσι διάφοροι—λέγω δὲ πρεσβύτης ἀνελεύ-
θερος καὶ τούτου παῖδες νεανίσκοι πίνειν καὶ
σπαθᾶν θέλοντες—τίς οὐκ ἂν τῶν ἄλλων οἰκετῶν
ὁμολογήσειεν ἀθλιωτέρους, ὅταν τοσούτους δέῃ
θεραπεύειν καὶ τούτων ἕκαστον ἄλλο τι βουλόμενον καὶ προστάττοντα;

---

[1] ἢ διανοίας Morel : ἢ ἀπονοίας, εὐτονίας Arnim.
[2] ζῶν] ζητῶν H.   [3] τοιαύτῃ Emperius : τῇ αὐτῇ.

riches or ancestry or the like or with physical or
mental excellence or who, at any rate, have acquired
a glib tongue, these, as if endowed with wings, are
all but carried to the stars, being called leaders of the
people and condottieri and sophists, courting communities and satraps and pupils ; but of the others,
who have no adventitious backing but are victims
of the same malady, each goes about living his life
with his eye on somebody else and concerned about
what people are saying of him, and if people speak
well of him, as he imagines, he is a happy man, cheerful of countenance, but otherwise he is depressed and
downcast and considers himself to be the sort of man
they say he is. Again, if he is involved in litigation
with any one before an arbitrator or a judge, he does
not expect the arbitrator or the judge to heed chance
witnesses, and yet he himself in matters which concern himself regards all and sundry as worthy of
credence.

What, then, is more ill-starred than human beings
who are at the mercy of others and in the power
of any one who meets them, always compelled to
keep their eye on him and to watch his countenance,
just as slaves must watch the countenance of their
masters ? Now any servitude is hard, but those whom
fate has doomed to servitude in a house in which
there are two or three masters, and masters, too,
who differ in both age and disposition—for example,
a niggardly old man and that man's youthful sons,
bent on drinking and extravagance—who would not
agree that slaves so placed are more wretched than
the others, seeing that they must serve so many
masters, each of whom desires and orders something
different ?

Εἰ δέ τις δημόσιος οἰκέτης εἴη πρεσβυτῶν,[1]
νεανίσκων, πενήτων, πλουσίων, ἀσώτων, φιλαργύ-
ρων, ποῖός τις ἂν ὁ τοιοῦτος εἴη; οἶμαι δέ, εἴ τις
ἐν τοιαύτῃ πόλει χρήματα ἔχων ἠναγκάζετο βιοῦν
ἐν ᾗ πᾶσιν ἐξῆν ἁρπάζειν τὰ τοῦ πέλας καὶ μηδεὶς
νόμος ἐκώλυε, παραχρῆμα ἂν ἀπέστη τῶν χρημάτων, εἰ καὶ φιλαργυρίᾳ τοὺς πώποτε ὑπερβε-
14 βλήκει. τοῦτο δὴ νῦν ἐπὶ τῆς δόξης ἐστίν. ἐφεῖται
γὰρ εἰς ταύτην τῷ βουλομένῳ τινὰ βλάπτειν καὶ
πολίτῃ καὶ ξένῳ καὶ μετοίκῳ.

15 Τοῖς ἀτίμοις ἀβίωτος εὐλόγως ὁ βίος φαίνεται,
καὶ πολλοὶ μᾶλλον αἱροῦνται θάνατον ἢ ζῆν τὴν
ἐπιτιμίαν ἀποβαλόντες, ὅτι τῷ ἐθελήσαντι τύπτειν
ἔξεστι καὶ κόλασις οὐκ ἔστιν ἰδίᾳ[2] τοῦ προπηλακί-
ζοντος. οὐκοῦν τὸν δυξυκύπυν ἅπασιν ἔξεστι
τύπτειν τῷ παντὶ χαλεπωτέρας πληγὰς τῶν εἰς
τὸ σῶμα· καίτοι τοὺς μὲν ἀτίμους οὐκ ἂν εὕροι
τις ῥᾳδίως ὑπό τινος τοῦτο πάσχοντας· τὸ γὰρ
νεμεσητὸν οἱ πολλοὶ καὶ τὸν φθόνον εὐλαβοῦνται
καὶ τὸ τελευταῖον ἐκ τῶν ἀσθενεστέρων αὐτοῖς
οὐδείς ἐστι κίνδυνος. τοῦ δὲ βλασφημεῖν μάλιστα
τοὺς δοκοῦντας ἐνδόξους οὐδεὶς φείδεται οὐδὲ
ἀδύνατος οὐδεὶς οὕτως,[3] ὅστις οὐκ ἂν ἰσχύσαι
16 ῥῆμα εἰπεῖν. τοιγαροῦν μέτριός τις τῶν ἀρχαίων
συνεχῶς τινος αὐτῷ προσφέροντος τοιούτους λόγους, Εἰ μὴ παύσῃ κακῶς ἀκούων ὑπὲρ ἐμοῦ,

[1] After πρεσβυτῶν Reiske deletes ἤ.
[2] ἰδίᾳ UBM] νὴ δία PH, οὐδεμία Pflugk.
[3] οὕτως added by Emperius.

But suppose a person were to be slave of a community consisting of old and young, of poor and rich, of wastrels and misers, what would the condition of such a person be? Again, methinks, if a man of wealth were forced to live in the kind of city in which all were free to plunder the possessions of their neighbours and there were no law to prevent it, he would renounce his wealth forthwith, no matter if he had surpassed all the world in avarice. This, in fact, is the case with popularity to-day. For in that respect licence has been granted to any one who so desires, whether citizen or alien or foreign resident, to injure any one.

To the disfranchised life seems with good reason not worth living, and many choose death rather than life after losing their citizenship, for whoever so desires is free to strike them and there exists no private means of punishing him who treats them with contumely. Well then, all are free to give the popularity-seeker blows altogether more grievous than those which are dealt the body. Yet the disfranchised, one would find, are not lightly subjected to this treatment by any one; for most men are on their guard against righteous indignation and ill will, and, finally, the disfranchised have naught to fear from any who are weaker than they. When it comes to vituperation, however, especially vituperation of those who are thought to enjoy esteem, no one forbears, and no one is so powerless as not to be able to utter some telling phrase. For that very reason a certain mild-tempered man of olden days, when somebody kept bringing him reports of that kind of language, was moved to say, " If you do not stop listening to bad words about me, I too shall listen to

κἀγώ, φησιν, ὑπὲρ σοῦ κακῶς ἀκούσομαι. βέλτιον
δὲ ἴσως ἦν, μηδὲ εἰ λέγει τὴν ἀρχὴν προσποι-
εῖσθαι.

Τὸν οἰκέτην πολλάκις ἀνειμένον καὶ παίζοντα
ὁ δεσπότης περιπεσὼν κλαίειν ἐποίησε· τὸν δὲ
τῆς δόξης ἥττονα ὁ βουλόμενος ἑνὶ ῥήματι συν-
έστειλεν. εἴ τις ἐπῳδὰς ἐπίστατο τοιαύτας παρὰ
τῆς Μηδείας μαθὼν ἢ παρὰ τῶν Θετταλῶν,[1] ὥστε
φθεγγόμενος τῶν ἀνθρώπων οὓς ἤθελε ποιεῖν
κλαίειν καὶ ὀδυνᾶσθαι μηδενὸς κακοῦ παρόντος,
οὐκ ἂν ἐδόκει τυραννὶς εἶναι ἡ τούτου δύναμις;
πρὸς οὖν τὸν ἐπὶ δόξῃ κεχαυνωμένον οὐκ ἔστιν
17 οὐδεὶς ὃς οὐκ ἔχει ταύτην τὴν ἰσχύν. δύο γὰρ ἢ
τρία ῥήματα εἰπὼν εἰς συμφορὰν καὶ λύπην
ἐνέβαλεν. καὶ μὴν εἴ γέ τις οὕτως ἐκ δαιμονίου
τινὸς ἔχοι τὸ σῶμα, ὥστε ἄν τις αὐτῷ καταράσηται,
παραχρῆμα πυρέττειν ἢ τὴν κεφαλὴν ἀλγεῖν, οὗτος
ἂν[2] ἀθλιώτερος ὑπῆρχε τῶν τρισαθλίων· εἰ δέ τις
οὕτως ἀσθενῶς ἔχοι τὴν διάνοιαν, ὥστε εἴ τις
λοιδορήσειεν αὐτὸν ἐξίστασθαι παραχρῆμα τὴν ψυ-
χήν, πῶς οὐχὶ τῷ τοιούτῳ φευκτὸς ὁ βίος;

Εἰ δέ τις κρίνοιτο καθ' ἑκάστην ἡμέραν περὶ
ὅτου δήποτε, ἢ περὶ τοῦ ζῆν ἢ περὶ τῶν χρημάτων,
ἆρ' οὐχὶ τῷ παντὶ βέλτιον ἐᾶσαι τοῦτο καὶ μηκέτι
τὸ λοιπὸν κινδυνεύειν,[3] εἰ μὲν περὶ χρημάτων,
18 τὰ χρήματα, εἰ δὲ περὶ τοῦ ζῆν, τὸν βίον; τί οὖν;
ὁ περὶ τῆς δόξης ἀγὼν οὐκ ἀεὶ τοῖς ἀνθρώποις[4]

---

[1] Θετταλῶν] Θετταλίδων Cobet.
[2] ἄν added by Pflugk.
[3] After κινδυνεύειν Arnim deletes καί.
τοῖς ἀνθρώποις] deleted by Wilamowitz.

bad words about you." But perhaps it would be better, in case some one starts using abusive language, not even to notice whether the man is speaking at all.

The slave who is unrestrained and given to jesting, if his master catches him at it, is often made to smart for it ; but the person who is subservient to public opinion is humbled by any one at all with a single word. If one were acquainted with spells learned from Medea or the Thessalians [1] which were so potent that by uttering them he could make any one he pleased weep and suffer pain though confronted by no misfortune, would not his power be regarded as tyranny ? Well, in dealing with one who has become puffed up by reputation there is none who does not have this power ; for by speaking two or three words you have plunged him into misery and anguish. Again, if because of some supernatural influence one's body were to be so constituted that, if any one should curse him, he would immediately have a fever or a headache, that man would be more wretched than the thrice wretched ; and if one were to be so feeble-minded that, in case some one should revile him, he would immediately become deranged, why would not life for such a man be a thing to shun ?

Or let us put it this way. Suppose one were to be put on trial every day concerning anything whatever, whether his life or his property, would it not be altogether preferable to renounce that thing and to cease being in jeopardy for the future—if it be property, then the property ; if it be life, then his life ? How then ? Is not the trial concerning reputation always in progress wherever there are

[1] The Thessalians were famed for their occult powers.

τοῖς ἀνοήτοις ἐνέστηκεν, οὐ μόνον[1] ἅπαξ τῆς
ἡμέρας, ἀλλὰ πολλάκις, οὐδὲ ἐφ᾽ ὡρισμένοις
δικασταῖς, ἀλλὰ πᾶσιν ἁπλῶς, καὶ τούτοις ἀνω-
μότοις καὶ μήτε μαρτύρων ἐπιστρεφομένοις μήτε
τεκμηρίων; μήτε γὰρ εἰδότες μήτε ἀκούοντες
μήτε λαχόντες δικάζουσι, καὶ οὐδὲν αὐτοῖς διαφέρει
πίνουσιν ἢ λουομένοις τὴν ψῆφον φέρειν· καὶ τὸ
πάντων δεινότατον· ὃν γὰρ ἂν ἀπολύσῃ τήμερον,
19 αὔριον καταδικάζει. οὐκοῦν ἀνάγκη τὸν ὑπὸ τῆς
νόσου ταύτης ἐχόμενον ὑπεύθυνον περιέρχεσθαι
καὶ προσέχειν ἑκάστῳ καὶ δεδοικέναι μή τινα
ἑκὼν ἢ ἄκων λυπήσῃ, μάλιστα τῶν ἑτοίμων[2] τινὰ
καὶ τῶν εὐτραπέλων. εἰ γὰρ καὶ σμικρόν, οἷα[3]
πολλὰ συμβαίνει, προσκρούσας τινὶ τύχοι, εὐθὺς
ἐπαφῆκε ῥῆμα[4] χαλεπόν· καὶ τοῦτο εἰπών, ἐὰν
μὲν ἀποτύχῃ πως, οὐδὲν[5] ἧττον ἐτάραξεν· ἐὰν δ᾽
ἐπιτύχῃ τοῦ καιρίου[6] παραχρῆμα ἀνῄρηκεν. πολλοὶ
μὲν γὰρ οὕτως ἔχουσιν ὥστε ὑπὸ παντὸς διατρέ-
πεσθαι καὶ διαρρεῖν.

20 Οὐ μὴν ἀλλὰ καὶ ἐνίοτε ἄλλα ἐπ᾽ ἄλλοις μᾶλλον
ἰσχύει· καθάπερ, οἶμαι, τῶν παιδαρίων ἕκαστον
ἰδιότροπόν τινα μορμὼ δέδοικε καὶ ταύτην συν-
είθισται φοβεῖσθαι—τὰ μὲν γὰρ φύσει δειλὰ πᾶν
ὅ τι ἂν δείξῃ τις ὡς φοβερὸν βοᾷ—πλὴν ἐπί γε
τούτων τῶν μειζόνων ὀνείδη[7] τινά ἐστι πρός τινας.

---

[1] οὐ μόνον: οἱ οὐ μόνον PH, μόνον οὐχ BM, οὐ μόνον οὐχ U.
[2] ἑτοίμων] ἰταμῶν Emperius.   [3] οἷα Emperius: ὅσα.
[4] ἐπαφῆκε ῥῆμα TU marg.: ἐσπάθησε ῥῆμα UBMP, εὐπα-
θείας ἔρημα H.   [5] οὐδὲν added by Wilamowitz.
[6] καιρίου Casaubon: κυρίου.   [7] ὀνείδη Sonny: ἤδη.

men—that is, foolish men—not merely once a day but many times, and not before a definite panel of judges but before all men without distinction, and, moreover, men not bound by oath, men without regard for either witnesses or evidence? For they sit in judgement without either having knowledge of the case or listening to testimony or having been chosen by lot, and it makes no difference to them if they cast their vote at a drinking bout or at the bath and, most outrageous of all, he who to-day is acquitted to-morrow is condemned. Accordingly, whoever is the victim of this malady of courting popularity is bound to be subject to criticism as he walks about, to pay heed to everyone, and to fear lest wittingly or unwittingly he give offence to somebody, but particularly to one of those who are bold and of ready wit. For if he should have the misfortune to have offended somebody never so little, as often happens, straightway the offended person lets fly a harsh word; and if with that word he perhaps misses his mark, nevertheless he causes dismay, while if he should hit the vital spot he has destroyed his victim forthwith. For the fact is, many are so constituted that they are overwhelmed and made to waste away by anything.

Not only so, but also sometimes one set of things is more potent with one kind of person and another with another; just as, I believe, each youngster fears some bogey peculiar to himself and is wont to be terrified by this—of course lads who are naturally timid cry out no matter what you produce to scare them—however, at least with these more important fellows, certain things are a source of shame with reference to certain persons. The beggar who is a

τὸν πτωχὸν τὸν[1] ἀλαζόνα καὶ θέλοντα φαίνεσθαι
Κροῖσον ἐξίστησιν ὁ Ἶρος· καὶ οὐδὲ τὴν Ὀδύσ-
σειαν ἀναγιγνώσκει διὰ τὸ

ἦλθε δ' ἐπὶ πτωχὸς πανδήμιος, ὃς κατὰ ἄστυ
πτωχεύεσκ' Ἰθάκης·

21 τὸν ἐκ δούλων ὁ Κέκροψ,[2] τὸν εὐτελῆ τὴν ὄψιν
καὶ καλὸν εἶναι βουλόμενον ὁ Θερσίτης. ἐὰν μὲν
γὰρ ὡς[3] λίχνον ἢ φιλάργυρον σκώψῃς ἢ κίναιδον
ἢ καθόλου πονηρὸν τὸν ἐπὶ τῇ σωφροσύνῃ κομῶντα
καὶ τὴν ἀρετὴν ἐπιγεγραμμένον, ὅλον ἀπολώλεκας.
ὁ Περσεὺς τὴν κεφαλὴν τῆς Γοργόνος περιφέρων
καὶ ταύτην τοῖς ἐχθροῖς δεικνὺς ἐποίει λίθους· οἱ
πολλοὶ δὲ ὑφ' ἑνὸς ῥήματος, ἐὰν ἀκούσωσι, λίθοι
γεγόνασι· καὶ τοῦτο οὐ δεῖ περιφέρειν, ἐν πήρᾳ
φυλάττοντα αὐτό.[4]

22 Καίτοι φέρε, εἰ καὶ τῶν ὀρνέων τὰς φωνὰς
συνίεμεν, τῶν κοράκων ἢ κολοιῶν, καὶ τῶν ἄλλων
ζῴων, οἷον βατράχων ἢ τεττίγων, δῆλον ὅτι καὶ
ταῖς τούτων φωναῖς ἂν προσείχομεν, τί λέγει περὶ
ἡμῶν ὁ κολοιὸς ὁ πετόμενος ἢ τί φησιν ἡ κίττα
καὶ τίνα ἔχει δόξαν. οὐκοῦν εὐτύχημα τὸ μὴ
ξυνιέναι. πόσοι δὴ τῶν ἀνθρώπων τῶν βατράχων
εἰσὶν ἀφρονέστεροι καὶ τῶν κολοιῶν; ἀλλ' ὅμως
κινεῖ τὰ παρὰ τούτων ἡμᾶς καὶ πάνυ κακῶς
διατίθησιν.

[1] τὸν Emperius : δὲ.
[2] Κέκροψ] Κέρκοψ Geel.
[3] ὡς Crosby : εἰς.
[4] φυλάττοντα αὐτό] φυλάττοντα αὐτήν H, φυλάττοντα Emperius, φυλαττόμενον Pflugk.

[1] *Odyssey* 18. 1-2.   Irus' humiliation at the hands of
Odysseus is a warning to braggarts.

braggart and seeks to appear a Croesus is confounded by Irus ; and he does not even read the *Odyssey* because of the lines which say

> In came a public beggar, who through the town
> Of Ithaca was wont to beg his way.[1]

Just so Cecrops confounds the man of servile parentage, and likewise Thersites confounds the man of shabby appearance but with ambition to be a beauty.[2] The fact is, if by calling him a glutton or a miser or a catamite or a general blackguard you jeer at the man who plumes himself on his temperance and who has enrolled under the banner of virtue, you have ruined him completely. By carrying around the Gorgon's head and displaying it to his foes Perseus turned them to stone ; but most men have been turned to stone by just one word, if it is applied to them ; besides, there is no need to carry this around, guarding it in a wallet.

And yet let me add this : if we understood also the cries of birds—for example, of the ravens or the jackdaws—and of the other creatures such as frogs or cicadae, of course we should pay heed to the cries of these as well, eager to learn what the jackdaw flying by is saying about us, or what the jay is saying and what he thinks about us. It is a lucky thing, then, that we do not understand. But how many human beings are more empty-headed than the frogs and the jackdaws ! Yet for all that, the words they speak excite us and make us utterly wretched.

---

[2] Cecrops and Thersites create confusion in different ways, the one because, as founder of Athens, his social position was secure, the other as a notorious example of an ill-favoured upstart humbled by his betters.

23 Οὐ μὴν ὅ γ' ἀφεὶς ἐλεύθερον ἑαυτὸν ἐπιστρέφεται
τῆς τῶν πολλῶν φλυαρίας, ἀλλὰ τῆς μὲν ἐκείνων
ἀδολεσχίας καταγελᾷ, πάλαι δὴ πρὸς ἅπαντας
εἰρηκώς,

οὐκ ἀλέγω, ὡσεί με γυνὴ βάλοι ἢ πάϊς ἄφρων·
κωφὸν γὰρ βέλος ἀνδρὸς ἀνάλκιδος οὐτιδανοῖο.

τὸν Ἡρακλέα τὸν τοῦ Διὸς πόσους οἴει βλασφημεῖν, τοὺς μὲν ὡς κλῶπα, τοὺς δὲ ὡς βίαιον, τοὺς
δὲ καὶ μοιχὸν λέγειν ἢ τεκνοκτόνον; ἀλλ' ὅμως
οὐδὲν αὐτῷ τούτων ἔμελεν· οὐδὲ ἦν ἴσως τις ὁ
ταῦτα φανερῶς λέγων, ἐπεὶ παραχρῆμα ἂν ὑπέσχε
τὴν δίκην.

24 Εἰ μὴ τῶν ἄλλων καταφρονῆσαι[1] πείσεις σαυτόν,
οὐδέποτε παύσῃ κακοδαιμονῶν, ἀλλ' ἀεὶ βίον
ἄθλιον ζήσεις καὶ χαλεπόν, πᾶσιν ὑποκείμενος
τοῖς βουλομένοις λυπεῖν, καὶ τοῦτο δὴ τὸ τοῦ
λόγου, λαγὼ βίον ζῶν. ἀλλ' ἐκεῖνοι μὲν τοὺς
κύνας καὶ τὰ δίκτυα καὶ τοὺς ἀετοὺς δεδοίκασι·
σὺ δὲ τοὺς λόγους ἐπηχὼς καὶ τρέμων περιελεύσῃ
μηδεμίαν φυλακὴν φυλάξασθαι δυνάμενος, μηδ'
ἂν ὁτιοῦν πράττῃς, μηδ' ἂν ὅπως βούλῃ διάγῃς.

25 ἀλλ' ἐὰν μὲν ἐμβάλλῃς συνεχῶς εἰς τὴν ἀγοράν,
ἀγοραῖος ἀκούσῃ καὶ συκοφάντης· ἐὰν δὲ τοὐναντίον
φυλάττῃ τὸ τοιοῦτον καὶ μᾶλλον ᾖς κατ' οἰκίαν
καὶ πρὸς τοῖς ἑαυτοῦ, δειλὸς καὶ ἰδιώτης καὶ
τὸ μηδέν· ἐὰν[2] παιδείας προνοῇ, εὐήθης καὶ μαλα-

---

[1] καταφρονῆσαι Casaubon : καταφρονήσας.
[2] After ἐὰν Arnim deletes δὲ, with some mss.

---

[1] *Iliad* 11. 389-390, spoken by Diomedes in scorn of the
wound just received from the arrow shot at him by Paris.
[2] Heracles might have been called ruffian on many an
occasion ; " thief " may allude to his theft of the dog

However, he who has asserted his independence pays no heed to the foolish talk of the crowd; rather he mocks at their loquacity, having indeed long since said in answer to them all,

> I care not; 'tis as if a woman threw
> At me, or else some witless lad; for blunt
> The missile of a feeble good-for-naught.[1]

Take Heracles, son of Zeus; how many, think you, were wont to disparage him, some dubbing him thief, some ruffian, some even adulterer or slayer of children?[2] Yet he was not at all disturbed by these taunts, though perhaps there was none who spoke them openly, since he would promptly have suffered for it.

Unless you bring yourself to look with scorn upon all others, you will never end your state of wretchedness; instead, you will always lead a pitiable, yes, a painful existence, being at the mercy of all who wish to hurt you and, as the saying goes, living a hare's life. Nay, hares fear the dogs and the nets and the eagles, but you will go about cowering and quaking before what people say, being utterly unable to provide yourself with any defence, no matter what you may be doing or if you spend your time in any way you please. If you are always rushing into the market-place you will hear yourself called a market idler and a shyster, whereas if, on the contrary, you are wary of that sort of thing and keep more at home and attend to your own affairs you will be called timid and an ignoramus and a nonentity; if you give thought to learning you will be called simple-minded

Cerberus; as for "slayer of children," in a fit of madness caused by Hera, his inveterate enemy, Heracles slew his own children, as we read in Euripides' *Heracles*.

111

κός· ἐὰν[1] ἐπ' ἐργασίας ἧς τινος, βάναυσος· ἐὰν
σχολάζων περιπατῇς,[2] ἀργός· ἐὰν ἐσθῆτα μαλα-
κωτέραν ἀναλάβῃς, ἀλαζὼν καὶ τρυφερός· ἐὰν
ἀνυπόδητος ἐν τριβωνίῳ, μαίνεσθαί σε φήσουσιν.
26 Σωκράτην διαφθείρειν τοὺς νέους ἔφασαν, εἰς τὸ
θεῖον ἀσεβεῖν· καὶ οὐκ εἶπον ταῦτα μόνον· ἧττον
γὰρ ἂν ἦν δεινόν[3]· ἀλλὰ καὶ ἀπέκτειναν αὐτόν,
ἀνυποδησίας δίκην λαμβάνοντες. Ἀριστείδην ἐξω-
στράκισαν Ἀθηναῖοι, καίτοι πεπεισμένοι σαφῶς
ὅτι δίκαιος ἦν. τί[4] δεῖ δόξης ἐπιθυμεῖν, ἧς καὶ
ἐὰν τύχῃ, πολλάκις οὐκ ἐπ' ἀγαθῷ[5] ἀπώνατο;[6]

Τῷ Βίωνι δοκεῖ μὴ δυνατὸν εἶναι τοῖς πολλοῖς
ἀρέσκειν εἰ μὴ πλακοῦντα γενόμενον ἢ Θάσιον·
εὐήθως,[7] ἐμοὶ δοκεῖν. πολλάκις γὰρ οὐδὲ ἐν
δείπνῳ δέκα ἀνθρώπων ὁ πλακοῦς ἤρεσε πᾶσιν,
ἀλλ' ὁ μὲν ἕωλον εἶναί φησιν, ὁ δὲ θερμόν, ὁ δὲ
λίαν γλυκύν· εἰ μὴ νὴ Δία Βίων φησιν ὅτι καὶ
θερμὸν πλακοῦντα καὶ ἕωλον δεῖ γενέσθαι καὶ
ψυχρόν.[8] καθόλου δὲ οὐ τοιοῦτόν ἐστι τὸ πρᾶγμα·
27 πόθεν; ἀλλὰ καὶ μύρον δεῖ καὶ αὐλητρίδα γενέσθαι
καὶ μειράκιον ὡραῖον καὶ Φίλιππον τὸν γελωτο-
ποιόν. λείπεται δὲ ἓν ἴσως, ὃ δεήσει γενέσθαι
τὸν θέλοντα ἀρέσαι τοῖς πολλοῖς, ἀργύριον. οὔκουν, κἂν ἀργύριον γένηταί τις, εὐθὺς ἤρεσεν·
ἀλλὰ δεῖ ῥάττεσθαι καὶ δάκνεσθαι. τί οὖν ἔτι

---

[1] After ἐὰν Arnim deletes δὲ, with some mss.
[2] περιπατῇς Jacobs : προπετῇς or προπέτης.
[3] δεινόν added by Arnim.
[4] After τί Arnim adds οὖν, Emperius δή.
[5] After ἀγαθῷ Arnim deletes πολλάκις.
[6] After ἀπώνατο the mss. read : δέον πολλάκις εὐλαβεῖσθαι,
κἂν ἄρα συμβαίνει τινί, which Emperius deleted. Arnim suspects a lacuna.
[7] After εὐήθως Casaubon deletes ὡς.

and effeminate ; if you are in some business, vulgar ;
if you stroll about at your leisure, lazy ; if you don
rather soft apparel, ostentatious and dandified ; if
you go barefoot and wear a ragged little coat they
will say you are crazy. Socrates, they said, corrupted
the young men, was irreverent toward religion ;
moreover, they did not merely say these things—
for that would have been less shocking—no, they
even killed him, exacting a penalty for his lack of
shoes ! Aristeides was ostracized by the Athenians,
although they were clearly persuaded that he was
just.[1] Why should one crave popularity, a thing from
which, even if attained, one often derives no profit ?

Bion [2] believes it impossible for one to please the
crowd except by turning into a cake or a jar of Thasian
wine—foolishly so believing, in my opinion. For
often even at a dinner of only ten guests the cake
does not please everybody, but, on the contrary, one
calls it stale, another hot, and another too sweet—
unless, by Heaven, Bion means that one must turn
into a cake which is both hot and stale and cold !
Nay, on the whole the case is not so simple as that ;
of course not. On the contrary, one must also turn
into perfume and a flute-girl and a lovely lad and a
Philip the jester.[3] However, one thing possibly still
remains which he who wants to please the mob will
have to turn into—silver. Nay, even if one turns
into silver one does not immediately satisfy ; instead,
one must also be struck and bitten.[4] Why then, you

---

[1] Aristeides' sobriquet was " the Just."
[2] Cynic philosopher of the third century B.C.
[3] For Philip see Xenophon, *Symposium* 1. 1. 11-16.
[4] As a test of genuineness.

---

[8] καὶ ψυχρόν deleted by Arnim, καὶ στρυφνόν Emperius.

διώκεις, ὦ κακόδαιμον, πρᾶγμα ἀκίχητον; οὔτε
γὰρ μύρον οὔτε στέφανος οὔτε οἶνος σὺ γένοιό
28 ποτ' ἂν οὔτ' ἀργύριον. κἂν ἀργύριον γένηταί τις,
χρυσίον ἐντιμότερον, κἂν χρυσίον, ἑψηθῆναι δεήσει.
τὸ γὰρ ᾧ διαφέρει[1] τῶν πλουσίων ἕκαστος ἔοικε
τῷ νομίσματι. καὶ γὰρ τοῦτο ἐπαινεῖ μὲν οὐδείς,
χρῆται δὲ ἕκαστος τῶν λαβόντων· ἔπειτα ὑπὸ τῶν
χρωμένων ἐκτρίβεται καὶ τελευταῖον ἐν τοῖς
ἀδοκίμοις ἐγένετο. κἀκεῖνος εἰς τοὺς πένητας
παρηγγυήθη[2] καὶ τοὺς ἀδοκίμους, καὶ οὐδεὶς ἔτι
τὸν τοιοῦτον προσίεται τῶν πρότερον τεθαυμακό-
των, ἀλλ' οὐδὲ στρέψας ἀπορρίπτει.[3]

29 Ταῖς τῶν τραγῳδῶν 'Ερινύσιν ἔοικεν ἡ δόξα·
τὸ μὲν γὰρ φαινόμενον αὐτῆς λαμπρὸν ὅμοιον τῇ
λαμπάδι, τὴν δὲ μάστιγα τοῖς κρότοις τις ἄν,
οἶμαι, καὶ τῇ βοῇ τῶν πολλῶν προσεικάσειε, τοῖς
δὲ ὄφεσι τοὺς ἐνίοτε συρίττοντας. πολλάκις οὖν
ἐν ἡσυχίᾳ τινὰ ὄντα καὶ μηδὲν ἔχοντα κακὸν
ἁρπάσασα καὶ τῇ μάστιγι ψοφήσασα ἐξέβαλεν
εἰς πανήγυρίν τινα ἢ θέατρον.[4]

[1] κἂν ἀργύριον . . . διαφέρει deleted by Arnim as being a
revised version of οὔκουν, κἂν ἀργύριον κ.τ.λ. preceding.
[2] παρηγγυήθη Pflugk : παρεγγυηθείς.
[3] κἂν ἀργύριον . . . ἀπορρίπτει deleted by Budé.
[4] κἂν ἀργύριον . . . θέατρον deleted by Emperius.

luckless creature, do you persist in pursuing a thing unattainable?[1] For you could never become either perfume or a crown or wine or yet silver. Besides, even if one should become silver, gold is more precious; and if gold, it will have to be refined. Indeed, each rich man resembles money, as far as any excellence is concerned. For while no one praises money, each one who gets it uses it; then it is worn out by those who use it and at last is found among the coins which do not pass current. So the rich man too comes to be reckoned among the poor and those who do not pass current and no one any longer receives a man like that of all who once were filled with admiration for him; instead, they do not even turn him over before casting him aside.

Again, reputation is like the Furies of the tragic poets—its seeming splendour is like their torch, while one might, I fancy, liken their whip to the clapping and the shouting of the crowd, and those who sometimes hiss might be likened to the Furies' snakes. Therefore, often when one is enjoying peace and quiet and is confronted by no evil, reputation lays violent hands on him, and, cracking her whip, drives him forth to some festal gathering or to the theatre.

[1] Possibly a reminiscence of *Iliad* 17. 75: Ἕκτορ, νῦν σὺ μὲν ὧδε θέεις ἀκίχητα διώκων.

THE SIXTY-SEVENTH DISCOURSE:
ON POPULAR OPINION

Although its Greek title is the same as that of the preceding Discourse, Or. 67 gives to the word a different meaning, that of opinion. It is argued that opinion is a poor guide and that, in order to discover the truth about external things, one must first obey the famous motto inscribed on Apollo's temple at Delphı—Know Thyself—the motto which formed the basic principle of the philosophy of Socrates. Proceeding from this fundamental concept, the author demonstrates the futility of being swayed by the opinions of others.

Here again we have what professes to be the report of a conversation between Dio and one of his followers. The abruptness with which it begins and ends has led Arnim to conclude that Dio did not intend it to be published, at least not in its present form. He regards it as what might be termed a stenographic record, which in some way or other found its way into the hands of Dio's editor.

67. ΠΕΡΙ ΔΟΞΗΣ ΔΕΥΤΕΡΟΣ

1 Τίνι γὰρ δοκεῖ σοι διαφέρειν μάλιστα ὁ σώφρων ἀνὴρ καὶ φιλόσοφος ἡμῶν τῶν πολλῶν τε καὶ εἰκῇ[1] φερομένων;

Δ.[2] Ἐμοὶ μέν, εἰ δεῖ οὕτως ἀποφήνασθαι φαύλως τε καὶ ἀκόμψως, ἀληθείᾳ δοκεῖ διαφέρειν καὶ τῷ ἐπίστασθαι οὐ μόνον τῶν πολλῶν, ἀλλὰ τῶν πάνυ ὀλίγων τε καὶ μακαρίων νενομισμένων, τὸν[3] φιλόσοφον.

Τῷ ὄντι[4] μέντοι φαῦλον καὶ ἄκομψον τὸ ῥῆμα.

Δ. Καί μοι τόδε εἰπέ, πρὸς θεῶν· ἄλλο τι ἢ ἀληθείᾳ φῂς διαφέρειν τῶν ἄλλων τὸν φιλόσοφον καὶ τῷ πρὸς ἀλήθειαν ἕκαστον ἀλλὰ μὴ κατὰ δόξαν σκοπεῖν;

2 Φαύλῳ γὰρ ἄν, ὦ ἄριστε, κανόνι καὶ παντάπασι σκολιῷ μὰ Δι' οὐ μίαν τινὰ καμπὴν ἔχοντι, μυρίας δὲ καὶ πάσας ὑπεναντίας,[5] τὰ πράγματα σταθμῷτο τῇ δόξῃ πειρώμενος ἀπευθύνειν αὐτά.

Δ. Πότερον οὖν τὰ μὲν ἄλλα πάντα πρὸς ἀλήθειαν σκοπεῖ, τὴν δόξαν οὐδαμῇ προσφέρων ὡς

---

[1] εἰκῇ added by Casaubon.
[2] Arnim distributes the parts differently in this first section, assigning to Δ the opening question.
[3] τὸν deleted by Arnim, who begins the following sentence with Φιλόσοφον.
[4] After ὄντι Arnim adds οὐ.
[5] ὑπεναντίας Emperius : ἀπεναντίας or ἐπεναντίας.

118

THE SIXTY-SEVENTH DISCOURSE:
ON POPULAR OPINION

Interlocutor. Well, in what particular does it seem to you that the man of self-control, the philosopher, most especially is superior to us who constitute the majority of mankind and are moved by random impulse ?

Dio. It seems to me, if one should express an opinion in such plain and unadorned terms, that he is superior in respect to truth and knowledge, not merely to the majority of mankind, but also to the very few, those who are regarded as favoured by fortune—the philosopher is, I mean.

Int. Indeed your statement is truly plain and un adorned.

Dio. Well, by Heaven, tell me this. You mean, do you not, that the philosopher is superior to all others in truth and in his examining each thing in the light of truth and not in accordance with opinion ?

Int. Why, my good sir, he would be using a poor straight-edge with which to gauge his problems, one altogether crooked, a straight-edge, by Zeus, with not just one bend but thousands, and all running counter to one another, if he tried to set things straight by means of opinion.

Dio. Well then, suppose that he views all else in the light of truth, never applying opinion as a gauge,

119

ψευδῆ τινα τῷ ὄντι καὶ ἀστάθμητον στάθμην καὶ
κανόνα τοιοῦτον, ὁποῖον ἄρτι εἴρηκας· αὐτὸς δὲ
αὐτὸν τούτῳ τῷ κανόνι καὶ ταύτῃ τῇ στάθμῃ
σταθμώμενος ἄξιος ἂν εἴη;

Οὐ μὰ Δί᾽ οὐδαμῶς.

Δ. Δῆλον γὰρ ὅτι οὐδέποτε γνοίη ἂν ἑαυτὸν
οὕτω σκοπῶν.

Οὐ γὰρ ἂν γνοίη.

3   Δ. Ὥστε οὐκ ἂν ἔτι πείθοιτο τῷ Δελφικῷ
προσρήματι κελεύσαντι παντὸς μᾶλλον γιγνώσκειν
αὑτόν;

Πῶς γὰρ ἂν πείθοιτο;

Δ. Οὔκουν[1] οὐδὲ τῶν ἄλλων οὐδὲν εἴσεται
πραγμάτων αὑτὸν ἀγνοῶν οὐδὲ δυνήσεται πρὸς
ἀλήθειαν ἐξετάζειν αὑτοῦ πρώτου[2] ἐσφαλμένος;

Παντάπασι μὲν οὖν.

Δ. Χαίρειν οὖν ἐάσει τιμὰς καὶ ἀτιμίας καὶ
ψόγον τε καὶ ἔπαινον τὸν παρὰ τῶν ἠλιθίων
ἀνθρώπων, ἐάν τε πολλοὶ τύχωσιν ὄντες ἐάν τε
ὀλίγοι μὲν ἰσχυροὶ δὲ καὶ πλούσιοι. τὴν δέ γε
καλουμένην δόξαν ἡγήσεται μηδὲν διαφέρειν σκιᾶς,
ὁρῶν ὅτι γίγνεται τῶν μεγάλων μικρὰ καὶ τῶν
μικρῶν μεγάλη· πολλάκις δὲ καὶ τῶν αὐτῶν ὁτὲ
μὲν πλείων, ὁτὲ δὲ ἐλάττων.

Εὖ πάνυ δοκεῖς[3] μοι προσεικάσαι.

4   Δ. Εἰ οὖν τις εἴη τοιοῦτος ἄνθρωπος οἷος ζῆν
πρὸς τὴν αὑτοῦ σκιάν, ὥστε αὐξομένης μὲν αὐτῆς

---

[1] Οὔκουν Dindorf : οὐκοῦν.
[2] αὑτοῦ πρώτου Emperius : αὐτὸν τοῦ πρώτου.

because he believes this to be, in fact, a false and untrustworthy measuring-line, a straight-edge such as you have just described it, yet if he should measure himself with that kind of straight-edge and that kind of measuring-line, would he be acclaimed as worthy ?

Int. No, by Heaven, not by any means.

Dio. Yes, it is plain that he could never come to know himself if he examined himself in that fashion.

Int. Why, of course he could not.

Dio. Consequently he would no longer be obeying the Delphic injunction, which has prescribed that, above all, a man must know himself.

Int. Why, of course he would not be obeying it.

Dio. Then he will not know any of the other things either, since he does not know himself, nor will he be able to examine things in the light of truth, since he has failed with himself to begin with ?

Int. Why, certainly.

Dio. Then he will bid farewell to honours and dishonours and to words of censure and of praise uttered by foolish persons, whether they chance to be many or whether they be few but powerful and wealthy. Instead, what is called popular opinion he will regard as no better than a shadow, seeing that sometimes the popular view makes much of small matters and little of great ones, and often concerning the same matters it is at one time greater and at another smaller.

Int. You seem to me to have made a very excellent comparison.

Dio. Suppose, then, there should be a person so constituted as to live with an eye to his own shadow, with the result that as it grew he would become

---

[3] Εὖ πάνυ δοκεῖς Selden : οὐ (or ᾧ) πάνυ δοκεῖ.

ἐπαίρεσθαι καὶ μεγαλαυχεῖσθαι καὶ τοῖς θεοῖς
θύειν αὐτός τε καὶ τοὺς φίλους κελεύειν, βραχυ-
τέρας δὲ γιγνομένης λυπεῖσθαί τε καὶ ὁρᾶσθαι
ταπεινότερος, καὶ τοσούτῳ μᾶλλον ὅσῳπερ ἂν
ἐλάττων γίγνηται, καθάπερ αὐτὸς φθίνων, θαυ-
μαστὴν ἄν, οἶμαι, παρέχοι διατριβήν.

Πολύ γε ἂν εἴη τοῦ Μαργίτου κωφότερος,[1]
ἀγνοοῦντος ὅ τι[2] χρὴ γήμαντα χρῆσθαι τῇ γυναικί.
5 Δ. Τῆς γὰρ αὐτῆς ἡμέρας ὁτὲ μὲν λυποῖτ' ἄν,
ὁτὲ δὲ χαίροι. πρωὶ μὲν ἐπειδὰν ἴδῃ[3] τὴν σκιὰν
ἑωθινὴν πάνυ μακράν, τῶν τε κυπαρίττων καὶ τῶν
ἐν τοῖς τείχεσι πύργων σχεδὸν μείζω, δῆλον ὅτι
χαίροι ἂν ὡς αὐτὸς ἐξαπίνης γεγονὼς τοῖς Ἀλωά-
δαις ἴσος καὶ εἰς τὴν ἀγορὰν βαδίζοι ἂν καὶ εἰς
τὰ θέατρα καὶ πανταχόσε τῆς πόλεως ὅπως ἂν
ὑπὸ πάντων βλέποιτο. περὶ δὲ πλήθουσαν ἀγορὰν
ἄρχοιτ' ἂν σκυθρωπότερος αὐτοῦ γίγνεσθαι καὶ
ἀναχωροίη. τῆς[4] δὲ μεσημβρίας αἰσχύνοιτ' ἂν
ὀφθῆναι ἀνθρώπῳ[5] τινὶ καὶ ἔνδον μένοι ἂν ἐγκλει-
σάμενος, ἐπειδὰν ἐν τοῖς ποσὶ βλέπῃ τὴν σκιάν·
πάλιν[6] δὲ περὶ δείλην ἀναλαμβάνοι ἂν αὐτὸν καὶ
γαυρότερος φαίνοιτ' ἂν ἀεὶ πρὸς ἑσπέραν.
6 Πάνυ μοι δοκεῖς ἄτοπον διάθεσιν καὶ ἄνδρα
διαπλάττειν ἠλίθιον.

[1] κωφότερος Valesius, μωρότερος Wilamowitz, ἀσοφώτερος
Meiser : σοφώτερος.
[2] ὅ τι Valesius : ὅτι.
[3] ἴδῃ Wilamowitz : ἴδοι.
[4] τῆς Reiske : τὰς.
[5] ἀνθρώπῳ] ἀνθρώπων Wilamowitz.
[6] βλέπῃ τὴν σκιάν· πάλιν Emperius : βλέπῃ τ. σ. πρὶν ἤ
MPH, βλέπειν τ. σ. παρῇ UB.

[1] Hero of a satiric poem of the same name sometimes

elated and boastful and not only offer a sacrifice of thanksgiving to the gods himself but also bid his friends to do so, while as his shadow diminished he would be grieved and show himself more humble, and the more so the smaller his shadow became, just as if he himself were wasting away, methinks he would afford wondrous amusement.

Int. Yes, he would be a much bigger booby than Margites,[1] who did not know how to treat his wife once he had married her.

Dio. Yes, for on the same day sometimes he would be sad and sometimes happy. For instance, early in the day, when he saw his shadow at dawn very long, almost larger than the cypresses or the towers on the city walls, manifestly he would be happy, supposing himself to have suddenly grown to the size of the sons of Aloeus,[2] and he would go striding into the market-place and the theatres and everywhere in the city to be observed by one and all. However, about the middle of the morning he would begin to grow more sad of countenance than he had been and would go back home. Then at noon he would be ashamed to be seen by anybody and would stay indoors, locking himself up, when he saw his shadow at his feet ; yet again, toward afternoon, he would begin to recover and would show himself ever more and more exultant toward evening.

Int. You certainly seem to me to be fashioning a strange disposition and a foolish kind of man.

ascribed to Homer by the ancients. Among the few lines now extant we get the following description of him : πόλλ' ἠπίστατο ἔργα, κακῶς δ' ἠπίστατο πάντα.

[2] They were said to have grown three cubits each year and, at the tender age of nine years, to have tried to scale the heavens by piling Ossa on Olympus and Pelion on Ossa.

Δ. Οὐκοῦν ὁ τῇ δόξῃ προσέχων οὐδέν τι βελτίων,
ἀλλὰ πολὺ ἀθλιώτερος. πολλάκις γὰρ ἂν πλείους
μεταβολὰς ἐν ἡμέρᾳ μιᾷ μεταβάλλοιτο, καίτοι
οὐχ, ὥσπερ ἐκεῖνος, ἐν τεταγμέναις ὥραις τισίν,
ἀλλὰ καὶ δείλης καὶ ἕωθεν οὐδὲν αὐτὸν κωλύσει
μὴ[1] δυστυχέστατον ἀνθρώπων εἶναι, νῦν μὲν φερόμενον καὶ πετόμενον ὑψηλότερον τῶν νεφῶν, ἂν
τύχωσι μετεωρίσαντες[2] αὐτόν τινες καὶ ἐπαινέ-
σαντες, νῦν δὲ συστελλόμενον καὶ ταπεινούμενον,
πολὺ πλείους αὐξήσεις τε καὶ φθίσεις τῆς ψυχῆς
αὐτοῦ λαμβανούσης, ἐμοὶ δοκεῖ,[3] τῶν τῆς σελήνης.
7 ἆρ' οὖν οὐκ ἀθλιώτερον πότμον καὶ μοῖραν εἴληχε
πολὺ δυστυχεστέραν ἢ φασι Μελέαγρον τὸν
Ἀλθαίας τε καὶ Οἰνέως τυχεῖν,[4] ᾧ δαλόν τινα
λέγουσι ταμιεύειν τὸν τῆς ζωῆς χρόνον· καὶ δὴ
λάμποντος αὐτοῦ καὶ τοῦ πυρὸς ἐν αὐτῷ δια-
μένοντος ζῆν τε καὶ ἀκμάζειν ἐκεῖνον, μαραινο-
μένου δὲ τοῦ δαλοῦ καὶ τὸν Μελέαγρον φθίνειν
ὑπὸ λύπης τε καὶ δυσθυμίας· σβεσθέντος δὲ οἴ-
χεσθαι ἀποθανόντα.

---

[1] μὴ omitted by MPH, bracketed by Arnim, Budé.
[2] μετεωρίσαντες Meiser, μακαρίσαντες Selden: μαρτυρήσαντες.
[3] δοκεῖ] δοκεῖν Dindorf.
[4] τυχεῖν deleted by Wilamowitz, λαχεῖν Pflugk.

THE SIXTY-SEVENTH DISCOURSE

Dio. Well then, he who pays heed to popular opinion is not a bit better, but rather far more pathetic.
For often he would undergo several changes on one
and the same day, yet not, like the man I have imagined, at certain definite times, but, alike in the
afternoon or in the early morning, nothing will keep
him from being the most unfortunate of mortals, now
being swept along and flying higher than the clouds,
if it so happen that any have sent him forth under full
sail and have praised him, now taking in his sails and
abasing himself, his spirit experiencing, methinks, far
more waxings and wanings than the moon. Has he
not, then, drawn a more wretched fate and a far more
luckless lot than they say fell to Meleager, son of Althaea and Oeneus, whose span of life, men say, was
in the keeping of a mere firebrand ? So long as the
brand blazed and the fire remained in it, just so long
Meleager lived and throve, but as the brand lost its
strength, he too wasted from grief and despondency,
and when the fire went out he died and was gone.[1]

[1] During the famous boar-hunt associated with his name,
by way of avenging a slight cast upon Atalanta by the
brothers of his mother Althaea, he slew them out of hand.
His mother, hearing of the deed, snatched the fatal brand
from its place in the ashes, hurled it into the flames, and
thus ended the life of her son.

THE SIXTY-EIGHTH DISCOURSE:
ON OPINION

In this Discourse Dio once more approaches the subject of opinion as contrasted with knowledge. Here, however, he is stressing the practical utility of knowledge in one's daily life and business pursuits, in other words, the impossibility of achieving success in any walk of life when led by mere opinion rather than by a clear understanding of the things to be avoided or attempted and of the reasons on which one's choice should be based. Although some attention is paid to the unwisdom of following the opinion of one's neighbours, the principal emphasis is laid upon the necessity in each instance of substituting knowledge for one's own untutored opinions.

68. ΠΕΡΙ ΔΟΞΗΣ ΤΡΙΤΟΣ

1 Οἱ πολλοὶ ἄνθρωποι ὁπόσα ἐπιτηδεύουσιν ἢ
ζηλοῦσιν, οὐδὲν αὐτῶν εἰδότες ὁποῖόν ἐστιν οὐδὲ
ἥντινα ἔχει ὠφέλειαν ἐπιτηδεύουσιν, ἀλλ' ὑπὸ
δόξης ἢ ἡδονῆς ἢ συνηθείας ἀγόμενοι πρὸς αὐτά·
οὐδ' αὖ ὅσων ἀπέχονται καὶ εὐλαβοῦνται μὴ
πράττειν, εἰδότες ἃ βλάπτει ἀπέχονται οὐδὲ
ὁποίαν τινὰ φέρει τὴν βλάβην, ἀλλὰ καὶ τούτων
ὅσα ὁρῶσι τοὺς ἄλλους εὐλαβουμένους ἢ περὶ ὧν
ἂν εἰς ἔθος καταστῶσιν ὥστε εὐλαβεῖσθαι, ἢ ἃ
νομίζουσιν ἀηδῆ ἔσεσθαι αὐτοῖς καὶ πόνον τινὰ
δοκεῖ ἔχειν, ὡς τὸ πολὺ ταῦτα ὑποπτεύουσιν.

2 Καὶ τὸ μὲν τῆς ἡδονῆς καὶ τὸ τοῦ πόνου πᾶσι
κοινόν· ἀλλ' οἱ μὲν ἧττον, οἱ δὲ[1] μᾶλλον ὑπ' αὐτῶν
δουλοῦνται· τὸ δὲ τῆς δόξης ἀνόμοιον καὶ οὐ ταὐτὸ
πᾶσιν. ὅθεν οἱ μὲν ταῦτα, οἱ δὲ ταῦτα ἐπαινοῦσι
καὶ ψέγουσι, πολλάκις τἀναντία. οἷον ἀλγεῖ μὲν
ὅ τε Ἰνδὸς καὶ ὁ Λάκων τιτρωσκόμενος ἢ καό-
μενος καὶ[2] ὅ τε Φρὺξ καὶ ὁ Λυδός· ἀλλ' ἐκεῖνοι
μὲν οὐχ ὑπείκουσι διὰ τὸ ἠσκηκέναι, οὗτοι δέ,

---

[1] οἱ δὲ Emperius : ἢ.
[2] καὶ added by Emperius.

THE SIXTY-EIGHTH DISCOURSE:
ON OPINION

Most men in all their pursuits and interests follow them in utter ignorance of what the nature of each is or even what practical value each has ; instead, they are drawn to them by opinion or pleasure or habit. Nor, on the other hand, in the case of those pursuits and interests from which they abstain and which they avoid engaging in, do they abstain because they know which are harmful or what is the nature of the harm which they entail ; instead, in these matters too, whatever they observe that their neighbours avoid or things which it has become their custom to avoid or which they suppose will be unpleasant for themselves and are reputed to be accompanied by some pain, these things they generally view with misgiving.

Moreover, while the sensations of pleasure and of pain are common to all men—though some are enslaved by them to a smaller and some to a greater degree—the matter of opinion varies and is not the same for all. Thus it happens that some praise or blame this and some that, frequently acting at variance in this regard. For example, pain is experienced by both the Indian and the Spartan when they are wounded or burnt, as well as by the Phrygian and the Lydian ; yet while the Indian and the Spartan refuse to flinch because they have been hardened

διὰ τὸ ἀσθενεῖς καὶ ἀνάσκητοι εἶναι. πάλιν ἥδεσθαι
μὲν ἀφροδισίοις καὶ σιτίοις καὶ ποτοῖς ἡδέσιν
ἀνάγκη τόν τε Ἴωνα καὶ τὸν Θετταλὸν καὶ τὸν
Ἰταλιώτην καὶ τὸν Γέτην καὶ τὸν Ἰνδὸν καὶ τὸν
Σπαρτιάτην· ἀλλ' οἱ μὲν οὐ πάνυ τι φροντίζουσι
τῶν ἡδέων, ἀρχὴν δὲ οὐδὲ πειρῶνται ἁπάντων·
οἱ δὲ ἀποθανεῖν ἕλοιντ' ἂν ὀλίγῳ πλέον ἡσθέντες.

3 Τὸ οὖν τῆς δόξης ἔοικεν εἶναι παντοδαπώτατον
καὶ πλείστη καὶ μεγίστη τούτου διαφορά. διὰ δὲ[1]
τοῦτο ἐν οὐδενὶ γένει τῶν ζῴων εὕροι τις ἂν
τοσαύτην στάσιν οὐδὲ οὕτως ἐναντίον αὑτῷ τι[2]
γένος, οἷον ἵππων ἢ κυνῶν ἢ λεόντων ἢ βοῶν ἢ
ἐλάφων, ἀλλὰ τρέφονταί τε ὁμοίως καὶ γεννῶσι
καὶ τρέφουσι καὶ ἐπὶ ταὐτὰ ὁρμῶσι καὶ τῶν αὐτῶν
ἀπέχονται τὰ ὅμοια. μόνῳ γὰρ ξυνέπονται ὡς
4 τὸ πολὺ τῷ ἡδεῖ καὶ τὸ ἀλγεινὸν φεύγουσιν. ἄνθρωπος δὲ φύσει φρονήσεως μετέχων, ἀπολειπό-
μενος δὲ αὐτῆς διὰ φαυλότητα καὶ ῥᾳθυμίαν,
δόξης καὶ ἀπάτης ἔνδοθεν μεστός ἐστι· καὶ πάντα
ἀλλήλοις διαφέρονται, καὶ περὶ ἐσθῆτος καὶ στολῆς
καὶ περὶ τροφῆς καὶ ἀφροδισίων καὶ περὶ τιμῆς
καὶ ἀτιμίας, κατὰ ἔθνη[3] καὶ πόλεις· ὁμοίως δὲ καὶ
ἐν τῇ[4] πόλει καθ' αὑτὸν ἕκαστος ἐσπούδακεν ὁ
μὲν γῆν ὡς πλείστην κτήσασθαι, ὁ δὲ ἀργύριον,
ὁ δὲ ἀνδράποδα, ὁ δὲ ξύμπαντα ταῦτα, ὁ δ' ἐπὶ
τῷ λέγειν θαυμάζεσθαι καὶ διὰ τοῦτο, τῶν ἄλλων

---

[1] διὰ δὲ Crosby : διά τε.
[2] αὑτῷ τι Reiske : αὐτῷ τι or αὐτῶν τι (or τό).
[3] καὶ περὶ τιμῆς καὶ ἀτιμίας, κατὰ ἔθνη Pflugk : καὶ περὶ
ἀτιμίας τὰ ἔθνη UBM, καὶ περὶ τιμῆς καὶ ἔθνη PH.

to it, the Phrygian and the Lydian do flinch, because
they are weak and not hardened. Again, while
pleasure inevitably is experienced in sexual relations and in food and drink which are pleasurable,
not only by the Ionian but also by the Thessalian,
the Italian Greek, the Getan, the Indian, and the
Spartan, yet some give no thought at all to such
gratifications and do not seek to know any of them
in the least, while the others would accept death as
the price of obtaining a little more pleasure.

Now apparently the matter of opinion is of every
conceivable kind and the differences to be found in
this matter are very numerous and very great. And
it is because of this fact that in no breed of animals
would one find so great dissension, nor would one
find any breed so at variance with itself—take, for
example, horses or dogs or lions or cattle or deer ;
on the contrary, animals that are alike behave alike
in feeding, in begetting, and in rearing their young,
and they have the same appetites and the same
aversions. The reason is that in general they follow
only what is pleasant and shun what is painful. But
the human race, which by nature partakes of wisdom,
though it falls short of it through bad judgement
and indifference, is inwardly full of opinion and self-
deception. Moreover, men differ with one another
in everything—in dress and apparel, in food and
sexual pleasures, in honour and dishonour—according
to nations and cities. And similarly also within the
city, each one has his own individual ambition—one
to obtain as much land as possible, another silver,
another slaves, another all these things together,
another to be admired for his eloquence and by this

---

[4] After τῇ Arnim adds αὐτῇ.

πλέον δύνασθαι, ὁ δὲ αὐτὸ μόνον δεινὸς εἶναι καὶ
τὴν ἐμπειρίαν τὴν περὶ τὰ πράγματα[1] ἐζήλωκεν,
ὁ δὲ ἀπ' ἄλλου τινὸς ἰσχύειν, ὁ δὲ τρυφὴν ὡς
πλείστην ἐπιτηδεύειν.[2]

5   Τούτων μὲν οὖν, ὅπερ ἔφην, οὐδὲν ἄν, ὡς εἰκός,
ὀρθῶς πράττοιεν οὐδὲ οἱ τὰ κράτιστα δοκοῦντες
ἐπιτηδεύειν. οὐ γὰρ εἰδότες τὸ βέλτιον ἢ τὸ
χεῖρον ἢ τὸ συμφέρον αἱροῦνται οὐδέν. ὅστις δ'
ἐπεθύμησε φρονήσεως καὶ διενοήθη πῶς[3] χρὴ
ἐπιμεληθέντα αὑτοῦ καὶ παίδευσιν τίνα[4] παιδευ-
θέντα γενέσθαι ἄνδρα ἀγαθὸν καὶ διαφέροντα τῶν
πολλῶν, τοῦτον ἐγώ φημι φύσεώς τε χρηστῆς
τυχεῖν καὶ τύχης ὁμοίας. ἐλπὶς γὰρ ζητοῦντα
καὶ παιδευόμενον ἐξευρεῖν τὸ δέον καὶ πρὸς τί
ὁρῶντα καὶ τί βουλόμενον πάντα τὰ ἄλλα χρὴ
πράττειν καὶ οἰκονομεῖν.

6   Ὁ δὲ τοῦτο συνεὶς ἅπαντα ἂν ἤδη καλῶς δια-
πράττοιτο καὶ τὰ μείζω δοκοῦντα καὶ τὰ σμικρό-
τερα· καὶ εἴτε ἱππικῆς ἐπιτηδεύοι ἀγωνίαν εἴτε
μουσικῆς εἴτε γεωργίας ἐπιμελοῖτο εἴτε στρατηγεῖν
ἐθέλοι ἢ ἄρχειν τὰς ἄλλας ἀρχὰς ἢ τὰ ἄλλα τὰ
κοινὰ ἐν τῇ πόλει πράττειν, εὖ πάντα ποιήσει[5]
καὶ περὶ οὐδὲν ἂν σφάλλοιτο. ἄνευ δὲ τούτου
καθ' ἕκαστον μὲν τῶν ἔργων ἐνίοτε αὑτῷ τε καὶ
τοῖς ἄλλοις φαίνοιτο ἂν κατορθῶν[6]· οἷον εἰ γεωργῶν
ἐπιτυγχάνοι περὶ τοὺς καρποὺς ἢ ἱππεύειν[7] ἐμπει-

[1] τὰ πράγματα Pflugk : τὸ πρᾶγμα.
[2] ἐπιτηδεύειν H : ἐπιτηδεύει.   [3] πῶς Emperius : ὡς.
[4] τίνα Emperius : τινα or τινα καί.
[5] εὖ πάντα ποιήσει M : καλῶς ἂν πάντα ποιήσοι PH, οὗτος
πάντα ποιήσει UB, καλῶς ἂν πάντα ποιήσειε Emperius.
[6] κατορθῶν] κατορθοῦν Emperius.
[7] ἱππεύειν Reiske : ἱππεύων.

means to have greater power than his fellows, another strives merely to be clever and to achieve experience in politics, another to have influence for some other reason, another to indulge in luxury to the fullest extent.

Now, as I was saying, in no one of these pursuits, in all likelihood, would even those who are reputed to be best in their line carry it on successfully. For, not knowing what is better or what is worse or what is advantageous, they exercise no choice at all. But he who has desired wisdom and has given thought to how he should look after himself and what education he should receive in order to become a good man and superior to the masses, he, I say, has been blest with a good character and with a corresponding fortune besides. For there is hope that, if he investigates and receives instruction, he will discover what is required and with what aim and purpose he should carry on and regulate all else.

But he who understands this would from that moment be successful in all things, both those which are thought to be more important and those which are thought to be less; and whether he were to follow horse-racing or to devote himself to music or to agriculture, or if he should wish to be a general or to hold the other offices or to conduct the other public business in his city, he will do everything well and would make no mistakes in anything. However, without this understanding, while in each of his labours he might sometimes seem both to himself and to his neighbours to be successful—for instance, if as a farmer he were to be fortunate with his crops, or if he were to have more than ordinary acquaintance with the handling of horses, or if he were to have

ρότερος εἴη ἢ τὰ[1] κατὰ μουσικὴν ἱκανῶς γιγνώσκοι[2]
ἢ ἀγωνιζόμενος δύναιτο τῶν ἀντιπάλων κρατεῖν,
τὸ δὲ σύμπαν ἁμαρτάνοι ἂν πρὸς οὐδὲν ἀγαθὸν
οὐδὲ ὥστε ὠφελεῖσθαι ταῦτα ἐργαζόμενος.

7 Οὔκουν δυνατός[3] ἐστιν εὐδαιμονεῖν, ὥσπερ οὐδ᾽
εὐπλοῆσαι δύναταί τις οὐκ εἰδὼς ἔνθα πλεῖ, μάτην[4]
ἐν τῷ πελάγει φερόμενος, νῦν μὲν ὀρθῆς πλεούσης
τῆς νεώς, ἂν οὕτω τύχῃ, νῦν δὲ ἀποκλινούσης,
καὶ νῦν μὲν οὐρίου φερομένου τοῦ πνεύματος,
πάλιν δὲ ἐναντίου. χρὴ δὲ ὥσπερ ἐν λύρᾳ τὸν
μέσον φθόγγον καταστήσαντες ἔπειτα πρὸς τοῦτον
ἁρμόζονται τοὺς ἄλλους· εἰ δὲ μή, οὐδεμίαν οὐδέποτε ἁρμονίαν ἀποδείξουσιν· οὕτως ἐν τῷ βίῳ
ξυνέντας τὸ βέλτιστον καὶ τοῦτο ἀποδείξαντας
πέρας πρὸς τοῦτο τἆλλα ποιεῖν· εἰ δὲ μή, ἀνάρμο-
στον αὐτοῖς καὶ ἐκμελῆ τὸν βίον εἰκός ἐστι
γίγνεσθαι.

---

[1] ἢ τὰ Reiske : εἴτε or ἤτε.
[2] γιγνώσκοι Wilamowitz : γιγνώσκων or γινώσκων.
[3] δυνατός Arnim : δυνατόν.
[4] After μάτην Emperius deletes δὲ ἄρτι with PH.

fairly good knowledge of music, or if in athletic contests he could overcome his competitors—still on the whole he would fail, since he would be working at these things to no good end nor in such a way as to derive benefit.

Therefore he is incapable of being prosperous, just as one cannot make a successful voyage if one does not know whither he is sailing, being carried along aimlessly on the sea, his ship at one moment sailing a straight course, should fortune so decree, but the next moment yawing, at one moment with the wind astern, the next with it dead ahead. Nay, just as with the lyre musicians first set the middle string and then tune the others to harmonize with that —otherwise they will never achieve any harmony at all—so with life, men should first come to understand what is best and then, having made this their goal, they should do everything else with reference to this ; otherwise their life will be out of harmony and out of tune in all likelihood.

THE SIXTY-NINTH DISCOURSE :
ON VIRTUE

THE theme of this Discourse is the doctrine that the virtuous life is the happy life. Dio bemoans the fact that most men give their whole attention to so-called practical pursuits to the neglect of their spiritual well-being and development. Striving to attain success in any number of material enterprises, they miss true happiness through their failure to see that character is its sure foundation. Without good character laws are of little avail, and happiness is the gift of the gods, who are not inclined to favour ignorance and inattention to the needs of the soul. It is interesting to find Dio here expressing the belief that those who would commit a crime but are prevented from so doing through fear are as guilty as those who actually yield to the temptation.

69. ΠΕΡΙ ΑΡΕΤΗΣ

1 Ἄπορόν μοι δοκεῖ εἶναι ὅτι οἱ ἄνθρωποι ἄλλα
μὲν ἐπαινοῦσι καὶ θαυμάζουσιν, ἄλλων δὲ ἐφίενται
καὶ περὶ ἄλλα ἐσπουδάκασιν. ἐπαινοῦσι μὲν γάρ,
ὡς ἔπος εἰπεῖν, πάντες καὶ θεῖα καὶ σεμνά φασιν
ἀνδρείαν καὶ δικαιοσύνην καὶ φρόνησιν καὶ συλ-
λήβδην ἀρετὴν πᾶσαν. καὶ οὓς ἂν ἡγῶνται τοιούτους εἶναι ἢ γεγονέναι ἢ ἐγγύς, θαυμάζουσι καὶ
ὑμνοῦσι· καὶ τοὺς μέν τινας θεούς, τοὺς δὲ ἥρωας
ἀποφαίνουσιν, οἷον Ἡρακλέα καὶ Διοσκούρους
καὶ Θησέα καὶ Ἀχιλλέα καὶ πάντας τοὺς ἡμιθέους
λεγομένους. οἷς ὅν[1] ἂν ὅμοιον ὑπολαμβάνωσιν,
ἕτοιμοί εἰσιν ἅπαντες ἐκείνῳ πείθεσθαι καὶ ὑπη-
ρετεῖν, ὅ τι ἂν προστάττῃ, καὶ βασιλέα καὶ ἄρχοντα
ἀποδεικνύναι ἑαυτῶν καὶ τὰ σφέτερα ἐπιτρέπειν
ὃν ἂν σώφρονα καὶ δίκαιον καὶ φρόνιμον ὄντως
ὑπολαμβάνωσι καὶ ἁπλῶς ἄνδρα ἀγαθόν.

2 Ὥστε ταύτῃ μὲν οὐκ ἄν τις αὐτοῖς μέμψαιτο
ὡς οὐκ αἰσθανομένοις ὅτι σεμνόν τι καὶ τίμιον
καὶ τοῦ παντὸς ἄξιον χρῆμα ἀρετή· ἐπιθυμοῦσί
γε μὴν πάντων μᾶλλον ἢ ἀγαθοὶ γενέσθαι καὶ
πράττουσι πάντα πρότερον ἢ ὅπως σωφρονήσουσι
καὶ φρόνιμοι ἔσονται καὶ δίκαιοι καὶ ἄνδρες
σπουδαῖοι, καλῶς μὲν αὐτῶν δυνάμενοι προΐστασθαι,

---

[1] οἷς ὅν Jacobs, ὧν ὅν Selden, καὶ ὅν Pflugk : ὅν or ὧν.

THE SIXTY-NINTH DISCOURSE:
ON VIRTUE

It seems to me a fact hard to explain, that people praise and admire one set of things yet aim at and have seriously pursued a different set. For instance, virtually all praise and refer to as " divine " and " august " such things as valour and righteousness and wisdom and, in short, every virtue. Moreover, whomever they believe to be, or to have been, characterized by such virtues, or nearly so, him they admire and celebrate in song ; and certain ones they represent as gods and others as heroes—for example, Heracles, the Dioscuri, Theseus, Achilles, and all the demigods, as they are called. And whomever they suppose to be like those beings they one and all are ready to obey and to serve, no matter what orders he may give, and they are ready to appoint as their king and ruler and to make the guardian of their possessions any man whom they suppose to be really prudent and righteous and wise and, in a word, a good man.

Therefore in this respect no one could censure them as not perceiving that virtue is something august and precious and all-important ; yet they really desire any and every thing in preference to becoming good, and they busy themselves with everything in preference to the problem of becoming self-controlled and wise and righteous and men of merit, competent

καλῶς δὲ οἶκον οἰκῆσαι, καλῶς δὲ ἄρξαι πόλεως,
εὖ δὲ πλοῦτον ἐνεγκεῖν, εὖ δὲ πενίαν, εὖ δὲ προσ-
ενεχθῆναι φίλοις, εὖ δὲ συγγενέσι, δικαίως δ’
ἐπιμεληθῆναι γονέων, ὁσίως δὲ[1] θεραπεῦσαι θεούς.
3 ἀλλ’ οἱ μέν τινες περὶ γεωργίαν πραγματεύονται,
οἱ δὲ περὶ ἐμπορίαν, οἱ δ’ ἐπὶ στρατείαν ὁρμῶσιν,
οἱ δ’ ἐπ’ ἰατρικήν, οἱ δὲ οἰκοδομικὴν ἢ ναυπηγικὴν
ἐκμανθάνουσιν, οἱ δὲ κιθαρίζειν ἢ αὐλεῖν ἢ σκυτο-
τομεῖν ἢ παλαίειν, οἱ δὲ ὅπως δεινοὶ δόξουσι περ
τὸ εἰπεῖν ἐν δήμῳ ἢ δικαστηρίῳ τὴν πᾶσαν σπουδὴν
ἔχουσιν, οἱ δὲ ὅπως ἰσχυροὶ ἔσονται τὰ σώματα.
καίτοι[2] τοὺς ἐμπόρους μὲν καὶ γεωργοὺς καὶ
στρατιώτας καὶ ἰατροὺς καὶ οἰκοδόμους καὶ κιθαριστὰς καὶ αὐλητὰς καὶ παιδοτρίβας, ἔτι δὲ τοὺς
λεγομένους ῥήτορας καὶ τοὺς πάνυ ἰσχύοντας τοῖς
σώμασιν, ἀθλίους καὶ δυστυχεῖς[3] πολλοὺς ἂν εὕροι
τις ἢ μικροῦ δεῖν ἅπαντας.
4 Ἂν δὲ ἡ ψυχὴ ἔμφρων γένηται καὶ ὁ νοῦς ἀγαθὸς
καὶ ἱκανοὶ ὦσι τά τε αὑτῶν πράγματα ὀρθῶς
πράττειν καὶ τὰ τῶν ἄλλων, τούτους ἀνάγκη καὶ
εὐδαιμόνως ζῆν, νομίμους ἄνδρας γενομένους καὶ
ἀγαθοῦ δαίμονος τυχόντας καὶ φίλους ὄντας τοῖς
θεοῖς. οὐ γὰρ ἄλλους μὲν φρονίμους εἰκὸς εἶναι,
ἄλλους δὲ ἐμπείρους τῶν ἀνθρωπίνων πραγμάτων,
οὐδὲ ἄλλους μὲν τἀνθρώπεια ἐπίστασθαι, ἄλλους
δὲ τὰ θεῖα, οὐδὲ ἄλλους μὲν εἶναι τῶν θείων ἐπι-
στήμονας, ἄλλους δὲ ὁσίους,[4] οὐδὲ ἄλλους μὲν[5]

---

[1] ὁσίως δὲ Emperius, ὁσίως τε Wyttenbach : ὅπως δὲ (τε).
[2] καίτοι Emperius : καὶ.

140

to govern themselves well, to manage a household well, to rule a city well, to endure well either wealth or poverty, to behave well toward friends and kinsmen, to care for parents with equity, and to serve gods with piety. But some busy themselves with farming, some with trading, some are devoted to military affairs, some to the medical profession, some acquire a thorough knowledge of carpentry or of ship-building, some of playing the lyre or the flute or of shoemaking or wrestling, some devote their whole attention to gaining a reputation as clever speakers in Assembly or in law-court, some to becoming strong in body. And yet the traders, farmers, soldiers, physicians, builders, lyre-players, flautists, athletic trainers, yes, and the orators, as they are called, and those who have great strength of body—all these one would find to be pitiable and unfortunate in many, or indeed in almost all, instances.

On the other hand, if their soul becomes rational and their mind really good, and if they are able to manage successfully their own affairs and those of their neighbours too, these men will necessarily also lead happy lives, having shown themselves to be law-abiding, having obtained a good genius to guard them, and being dear to the gods. For it does not stand to reason that one set of men are wise and another set versed in human affairs, nor yet that some are conversant with human affairs and some with affairs divine, nor that some men have knowledge of divine things and others are pious, nor that some

---

³ After δυστυχεῖς Pflugk adds τούς.

⁴ After ὁσίους UB add οὐδὲ ἄλλους μὲν δικαίους ἄλλους δὲ ὁσίους, M οὐδὲ ἄλλους δικαίους καὶ ἄλλους ὁσίους.

⁵ After μὲν PH add καὶ δικαίους.

ὁσίους, ἄλλους δὲ θεοφιλεῖς· οὐδὲ ἕτεροι μὲν
ἔσονται θεοφιλεῖς, ἕτεροι δὲ εὐδαίμονες. οὐδὲ
ἕτεροι μέν εἰσιν ἄνθρωποι ἄφρονες, ἕτεροι δ᾽
ἀγνοοῦσι τὰ καθ᾽ αὑτοὺς πράγματα· οὐδὲ οἳ τὰ
σφέτερα πράγματα ἀγνοοῦσι, τὰ θεῖα ἴσασιν· οὐδὲ
οἱ φαύλως περὶ τῶν θείων ὑπειληφότες οὐκ ἀνόσιοί
εἰσιν. οὐδέ γε τοὺς ἀνοσίους οἷόν τε φίλους εἶναι
θεοῖς, οὐδὲ τοὺς μὴ φίλους θεοῖς μὴ δυστυχεῖς
εἶναι.

Διὰ τί ποτ᾽ οὖν οἱ[1] ὀρεγόμενοι ὅπως εὐδαιμονή-
σουσιν οὐ προθυμοῦνται[2] τοιούτους παρέχειν σφᾶς
αὑτούς, ἃ δὲ πράττοντας οὐδὲν αὑτοὺς κωλύει
κακῶς καὶ ἀθλίως ζῆν, πᾶσαν τούτων ἐπιμέλειαν
5 ποιοῦνται; καίτοι ἄνευ μὲν αὐλητῶν καὶ κιθα-
ριστῶν καὶ σκυτοτόμων καὶ παιδοτριβῶν καὶ
ῥητόρων καὶ ἰατρῶν οὐκ ἀδύνατον ἀνθρώποις
βιοῦν πάνυ καλῶς καὶ νομίμως, οἶμαι δ᾽ ἐγὼ καὶ
6 δίχα γεωργῶν καὶ οἰκοδόμων. Σκύθαι γοῦν οὐδὲν
κωλύονται οἱ νομάδες μήτε οἰκίας ἔχοντες μήτε
γῆν σπείροντες ἢ φυτεύοντες δικαίως καὶ κατὰ
νόμους πολιτεύεσθαι· ἄνευ δὲ νόμου καὶ δικαίου
μὴ κακῶς ζῆν ἀνθρώπους καὶ πολὺ τῶν θηρίων
ὠμότερον[3] οὐ δυνατόν. ἔτι δ᾽ ὅπου μὲν φαῦλοι
σκυτοτόμοι εἰσὶ καὶ γεωργοὶ καὶ οἰκοδόμοι, οὐδὲν
ἐκεῖ διὰ τοῦτο συμβαίνει χαλεπόν, ἀλλὰ τὰ ὑποδήματα χείρω[4] καὶ πυροὶ ἐλάττους καὶ κριθαί·
ὅπου δὲ ἄρχοντες χείρους καὶ δικασταὶ καὶ νόμοι,

---

[1] After οἱ Emperius deletes μέν.
[2] After προθυμοῦνται Emperius adds μέν.
[3] ὠμότερον UB : ἀνομώτερον MPH.

are pious and others dear to the gods ; nor will a separate group be dear to the gods and another group be favoured by fortune. Nor is there one class of men who are fools but another class ignorant of their own affairs ; nor are those who are ignorant of their own affairs informed about things divine ; nor are those who have formed mistaken opinions about things divine free from impiety. And surely those who are impious cannot be dear to the gods nor those who are not dear to the gods be other than unfortunate.

Why in the world, then, do not those who aim to attain a happy life do their best to make themselves happy instead of devoting their entire attention to things which do not at all prevent their leading a bad, yes wretched, existence ? Yet without flute-players and lyre-players and shoemakers and athletic trainers and orators and physicians it is not impossible for men to live very good and ordered lives, and, I fancy, even without farmers and builders. At any rate the Scythians who are nomads, though they neither have houses nor sow seed nor plant trees and vines, are by no means prevented from playing their part as citizens with justice and in accordance with law; yet without law and justice men cannot avoid living badly and in much more savage fashion than the wild beasts. Moreover, where shoemakers and farmers and builders are of inferior quality, no serious harm results on that account ; it is merely that the shoes are inferior and the wheat and barley scarcer. On the other hand, where rulers and judges and laws are inferior, the

---

[4] χείρω added by Reiske, χείρω καὶ τὰ οἰκοδομήματα Wenkebach.

τὰ πράγματα κάκιον ἔχει τῶν ἀνθρώπων ἐκείνων
καὶ ὁ βίος δυστυχέστερος καὶ στάσεις καὶ ἀδικίαι
καὶ ὕβρεις καὶ ἀσέβεια πολλὴ φύεται παρ' αὐτοῖς.
7 Ἔτι δὲ σκυτοτόμον μὲν αὐτὸν οὐκ ὄντα λυσιτελεῖ
παρ' ἄλλου πρίασθαι ὑποδήματα, καὶ οἰκοδομεῖν
οὐκ ἐπιστάμενον ἄλλον ἐπὶ τούτῳ μισθώσασθαι,
καὶ γεωργὸν μὴ ὄντα σῖτον πρίασθαι καὶ ὄσπρια·
ἄδικον δὲ αὐτὸν ὄντα οὐ λυσιτελεῖ τῶν δικαίων
παρ' ἄλλου τυγχάνειν οὐδὲ ἄφρονα καὶ ἀγνοοῦντα
ἃ δεῖ ποιεῖν καὶ ὧν ἀπέχεσθαι, μετανοοῦντα[1] ἐφ'
ἑκάστῳ πρὸς ἕτερον ἰέναι. πρὸς γὰρ τοῖς ἄλλοις
ὁ μὲν ἀργυρίου δεόμενος ἢ ἱματίων ἢ οἰκίας ἢ
ἄλλου του ἐπίσταταί τε καὶ ζητεῖ παρὰ τῶν
ἐχόντων λαβεῖν· ὁ δὲ νοῦν οὐκ ἔχων οὐδὲ αὐτὸ
τοῦτο ἐπίσταται ὅτι οὐκ ἔχει νοῦν· ἀλλ' αὐτός
φησιν ἱκανὸς εἶναι καὶ ἰσχυρίζεται τῇ[2] ἀφροσύνῃ,
πάντα πράττων καὶ λέγων ἀφρόνως, καὶ οὔ φησιν
ἄδικος εἶναι οὐδὲ ἀνόητος οὐδὲ ἀκόλαστος, ἀλλ'
ὡς οἷόν τε ἱκανῶς περὶ ταῦτα ἔχειν, ὧν οὐδεμίαν
πώποτε ἐπιμέλειαν ἐποιήσατο οὐδὲ ἔμαθεν οὐδὲν
τούτων ἕνεκεν.
8 Οὐδὲ γὰρ ἐπιστήμην εἶναι νομίζουσι, καθ' ἣν
εἴσονται τί πρακτέον αὐτοῖς ἢ τί μὴ πρακτέον καὶ
πῶς βιώσονται ὀρθῶς· ἀλλὰ τοὺς νόμους αὐτοῖς
ἱκανοὺς εἶναι πρὸς τοῦτο τοὺς γεγραμμένους·
ὅπως δὲ πείσονται τοῖς νόμοις καὶ ἑκόντες ποιή-

---

[1] μετανοοῦντα] μετὰ νοῦν Arnim.
[2] τῇ added by Emperius.

affairs of those people are in worse condition and their life is more unfortunate, and factions, injustices, deeds of arrogance, and impiety flourish in abundance with them.

Furthermore, though when one is not himself a shoemaker it is profitable to purchase shoes from another person, and when one does not understand building, to hire another person for that work, and when one is not a farmer, to purchase grain and pulse ; on the other hand, when one is himself unjust, it is not profitable to get his justice from another, nor, when one lacks wisdom and does not know what he ought to do and what he ought to refrain from doing, to be constantly regretting every single act and resorting for knowledge to another person. For, in addition to all the other considerations, he who needs money or clothing or house or anything else not only knows that fact but also seeks to get these things from those who have them ; whereas he who has no sense does not even know just this very fact, that he has no sense ; instead, he himself claims to be competent and obstinately persists in his folly, everything he does or says being witless, and he denies that he is unjust or foolish or lawless but insists that he is ever so competent in these matters, though he has never paid any attention to them or learned anything as far as those things are concerned.

In fact, these men do not even believe in the existence of a knowledge in accordance with which they will know what they ought to do or what they ought not to do and how they will live correctly ; nay, they believe that the laws are sufficient for them for that purpose, the laws on the statute books ; but how they are to obey the laws and voluntarily do

145

DIO CHRYSOSTOM

σουσι τὰ ἐκείνοις δοκοῦντα οὐδὲν φροντίζουσιν.
καίτοι τί ἧττον ὁ φόβῳ τοῦ κλέπτειν ἀπεχόμενος,
εὐδοκῶν¹ ἀλλὰ μὴ μισῶν τὸ πρᾶγμα καὶ κατα-
γιγνώσκων, κλέπτης τῶν ὑφαιρουμένων ἐστίν·
εἰ μὴ καὶ τὸν ἡμέρας οὐ κλέπτοντα, ἀλλὰ νυκτὸς
γενομένης, κλέπτην οὐ φήσομεν ἐν τῇ ἡμέρᾳ,
ἀλλὰ δίκαιον εἶναι; ἔπειτα δέονται πολλῶν τῶν
ἀπειλούντων καὶ κολαζόντων, ὡς οὐ δυνάμενοι
αὐτοὶ ἀπέχεσθαι τῶν ἀδικημάτων, ἀλλὰ καὶ οἴκοι
τοιοίδε² ὄντες· τοιοῦτοι δὲ ὄντες αἱροῦνται τοὺς
νομοθέτας καὶ κολάζουσι τοὺς ἀνόμους,³ ὥσπερ
εἰ ἄμουσοι ὄντες ᾑροῦντο τοὺς μουσικοὺς καὶ
οὐδὲν ἐπαΐοντες περὶ γεωμετρίας τοὺς γεωμέτρας.
9 Σημεῖον δὲ τῆς πονηρίας τῆς τῶν ἀνθρώπων·
εἰ γὰρ ἀνέλοιεν τοὺς νόμους καὶ ἄδεια γένοιτο τοῦ
τύπτειν ἀλλήλους καὶ ἀποκτείνειν καὶ ἁρπάζειν
τὰ τῶν πέλας καὶ μοιχεύειν καὶ λωποδυτεῖν, τίνας
ἔσεσθαι οἰητέον τοὺς ἀφεξομένους τούτων καὶ μὴ⁴
πάνυ ῥᾳδίως τε καὶ ἑτοίμως ἅπαντα ἐξαμαρτεῖν
βουλομένους; ὡς⁵ τὸ νῦν γε οὐδὲν ἧττον λανθά-
νομεν μετὰ κλεπτῶν καὶ ἀνδραποδιστῶν καὶ
μοιχῶν ζῶντες καὶ συμπολιτευόμενοι καὶ κατὰ
τοῦτο οὐδὲν βελτίους τῶν θηρίων ἐσμέν· καὶ γὰρ
ἐκεῖνα ἂν φοβηθῇ ἀνθρώπους φυλάττοντας ἢ
κύνας, ἀπέχεται τοῦ ἁρπάζειν.

¹ ἀπεχόμενος, εὐδοκῶν Capps : ἀπεχόμενος δοκῶν UBM, ἀπέχεσθαι δοκῶν PH, δοκῶν deleted by Arnim.
² καὶ οἴκοι τοιοίδε PH : καὶ οἴκοι UBM, κακοὶ Selden.
³ ἀνόμους Post : νόμους.
⁴ τούτων καὶ μὴ] τοῦ μὴ Arnim.
⁵ ὡς] καὶ Arnim.

146

what those laws prescribe is a matter to which they give no serious thought. And yet how is he any less a thief who refrains from thieving out of fear, if he approves but does not loath and condemn the business, than those who actually commit theft—unless also he who does not do his thieving by day, but only after nightfall, is to be called no thief in daytime, but rather a man of probity? Besides, such persons require the presence of many to threaten and restrain them, since they are not able of themselves to refrain from their misdeeds, but even when at home are men of thievish disposition. However, though they are of such character, they choose the law-givers and punish the lawless, just as if persons who are unmusical were to choose the musicians, or as if those who know nothing of surveying were to choose the surveyors!

And here is an indication of the depravity of mankind. If men were to do away with the laws and licence were to be granted to strike one another, to commit murder, to steal the property of one's neighbours, to commit adultery, to be a footpad, then who must we suppose would be the persons who will refrain from these deeds and not, without the slightest scruple or hesitation, be willing to commit all manner of crimes? For even under present conditions we none the less are living unwittingly with thieves and kidnappers and adulterers and joining with them in the activities of citizenship, and in this respect we are no better than the wild beasts; for they too, if they take fright at men or dogs set to guard against them, refrain from thieving.

THE SEVENTIETH DISCOURSE:
ON PHILOSOPHY

This brief dialogue, like others in our collection, both begins and ends abruptly. It has the appearance of being an excerpt from a lengthier discussion, probably selected for publication because it contained a noteworthy tribute to the essential nature of philosophy. The rôle of the student in this document—if it was a student—is decidedly minor, consisting chiefly in assenting to the statements made by the principal speaker. Dio is emphasizing the crucial difference between pseudo-philosophers and those who are philosophers in deed as well as in word. In truly Socratic fashion he leads up to his main thesis by citing examples of pretence in fields such as farming, trading, hunting, and the like, showing in each instance that no one is misled by profession of interest unaccompanied by fitting conduct.

70. ΠΕΡΙ ΦΙΛΟΣΟΦΙΑΣ

1 Δ. Φέρε, εἴ τινος ἀκούοις λέγοντος ὅτι βούλεται
γεωργεῖν, μηδὲν δὲ πρὸς τοῦτο πράττοντα ὁρῷης
αὐτόν, μήτε βοῦς ὠνούμενον ἢ τρέφοντα μήτε
ἄροτρα κατασκευαζόμενον μήτε τὰ ἄλλα τὰ πρὸς
τὴν γεωργίαν σκεύη, μηδὲ ἐνοικοῦντα ἐν ἀγρῷ
αὐτὸν ἢ[1] κεκτημένον ἢ[2] παρ' ἄλλου μισθωσάμενον,
ἀλλ' ἐν ἄστει τὰ πολλὰ διατρίβοντα περὶ τὴν
ἀγορὰν καὶ τὸ γυμνάσιον καὶ περὶ πότους ὄντα
καὶ ἑταίρας καὶ τὴν τοιαύτην ῥαθυμίαν, πότερον
προσέξεις οἷς λέγει μᾶλλον ἢ τοῖς πραττομένοις
ὑπ' αὐτοῦ; καὶ πότερα φήσεις γεωργὸν εἶναι τὸν
ἄνθρωπον καὶ ἐργάτην ἢ τῶν ἀργῶν καὶ ῥαθύμων;
    Δῆλον ὅτι τῶν ἀργῶν.

2 Δ. Εἶεν· εἰ δὲ κυνηγέτης εἶναι λέγοι τις καὶ τὸν
Ἱππόλυτον αὐτὸν ἢ Μελέαγρον ὑπερβάλλειν τῇ
τε ἀνδρείᾳ καὶ τῇ φιλοπονίᾳ, μηδὲν δὲ φαίνοιτο
πράττων ὅμοιον, μήτε κύνας κεκτημένος μήτε λίνα
μήτε ἵππον μήτε ὅλως ἐπὶ θήραν ἐξιών, ἀλλὰ μήτε[3]
ὑπὸ ἡλίου τὸ σῶμα ἐπικεκαυμένος μήτε ψύχους
ἀνέχεσθαι δυνάμενος, ἐσκιατραφημένος δὲ καὶ
ἁπαλὸς καὶ μάλιστα ἐοικὼς ταῖς γυναιξίν, ἔσθ'

---

[1] After ἢ Crosby deletes αὐτὸν μὴ, Wilamowitz also ἢ.
[2] ἢ added by Arnim.

150

THE SEVENTIETH DISCOURSE :
ON PHILOSOPHY

Dio. Come now, suppose you should hear some one say that he wants to be a farmer, but should observe that he is doing nothing toward that end, neither buying or raising cattle nor preparing ploughs or the other equipment needed in farming, nor even living on a farm himself, either as owner or as tenant of another, but rather in town, spending his time principally about the market-place and the gymnasium and occupied with drinking parties and courtesans and that sort of frivolity—in such a case will you treat seriously what he says rather than what he does ? And will you say the fellow is a farmer and a producer, or one of the lazy and frivolous set ?

Interlocutor. One of the lazy set, of course.

Dio. Very good. But suppose a man were to say that he is a huntsman, and that he surpasses Hippolytus himself or Meleager in both his valour and his diligence, but it should be obvious that he is engaged in no activity of that nature, since he has acquired neither dogs nor hunting-nets nor a horse and never goes out after game at all but, on the contrary, neither has been tanned by the sun nor is able to endure cold, but has been reared in the shade and is soft and very like the women, could you pos-

---

³ μήτε Emperius : μηδὲ.

ὅπως ὑπολάβοις ἂν τἀληθῆ λέγειν τοῦτον καὶ
προσήκειν τι αὐτῷ κυνηγεσίων;

Οὐκ ἔγωγε.

3 Δ. Ἄτοπον γὰρ ἀπὸ τῶν λόγων μᾶλλον οὓς
λέγει τις ἢ ἀπὸ τῶν ἔργων εἰδέναι καὶ τεκμαίρεσθαι
τὸν ἑκάστου βίον. εἰ δέ τις ἐπαγγέλλοιτο μὲν[1]
ὡς μουσικὴν ἄριστα ἐπιστάμενος καὶ περὶ τοῦτο
διατρίβων, μήτε δὲ αὐτοῦ κιθαρίζοντος μηδεὶς
πώποτε ἀκοῦσαι, ἀλλὰ μηδὲ κιθάραν ἢ λύραν
ἔχοντα ὁρῴη τις, μήτε[2] λόγον τινὰ διεξιόντα τῶν
κατὰ μουσικὴν δίχα γε τῆς ἐπαγγελίας καὶ τοῦ
ἐπίστασθαι φάσκειν τοῦ Ὀρφέως ἄμεινον καὶ τοῦ
Θαμύρα, βλέποι δ' αὐτὸν ἀλεκτρυόνας ἢ ὄρτυγας
θεραπεύοντα καὶ τρέφοντα καὶ μετὰ τῶν τοιούτων
ἀνθρώπων ὡς τὸ πολὺ διατρίβοντα, πότερον τῶν
μουσικῶν τοῦτον δεῖ ὑπολαμβάνειν ἢ τούτων τῶν
ἀνθρώπων μεθ' ὧν ἐστι καὶ οἷς ταῦτα ἐπιτηδεύει;

Δῆλον ὅτι τούτων.

4 Δ. Ἐὰν δὲ ἀστρονόμος εἶναί τις ὑπισχνῆται
καὶ σαφέστατα ἐπίστασθαι τὰς περιόδους καὶ
πορείας καὶ τὰ ἀποστήματα πῶς ἔχουσι πρὸς
ἄλληλα ἡλίου τε καὶ σελήνης καὶ τῶν τοιούτων
ἄστρων καὶ τὰ οὐράνια πάθη, μηδὲν δὲ τοιοῦτον ἢ
προῃρημένος μηδὲ περὶ ταῦτα φροντίζων, ἀλλὰ
μᾶλλον συνὼν[3] τοῖς κυβεύουσι καὶ μετ' ἐκείνων
ἑκάστοτε ζῶν καὶ βλεπόμενος, ἀστρονόμον τοῦτον
φήσεις ἢ κυβευτήν;

---

[1] μὲν Emperius : τι or τις.
[2] μήτε Emperius : μηδὲ.
[3] συνὼν Reiske : σύν.

---

[1] Like the more famous Orpheus, Thamyras—or Thamyris,
as the name is sometimes given—was reputed to have been a

152

sibly believe that this man is telling the truth and that he has anything to do with hunting ?

Int. Not I.

Dio. Correct; for it is absurd that we should know and pass upon every man's life on the strength of what he says rather than of what he does. Again, if some one should offer his services as an expert in music and as one who devotes his time to this, and yet no one should ever hear him either playing the cithara, nay, even see him holding a cithara or a lyre, or descanting on any subject related to music—that is, apart from his offering his services and saying that he has a better knowledge of music than Orpheus and Thamyras [1]—but if one should see him training and rearing game-cocks or quails and spending his time for the most part in company with those of like interests, ought one to conclude that he is a musician, or, on the contrary, one of the set with which he associates and whose pursuits are the same as his ?

Int. Evidently one of that set.

Dio. Again, if one were to profess that he is an astronomer and that he knows most accurately how the orbits and courses and the intervening distances stand with relation to one another in the case of sun and moon and similar heavenly bodies, and also celestial phenomena, and yet the man has shown no predilection of this sort and has no serious interest in these matters, but rather prefers to associate with gamblers, lives his life in their company, and is seen with them day after day, will you call this man an astronomer or a gambler ?

Thracian bard of extraordinary skill. He is said to have challenged the Muses to a competition and, when defeated, to have been deprived of his sight.

Οὐ μὰ τὸν Δί᾽ ἀστρονομίας ἡγησαίμην ἂν ἔγωγε προσήκειν αὐτῷ τι, πολὺ δὲ μᾶλλον κυβείας.

5   Δ. Δύο δέ τινων τοῦ μὲν λέγοντος ὅτι πλευσεῖται τὴν ταχίστην καὶ πολλὰ κερδανεῖ χρήματα ἀπὸ ἐμπορίας, μήτε δὲ ναῦς μήτε ναύτας παρεσκευασμένου μήτε φόρτον ἔχοντος μηδένα,[1] ἀλλὰ μηδὲ προσιόντος ὅλως τῷ λιμένι μηδὲ τῇ θαλάττῃ, τοῦ δὲ πραγματευομένου περὶ ταῦτα καὶ πλοῖον περισκοποῦντος καὶ κυβερνήτην καὶ χρήματα ἐμβαλλομένου· πότερον αὐτῶν φήσεις ἐμπορίᾳ προσέχειν τὸν νοῦν; τὸν λέγοντα ἢ τὸν πράττοντα καὶ παρασκευαζόμενον τὰ τοῦ πλοῦ καὶ τὰ τῆς ἐμπορίας;

Ἐγὼ μὲν τοῦτον.

6   Δ. Ἐπὶ παντὶ ἄρα τὸν μὲν λόγον, εἰ καθ᾽ αὑτὸν λέγοιτο, μηδενὸς ἔργου προσόντος,[2] ἄκυρον ἡγήσῃ καὶ οὐ πιστόν· τὸ δ᾽ ἔργον αὐτὸ πιστόν τε καὶ ἀληθές, ἐὰν καὶ μὴ προάγῃ λόγος;

Οὕτως.

Δ. Πότερον οὖν γεωργίας ἐστί[3] τινα ἔργα καὶ σκεύη[4] ἢ ναυτιλίας καὶ ἄλλα τῷ κυνηγέτῃ προσήκοντα καὶ τῷ ἀστρονόμῳ καὶ ἔτι[5] τοῖς ἄλλοις ἅπασι, φιλοσοφίας δὲ οὐδέν ἐστιν οἰκεῖον ἔργον οὐδὲ πρᾶγμα οὐδὲ παρασκευή;

Πάνυ μὲν οὖν.

7   Δ. Ἀλλὰ ταῦτα μὲν ἄδηλα τὰ προσήκοντα τῷ φιλοσόφῳ καὶ φιλοσοφίᾳ, τὰ δὲ τῶν ἐμπόρων

---

[1] μηδένα Reiske : μηδέν.
[2] μηδενὸς ἔργου προσόντος Jacobs : μηδὲν περὶ τοῦ προσόντος

Int. Nay, by heaven, I would not consider that he had anything at all to do with astronomy, but much rather with gambling.

Dio. Again, given two persons, one of whom says he intends to sail immediately and will gain much profit from trading, although he has not provided himself with either ship or sailors, has no cargo whatever, but, in fact, never goes near the harbour at all, or even the sea ; whereas the other occupies himself constantly with these matters, examining thoroughly a boat and putting on board a pilot and a cargo—which of the two will you say is seriously interested in trading ? The one who says he is, or the one who works at it and provides himself with all that the voyage and the business of trading demand ?

Int. I should say the latter.

Dio. In every matter, then, will you consider that the word alone, unaccompanied by any act, is invalid and untrustworthy, but that the act alone is both trustworthy and true, even if no word precedes it ?

Int. Just so.

Dio. Well then, if there are certain functions and articles of equipment peculiar to farming or to seafaring and different ones appropriate to the hunter, the astronomer, and all other professions as well, then has philosophy no function peculiar to itself, no activity, no equipment ?

Int. Most assuredly it has.

Dio. Well, are those things obscure which belong to the philosopher and to philosophy, while those

---

M, μηδὲν ἔχων περὶ τοῦ προσόντος UB, περὶ τοῦ προσόντος μηδὲν PH.   ³ ἐστί Reiske : εἶναι.

⁴ σκεύη] περὶ σκεύη MH, παρασκευὴ Jacobs.

⁵ ἔτι PH : ἐπὶ UBM, which Wilamowitz deletes.

καὶ γεωργῶν καὶ μουσικῶν καὶ ἀστρονόμων καὶ ὧν νῦν δὴ εἶπον ἔκδηλα καὶ φανερά;

Οὔ μοι δοκεῖ.

Δ. Ἀλλὰ δὴ καὶ λόγοι τινές εἰσιν ὧν δεῖ τὸν φιλοσοφοῦντα ἀκούειν, καὶ μαθήματα ἃ δεῖ μανθάνειν, καὶ δίαιτα ἣν δεῖ διαιτᾶσθαι, καὶ καθόλου βίος ἄλλος μὲν τοῦ φιλοσοφοῦντος, ἄλλος δὲ τῶν πολλῶν ἀνθρώπων· ὁ μὲν πρὸς ἀλήθειαν καὶ φρόνησιν τείνων[1] καὶ θεῶν ἐπιμέλειαν καὶ θεραπείαν καὶ[2] τῆς αὑτοῦ[3] ψυχῆς—μακρὰν ἀπ᾽[4] ἀλαζονείας καὶ ἀπάτης καὶ τρυφῆς—εὐτέλειάν τε καὶ σωφροσύνην.

8 Καὶ γὰρ στολὴ ἑτέρα μὲν τοῦ φιλοσοφοῦντος, ἑτέρα δὲ τῶν ἰδιωτῶν καὶ κατάκλισις καὶ γυμνάσια καὶ λουτρὰ καὶ ἡ ἄλλη δίαιτα, καὶ τὸν μὲν ἀκολουθοῦντα καὶ[5] χρώμενον τούτοις δεῖ νομίζειν ὡς φιλοσοφίᾳ προσέχοντα τὸν νοῦν· τὸν δὲ ἐν μηδενὶ τούτων διαφέροντα μηδὲ ὅλως ἕτερον ὄντα τῶν πολλῶν οὐχ[6] ἕνα ἐκείνων θετέον, κἂν μυριάκις εἴπῃ τε καὶ ἐπαγγείληται φιλοσοφεῖν ἐναντίον τοῦ δήμου τοῦ Ἀθηναίων ἢ Μεγαρέων ἢ παρὰ τοῖς Λακεδαιμονίων βασιλεῦσιν· ἀλλ᾽ ὠστέον τοῦτον τὸν ἄνθρωπον εἰς τοὺς ἀλαζόνας καὶ ἀνοήτους καὶ τρυφερούς.

9 Καίτοι μουσικὸν μὲν οὐκ ἀδύνατον εἶναι μὴ πράττοντα τὰ τοῦ μουσικοῦ· ἡ γὰρ μουσικὴ οὐκ ἀναγκάζει[7] προσέχειν[8] αὐτῇ[9] τὸν νοῦν καὶ μηδὲν ἄλλο ποιεῖσθαι περὶ πλείονος· καὶ ἀστρονόμον

---

[1] τείνων Selden : τιμῶν. [2] καὶ omitted by MPH.
[3] αὑτοῦ Emperius : αὐτοῦ.
[4] ἀπ᾽ added by Capps.
After καὶ Emperius deletes τὸν.
[6] οὐχ added by Arnim.

which belong to the traders and farmers and musicians and astronomers and those whom I have just named are conspicuous and manifest ?

Int. No, I think not obscure.

Dio. But surely there are certain words which one who goes in for philosophy must hear, and studies which he must pursue, and a regimen to which he must adhere, and, in a word, one kind of life belongs to the philosopher and another to the majority of mankind : the one tends toward truth and wisdom and toward care and cultivation of the gods, and, as regards one's own soul, far from false pretence and deceit and luxury, toward frugality and sobriety.

And, in fact, there is one kind of dress for the philosopher and another for the layman, and the same holds good as to table manners and gymnasia and baths and the mode of living generally, and he who is guided by and employs these distinctions must be thought to be devoted to philosophy ; whereas he who does not differ in any of these matters and is not at all unlike the world in general must not be classified as a philosopher, not even if he says he is a thousand times and makes public profession of philosophy before the popular assembly of Athens or of Megara or in the presence of the kings of Sparta ; instead, we must banish this man to the company of impostors and fools and voluptuaries.

And yet it is not impossible to be musical without engaging in musical activities ; for the art of music does not compel one to devote his attention to it and to regard nothing else of greater moment. Again,

---

[7] ἀναγκάζει Reiske : ἀνάγκη B, ἀναγκάσει UMPH.
[8] After προσέχειν Jacobs adds ἀεί.
[9] αὐτῇ Emperius : αὐτῇ or αὐτή.

157

ὄντα οὐδὲν ἴσως κωλύει τρέφειν ἀλεκτρυόνας ἢ
κυβεύειν· οὐδὲν γὰρ ἡ ἀστρονομία ἐμποδών ἐστι
τῷ μὴ τὰ δέοντα ποιεῖν· καὶ νὴ Δία ἱππικὸν
γενόμενον ἢ κυβερνήτην ἀγαθὸν ἢ γεωμέτρην ἢ
γράμματα εἰδότα οὐδὲν θαυμαστὸν ἢ[1] παρὰ ταῖς
ἑταίραις ἢ ταῖς αὐλητρίσιν ὁρᾶσθαι. τὸ γὰρ ταῦτα
ἐπίστασθαι οὐδὲν ποιεῖ βελτίω τὴν τοῦ ἀνθρώπου
10 ψυχὴν οὐδὲ ἀποτρέπει τῶν ἁμαρτημάτων· φιλοσοφίᾳ δὲ προσέχων τις καὶ μετασχὼν τούτου τοῦ
μαθήματος οὐκ ἂν ποτε ἀποσταίη τῶν βελτίστων,
οὐδὲ τούτων ἀμελήσας αἰσχρόν τι καὶ φαῦλον
προέλοιτ' ἂν πράττειν οὐδὲ ἀργεῖν καὶ ὀψοφαγεῖν
καὶ μεθύσκεσθαι. τὸ γὰρ ταῦτα μὴ[2] θαυμάζειν
καὶ τὴν τούτων ἐπιθυμίαν ἐξαιρεῖν[3] τῆς ψυχῆς καὶ
τοὐναντίον εἰς μῖσος αὐτῶν καὶ κατάγνωσιν
προάγειν[4] φιλοσοφία ἐστίν.[5] τὸ δέ γε φῆσαι
ψιλοσοφεῖν καὶ ἀλαζονεύεσθαι καὶ αὐτὸν ἐξαπα-
τῆσαι καὶ τοὺς ἄλλους οὐδὲν ἴσως κωλύει.

[1] ἢ omitted by M.
[2] μὴ deleted by Wilamowitz with M.
[3] ἐξαιρεῖν] ἐξαιρεῖ Wilamowitz, ἐξαίρειν BM.
[4] προάγειν] προάγει Wilamowitz with M.
[5] φιλοσοφία ἐστίν deleted by Wilamowitz with M.

if one is an astronomer, possibly nothing prevents his keeping game-cocks or throwing dice ; for in no wise does astronomy prevent his doing what is not right ! Furthermore, by Heaven, if one has become an expert horseman, or a good pilot, or a surveyor, or a literary critic, it is nothing surprising that he should be seen in the apartments of either the courtesans or the flute-girls. For the knowledge of those skills does not make the human soul one whit better or turn it aside from its errors ; but if one is devoted to philosophy and partakes of this study, one could never desert the highest things, nor, neglecting these things, could he prefer to engage in anything which is shameful and low, or to be lazy and gluttonous and drunken. For to refuse to admire these things and to banish the desire for them from the soul and on the other hand, to lead the soul to hate and condemn them, is the essence of philosophy. However, possibly there is nothing to prevent one's claiming to be a philosopher and at the same time playing the impostor and deceiving himself and everybody else.

THE SEVENTY-FIRST DISCOURSE:
ON THE PHILOSOPHER

In this Discourse Dio examines the statement that "the philosopher should be remarkable in everything." As examples of versatility he considers Hippias of Elis, the well-known sophist, and Odysseus, each of whom exhibited a high degree of skill in both intellectual and manual pursuits. While admitting their claim to excellence, Dio maintains that the philosopher should be able to excel all men above all in " acting, or not acting, advantageously, and in knowing when to act and where and the right moment better than the craftsman, and also in knowing what is possible of achievement." This dictum (§ 6) is illustrated by reference to Daedalus and other skilled artificers, who failed of real excellence because they were ignorant in just those respects. The Discourse concludes with a sarcastic allusion to Nero's varied ambitions.

71. ΠΕΡΙ ΦΙΛΟΣΟΦΟΥ

1   Εἰσὶν οἴ φασι δεῖν πάντα ἐν πᾶσιν εἶναι περιττὸν
τὸν φιλόσοφον· καὶ ὁμιλῆσαι ἀνθρώποις φασὶ δεῖν
εἶναι δεινότατον καὶ μηδέποτε σιγᾶν μηδὲ ἀπορεῖν
λόγων τοιούτων πρὸς τοὺς παρόντας οἳ δυνήσονται
τέρπειν αὐτούς· εἰ δὲ μή, φασὶν ἰδιώτην εἶναι τὸν
μὴ παρεσκευασμένον οὕτως καὶ ὀλίγου ἄξιον.
ἐγὼ δέ φημι τὰ μὲν δίκαια καὶ ἀληθῆ λέγειν
2 αὐτούς, τὰ δὲ οὔ. τὸ μὲν γὰρ διαφέρειν πανταχοῦ
τὸν φιλόσοφον τῶν ἄλλων δοκοῦσί μοι ὀρθῶς
ἀξιοῦν· πλὴν εἰ μή γε¹ καὶ τὰς τέχνας φασὶ δεῖν
αὐτὸν ἁπάσας εἰδέναι καὶ βέλτιον κατὰ τὴν τέχνην
ἅπαντα ποιεῖν τῶν δημιουργῶν, οἰκίας τε οἰκοδο-
μούμενον καὶ πλοῖα ναυπηγούμενον καὶ χαλκεύοντα
καὶ ὑφαίνοντα καὶ γεωργοῦντα· ὥσπερ ὁ Ἠλεῖος
Ἱππίας ἠξίου σοφώτατος εἶναι τῶν Ἑλλήνων, οὐ
μόνον ποιήματα πανταπὰ καὶ λόγους αὐτοῦ
ποικίλους προφέρων Ὀλυμπίασί τε καὶ ἐν ταῖς
ἄλλαις πανηγύρεσι τῶν Ἑλλήνων, ἀλλὰ καὶ ἄλλα
ἐπιδεικνὺς² ἔργα, τόν τε δακτύλιον καὶ τὴν λή-
κυθον καὶ στλεγγίδα καὶ τὸ ἱμάτιον³ καὶ τὴν

¹ μή γε Emperius : μήτε, μή τι, or μή.
² ἐπιδεικνὺς deleted by Arnim.

162

THE SEVENTY-FIRST DISCOURSE :
ON THE PHILOSOPHER

THERE are those who say that the philosopher should be remarkable in everything in any surroundings ; moreover, they say that he should be very able in conversation with men and never keep silent or be at a loss before those in his company for lack of such language as will be capable of pleasing them ; otherwise, they say, he who is not thus equipped is an ignoramus and worth but little. But I say that, though some of their statements are just and truthful, some are not. For that the philosopher should in every situation be superior to all others, it seems to me they are right in demanding—unless they mean that he must not only know all the crafts but also, in accordance with the rules of the craft, produce everything better than the craftsmen, both building houses and making boats and working as a smith and weaving and farming. For example, Hippias of Elis claimed to be the wisest of the Greeks, for both at the Olympic Games and at the other national gatherings of the Greeks he produced poems of every style and speeches which he had composed of divers kinds, but he also displayed other products of his——his ring, his oil-flask and strigil, his mantle, and

---

³ τὸ ἱμάτιον Wilamowitz : ἱμάντα or ἵμα.

ζώνην ὡς ἅπαντα πεποιηκὼς αὐτός, οἷον ἀπαρχὰς
τῆς σοφίας τοῖς Ἕλλησιν ἐπιδεικνύων.

3 Σχεδὸν δὲ καὶ Ὅμηρος Ὀδυσσέα πεποίηκεν
οὐ μόνον γνώμῃ διαφέροντα καὶ τῷ δύνασθαι περὶ
πραγμάτων βουλεύεσθαι καὶ λέγειν δεινότατον[1] ἔν
τε πλήθει καὶ πρὸς ὀλίγους καὶ πρὸς ἕνα, καὶ
νὴ Δία γε ἐν ἐκκλησίᾳ τε καὶ παρὰ πότον καὶ εἰ
τύχοι μετά τινος βαδίζων ὁδόν, καὶ πρὸς βασιλέα
καὶ πρὸς ἰδιώτην, καὶ πρὸς ἐλεύθερον καὶ πρὸς
δοῦλον, καὶ αὐτὸν ἔνδοξον[2] ὄντα καὶ βασιλέα καὶ
αὖ πάλιν ἀγνοούμενον καὶ πτωχόν, καὶ πρὸς
ἄνδρα τε ὁμοίως καὶ γυναῖκα καὶ κόρην, ἔτι δὲ
μάχεσθαι ἐπιστάμενον, ἀλλὰ καὶ τῶν τοιούτων
ἁπάντων ἔμπειρον, τεκτονικῆς καὶ οἰκοδομίας καὶ
4 ναυπηγικῆς. πῶς γὰρ ἂν τὸ λέχος ἐποίησεν
ἀποκόψας τὸν[3] τῆς ἐλαίας θαλλόν, εἰ μὴ τεκτονικῆς ἐπιστήμων ἦν; πῶς δ' ἂν περιέβαλε τὸν
θάλαμον, εἰ μὴ καὶ οἰκοδομῆσαι ἠπίστατο; πῶς
δ' ἂν εἰργάσατο τὴν σχεδίαν οὐκ ὢν ἔμπειρος
ναυπηγίας; τὰ δὲ περὶ φυτείαν καὶ γεωργίαν
εὐθὺς ἐκ παιδὸς[4] ἐσπουδακὼς φαίνεται παρὰ τοῦ
πατρὸς δένδρα αἰτῶν καὶ ἀμπέλους· ἄλλως τε καὶ
τοῦ πατρὸς γεωργοῦ ὄντος πάνυ ἐπιμελοῦς τε καὶ

---

[1] δεινότατον Arnim : δεινότατα.

[2] καὶ αὐτὸν ἔνδοξον Emperius : καὶ τὸν ἔνδοξον UB, τὸν
ἔνδοξον M, καὶ πρὸς ἔνδοξον PH.

[3] τὸν Reiske with C : τόν γε or τόν τε.

[4] παιδὸς Capps : παίδων.

---

[1] The versatility of Hippias, well-known sophist of the
fifth century, was a familiar topic ; cf. Plato, *Hippias
Minor* 368 B–D.

his girdle—boasting that he had made them all himself, displaying them to the Greeks as a kind of firstfruits of his wisdom.[1]

And Homer too, I venture to remark, has represented Odysseus, not merely as pre-eminent in judgement and in his ability to plan concerning practical matters, not merely as a most able speaker,[2] whether in a crowd or before a few or before only one person—yes, by Heaven, both in assembly and over the wine-cups and on occasions when walking with somebody on a journey—whether in the presence of king or of commoner, freeman or slave, no matter whether he was himself held in honour and recognized as king or, on the other hand, unknown and a beggar, and, moreover, alike when addressing either man or woman or maiden; but he also makes him pre-eminent for his knowledge of the art of combat, and he has even represented him as skilled in all such crafts as those of the joiner, the carpenter, and the shipwright. For instance, how could Odysseus have constructed his bed by cutting off the trunk of an olive tree if he were not acquainted with the joiner's art?[3] How could he have enclosed his bed-chamber if he had not been acquainted with the builder's art? How could he have built his raft if he had not understood ship-building?[4] As for the operations connected with planting and husbandry, he obviously had shown a serious interest in all that from his very boyhood, since he begged his father for trees and vines[5]; and especially, since his father was a very careful and experienced farmer, it was to be

[2] See especially Homer's tribute to his oratory in *Iliad* 3. 216-224.
[3] *Odyssey* 23. 184-204.
[4] *Ibid*. 5. 234-261.
[5] *Ibid*. 24. 336-344.

ἐμπείρου εἰκὸς ἦν αὐτὸν ταῦτα μὴ ἀγνοεῖν, ὅπου
γε καὶ προκαλεῖται τὸν Εὐρύμαχον καὶ ἀμῆσαι
καὶ ἀρόσαι. ἀλλά φησι καὶ τῶν τοιούτων ἔμπειρος εἶναι, μαγειρικῆς τε καὶ οἰνοχοΐας καὶ τῆς
ἄλλης ἁπάσης διακονίας, ἅ φησι τοὺς χείρονας
τοῖς ἀγαθοῖς διακονεῖσθαι.

5 Ταῦτα μὲν οὖν ἴσως Ἱππίας καὶ Ὀδυσσεὺς
δεινὼ ἤστην· ἐγὼ δέ φημι τὸν φιλόσοφον τὰς μὲν
τέχνας οὐχ οἷόν τε εἶναι πάσας εἰδέναι—χαλεπὸν
γὰρ καὶ μίαν ἀκριβῶς ἐργάσασθαι—ποιῆσαι δ' ἂν
ἅπαντα βέλτιον ὅ τι ἂν τύχῃ ποιῶν τῶν ἄλλων
ἀνθρώπων, καὶ τὰ κατὰ τὰς τέχνας, ἂν ἄρα
ἀναγκασθῇ ποτε ἅψασθαι τοιούτου τινός, οὐ κατὰ
τὴν τέχνην διαφέροντα· τοῦτο γὰρ οὐχ οἷόν τε,
τοῦ τέκτονος τὸν ἰδιώτην ἄμεινον ποιῆσαί τι κατὰ
τὴν τεκτονικὴν ἢ τοῦ γεωργοῦ τὸν οὐκ ὄντα
γεωργίας ἔμπειρον ἐν τῷ ποιεῖν τι τῶν γεωργικῶν
ἐμπειρότερον φανῆναι.

6 Ποῦ δ' ἂν διαφέροι; τῷ συμφερόντως ποιεῖν
ἢ μὴ ποιεῖν καὶ ὅτε δεῖ καὶ ὅπου καὶ τὸν καιρὸν
γνῶναι τοῦ δημιουργοῦ μᾶλλον καὶ τὸ δυνατόν.
αὐτίκα οὐ δοκεῖ μοι Δαίδαλος καλῶς εἰργάσθαι
ἐν Κρήτῃ τὸν Λαβύρινθον, οὗ εἰσερχόμενοι ἀπώλ-
λυντο οἱ πολῖται αὐτοῦ καὶ αἱ πολίτιδες· οὐ γὰρ[1]
δικαίως εἰργάσατο. συμπράττων δ' αὖ[2] τῇ νόσῳ
τῆς Πασιφάης οὐκ ὀρθῶς εἰργάσατο· οὐ γὰρ

---

[1] οὐ γὰρ] οὐδ' αὖ Jacobs.
[2] συμπράττων δ' αὖ, with full stop after εἰργάσατο, Arnim,
οὐδὲ συμπράττων Emperius : συμπράττων.

expected that Odysseus would not be ignorant of these matters, yes, he even challenges Eurymachus to a contest in both reaping and ploughing.[1] Why, Odysseus claims to be acquainted also with such matters as cookery and wine-serving and all other departments of domestic service, matters wherein he says that those of lower rank serve the nobles.[2]

Very well, in these respects no doubt Hippias and Odysseus were a clever pair; but I say that the philosopher, while unable to know every one of the crafts—for it is difficult to be thoroughly proficient in the practice of even one—nevertheless could do everything, no matter what he might be doing, better than anybody else, even though from the point of view of the crafts, if he really is ever compelled to tackle anything of that nature, he is not superior when measured by the standard of craftsmanship. For this is an impossibility, that the layman should produce anything better than the joiner by the standard of the joiner's craft, or that one who lacks experience in farming should be found more expert than the farmer in performing any of the tasks of the farmer.

Wherein, then, would the philosopher be superior? It would be in his acting, or not acting, advantageously, and in his knowing when to act and where and the right moment better than the craftsman, and also in his knowing what is possible of achievement. For instance, I believe that Daedalus did not build his Labyrinth in Crete well—entering which his fellow citizens, both male and female, met their death[3]—for he did not build it justly. And besides, in abetting the malady of Pasiphaë he wrought not

[3] The Athenian youths and maidens sent every ninth year to King Minos.

συνέφερεν οὐδὲ ἦν δίκαιον οὐδὲ καλὸν τοιαῦτα συμπράττειν οὐδὲ μηχανὰς εὑρίσκειν ἐπὶ τὰ αἰσχρὰ καὶ ἀνόσια. οὐδὲ ὡς τὸν Ἴκαρον ἐπτέρωσεν, εἰ χρὴ πιστεύειν τῷ μύθῳ, καλῶς ἐξευρεῖν φημι τήνδε τὴν μηχανήν· οὐ γὰρ δυνατὰ ἐμηχανᾶτο πτέρυγας ἀνθρώπῳ προστιθείς. οὐκοῦν διέφθειρε τὸν υἱόν.

7 Ἔοικε δὲ καὶ Ὅμηρος λοιδορεῖν τινα τέκτονα τῶν Τρώων, ὡς[1] οὐ καλῶς ἐργασάμενον τὰς ναῦς τῷ Ἀλεξάνδρῳ αἷς ἔπλευσεν[2] εἰς τὴν Ἑλλάδα, οὐδὲν ἔχων αἰτιάσασθαι κατὰ τὴν τέχνην. φησὶ γάρ,

ὃς καὶ Ἀλεξάνδρῳ τεκτήνατο νῆας ἐΐσας,
ἀρχεκάκους,

οὐκ ἐγκωμιάζων αὐτὸν ἐπὶ[3] τῇ ποιήσει τῶν νεῶν, ἀλλὰ ψέγων πολὺ μᾶλλον ἢ εἰ λέγων αὐτὸν ποιῆσαι τὰς ναῦς ἢ βραδείας ἢ ἄλλο τι ἁμάρτημα ἐχούσας ᾐτιᾶτο περὶ τὴν ναυπηγίαν. ψέγει δὲ ὁμοίως καὶ κυνηγέτην τινὰ καὶ καταγελᾷ τῆς ἐμπειρίας, ὅτι εἰς οὐδὲν δέον ἐκέκτητο αὐτήν, ἀλλὰ τὰ μὲν θηρία ἠπίστατο βάλλειν, ἐν δὲ τῷ πολέμῳ οὐκ ἐτύγχανεν οὐδενός, ἀλλ' ἀχρεῖος ἦν διὰ τὴν δειλίαν,

---

[1] ὡς added by Crosby.
[2] ἔπλευσεν Reiske, ἐπέπλευσεν Gasda : εἰσέπλευσεν.
[3] ἐπὶ Arnim : ἐν.

---

[1] Pasiphaë, wife of Minos, had been cursed by Poseidon with unnatural lust for the bull which he had sent Minos. Daedalus helped her to satisfy that lust ; cf. Apollodorus, *Bibliotheca* 3. 1. 4.

rightly; for it was not advantageous nor was it just or honourable to lend such aid or to invent devices for ends which were shameful and impious.[1] And even when he equipped Icarus with wings—if we are to believe the tale—I say he did not do well to invent this device; for he was attempting the impossible when he attached wings to a human being. Accordingly he wrought the death of his son.

But apparently Homer too says harsh things of a certain builder among the Trojans, as not having done well when he built for Alexander the ships with which he sailed to Hellas—though he has no fault to find with him on the score of craftsmanship. For this is what he says:

> Who built for Paris well-proportioned ships,
> Sources of ill,[2]

not lauding him for his construction of the ships, but rather censuring him much more severely than if, by saying that he had made the ships either slow or with some other defect, he had censured him for his ship-building. And Homer in similar fashion censures also a certain huntsman [3] and ridicules his skill, because he had acquired it to no good purpose, but, on the contrary, while the man knew how to shoot wild beasts, in warfare he could not hit any one but was useless because of his cowardice, and

---

[2] *Iliad* 5. 62-63, speaking of Phereclus. The context (59-64) does testify to his skill, for the poet troubles to give his lineage—" son of Carpenter, son of Joiner," and it is said that " Athena loved him exceedingly "; he is excused on the ground that he did not know the will of the gods.

[3] Scamandrius; cf. *Iliad* 5. 49-58. Artemis had taught him the art of hunting. As to his cowardice, Homer only says that he fled before Menelaüs, as did many another.

169

καὶ οὔ φησιν αὐτῷ τότε βοηθῆσαι τὴν Ἄρτε-
μιν.

8   Οὐκοῦν ἐκ τούτων δῆλον ὅτι δεῖ φρονήσεως καὶ
ἀρετῆς καὶ πρὸς ἃ ἐπίστανται οἱ ἄνθρωποι καὶ
πρὸς ἃ οὐκ ἐπίστανται· καὶ οὕτως ἂν ἅπαντα
διαφέροι πάντων ὁ σώφρων, οἷον χρὴ εἶναι τὸν
φιλόσοφον, καὶ ποιῶν τι τούτων καὶ μὴ ποιῶν,
κἂν ὁπωσοῦν ποιῇ κατὰ τὴν τέχνην. ὡς δὲ τῶν
ζωγράφων γράψει κρεῖττον οὐκ ὢν ζωγράφος,
ἢ τῶν ἰατρῶν ἄμεινον θεραπεύσει κατὰ τὴν ἰατρικήν[1] οὐκ ὢν ἰατρός, ἢ τῶν μουσικῶν μουσικώτερον
ᾄσεται οὐκ ὢν ἔμπειρος μουσικῆς ἢ μετρίως
ἔμπειρος γεγονώς, ἢ τῶν ἀριθμητικῶν περὶ τοὺς
ἀριθμοὺς ἢ τῶν γεωμετρῶν ἐμπειρότερος φανεῖται
περὶ γεωμετρίαν ἢ περὶ φυτείαν τῶν γεωργῶν
ἢ περὶ κυβερνητικὴν τῶν κυβερνητῶν, ἢ σφάξει[2]
θᾶττον τῶν μαγείρων ἢ διελεῖ[3] δέον διελεῖν τῶν
αὐτὸ τοῦτο ἔργον πεποιημένων, οὐ χρὴ διανοεῖ-
σθαι.

9   Καίτοι τῶν νῦν βασιλέων τις ἐπεθύμει σοφὸς
εἶναι τὴν τοιαύτην σοφίαν, ὡς πλεῖστα ἐπιστάμενος·
οὐ μέντοι τὰ τοιαῦτα ἃ μὴ θαυμάζεται παρὰ
τοῖς ἀνθρώποις, ἀλλὰ ἐφ' οἷς στεφανωθῆναι ἔστι,
κηρύττειν καὶ ᾄδειν πρὸς κιθάραν καὶ τραγῳδεῖν
καὶ παλαίειν καὶ παγκρατιάζειν. φασὶ δὲ καὶ

---

[1] κατὰ τὴν ἰατρικὴν deleted by Arnim.
[2] σφάξει Dindorf : σφάζειν or σφάξειν or σφάζιν.
[3] διελεῖ Dindorf : διελεῖν.

he adds that on the occasion in question Artemis did not aid him.

From these illustrations, therefore, it is evident that there is need of wisdom and virtue as applied both to what men know and also to what they do not know; and thus it is that the prudent man, such as the philosopher should be, would in everything be superior to all the world, whether in doing any of these things or in not doing, no matter how he performs according to the standards of the craft. But that he will paint better than the painter when not himself a painter; or that he will tend the sick better than the physician, as measured by the standards of the art, when not himself a physician; or that he will sing more musically than the musicians when unacquainted with the art of music or only slightly acquainted; or that he will show himself better versed than the arithmeticians in the theory of numbers, or than the surveyors in surveying, or than the farmers in planting, or than the pilots in piloting; or that he will slaughter an animal more expeditiously than the butchers, or, should it be necessary to cut it up, do so more expeditiously than those who have made this very thing their profession such things are not to be expected.

And yet a certain king of our times had the ambition to be wise in this sort of wisdom,[1] believing that he had knowledge of very many things—not, however, of such things as do not receive applause among men, but rather those for which it is possible to win a crown—I mean acting as a herald, singing to the cithara, reciting tragedies, wrestling, and taking part in the pancration. Besides, they say that he could

[1] Nero.

171

γράφειν καὶ πλάττειν ἱκανὸν αὐτὸν εἶναι καὶ αὐλεῖν τῷ τε στόματι καὶ ταῖς μασχάλαις ἀσκὸν
ὑποβάλλοντα, ὅπως διαπεφευγὼς ἦ τὸ αἰσχρὸν
τὸ τῆς Ἀθηνᾶς. οὔκουν ὑπῆρχε σοφός;

---

[1] Evidently a sort of bagpipe; cf. Guhl and Koner, *Life of the Greeks and Romans*, fig. 242.

[2] Aphroditê joked Athena because her piping made her

paint and fashion statues and play the pipe, both by means of his lips and by tucking a skin beneath his armpits [1] with a view to avoiding the reproach of Athena ! [2]   Was he not, then, a wise man ?

puff out her cheeks and thus spoiled her beauty, whereupon Athena in disgust cast the pipes on the ground.   The bagpipe enabled Nero to avoid such facial distortion.

THE SEVENTY-SECOND DIS-
COURSE: ON PERSONAL AP-
PEARANCE

In this Discourse Dio is defending what he considers to be the typical appearance of philosophers—the himation, or cloak, unaccompanied by the tunic generally worn next to the body, and long hair and beard. We learn that those who presented such an appearance were commonly subjected to insult and mockery and even to physical violence. And yet, as he tells us, philosophers—or pseudo-philosophers— were a more familiar spectacle with his hearers than shoe-makers or fullers or jesters or the followers of any other calling. It is argued that the philosopher can find a precedent for his appearance in the statues of both gods and generals and kings, none of which excites amusement or resentment on the part of the beholder. Furthermore, the city in which he is speaking tolerates the sight of many outlandish cos-tumes. This leads to the conjecture that the reason why the philosopher is singled out for insult is that men are in-clined to view him with distrust, feeling that he is critical of them, and being actuated, as one might say, by an inferiority complex. Sometimes also the philosopher is subjected to annoyance by those who expect to hear from him words of wisdom. Reference to this type of annoyance leads naturally to the telling of the fable of the owl and the birds, a fable more briefly sketched in Or. 12. 7 but preserved nowhere else. The moral of the fable is that it is risky to trust to appearances, for, though the owl of the fable was truly wise, the owl of Dio's day resembled her only in " feathers, eyes, and beak," and actually served as decoy for other fowl.

In what city was this Discourse delivered? Arnim argues

with much plausibility that it must have been Rome ; for in §§ 3-4 we are told that foreigners in most outlandish dress, who came from remote parts of the empire, were a common spectacle about the streets ; furthermore, we are told in § 5 that the local type of cult statue differed from that found in Egypt and Phoenicia but was identical with the Greek type ; and, lastly, § 6 shows clearly that the city in question was not Greek. No other city seems to suit these clues so well as Rome. It is suggested that Dio is speaking there on his first visit following his return from exile.

72. ΠΕΡΙ ΤΟΥ ΣΧΗΜΑΤΟΣ

1 Διὰ τί ποτε οἱ ἄνθρωποι, ὅταν μέν τινα ἴδωσιν
αὐτὸ μόνον χιτῶνα ἔχοντα, οὔτε προσέχουσιν οὔτε
διαγελῶσι; λογιζόμενοι τυχὸν ὅτι[1] ναύτης ἐστὶν
ὁ ἄνθρωπος καὶ ὅτι οὐδὲν δεῖ καταγελᾶν τούτου
ἕνεκα. ὁμοίως οὐδ᾽ εἴ τινα ἴδοιεν γεωργοῦ στολὴν
ἔχοντα ἢ ποιμένος, ἐξωμίδα ἔχοντα ἢ διφθέραν
ἐνημμένον ἢ κοσύμβην ὑποδεδυκότα[2] οὐ χαλεπαί-
νουσιν, ἀλλ᾽ οὐδὲ προσποιοῦνται τὴν ἀρχήν,
ἡγούμενοι προσήκειν τὴν στολὴν τῷ τοιοῦτόν τι
2 πράττοντι. τούς γε μὴν καπήλους ἑκάστοτε
ὁρῶντες πρὸ τῶν καπηλείων ἀνεζωσμένους οὐδέποτε τωθάζουσι, καταγελῷεν δ᾽ ἂν τοὐναντίον
εἰ μὴ οὕτως ἐνεσκευασμένοι εἶεν, ὡς οἰκείου τοῦ
σχήματος ὑπάρχοντος τῇ ἐργασίᾳ ἣν μεταχειρί-
ζονται. ἐπειδὰν δέ τινα ἴδωσιν ἀχίτωνα ἐν ἱματίῳ
κομῶντα τὴν κεφαλὴν καὶ τὰ γένεια, οὐχ οἷοί τέ
εἰσι πρὸς τούτους τὴν ἡσυχίαν ἄγειν οὐδὲ σιγῇ
παρέρχεσθαι, ἀλλ᾽ ἐφίστανται καὶ ἐρεθίζουσι καὶ
ἤτοι κατεγέλασαν ἢ ἐλοιδόρησαν ἢ[3] ἐνίοτε ἕλκουσιν

---

[1] ὅτι added by Arnim.
[2] ὑποδεδυκότα] ἀποδεδυκότα M, ἐπενδεδυκότα Naber.
[3] ἢ] καὶ Arnim.

---

[1] A variety of tunic which left the right shoulder bare and therefore was appropriate for most labourers.
[2] This word occurs nowhere else except in the lexica. The

176

THE SEVENTY-SECOND DISCOURSE:
ON PERSONAL APPEARANCE

WHY on earth is it that, whenever men see somebody wearing a tunic and nothing more, they neither notice him nor make sport of him? Possibly because they reason that the fellow is a sailor and that there is no occasion to mock him on this account. Similarly, if they should spy some one wearing the garb of a farmer or of a shepherd—that is, wearing an exomis [1] or wrapped in a hide or muffled in a kosymba [2]—they are not irritated, nay, they do not even notice it to begin with, feeling that the garb is appropriate to the man who follows such a calling. Take our tavern-keepers too; though people day after day see them in front of their taverns with their tunics belted high, they never jeer at them but, on the contrary, they would make fun of them if they were not so attired, considering that their appearance is peculiarly suited to their occupation. But when they see some one in a cloak but no tunic,[3] with flowing hair and beard, they find it impossible to keep quiet in his presence or to pass by in silence; instead, they step up to him and try to irritate him and either mock at him or speak insultingly, or sometimes they catch hold

context and the meaning attached to a few related words suggest a sort of poncho with a tasselled border.

[3] Socrates is reported to have followed this custom.

ἐπιλαβόμενοι, ὅταν τινὰ ὁρῶσι μὴ πάνυ ἐρρωμένον
αὐτὸν μηδὲ ἄλλον μηδένα παρόντα τὸν ἐπιβοηθή-
σοντα, καὶ ταῦτα εἰδότες ὅτι τοῖς καλουμένοις
φιλοσόφοις ξυνήθης ἐστὶν ἡ στολὴ αὕτη καὶ τρόπον
τινὰ ἀποδεδειγμένη.

3 Ὁ δὲ ἔτι τούτου παραδοξότερον· ἔνθα γὰρ ἐνίοτε
βλέπουσιν ἀνθρώπους, τοὺς μέν τινας πίλους ἐπὶ
ταῖς κεφαλαῖς ἔχοντας, ὡς νῦν τῶν Θρᾳκῶν τινες
τῶν Γετῶν λεγομένων, πρότερον δὲ Λακεδαιμόνιοι
καὶ Μακεδόνες, ἄλλους δὲ τιάραν καὶ ἀναξυρίδας,
καθάπερ, οἶμαι, Πέρσαι τε καὶ Βάκτριοι καὶ
Παρθυαῖοι καὶ ἄλλοι πολλοὶ τῶν βαρβάρων· οἱ
δὲ ἔτι τούτων ἀτοπώτεροι εἰώθασιν ἐπιδημεῖν
πτερὰ ἔχοντες ἐπὶ ταῖς κεφαλαῖς ὀρθά, ὥσπερ
Νασάμωνες· οὐκοῦν οὐδὲ τούτοις πάνυ τι τολμῶσι
πράγματα παρέχειν οὐδ' ἐνοχλεῖν προσιόντες.
καίτοι Γέτας μὲν ἢ Πέρσας ἢ Νασάμωνας, τοὺς
μὲν οὐ πολλοὺς βλέπουσι, τοὺς δὲ σπανίως ἐπι-
4 δημοῦντας, τῶν δὲ τοιούτων ἀνθρώπων ὀλίγου
νῦν μεστὰ πάντα, καὶ σχεδὸν πλείους γεγόνασι
τῶν σκυτοτόμων καὶ κναφέων καὶ τῶν γελωτο-
ποιῶν[1] ἢ ἄλλην ὁποίαν βούλει τέχνην ἐργαζομένων·
ὥστε καὶ ἐφ' ἡμῶν ἴσως ῥηθῆναι εἰκότως ὅτι πλεῖ
πάντα ὁμοίως ἀκάτια καὶ πᾶσα βοῦς ἀροτριᾷ.

---

[1] γελωτοποιῶν] γελγοπωλῶν Naber.

---

[1] Presumably Rome ; cf. Introduction.
[2] A tribe in southern Russia which seems to have piqued
the curiosity of Dio. He wrote a special treatise on them,
but it is no longer extant.
[3] A people occupying part of the Libyan coast between
the modern towns of Tripoli and Bengazi. Herodotus speaks
of them in his account of Egypt (2. 32).

of him and try to drag him off, provided they see one who is not himself very strong and note that no one else is at hand to help him ; and they do this although they know that the garb he wears is customary with the philosophers, as they are called, yes, as one might say, has been prescribed for them.

But what is even more astounding still is this. Here in your city [1] from time to time are to be seen persons, some of whom are wearing felt caps on their heads—as to-day certain of the Thracians who are called Getae [2] do, and as Spartans and Macedonians used to do in days gone by—and others wearing a turban and trousers, as I understand Persians and Bactrians and Parthians and many other barbarians do ; and some, still more outlandish than these, are accustomed to visit your city wearing feathers erect on their heads, for instance the Nasamonians [3] ; yet the citizens do not have the effrontery to make any trouble at all even for these, or to approach and annoy them. And yet as for Getae or Persians or Nasamonians, while some of them are seen here in no great numbers and others rarely visit here, the whole world to-day is virtually crowded with persons such as I have described,[4] yes, I might almost say that they have grown more numerous than the shoemakers and fullers and jesters or the workers at any other occupation whatever. Therefore in our day too possibly it could be said with good reason that every catboat is under sail and every cow is dragging a plow.[5]

---

[4] The philosophers with their long hair and beard and no tunic.

[5] A manifest proverb whose present aim is to ridicule the prevalence of the so-called philosophers of § 2.

5 Οὐ τοίνυν κατὰ τοῦτο μόνον ξυνήθης αὐτοῖς ἡ ὄψις, ἀλλὰ καὶ τὰ ἀγάλματα ὁρῶσιν ἐν τοῖς ναοῖς, οἷον Διὸς καὶ Ποσειδῶνος καὶ ἄλλων πολλῶν θεῶν ἀγάλματα, ἐν τοιαύτῃ διαθέσει τοῦ σχήματος. παρὰ μὲν γὰρ Αἰγυπτίοις καὶ Φοίνιξι καὶ ἑτέροις τισὶ τῶν βαρβάρων οὐχ ὁ αὐτὸς τύπος τῶν ἀγαλμάτων, ὥσπερ, οἶμαι, παρὰ τοῖς Ἕλλησιν, ἀλλὰ πολὺ διαφέρων, ἐνθάδε δὲ ὁ αὐτός ἐστιν. καὶ ἀνδρῶν εἰκόνας ὁρῶσι πολιτῶν τῆς πόλεως καὶ ἐν τῇ ἀγορᾷ καὶ ἐν τοῖς ἱεροῖς, στρατηγῶν καὶ βασιλέων, οὕτως ἀνακειμένας,[1] γένεια καθεικότων. ἀλλὰ
6 τί δεῖ ταῦτα λέγειν; σχεδὸν γάρ τι καὶ τῶν Ἑλλήνων οἱ πλείους ὁμοίως πρὸς τοῦτο ἔχουσι, καὶ οὐδὲν αὐτοὺς ἡ ξυνήθεια ἀποκωλύει τὸ μὴ οὐκ ἐρεσχηλεῖν μηδὲ ὑβρίζειν ἐπειδάν τινα ἴδωσι τοιοῦτον, λέγω δὲ τῶν πολλῶν καὶ ἀδόξων, οὓς μὴ δεδοίκασιν ὡς ἱκανοὺς ἀμύνεσθαι· ἐπεὶ τούς γε τοιούτους σχεδὸν δυσωποῦνται καὶ θαυμάζουσιν.

Τυχὸν οὖν τοιοῦτόν ἐστι τὸ γιγνόμενον. τοὺς μὲν ναύτας καὶ τοὺς γεωργοὺς καὶ ποιμένας, ἔτι δὲ Πέρσας καὶ Νασάμωνας, οὐκ οἴονται καταφρονεῖν αὐτῶν οὐδὲ εἶναι πρὸς αὐτοὺς οὐδένα ἐκείνοις
7 λόγον, ὅθεν οὐδὲν φροντίζουσι. τοὺς μέντοι φιλοσόφους ὑπονοοῦσιν, ὡς καταφρονοῦντας αὐτῶν[2] καὶ καταγιγνώσκοντας πολλὴν ἀμαθίαν καὶ δυστυχίαν, καὶ ὅτι φανερῶς μὲν οὐ καταγελῶσιν, ἰδίᾳ δὲ παρ' αὑτοῖς οὕτως ἔχουσιν, ὡς πάντας

---

[1] ἀνακειμένας Reiske : ἀνακείμενα.
[2] αὑτῶν Crosby : αὐτῶν.

---

[1] Greek statues of male deities, when clad at all, wore only a cloak (*himation*), usually loosely draped ; female deities were rarely represented in the nude, their statues

180

Moreover, it is not for the above reason alone that this spectacle is familiar to them, nay, they also have before their eyes the statues in the temples—as, for example, statues of Zeus and Poseidon and many other gods—arrayed in this type of costume.[1] For while among Egyptians and Phoenicians and certain other barbarians you do not find the same type of statues as you do, I believe, among the Greeks, but far different, here you find the same. Likenesses of men too, citizens of your city, they have before their eyes both in the market-place and in the temples, likenesses of generals and kings set up in this guise with flowing beards. But why need I tell all this? For I might almost say that most of the Greeks also feel as you do about this matter, and their familiarity with the sight does not keep them from teasing or even insulting whenever they spy a man of that appearance—I mean, whenever they see one of the common sort of no repute, whom they do not fear as being able to retaliate; for of course those who have that ability they virtually cringe before and admire!

Well, possibly what goes on is like this: the sailors and the farmers and shepherds, yes, and the Persians and Nasamonians too, the people believe do not look down on them or have any concern with them, and so they do not give them a thought. The philosophers, however, they view with misgivings, suspecting that they scorn them and attribute to them vast ignorance and misfortune; and they suspect that, though the philosophers do not laugh at them in public, privately among themselves they view them in that light,

commonly wearing the tunic, over which in many instances was draped the himation.

DIO CHRYSOSTOM

ἀθλίους ὄντας τοὺς ἀπαιδεύτους, ἀρξαμένους ἀπὸ
τῶν πλουσίων δὴ καὶ μακαρίων δοκούντων, οὓς
αὐτοὶ ζηλοῦσι καὶ σμικρὸν διαφέρειν οἴονται τῶν
θεῶν εὐδαιμονίας ἕνεκεν· καὶ ὅτι ἀτιμάζουσι καὶ
διαγελῶσιν[1] ὡς[2] πολυτελῶς ἐσθίοντάς τε καὶ πίνον-
τας καὶ καθεύδειν μαλακῶς βουλομένους καὶ μετὰ
γυναικῶν ἑκάστοτε ὡραίων καὶ παίδων ἀναπαύε-
σθαι καὶ πολλὰ χρήματα ἔχειν καὶ θαυμάζεσθαι
ὑπὸ τοῦ πολλοῦ ὄχλου καὶ περιβλέπεσθαι· ὧν οὐδὲν
ἡγοῦνται μεῖζον οὐδὲ κάλλιον.

8   Διὰ δὴ ταύτην τὴν ὑποψίαν δυσχεραίνουσι τοὺς
μὴ ταὐτὰ σφίσι θαυμάζοντας μηδὲ τιμῶντας μηδὲ
τὴν αὐτὴν περὶ τῶν μεγίστων ἔχοντας διάνοιαν.
οὐκοῦν προκαταλαμβάνουσιν αὐτοὶ λυιδοροῦντες
καὶ τωθάζοντες ὡς ἀθλίους καὶ ἀνοήτους, εἰδότες
ὅτι, εἰ μὲν τούτους ἀποφανοῦσιν ἄφρονας καὶ
μαινομένους, ἅμα καὶ αὑτοὺς ἀποδείξουσι σωφρο-
νοῦντας καὶ νοῦν ἔχοντας· εἰ δὲ παραχωρήσουσιν,
ὡς τούτων ἃ χρὴ γιγνωσκόντων καὶ πολλοῦ ἀξίων,
ἅμα καὶ αὑτοὺς ὁμολογήσουσι δυστυχεῖς καὶ
ἀναισθήτους καὶ οὐδὲν εἰδότας ἁπλῶς ὧν προσήκει
ἀνθρώπους ἐλευθέρους εἰδέναι.

9   Ἔτι δὲ ἐὰν μέν τινα ἴδωσιν ὡς ναύτην ἐσταλ-
μένον, ἴσασι τοῦτον πλευσούμενον, κἂν ὡς γεωργὸν
ἕτερον, γεωργήσοντα· τόν γε μὴν ποιμένος ἔχοντα
στολὴν ἴσασι καὶ τοῦτον ὅτι ἄπεισιν ἐπὶ τὰ πρό-

---

[1] ἀτιμάζουσι καὶ διαγελῶσιν Reiske : ἀτιμάζοιεν καὶ διαγελῷεν.
[2] ὡς] τοὺς Arnim, ὁρῶντες Reiske.

182

holding that the unenlightened are all pitiable creatures, beginning, in fact, with those who are reputed to be rich and prosperous, persons whom these mockers themselves envy and believe to be little different from the gods in felicity ; furthermore, they suspect that these philosophers disparage and ridicule them as being extravagant in eating and drinking, as wanting a soft bed to sleep on and the company of young women and boys whenever they repose, and plenty of money, and to be admired and looked up to by the mob, things which they believe to be more important and better than anything else.

Because of this suspicion they of course dislike those who do not admire or prize the same things as they do and do not hold the same opinion about the things of chief importance. Therefore they seize for themselves the initiative in reviling and jeering at the philosophers as being luckless and foolish, knowing that if they succeed in showing that the philosophers are senseless and daft they will at the same time also prove themselves to be prudent and sensible ; whereas if they give way to them, recognizing that the philosophers know what they should and are highly estimable, at the same time they will be admitting that they themselves are luckless and thick-witted and know absolutely none of the things free men should.

Again, if they see a man rigged out as a sailor, they know that he is about to put to sea, and if they see some one else rigged out as a farmer, they know that he is about to engage in farming, and of course they know also that he who is clad in shepherd's garb is on his way to his sheep and will spend his

βατα καὶ περὶ ἐκεῖνα διατρίψει,[1] ὥστε ὑπ' οὐδενὸς
λυπούμενοι τούτων ἐῶσιν αὐτούς· ὅταν δέ τινα
ἴδωσι τὸ σχῆμα ἔχοντα τὸ τοῦ φιλοσόφου, λογί-
ζονται ὅτι οὗτος οὔτε πρὸς τὸ πλεῖν[2] οὔτε πρὸς
γεωργίαν οὔτε προβάτων ἕνεκεν οὕτως ἔσταλται,
ἀλλ' ἐπ' ἀνθρώπους παρεσκεύασται, ὡς νουθετή-
σων τε καὶ ἐξελέγξων καὶ οὐδέν τι θωπεύσων
οὐδένα αὐτῶν οὐδὲ φεισόμενος οὐδενός, τοὐναντίον
δὲ κολάσων ὡς ἂν δύνηται αὐτοὺς μάλιστα τῷ
10 λόγῳ καὶ ἐπιδείξων οἷοί εἰσιν. οὔκουν δύνανται
ἡδέως ὁρᾶν αὐτούς, ἀλλὰ προσκρούουσι καὶ δια-
μάχονται, ὥσπερ οὐδ' οἱ παῖδες ἡδέως ὁρᾶν
δύνανται οὓς ἂν ἴδωσι παιδαγωγῶν σχῆμα ἔχοντας
καὶ παρεσκευασμένους οὕτως ὡς ἐπιπλήξοντας
αὐτοῖς καὶ οὐκ ἐπιτρέψοντας ἁμαρτάνειν οὐδὲ
ῥᾳθυμεῖν. εἰ γάρ τοι καὶ τοῖς παισὶν ἐξῆν τῶν
τοιούτων καταγελᾶν καὶ ὑβρίζειν, οὐδὲν ἂν πρότερον τούτου ἐποίουν.

Οὐ μέντοι ἅπαντες ἀπὸ ταύτης τῆς διανοίας
προσέρχονται καὶ ἐνοχλοῦσιν, ἀλλ' ἔστι γένος
ἀνθρώπων πολυπραγμονοῦν τοιαύτην πολυπραγμο-
11 σύνην καὶ τρόπον τινὰ οὐ πονηρόν· οὗτοι προσίασιν[3] οὓς ἂν ἡγῶνται φιλοσόφους ἀπὸ τῆς
στολῆς, ὡς ἀκουσόμενοί τι παρ' αὐτῶν σοφὸν
ὃ οὐκ ἂν παρ' ἑτέρου ἀκούσειαν, πυνθανόμενοι
καὶ περὶ Σωκράτους ὅτι σοφός τε ἦν καὶ διελέγετο[4]
τοῖς προσιοῦσι λόγους φρονίμους, καὶ περὶ Διογένους, ὅτι καὶ αὐτὸς πρὸς ἅπαντα εὐπόρει λόγου
καὶ ἀποκρίσεως. καὶ τὰ μὲν τούτου καὶ διαμνη-

---

[1] διατρίψει Reiske : διατρίψοι.
[2] After πλεῖν Arnim deletes ἐστιν.
[3] After προσίασιν Herwerden adds πρὸς.

time attending to them, and so, since they are not
irritated by any of these, they let them alone ; but
when they see a man in the garb of the philosopher,
they reason in his case that it is not for sailing or for
farming or for tending sheep that he is thus arrayed,
but rather that he has got himself ready to deal with
human beings, aiming to admonish them and put
them to the test and not to flatter or to spare any one
of them, but, on the contrary, aiming to reprove
them to the best of his ability by his words and to
show what sort of persons they are. They cannot,
therefore, look upon the philosophers with any
pleasure, but instead they clash with them and
fight with them, just as boys too cannot look with
pleasure upon any whom they see in the guise of
tutors and prepared as if they meant to rebuke them
and not to allow them to go astray or be careless.
In truth, if the boys were at liberty to mock at
and insult such persons, there is nothing they would
rather do than that.

However, not all have this motive in coming up
and making themselves a nuisance ; on the contrary,
there are persons who indulge in this kind of
curiosity and, in a way, are not bad persons either.
These approach any whom, because of their dress,
they take to be philosophers, expecting to hear from
them some bit of wisdom which they could not hear
from any one else, because they have heard regarding
Socrates that he was not only wise but also accustomed to speak words of wisdom to those who approached him, and also regarding Diogenes, that
he too was well provided with statement and answer
on each and every topic. And the masses still

μονεύουσιν οἱ πολλοί, τὰ μέν τινα ἴσως εἰπόντος
αὐτοῦ, τὰ δὲ καὶ ἄλλων συνθέντων.

12 Τῶν γε μὴν ἑπτὰ σοφῶν τὰς γνώμας ἀκούουσι
καὶ ἐν Δελφοῖς ἀνατεθῆναι πρότερον, οἷον ἀπαρχάς
τινας τῆς σοφίας τῆς ἐκείνων καὶ ἅμα τῆς τῶν
ἀνθρώπων ἕνεκεν ὠφελείας, ὡς τῷ ὄντι δὴ θεῖα
ταῦτα καὶ σχεδόν τι τῶν χρησμῶν θειότερα οὓς
ἡ Πυθία ἔχρα καθίζουσα ἐπὶ τοῦ τρίποδος, ἐμ-
πιμπλαμένη τοῦ πνεύματος. τὸ γὰρ αὑτῷ χρησθὲν
ἕκαστος ἀκούσας ἄπεισι, καὶ οὐκ ἀνατίθεται ταῦτα, ὥστε δὴ καὶ πᾶσιν ἀνθρώποις εἶναι γνώριμα·
τὰ δὲ ἐκείνων δόγματα κοινὰ ἀπεδείχθη τοῖς
ἀφικνουμένοις παρὰ τὸν θεόν, ὡς ὁμοίως ξυμφέρον
πᾶσιν εἰδέναι καὶ πείθεσθαι.

13 Εἰσὶ δὲ οἳ καὶ τὸν Αἴσωπον οἴονται τοιοῦτόν
τινα γενέσθαι, σοφὸν μὲν καὶ φρόνιμον, αἱμύλον
δὲ ἄλλως καὶ ξυνθεῖναι λόγους ἱκανὸν οἵων αὐτοὶ
ἥδιστ᾽ ἂν ἀκούοιεν. καὶ τυχὸν οὐ[1] παντάπασι
ψευδῆ οἴονται καὶ[2] τῷ ὄντι Αἴσωπος τοῦτον τὸν
τρόπον ἐπειρᾶτο νουθετεῖν τοὺς ἀνθρώπους καὶ
ἐπιδεικνύναι αὐτοῖς ἄττα ἁμαρτάνουσιν, ὡς ἂν
μάλιστα ἠνείχοντο αὐτόν, ἡδόμενοι ἐπὶ τῷ γελοίῳ
καὶ τοῖς μύθοις· ὥσπερ τὰ παιδία ταῖς τίτθαις
μυθολογουμέναις προσέχουσί τε καὶ ἥδονται. ἀπὸ
δὴ τῆς τοιαύτης δόξης, ὡς καὶ παρ᾽ ἡμῶν ἀκουσό-

---

[1] οὐ added by Selden.   [2] καὶ Arnim: εἰ or ἦ or ἡ.

---

[1] Cf. Plato, *Protagoras* 342 E—343 B, which Dio seems to
have in mind, and Pausanias 10. 24. 1. The only sayings
expressly stated to have been inscribed at Delphi are the most
famous of all—KNOW THYSELF and NOTHING IN EXCESS.

[2] Aesop was frequently associated with the Seven Sages.
The homely wisdom of his beast fables appealed strongly to
the Greeks. Aristophanes drew upon them from time to

remember the sayings of Diogenes, some of which he may have spoken himself, though some too were composed by others.

Indeed, as for the maxims of the Seven Sages, they hear that these were even inscribed as dedications at Delphi in days gone by, firstfruits, as it were, of the wisdom of those men and at the same time intended for the edification of mankind, the idea being that these maxims were truly divine, and if I may say so, even more divine than the responses which the Pythian priestess was wont to give as she sat upon her tripod and filled herself with the breath of the god. For the response which is made to each for himself he listens to and then goes his way, and such responses are not dedicated and thereby made known to all mankind too ; but the maxims of the Seven Sages have been appointed for the common use of all who visit the god, as being profitable for all alike to know and to obey.[1]

And there are those who think that Aesop too was somewhat like the Seven Sages, that while he was wise and sensible, yet he was crafty too and clever at composing tales such as they themselves would most enjoy to hear.[2] And possibly they are not wholly mistaken in their suppositions and in reality Aesop did in this way try to admonish mankind and show them wherein they were in error, believing that they would be most tolerant toward him if they were amused by his humour and his tales—just as children, when their nurses tell them stories, not only pay attention to them but are amused as well. As the result, then, of this belief,

time. The earliest known example of this type of fable is Hesiod's Hawk and Nightingale, *Works and Days* 202-212.

μενοί τι τοιοῦτον οἷον Αἴσωπος ἔλεγεν ἢ ὁποῖον
Σωκράτης ἢ ὁποῖα Διογένης, προσίασι καὶ ἐν-
οχλοῦσι καὶ οὐ δύνανται ἀπέχεσθαι ὃν ἂν ἴδωσιν
ἐν τούτῳ τῷ σχήματι, οὐ μᾶλλον ἢ τὰ ὄρνεα
ἐπειδὰν ἴδωσι γλαῦκα.

14 Ἐφ' ᾧ καὶ ξυνετίθει λόγον Αἴσωπος τοιοῦτον,
ὡς τὰ ὄρνεα ξυνῆλθε πρὸς τὴν γλαῦκα καὶ ἐδεῖτο
τῆς μὲν ἀπὸ τῶν οἰκοδομημάτων σκέπης[1] ἀπαν-
ίστασθαι, πρὸς δὲ τὰ δένδρα τὴν καλιάν, ὥσπερ
καὶ αὐτά, καὶ τοὺς τούτων μεταπήγνυσθαι κλῶνας,
ἀφ' ὧν καὶ ᾄδειν ἔστιν εὐσημότερον· καὶ δὴ καὶ
πρὸς δρῦν ἄρτι τότ' ἤδη[2] φυομένην, ἐπειδὰν πρὸς
ὥραν ἀφίκηται, ἑτοίμως ἔχειν ἱζάνειν καὶ τῆς
χλοερᾶς κόμης ἀπόνασθαι. ἀλλ' οὖν τήν γε
γλαῦκα μὴ τοῦτο τοῖς ὀρνέοις ποιεῖν παραινεῖν
μηδὲ φυτοῦ βλάστῃ ἐφήδεσθαι ἰξὸν πεφυκότος
15 φέρειν, πτηνοῖς ὄλεθρον. τὰ δὲ μήτε τῆς ξυμ-
βουλῆς ἀπεδέχετο[3] τὴν γλαῦκα, τοὐναντίον δὲ
ἔχαιρε τῇ δρυΐ φυομένῃ, ἐπειδὴ δὲ[4] ἱκανὴ ἦν,
καθίσαντα ἐπ' αὐτὴν ᾖδεν. γενομένου δὲ τοῦ
ἰξοῦ ῥᾳδίως ἤδη ὑπὸ τῶν ἀνθρώπων ἁλισκόμενα
μετενόουν καὶ τὴν γλαῦκα ἐθαύμαζον[5] ἐπὶ τῇ
ξυμβουλῇ. καὶ νῦν ἔτι οὕτως ἔχουσιν, ὡς δεινῆς
καὶ σοφῆς οὔσης αὐτῆς, καὶ διὰ τοῦτο ἐθέλουσι
πλησιάζειν, ἡγούμενα ἀγαθόν τι ἀπολαύειν τῆς
ξυνουσίας· ἔπειτα, οἶμαι, προσίασι μάτην ἐπὶ
κακῷ. ἡ μὲν γὰρ ἀρχαία γλαὺξ τῷ ὄντι φρονίμη

---

[1] σκέπης Reiske : ὀπῆς.
[2] ἄρτι τότ' ἤδη Post, ταυτηνὶ ἄρτι Reiske : ἄρτι ταυτηνὶ.

that they are going to hear from us too some such saying as Aesop used to utter, or Socrates, or Diogenes, they draw near and annoy and cannot leave in peace whomever they may see in this costume, any more than the birds can when they see an owl.

Indeed, this is why Aesop composed a fable which I will relate. The birds came together to call upon the owl, and they begged her to withdraw from the shelter afforded by the human habitations and to transfer her nest to the trees, just like themselves, and to their branches, " whence," they declared, " it is actually possible to sing a clearer note." And in fact, as the fable has it, they stood ready to settle upon an oak, which was then just starting to grow, as soon as it should reach its prime, and to enjoy its green foliage. However, the story continues, the owl advised the birds not to do this and not to exult in the shoot of a plant whose nature it is to bear mistletoe, a bane to feathered folk. But the birds not only did not applaud the owl for her advice, but, quite the reverse, they took delight in the oak as it grew, and when it was of proper size they alighted on it and sang. But because the mistletoe had grown on it, they now were easily captured by the men and repented of their conduct and admired the owl for her advice. And even to this day they feel this way about her, believing her to be shrewd and wise, and on this account they wish to get near her, believing that they are deriving some benefit from association with her ; but if they do, they will approach her, I fancy, all in vain and to their cost. For though that

---

³ ἀπεδέχετο Reiske : ἀποδέχεσθαι.
⁴ ἐπειδὴ δέ] ἐπειδή τε Emperius.
⁵ ἐθαύμαζον editio princeps : ἐθαύμαζεν.

τε ἦν καὶ ξυμβουλεύειν ἐδύνατο, αἱ δὲ νῦν μόνον
τὰ πτερὰ ἔχουσιν ἐκείνης καὶ τοὺς ὀφθαλμοὺς
καὶ τὸ ῥάμφος, τὰ δὲ ἄλλα ἀφρονέστεραί εἰσι
16 τῶν ἄλλων ὀρνέων. οὐκοῦν οὐδὲ ἑαυτὰς δύνανται
οὐδὲν ὠφελεῖν· οὐ γὰρ ἂν παρὰ τοῖς ὀρνιθοθήραις
ἐτρέφοντο δεδεμέναι καὶ δουλεύουσαι.[1]

Καὶ ἡμῶν ἕκαστος τὴν μὲν στολὴν ἔχει τὴν
Σωκράτους καὶ Διογένους, τὸ δὲ φρονεῖν πολλοῦ
δέομεν ὅμοιοι εἶναι τοῖς ἀνδράσιν ἐκείνοις ἢ ζῆν
ὁμοίως αὐτοῖς ἢ λόγους τοιούτους διαλέγεσθαι.
τοιγάρτοι οὐδὲν ἄλλο ἢ βλεπόμενοι ὥσπερ αἱ
γλαῦκες ὄχλον πολὺν ξυνάγομεν τῷ ὄντι ὀρνέων,
αὐτοί τε ὄντες ἠλίθιοι καὶ ὑφ' ἑτέρων τοιούτων
ἐνοχλούμενοι.

---

[1] δουλεύουσαι] παλεύουσαι Herwerden.

owl of olden days was really wise and able to give
advice, those of to-day merely have her feathers,
eyes, and beak, but in all else they are more foolish
than the other birds. Therefore they cannot benefit
even themselves ; for otherwise they would not be
kept at the bird-catcher's, caged and in servitude.[1]

Just so, though each of us has the garb of Socrates
and Diogenes, in intellect we are far from being like
those famous men, or from living as they did, or
from uttering such noble thoughts. Therefore, for no
other reason than because of our personal appearance,
we, like the owls, collect a great company of those
who in truth are birds, being fools ourselves besides
being annoyed by others of like folly.

[1] Dio employs this fable of Aesop's also in Or. 12. 6-8.

THE SEVENTY-THIRD DISCOURSE:
ON TRUST

ALTHOUGH this Discourse begins with no formal address, it presents the appearance of a letter, for in the final paragraph the author applies his remarks to some one individual, whose name, unfortunately, is not given. Certainly, if we were to assume that we had before us an oral communication, we should expect to find now and then some appeal to the listener and an occasional response, however brief and perfunctory.

Dio appears to be writing to some acquaintance, possibly a former pupil, who seems to be considering acceptance of some responsibility, the nature of which it is idle to conjecture. All but the final paragraph is devoted to an exposition of the discomforts and even dangers attendant upon such a decision. As horrible examples of the ingratitude of both state and private citizen Dio passes in review some of the most notable personages of myth and history, besides calling attention to the many nameless persons who were repaid for their services as guardians or trustees by reproach or even by prosecution in the courts. We infer that he would have his anonymous acquaintance remain true to philosophy.

73. ΠΕΡΙ ΠΙΣΤΕΩΣ

1 Ἆρά γε τὸ πιστεύεσθαι τοῖς πιστευομένοις
ἀγαθόν ἐστι καὶ τοιοῦτον οἷον τὸ πλουτεῖν καὶ τὸ
ὑγιαίνειν καὶ τὸ τιμᾶσθαι τοῖς τιμωμένοις καὶ
ὑγιαίνουσι καὶ πλουτοῦσιν, αὐτοῖς ἐκείνοις τινὰ
φέρον ὠφέλειαν; λέγω δὲ οἷον εἴ τις δημοσίᾳ
τύχοι πιστευόμενος ὑπὸ τῆς αὑτοῦ[1] πόλεως ἢ ἑτέρας
στρατιὰν[2] ἢ χρήματα ἢ τείχη, καθάπερ ἤδη πολλοὶ
τὰ τοιαῦτα ἐπετράπησαν, οἱ δὲ καὶ αὐτὰς τὰς
πόλεις μετὰ παίδων καὶ γυναικῶν εἰρήνης τε
2 οὔσης καὶ πολέμου καταλαβόντος ἐνίοτε· καὶ νὴ
Δία εἴ τις ὑπ᾽[3] ἀνδρὸς βασιλέως ἢ τυράννου
πιστεύοιτο χρυσίον ἢ ἀργύριον ἢ ναῦς ἢ ὅπλα ἢ
ἀκρόπολιν ἢ ξύμπασαν τὴν ἀρχήν, ὥσπερ Λεπτίνης
μὲν παρὰ τοῦ ἀδελφοῦ πολλάκις Συρακούσας
παρέλαβε, Φίλιστος δὲ παρὰ τοῦ νεωτέρου Διονυ-
σίου, μάγοι δὲ παρὰ Καμβύσου τὰ Περσῶν βασίλεια, ὅτε εἰς Αἴγυπτον ἐστρατεύετο, παρὰ δὲ

---

[1] αὑτοῦ Emperius : αὐτοῦ.
[2] στρατιὰν Emperius : στρατείαν.
[3] ὑπ᾽ Emperius : ἀπ᾽.

---

[1] Dionysius the Elder, who banished Leptines for marrying without his consent, but later recalled him.
[2] Philistus was both soldier-politician and historian.

THE SEVENTY-THIRD DISCOURSE:
ON TRUST

Do you really mean to say that being trusted is a good thing for those who are trusted and comparable to being wealthy or healthy or honoured for those who are honoured or healthy or wealthy, because it brings to those persons themselves some benefit? I mean, for instance, if a person should chance to be trusted in an official capacity, by his own state or by another, with an army or money or fortifications, just as in the past many have had such things entrusted to them, and in some instances even the cities themselves, women and children and all, not only in times of peace, but also sometimes when in the grip of war. And, by Heaven, if a person were to be trusted by a king or a tyrant with gold or silver or ships or arms or a citadel or the supreme command —for example, Leptines often received command of Syracuse from his brother,[1] and Philistus received it from the younger Dionysius,[2] and the Magi received from Cambyses charge of his palace in Persia at the time when he was campaigning against Egypt,[3]

Exiled by Dionysius the Elder along with Leptines, he was recalled sixteen years later on the accession of Dionysius II, but finally fell by his own hand when defeated in the attempt to save his master's power.

[3] One of the most famous tales in Herodotus (3. 61-80). The Magi paid with their lives for their conspiracy.

DIO CHRYSOSTOM

Δαρείου Μιθράνης τὴν Σάρδεων ἀκρόπολιν, Περσαῖος δὲ παρὰ ᾽Αντιγόνου τὸν ᾽Ακροκόρινθον, πολὺ δὲ τούτων πρότερον ᾽Ατρεὺς παρ᾽ Εὐρυσθέως τὸ ῎Αργος ὅτε Εὐρυσθεὺς ἐπ᾽ ᾽Αθήνας ἐστρατεύετο οὐκ ἐκδιδόντων ᾽Αθηναίων τοὺς ῾Ηρακλέους παῖδας· ὁ δὲ υἱὸς αὐτοῦ ὁ ᾽Αγαμέμνων, ἡνίκα ἐπὶ Τροίαν ἔπλει, μουσικῷ ἀνδρὶ ἐπίστευσε τὴν γυναῖκα καὶ
3 τὴν οἰκίαν—τούτους ἅπαντας φῶμεν τοὺς πιστευομένους ἀγαθόν τι ἀπολαύειν καὶ αὐτοὺς τῆς πίστεως;

Καὶ αὖ τοὺς ὑπὸ τῶν ἰδιωτῶν πιστευομένους ἢ γυναῖκας ἢ παῖδας ἢ τὴν οὐσίαν, καθάπερ, οἶμαι, πολλοὶ ἐπιτρόπους καὶ κηδεμόνας καταλείπουσιν, οἱ μὲν ἀποδημοῦντες, οἱ δὲ ἀποθνήσκοντες, οἱ δὲ παρακαταθήκας διδόασιν ἄνευ μαρτύρων, οὐ δεδιότες μὴ ἀφαιρεθῶσιν, ἔνιοι δὲ τῶν νόμων ἀπαγορευόντων μὴ καταλιπεῖν κληρονόμους οὓς αὐτοὶ βούλονται, ἑτέρους καταλείπουσιν, ἐντειλάμενοι τὰ χρήματα ἀποδοῦναι τοῖς αὐτῶν[1] ἐπι-
4 τηδείοις—τούτοις δὴ πᾶσι λυσιτελεῖν φῶμεν τὸ πρᾶγμα καὶ τὴν δόξαν, ἣν ἔχοντες περὶ αὐτῶν ἐπιτρέπουσιν αὐτοῖς οἱ τὰ σφέτερα ἐπιτρέποντες,

---

[1] αὐτῶν Emperius : αὑτῶν.

---

[1] Satrap under Darius III, Mithranes surrendered Sardis to Alexander the Great, who later put him in charge of Armenia ; cf. Diodorus 17. 21. 7 and 17. 64. 6.
[2] A distinguished pupil of Zeno, the Stoic philosopher. Antigonus Gonatas put him in charge of Acrocorinth.

196

and Mithranes [1] received from Darius the citadel of Sardis, and Persaeus [2] received Acrocorinth from Antigonus, and, much earlier than these, Atreus received Argos from Eurystheus, when Eurystheus was campaigning against Athens for refusing to surrender the children of Heracles,[3] and, further- more, the son of Atreus, Agamemnon, when setting sail for Troy, entrusted to a musician his wife and his house [4]—shall we say that all those who were trusted themselves derived some good from the trust?

Again, how about those who are entrusted by men in private station with either wives or children or estate? For instance, many, I fancy, leave behind them guardians and protectors, some when going on a journey and others when dying; and some place deposits in trust without the presence of witnesses, having no fear of being defrauded; and some, because the laws forbid their naming as heirs those whom they themselves prefer,[5] name others, in- structing them to turn over the property to the friends of the deceased—are we to say that all such derive an advantage from the transaction and from the high opinion about them which leads those who do so to entrust them with their possessions, but

When Aratus snatched it from him he managed to escape with his life.

[3] When Heracles died, his children, fearing Eurystheus, fled to Athens.

[4] Homer relates (*Odyssey* 3. 267-272) that, in order to effect his seduction of Clytaemnestra, Aegisthus removed the nameless bard to a desert island and left him there to become a prey to the birds.

[5] According to Attic law, if a man had sons born in lawful wedlock, he must leave his estate to them; if he had a daughter but no sons, her husband, preferably a relative, was given charge of the inheritance.

μάλιστα δὲ¹ τοῖς τελευταίοις τοῖς παρανόμως
πιστεύεσθαι δοκοῦσιν· ἢ τοὐναντίον χαλεπὸν εἶναι
τὸ τοιοῦτον καὶ πολλῆς ἀσχολίας καὶ φροντίδων
αἴτιον, ἐνίοτέ γε² μὴν καὶ κινδύνων τῶν μεγίστων;

Ἔξεστι δὲ σκοπεῖν εὐθὺς ἀπὸ τῶν δοκούντων
εἶναι μεγίστων· οὗτοι γὰρ τῶν μὲν ἰδίων ἐξ
ἀνάγκης ἀμελοῦσι καὶ χρημάτων καὶ τέκνων,
προσέχουσι δὲ τοῖς κοινοῖς καὶ ἐπὶ τούτων εἰσί·
καὶ πολλάκις μὲν ὑπὸ τῶν ἐπιβουλευόντων ταῖς
πόλεσιν ἢ πολεμίων ἢ πολιτῶν τινων ἀπόλλυνται,
πολλάκις δὲ ὑπ' αὐτῶν τῶν πόλεων ἀδίκως δια-
βληθέντες. οἱ μὲν γὰρ οὐσίας ἀφῃρέθησαν, τοὺς
δὲ καὶ ὀνείδη συνέβη κτήσασθαι καταδικασθέντας
κλοπῆς· οἱ δὲ ἐξέπεσον ἐκ τῶν πατρίδων, οἱ δὲ
καὶ ἀπέθανον.

5 Ὥσπερ οὖν λέγουσι Περικλέα μὲν ἁλῶναι
κλοπῆς παρὰ Ἀθηναίοις τὸν κάλλιστα καὶ ἄριστα
προστάντα τῆς πόλεως, Θεμιστοκλέα δὲ ἐκπεσεῖν
ὡς προδιδόντα, ὃς παραλαβὼν αὐτοὺς οὐ δυνα-
μένους τὸ ἔδαφος τῆς πατρίδος οἰκεῖν, ἀλλὰ
παραχωροῦντας τοῖς πολεμίοις αὐτοῦ τοῦ ἄστεος
καὶ τῶν ἱερῶν, οὐ μόνον ταῦτα πάντα ἀπέδωκεν,
ἀλλ' ἔτι καὶ τῶν Ἑλλήνων ἡγεμόνας ἐποίησεν,

¹ δὲ Pflugk : δή.
² γε added by Reiske.

---

¹ In reporting what presumably was the gossip of the
comic poets, Plutarch, *Pericles* 32. 2-3, relates that, wishing
to discredit Pericles with the people, Dracontides sponsored
a bill providing that Pericles should deposit his accounts of
public moneys with the prytanes and defend them in court,
and that, because he had previously come into collision with

particularly in the case of those last mentioned, who seem to be trusted in violation of the laws? Or, on the contrary, shall we say that such a responsibility is vexatious and the source of much trouble and many worries, sometimes indeed even of the greatest perils?

But we may examine the question by beginning immediately with those who are thought to be of highest rank; for these of necessity neglect their private interests, both property and children, and devote their attention to the public interests and are absorbed in them; and often at the hands of those who plot against their cities, whether foreign foes or some of their fellow citizens, they meet with disaster, and often, too, at the hands of the cities themselves, because of unjust accusation. For some have been deprived of property, and some even have suffered disgrace of various kinds, having been convicted on a charge of embezzlement, others have been banished from their native land, and others have even been put to death.

For example, they say that Pericles was convicted of embezzlement in an Athenian court,[1] the noblest and best champion the city ever had; and that Themistocles was banished on a charge of treason, the one who, after having taken charge of the Athenians at a time when they were no longer able to occupy the soil of their native land but were yielding to the foe their city itself and their shrines, not only restored all these things, but even made the Athenians leaders of the Greeks, wresting the leader-

the people in the case of Pheidias, Pericles feared to appear before a jury and avoided trial by hastening the outbreak of the Peloponnesian War.

199

ἀφελόμενος Λακεδαιμονίους ἐξ ἀρχῆς ἔχοντας τὴν τιμὴν ταύτην.

6 Μιλτιάδης δὲ ὁ πρῶτος νικήσας τοὺς βαρβάρους μετὰ μόνων τῶν πολιτῶν καὶ τὸ Περσῶν φρόνημα καθελών, ὃ πρότερον εἶχον ὡς ἁπάντων ἀνθρώπων κρείττους ὄντες, οὗτος μετ' οὐ πολὺν χρόνον εἰς τὸ δεσμωτήριον ὑπ' αὐτῶν ἐνέπεσε, καὶ προσέτι ὁ υἱὸς αὐτοῦ Κίμων ἄτιμος ἦν ἂν τὸν ἅπαντα χρόνον, εἰ μὴ τὴν ἀδελφὴν Ἐλπινίκην ἐξέδωκεν ἀνδρὶ ταπεινῷ[1] χρήματα δ'[2] ἔχοντι, ὃς ὑπὲρ αὐτοῦ τὴν ζημίαν κατέβαλε τὰ πεντήκοντα τάλαντα. καίτοι Κίμων ὕστερον Ἀθηναίοις Κύπρον ἐκτήσατο καὶ πεζῇ ἅμα καὶ ναυσὶν ἐνίκησε τοὺς βαρβάρους περὶ Παμφυλίαν· ἀλλ' ὅμως τὸν τοιοῦτον αὐτὸν ὄντα καὶ τοιούτου πατρός, εἰ μὴ χρημάτων εὐπόρησεν, ἄτιμον ἂν[3] εἴων ἐν τῇ πόλει.

7 Φωκίωνα δὲ ὕστερον τὸν ὑπὲρ ὀγδοήκοντα ἔτη βιώσαντα, τούτων δὲ τὰ πλείω στρατηγήσαντα καὶ τὴν πόλιν διαφυλάξαντα ἐν τοῖς χαλεπωτάτοις καιροῖς καὶ χρηστὸν ὑπ' αὐτῶν ἐκείνων ὀνομασθέντα, τοῦτον οὐκ ἤρκεσεν αὐτοῖς ἀποκτεῖναι μόνον, ἀλλ' οὐδὲ νεκρὸν εἴασαν ἐν τῇ Ἀττικῇ,

---

[1] καί after ταπεινῷ deleted by Emperius.
[2] δ' added by Capps.
[3] ἄν added by Dindorf.

---

[1] Aristophanes (*Knights* 813-819) pays high tribute to Themistocles.

[2] At Marathon. One thousand Plataeans are said to have aided Athens.

[3] He incurred the displeasure of Athens for his failure to take Paros. Herodotus (6. 136) speaks only of his being fined, but Diodorus and others add that he was imprisoned.

[4] Callias, a familiar figure in Greek literature, famed alike for his great wealth and for his profligacy.

ship from the Spartans, who had held this honour from the beginning.[1]

Again, Miltiades, who had been the first to vanquish the barbarians, with only his fellow citizens to aid him, and to humble the pride of the Persians,[2] a pride which they formerly held, believing themselves to be superior to all other men—this man, I say, not much later was cast into prison by the Athenians[3]; and, besides, his son Cimon would have been deprived of civic rights for the rest of his life if he had not given his sister Elpinicê in marriage to a man of humble origin but great wealth, who in his behalf paid the fine of fifty talents.[4] And yet later on Cimon gained Cyprus for the Athenians, and in a joint attack by land and sea vanquished the barbarians in the neighbourhood of Pamphylia. Still, though so remarkable himself and the son of so remarkable a father, if he had not secured considerable money the Athenians would have suffered him to be without civic rights in his city.[5]

And take the case of Phocion of a later period, who lived to be more than eighty years of age, and who for most of those years had served as general, had preserved the state in its moments of direst need, and had been dubbed excellent[6] by those very Athenians—this man they were not content merely to put to death, nay, they would not even permit his corpse to rest in Attic soil, but cast it forth beyond

[5] Since Miltiades had died a debtor to the state, the son was deprived of civic rights until his father's debt was paid.

[6] The word χρηστός is frequent in honorific inscriptions. In the case of Phocion it would seem to have been his sobriquet; cf. Plutarch, *Phocion* 10. 2. Phocion was born c. 402 B.C. and was executed in 318 on a charge of treason. He had been made general forty-five times.

ἀλλ' ὑπὲρ τοὺς ὅρους ἐξέβαλον. Νικίας δὲ ὁ
Νικηράτου διὰ τὸ πιστεύεσθαι ὑπὸ τῶν πολιτῶν,[1]
ἐπιστάμενος τὴν ἐν Σικελίᾳ στρατείαν οἷα ἔσοιτο
καὶ ἀπὸ τοῦ θεοῦ καὶ τῷ λογίζεσθαι, ὅμως ἠναγ-
κάσθη στρατεύσασθαι νοσῶν διὰ τὴν πίστιν ταύτην.
καὶ εἰ μὲν ἀποβαλὼν τὴν στρατιὰν ἢ μέρος αὐτῆς
αὐτὸς γοῦν ἐσώθη, δῆλον ὅτι οἴκοι ἀφικόμενος
ἀπολώλει ἄν. ἐπεὶ δὲ τοῦτο εἰδὼς προσελιπάρει
πάντα τρόπον, ληφθεὶς ὑπὸ τῶν πολεμίων τοῦτο
ἔπαθεν.

8 Καὶ ταῦτα ἐμοὶ περὶ μιᾶς πόλεως εἴρηται καὶ
τῶν ἐν μιᾷ πόλει πολιτευομένων, οὐδὲ τούτων
ἁπάντων. τοὺς δὲ παρὰ τοῖς τυράννοις δοκοῦντας
πιστοὺς εἰ ἐπεξίοιμι οἵων δὴ τετυχήκασι, πολλῶν
ἂν ἴσως μοι δεήσαι πάνυ ἡμερῶν. σχεδὸν γὰρ
τὸ γεγηθέναι[2] ἐκείνους ἀδύνατόν ἐστιν. οἳ μὲν
γὰρ ἂν παράσχωσι καθ' αὑτῶν αἰτίαν, ὡς ἀδική-
σαντες, διὰ τοῦτο ἀπόλλυνται καὶ οὐκ ἔστιν οὐδεμιᾶς συγγνώμης τυχεῖν· οἳ δ' ἂν ἄνδρες ἀγαθοὶ
φανῶσι καὶ διαφυλάττειν δυνάμενοι τὰ πιστευθέντα,
παραχρῆμα μὲν τιμῆς τινος ἔτυχον, μετ' οὐ πολὺ
δὲ ἀπόλλυνται φθονούμενοι καὶ ὑποπτευόμενοι.

9 οὐ γὰρ δοκεῖ λυσιτελεῖν τοῖς μονάρχοις οὐδέν'
ἄνδρα ἀγαθὸν εἶναι παρ' αὐτοῖς οὐδ' εὐδοκιμοῦντα
φαίνεσθαι παρὰ τῷ πλήθει. αἱ δὲ παρὰ τῶν
ἰδιωτῶν πίστεις κινδύνους μὲν ἥττους ἴσως ἔχουσιν,

---

[1] διὰ τὸ . . . πολιτῶν] deleted by Emperius.
[2] γεγηθέναι] γε σωθῆναι Wilamowitz.

---

[1] The tragic story is vividly told by Thucydides. The
whole of book VII is a tribute to the loyalty and dogged
determination of Nicias in the face of disease and crushing
misfortune.

their borders. Or take Nicias son of Niceratus—
because he was trusted by his fellow citizens, though
he knew full well what the campaign in Sicily would
be like, both from the warnings of the god and from
his own reasoning, still he was compelled to make
the expedition, ill as he was, because of this trust of
theirs. Moreover, if after losing his army or a portion
of it he himself had come back in safety, clearly on
reaching home he would have been put to death.
But since, knowing this, he persevered in every way,
he was taken captive and suffered that fate at the
hands of the enemy.[1]

Now these observations of mine have been made
about a single city and about the statesmen in a
single city, nor have all of these been named. But
as to those who at the courts of the tyrants enjoyed
a reputation for trustworthiness, were I to recount
fully what sort of fate has been theirs I should perhaps
need very many days. For one might almost say
that it is impossible for such men to go scot free.
For any who lay themselves open to a charge of
misconduct are put to death on that account, and
there is no chance of obtaining any pardon ; while
those who show themselves to be good men and
competent to safeguard what has been entrusted to
them, though at the moment they obtain a certain
honour, not much later they meet with disaster,
being victims of envy and suspicion. It does not,
you see, seem to be advantageous to absolute
monarchs that any man in their service should be
good, or that any man should patently stand high
in the esteem of the masses. On the other hand,
trusts bestowed by men in private life, though
possibly they involve less risk, because the business

ὅτι καὶ τὰ πράγματα ἐλάττω ἐστίν, ἀσχολίαν δὲ
μυρίαν καὶ πόνους, καὶ πολλάκις οὐδὲ χάρις οὐδ'
ἡτισοῦν συνέπεται. πολλάκις δὲ συμβαίνει παρ'
αὐτῶν τῶν εὖ παθόντων αἰτίαν ἔχειν, ὡς οὐ δικαίως
οὐδὲ καθαρῶς ἅπαντα ἀποδόντας.[1]

10 Τί δὴ βουλόμενος ταῦτα ἐγὼ διῆλθον; οὐ γὰρ
δὴ νουθετῶν σε τοιαύτην νουθεσίαν οὐδὲ ἀποτρέπων
τοῦ πιστὸν εἶναι. πολὺ γὰρ ἂν εἴην τοῦ Ζήθου
φαυλότερος τοιαῦτα ἐπιτιμῶν, ὡς ἐκεῖνος ἐνου-
θέτει τὸν ἀδελφὸν οὐκ ἀξιῶν φιλοσοφεῖν αὐτὸν
οὐδὲ περὶ μουσικὴν διατρίβειν, ἐάσαντα τὴν τῶν
ἰδίων ἐπιμέλειαν· ἔφη δὲ αὐτὸν ἄτοπόν τινα καὶ
ἀσύμφορον μοῦσαν εἰσάγειν. ὥσπερ ἂν τυχὸν
εἴποι τις καὶ σὲ τοιαύτην προῃρῆσθαι πρᾶξιν, οὐκ
ἀργὸν οὐδὲ φίλοινον οὐδαμῶς, χρημάτων μέντοι
τῶν αὑτοῦ ἀτημελῆ ἴσως· καὶ νὴ Δία λέγοι ἂν
καὶ τόδε τὸ ἔπος·

ἐξ ὧν κενοῖσιν ἐγκατοικήσεις δόμοις.

---

[1] ἀποδόντας Emperius : ἀποδόντων.

---

[1] Zethus and Amphion, sons of Antiopê and Zeus, were
exposed in infancy and reared by shepherds. Zethus busied
himself with hunting and sheep-tending, while Amphion
became a very famous musician, by the magic of whose
strains the very stones which were to form the walls of
Thebes moved into place. The controversy between the two
brothers occupies several fragments of the *Antiopê* of

in hand is less important, still entail untold trouble and labours, and often not even gratitude, however slight, is their reward. On the contrary, it often happens that the very men who have received benefits at their hands charge them with not having paid all that is due with justice and clean hands.

Now with what purpose have I rehearsed these matters? Surely not because I was making you the object of such admonition, or because I aimed to dissuade you from being true to a trust. For I should be far worse than Zethus was if I subjected you to such criticism, for he admonished his brother because he did not deem it fitting for him to devote himself to the pursuit of wisdom or to waste time on music to the neglect of his own affairs; and he said that his brother was introducing an absurd and unprofitable Muse. Just as if perchance some one were to say that you too had chosen that sort of occupation, not one of idleness or of drunkenness by any means, and yet one involving neglect of your own estate quite possibly; and, by Zeus, he might even recite this line:

Wherefore an empty house shall be thy home.[1]

Euripides. Dio here paraphrases one fragment and quotes from another; cf. Nauck, *T.G.F.*, Euripides, fragg. 184, 188; fragments of Pacuvius' *Antiopa* (based on Euripides) in *Remains of Old Latin*, L.C.L., vol. II, pp. 158-171.

THE SEVENTY-FOURTH DIS-
COURSE : ON DISTRUST

This Discourse, as its title suggests, approaches the question of human relationships from a different angle from that observed in Or. 73. There the speaker was stressing the annoyances and misfortunes resulting from being trusted ; here he produces a wealth of examples to show that it is dangerous to trust any one. That note of cynicism is maintained with remarkable consistency to the very end, and there is a ring of conviction about it all which suggests strongly that Dio is speaking out of the bitterness of his own heart. Arnim places the Discourse among those delivered during the period of Dio's exile. Because the element of dialogue is found only at the very opening of the document, he infers that Dio was addressing a group of listeners, one of whom bore to the speaker a closer relationship and therefore was helpful in launching the discussion. The abruptness with which the Discourse opens and closes is held to indicate, as in some other instances, that our text has been separated from its original setting, or possibly that the reporter chose only this much for preservation.

74. ΠΕΡΙ ΑΠΙΣΤΙΑΣ

1 Δ. Ἐπίστασαί τινας ἤδη βλαβέντας ὑπὸ ἐχθρῶν;
Πῶς γὰρ οὔ;

Δ. Τί δέ; ὑπὸ τῶν καλουμένων φίλων καὶ
συνήθων ἢ καὶ ὑπὸ συγγενῶν τινων, ἐνίους δὲ καὶ
ὑπὸ τῶν ἔγγιστα, ἀδελφῶν ἢ υἱῶν ἢ πατέρων;
Ἔγωγε πολλούς.

Δ. Τίς οὖν ἡ αἰτία, δι' ἣν οὐ μόνον οἱ ἐχθροὶ
τοὺς ἐχθροὺς ἀδικοῦσιν, ἀλλὰ καὶ οἱ λεγόμενοι
φίλοι ἀλλήλους καὶ νὴ Δία πολλοὶ καὶ τῶν οὕτως
ἀναγκαίων;

Δῆλον ὡς ἡ κακία τῶν ἀνθρώπων, ὑφ' ἧς
ἕκαστος, οἶμαι, καὶ αὐτός ἐστιν αὑτῷ βλαβερός.

Δ. Πάντας ἄρα δεῖ[1] ἐπ' ἴσης φυλάττεσθαι καὶ
μὴ πιστεύειν μηδὲν μᾶλλον, κἂν[2] φίλος ἢ συνήθης
ἢ πρὸς αἵματος εἶναι δοκῇ;
Πάντας, ὡς ὁ λόγος οὗτός φησιν.

Δ. Οὐκοῦν ὀρθῶς ἔγραψεν ὁ τοῦτο γράψας τὸ
ἔπος·

νᾶφε καὶ μέμνασ'[3] ἀπιστεῖν· ἄρθρα ταῦτα τᾶν
φρενῶν;

2 Ἴσως ὀρθῶς.

---

¹ After δεῖ Pflugk deletes τοὺς φίλους.
² κἂν Casaubon : ἢ ἂν.   ³ μέμνασ' Emperius : μέμνησο.

---

¹ Kaibel, *C.G.F.*, Epicharmus, frag. 250.

208

THE SEVENTY-FOURTH DISCOURSE : ON DISTRUST

Dio. Are you aware that in the past there have been persons who have been harmed by enemies ?

Interlocutor. Why, of course.

Dio. Well then, have they been harmed by so-called friends and close acquaintances, or even by certain kinsmen, some even by the very closest, brothers or sons or fathers ?

Int. Yes indeed, many have been.

Dio. What is the reason, then, that not only do enemies injure their enemies but also the so-called friends injure one another, and, by Heaven, that many even of those who are so closely related act so ?

Int. Clearly the reason is found in the depravity of mankind, because of which each, I imagine, is also himself harmful to himself.

Dio. Toward all men, then, one should be equally on his guard, and not be one whit more trustful even if a person is held to be a friend or a close acquaintance or a blood-relative ?

Int. Toward all, as this statement of yours declares.

Dio. Then was the author of this verse right when he wrote,

Keep sober and remember to distrust ;
These are the joints essential to the mind ? [1]

Int. Probably he was.

DIO CHRYSOSTOM

Δ. Καὶ μὴν δῆλος¹ ὁ ποιητὴς οὐ πρὸς τοὺς ἐχθροὺς ταῦτα ὑποτιθέμενος, ἀλλὰ πρὸς τοὺς νομιζομένους φίλους. οὐ γὰρ δὴ² ὑφ᾽ ὧν τις μισούμενος ἐπίσταται, τούτοις ἂν ἐξουσίαν δοίη καθ᾽ αὑτοῦ. πῶς ἂν οὖν διακελεύοιτο ἀπιστεῖν, οἷς μηδὲ³ πιστεύει;

Φέρε τοίνυν κἀκεῖνο ἴδωμεν. ὑπὸ τίνων πλείους ἀπολώλασι, πότερον ὑπὸ τῶν ὁμολογουμένων ἐχθρῶν ἢ τοὐναντίον ὑπὸ τῶν προσποιουμένων εἶναι φίλων; ἐγὼ μὲν γὰρ ὁρῶ καὶ τῶν πόλεων τῶν ἁλουσῶν πλείονας ὑπὸ τῶν προδοτῶν ἀπολομένας ἢ ὑπὸ τῶν πολεμίων εἰλημμένας κατὰ κράτος, καὶ τῶν ἀνθρώπων πλείους τῷ παντὶ τοῖς φίλοις καὶ τοῖς συνήθεσιν ἐγκαλοῦντας τῶν αἰτιωμένων τοὺς ἐχθροὺς ἐπὶ ταῖς συμφοραῖς· ἔτι δὲ πρὸς μὲν τοὺς πολεμίους ἅπασι τείχη καὶ φρούρια κατεσκευασμένα, καὶ τούτων ἐνίοτε πολλῶν ἐτῶν μηδεμίαν χρείαν γενομένην· πρὸς δὲ τοὺς συμπολιτευομένους καὶ τῶν αὐτῶν κοινωνοῦντας ἱερῶν καὶ θυσιῶν καὶ γάμων καὶ φυλέτας ὄντας ἀλλήλων καὶ δημότας καὶ συγγενεῖς τὰ δικαστήρια καὶ τοὺς νόμους καὶ τὰ ἀρχεῖα. καὶ ταῦτα οὐδέποτε ἠρεμεῖ. μεσταὶ γοῦν αἱ πόλεις αἰεὶ κατηγορούντων, ἀπολογουμένων, δικαζόντων, δικαζομένων, καὶ οὐδὲ⁴ ἐν ταῖς ἱερομηνίαις ἢ ταῖς σπονδαῖς ἀλλήλων ἀπέχεσθαι δύνανται. τίθενται γοῦν⁵ ἑτέρους νόμους ὑπὲρ τῶν ἀδικημάτων τῶν ἐν ταῖς ἑορταῖς καὶ τούτους ἱεροὺς καλοῦσιν, ὥσπερ τὸ ὄνομα ὠφελοῦν.

---

¹ δῆλος Pflugk : οὗτος.
² οὐ γὰρ δὴ² Wilamowitz, οὐδὲ γὰρ Emperius, οὐ γὰρ Reiske : οὐ δὴ or οὐδὲ.   ³ μηδὲ] μηδεὶς Arnim.
⁴ οὐδὲ Emperius : οὔτε.   ⁵ γοῦν Arnim : οὖν.

Dio. Furthermore, manifestly the poet is giving this advice, not to his enemies, but rather to those whom he considers friends. For surely those by whom one knows himself to be hated one would not entrust with power against himself. How, then, could the poet be urging those to be distrustful whom he does not himself trust ?

Well then, let us consider the following question also. By whom have more persons been ruined— by those who are admittedly enemies, or, on the contrary, by those who profess to be friends ? As for myself, I observe that of the cities which have been captured those which have been destroyed by traitors are more numerous than those which have been forcibly seized by the foe, and also that with human beings those who lodge complaints against their friends and close acquaintances are altogether more numerous than those who blame their enemies for their misfortunes ; and, furthermore, that whereas against the foe walls and fortresses have been provided for all—though sometimes no use has been made of these for many years—yet against their fellow citizens, against men who have a common share in the same sanctuaries and sacrifices and marriage rites, men who are fellow tribesmen with one another, fellow demesmen and kinsmen, the courts, the laws, and the magistracies have been provided. Furthermore, these institutions are never idle. At any rate the cities are always crowded with plaintiffs and defendants, with juries and litigants, and not even during their solemn festivals or in times of truce can men keep their hands off one another. At least they pass special laws regarding crimes committed during festivals, and they call these " holy laws," as if the

ὁ γὰρ τῆς κακίας πόλεμος[1] διηνεκὴς ἅπασι πρὸς
4 ἅπαντας, ἄσπονδος ὢν καὶ ἀκήρυκτος· μάλιστα
δὲ οὗτος συνέστηκε τοῖς ἐγγὺς πρὸς ἀλλήλους.

Τὸν μὲν οὖν ἐν εἰρήνῃ βουλόμενον βιοῦν καὶ
μετ' ἀσφαλείας τινὸς εὐλαβεῖσθαι δεῖ τὴν πρὸς
ἀνθρώπους κοινωνίαν καὶ τὴν φύσιν ἐπίστασθαι
τῶν πολλῶν ἑτοίμην οὖσαν πρὸς τὸ μεταδοῦναι
κακίας τινός, καὶ μηδὲ ἂν μυριάκις λέγῃ φίλος
εἶναι πιστεύειν. οὐ γάρ ἐστι παρ' αὐτοῖς βέβαιον
οὐθὲν οὐδὲ[2] ἀληθές· ἀλλ' ὃν ἂν ἁπάντων προτιμῶσιν
ἤδη καὶ τοῦ ζῆν ἐὰν οὕτω τύχῃ, μετὰ μικρὸν
ἔχθιστον νομίζουσι καὶ οὐδὲ τοῦ σώματος ἀπέχονται
5 πολλάκις. ὁ γοῦν ἐραστὴς τὸν ἐρώμενον ἀπο-
σφάττει διὰ τὸ λίαν φιλεῖν, ὡς οἴεται, παροξυνθεὶς
ἐκ τῆς τυχούσης αἰτίας. ἕτεροι δ' ἑαυτοὺς ἀπο-
κτιννύασιν, οἱ μὲν ἄκοντες δι' ἀκρασίαν, οἱ δὲ
ἑκόντες, μηδενὸς ὄντος αὐτοῖς ἀτοπωτέρου[3] κατὰ
τὸν βίον ἢ τῆς ἐν αὐτοῖς μοχθηρίας. τὰς μὲν
γὰρ ἄλλας βλάβας τὰς εἰς ἑαυτὸν ἑκάστου δῆλον
ὡς οὐκ ἐπεξελθεῖν ἔστιν.

Ποία δὴ πίστις πρὸς τοὺς τοιούτους ἢ τίς ἀσφά-
λεια; ἢ πῶς ἂν ἐμὲ ἀγαπήσειεν ὁ μηδ' αὐτὸν
ἀγαπῶν; τὸ γὰρ πρὸς τοὺς Ἀθηναίους ῥηθέν, ὅτε
ἐν ἐσχάτοις ὄντες ἠξίουν τι περὶ Σάμου, καλῶς
ἄν, οἶμαι, λεχθείη πρὸς τοὺς φιλίαν ὑπερχομένους

---

[1] πόλεμος Reiske : ἔπαινος.   [2] οὐδὲ Emperius : οὔτε.

name did any good! Yes, the war against depravity
is unremitting for all against all, a war without truce
and without herald; but above all this war is joined
between those who are close to one another.

Accordingly those who wish to live at peace and
with some degree of security must beware of fellowship with human beings, must recognize that the
average man is by nature prone to let others have
a share in any evil, and that, no matter if one claims
a thousand times to be a friend, he is not to be trusted.
For with human beings there is no constancy or
truthfulness at all; on the contrary, any man whom
at the moment they prize above everything, even,
it may be, above life itself, after a brief interval they
deem their bitterest foe, and often they cannot refrain even from attacking his body. For example,
the lover slays his beloved because he loves him too
much, as he imagines, but really because he has
become enraged over some trivial matter. Others
slay themselves, some involuntarily because of
incontinence, and some voluntarily, since there is
nothing in their life more extraordinary than their
innate depravity. But enough of this, for the other
injuries which each inflicts upon himself it obviously
is impossible to examine in detail.

Then what kind of trust can one have in dealing
with men like these, or what assurance? Or how
could a person love me who does not love even
himself? For the reply which was made to the
Athenians on the occasion when, being in dire straits,
they made some request concerning Samos, might
well, I think, be made to those low persons who try
to worm their way into one's friendship: "If one

---

³ ἀτοπωτέρου Crosby : ἀτόπου.

τῶν φαύλων· ὃς αὐτὸς αὑτὸν οὐ φιλεῖ, πῶς ἄλλον φιλεῖ, ἢ ξένον ἢ τέκνον ἢ ἀδελφόν;

6 Τί οὖν, ὅταν τις φιλοφρονῆται καὶ καθ᾽ ἱερῶν ὀμνύῃ καὶ μόνον οὐ κατατέμνειν αὑτὸν ᾖ πρόθυμος; ἀκούειν μὲν ἤδη τούτων ἐξ ἀνάγκης καὶ νὴ Δία ἴσως κατανεύειν· εἰδέναι μέντοι σαφῶς ὅτι μηδὲν αὐτῶν ἐστιν ἰσχυρόν. Ἠλέκτρα τὸν Ὀρέστην δακρύοντα ὁρῶσα καὶ προσαγόμενον αὐτήν, τότε[1] μὲν ᾤετο ἄνεσίν τινα αὐτῷ γεγονέναι, τοῦ μέντοι παντάπασι πιστεύειν πολὺ ἀπεῖχεν. ὁρῶσα γοῦν μετ᾽ ὀλίγον παρακινοῦντά φησιν,

οἴμοι, κασίγνητ᾽, ὄμμα σὸν ταράσσεται,
ταχὺς δὲ μετέθου.

7 Τὴν θάλασσαν οὕτως ἠρεμοῦσαν πολλάκις ἰδεῖν ἔστιν, ὥστ᾽, οἶμαι, καὶ τὸν δειλότατον καταφρονῆσαι. τί οὖν; διὰ τοῦτο πιστεύειν δεῖ καὶ μήτε ἀγκύρας ἔχοντα μήτε πηδάλιον μήτε τἆλλα τὰ πρὸς τὴν σωτηρίαν ἀνάγεσθαί ποτε; ὄψει γάρ, ἂν οὕτω τύχῃ, μετ᾽ ὀλίγον κατερείσαντος ἀνέμου κλύδωνα ἰσχυρὸν καὶ

κύματά τε[2] τροφόεντα, πελώρια ἶσα ὄρεσσι,
κυρτὰ φαληριόωντα·

καὶ τὸν νῦν σοι φαινόμενον πρᾶον καὶ πολλὴν ἐνδεικνύμενον εὔνοιαν καὶ σπουδὴν τῆς τυχούσης αἰτίας καταλαβούσης ἄγριον εὑρήσεις καὶ χαλεπὸν καὶ πᾶν ὁτιοῦν κακὸν ἕτοιμον ἐργάσασθαι.

8 Πόσα δοκεῖς τὴν Μήδειαν εὔξασθαι τοῖς θεοῖς

---

[1] τότε Reiske : ποτέ.   [2] τε with P.

---

[1] Euripides, *Orestes* 253-254.
[2] This is a cento, consisting of *Odyssey* 3. 290 and *Iliad* 13. 799. Though familiar with the sea and largely dependent

does not love himself, how can he love another, whether stranger or son or brother?"

What, then, must one do when some one makes a show of friendship, takes a solemn oath at the altar, and is almost eager to butcher himself there? He must listen, of course, immediately, and, by Zeus, possibly nod assent; yet at the same time be quite certain that not one of his protestations is valid. For example, when Electra beheld Orestes weeping and striving to draw her to him, at the moment she supposed that he had experienced some abatement of his madness, and yet she was far from trusting him entirely. At any rate shortly afterward, seeing him sore distraught, she exclaimed,

Ah me, dear brother, how confused thy glance,
How swiftly thou hast changed! [1]

Again, one may often behold the sea so calm that, methinks, even the most timid would scorn it. What then? On that account should one have faith in it, and with neither anchors nor rudder nor all the other aids to safety ever put to sea? Nay, if Fortune so decrees, presently a gale will swoop down upon you and you will behold a mighty surge and

Enormous billows, huge as mountains are,
Curling and topped with foam [2];

and the man who but now seems to you gentle and who makes much display of kindliness and zeal, when some chance occasion overtakes him you will find is savage and harsh and ready to work any and every mischief.

How many prayers do you suppose Medeia offered

on it for a living, the Greeks felt toward it a wholesome respect, and their writings show little, if any, trace of joy in sailing or in the sea.

ὑπὲρ τῶν τέκνων ἢ ποσάκις ἀγωνιᾶσαι νοσούντων
ἢ ποσάκις ἀντ' ἐκείνων αὐτὴν ἂν ἑλέσθαι τελευτᾶν;
ἀλλ' ὅμως αὐτόχειρ αὐτῶν ἐγένετο. νὴ Δία, ἐρεῖ
τις, ὀργιζομένη καὶ ζηλοτυποῦσα. τοὺς πολλοὺς
δὲ οὐκ ἂν οἴει καὶ¹ ζηλοτυπῆσαι; τί δέ; φθο-
νῆσαι; τί δέ; ἐλπίσαι; σχεδὸν γὰρ αἰεὶ καὶ
συνεχῶς ἐν τούτοις εἰσίν. μὴ τοίνυν πίστευε τοῖς
εὐνοεῖν φάσκουσι καὶ μηδέποτε ἂν² ἐγκαταλιπεῖν
τὴν πρὸς σὲ φιλίαν. ὥσπερ γὰρ αἱ τὸν ἄνεμον
σημαίνουσαι ταινίαι κατὰ τὴν στάσιν αἰεὶ τοῦ
πνεύματος αἰωροῦνται, νυνὶ μὲν οὕτως, πάλιν
δὲ ἐπὶ θάτερα, τὸν αὐτὸν τρόπον ἡ τῶν φαύλων
διάνοια πρὸς πᾶσαν φορὰν οὕτως³ ἔχει.

9 Τοῖς δούλοις οὐδεὶς πιστεύει συντιθεμένοις διὰ
τὸ μὴ κυρίους ἑαυτῶν εἶναι· πολὺ μᾶλλον οὐ χρὴ
προσέχειν ταῖς τῶν τοιούτων ὁμολογίαις. τῷ
παντὶ γὰρ πλεῖον ἀπέχουσι τῆς ἐλευθερίας διὰ
τὴν κακίαν οἱ ἄνθρωποι. τοῖς νεωτέροις τοσούτων
ἐτῶν νόμος οὐκ ἐᾷ συμβάλλειν ὡς ἀπίστοις οὖσιν,
οὐδὲ γυναικὶ παρ' Ἀθηναίοις συναλλάσσειν πλὴν
ἄχρι μεδίμνου κριθῶν, διὰ τὸ τῆς γνώμης ἀσθενές.
τῶν μὲν γὰρ πάνυ νέων⁴ οὐθὲν διαφέρουσιν οἱ
φαῦλοι, μᾶλλον δὲ οὐδὲ τῶν παιδαρίων, πλὴν τῷ

---

¹ καὶ deleted by Dindorf, Emperius reads ὀργίσασθαι καὶ.
² ἂν added by Madvig.
³ After οὕτως Sonny adds ἢ οὕτως.
⁴ νέων Arnim : νεωτέρων or μετεώρων.

---

¹ In Euripides' *Medeia* the heroine has two children, sons
of Jason, whom she had helped to gain the Golden Fleece.

to the gods in behalf of her children, or how many times did she suffer agony when they were ill, or how often would she have chosen to give her own life in their stead ? Yet she became their murderer.[1] " Aye, by Zeus," some one will say, " in a fit of anger and jealousy." But do you not suppose that most of mankind could also become jealous, envious, apprehensive ? Why, one might almost say that they are always and unceasingly in the grip of these emotions. Do not, therefore, trust those who say that they feel kindly toward you and that they never would abandon their affection for you. For just as the streamers which mark the breeze always flutter according to the quarter from which it blows, now in this direction and now in the opposite direction, in the same way the mood of the common herd shifts in response to each and every emotion.

Nobody trusts slaves when they make an agreement, for the reason that they are not their own masters ; far more should one pay no heed to the agreements of such persons as I am describing. For in every respect human beings, because of their depravity, are farther removed from a state of freedom. The law does not permit one to make a contract with persons younger than a specified age on the ground that they are untrustworthy, nor, at Athens, may one have business dealings with a woman except to the extent of a measure of barley because of the weakness of female judgement. In fact, ordinary persons are no better than the very young, or rather than even the little boys, except in their bodily

For reasons of state he abandoned Medeia and married a Corinthian princess, whereupon Medeia slew her children and the princess, and sought refuge in Athens.

δύνασθαι καὶ τῇ πανουργίᾳ· διὸ μᾶλλον αὐτοῖς
ἀπιστεῖν ἐκείνων προσήκει.

10 Μακάριον γὰρ ἂν ἦν, εἰ καθάπερ παῖδα καὶ
μειράκιον καὶ νεανίσκον καὶ πρεσβύτην χρόνος
ποιεῖ, καὶ φρόνιμον οὕτως καὶ δίκαιον καὶ πιστόν.
καὶ μὴν τῶν γυναικῶν τῶν φαύλων οὐδέν εἰσι
βελτίους οἱ ἄνδρες οἱ μοχθηροί. κατὰ γὰρ τὸ
σῶμα διαφέρουσιν, οὐ κατὰ τὴν διάνοιαν. καθάπερ οὖν πρὸς οὐδὲν ἐκείνας ἐᾷ προσίεσθαι τῶν
πλείονος ἀξίων ὁ νόμος, ἀλλ' ὥρισται μέχρι τίνος
προσήκει· τὸν αὐτόν, οἶμαι, τρόπον καὶ τοῖς
πολλοῖς μέχρι τῶν ἐλαχίστων κοινωνητέον· πρά-
ξεων δὲ μειζόνων ἢ λόγων ἀναγκαίων ἢ τῆς
11 ἀσφαλείας τῆς περὶ τὸν βίον οὐδέποτε. καὶ γὰρ
εἴ ποτε ἀπέχονται τοῦ κακῶς ποιεῖν δι' ἢν δήποτ'
αἰτίαν, ὥσπερ τὰ θηρία πολλάκις ἠρεμεῖ κοιμώμενα
ἢ ἐμπεπλησμένα, τὴν μέντοι φύσιν οὐκ ἀπο-
βέβληκε τὴν αὐτῶν, παραπλησίως δὴ κάκεῖνοι
χρόνον τινὰ οὐκ ἔβλαψαν, ἔπειτα συμβάσης προ-
φάσεως καὶ τὸν[1] τόκον, φασί, καὶ τὸ κεφάλαιον τῆς
πονηρίας ἐκτίνουσιν.

Ὁ Λάκων, ἐν ὁμιλίαις τινῶν συντιθεμένων αὐτῷ
καὶ ἀξιούντων παρ' αὐτῶν λαμβάνειν ἢν ἂν προ-
αιρῆται πίστιν ὑπὲρ τῆς φιλίας, μίαν ἔφη πίστιν
εἶναι τὸ ἐὰν θέλωσιν ἀδικῆσαι μὴ δύνασθαι, τὰς
δὲ λοιπὰς πάσας εὐήθεις καὶ τελέως ἀσθενεῖς.
12 ταύτην μόνην παρὰ τῶν πολλῶν τὴν πίστιν δεῖ
λαμβάνειν, ἑτέραν δὲ οὐδεμίαν. ἢ γὰρ ἐκ τῶν

---

[1] τὸν added by Reiske.

strength and their rascality; consequently they deserve to be distrusted more than those others.

It would indeed be a blessing if, just as one becomes successively a lad, a stripling, a youth, and an old man by the passing of time, one might also in the same way become wise and just and trustworthy. Yet it must be said that not one whit better than women of the meaner sort are the men who are depraved. They differ in body, not in mind. Accordingly, just as the women are not allowed by law to accept agreements involving too large a sum, but a limit has been set defining the amount to which they may do so, in the same way, I believe, we should also have dealings with the ordinary run of men so far as the things of least importance, but in actions of greater importance or in discussions about urgent matters or in the safeguarding of one's existence, never! For the fact is, if they ever refrain from doing mischief for whatever reason, just as the wild beasts often are quiet when asleep or sated with food, though they have not discarded their own peculiar nature, similarly the masses too for a time do no harm, yet later when some pretext is presented they pay in full, as the saying goes, both the interest and the principal of their villainy.

The Spartan, when in social gatherings certain persons offered to make a compact with him and invited him to take as a guarantee of their friendship whatever he might choose, replied that there was only one guarantee, namely, their inability to do harm even if they wished, but that all other guarantees were foolish and absolutely good for nothing. That guarantee alone should one accept from the masses, no other. For the guarantee which consists in

DIO CHRYSOSTOM

λόγων καὶ τῆς συνηθείας καὶ τῶν ὅρκων καὶ τοῦ γένους καταγέλαστος. ὁ Ἀτρεὺς ἀδελφὸς ἦν τοῦ Θυέστου καὶ τῶν παιδαρίων, ἃ κατέκοψεν, θεῖος· ὁ Ἐτεοκλῆς καὶ ὁ Πολυνείκης οὐ μόνον ἀδελφοὶ κατὰ τὸν νόμον, ἀλλὰ καὶ ἐξ υἱοῦ καὶ μητρὸς γεγονότες τῶν ξυγγενεστάτων· ὥστ', εἴπερ ὠφέλει τι τὸ γένος, οὗτοι μάλιστα ἁπάντων ἀλλήλους[1] ὤφειλον ἀγαπᾶν· ἀλλ' ὁ πιστευθεὶς πρῶτον τὸν
13 πιστεύσαντα ἐξέβαλε καὶ τῆς πατρίδος ἀπεστέρει καὶ μετὰ ταῦτα ἀλλήλους ἀπέκτειναν. ὁ Θησεὺς τὸν Ἱππόλυτον, πατὴρ ὢν καὶ Ποσειδῶνος υἱός, διαβολαῖς πεισθεὶς ἀπέκτεινε καταρασάμενος. ὁ Πρίαμος πρότερον εὐδαιμονίᾳ διαφέρων καὶ τοσούτων ἐθνῶν καὶ τηλικούτου τόπου βασιλεύων,

> ὅσσον Λέσβος ἄνω Μάκαρος ἕδος ἐντὸς ἐέργει
> καὶ Φρυγίη καθύπερθε καὶ Ἑλλήσποντος ἀπείρων

διὰ τὸν υἱὸν καὶ τὴν ἀκρασίαν τὴν ἐκείνου πάντων ἀθλιώτατος ἐγένετο. καὶ οὗτοι μὲν ἐπίσημοι. πόσον δέ, οἴει, πλῆθος ἐν ἑκάστῃ πόλει τῶν ἀφανῶν καὶ δημοτικῶν Ἀτρέων καὶ Θυεστῶν, τῶν μὲν καὶ ἀποκτιννύντων κρύφα, τῶν δὲ εἰς ἄλλα ἐπιβου-

---

[1] After ἀλλήλους Pflugk deletes μᾶλλον.

---

[1] This is but one chapter in the scandalous tale of the dealings of these two brothers, a tale that forms the background of many a Greek tragedy ; cf. Apollodorus, *Bibliotheca*, epitome 2. 10-14. In revenge for the seduction of his wife Atreus slew the children of Thyestes and served their flesh as food for their father to eat.

[2] Oedipus unwittingly married his mother Jocasta, and by her he became the father of Eteocles and Polyneices. When Oedipus discovered his sin and gave up his throne in Thebes, Eteocles expelled his brother, but Polyneices led an army against Thebes, and in the ensuing battle each slew the other.

phrases, in acquaintanceship, in oaths, in kinship is laughable. Atreus was the brother of Thyestes and the uncle of the little boys whom he slaughtered[1]; Eteocles and Polyneices were not only brothers according to the law, but also children of a son and his mother, the closest relationship possible ; wherefore, if there were any utility in birth, these most of all should have loved each other ; whereas, in the first place, he who had been trusted expelled the brother who had trusted him and robbed him of his country, and after that they slew each other.[2] Although Theseus was the father of Hippolytus and the son of Poseidon, persuaded by slanders he cursed his son and brought about his death.[3] Priam, who previously had been notable for good fortune and who was king over so many tribes and so wide a domain—

> Seaward as far as Lesbos, the abode
> Of Macar, landward to Phrygia and the stream
> Of boundless Hellespont [4]—

all because of his son [5] and that son's incontinence became the most wretched man of all. Now these were men of mark, but how great a multitude do you suppose can be found in every city of the obscure and plebeian Atreuses and Thyesteses, some actually committing murder undetected, and some making

---

[3] Phaedra, the step-mother of Hippolytus, thwarted in her passion for the youth, committed suicide, and Theseus, betrayed by the false charges she left behind, cursed his son and caused his death. The tale is told by Euripides in his *Hippolytus*.

[4] *Iliad* 24. 544-545, quoted with some variation in Or. 33. 19.

[5] Paris.

14 λευόντων; Ἀερόπας μέν γε καὶ Κλυταιμνήστρας
καὶ Σθενεβοίας οὐδὲ εἰπεῖν ἔστιν.[1]

Ἀλλὰ τὰ μὲν τοῦ γένους καὶ τῆς οἰκειότητος
τοιαῦτα, τὰ δὲ τῶν ὅρκων ποῖα;[2] ὁ Πάνδαρος
ὤμοσε τῷ Μενελάῳ, ὥσπερ καὶ οἱ λοιποὶ Τρῶες,
ἀλλ' οὐδὲν ἧττον ἔτρωσεν αὐτόν. Τισσαφέρνης
οὐκ ὤμοσε τοῖς περὶ Κλέαρχον; τί δέ; ὁ βασιλεὺς οὐχὶ καὶ τοὺς βασιλείους θεοὺς καὶ τὴν δεξιὰν
ἀπέστειλε; Φίλιππος δὲ ὁ Μακεδὼν οὐ διετέλει
καθάπερ ἄλλο τι τῶν εἰς τὸν πόλεμον εὐχρήστων
καὶ τὴν ἐπιορκίαν παρεσκευασμένος καὶ δυσὶ
τούτοις τὰς πόλεις αἱρῶν, τῷ τε παρασπονδεῖν
καὶ τῷ τοὺς προδώσοντας παρασκευάζειν; τῷ
παντὶ πρὸς ἐκεῖνον τὸν τρόπον οἰκειότερον εἶχε[3]·
τοῖς μὲν γὰρ προδόταις ἀργύριον ἦν ἀνάγκη
διδόναι, τοῖς θεοῖς δὲ περὶ ὅρκων[4] οὐθὲν ἐτέλει.

15 τὸν δὲ Λύσανδρον τὸν Λακεδαιμόνιον γνώμην ἀπο-
φαίνεσθαι λέγουσιν ὅτι τοὺς μὲν παῖδας ἀστρα-
γάλοις καὶ σφαίραις ἐξαπατᾶν δεῖ, τοὺς δὲ ἄνδρας
ὅρκοις καὶ ῥήμασιν.[5] ἡ κερδαλῆ δὲ ἀλώπηξ ἑτέρα
τίς ἐστι παρὰ Ἀρχιλόχῳ; τὸν δὲ τοῦ Γλαύκου

---

[1] οὐδὲ εἰπεῖν ἔστιν] ὅσας οὐδὲ εἰπεῖν Hertlein, οὐδὲ εἰπεῖν
ἔστιν ὅσαι Arnim.
[2] ποῖα added by Arnim.
[3] εἶχε Capps, ἔχων Casaubon : ἔχειν.
[4] περὶ ὅρκων] ἐπιορκῶν Gasda.
[5] ῥήμασιν Emperius : χρήμασιν.

---

[1] Notorious examples of marital infidelity. Aëropê, wife
of Atreus, had an affair with his brother; Clytaemnestra,
wife of Agamemnon, lived in adultery with his kinsman
Aegisthus, with whose aid she slew her husband on his

plots of other kinds ?   As for the Aëropês and Cly-
taemnestras and Stheneboeas, they are too numerous
to mention.[1]

Well, such are the facts about family and domestic
ties, but how about oaths ?   Pandarus gave an oath
to Menelaüs, as did the other Trojans too, but none
the less he wounded him.[2]   Did not Tissaphernes
give an oath to Clearchus and his men ?   What !
did not the Great King send them the royal gods
and his plighted word ?[3]   Again, take Philip of
Macedon ;   just as any other weapon which was
serviceable for his warfare, was he not always
equipped with perjury too ;   and was he not always
seizing the cities by means of these two devices,
either violation of treaties or suborning of traitors ?[4]
He found the former altogether more congenial ;
for while he had to give money to the traitors, to the
gods he paid nothing in connexion with oaths.   As
for Lysander the Spartan, they say that he gave as
his opinion that boys should be deceived with knucklebones and balls, but men with oaths and phrases.[5]
But is the crafty fox at all different, as portrayed
by Archilochus ?[6]   And as for the oracle received

return from Troy ; Stheneboea, having failed to seduce her
husband's guest, Bellerophon, falsely accused him and
plotted his death.

[2] Pandarus shared in the oath given in behalf of all the
Trojans (*Iliad* 3. 298-301) and was led by Athena to violate
it (*ibid.* 4. 86-140).

[3] Cf. Xenophon, *Anabasis* 2. 3. 26-28 ; 2. 4. 1 ; 2. 5. 27 ff.

[4] On his bribery, cf. Demosthenes, *de Falsa Leg.* 265-268.

[5] Cf. Plutarch, *Lysander* 8.

[6] The fragments of his poem are in Edmonds, *Elegy and
Iambus* II, p. 145 (L.C.L.) ; cf. Aesop 44 for a prose version.
The fox tricked the ape by playing upon his cupidity and
pride.

χρησμὸν οὐκ οἴει πρότερον δεδωκέναι[1] τοὺς
πλείστους τῶν ἀνθρώπων, ὀμνύειν

ἐπεὶ θάνατός γε καὶ εὔορκον μένει ἄνδρα.

καὶ τούτους μὲν τοὺς προειρημένους καὶ τοιούτους
ἑτέρους διὰ τὰς περιστάσεις συμβέβηκεν ἐνδόξους
γεγονέναι, τῶν δὲ ἀφανεστέρων Γλαύκων ἢ
Πανδάρων μεσταὶ μὲν ἀγοραὶ ἀνθρώπων, μεσταὶ
δὲ ἀγυιαί. διὸ μήτε τὸν Ἀπόλλωνα μήτε τὴν
Ἀθηνᾶν σύμβουλον τῆς ἐπιορκίας λαμβάνουσιν.

16 Ἀλλ' ἡ συνήθεια τοῖς ἀνθρώποις μέγα δίκαιον
τοῦ μηθὲν ἀδικεῖν καὶ σπονδαὶ καὶ τράπεζαι. τὸν
Εὔρυτον ἀπέκτεινεν ὁ παρ' αὐτῷ ξενίσας,[2]

σχέτλιος, οὐδὲ θεῶν ὄπιν ᾐδέσατ' οὐδὲ τράπεζαν,
τὴν ἥν οἱ παρέθηκεν· ἔπειτα δὲ πέφνε καὶ αὐτόν.

καίτοι θεὸς ἔδοξεν οὗτος[3] τὴν τῶν θεῶν ὄπιν οὐκ
αἰδεσάμενος οὐδὲ τὴν τράπεζαν καὶ

τέρπεται ἐν θαλίη, κατέχων καλλίσφυρον Ἥβην.

τὸν Ἀρχίλοχον οὐδὲν ὤνησαν οἱ ἅλες καὶ ἡ τρά-
πεζα πρὸς τὴν ὁμολογίαν τῶν γάμων, ὥς[4] φησιν

---

[1] πρότερον δεδωκέναι] πρότερον δεδαηκέναι Emperius, Ἡρόδοτον διαδεδωκέναι τοῖς πλείστοις or Ἡρόδοτον δεδιδαχέναι τοὺς
πλείστους Arnim.
[2] αὐτῷ ξενίσας Arnim : αὐτῷ ξενισθείς.
[3] After οὗτος Reiske adds ὁ.   [4] ὥς Dindorf : ὧν.

---

[1] For the complete response of the Pythia, see Herodotus
6. 86.
[2] Aratus, *Phaenomena* 2-3.
[3] Since Pandarus and Glaucus did not gain by consulting
Athena and Apollo, later perjurers avoided these gods.

by Glaucus, do you not imagine that most men had given that advice ere then, namely, to swear,

> Since death awaits as well the man who keeps
> His oath ? [1]

Furthermore, while it has so happened that the persons just named and others like them achieved notoriety because of the great events in which they took part, with the less illustrious Glaucuses or Pandaruses " the marts are thronged and thronged the ways." [2] This explains why they take neither Apollo nor Athena as counsellor in their perjury. [3]

But, you say, familiar acquaintance constitutes for mankind a great moral bar against any injury, as also do treaties and hospitality. Eurytus was slain by the man who had entertained him in his house,

> The daring one, who feared not Heaven's wrath,
> Nor reverenced the table he had spread,
> But later even slew his guest. [4]

And yet he came to be thought a god, though he had shown no reverence for the anger of the gods or for the table of hospitality, and he

> Delighteth in the feast and hath for wife
> Fair-ankled Hebê. [5]

As for Archilochus, his salt and table availed him naught for the fulfilment of his marriage contract,

---

[4] *Odyssey* 21. 28-29. Dio seems to be quoting from memory, for he has confused Eurytus with his son Iphitus, who went to the house of Heracles in quest of his stolen mares and there met death. Dio's error may be due to the fact that Homer is speaking of the bow used by Odysseus, commonly called " the bow of Eurytus."

[5] *Ibid.* 11. 603. Upon his death Heracles was raised to godhead.

17 αὐτός. ὁ Λυκάων[1] ἀνόητος[2] εἰς τὸν Ἀχιλλέα δεύτερον ἐμπεσών, δέον αὐτὸν ἢ μάχεσθαι προθύμως
ἢ φεύγειν τάχιον,

πὰρ γὰρ σοὶ πρώτῳ, φησί, πασάμην Δημήτερος
ἀκτήν.

τοιγαροῦν πρότερον, ὁπότε οὐδέπω μετειλήφει τῆς
παρ᾽ αὐτῷ τροφῆς, εἰς Λῆμνον ἀπεμποληθεὶς
ἐσώθη· τότε δὲ ληφθεὶς ἀπεσφάγη. τοσοῦτον
αὐτὸν ὤνησεν ἡ Δημήτηρ. τὰς νήττας καὶ τὰς
πέρδικας οὐ πρότερον θηρεύομεν, πρὶν ἂν φάγωσι
18 παρ᾽ ἡμῶν. ὁ δὲ Αἴγισθος τὸν Ἀγαμέμνονα

δειπνίσσας ὥς τίς τε κατέκτανε βοῦν ἐπὶ φάτνῃ.

καὶ ὑπὸ μὲν τῶν Τρώων οὐδὲν ἔπαθεν ἐν δέκα ἔτε-
σιν οἷς ἐπολέμει καὶ οὐδεπώποτε αὐτοῖς συνέστιος
ἐγένετο· εἰς δὲ τὴν οἰκίαν ἐλθὼν διὰ τοσούτου
χρόνου, θύσας τοῖς θεοῖς, καὶ τὴν αὐτοῦ τράπεζαν παραθέμενος, ὑπὸ τῆς ἰδίας γυναικὸς οὕτως
ὠμῶς ἀνῃρέθη. καὶ μετὰ ταῦτα κάτω περιτυχὼν
19 τῷ Ὀδυσσεῖ μέμφεται Κλυταιμνήστραν· μηδὲ γὰρ
τοὺς ὀφθαλμοὺς αὐτοῦ τελευτῶντος συγκλεῖσαι·
πρὸς δὲ τούτοις παρακελεύεται μηδέποτε πιστεύειν γυναικί,

---

[1] After Λυκάων Emperius deletes ὤν.
[2] ἀνόητος] ἀνοήτως Arnim.

---

[1] Cf. Edmonds, *op. cit.* II. pp. 146-153, especially fragg.
96 and 97A. According to tradition, when Lycambes gave
to another the daughter he had promised to Archilochus, the
poet attacked him and his family with such savage verses
that they committed suicide.

as he says himself.[1]   Lycaon, fool that he was, having
encountered Achilles a second time, though he
should either fight with vigour or else flee with all
speed, urges the plea,

> For with thee first I ate Demeter's grain.[2]

Well then, previously, when he had not yet partaken
of Achilles' food, he was sold into Lemnos and thus
saved ; but this time when taken captive he was
slaughtered.   That was all the good Demeter did
him.   As for the ducks and partridges, we do not
hunt them until they have eaten of our food.   Take
Aegisthus ; he slew Agamemnon,

> First feeding him, as he who slays an ox
> Hard by the crib.[3]

And although Agamemnon had suffered no harm at
the hands of the Trojans during the ten years in
which he had been at war with them and had never
sat at meat with them ; on the other hand, when
he had come home after so long an absence, had
sacrificed to the gods, and had caused his own table
to be spread before him, his own wife slew him so
cruelly.   Yes, afterwards, when at the gates of Hades
he encountered Odysseus, he denounces Clytaemnestra, for he says she did not even close his eyes
when he was dead[4] ; and, furthermore, he urges
Odysseus never to trust a woman,

---

[2] *Iliad* 21. 76.   Though a prisoner of war and destined
for the slave market of Lemnos, *loc. cit.* 77-79, Lycaon was
a son of Priam and for that reason, no doubt, ate at the
table of Achilles after his capture.   He seems to make a
point of the fact that Achilles was the first Greek with whom
he ate.

[3] *Odyssey* 4. 535 and 11. 411.

[4] *Ibid.* 11. 423-426.

μηδέ οἱ ἐκφάσθαι πυκινὸν ἔπος.

Καίτοι ἡ Κλυταιμνήστρα οὐχ ὅτι γυνὴ ἦν ταῦτα διέθηκεν αὐτόν, ἀλλ' ὅτι πονηρά· καὶ οὐδὲν μᾶλλον 20 οὐ χρὴ γυναικὶ ἤπιον εἶναι ἢ ἀνδρί. ἀλλ', οἶμαι, τῶν περιπεσόντων ἕκαστος, ὑφ' οὗ πέπονθε κακῶς, ἐκεῖνο μάλιστα ὑφορᾶται καὶ προλέγει φυλάττεσθαι τοῖς ἄλλοις, ὁ μὲν ὑπὸ ἔχεως πληγεὶς ὄφιν,[1] ὁ δὲ ὑπὸ σκορπίου σκορπίον· ὃν δ' ἂν κύων δάκῃ, ὄψει βακτηρίαν ἀεὶ περιφέροντα· τὸ αὐτὸ δὴ τοῦτο καὶ πρὸς ἀνθρώπους πεπόνθασιν οἱ πολλοί. τῷ μὲν ἐκ γυναικός τι συνέβη δεινόν· οὗτος δὴ κέκραγεν·

ὦ Ζεῦ, τί δὴ κίβδηλον ἀνθρώποις κακὸν
γυναῖκας εἰς φῶς ἡλίου κατῴκισας;

ἄλλον ὑποδεχθεὶς ξένος ἐλύπησεν, ὡς Ἀλέξανδρος τὰ τοῦ Μενελάου κτήματα καὶ τὴν γυναῖκα ὑφελό-μενος. ὁ τοιοῦτος πρὸς τοὺς ξένους διαβέβληται, πρὸς ἀδελφὸν ἕτερος, ἄλλος πρὸς υἱόν.

21 Τὸ δὲ πρᾶγμα οὐ τοιοῦτόν ἐστιν· οὐ γὰρ ὁ ἀδελφὸς οὐδὲ ὁ συγγενὴς οὐδὲ ὁ ξένος πέφυκεν ἀδικεῖν, ἀλλ' ὁ μοχθηρὸς ἄνθρωπος· τοῦτο δὲ μικροῦ δεῖν ἐν πᾶσίν ἐστιν· ἀλλ' εἰ νοῦν ἔχεις, πάντας εὐλαβοῦ. ξένος· εὐλαβοῦ. μέτριος εἶναί φησι· μᾶλλον εὐλαβοῦ. τοῦτο ἀκίνητον ὑπαρχέτω. νὴ Δί', ἀλλ' ἐπιδείκνυται δεξιοῦ τινος εὔνοιαν. οὐκοῦν ἀποδέχου τοῦτον, τοῖς θεοῖς εἰδὼς χάριν,

---

[1] ὄφιν] ἔχιν Emperius.

---

[1] Dio must have in mind *Odyssey* 11. 441-443, as indicated by the similarity of sentiment and by the word ἤπιον in the next sentence, yet the wording is quite different from our text of the *Odyssey* passage.

[2] Euripides, *Hippolytus* 616-617. Hippolytus cries out against the wickedness of his step-mother Phaedra.

THE SEVENTY-FOURTH DISCOURSE

Or ever tell to her a crafty plan.[1]

Yet Clytaemnestra treated him as she did, not because she was a woman, but because she was a wicked woman ; and there is no more reason for not being kind to a woman than to a man. However, I fancy, each one who has encountered misfortune distrusts particularly that because of which he has suffered and warns all others to beware of it. For instance, he who has been bitten by a viper warns against snakes, another who has been bitten by a scorpion warns against scorpions, and if a man has been bitten by a dog, you will see him always carrying a cane ; in just that way most men behave toward human beings. One man has met with some dreadful misfortune because of a woman ; so he cries to Heaven,

O Zeus, why hast thou brought to light of day
The breed of women, snare and curse to men ? [2]

Another, a stranger who has been received as a guest, brings grief to his host, as Alexander did by stealing from Menelaüs his wealth and his wife. The man so treated has been made distrustful toward strangers, another toward a brother, another toward a son.

But the case is not so simple ; for it is not the brother as such or the kinsman or the stranger who is by nature prone to do wrong, but rather the wicked man ; but wickedness is found in almost all ; aye, if you have good judgement, beware of all. A stranger ? Beware. A fair and moderate man, he says ? Beware still more. Let this principle be inviolate. " Yes," you counter, " but he shows the kindly disposition of a man of courtesy." Very well, accept him, with gratitude to the gods—or, so please

εἰ βούλει δέ, κἀκείνῳ· πρὸς δὲ τὸ μέλλον φυλάττεσθαι χρὴ αὐτόν. ὃ γάρ τις ἐπὶ τῆς τύχης εἶπε, πολὺ μᾶλλον ἂν ἐπ' ἀνθρώπων τοῦτο ῥηθείη, τὸ μηδένα εἰδέναι περὶ μηδενός, εἰ μέχρι τῆς αὔριον

22 διαμενεῖ τοιοῦτος. τὰς γοῦν πρὸς αὐτοὺς[1] παραβαίνουσι συνθήκας καὶ συμβουλεύουσιν αὐτοῖς[2] ἕτερα, καὶ ἄλλα συμφέρειν νομίζοντες ἄλλα πράττουσιν. ὅθεν ὅταν τις ἐκ τοῦ πιστεύειν περιπέσῃ τινὶ τῶν δυσκόλων, γελοῖός ἐστιν αἰτιώμενος ἐκεῖνον ἑαυτὸν δέον, καὶ θεοὺς ἐνίοτε ἐπιβοώμενος, ὑπ' ἀνδρὸς ἀπατηθεὶς φίλου καὶ συνήθους. οἱ δὲ θεοὶ καταγελῶσιν, εἰδότες ὅτι ἑαυτὸν ἐξηπάτησεν ἐπ' ἄλλῳ ποιησάμενος. οἱ προσπταίοντες ἐν ταῖς ὁδοῖς ἢ νὴ Δία ἐμπεσόντες εἰς πηλὸν ἢ βόθρον οὐκ ὀργίζονται τοῖς λίθοις ἢ τῷ πηλῷ· τελέως γὰρ ἂν ἦσαν ἀπόπληκτοι, δέον αὐτοὺς αἰτιᾶσθαι καὶ τὸ μὴ προσέχειν.

23 Τί οὖν; φήσει τις, δεῖ θηρίου βίον προαιρεῖσθαι καὶ ζῆν ἔρημον; οὐ θηρίου, ἀλλ' ἀνδρὸς φρονίμου καὶ ζῆν ἀσφαλῶς ἐπισταμένου. πολὺ γὰρ ἀσφαλεστέρα καὶ κρείττων ἡ ἐρημία τῆς πρὸς ἀνθρώπους κοινωνίας, ἐὰν ἀδεῶς γίγνηται καὶ χωρὶς κοινῶν προσοχῆς. ὥσπερ, οἶμαι, τοῖς πλέουσι τὸ πέλαγος συμφέρει μᾶλλον τῆς γῆς, εἰ μή τις ἐν εὐδίᾳ πλέοι καὶ σαφῶς εἰδὼς τοὺς τόπους· ἐν μὲν γὰρ τῷ πελάγει σπάνιον εἴ που διεφθάρη[3] ναῦς, πρὸς δὲ

[1] αὐτοὺς Emperius : αὑτούς.   [2] αὐτοῖς Emperius : αὑτοῖς.
[3] διεφθάρη Emperius : διαφθαρῇ.

you, to him as well—yet for the future you must watch him. For what some one has said about Fortune might much rather be said about human beings, namely, that no one knows about any one whether he will remain as he is until the morrow. At any rate, men do violate the compacts made with each other and give each other different advice and, believing one course to be expedient, actually pursue another. Thus it comes to pass that when a man, through trusting another, gets involved with one of those troublesome fellows, he makes himself ridiculous if he lays the blame on him when he should blame himself, and if he now and then cries out against the gods, when it is a man by whom he has been duped, a friend and close acquaintance. But the gods laugh at him, knowing as they do that he had duped himself by putting himself in another's power. Those who stumble on the street or, by Zeus, fall into a mud-puddle or a pit are not angry at the stones or at the mud ; for they would be absolutely crazy if they did, seeing that they ought to blame themselves and their heedlessness.

"What !" some one will say, "must we choose the existence of a wild beast and live a solitary life ? " No, not that of a wild beast, but rather that of a prudent man and of one who knows how to live in safety. For far safer and better is solitude than association with mankind, if only solitude be found apart from fear and devoid of solicitude for things of common interest. Just as, in my opinion, for persons making a voyage the open sea is more to their advantage than the coast, unless one be sailing in fair weather and be well acquainted with the region; for in the open sea rarely, if ever, is a ship wrecked,

ταῖς ἀκταῖς καὶ περὶ τὰς ἄκρας ἰδεῖν ἔστι τὰ
24 ναυάγια. τοιγαροῦν, ὅταν χειμὼν καταλάβῃ, τῶν
μὲν ἀπείρων ἕκαστος ἐπιθυμεῖ τῆς γῆς, ὁ δὲ κυβερνήτης ὡς πορρωτάτω φεύγει. καίτοι λιμένας
μὲν εὕροι τις ἂν ἀκλύστους, οἷς ἔνεστι πιστεύσαντας
ἀσφαλῶς ὁρμεῖν, ἡλίκον ἄν ποτε ἀρθῇ τὸ πνεῦμα·
τῶν δὲ ἀνθρώπων οἱ μετριώτατοι τοῖς θερινοῖς
ὅρμοις ἐοίκασιν, οἵτινες πρὸς τὸ παρὸν σκέπουσι·
κἀκείνων γὰρ ἕκαστος πρὸς ἕν τι τῶν κατὰ τὸν
βίον ἐπιεικής, οὐ μέντοι καὶ πρὸς τἆλλα ὑπάρχει.
χρημάτων μὲν γὰρ ἕνεκεν οὐδέν σε ἀδικήσειεν ἄν[1]·
ἔστω γὰρ εἶναί τινα τοιοῦτον· ἀλλὰ τάχ' ἂν ὀργῆς
ἢ φιλοτιμίας καταλαβούσης οὐκ ἂν ἐπιγνοίης
αὐτὸν ἀσάλευτον καὶ πιστόν.[2]
25 Οὐκοῦν τοῖς γε τοιούτοις ὅσον ὑπὸ ἀνάγκης καὶ
τελέως ὀλίγον δεῖ χρῆσθαι, τὸ πλέον αὐτὸν ἐγρη-
γορότα καὶ φυλάττοντα, ὡς τοὺς Ἀχαιοὺς τὸν
Ἕκτορά φησιν ὁ ποιητής·

ὁ δὲ ἰδρείῃ πολέμοιο
ἀσπίδι ταυρείῃ κεκαλυμμένος εὐρέας ὤμους
σκέπτετ' ὀιστῶν τε ῥοῖζον καὶ δοῦπον ἀκόντων.

ὁμοίως ἐν τῷ βίῳ δεῖ τὴν φρόνησιν καὶ τὴν ἐπιστήμην προβεβλημένους καὶ καλυφθέντας αὐτῇ
φεύγειν καὶ φυλάττεσθαι τὴν τῶν ἀνθρώπων
κακίαν καὶ τὰς τέχνας καὶ τὰς ἐπιβουλὰς αἷς
εἰώθασι χρῆσθαι.
26 Καθόλου δὲ θαυμαστόν, εἰ τὸ μὲν φαγεῖν ἀπὸ
τῆς αὐτῆς τραπέζης ἐμποδὼν ἔσται τῇ πονηρίᾳ

---

[1] ἄν added by Emperius.
[2] After πιστόν the mss. read ἄλλως (or ἀλλ' ὡς) ὑπὸ μηδενὸς
πάθους κινούμενον, ἐφ' ᾧ τις ἂν πιστεῦσαι βεβαίως δύναιτο:

but it is close to the shores and near the capes that
the wreckage may be seen. Therefore, when storm
overtakes a ship, though every landlubber longs for
the land, the skipper flees from it as far as possible.
Yet havens free from billows can be found, trusting
which men may safely ride at anchor, however high
the gale may rise. But with human beings, the most
temperate are like our summer anchorages, which
afford shelter for the moment only ; for with men
of that type also the individual is a reasonable person
with regard to some one of life's problems, but with
regard to the rest he is not. In money matters, for
instance, he might never wrong you—granted, of
course, that a man of that sort exists—but let a fit
of rage or jealous rivalry seize him and you would
perhaps not find him unshaken and trustworthy.

Accordingly, one should have dealings with such
persons only in so far as one is compelled to do so
and extremely little at that, what is more, keeping
wide awake one's self and on guard, as the poet says
of the Achaeans and Hector,

But he, experienced in war, with shield
Of ox-hide covered his shoulders broad and watched
The whir of arrows and the thud of darts.[1]

Similarly in our life we must employ prudence and
understanding as a shield and, covered by it, flee and
guard against men's villainy and the tricks and plots
which they are wont to use.

But, speaking generally, it would be surprising if
eating from the same table were to prove a bar to

[1] *Iliad* 16. 359-361.

---

*in other words, one moved by no unhappy experience, one you
could trust with confidence*, which Emperius deletes.

καὶ νὴ Δία τὸ πιεῖν ἀπὸ τοῦ αὐτοῦ κρατῆρος καὶ
τὸν αὐτὸν λύχνον ὁρᾶν· τὸ δὲ τὸν ἥλιον βλέπειν
τὸν αὐτὸν καὶ ἀπὸ τῆς αὐτῆς τρέφεσθαι γῆς οὐδεὶς ὑπολογίζεται τῶν πονηρῶν· ἀλλὰ τὸ μὲν
πανδοκεῖον ἢ νὴ Δία οἶκος ἕτερος ἐκ λίθων καὶ
ξύλων ᾠκοδομημένος συγκίρνησιν ἀνθρώπους καὶ
δύναται συνάγειν εἰς φιλίαν, ὥσπερ Ὀδυσσεὺς
ἀξιοῖ·

αἰδεῖσθαι δὲ μέλαθρον· ὑπωρόφιοι δέ τοί εἰμεν.

οὕτως ἡγεῖται τὴν σκηνὴν ἀξιωτέραν[1] αἰδοῦς, καὶ
ταῦτα ἐκ ξύλων τῶν ἐν τῇ πολεμίᾳ γεγονυῖαν,
ἥπερ αὐτούς. ὁ δὲ σύμπας οὐρανός, ὑφ' ᾧ πάντες
ἐσμὲν ἀρχῆθεν, οὐδὲν ὠφελεῖ πρὸς ὁμόνοιαν οὐδὲ
ἡ τῶν ὅλων κοινωνία θείων οὖσα καὶ μεγάλων, ἀλλὰ τοὐναντίον ἡ τῶν μικρῶν καὶ οὐδενὸς
ἀξίων.

27 Καὶ ὁ μὲν ἴδιος ἑκάστῳ πατήρ, πολλάκις οὐδενὸς
ἄξιος πρεσβύτης, μέγα δίκαιον ὥστε μὴ ἐπιβου-
λεύειν ἀλλήλοις τοὺς ἐκ τοῦ αὐτοῦ γένους· ὁ δὲ
κοινὸς ἁπάντων " ἀνδρῶν τε θεῶν τε," ἐξ οὗ πάντες
γεγόναμεν, οὐ κατὰ Λάχητα ὢν οὐδὲ κατὰ Σίμωνα,
οὐ δύναται κατασχεῖν οὐδὲ κωλῦσαι τὴν ἀδικίαν
τῶν ἀνθρώπων. καὶ μὴν ὅτι γε τοῖς λόγοις οὐκ
ἂν πιστεύοι τις τοῖς ὑπὲρ τῆς φιλίας, τοῦτο γὰρ
28 λοιπόν ἐστι, φανερὸν δήπου. γελοῖον γὰρ ἀργύριον
μὲν δανείζοντα τοῖς πέλας[2] μὴ ῥᾳδίως ἄν τινα
πιστεῦσαι λόγῳ μόνῳ, ἀλλὰ μαρτύρων δεῖσθαι

---

[1] ἀξιωτέραν Geel : ἀξίαν.

villainy, and, forsooth, drinking from the same mixing-bowl and seeing the same lamp, when, on the other hand, seeing the same sun and being nourished by the same earth does not enter into the reckoning of any rogue ; why, the tavern or, by Zeus, any other house made of stones and timbers mixes human beings together and can bring them together in friendship, just as Odysseus thinks is proper :

Respect the house ; we're underneath thy roof.[1]

Thus he thinks that the hut—a hut, too, built of wood grown on hostile soil—is worthier of respect than the men themselves. Yet the whole sky, beneath which we all have been from the beginning, is of no avail toward producing concord, neither is our partnership in the universe, a partnership in things divine and majestic, but only, on the contrary, our partnership in things which are petty and worthless.

Again, every man's own father—often an ineffectual old man—is a great force for righteousness to prevent those of the same family from plotting against each other ; while the common father of all, of " both men and gods," he from whom we all have our being, not a creature such as Laches or Simon,[2] cannot check or prevent the unrighteousness of men ! Indeed, that one could not trust mere words about friendship—for this is the only point remaining— is no doubt clear. For it is absurd that, when lending money to one's neighbours, no one would lightly put faith in word alone, but instead requires witnesses

[1] *Iliad.* 9. 640. But it is Ajax, not Odysseus, who is complaining of Achilles' lack of hospitality.
[2] Seemingly equivalent to our " Smith or Jones."

---

[2] πέλας Emperius : πολλοῖς.

καὶ γραμμάτων καὶ πολλοὺς καὶ ταῦτα παραβαίνειν.[1]

Τί οὖν; φησί τις,[2] οὐκ ἤδη τινὲς ἐγένοντο φίλοι
τῶν πρότερον; οἷον πῶς[3] ἂν λέγοις[4] τοὺς ἡμιθέους[5] θρυλουμένους τούτους, Ὀρέστην καὶ Πυλά-
δην καὶ Θησέα καὶ Πειρίθουν καὶ Ἀχιλλέα καὶ
Πάτροκλον; εἰ δ' οὖν τις συγχωρήσειεν ἀληθῆ
τὴν δόξαν εἶναι ταύτην, δῆλον ὡς τρεῖς ἂν εἶεν
φιλίαι γεγονυῖαι ἐν τοσούτῳ χρόνῳ, ἐν ὅσῳ πλεο-
νάκις ἂν εἴποι τὸν ἥλιον ἐκλελοιπέναι.

[1] After παραβαίνειν Reiske noted a lacuna.
[2] φησί τις Capps : φησίν.   [3] πῶς] πᾶς Arnim.
[4] λέγοις Crosby : λέγοι.   [5] ἡμιθέους deleted by Arnim.

and writings—and many do violence to even these—
[and, on the other hand, that the mere profession of
friendship should suffice [1]].

" What ! " somebody objects, " did not the men
of former times have any friends ? For instance,
what would you say of these demigods that are on
the lips of all : Orestes and Pylades, Theseus and
Peirithoüs, Achilles and Patroclus ? " [2] Well, if one
were to admit that the popular belief about these
is true, there would be three friendships that had
occurred in a period of time so extensive that in it
one could say that the sun had gone into an eclipse
quite a number of times.

[1] The words " and, on the other hand, . . . should
suffice " have been supplied from the context to fill out a
lacuna.
[2] Typical pairs of devoted friends, each pair as famous as
the biblical David and Jonathan.

THE SEVENTY-FIFTH DISCOURSE:
ON LAW

Oₙ stylistic grounds this Discourse has been assigned to
the sophistic period of Dio's career. It is an encomium such
as is familiar in sophistic literature, and it exhibits both the
merits and the defects of that form of composition. Careful
attention is paid to matters of detail connected with rhetorical
effect, but one misses the note of sincere conviction to be
found in many other writings of our author.

The topic chosen for eulogy is νόμος. As is well known,
that word covers a wide range, meaning at one time usage
sanctified by long tradition, at another divine ordinance, and
at another statutory law. Dio treats all three varieties im-
partially, passing lightly from one to another and back
again. The opening phrase, ἔστι δέ, suggests that our
Discourse was preceded by an introductory composition no
longer extant.

75. ΠΕΡΙ ΝΟΜΟΥ

1 Ἔστι δὲ ὁ νόμος τοῦ βίου μὲν ἡγεμών, τῶν πόλεων δὲ ἐπιστάτης κοινός, τῶν δὲ πραγμάτων κανὼν δίκαιος, πρὸς ὃν ἕκαστον ἀπευθύνειν δεῖ τὸν αὑτοῦ τρόπον· εἰ δὲ μή, σκολιὸς ἔσται καὶ πονηρός. οἱ μὲν οὖν τοῦτον φυλάττοντες ἔχονται τῆς σωτηρίας· οἱ δὲ παραβαίνοντες πρῶτον μὲν αὑτοὺς ἀπολλύουσιν, ἔπειτα καὶ τοὺς ἄλλους, παράδειγμα καὶ ζῆλον αὐτοῖς ἀνομίας καὶ βίας παρέχοντες. ὥσπερ δὲ τῶν πλεόντων οἱ τοῦ πυρσοῦ μὴ διαμαρτάνοντες, οὗτοι μάλιστα σώζονται καὶ τοὺς λιμένας εὑρίσκουσιν, οὕτως οἱ κατὰ τὸν νόμον ζῶντες ἀσφαλέστατα πορεύονται διὰ τοῦ βίου καὶ τῆς καταγωγῆς τῆς δεούσης 2 τυγχάνουσιν. ἀνθρώπῳ μὲν οὖν ἤδη τις συμβούλῳ χρησάμενος μετενόησεν, οὐ μέντοι νόμῳ. τοσούτῳ δὲ τῶν τειχῶν ταῖς πόλεσι χρησιμώτερός ἐστιν, ὥστε ἀτείχιστοι μὲν πολλαὶ τῶν πόλεων διαμένουσι, νόμου δὲ χωρὶς οὐκ ἔστιν οὐδεμίαν οἰκεῖσθαι πόλιν.

Οὐ μόνον δὲ συμφέρει τοῖς θνητοῖς, ἀλλὰ καὶ τοῖς θεοῖς. ὁ γοῦν κόσμος ἀεὶ τὸν αὐτὸν νόμον ἀκίνητον φυλάττει καὶ τῶν αἰωνίων οὐδὲν ἂν παραβαίη τοῦτον. ὅθεν, οἶμαι, καὶ βασιλεὺς εἰ-

THE SEVENTY-FIFTH DISCOURSE :
ON LAW

THE law is for life a guide, for cities an impartial overseer, and for the conduct of affairs a true and just straight-edge by which each must keep straight his own conduct ; otherwise he will be crooked and corrupt. Accordingly, those who strictly observe the law have firm hold on safety ; while those who transgress it destroy first of all themselves and then their fellows too, providing them with an example and pattern of lawlessness and violence. Yes, just as at sea those who do not miss the beacon are most likely to come through with their lives and to find their havens, so those who live according to the law journey through life with maximum security and reach the right destination. There have been, it is true, instances in which one who has used a human being as counsellor has done so to his sorrow, but not so with the law. So much more serviceable is it for our cities than their walls that many of them still remain unwalled, but without law no city can be administered.

But the law is of advantage not only to mortals, but to the gods as well. At any rate the universe always preserves the same law inviolate, and nothing which is eternal may transgress it. It is for that reason, methinks, that the law has appropriately

κότως ἀνθρώπων καὶ θεῶν κέκληται, τὴν μὲν
βίαν καταλύων, τὴν δὲ ὕβριν καθαιρῶν, τὴν δὲ
ἄνοιαν σωφρονίζων, τὴν δὲ κακίαν κολάζων, ἰδίᾳ
δὲ καὶ κοινῇ πάντας τοὺς δεομένους ὠφελῶν, τοῖς
μὲν ἀδικουμένοις βοηθῶν, τοῖς δὲ ἀπορουμένοις
3 περί τινος μηνύων τὸ δέον. ὅταν γάρ τις συμ-
βάντος τινὸς αὐτῷ δυσκόλου πράγματος ζητῇ τὸ
συμφέρον, οὐδέν, οἶμαι, δεῖ φίλους παρακαλεῖν
οὐδὲ συγγενεῖς, ἀλλὰ ἐλθόντα παρὰ τοὺς νόμους
πυνθάνεσθαι. καὶ γὰρ[1] οὐκ ἂν τὸ οἰκεῖον σκοπῶν
χεῖρον ἐκείνῳ παραινέσειεν οὐδὲ[2] ἀγνοήσας τὸ
βέλτιον, οὐδὲ[3] δι᾽ ἀσχολίαν τινὰ ἢ τὸ μὴ φροντίζειν
τοὺς σκεπτομένους[4] παραιτήσαιτ᾽ ἄν. τοὐναντίον
γὰρ ἁπάντων ὁμοίως κήδεται καὶ σχολὴν ἄγει
πρὸς τὰ τῶν ἄλλων πράγματα καὶ οὐδὲν ἴδιον
οὐδὲ ἐξαίρετόν ἐστιν αὐτῷ.

4 Καὶ μὴν τοσούτῳ γε τῆς παρὰ τῶν θεῶν μαντείας
ὠφελιμώτερός ἐστι νόμος, ὅσῳ τοὺς μὲν χρησμοὺς
ἤδη τινὲς ἠγνόησαν καὶ δοκοῦντες πράττειν κατ᾽
αὐτοὺς τἀναντία ἐποίησαν, ὅθεν, οἶμαι, συμφοραῖς
ἐχρήσαντο· παρὰ τοῦ νόμου δὲ οὐδέν ἐστι σκολιὸν
οὐδὲ ἀμφίβολον, ἀλλ᾽ ἁπλῶς ἅπαντα ἃ προσήκει
τοῖς δεομένοις φράζει. ἄρχων δὲ ἁπάντων καὶ
κύριος ὢν χωρὶς ὅπλων καὶ βίας κρατεῖ· τοὐναντίον γὰρ αὐτὸς καταλύει τὴν βίαν· ἀλλὰ μετὰ

---

[1] γὰρ added by Crosby.
[2] οὐδὲ Emperius : οὔτε.
[3] οὐδὲ Emperius : οὔτε.
[4] σκεπτομένους Morel : κλεπτομένους.

been called "king of men and gods"[1]; for law does away with violence, puts down insolence, reproves folly, chastises wickedness, and in private and public relations helps all who are in need, succouring the victims of injustice, and to those who are perplexed about a course of action making known what is their duty. Whenever, for instance, a man is confronted by a perplexing situation and is seeking to discover what is expedient for him, he need not, I believe, call in friends or kinsmen, but rather go to the laws and pose his question. For the law would not, having an eye to its own advantage, give him inferior advice, nor yet through ignorance of the better course, nor would it because of some engagement or lack of interest beg its consultants to let it be excused. For, on the contrary, it has regard for all alike, and it has leisure for the problems of all others, and for it there is no private or special interest.

Again, law is more serviceable than the oracular responses of the gods in that, while there have been some who did not understand the oracles, and, supposing that they were acting in harmony with them, have done the very opposite—which accounts, I imagine, for their having met with disaster—from the law there proceeds nothing which is tortuous or ambiguous, but, instead, it puts in simple phrases everything which is appropriate for those who are in need. Besides, though ruler and master of all things, it exercises its authority without the use of arms and force—on the contrary, law itself does away with force; nay, it rules by persuasion and governs

[1] Cf. Pindar, frag. 169. Dio here puts into prose the most significant part of the passage; Plato quotes several lines from it in *Gorgias* 484 в.

πειθοῦς καὶ βουλομένων προέστηκεν. πείσας γὰρ
πρότερον καὶ δοκιμασθεὶς οὕτως γίγνεται καὶ τὴν
ἰσχὺν τὴν αὑτοῦ λαμβάνει.

5 Τηλικαύτην δὲ ἔχει δύναμιν ὥστε καὶ τοῖς θεοῖς
οὗτός ἐστιν ὁ βοηθῶν. τοὺς γὰρ ἱεροσύλους καὶ
τοὺς παραβαίνοντας τὴν πρὸς αὐτοὺς εὐσέβειαν
κολάζει. καὶ μὴν αὐτόν γε οὐδὲ εἷς οἷός τέ ἐστιν
ἀδικῆσαι. τῶν γὰρ παραβαινόντων τὸν νόμον
6 ἕκαστος οὐκ ἐκεῖνον, ἀλλ' ἑαυτὸν βλάπτει. τοσαύ-
της δὲ δικαιοσύνης καὶ φιλανθρωπίας μεστός
ἐστιν, ὥστε καὶ τοῖς ἀτυχοῦσι χρησιμώτερος
καθέστηκε τῶν γένει προσηκόντων καὶ τοῖς ἀδικουμένοις ἰσχυρότερος τῆς αὐτῶν ἐκείνων ῥώμης, καὶ
πατράσιν υἱέων εὐνούστερος καὶ παισὶ γονέων
καὶ ἀδελφοῖς ἀδελφῶν. πολλοὶ γοῦν ὑπὸ τῶν
φιλτάτων ἀδικούμενοι πρὸς τοῦτον καταφεύγουσιν.
ἔτι[1] δὲ καὶ μηδὲν ὑπὸ μηδενὸς εὖ πεπονθὼς ὁ
νόμος πᾶσιν ὧν ἂν εὐεργετήσωσιν ἑτέρους ἐκτίνει
τὰς χάριτας, καὶ γονεῦσι παρὰ παίδων τὰς ὁμοίας
κομιζόμενος καὶ τοῖς ἰδίᾳ τινῶν εὐεργέταις παρὰ
τῶν εὖ παθόντων καὶ τοῖς κοινῇ φιλοτιμουμένοις
παρὰ τῆς πόλεως.

7 Κάλλιστα δὲ τὰ ἆθλα[2] τῶν εὐεργεσιῶν πεποίηκε,
στεφάνους καὶ κηρύγματα καὶ προεδρίας ἐξευρών·
ἃ τοῖς μὲν παρέχουσιν οὐδεμίαν φέρει δαπάνην,
τοῖς δὲ τυγχάνουσι τοῦ παντὸς ἄξια καθέστηκεν.
ὅ τι δ' ἂν ἐθέλῃ τῶν εὐτελεστάτων, εὐθὺς τοῦτο
μέγα καὶ τίμιον ἐποίησεν. οὗτός ἐστιν ὁ τὸν

---

[1] ἔτι Arnim : εἰ.　　　[2] τὰ ἆθλα Casaubon : τὰς ἄλλας.

willing subjects. For it is because it first persuades men and secures their approval that law comes into being and acquires its own power.

But so great is the power it possesses, that it is the law which assists even the gods. For example, the sacrilegious and those who violate the reverence due to the gods it punishes. Moreover, the law itself no one has the power to injure. For every one who transgresses the law harms, not the law, but himself. But such is the righteousness and benevolence which pervades the law, that for the unfortunate it has proved even more helpful than their blood relatives ; and for the victims of injustice it has proved more potent than their own might ; and for fathers, more kindly than their sons ; for sons, more kindly than parents ; for brothers, than brothers. At any rate many, when wronged by their closest kin, seek refuge with the law. Then too, though it has experienced no kindness at the hands of any one, the law renders thanks in full to all for the kindnesses which they show to others, exacting thanks alike for fathers from their sons, for those who have in private done some deed of kindness from those whom they have benefited, and for those who display public spirit in municipal affairs from their city.

Furthermore, most beautiful are the rewards which it has established for their benefactions, having devised crowns and public proclamations and seats of honour, things which for those who supply them entail no expense, but which for those who win them have come to be worth everything. Indeed, whatever it so desires, however inexpensive it may be, the law immediately renders important and precious. It is the law which has made the wild olive so im-

κότινον οὕτως μέγα καὶ τηλικαύτης ἄξιον σπουδῆς
8 ἀποδείξας καὶ τὰ σέλινα καὶ τὴν πίτυν καὶ τὸν
τοῦ θαλλοῦ στέφανον· οὗτος ὁ τὰ τρία ῥήματα,
οἷς ἕκαστος κηρύττεται τῶν ἀγαθῶν, πολλοῖς
ἀποφήνας τοῦ ζῆν τιμιώτερα. οὗτός ἐστιν ὁ τὰς
πανηγύρεις συνάγων, ὁ τοὺς θεοὺς τιμῶν, ὁ τὴν
ἀρετὴν αὔξων· οὗτος ὁ τὴν θάλατταν καθαίρων,
ὁ τὴν γῆν ἥμερον ποιῶν, ὁ τοῦ Διὸς ὄντως[1] υἱός,
ὁ τὴν ἀήττητον καὶ ἀνυπέρβλητον ἰσχὺν ἔχων·
τοσοῦτον ἁπάντων σωφροσύνῃ καὶ πίστει διαφέρων ὥστε καὶ γυναικῶν κοινωνίαν καὶ παρθένων
ὥραν καὶ παίδων ἀκμὴν τούτῳ πάντες πεπιστεύ-
καμεν. ἔτι δὲ καὶ παρθένου τῆς Δίκης οὔσης
μόνος αὐτῇ διὰ σωφροσύνην σύνεστιν.

9 Οὗτος ἐπίκουρος γήρως, διδάσκαλος νεότητος,
πενίας συνεργός, φύλαξ πλούτου, τῇ μὲν εἰρήνῃ
σύμμαχος, τῷ δὲ πολέμῳ ἐναντίος. οὐ μὴν ἀλλὰ
καὶ ἐν αὐτῷ τούτῳ πλέον[2] ἰσχύει. τὸν γοῦν παρὰ
τῶν ἐχθίστων κήρυκα πεμπόμενον οὗτός ἐστιν ὁ
σῴζων καὶ διαφυλάττων, παντὸς θώρακος καὶ
πάσης ἀσπίδος ἰσχυρότερον αὐτῷ δοὺς ὅπλον τὸ
κηρύκειον· ἔστι δὲ τοῦ νόμου σύμβολον.[3] διὰ τοῦτον τοὺς ἀποθανόντας οὐδεὶς ἔτι κρίνει πολεμίους
οὐδὲ τὴν ἔχθραν καὶ τὴν ὕβριν εἰς τὰ σώματα αὐτῶν
ἐπιδείκνυνται.

10 Τοσούτῳ δὲ ταῖς[4] πόλεσι χρησιμώτερός ἐστιν

---

[1] ὄντως Sonny : ἐστὼς BMPH, ἐτεὸς U.
[2] πλέον] πλεῖστον Emperius.
[3] ἔστι δὲ . . . σύμβολον suspected by Geel.
[4] ταῖς Morel : τὸ M, omitted by UBPH.

---

[1] The crown of wild olive was awarded at the Olympic
Games, the parsley at Nemea, and the pine at the Isthmus.

portant, worth so much devoted effort, just as also with the parsley, the pine, and the olive crown [1]; it is the law which has made the three words with which each good man is publicly acclaimed [2] more precious to many than life itself. It is the law which convenes the national festive gatherings, which honours the gods, which exalts virtue; it is the law which purges the sea,[3] makes civilized the land, is the veritable son of Zeus, the possessor of invincible, insuperable might [4]; for it is so far superior to all else in temperance and trustworthiness that not only partnership with women but also the bloom of maidens and the prime of lads we all have entrusted to the law. Besides, though Justice is a virgin, such is his continence that Law dwells with her without a chaperon.

Law is a protector of old age, a schoolmaster of youth, of poverty a fellow labourer, a guard of wealth, to peace an ally, to war a foe. Nay, even in war itself law has the greater might. For instance, the herald who is dispatched from one's bitterest foes the law protects and guards, giving him as a weapon more mighty than any corselet or any shield the herald's staff—in fact, this is a symbol of the law. Because of the law the slain are deemed no longer to be foes, nor are hatred and insult wreaked upon their bodies.

Again, so much more useful is the law to our cities

Distinguished public service at Athens was also rewarded by " the olive crown "; cf. Aeschines 3. 187.

[2] The words in question may be ἀνὴρ ἀγαθός ἐστι, a phrase which occurs with great regularity in honorific decrees.

[3] That is, rids it of pirates.

[4] The law is here being compared to Heracles, whose labours consisted largely in ridding civilization of its foes.

ἥπερ τὰ πηδάλια ταῖς ναυσίν, ὥστε ἡ μὲν ἀποβαλοῦσα[1] τοὺς οἴακας ναῦς οὐκ ἂν ἀπόλοιτο μὴ
χειμῶνος καταλαβόντος, πόλιν δ' οὐκ ἔνι σωθῆναι
τοῦ νόμου λυθέντος, οὐδ' ἂν μηδὲν ἔξωθεν συμβαίνῃ
δεινόν. ὥσπερ δὲ ὑπὸ τῆς ἐν αὐτῷ διανοίας δι-
οικεῖται καὶ σῴζεται τῶν ἀνθρώπων ἕκαστος, ἡ
δὲ ταύτης διαφθορὰ μανίαν καὶ παρακοπὴν φέρει,
παραπλησίως, ἄν τις ἀνέλῃ τὸν νόμον ἐκ τοῦ βίου,
καθάπερ, οἶμαι, τὸν νοῦν ἀπολωλεκὼς εἰς παντελῆ
μανίαν καὶ ταραχὴν περιστήσεται.

---

[1] ἀποβαλοῦσα Pflugk : ἀποβάλλουσα.

than rudders are to our ships that, whereas a ship which has lost its rudders [1] would not perish unless a storm should overtake it, a city cannot be saved if the law has been destroyed, not even when no dire disaster befalls it from without. But just as each of us is governed and safeguarded by the intelligence which is in him, while its destruction entails madness and insanity, similarly, if one expels the law from his life, just as if he had lost his mind, I believe he will be brought into a state of utter madness and confusion.

[1] Greek ships commonly had two rudders, one on each side.

THE SEVENTY-SIXTH DISCOURSE:
ON CUSTOM

THIS is another sophistic exercise. Comparison with the preceding Discourse will show with what ease the sophist could shift his ground. In Or. 75 law is eulogized as a beneficent influence in human affairs; here custom has taken its place. Contradictions between the two documents abound, but perhaps none more striking than the two statements that follow: " from the law there proceeds nothing which is tortuous or ambiguous, but, instead, it puts in simple phrases everything which is appropriate for those who are in need " (Or. 75. 4) and " some laws have not been clearly written, and they are often warped and twisted by the eloquence of the orators; but our customs are never ambiguous or crooked, and oratory could not get the upper hand with them " (Or. 76. 4).

76. ΠΕΡΙ ΕΘΟΥΣ

1 Ἔστι δὲ τὸ ἔθος γνώμη μὲν τῶν χρωμένων κοινή, νόμος δὲ ἄγραφος ἔθνους ἢ πόλεως, δίκαιον δὲ ἑκούσιον, κατὰ ταὐτὰ¹ πᾶσιν ἀρέσκον, εὕρεμα δὲ ἀνθρώπων οὐδενός, ἀλλὰ βίου καὶ χρόνου. τῶν μὲν οὖν ἄλλων νόμων ἕκαστος ἅπαξ δοκιμασθεὶς ἔλαβε τὴν ἰσχύν· τὸ δὲ ἔθος ἀεὶ δοκιμάζεται. καὶ νόμος μὲν οὐδεὶς ῥᾳδίως ὑπὸ πάντων κριθήσεται²· ταῖς γὰρ τῶν πλειόνων δόξαις κυροῦται· ἔθος δὲ οὐκ ἐνῆν γενέσθαι μὴ προσδεχθὲν ὑπὸ πάντων. κἀκεῖνος ἀπειλῶν καὶ βιαζόμενος μένει κύριος, ὑπὸ δὲ τῶν ἐθῶν πειθόμενοι καὶ καλὰ καὶ συμφέροντα κρίνομεν αὐτά.

2 Διό μοι δοκεῖ τις ἂν προσεικάσαι τὸν μὲν ἔγγραφον νόμον τῇ δυνάμει τῆς τυραννίδος, φόβῳ γὰρ ἕκαστον καὶ μετὰ προστάγματος διαπράττεται· τὸ δὲ ἔθος μᾶλλον τῇ φιλανθρωπίᾳ τῆς βασιλείας, βουλόμενοι γὰρ αὐτῷ πάντες καὶ δίχα ἀνάγκης ἕπονται.³ καὶ νόμους μὲν ἴσμεν πολλοὺς ἀνῃρημένους ὑπὸ τῶν θέντων αὐτούς, ὡς πονηρούς·

---

¹ κατὰ ταὐτὰ Dindorf: καὶ κατὰ ταὐτὰ PH, καὶ ταὐτὰ B, καὶ ταῦτα UM.
² κριθήσεται] ἐγκριθήσεται Arnim.
³ ἕπονται Geel: οἴονται.

252

THE SEVENTY-SIXTH DISCOURSE:
ON CUSTOM

CUSTOM is a judgement common to those who use it, an unwritten law of tribe or city, a voluntary principle of justice, acceptable to all alike with reference to the same matters, an invention made, not by any human being, but rather by life and time. Therefore, while of the laws in general each obtains its power through having been approved once and for all, custom is constantly being subjected to scrutiny. Moreover, while no law will readily be chosen by everybody—for it is by the opinions of the majority that it is ratified—yet a custom could not come into being if not accepted by all. Again, while law by threats and violence maintains its mastery, it is only when we are persuaded by our customs that we deem them excellent and advantageous.

Therefore it seems to me that we might liken the written law to the power of tyranny, for it is by means of fear and through injunction that each measure is made effective; but custom might rather be likened to the benevolence of kingship, for of their own volition all men follow custom, and without constraint. Again, we know of many laws which have been repealed by those who made them, because they judged them to be bad; but no one could

ἔθος δὲ οὐκ ἂν οὐδεὶς ῥᾳδίως δείξειε λελυμένον.
καὶ μὴν τῷ παντὶ ῥᾷον[1] ἐστιν ἀνελεῖν ὅ τι βούλει
3 τῶν ἐγγράφων ἢ τῶν ἐθῶν. τὰ μὲν γὰρ ἂν
ἀπαλείψῃς ἅπαξ, ἡμέρᾳ μιᾷ λέλυται· συνήθειαν
δὲ πόλεως οὐκ ἔστιν ἐν πάνυ πολλῷ καταλῦσαι
χρόνῳ. κἀκεῖνοι μὲν ἐν σανίσιν ἢ στήλαις φυλάτ-
τονται· τῶν δὲ ἕκαστον ἐν ταῖς ἡμετέραις ψυχαῖς.
ἀσφαλεστέρα δὲ καὶ κρείττων ἡ τοιαύτη φυλακή.
καὶ μὴν ὁ μὲν ἔγγραφος νόμος αὐστηρός ἐστι
καὶ ἀπηνής, ἔθους δὲ οὐδὲν ἥδιον. ἔπειτα τοὺς
νόμους παρ' ἄλλων πυνθανόμεθα, τὰ δὲ ἔθη πάντες
ἐπιστάμεθα.

4   Κἀκείνων μέν εἰσιν οὐ σαφῶς ἔνιοι γεγραμμένοι
καὶ διαστρέφονται πολλάκις ὑπὸ τῆς τῶν ῥητόρων
δυνάμεως· τῶν δὲ ἐθῶν οὐδὲν ἀμφίβολον οὐδὲ
σκολιόν, οὐδ' ἂν περιγένοιτ' αὐτῶν λόγος. κἀκείνων μὲν ἀεὶ δεῖ μνημονεύειν, εἰ μέλλοιμεν
αὐτοῖς ἐμμένειν· τοῦ δὲ ἔθους οὐκ ἔστιν οὐδὲ
βουλομένους ἐπιλαθέσθαι· τοιαύτην γὰρ ἔχει[2] φύσιν ὥστε ἀεὶ ὑπομιμνήσκειν αὐτούς.[3]

Καθόλου δὲ τοὺς μὲν νόμους φαίη τις ἂν ποιεῖν
δούλων πολιτείαν, τὰ δὲ ἔθη τοὐναντίον ἐλευθέρων.
ἐκεῖνοι μὲν γὰρ ποιοῦσιν[4] εἰς τὰ σώματα κολάσεις·
παραβαινομένου δὲ ἔθους τὴν ζημίαν εἶναι συμβέβηκεν αἰσχύνην. ὥστε ἐκεῖνος μὲν φαύλων, οὗτος δὲ ἀγαθῶν ἐστι νόμος. εἰ γὰρ ἅπαντες ἦσαν
ἀγαθοί, δῆλον ὅτι τῶν ἐγγράφων ἡμῖν οὐδὲν ἂν ἔδει
νόμων. ἔτι δὲ[5] τῶν μὲν νόμων εἰσὶν οἱ βασιλεῖς

---

[1] ῥᾷον Morel : ῥᾴδιον.   [2] γὰρ ἔχει Emperius : παρέχει.
[5] αὐτούς] αὐτοῦ Emperius.

readily point to a custom which had been dissolved. Nay, it is altogether easier to do away with any written ordinance you please than to do away with any custom. For written ordinances, once the writing is erased, are done for in a single day ; but a city's usage it is impossible to destroy in a very long period of time. Besides, while laws are preserved on tablets of wood or of stone, each custom is preserved within our own hearts. And this sort of preservation is surer and better. Furthermore, the written law is harsh and stern, whereas nothing is more pleasant than custom. Then too, our laws we learn from others, but our customs we all know perfectly.

Again, some laws have not been clearly written, and they are often warped and twisted by the eloquence of the orators ; but our customs are never ambiguous or crooked, and oratory could not get the upper hand with them. Also the laws must be kept constantly in mind if we are to abide by them ; whereas a custom men cannot forget, even if they would ; for such is its nature that it is constantly reminding them.

And, speaking generally, while one might say that the laws create a polity of slaves, our customs, on the contrary, create a polity of free men. For the laws inflict punishment upon men's bodies ; but when a custom is violated, the consequent penalty has always been disgrace. Therefore the one is a law for bad persons, the other for good persons. Indeed, if all men were good, evidently we should have no need of the written laws. Furthermore, although our

---

⁴ ποιοῦσιν] ἀπειλοῦσιν Arnim. ⁵ δὲ added by Emperius.

ἐπάνω καὶ πολλὰ πράττουσι παρ' αὐτούς, τοῖς δὲ
ἔθεσι κἀκεῖνοι κατακολουθοῦσιν.

5 Καὶ τῶν μὲν ἐγγράφων οὐδὲν ἐν τοῖς πολέμοις
ἰσχύει, τὰ δὲ ἔθη φυλάττεται παρὰ πᾶσι, κἂν εἰς
ἐσχάτην ἔχθραν προέλθωσιν. τὸ γοῦν μὴ κωλύειν
τοὺς νεκροὺς θάπτειν οὐδαμῇ γέγραπται· πῶς
γὰρ ἂν ὑπήκουον οἱ κρατοῦντες τοῖς τῶν ἡττω-
μένων ἐπιτάγμασιν; ἀλλ' ἔθος ἐστὶ τὸ ποιοῦν τῆς
φιλανθρωπίας ταύτης τοὺς κατοιχομένους τυγχάνειν. ὁμοίως τὸ τῶν κηρύκων ἀπέχεσθαι καὶ
μόνοις τούτοις πολλὴν ἀσφάλειαν εἶναι βαδίζουσιν.
τῶν μὲν οὖν νόμον παραβαινόντων οὐδεὶς ἂν
ἐπιδείξειεν οὐδένα, οἶμαι, φανερῶς ὑπὸ τῶν θεῶν
κεκολασμένον· Λακεδαιμόνιοι δ' ἐπεὶ παρέβησαν
τὸ κηρύκων ἔθος, τοὺς παρὰ βασιλέως ἐλθόντας
ἀνελόντες, ἐκολάσθησαν ὑπ' αὐτοῦ τοῦ δαιμονίου.

---

[1] Herodotus tells the tale (7. 133-137). When the heralds
came demanding earth and water as tokens of submission
to Persia, the Spartans cast them into a well, telling them to
get their earth and water there. For a long time afterwards
Sparta could not obtain favourable omens, until finally two

kings are above the laws and do many things in violation of them, even they follow the customs.

Again, of the written laws, not one is in force in time of war, but the customs are observed by all, even if men proceed to the extremity of hatred. For example, the provision that no one shall prevent the burial of the dead has nowhere been put in writing, for how could the victors obey the injunctions of the vanquished ? Nay, it is custom which brings it to pass that the departed are granted that act of humanity. It is the same with the provision that no one shall lay hands on heralds, and that they alone enjoy complete security on their missions. Finally, from among those who transgress law, I believe that not one could be shown to have been punished openly by the gods ; yet the Spartans, when they had transgressed the custom regarding heralds, having slain the heralds who came from the Great King, were punished by the divine power itself.[1]

nobles volunteered to offer themselves to the Great King in expiation of the crime against the sanctity of heralds. The king magnanimously spared their lives.

THE SEVENTY-SEVENTH/EIGHTH DISCOURSE : ON ENVY

In enumerating the eighty items which he found in his copy of Dio, Photius lists next in order after Or. 76 two speeches entitled περὶ φθόνου. Some support is given Photius in that connexion by our manuscripts, for UB place at the beginning of the document before us the heading περὶ φθόνου α, and, to introduce § 15, a second heading, περὶ φθόνου β, while PH have preserved for us only §§ 1-14. These facts account for the double number attached to the present Discourse in editions of our author. How it came to be viewed as two separate documents is difficult to understand, for both parts deal with the same theme, the second part follows naturally upon the first, and there is no perceptible break between them. To be sure, dialogue predominates in the first part, while in the second there is almost unbroken exposition, but that is a phenomenon noticed in other specimens of Dio's teaching.

Arnim assigns this Discourse to the period of Dio's exile and regards it as a trustworthy and significant illustration of the way in which at that period he sometmes imparted instruction. The dialogue begins abruptly, the opening words revealing that the discussion is already under way. Almost immediately Dio's partner calls attention to the presence of a large company of listeners, who might find a detailed discussion irksome. Dio counters by asking if they have not assembled for the express purpose of listening to " wise words and about wise words," and he proceeds to test the sincerity of their interest by continuing the argument. But by the time we reach § 9 we find that—possibly because he has taken to heart the warning about his audience—he begins to abandon dialectic and to launch forth into rather continuous exposition. One is reminded of the Borysthenitic

Discourse (Or. 36), in which we are told that a large crowd has assembled to hear their visitor, and Dio, after a preliminary skirmish with the young Callistratus, directs his further remarks to his audience at large. The setting of our present Discourse cannot be determined with precision, but that it was delivered in some large city may be inferred from § 8. Furthermore, the size of the audience and the reference (§ 15) to a discussion which had taken place the day preceding suggest that Dio had been in residence long enough to have attracted some attention.

77. 78. ΠΕΡΙ ΦΘΟΝΟΥ[1]

1 Δ. Ἆρα διὰ ταῦτα καὶ τὰ τοιαῦτα ἐνομίσθη σοφὸς ἐν τοῖς Ἕλλησιν Ἡσίοδος καὶ οὐδαμῶς ἀνάξιος ἐκείνης τῆς δόξης, ὡς οὐκ ἀνθρωπίνῃ τέχνῃ τὰ ποιήματα ποιῶν τε καὶ ᾄδων, ἀλλὰ ταῖς Μούσαις ἐντυχὼν καὶ μαθητὴς αὐτῶν ἐκείνων γενόμενος; ὅθεν[2] ἐξ ἀνάγκης ὅ τι ἐπῄει αὐτῷ πάντα μουσικά τε καὶ σοφὰ ἐφθέγγετο καὶ οὐδὲν μάταιον, ὧν δῆλον ὅτι καὶ τοῦτο τὸ ἔπος ἐστίν.

Τὸ ποῖον;

Δ. Καὶ κεραμεὺς κεραμεῖ κοτέει καὶ τέκτονι τέκτων.

2 Πολλὰ μὲν καὶ ἄλλα φανήσεται τῶν Ἡσιόδου πεποιημένα καλῶς περί τε ἀνθρώπων καὶ θεῶν σχεδόν τι καὶ περὶ μειζόνων πραγμάτων ἢ ὁποῖα τὰ λεχθέντα νῦν· ἀτὰρ οὖν καὶ ταῦτα ἀπεφήνατο μάλ' ἀληθῶς τε καὶ ἐμπείρως τῆς ἀνθρωπίνης φύσεως.

Δ. Βούλει οὖν ἐπιμελέστερον σκοπῶμεν αὐτά;

Καὶ πῶς ἡμᾶς ἀνέξονται τοσοῦτος ὄχλος περὶ τοιούτων διαλεγομένους;

---

[1] περὶ φθόνου MH, περὶ φθόνου a UB ; see Introduction.
[2] ὅθεν Casaubon : ὃ ἦν (ἦν).

THE SEVENTY-SEVENTH/EIGHTH DISCOURSE : ON ENVY

Dio. Is it really for these and similar reasons that Hesiod came to be regarded as a wise man among the Greeks and by no means unworthy of that reputation, as being one who composed and chanted his poems, not by human art, but because he had held converse with the Muses and had become a pupil of those very beings ? [1] Whence it inevitably follows that whatever entered his mind he always expressed with both music and wisdom and in no instance without a purpose, as is clearly illustrated by the verse I have in mind.

Interlocutor. What verse ?

Dio. Both potter at potter doth rage and joiner at joiner.[2]

Int. Many other verses of Hesiod's will be seen to have been well expressed about both men and gods, and, I may almost add, about more important matters than the sort just mentioned ; yet here too, no doubt, he has expressed himself very truthfully as well as with experience of human nature.

Dio. Shall we, then, consider them more carefully ?

Int. Why, how will so large a gathering bear with us if we discuss such matters ?

---

[1] Hesiod tells of his encounter with the Muses in *Theogony* 22-34.
[2] Hesiod, *Works and Days* 25.

Δ. Τί δέ; οὐ σοφὰ καὶ περὶ σοφῶν ἥκουσιν ἀκουσόμενοι;

Φαῖεν ἄν, ὥς μοι δοκοῦσιν.

Δ. Ἀλλὰ μὴ τὸν Ἡσίοδον φαῦλον ἡγοῦνται καὶ ὀλίγου ἄξιον;

Οὐδαμῶς.

Δ. Ἀλλὰ περὶ φθόνου καὶ ζηλοτυπίας καὶ τίνες εἰσὶν οἱ πρὸς ἀλλήλους οὕτως ἔχοντες καὶ ἐπὶ τίσιν οὐ χρήσιμον αὐτοῖς ἀκροᾶσθαι;

Πάντων μὲν οὖν χρησιμώτατον.

3 Δ. Οὐκοῦν χρήσιμον[1] ἤδη καὶ ἀποπειρᾶσθαι τῶν ἀνδρῶν. φέρε δή, δι' ἄλλο τί φησι τούτους Ἡσίοδος εἶναι φθονεροὺς καὶ δυσκόλως ἀλλήλοις ἔχειν ἢ διότι ἧττον ἂν[2] ἐργάζοιτο[3] ἐκ τοῦ πράγματος ἕκαστος, ὅτου ἂν τύχῃ πράττων, πολλῶν ὄντων ὁμοίων;

Διὰ τί γὰρ ἄλλο;

Δ. Πότερον οὖν κεραμεῖ μὲν λυσιτελεῖ μηδένα ἄλλον εἶναι κεραμέα ἐν τῇ αὐτῇ πόλει τε καὶ κώμῃ, μαγείρῳ δὲ τοῦτο οὐ λυσιτελές, ὅπως ἐξῇ αὐτῷ ἀποδίδοσθαι ὁποῖ' ἂν ἔχῃ τὰ κρέα τοῖς δεομένοις, ἂν καὶ πάνυ λεπτὸν ἱερεῖον ἢ πρεσβύτερον τύχῃ πριάμενος;

Δῆλον ὅτι καὶ μαγείρῳ.

4 Δ. Τί δέ; βαφεῖ τὴν βαφικὴν ἐργάζεσθαι τέχνην οὐ μόνῳ αὐτῷ ἄμεινον ἢ μεθ' ἑτέρων ἀντιτέχνων, ἵνα ὁποιαοῦν ἀποδιδῶται τὰ βάμματα ταῖς γυναιξίν; ἀγαπήσουσι γὰρ ὠνούμεναι κἂν ὀλίγῳ βελτίω ἢ ὁποῖα εἰώθασιν αὐταὶ βάπτειν ἐν τοῖς

---

[1] χρήσιμον] χρὴ Arnim.
[2] ἂν Geel : ἐν M, omitted by UBPH.

Dio. Why not ; have they not come to hear wise words and about wise words ?

Int. They would say so, it seems to me.

Dio. But they do not regard Hesiod as commonplace and of small account, do they ?

Int. By no means.

Dio. Well, is it not useful for them to hear about envy and jealousy, and who those are who are envious and jealous of one another, and for what reasons ?

Int. Of course, most useful of all.

Dio. Then it is useful also to test the patience of the gentlemen without delay. Well now, does Hesiod have any other reason for saying that these men of his are envious and ill-disposed toward one another than because each would make less profit from his occupation, whatever that occupation may be, if there were many of a similar occupation ?

Int. Why, what other reason could it be ?

Dio. Then, if it is profitable for a potter that there should be no other potter in the same city or village, is this not profitable for a butcher, to the end that he may have the opportunity to sell whatever kind of meat he has to those who need it, even if by chance he has bought a very lean or oldish carcass ?

Int. Evidently it is profitable for a butcher too.

Dio. Well then, is it not preferable for a dyer to ply his trade as dyer all by himself rather than in competition with other craftsmen, so that he may be able to sell his dyes, of whatever quality they may be, to the women ? For they will then be satisfied to buy dyes even slightly better than the kind they are themselves accustomed to use for dyeing on their

---

³ After ἐργάζοιτο Geel deletes τῆς αὐτοῦ τέχνης (τὸ τῆς αὐτοῦ τέχνης UB, τὴν αὐτοῦ τέχνην PH).

ἀγροῖς ὡς ἔτυχε, καὶ οὐ ζητήσουσι δευσοποιὰ καὶ ἁλουργῆ.

Πῶς γὰρ ζητήσουσι;[1]

Δ. Φέρε, πορνοβοσκῷ δὲ οὐ κερδαλεώτερόν τε καὶ ἄμεινον πρὸς τὴν ἐμπολὴν μόνον ἔχειν τοῦτο τὸ[2] ὄνειδος καὶ μόνον αὐτὸν ἀκούειν κακῶς ἢ σὺν ἑτέροις, ὁμοίως μὲν ἐν πόλει τρέφοντα καὶ ἀσκοῦντα τοιοῦτον θρέμμα, ὁμοίως δὲ εἰς Πυλαίαν καὶ τὰς ἄλλας πανηγύρεις πορευόμενον καὶ περιάγοντα;

Καὶ πάνυ μοι δοκεῖ πορνοβοσκὸς εὔξασθαι ἂν ἀνδρῶν ὁμοτέχνων πολλὴν ἐρημίαν.

5 Δ. Ἆρ' οὖν καὶ περὶ πάντων ἁπλῶς οὕτως ὑπελάμβανε τῶν τὰς αὐτὰς ἐργασίας ἐργαζομένων, ὡς βλαβεροὺς ὄντας ἀλλήλοις καὶ ἐμποδὼν πρὸς τὸν βίον;

Περὶ πάντων, ὡς τὸ εἰκός.

Δ. Ἀλλ' οὐκ ἔπρεπεν, οἶμαι, καθ' ἕκαστον ἐπεξιέναι. καὶ γὰρ ἐπ' ἄλλοις ἔθος ἐστὶν αὐτῷ περὶ ὅλου τοῦ πράγματος φράζειν ἐφ' ἑνὸς ἢ δυοῖν· οἷον ὅταν φῇ μηδ' ἂν βοῦν ἀπολέσθαι τινὶ ἄνευ τῆς τοῦ γείτονος πονηρίας, οὐ δήπου φησὶν ὅτι βοῦν μὲν ἀπολέσαι ἂν γείτων πονηρὸς ἢ ἄλλοις[3] συγγνοίη, πρόβατον δὲ οὐκ ἂν ὑφέλοιτο,[4] ἐὰν δύνηται λαθεῖν, οὐδὲ αἶγα τῶν καλῶν τῶν πολὺ ἀμελγομένων καὶ διδυμοτοκουσῶν· ἀλλὰ δῆλον ὅτι ὡς πρὸς συνιέντας λέγει τοὺς ἐντυγχάνοντας τοῖς

---

[1] ζητήσουσι Reiske : ζητοῦσι.
[2] τὸ added by editio princeps.
[3] ἄλλοις Selden : ἄλλως.　　[4] ὑφέλοιτο Reiske : ἀπόλοιτο.

farms, dyes picked up at random, and they will not demand fast colours and royal purples.

Int. Of course they will not.

Dio. Well, how about a brothel-keeper? Is it not more profitable and better with a view to his earnings that he alone should have this reproach and alone be called vile names rather than in company with others, alike whether supporting and training that kind of cattle in the city or taking to the road and dragging his stock about to the congress at Thermopylae [1] and to the other great festive gatherings as well?

Int. Indeed I am quite sure that the brothel-keeper would pray that fellow artists might be very scarce.

Dio. Then, was it about all, that is, all who are engaged in the same line of business, that he was making an assumption in terms so sweeping, believing that all are detrimental to one another and a hindrance in the gaining of their living?

Int. Yes, he meant all, most likely.

Dio. Aye, it was not like him, I suppose, to take them up one by one. For certainly in other matters it is his custom to treat of the whole topic by means of one or two examples. For instance, when he says that a man would not even lose an ox except for the depravity of his neighbour,[2] he surely does not mean that, while a bad neighbour would destroy an ox or condone the crime in others, he would not steal a sheep, provided he could escape detection, or one of the fine goats which yield abundant milk and bear twins; nay, manifestly he speaks to those who read

---

[1] Thermopylae was the meeting place of the Delphic Amphictyony. [2] *Works and Days* 348.

6 ποιήμασιν. οὐκοῦν περὶ πάντων αὐτὸν ἑνὶ λόγῳ
φῶμεν ἐν βραχεῖ λέγειν οὕτως τῶν ὁμοτέχνων,
ὡς οὔτε φιλούντων αὑτοὺς οὔτε λυσιτελούντων
ἀλλήλοις;

Πάνυ μὲν οὖν.

Δ. Φέρε δὴ πρὸς θεῶν, ἡ ναυτικὴ τέχνη ἐστίν,
ἢ ἧττόν[1] τι τῆς κεραμευτικῆς ἢ τῆς μαγειρικῆς
τυγχάνοι ἂν τοῦδε τοῦ ὀνόματος;

Οὐχ ἧττον ἴσως.

Δ. Ἆρ᾽[2] οὖν ἐν νηὶ μεγάλῃ πολλὰ ἱστία ἐχούσῃ
καὶ φόρτον πολὺν καὶ ἀνθρώπων ἐπιβατῶν ὅμιλον
εἷς ναύτης καλῶς πράττοι ἄν, καὶ συμφέροι αὐτῷ
μηδένα ἄλλον ἐν τῇ νηὶ πλεῖν μήτε μᾶλλον αὐτοῦ
μήτε ἔλαττον ἐπιστάμενον τὰ ναυτικά, ἂν δὲ πολλοὶ ὦσιν, ἀσύμφοροι ἀλλήλοις ἔσονται καὶ πρὸς
βλάβης, καὶ διὰ τοῦτο ἐν νηὶ μισοῦσιν ἀλλήλους οἱ πλείονες ναῦται;

7 Τοῦτο μὲν ἕτερον τὸ τῶν ναυτῶν. ἀλλὰ κυβερνήτης γε, οἶμαι, κυβερνήτην οὐκ ἂν ἥδοιτο[3] ὁρῶν
συμπλέοντα αὐτῷ.

Δ. Πότερον ὅταν χειμὼν ἰσχυρὸς ᾖ καὶ μὴ
κατισχύῃ τοῖν πηδαλίοιν ἑκατέρου διὰ γῆρας ἢ
διὰ βίαν τῆς θαλάττης, οὐδὲ τότε φιλεῖ κυβερνήτην ἄλλον οὐδ᾽ εὔχεται φανεῖσθαι τὸν διαδεξόμενον,
οὐδ᾽ ὅταν κατακοιμηθῆναι δέηται, πολλὰς ἐφεξῆς
ἀγρυπνῶν νύκτας καὶ ἡμέρας, ἀλλὰ καὶ τότε
ὁμοίως μισεῖ καὶ ζημίαν αὐτοῦ νενόμικεν εἰ
κυβερνήτης ἐν τῇ νηὶ ἕτερός ἐστιν;

[1] ἢ ἧττόν Arnim : ἀλλ᾽ ἧττόν UBM, ἧττόν PH.

his poems as to intelligent persons. Are we, then, putting it concisely, to say that the poet, speaking thus briefly, refers to all who belong to the same craft as not loving one another and not benefiting one another ?

Int. Most assuredly.

Dio. Well now, in Heaven's name, is seafaring a craft, or would it receive that label in any degree less than the craft of the potter or of the butcher ?

Int. Not less, I suppose.

Dio. Then in a large ship with many sails and a large cargo and a crowd of passengers would a single sailor be successful, and would it be to his advantage to have no other sailor on board, be his knowledge of nautical affairs either greater or less than his own ; and, on the other hand, if there are many of them, will they be detrimental to one another and harmful, and on that account on a ship do the majority of the sailors hate each other ?

Int. This matter of the sailors is a different story. Yet at any rate a pilot, I fancy, would not enjoy seeing another pilot sailing with him.

Dio. When there is a violent storm and the pilot cannot control each of his two rudders because of old age or the violence of the sea, even at such a time does he not like another pilot or pray that the one to relieve him may make his appearance ; or, again, when he needs to sleep, having been without sleep for many nights and days together, even in such circumstances too does he feel the same hatred, and does he consider it his loss if a second pilot is on board ?

---

² ἴσως. Δ. Ἀρ' Pflugk : ἴσως γάρ.
³ ἥδοιτο Selden : ἡγοῖτο.

Οὐκ ἂν ἴσως τότε μισοῖ· πῶς γάρ; ἀλλ' ἡμεῖς οὐ περὶ ναυτιλίας οὐδὲ περὶ τῶν ἐν θαλάττῃ λεγόμεν.

8 Δ. Εἶεν· οὐκοῦν ὅ γε ἰατρὸς ἐπὶ γῆς ἰᾶται καὶ τέχνην οὐδὲν ἐλάττονα ἔχει τῶν τεκτόνων.

Τί οὖν δὴ τοῦτο;

Δ. Ἆρά γε δοκεῖ σοι βούλεσθαι μόνος ἂν εἶναι τὴν τέχνην ἐπιστάμενος ἐν πόλει τηλικαύτῃ τὸ μέγεθος, καὶ ταῦτα πολλῶν νοσούντων;

Τί δὲ κωλύει βούλεσθαι μόνον εἶναι; τοῖς μὲν γὰρ ἄλλοις ἴσως χεῖρον οὐ δυναμένοις ὑφ' ἑνὸς ἰατρεύεσθαι, τὸ δέ γε ἐκείνου τιμιώτερον οὕτως. οὐδὲ γὰρ εἰπεῖν ἔστιν ἡλίκων ἂν καὶ ὅσων μισθῶν τυγχάνοι μόνος ἐν τοσούτοις νοσοῦσιν ἱκανὸς ὢν ἰᾶσθαι.

Δ. Ἀλλ' οὐ μαινόμενον ἰατρὸν λέγω σοι.

9 Τί δέ; μαινομένου σοι δοκεῖ τὸ ἐπιθυμεῖν σφόδρα τιμᾶσθαι καὶ πολλὰ χρήματα λαμβάνειν;

Δ. Ὅταν γε αὐτὸς ὑπὸ ληθάργου ἐχόμενος ἢ φρενίτιδι περιπεσὼν χαίρῃ, ὅτι οὐδένα ἔχει[1] τὸν ἰασόμενον οὐδὲ τὸν δώσοντα μανδραγόραν πιεῖν ἢ ἄλλο φάρμακον ὑγιεινόν, ἵνα δὴ μόνος ἔχῃ τοὺς ἐν τῇ πόλει μισθούς τε καὶ τιμάς. εἰ δὲ δὴ σὺν αὐτῷ καὶ τὰ παιδία νοσοῖ καὶ ἡ γυνὴ καὶ οἱ φίλοι πάντες ἐπισφαλῶς, ἆρα καὶ τότε εὔχοιτ' ἂν μηθένα ἄλλον ἰατρὸν εὑρεθῆναι τὸν βοηθήσοντα

[1] ἔχει Reiske : ἔχοι.

SEVENTY-SEVENTH/EIGHTH DISCOURSE

Int. Perhaps he would not hate him then ; how could he ? Still, we are not speaking of a sailor's craft or of nautical affairs either.

Dio. Very well. The physician, at any rate, practises his healing art on land and has a profession not inferior to that of the joiners.

Int. Well, what of that ?

Dio. Do you really suppose he would like to be the only one acquainted with his art in a city as large as this, particularly if many are ill ?

Int. What is to prevent his wishing to be the only one ? For though for everybody else the situation may be worse, since they cannot all be treated by a single physician, still his work is prized more highly under these conditions. Nor can one tell the amount and the number of the fees he might take in if he, single-handed in the midst of so many sick, were able to provide treatment.

Dio. But I am not speaking to you of a physician who is crazy.

Int. What ! Do you consider it the mark of insanity in a man to wish to be very highly prized and to amass great wealth ?

Dio. Yes, if when he himself is a victim of lethargic fever or has an attack of inflammation of the brain he is delighted that he has no one to cure him and give him a potion of mandragora [1] to drink or some other healthful drug, his purpose being, forsooth, to be the only one to get the fees and honours in the city. But if, then, besides himself, his children also and his wife and his friends should be ill, all dangerously ill, would he even then pray that no other physician be found to come to his rescue ; and if

[1] Mandragora was a recognized sedative.

ἐὰν δὲ φανῇ τις, κατὰ τὸν Ἡσίοδον κοτέειν μέλλει
καὶ ἐχθρὸν ἡγεῖσθαι τὸν αὑτοῦ σωτῆρα καὶ τῶν
φιλτάτων;

10   Φέρε, ἐὰν δὲ συμβῇ πρᾶγμα τοιοῦτον ὁποῖόν
ποτε συνέτυχε περὶ τοὺς Αἰγυπτίους ἰατρούς·
ἐκεῖνοι γὰρ ἰώμενοι Δαρεῖον τὸν Πέρσην—ὡς
ἔτυχεν αὐτῷ πεσόντι ἀπὸ τοῦ ἵππου μεταχωρήσας
ὁ ἀστράγαλος—οὐχ οἷοί τε ἦσαν ἰᾶσθαι κατὰ τὴν
αὑτῶν τέχνην, ἀλλ᾽ εἰς ἀγρυπνίας τε καὶ ἀλγηδόνας
δεινὰς ἐνέβαλον αὐτόν, ἕλκοντες καὶ βιαζόμενοι
τὸ ἄρθρον. τούτους μὲν οὖν ἐκέλευσε φυλάττειν,
ὅπως ἀποθάνοιεν στρεβλωθέντες. πυθόμενος δ᾽
ἐν τοῖς αἰχμαλώτοις εἶναί τινα Ἕλληνα ἐπιχειροῦντα ἰᾶσθαι, καλέσας αὐτὸν ὑπὸ ἀμηχανίας
11 ἐκέλευσεν, εἴ τι ἔχοι, βοηθεῖν. ἦν δὲ ἄρα Δημοκήδης[1] ὁ Κροτωνιάτης, ὅσπερ ἄριστος ἐδόκει τῶν
τότε ἐν τοῖς Ἕλλησιν ἰατρῶν· ὃς καὶ παραχρῆμα
μὲν καθυπνῶσαι αὐτὸν ἐποίησεν, εἶτα καταπλάτ-
των καὶ καταιονῶν καὶ τἆλλα ἐπιμεληθεὶς ὀλίγων
ἡμερῶν ὑγιῆ ἀπέδειξεν. κελεύσαντος δὲ Δαρείου
λαβεῖν ὅ τι βούλεται, τοὺς ἰατροὺς παρῃτήσατο
ἀφεῖναι αὐτόν. καὶ μέντοι ἀφείθησαν, ἐκείνου
δεηθέντος. πότερον οὖν τότε ἐφθόνουν τῷ Δημοκήδει[2] καὶ ἐχθρὸν ἡγοῦντο, ᾗ φησιν Ἡσίοδος
ἐπὶ τῶν κεραμέων ἢ τεκτόνων, λυσιτελεῖν νομίζοντες αὑτοῖς εἰ μηδεὶς ἄλλος ἰατρὸς ἐφάνη

─────────────────────────
[1] Δημοκήδης Dindorf: δημοδόκης or δημόδοκος.

one does make his appearance, is the physician likely, as Hesiod puts it, to rage and to regard as an enemy his own saviour and the saviour of those dearest to him ?

Again, suppose there should occur some such thing as once befell the Egyptian physicians. You see, they tried to cure Darius the Persian—for in falling from his horse his ankle bone happened to slip out of place—and they were unable by means of their own art to correct the injury, but, instead, they brought upon him insomnia and awful pains by pulling the joint and trying to force it into place. So Darius gave orders to keep these men in prison, intending that they should be tortured to death. But learning that among his captives there was a certain Greek who endeavoured to heal people, summoning him in desperation he ordered him to help him if he could. Now the man was Democedes of Croton, who was considered the ablest of the Greek physicians of that day. And he did immediately cause him to fall asleep, and then by means of poultices and fomentations and so forth within a few days he made him sound and well. But when Darius bade him take as reward anything he pleased, he besought him to release the physicians. And, indeed, they were released, because Democedes had requested it.[1] Now I ask you whether in such circumstances they were jealous of Democedes and regarded him as an enemy, as Hesiod says is true with the potters or the joiners, because they believed it to be to their advantage if no other physician turned up and cured

[1] For a fuller narrative of this episode, see Herodotus 3. 125 and 129-132.

---

[2] Δημοκήδει Dindorf: Δημοδόκῳ.

βασιλέα ἰασάμενος, ἢ σφόδρα ἠγάπων καὶ χάριν
ᾔδεσαν;

Εἰκὸς μὲν ἦν χάριν εἰδέναι.

12 Δ. Καὶ μὴν θωρακοποιοί εἰσιν ἐν ταῖς πόλεσι
καὶ κρανοποιοὶ καὶ τειχοποιοὶ καὶ δορυξόοι καὶ
ἕτεροι πλείους· εἰ οὖν τούτοις λυσιτελεῖ ἕνα
ἕκαστον ἐν ἑκάστῃ τῶν πόλεων εἶναι τῆς τέχνης
δημιουργὸν μᾶλλον ἢ τοὺς ἱκανοὺς ἡδέως ἔγωγ᾽
ἂν πυθοίμην. δῆλον γὰρ ὡς πολεμίων ἐπιόντων,
καὶ μήτε τῶν τειχῶν ἑστηκότων μήτε ὡπλισμένων
ἁπάντων, ἀναγκάζοιντ᾽ ἂν ἄνοπλοι καὶ ἀτείχιστοι
13 διακινδυνεύειν. ὥστε ἁλούσης τῆς πόλεως οὐκ
ἂν ἴσως οὗτοί γε ἀποθάνοιεν, ληφθέντες δὲ καὶ
δεθέντες προῖκα ἂν ἐργάζοιντο τοῖς πολεμίοις
πρὸς ἀνάγκην, ἀνθ᾽ ὧν πρότερον θρυπτόμενοι
πολλῆς τιμῆς ἀπεδίδοντο τούς τε θώρακας καὶ τὰ
κράνη καὶ τὰ δόρατα, καὶ γνοῖεν ἂν ὅτι οὐκ ὀρθῶς
οὐδ᾽ ἐπ᾽ ἀγαθῷ ἐφθόνει καὶ ἐμήνιε διὰ τὴν τέχνην
οὔτε χαλκεὺς χαλκεῖ οὔτε τέκτονι τέκτων, οὐδὲ
λῷόν τε καὶ ἄμεινον ἦν αὐτῷ μόνον[1] ἢ σὺν ὀλίγοις
εἶναι τῆς τέχνης ἐργάτην.[2]

14 Ἀλλὰ δὴ τοῖς μὲν ἄλλοις σχεδὸν οὐκ ἀεὶ βέλτιον
ὅ φησι[3] βούλεσθαι αὐτοὺς Ἡσίοδος, μόνοις δὲ
τοῖς κεραμεῦσι καὶ μαγείροις τε καὶ βαφεῦσι καὶ
πορνοβοσκοῖς. οὐκοῦν ἡ ζηλοτυπία καὶ ὁ φθόνος
καὶ τὸ μηδένα ἄλλον ἐθέλειν πράττειν τὸ αὐτὸ
ἔργον μαγειρικόν τε καὶ βαφικὸν καὶ κεραμευτικὸν
καὶ ἔτι[4] μᾶλλον πορνοβοσκοῖς προσῆκον ἤπερ

---

[1] μόνον] μόνῳ Pflugk.
[2] ἐργάτην Emperius : ἐργάταις.
[3] βέλτιον, ὅ φησι Arnim, βέλτιον ὡς φησι Selden : βελτίους
φησὶ (φήσει).
[4] ἔτι deleted by Arnim.

the king, or whether they felt a strong affection for Democedes and were grateful to him.

Int. It would be reasonable to suppose they were grateful.

Dio. Again, there are corselet-makers in the cities and helmet-makers and wall-builders and spear-polishers and many others; whether, therefore, it is to their advantage that only one in each city should be a worker at each craft rather than enough to do the work is a matter I would gladly learn. For it is clear that, if enemies attack at a time when the walls have not been completed and not all the citizens have been equipped with arms, then they would be forced to hazard all without arms and walls. Therefore, if the city were taken, though possibly these craftsmen might escape with their lives, still, taken captive and in chains, they would work for the foe without pay and at forced labour, all because previously they had lived pampered lives and sold their corselets and helmets and spears at an excessive price, and they would recognize that it was not right nor for their own good for a craftsman to be jealous or angry because of his craft, whether it was black-smith against blacksmith or joiner against joiner, and that it was not more profitable or better for him to be the only worker at his craft than to have a few fellow workers.

Well then, for the others, I dare say, what Hesiod says they desire is not always preferable, but only for the potters and butchers and dyers and brothel-keepers. Then jealousy and envy and the desire that no one else shall ply the same trade, whether it be that of the butcher or the dyer or the potter, are even still more suitable for the brothel-keepers

ἰατροῖς τε καὶ κυβερνήταις ἢ ἄλλο τι σπουδαιότερον πράττουσιν.

Εἶεν. ἀλλ᾽ εἰ κυβερνήταις τε καὶ ἰατροῖς καὶ οἷς νῦν δὴ ἐλέγομεν οὐ βέλτιον ἐν σπάνει τῶν ὁμοτέχνων ζῆν, ἦπου τοῖς γε φρονίμοις καὶ σοφοῖς ἀνδράσι λῷόν τε καὶ ἄμεινον ὁρᾶσθαι μόνοις;

Οὐδαμῶς.[1]

15 Δ. Ὅτι πρὸς τῷ μεγαλόφρων τε εἶναι καὶ ἄλυπος ὁ νοῦν ἔχων καὶ φιλάνθρωπος, καὶ τὴν ἀρετὴν ἐπίστασθαι συμφέρουσαν αὑτῷ, τήν τε αὑτοῦ καὶ τὴν τῶν πέλας, καὶ μηδέποτε ἂν ὑπὲρ τούτων μηδένα μηδὲ τῶν φαυλοτέρων ἄλλον ἄλλῳ φθονεῖν,[2] ἃ κοινὰ ὑπάρχει πᾶσιν ἀγαθά· πρὸς τούτοις πᾶσιν οὐδὲ τῶν ἄλλων ἐφ᾽ οἷς ὅ τε φθόνος γίγνεται καὶ τὸ βασκαίνειν ἀλλήλοις τοὺς πολλούς, οὔτε θαυμάζει τὸ παράπαν οὐδὲν οὔτε ἄξιον σπουδῆς νενόμικεν, οἷον δὴ χθὲς περὶ πλούτου ἐλέγομεν.

16 ὥστε οὐδ᾽ ἂν φθονήσειεν οὐδενὶ χρυσοῦ ἢ ἀργύρου ἢ βοσκημάτων ἢ οἰκίας ἢ ἄλλου τῶν τοιούτων, ὑπὲρ ὧν ἐλέγομεν· ὥς φησιν ἕτερος ποιητής, οὐχ αὑτοῦ γνώμην ἀποφαινόμενος, ἀλλὰ τὴν τῶν ἀνθρώπων ἐξηγούμενος δόξαν·

οἷσίν τ᾽ εὖ ζώουσι καὶ ἀφνειοὶ καλέονται·

ὡς μόνον καλουμένων αὐτῶν ἀφνειῶν, ἀλλ᾽ οὐκ ὄντων κατ᾽ ἀλήθειαν.

17 Εἶεν· οὐκοῦν χρημάτων μὲν κρείττων ὁ γενναῖος καὶ τέλειος ἀνὴρ ἡμῖν δοκεῖ· περὶ δὲ δόξης τυχὸν

---

[1] What follows is found only in UBM and is preceded by the heading περὶ φθόνου β or περὶ φθόνου. See Introduction.
[2] φθονεῖν Wyttenbach : φρονεῖν.

---

[1] *Odyssey* 17. 423.

than for physicians and pilots or for those who are
engaged in any other more serious pursuit.

Very good. But if for pilots and physicians and
those just mentioned it is not better to live where
there is a shortage of their fellow craftsmen, can it
be that for men of prudence and wisdom it is better
and more profitable to find themselves without
associates ?

Int. By no means.

Dio. Yes, because with the man of intelligence and
benevolence, in addition to his being magnanimous
and inoffensive, in addition to his knowing that virtue
is beneficial to him, both his own virtue and that of
his neighbours, and in addition to the unlikelihood
that any one, even of the commoner sort, would ever
be jealous one toward another regarding these things
which are the common blessings of all mankind—
in addition, I say, to all this, of the other things which
are the occasion of envy and reciprocal ill-will among
the masses, not only does he not admire a single one,
but he does not consider any to deserve serious regard,
just as yesterday we were saying with reference to
wealth. Consequently, neither would he envy any
one gold or silver or cattle or house or any other
thing such as we were speaking of—as another poet
says, not expressing his own private sentiment but
expounding the opinion of mankind,

> The things whereby men live at ease and gain
> The epithet of affluent,[1]

his idea being that they merely are called affluent,
but are not truly so.

Very well ; then, we are agreed, the high-minded,
perfect man is above material wealth ; but in the

275

ἐρίζοι ἂν[1] καὶ φθονοῖ οὓς ἂν τιμωμένους μᾶλλον
παρὰ τῷ πλήθει βλέπῃ καὶ μειζόνων ἐπαίνων
τυγχάνοντας; ἢ οὐκ ἀγνοεῖν φήσομεν ὡς ἔστιν
ἡ δόξα ὁ παρὰ τῶν πολλῶν ἔπαινος· εἰ δὲ τῶν
πολλῶν, δῆλον ὅτι τῶν οὐκ εἰδότων;

Οὐδαμῶς τοῦτό γε εἰκὸς αὐτὸν ἀγνοεῖν.

18 Δ. Φέρε οὐκοῦν[2] δοκεῖ σοι ἀγαθὸς αὐλητὴς
ἥδεσθαι ἐπὶ τῇ τέχνῃ καὶ μέγα φρονεῖν ὑπὸ ἀμού-
σων καὶ ἀτέχνων ἐπαινούμενος, κἂν εἰ περιστάντες
αὐτὸν παῖδες συφορβοὶ καὶ ποιμένες θαυμάζοιεν
καὶ κροτοῖεν, ἐπαίρεσθαι ἐπ' αὐτῷ τούτῳ καὶ τοῦ[3]
παντὸς ἄξιον ἡγεῖσθαι τὸν παρ' ἐκείνων ἔπαινον;
ἀλλὰ μὴν ἐδήλωσεν ὁ Θηβαῖος αὐλητὴς οὔτε[4]
τῷ θεάτρῳ πάνυ προσέχων τὸν νοῦν οὔτε[5] τοῖς
κριταῖς ἀπείροις οὖσιν αὐλήσεως, καὶ ταῦτα περὶ
ἄθλου καὶ νίκης ἀγωνιζόμενος· ἀλλ' ὅμως οὐδὲ
μικρὸν ἐκβῆναι τοῦ ῥυθμοῦ τοῦ πρέποντος ἐτόλ-
μησεν, αὑτῷ δὲ καὶ ταῖς Μούσαις αὐλεῖν ἔφη.

19 τί οὖν; οἴει τὸν Ὀρφέα, τὸν τῆς Μούσης υἱόν,
εἰ ἀληθὴς ὁ κατ' αὐτὸν μῦθος, μᾶλλον ἂν χαίρειν
τῶν ὀρνίθων καταπετομένων πρὸς αὐτὸν ᾄδοντα
καὶ τῶν θηρίων κηλουμένων ὑπὸ τῆς φωνῆς καὶ
παρεστηκότων πρᾴως καὶ ἀθορύβως ὁπότε ἄρξαιτο
μελῳδεῖν, ἔτι δὲ τῶν δένδρων προσιόντων ἅμα
τῷ καρπῷ τε καὶ ἄνθει, καὶ τῶν λίθων κινουμένων
καὶ ξυνιόντων, ὥστε μεγάλα ἕρματα ἀθροίζεσθαι
λίθων πλησίον αὐτοῦ, μᾶλλον ἐπὶ τούτοις γιγνο-
μένοις ὁρῶντα τέρπεσθαι καὶ μεγαλαυχεῖσθαι,

---

[1] ἐρίζοι ἂν Emperius : ἐριζοίαν Μ, ἐρίζοι UB.
[2] οὐκοῦν] οὖν Arnim.
[3] τοῦ Reiske : τοῦτο Μ, τούτῳ UB.
[4] οὔτε Crosby : οὐδὲ.
[5] οὔτε Crosby : οὐδὲ.

matter of reputation would he perhaps quarrel with and envy those whom he sees more highly honoured by the crowd and winning greater plaudits? Or shall we say that he is not unaware that fame is the praise bestowed by the masses; but if the masses, evidently the unintelligent?

Int. By no means is it likely that he is ignorant of that.

Dio. Well then, do you believe that a good flautist takes pleasure in his skill and is proud when praised by unmusical and unskilled persons, and that, if youthful swineherds and shepherds crowding around him express their admiration and applaud him, he is elated over this thing itself and feels that praise from those persons is worth everything? Why, the Theban flautist made it plain that he did not pay very much attention either to the audience in the theatre or to the judges, inexperienced in flute-playing as they were—and that, too, although he was contending for a prize and victory—but for all that, he did not venture to depart even slightly from the proper rhythm, but he said that he was piping for himself and the Muses. What then! Do you suppose that Orpheus, the son of the Muse—if the tale about him is true—would rejoice more when the birds flew down to him as he sang and the wild beasts were entranced by his voice and stood by tamely and quietly every time he began to make melody, and when, moreover, the trees came toward him with their fruit and flowers, and when the stones moved and came together, so that great cairns of stones were collected near him—do you suppose, I say, that at the sight of these doings he was delighted and proud, believing that he had reached

νομίζοντα τῆς μουσικῆς ἥκειν ἐπ' ἄκρον, ἢ εἴπερ
ἡ μήτηρ αὐτὸν ἡ Καλλιόπη κιθαρίζοντα ἐπήνεσέ
τε καὶ εἶπε καταψήσασα ἅμα τὴν κεφαλήν, ὡς
ἱκανῶς ἔχοι μουσικῆς καὶ σοφώτατος εἴη τὰ τῆς
20 τέχνης; ἐγὼ μὲν γὰρ οἶμαι μᾶλλον ὑπὸ Φιλάμ-
μωνος αὐτὸν ἐθέλειν ἐπαινεθῆναι περὶ μουσικὴν ἢ
εἴ τις ἦν τῶν τότε ἔμπειρος κιθαρῳδίας ἢ ξυμ-
πάντων ἁπλῶς τῶν θηρίων τε καὶ ὀρνέων· ἀλλ'
οὐδὲ τῶν κύκνων ἐπιβοώντων καὶ συμφθεγγομένων[1]
φροντίσαι ἂν οὐδέν, ὅτι οὐκ εἶχον τέχνην οὐδὲ
ἐπιστήμην περὶ τὸ μελῳδεῖν.

Εἶεν· τί δέ; ὑγιείας μάρτυρα καὶ ἐπαινέτην
βούλοιτ' ἂν ὁ νοῦν ἔχων ἀνὴρ ἕνα λαβεῖν, ὅστις
ἰατρικὸς καὶ περὶ σώματος θεραπείας ἔμπειρος,
ἢ πολλὰς μυριάδας ἀνθρώπων οὐδὲν ἐπαϊόντων,
οἵ, ἂν[2] οὕτω τύχῃ, πεπρημένον ὁρῶντες αὐτὸν ὑπὸ
νόσου καὶ οἰδοῦντα καὶ ὕπουλον, μακαρίζοιεν ὡς
Πουλυδάμαντα τὸν Θετταλὸν καὶ Γλαῦκον τὸν
21 Καρύστιον ἡγούμενοι διαφέρειν εὐεξίᾳ; ἀλλὰ εἰς
μὲν αὔλησιν καὶ κιθαρῳδίαν καὶ τὸ[3] περιεῖναι παλαί-
οντα ἢ πυκτεύοντα τῶν ἄλλων ἁπάντων[4] ὁ τῶν ἐπι-
σταμένων ἔπαινος ἥδιστος τοῖς εἰδόσι καὶ πλείστης
σπουδῆς ἄξιος· εἰς δὲ φρόνησιν καὶ δικαιοσύνην
καὶ ξύμπασαν ἀρετὴν ἱκανὸς εὐφρᾶναι τὸν νοῦν

---

[1] συμφθεγγομένων Selden : συμφθειρομένων.
[2] οἵ, ἂν Casaubon : οἱ ἂν M, ᾧ ἂν U, ὦ ἂν B.
[3] τὸ added by Reiske.
[4] After ἁπάντων Morel deletes οὐδαμῶς.

---

[1] Father of Thamyris and contemporary with Orpheus.
278

the pinnacle of musical success, more than if his mother Calliopê had praised his playing the cithara and had stroked his head and said that he was fairly competent in music and very skilful in the fine points of his art ? I fancy he would rather be praised by Philammon [1] for musical skill or by any one then living who was acquainted with the art of singing to the cithara, than by absolutely all the beasts and birds together ; nay, even if the swans had uttered cries of praise and had accompanied him with their notes, he would not have given them a moment's notice, because they did not possess skill, or even knowledge, about the art of making melody.

Very good ; what then ? In the matter of health would the man of sound judgement desire to win the testimony and commendation of a single individual who is a skilled physician and conversant with care of the body, or, instead, that of countless thousands who have no understanding, who, as likely as not, on seeing him bloated with disease and swollen and ulcerous, would congratulate him as they would Pulydamas the Thessalian and Glaucus the Carystian,[2] supposing him to be in prime condition ? Well, if as regards flute-playing and singing to the cithara and pre-eminence as a wrestler or a boxer the praise of experts above all others is sweetest to the ears of connoisseurs and worth the most serious attention, as regards wisdom and justice and virtue as a whole

said to have won a prize for singing at the Pythian Games ; cf. Pausanias 10. 7. 2.

[2] Both were unusually tall and strong and both had statues at Olympia, Pulydamas having won in wrestling in 408 B.C. and Glaucus in boxing in 480 B.C. ; cf. Pausanias 6. 5 and 6. 10. 1. Greek athletes were commonly of heavy build.

ἔχοντα καὶ ἀποπληρῶσαι τὴν διάνοιαν ὁ[1] τῶν
ἠλιθίων καὶ τῶν ἐπιτυχόντων;

Οὐδαμῶς.[2]

22 Δ. Καὶ πότερον οἴει τὸν ἔμπειρον τῆς τεκτονικῆς τέχνης, εὐθύ τι ἐργάσασθαι βουλόμενον, ἑνὶ
προσαρμόσαντα κανόνι καὶ μιᾷ στάθμῃ σταθμη-
σάμενον ἥδιον ἔχειν καὶ πεποιθέναι περὶ τῆς
ὀρθότητος μᾶλλον ἢ πολλοῖς τε καὶ ἀνωμάλοις
ξύλοις ἀπευθύνοντα καὶ καταμετροῦντα;

Φέρε πρὸς Διός, ἆρα ἀκήκοας ζωγράφου χαρίεν-
τος ἔργον γραφήν τινα προθέντος εἰς τὸ φανερὸν
23 ἵππου, θαυμαστήν τε καὶ ἀκριβῶς ἔχουσαν; φασὶ
γὰρ αὐτὸν κελεῦσαι παραφυλάττειν τὸν παῖδα τοὺς
ὁρῶντας, εἰ ψέγοιεν ἢ ἐπαινοῖεν, καὶ μνημονεύ-
σαντα ἀπαγγεῖλαι πρὸς αὐτόν. τῶν δὲ ἕκαστον
ἄλλον ἄλλο τι λέγειν περὶ τῆς γραφῆς καὶ αἰτιᾶσθαι,
τὸν μέν τινα, οἶμαι, τὴν κεφαλήν, τὸν δὲ τὰ ἰσχία,
τὸν δὲ περὶ τῶν σκελῶν, ὡς, εἰ τοιαῦτα ἐγεγόνει,
πολὺ κάλλιον ἂν εἶχεν. ἀκούσαντα δὲ τὸν γραφέα
τοῦ παιδός, ἐργασάμενον ἄλλην γραφὴν κατὰ τὴν
τῶν πολλῶν δόξαν καὶ ἐπίνοιαν, κελεῦσαι θεῖναι
παρὰ τὴν πρότερον. εἶναι οὖν πολὺ τὸ διαφέρον·
τὴν μὲν γὰρ ἀκριβέστατα ἔχειν, τὴν δὲ αἴσχιστα
καὶ γελοιότατα καὶ πᾶσι μᾶλλον ἢ ἵππῳ ἐοικέναι.

24 Δῆλον οὖν ὡς εἰ σφόδρα προσδεήσεται τοῦ παρὰ

---

[1] ὁ added by Reiske.
[2] Οὐδαμῶς added by Reiske.

is the praise of fools and nobodies sufficient to cheer the heart of the man of sense and to satisfy his intelligence?

Int. By no means.

Dio. Again, do you think that he who is acquainted with the joiner's art, when he wants a piece of furniture to be made true and straight, after he has fitted his work together by applying one straight-edge and one gauge is happier and more confident of the accuracy of his work than if he had done the adjusting and the measuring with several different and uneven strips of wood?

By Heaven, have you heard about the doings of an accomplished painter who had exhibited in public a painting of a horse, a wonderful work of art and true to life? They say, you remember, that he ordered his servant to observe those who looked at it, to see if they found fault with it or praised it, and to remember what they said and report back to him. The story goes on to relate that every man of them had something different to say about the painting and criticized it, one, I imagine, finding fault with the head, another with the haunches, another with the legs, to the effect that, if these parts had been done so and so, the work would be much better. And when the painter heard what his servant had to report, he made another painting, which conformed with the judgement and conception of the crowd, and he gave orders to place it beside the earlier one. Now the difference between the two was great; for the one was quite true to life, while the other was extremely ugly and ludicrous and resembled anything at all rather than a horse.

Clearly, therefore, if a person is going to be ex-

τῶν πολλῶν ἐπαίνου, τῆς αὑτοῦ[1] γνώμης ἡγούμενος κυριώτερον τὸν ἐκείνων ψόγον τε καὶ ἔπαινον, οὕτως ἕκαστα πράξει καὶ προθυμήσεται τοιοῦτον παρέχειν ἑαυτὸν ὁποῖον ἀξιοῦσιν οἱ πολλοί.
καὶ δῆλον ὅτι ἔσται ταχὺ μάλα ἐοικὼς ἀντ᾽ ἐκείνου
τοῦ πρότερον ἵππου, τοῦ φαύλως καὶ κατὰ τὴν
τοῦ ἑνὸς εἰργασμένου τέχνην, τῷ θαυμαστῷ καὶ
πολυτέχνῳ δημιουργήματι, μηδὲ αὐτοὺς ἐκείνους
ἀρέσκοντι τοὺς δημιουργούς, ὑπὸ τῆς ἁπάντων ἐπινοίας καὶ δημιουργίας συγκειμένῳ.

25   Καθάπερ ὁ μῦθός φησι τὴν Πανδώραν οὐχ ὑφ᾽
ἑνὸς τῶν θεῶν πεπλασμένην, ἀλλὰ κοινῇ ὑπὸ
πάντων, ἄλλο ἄλλου δωρουμένου καὶ προστιθέντος,
οὐδαμῶς σοφὸν οὐδ᾽ ἐπ᾽ ἀγαθῷ τὸ πλάσμα γενόμενον, παντοδαπὸν δὲ καὶ ποικίλον τοῖς λαβοῦσιν
ἀποβῆναι κακόν. ὅπου δὲ θεῶν ὄχλος καὶ δῆμος
κοινῇ δημιουργῶν καὶ ἐργαζόμενος οὐχ οἷός τε
ἐγένετο καλῶς τε καὶ ἀμέμπτως ἐργάσασθαι, τί
ἂν φαίη τις τὸν ὑπό γε ἀνθρωπίνης δόξης πλαττό-
μενον καὶ δημιουργούμενον βίον τε καὶ ἄνδρα;
δῆλον οὖν ὡς εἴ τις ἔφυ τῷ ὄντι φρόνιμος, οὐδὲν
ἂν προσέχοι τῷ λόγῳ τῶν πολλῶν οὐδὲ θεραπεύοι
τὸν παρ᾽ ἐκείνων ἔπαινον ἐξ ἅπαντος, ὥστε[2] οὐδὲ[3]
μέγα οὐδὲ τίμιον οὐδὲ ἀγαθόν, ὡς ἔπος εἰπεῖν,

---

[1] αὑτοῦ Dindorf : αὐτοῦ.   [2] ὥστε] ὅς γε Emperius.

ceedingly anxious to win the praise of the crowd as well, believing that its praise or censure has more weight than his own judgement, his every act and wish will be aimed to show himself the sort of person that the crowd expects. And manifestly he will presently be very like, not that first horse, which was executed with sincerity and in harmony with one man's conception of his art, but like that amazing product of multiple workmanship, not pleasing even to those men themselves, its creators, having been put together by the conception and workmanship of all the world !

Just so the myth says of Pandora, that she was fashioned, not by a single one among the gods, but jointly by them all, one contributing one gift and adding it to the whole, another another, the form thus fashioned proving to be by no means wise or destined for a good end either, but, as it turned out, a heterogeneous and complicated plague to those who got her.[1] But when a multitude of gods, yes, a democratic rabble, jointly creating and labouring at their task, proved unable by all their labour to turn out an excellent and faultless work, what would one say of that which is fashioned and created by human opinion, be it a way of life or a man ? Evidently, then, if one is by nature really prudent, he would pay no heed at all to the talk of the masses, nor would he court their praise by any and every means, and consequently he will never regard this praise as

[1] The famous story of Pandora occurs first in Hesiod, *Theogony* 570-602 and *Works and Days* 54-89. She proved a plague first of all to Epimetheus and then, through him, to mankind in general.

---

[3] οὐδὲ] οὐδὲν Gasda.

τοῦτό¹ ποτε ἡγήσεται. μὴ νομίζων δὲ ἀγαθὸν
βασκαίνειν ἐπ' αὐτῷ τοῖς ἔχουσιν ἀδύνατος.²

26 Οὔκουν τοιοῦτος ἡμῖν ὁ γενναῖος καὶ σώφρων
καὶ κεκολασμένος ἀνήρ, πλούτους τε καὶ ἐπαίνους
καὶ στεφάνους Ὀλυμπικούς τε καὶ Πυθικοὺς καὶ
γράμματα ἐν στήλαις καὶ μαρτυρίας ἐγγράφους
δήμων καὶ βασιλέων διώκων, ὅπως ἂν ᾖ περί-
βλεπτος καὶ φανερός, ἀλλ' εὐσταλής τε καὶ ἄτυφος
ὡς οἷόν τε χωρῶν διὰ τοῦ βίου, ταπεινὸς καὶ
κεκολασμένος αὐτὸς ὑφ' αὑτοῦ³ καὶ τῆς αὑτοῦ⁴
διανοίας, οὐθενὸς ἔξωθεν κόσμου προσδεόμενος
οὐδὲ ἐπιθέτου τιμῆς οὐδὲ φαλάρων καὶ πτερῶν,
ὥσπερ οἱ κακοὶ μισθοφόροι πτερὰ καὶ λόφους
ἀναλαβόντες καὶ Γοργόνας ἐπὶ τῶν ἀσπίδων καὶ
τοῖς δορατίοις ψοφοῦντες ἔπειτα φεύγουσιν, εἰ
μικρὸς καταλάβοι κίνδυνος.

27 Οἵους πολλοὺς ἰδεῖν ἔστι τῶν οἰομένων εἶναι
μακαρίων, ξεναγούς τινας καὶ δημαγωγοὺς καὶ σοφιστάς, ἐν θεάτροις καὶ παρὰ τοῖς μαθηταῖς καὶ
κατὰ σκηνὰς ἐντὸς στρατοπέδου μεγαλαυχουμέ-
νους, ὅταν τύχωσιν ὑποπιόντες⁵ τῆς μεσημβρίας,

Τρώων ἀνθ' ἑκατόν τε διηκοσίων τε ἕκαστος
στήσεσθαι·

τοὺς δὲ αὐτοὺς τούτους ἑνὸς ἀνθρώπου κατατρέ-

---

¹ τοῦτό] τοῦτόν Emperius.
² ἀδύνατος Emperius : ἀδύνατον.
³ ὑφ' αὑτοῦ Dindorf : ὑπ' αὐτοῦ.
⁴ αὑτοῦ Dindorf : αὐτοῦ.
⁵ ὑποπιόντες Emperius : ὑποπίνοντες.

important or valuable or, if I may say so, good. But not regarding it as a good, he will be incapable of viewing with malice on that account those who have it.

Accordingly, so high-minded, sane, and chastened a man as the one we have in mind is not the sort that chases after riches and praise and Olympic or Pythian crowns, nor after letters carved on tablets of stone and written testimonials of communities and kings, with a view to being universally admired and conspicuous; instead, he journeys through life without ostentation and free from arrogance, so far as possible, humble and chastened by himself and by his own conscience, having no need of any extraneous adornment or adventitious honour, nor of trappings and plumes, like your cowardly hireling soldiers, who affect plumes and crests and Gorgons on their shields, who rattle their little lances and then take to their heels if some trifling danger overtakes them.

Persons of this description are to be seen in large numbers among the would-be great—*condottieri* of a sort, popular leaders, and sophists, in theatres or before their pupils or among the tents inside a camp, uttering loud boasts on occasions when they chance to be tipsy at mid-day,[1]

> That each will be a match for one, yes, two
> Full companies of Trojan men [2];

yet these same persons, if a single human being runs

---

[1] It was not thought respectable to begin drinking so early in the day.

[2] *Iliad* 8. 233-234. Agamemnon upbraids his forces for cowardice in the face of Hector. More of the passage might well have been quoted, for it deals with boasting after immoderate eating and drinking.

χοντος καὶ διώκοντος προτροπάδην φεύγοντας,
ξύμπαντας οὐ φαινομένους ἐκείνου γ᾽[1] ἀξίους.

28 Ἀλλὰ μὴν οὐδ᾽ ἂν[2] ἡδονάς τινας, σίτων ἢ ποτῶν
ἢ ἀφροδισίων, ἢ γυναικὸς κάλλος ἢ παιδὸς ὥραν
τεθαυμακὼς καὶ τούτων ἐπιθυμῶν καὶ μεγάλα
ἡγούμενος, εὐδαιμονίζοι τοὺς τυγχάνοντας αὐτῶν,
σατράπας καὶ δυνάστας καὶ νὴ Δία βαναύσους
τινὰς καὶ οἰκότριβας πεπλουτηκότας, τοὺς μὲν
ἀπὸ τῆς τέχνης, τοὺς δὲ τὰ τῶν δεσποτῶν ὑφαιρου-
μένους· αὐτὸν δὲ οἰκτείροι τῆς ἀπορίας τε καὶ
ἐρημίας τούτων τῶν ἀγαθῶν[3] καὶ ἡγοῖτο οὐ τῶν
εὐτυχῶν· διὰ δὲ τοῦτο ἐκείνοις[4] φθονοῖ καὶ ἐπι-
βουλεύοι πάντα τρόπον καὶ εὔχοιτ᾽ ἂν ἀπολέσθαι
αὐτούς.

29 Ἦ καὶ συγχωρήσωμεν τὸν γενναῖον ἄνδρα καὶ
μεγαλόφρονα τὸ τῶν κυνῶν τε καὶ ἵππων καὶ
ἄλλων θηρίων πεπονθέναι πάθος, ἃ οὐ δύναται
κατέχειν ἑτέρων ἐμπιμπλαμένων τε καὶ ὀχευόντων,
ἀλλὰ χαλεπαίνει καὶ ἀγανακτεῖ καὶ ὀργίζεται τοῖς
ἀπολαύουσι καὶ ἕτοιμα ἐπιπηδᾶν καὶ δάκνειν καὶ
κυρίττειν καὶ πάντα τρόπον ἀλλήλοις πολεμεῖν
ἐστι[5] περὶ τῶν ἡδονῶν· κἀκεῖνον[6] οὕτως ἔχειν φῶμεν, ὡς ὁμολογοῦντα τούτων εἶναί τι σπουδαῖον
καὶ τὸν Σαρδανάπαλον ἡγούμενον ζηλωτόν, ὃς ἔφη
διατελέσαι τὸν βίον εὐωχούμενός τε καὶ ὑβρίζων
μετὰ εὐνούχων καὶ γυναικῶν, καὶ διὰ τοῦτο ζηλο-

---

[1] ἐκείνου γ᾽ Post, ἐκείνου Casaubon : ἐκείνους.
[2] ἂν added by Post.
[3] ἀγαθῶν Geel : ἀνθρώπων.
[4] ἐκείνοις Casaubon : ἐκεῖνος.
[5] ἐστι Reiske : ἔτι.   [6] κἀκεῖνον Casaubon : κἀκεῖνο.

at them and offers to give chase, will be seen to flee
in utter rout, the pack of them not showing themselves
a match for that lone man.

Nay more ; as for certain pleasures of food or
drink or fornication, or as for a woman's beauty or
the bloom of a boy, he would not, through having
become infatuated with these things and lusting after
them and counting them important, deem fortunate
those who get them—satraps and princes and, forsooth, vulgarians and flunkies who have become
wealthy, the former by the practice of their craft, the
latter by filching their masters' property—nor would
he pity himself for his poverty and for his lack of
these good things and look upon himself as not one
of the fortunate class ; nor would he on this account
envy the persons whom I have named, plot against
them in every way, and pray for their ruin.

Or shall we go so far as to acknowledge that our
noble, our magnanimous man is in no better case
than dogs and horses and the other beasts, which
cannot contain themselves when the other beasts
are stuffing their bellies or copulating, but are resentful and indignant and enraged against those which
are enjoying themselves, and are ready to pounce
upon and bite and butt and to wage all manner
of warfare against each other for the enjoyment of
these pleasures ; shall we say that he too is in that
condition, as though admitting that any of these
pleasures is of real importance, and that he regards
Sardanapalus as one to be envied, who declared that
he spent his life in feasting and in playing the wanton
with eunuchs and women,[1] and shall we say that on

[1] Strabo (14. 5. 9) reports that such a statement was
inscribed on a funeral monument of Sardanapalus.

287

τυπεῖν αὐτὸν τὴν τῶν τράγων τε καὶ ὄνων
εὐδαιμονίαν;

30 Μὴ γὰρ οὐδὲ εὐσεβὲς τὰ τοιαῦτα περὶ τοῦ
μετρίου καὶ πεπαιδευμένου διανοηθῆναί ποτε
ἀνδρός.

Δ. Οὐκοῦν εἰ μήτε διὰ δόξαν μήτε διὰ χρήματα
μήτε δι' ἡδονὰς βρώσεων ἢ πόσεων ἢ μίξεων
αὐτὸν ἢ ἄλλον οἴεται μακάριον μηδὲ ὅλως εἶναί
τι τῶν τοιούτων περιμάχητον ἢ τίμιον, οὐκ ἂν
διαφέροιτο περὶ αὐτῶν οὐδ' ἂν φθονήσειεν οὐδενὶ
ἐκείνων, οὐ μᾶλλον¹ ἢ τῆς ψάμμου τῆς ἐπὶ τοῖς
αἰγιαλοῖς ἢ τῶν κυμάτων τοῦ ψόφου τε καὶ ἤχου
31 τοῖς πρὸς τῇ θαλάττῃ οἰκοῦσιν· οὐδ' εἴ τῳ χρυσίον
αὐτόματον ἐκ τοῦ οὐρανοῦ τὸν κόλπον ἐμπλήσειεν,
ὥσπερ τῇ Δανάῃ δή ποτε λέγουσιν ἐν οἰκήματι
χαλκῷ φυλαττομένῃ χρυσίον ἐξαίφνης ἄνωθεν
εἰσρυῆναι διὰ τὸ κάλλος αὐτῆς, οὐδὲ εἰ χειμάρρους
αὐτῷ ποθεν ἐπέλθοι χρυσὸν πολὺν καὶ ἄθρουν
καταφέρων, ὥσπερ ἰλύν· καθάπερ, οἶμαί, φασι
Κροίσῳ πρότερον τὸν Πακτωλὸν διὰ μέσων
ἀφικνούμενον Σάρδεων ἕτοιμα χρήματα κομίζειν,
πλείω φόρον τε καὶ δασμὸν ἢ ξύμπασα Φρυγία
καὶ Λυδία καὶ² Μαίονές τε καὶ Μυσοὶ καὶ ξύμπαντες
οἱ νεμόμενοι τὴν ἐντὸς Ἅλυος.

32 Οὐδέ γε τὸν λαβόντα παρὰ Κροίσου τὴν δωρεὰν
ἐκείνην³ Ἀλκμέωνα ἐζήλωσεν οὔτε Σόλων οὔτε
ἄλλος οὐδεὶς τῶν τότε σοφῶν ἀνδρῶν, ᾧ φασι τὸν
Λυδὸν ἐπιτρέψαι τοὺς θησαυροὺς ἀνοίξαντα φέρειν

---

¹ οὐ μᾶλλον added by Reiske.
² καὶ added by Emperius.   ³ ἐκείνην Crosby : ἐκεῖνον.

this account he envies the happiness of goats and asses ?

Int. Why, it would perhaps be even impious ever to entertain such thoughts concerning the temperate man of cultivation.

Dio. Well then, if neither fame nor wealth nor pleasures of eating or drinking or copulation lead him to regard himself or any one else as fortunate or to suppose that any such thing at all is worth fighting over or valuable, he would not wrangle over them or begrudge any one those things any more than he would begrudge those who dwell near the sea either the sand upon the beaches or the roar and reverberation of the waves ; nay, not even if gold of its own accord were to fall from the sky and fill the fold of his garment, just as they say that once upon a time, when Danaë was being closely guarded in a bronze chamber, gold suddenly rained down upon her from above, drawn by her beauty [1] ; nay, not even if a torrent were to come from somewhere, sweeping down to him a flood of gold in a mass like mud, as, I believe, it is said that to Croesus in days of old the Pactolus, making its way through the midst of Sardis, brought ready wealth, a larger revenue and tribute than all Phrygia and Lydia, yes, and the Maeonians and Mysians and all who occupy the land this side the Halys River, brought him. [2]

Nay, not even the man who received from Croesus that famous gift did either Solon or any other of the wise men of that day envy, Alcmaeon, whom they say the Lydian allowed to open his treasuries and

---

[1] Zeus visited Danaë as a shower of gold and begot Perseus.

[2] Cf. Or. 33. 23 and Herodotus 5. 101.

DIO CHRYSOSTOM

αὐτὸν ὁπόσον βούλεται τοῦ χρυσοῦ. καὶ τοῦτον[1]
εἰσελθόντα πάνυ ἀνδρείως ἐμφορήσασθαι τῆς βασι-
λικῆς δωρεᾶς, χιτῶνά τε ποδήρη καταζωσάμενον
καὶ τὸν κόλπον ἐμπλήσαντα γυναικεῖον καὶ βαθὺν
καὶ τὰ ὑποδήματα ἐξεπίτηδες μεγάλα καὶ κοῖλα
ὑποδησάμενον, τέλος δὲ τὴν κόμην διαπάσαντα
καὶ τὰ γένεια τῷ ψήγματι καὶ τὸ στόμα ἐμπλήσαντα καὶ τὰς γνάθους ἑκατέρας μόλις ἔξω βαδί-
ζειν, ὥσπερ αὐλοῦντα τὴν τῆς Σεμέλης ὠδῖνα,
γέλωτα καὶ θέαν Κροίσῳ παρέχοντα καὶ Λυδοῖς.
33 καὶ ἦν τότε Ἀλκμέων οὐδεμιᾶς ἄξιος δραχμῆς,
ὡς εἶχεν ἱστάμενος.

Οὔτε οὖν ἐπὶ τούτοις, ὡς ἔφην, ζηλοτυπήσειεν
ἄν, οὔτε εἴ τινα βλέποι θαυμαζόμενόν τε καὶ
ὑμνούμενον ὑπὸ ἀνθρώπων μυρίων ἢ δισμυρίων,
εἰ δὲ βούλει,[2] κροτούμενον καὶ ταινιούμενον, κορω-
νιῶντα καὶ γαυριῶντα, καθάπερ ἵππον ἐπὶ νίκῃ,
παραπεμπόμενον ὑπὸ πλειόνων ἢ ὁπόσοι προ-
πέμπουσι τοὺς νυμφίους· αὐτὸς δὲ ἀδοξότερος μὲν
εἴη τῶν πτωχῶν, ἐρημότερος δὲ τῶν ἐν ταῖς ὁδοῖς
ἐρριμμένων, μηδενὸς δὲ ἀξιούμενος παρὰ μηδενὶ
λόγου, καθάπερ Μεγαρέας ποτέ φασι, διὰ τὸ μὴ
δύνασθαι θεραπεύειν μηδὲ πρὸς χάριν ὁμιλεῖν, ἅτε
αὐστηρὸς ὢν τὴν φύσιν καὶ ἀληθείας φίλος, οὐδὲν

---

[1] τοῦτον Crosby : τὸν.　　[2] βούλει Pflugk : βούλεται.

[1] Alcmaeon gave his name to the aristocratic house to
which Pericles belonged. This humorous tale of the origin
of his great wealth is told with evident relish by Herodotus
(6. 125), whom Dio follows closely. Croesus was repaying
Alcmaeon for his kindness to Lydian envoys who consulted
the oracle at Delphi.

carry off on his own person as much of the gold as
he wished.[1] And yet, so the story runs, he entered
in and set to work right manfully to load himself
with the king's bounty, girding about him a long,
trailing tunic and filling its womanish, deep fold and
the huge, capacious boots which he had put on for
that express purpose and finally, after sprinkling
the gold dust in his hair and beard and stuffing with
it his cheeks and mouth, with difficulty he came
walking out, the very image of a piper piping the
birth-pangs of Semelê,[2] thereby presenting a ludicrous
spectacle for Croesus and his Lydians. Moreover,
at that moment Alcmaeon was not worth a single
drachma, standing there in that condition.

So, as I was saying, our man of prudence would
not be moved to envy, either by these things or if
he were to see a man admired and extolled by ten
or twenty thousand human beings, or, if you please,
applauded and bedecked with ribbons, arching his
neck and prancing like a horse exulting in a victory,
escorted by more people than the crowds which
escort a bride and groom ; on the contrary, he might
himself be more inglorious than the beggars, more
destitute than the wretches who lie prostrate in the
streets, held worthy of no consideration at all by
anybody—just as they say was true of the Megarians
once on a time [3]—because of his inability to court
favour or to be agreeable in converse, being austere
by nature and a friend of truth, making no secret

[2] The story of Semelê, the Theban princess who died in
giving birth to the god Dionysus, occurred often in Greek
tragedy, but Dio's piper may well have performed in a
Semelê pantomime.

[3] Athenians spoke of the boorishness of Megarians, just
as they did of Boeotians.

ἀποκρυπτόμενος· οὐδὲ οὕτως πείσεται τὸ τῶν κεραμέων τε καὶ τεκτόνων καὶ ἀοιδῶν οὐδὲ[1] καμφθήσεταί ποτε δι' ἔνδειαν ἢ δι' ἀτιμίαν οὐδὲ μεταβαλεῖ τὸν αὑτοῦ τρόπον, κόλαξ καὶ γόης ἀντὶ γενναίου καὶ ἀληθοῦς φανείς.

34 Καίτοι τί ποτε βούλονται τῶν μακαρίων τινὲς θεραπεύεσθαι πρὸς ἀνθρώπων ἐλευθέρων εἶναι φασκόντων καὶ τοὺς καλουμένους φιλοσόφους ἐπὶ θύραις αὐτῶν[2] ὁρᾶσθαι ταπεινοὺς καὶ ἀτίμους, καὶ νὴ Δία[3] καθάπερ ἡ Κίρκη ἐβούλετο τὴν οἴκησιν αὐτῆς φυλάττεσθαι ὑπὸ λεόντων δειλῶν καὶ κατεπτηχότων; οὔκουν οὐδὲ ἐκεῖνοι λέοντες ὄντες ἐφύλαττον αὐτήν, ἀλλὰ δύστηνοι ἄνθρωποι καὶ ἀνόητοι, διεφθαρμένοι διὰ τρυφὴν καὶ ἀργίαν. 35 οὐκοῦν ὅταν ἴδῃ τις τῶν φιλοσόφων τινὰ καλουμένων περὶ τὰς αὐλὰς καὶ πρόθυρα σαίνοντα καὶ ταπεινὸν ἐκείνων, ἄξιον ἀναμνησθῆναι τῶν λεόντων, κυσὶν ὁμοίων πεινῶσι καὶ δειλοῖς, ὠρυομένων ὀξύτατον, ἅτε ὑπὸ φαρμάκων διεφθαρμένων.

Ἀλλὰ δή ἐστιν οὐκ οἶδ' ὁποῖόν τι ἡ τοιαύτη ἐπιθυμία. μυρίοι μὲν γάρ εἰσιν οἳ ἑκόντες καὶ πάνυ προθύμως θεραπεύουσι τοὺς πλουσίους καὶ δυνατοὺς καὶ μεστὰ πάντα κολάκων ἐστὶ καὶ μετ' 36 ἐμπειρίας καὶ τέχνης αὐτὸ πραττόντων. ὥστε οὐκ ἀπορίᾳ τοῦδε τοῦ χρήματος ζητοῦσι παρὰ τῶν εὖ[4] πεφυκότων, ἀλλ' ἔστιν ὅμοιον τοῦτο ἑτέρῳ ἐπι-

[1] οὐδὲ Arnim : οὐ.   [2] αὐτῶν Dindorf : αὑτῶν.
[3] καὶ νὴ Δία Emperius, καὶ Reiske : καὶ μὴ.
[4] εὖ] οὐ Emperius.

of his thoughts ; still, not even so will he behave like the potters and joiners and bards,[1] nor will he ever be warped through want or dishonour or change his own character, becoming a toady and cheat instead of noble and truthful.

And yet why on earth do some of the prosperous wish to be courted by persons who claim to be free men, and why do they wish the so-called philosophers to be seen at their doors, humble and unhonoured, just as, so help me, Circê wished her dwelling to be guarded by lions that were timid and cringing ?[2] Nay, it was not even real lions that guarded her, but wretched, foolish human beings, who had been corrupted by luxury and idleness.[3] Therefore, whenever any one beholds one of the so-called philosophers fawning about the courtyards and vestibules and grovelling, it is fitting to recall those lions of Circê's, which resembled hungry, cowardly curs, howling most shrilly, since they had been perverted by sorcery.[4]

Nay, to such a desire as I have mentioned I know not what name to give. For there are thousands who willingly, yes, very eagerly, cultivate the rich and influential, and all the world is full of flatterers, who ply that calling with both experience and skill. Therefore it is not for lack of this line of goods that men seek to obtain it from persons of good breeding ; rather this is like another enterprise of the very

---

[1] Here for the first time Dio includes the bards, who are coupled by Hesiod with the potters, joiners, and beggars, *Works and Days* 26.   [2] Cf. *Odyssey* 10. 212-219.

[3] An instance of the allegorical interpretation of Homer that was growing in popularity.

[4] *Odyssey* 10. 212-219. Homer mentions also wolves, and he says nothing of the howling.

χειρήματι τῶν σφόδρα ἀκολάστων, οἳ γυναικῶν
ἀφθόνων οὐσῶν δι' ὕβριν καὶ παρανομίαν ἐπιθυμοῦσιν ἐκ τῶν ἀνδρῶν γυναῖκας σφίσι γενέσθαι
καὶ λαβόντες παῖδας ἐξέτεμον. ὅθεν πολὺ κάκιον
καὶ δυστυχέστερον γένος¹ ἐγένετο, ἀσθενέστερον
τοῦ γυναικείου καὶ θηλύτερον.

37 Ἀλλ' ὅ γε πρὸς ἀλήθειαν ἀνδρεῖος καὶ μεγαλόφρων οὐκ ἄν ποτε πάθοι τοιοῦτον οὐδὲν οὐδ'
ἂν πρόοιτο τὴν ἐλευθερίαν τὴν αὑτοῦ καὶ τὴν
παρρησίαν τιμῆς τινος ἀτίμου χάριν ἢ δυνάμεως
ἢ χρημάτων, οὐδ' ἂν φθονοῖ τοῖς μεταβαλλομένοις
τε καὶ μεταμφιεννυμένοις ἐπὶ τοιαύταις δωρεαῖς,
ἀλλ' ἡγοῖτ' ἂν ὁμοίους² τοῖς μεταβάλλουσιν ἐξ
ἀνθρώπων εἰς ὄφεις ἢ³ ἄλλα θηρία· ἐκείνους μὲν
οὐ ζηλῶν οὐδὲ βασκαίνων αὐτοῖς τῆς τρυφῆς,
ἀλλὰ τοὐναντίον ὀλοφυρόμενος καὶ ἐλεῶν, ὅταν
ἐπὶ δώροις, ὥσπερ οἱ παῖδες, ἀποκείρωνται, καὶ
38 ταῦτα τὰς πολιάς· αὐτὸς δὲ τὸ καθ' αὑτὸν πειρά-
σεται διαφυλάττειν εὐσχημόνως καὶ βεβαίως,
μηδέποτε λείπων τὴν αὑτοῦ⁴ τάξιν, ἀρετὴν δὲ
καὶ σωφροσύνην τιμῶν ἀεὶ καὶ αὔξων καὶ πάντας⁵
ἐπὶ ταῦτα⁶ ἄγων, τὰ μὲν πείθων καὶ παρακαλῶν,
τὰ δὲ λοιδορούμενος καὶ ὀνειδίζων, εἴ τινα δύναιτο
ἐξελέσθαι ἀφροσύνης καὶ φαύλων ἐπιθυμιῶν καὶ
ἀκρασίας καὶ τρυφῆς, ἰδίᾳ ἕκαστον ἀπολαμβάνων
καὶ ἀθρόους νουθετῶν, ὁσάκις ἂν καιροῦ τύχῃ
τινός,

¹ After γένος Arnim deletes εὐνούχων.
² ὁμοίους Casaubon : ὁμοίως.
³ εἰς ὄφεις ἢ Emperius : ἐπ' ὄφεις ἢ UB, ἐποφθείση M.
⁴ αὑτοῦ Emperius : αὐτοῦ.

dissolute, who, although there are women in abundance, through wantonness and lawlessness wish to have females produced for them from males, and so they take boys and emasculate them. And thus a far worse and more unfortunate breed is created, weaker than the female and more effeminate.

But he who in very truth is manly and high-minded would never submit to any such things, nor would he sacrifice his own liberty and his freedom of speech for the sake of any dishonourable payment of either power or riches, nor would he envy those who change their form and apparel for such rewards ; on the contrary, he would think such persons to be comparable to those who change from human beings into snakes or other animals, not envying them, nor yet carping at them because of their wantonness, but rather bewailing and pitying them when they, like the boys, with an eye to gifts have their hair cut off, and grey hair at that ! [1] But as for himself, the man of whom I speak will strive to preserve his individuality in seemly fashion and with steadfastness, never deserting his post of duty, but always honouring and promoting virtue and sobriety and trying to lead all men thereto, partly by persuading and exhorting, partly by abusing and reproaching, in the hope that he may thereby rescue somebody from folly and from low desires and intemperance and soft living, taking them aside privately one by one and also admonishing them in groups every time he finds the opportunity,

[1] Long hair was the outward and visible sign of the philosopher.

---

5 πάντας Arnim : πάντα.
6 ταῦτα] ταύτην Reiske.

ἄλλον μειλιχίοις, ἄλλον στερεοῖς ἐπέεσσι,

39 μέχρι ἄν, οἶμαι, διέλθῃ τὸν βίον κηδόμενος[1] ἀνθρώπων, οὐ βοῶν οὐδὲ ἵππων οὐδὲ καμήλων τε καὶ
οἰκημάτων, ὑγιὴς μὲν ἐν λόγοις ὑγιὴς δὲ ἐν ἔργοις,
ἀβλαβὴς μὲν συνοδοιπόρος ὅτῳ γένοιτο ἢ σύμ-
πλους, ἀγαθὸς δὲ σύμβολος[2] θύουσι φανείς, οὐ
στάσιν ἐγείρων οὐδὲ πλεονεξίαν οὐδὲ ἔριδας καὶ
φθόνους καὶ αἰσχρὰ κέρδη, σωφροσύνης δὲ ὑπο-
μιμνήσκων καὶ δικαιοσύνης καὶ ὁμόνοιαν αὔξων,
ἀπληστίαν δὲ καὶ ἀναίδειαν καὶ μαλακίαν ἐξε-
λαύνων ὅσον δυνατόν, πολὺ τῶν σπονδοφόρων καὶ
τῶν κηρύκων τῶν ἐν τοῖς πολέμοις ἐκεχειρίας
κομιζόντων ἱερώτερος.

40 Βούλεται μὲν οὖν καὶ προθυμεῖται καθ' ὅσον
οἷός τέ ἐστι βοηθεῖν ἅπασιν· ἡττᾶται δ' ἑτέρων
ἐνίοτε ἀνθρώπων καὶ ἐπιτηδευμάτων καὶ οὐδὲν ἢ
μικρὸν ἰσχύει παντελῶς. λοιπὸν δὲ τὴν αὑτοῦ
διάνοιαν καθαίρει τῷ λόγῳ καὶ πειρᾶται παρέχειν
ἀδούλευτον, πολὺ μᾶλλον περὶ τῆς ἐλευθερίας
μαχόμενος ἡδοναῖς[3] τε καὶ δόξαις καὶ ἀνθρώποις
ἅπασι μετ' ὀλίγων τῶν βουλομένων ἢ Λακεδαιμό-
νιοί ποτε τὰ στενὰ καταλαβόντες ἐμάχοντο πρὸς
ἅπαντας τοὺς ἐκ τῆς Ἀσίας, ὀλίγοι τὸν ἀριθμὸν
ὄντες, τρεῖς ἐφεξῆς νύκτας τε καὶ ἡμέρας, μέχρι
κυκλωθέντες δι' ἑνὸς ἀνδρὸς προδοσίαν ἐν ταὐτῷ
41 μένοντες κατεκόπησαν[4]· τὸ δὲ σῶμα ἀσκῶν καὶ

---

[1] κηδόμενος Casaubon : ἡδόμενος.
[2] ἀγαθὸς δὲ σύμβολος Emperius : ἀβλαβὴς δὲ σύμβουλος,
ἀγαθὸς δέ.
[3] ἡδοναῖς Geel : ἢ ὀδύναις.
[4] After κατεκόπησαν Hertlein deletes οἳ τὴν Σπάρτην ἐνόμιζον
ἐλευθέραν διαφυλάττειν ἀτείχιστον οὖσαν: who believed that they
were preserving Sparta in its freedom, unwalled as it was.

With gentle words at times, at others harsh,[1]

until, methinks, he shall have spent his life in caring
for human beings, not cattle or horses or camels and
houses, sound in words and sound in deeds, a safe
travelling companion for any one to have on land
or sea and a good omen for men to behold when
offering sacrifice, not arousing strife or greed or
contentions and jealousies and base desires for gain,
but reminding men of sobriety and righteousness
and promoting concord, but as for insatiate greed
and shamelessness and moral weakness, expelling
them as best he can—in short, a person far more
sacred than the bearers of a truce or the heralds who
in times of war come bringing an armistice.

Therefore he wishes, yes, is eager, in so far as he
can, to aid all men ; though sometimes he is defeated
by other men and other practices and has little or
no power at all. Finally, he purges his own mind
by the aid of reason and tries to render it exempt
from slavery, fighting in defence of freedom a much
more stubborn battle against lusts and opinions and
all mankind, aided by the few who wish to help him,
than once the Spartans fought when, having seized
the pass, they gave battle to all the hordes from
Asia, few though those Spartans were, for three
nights and days in succession until, having been en-
veloped through one man's treachery, they stood
their ground and were hacked to pieces.[2] More-

---

[1] *Iliad* 12. 267, spoken of the chiding administered by
the two Ajaxes to their laggard fellow soldiers.

[2] At Thermopylae the traitor Ephialtes led the Persians
over a mountain trail to the rear of the Spartans. However,
Leonidas and his little band refused to flee, but fought to
the last.

συνεθίζων κατὰ τὴν ἑαυτοῦ δύναμιν πονεῖν, οὐκ
ἐῶν θρύπτεσθαι λουτροῖς τε καὶ ἀλείμμασι καὶ
μύροις, μέχρι ἂν γένηται μαλακώτερον καὶ σαθρό-
τερον, ὥσπερ κακὸν σκεῦος. ταῦτα δὲ ὁρῶντες
ἔνιοι δι' εὐήθειαν αὐτὸν ἐπιτηδεύειν καὶ ἀφροσύνην
φασί, τὸ πλουτεῖν ἐάσαντα καὶ τὸ τιμᾶσθαι καὶ
τὸ διὰ παντὸς ἥδεσθαι, καὶ[1] καταφρονοῦσι καὶ
42 μαίνεσθαι νομίζουσι καὶ ἀτιμάζουσιν. ὁ δὲ οὐκ
ὀργίζεται πρὸς αὐτοὺς οὐδ' ἔχει χαλεπῶς, ἀλλ'
ἔστιν, οἶμαι, καὶ πατρὸς εὐνούστερος ἑκάστῳ
καὶ ἀδελφῶν καὶ φίλων· καὶ δὴ καὶ τοὺς πολίτας
τοὺς αὐτοῦ[2] καὶ φίλους καὶ συγγενεῖς αἰδούμενος
μέν, οὐκ ἀποκρυπτόμενος δέ,[3] τοσούτῳ μᾶλλον
ὅσον τῶν ἄλλων οἰκειοτέρους τε καὶ ἀναγκαιοτέ-
ρους νενόμικεν, ὡς οἷόν τε ἐπιτείνας τοὺς λόγους
καὶ σφοδροτέραν τὴν νουθεσίαν καὶ παρακέλευσιν
ποιούμενος αὐτῷ τε κἀκείνοις.

43 Οὐδὲ γὰρ ἰατρός, ὅτῳ ἀνάγκη πατέρα ἢ μητέρα
ἢ τοὺς ἑαυτοῦ παῖδας ἰᾶσθαι νοσοῦντας ἢ καὶ
αὐτὸν διὰ σπάνιν τε καὶ ἐρημίαν ἄλλων ἰατρῶν,
εἰ δέοι τέμνειν ἢ καίειν, ὅτι φιλεῖ τὰ τέκνα καὶ
τὸν πατέρα αἰσχύνεται καὶ τὴν μητέρα, διὰ τοῦτο
ἀμβλυτέρῳ τῷ σιδήρῳ τέμοι ἂν καὶ χλιαρωτέρῳ
τῷ πυρὶ καίοι, τοὐναντίον δὲ ὡς οἷόν τε ἰσχύοντι
44 καὶ ἀκμαίῳ. τὸν γοῦν Ἡρακλέα φασίν, ἐπειδὴ
οὐκ ἐδύνατο ἰάσασθαι τὸ σῶμα ὑπὸ νόσου δεινῆς
κατεχόμενον, τοὺς υἱοὺς καλέσαι πρώτους κε-

---

[1] καὶ added by Jacobs.
[2] αὐτοῦ Dindorf : αὑτοῦ.
[3] After δέ Geel adds νουθετεῖ.

---

[1] Heracles was in torment from the poisoned " shirt of
Nessus " which his jealous wife had sent him in the hope

over, he trains his body, inuring it to labour with all his might, not allowing it to become enervated by baths and ointments and perfumes until it becomes too soft and as unsound as a bad vessel. But some who see him say that he follows these practices out of foolishness and stupidity, having neglected the opportunity to be rich, to be honoured, and to live a life of continual pleasure, and they scorn him, think him insane, and esteem him lightly. Yet he is not enraged at them or vexed ; on the contrary, I believe he is kinder to each one than even a father or brothers or friends. And in fact, though he shows respect for his own fellow citizens and friends and kinsmen, still he does not hide his thoughts from them—all the more so because he believes them to be closer to him than all others through home ties and relationship—stressing his words as much as possible and increasing the vehemence of his admonition and exhortation for himself and them alike.

Take, for example, the physician ; if he should find it necessary to treat father or mother or his children when they are ill, or even himself through scarcity or lack of other physicians, in case he should need to employ surgery or cautery, he would not, because he loves his children and respects his father and his mother, for that reason cut with a duller knife or cauterize with milder fire, but, on the contrary, he would use the most potent and vigorous treatment possible. For example, they say of Heracles, that when he was unable to heal his body, which had become the victim of a dread malady,[1] he called his sons first of all and ordered them to set

of recovering his love and loyalty ; cf. Or. 60 and Sophocles, *Trachiniae* 1046-1057.

λεύοντα ὑποπρῆσαι λαμπροτάτῳ πυρί· τῶν δὲ
ὀκνούντων καὶ ἀποστρεφομένων, λοιδορεῖν αὐτοὺς
ὡς μαλακούς τε καὶ ἀναξίους αὐτοῦ[1] καὶ τῇ μητρὶ
μᾶλλον ἐοικότας, λέγοντα, ὡς ὁ ποιητής φησι,

> ποῖ μεταστρέφεσθ᾽, ὦ κακοὶ
> καὶ ἀνάξιοι τῆς ἐμῆς σπορᾶς,
> Αἰτωλίδος ἀγάλματα μητρός;

45   Οὐκοῦν αὐτῷ[2] πρώτῳ χρὴ καὶ τοῖς φιλτάτοις
καὶ ἐγγυτάτω μετὰ πλείστης παρρησίας τε καὶ
ἐλευθερίας προσφέρεσθαι, μηδὲν ἀποκνοῦντα μηδὲ
ὑφιέμενον ἐν τοῖς λόγοις.   πολὺ γὰρ χεῖρον[3]
διεφθαρμένου σώματος καὶ νοσοῦντος ψυχὴ διεφθαρμένη, μὰ Δία, οὐχ ὑπὸ φαρμάκων χριστῶν[4]
ἢ ποτῶν οὐδὲ ὑπὸ ἰοῦ τινος διεσθίοντος, ἀλλ᾽ ὑπό
τε ἀγνοίας καὶ πονηρίας καὶ ὕβρεως καὶ φθόνου
δὴ καὶ λύπης καὶ μυρίων ἐπιθυμιῶν.   τοῦτο τὸ
νόσημα καὶ τὸ πάθος χαλεπώτερον ἐκείνου καὶ
πολὺ μείζονος καὶ λαμπροτέρου δεόμενον ἐμπρη-
σμοῦ· ἐφ᾽ ἣν ἴασιν καὶ ἀπόλυσιν χρὴ παρακαλεῖν
ἀπροφασίστως καὶ πατέρα καὶ υἱὸν καὶ ξυγγενῆ
καὶ ἀλλότριον καὶ πολίτην καὶ ξένον.

---

[1] αὑτοῦ Dindorf : αὐτοῦ.   [2] αὑτῷ Emperius : αὐτῷ.
   [3] After χεῖρον Reiske deletes καί.
      [4] χριστῶν Casaubon : χρειστῶν or χρηστῶν.

fire to him with most brilliant flame ; but when they were reluctant and shrank from the ordeal, he abused them as weaklings and unworthy of him and more like their mother, saying, in the words of the poet,

> Whither away, ye cravens and disgrace
> To my engendering, ye likenesses
> Of her, your mother, whom Aetolia bore ? [1]

Therefore toward oneself first of all, and also toward one's nearest and dearest, one must behave with fullest frankness and independence, showing no reluctance or yielding in one's words. For far worse than a corrupt and diseased body is a soul which is corrupt, not, I swear, because of salves or potions or some consuming poison, but rather because of ignorance and depravity and insolence, yes, and jealousy and grief and unnumbered desires. This disease and ailment is more grievous than that of Heracles and requires a far greater and more flaming cautery ; and to this healing and release one must summon without demur father or son, kinsman or outsider, citizen or alien.

[1] Nauck, *T.G.F.*, adespota 99. The mother of Heracles' sons was Deïaneira, daughter of Oeneus, king in Calydon, and sister of the famous Meleager.

THE SEVENTY-NINTH DISCOURSE:
ON WEALTH

THE title of this Discourse as preserved in Parisinus 2985 is περὶ πλούτου τῶν ἐν Κιλικίᾳ, but the other manuscripts give merely περὶ πλούτου. What is the explanation of the additional phrase contained in the Paris manuscript? Cilicia is not named in the document before us, and a careful scrutiny of the speech fails to reveal any clear clue to the place of its delivery. One may reasonably infer from the choice of subject that Dio was addressing an audience in some wealthy city. His opening sentence might suggest Rome as the setting, but, were that the case, one may question whether he would have identified himself with his hearers as he does in § 5. The logical conclusion would seem to be that the scribe of the Paris manuscript has preserved for us a genuine tradition, based upon some memorandum left by the author, or else, possibly, upon the circumstances attending the discovery of the speech by his editor.

Assuming the accuracy of the title referred to, one would naturally think of Tarsus as the city in which Dio was speaking, for two of the speeches in our collection were certainly delivered in that city (33 and 34), and Dio calls Tarsus " the greatest of all the cities of Cilicia and a metropolis from the outset " (Or. 34. 7).

The argument of our Discourse is, in brief, that wealth confers upon its owners no desirable distinction, possesses no real utility, is transitory in its nature, and leads to vulgar extravagance, in the course of which Celts, Indians, Iberians, Arabs, and Babylonians " take tribute " from the stupid and self-indulgent persons who covet their exotic products. That for which a city really merits commendation and congratulation is the excellence of its laws, the probity of its citizens, and the moderation of its rulers.

79. ΠΕΡΙ ΠΛΟΥΤΟΥ

1 Φέρε πρὸς θεῶν, ἐπὶ τίνι μάλιστα θαυμάζειν καὶ
ἐπὶ τῷ μέγα φρονεῖν καὶ μακαρίζειν ἄξιον πόλιν
ἁπασῶν μεγίστην καὶ δυνατωτάτην; πότερον ἐπὶ
νόμων ἀρετῇ καὶ πολιτῶν ἐπιεικείᾳ καὶ σωφροσύνῃ τῶν ἀρχόντων, ἢ ταῦτα μὲν μικρὰ καὶ
οὐδενὸς ἄξια καὶ ῥᾴδια τοῖς τυχοῦσιν, ἐπὶ δὲ ἀνθρώπων πλήθει καὶ ἀγορᾶς ἀφθονίᾳ καὶ τῇ πολυ-
τελείᾳ τῶν οἰκοδομημάτων δεῖ μακαρίζειν αὐτὴν
καὶ τοῖς Σύρων[1] καὶ Βαβυλωνίων ὑφάσμασι, καὶ ὅτι
χρυσῷ τὰς οἰκίας ἐρέπτουσι, καὶ μεστὰ πάντα ἀργύρου καὶ ἠλέκτρου καὶ ἐλέφαντος, ὁποῖα Ὅμηρος
εἴρηκε τὰ Ἀλκινόου καὶ τὰ Μενελάου βασίλεια
ὑπερβάλλων τό τε ἀληθὲς καὶ τὸ δυνατὸν σχεδόν, οὕτως ἅπασαν[2] ἠσκημένην τὴν πόλιν· καὶ νὴ
Δία ἐπὶ ταῖς γραφαῖς καὶ τοῖς ἀνδριᾶσιν, ὧν οὐδὲν ὤνησε τοὺς πρότερον ἔχοντας, ἀλλὰ παρ' ὧν
ἐκεῖνα ἐκομίσθη,[3] τούτους ἴδοι τις ἂν δούλους καὶ
ταπεινοὺς καὶ πένητας;

2 Εἰ γὰρ ἦν ὄφελός τι χαλκοῦ καλῶς κεκραμένου

---

[1] Σύρων] Σήρων Reiske.
[2] After ἅπασαν Casaubon adds πλάσας.
[3] ἐκομίσθη Emperius : ἐκοσμήθη.

---

[1] For his description, see *Odyssey* 7. 84-97 and 4. 71-75
respectively. In *Odyssey* 4. 73 ἠλέκτρου may mean a natural

THE SEVENTY-NINTH DISCOURSE:
ON WEALTH

Come now, in Heaven's name do tell me: on what account above all is it fitting to admire, yes, to feel proud of and to congratulate, a city which is the greatest and the most powerful of all? Is it for excellence of laws, for probity of citizens, and for moderation of its rulers; or are these things trifles and worthless and easy to come by for ordinary people, and is it rather for multitude of inhabitants, lavishness of market-place, and sumptuousness of its edifices that one should congratulate it, for its Syrian and Babylonian fabrics, and because its citizens roof their houses with gold and the whole place teems with silver and amber and ivory, like the palaces of Alcinoüs and Menelaüs which Homer has described [1] —overstepping the reality and the possibility too, one may venture to suggest—the city, I mean, having been equipped throughout in that fashion? Would it be, in Heaven's name, for its paintings and its statues, none of which had been of any service to their former owners; on the contrary, those from whom these things were obtained would be found to be slaves, of low estate, and poor?

For example, if there were any utility in bronze

alloy of gold and silver rather than amber, which is its usual meaning and the one required in § 4.

καὶ κρατήρων καὶ βωμῶν καὶ θυμιατηρίων
περιττῶς εἰργασμένων, ἡ Κορινθίων πόλις ἂν
εὐδαίμων ἦν καὶ πολὺν ᾠκεῖτο ἂν χρόνον, σῴ-
ζουσα τοὺς ἑαυτῆς οἰκήτορας καὶ πολίτας· εἰ δ'
αὖ λίθων εὐχρόων καὶ ποικίλων, ἡ[1] Τηίων ἢ
Καρυστίων καί τινων Αἰγυπτίων καὶ Φρυγῶν
παρ' οἷς ἐστι τὰ ὄρη ποικίλα· ἀκούω δ' ἔγωγε
τῶν σορῶν[2] τὰς πάνυ παλαιὰς τῆς αὐτῆς εἶναι
πέτρας· ἀλλ' ὅμως οὐδενός εἰσι βελτίους οὐδ' εὐ-
τυχέστεροι τῶν πάνυ ταπεινῶν[3] τε καὶ ἀθλίων.

3   Εἰ δέ γε ὠφέλει τὸ κεκτῆσθαι χρυσίον οὐδὲν
ἐκώλυεν Αἰθίοπας τοὺς ἄνω μακαριωτάτους εἶναι
δοκεῖν, ὅπου τὸ χρυσίον ἀτιμότερον ἢ παρ' ἡμῖν
ὁ μόλιβδος, καί φασιν αὐτόθι τοὺς κακούργους
ἐν παχείαις χρυσαῖς[4] δεδέσθαι πέδαις, ἀλλ' οὐδὲν
ἧττόν εἰσι δεσμῶται καὶ πονηροὶ καὶ ἄδικοι. τὸ
δὲ μακαρίζειν τοὺς πλουσίους καὶ πολλὰ χρήματα
ἔχοντας, τὰ δὲ ἄλλα μηδὲν διαφέροντας τῶν πάνυ
φαύλων, ὅμοιον οἷον[5] εἴ τις τοὺς ἐκεῖ δεσμώτας
ἰδὼν προϊόντας ἐκ τῆς εἰρκτῆς ἐζήλου, καὶ πάντων
εὐδαιμονέστατον ἔκρινε τὸν ἔχοντα τὰς μείζους
πέδας.

4   Εἰ δὲ ἐλέφας θαυμαστὸν κτῆμα καὶ περιμάχητον,

---

[1] ἡ Casaubon : ἦ.   [2] σορῶν Post : ὀρῶν.
[3] ταπεινῶν Pflugk, ταλαιπώρων Emperius, φαύλων Selden :
παλαιῶν.   [4] χρυσαῖς added by Casaubon.
[5] οἷον added by Emperius, ὡς Casaubon.

---

[1] Corinth for centuries led in art and commerce, but it was
destroyed by Mummius in 146 B.C. Julius Caesar revived it

well blended and in mixing-bowls and altars and censers of cunning workmanship, the Corinthians' city would have been prosperous and have long maintained its existence as a state, safeguarding its own settlers and citizens.[1] And again, if there were utility in beautifully coloured and variegated marbles, the same statement could be made about the cities of Teos and Carystus,[2] as well as about certain Egyptian and Phrygian cities in whose vicinity the mountains are of variegated stone—in fact, I hear that among their sarcophagi the very ancient ones are of this same rock—yet, for all that, they are no better or more fortunate than any of the very lowly and pitiful cities.

Furthermore, if it were advantageous to possess gold, there was nothing to prevent the Ethiopians of the interior from being deemed most fortunate, for in their land gold is less highly prized than lead is with us, and it is said that in that region the criminals have been bound with heavy fetters of gold,[3] yet they are none the less prisoners and depraved and evildoers. But to congratulate the wealthy and men of great riches, when in all other respects they are no better than very ordinary folk, is as if, on seeing the prisoners of Ethiopia emerge from their prison, one were to envy them and judge the most fortunate of all to be the one with the heaviest fetters.

Again, if ivory is a marvellous possession and worth

as a Roman colony more than a century prior to our Discourse and it was again rich and populous.

[2] Teos was midway between Smyrna and Ephesus, Carystus was in Euboea. We hear little of Tean marble, but Roman writers often speak of the green marble of Carystus, which was very popular.   [3] Cf. Herodotus 3. 23.

Ἰνδοὶ πολὺ πάντων ὀλβιώτατοι καὶ ἄριστοι, παρ'
οἷς ἔρριπται τὰ τῶν ἐλεφάντων ὀστᾶ καὶ οὐδεὶς
πρόσεισιν, ὥσπερ ἐνθάδε τὰ τῶν βοῶν τε καὶ
ὄνων· καὶ πολλαχοῦ φασιν ἐν τοῖς τοίχοις ἐνοικο-
δομεῖσθαι τὰ κρανία τῶν ἐλεφάντων αὐτοῖς ὀδοῦ-
σιν. τί δὲ χρὴ περὶ Κελτῶν λέγειν, ὅπου φασὶ
ποταμόν τινα καταφέρειν τὸ ἤλεκτρον καὶ πολὺ
πανταχοῦ κεῖσθαι παρὰ ταῖς ὄχθαις ἐκβεβρασμέ-
νον, ὥσπερ αἱ ψῆφοι παρ' ἡμῖν ἐπὶ τῶν αἰγιαλῶν;
καὶ πρότερον μὲν οἱ παῖδες παίζοντες διερρίπτουν[1]·
νῦν δὲ κἀκεῖνοι συλλέγουσι καὶ φυλάττουσιν αὐτό,
παρ' ἡμῶν μεμαθηκότες ὅτι εἰσὶν εὐδαίμονες.

5 Ἆρα ἐνθυμεῖσθε ὅτι πάντες οὗτοι, λέγω δὲ τοὺς
Κελτοὺς καὶ Ἰνδοὺς καὶ Ἴβηρας[2] καὶ Ἄραβας καὶ
Βαβυλωνίους, φόρους παρ' ἡμῶν λαμβάνουσιν,
οὐ τῆς χώρας οὐδὲ τῶν βοσκημάτων, ἀλλὰ τῆς
ἀνοίας τῆς ἡμετέρας; οὐ γάρ, ἂν μὲν τοῖς ὅπλοις
κρατήσαντές τινες ἀναγκάσωσιν αὐτοῖς ἀργύριον
ὑποτελεῖν τοὺς ἡττημένους, τοῦτο ὀνομάζεται
φόρος, καὶ ἔστιν ἀνθρώπων οὐ σφόδρα εὐτυχῶν
οὐδὲ ἀνδρείων δασμὸν ἑτέροις παρέχειν· ἐὰν δέ
τινες, μήτε ἐπιστρατευσαμένου μηδενὸς μήτε
ἀναγκάσαντος, δι' εὐήθειαν δὲ καὶ τρυφήν, ὃ περὶ
πλείστου ποιοῦνται ἁπάντων, ἀργύριον πέμπωσιν
ἑκόντες, διὰ μακρᾶς μὲν ὁδοῦ πολλῆς δὲ θαλάττης,

---

[1] παίζοντες διερρίπτουν Emperius : ἔπαιζον τὰ δὲ ἐρρίπτουν.
[2] Ἴβηρας] Σῆρας Emperius.

---

[1] Amber was found at Olbia, near the mouth of the
Dnieper, and also at Marseilles, at the mouth of the Rhône.

fighting for, the Indians are of all men most blest
and pre-eminent by far, for in their land the bones
of the elephants are tossed aside and no one troubles
to go near them, just as in our land the bones of
cattle and of asses are treated ; they even say that
in many places the skulls of the elephants, tusks and
all, are built into their house walls. But what should
we say of the Celts, in whose country, according to
report, a certain river carries the amber down with
its waters and the amber is found in abundance
everywhere by the river banks, cast ashore like the
pebbles on the beaches in our country ? [1] Indeed, in days gone by their children at play used to
toss it about, though now they too collect and
treasure it, having learned from us how fortunate
they are.

Are you aware that all these peoples—the Celts,
Indians, Iberians, Arabs,[2] and Babylonians—exact
tribute from us, not from our land or from our flocks
and herds, but from our own folly ? For if, when by
force of arms any people get the upper hand and compel the vanquished to pay them silver, this is called
tribute, and it is a sign that people are not very
fortunate or brave if they pay tribute to others, then
is it not true that if, though no one has attacked
or compelled them, but because of stupidity and self-
indulgence, a certain people take that which they
prize most highly, silver, and of their own volition
send it over a long road and across a vast expanse

Dio may have the latter in mind, for his " Celts " may refer
to the Celtiberians of that general region, both Celts and
Iberians being listed in the next section.

[2] The Iberians and Arabs have not been mentioned previously in this speech. Their inclusion here may betoken
ex-tempore delivery.

τοῖς μηδὲ ἐπιβῆναι ῥᾳδίως δυναμένοις τῆς ἡμετέρας
γῆς, οὐ τῷ[1] παντὶ κάκιόν τε καὶ αἴσχιον τὸ γιγνό-
6 μενον; πλὴν ὅτι λίθους μικροὺς καὶ ἀσθενεῖς
καί, νὴ Δία, θηρίων ὀστᾶ διδόντες λαμβάνουσιν
ἀργύριον καὶ χρυσίον, ἀντὶ χρηστῶν ἄχρηστα
ἀντικαταλλαττόμενοι. μάλιστα δὲ θαυμάζω πολλάκις ἐννοῶν[2] ὅτι Μῆδοι μὲν τὰ Σύρων λαβόντες
ἠγάπων καὶ ἔχαιρον, Πέρσαι δὲ τὰ Μήδων,
Μακεδόνες δὲ τὰ Περσῶν, καὶ τότε ᾤοντο εὐτυχεῖς
γεγονέναι καὶ πράττειν ἄμεινον, ὅτε εἶχον τὰ τῶν
ἀθλίων καὶ δυστυχούντων κτήματα.

Ταῦτα δὲ οὐκ ἄλλως ἔγωγε ληρῶν εἶπον, ἀλλ᾽
ὅτι τῶν τοιούτων, ὑπὲρ ὧν ἔχουσι τὴν πᾶσαν
σπουδὴν καὶ ἐφ᾽ οἷς θαυμάζουσιν οἱ πολλοὶ τοὺς
κεκτημένους, οὐδέν ἐστιν ὄφελος, ἀλλ᾽ οὐδεμιᾶς
ἄξια δραχμῆς τὰ σύμπαντα· οὐδ᾽ ἂν γένοιντο
ἄνθρωποί ποτε εὐδαίμονες ἀνόητοι καὶ ἄφρονες,
οὐδ᾽ ἂν τὸν ἐν Σούσοις παράδεισον οἰκήσωσιν,[3]
ὃς ἦν, ὥς φασι, μετέωρος ἅπας.

---

[1] οὐ τῷ Casaubon : οὕτω or οὕτως.
[2] ἐννοῶν Reiske : ἐνίων.
[3] οἰκήσωσιν Dindorf, ἐνοικήσωσιν Reiske, ἀνοικοδομήσωσιν
Post : οἰκοδομήσουσιν or οἰκοδομήσωσιν.

---

[1] Bits of amber. Theophrastus, De Lapidibus 29, classifies
amber as a λίθος.
[2] By " Syrian " Dio is thought to have meant Assyrian ;
Herodotus (7. 63) says Syrian was the Greek term, Assyrian
the barbarian. Cyaxares the Mede at the close of the
seventh century took part in the sack of Nineveh.

of sea to those who cannot easily even set foot upon
our soil, such conduct is altogether more cowardly
and disgraceful ? Except for one thing, that they
do offer tiny, fragile pebbles [1] and, forsooth, bones
of wild beasts when they take our silver and gold,
exchanging useless things for useful ! But I am
often most astonished when I reflect that the Medes
were well content, yes, delighted at having got the
Syrian [2] riches, and the Persians in turn at having
got that of the Medes, and the Macedonians that
of the Persians, and that they thought they had
at last become Fortune's darlings and were more
prosperous at the moment when they had in their
possession what once had belonged to those wretched
and unfortunate peoples.

But these words I have spoken, not in a spirit
of idle folly, but because such goods, on the possession of which they have set their hearts and for
which most men admire those who have acquired
them, are good for nothing, nay, are not worth a
single drachma when lumped together ; nor can
human beings ever become fortunate if ignorant
and empty-headed, not even if they make the park
at Susa their dwelling-place, a park which was, we
are told, wholly up in the air.[3]

[3] At Susa the Persian monarch had his chief palace,
which, like the palace of Xerxes at Persepolis, was built on
lofty artificial terraces, in imitation of Babylon. In speaking
of " the park at Susa " Dio may have had in mind the
" hanging gardens " of Babylon, which Diodorus himself
calls a παράδεισος.

THE EIGHTIETH DISCOURSE:
ON FREEDOM

Conditions surrounding the Greek title of this Discourse are the opposite of those noted in connexion with that of the one preceding, for in the present instance all manuscripts except Parisinus 2985 add the phrase τῶν ἐν Κιλικίᾳ. What was said in the Introduction to Or. 79 regarding the problem presented by that phrase is equally appropriate here, for once more we get no clue to the place of delivery.

The freedom which the speaker has chosen as his theme is the freedom which characterizes himself, the philosopher— freedom to come and go as suits his fancy, freedom from the anxieties and inconveniencies that harass mankind at large, freedom from the temptations which assail seekers after riches or fame or self-indulgence. Such freedom belongs to him who leads the simple life, obedient to the ordinances of Zeus rather than to those of some imperfect, earthly law-giver. This creed is abundantly fortified with illustrations drawn from Greek myth and history.

80. ΤΩΝ ΕΝ ΚΙΛΙΚΙΑΙ ΠΕΡΙ ΕΛΕΥΘΕΡΙΑΣ

1 Ὑμεῖς μὲν ἴσως θαυμάζετε καὶ παράδοξον ἡγεῖσθε καὶ οὐδαμῶς σωφρονοῦντος ἀνδρός, ὅστις ἁπάντων ἀποστὰς περὶ ἃ οἱ πολλοὶ σπουδάζουσι, καὶ τρόπον τινὰ ἐάσας κατὰ ῥοῦν φέρεσθαι χρήματά τε καὶ δόξας καὶ ἡδονάς, οὔτε γεωργὸς οὔτε ναύκληρος οὔτε στρατιώτης οὔτε στρατηγὸς περίεισιν, οὐ σκυτοτόμος, οὐ τέκτων, οὐκ ἰατρός, οὐ ῥήτωρ, οὐκ ἄλλο τι σύνηθες πρᾶγμα ποιῶν,[1] οὑτωσὶ δὲ ἀτόπως ἰών τε καὶ ἀπιὼν καὶ παριστάμενος ἔνθα μηδὲν αὐτῷ πρᾶγμά ἐστιν, ἀλλ' 2 ὡς ἂν τύχῃ τε καὶ ὁρμήσῃ· βουλευτήρια μὲν καὶ θέατρα καὶ συλλόγους ἀτιμάσας, ἐκκλησιάζων δὲ μόνος αὐτός· καὶ θεωρῶν οὐκ ὀρχουμένους οὐδὲ ᾄδοντας οὐδὲ πυκτεύοντας οὐδὲ παλαίοντας, ἀλλ' ὠνουμένους καὶ βαδίζοντας καὶ λαλοῦντας καὶ μαχομένους, ποτὲ μὲν τούτοις ἅπασι προσέχων εὖ μάλα καὶ τερπόμενος πολὺ μᾶλλον ἢ παῖδες ἐν ἀγῶσι καὶ θεάτροις, οὐ προκαταλαμβάνων οὐδὲ ἀγρυπνῶν οὐδὲ θλιβόμενος, ποτὲ δὲ αὖ[2] μήτ' ἀκούων μηδενὸς μήθ' ὁρῶν, ἀλλὰ μηδ' εἶναι[3] νομίζων αὐτούς, ἐννοῶν ὃ βούλεται καὶ πράττων ἀδεῶς.

---

[1] ποιῶν Emperius : κοινόν.   [2] αὖ Casaubon : ἂν.
[3] ἀλλὰ μηδ' εἶναι Emperius : ἀλλὰ μηδ' εἰδέναι UB, μὴ δ' εἰδέναι M.

THE EIGHTIETH DISCOURSE:
ON FREEDOM

You perhaps are surprised and consider it past all belief and a mark of one who is by no means of sound judgement if a person abandons all that most men view with serious regard and, as one might say, permits riches and fame and pleasures to drift downstream but goes about as neither farmer nor trader nor soldier nor general, nor as shoemaker or builder or physician or orator, nor as one engaged in any other customary occupation, but, on the other hand, comes and goes in this strange fashion and puts in an appearance in places where he has no business at all but rather where chance and impulse may lead him. Council chambers and theatres and assemblies he has held in light esteem, and yet he conducts a popular assembly all by himself; the spectacles which attract his gaze are not dancers or singers or boxers or wrestlers, but buyers and strollers and talkers and fighters; sometimes all these receive his very strict attention, and he derives from them much more enjoyment than do boys at athletic contests and theatrical performances, although he does not come ahead of time or keep awake all night to get a seat or get crushed by the crowd; at other times, on the contrary, he neither hears nor sees any single one of them, but ignores their existence, thinking of anything that suits his fancy and acting without fear.

3 Ἐγὼ δὲ τοῦτο μὲν λαμπρὸν ἡγοῦμαι καὶ μακάριον, εἴ τις ἐν οἰκέταις[1] ἐλεύθερος εἶναι δύναται
καὶ ἐν ὑπηκόοις αὐτόνομος· ὑπὲρ οὗ[2] πολλὰ μὲν
Λυδοὶ Φρυξί, πολλὰ δὲ Φρύγες Λυδοῖς ἐπολέμησαν,
πολλὰ δ' Ἴωνές τε καὶ Δωριεῖς καὶ ξύμπαντα
γένη, ἀλλὰ νοητοειδοῦς[3] αὐτονομίας ἔρωτι οὐδεὶς[4]
ἐγκεχείρηκεν τοῖς αὐτὸς αὑτοῦ χρῆσθαι[5] νόμοις,
οἱ δὲ ξύμπαντες περὶ τῶν Σόλωνος καὶ Δράκοντος
καὶ Νόμα καὶ Ζαλεύκου νόμων ἐρίζουσιν, ὅπως
τούτοις ἀλλὰ μὴ τούτοις ἕπωνται, μηδενὸς αὖ
μηδὲ ἐκείνων οἷα ἐχρῆν θέντος.[6] Σόλωνα μέντοι
καὶ αὐτὸν εἰρηκέναι[7] φασὶν ὡς[8] αὐτῷ μὴ ἀρέσκοντα
εἰσηγεῖτο Ἀθηναίοις, ἀλλ' οἷς αὐτοὺς ὑπελάμβανε
χρήσεσθαι.

4 Δῆλον οὖν ὅτι πονηροὺς ἔγραφε νόμους, εἴπερ
τοὺς ἀρέσοντας πονηροῖς ἔγραφεν· ἀλλ' ὅμως καὶ
αὐτὸς τούτοις ἐχρῆτο πονηροῖς τε οὖσι καὶ οὐκ
ἀρέσκουσιν αὐτῷ. δῆλον οὖν ὅτι τούτων μὲν
οὐδενὶ μετῆν αὐτονομίας, οὐδὲ ἐσπούδαζον οὐδὲ

---

[1] οἰκέταις Casaubon : οἰκίαις or οἰκείαις.
[2] After οὗ Emperius adds δὲ.
[3] ἀλλὰ νοητοειδοῦς Post : ἀνόητοι εἴδους.
[4] ἐρῶντες. οὐδεὶς δ' Crosby, οὗ ἔρωτι Sonny.
[5] χρῆσθαι Morel : χρᾶσθαι.
[6] θέντος Emperius : τιθέντων.
[7] εἰρηκέναι Jacobs : εἰδέναι.
[8] After ὡς Jacobs deletes ὅτι.

---

[1] How much did Dio know of this warfare ? Herodotus
begins his account of Lydia at the point where all the country
west of the Halys River was subject to the Lydians.

[2] The casual reference to Numa, legendary king and law-
giver of Rome, suggests that the audience either was well

316

As for myself, however, I regard it as a splendid and blessed state of being, if in the midst of slaves one can be a free man and in the midst of subjects be independent. To attain this state many wars were waged by the Lydians against the Phrygians and by the Phrygians against the Lydians,[1] and many, too, by both Ionians and Dorians and, in fact, by all peoples, yet no one has ever, because he was enamoured of independence in the spiritual sense, undertaken to use his own personal laws ; instead they all wrangle over the laws of Solon and Draco and Numa and Zaleucus,[2] bent on following the one code but not the other, though, on the other hand, not even one of these law-givers had framed the sort of laws he should. Why, Solon himself, according to report, declared that he was proposing for the Athenians, not what satisfied himself, but rather what he assumed they would accept.[3]

Evidently, therefore, he composed bad laws, if indeed he composed the laws which would satisfy bad men ; but, for all that, even Solon himself used these laws, bad as they were and not satisfactory to himself. Clearly, then, not one of these law-givers had any claim to independence, nor did they exert themselves or wage war for the purpose of

educated or else contained persons with a Roman background. To be sure, at about this time Plutarch was composing his life of Numa, but the name appears rarely in Greek writings. Zaleucus, early law-giver of Locri in Italy, had been discussed by Ephorus (4th century B.C.) in his *Universal History*.

[3] The fragments of Solon's poems bearing upon his legislation testify to his pride in the achievement ; however, Plutarch reports (*Solon* 15. 2) that, in defence of his laws, Solon once said that they were " the best laws the Athenians would have accepted."

ἐπολέμουν ὅπως ὦσιν ἐλεύθεροι· ἀλλὰ γὰρ ἄφθονόν
τε καὶ πολλὴν δουλείαν ἐντὸς τῶν τειχῶν ἐγκαθείρ-
ξαντες ἔπειτα ἐπάλξεσι καὶ πύργοις καὶ βέλεσιν
ἠμύνοντο, ὅπως μὴ εἰσίοι ἔξωθεν παρ' αὐτούς,
ὥσπερ εἴ τις νεὼς διερρηγμένης κλύδωνος ἔνδον
ὄντος φυλάττοιτο καὶ πράγματα ἔχοι, μήποτε
ἄνωθεν ὑπερβάλῃ. καθάπερ οὖν φασι τοὺς Τρῶας
ὑπὲρ τῆς Ἑλένης πολιορκεῖσθαι καὶ ἀποθνήσκειν
οὐκ ἔνδον οὔσης ἀλλ' ἐν Αἰγύπτῳ, ταὐτὸ πάθος
οὗτοι πεπόνθασιν[1]· ὑπὲρ τῆς ἐλευθερίας ἐμάχοντο
καὶ ἠγωνίων, οὐκ οὔσης παρ' αὐτοῖς.

5 Ἀλλ' ὅμως ἐκεῖνοί τε ἔλεγον πάντα πάσχειν
ὑπὲρ τῶν νόμων, καὶ νῦν φασιν ἐν τούτοις εἶναι
τὴν δίκην, ὁπόσ' ἂν[2] αὐτοὶ δυστυχεῖς ὄντες συγ-
γράφωσιν ἢ παρ' ἄλλων ὁμοίων[3] παραλάβωσιν.
νόμον δὲ τὸν ἀληθῆ καὶ κύριον καὶ φανερὸν οὔτε
ὁρῶσιν οὔτε ἡγεμόνα ποιοῦνται τοῦ βίου. τοιγαροῦν ὥσπερ ἐν μεσημβρίᾳ λάμποντος ἡλίου
δᾷδας ἴασι καὶ δαλοὺς ἀράμενοι, τὸ μὲν θεῖον φῶς
ἐάσαντες,[4] καπνῷ δὲ ἑπόμενοι κἂν μικρὸν αἴθυγμα
δεικνύντι πυρός. ὁ μὲν οὖν τῆς φύσεως νόμος
ἀφεῖται καὶ ἐκλέλοιπε[5] παρ' ὑμῖν, ὦ κακοδαίμονες·
ἄξονας δὲ καὶ γραμματεῖα καὶ στήλας φυλάττετε
καὶ ἀνωφελῆ στίγματα.

6 Καὶ τὸν μὲν τοῦ Διὸς θεσμὸν πάλαι παρέβητε,

---

[1] πεπόνθασιν] πεπόνθεσαν Arnim.
[2] ὁπόσ' ἂν Pflugk : ὁπότ' ἂν or ὁπόταν.
[3] ὁμοίων Morel : ὁμοίως.
[4] ἐάσαντες Morel : ἐλάσαντες.
[5] ἐκλέλοιπε Emperius : λέλοιπε.

---

[1] Stesichorus is said to have invented this version of the
Helen story, incorporating it in his famous palinode, four

318

being free ; on the contrary, after they had gathered within the compass of their city walls slavery without bound or limit, thereupon with ramparts and towers and missiles they tried to protect themselves against the chance that slavery might make its entry among them from without, just as if, when a ship's seams have opened up and the hold is already taking water, one were to take measures of prevention and be concerned lest perchance the sea might sweep over from above. Accordingly, just as it is said that the Trojans for Helen's sake endured siege and death, although she was not at Troy but in Egypt,[1] just so has it been with these men—in behalf of their freedom they fought and struggled, when all the while they had no freedom.

Yet not only did these men of old profess to be enduring all things in defence of the laws, but even now men say that justice resides in whatever laws they themselves, luckless creatures that they are, may frame or else inherit from others like themselves. But the law which is true and binding and plain to behold they neither see nor make a guide for their life. So at noon, as it were, beneath the blazing sun, they go about with torches and flambeaux in their hands, ignoring the light of heaven but following smoke if it shows even a slight glint of fire. Thus, while the law of nature is abandoned and eclipsed with you, poor unfortunates that you are, tablets and statute books and slabs of stone with their fruitless symbols are treasured by you.

Again, while the ordinance of Zeus you transgressed

lines of which have been preserved by Plato (*Phaedrus* 243 A). Herodotus tells the story in great detail (2. 112-119), and Euripides used that version for the framework of his *Helen*.

τὸν δὲ τοῦ δεῖνος ἢ τὸν τοῦ δεῖνος ὅπως μηδεὶς
παραβήσεται σκοπεῖσθε. καὶ τὴν ἀρὰν ἣν Ἀθηναῖοι
περὶ τῶν Σόλωνος ἔθεντο νόμων τοῖς ἐπιχειροῦσι
καταλύειν ἀγνοεῖτε κυριωτέραν οὖσαν ἐπὶ τοῖς
ἐκείνου νόμοις· πᾶσα γὰρ ἀνάγκη τὸν συγχέοντα[1]
τὸν[2] θεσμὸν ἄτιμον ὑπάρχειν[3]· πλὴν παῖδας καὶ
γένος οὐκ ἐπέξεισιν, ὡς ἐκεῖ, τῶν ἁμαρτανόντων,
ἀλλ' ἕκαστος αὑτῷ[4] γίγνεται τῆς ἀτυχίας αἴτιος.
τὸν οὖν ἐπιχειροῦντα τοῦτον ἀνασῴζειν[5] ὡς ἂν οἷός
τε ᾖ καὶ τό γε καθ' αὑτὸν φυλάττειν οὐδέποτε
ἂν μὴ φρονεῖν φαίην ἔγωγε.

7 Πολὺ δὲ μᾶλλον ὑμᾶς θαυμάζω καὶ ἐλεῶ τῆς
χαλεπῆς καὶ παρανόμου δουλείας ἐν ᾗ ζεύξαντες
αὑτοὺς ἔχετε, οὐχ ἑνὶ δεσμῷ μόνον περιβαλόντες[6]
οὐδὲ δυσίν, ἀλλὰ μυρίοις, ὑφ' ὧν ἄγχεσθε καὶ
πιέζεσθε πολὺ μᾶλλον τῶν ἐν ἁλύσει τε καὶ κλοιῷ
καὶ πέδαις ἑλκομένων. τοῖς μὲν γὰρ ἔστι καὶ
ἀφεθῆναι καὶ διακόψασι φυγεῖν, ὑμεῖς δὲ ἀεὶ
μᾶλλον κρατύνεσθε τὰ δεσμὰ καὶ πλείω καὶ
ἰσχυρότερα ἀπεργάζεσθε. καὶ μή, ὅτι οὐχ ὁρᾶτε
αὐτά, ψευδῆ καὶ ἄπιστον ἡγεῖσθε τόνδε τὸν λόγον·
σκοπεῖτε δὲ Ὁμήρου τοῦ καθ' ὑμᾶς[7] σοφωτάτου
ποῖ' ἄττα δεσμὰ τὸν Ἄρη φησὶ[8] κατασχεῖν,

---

[1] συγχέοντα Casaubon : συνέχοντα.
[2] τὸν with UB, τόνδε τὸν Emperius, τὸ πᾶν Arnim ; τὸν
δὲ M.
[3] ἄτιμον ὑπάρχειν Emperius, ἀραῖον ὑπάρχειν Arnim : ἀθηναῖον
ἐπάρχειν.   [4] αὑτῷ Reiske : αὑτῶν.
[5] ἀνασῴζειν Casaubon : ἂν σῴζειν.
[6] περιβαλόντες Pflugk : περιβάλλοντες.

long ago, the ordinance of this man or of that you make it your aim that no man shall transgress. Moreover, the curse which the Athenians established in connexion with Solon's laws against all who should attempt to destroy them [1] you fail to see is more valid touching the laws of Zeus, for it is wholly inevitable that he who attempts to nullify the ordinance of Zeus shall be an outlaw—except that in this instance children and kinsmen of the guilty are not included in the punishment, as they were at Athens; instead, each is held accountable for his own misfortune. Whoever, therefore, tries to rescue this ordinance as best he can and to guard his own conduct I for my part would never say is lacking in judgement.

But much more do I marvel at and pity you [2] for the grievous and unlawful slavery under whose yoke you have placed your necks, for you have thrown about you not merely one set of fetters or two but thousands, fetters by which you are throttled and oppressed much more than are those who drag themselves along in chains and halters and shackles. For they have the chance of release or of breaking their bonds and fleeing, but you are always strengthening your bonds and making them more numerous and stronger. Moreover, merely because you do not see your bonds, do not think that these words of mine are false and untrustworthy; nay, consider Homer— who in your estimation is wisest of all—and what kind of bonds he says made Ares captive,

[1] Cf. Aristotle, *Athen. Pol.* 16. 10.
[2] Dio here recalls his opening statement, that his hearers may be surprised at his conduct.

---

[7] ὑμᾶς Emperius: ἡμᾶς.   [8] φησὶ Morel: φασὶ.

ὠκύτατόν περ ἐόντα θεῶν, οἳ Ὄλυμπον ἔχουσιν,
ἠΰτ' ἀράχνια λεπτά, τά γ' οὔ κέ τις οὐδὲ ἴδοιτο.

8 Μὴ οὖν οἴεσθε τὸν μὲν Ἄρη, θεὸν ὄντα καὶ
ἰσχυρόν, οὕτως ὑπὸ λεπτῶν τε καὶ ἀοράτων
πεδηθῆναι δεσμῶν, αὐτοὺς δέ, πάντων θηρίων
ἀσθενεστάτους ὄντας, μὴ ἄν ποτε ἁλῶναι δεσμοῖς
ἀφανέσιν, ἀλλ' εἰ μὴ σιδήρου τε καὶ ὀρειχάλκου
εὖ[1] πεποιημένα εἴη. τὰ μὲν οὖν σώματα ὑμῶν,
οἷα δὴ στερεὰ καὶ τὸ πλέον γῆς γέμοντα,[2] τοιούτων[3]
δεῖται[4] τῶν κρατησόντων· ψυχὴ δὲ ἀόρατός που
καὶ λεπτὴ φύσει πῶς οὐκ[5] ἂν δεσμῶν τοιούτων
τυγχάνοι;[6] ὑμεῖς δὲ στερροὺς καὶ ἀδαμαντίνους
πεποίησθε πάσῃ μηχανῇ πλεξάμενοι, καὶ τὸν
Δαίδαλον[7] αὐτὸν ὑπερβεβλημένοι τῇ τέχνῃ τε καὶ
σπουδῇ πρὸς τὸ πᾶν ὑμῶν μέρος τῆς ψυχῆς κατα-
δεδέσθαι καὶ μηδὲν ἐλεύθερον εἶναι μηδὲ αὐτόνομον.
9 τί γὰρ ἦν ἡ Κνωσίων εἱρκτὴ καὶ τὸ τοῦ Λαβυρίνθου
σκολιὸν πρὸς τὴν σκολιότητα καὶ τὸ δυσεύρετον
τῆς ἀφροσύνης; τί δ' ἡ Σικελικὴ φρουρὰ τῶν
Ἀττικῶν αἰχμαλώτων, οὓς εἰς πέτραν τινὰ ἐνέβαλον; τί δ' ὁ Λακώνων Κεάδας καὶ τὸ παρὰ

---

[1] εὖ deleted by Reiske.
[2] γῆς γέμοντα with M, ἐκ γῆς γεγονότα Arnim : ὀργῆς
γέμοντα UB.
[3] τοιούτων Emperius : τοσούτων.
[4] δεῖται Geel : δεῖ.
[5] οὐκ added by Geel.
[6] After τυγχάνοι Geel deletes κατὰ τὸν Ἥφαιστον αὐτόν.
[7] Δαίδαλον] Ἥφαιστον Emperius.

---

[1] A fusion of *Odyssey* 8. 331 and 8. 280.

Although the fleetest of the gods who hold
Olympus, bonds like filmy spider-webs,
Which no man e'en could see.[1]

Then, think not that Ares, god that he was and
mighty, was made captive by bonds so delicate and
invisible withal, and yet that you yourselves, of all
creatures the weakest, could never be made captive
by means of bonds that are invisible but only by such
as have been well made of steel and brass.[2] Your
bodies, to be sure, being solid and for the most part
composed of earth,[3] require bonds of that kind to
master them ; but since soul is invisible and delicate
by nature, why might it not get bonds of like description ? But you have made for yourselves stubborn, adamantine bonds, contriving them by any and
every means, surpassing even Daedalus himself in
your craft and in your eagerness to insure that every
particle of your soul shall have been fettered and
none of it be free or independent. For what were
the dungeon of the Cnossians and the crooked wind-
ings of the Labyrinth compared to the crookedness
and the intricacy of folly ? What was the Sicilian
prison of the Athenian captives, who were cast into
a sort of rocky pit ?[4] What was the Ceadas of the
Spartans,[5] or the ash-filled room that the Persians

---

[2] Literally, mountain-copper, mentioned as early as the
Hesiodic *Shield of Heracles* (122), the greaves of the hero
being of that material.

[3] Possibly an allusion to the tradition that Prometheus
formed the human race of clay ; cf. Pausanias 10. 4. 4.

[4] After the collapse of the Sicilian Expedition in 413 B.C.,
the Athenian captives were thrown into the quarries of
Syracuse ; cf. Thucydides 7. 86-87.

[5] A chasm or ravine into which great criminals were
hurled ; cf. Thucydides 1. 134 and Pausanias 4. 18. 4.

Πέρσαις οἴκημα μεστὸν τέφρας, ἢ νὴ Δία εἴ τινας[1]
κόρας χαλεποὶ πατέρες, ὡς ὁ τῶν ποιητῶν λόγος,

χαλκέων περιβόλων ἐφρούρησαν εἱρκταῖς.

Οὐδ' ἐγὼ[2] νήφειν ἐν τοῖς λόγοις ἔτι μοι δοκῶ
τῶν ἀνθρωπίνων συμφορῶν μνησθεὶς ἐπὶ πλέον
ἢ[3] τῆς αἰσχρᾶς καὶ δυσχεροῦς δουλείας ἣν δεδού-
λωσθε πάντες· ὅθεν οὐ νημάτων ἔστι λεπτῶν[4]
εὐπορήσαντας ἐξελθεῖν βοηθείᾳ κόρης ἄφρονος,
ὥσπερ ἐκεῖνον Θησέα φασὶν ἐκ Κρήτης σωθῆναι,
εἰ μή τι αὐτῆς,[5] οἶμαι, τῆς Ἀθηνᾶς παρισταμένης
10 καὶ σωζούσης ἅμα. εἰ γὰρ ἐθέλοιμι πάσας εἰπεῖν
τὰς εἱρκτὰς καὶ τὰ δεσμὰ τῶν ἀνοήτων[6] τε καὶ
ἀθλίων ἀνθρώπων οἷς ἐγκλείσαντες αὐτοὺς ἔχετε,[7]
μὴ σφόδρα ὑμῖν ἀπηνής τε καὶ φαῦλος δόξω
ποιητής, ἐν οἰκείοις τραγῳδῶν πάθεσιν. οὐ γὰρ
μόνον, ὡς οἱ δόξαντες ὑμῖν κακοῦργοι πιεζοῦνται,[8]
τραχήλου τε καὶ χειρῶν καὶ ποδῶν, ἀλλὰ γαστρὸς
καὶ τῶν ἄλλων μερῶν ἑκάστου[9] ἰδίῳ δεσμῷ τε
καὶ ἀνάγκῃ κατειλημμένοι εἰσὶ[10] ποικίλῃ τε καὶ

---

[1] εἴ τινας Morel : οἴ τινας M, εἴ τινες UB.
[2] οὐδ' ἐγὼ Geel : οὐδέ τῳ.
[3] ἢ Capps : καὶ.
[4] οὐ νημάτων ἔστι λεπτῶν Casaubon : νημάτων ἐστὶν οὐ λεπτῶν.
[5] εἰ μή τι αὐτῆς Dindorf, ἀλλ' οὐδὲ αὐτῆς Arnim : εἰ μή τις αὐτῆς.
[6] ἀνοήτων Emperius : θνητῶν.
[7] ἔχετε] ἔχουσι Reiske.
[8] πιεζοῦνται] πιέζονται Morel.
[9] ἑκάστου Casaubon : ἕκαστον.

had,[1] or, by Zeus, what were the cruel fathers of certain maidens, who, as the poets tell us,

Immured them in prison cells of encircling bronze ?[2]

But, methinks, I too am no longer acting sensibly in giving more space in my remarks to the misfortunes of mankind than to the disgraceful, odious slavery in which you all have been enslaved, a slavery from which men cannot escape by providing themselves with fine threads by the aid of a foolish maiden, as the famous Theseus is said to have escaped in safety from Crete[3]—at least, I fancy, not unless Athena herself were to lend her aid and join in the rescue. For if I should wish to name all the prisons and the bonds of witless, wretched human beings by means of which you have made yourselves prisoners, possibly you would think me an exceedingly disagreeable and sorry poet for composing tragedies on your own misfortunes.[4] For it is not merely with bonds such as confine those whom you consider criminals—bonds about neck and arms and legs—but with a special bond for the belly and for each of the other parts that they have been made captive, and with a constraint which is both varied and complex ;

[1] Referred to by Ctesias (48, 51, 52).
[2] Attributed by Wilamowitz to Euripides' *Danaë* ; but Sophocles also dealt with the same theme.
[3] Ariadnê, daughter of Minos, gave Theseus the thread by which he made his escape after slaying the Minotaur.
[4] Possibly a reminiscence of the affair of the tragic poet Phrynichus, whom the Athenians fined one thousand drachmas because by his *Capture of Miletus* he had revived their sorrow over the fate of their Ionian kinsmen : cf. Herodotus 6. 21.

---

[10] κατειλημμένοι εἰσὶ Arnim : κατειλημμένον. οἱ δ᾽ εἰσὶ.

πολυτρόπω[1]· καί μοι δοκεῖ τις ἂν ἰδὼν τῇ[2] ὄψει
τερφθῆναί τε καὶ σφόδρα ἄγασθαι τὴν ἐπίνοιαν.

11 Πρώτη μὲν γάρ, οἶμαι, πρὸς ἕκαστον ἔστη[3]
δέσποινα χαλεπὴ μὲν ἄλλως καὶ δυσμενὴς καὶ
ἐπίβουλος, ἰδεῖν δὲ ἱλαρὰ[4] καὶ μειδιῶσα πρὸς
ἅπαντας

σαρδάνιον μάλα τοῖον

καὶ[5] φέρει[6] δεσμὰ κατὰ τὴν αὑτῆς φύσιν εὐανθῆ
καὶ μαλακὰ τὴν πρώτην, οἷς[7] εἰκός ἐστι κατα-
δεῖσθαι βασιλεῖς ἢ τυράννους καὶ πάντας[8] ὅσοι
μακαρίων παῖδες κέκληνται· τούτων δὲ χαλεπώτερον οὐδὲν οὐδὲ μᾶλλον ἐμφύεται καὶ πιέζει.

12 μετὰ δὲ ταύτην ἦλθεν ἑτέρα, κλοιόν τινα φέρουσα
χρυσοῦν ἢ ἀργυροῦν. τοῦτον δὲ περιθεῖσα ἕλκει
μὲν ἰδιώτας περὶ πᾶσαν γῆν καὶ θάλασσαν, ἕλκει
δὲ βασιλεῖς καθ' Ἡσίοδον, σύρει δὲ πόλεων στρα-
τηγοὺς ἐπὶ πύλας, ὥστε ἀνοίγειν καὶ προδιδόναι.
φησὶ δὲ κήδεσθαι[9] τούτων οὓς ἂν ἀπολύῃ, καὶ
ποιεῖν εὐδαίμονας· ὥσπερ Ἀστυάγην ποτὲ Κῦρος
ἐν χρυσαῖς ἔδησε πέδαις, ὡς ἂν δῆλον ὅτι πάππου
κηδόμενος.

13 Πολὺ δ' ἂν ἔργον εἴη διεξιέναι πάσας τὰς ἰδέας

[1] ποικίλη τε καὶ πολυτρόπῳ Arnim : ποικίλοι τε καὶ πολύ-
τροποι.
[2] τῇ added by Emperius.
[3] ἕκαστον ἔστη Reiske : ἕκαστόν ἐστι.
[4] ἰδεῖν δὲ ἱλαρὰ Wilamowitz : ἰδεῖν· εἰ δ' ἄρα.
[5] Before καὶ Emperius deletes χαλεπὴ δὲ ἡδονὴ.
[6] φέρει Geel : φέρειν.
[7] οἷς] οἵοις Arnim.
[8] πάντας Morel : πάντες.
[9] φησὶ δὲ κήδεσθαι Casaubon : φασὶ δὲ καὶ δεῖσθαι.

moreover, I believe that any one who had seen the
spectacle would have been delighted by it and would
exceedingly admire the conceit.

For first, I fancy, there comes to each a mistress
who is in other respects harsh and ill-disposed and
treacherous, but in appearance cheerful and with a
smile for all,

A smile of portent grim,[1]

and in her hands she bears fetters to match her
nature, flowery and soft at first glance, such as those
with which one might expect that kings or tyrants
and all who have been called " sons of the Blest "
have been bound ; yet nothing is more grievous than
these bonds, nothing clings more closely and exerts
more pressure. After her there comes a second,
bearing a sort of collar of gold or silver. Having
put this about their necks, she drags men in private
station around every land and sea, yes, and kings as
well, according to Hesiod,[2] and she drags generals of
cities to the gates, so as to open them and act the
traitor. And yet she professes to be solicitous for
these whom she destroys, and to be making them
happy—just as once upon a time Cyrus bound
Astyages with golden fetters, as being, evidently,
solicitous for his grandfather ![3]

But it would be a huge undertaking to enumerate

[1] *Odyssey* 20. 302, spoken of Odysseus when he had
dodged the ox-hoof hurled at him by Ctesippus.

[2] In his *Works and Days* (38-39 and 263-264) he calls
them δωροφάγοι.

[3] Herodotus devotes much space (1. 107-129) to the tale
of Cyrus and Astyages, but he says nothing of golden
fetters. Dio may be hinting that gold was used by Harpagus
and Cyrus to corrupt the soldiers of Astyages, who in the
final battle were strangely ready to desert.

τῶν δεσμῶν. ἕνα[1] δ' οὖν ἄξιον μὴ παρεῖναι τὸν
παραδοξότατον αὐτῶν καὶ ποικιλώτατον, ὃν ἡ
χαλεπωτάτη φέρει δέσποινα, χρυσῷ καὶ ἀργύρῳ
καὶ παντοίοις λίθοις τε καὶ ψήφοις καὶ ζῴων
κέρασι καὶ ὀδοῦσι καὶ ὀστράκοις, ἔτι δὲ ἁλουργέσι
βαφαῖς καὶ ἑτέροις μυρίοις τισὶν ὥσπερ ὅρμον
πολυτελῆ καὶ θαυμαστὸν ἀσκήσασα καὶ πολλά
τινα ἐν αὐτῷ σχήματά τε[2] καὶ μορφὰς μιμησαμένη,
στεφάνους τε καὶ σκῆπτρα καὶ τιάρας καὶ θρόνους
ὑψηλούς· καθάπερ οἱ περιττοὶ τεχνῖται κλίνας
τινὰς ἢ θύρας ἢ ὀροφὰς οἰκιῶν κατασκευάζοντες
ἕτερ' ἄττα μηχανῶνται φαίνεσθαι, λέγω δὲ οἷον
θυρῶν ἐξοχὰς θηρίων κεφαλαῖς[3] ἀπεικάσαντες
14 καὶ κιόνων ὁμοίως· ἔτι δὲ καὶ ἦχος ἐν τούτῳ καὶ
φωνὴ παντοία κρότων τε καὶ ποππυσμῶν.[4] πάλιν
οὖν τοῦτον περιβάλλει δημαγωγοῖς τε καὶ βασιλεῦ-
σιν. ἀλλ' ὅπως μὴ πόρρω που αὐτοὶ φερώμεθα
ὑπὸ τῆς εἰκόνος, ὥσπερ ὄντως εἰδώλῳ τινὶ λόγου
ἐπακολουθοῦντες, ὡς Ὅμηρος Ἀχιλλέα ἐποίησε
τῷ τοῦ Ἀγήνορος[5] ἑπόμενον μακρὰν ἀπελθεῖν.
ἱκανῶς ἔχει.

[1] ἕνα Morel : ἔνθα.
[2] σχήματά τε Wyttenbach : ὀχήματά τε UB, ὄχημα τε M.
[3] κεφαλαῖς Reiske : κεφαλὰς.
[4] After ποππυσμῶν Emperius deletes καὶ ἠχεῖ ταῦτα τὰ
δεσμά.
[5] Ἀγήνορος Morel : ἀντήνορος.

all the varieties of the fetters. Still, one variety deserves not to be overlooked, the most amazing of them all and the most complicated, one carried by the harshest mistress, a combination of gold and silver and all sorts of stones and pebbles and horns and tusks and shells of animals and, furthermore, purple dyes and countless other things, a sort of costly, marvellous necklace which she had contrived, imitating in it many patterns and forms—crowns and sceptres and diadems and lofty thrones—just as the over-subtle craftsmen in fashioning certain couches or doors or ceilings of houses contrive to make them appear something different from what they are ; I mean, for example, making bosses on doors resemble heads of animals, and likewise with bosses on columns. And, furthermore, in this collar are found noise and sound of every kind, both of clapping hands and of clucking tongues.[1] So this collar, in turn, is placed about the necks of both demagogues and kings. But let us not ourselves be carried along too far by our simile, as if actually following a word-phantom, as Homer caused Achilles to go a long way off in following the phantom of Agenor.[2] This will suffice.

[1] The word ποππυσμός signified the noise Greeks made with their lips to express surprise and admiration.
[2] *Iliad* 21. 595-605.

ENCOMIUM ON HAIR

THIS short composition—preserved embedded in Synesius'
Encomium on Baldness—like Dio's *Praise of the Gnat* and
Praise of the Parrot, whose titles alone have come down to
us, is clearly a sophistic exercise. Its opening sentence bears
some resemblance to the proem of Or. 52 and might suggest
as the time of its composition the same general period in
Dio's career. The abruptness with which the composition
closes is indeed striking, and that, together with what has
been regarded as rather inadequate handling of an attractive
theme, has led to the supposition that we have but a fragment of the original work. However, Synesius seems to
view it as complete and himself remarks that " it does not
contain many lines."

Synesius was born at Cyrenê about A.D. 370 and cannot
be traced beyond the year 413. He was a pupil of the
learned Hypatia at Alexandria, and we are told that he
inherited a library from his father. His interest in Dio
Chrysostom is attested, not only by his *Encomium on
Baldness*, but also by reminiscences of Dio in a speech
delivered at Constantinople about the year 400 and by his
Dio, composed about five years later, a considerable portion
of which will be found on pages 365-387.

ΔΙΩΝΟΣ ΚΟΜΗΣ ΕΓΚΩΜΙΟΝ

Ex Synesii Encomio Calvitii pp. 63 sqq. Petav.

Δίωνι τῷ χρυσῷ τὴν γλῶτταν ἐποιήθη βιβλίον,
Κόμης Ἐγκώμιον, οὕτω δή τι λαμπρὸν ὡς ἀνάγκην
εἶναι παρὰ τοῦ λόγου φαλακρὸν ἄνδρα αἰσχύνεσθαι.
συνεπιτίθεται γὰρ ὁ λόγος τῇ φύσει· φύσει δὲ
ἅπαντες ἐθέλομεν εἶναι καλοί, πρὸς ὃ μέγα μέρος
αἱ τρίχες συμβάλλονται, αἷς ἡμᾶς ἐκ παίδων ἡ
φύσις ᾠκείωσεν. ἐγὼ μὲν οὖν καὶ ὁπηνίκα τὸ
δεινὸν ἤρχετο καὶ θρὶξ ἀπερρύη μέσην αὐτὴν
δέδηγμαι τὴν καρδίαν, καὶ ἐπειδὴ προσέκειτο μᾶλλον, ἄλλης ἐπ' ἄλλῃ πιπτούσης, ἤδη δὲ καὶ σύνδυο
καὶ κατὰ πλείους καὶ ὁ πόλεμος λαμπρὸς ἦν,
ἀγομένης καὶ φερομένης τῆς κεφαλῆς, τότε δὴ
τότε χαλεπώτερα πάσχειν ᾤμην ἢ ὑπ' Ἀρχιδάμου
τοὺς Ἀθηναίους ἐπὶ τῇ δενδροτομίᾳ τῶν Ἀχαρνῶν,
ταχύ τε ἀπεδείχθην ἀνεπιτήδευτος Εὐβοεύς, οὓς
ὄπιθεν κομόωντας ἐστράτευσεν ἐπὶ Τροίαν ἡ
ποίησις.

---

[1] Acharnae, largest of the Attic demes, situated about
seven miles north of Athens, suffered severely in the first
year of the Peloponnesian War (431 B.C.). Thucydides
(2. 19-22) records that the Spartan king Archidamus camped
there for some time and laid waste the countryside. Aristophanes in his *Acharnians* mentions especially the destruction
of the vineyards.

ENCOMIUM ON HAIR

SYNESIUS' *Encomium on Baldness* : Dio of the golden tongue has composed a discourse entitled *An Encomium on Hair,* which is a work of such brilliance that the inevitable result of the speech is to make a bald man feel ashamed. For the speech joins forces with nature ; and by nature we all desire to be beautiful, an ambition whose realization is greatly assisted by the hair to which from boyhood nature has accustomed us. In my own case, for example, even when the dreadful plague was just beginning and a hair fell off, I was smitten to my inmost heart, and when the attack was pressed with greater vigour, hair after hair dropping out, and ultimately even two or three together, and the war was being waged with fury, my head becoming utterly ravaged, then indeed I thought myself to be the victim of more grievous injury than the Athenians suffered at the hands of Archidamus when he cut down the trees of the Acharnians,[1] and presently, without my so intending, I was turned into a Euboean, one of the tribe which the poet marshalled against Troy " with flowing locks behind." [2]

---

[2] *Iliad* 2. 542 : τῷ δ' ἅμ' Ἄβαντες ἕποντο θοοί, ὅπιθεν κομόωντες. The peculiarity here referred to consisted not in wearing long hair—the Achaeans frequently are termed κάρη κομόωντες—but in shaving all but the back hair. This, of course, is the point in Synesius' allusion.

Ἐν ᾧ τίνα μὲν θεῶν, τίνα δὲ δαιμόνων παρῆλθον ἀκατηγόρητον; ἐπεθέμην δὲ καὶ Ἐπικούρου τι γράφειν ἐγκώμιον, οὐ κατὰ ταὐτὰ περὶ θεῶν διακείμενος, ἀλλ' ὡς ὅ τι κἀγὼ δυναίμην ἀντιδηξόμενος. ἔλεγον γὰρ ὅτι ποῦ τὰ τῆς προνοίας ἐν τῷ παρ' ἀξίαν ἑκάστου; καὶ τί γὰρ ἀδικῶν ἐγὼ φανοῦμαι ταῖς γυναιξὶν ἀειδέστερος; οὐ δεινὸν εἰ ταῖς ἐκ γειτόνων· τὰ γὰρ εἰς Ἀφροδίτην ἐγὼ δικαιότατος κἂν τῷ Βελλεροφόντῃ σωφροσύνης ἀμφισβητήσαιμι. ἀλλὰ καὶ μήτηρ, ἀλλὰ καὶ ἀδελφαί, φασί, τῷ κάλλει τι νέμουσι τῶν ἀρρένων. ἐδήλωσε δὲ ἡ Παρύσατις, Ἀρταξέρξην τὸν βασιλέα διὰ Κῦρον τὸν καλὸν ἀποστέρξασα.

Ταῦτ' ἄρα ἐποτνιώμην, καὶ μικρὸν οὐδὲν ἐπενόουν περὶ τῆς συμφορᾶς. ἐπεὶ δὲ ὅ τε χρόνος αὐτὴν συνηθεστέραν ἐποίησε καὶ ὁ λόγος ἀντεισιὼν κατεξανέστη τοῦ πάθους, τὸ δὲ κατὰ μικρὸν ὑπεξίστατο, ἤδη διὰ ταῦτα ῥᾴων ἦν καὶ ἀνέφερον· νυνὶ δὲ ἀνθυπήνεγκεν αὐτὸ ῥεῦμα ἕτερον οὗτος αὐτὸς ὁ Δίων, καὶ ἐπανήκει μοι μετὰ συνηγόρου. πρὸς δύο δέ, φησὶν ὁ λόγος, οὐδ' Ἡρακλῆς, εἰ τοὺς Μολιονίδας ἐκ λόχου προσπεσόντας οὐκ

---

[1] While not denying the existence of gods, Epicurus held that they dwelt far off and had no concern for mortals.

[2] The Bellerophon story appears for the first time in *Iliad* 6. 156-195. It is the Greek counterpart of the story of Joseph and Potiphar's wife.

[3] Parysatis, wife of Darius II, was the mother of Artaxerxes and Cyrus. Xenophon states (*Anabasis* 1. 1. 4) that she loved Cyrus more than Artaxerxes, but he does not tell why. One might conclude from his obituary of Cyrus (*op. cit.* 1. 9) that character rather than physical beauty determined her preference.

ENCOMIUM ON HAIR

At this stage what god, what spirit, did I pass by without arraignment? I even set myself to composing a eulogy of Epicurus, not that I held the same views about the gods as he,[1] but rather because I aimed to make them smart for it to the best of my poor powers. For I said, "Where are the tokens of their providence in their treating the individual contrary to his deserts? For what crime of mine dooms me to appear less comely in women's eyes? It is nothing terrible if I am to appear so to the women of the neighbourhood—for so far as love is concerned I might with fullest justice lay claim to the prize for continence, even against Bellerophon[2] —but even a mother, yes, even sisters, I am told, attach some importance to the beauty of their men. And Parysatis made this plain by growing cold toward Artaxerxes who was king because of Cyrus who was beautiful."[3]

Thus, then, I cried aloud in indignation, and I made no light matter of my misfortune. But when time had made it more familiar and reason, too, entering as contender, rose up to give battle against my suffering, and when little by little that suffering was yielding ground, then at last for these reasons I was more at ease and beginning to recover; but now this very Dio has caused the flood of my distress to flow afresh, and it has returned to attack me in company with an advocate. But against two adversaries, as the saying is, not even Heracles could contend, since when the Molionidae[4] fell upon him from

[4] Eurytus and Cteatus, sons of Molionê and Poseidon and nephews of Augeas, who was responsible for their conflict with Heracles. According to Pindar, *Olymp.* 10. 29-38, Heracles attacked from ambush and slew them both.

ἤνεγκεν. ἀλλὰ καὶ πρὸς τὴν Ὕδραν ἀγωνιζόμενος, τέως μὲν εἷς ἑνὶ συνειστήκεσαν· ἐπεὶ δὲ ὁ καρκίνος αὐτῇ παρεγένετο, κἂν ἀπεῖπεν, εἰ μὴ τὴν Ἰόλεω συμμαχίαν ἀντεπηγάγετο. κἀγώ μοι δοκῶ παραπλήσιόν τι παθεῖν ὑπὸ Δίωνος, οὐκ ἔχων ἀδελφιδοῦν τὸν Ἰόλεων. πάλιν οὖν ἐκλαθόμενος ἐμαυτοῦ τε καὶ τῶν λογισμῶν ἐλεγεῖα ποιῶ, θρηνῶν ἐπὶ τῇ κόμῃ.

Σὺ δὲ ἐπειδὴ φαλακρῶν μὲν ὁ κράτιστος εἶ, δοκεῖς δέ τις εἶναι γεννάδας, ὃς οὐδὲ ἐμπάζει τῆς συμφορᾶς, ἀλλὰ καὶ ὅταν ἔτνους προκειμένου μετώπων ἐξέτασις γίνηται, σαυτὸν ἐπιλέγεις, ὡς ἐπ᾽ ἀγαθῷ δή τινι φιλοτιμούμενος, οὐκοῦν ἀνάσχου τοῦ λόγου, καὶ τήρησον ἐν πείσῃ, φασί, τὴν καρδίαν, ὥσπερ ὁ Ὀδυσσεὺς πρὸς τὴν ἀναγωγίαν τῶν γυναικῶν ἀνέκπληκτος ἔμεινε· καὶ σὺ πειρῶ μηδὲν ὑπὸ τούτου παθεῖν. ἀλλ᾽ οὐκ ἂν δύναιο. τί φῄς; καὶ μὴν δυνήσει; τοιγαροῦν ἄκουε. δεῖ δὲ οὐδὲν ἐξελίττειν τὸ βιβλίον, ἀλλ᾽ αὐτὸς ἐρῶ. καὶ γὰρ οὐδὲ πολύστιχόν ἐστι. γλαφυρὸν μέντοι, καὶ τὸ κάλλος αὐτοῦ προσιζάνει τῇ μνήμῃ, ὥστε οὐδὲ βουλόμενον ἐπιλαθέσθαι με οἷόν τε.

"Ἀναστὰς ἕωθεν καὶ τοὺς θεοὺς προσειπὼν ὅπερ εἴωθα, ἐπεμελούμην τῆς κόμης· καὶ γὰρ ἐτύγχανον μαλακώτερον τὸ σῶμα ἔχων· ἡ δὲ ἠμέλητο ἐκ πλείονος. πάνυ γοῦν συνέστραπτο καὶ συνεπέπλεκτο τὰ πολλὰ αὐτῆς, οἷον τῶν οἰῶν

---

[1] Apparently for the purpose of deciding, on the basis of age, who should help himself first.

[2] A reminiscence of *Odyssey* 20. 23, τῷ δὲ μάλ᾽ ἐν πείσῃ κραδίη μένε τετληκυῖα, referring to the behaviour of Odysseus as he noted with irritation that his maidservants were on their way to meet their lovers among the suitors.

ambush he did not endure the attack. Nay, even in his struggle with the Hydra, though for a time they were locked in single combat, yet when the crab came to her aid Heracles might even have cried quits, had he not enlisted Iolaüs against them as ally. I too, methinks, have had much the same experience at the hands of Dio, though I have no nephew Iolaüs. Once more, therefore, quite forgetful of myself and my reasonings, I am composing laments, mourning my lost head of hair.

But since you are the most excellent of bald-heads and are apparently a man of mettle, seeing that you do not even give a thought to your misfortune but, when pease porridge has been served and an inspection of foreheads is in progress,[1] even call attention to yourself, as if priding yourself, forsooth, upon some blessing, therefore endure with patience Dio's discourse and, as the saying goes, keep your heart in obedience,[2] just as Odysseus when confronted with the misconduct of the women remained undaunted ; so do you too endeavour to be undismayed by Dio. Ah, but you couldn't. What's that you say ? You will indeed be able ? Well then, listen. But there is no need to unroll the parchment ; instead I will recite the speech myself. For in fact it does not contain many lines ; yet it is a polished composition, and its beauty lingers in my memory, so that not even if I wished to do so could I forget.

Dio's *Encomium on Hair* : " Having arisen at dawn and having addressed the gods, as is my wont, I proceeded to attend to my hair ; for in truth my health, as it happened, was rather feeble and my hair had been too long neglected. At any rate, most of it had become quite matted and tangled, as happens

τὰ περὶ τοῖς σκέλεσιν αἰωρούμενα· πολὺ δὲ ταῦτα
σκληρότερα ὡς ἂν ἐκ λεπτοτέρων συμπεπλεγμένα
τῶν τριχῶν.

"Ἦν οὖν ὀφθῆναί τε ἀγρία ἡ κόμη καὶ βαρεῖα,
μόλις δὲ διελύετο καὶ τὰ πολλὰ αὐτῆς ἀπεσπᾶτο
καὶ διετείνετο. οὐκοῦν ἐπῄει μοι τοὺς φιλοκόμους
ἐπαινεῖν, οἳ φιλόκαλοι ὄντες καὶ τὰς κόμας περὶ
πλείστου ποιούμενοι ἐπιμελοῦνται οὐ ῥᾳθύμως,
ἀλλὰ κάλαμόν τινα ἔχουσιν ἀεὶ ἐν αὐτῇ τῇ κόμῃ,
ᾧ ξαίνουσιν αὐτήν, ὅταν σχολὴν ἄγωσι· καὶ τοῦτο
δὴ τὸ χαλεπώτατον, χαμαὶ κοιμώμενοι φυλάττουσιν ὅπως μηδέποτε ἅψωνται τῆς γῆς, ὑπερεί-
δοντες ὑπὸ τὴν κεφαλὴν μικρὸν ξύλον, ὅπως
ἀπέχῃ τῆς γῆς ὡς πλεῖστον, καὶ μᾶλλον φροντίζουσι τοῦ καθαρὰν φέρειν τὴν κόμην ἢ τοῦ ἡδέως
καθεύδειν· ἡ μὲν γὰρ καλούς τε καὶ φοβεροὺς
ἔοικε ποιεῖν, ὁ δὲ ὕπνος, κἂν πάνυ ἡδὺς ᾖ, βραδεῖς
τε καὶ ἀφυλάκτους.

"Δοκοῦσι δέ μοι καὶ Λακεδαιμόνιοι μὴ ἀμελεῖν
τοῦ τοιούτου πράγματος, οἳ τότε ἥκοντες πρὸ τῆς
μάχης τῆς μεγάλης τε καὶ δεινῆς, ὅτε μόνοι τῶν
Ἑλλήνων ἔμελλον δέχεσθαι βασιλέα, τριακόσιοι
τὸν ἀριθμὸν ὄντες, ἐκάθηντο ἀσκοῦντες τὰς κόμας.
δοκεῖ δέ μοι καὶ Ὅμηρος πλείστης ἐπιμελείας
ἀξιοῦν τὸ τοιοῦτον. ἀπό γε μὲν ὀφθαλμῶν οὐ
πολλάκις ἐπαινεῖ τοὺς καλούς, οὐδὲ ἀπὸ τούτου
μάλιστα ἡγεῖται τὸ κάλλος ἐπιδείξειν. οὐδενὸς
οὖν τῶν ἡρώων ὀφθαλμοὺς ἐγκωμιάζει ἢ Ἀγα-

---

[1] Herodotus (7. 208) relates that a Persian scout, sent to
spy out the Greek camp before the battle of Thermopylae,
was amazed to find some of the Spartans combing their hair.

with the knots of wool that dangle about the legs of sheep—though these, of course, are far more stubborn, having been twisted together out of strands that are finer.

"Well, my hair was a wild and grievous sight to behold, and it was proving difficult to get it loosened up, and most of it threatened to tear out and resisted my efforts. Accordingly it occurred to me to praise the hair-lovers, who, being beauty-lovers and prizing their locks most of all, attend to them in no casual manner, but keep a sort of reed always in the hair itself, wherewith they comb it whenever they are at leisure ; moreover—the most unpleasant thing of all —while sleeping on the ground they are careful never to let their hair touch the earth, placing a small prop of wood beneath their head so as to keep it as far as possible from the earth, and they are more concerned to keep their hair clean than they are to enjoy sweet sleep. The reason, it would seem, is that hair makes them both beautiful and at the same time terrifying, while sleep, however sweet it be, makes them both sluggish and devoid of caution.

"And it seems to me that the Spartans, too, do not disregard a matter of such importance, for on that memorable occasion, on their arrival before the great and terrible battle, at a time when they alone among the Greeks were to withstand the attack of the Great King, three hundred in number as they were, they sat down and dressed their locks.[1] And Homer, too, methinks, believed that sort of thing deserved fullest attention. At least he does not often praise his beauties for their eyes, nor does he think that by so doing he will best set forth their beauty. Accordingly, he praises the eyes of none of his heroes

339

μέμνονος, ὥσπερ καὶ τὸ ἄλλο σῶμα ἐπαινεῖ αὐτοῦ·
καὶ οὐ μόνον τοὺς Ἕλληνας ἑλίκωπας καλεῖ· ἀλλ'
οὐδὲν ἧττον καὶ τὸν Ἀγαμέμνονα τὸ κοινὸν ἐπὶ
τοῖς Ἕλλησιν· ἀπὸ δὲ τῆς κόμης πάντας· πρῶτον
μὲν Ἀχιλλέα,

> ξανθῆς δὲ κόμης ἕλε Πηλείωνα·

ἔπειτα Μενέλαον ξανθὸν ἐπονομάζων ἀπὸ τῆς
κόμης· τῆς δὲ Ἕκτορος χαίτης μέμνηται,

> ἀμφὶ δὲ χαῖται
> κυάνεαι πεφόρηντο.

Εὐφόρβου γε μὴν τοῦ καλλίστου τῶν Τρώων
ἀποθανόντος οὐδὲν ἄλλο ὠδύρετο λέγων,

> αἵματί οἱ δεύοντο κόμαι Χαρίτεσσιν ὁμοῖαι,
> πλοχμοί θ' οἳ χρυσῷ τε καὶ ἀργύρῳ ἐσφήκωντο·

καὶ τὸν Ὀδυσσέα ὅταν ἐθέλῃ καλὸν γεγονότα ὑπὸ
τῆς Ἀθηνᾶς ἐπιδεῖξαι· φησὶ γοῦν,

> κυάνεαι δ' ἐγένοντο ἔθειραι.

πάλιν δ' ἐπὶ τοῦ αὐτοῦ,

> κὰδ δὲ κάρητος
> οὔλας ἧκε κόμας, ὑακινθίνῳ ἄνθει ὁμοίας.

" Καὶ πρέπειν γε μᾶλλον τοῖς ἀνδράσι φαίνεται
καθ' Ὅμηρον ὁ κόσμος ὁ τῶν τριχῶν ἢ ταῖς

---

[1] Iliad 2. 478-479 ; ὄμματα καὶ κεφαλὴν ἴκελος Διὶ τερπι-
κεραύνῳ, Ἄρεϊ δὲ ζώνην, στέρνον δὲ Ποσειδάωνι, " in eyes and head
like unto Zeus who delights in the thunder, in waist to Ares,
in chest to Poseidon."
[2] Iliad 1. 197.   Athena checks Achilles' rage.
[3] One of the commonest epithets applied to Menelaüs.
[4] Iliad 22. 401-402.

except Agamemnon, just as he praises the rest of
his body also [1]; moreover, he applies the term
'flashing-eyed,' not to the Greeks alone, but just
as much to Agamemnon himself, using the epithet
common to the Greeks in general; on the other
hand, he praises everybody for his hair. First of all
take Achilles, of whom he says,

> She seized Peleides by his flaxen hair, [2]

then Menelaüs, whom he calls 'blonde' [3] for his hair.
And Hector's hair he mentions in these words,

> And all about his blue-black tresses swept. [4]

Indeed, on the death of Euphorbus, the most beautiful
of the Trojans, Homer mourned nothing else of his,
for he said,

> His locks, so like the Graces', were wet with blood,
> His braids with gold and silver tightly claspt. [5]

The same is true of Odysseus, when the poet wishes
to exhibit him rendered beautiful by Athena; at
any rate he says,

> Blue-black his locks had grown. [6]

And again of the same person,

> Down from his head she caused the curly locks
> To fall, like bloom of hyacinth. [7]

"Moreover, the adornment afforded by the hair, to
judge by Homer, seems to be more suited to the men

[5] *Ibid.* 17. 51-52.
[6] Dio must have *Odyssey* 16. 176 in mind, but he has
substituted ἔθειραι for γενειάδες (beard). Odysseus' hair was
blonde; cf. *Odyssey* 13. 399.
[7] *Odyssey* 6. 230-231.

γυναιξί. γυναικῶν γοῦν περὶ κάλλους διεξιὼν οὐ
τοσαυτάκις φαίνεται κόμης μεμνημένος· ἐπεί τοι
καὶ τῶν θεῶν τὰς μὲν θηλείας ἄλλως ἐπαινεῖ—
χρυσῆν γὰρ Ἀφροδίτην καὶ βοῶπιν Ἥραν καὶ
Θέτιν ἀργυρόπεζαν—τοῦ Διὸς δὲ μάλιστα ἐπαινεῖ
τὰς χαίτας·

ἀμβρόσιαι δ' ἄρα χαῖται ἐπερρώσαντο ἄνακτος.''

Ταυτὶ μέν σοι τὰ Δίωνος.

than to the women. At any rate, when descanting on feminine beauty, he is not found to mention hair so often; for even with the gods he praises the female deities in different fashion—for it is ' golden Aphroditê ' and ' great-eyed Hera ' and ' Thetis of the silver feet '—but with Zeus he praises most of all his hair :

And toward her streamed the god's ambrosial locks." [1]

There you have the words of Dio.

[1] *Iliad* 1. 529.

FRAGMENTS

*We are indebted for the following brief fragments to the
anthologies of Stobaeus (c. A.D. 450) and Maximus the
Confessor (A.D. 580–662). Stobaeus names as his sources two
works nowhere else listed under the name of Dio, namely,
Sayings and Domestic Affairs ; Maximus does not tell us
the titles of the works from which he drew his quotations.
It is manifest that our manuscripts of Dio have preserved
for us only a portion of Dio's writings, and the Sayings
was probably a compilation made by an admirer of Dio, who
drew upon works now lost. At all events, both Stobaeus and
Maximus bear witness to the enduring fame and influence of
our author.*

DIONIS FRAGMENTA

I. Stob. Flor. 3, VII 28 p. 316 Hense
(VII 29 Meineke).

Ἐκ τῶν Δίωνος Χρειῶν·

Λάκαινα γυνὴ τοῦ υἱοῦ αὐτῆς ἐν παρατάξει χωλωθέντος καὶ δυσφοροῦντος ἐπὶ τούτῳ, Μὴ λυποῦ, τέκνον, εἶπεν· καθ᾽ ἕκαστον γὰρ βῆμα τῆς ἰδίας ἀρετῆς ὑπομνησθήσῃ.

II. Stob. Flor. 3, XIII 42 p. 462 Hense
(XIII 24 Mein.).

Ἐκ τῶν Δίωνος Χρειῶν·

Τὴν ἐπιτίμησιν ὁ Διογένης ἀλλότριον ἀγαθὸν ἔλεγεν εἶναι.

III. Stob. Flor. 3, XXXIV 16 p. 686 Hense
(XXXIV 16 Mein.).

Ἐκ τῶν Δίωνος Χρειῶν·

Τῶν συνόντων τις μειρακίων Διογένει ἐρωτώμενος ὑπ᾽ αὐτοῦ ἐσιώπα. ὁ δὲ ἔφη, Οὐκ οἴει τοῦ αὐτοῦ εἶναι εἰδέναι ἅ τε λεκτέον καὶ πότε καὶ τίνα σιωπητέον καὶ πρὸς τίνα;

FRAGMENTS
SAYINGS

1. A SPARTAN woman, when her son had been lamed on the field of battle and was chafing on that account, remarked, " Grieve not, my child, for at every step you will be reminded of your own valour."

2. " REPROOF," Diogenes was wont to say, " is another's blessing."

3. ONE of the youths who were disciples of Diogenes, when questioned by him, remained silent. But Diogenes remarked, " Do you not believe that it is to be expected of the same man that he should know, not only what he should say and when, but also what he should refrain from saying and before whom ? "

IV. Stob. Flor. 3, XLII 12 p. 762 Hense
(XLII 12 Mein.).

Δίωνος ἐκ τοῦ Οἰκονομικοῦ·

Ἀρξόμεθα δὲ ἀπὸ τοῦ μάλιστα ὠφελοῦντος
οἰκίαν· εἴη δ' ἂν τοῦτο ἐπιτίμησις διαβολῆς·
διαβολὴ γὰρ κακῶν τὸ ὀξύτατον καὶ ἐπιβουλότατον.

V. Stob. Flor. 4, XIX 46 p. 430 Hense
(LXII 46 Mein.).

Δίωνος ἐκ τοῦ Οἰκονομικοῦ·

Χρὴ οὖν δεσπόζειν ἐπιεικῶς καὶ ἀνεθῆναί ποτε
βουλομένοις ἐπιτρέπειν. αἱ γὰρ ἀνέσεις παρα-
σκευαστικαὶ πόνων εἰσί, καὶ τόξον καὶ λύρα καὶ
ἄνθρωπος ἀκμάζει δι' ἀναπαύσεως.

VI. Stob. Flor. 4, XXIII 59 p. 588 Hense
(LXXIV 59 Mein.).

Δίωνος ἐκ τοῦ Οἰκονομικοῦ·

Εὐσέβεια δὲ γυναικεία ὁ πρὸς τὸν ἄνδρα ἔρως.

VII. Stob. Flor. 4, XXIII 60 p. 588 Hense
(LXXIV 60 Mein.).

Ἐν ταὐτῷ·

Γέλως δὲ συνεχὴς καὶ μέγας θυμοῦ κακίων· διὰ
τοῦτο μάλιστα ἑταίραις ἀκμάζων καὶ παίδων τοῖς
ἀφρονεστέροις. ἐγὼ δὲ κοσμεῖσθαι πρόσωπον
ὑπὸ δακρύων ἡγοῦμαι μᾶλλον ἢ ὑπὸ γέλωτος.
δάκρυσι μὲν γὰρ ὡς ἐπὶ τὸ πλεῖστον σύνεστι καὶ
μάθημά που χρηστόν, γέλωτι δὲ ἀκολασία. καὶ
κλάων μὲν οὐδεὶς προυτρέψατο ὑβριστήν, γελῶν
δὲ ηὔξησεν αὐτοῦ τὰς ἐλπίδας.

FRAGMENTS

DOMESTIC AFFAIRS

1. WE shall begin with that which especially benefits a household ; and that would be reproof of slander, for slander is the most painful of all evils and the most insidious.

2. THEREFORE one ought to act the master with moderation and permit any who so desire to relax at times. For intervals of relaxation are preparatory for labours—both bow and lyre and men as well are at their best through relaxation.

3. BUT wifely piety is love of husband.

4. BUT laughter which is continuous and boisterous is worse than anger ; therefore it abounds especially among courtesans and the more foolish of children. As for myself, I hold that a face is adorned by tears more than by laughter. For with tears as a rule there is associated some profitable lesson, but with laughter licence. Moreover, by tears no one gives encouragement to a licentious person, whereas by laughter one fosters his expectations.

DIO CHRYSOSTOM

VIII. Stob. Flor. 4, XXVIII 12 p. 679 Hense
(LXXXV 12 Mein.).

Δίωνος ἐκ τοῦ Οἰκονομικοῦ·
Μέγα γὰρ δυσώπημα σωφροσύνης τέκνωσις.

IX. Stob. Flor. 4, XXVIII 13 p. 679 Hense
(LXXXV 13 Mein.).

Ἐν ταὐτῷ·
Τὸ μὲν γὰρ τίκτειν ἀνάγκης ἐστὶν ἔργον, τὸ δὲ
ἐκτρέφειν φιλοστοργίας.

X. Maxim. Flor. (Vatic. gr. 397 f. 81b).

Δίωνος τοῦ Χρυσοστόμου·
Πῶς οὐ δεινὸν τοῖς μὲν θεοῖς ἐνοχλεῖν, αὐτοὺς
δὲ μὴ βούλεσθαι πράττειν ἅ γε ἐφ' ἡμῖν εἶναι δοκεῖ
τοῖς θεοῖς.

XI. Maxim. Flor. (Vatic. gr. 397 f. 159b).

Δίωνος τοῦ Χρυσοστόμου·
Κινδύνων ἐλπὶς ἄνευ κινδύνων τίθησι τὸν ἐλπίζοντα τῷ προησφαλίσθαι τῶν δυσχερῶν τῇ δοκήσει
τὰ πράγματα.

XII. Maxim. Flor. (Vatic. gr. 739 f. 217a).

Δίωνος τοῦ Χρυσοστόμου·
Πονηρίαν γὰρ ἀρχομένην μὲν κωλῦσαι τάχα
τις κολάζων ἄν¹ δυνηθείη· ἐγκαταγεγηρακυῖαν δὲ
καὶ γεγενημένην τῶν εἰθισμένων διὰ² τιμωριῶν
ἀδύνατον εἶναι λέγουσιν.

FRAGMENTS

5. For great humiliation is the engendering of self-control.

6. For while the begetting of offspring is an act of necessity, their rearing is an act of love.

MISCELLANEOUS

1. Surely it is shocking to importune the gods and yet to be unwilling ourselves to do the things which by the gods' decree are in our power.

2. Expectation of dangers exempts from dangers him who expects them, since his affairs are made secure beforehand by reason of his anticipation of the difficulties.

3. For though wickedness, when incipient, might possibly be checked by repression, when chronic and established as a thing to which we have grown accustomed, it cannot, they say, be checked through penalties.

---

[1] ἄν added by Arnim.
[2] διά added by Crosby, κρατῆσαι διά τινων ἐπικειμένων Arnim.

LETTERS

Five letters included by Hercher in his Epistolographi Graeci, *page 259, have been associated with the name of Dio. Their contents afford no sure clue as to authorship, but there seems to be no good reason for refusing to attribute them to Dio. The Rufus to whom the first two are addressed may have been the Musonius Rufus who was the only philosopher at Rome to escape the wrath of Vespasian in the expulsions of* A.D. 71. *In a writing no longer extant,* πρὸς Μουσώνιον, *Dio seems to have made him the recipient of a violent attack upon the philosophers of that day, but if the unstinted commendation of an unnamed philosopher bestowed by Dio in his* Rhodian Discourse (§ 122) *refers to Musonius, as is generally believed, Dio clearly either had never borne him any malice or else had repented of it. It may very well be that friendship for Musonius was at least partially responsible for Dio's conversion to philosophy. As for the identity of the persons to whom the other letters are addressed, it seems idle to speculate, since neither the letters themselves nor any external evidence affords a clue.*

ΔΙΩΝΟΣ ΕΠΙΣΤΟΛΑΙ

α΄. Ῥούφῳ

Συνίστημί σοι τὸν φέροντα τὴν ἐπιστολὴν ἄνδρα
πράγματα μὲν ἔχοντα δι᾽ ἀντιδίκου φιλονεικίαν,
αὐτὸν δὲ τοῖς φίλοις παρέχειν οὐ βουλόμενον. ἔτι
δὲ καὶ τἆλλα οἷον ἂν σὺ ἐπαινέσειας, μέτριος καὶ
ἐπιεικής· τὸ γὰρ τοῦ γένους καὶ πολιτικοῦ ἀξιώ-
ματος οὐδ᾽ οἶμαί[1] σε δεῖσθαι πυνθάνεσθαι, καὶ γὰρ
καὶ ταῦτα αὐτῷ ὑπάρχει.

β΄. Ῥούφῳ

Ἐρέννιον[2] τὸν ἐμὸν ἑταῖρον φθάνεις μὲν ἐπιστάμενος, οὔπω δὲ ἱκανῶς, ὅσον ἐγὼ βούλομαι.
οὐδὲ γὰρ νῦν ἂν δυναίμην ἴσως εἰπεῖν ἅπαντα τὰ
προσόντα αὐτῷ. τοσαῦτα μέντοι ἄξιον αὐτὸν
μαρτυρῆσαι, ὡς καὶ γέγονεν ἡμῖν ἐκ πλείονος
φίλος καὶ[3] πεῖραν ἤδη τῷ χρόνῳ δέδωκε, καὶ περὶ
τοὺς λόγους πρότερον μὲν ἐζήλωσε, νῦν δὲ καὶ
ὑπερεβάλετο. ἔστι γὰρ ῥήτωρ ἀγαθός, ἔτι δ᾽ ἂν
γένοιτο βελτίων σοὶ συνὼν καὶ ὑπὸ σοῦ προαγό-
μενος. σὺ δέ μοι[4] πολλὰ περὶ πολλῶν χαριζόμενος

---

[1] οὐδ᾽ οἶμαί Emperius : οὐ δέομαι.
[2] Ἐρέννιον Hercher, Τερέντιον Emperius : Τερένιον.
[3] καὶ Crosby, ὥστε Emperius : καὶ ὅσα.
[4] After μοι Crosby deletes τὰ.

LETTERS

1. *To Rufus*

THE bearer of the letter I introduce to you as a man who, though in trouble because of an adversary's contentiousness, does not himself wish to make trouble for his friends. Moreover, in all other respects as well he is the kind of man you would approve— moderate and reasonable ; as for his birth and social standing, I think you need not even inquire, for he has those requisites to commend him also.

2. *To Rufus*

You already are acquainted with my good friend Herennius, though not yet sufficiently, not to the extent that I desire. In fact, I could not even now, perhaps, tell all his attributes. This much, however, it is fitting that I myself should testify : not only has he been a friend of mine for some time, but also he has stood the test of time. Besides, though he had been a devoted student of the art of public speaking previously, now he has actually surpassed himself. For in truth he is an excellent orator, but he might become still better through association with you and through your guidance. But though you do me many favours in many matters, you

355

ἐν τοῖς μάλιστα ἂν χαρίζοιο καὶ Ἑρέννιον[1] σαυτοῦ
νομίζων.

γ΄. Εὐσεβίῳ

Παρόντα σε βλέπειν οἶμαι ταῖς ἐπιστολαῖς
ἐντυγχάνων αἷς ἐπιστέλλεις, ὥστ᾽ εἰ γράφοις μοι
συνεχέστερον ἥκιστ᾽ ἂν ἐπὶ τῇ ἀπουσίᾳ δυσχεραί-
νοιμι.

δ΄. τῷ αὐτῷ

Ἀνιαρὰ μὲν εἶναι τὰ συμβάντα Δρακοντίῳ[2] καὶ
κακῶν ἔσχατα[3] τίς οὐκ ἂν ὁμολογήσειεν, ἀνθρώπινα
δὲ καὶ πολλοῖς ἤδη γεγενημένα. διὸ καρτερεῖν
μὲν ἐπ᾽ ἐκείνοις ἀνάγκη καὶ φέρειν ἑκόντα[4]· δεῖ
γάρ, κεἰ ἄλλως ἔχοι,[5] κεἰ σφόδρα τοῦ πάθους
ἡττῷτο,[6] ὑπὲρ τῶν ὄντων ὁρᾶν ὀρθῶς, ἵνα μὴ[7]
τὰς μὲν συμφορὰς ἄριστα διηνυκέναι δοκῇ,[8] περὶ
δὲ τοῦ ζῶντος οὐκ[9] ἄριστα φρονεῖν.

ε΄. Σαβινιανῷ[10]

Οὐκ ὄκνῳ τοῦ γράφειν οὐδ᾽ ὑπεροψίᾳ τινὶ σε-
σιώπηταί μοι τὰ πρότερον. καί σοι ἂν ὡμολόγουν[11]

---

[1] Ἑρέννιον Hercher, Τερέντιον Emperius : Τερένιον.
[2] Δρακοντίῳ Hercher, Δράκοντι Emperius : δράκοντα.
[3] ἔσχατα Emperius : ἔσχοντα.
[4] ἑκόντα Emperius : ἑκόντας.
[5] κεἰ . . . ἔχοι Emperius, κἂν . . . ἔχῃς Hercher : κἂν
. . . ἔχοι.
[6] κεἰ . . . ἡττῷτο Emperius, κἂν . . . ἡττᾷ Hercher κἂν
. . . ἡττῷτο.
[7] μὴ added by Hercher.
[8] δοκῇ] δοκῇς Hercher.

would favour me especially if you would consider
Herennius, too, a friend of yours.

3. *To Eusebius*

I FANCY that I am beholding your very presence
when I read the letters you send me, and so if you
were to write me more often, I should be least vexed
at your absence.

4. *To the same*

THE misfortunes which have befallen Dracontius
are, to be sure, painful and evil in the extreme, as
every one would admit, and yet they are such as
mankind is subject to and as have ere now befallen
many. Wherefore he must be steadfast in those
tribulations and endure them with set purpose. For
even if conditions should be otherwise, even if he
should be exceedingly overcome by his experience,
he must maintain a correct view regarding the facts,
lest he be thought to have come through his misfortunes most nobly and yet not be most nobly
minded regarding the living.

5. *To Sabinianus*

NOT because of reluctance to write or because of
any disdain have I hitherto kept silence. And I

---

⁹ οὐκ omitted by Emperius.
¹⁰ Σαβινιανῷ Boissonadiana: Σασιανῷ, Σαβιανῷ, or Σταβι-
ανῷ.
¹¹ ὡμολόγουν Hercher: ὡμολογούμην or ὁμολογούμενον.

εἶναι σχετλιώτατος ἀνθρώπων, εἰ τέχνῃ μὲν τὸ
λέγειν ἀσκήσας ἐπιστέλλειν οὐκ ἐβουλόμην, ἠμέ-
λουν δὲ φίλου ᾧ καὶ συνεχόρευσα τὰ τῶν Μουσῶν
καὶ τὰ ἱερὰ συνετελέσθην ὅσα δὴ πάντων ἐν
Ἕλλησιν ἁγιώτατα.

would agree with you that I am the wickedest of mortals if, after having cultivated eloquence as an art, I refused to write a letter and, instead, neglected a friend with whom I had joined in song and dance in honour of the Muses and with whom I had been initiated into all the religious rites of greatest sanctity among the Greeks.

TESTIMONY REGARDING DIO'S LIFE AND WRITINGS

Although Dio's claim to a place in the history of Greek literature has long been based upon the eighty Discourses that bear his name, the testimony of certain scholars, critics, and book-lovers of later ages reveals the high esteem which his work in general continued to enjoy and enables us to piece out the story of his life, supplying also at least the titles of certain works now lost. The more significant portions of this testimony are recorded on the following pages.

DE VITA ET SCRIPTIS DIONIS
TESTIMONIA ET IVDICIA

1. Philostratus

Philostratus, one of the most distinguished sophists of the third century of our era, is perhaps our most important witness. In his Lives of the Sophists *he testifies to Dio's effectiveness as a public speaker, his intimacy with Trajan, and his sincerity of purpose, explaining that the* Praise of the Parrot, *now lost, was a typically sophistic exercise, belonging to Dio's earlier career. He also adds some interesting details*

2. Lucianus Peregrin. c. 18

Lucian, whose literary career followed that of Dio after an interval of only a few years, has left us one brief reference to our author, but that he regarded Dio as a philosopher worthy

Πλὴν ἀλλὰ καὶ τοῦτο κλεινὸν αὐτοῦ καὶ διὰ στόματος ἦν ἅπασιν, ὁ φιλόσοφος διὰ τὴν παρρησίαν καὶ τὴν ἄγαν ἐλευθερίαν ἐξελαθείς· καὶ προσήλαυνε κατὰ τοῦτο τῷ Μουσωνίῳ καὶ Δίωνι καὶ Ἐπικτήτῳ καὶ εἴ τις ἄλλος ἐν περιστάσει τοιαύτῃ ἐγένετο.

3. Themistius Orat. V, p. 63 d

Themistius, whose career covered most of the fourth century, is perhaps best known for his Paraphrases *of Aristotle, but he achieved eminence as a public speaker at Constantinople,*

Οὕτω καὶ οἱ πατέρες τῆς σῆς βασιλείας τοὺς

---

[1] For Philostratus' testimony regarding Dio the reader

TESTIMONY REGARDING DIO'S
LIFE AND WRITINGS

1. Philostratus

concerning Dio's exile, for example, that he carried with him
Plato's Phaedo *and* Demosthenes' On the False Embassy,
information presumably gleaned from writings since lost.
Scattered allusions to Dio in Philostratus' Life of Apollonius,
though in themselves less significant and possibly somewhat
fanciful, reinforce what is told in the Lives of the Sophists.[1]

2. Lucian

of respect may be inferred from his having coupled him with
Musonius and Epictetus.

Peregrinus : However, this too brought him (Peregrinus) renown, and he was on everybody's tongue,
" the philosopher who was exiled for his frankness
and extreme independence " ; and in this particular
he came close to Musonius and Dio and Epictetus
and any one else who found himself in like situation.

3. Themistius

and the following testimony to Trajan's fondness for Dio
comes from one of his addresses. It is noteworthy chiefly as
an early allusion to Dio's title, Chrysostomos.

Discourses : Thus also the fathers of your empire

may consult Wright's *Philostratus and Eunapius* (L.C.L.),
pp. 16-23, and Conybeare's *Life of Apollonius of Tyana*
(L.C.L.), vol. I, pp. 522-523, 532-545, 558-559, 562-565, and
vol. II, pp. 296-297.

προγόνους ταύτης τῆς τέχνης προῆγον, τὸν Ἄρειον
ἐκεῖνον ὁ Σεβαστός, ὁ Τιβέριος τὸν Θρασύλον,
Τραιανὸς ὁ μέγας Δίωνα τὸν χρυσοῦν τὴν γλῶτταν, κτλ.

4. Menander περὶ ἐπιδεικτικῶν Rhetor. Gr. III
p. 389, 30 Spengel

*The Menander to whom we are indebted for the following
brief references, whose significance consists in the linking of
Dio with Plato, Xenophon, Nicostratus, and Philostratus as*

Ὅταν μὴ τραχείᾳ χρώμεθα τῇ ἀπαγγελίᾳ μηδὲ
περιόδους ἐχούσῃ καὶ ἐνθυμήματα, ἀλλ᾽ ὅταν
ἁπλουστέρα τυγχάνῃ καὶ ἀφελεστέρα, οἷα ἡ
Ξενοφῶντος καὶ Νικοστράτου καὶ Δίωνος τοῦ
Χρυσοστόμου καὶ Φιλοστράτου τοῦ τῶν Ἡρωικῶν
τὴν ἐξήγησιν καὶ τὰς Εἰκόνας γράψαντος, εἰρομένη
καὶ ἀκατασκεύαστος.

Ibid. p. 411, 29. Γένοιτο δ᾽ ἂν καὶ ἀπὸ λέξεως
ἐπιτετηδευμένης καὶ κεκαλλωπισμένης χάρις ἐν
λόγῳ, οἷα ἐστὶν ἡ Πλάτωνος καὶ Ξενοφῶντος καὶ
τῶν νεωτέρων, Δίωνος καὶ Φιλοστράτου καὶ τῶν
σοφιστῶν ὅσοι καὶ συντιθέναι τὸ συγγραφικὸν
εἶδος ἔδοξαν χαριέντως.

5. Synesii Dio, cap. 1, pp. 35 sqq. Petav.

*The literary activity of Synesius falls in the opening years
of the fifth century. From his father he inherited a library,
and also, it would seem, the love of books. He exhibits familiarity of a non-professional nature with many of the great
Greek writers of the classic period, Plato being apparently
his favourite. But Dio seems to have held for him a special
attraction, for he incorporated Dio's Encomium on Hair in*

showed preference for the founders of this art—
Augustus for the famous Areius, Tiberius for Thrasylus, the mighty Trajan for Dio of the golden
tongue . . .

4. Menander

*exponents of simple, graceful prose, is probably the rhetorician
who lived in the third century.*

On Declamation : Whenever the recital we employ
is not harsh or teeming with periods or enthymemes
but, as it happens, is more simple and artless, like
that of Xenophon and Nicostratus [1] and Dio Chrysostom and Philostratus, who wrote the *Heroica* and the
Imagines,[2] it is a running and natural style.

(*The same*) : Even from a style involving conscious
art and embellishment there might arise grace of
expression, like the style of Plato and Xenophon and
the later writers, Dio and Philostratus and all the
sophists who have gained a reputation for composing
graceful prose.

5. Synesius

his own Encomium on Baldness,[3] *and he even composed a
treatise entitled* Dio, *which he professes to have intended for
the edification of his son-to-be.*

In his Dio *he discriminates between Dio the sophist and
Dio the philosopher, and he reproves Philostratus for a certain
confusion or inconsistency in that regard. Synesius makes
the practical suggestion that it would be helpful to label each
of Dio's writings either " pre-exile " or " post-exile " as the
case might be, Dio's exile marking his transformation from*

---

[1] A rhetorician contemporary with Marcus Aurelius.
[2] Nephew of the author of the *Lives of the Sophists*.
[3] See pages 332-343.

*sophist to philosopher and statesman. In the course of this
work Synesius mentions, sometimes with suggestive comment,*

Φιλόστρατος μὲν ὁ Λήμνιος ἀναγράφων τοὺς
βίους τῶν μέχρις αὑτοῦ σοφιστῶν ἐν ἀρχῇ τοῦ
λόγου δύο μερίδας ποιεῖ, τῶν τε αὐτὸ τοῦτο
σοφιστῶν καὶ τῶν ὅσοι φιλοσοφήσαντες διὰ τὴν
εὐστομίαν ὑπὸ τῆς φήμης εἰς τοὺς σοφιστὰς
ἀπηνέχθησαν· καὶ τάττει τὸν Δίωνα μετὰ τούτων,
ἐν οἷς Καρνεάδην τε καταλέγει τὸν Ἀθηναῖον καὶ
Λέοντα τὸν Βυζάντιον, καὶ συχνοὺς ἄλλους, κατα-
βιώσαντας μὲν ἐπὶ φιλοσόφου προαιρέσεως, λόγου
δὲ ἰδέαν σοφιστικὴν ἡρμοσμένους, ἐν οἷς ἀριθμεῖ
καὶ τὸν Κνίδιον Εὔδοξον, ἄνδρα τὰ πρῶτα τῶν
Ἀριστοτέλους ὁμιλητῶν, ἀλλὰ καὶ ἀστρονομίας εὖ
ἥκοντα, ὁπόσην ὁ τότε χρόνος ἐπρέσβευεν.

Ἡμῖν δὲ ὁ Δίων τῇ μὲν περιβολῇ τῆς γλώττης,
ἣν χρυσῆν εἶχεν, ὥσπερ καὶ λέγεται, σοφιστὴς
ἔστω διὰ πάντων τῶν ἑαυτοῦ, εἴ τις ἀξιοῖ τὴν
ἐπιμέλειαν τῆς φωνῆς σοφιστικὸν ἀγώνισμα οἴε-
σθαι· καίτοι καὶ τοῦτο μετὰ μικρὸν ὁποῖόν ἐστιν
ἐξετάσομεν· τὴν δὲ προαίρεσιν οὐχ εἷς ὁ Δίων,
οὐδὲ μετὰ τούτων τακτέος, ἀλλὰ μετ' Ἀριστο-
κλέους, ἀπ' ἐναντίας μέντοι κἀκείνῳ. ἄμφω μέν
γε μεταπεπτώκασιν· ἀλλ' ὁ μὲν ἐκ φιλοσόφου καὶ
μάλα ἐμβριθοῦς καὶ πρόσω καθεικότος τὸ ἐπι-
σκύνιον ἐτέλεσεν εἰς σοφιστάς, καὶ τρυφῆς ἁπάσης
οὐχ ἥψατο μόνον, ἀλλὰ καὶ εἰς ἄκρον ἐλήλακεν·
ἐννεάσας δὲ τῇ προστασίᾳ τῶν ἐκ τοῦ περιπάτου

certain of Dio's writings no longer extant, whence we learn that the corpus of Dio's writings had not yet been reduced to its present compass.

Dio : Philostratus of Lemnos, when recording the lives of the sophists down to his own time, in the beginning of his account establishes two categories, namely, the genuine sophists and those who, though they had devoted themselves to philosophy, yet because of the beauty of their language were by common report classed among the sophists. And he puts Dio among the latter, among whom he lists not only Carneades the Athenian and Leon the Byzantine but many others as well, men who had lived their lives as professing philosophers and yet had adopted a style characteristic of the sophists. Among these he numbers also Eudoxus of Cnidus, a man who holds first place among the disciples of Aristotle but also was well versed in astronomy, to the extent to which it was then cultivated.

As for myself, though in the dress affected by his tongue—and he had a tongue of gold, as is actually said—it may be conceded that Dio was a sophist in all his writings, provided one sees fit to suppose that attention to the sound is a sophistic aim, though the nature of this, too, I shall shortly examine, still in his purpose Dio is not one kind of person, nor should he be classed with these men, but rather with Aristocles, although he presents a striking contrast even with him. To be sure, they both underwent a change ; but Aristocles, after having been a philosopher, both very grave and deeply frowning, took his place among the sophists, and he not only tasted every form of luxury but even went to the extreme. And after spending his youth in defence of the

δογμάτων, καὶ συγγράμματα ἐξενηνοχὼς εἰς τοὺς
Ἕλληνας ἄξια φιλοσόφου σπουδῆς, οὕτω τι ἥττων
ἐγένετο δόξης σοφιστικῆς, ὡς μεταμέλειν μὲν
αὐτῷ γηρῶντι τῆς ἐν ἡλικίᾳ σεμνότητος, κόψαι
δὲ τὰ Ἰταλιωτικά τε καὶ Ἀσιανὰ θέατρα μελέταις
ἐναγωνιζόμενον· ἀλλὰ καὶ κοττάβοις ἐδεδώκει,
καὶ αὐλητρίδας ἐνόμιζε, καὶ ἐπήγγελλεν ἐπὶ τούτοις συσσίτια· ὁ δὲ Δίων ἐξ ἀγνώμονος σοφιστοῦ
φιλόσοφος ἀπετελέσθη· τύχῃ δὲ μᾶλλον ἢ γνώμῃ
χρησάμενος τὴν τύχην αὐτὸς διηγήσατο. ἦν δὲ
δὴ καὶ τοῦ γράφοντος βίον διηγήσασθαι τὴν περὶ
τὸν ἄνδρα διπλόην, ἀλλὰ μὴ ἁπλῶς οὕτω συγκατ-
αριθμῆσαι τοῖς ἀμφὶ Καρνεάδην καὶ Εὔδοξον·
ὧν ἥντινα ἂν λάβῃς ὑπόθεσιν, φιλόσοφός ἐστι,
μετακεχειρισμένη σοφιστικῶς, τοῦτ᾽ ἔστι λαμπρῶς
ἀπηγγελμένη καὶ δεξιῶς καὶ πολλὴν τὴν ἀφροδίτην
ἐπαγομένη. ταύτῃ καὶ παρὰ τῶν ἀνθρώπων, οὓς
λέγοντες ἐκήλουν τῷ κάλλει τῶν ὀνομάτων,
ἠξιοῦντο τῆς προσηγορίας τοῦ σοφιστοῦ· αὐτοὶ
δ᾽ ἂν ἀπαξιῶσαί μοι δοκοῦσι καὶ οὐδὲ διδόμενον
δέξασθαι, φιλοσοφίας ἐν ὀνείδει τὸ τοιοῦτον
τιθείσης ἄρτι, τοῦ Πλάτωνος ἐπαναστάντος τῷ
ὀνόματι. ὁ δὲ προύστη τε λαμπρῶς τοῖν βίοιν
ἑκατέρου χωρίς, καὶ ταῖς ὑποθέσεσι μάχεται ταῖς
αὐτὸς ἑαυτοῦ, λόγους ἐξενεγκὼν ἀπὸ τῶν ἐναντίων
ἐνστάσεων.

Χρὴ δήπου καὶ δι᾽ αὐτὴν οὐχ ἥκιστα τὴν ἐν τοῖς

---

[1] The school of Aristotle.
[2] A game of chance popular at drinking parties.

doctrines of the Peripatos [1] and after publishing among the Greeks treatises worthy of a philosopher's serious attention, he became so enslaved to the reputation of a sophist as to repent, as he grew older, of the solemnity that marked his prime and to knock for admission to the theatres of Magna Graecia and Asia, entering into competitions in declamation. Why, he even indulged in the cottabus,[2] and he employed flute-girls, and he issued invitations to dinner parties with these attractions. Dio, on the contrary, after having been a headstrong sophist, ended by becoming a philosopher ; yet this was the result of chance rather than of set purpose, as he himself has narrated. But it was to be expected also of the biographer that he should describe the twofold nature of Dio, instead of merely cataloguing him along with Carneades and Eudoxus and their following. For no matter what treatise of theirs you may take, it is philosophic in nature, though handled in sophistic fashion, that is, phrased brilliantly and cleverly and provided with charm in abundance. In this way, too, they were deemed worthy of the title sophist by the persons whom they beguiled in their speeches by the beauty of their language. And yet they themselves would have rejected that title, methinks, and would not have accepted it when offered, philosophy having lately made it a term of reproach, since Plato had rebelled against the name. Dio, on the contrary, not only championed in brilliant fashion each of the two types of career separately, but he also is at variance with his own principles, having published treatises based upon the opposite foundations.

Surely, not least of all by reason of the very

λόγοις διαφορὰν μὴ σεσιγῆσθαι τὰ περὶ τὸν ἄνδρα. ὅπερ γὰρ ἐν τοῖς μετὰ ταῦτά φησιν, ἀπολύων αὐτὸν αἰτίας συνθέντα ἔπαινον ἐπὶ ψιττακῷ τῷ ὄρνιθι· σοφιστοῦ γὰρ εἶναι μηδὲ τούτων ὑπεριδεῖν· αὐτοῦ μὲν ἂν ἔλεγχος εἶναι δόξειε, προειπόντος ὅτι τῶν συκοφαντουμένων ἐστὶν ὁ ἀνήρ, ὅστις φιλόσοφος ὢν εἰς τὸν σοφιστὴν ἕλκεται. λέγει γὰρ οὕτω· Σοφιστὰς δὲ οἱ παλαιοὶ ἐπωνόμαζον οὐ μόνον τῶν ῥητόρων τοὺς ὑπερφωνοῦντάς τε καὶ λαμπρούς, ἀλλὰ καὶ τῶν φιλοσόφων τοὺς σὺν εὐροίᾳ ἑρμηνεύοντας, ὑπὲρ ὧν ἀνάγκη πρότερον εἰπεῖν, ἐπειδὴ οὐκ ὄντες σοφισταί, δόξαντες δέ, παρῆλθον εἰς τὴν ἐπωνυμίαν ταύτην· εἶτα σαφῶς φιλοσόφους ἄνδρας ἐξαριθμεῖται· μεθ' ὧν δὴ καὶ τὸν Δίωνα, καὶ μετὰ Δίωνα ἄλλους, ὧν περὶ τοῦ τελευταίου παυόμενος, Τοσαῦτα, φησί, περὶ τῶν φιλοσοφησάντων ἐν δόξῃ τοῦ σοφιστεῦσαι· ταύτὸν ἑτέρως εἰπών, ὅτι μὴ ὄντες σοφισταὶ τοῦ ὀνόματος ἐπεβάτευσαν. καίτοι μεταξύ πού φησιν ἀπορεῖν οἷ χοροῦ τάξει τὸν ἄνδρα, περιδέξιον δή τινα ὄντα. τί οὖν προεῖπας, τί δὲ ἐπεῖπας, ὅτι τοῦτο μὲν ἔστιν, ἐκεῖνο δὲ φαίνεται;

'Αλλ' ἔγωγε οὐ μικρολογοῦμαι πρὸς τὰς ἐναντιολογίας· συγχωρῶ δὲ τὸν Δίωνα φιλόσοφον ὄντα παῖξαι τὰ σοφιστῶν, εἰ μόνον πρᾶός ἐστι καὶ ἵλεως φιλοσοφίᾳ, καὶ μηδαμοῦ μηδὲν ἐπηρέακεν

---

[1] No longer extant.

difference found among Dio's discourses, the facts about him ought not to have been kept silent. For what Philostratus says later on, when he tries to excuse Dio for having composed a eulogy on the parrot,[1] namely, that it is to be expected of a sophist that he should not disdain even these topics, might seem to be a refutation of himself, since previously he had said that Dio is one of those who are the victims of false charges, since, though a philosopher, he is forced into the category of the sophist. These are his words : " Sophist is the name the men of old applied, not only to those orators who excelled in delivery and in brilliance, but also to those philosophers who expressed themselves fluently ; and I must treat them first, since, though they were not sophists, but only so regarded, they have come to receive that title." Then he enumerates men who were clearly philosophers—among whom, of course, he places Dio, and after Dio others—and in concluding his remarks about the last in his list he says : " So much for those who practised philosophy but were thought to have been sophists," which was another way of saying that, though not sophists, they usurped the title. Yet somewhere between he says that he is at a loss to decide in what class to place Dio, since, forsooth, Dio is exceedingly clever. Why then did you say at the beginning and at the end that he really is the one, but seems to be the other ?

However that may be, I for my part do not split hairs regarding the contradictions ; on the contrary, I am willing to admit that Dio, though a philosopher, indulged in the tricks of the sophists, provided only that he is kindly and gracious toward philosophy and

DIO CHRYSOSTOM

αὐτῇ, μηδ' ἐπ' αὐτὴν συντέθεικε λόγους ἰταμούς
τε καὶ κακοήθεις. ἀλλ' οὗτός γε πλεῖστα δὴ καὶ
μάλιστα σοφιστῶν εἰς φιλοσόφους τε καὶ φιλοσοφίαν ἀπηναισχύντηκεν. ἅτε γάρ, οἶμαι, φύσεως
λαχὼν ἐχούσης ἰσχύν, καὶ τὸ ῥητορεύειν αὐτὸ
ἠλήθευεν, ἄμεινον ἀναπεπεισμένος εἶναι τοῦ ζῆν
κατὰ φιλοσοφίαν τὸ ζῆν κατὰ τὰς κοινὰς ὑπο-
λήψεις· ὅθεν ὅ τε κατὰ τῶν φιλοσόφων αὐτῷ λόγος
ἐσπουδάσθη, σφόδρα ἀπηγκωνισμένος καὶ οὐδὲν
σχῆμα ὀκνήσας, καὶ ὁ πρὸς Μουσώνιον ἕτερος
τοιοῦτος, οὐ προσγυμναζομένου τῷ τόπῳ τοῦ
Δίωνος, ἀλλ' ἐκ διαθέσεως γράφοντος, ὡς ἐγὼ
σφόδρα διισχυρίζομαι· πείσαιμι δ' ἂν καὶ ἄλλον,
ὅστις εὔστοχος ἤθους εἰρωνείαν τε καὶ ἀλήθειαν
ἐκ παντοδαποῦ λόγου φωρᾶσαι.

Ἐπειδή τε ἐφιλοσόφησεν, ἐνταῦθα δὴ καὶ
μάλιστα ἡ ῥώμη τῆς φύσεως αὐτοῦ διεδείχθη.
ὥσπερ γὰρ ἐπιγνούσης ὀψὲ τῆς φύσεως τὸ οἰκεῖον
ἔργον, οὐ κατὰ μικρόν, ἀλλ' ὅλοις τοῖς ἱστίοις
ἀπηνέχθη τῆς σοφιστικῆς προαιρέσεως· ὅς γε καὶ
τὰς ῥητορικὰς τῶν ὑποθέσεων οὐκέτι ῥητορικῶς,
ἀλλὰ πολιτικῶς μετεχειρίσατο. εἴ τις ἀγνοεῖ τὴν
ἐν ταὐτῷ προβλήματι διαφορὰν τοῦ πολιτικοῦ καὶ
τοῦ ῥήτορος, ἐπελθέτω μετὰ νοῦ τὸν Ἀσπασίας
τε καὶ Περικλέους ἐπιτάφιον Θουκυδίδου καὶ
Πλάτωνος, ὧν ἑκάτερος θατέρου παρὰ πολὺ
καλλίων ἐστί, τοῖς οἰκείοις κανόσι κρινόμενος.

Ὁ δ' οὖν Δίων ἔοικε θεωρήμασι μὲν τεχνικοῖς

---

[1] The two compositions here mentioned are not extant.
[2] Pericles' famous oration (Thuc. 2. 35-46) is statesman-
like, while Aspasia's (Plato, *Menexenus* 236 D—249 c) is a
model of rhetorical composition.

nowhere has dealt despitefully with it or has composed
against it speeches which are both reckless and
malicious. Yet the fact is that Dio has behaved with
more copious and vehement effrontery toward both
philosophers and philosophy than any of the sophists.
The reason, I fancy, is that, being endowed with a
forceful disposition, he was frank also in his behaviour
as a public speaker, having been convinced that it
is better to live in accord with common notions than
in accord with philosophy. Therefore not only was
his diatribe *Against the Philosophers* a serious composition on his part, utterly unabashed and shrinking
from no rhetorical device, but also his *Reply to
Musonius* [1] was another of the same character, for Dio
was not employing the occasion to exercise his talents,
but rather writing from conviction, as I emphatically
maintain, and I could convince any one else who is
skilful at detecting both irony and sincerity of
character in every sort of composition.

Furthermore, when Dio took up philosophy, then
indeed most of all the vigour of his nature was displayed. For as if his nature had been late in recognizing its proper function, not little by little but
under full sail he was swept away from the calling of
a sophist. At any rate, those subjects which were
rhetorical he no longer handled like a rhetorician but
rather like a statesman. If a person is ignorant of the
difference between the statesman and the rhetorician
in dealing with the same problem, let him review the
funeral orations of Aspasia and Pericles as recorded
by Thucydides and by Plato, each of which is far
more beautiful than the other when judged by its
own special standards. [2]

Well then, in philosophy Dio apparently did not

373

ἐν φιλοσοφίᾳ μὴ προσταλαιπωρῆσαι μηδὲ προσ-
ανασχεῖν φυσικοῖς δόγμασιν, ἅτε ὀψὲ τοῦ καιροῦ
μετατεθειμένος· ὀνάσθαι δὲ τῆς στοᾶς ὅσα εἰς
ἦθος τείνει καὶ ἠρρενῶσθαι παρ' ὁντινοῦν τῶν ἐφ
ἑαυτοῦ, ἐπιθέσθαι δὲ τῷ νουθετεῖν ἀνθρώπους
καὶ μονάρχους καὶ ἰδιώτας καὶ καθ' ἕνα καὶ
ἀθρόους, εἰς ὃ χρήσασθαι προαποκειμένῃ τῇ
παρασκευῇ τῆς γλώττης. διό μοι δοκεῖ καλῶς
ἔχειν ἐπιγράφειν ἅπασι τοῖς Δίωνος λόγοις, ὅτι
πρὸ τῆς φυγῆς ἢ μετὰ τὴν φυγήν, οὐχ οἷς ἐμφαί-
νεται μόνοις ἡ φυγή, καθάπερ ἐπέγραψαν ἤδη
τινές, ἀλλ' ἀπαξάπασιν. οὕτω γὰρ ἂν εἴημεν
τούς τε φιλοσόφους καὶ τοὺς αὐτὸ τοῦτο σοφι-
στικοὺς λόγους διειληφότες ἑκατέρους χωρίς, ἀλλ'
οὐχ ὥσπερ ἐν νυκτομαχίᾳ περιτευξόμεθα αὐτῷ
νῦν μὲν βάλλοντι Σωκράτην καὶ Ζήνωνα τοῖς ἐκ
Διονυσίων σκώμμασι καὶ τοὺς ἀπ' αὐτῶν ἀξιοῦντι
πάσης ἐλαύνεσθαι γῆς καὶ θαλάττης, ὡς ὄντας
Κῆρας πόλεών τε καὶ πολιτείας, νῦν δὲ στεφα-
νοῦντί τε αὐτοὺς καὶ παράδειγμα τιθεμένῳ γενναίου
βίου καὶ σώφρονος.

Φιλόστρατος δὲ καὶ τοῦτο ἀπεριμερίμνως τὸν
ἔπαινον τοῦ ψιττακοῦ καὶ τὸν Εὐβοέα τῆς αὐτῆς
προαιρέσεως οἴεται, καὶ ὑπὲρ ἀμφοῖν ὁμοίως εἰς
ἀπολογίαν καθίσταται τὴν ὑπὲρ τοῦ Δίωνος, ὡς
μὴ ἐπὶ τοῖς τυχοῦσιν ἐσπουδακέναι δοκεῖν. τοῦτο
δ' ἤδη πλέον ἐστὶ ποιήσασθαι θάτερον. ὁ γὰρ
ἀναγορεύσας αὐτὸν ἐν τοῖς δι' ὁλοκλήρου τοῦ

---

[1] The Stoic school.
[2] Synesius refers to the licence of comedy.
[3] No longer extant.
[4] Or. 7.

persevere in technical speculations, nor did he devote himself to physical dogmas, because he had shifted his position late in his career ; on the contrary, he seems to have profited from the Porch [1] in all that pertains to character, and to have become more manly than any person of his own day ; furthermore, he applied himself to the task of admonishing mankind, whether monarchs or men in private station, whether singly or in groups, to which end he utilized the training in oral expression which he had acquired previously. For this reason I think it well to make the notation " before his exile " or " subsequent to his exile " on all Dio's speeches, not alone on those in which his exile is reflected, as some have done in the past, but on one and all. For by so doing we should have separated the philosophic speeches and the truly sophistic, each variety by itself, and we shall not, as in a nocturnal engagement, find him at one moment hurling at Socrates and Zeno the coarse jests of the Dionysiac festival [2] and demanding that their disciples be expelled from every land and sea in the belief that they are Messengers of Death to states and civic organization alike, and at another moment find him crowning them with garlands and making them his pattern of a life of nobility and sobriety.

Philostratus, however, and without due consideration, imagines the *Encomium on the Parrot* [3] and the *Euboean Discourse* [4] to belong to the same school, and regarding both alike he enters the lists in the defence of Dio, to save him from the imputation of having paid serious attention to ordinary matters. But this actually is rather to achieve for himself the other alternative. For he who had publicly proclaimed

375

βίου φιλοσοφήσασι προϊὼν οὐ μόνον ἐνδέδωκε
πρὸς τὸ καὶ σοφιστικόν τι ἔργον εἰργάσθαι τὸν
Δίωνα, ἀλλὰ προσαποστερεῖ τὸν ἄνδρα καὶ τῶν
ὄντων ἐκ τῆς φιλοσόφου μερίδος, προσνέμων αὐτὰ
τοῖς σοφιστικοῖς. εἰ γὰρ τὸν Εὐβοέα τις ἀφαι-
ρήσεται τοῦ σπουδαῖον εἶναι καὶ ὑπὲρ σπουδαίων
συγκεῖσθαι, οὔ μοι δοκεῖ ῥᾷστ' ἂν ὁ τοιοῦτος
ἐγκρῖναί τινα λόγον τῶν Δίωνος ὥστε καὶ φιλόσοφον ὑπ' αὐτοῦ προσειρῆσθαι. ὡς οὗτός γε ὁ
λόγος ὑποτύπωσίς ἐστιν εὐδαίμονος βίου, πένητι
καὶ πλουσίῳ τοῦ παντὸς ἀνάγνωσμα ἀξιώτατον.
ᾠδηκός τε γὰρ ἦθος ὑπὸ πλούτου καταστέλλει,
τὸ εὔδαιμον ἑτέρωθι δείξας, καὶ τὸ καταπεπτωκὸς
ὑπὸ πενίας ἐγείρει καὶ ἀταπείνωτον εἶναι παρα-
σκευάζει, τοῦτο μὲν τῷ καταμελιτοῦντι τὰς
ἁπάντων ἀκοὰς διηγήματι, ὑφ' οὗ κἂν Ξέρξης
ἀνεπείσθη, Ξέρξης ἐκεῖνος ὁ τὴν μεγάλην στρατιὰν
ἐλάσας ἐπὶ τοὺς Ἕλληνας, μακαριώτερον ἑαυτοῦ
γεγονέναι κυνηγέτην ἄνδρα ἐν τῇ ὀρεινῇ τῆς
Εὐβοίας κέγχρους ἐσθίοντα, τοῦτο δὲ ταῖς ἀρίσταις
ὑποθήκαις, αἷς χρώμενος οὐδεὶς αἰσχυνεῖται πενίαν,
εἰ μή γε καὶ φεύξεται.

Διὸ βελτίους οἱ τάττοντες αὐτὸν μετὰ τὸν
ἔσχατον περὶ βασιλείας, ἐν ᾧ τέτταρας ὑποθέμενος
βίους καὶ δαίμονας, τὸν φιλοχρήματόν τε καὶ τὸν
ἀπολαυστικὸν καὶ τρίτον τὸν φιλότιμον, τελευταῖον
δὲ καὶ ἐπὶ πᾶσι τὸν εὔφρονα καὶ σπουδαῖον,

---

[1] Or. 4.
[2] This is not strictly true, for the fourth life and spirit is
merely promised (Or. 4. 139), as Synesius himself proceeds
to point out.

TESTIMONY

Dio to be among those who had practised philosophy
all their lives has not only later on yielded to the
idea that Dio had also done work of a sophistic
nature, but he goes so far as to defraud him also of
the possessions which come from the philosophic
category, since he assigns them to those that are
sophistic. For if a person is going to rob the *Euboean
Discourse* of its claim to be a serious work and to
have been composed on serious topics, in my opinion
such a person would not very easily accept any of
Dio's speeches to the extent of having it labelled by
him actually philosophic. For certainly this discourse
constitutes a pattern of a happy life, a work of literature of the very highest value for rich or poor alike.
For not only does it deflate a character that has
become puffed up by riches, pointing out that happiness is to be found elsewhere, but it also arouses a
character that has been cast down by poverty and
restores its self-respect, partly by means of his tale
that fills the ears of all with sweetness, a tale by
which even Xerxes, the famous Xerxes who marched
his mighty host against the Greeks, might have been
persuaded that a huntsman who fed on millet amid
the mountains of Euboea had been more blessed than
himself, and partly by his most excellent precepts,
which will not allow any one who follows them to be
ashamed of poverty, unless of course he is also to be
an exile.

Therefore those are better critics who place the
Euboean after the last discourse *On Kingship*,[1] in
which, after having set forth lives and spirits of four
kinds [2]—the avaricious, the pleasure-loving, thirdly
the ambitious, and finally, to cap them all, the
gracious and serious—he describes and sketches the

ἐκείνους μὲν τοὺς κατὰ τὴν ἀλογίαν ἅπαντας
γράφει τε καὶ σχηματίζει, παύεται δὲ τοῦ βιβλίου,
τὸν λοιπὸν ἐπαγγειλάμενος αὐτίκα ἀποδώσειν,
ὅτῳ ποτὲ πεπρωμένος ἐκ θεῶν ἐγένετο. χωρὶς
οὖν τιθέντι τοὺς ἐν τοῖς συχνοῖς λόγοις Διογένας
τε καὶ Σωκράτας, οἳ καὶ περιττοὶ τὴν φύσιν
ἔδοξαν· καὶ οὐχ ἅπαντός ἐστιν ὁ τοῖν ἀνδροῖν
τούτοιν ζῆλος, ἀλλ' ὅστις εὐθὺς αἵρεσίν τινα τῶν
κατὰ φιλοσοφίαν ὑπέσχετο· τὸν δὲ κατὰ τὴν
κοινὴν φύσιν ζητοῦντι καὶ τὸν ἅπασιν ἐγχωροῦντα,
δίκαιον, ὅσιον, αὐτουργόν, ἀπὸ τῶν ὄντων φιλάν-
θρωπον, οὐκ ἂν ἕτερος ἀντὶ τοῦ Εὐβοέως ἀπο-
δεδομένος εἴη βίος εὐδαιμονικός.

Ἔτι καὶ τοὺς Ἐσσηνοὺς ἐπαινεῖ που, πόλιν
ὅλην εὐδαίμονα τὴν παρὰ τὸ νεκρὸν ὕδωρ ἐν τῇ
μεσογείᾳ τῆς Παλαιστίνης κειμένην παρ' αὐτά
που τὰ Σόδομα. ὁ γὰρ ἀνὴρ ὅλως, ἐπειδὴ τοῦ
φιλοσοφεῖν ἀπήρξατο καὶ εἰς τὸ νουθετεῖν ἀνθρώπους ἀπέκλινεν, οὐδένα λόγον ἄκαρπον ἐξενήνοχε.

Τῷ δὲ μὴ παρέργως ἐντυγχάνοντι δήλη καὶ ἡ
τῆς ἑρμηνείας ἰδέα διαλλάττουσα καὶ οὐκ οὖσα
μία τῷ Δίωνι κατά τε τὰς σοφιστικὰς ὑποθέσεις
καὶ κατὰ τὰς πολιτικάς. ἐν ἐκείναις μὲν γὰρ
ὑπτιάζει καὶ ὡραΐζεται, καθάπερ ὁ ταῶς περιαθρῶν
αὑτὸν καὶ οἷον γανύμενος ἐπὶ ταῖς ἀγλαΐαις τοῦ
λόγου, ἅτε πρὸς ἓν τοῦτο ὁρῶν καὶ τέλος τὴν
εὐφωνίαν τιθέμενος. ἔστω παράδειγμα ἡ τῶν
Τεμπῶν φράσις καὶ ὁ Μέμνων. ἐν τούτῳ μέν γε

---

[1] The Essenes were a Jewish sect. Synesius is our only
witness to the existence of this writing.

[2] Neither work now extant. The former presumably

first three, which are all marked by lack of reason, but concludes his treatise with the announcement that the one yet remaining he will presently display for him, whoever it may be, for whom it has been destined by the gods. Accordingly, if one sets aside the Diogeneses and Socrateses that are found in many of his discourses, who actually have been thought unusual in their nature—and it is not every one who can imitate those two men, but only he who from the outset has professed some one of the philosophic creeds—and if he seeks after the life which accords with our common nature and which is possible for us all—righteous, pious, industrious, generous with its possessions—no other life would be displayed instead of the Euboean as a life of happiness.

Furthermore, Dio somewhere praises the Essenes,[1] a community of complete happiness, situated beside the Dead Sea in the interior of Palestine somewhere near Sodom itself. For when once he had started on his career as a philosopher and had turned to admonishing mankind, Dio never produced any discourse at all which was unprofitable.

But to one who is not a superficial reader it is plain that Dio's form of expression varies and is not uniform, according as his themes are sophistic or political. For in the sophistic he struts and plumes himself, looking himself over like the peacock and, as it were, exulting in the splendours of his eloquence, since he has eyes for that alone and makes euphony his goal. Take, for example, his *Tempê* and his *Memnon*.[2] In the latter, certainly, his style is actually

dealt with the famous Vale of Tempê in northern Greece; the latter has been associated with the Memnon statues at Egyptian Thebes.

καὶ ὑπότυφός ἐστιν ἡ ἑρμηνεία· τὰ δὲ τοῦ δευτέρου
χρόνου βιβλία, ἥκιστ᾽ ἂν ἐν αὐτοῖς ἴδοις χαῦνόν
τι καὶ διαπεφορημένον. ἐξελαύνει γάρ τοι φιλοσοφία καὶ ἀπὸ γλώττης τρυφήν, τὸ ἐμβριθές τε
καὶ κόσμιον κάλλος ἀγαπῶσα, ὁποῖόν ἐστι τὸ
ἀρχαῖον, κατὰ φύσιν ἔχον καὶ τοῖς ὑποκειμένοις
οἰκεῖον, οὗ μετὰ τοὺς λίαν ἀρχαίους καὶ Δίων
ἐπιτυγχάνει, διὰ τῶν πραττομένων ἰών, κἂν λέγῃ
κἂν διαλέγηται.

Ἔστω παράδειγμα τῆς ἀφελοῦς καὶ κυρίως
ἐχούσης ἑρμηνείας ὁ ἐκκλησιαστικός τε καὶ ὁ
βουλευτικός· εἰ δὲ βούλει, καὶ ὁντινοῦν τῶν πρὸς
τὰς πόλεις εἰρημένων τε καὶ ἀνεγνωσμένων προ-
κεχειρισμένος, ἴδοις ἂν ἑκατέραν ἰδέαν ἀρχαϊκήν,
ἀλλ᾽ οὐ τῆς νεωτέρας ἠχοῦς τῆς ἐπιποιούσης τῷ
κάλλει τῆς φύσεως, ὁποῖαι αἱ διαλέξεις, ὧν πρόσθεν
ἐμνημονεύσαμεν, ὁ Μέμνων τε καὶ τὰ Τέμπη,
λόγος τε οὗτος ὁ κατὰ τῶν φιλοσόφων. κἂν γὰρ
ἀποπροσποιῆται, πάνυ τοῦ θεάτρου γίνεται καὶ
τῆς χάριτος· καὶ οὐκ ἂν εὕροις ῥητορείαν ἐπαφρο-
διτοτέραν παρὰ τῷ Δίωνι· ὃ καὶ θαυμάσας ἔχω
τὴν τύχην φιλοσοφίας, εἰ μήτε κωμῳδία τῶν
Νεφελῶν μᾶλλον εὐδοκιμεῖ· οὐδὲ γὰρ ἔστιν ἥντινα
μετὰ τῆς ἴσης δυνάμεως Ἀριστοφάνης ἀπήγγελκε·
τεκμήριον ποιοῦ τοῦ στρογγύλως καὶ σὺν εὐροίᾳ
προενηνέχθαι,

κηρὸν διατήξας, εἶτα τὴν ψύλλαν λαβὼν
ἐνέβαψεν εἰς τὸν κηρὸν αὐτῆς τὼ πόδε·

---

[1] We do not know to what speeches Synesius refers.

bombastic. But in the works of his second period by no means would you find anything conceited and diffuse. For, you see, philosophy banishes luxuriousness even in the field of eloquence, being fond of a beauty which is grave and orderly, the ancient form, natural and germane to the subject, a form which Dio, too, achieves, second only to the very ancient writers, proceeding as he does through the matters in hand, whether he is delivering a speech or conducting a discussion.

Take as samples of his unaffected and literal style his *Ecclesiasticus* and his *Bouleuticus*.[1] Or, if you wish, take any one at all of his addresses to the cities, whether orally delivered or read, and you would find in each an old-fashioned style rather than that of the more modern note which makes additions to the beauty of nature, as in the case of the discourses already mentioned, the *Memnon* and the *Tempê*, and in this one, too, *Against the Philosophers*. For even if he disclaims it, this speech belongs wholly to the theatre and the desire to please ; furthermore, you could not find a more charming display of rhetoric in Dio. In this connexion I have marvelled at the good fortune of philosophy if, in the first place, no comedy is more in favour than the *Clouds*,[2] for there is none which Aristophanes has composed with equal power. As witness to his compact and flowing style, take these lines :

> He melted wax, and then he took the flea
> And dipt its two feet in the wax ; and then,

Or. 47 and Or. 48 were delivered before the *Ecclesia*, and the next two before the *Boulê*.

[2] The popularity of the *Clouds* is attested by the number of the manuscripts in which it is found.

κᾆτα ψυγείσῃ περιέφυσαν Περσικαί.
ταύτας ὑπολύσας ἀνεμέτρει τὸ χωρίον.

Ἀριστείδην τε ὁ πρὸς Πλάτωνα λόγος ὑπὲρ
τῶν τεσσάρων πολὺν ἐκήρυξεν ἐν τοῖς Ἕλλησιν·
οὗτος μὲν καὶ τέχνης ἁπάσης ἀμοιρῶν ὅν γε οὐδ'
ἂν ἐπαγάγοις εἴδει ῥητορικῆς, οὔκουν ἐκ τοῦ δικαίου γε καὶ τῶν νόμων τῆς τέχνης· συγκείμενος
δ' οὖν ἀπορρήτῳ κάλλει καὶ θαυμαστῇ τινι χάριτι,
εἰκῇ πως ἐπιτερπούσῃ τοῖς ὀνόμασι καὶ τοῖς
ῥήμασιν· οὗτός τε ὁ Δίων ἤκμασε μάλιστα ἐν τῷ
κατὰ τῶν φιλοσόφων, ἥντινα καὶ καλοῦσιν ἀκμὴν
οἱ νεώτεροι· τοῦτ' ἔστιν ἡρμόσατο πανηγυρικώ-
τερον ἀνδρὸς ἀφελοῦς, καὶ μέντοι γε εἰς τὴν
τοιαύτην ἰδέαν αὐτὸς αὑτοῦ ταύτῃ κράτιστος
ἔδοξεν.

Οὐ μέντοι τοσοῦτον ὁ Δίων ἐξωρχήσατο τὴν
ἀρχαίαν ῥητορικὴν ἐν οἷς καὶ δοκεῖ σαφῶς ἀνα-
χωρεῖν τῶν οἰκείων ἠθῶν, ὡς ἂν καὶ λαθεῖν ὅτι
Δίων ἐστί, παρακινήσας εἰς τὸ νεώτερον· ἀλλ'
εὐλαβῶς ἅπτεται τῆς παρανομίας, καὶ αἰσχυνομένῳ
γε ἔοικεν, ὅταν τι παρακεκινδυνευμένον καὶ
νεανικὸν προενέγκηται· ὥστε κἂν αἰτίαν φύγοι
δειλίας, εἰ πρὸς τὴν ὕστερον ἐπιπολάσασαν τῶν
ῥητόρων τόλμαν αὐτὸν ἐξετάζοιμεν, τοῖς πλείστοις
δὲ τῶν ἑαυτοῦ, καὶ παρὰ βραχὺ τοῖς ἅπασι μετ'
ἐκείνων ταττέσθω τῶν ἀρχαίων τε καὶ στασίμων
ῥητόρων, παρ' ὁντινοῦν καὶ δήμῳ διαλεχθῆναι

---

[1] *Clouds* 149-152.

When cooled, about it Persian shoes had formed.
Removing these, he fell to measuring the space.[1]

Again, the address *To Plato in Defence of the Four*
heralded the fame of Aristeides far and wide among
the Greeks.[2] This work, while actually devoid of all
artifice, one which surely you could not even assign
to the category of rhetoric, at least justly and on
the basis of the laws of the art, is composed with
an ineffable beauty and wondrous charm, one that
seemingly without premeditation delights by means
of its nouns and verbs. And lastly, our Dio was at
his prime in his *Against the Philosophers*, to use the
term prime as the moderns do ; that is, he composed
in a more showy manner than a plain man would,
and yet for such a style Dio was thought to be at his
best in this.

However, in the works in which he seems clearly
to depart from his own special habits Dio did not
display such scorn for the old-fashioned rhetoric as
to disguise the fact that it is Dio, though he did
move in the direction of the more modern ; on the
contrary, he is discreet when he violates his standards,
and he actually seems to be ashamed whenever he
has used any daring or audacious expression. Therefore he might even be taken to task for cowardice, if
we were to scrutinize him in the light of the audacity
which later became the vogue among the orators.
But in most of his own work, yes, in very nearly all,
let him be ranked with those old-fashioned and steady
orators, since, compared with any one at all, he is
wholly fit to address either a community or a person

[2] Aelius Aristeides (A.D. 129–189) in the work in question
praises Themistocles, Miltiades, Pericles, and Cimon.

καὶ ἰδιώτῃ τοῦ παντὸς ἄξιος. οἵ τε γὰρ ῥυθμοὶ
τοῦ λόγου κεκολασμένοι καὶ τὸ βάθος τοῦ ἤθους
οἷον σωφρονιστῇ τινι καὶ παιδαγωγῷ πρέπον
πόλεως ὅλης ἀνοήτως διακειμένης. ὥσπερ δὲ
τὴν ἑρμηνείαν οὔτε μίαν ἔφαμεν πάντως οὔτε
ἀνεπίγνωστον ὅτι Δίωνός ἐστιν ἑκατέρα, νῦν μὲν
ῥήτορος ἀνδρός, νῦν δὲ πολιτικοῦ, οὕτω καὶ τὰς
διανοίας, ὅστις οὐκ αὐτὸς δίχα διανοίας ἐπιβάλλει
τὰς ὄψεις ὅτῳ δὴ τῶν βιβλίων αὐτοῦ, ἐπιγνώσεται
Δίωνος οὔσας ἐν ταῖν δυοῖν ἰδέαιν τῶν ὑποθέσεων·
κἂν τὸ φαυλότατον προχειρίσῃ, τὸν Δίωνα ὄψει
τὸν πορισμώτατον τῇ ῥητορείᾳ παντὸς ἐξευρεῖν
λόγους· μακρῷ γὰρ δὴ σοφιστῶν κατὰ τὸ ἐπι-
χειρῆσαι διήνεγκεν. εἰ δέ τις καὶ ἕτερος σοφιστὴς
ἦν εὔπορος, ἀλλὰ πολλοῦ γε καὶ δεῖ παραβάλλεσθαι
πρὸς τὴν τοῦδε πυκνότητα· ἅμα δὲ καὶ θαυμαστή
τις ἰδιότης χαρακτηρίζει τὰς Δίωνος ἐπινοίας.
δηλούτω σοι τὸν ἄνδρα ὁ Ῥοδιακός τε καὶ ὁ
Τρωικός· εἰ δὲ βούλει, καὶ ὁ τοῦ κώνωπος ἔπαινος.
ἐσπουδάσθη γὰρ τῷ Δίωνι καὶ τὰ παίγνια, πανταχοῦ τῇ φύσει χρωμένῳ· καὶ οὐκ ἂν ἀπιστή-
σαις αὐτὰ τῆς αὐτῆς εἶναι παρασκευῆς τε καὶ
δυνάμεως.

Ταῦτά μοι περὶ Δίωνος εἰπεῖν ἐπῆλθε πρὸς τὸν
ὕστερόν ποτε παῖδα ἐσόμενον, ἐπεί μοι καὶ διεξ-
ιόντι τοὺς παντοδαποὺς αὐτοῦ λόγους μεταξὺ τὸ
μάντευμα γέγονε. πατρικὸν δὴ πέπονθα, καὶ ἤδη
συνεῖναι τῷ παιδὶ βούλομαι καὶ διδάσκειν ἅττα
μοι φρονεῖν ἔπεισι περὶ ἑκάστου συγγραφέως τε
καὶ συγγράμματος, συνιστὰς αὐτῷ φίλους ἄνδρας

in private station. For the rhythms of his speech are restrained and the gravity of his style is such as would befit any supervisor and guardian of a state wholly inclined to folly. But just as I have said of his style, that it is not by any means uniform, and yet that unmistakably each style is Dio's, now as orator and now as statesman, so also regarding his thoughts—whoever not without thought himself casts his eyes on any of Dio's writings will see that the thoughts are Dio's in both varieties of his speeches; and even if you select the most trivial of them, you will find Dio to be the most resourceful in his oratory at finding words for everything, for he is far superior to the sophists in dialectic argument. Nay, if any other sophist was resourceful, still he is far from deserving comparison with Dio in regard to the latter's sagacity; and at the same time a wondrous individuality marks his thoughts. Let both his *Rhodian* and his *Trojan* [1] discourses reveal him to you; or, if you wish, include his *Eulogy of the Gnat*.[2] For even his sportive compositions were treated seriously by Dio, who indulged his natural propensities in every field; moreover, you would not doubt that they were the product of the same training and faculty.

This is what it has occurred to me to say about Dio to him who some day in the future is to be my son, for even as I was going through Dio's speeches of every kind I received the prophecy. Already I feel like a father, and I want to be with my son at once and to teach him whatever occurs to me to think about each writer and each work of literature, introducing to him men who are my friends, along with

---

[1] Or. 11 and Or. 31 respectively.
[2] No longer extant.

μετὰ τῆς προσηκούσης ἕκαστον κρίσεως· ἐν οἷς
ἔστω καὶ Δίων ὁ Προυσαεύς, περιττὸς ἀνὴρ εἰπεῖν
τε καὶ γνῶναι. καὶ τοῦτον οὖν ἐπαινέσας αὐτῷ
παραδίδωμι, ἵνα μοι μετὰ τοὺς τῆς γενναίας
φιλοσοφίας προστάτας ἀπάρχοιτό ποτε καὶ τοῖς
πολιτικοῖς τοῦ Δίωνος γράμμασι, μεθόριον αὐτὰ
ἡγούμενος τῶν προπαιδευμάτων τε καὶ τῆς ἀλη-
θινωτάτης παιδείας.

6. Photius Bibl. cod. 209

*Photius, the learned Patriarch of Constantinople of the
ninth century, was an omnivorous reader, and his observations
on what he read are embodied in a digest entitled* Bibliotheca.
*His discussion of Dio's writings, which is confined to the
eighty discourses that make up our own collection, opens with
a few details regarding the life and personal characteristics
of Dio, followed by general remarks concerning his literary
qualities. Photius then proceeds to list, title by title, all*

Ἀνεγνώσθη Δίωνος βιβλίον ἐν λόγοις πʹ. οὗτος
ἔστι μὲν τὴν πατρίδα Προυσαεύς, φυγὰς δ' ἐγεγόνει ταύτης, τυραννίδος ἐκκλίνων δουλείαν, καὶ
πολλὴν ἐπῆλθε πλανώμενος γῆν. δεξιὸς δὲ περὶ
τοὺς λόγους ἔδοξεν εἶναι, καὶ μάλιστα τοὺς ὅσοι
ῥυθμίζειν συμβουλεύουσι τὰ ἤθη. ἤκμασε δὲ κατὰ
τοὺς χρόνους τοῦ βασιλέως Τραιανοῦ, καὶ πλεῖστον διέτριψε χρόνον παρ' αὐτῷ καὶ τῆς ὅτι
μάλιστα τιμῆς καὶ δεξιώσεως ἔτυχεν, ὡς καὶ συγκαθέζεσθαι αὐτὸν τῷ βασιλείῳ ὀχήματι. παῖς
μὲν ἦν οὗτος Πασικράτους, σοφιστὴς δὲ καὶ
φιλόσοφος τὸ ἐπιτήδευμα. ἐπὶ τοσοῦτον δ' αὐτὸν
τῆς κατὰ τὸ σχῆμά φασι σεμνότητος ἀντιποιεῖσθαι
ὡς καὶ λεοντὴν πολλάκις ἐνημμένον ποιεῖσθαι τὴν

the critical appraisal befitting each. And among these let Dio of Prusa, too, have his place, a man remarkable in both speech and discernment. And so, having praised Dio, I entrust him to my son, that having cultivated the champions of genuine philosophy, he may some day, I trust, pay tribute also to the political writings of Dio, believing them to be a border-land between the preparatory subjects of instruction and the most genuine education.

6. Photius

eighty discourses that had come to his attention, usually adding a few words to indicate the contents and occasionally including remarks by way of critical appraisal. His literary judgement does him credit. It should be noted that the order in which Photius presents the discourses differs markedly from that followed in the present edition, the same difference being observable to-day between the two main families of Dio manuscripts.

Bibliotheca : We have read a work of Dio's consisting of eighty speeches. Dio is by birth a citizen of Prusa, but he was banished from there because he shunned being in slavery to a tyrant, and he covered much territory in his wanderings. He gained a reputation for being clever in his speeches, and especially in those which advise men to amend their ways. He flourished in the time of the emperor Trajan, and he spent a great deal of time in his society and gained from him the very highest honour and hospitality, even to the extent of sitting beside Trajan in his imperial carriage. Dio was the son of Pasicrates, and a sophist and philosopher by profession. It is said that he made such pretensions to dignity of appearance as even to appear frequently

DIO CHRYSOSTOM

πρόοδον. φωνὴν δ' ἠρεμαίαν ἠφίει καὶ σταθεράν·
καὶ σχολαῖον μέν, ἀλλ' οὐκ ἀναβεβλημένον βάδισμα,
καὶ τἆλλα τῶν κινημάτων οὐκ ἀσύμφωνα· ἰσχνὸς
δ' ἦν καὶ οὐδὲ μέγας τὸ σῶμα.

Τοῦτον πολλούς φασι καὶ ποικίλους γράψαι
λόγους· οἱ δ' εἰς ἡμετέραν φθάσαντες γνῶσιν τὸν
π' ἐπλήρουν ἀριθμόν.¹ Χρυσόστομον δ' αὐτὸν οἱ
λόγοι τῇ κατ' αὐτὸν γενεᾷ δεδώκασιν ἐπονομάζειν.
ἔστι μὲν οὖν, ὅπερ ἔφην, τὸ πλεῖστον αὐτοῦ τῶν
λόγων, οὓς ἡμεῖς ἴσμεν, συμβουλευτικόν· οἷα δ'
εἰκός, καὶ τῷ συμβουλευτικῷ παραπλεκόμενον τὸ
οἷον δικανικὸν παραπλήσιον τὴν ἀρετὴν κἂν τῷ
μέρει τῷδε τοῦ λόγου δεικνύει, καὶ μάλιστα τῶν
ἄλλων ὁ Ῥοδιακός.² δριμύς τε γάρ ἐστι τοῖς
ἐνθυμήμασι καὶ τὸ συνεστραμμένον πρός γε τὸν
αὐτοῦ χαρακτῆρα τῶν λόγων ἔχων καὶ τὸ ἔντονον
μετὰ τοῦ γονίμου πλουτῶν· ἄριστος δὲ τοῖς παρα-
δείγμασι καὶ πολύς ἐστι πανταχοῦ, καὶ ποικίλης
ὕλης λαμβάνων αὐτὰ καὶ προσφυῶς ἁρμοζόμενος.
χαίρει δὲ μάλιστα καὶ μυθολογήμασι τὰς παραι-
νέσεις συνδιαπλέκειν· διὸ καὶ τὸ ἀφελὲς διώκειν
δοκεῖ. σπάνιον γὰρ εἴ τις εὕροι κατὰ τὸν Πλατωνικὸν ζῆλον τοῖς διάρμα καὶ ὄγκον ἐνεργαζομένοις
τῷ λόγῳ, ὥσπερ ἐν τῷ Βορυσθενιτικῷ, μύθοις
αὐτὸν ἀποχρώμενον. ἀφελὴς μὲν οὖν ἐστι τὰ
πολλά, ὡς ἔφθην εἰπών, ταῖς ἐννοίαις, καὶ τῶν τε
καθωμιλημένων αὐτῷ καὶ ἐπιπολαζουσῶν αἱ λέξεις,
καὶ οὐδὲν οὐδ' ἡ σύνταξις οὔτ' ἐπὶ τὸ βαθύτερον
οὔτ' ἐπὶ τὸ καθηδυνόμενον ἐκνεωτερίζει. καὶ
τό γε ἐπὶ τοῖς ῥήμασι καὶ τῇ συμπλοκῇ τῶν

---

¹ Or. 31.
² Or. 36.

in public clad in a lion's skin. His manner of speaking was quiet and deliberate ; his gait was leisurely, though not slow, and his other movements were not out of harmony with his gait ; he was spare of frame and not tall of stature.

It is said that Dio composed many speeches and of many kinds ; but those that have come to my attention amounted to an even eighty. Chrysostom is the sobriquet which his speeches have caused his generation to apply to him. Now, as I was saying, most of Dio's speeches with which I am familiar are deliberative ; but, as was to be expected, intertwined with the deliberative, his quasi-forensic product too shows his excellence in this branch of oratory as well to be nearly as great, and most of all the *Rhodian Discourse*.[1] For he is sagacious in his reasoning, and he possesses the quality of pithiness, at least with regard to his own style of oratory, and he has a wealth of intensity combined with originality. Again, he is excellent in his illustrations from history and abounds in them everywhere, not only culling his illustrations from various sources but also fitting them in appropriately. But especially he delights to inter-weave his exhortations with mythological narratives ; and this seems to be his reason for aiming also at simplicity. For example, one would rarely find him following the pattern of Plato and using myths which impart elevation and dignity to his eloquence, as is the case in his *Borysthenitic Discourse*.[2] So, as I have just said, for the most part he is simple in his con-ceptions and his phrases are such as were current and popular in his day ; nor does his syntax attempt any innovation in the direction of either profundity or ornamentation. Furthermore, in the matter of his

ὀνομάτων τοῦ σαφοῦς ἄν τις ἐλπίσειε τὸν συγ-
γραφέα κατεστοχάσθαι· ἀλλὰ τό γε διὰ μακροῦ
τὴν τῆς διανοίας ἀπόδοσιν προϊέναι, καὶ ταῖς
ἐπιβολαῖς ἐκ τοῦ ἐπὶ πλεῖστον τὸν λόγον διαπε-
πλέχθαι, οὐκ ἐπὶ μικρῷ τῆς τοιαύτης αὐτὸν
ἐκκλείει ἰδέας. ἀλλὰ ταῦτα μὲν παραλλαγὴ ἰδέας
καὶ χαρακτῆρος ἰδίωμα, ἀλλ' οὐκ αἰτίας ἴσως
ἔνδειξιν ἔχει· τὸ δ' ἐπὶ μακρότατον ἀποτείνειν
τὰ προοίμια ἢ τὰ οἷον προοίμια οὐκέτι ἀφίησιν
αὐτὸν τὸ μὴ οὐχὶ ἀντὶ πολιτικοῦ καὶ συγγραφικοῦ
τύπου τὸν ἐπὶ ταῖς συνουσίαις ἀλλάξασθαι παρα-
δεδυκότα καὶ μείζω τὴν κεφαλὴν τὴν ὡς ἐν λόγῳ
τοῦ λοιποῦ σώματος διαπλάττειν.

Τῶν τοίνυν λόγων αὐτοῦ δ' περὶ βασιλείας μέν
εἰσιν εἰρημένοι. καὶ ὁ ε' δέ, Λιβυκὸς ἐπιγραφόμενος, μῦθον μὲν Λίβυν ἀπαγγέλλει, ἐκείνων δ'
ἐστὶν ἐξημμένος. ὁ δ' ἕκτος περὶ τυραννίδος
δίεισι, καὶ περὶ ἀρετῆς ὁ ἐπὶ τούτῳ. ὁ δὲ η'
Διογένης μὲν ἢ Ἰσθμικὸς ἐπιγραφὴν ἔχει, πρᾶξιν
δέ τινα καὶ λόγους Διογένους κατὰ τὰ Ἴσθμια
διαγγέλλει. καὶ ὁ θ', Διογένης ἢ περὶ οἰκετῶν,
παραινεῖ μὲν ἅπαντας δι' ἑνὸς προσώπου αὐτοῦ
μὲν ἕκαστον πολλὴν ἐπιστροφὴν καὶ ἐπιμέλειαν
ποιεῖσθαι, ὀλίγην δὲ τῶν ἔξωθεν συμπιπτόντων·
καὶ μὴ χρῆναι φεύγοντα διώκειν οἰκέτην· ἄτοπον
γὰρ ἐκείνους μὲν κακοὺς ὄντας ἐλπίζειν ἄνευ τῶν
δεσποτῶν ἄμεινον βιώσεσθαι, τοὺς δεσπότας δὲ
μὴ ἀξιοῦντας φαύλους εἶναι μὴ νομίζειν ἄμεινον
διάξειν, εἰ μὴ παραπολαύοιεν τῆς τῶν δραπετῶν

---

[1] In our collection the *Euboean Discourse*, which Photius
makes number thirteen, precedes *On Virtue*; consequently

verbs and the intertwining of his nouns one might expect the prose writer to have aimed at clarity ; yet Dio's long postponement of the conclusion of his thought and his extreme use of repetition in weaving the pattern of the discourse in no small measure exclude it from such a category. But while these matters constitute a difference of literary form and a peculiarity of style, they possibly do not afford occasion for censure ; yet his prolonging his proems, or his quasi-proems, to great length does not any longer permit him to escape the charge of having substituted for a political and literary type the conversational, into which he has slipped, and of making the head, as one might say, larger than the rest of the body.

Now then, among his speeches four are entitled *On Kingship.* The fifth, entitled *Libyan,* recounts a Libyan myth, but it is a pendant of those four. The sixth is *On Tyranny,* and the one following is *On Virtue.*[1] The eighth has the title *Diogenes or Isthmian,* and it reports an experience which Diogenes had and things which he said at the Isthmian Games. The ninth, *Diogenes or On Servants,* exhorts all mankind, through a single illustration, to give much heed and care to themselves individually, but little to what befalls them from without ; also it states that one ought not to pursue a runaway servant, because it is absurd that, while servants, who are base, hope to live a better life apart from their masters, the masters, who do not think poorly of themselves, should fail to hold that they will live a better life if they do not share the fruits of the fugitives' stupidity.

Photius' numbering of the next few discourses does not correspond to ours.

σκαιότητος. ὁ δὲ ι΄ Τρωικὸς μὲν ἕλκει τὴν
ἐπιγραφήν, ὑπὲρ τοῦ μὴ ἁλῶναι δὲ τὸ Ἴλιον διε-
σπούδασται, Ὁμήρῳ τε κατὰ τὸ τραχύτερον προσ-
φέρεται, καὶ ὅσα ἄλλα κατὰ τὴν Ἰλιάδα αὐτῷ
πεποίηται, τἀναντία τούτοις πραγματεύεται. ὁ
δὲ Ὀλυμπικὸς ἢ περὶ τῆς πρώτης τοῦ θεοῦ
ἐννοίας, αὐτὸ τοῦτο πειρώμενος ἐπιδεικνύειν, ἑνδέ-
κατός ἐστιν. ὁ δὲ ιβ΄, ἐν Ἀθήναις περὶ φυγῆς
ἐπιγραφὴν ἔχων, εἴρηται μὲν ἐν αὐταῖς, δίεισι δὲ
ὡς οὐδὲν ἡ φυγὴ χαλεπόν, καὶ ὡς πλοῦτος μὲν
καὶ δόξα καὶ δυναστεία θᾶττον ἀπὸ τῶν ἐχόντων
ἐπὶ τοὺς μηδ᾽ ἐλπίσαντας μεταρρεῖ, τὸ δὲ φιλοσοφεῖν καὶ τὴν ἀρετὴν ἀσκεῖν διὰ βίου τε κτῆμα
διαμένει ἀγαθὸν καὶ ἀποιχομένοις συνέπεται. ὁ
δὲ ιγ΄ Εὐβοϊκὸς ἢ κυνηγετικὸς ἔλαχεν ἐπιγραφήν,
εἰσάγει δέ τινας ἐν Εὐβοίᾳ τοιοῦτον βίον βιοῦντας·
δι᾽ ὧν κατασκευάζει ὡς ὁ ἀπράγμων βίος, εἰ καὶ
πενόμενος εἴη, πολλῷ τῶν ἐν ἄστει θορυβουμένων
τε καὶ τρυφώντων ἡδίων τε καὶ λυσιτελέστερος.
Ῥοδιακὸς δὲ ὁ ιδ΄ ἐπιγράφεται ἐν τούτῳ ἔθος
ἄλογον παρὰ Ῥοδίοις ἐπιτιμᾷ ἐπιπολάσαν. τὸ δ᾽
ἦν, οὓς ἐβούλοντο τιμᾶν ἀνδριᾶσι, τούτοις μὲν
ἀνδριάντα ἀνίστασαν οὐδένα· τοὺς δὲ τοῖς πάλαι
ἀνεστηκότας, τούτων ἄρα ἢ τὰς ἐπιγραφὰς μετα-
ξέοντες εἰς τὰ τῶν μελλόντων τιμηθῆναι ὀνόματα,
ἢ τῷ χρόνῳ μηδὲ φαινομένων ἐπιγράφοντες, τῶν
τε οἰχομένων τό γε ἐπ᾽ αὐτοῖς τὴν τιμὴν ἐλυμαί-

---

[1] In our collection the *Rhodian Discourse* is number
thirty-one ; Photius places Orr. 14-30 at the end of his
enumeration.

The tenth bears the title *Trojan*, and the author has taken great pains to prove that Ilium was not captured. Not only does he handle Homer rather roughly, but everything else that Homer has put into his *Iliad* is treated contrary to the poet's version. The *Olympic or On the First Conception of God*, whose aim is to point out precisely that, is number eleven. The twelfth, whose title is *In Athens, On Banishment*, was delivered in Athens, and it argues that banishment is no hardship, also that wealth and fame and power rather speedily desert those who possess them and change over to those who never even expected to have them, whereas the pursuit of wisdom and the cultivation of virtue not only through life remain a noble possession, but also accompany men when they die. The thirteenth has drawn the title *Euboean or On the Hunter*, and it introduces certain persons who follow that sort of career in Euboea. By means of these persons the discourse seeks to prove that the care-free life, even though it be a life of poverty, is far more pleasant and also more profitable than the life of those who in a city are surrounded by confusion and luxury. *Rhodian* is the title of the fourteenth.[1] In this the author reproves an absurd practice prevalent among the Rhodians. That is to say, when they wanted to honour persons with statues, their practice was, not to erect any statue for them, but to take the statues which had been erected for men of former days and either erase what had been inscribed upon them and substitute the names of the persons now to be honoured, or else, if through lapse of time the original inscription was not even legible, inscribing a new one. Thus, at least in so far as they were able, they would outrage the honour belonging to

νοντο, καὶ οὓς τιμᾶν ὑπεπλάττοντο, ἀλλοτρίαις καὶ κατ' οὐδὲν ἐοικυίαις εἰκόσιν ἐνύβριζον. ἐν τῷδε τῷ λόγῳ μεγάλη τοῦ ἀνδρὸς τῆς ἀνασκευαστικῆς ἰσχύος ἡ ἀρετὴ διαφαίνεται. ὁ δὲ ιε΄ πρὸς Ἀλεξανδρεῖς μὲν ἐπιγέγραπται, δήμου δὲ φύσιν ἀναπτύσσων ταύτης κατατρέχει· καὶ ὅτι μὴ χρὴ τὸν Ἀλεξανδρέων δῆμον, ἴδια πολλὰ τὰ πρὸς ἀρετὴν παρακαλοῦντα ἔχοντα, τῆς ἐν τῷ κοινῷ ἐπιπολαζούσης ταραχῆς καὶ ἀταξίας καὶ αὐτὸν εἶναι ἀνδράποδον, μάλιστα δὲ παραφυλάττεσθαι τὸ ἁμάρτημα κατὰ τὰς δημοτελεῖς πανηγύρεις καὶ τὰ θέατρα. Ταρσικοὶ δὲ δύο ἐφεξῆς ἐπιγραφῆς ἔτυχον, ὧν ὁ μὲν α΄ ἔπαινόν τινα τῆς πόλεως ἐπιτρέχων οὐκ εὐδαίμονας ἐκείνας ἀποφαίνει τῶν πόλεων, ὅσαι κρήνας καὶ ποταμοὺς καὶ κάλλη στοῶν καὶ οἰκοδομημάτων καὶ καρπῶν ἀφθονίαν καὶ τὰ παραπλήσια προβάλλονται, ἀλλ' ἐν ὅσαις τάξις καὶ ἀρετὴ τῶν πολιτευομένων διαδείκνυται. οὗτος ὁ λόγος καὶ παράλογόν τι καὶ ἐφύβριστον ἔθος κατὰ φωνῆς ἀπήχησιν τοῖς Ἀλεξανδρεῦσι πραττόμενον εὐθύναις ὑπάγει, παραινῶν ἀποσχέσθαι τοὺς χρωμένους ἢ μᾶλλον αὐτῶν πληκτικώτερον καθαπτόμενος. ὁ δὲ δεύτερος παραινεῖ μὴ συκοφαντικῶς πρὸς τοὺς ἄρχοντας διακεῖσθαι, μηδ' ἐπὶ τοῖς βραχέσι τῶν παραλυπούντων εὐθὺς ἀνερεθίζεσθαι καὶ ἐπαιτιᾶσθαι τούτους. ὁ δὲ ιη΄, ὃς

---

[1] For the sound in question, see Or. 33. 31-56 and Campbell Bonner's valuable article (*Harv. Theol. Rev.* xxxv, pp.

the departed and at the same time they would insult
those whom they were pretending to honour by
means of statues to which they had no claim and
which in no wise resembled the recipient. In this
discourse the excellence of Dio's destructive power
is conspicuously great. The fifteenth discourse is
entitled *To the Alexandrians,* and it lays bare the
nature of the populace and inveighs against it.
Furthermore, it states that the populace of Alexandria, since it has many special incentives to virtue,
should not itself be a slave to the confusion and disorder prevalent in the community, but should most
of all guard against the misconduct encountered in
the popular gatherings and in the theatres. Two
discourses that follow have been labelled *Tarsic,* the
first of which, while dealing lightly with a sort of
laudation of Tarsus, seeks to prove that the fortunate
cities are not those which offer in evidence fountains
and rivers, beautiful colonnades and edifices, and
abundance of crops and the like, but rather those in
which orderliness and virtue are conspicuous on the
part of those who administer the government. This
oration also subjects to scrutiny a certain surprising
and wanton habit of the Alexandrians in connexion
with a resonant vocal sound, advising those who
indulge in it to refrain, or, more properly speaking,
attacking them quite vehemently.[1] The second *Tarsic* advises against being disposed to employ captious
charges with reference to their magistrates and
against a readiness to grow excited over trifling
annoyances and to find fault with these magistrates.
The eighteenth discourse, which bears no title, was

1-11). Alexandrians has carelessly displaced Tarsians, as is
clear from both the content and the context of this sentence.

οὐκ ἐπιγέγραπται, ἐν Κελαιναῖς ἐρρήθη τῆς Φρυγίας. διαλαμβάνει δὲ ὡς οὐκ ἀρετῆς εἴη σημεῖον τὸ κομᾶν, ὥσπερ οὐδ' ἄλλο τι τῶν σχημάτων τῶν περὶ τὸ σῶμα, ὥσπερ οὐδὲ τούτων τὰ ἐναντία· διαπλέκεται δ' αὐτῷ καὶ τῆς πόλεως ἔπαινος. τὸν δὲ ιθ' μηνύει ἡ ἐπιγραφὴ ῥηθῆναι μὲν ἐν τῷ Βορυσθένει, ἀναγνωσθῆναι δὲ ἐν τῇ πατρίδι· ἐν ᾧ ἄλλα τε δίεισιν ὁ συγγραφεὺς καὶ κατὰ τὸν Πλατωνικὸν συνομολογεῖ ζῆλον περί τε τοῦ δημιουργοῦ τῶν ὅλων τοῖς Βορυσθενίταις διειλέχθαι τῆς τε τοῦ παντὸς διακοσμήσεως καὶ κινήσεως καὶ τῶν ἐν αὐτῷ στοιχείων. ἔχεται δέ τινος λαμπρότητος καὶ σεμνότητος οὗτος ὑπὲρ τοὺς ἄλλους ὁ λόγος. καὶ ὁ Κορινθιακὸς δέ, κ' ὤν, ἐν Κορίνθῳ μὲν ἐρρήθη, ἐπιτίμησιν δ' αὐτῶν διαπεραίνει ἀνθ' ὧν εἰκόνι τὰ πρῶτα τιμήσαντες αὐτὸν ὕστερον ἀποδημήσαντος ἐκ διαβολῆς οὐ δικαίας περιείλοντο τὸ γέρας. ἐγγὺς δ' ἐστὶ τοῦ Ῥοδιακοῦ κατὰ τὴν ἐν λόγοις ῥώμην καὶ ἀρετὴν οὗτος· ἡ δὲ τοῦ οἷον προοιμίου παράτασις κἀνταῦθα, ὡς καὶ παρὰ μικρὸν πανταχοῦ, τῆς ἀρετῆς οὐ μετέχει. τοῦ δὲ κα' ἡ ἐπιγραφὴ περὶ τῆς πρὸς Νικαεῖς ὁμονοίας τῶν Νικομηδέων ἐστί· καὶ τοῦτον ὑπέρχεται τὸν ἀγῶνα ὁ λόγος εὐκαίρως διὰ τῆς ἡδονῆς προενηνεγμένος· μᾶλλον γὰρ οὕτω ταῖς ψυχαῖς τὸ πιθανὸν ἐθέλει διαδύειν. τὸν δὲ β' καὶ κ' ἐν Νικαίᾳ εἰρῆσθαι ἡ ἐπιγραφὴ δηλοῖ περὶ ὁμονοίας, πεπαυμένης τῆς στάσεως· αὐτὸ δὲ τοῦτο διατίθησιν ὁ ἀνήρ, ἔπαινον τοῦ γεγονότος. ὁ δὲ κγ' περὶ τῆς πρὸς Ἀπαμεῖς ὁμονοίας εἴρηται

delivered in Celaenae in Phrygia. It maintains that
it is no sign of virtue to wear long hair, any more
than any other bodily characteristics, or their oppo-
sites. Interwoven with it also is a laudation of the
city. The title of the nineteenth reveals that it had
been delivered in Borysthenes, but that it was given
as a public reading in Dio's native city. In this
speech the author, in addition to other matters,
admits that he had in emulation of Plato discoursed
to the citizens of Borysthenes regarding the creator
of the universe and also regarding the orderly arrangement and movement of the universe and the elements
of which it is composed. A certain brilliance and
solemnity mark this discourse above all others. The
Corinthian discourse, which is the twentieth, was delivered in Corinth and is a thorough-going reproval
of the people for having at first honoured the speaker
with a statue and then, after he had left the city,
having removed the mark of distinction because of
a malicious rumour without any justification. This
speech is close to the *Rhodian* in the vigour and the
high quality of its eloquence ; however, the prolonga-
tion of what may be termed its proem, here as
practically everywhere, does not partake of that high
quality. The title of number twenty-one is *On
Concord between Nicaea and Nicomedia* ; and the
speech approaches this theme propitiously, having
been delivered in an indulgent spirit, for in this way
persuasion is more likely to penetrate men's souls.
The title of number twenty-two reveals that it was
delivered in Nicaea upon the subject of concord after
the cessation of civil strife ; and this is precisely what
the author makes his theme, a laudation of what
has taken place. Number twenty-three, *On Concord*

ἐν τῇ πατρίδι· αὐτὸ δὲ διαπράττεται τοῦτο. καὶ
ὁ ἐφεξῆς δὲ περὶ ὁμονοίας τῆς πρὸς τοὺς Πρου-
σαεῖς παρακαλεῖ τοὺς Ἀπαμέας. ὁ δὲ κε΄ διάλεξίς
ἐστιν ἐν τῇ πατρίδι. ἄγνοιαν δὲ ὑποπλάττεται
τῆς αἰτίας ὁ διαλεγόμενος, δι᾽ ἣν μηδὲν χρήσιμον
αὑτοῦ τῶν λόγων προβεβλημένων ἡδέως καὶ
ποθοῦντες ἀκούουσι. πολιτικὸς δέ ἐστι τῷ κϛ΄
ἡ ἐπιγραφή, καὶ εἴρηται ἐν τῇ πατρίδι, ὥσπερ
καὶ ὁ ἐφεξῆς, φιλοφρονητικὸς ὑπάρχων αὐτῇ ἀνθ᾽
ὧν τιμαῖς τὸν φιλοφρονούμενον ἐδεξιοῦτο. ἀπο-
λογισμὸς δέ ἐστιν ὁ μετ᾽ αὐτούς, ὅπως διέκειτο
πρὸς τὴν πατρίδα. ὁ δὲ θ΄ καὶ κ΄ πρὸ τοῦ φιλοσοφεῖν μὲν ἐν τῇ πατρίδι ἐπιγράφεται, τοὺς δ᾽
ἐπιχειρήσαντας καταλεύειν αὐτόν τε καὶ σὺν αὐτῷ
ἕτερον, εἶτα δὲ καὶ πυρὶ τὴν οἰκίαν δοῦναι, τούτους ἠρέμα πως ἐπιτιμῶν, τὸ πλανᾶσθαι ἐπὶ τῆς
ξένης τῆς οἴκοι διατριβῆς διὰ τὰς ἐν πόλει ἀταξίας
ἄμεινον κατασκευάζει. ἡ δὲ τῶν πολιτῶν ὀργὴ
κατ᾽ αὐτοῦ, διότι, φησί, καταρρέουσαν ἐπὶ τὸ
βέλτιον ἀνέλαβε τὴν οἰκίαν. καὶ ὁ λ΄ δέ, δημη-
γορία ἐν τῇ πατρίδι τὴν ἐπιγραφὴν φέρων, εἰς τὴν
αὐτὴν ὑπόθεσιν ἀποβλέπει. καὶ ὁ α΄ καὶ λ΄ ἐν τῇ
πατρίδι μὲν ἐλέχθη, πολιτικὸς δ᾽ ἐπιγέγραπται
ἐν ἐκκλησίᾳ, καὶ συμβουλεύει τῶν εἰς ἀλλήλους
ὕβρεων ἀποσχομένους καὶ προπηλακισμῶν τὴν
στάσιν εἰς ὁμόνοιαν διαλύειν. ὡσαύτως ἐν τῇ
πατρίδι μὲν ἐλέχθη καὶ ὁ ἐφεξῆς, ὃ δὲ ἐπιγράφεται,
398

with Apameia, was delivered in his native city, and this is precisely what the speaker seeks to achieve. The following discourse also is an appeal to the Apameians for concord with the people of Prusa. Number twenty-five is *An Address in his Native City*. The speaker professes ignorance of the reason why, although his speeches have contributed nothing useful, his audience is glad, yes, longs to hear him. The title of twenty-six is *A Political Address*, and it was delivered in his native city, as was also the one that follows, which is an address of friendship toward Prusa for receiving with honours the man who is making the address of friendship. The speech that follows these is a defence of his attitude toward his native city in the past. Number twenty-nine has the title, *Prior to his Philosophical Career, in his Native City*. Those who had tried to stone Dio to death, and with him also a second person, and then also to give his house to the flames, the speech reproves rather mildly and it maintains that the life of a wanderer in foreign lands is preferable to living at home because of the disorder prevalent in the city. The speaker says that the anger directed against him by his fellow-citizens was occasioned by his repairing his house, which had been falling in ruins. The thirtieth speech, which bears the title, *A Speech in the Public Assembly in his Native City*, is also directed toward the same theme. Number thirty-one, delivered in his native city, is entitled *A Political Address in Assembly*, and it advises his hearers to desist from their deeds of reciprocal violence and their insults and to turn their party strife into concord. Similarly the next also was delivered in his native city, and its title, *A Refusal of Office*,

παραίτησις ἀρχῆς ἐν τῇ βουλῇ, τοῦτο καὶ ἐνδείκνυ-
ται· ἐκ ψηφίσματος γὰρ ἄρχειν ὁ συγγραφεὺς
ᾑρημένος παραιτεῖται. ὁ δὲ λγ΄, περὶ τῶν ἔργων
ἐν βουλῇ τὴν ἐπιγραφὴν παρέχων, ἔπαινον μέν
τινα τῆς βουλῆς ἐπιτρέχει, ἀπολογεῖται δὲ καὶ
ὑπὲρ ὧν ὁ Δίων ὑπενοεῖτο, ὡς μὴ τὰ τοῦ παιδὸς
ἔργα καὶ αἱ πράξεις αἱ κατὰ τὴν πόλιν τῆς πατρικῆς
εἰσι βουλῆς ἐξημμέναι. ὁ ἐφεξῆς δὲ πρὸς Διόδωρον ἐπιγραφόμενος, προτροπὴν μέν τινα ἐπ᾽
ἀρετὴν εἰσάγει, ἐπαινεῖν δὲ τὴν πόλιν φησὶ δι᾽ ὧν
τὸν ἐγκωμιάσαντα Διόδωρον ἐπαίνοις περιβάλλει.
ὁ δὲ λε΄, περὶ Αἰσχύλου καὶ Σοφοκλέους καὶ
Εὐριπίδου ἢ περὶ τῶν Φιλοκτήτου τόξων ἐπιγεγραμμένος, τὴν τοῦ Φιλοκτήτου πλάττει ἐξαπάτην,
ἣν προβεβλημένος Ὀδυσσεὺς λαβὼν ᾤχετο τὰ
τόξα. τῷ δὲ ς΄ καὶ λ΄ λόγῳ ἡ μὲν ἐπιγραφὴ περὶ
Ὁμήρου λέγει, ἔπαινος δέ τις τοῦ ποιητοῦ διυ-
φαίνεται, ὥσπερ καὶ τῷ περὶ Σωκράτους ἐπιγραφο-
μένῳ τοῦ φιλοσόφου. ὁ δὲ περὶ Ὁμήρου καὶ
Σωκράτους, λη΄ λόγος ὤν, ζηλωτὴν Ὁμήρου
Σωκράτην καὶ μαθητὴν ἐπιδείκνυσι, καὶ τό τε
οἰκεῖον τῆς τῶν παραδειγμάτων μεταχειρίσεως
ἐκεῖθεν ἀναμαθεῖν τὸν φιλόσοφον ἐπιδεικνύει, καὶ
τὴν ἄλλην τοῦ λόγου χάριν καὶ δύναμιν ἐναπο-
μάξασθαι. ὁ δὲ λθ΄, Ἀγαμέμνων ἢ περὶ βασιλέως
ἐπιγραφόμενος, διέξεισιν ὡς δεῖ συμβούλων τοῖς
ἀρίστοις τὸν βασιλέα κεχρημένον ἐκείνοις τε πείθεσθαι καὶ μὴ κατὰ τὸ δοκοῦν ἀπαυθαδιάζειν.
καὶ ᾧ δὲ Νέστωρ ἡ ἐπιγραφή, ὅπως κεχρῆσθαι
προσῆκε τῇ πρὸς τοὺς βασιλεῖς παραινέσει περι-

before the Council, is self-explanatory, for the author
had by official ballot been elected archon but begs
to be excused. Number thirty-three, which provides
the title, *Concerning his Past Record, before the Council,* deals lightly with a laudation of the Council, but
it also contains a defence regarding matters about
which Dio was the subject of suspicion, setting forth,
as it does, that his son's actions and the administration of the city's affairs did not depend upon the
advice of the father. The one following, entitled *In
Reply to Diodorus,* introduces what may be termed
an exhortation to virtue, but Dio says that he is
praising the city by covering with praises Diodorus,
who had eulogized it. Number thirty-five, entitled
*On Aeschylus and Sophocles and Euripides or On the
Bow of Philoctetes,* depicts the deception of Philoctetes,
under cover of which Odysseus seized and carried off
the bow. The title of number thirty-six reads : *On
Homer,* and it is interwoven with a laudation of the
poet, just as there is laudation of the philosopher in
the discourse labelled *On Socrates.* The discourse *On
Homer and Socrates,* which is number thirty-eight,
depicts Socrates as an imitator and disciple of Homer
and seeks to show both that the philosopher's own
peculiar manner of handling his illustrations had
been learned from Homer and also that the rest of
the charm and force to be found in his language had
received the imprint of Homer. Number thirty-nine,
labelled *Agamemnon or On the King,* argues that the
king must employ the best of counsellors and must
not only follow their advice but also not act arbitrarily to suit his own opinion. Again, the discourse
entitled *Nestor* contains the doctrine that it was
proper to employ Nestor's advice to the kings. In

λαμβάνεται. ὁ δὲ ἐφεξῆς, Ἀχιλλεὺς οὐ πειθό-
μενος τῷ Χείρωνι, προνοίᾳ καὶ τέχνῃ, ἀλλὰ μὴ
θράσει καὶ χειρῶν ἰσχύϊ συμβουλεύοντι μετα-
χειρίζεσθαι πόλεμον, ὕστερον οὐκ ἀπώνατο τῆς
ἀπειθείας. καὶ ὁ Φιλοκτήτης δὲ παράφρασίς ἐστι
τοῦ κατ᾽ αὐτὸν ἀτυχήματος. ἐφ᾽ οἷς ὁ Νέσσος ἢ
Δηιάνειρα τῶν ἀπιθάνως περὶ αὐτοὺς πεπλασμένων
διά τινος θεραπείας εἰς εἱρμόν τινα καὶ τάξιν δοκεῖ
τὸ ἀπίθανον μεταρρυθμίζειν. καὶ ὁ Χρυσηῒς
ἔπαινός ἐστι Χρυσηΐδος. ὁ δὲ περὶ βασιλείας καὶ
τυραννίδος περὶ αὐτῶν τούτων διαλαμβάνει. καὶ
οἱ ἐφεξῆς δὲ γ΄ περὶ τύχης λόγοι χαρίεντά τινα
καὶ φιλοσοφίας ἅμα ἐχόμενα θεωρήματα διατυ-
ποῦσιν. ὡσαύτως καὶ οἱ μετὰ τούτους περὶ δόξης
γ΄ λόγοι συμβουλεύουσι καὶ παραινοῦσι μηδένα
λόγον τῆς τῶν πολλῶν δόξης ποιεῖσθαι· καλὰ δὲ
καὶ ὠφέλιμα τῇ παραινέσει συνδιαπλέκεται θεωρήματα. ὁ δὲ νβ΄ περὶ ἀρετῆς καὶ ἐπιγράφεται καὶ
δίεισι. περὶ φιλοσοφίας δέ ἐστιν ὁ γ΄ καὶ ν΄. ὁ
δὲ νδ΄ περὶ τοῦ φιλοσόφου· ὁ δὲ ε΄ καὶ ν΄ περὶ τοῦ
σχήματος ἐπιγεγραμμένος δείκνυσιν ὡς οὐ χιτῶνι
καὶ ὑποδήματι φιλοσόφων ὁ κατεσχηματισμένος
ἤδη καὶ τὸν βίον φιλόσοφός ἐστιν. ὁ δὲ ϛ΄ καὶ
ν΄ περὶ πίστεως ἐπιγραφῆς τυχών, καὶ ὁ ἐφεξῆς
περὶ ἀπιστίας, προτρέπονται φυλάσσεσθαι τὸ
θαρρεῖν καὶ καταπιστεύειν καὶ τοῖς μάλιστα φιλεῖν
δοκοῦσι· πολλοῖς γὰρ πιστεύσασι μὲν μεγάλη ἀπ-
ήντησε συμφορά, ἀπιστίᾳ δὲ φραξαμένοις λαμπρὰ
περιγέγονε σωτηρία. ἀλλὰ ταῦτα μὲν ὁ περὶ

---

[1] The centaur to whom the youthful Achilles had been
entrusted.

the next we find Achilles refusing to obey Cheiron,[1] who was advising him to practise warfare with prudence and craft, instead of with daring and strength of arm, a refusal which subsequently he had occasion to repent. The *Philoctetes* is a paraphrase of that hero's misfortune. Next comes the *Nessus or Deïaneira*, which seems to transform the improbability of the unconvincing fictions regarding those two characters into a sort of orderly sequence through the operation of a kind of healing process. Again, the *Chryseïs* is a laudation of Chryseïs. The discourse *On Kingship and Tyranny* deals with these very topics. The three speeches *On Fortune* that follow give expression to certain clever and at the same time rather philosophic observations. Likewise also the next three *On Opinion* counsel and exhort the listener not to pay any heed to the opinion of the masses ; noble and useful observations also are interwoven with the exhortation. Number fifty-two, both in title and in content, is *On Virtue*. Fifty-three is *On Philosophy* ; fifty-four is *On the Philosopher* ; and fifty-five, which is entitled *On Personal Appearance*, points out that it is not the person who has dressed himself up with tunic and sandal of the philosophers who is by virtue of that fact a philosopher in his life as well. Number fifty-six, which is called *On Trust*, and the one following, *On Distrust*, urge mankind to guard against having confidence and trusting even those who most of all are thought to be friends ; for while many who have bestowed their trust have encountered great misfortune, those who have hedged themselves about with distrust have found notable safety to be the outcome. However, these things constitute the

403

ἀπιστίας λόγος· ὁ δὲ πρὸ αὐτοῦ διέξεισιν ὡς καὶ
τὸ πιστεύεσθαι ὡς ἐπίπαν μεγάλα τοὺς πιστευομένους ἐζημίωσεν. ἡ δ' ὑπόθεσις τοῦ νη' λόγου,
ὥσπερ καὶ ἡ ἐπιγραφή, περὶ νόμου ἐστίν· ὡς καὶ
ἡ τοῦ νθ' περὶ ἔθους, ὃ πράττειν μὲν ὅσα ὁ νόμος
ἀποδείκνυσι, μεθ' ἡδονῆς δὲ καὶ πειθοῦς μᾶλλον
ἢ βίας, καὶ ἀσφαλέστερον. δύο δὲ οἱ ἐφεξῆς περὶ
φθόνου διαλαμβάνουσι. καὶ ὁ β' καὶ ξ' περὶ
πλούτου, τὸ ὀχληρὸν αὐτοῦ καὶ ἐπίβουλον στηλι-
τεύων, καὶ πολλῷ λυσιτελεστέραν αὐτοῦ παριστῶν
τὴν μετὰ δικαιοσύνης πενίαν. ὁ δὲ γ' καὶ ξ'
ἐπιγράφεται τῶν ἐν Κιλικίᾳ περὶ ἐλευθερίας,
ἐκεῖνον δὲ ἐλεύθερον παριστᾷ, ὃς τῶν ἐν αὐτῷ
κύριος εἴη παθῶν, κἂν μυρίοι ἔξωθεν αὐτοῦ τοῦ
σώματος ὦσι δεσπόται, καὶ δοῦλον ἐκεῖνον, ὃς
ἀνδράποδόν ἐστι παθῶν, εἰ καὶ συμπάσης ἄρχειν
τῆς οἰκουμένης δοκεῖ. εἰς τὴν αὐτὴν δ' ἀναφέρεται
διάνοιαν καὶ ὁ ἐφεξῆς, περὶ δουλείας καὶ ἐλευθερίας ἐπιγραφὴν ἔχων, ὥσπερ καὶ ὁ ἐφεξῆς
δεύτερος, περὶ δούλων ὤν. καὶ ὁ μετ' αὐτὸν δέ,
περὶ λύπης, ὡς οὐ χρὴ παρεγγυᾶται τὸν γενναῖον
καὶ νοῦν ἔχοντα ἄνδρα ὑποκατακλίνεσθαι τῷ πάθει,
περιορᾶν δὲ μᾶλλον καὶ ἀποτρίβεσθαι. καὶ ὁ περὶ
πλεονεξίας, ζ' καὶ ξ' ὤν, ἀποτρέπεσθαι ταύτην
παρεγγυᾷ. καὶ ὁ ξη', ὥσπερ ἐπιγέγραπται περὶ
λόγου ἀσκήσεως, τοιαύτην καὶ τὴν ὑπόθεσιν ὑπο-
βάλλει. περὶ δὲ τῆς αὐτοῦ φιληκοΐας ὁ ξθ' καὶ
ἐπιγράφεται καὶ διαλαμβάνει. ὁ δὲ ο' ἐπιγραφῆς
μὲν περὶ ἀναχωρήσεως τυγχάνει, κατασκευάζει
δὲ ὡς οὐχὶ τὸ τὰς ἐρήμους διώκειν ἀναχώρησίς
ἐστι παθῶν καὶ τῶν ἐν βίῳ θορύβων, ἀλλὰ τὸ εἰς

speech *On Distrust*; the speech which precedes it
describes in detail how even being trusted as a rule
has brought great losses on those trusted. The
theme of fifty-eight, as also its title, is *On Law*;
so, too, number fifty-nine is *On Custom*. The latter
proves that custom accomplishes as much as law,
but that it operates by means of pleasure and
persuasion rather than by means of force, and with
greater certainty. The two speeches following are
treatises *On Envy*. Number sixty-two is *On Wealth*,
a discourse which holds up to public ridicule the
vexatiousness and fickleness of wealth and shows
that much more profitable is poverty joined to
righteousness. Number sixty-three is labelled *One
of the Addresses in Cilicia, On Freedom*, and it seeks
to show that that person is free who is master of
the emotions within him, even though ten thousand
persons outside him may be masters of his body;
and, on the other hand, that he is a slave who is
slave to his emotions, even if he is thought to be
lord of all the world. The next discourse also, with
the title *On Slavery and Freedom*, refers to the same
notion, just as does also the next in order, which is
On Slaves. The one after that, *On Pain*, exhorts the
high-born man who has intelligence not to give
way to suffering, but rather to disregard and abolish
it. *On Covetousness*, number sixty-seven, also is
an exhortation to avoid this fault. The theme of
number sixty-eight is, like its title, *On Training for
Public Speaking*. *On Dio's Love of Listening* is both
the title and the theme of number sixty-nine.
Number seventy has the title *On Retirement*, and it
seeks to prove that hunting for places of seclusion is
not retirement from sufferings and from the turmoils

ἑαυτὸν ἐπεστράφθαι καὶ σπεύδειν γνῶναι ἑαυτόν,
τῆς ἀπὸ τῶν ἄλλων κακίας συμφορῶν ὀλίγον
ἔχοντα λόγον. περὶ κάλλους δὲ ὁ μετὰ τοῦτον
λόγος, ὃν ἐπιγέγραπται τρόπον, τὸν αὐτὸν καὶ
περὶ νεανίσκου διέξεισιν· ἐν ᾧ ὡς οὐ παρὰ πᾶσιν
ἔθνεσι καὶ βαρβάροις τὸ αὐτὸ νομίζεται κάλλος,
ἄλλο δὲ παρ' ἄλλοις νικᾷ. ὁ δὲ οβ' περὶ εἰρήνης
καὶ πολέμου τήν τε ἐπιγραφὴν προβάλλεται καὶ
διαλαμβάνει. ὁ δὲ γ' καὶ ο', ὅτι εὐδαίμων ὁ σοφός,
καὶ ὁ ἐπ' αὐτῷ περὶ εὐδαιμονίας· ὁ δὲ ἐπὶ τούτοις
περὶ τοῦ δαίμονος. δαίμονας δὲ καλεῖ τοὺς ὅσοι
λαχόντες ἄρχειν ἑτέρων ἄμεινον πράττειν τοὺς
ἀρχομένους ἢ καὶ χεῖρον συμμετεσκεύασαν. περὶ
δὲ τοῦ βουλεύεσθαι ὁ ϛ' καὶ ο' διαλαμβάνει. ὁ δὲ
ζ' καὶ ο' διατριβὴ περὶ τῶν ἐν συμποσίῳ τὴν
ἐπιγραφὴν πεποιημένος τινὰ τῶν ἐν αὐτῷ διέξεισι
συμπιπτόντων, καὶ ὡς ὁ πολὺς ἄνθρωπος τηνι-
καῦτα πρὸς φιλοσοφίαν ὁρᾶν εἴωθεν, ἡνίκα αὐτοῦ
ὁ βίος ἀνίαις περιρρεῖται. ὁ δὲ η' καὶ ο' καὶ ὁ
μετ' αὐτὸν Μελαγκόμας α' καὶ β' ἐπιγεγραμμένοι
ἔπαινόν τε διαγράφουσι τοῦ νεανίσκου καὶ μνήμην
ἐπὶ χρηστοῖς τελευτήσαντος καὶ λύπην. ὁ δὲ π',
Χαρίδημος μὲν αὐτῷ ἡ ἐπιγραφή, ἔπαινον δὲ καὶ
πένθος ἐπὶ τελευτήσαντι συνδιαπλέκει τῷ νέῳ.

7. Arethae Archiepiscopi Dio

*Arethas, Bishop of Caesarea in Cappadocia, was a pupil
of Photius and shared his enthusiasm for Greek literature.
He was exceedingly active in collecting manuscripts, and we
possess some that were copied at his expense, notably the*

of life, but rather retirement is turning one's mind inward upon oneself and seeking to know oneself, paying little heed to misfortunes which result from the wickedness of others. *On Beauty*, which comes next, in keeping with its title discusses the beauty of a youth. In this discourse it is pointed out that not among all nations alike, including barbarians, is the same thing held to be beauty, but that one thing is preferred here and another there. *On Peace and War* is both the title and the subject matter of seventy-two. Seventy-three has the title, *That the Wise is Fortunate and Happy* ; next comes *On Happiness* ; and the next is *On the Guardian Spirit*. The author applies the term guardian spirit to all who, having been chosen to govern others, help to cause those whom they govern to fare better or worse. *On Deliberation* is the theme of seventy-six. Seventy-seven, *A Short Talk on What Takes Place at a Symposium*, discusses some of the things that occur at a symposium and maintains that the time when most men are wont to turn their attention to philosophy is when their lives are engulfed in troubles. Number seventy-eight and the one which follows, which are entitled *Melancomas I* and *II* respectively, contain a laudation of the youth, a reminder of the noble career that preceded his death, and an expression of the grief which his death occasioned. Number eighty has the title *Charidemus*, and it combines praise and sorrow over the death of the young man.

7. Arethas

Bodleian Plato known as Clarkianus. *Some of his annotations on Greek authors have been preserved, Dio being included in that number.*

DIO CHRYSOSTOM

The rather lengthy note on Dio that we present first is a scholium on the discourses On Kingship. *Arethas seeks to defend Dio against the imputation of arrogance in those four compositions by citing the conduct of Nestor in the famous scene in* Iliad 1 *in which Nestor recounts glorious exploits of his younger days for the purpose of securing the obedience of Agamemnon and Achilles. The appeal to the authority of Homer is quite in the spirit of Dio himself.*

It will be observed that Arethas has the false impression

Σοφὸς οὑτοσὶ τῷ ὄντι Δίων ὁ Προυσαεὺς καὶ τἄλλα μὲν τὰ περὶ λόγων ἀσκήσεως, μάλιστα δὲ τοὺς προκειμένους περὶ βασιλείας φρονήσει διαρκεστάτῃ ἐξυφαινόμενος. Οὐεσπασιανὸς ὁ αὐτοκράτωρ τῆς βιωφελοῦς τούτων γνώμης ἐπήβολος. οἷς γὰρ ἠπόρει τῇ ἐπικρατούσῃ ταῖς τῶν συμβούλων εἰς ὕπαιθρον χρῆσθαι μεθόδοις περιαυτολογίᾳ, φησὶ τὸν εἰσηγεῖσθαι τεταγμένον σεμνολογήσασθαι, ὡς ἂν ᾖ ταύτῃ τὸ εὐπαράδεκτον αὐτῷ τῶν ὑποτιθεμένων κατανυόμενον, ἐπεί τοι καὶ λόγος δραστικώτερος ὁ τοῦ κρείττονος. ἀφ' οὗ δοκεῖ μοι καὶ Ὅμηρος ὁ ἐποποιός, ἐνευδοκιμῶν τὰ τοιαῦτα οὐ κατὰ τοὺς πολλοὺς καίριόν τι τοῖς μετ' αὐτὸν ἐν τοῖς ὁμοίοις παραδεικνὺς μάθημα, τὸν Πύλιον παρεισήγαγε Νέστορα ὑπὸ Δρύαντος Καινέως τε μετακαλούμενον καὶ Ἐξαδίου τῆς τ' ἄλλης κατ' ἐκείνους φρατρίας ἀρχὴν μὲν ἐκβοηθεῖν, εἶτα τούτου λαβόμενον Νέστορα τῇ ἐξαγγελίᾳ, ἅτε δὴ τῇ κατὰ χεῖρα βοηθείᾳ τοσούτοις τὸ ἐννάλιον ἀνδράσι χρειωδέστατον δόξαντα, προσθεῖναι τὸ ἀπὸ τοῦδε οὐκ ὠκνηκότα τί; τοῦτο τὸ καιριώτατον λέγω τῆς συμβουλῆς. τί γάρ φησι;

καὶ μέν μευ βουλέων ξύνιον πείθοντό τε μύθῳ.

---

[1] *Iliad* 1. 273.

that the discourses On Kingship *were composed for Vespasian.
Probably that error, as also the error of making Nero the
author of Dio's exile, was due to a misunderstanding of his
teacher Photius, whom he echoes in a passage we have omitted.
Arethas also gives to the epithet Chrysostomos a novel
meaning, which he supports by citing some amusing verses of
an unknown versifier, whose gossip resembles Lucian's anecdote
(Hermotimus 34) about the Sicilian tyrant Gelon.*

This Dio of Prusa was truly wise in general in
his practice of oratory, but particularly when, with
consummate wisdom, he wove the present speeches
On Kingship. The emperor Vespasian had grasped
the practical wisdom which characterizes them ; for
when he was at a loss how to deal with the undisguised
egotism dominant in the methods of his counsellors,
he says that the counsellor who had been appointed
to make a proposal resorted to grandiloquence, in
order that in this way he might insure that the
acceptability of his proposals might be achieved, for
of course an utterance is more cogent when it is that
of a superior person. This, in my opinion, is the
reason why Homer the epic poet, who enjoys a high
reputation in such matters not matched by most men,
when handing down to his successors a timely lesson
to serve them in like circumstances, introduced into
his narrative the statement that Pylian Nestor, when
summoned by Dryas and Caeneus and Exadius and
the rest of their clan, first of all came to their aid,
and then, after Nestor had dealt with that exploit,
since of course by his active assistance to so many
men in war he had gained a reputation for being
most indispensable, that he added to his declaration
without any hesitation—what ? This I claim is the
most vital point in his counsel. For what does he say ?

They heard my counsels and obeyed my word.[1]

409

καὶ ἐπειδήπερ ἐπὶ τοσοῦτον τὸ ἑαυτοῦ μεγαλο-
πρεπὲς ὑπεστήσατο, ὡς ἂν ἤδη μετεωρίσας τὸ
ἔργον ἀπὸ τοῦ τοιούτοις ὑπερφυέσιν ἀξιόχρεως
νομισθῆναι, οὓς καὶ πειθηνίους τῶν ἑαυτοῦ βου-
λευμάτων ἐξέφηνε, πεποιθότως ἐντεῦθεν ἐπήνεγκεν·

ἀλλὰ πίθεσθε καὶ ὔμμες, ἐπεὶ πείθεσθαι ἄμεινον,[1]

μόνον οὐχὶ λέγων· ὁρᾶτε οὓς ἐγὼ τοιούτους ἔσχηκα
κατηκόους; οὔκουν ἀκλεὲς οὐδὲ ἀσύμφορον καὶ
ὑμᾶς ἐμοὶ πείθεσθαι.

Ὁ μὲν οὖν οὕτω σαφῶς τὴν περίνοιαν δηλοῖ,
τῇ πράξει τὴν μέθοδον ἐμπεδώσας, ἀλλ᾽ οὐχ ὁ
Προυσαεὺς οὗτος τοιοῦτος, διόπερ οὐκ ἔχων
τοιούτοις καὶ οὗτος ἐγκαλλωπίσασθαι ἑτέρως
μέτεισι τὴν χρείαν. ἐπεὶ γὰρ ἤδει τὴν ὁμογνω-
μοσύνην ταυτότητι τρόπων τοὺς ὁμογνωμονοῦντας
συνδέουσαν, ὅ γε λοιπὸν καὶ τὴν ἰσονομίαν βρα-
βεύειν ἐπίσταται, ἐκείνους ἀθροίσας ὅσοι τὰς
βασιλείους οἴμους κατειληφότες γνωρίζειν τοῖς
ἔρχεσθαι ταύτας ἀσφαλέστατα βουλομένοις θεσπί-
ζουσι, τὸν Μελητιάδην Ὅμηρον λέγω, Σωκράτη
τε τὸν Σωφρονίσκου καὶ Φαιναρέτης, πρὸς δὲ
καὶ Διογένη τὸν Σινωπέα, καὶ μέντοι πλασάμενός
τι μεταξὺ τῶν λόγων καὶ αὐτός, ἐκ Πελοποννησίας
γραός, Ἀρκαδικῆς μὲν τὴν οἴκησιν, νομαδικῆς
δὲ τὸν βίον, καὶ περὶ τὸ ἐνθουσιᾶν προσευκαιρούσης,
ταύτης ἀκηκοέναι περὶ τοῦ ἐκ Σεμέλης Ἡρακλέους[2]
τίς τε οὗτος εἴη ὁ ἐκ Σεμέλης καὶ οἷος τὸν βίον,

---

[1] *Iliad* 1. 274.   [2] Cf. Or. 1. 49 ff.   Arethas is in error.

And when Nestor had established his own importance to that extent, as if he had already exalted his achievement through having been deemed trustworthy by such extraordinary beings, whom he declared also to have been obedient to his desires, he thereupon added with confidence,

But ye too harken, for 'tis better so,[1]

all but saying, " Do you see how wonderful these men were whose obedience I have had ? Then it is not ignominious or disadvantageous for you also to obey me."

Well then, this is the way in which Nestor clearly reveals his intellectual superiority, having established doctrine by achievement ; but this man from Prusa was not another Nestor, wherefore, not being able to boast of exploits such as his, he pursues his purpose differently. For since he knew that like-mindedness by identity of manners binds together the like-minded, he therefore knows how to judge equality as well, and he assembles all those famous men who, having comprehended how to recognize the paths of kingship, lay down the law for those who wish to tread them most securely—I refer to Homer son of Meles, Socrates son of Sophroniscus and Phaenaretê, and also Diogenes of Sinopê. Moreover, he too resorted to a bit of invention in the midst of his speeches, namely, the fiction that from an old woman of the Peloponnese—who was an Arcadian by domestic ties but lived a roving life and also found leisure for ecstatic experience—that from her, I say, he had heard about Heracles son of Semelê, not only who this son of Semelê was but also what kind of life he lived.[2] Nay more, he claimed

411

ἀλλά γε καὶ ὅτι ὑπ' αὐτῆς ἀπαγγέλλειν ταῦτα
προστέτακται ὅτῳ ἔστιν ὅτε συγκυρήσοι ἀξίῳ τοῦ
βασιλείου ἐπιτηδεύματος, καὶ τούτοις οὐ μόνον
ἐπιρρώσας τὸ ἑαυτῷ σπουδαζόμενον, εἰ μή που
καὶ ὡς ὁμόγλωσσον ἑαυτὸν τούτοις ἐν ταῖς προ-
κειμέναις ὑποθέσεσιν ἀποφήνας ἀνεπαχθέστατα τὸ
ἔργον συνεπεράνατο. ἃ γὰρ οὗτος τὰ νῦν συμβου-
λεύειν προείλετο, ἐκείνοις προδιηγορευμένα ὑπέφη-
νεν, λεληθότως ἐκ τούτων φιλοτιμούμενος ἑαυτὸν
παρισῶσαι τοῖς προεφωδευκόσι τὰ νῦν αὐτῷ
πρεσβευόμενα. τοιγὰρ τῇ πρὸς τούτους κοινο-
λογίᾳ, ἐν οἷς τῆς βασιλείου βιοτῆς τε καὶ τάξεως
τὰ παράσημα διεξῄεσαν, οὐχ ἧττον καὶ οὗτος τὸ
μεγαλαυχεῖν ἐπεσπάσατο, πεφυκότος εἰς ἅπαν τοῦ
κατ' οὐδὲν ὑπαλλάσσειν τὴν εἰσήγησιν τῶν ἐν
τῷ ζῆν προτερημάτων ἐνάμιλλον παριστάνειν καὶ
τοῦτον ἐκείνων τῶν προκαταρξάντων βιωφελῶν
οὕτω ῥημάτων. τί γάρ φησιν ὁ Ἀσκραῖος ποιμήν;
ἐσθλὸς δ' αὖ κἀκεῖνος, ὃς ἄλλου εὖ εἰπόντος
πείθεται.

Συντόμως τὸ προκείμενον τοῦ εὐπαρακολουθήτου
ἕνεκα οὕτω προσακτέον. Δίων οὗτος ὁ Προυσαεὺς
οἷς οὐκ εἶχεν ἐγκαλλωπίσασθαι περιαυτολογίᾳ,
φημὶ ὥσπερ ὁ Πύλιος Νέστωρ, ἐπεὶ καὶ τοῦτο
εἰς ἀναντίρρητον τοῖς συμβουλεύουσιν ἐπακολουθεῖ
ὑπὲρ τοῦ εὐπαράδεκτον εἶναι τὴν ἀπὸ τῶν κρειτ-
τόνων παράκλησιν. οἷς οὖν οὕτω προάγειν οὐκ
εἶχε, τέχνῃ τοῦτο κατήνυσεν, σύμφωνον ἑαυτὸν
ἀποφαίνων τοῖς περὶ βασιλείας εἰρηκόσι σοφοῖς
καὶ ὅπως χρὴ βασιλείαν μετιέναι. τὸ γὰρ ὁμό-

---

[1] Hesiod, *Works and Days* 295.

that he had been appointed by this old woman to report these things to any one whom he might encounter from time to time who was worthy of the kingly office, and in such cases not merely lending strength to his own special interest, unless perchance by proving that he spoke the same language as they did on the subjects under discussion, he accomplished his task with the least offence. For the advice which he chose to give on such an occasion he revealed as having been previously delivered by those men of old, secretly aspiring in this way to place himself on the same level with those who had led the way in the matters then advocated by him. Therefore in his discussions with these men, while they were going through the spurious elements in the kingly life and order, nevertheless he too induced boasting, since it was wholly natural that his failure to alter in any wise his recommendation of the advantages in his mode of life should result in his presenting himself too as a rival of those men of old who had first uttered sayings of such practical utility. For what says the shepherd of Ascra? " He too is noble who heeds another who has spoken wisely."[1]

In short, the subject under discussion must, for the sake of clearness, be presented as follows. This Dio of Prusa, in matters wherein he was unable to boast of personal exploits—I mean as Pylian Nestor did, since this too results in making unanswerable the words of the counsellor regarding the acceptability of the exhortation offered by those who are superior—in matters, then, wherein he could not persuade in this way, he achieved his aim by artifice, representing himself as in agreement with the sages who have told about kingship and how it should be

γνωμον καὶ ἰσότιμον τοῖς προαπηγγελκόσι τὰ
κεδνὰ ταῦτα βουλεύματα, εἴ τι τῷ Ἀσκραίῳ
πιστεύειν δεῖ ποιμένι. . . .

Περὶ Δίωνος καὶ τῶν κατ' αὐτὸν καὶ τῆς τοῦ
λόγου αὐτοῦ ἰδέας. Ὁ Δίων οὗτος ἦν μὲν Προυσαεύς, Προύσης τῆς πρὸς τῷ Μυσῷ Ὀλύμπῳ,
πρὸς δὲ τῇ ἄλλῃ σοφίᾳ καὶ τὰ περὶ λόγους ἐπήσκητο
καὶ λέγειν σχεδίως εἰς ἄκρον τῶν καθ' ἑαυτὸν
παρεσκευασμένος ζηλωτὸς ἅπασι καὶ ἀπόβλεπτος
ἦν. ταύτῃ τοι καὶ τῇ τοῦ λόγου χρησάμενος ῥύ-
μῃ, καὶ πρὸς Νέρωνα ὑπὲρ τῶν ἑαυτοῦ παρρη-
σιασάμενος φίλων, ἀειφυγίᾳ κατεδικάσθη καὶ ἦν
τῷ ζημιώματι ἐπίτιμος τούτῳ ἐς ὅτε Οὐεσπασια-
νὸν ἡ Ῥωμαίων εὐτυχεῖ πολιτεία, ᾧ συγγε-
νόμενος κατὰ τὴν Νειλῴαν Ἀλεξάνδρειαν καὶ πολλὰ
τῶν βασιλεῖ ὑποθέμενος ἀνηκόντων τέλος καὶ τοὺς
παρόντας βασιλικοὺς λόγους αὐτῷ ἐξεπόνησε.

Χρυσόστομος δὲ κατὰ τὸν λόγον οὐχ οὕτως ὅσον
διά τι σύμπτωμα ἐπὶ τὸ εὐσχημονέστερον μετα-
ποιούμενον ἐκλήθη. τῇ γὰρ ἀπὸ τοῦ στόματος
ἀποφορᾷ οὐ πάνυ εὐτυχεῖ ἐχρῆτο, ὡς δὴ καὶ ἄλλοι
πολλοί, καὶ ὁ τοὺς λόγους θεῖος ἀπαγγέλλει ἀνήρ.
φησὶ γὰρ περὶ αὐτοῦ ἐν ἰαμβείοις αὐτοῦ οὕτω.

Δίων ἀνέπνει, φασίν, οὐ μάλ' ἡδύ τι·
τοῦτον λέγω Δίωνα, οὗ πολὺς λόγος.
καὶ τοῦτ' ἐκερτόμησε τῶν τις ἀστικῶν.
τὸν δ' ὡς ἰδεῖν γυναῖκα τὴν αὐτοῦ, φράσαι·

---

[1] Arethas is at fault in this account of Dio's exile and
return to imperial favour. Dio is critical of Nero, but it
was Domitian who caused his exile and whose death made
possible his return. Furthermore, the discourses *On Kingship*
are believed to have been addressed to Trajan.

practised. For like-mindedness is also equality in honour with those who previously have announced these sage counsels, if we should give any credence to the shepherd of Ascra. . . .

Concerning Dio, the facts about him, and the style of his eloquence : This Dio was a native of Prusa, the Prusa near Mysian Olympus. In addition to his wisdom in general, he had cultivated also the art of public speaking and, having prepared himself for extempore speaking to a point surpassing those of his own day, he was envied and admired by all. In this way, you see, having indulged in the vehemence of his language and having expressed himself freely in the presence of Nero in behalf of his own friends, he was sentenced to lifelong banishment, and he remained under this sentence until the Roman state secured Vespasian as emperor. Having met Vespasian in Alexandria on the Nile and having instructed him in many of the matters pertaining to a king, he finally worked out for him the present discourses *On Kingship*.[1]

He was called Golden-mouthed, not so much to accord with his eloquence, as on account of a certain physical peculiarity the name of which was altered in the direction of greater respectability. For he was not at all fortunate in the effluvia that issued from his mouth, as indeed many others report and in particular the man of divine utterance. For he speaks of Dio in his iambics as follows.

'Tis said that Dio's breath was nothing sweet—
I mean that Dio of whom there's so much talk.
A city fellow told this mocking tale.
He said when Dio saw his wife he cried,

415

DIO CHRYSOSTOM

Τί τοῦτο; οὐ γὰρ ἔφρασάς μοι τὴν νόσον.
καὶ τὴν σὺν ὅρκῳ, Τοῦτο πάντων ἀρρένων,
εἰπεῖν, τὸ σύμπτωμ᾽ ᾠόμην, οὐ σοῦ μόνου·
τοσοῦτον ἀνδρῶν καὶ φίλων ἀπεστάτει.
ὁ γὰρ λόγος δίδαγμα τοῦ σεμνοῦ τρόπου.

ἀντὶ τοίνυν τοῦ ᾽Οζόστομος ἐλέχθη εὐφήμως Χρυσόστομος.

᾽Ιδέᾳ δὲ κέχρηται συγκράτῳ τοῦ λόγου Πλατωνικῇ
καὶ Λυσιακῇ, οὔτε τὸ διηρμένον τοῦ Πλάτωνος τῆς
Λυσιακῆς ἀπολύων ἁπλότητος, οὔτε τὸ Λυσιακὸν
εἰς ἁπλότητα ἐπιτετηδευμένον τῆς Πλατωνικῆς
σεμνότητος ἀποστερῶν, ἀλλὰ καὶ σεμνολογῶν μετὰ
ἀφελείας καὶ τὴν ἀφέλειαν ἐξαίρων διὰ σεμνότητος.

8. Suidas Lexic. s.v.

*Suidas is the author of a famous lexicon, probably composed
in the third quarter of the tenth century, which is especially
valuable for its information on literary matters. In the
following entry regarding Dio it will be noted that the bio-*

Δίων ὁ Πασικράτους, Προυσαεύς, σοφιστὴς καὶ
φιλόσοφος, ὃν Χρυσόστομον ἐκάλεσαν. ἀντε-
ποιεῖτο δὲ σεμνότητος, ὡς καὶ λεοντῆν φορῶν
προϊέναι. ἦν δὲ λεπτὸς τὸ σῶμα, καὶ διέτριψε τὸ
πλεῖστον παρὰ Τραιανῷ τῷ Καίσαρι, ὡς καὶ
συγκαθέζεσθαι ἐν τῷ βασιλικῷ ὀχήματι. ἔγραψεν,
Εἰ φθαρτὸς ὁ κόσμος, ᾽Εγκώμιον ῾Ηρακλέους
καὶ Πλάτωνος, ῾Υπὲρ ᾽Ομήρου πρὸς Πλάτωνα
δ᾽, Περὶ τῶν ᾽Αλεξάνδρου ἀρετῶν η᾽.

9. C. Plini et Traiani Epistulae LXXXI—LXXXII

Pliny, Letters x. 81 and 82, a communication from Pliny

" How's this ?   You never mentioned my disease."
And she with solemn oath replied, " I thought
That symptom was the nature of all males,
And not of you alone."   So far removed
Was she from men and friends.   The story serves
To indicate the man's majestic ways.

So it is that, instead of Foul-mouthed, through
euphemism he was termed Golden-mouthed.

Dio uses a literary style that is a blend of the
styles of Plato and of Lysias, for he neither frees
the sublimity of Plato from the simplicity of Lysias
nor deprives of Plato's solemnity that trait of Lysias
which cultivated simplicity ; on the contrary, he not
only talks solemnly with simplicity but also elevates
his simplicity by means of solemnity.

8. Suidas

*graphical details are those earlier recorded by Photius.   In
view of that, it is noteworthy that the only works listed for
Dio by Suidas are four that are mentioned nowhere else.*

Lexicon : Dio son of Pasicrates, citizen of Prusa,
sophist and philosopher, whom men called Chrysostom.
He affected solemnity to the extent of actually appearing in public wearing a lion's skin.   He had a
lean body.   He spent his time for the most part in
the society of the emperor Trajan, so that he even
sat beside him in the imperial carriage.   Writings :
Is the Universe Perishable? ; *In Praise of Heracles and
Plato* ; *Against Plato in Defence of Homer*, four books ;
On the Virtues of Alexander, eight books.

9. Correspondence of Pliny and Trajan

the Younger to the emperor Trajan and the emperor's reply,

*are of interest for several reasons. Both documents belong
to the year 112, when Pliny was proconsul of Bithynia, and
they supply for Dio's career the latest date for which we have
sure evidence. They also confirm Dio's words as to the
political tension prevalent in Prusa and the petty jealousies
and bickering which he encountered upon his return from
exile. They are of special interest in connexion with Or. 45
and Or. 47, which deal with the building project to which Pliny*

LXXXI [LXXXV]
C. Plinius Traiano Imperatori

Cum Prusae ad Olympum, domine, publicis negotiis
intra hospitium eodem die exiturus vacarem, Asclepiades magistratus indicavit appellatum me a
Claudio Eumolpo. Cum Cocceianus Dion in bule
adsignari civitati opus cuius curam egerat vellet, tum
Eumolpus adsistente Flavio Archippo dixit exigen-
dam esse a Dione rationem operis, ante quam rei
publicae traderetur, quod aliter fecisset ac debuisset.
Adiecit etiam esse in eodem opere positam tuam
statuam et corpora sepultorum, uxoris Dionis et filii,
postulavitque, ut cognoscerem pro tribunali. Quod
cum ego me protinus facturum dilaturumque profectionem dixissem, ut longiorem diem ad instruendam
causam darem, utque in alia civitate cognoscerem,
petiit. Ego me auditurum Nicaeae respondi. Ubi
cum consedissem cogniturus, idem Eumolpus tam-
quam adhuc parum instructus dilationem petere

refers and give a vivid picture of the hostile opposition against which Dio had to struggle, one specimen of which is contained in the Pliny-Trajan correspondence. Trajan's rather brusque reply may indicate impatience over the attempt to harass his old friend Dio, an impatience in no wise diminished, no doubt, because the Archippus who instigated the present trouble had previously been the occasion of annoyance to the emperor, as we learn from Pliny, Letters x. 58-60.

LXXXI [LXXXV]

Gaius Pliny to the Emperor Trajan

While at Prusa near Olympus, sire, I was in my quarters attending to public business, planning that same day to take my departure, Asclepiades the magistrate made known that an appeal had been made to me by Claudius Eumolpus. When Cocceianus Dio in the Council desired to have turned over to the municipality a work which he had had in charge, Eumolpus, acting in the interest of Flavius Archippus, said that an accounting for the work should be demanded of Dio before it was turned over to the commonwealth, alleging that Dio had acted otherwise than he should have done. He added that the same structure contained a statue of you and also corpses which had been interred there, to wit, those of Dio's wife and son, and he demanded that I conduct a judicial investigation. When I said I would do so forthwith and would postpone my departure, he begged that I allow him more time to prepare his case and that I hold the hearing in a different city. I replied that I would hear the case at Nicaea. When I took my seat there to hold the hearing, the aforesaid Eumolpus, as if still insufficiently prepared, began to ask for postponement;

419

coepit, contra Dion, ut audiretur, exigere. Dicta
sunt utrimque multa etiam de causa. Ego cum
dandam dilationem ad te consulendum existimarem
in re ad exemplum pertinenti, dixi utrique parti, ut
postulationum suarum libellos darent. Volebam
enim te ipsorum potissimum verbis ea quae erant
proposita cognoscere. Et Dion quidem se daturum
dixit, at Eumolpus respondit complexurum se libello
quae rei publicae peteret, ceterum quod ad sepultos
pertineret non accusatorem se sed advocatum Flavi
Archippi, cuius mandata pertulisset. Archippus,
qui Eumolpo sicut Prusiade adsistebat, dixit se
libellum daturum. At[1] nec Eumolpus nec Archippus
quamquam plurimis diebus expectatis adhuc mihi
libellos dederunt ; Dion dedit, quem huic epistulae
iunxi. Ipse in re praesenti fui et vidi tuam quoque
statuam in bibliotheca positam, id autem, in quo
dicuntur sepulti filius et uxor Dionis, in area collocatum, quae porticibus includitur. Te, domine,
rogo, ut me in hoc praecipue genere cognitionis
regere digneris, cum alioqui magna sit expectatio,
ut necesse est in ea re, quae et in confessum venit
et exemplis defenditur.

LXXXII [LXXXVI]
Traianus Plinio S.

Potuisti non haerere, mi Secunde carissime, circa
id de quo me consulendum existimasti, cum pro-

---

[1] *At* Schaefer : *Ita.*

Dio, on the contrary, demanded that the hearing proceed. Many statements were made by both parties, even about the case. Since I believed that a postponement should be granted in order to consult you in a matter bearing on precedent, I told both parties to present their demands in writing. You see, I wanted you to learn from their own words preferably the claims which had been put forward. And Dio, indeed, said that he would do as requested, but Eumolpus answered that he would put in writing what he was asking in behalf of the commonwealth, but that with regard to the buried bodies he was not the accuser but rather the attorney of Flavius Archippus, whose orders he had executed. Archippus, who was assisting Eumolpus as he had at Prusa, said that he would present the memorial. However, neither Eumolpus nor Archippus, despite very many days of waiting, has up to the present handed me the memorials ; Dio has presented his, and I append it to this letter. I myself visited the spot, and I saw your statue also in position in the library ; however, the place where the bodies of Dio's son and wife are said to have been buried is located in a vacant space surrounded by colonnades. I ask you, sire, to see fit to direct me in this kind of inquiry especially, since of itself the case has aroused great public interest, as is inevitable in a matter which is both well known and supported by precedents.

LXXXII [LXXXVI]

Trajan to Pliny, greetings

You might have suffered no perplexity, my very dear Secundus, regarding the matter about which

positum meum optime nosses non ex metu nec terrore hominum aut criminibus maiestatis reverentiam nomini meo adquirendi. Omissa ergo ea quaestione, quam non admitterem, etiam si exemplis adiuvaretur, ratio potius operis effecti sub cura Cocceiani Dionis excutiatur, cum et utilitas civitatis exigat, nec aut recuset Dion aut debeat recusare.

you thought I should be consulted, since you knew very well my purpose not to secure respect for my name through men's fear or dread or by means of charges of high treason. Putting aside, therefore, that point at issue, which I would not entertain even if it were sustained by precedents, rather let the accounting for the work executed under the supervision of Cocceianus Dio be thoroughly investigated, since the advantage of the municipality demands it and Dio neither refuses nor should refuse.

INDEX

The numbers refer to volume and page of this edition

Abdera, seaport in Thrace, birthplace of Protagoras 4 373

Academy, grove and gymnasium in the suburbs of Athens, had lost its characteristic quality 3 167, visited by Socrates 4 427, a short distance from Lyceum *ibid.* and n. 1

Acanthus, town in Chalcidicê, scene of Athenian defeat 2 157

Achaeans, term used for the Greeks besieging Troy, contrasted with Trojans 1 85, chant paean over Hector's body 87, slew Polyxena at tomb of Achilles 261, brought 1200 ships to Troy 491, landing opposed by Trojans 503, wall and trench 505, did not control environs of Troy 505 f., tilled Chersonese 507, sought wine at Lemnos *ibid.*, routed 509, withdrew to Chersonese 533, 543, many lost returning from Troy 545, expelled from Peloponnese 549, founded

Lesbos while fleeing from Dorians 555, stoned to death Palamedes 2 109, marvelled at Hector's beauty 289, 5 233

Achaia, birthplace of Clytemnestra and Helen 5 11

Acharnians, members of deme in Attica, lost trees in Archidamian war 5 333

Acheloüs, river-god, wooed Deïaneira and overcome by Heracles 4 453, lost horn in fight with Heracles 5 41

Achilles, compared with Alexander the Great 1 59, pupil of Phoenix 59, 63, subject to orders 61, made Alexander jealous 71, voice routed Trojans 87, bade Achaeans chant paean over Hector's body *ibid.*, his ghost 191, 261, pursued Hector all day 413, death not narrated by Homer 471, 531, 543, battle with Penthesilea 471, battle with river *ibid.*, 485, clever at ambush 505, nearly captured Aeneas *ibid.*, entreated 511, 515, 517, wounded by Asteropaeus 519, fought Aeneas *ibid.*, could not overtake Agenor *ibid.*, pursued and slain by Hector *ibid.*, warned by Thetis about Patroclus 523, not slain by Paris 527, exploits garbled 527 f., duel with Hector 529, entertained Priam 563, built funeral pyre for Patroclus 2 121, 287, not described by Homer 289, died young 371, 391, beautiful and brave 389, preferred honour to long life 3 23, elated by new armour 397, worshipped at Borysthenes 435, his holy isle 443, 447, his wrath 4 347, valour well known in India 363, horses coveted by Dolon 391, 395, offered satisfaction by Agamemnon 413 f., admonished by Nestor 419, arrogant 423, son of Peleus and Thetis *ibid.*, Discourse on 431-437, early years as told by Apollodorus 431, argues with Cheiron 433 f., spoiled by parents 437, 5 139, slew Lycaon 227, friendship with Patroclus proverbial 237, tricked by phantom of Agenor 329, had flaxen hair 341

Acratus, agent of Nero, did not seize Rhodian statues 3 153

Acrocorinth, overshadows

Corinth 1 253, held by Persaeus 5 197

Acropolis, at Athens, more beautiful than Ecbatana and Babylon 1 253, above theatre of Dionysus 3 127, despoiled by Nero 151

Actaeon, slain by his own dogs 1 421, saw Artemis naked 4 33

Actor, name of a Lemnian in Euripides' *Philoctetes* 4 345

Actors, poor people should not be 1 353, compared with orators 2 241, hissed 3 123, 157, afford pleasure and profit 4 85

Adana, town in Cilicia, hostile to Tarsus 3 321, 349

Adeimantus, Corinthian general, maligned by Herodotus 4 11, commemorated by Simonides 21

Admiral, leader of a fleet 4 405

Adonis, famed for beauty 2 389, lamented by women 5 29 and n. 3

Adrastus, king of Argos, son of Talaüs 4 403

Adriatic territories, held by Antenor 1 553

Aegae, ancient capital of Macedonia, seized by Alexander 2 331

Aegae, town in Cilicia 3 321, quarrels with Tarsus 347, 349 f.

Aegina, island near Athens 2 247

Aegisthus, slew Agamemnon

and seized his throne **1** 547, paramour of Clytemnestra **2** 149, offspring of incestuous union and accomplice of Clytemnestra **5** 95, fed Agamemnon before slaying him 227

Aegospotami, Athenian navy defeated at **5** 59 n. 2

Aeneas, eluded Achilles **1** 505, conquered by Diomede 511, 513, fought Achilles 519, sent by Hector with large fleet and occupied Italy 551, founded Rome 553 f., aided Diomede 555

Aeolians, ruled by Aeolus **4** 407

Aeolis, district in Asia Minor, made subject to Mytilenê **4** 221

Aeolus, ruled Aeolians **4** 407, fortunate in his children **5** 51 and n. 3

Aëropê, wife of Atreus, seduced by Thyestes **2** 149, typifies marital infidelity **5** 223

Aeschines, Athenian orator and politician, orations superior to those of Demosthenes and Lysias **2** 223

Aeschines, disciple of Socrates **1** 377

Aeschylus, compared with Sophocles and Euripides **4** 339 ff., his *Philoctetes* 339, competed with Sophocles 341, heroes true to ancient type *ibid.*, his Odysseus analysed 341 f.,

did not have Athena disguise Odysseus 343, his chorus in *Philoctetes* compared with that of Euripides *ibid.*, not inconsistent 345 f., lacked sagacity of Euripides 347, compared with Sophocles 351, *Oresteia* overlooked by Dio **5** 95 n. 1

Aesop, his fable of the Owl **2** 11 f., **5** 189 f., a Phrygian kinsman tells of Orpheus **3** 235 f., fable of the Eyes 289, fable of the Fox and the Oak **4** 265, compared with Seven Sages **5** 187

Aethiopis, cyclic poem, recounted slaying of Achilles by Paris **4** 437 n. 4

Aethra, depicted on chest of Cypselus **1** 481, mother of Theseus 491, daughter of Pittheus 493, slave in Sparta *ibid.*, followed Paris and Helen to Troy *ibid.*, 501

Aetolians, did not overcome Alexander **5** 65

Agamemnon, **1** 59, praised Nestor 63, could not control army 65, fed troops on beef 79, honoured Ajax with chine of ox *ibid.*, only hero to wear purple robe 81, described by Homer 93, associated with Argos 355, married Clytemnestra 481, sought to wed Helen to Menelaüs *ibid.*, a Phrygian from Mt. Sipylus 485, fearing Paris, prepared

427

suitors for war 493 f., assembled troops 507, impugned honesty of Calchas *ibid.*, held midnight council 511, appealed to Achilles *ibid.*, fled before Hector 513, 531, despised by wife 547, slain and supplanted by Aegisthus *ibid.*, wed Cassandra 563 f., compared by Homer to Zeus 2 67, 5 9, in tragedy 1 107, actors in rôle of 4 85, relied on Nestor 297, 395, 403, 409 f., ruled Achaeans and Argives at Ilium 409, relied on council of elders 411, treatment of Briseïs 411 f., offered Achilles satisfaction 413 f., admonished by Nestor 419, arrogant 423, sole ruler of Greeks *ibid.*, praised intelligence of Chryseïs 5 3, powerful and ambitious 7, disparaged Clytemnestra 13, slain by Clytemnestra 15, displeased Chryseïs *ibid.*, arrogant 17, his passion for Cassandra 19, his thousand ships 53, entrusted wife to musician 197 and n. 4, complained about Clytemnestra to Odysseus 227, body praised by Homer 339 f.

Agaristê, daughter of Cleisthenes 1 481 and n. 1

Agenor, escaped from Achilles 1 519, phantom led Achilles astray 5 329

Agesilaüs, king of Sparta, refused to have likeness made 4 41 f., recalled by ephors from Asia Minor 407

Aglaophon, Thasian artist 2 51, father and teacher of Polygnotus and Aristophon 4 381

Ahenobarbus, Latin equivalent of Greek Chalcopogon, name attached to statue of Alcibiades 4 39 and n. 4

Ajax, 1 63, honoured with chine of ox 79, death not narrated by Homer 471, duel with Hector 509, valour 511, fled before Hector 513, defeated at the ships *ibid.*, rescued body of Achilles 519, committed suicide 527, slain by Hector 535, 543, his grave *ibid.*, his madness 563, complained of Achilles' lack of hospitality 5 235 n. 1

Ajax, the Locrian, abused Idomeneus at Funeral Games 3 251, punished for impiety *ibid.*

Alcaeus, lyric poet, his statue at Thebes 3 97 and n. 2

Alcamenes, sculptor, pupil of Pheidias 2 49

Alcibiades, son of Cleinias and nephew of Pericles, still talked about 2 283, guiding spirit of Athens 329, statue labelled Chalcopogon 4 39, statue mutilated *ibid.*, used as type by

INDEX

Socrates 389, his beauty 5 71

Alcinoüs, king of the Phaeacians, palace described 1 75, heard tale of Odysseus 473, palace 5 305

Alcmaeon, ancestor of Pericles, wandering of 5 47 and n. 4, his greed 289 f.

Alcmenê, mother of Heracles 1 31, 245

Alector, Castle of, near mouth of Borysthenes 3 423

Alexander, son of Priam, see Paris

Alexander the Great, exalted by music of Timotheüs 1 3, passionate 5, disdained father *ibid.*, as a lad joined Philip on campaign 51, responsible for battle of Chaeronea *ibid.*, discussed poets with father 53 ff., preferred Homer 55, superior to Achilles and other heroes 59, slighted poets other than Homer 71, jealous of Achilles *ibid.*, spared house of Pindar *ibid.*, conversed with Diogenes 169-205 *passim*, ambitious 169 f., admired Diogenes 171, visited Diogenes at Corinth 173 f., called a bastard 177, knew by heart the *Iliad* and much of the *Odyssey* 187, wanted to rule the world 191, slave of glory 197, descendant of Heracles 201, descendant of Archelaüs *ibid.*, his Asiatic campaign topic for orators 2 297, guiding spirit of Macedonians 331, annexed Egypt, Babylon, Susa, and Ecbatana *ibid.*, deprived Macedonians of Aegae, Pella, and Dium 331 f., claimed to be son of Zeus 3 263, taught by Aristotle 4 255, 297, his death 5 63 f., father of Heracles 67 and n. 9, received obeisance of Darius' mother *ibid.*

Alexander the Philhellene, extolled by Pindar 1 71

Alexandria, in Egypt, cult of Serapis 3 183, has wonderful water but foul canals 187, importance of 205 f., world centre 207, 209, 217, not wholly self-sustaining 231, 5 415

Alexandrians, Discourse on 3 171-271, lack seriousness 173, at the theatre 175, 191, 193, excitable 201, despised by rulers *ibid.*, eager for " bread and the games " *ibid.*, as viewed by strangers 211 f., passion for gymnasium and hippodrome 213 ff., passion for music 217 f., extravagant enthusiasm 221 f., crazed by song 225, used music in all pursuits 239, contrasted with Spartans 241, affair with Conon 243, behaviour in stadium 245 ff.

Aloeus, mythical hero, sons of 5 123

Alpheüs, river in Elis near Pisa 1 29

Althaea, mother of Meleager, caused son's death 5 125

Amaltheia, horn of, awarded to Acheloüs by Heracles 4 452, 5 41

Amasis, king of Egypt, his corpse mistreated by Cambyses 4 43

Amazons, vanquished by Heracles 1 201, 5 39, expedition against Achaeans not narrated by Homer 1 471, aid omitted by Homer 531, came from Pontus to aid Troy 533, 535

Amber, adorned palaces of Alcinoüs and Menelaüs 5 305, 311 n. 1

Ammon, Egyptian deity, said by Olympias to be father of Alexander 1 177, his oracle 247

Amoebeus, famous singer 5 99

Amphictyons, their influence at Delphi 4 29

Amphion, founder of Thebes 1 453, children slain by Apollo and Artemis *ibid.*, son of Antiopê and Zeus 2 153, built walls of Thebes 3 233, 5 65, censured by Zethus for devotion to music 205

Amphipolis, town in Thrace won by Philip 1 63

Amyntas, father of Philip of Macedon 4 41

Amyntor, father of Phoenix 1 59

Anacharsis, Scythian traveller, criticized the Greeks 3 213 f.

Anacreon of Teos, his poetry not suitable for kings 1 67, quoted 91

Anaxagoras of Clazomenae, philosopher, not overcome by loss of son 4 37, taught Pericles 299

Anaxarchus of Abdera, philosopher, unmoved by torture and death 4 43 f., his luck 5 61

Andromachê, wife of Hector, her story known in India 4 363

Andros, Aegean island 3 155

Animals, incest among 1 441, obey will of Zeus 2 39, their fat used to cure disease 3 191, friendly toward one another 4 145 f., their curative properties 169, like species behave alike 5 131, fear of dogs prevents thieving 147, heads used as architectural embellishment 329

Antenor, Trojan sage 1 489, gained dominion over Heneti 553, emulated Aeneas 555

Anthropomorphism, an attempt to portray the unportrayable 2 63

Anthropos, defined 3 439

Antigonus, a general of Alexander, melted down the golden plane-tree 4 429 n. 3

Antigonus Gonatas, put Persaeus in charge of Acro-corinth **5** 197

Antilochus, his death not told by Homer **1** 471, 485, died for Nestor 525, slain by Memnon 535, died young **2** 391

Antinoüs, upbraided by Odysseus **1** 333, **2** 141, used by Homer to typify braggadocio **4** 395 f., smitten through the throat 397

Antioch, at variance with Apameia **3** 383, active in civic improvement **4** 119, 261, 263

Antiochus, Arcadian envoy, ridiculed golden plane-tree **4** 429 n. 3

Antiochus II, surnamed Divine **4** 9

Antiochus III, overcome by Rhodes **3** 117

Antipater, a general of Alexander, who planned his death **5** 63 and n. 8

Antipater, a late rhetorician, worth reading **2** 223 f.

Antispast, a metrical foot, used in a simile **4** 39

Antisthenes, Cynic philo-sopher, associated with Diogenes **1** 377, anticipated Zeno regarding inconsis-tencies in Homer **4** 361

Ants, dig gold **3** 413 f., be-have sensibly **4** 139, 145, 291

Anytus, wealthy Athenian politician, used by Socra-tes as a type **4** 389, 399

Apameia (Apameians), at variance with Antioch **3** 383, at variance with Prusa **4** 123 ff., invited Dio to pay a visit 123, 151, gave citi-zenship to Dio's father 155, refounded by Rome 157

Apelles, his painting of a horse **5** 37 f.

Aphroditê, **1** 259, "golden" 261, **2** 263, **5** 343, patroness of lawful love **1** 365, con-testant for prize of beauty 455, sister of Helen *ibid.*, urged by Hera to help deceive Zeus 461, promised Paris loveliest woman 483, wounded by Diomede 513, preserved Hector's body 525, not more beautiful than Cassandra **3** 293, punished Lemnian women 321, connected with gen-eration 471, slandered **4** 33, at Corinth *ibid.*, Fos-terer of Friendship 103, made sport of Athena **5** 173 n. 2

Apis, Egyptian deity, his oracle at Memphis **3** 185

Apollo, invoked by Dio **1** 7, enjoined self-knowledge 195, slew Amphion's chil-dren 453, preserved Hec-tor's body 525, pursued by Achilles 529, his response to Croesus **2** 95, called Socrates wisest of men 115, 155, identified with Helius and Dionysus **3** 17, for-bade removing nestlings 95, advised Athenians 175,

Healer and Averter-of-Evil 227, honoured Archilochus 285, helped build walls of Troy 293, honoured at Tarsus 315, 475, 4 31, hymned by Socrates 185, connected with Colophon 251, inspired poets 363, his fillets create awe 5 19, worked for hire 65 and n. 7, temple at Delphi 117, avoided by perjurers 225 and n. 3

Apollodorus, tyrant of Cassandreia 1 99

Apollonia, Black Sea settlement 3 425

Apollonius of Tyana, philosopher, announced in Ephesus Domitian's death as it was taking place at Rome 5 87

Arabia, the fragrant herbs of 3 301

Arabs, in Persian army of invasion 1 189, at Alexandria 3 211, their garb 393, enriched through trade 5 309

Aradians, islanders near Phoenicia 3 311, 313

Aratus, didactic poet, quoted 5 225 n. 2

Aratus of Sicyon, seized Acrocorinth from Persaeus 5 197 n. 2

Arbitrators, do not incur enmity for adverse decisions 1 455

Arcadia, 1 27, its horses 2 171, coveted by Sparta 201, its caps 3 403, 5 67,

a fictitious old woman from 411 f.

Arcadians, driven from home 3 297, from Pheneus 4 41, in Agamemnon's army 409

Archelaüs, founder of Aegae, ancestor of Alexander, once goat-herd 1 201, invited Socrates to visit Macedonia 2 115

Archelaüs, pupil of Anaxagoras and teacher of Socrates 4 383 and n. 1

Archidamus, Spartan general, destroyed trees of Acharnians 5 333

Archilochus, ranked with Homer 3 283, censorious 285, honoured highly by Apollo *ibid.*, quoted 291, 331, his metres not like Homer's 4 385, his fable of the fox 389, 5 223, his tale of Nessus and Deïaneira 4 451 f., his quarrel with Lycambes 5 225 f. and n. 1

Archippus, Flavius, prosecuted Dio before Pliny 5 419 f.

Architecture, simplicity commended 1 353

Areius, friend and preceptor of Augustus 5 365

Areopagus, respected even by demagogues 4 313 f.

Ares, his battle song 1 87, 511, wounded by Diomede 513, bonds of 5 321 f.

Arethas, bishop of Caesarea in Cappadocia, notes

on Dio **5** 406-417, gives garbled account of Dio's life 415, novel explanation of Dio's surname 415 f., calls Dio's style a blend of Plato and Lysias 417

Argives, cherish myths about ancestors **1** 451, fallen on evil days **3** 161, ancestors of Tarsians 275, did not aid Heracles **4** 251, 409

Argo, ship of Jason **1** 223, victorious at Isthmian Games **4** 17, dedicated to Poseidon at Isthmus *ibid.*

Argos, ruled by Heracles **1** 31, 355, exiled Diomede 555, **3** 311, belongs to Hera **4** 13, prominence in Greece 195, 249, **5** 11, 17, entrusted to Atreus by Eurystheus 197

Ariadnê, saved Theseus with ball of thread **5** 325 n. 3

Arion, early lyric poet **2** 237 n. 3, 239, encounter with pirates **4** 5 f., invented dithyramb and presented chorus at Corinth 5, acquired wealth in Magna Graecia *ibid.*, bronze image at Taenarum 7

Aristarchus, Alexandrian scholar, interpreted Homer **4** 357

Aristeas, of Proconnesus, his supernatural experience **4** 45

Aristeides, Aelius (A.D. 129–189), *To Plato in Defence of the Four* **5** 383

Aristeides, the Just, a philosopher in politics **2** 293, benefactor of Athens **4** 299, upright **5** 71, ostracized 113

Aristippus, philosopher from Cyrenê, friend of Socrates **1** 377

Aristocles, Peripatetic philosopher, deserted philosophy for sophistic and luxurious living **5** 367 f.

Aristocracy, defined **1** 125

Aristodicus, of Cymê, forbidden to remove nestlings from temple of Apollo **3** 95 and n. 2

Aristogeiton, tyrannicide, honoured by Athens **1** 559, descendants exempt from liturgies **3** 135 f., statue in Persia **4** 39

Aristomenes, Messenian hero, shaggy heart of **3** 393

Aristophanes, poet of Old Comedy, quoted (*Knights* 42 f.) **3** 177, (frag. 581) **4** 353, (*Clouds* 149-152) **5** 381 f., enjoyed licence at Athens **3** 281, 333

Aristophon, brother of Polygnotus, son and pupil of Aglaophon **4** 381

Aristotle, teacher of Alexander **1** 59, **4** 297, honoured by Philip **1** 101, interpreted Homer *ibid.*, rebuilt Stageira *ibid.*, **4** 255, complained of fellow townsmen *ibid.*, 259, founded literary criticism 357, death planned by Alexander **5** 63 and n. 8, taught Eudoxus 367

INDEX

Arithmeticians, expert in theory of numbers 5 171

Artaphernes, Persian general sent against Naxos and Eretria 1 559, lost ships on coast of Attica *ibid.*

Artaxerxes, brother of Cyrus the Younger, not loved by mother because less beautiful 5 335

Artemis, protectress of child-bed 1 365, slew Amphion's children 453, her temple at Ephesus a depository for states and private citizens 3 59 f., slandered 4 33, temple at Ephesus 117, hymned by Socrates 185, taught Scamandrius hunting 5 169 n. 3

Artists, depict gods and forces of nature in human form 1 207, inspire belief in gods 2 49 f., occasionally contribute ideas not found in myths 51, handicaps 73 f., limitations of material 83

Asclepiades, magistrate at Prusa 5 419

Asclepius, his sons healers 1 263

Ascra, home of Hesiod 5 413 f.

Asia, ruled by Persia as far as the Indies 1 121, 191, 193, subject to others (i.e. Rome) 561, invaded by Macedonians 3 299, 4 211, its cities progressive 257, overrun by Agesilaüs 407, 5 7, the hordes of 297, theatres sponsored competitions in declamation 369

Asius, son of Hyrtacus, used by Homer to typify disobedience and boastfulness 4 393 f.

Aspasia, of Miletus, wife of Pericles, her funeral oration 5 373 and n. 2

Asses, relations with horses 2 277, " ass's shadow " 3 383, their braying 393, mated with mares 403

Assurbanipal, Assyrian ruler 5 29 n. 1, sometimes confused with Sardanapallus 31 n. 1

Assyrians, ruined by luxury 3 299, confused with Syrians 311 n. 2

Asteropaeus, son of Paeon, wounded Achilles 1 519

Astronomers, their knowledge 5 153, function and equipment 155 f., 159

Astyages, maternal grandfather of Cyrus 2 165, censured Fortune 5 45 and n. 3, bound with golden fetters 327 and n. 3

Astyanax, son of Hector, hurled to death from walls of Troy 1 563

Atalanta, avenged by Meleager 5 125 n. 1

Athena, martial strain of 1 3, destroyed her own city (Troy) 453, in guise of Deïphobus tricked Hector 529, Trojan sanctuary 563, fairest and wisest 2 9, statue by Pheidias *ibid.*, contestant for prize of beauty 265, affronted by

INDEX

Ajax the Locrian **3** 251, honoured at Tarsus 315, patron of Athens **4** 13, slandered 33, 103, in Homer and Euripides disguised Odysseus but not in Aeschylus' *Philoctetes* 343, 349, shrine at Sparta refuge of Pausanias 407, Promachus 418 n. 1, disguised Odysseus 443, her reproach **5** 173 and n. 2, avoided by perjurers 225 and n. 3, 325, made Odysseus beautiful 341

Athenians, embellished Athens **1** 73, martial exploits *ibid.*, sword of Mardonius and shields from Pylos dedicated *ibid.*, resettled by Peisistratus 345 f., interested in drama 355, honoured tyrannicides 559, hall of initiation **2** 37, conflicts with Persia 113, victory off Cnidos *ibid.*, intercourse with maid-servants 149, slaves in Sicily and Peloponnese 157, defeat at Acanthus *ibid.*, freed slaves 163, consulted Apollo about Sicilian expedition 203, interregnum 275, chose Critias lawgiver *ibid.*, influenced by Peisistratus 327, under leadership of Themistocles 329, court Romans **3** 109, not wealthy 111, gladiatorial shows in theatre 125 f., scrupulous as to statues 129, lost primacy 135, convicted Leptines *ibid.*, fallen on evil days 161, misunderstood oracle 175, comic licence 177, cultivated physical prowess 261, admired for devotion to oratory, poetry and love of drama *ibid.*, tolerated comic abuse 281, punished Socrates 281 f., desecrated statues of Demetrius and Philip **4** 39, deified Philip 39 f., gave Socrates a hearing 187, ancient glory due to morality and love of learning 201, civil war 287, benefited by Solon, Aristeides, and Pericles 299, most democratic 313 f., executed Socrates 333, captured **5** 49 and n. 5, autochthonous, migrated to Euboea and later Naples 55, no longer masters 59, ancestors of Neapolitans 59, 71, ostracized Aristeides 113, met death in Labyrinth 167 and n. 3, ingratitude toward leaders 199 f., made request regarding Samos 213, cursed violators of Solon's laws 321

Athenodorus, pancratiast **2** 367

Athenodorus, Stoic philosopher, honoured by Augustus **3** 319

Athens, embellished **1** 73, visited by Diogenes 251, 377, its topography *ibid.*, extent 253, destroyed by Xerxes 559, colonized Ionia

435

2 103, walls destroyed 113, refused citizenship to slaves 159, 253, attacked by Darius 331, colonized Cythnos and Seriphos 421, removes name of condemned from citizen roll 3 89, decline 121, sanctuary of Horse and Maiden 249 and n. 1, rival of Sparta 383, belongs to Athena 4 13, freed by Corinth 17, attempt to tyrannize over Hellas foiled by Corinth 17 f., fought Sparta for primacy 73, 83, prominence in Greece 195, exalted by Theseus 221, Painted Porch 263, dramatic contests 341, Hephaesteüm 418 n. 1, overwhelmed by Dioscuri 5 13, wronged by orators 37 and n. 1, fallen on evil days 59, bad climate *ibid.*, popular assembly 157, attacked by Eurystheus 197, sheltered Heracleidae *ibid.*

Athletes, Isthmian victor idolized 1 411, training 2 217, endure even death 3 25, scourged for quitting contest 123, proper conduct 133, degenerate kind 191, in simile 4 35

Athletics, for leisured class 1 159, compared with warfare 2 381, 387, corruption 3 123, effect upon country people 165, size a handicap 349

Athos, promontory in Thrace, severed by Xerxes 1 119

Atreidae, humoured by Homer 1 473, connected with Trojans 539, dominated by wives 5 11, descended from Pelops *ibid.*

Atreus, wife defiled by Thyestes 1 451, 2 149, served up Thyestes' children at banquet 1 451, 5 221, hero in tragedy 2 107, given charge of Argos by Eurystheus 5 197

Attendant Spirit, explained by Diogenes 1 203 f.

Attic Dialect, employed by Homer 2 69

Attica, topography and climate 1 251, etymology of name *ibid.*, threatened 2 247, planted with olive trees by Peisistratus 327, produces purest honey 3 267, united by Theseus 4 221, thrifty 5 57 and n. 2

Auctioneers, decried 1 357

Augê, mother of Telephus 2 153

Augeas, king in Elis, stables cleansed by Heracles 1 397, 4 249

Augustus, honoured Athenodorus 3 319, "the second Caesar," favoured Tarsus 343, 361, fond of Areius 5 365

Aulis, Iphigeneia sacrificed at 1 339

Autolycus, grandfather of Odysseus, learned perjury from Hermes 1 457

Babês, servant of Hippaemon 4 37

Babylon, 1 193, 215, winter residence of Persian king 251, twice the size of Athens 253, walls of 271, founded by Ninus and Semiramis 2 13 and n. 3, 253, taken by Alexander 331, costly buildings 3 295, ruled by Sardanapallus 5 29, scene of Alexander's death 65, overcome by Zopyrus 67

Babylonian, fabrics 5 305, trade 309

Bacchants, maddened by song 3 229, carry lions *ibid.*, miraculously supplied with wine, milk, and honey 229 f., leap about Dionysus 399

Bacchic, fawn-skin and thyrsus 3 229, revels 231, rites 453

Bacis, prophet 2 121, 3 391

Bactra, Persian city, walls 1 193, winter resort of Persian king 251, 2 13

Bactrians, visit Alexandria 3 211, horsemen 213, wear turban and trousers 5 179, seen in Rome *ibid.*

Balls, coloured 1 385, beguile lads 5 223

Banishment, Discourse on Dio's 2 89-121

Banquet, allegory of 2 423 ff., behaviour at 3 223 f., 4 277, carping guests 5 113

Barbarians, conduct in *Iliad* 1 83, portray gods as animals 2 63, worship mountains, trees, and stones 65, their words in Homer 69, differ from Greeks in beauty, dress, and language 287, wear long hair 3 401

Barsinê, mother of Heracles son of Alexander 5 67 n. 9

Baths, cure indigestion 1 257, 5 157

Batieia, mound near Ilium, called Sema Myrines by the gods 1 435, 463

Beacons, invented by Palamedes 2 109

Bears, constellation, not visible in India 4 363

Beasts, quiet when asleep or well fed 5 219

Beauty, Discourse on 2 271-289, masculine declining, feminine increasing 273, types 287, Hector's beauty 289, masculine beauty admired by women 5 335

Bees, illustrate essentials of good government 1 127, king has no sting 197, sensible 4 145, devoted to hive 197, carry pebbles for ballast *ibid.*, treatment by farmers *ibid.*

Beetles, do not taste Attic honey 3 267

Beggars, not trustworthy 1 457, shamed by episode of Irus 5 109

Bellerophon, courageous 3 199, continent 5 335

Bion, Cynic philosopher, regarding popularity 5 113

Bird-lime, procured from oak 2 11

Birds, attracted by owls 2 5, 13, 3 403, concord 4 145, fable of Birds and Owl 2 11 f., 5 189 f., caught by mistletoe 189, kept in cages 191

Bithynia, in Asia Minor, tithes 4 73, 87

Black Sea, visited by Rhodian warships 3 107

Boars, come close when exhausted 2 385

Boatrace, at Isthmian Games 4 71

Boatswains, not competent to command or pilot trireme 2 109

Body, contrasted with soul 1 137, 4 43, at war with soul 2 411, afflictions 411 f., composition 413, compared to tomb 5 35

Boeotia, haunt of Muses 1 31, 419, 539, unified by Epaminondas 4 221, 5 67

Boeotians, stupid 1 441 f., 5 55, allies of Theseus 1 501 f., 2 55, appearance 287, in Agamemnon's army 4 409

Books, reading essential to education 1 181, old books preferred because better written and on better paper 2 283, new books disguised as old *ibid.*, purchase 4 171

Booksellers, counterfeit old books 2 283

Boreas, sons sailed on the Argo 1 223

Borysthenes, town in Thrace, inhabitants visit Isthmian Games to hear Diogenes 1 405, visited by Dio 3 421, named for river but situated on Hypanis *ibid.*, history and present state 423 ff., welcomed Dio 427, inhabitants wear black 427 f., colony of Miletus 429 and n. 2, interested in Homer 429, reveres Achilles *ibid.*, speaks poor Greek 431, knows *Iliad* by heart *ibid.*, attacked by Scythians 435, assembly by temple of Zeus 437, people wear long hair and beards *ibid.*, ancient Greek city *ibid.*, some inhabitants love Plato 445

Borysthenes, the river Dnieper, large and beautiful 3 421, topography 421 f., salt-works 423

Borysthenitic Discourse 3 417-475

Boxing, tactics 1 387, 2 365, laborious 383

Boys, play "Kings" 1 189 f., share citizenship 3 441 f., sing cheap ditties 4 169, would like to mock teachers 5 185, deceived with knucklebones and balls 223, bribed to have hair cut 295, delight in athletic contests and theatre 315

Brachmanes, devoted to contemplation 3 411, endurance *ibid.*, advise Indian monarchs 4 301, self-con trol, righteousness, and knowledge of future *ibid.*

Briseïs, loved by Achilles **1** 69, treatment by Agamemnon **4** 411 f., **5** 1, fond of Achilles 9, departed in sorrow 17

Brothel, **3** 307

Brothel-keepers, disgraceful **1** 363 f., tolerated 367, scorned **2** 131, called vile names **5** 265, attend great national gatherings *ibid.*, 273

Builders, **5** 141, not indispensable 143

Bulls, contrasted with other animals **1** 95 ff., symbolic of kingship *ibid.*

Burial, denied traitors **3** 89 f., under auspices of the state 99 and n. 1

Busiris, mythical king of Egypt, encounter with Heracles **1** 395, **3** 317

Butchers, expert craftsmen **5** 171, 263, 273

Byzantium, courts Romans **3** 109, near Pontus 297, finds fish cast ashore *ibid.*, 415

Cadmea, citadel of Thebes, survived destruction **1** 355

Caeneus, Lapith king, summoned Nestor **5** 409

Caesar, " the second " (Augustus) favoured Tarsus **3** 343, 361, property claimed for **4** 235

Caesarea, unidentified city, smaller than Prusa but very Greek **4** 257

Calaïs, athletic son of Boreas **1** 391, won footrace at Isthmian Games **4** 15

Callias, wealthy Athenian, son a slave in Thrace **2** 157, estate claimed by impostor 159, wed Elpinicê and paid debt of Miltiades **5** 201

Calliopê, muse of oratory and epic poetry **1** 65, mother of Orpheus **3** 235, **5** 279, had Zeus change animals into human form **3** 235

Callisthenes, sophist, slain by pupil Alexander **5** 63 and n. 8

Callistratus, inhabitant of Borysthenes, fond of Homer **3** 427 f.

Calydonian Boarhunt, **5** 13 n. 4

Calymnians, islanders near Cos **3** 55 and n. 2

Calypso, her grotto **1** 77, told Odysseus about debates of gods 461, visited by Hermes **3** 193.

Cambyses, son of Cyrus the Great, unwise ruler **2** 331, abused corpse of Amasis **4** 43, entrusted palace to Magi **5** 195

Candaules, king of Lydia, ruined by infatuation for wife **5** 69 and n. 6

Capaneus, father of Sthenelus **5** 59 n. 7

Caphereus, cape of Euboea **1** 305, 307, 317

Cappadocians, market in Celaenae **3** 405

INDEX

Caps, felt 3 403, Arcadian or Laconian *ibid.*

Captain, defined 4 405

Caria, home of Melancomas the Elder 2 367, property of Rhodes 3 51, supplied revenue for Rhodes 105, protected by Celaenae 405

Carian, rebuked by Homer for extravagance in dress 1 83, dogs 2 171

Carion, drunken character in comedy 3 263

Carneades, philosopher who for his charming style was commonly considered sophist 5 367, contrasted with Dio 369

Carpathos, island near Rhodes 3 53

Carthaginians, guided by Hanno and Hannibal 2 331 f., controlled Italy seventeen years *ibid.*, driven from Carthage *ibid.*, war with Syracuse 4 21

Carystus, town in Euboea, exported variegated marbles 5 307

Cassandra, divinely inspired 1 489, 5 19 and n. 2, priestess of Apollo, outraged in Athena's sanctuary 1 563, wedded by Agamemnon 563 f., not inferior to Aphroditê in beauty 3 293, slain by Clytemnestra 5 15 n. 1, 17, loved by Agamemnon 19

Castalia, fountain at Delphi, clear waters 3 295

Castor, not at Troy 1 501, brother of Helen 2 263, won footrace at Isthmian Games 4 15, family connexions 5 13, overwhelmed Athens *ibid.*

Catalogue of Fair Women, poem of Hesiod 1 59

Catamites, 3 323, 325, term of reproach 5 109

Catboat, proverb 5 179

Cattle, illustrate essentials of good government 1 127, tender hooves 3 289, 4 145, resent neglect 295, decoyed by sprig of green 5 89

Caunians, in Asia Minor, foolish 3 55 and n. 3, scorned 131, afflicted with fever 261

Cautery, used by physicians 2 129, 4 315, 423

Ceadas, chasm into which Spartans cast criminals 5 323 and n. 4

Cecrops, mythical king of Athens, shames men of low birth 5 109

Celaenae, city in Phrygia, Discourse delivered in 3 389-415, advantages 403 ff., rivers 405, market centre *ibid.*, taxes *ibid.*, court business 405 f., bulwark of Phrygia, Lydia, and Caria 405

Celts, 4 27, Druids advised kings 301, have much amber 5 309 and n. 1

Cenchreae, port of Corinth 4 11

Centaurs, progeny of Ixion

1 229, invented by poets and artists 3 199, banquet 225, drunken and amorous 263, fight with Lapiths 2 351 and n. 1, 4 418 n. 1

Centipedes, slowest of creeping things 1 425

Cephallenians, courted Penelopê 1 549

Cercopes, term applied to Tarsians 3 309

Chaeronea, battle of 1 51, 2 163

Chalcis, town in Euboea, founded Cumae 5 55 n. 4

Chalcopogon, Greek equivalent of Ahenobarbus, label attached to statue of Alcibiades 4 39 and n. 4

Chalkis, divine name for bird kymindis 1 435, 463

Charicles, 2 341

Charidemus, Discourse entitled 2 395-435, imitated Dio 403

Chariots, essential knowledge of driver 1 179, statue by Lysippus 3 91 and n. 1, success in race or war demands concord 4 101 f., simile 5 31

Charixenus, 2 341

Chastity, imperilled through tolerance of brothels 1 367 ff.

Cheiron, healer 1 263, tutor of Achilles 4 431, argues with Achilles 433 ff., called sophist by Achilles 435

Chersonese, Tauric, gets salt from Borysthenes 3 423

Chersonese, Thracian, burial

place of Protesilaüs 1 503, tilled by Achaeans 507, Achaeans withdraw to 531

Chestnuts, fed to swine 1 327

Children, identified by necklaces 1 179, deterred by hobgoblins 243, afraid of dogs 407, spoiled by servants 427, supposititious 447, 2 149 f., 3 157, play with fire 2 179, drive men mad 397, learning to talk 399, ashamed to make up quarrels 4 69, undiscriminating 83, reported to teachers for bad behaviour at home 241, prayed for 285, beguiled by tales of Lamia 389, fears 5 107, amused and guided by nurses' tales 187

Chimaera, invented by poets and artists 3 199

Chios, wine 1 259, 287, reputed birthplace of Homer 355 and n. 1, not much talked about 4 251

Choregus, functionary of dramatic festivals 4 341 and n. 3

Choruses, introduced by herald 1 223, contesting 353, sacred *ibid.*, obey leader 2 127, unison essential 3 173, 4 101, 281, reproved audience 3 179, 441, in tragic contests 4 341, leaders of 405

Chrysa, town near Troy, altar of Apollo 4 447 and n. 2, 5 7 and n. 1

Chryseïs, 1 475, 4 447 n. 2,

Discourse entitled 5 1 ff., story not used by dramatists 1, prized by Agamemnon 3, 5, singular conduct 7, had no grievance against Agamemnon 9, motives for urging intervention of Chryses 11, displeased by Agamemnon 15, prudent 17, restored to father by Odysseus *ibid.*, 21

Chryses, 1 475, conduct regarding daughter 5 5 f., subject to Achaeans *ibid.*, visited camp in tenth year of war 7, bidden by Chryseïs to entreat Achacans 11

Chrysippus, philosopher, inconsistent with professions 4 249

Chrysippus, son of Pelops, loved by Laïus 1 437

Cicadae, sing when thirsty 4 261, 5 109

Cilicia, visited by Rhodian warships 3 107, 165, people visit Alexandria 211, Tarsus capital 289, Tarsus metropolis 343, cities progressive 4 257

Cimon, son of Miltiades, cancelled father's debt by marrying Elpinicê to Callias 5 201 and n. 4, victorious at Cyprus 201

Cinyras, mythical king of Cyprus, famed for wealth and beauty 1 393

Circê, fed victims cornel berries 1 283, drugged companions of Odysseus 389, 391, magic 473, turned men into swine and wolves 3 327, her cowardly lions 5 293

Cithara, 4 75, 5 153, Nero sang to 171

City, defined 3 439, 449, cannot be administered without law 5 241, some cities unwalled *ibid.*

Cleanthes, philosopher, contradicts Euripides and Sophocles about wealth 1 343 and n. 2, inconsistent with professions 4 249

Clearchus, Spartan general, treacherously slain by Tissaphernes 5 223

Cleinias, father of Alcibiades 2 329, 4 39

Cleisthenes, Athenian statesman 2 293

Cleisthenes, tyrant of Sicyon, called oppressor by Apollo 1 123 and n. 1, daughter of 481

Cleitus, Macedonian officer, slain by Alexander 5 63 and n. 8

Cleombrotus, Spartan, father of Pausanias 4 407

Cleomenes, Spartan king, expelled from Athens by Corinthians 4 17

Cleon, guiding spirit of Athens 2 329, demagogue 4 313

Clerks, decried 1 347

Cloaks, occasion ridicule if worn alone 5 177 f., regularly worn alone by philosophers 179

INDEX

Clytemnestra, daughter of Tyndareüs and Leda 1 479, 5 11, seduced by Aegisthus 2 149, compared with Chryseïs by Agamemnon 5 3, cruel and bold 11, sister of Dioscuri 13, disparaged by Agamemnon *ibid.*, slew Agamemnon and Cassandra 15 n. 1, helped Aegisthus slay Agamemnon 95, slain by Orestes *ibid.*, typifies marital infidelity 223, denounced by Agamemnon in Hades 227 f.

Cnidus, scene of Athenian victory 2 113

Cnossians, dungeon and Labyrinth 5 323

Coats, of goat-skin 3 403

Cobblers, used by Socrates as illustrations 1 115

Cocks, presented by paederasts 5 99, 153

Coins, falsely struck 3 29, counterfeit 37, tests of genuineness 5 113, discarded when worn out 115

Colchis, sown with dragon's teeth by Jason 2 305

Colonel, defined 4 405

Colonies, relation to parent city 2 421

Colophon, reputed birthplace of Homer, not much talked about 4 251, can boast of Apollo *ibid.*

Colts, badly broken in 4 359

Comedy, treats of supposititious children 2 151, now confined to " ancient " productions 241, licence 3 177, anonymous author quoted 195, characters 263, made truths palatable by laughter 283, revival of old comedies 4 427 and n. 2

Concord, Discourses on 4 48-93, 94-105, 106-147, 149-163, lauded 55 ff., between Nicomedia and Nicaea 57, praised by poets, philosophers, and historians 59, unites the elements 61 essential in the home 63 f., practical advantages 79 f., 87 f., more precious than wealth 101 f., gods and universe 141 ff., praised 161 f., essential to men and gods 289

Condottieri, 5 101, boastful when drunk 285 f.

Conflagration, simile of 3 213

Conon, an official at Alexandria 3 243

Conon, Athenian general, victorious off Cnidus 2 113

Conon, late grammarian (?), worth reading 2 223 f.

Constellations, 3 461 and n. 3

Convulsions, afflict the body 2 411

Corinth, visited by Alexander 1 173, visited by Diogenes 251, breezy 253, home of Diogenes 379, harbours and hetaerae draw crowds *ibid.*, " crossroads of Greece " *ibid.*, 2 253, visited by Rhodian warships 3 107, fountain made

443

by Pegasus 463, dithyrambic chorus of Arion 4 5 f., visited by Solon 7, "the promenade of Hellas" 9, visited by Herodotus 9 f., library contained statue of Favorinus 11, Poseidon vies with Helius for possession 13 f., refuge of Dionysius 21, hellenized 25 f., favoured by Aphrodité 33, " both prow and stern of Hellas " 35, envy of all *ibid.*, famous for art work 5 307 and n. 1

Corinthians, preside at Isthmian Games 1 385, disregarded Diogenes 405, forbade Diogenes to wear crown of pine 409, gladiatorial shows 3 125 f., fallen on evil days 161, cultivated physical prowess 261, once pre-eminent for justice 4 17, freed Athens *ibid.*, freed Hellas from Athens and Sparta 17 f., with Thebes and Elis opposed Sparta 19, valour at Thermopylae and Salamis *ibid.*, dead at Salamis commemorated by Simonides *ibid.*, freed Sicily from Carthage and Syracuse from tyrants 21, colonized Syracuse *ibid.*

Cormorants, 3 297

Corselet-makers, 5 273

Corybantes, possess the Alexandrians 3 229

Coryza, 1 381

Cosmetics, decried 1 353

Council of Six Hundred, at Athens 4 313 f.

Courtesans, 5 151, 159

Courts, attract motley throng 3 405 f.

Covetousness, Discourse on 2 187-207

Cow and Plough, proverb 5 179

Crab, assisted Hydra against Heracles 5 337

Craneion, gymnasium at Corinth 1 173, admired 253, home of Diogenes 379, 405

Cranes, simile in Homer 1 83, mode of flight 193, migrate in search of food 267

Crates, of Mallos, interpreted Homer 4 357

Cratinus, comic poet, enjoyed licence 3 281, quoted 4 403

Crete, supplied Lycurgus with Homeric poems 1 79, 539, Labyrinth 5 167, Theseus' escape from 325

Criers, proclaim rewards for thieves and runaways 1 357

Critias, Athenian politician, one of the Thirty 2 275, views on beauty *ibid.*, chosen lawgiver *ibid.*

Critics, 5 159

Croesus, misunderstood oracle 1 437, visited by Solon 439, 5 49, 69, 109, warned by Apollo 2 95, generous toward oracle 97, made sport of greedy men 207, 4 259, blamed Fortune for loss of son 5 45 and n. 2, derived great wealth from Pactolus 289, generous toward Alcmaeon 289 f.

Cronus, father of Hera 1 455, mutilated Uranus 559, mutilated by Zeus *ibid.*, eldest king of the gods 2 139, in bondage *ibid.*

Croton, Greek colony in Italy, desolate 3 297, idleness 5 57, Democedes 271

Crowns, lure seekers after reputation 5 89 and n. 2, made of olive, oak, ivy, myrtle 91 and n. 1, 115, of athletic victors 93 and n. 2, Olympic or Pythian 285

Ctesias, historian, regarding Sardanapallus 5 29 n. 1

Ctesias, son of Ormenus, father of Eumaeus 2 157

Cumae, settled Naples 5 43, founded by Chalcis 55 n. 4

Custom, Discourse on 5 251-257, defined 253, subject to constant scrutiny *ibid.*, gains voluntary obedience *ibid.*, creates polity of free men 255, valid even in war 257

Cyaxares, king of Medes, helped sack Nineveh 5 311 n. 2

Cyclones, visit the universe 2 409

Cyclopes, island of 3 311, in Homer 4 389, life of 5 51 and n. 6

Cyclops, the, story of 1 473, drunken and amorous 3 263

Cydippê, Argive priestess, mother of Cleobis and Biton 5 51 and n. 2

Cydnus, river in Tarsus 3 275 f.

Cymê, home of Aristodicus 3 95 and n. 2

Cynics, bad influence in Alexandria 3 181, punning reference 233, viewed with scorn 337 f.

Cynosarges, gymnasium at Athens, frequented by non-Athenians 2 147

Cyprus, visited by Rhodian warships 3 107, tale of 5 47, won for Athens by Cimon 201

Cypselus, tyrant of Corinth, dedicated chest at Olympia 1 479, father of Periander 4 5, statue of beaten gold at Olympia 193 and n. 1

Cyrus the Elder, founded Persian empire and fostered by Zeus 1 101, captured Babylon *via* the river 193, vassal of Astyages 2 163, freed Persians *ibid.*, 320, still talked about 283, guiding spirit of Persians 329, ruled Persians 4 405, slain by Tomyris 5 45 and n. 5, 49, conquered Medes 67, rescued by Spako *ibid.* n. 7, bound Astyages with golden fetters 327 and n. 3

Cyrus the Younger, campaign of 1 377, preferred by Parysatis because of beauty 5 335 and n. 3

Cythera, founded by Sparta 2 421

Cythnos, Aegean island, colonized by Athens 2 421

Cyzicus, on the Propontis, visited by Dio 2 237 f.

Daedalus, mythical artist 2 51, deceived bull 277, imparted motion to statues 4 13, 17, 43, 5 161, criticized 167 f., clever artificer 323

Danaë, daughter of Acrisius, shower of gold 5 289

Dancing, indecency decried by Alexander 1 87, 89, of Kouretes *ibid.*, not approved for the poor 353, in Hippodrome 2 255, of the heavenly host 3 441

Dardanus, ruled the Phrygians 4 407

Darius I, palace 1 75, motley army 189, called shopkeeper 215, 559, treatment of Egyptian physicians 2 129, guiding spirit of Persia 331, wars *ibid.*, 4 259, cured by Democedes 5 271

Darius Codomannus, last king of Persia 1 175 and n. 1, 191 f., failed to overcome Alexander 5 65, mother made obeisance to Alexander and Hephaestion 67 and n. 10, made Mithranes ruler of Sardis 197

Darius Nothus, king of Persia (424-405 B.C.) 1 105

Datis, dispatched against Naxos and Eretria 1 559,
lost ships on Attic coast *ibid.*

Davus, slave rôle in comedy 3 263

Dead Sea, in interior of Palestine 5 379

Death, a release from prison house of life 2 409

Debts, cancellation sometimes justified 3 75, cancellation forbidden 77

Decarchy, 3 451

Deer, migrate 1 267

Deïaneira, Discourse on 4 451-461, narrated by Archilochus and Sophocles 4 451, sister of Meleager 453 n. 1, shirt of 459 and n. 2

Deinomenes, father of Gelon 4 23

Deïoces, founder of Median empire, fostered by Zeus 1 101, ruled Medes 4 405, toiled to found empire 5 65

Deïphobus, brother of Hector, married Helen 1 497, 501, 541, 555, counterfeited by Athena 529

Deliberation, Discourse on 2 337-345

Delphi, oracle at 1 419, inscription at 435, visited by Laïus 437, enriched by Croesus 2 97, despoiled by Nero 3 151, statue of Gorgias 4 27, statue of Phrynê 29, impoverished 35, Apollo's temple 5 117, maxims on temple 187 and n. 1

Delphic injunction, 5 121

Demeter, slandered 4 33,

Damater 179, farmers' name for Fortune 5 51, 227

Demetrius of Phalerum, 1500 statues destroyed by Athenians in single day 4 39

Demetrius Poliorcetes, taken captive and died from drunkenness 5 65

Demigods, honoured for virtues 5 139

Demiurgos, official at Tarsus 3 367

Democedes of Croton, famous physician, healed Darius 5 271

Democracy, impracticable form of government 1 125 f., rule of majority 3 11, analysed 197 f., licence to criticize 4 153, strength depends on wisdom and fair dealing 229

Democritus, philosopher, called Homer " divinely inspired " 4 357

Demodocus, Homeric bard, sings of Wooden Horse 1 473

Demonassa, story of 5 47 f., statue and epitaph *ibid.*

Demosthenes, orator, opposed Philip 1 63, excels in vigour, impressiveness of thought, and copiousness of diction 2 223, imprisoned 5 37 and n. 1, quoted 67 n. 3

Dentist, 1 381

Deucalion, the Greek Noah, saved the race from destruction 3 465

Deus ex machina, Socrates 2 101

Dicing, 1 385, 2 427, 5 159

Dictation, 2 405

Didymeium, Apollo's temple near Miletus 4 115

Dio of Prusa, wanderer and self-taught 1 7, visited Peloponnese as exile 27 f., intimate acquaintance with Trajan 105, boldness toward Domitian 111, 4 207, 319, independent and generous *ibid.*, repeated discourses on several occasions 1 449 f., 4 417, 5 23, ill-health 2 15, 4 103, 281, 339, 5 337, wore long hair 2 19, 391, visited Getae 2 21 f., exiled for friendship with Sabinus 91 and n. 1, consulted Delphic oracle 97, became philosopher during exile 99, visited Rome 115, visited Cyzicus 235, fond of music 239, not fond of tragedy 283, contemporaries prefer men of old *ibid.*, taciturn 403, describes himself 3 285, dressed like Cynics 337, visited Borysthenes 421, received citizenship from Nicomedia 4 51, unsociable *ibid.*, on return from exile wished to attend to private affairs 109 ff., distrusted by Prusa *ibid.*, fortunes impaired by exile 109 f., inured to poverty and hardship 111, son courageous *ibid.*, received letter from Emperor 113 and n. 2, connexion with public works at Prusa 113 f., 119 f., 221 f., 257 ff., relations with Apameia 123 f., 153 f., 157, friendly reception during exile 151, family honoured with citizenship in Rome and Apameia 155, popularity and fate of speeches 169 f., dealings with Prusa 175, 181, 185 f., 209 f., 215 f., 219, 233 f., 315 ff., about to leave Prusa 183, 207, 319, family honoured by Prusa 193, grandfather planned to get independence for Prusa from Emperor 195, declined many invitations to live abroad *ibid.*, honoured by Emperor 197, son and nephew ambitious and patriotic 197 f., declined invitation to visit Emperor 203, conduct in exile 207, illness prevented visiting Nerva 209, Trajan friendly *ibid.*, reputation of father and grandfather 231, financial status *ibid.*, 267, improved real estate 235, attacked by mob 241, called nightingale 261, influence at Rome 267, personal habits 271, son elected archon 291 n. 3, declines election 307 f., did not rely on political clubs 315, son 317, father and grandfather 319, did not interfere with son's administration 321 f., morning routine 339, admirer of Socrates 381, paraphrases *Iliad* (1. 269 f.) 420 n. 1, addressed Emperor 429, his *Achilles* resembles dramatic dialogues of Lucian 431, his *Philoctetes* paraphrases Euripides' prologue 438 f., *Encomium on Hair* 5 331-343, Fragments 345-351, Letters 353-359, Testimonia 361-423, carried into exile Plato's *Phaedo* and Demosthenes' *Against the Embassy* 363, coupled by Lucian with Musonius and Epictetus *ibid.*, earliest known reference to "golden tongue" 365, compared with Xenophon, Nicostratus, and Philostratus for simple, artless prose *ibid.*, "tongue of gold" 367, compared with Aristocles *ibid.*, abandoned sophistics for philosophy 369, contrasted with Carneades and Eudoxus *ibid.*, composed both sophistic and philosophic treatises *ibid.*, perplexed Philostratus 371, attacked philosophy in his *Against the Philosophers* and *Reply to Musonius* 373, speeches should be labelled either pre-exilic or post-exilic 375, sometimes attacked Socrates and Zeno with coarse jests *ibid.*, *Encomium on the Parrot* and *Eu-*

boean Discourse not of the same school, as imagined by Philostratus *ibid.*, *Euboean Discourse* praised 377, praised Essenes 379, *Tempê*, *Memnon*, and *Against the Philosophers* contrasted with *Ecclesiasticus* and *Bouleuticus* 379 f., *Against the Philosophers* praised 383, superior to sophists in dialectic 385, *Rhodian* and *Trojan* discourses and *Eulogy of the Gnat ibid.*, life and personality 387 ff., speeches *On Kingship* display great wisdom 409 f., interview with old woman an invention 411 f., compared with Nestor 413, career garbled by Arethas 415, novel explanation of sobriquet 415 f., style a blend of Plato and Lysias 417, briefly mentioned by Suidas, who lists four works otherwise unknown *ibid.*, called Cocceianus by Pliny and Trajan 419, 423, on trial before Pliny 419 f., buried wife and son in Prusa 421

Diodorus, Discourse in Reply to 4 324-335

Diogenes, Cynic philosopher, an exile from Sinopê 1 169, 377, conversed with Alexander 169 ff., admired by Alexander 171, fame *ibid.*, independence *ibid.*, homeless wanderer 173, Discourse on 249-283, divided time between Corinth and Athens 251, 283, 419, personal habits 255 ff., diet 283, went to Corinth after death of Antisthenes 283, camped out in Craneion *ibid.*, attended Isthmian Games *ibid.*, 403, disregarded by Corinthians 405, attracted visitors from afar *ibid.*, compared to Odysseus 407, insolent toward Fortune 5 61, exile, arrival in Athens, introduction to Antisthenes, and slavery in Crete *ibid.*, wisdom 185, "sayings" not all authentic but still remembered 187 ff., quoted 347, 411

Diomede, eloquence 1 63, as portrayed by Homer 79, 485, conquered Aeneas 511, wounded Ares and Aphroditê 513, aided Nestor and then fled *ibid.*, 531, exiled 549, aided by Aeneas 555, accompanied Odysseus to Lemnos 4 349

Diomede the Thracian, slain by Heracles 1 395, 3 317, admonished by Heracles 5 39

Dionysia, annual festival 2 107

Dionysius I, statue spared by Syracuse 4 23, relations with Leptines 5 195 n. 1

Dionysius II, fled to Corinth 4 21, 5 61, relations with Philistus 195 and n. 2

INDEX

Dionysus, child of lightning and thunder, fills votaries with fire 2 349 f., " harmost " from the gods 423, identified with Apollo and Helius 3 17, statue in orchestra at Athens 127, Bacchants 399, attributes given statues of Dionysius I and II 4 23, progenitor of Nicaeans 103, abused by Alexander 5 63

Dionysus, sobriquet of Mithridates Eupator 4 9

Dioscuri, sons of Tyndareüs and Leda 1 479, invaded Athens, recovered Helen, captured Theseus' mother *ibid.*, depicted on chest of Cypselus 479 f., 491, did not go to Troy 501, pilots' name for Fortune 5 51, scorned by Alexander 63, 139

Disfranchisement, evils of 5 103

Distrust, Discourse on 5 207-237, aimed at what has caused misfortune 229

Dithyrambic Poetry, valuable for men of leisure 2 221

Dium, town in Pieria 1 51, taken from Macedonians by Alexander 2 333

Divination, by clods or stones 2 91, hindered by disappearance of bird 3 475

Dogs, love hunters they serve 1 13, prey upon fold when neglected 17, impetuous when young 51, behaviour when untrained 183 f., thievish 213, Laconian breed 383, 387, at festivals 403, scare children 407, various breeds 2 171, well trained *vs.* untrained 257 f., develop in proportion to legs when young 4 261, frighten predatory beasts 5 147, warded off by carrying cane 229

Dolls, easily broken 3 157

Dolon, used by Homer to typify cowardice and love of notoriety 4 391

Dolphins, rescued Arion 3 231 f., 4 7

Domitian, 1 293 n. 1, Dio's behaviour toward 4 207 and n. 2, deified *ibid.*, death 209, not flattered by Dio 319, assassination foretold 5 87, now in jeopardy 95 and n. 4

Dorian Mode, once dominant in music 3 313

Dorians, entered Peloponnese with Heracleidae 1 549, in Sicily and Italy 4 25, ruled by Dorus 407, wars with Ionians 5 317

Doric Dialect, 1 435, in Homer 2 69, used by a Lucanian 4 23 f.

Dorieus, Rhodian athlete 3 133 and n. 2

Dorus, ruled Dorians 4 407

Draco, Athenian lawgiver 5 317

Dracontides, Athenian politician, attacked Pericles 5 199 n. 1

INDEX

Dracontius, unidentified acquaintance of Dio 5 357

Dragons, hiss 1 241

Drama, messenger in 2 69

Draughts, game 2 427

Dromon, Athenian shopkeeper 1 213

Drugs, evaporate and lose power 2 101

Druids, have prophetic art and advise Celtic kings 4 301

Dryas, Lapith, superior to Agamemnon and Achilles 4 419, summoned Nestor 5 409

Ducks, decoyed by food 5 227

Dyers, sell to women 5 263, 273

Dyes, used by women 5 263 f.

Eagle, sobriquet of Pyrrhus 5 65 and n. 3

Eagles, birds of augury 3 341

Earrings, suitable for girls or sons of Lydians and Phrygians 3 175

Ears, compared with eyes 2 75, King's Ears 4 429 and n. 2

Ease, contrasted with toil 1 143, 159

Ecbatana, 1 193, summer residence of Persian king 251, seized by Alexander 2 331

Ecclesiasts, members of popular assembly at Athens, degenerate 1 347

Echo, nymph, vainly pursued by Pan 1 261

Education, subject of pun 1 181 and n. 2, analysed 181 ff., scrutinized by Socrates 2 103 f., Persian 277, cures human ills 3 187

Eëtion, father of Andromachê, slain by Achilles 1 69

Egypt, earlier kings fostered by Zeus 1 101, temples bear historical records 475, Menelaüs in 549, sunny and balmy 551, " city of shopkeepers " (Naucratis) 2 103 and n. 1, taken by Alexander 331, statue of Memnon 3 97, visited by Rhodian warships 107, 117, " framework " of Alexandria 205, experience of early musician 269 f., costly buildings 295, King Amasis 4 43, subjugated by Heracles 249, invaded by Cambyses 5 195, ancient sarcophagi of variegated stone 307, Helen 319 and n. 1

Egyptians, in Persian army 1 189, have no poetry 477, claim Achaean wall unfinished 505, treat Darius for dislocation 2 129, 3 297, 4 43, made priests advisors of king 301, farm for others 5 57, sculpture different from Greek and Roman 181

Eileithyiae, daughters of Hera, preside over birth 1 365

Elders, political organization at Tarsus 3 351 and n. 2

INDEX

Eleans, preside over Olympic Games 1 385, 2 27, spent money for statue by Pheidias 55, receive letters recommending athletes 3 115, self-esteem *ibid.*, altar to Poseidon Taraxippus 247

Electra, mourns for Orestes 2 93, disturbed by Orestes' behaviour 5 215

Elegiac Poetry, not essential for orators 2 221

Elephants, heads built into Indian house walls 5 309

Eleusinian Mysteries, 2 35 and n. 1, 3 97

Eleusis, way-station between Corinth and Athens 1 255

Eleutherae, border town of Attica, home of Oeneus' herdsman 2 151

Elis, 1 27, with Thebes and Corinth opposed Sparta 4 19, home of sophist Hippias 373, 5 161

Elpinicê, sister of Cimon, married Callias 5 201

Elpis (Hope), a phase of Fortune 5 51

Elysian Fields, received Menelaüs 1 551, Homer's name for Egypt *ibid.*

Empedocles, philosopher of Agrigentum, pupil of Pythagoras 4 381

Emperor (Roman), restraining influence 4 35, gave citizenship in Rome and Apameia to Dio's mother and grandfather 155, received embassies from Prusa 335

Enhoplic, dance connected with religion and war 1 89, performed by Meriones *ibid.*

Enthronement, rite of 2 35 f.

Envoys, enjoy safe conduct 4 67

Envy, Discourse on 5 258-301

Eos, goddess, slandered 4 33

Epaminondas, Theban general and statesman, a philosopher in politics 2 293, organized Sacred Band 295, replied to abuse 4 177 f., unified Boeotia under Thebes 221, knew Philip 299, overthrew Spartans *ibid.*, conversed with Lysis *ibid.*, benefited Thebes *ibid.*

Ephebes, young men in state schools at Prusa 4 335

Ephesians, preserved wealth of states and individuals in temple of Artemis 3 59, kept official record of deposits 59 f., less prosperous than Rhodes 61, 69 f., at variance with Smyrna 383

Ephesus, Artemis' temple 4 117, cited as example 119, home of Heracleitus 381

Ephialtes, Boeotian famed for height and beauty 2 391

Ephors, Spartan officials 4 313, established under Theopompus 407, more powerful than Spartan kings *ibid.*, treatment of Pausanias *ibid.*, brought Agesilaüs home *ibid.*

Ephorus, historian, useful but tedious 2 223

Epicharmus, comic poet, quoted 5 209

Epictetus, coupled by Lucian with Dio and Musonius 5 363

Epicureans, deify pleasure 2 39 f., banish the gods 41

Epicurus, attitude toward the gods 5 335 and n. 1

Epidaurus, cult centre of Asclepius in Argolid 3 155

Epilepsy, 2 411

Epirus, in north-eastern Greece, ruled by Helenus 1 551

Eretria, seaport in Euboea, attacked by Persians 1 559

Eris, goddess of discord, size suggested by Homer 2 75

Erymanthus, mountain in Arcadia, the boar of 5 39

Essenes, Jewish sect, praised by Dio 5 379 and n. 1

Eteocles, son of Oedipus, addressed by Iocasta 2 195, 5 69 n. 3, dealings with Polyneices 221 and n. 2

Ethiopia, limit of Paris' empire 1 483, 533, source of Nile 3 209

Ethiopians, ruled by Memnon 1 483, 2 289, in Alexandria 3 211, rich in gold 5 307

Euboea, Hollows of 1 287, 291, 307, 539, disastrous to Greeks returning from Troy 545, Persian fleet lay off coast 559, received colonists from Athens 5 55, rugged 55 and n. 2

Euboean Discourse, 1 285-373

Euboeans, wore hair long in back 1 289, 5 333 and n. 2

Eucleides, philosopher of Megara, pupil of Socrates 1 377

Eudorus, son of Hermes and Polydora 1 371

Eudoxus, native of Cnidus, disciple of Aristotle but commonly regarded as sophist because of charm 5 367, contrasted with Dio 369

Eumaeus, swineherd of Odysseus 1 333, son of Ctesias, son of Ormenus, served Odysseus and Laërtes 2 157, 3 311, 4 349

Eumelus, Homeric hero, horses of 3 251

Eumenes I, wagoner's son, became king of Pergamum 5 67 and n. 8

Eumolpus, Claudius, obscure foe of Dio, appeals to Pliny 5 419 f.

Eunuchs, likened to ignorant sophists 1 185, wanton impotence ibid., 271, 2 275 f., shrill-voiced 5 29, created to satisfy men's wantonness 295, weaker than females ibid.

Euphorbus, Trojan, hair mentioned by Homer 2 289, most beautiful of Trojans 5 341

Euphranor, Corinthian sculptor, statue of Hephaestus 4 41

Eupolis, poet of Old Comedy, quoted 3 177

Euripides, alludes to effeminacy of Menelaüs 1 77, contradicted regarding wealth 343, second to none in reputation 2 195, good training for orators 219, preferred to earlier tragedians *ibid.*, compared with Aeschylus and Sophocles 339 ff., competed with Sophocles but not with Aeschylus 341, imitated Homer in having Athena disguise Odysseus 343, chorus of his *Philoctetes* compared with that of Aeschylus *ibid.*, introduced in *Philoctetes* Lemnian named Actor 345, antithesis of Aeschylus in sagacity and attention to detail 347 f., synopsis of *Philoctetes* prologue 347 f., compared with Homer 349, virtues of *Philoctetes* summarized 349 f., compared with Sophocles 351 f., son of Mnesarchides 5 53, praised 95, quoted : *Orestes* (349 ff.) 1 17, *Orestes* (1-3) 205, *Electra* (424 f.) 331, *Electra* (233 ff.) 93 f., *Phoenissae* (531-540) 2 195, *Cresphontes* (frag. 452) 303, *Hecuba* (607) 3 255, *Heracles* (947 ff.) 263, *Heracles* (673 ff.) 269, *Protesilaüs* (frag. 655) 4 45, *Phoenissae* (395) 327, *Philoctetes* (frag. 788. 1) 349, *Antigonê* (frag. 157) 5 49, (frag. 921) 53, *Orestes* (253 f.) 215, *Hippolytus* (616 f.) 229

Euripus, strait between Euboea and mainland, shifting currents 5 55 and n. 3

Europe, 1 191, Greeks in 2 55, no longer has lions 273, nearly all conquered by Philip 331

Eurybates, type of rascality 4 345

Eurymachus, suitor of Penelopê 2 141

Eurypylus, Homeric hero, brave in battle 1 511, 2 289

Eurystheus, mythical king of Argos, rule misunderstood 1 33, ordered Heracles about 393, entrusted Argos to Atreus 5 197

Eurytus, mythical hero, bow of 1 335, 3 447, slain by host 5 225 and n. 4

Eusebius, unidentified correspondent of Dio 5 357

Euthyphro, character used as type by Socrates 4 389

Euxine Sea, shores held by Thracians and Scythians 4 249

Exadius, Lapith, summoned Nestor 5 409

Exile, appraised 2 91 ff.

Exomis, variety of tunic 5 177 and n. 1

Eye, King's 1 157

Eyes, compared with ears 2 75, sore eyes 4 281 f., King's Eyes 4 429 n. 2

Falcons, birds of omen 3 341

Farmers, 1 131, graft trees 237, wear long hair 3 401, treatment of bees 4 289 f., 5 141, not indispensable 143, activities 151, function and equipment 155´f., 171, garb 177, not distrusted 181, 183

Fates, kindly spirits 1 233, bringers of fulfilment 365

Fathers, have absolute authority 2 161, reinforce admonition with prayers 4 103

Favorinus, sophist from Arelatê, devoted to Greek ways 4 25 f., honoured everywhere 35 f.

Felt, caps worn by Getae and formerly by Spartans and Macedonians 5 179

Festivals, reveal character 2 349, activities 351 f.

Fever, prevalent 3 261, treatment 4 287, lethargic fever 5 269, brain fever *ibid.*

Figurines, makers of, compared to philosophers 4 461

File, parable of 2 417 f.

Filial Piety, betokens good citizen 4 153 f.

Fire, source of human frailty 1 263, discovered by Prometheus *ibid.*, not made with green logs 4 275

Fish, abundant in Hellespont 1 81, not eaten by Homeric heroes *ibid.*, compared with erotic men 261

Flatterers, 1 111 ff., 4 53, numerous 5 293

Flute-players (flautists), contend in theatre 1 355, hold school in street 2 253, in Hippodrome 255, 4 75, entertain mob 5 97, 113, 141, not indispensable 143

Flutes, unfit for kings 1 85

Fomentations, not immediately effective 2 193

Fortune, sometimes gives good guardian spirit, sometimes bad 2 309, Discourses on : I 5 33-41, II 43-71, III 73-85, essential in all human activities 5 35 f., resourceful 37, representations in art 41, 49 f., unjustly censured 45 f., many names 51, saviour of mankind 53, 231

Fox, Archilochus' fable 4 263, 389, 5 223 and n. 6

Freedom, Discourse on 5 313-329

Friendship, lauded 1 145 ff., " Common are the possessions of friends " 153, 161 f., defined 187, old friends best 3 83, Discourse on 4 189-203

Frogs, tough 1 265, scared by water snake 399, 5 109

Fullers, numerous 5 179

Furies, transformed Hecuba 3 329, simile 5 115

Gamblers, 5 153

Game-cocks, aroused by blow 2 145, 5 153, 159

Ganymede, famed for beauty, vanished in youth 2 389, Zeus' cupbearer 3 293, 295

INDEX

Gelon, tyrant of Syracuse, son of Deinomenes, statue spared by Syracuse **4** 23

Generals, responsibilities of **1** 135 f., lead armies as a whole **4** 405

Geryones, encounter with Heracles **1** 395, **5** 39'

Getae, called Mysians by Homer **2** 21, visited by Dio 21 f., **3** 421, captured Borysthenes and Pontic cities 425, reviled **4** 279, pleasure-loving **5** 131, wore felt caps 179 and n. 2, seen in Rome *ibid.*

Giants, not progenitors of man **2** 421

Glaucus, famous Carystian boxer **5** 279 and n. 2

Glaucus, Spartan, false to his oath **5** 223 f.

Glutton, term of reproach **5** 109

Goats, live peacefully with sheep **4** 145, resent bad masters 295, do not dislike wild olive **5** 93, bear twins 265

God (Theos), sobriquet of Antiochus II **5** 65 and n. 3

Gods, live at ease **1** 267, language 435, believed in by all rational beings **2** 43, how portrayed 63, progenitors of man 421, once visited mankind in person 421 f., syncretism **3** 17, regard worshippers' intent 19 f., responsible for all blessings 185 f., harmony 441 f., fellowship with mankind 455, slandered **4** 31 f., warnings disregarded 65, blamed for pestilence or earthquake 67

Gold, more precious than silver **5** 115, used to roof houses 305

Golden Age, **5** 51

Golden Lamb, myth **2** 107 and n. 1, **5** 93 f.

Gorgias, Sicilian sophist, vain **2** 19, statue at Delphi **4** 27, won fame and wealth 373, used as type by Socrates 389

Gorgon, head turned Perseus' foes to stone **5** 109, device on shields 285

Gourmets, satisfied with single fish **5** 95 f.

Gout, **1** 381

Government, defined **1** 125

Graces, considered goddesses **3** 41, 269

Grafting, fruit trees **1** 237

Great King, tall tiara **2** 137, defeated by Agesilaüs near Sardis **4** 407

Greece, not in Persian domain **1** 121, declined after Trojan War 551, subject to others (i.e. Romans) 561, all but Rhodes fallen on evil days **3** 161, ancient glory attested only by ruins of buildings 163, licentious **4** 33

Greeks, use poetry as evidence in disputes **1** 477, sacrifice to tragic heroes **2** 153, differ from barbarians in beauty, dress, and lan-

INDEX

guage 287, at Alexandria
3 211, vanquished by
Macedonians 299, ape Ro-
man ways 4 25, ruled by
Agamemnon 423, statues
like Roman but not like
Egyptian and Phoenician
5 181, insult philosophers
ibid.

Guardian (Guiding) Spirit,
1 233, 2 307 ff., Discourse
on 323-335

Gulls, float on waves 2 257

Gyges, Lydian king, suc-
ceeded Candaules 5 69
n. 6

Gymnasiarch, official at Tarsus 3 367

Gymnasium, scene at a 2
361, haunt of idlers 5 151,
157

Hades, visited by Odysseus
1 185, 279, visited by Heracles 4 249, Odysseus meets
Agamemnon at gates 5
227

Hair, worn long by philo-
sophers 3 391, Aristomenes
393, 401 f., worn short by
most Greeks 403, Dio's
Encomium on Hair 5 331-
343, odd customs 339,
productive of both beauty
and terror *ibid.*, special
subject of praise in Homer
341 f., most essential to
male beauty 343

Halys, river in Asia Minor,
crossed by Croesus 1 437,
boundary of Croesus' em-
pire 5 289

Hands, extra fingers 1 425

Hannibal, guiding spirit of
Carthage 2 331, confused
with Mago 5 69 n. 1, com-
mitted suicide in Bithynia
ibid.

Hanno, guiding spirit of
Carthage 2 331

Happiness, Discourse on 2
317-321

Hares, migrate 1 267, sleep
with eyes open 3 303 and
n. 1, shaggy coats 401,
typify timidity 5 111

Harlots, 1 247, licentious
language 4 135, 5 97

Harmodius, Athenian ty-
rannicide, honoured by
Athenians 1 559, descend-
ants exempt from liturgies
3 135 f., statue in Persia
4 39

Harmony, invoked as god-
dess 4 103

Harmosts, sent by the gods
2 421 f. and n. 1

Harp, regarded by Alexander
unfit for kings 1 85

Harpalus, Alexander's treasurer, affair of 5 37 n. 1

Harpists, contend in theatre
1 355, tuning harps 379,
at Alexandria were once
dogs charmed by Orpheus
3 237, admired at Alex-
andria 267, employed to
gain popularity 5 97

Health, greatest of blessings
4 61, 101

Hebê, wife of Heracles 1 393

Hecataeus, recorded own
name in history 4 363

457

Hecatê, goddess of underworld, appeased 1 209

Hector, son-in-law of Eëtion 1 69, prized armour of victims 73, dragged to Greek camp to accompaniment of paean 87, death not in original plan of *Iliad* 473, brought country folk into city 505, upbraided Paris 507, duel with Ajax false 509, compared to Ares 511, aided by Apollo and Zeus *ibid.*, twice conquered by Ajax *ibid.*, fights at Greek camp 513, tomb venerated 525, body preserved by gods and restored to Priam by command of Zeus *ibid.*, really slew Achilles 527, 531, slew Ajax 535, 537, gave Helen in marriage to Deïphobus 541, died at ripe old age, leaving throne to Scamandrius *ibid.*, 543, sent Aeneas to occupy Italy 551, 2 287, died young 371, preferred honour to long life 3 23, almost burned Greek naval station 4 347, valour known in India 363, 395, defeated by Ajax 5 69 and n. 4, hair praised by Homer 341

Hecuba, wife of Priam, became Odysseus' slave and was changed into a dog 1 563, transformed by Furies 3 329, wailings known in India 4 363

Hegias, sculptor, taugh Pheidias 4 381

Helen, maligned by Stesichorus 1 59, gave gifts to Telemachus 339, sister of Aphroditê 455, unjustly maligned *ibid.*, deified *ibid.*, 475, went to Egypt, not Troy 477, 5 13 and n. 1, daughter of Tyndareüs and Leda 1 479, 5 11, carried off by Theseus 1 479, 2 389, 5 13 n. 3, rescued by Dioscuri 1 479, many suitors 481, married Deïphobus 497, 541, surprised at absence of Dioscuri 501, lamented before Priam 507, disappeared 551, 2 199, family 263, 267, courted by noblest Greeks 5 11, sister of Castor and Polydeuces 13 and n. 2, chose Asia in preference to Greece *ibid.*, pampered by Menelaüs 13 and n. 5

Helenus, Trojan seer 1 489, became king of Molossians and eastern Epirus 551, colonized because jealous of Deïphobus 555, ablest prophet among Phrygians 4 443

Helicon, mountain in Boeotia, had tripod commemorating victory of Hesiod over Homer 1 57, scene of Hesiod's inspiration by the Muses 4 381

Helius, identified with Apollo and Dionysus 3 17, children 97, father of Pasiphaë

247, **chariot** 455 f., horse maintained by Magi 459, 465, contended for Corinth 4 13, patron of Rhodes 13 f.

Hellas, Hellenes : see Greece, Greeks

Hellen, eponymous ruler of Hellenes 4 405 f.

Hellespont, "fish-abounding" 1 81, 3 383, subject to Mytilenê 4 221, scene of Athenian naval defeat 5 59 and n. 2

Helmet-makers, 5 273

Helots, Messenians 2 169, threaten Sparta 3 455

Heneti, had best land on Adriatic 1 553, ruled by Antenor *ibid.*

Hephaesteüm, temple at Athens, decoration 4 419 n. 1

Hephaestion, general of Alexander, received obeisance of Darius' mother 5 67 and n. 10

Hephaestus, battles with Scamander 1 471, made Achilles' armour 527, art critic 2 57, limitations as craftsman 85, connexion with Athena 4 33, statue by Euphranor 41, gave sword to Peleus 5 71 n. 1

Hera, in art 1 37, beloved of Ixion 229, goddess of marriage 365, sent Sphinx against Thebes 451, contestant for prize of beauty 453 f., 2 265, eldest child of Cronus 1 455, deceived Zeus 459, urged Aphrodité to help deceive Zeus 461, temple at Olympia 479, horse 3 461 f. and n. 4, marriage with Zeus 471, patron of Argos 4 13, "great-eyed" 5 343

Heracleidae, descendants of Heracles, ruled Lacedaemon 4 407, took refuge in Athens 5 197 and n. 3

Heracleides of Pontus, moralist, admired Homer 4 357

Heracleitus of Ephesus, philosopher, claimed to have had no teacher 4 381

Heracles, myth of 1 27 ff., rustic shrine in Elis 29, son of Zeus and Alcmena 31, 245, 3 263, king of all Greece 1 31, attributes 33, generous *ibid.*, reared at Thebes 35, "Choice" 35 ff., ancestor of Philip and Alexander 101, 183, 201, self-immolation 183, 397, 5 63, vanquished Amazons 1 201, slew Libyan monsters 245, statue in theatre 309, 391, deified 393, wed Hebê *ibid.*, roved over Europe and Asia *ibid.*, subject to Eurystheus 393, 4 251, slew Diomede the Thracian 1 395, slew Geryones *ibid.*, defeated Busiris *ibid.*, affair with Hippolytê *ibid.*, rescued Prometheus 395 f., apples of Hesperides 397, Augean stables *ibid.*, bow and arrows 411 f., exploits at Troy 485 ff., comrade of

INDEX

Theseus 501, intercourse with slave woman **2** 149, father of Telephus 153, his arcade 361, " harmost " 423, laboured in behalf of virtue **3** 21, statues 97, in comedy 263, in Euripides *ibid.*, honoured at Tarsus 275, 315 f., victor at Isthmian Games **4** 15, founded Nicaea 103, conquered Egypt, Libya, Thrace, Scythia, and Troy, yet did menial tasks in Argos 249, his bow essential to capture of Troy 443, vanquished Centaurs 455 and n. 2, shot Nessus 457, captured Oechalia 459, labours **5** 39 and n. 1, horn 51 and n. 5, indifferent toward abuse 111 and n. 2, 139, slew Eurytus 225 and n. 4, called sons cowards 299 f., no match for more than one at a time 335 f., 411

Heracles, son of Alexander the Great, murdered **5** 67 and n. 9

Heraea, town near Pisa in Elis **1** 29

Heraeum, sanctuary of Hera in Samos **4** 115

Heralds, introduce the chorus **1** 223, staff of office a safeguard in war 281, 293, proclaim peace but not war **4** 67, Nero a herald **5** 171, sacred 297

Herdsmen, take best care of cattle **1** 11, treatment of bull 97 f.

Herennius, unidentified friend of Dio **5** 355 f.

Hermes, visited Thebes to instruct Heracles **1** 35 ff., father of Pan 261, taught Pan masturbation *ibid.*, statue at Thebes 355, father of Eudorus 371, taught Autolycus perjury 457, excused himself to Calypso **3** 193

Herodotus, delightful for leisure hours **2** 221, visited Corinth **4** 9 f., falsified rôle of Corinthians at Salamis 11 and n. 1, 19, recorded own name in his history **4** 365, refers to wealth of Sardanapallus **5** 29 n. 1

Heroes, enjoy mystic rites **3** 87

Hesiod, useful for shepherds, carpenters, and farmers **1** 55, defeated Homer 57, composed *Catalogue of Fair Women* 59, his " Homeric " passages valuable for kings 67, commends all work 349, decries idleness 351, beloved of the Muses **2** 25, invocation of Muses *ibid.*, tells of Cronus' bondage 139, possessed by Muses **3** 453, divinely inspired on Helicon **4** 381, lists Tychê among offspring of Tethys and Oceanus **5** 33, tale of Hawk and Nightingale 187 n. 2, esteemed for wisdom 261, conveys general truth by

INDEX

one or two examples 265,
" shepherd of Ascra,"
quoted : *Works and Days*
(383 f.) **1** 55, (1-8) **2** 27,
(763 f.) **4** 47, (6 f.) **5** 53,
(25) 263, (348) 265, (295,
paraphrased) 413, *Theogony* (80-82) **1** 65

Hesionê, daughter of Laomedon, married Telamon
1 485

Hesperides, apples of **1** 397

Hestia, goddess of the hearth,
horse of **3** 463

Hetaerae, attract visitors to
Corinth **1** 379

Hides, as clothing **5** 177

Hierophant, in theatre at
Athens **3** 127

Hieroson, Homer enthusiast
at Borysthenes **3** 447

Hippaemon of Magnesia,
epitaph **4** 37

Hippias, tyrant of Athens,
expelled by Corinthians **4**
17

Hippias of Elis, sophist, encounters Socrates **1** 115 f.,
vanity **2** 19, won fame and
wealth **4** 373, **5** 161, versatility 163 f. and n. 1, 167

Hippodameia, wife of Pelops
1 481

Hippodrome, scene of varied
activity **2** 255, **3** 463

Hippolaüs (Cape), near Borysthenes **3** 421

Hippolytê, Amazon defeated
by Heracles **1** 395

Hippolytus, son of Theseus,
huntsman **2** 391, died
young *ibid.*, slandered by

Phaedra and cursed by
Theseus **5** 221 and n. 3

Historians, have practical
purpose **4** 59, 389

History, knowledge of **1** 557,
requisite preparation for
orators **2** 221

Hobgoblins, used to repress
children **1** 243

Homer, wisdom **1** 9, concept
of kingship 11 ff., favourite
poet of Alexander 53 ff.,
71, defeated by Hesiod 57,
avenged himself on Euboeans *ibid.*, prized oratory 65, most valuable for
kings 67, better than
Tyrtaeus for military
ends 69, described palaces
of Alcinoüs and Menelaüs
75 f., never spoke aimlessly
ibid., described Calypso's
grotto 77, provides instruction for kings and
heroes 79, responsible for
mess at Sparta *ibid.*, poems
brought from Crete by
Lycurgus *ibid.*, portrayal
of Diomede *ibid.*, diet of
heroes *ibid.*, calls Hellespont " fish-abounding " 81,
suitors do not eat fish *ibid.*,
heroes epicures *ibid.*, interested in apparel 81 f.,
disapproves of gold ornaments for men 83, rebukes
a Carian *ibid.*, disciplinarian 85, describes Agamemnon 93, commends
by phrase " shepherd of
peoples " 189, endows Scamander with speech 207,

461

says gods live at ease 267, 283, 289, calls cities " well inhabited " 345, associated with Chios and Smyrna 355, mentions Eudorus 371, bilingual 435 f., begged throughout Greece 457, madman *ibid.*, lied about gods 457 f., related conversations he could not have heard 459 f., professed knowledge of language of gods 463, used Aeolic, Doric, and Ionic *ibid.*, did not begin tale at the beginning so as to escape detection as liar 465, did not tell end of Trojan War 467, had Priam foretell final catastrophe 469, used Odysseus and Demodocus as mouthpiece for lies 471 f., purposely omitted many things *ibid.*, 'nvented incidents to humour listeners 473, had abduction of Helen told by others 507 f., first to narrate Trojan story 515, composed *Iliad* long after the events *ibid.*, wished to hide fact of Achilles' death at Troy 525, knew Menelaüs stayed in Egypt 549 f., inspired Pheidias 2 29, 39, portrayer of gods 65 f., compared Agamemnon to Zeus 67, used mixture of Doric, Ionic, and Attic, as well as foreign words 69 f., artistic in diction 71 f., meta-

phors *ibid.*, praised 75 f., tells of Cronus' bondage 139, best preparation for orators 219, 267, described Hector but not Achilles 289, views on man's existence 303, defended 307, 407, calls mob " unruly " 3 193 f., describes effects of storm 201, 209, 249, portrayal of Thersites 269, 275 f., surpassed all poets but Archilochus 283, lavish with praise *ibid.*, his witness 291 ff., 331, 397, honoured at Borysthenes 429 f., compared with Phocylides 431 ff., known by all men 431, inspires troops *ibid.*, blind *ibid.*, used 5000 verses on single battle 433, never named himself *ibid.*, venerated at Borysthenes 435, 445, compared with Plato 447, possessed by Muses 453, wandering minstrel, pretending madness 4 251, widely known *ibid.*, Ios, Chios, and Colophon claimants as birthplace *ibid.*, used Odysseus to express love of fatherland 253, had Athena disguise Odysseus 343, praised by Democritus 357, interpreted by Aristarchus, Crates, Aristotle, Heracleides of Pontus *ibid.*, appraised by Plato 357 f., allegorically interpreted 359, highly regarded by Zeno 361, extent and dura-

tion of influence 363 f.,
well known in India
through translation 363,
surpassed Sirens and Or-
pheus 363 f., name known
by barbarians ignorant of
meaning 365, career and
conduct *ibid.*, always useful 367, private life un-
known 383, teacher of
Socrates *ibid.*, supreme
poet 385, influenced Stesichorus *ibid.*, resembles
Socrates in character and
methods 385 ff., did not
refer to self 387, concerned
with morals *ibid.*, effective
in similes 387 f., used
specific persons as types
391 ff., always purposeful
397, 405, praised but not
read 5 3, excels in know-
ledge of human passions
ibid., silent regarding
words and deeds of Chry-
seïs 5, compares Agamem-
non to Zeus 9, left some
things to perception of
readers *ibid.*, portrayal of
Odysseus 165, criticized
Phereclus 169 and n. 2,
censured Scamandrius 165
n. 3, exaggerated 305, described Ares' bonds 321 f.,
led Achilles astray with
phantom of Agenor 329,
refers to long hair of
Abantes 333 n. 2, praised
hair especially 339 ff., used
Nestor to illustrate diplo-
macy 409 f., " son of
Meles " 411

Iliad—
A (1-5) **4** 473, (29-31) **5** 15,
(154) **4** 183, (156) **4** 43,
(249) **1** 63, (260-268) **4**
419, (269 f.) **4** 420 n. 1,
(273) **5** 409, (273 f.) **4**
419, (274) **5** 411, (288)
1 53, (446 f.)·**5** 17, (528-
530) **2** 29
B (24 f.) **1** 9, (144-146)
3 195, (204 f.) **1** 125,
(205 f.) **1** 9, (214-216) **3**
269, (363) **3** 409, (412-
418) **1** 93, (478) **2** 67,
(480-483) **1** 93, (489-
492) **3** 205, (542) **1** 57,
(872-875) **1** 83
Γ (39 f.) **1** 489, (54 f.)
ibid., (179) **1** 85
Δ (59) **1** 455, (362 f.) **3**
435, (431) **1** 83, (443) **2**
75
E (62 f.) **5** 169, (640-642)
1 489
H (83) **1** 73, (171 f.) **3** 69,
(351 f.) **3** 393
Θ (233) **5** 285
I (106-112) **3** 413, (383 f.)
3 57, (443) **1** 63, (640)
5 235, (649) **3** 425
K (13) **1** 85, **5** 99
Λ (67-71) **1** 57, (389 f.) **5**
111
M (112-115) **3** 393, (267) **5**
297
N (799) **5** 215
O (696) **1** 389, (711 f.) *ibid.*
Π (180) **1** 371, (359-361) **5**
233, (617 f.) **1** 89
P (75) **5** 115, (177 f.) **3**
193, (447) **2** 303, (474 f.)
2 85, (541 ff. **1** 57

INDEX

Τ (386) 3 397
Υ (52) 1 87, (248 f.) 2 69, (252-255) 3 135
Φ (76) 5 227, (279) 1 561, (389 f.) 3 475
Χ (370 f.) 2 289, (391-394) 1 87
Ψ (368-372) 3 249
Ω (527) 5 69, (544 f.) 3 291
Centos : 3 175, 251 ff.

Odyssey—
α (376) 2 19
γ (290) 5 215
δ (45 f.) 1 75, (73) *ibid.*, (85) 5 57, (221) 2 57, (244-246) 3 287, (535) 5 227, (604) 3 403, 433
ε (99-101) 2 193, (377 f.) 5 55
ζ (162) 5 55
θ (223) 3 447, (280) 5 323, (331) *ibid.*
ι (8-10) 5 99, (27) 5 55, (34) 4 191
κ (239 f.) 3 327, (38 f.) 4 269, (10 f.) 5 99
λ (222) 4 11, (303 f.) 3 187, (441-443) 5 229, (490 f.) 1 191, (603) 5 225
ο (330-332) 3 287
ρ (222) 1 27, (266-268) 79, (269) 3 311, (423) 5 275, (455-457) 1 333
σ (1 f.) 5 109, (406 f.) 3 245
τ (114) 1 109, (329-334) 25 f.
υ (302) 5 327
φ (28 f.) 5 225
ω (249 f.) 2 87
Cento : 3 175

Honey, Pontic 1 405, purest in Attica 3 267, cleansing power 4 425
Honour, inspires heroism 3 21 f., revoked 31
Hoopoe, once a man 1 413
Hoops, as playthings 2 41
Horsemen, prefer mettlesome horses 1 377 f., 5 159
Horses, best handled by master of large drove 1 11, Nisaean 161, Thessalian *ibid.*, proverb 273, behaviour before race 2 23, breeds 171, relations with asses 277, 4 145, colts develop in proportion to legs 261 and n. 1, intractable 287, resent mistreatment 295, Thracian horses of Rhesus 391
Horus, author of *Dreams* 1 545
Hunters, loved by dogs 1 13, 131, conduct 361, equipment and characteristics 5 151, 155
Hunting, best recreation for kings 1 163, Persian style scorned *ibid.*, no proof of courage 2 391
Hydra, Lernaean 4 249, 5 39, assisted by crab 337
Hypanis, river in Scythia 3 421
Hyperbolus, Athenian demagogue 2 329, 4 313
Hypereides, Attic orator, better than Demosthenes and Lysias as training in oratory 2 223
Hyrtacus, father of Asius 4 393

Iambic Poetry, not necessary for orators 2 221

Iardanus, unidentified oriental whose slave became mother of kings of Sardis 2 149

Iatrocles, athlete 2 363

Iberians, enriched through trade 5 309

Icarius, father of Penelopê 1 335, 2 147

Icarus, son of Daedalus, gave name to sea into which he fell 1 225, wings 5 169

Ida, mountain in Troad, shepherds of 1 455, scene of attack on Aeneas 505, 2 67, Paris tends herds on 261, 3 293

Idanthyrsus, Scythian ruler, fostered by Zeus 1 101

Idomeneus, Cretan king, fled before Hector 1 513, abused by Ajax the Locrian 3 251

Ilium, capture not in original plan of *Iliad* 1 473, " beloved of the gods " 509, 2 263, people reproved 3 281, 295, 5 7, 11

Illness, from excess of blood or pressure of warm breath 2 205

Illyrians, once served by Macedonians 1 55, ruled by Philip 4 297

Immorality, successive stages 3 331 f.

Incest, not repulsive to animals or Persians 1 441, 2 277

India, has superior hounds 1 161, king ruined by luxury 171, fragrant herbs 3 301

Indian Ocean, once rarely mentioned, controlled by Alexandria 3 207

Indians, king of 1 193, empire *ibid.*, in Alexandria 3 211, 299, idyllic existence 407-413, appointed Brachmans advisors to royalty 4 301, translated Homer 363, do not see same stars as Greeks *ibid.*, ruled by barber 5 63, reaction to pleasure and pain 129 f., think little of ivory 307 f.

Infanticide, practised by slave mothers 2 151

Inheritance, laws evaded 5 197 and n. 5

Interregnum, at Athens 2 275 and n. 1

Intoxication, from fumes of an incense 3 227

Io, came to Egypt 1 481, not maddened by gadfly *ibid.*

Iocasta, wife of Oedipus, addresses Eteocles 2 195, mutual slaughter of sons 199

Iolaüs, nephew of Heracles, helped in fight against Hydra 5 337

Iolê, princess of Oechalia, beloved of Heracles 4 459 and n. 1

Ionia, supplied Lycurgus with Homeric poems 1 79, colonized from Athens 2 103

Ionian, once dominant musical mode 3 313

Ionians, luxurious **1** 81, at Isthmian Games 405, **2** 55, forbid accusations **3** 373, 383, sensuous **5** 131, war with Dorians 317

Ionic Dialect, used by Homer **2** 69

Ios, Aegean island, reputed birthplace of Homer, scarcely heard of **4** 251

Iphitus, re-established Olympic Games **2** 59, confused with his father Eurytus **5** 225 n. 4

Irus, beggar at Ithaca, fought Odysseus **4** 305, warning to braggarts **5** 109

Isagoras, Athenian rival of Cleisthenes **4** 19

Isles of the Blest, **5** 51

Ismenias, famous piper **3** 231, scorned pipers at funerals **4** 305

Ister, Danube, visited by Dio **2** 21

Isthmia (Poseidon), statue carried to Rome by Mummius **4** 41

Isthmian Discourse, **1** 401-415

Isthmian Games, **1** 379, attract motley crowd 381, 403, attended by men from afar 405, founded by Poseidon and Helius **4** 15, pine crown **5** 93 and n. 3

Isthmus of Corinth, **1** 379, visited by Diogenes 403

Italians, in Alexandria **3** 211

Italiots, Greeks of Magna Graecia, luxurious **1** 81, at Isthmian Games 405, prospered under Pythagoras **4** 299 f., sensuous **5** 131

Italy, not in Persian domain **1** 121, man from 481, occupied by Aeneas 551, 553, controlled by Carthage seventeen years **2** 333, **3** 297, wars on Syracuse **4** 21, **5** 67

Ithaca, home of Odysseus, suitors on **1** 81, 471, 539, sailors resist song of Sirens **2** 39, 157, " tiny, inglorious island " **3** 257, 295, loved by Odysseus **4** 253

Itys, mythical Thracian, mourned by nightingales in spring **2** 305

Ivory, adorned palaces of Alcinoüs and Menelaüs **5** 305, not valued highly by Indians 307 f.

Ivy, crowns **5** 91 and n. 1

Ixion, impious Lapith, punished on the wheel **1** 225, **3** 245, myth of 229, father of Centaurs *ibid.*

Jackdaws, idle chatterers **1** 175, **5** 109

Jason, leader of Argonauts, admired for wealth and beauty **1** 393, protected by salve **2** 183, sowed dragon's teeth 305, dedicated Argo to Poseidon **4** 17, unfaithful **5** 217 n. 1

Jay, a chatterer **5** 109

Jesters, numerous **5** 179

Jocasta, see Iocasta

Jockeys, admired at Alexandria **3** 267

INDEX

Joiners, jealous of one another 5 261, 273, use straight-edge and gauge 281

Judges, in dramatic contests 4 341

Jugglers, in Hippodrome 2 255, 3 179, means of courting popularity 5 97

Jurymen, decried 1 347

King of Persia, gave plighted word to Clearchus 5 223, his heralds slain by Spartans 257 and n. 1, 339

Kings, discussed 1 1-233 *passim*, game called " kings " 189 f., qualities and responsibilities 5 31, headband 93, above law but obedient to custom 255 f.

Kingship, Discourses on: 1 1-47, 49-101, 103-165, 167-233; 4 401-415, 5 23-31

Kissing, not practised in cities 1 319

Knucklebones, used to deceive boys 5 223

Kosymba, article of dress 5 177 and n. 2

Kouretes, Cretan demi-gods, danced a native war dance 1 89

Kymindis, bird, called chalkis by gods 1 435, 463

Labourers, lighten toil by song 1 7

Labyrinth, not built justly 5 167, 323

Lacedaemon, 3 431, ruled by Heracleidae 4 407

Lacedaemonians, had no Scirite band 1 557, defeated at Thermopylae 559, aided by Persia in Peloponnesian War 2 113

Laches, Athenian patriot, used by Socrates as a type 4 389

Laches, name used to betoken ordinary man 5 235 and n. 2

Laconic expressions, 5 61

Ladon, river in Arcadia 3 297

Laërtes, father of Odysseus, served by Eumaeus 2 157

Laïus, father of Oedipus, lover of Chrysippus 1 437, misinterpreted oracle *ibid.*, exposed Oedipus *ibid.*, slain by Oedipus *ibid.*, 451

Lamia, mythical monster, used by nurses to beguile children 4 389

Lamprocles, lyric poet, quoted 2 105

Land, redistribution forbidden 3 77

Laodameia, wife of Protesilaüs, portrayed by Euripides 4 45

Laomedon, Trojan king, married Hesionê to Telamon 1 485, failed to pay Heracles 489

Lapiths, fight with Centaurs at wedding of Peirithoüs 4 418 and n. 1

Lard, used as ointment 1 385

Law, ordains recovery of cost by persons dispossessed 3 65, forbids cancellation of debts and redistribution of land 77, punishes by death mutilation of official records 91, provides for trial of inanimate objects 101, of Leptines 135 f., pride of Rhodians 149, essential to civilized life 5 143, " holy law " 211, forbids contracts with minors 217, limits business dealings with women *ibid.*, Discourse on 239-249, essential to human welfare 239, cosmic law inviolate *ibid.*, " king of men and gods " (Pindar) 241 and n. 1, more serviceable than oracles *ibid.*, owes existence to persuasion 245, transgression harms transgressor 245, more valuable than kinsmen *ibid.*, rewards *ibid.*, compared to Heracles 247 n. 4, protects heralds 247, more essential to a city than rudders to a ship 247 f., contrasted with custom 253-257, repeal 253 f., on tablets of wood or stone 255, sometimes obscure *ibid.*, creates polity of slaves *ibid.*, invalid in war 257

Lawgivers, inspire belief in gods 2 45 ff.

Lawsuits, occasion of war between Athens and islanders 4 73

Lawyers, unscrupulous 1 357

Lechaeum, harbour of Corinth 1 253

Leda, mother of Helen, Dioscuri, and Clytemnestra 1 479, 5 11

Lemnians, formed chorus in *Philoctetes* of Aeschylus and Euripides 4 343

Lemnos, supplied Achaeans with wine 1 507, women punished by Aphroditê 3 321, visited by Odysseus 4 441, Lycaon sold 5 227

Leon of Byzantium, a philosopher regarded as sophist because of literary charm 5 367

Leon of Salamis, arrest ordered by the Thirty 4 183

Leonidas, Rhodian athlete 3 133 and n. 3

Leonidas, Spartan king, slain by Persians 1 559

Leonteus, Achaean hero in *Iliad* 4 393 n. 7

Leontini, city in Sicily, home of Gorgias 4 373

Leptines, Athenian politician, convicted of illegal proposal 3 135 f.

Leptines of Sicily, brother of Dionysius the Elder 5 195 and n. 1

Lesbos, wine 1 259, founded by fugitive Achaeans 555, 2 263, united under Mytilenê 4 221, girls of 5 97

Leucon, king of Bosporus, fostered by Zeus 1 101

Leucothea, sailors' name for Fortune 5 51

Leuctra, battle of 2 169, 295

Libel, law regarding 2 151

Libya, 1 191, produces animals of all kinds 239, 243, 2 333, 3 117, 317, subjugated by Heracles 4 249

Libyan, myth 1 203, Discourse on myth 235-247, monster 239 f.

Libyans, 1 241, women cover their heads 247, at Isthmian Games 405, Carthaginians become Libyans 2 333, in Alexandria 3 211, king sacked 500 cities of the Romans and displayed rings taken from the slain 5 67, king died an ignominious death 69 and n. 1

Linen-workers, cause trouble at Tarsus 3 357 f.

Linus, mythical bard, heard the Muses 1 31 and n. 2

Lions, their keepers 1 281, extinct in Europe, though once in Macedonia 2 273, carried by Bacchants 3 229

Listening, Discourse on Dio's Fondness for 2 235-243

Literature, acquaintance with, a mark of education 1 181

Liturgies, imposed on rich 2 247, exemption attacked by Leptines 3 135 ff., demand men of wealth 4 53

Lot, used in filling offices and in division of patrimony 5 69 and n. 2

Lovers, suspicious and prone to anger 5 3 f., self-indulgent in private but embarrassed in public 19

Lucanian, rewarded by Syracuse for speaking Doric 4 23 f.

Lucian, satirist, dramatic dialogues similar to Dio's *Achilles* 4 431, coupled Dio with Musonius and Epictetus 5 363

Lycambes, broke marriage contract of Archilochus 5 227 n. 1

Lycaon, Trojan prince, slaughtered by Achilles on second encounter 5 227 and n. 2

Lyceum, gymnasium at Athens, visited by Socrates 2 101, 4 427, lost its individuality 3 167, near Academy 4 427 and n. 1

Lycia, in Asia Minor, partially tributary to Rhodes 3 105

Lycians, ruled by Sarpedon 1 517

Lycomedes, received youthful Achilles on Scyros 4 431

Lycon, used by Socrates to typify litigation 4 399

Lycurgus, Athenian orator, recommended as training in oratory because of lightness of touch 2 223

Lycurgus, Spartan law-giver, possibly derived common mess from Homer 1 79, introduced Homer's poems to Greece *ibid.*, his polity 89, re-established Olympic Games 2 59 and n. 3, philosopher in politics 293 f., guiding spirit of Spartans 327

469

Lydia, women despised by Paris 2 263, protected by Celaenae 3 405, luxurious 5 57, 289

Lydian, musical mode 3 313, 4 175

Lydians, ruled by Croesus 2 95, sons effeminate 3 175, once got gold from Pactolus 295, ruined by luxury 299, ruled by shepherd 5 63 and n. 3, reaction to pain 129 f., wars with Phrygians 317

Lyre, tuning 5 135, players 141, 153

Lyric Poetry, not essential for training of orators 2 221

Lysander, Spartan general, destroyed Athenian navy 5 59 and n. 2, a saying of 223

Lysias, Attic orator, excels in brevity, simplicity, coherence, and disguised cleverness 2 223, simplicity 5 417

Lysicles, used by Socrates to typify sheep dealers 4 399

Lysippus, sculptor, statue of chariot at Rhodes 3 91 and n. 1

Lysis, disciple of Pythagoras, conversed with Philip 4 299

Macedonia, not less powerful than Phthia 1 59, subject to Persia 121, invited Socrates to visit 2 115, once had lions 273

Macedonian Phalanx, 1 171

Macedonians, once herdsmen and farmers for Illyrians and Triballians 1 55, became masters of nearly all Europe 2 331, gained Egypt, Babylon, Susa, and Ecbatana but lost Aegae, Pella, and Dium 331 f., certain Macedonians, sprung from animals charmed by Orpheus, settled Alexandria 3 237, rise and decline 299, 4 297, once wore felt caps 5 179, despoiled Persians 311

Macrinus, resident of Prusa, removed from marketplace the tomb and statue of King Prusias 4 261

Maeander, winding river 3 405

Maeonians, tributary to Croesus 5 289

Magi, Persian priests, their cosmic myth 3 455-475, secret rites 455, defined 457, follow sacred sayings *ibid.*, identified with wizards by the Greeks *ibid.*, maintain team of Nisaean horses for Zeus but a single horse for Helius 457 f., counsellors of Persian kings 4 301, in charge of Cambyses' palace 5 195 and n. 3

Magna Graecia, sponsored competitions in declamation 5 369

Magnesia, home of Hippaemon 4 37

Magnetic Stone, 1 211

INDEX

Mago, Hannibal's brother, said to have dumped Roman rings before senate house in Carthage 5 69 n. 1

Mallus, quarrels with Tarsus 3 347 ff., 377 ff.

Mandragora, used as sedative 5 269 and n. 1

Mankind, its lot 1 137 f., 2 308, primitive state 265, 31 ff., harmed by civilization *ibid.*, commits suicide through fear of death 273, gullible and obstinate 447, innate belief in gods 43, span of life seventy years 205, beloved of the gods have short life 369, 391, offspring of Titans 409, suffer for sins of Titans *ibid.*, usually not released from prison house of life until offspring supplied 413, fetters described 415 ff., peasant version of lot 419 ff., invited by Zeus to banquet 423 ff., progressive deterioration 3 81 f., seek to attain goodt and avoid ill 4 75, arrogany in victory but swayed by religion in war 5 11, subject to opinion or pleasure or habit 129 ff., individual differences 131 f., composed mostly of earth 323 and n. 3

Mardian, overcame Sardis 5 67

Mardonius, Persian general, sword dedicated in Parthenon 1 73 and n. 2

Mares, have manes shorn before mating with asses 3 403

Margites, satiric epic, quoted 1 351, work of Homer's youth 4 359 f., hero did not know how to treat wife 5 123 and n. 1

Marines, not competent to pilot or command triremes 2 109

Market-place, haunt of idlers 5 151

Marriage, sanctity of 3 47

Marsyas, river in Celaenae 3 405

Marsyas, satyr, skilled with flute 1 3

Massilia (Marseilles), represented at Isthmian Games 1 405

Master of the Games, 4 35, 41

Maxims : do not judge before hearing both sides 5 9 and n. 5

Measuring-line, simile of 5 121

Measuring-rod, must be even 5 31

Meat, without salt 2 237

Medea, gave Jason magic salve 2 183, name means Meditation *ibid.*, blamed Fortune for her passion 5 47 and n. 1, her spells 105, slew children 215 f.

Medes, luxurious 1 75, wealthy 173, in armies of invasion 189, enslaved Persians 2 329, ruined by luxury 3 299, garb 393, ruled by Deïoces 4 405,

471

5 49, failed to overcome Alexander 65, conquered by Cyrus 67, got Syrian riches 311 and n. 2, despoiled by Persians *ibid.*

Media, horses from 2 171

Megara, 1 255, 2 247, 3 155, its pine not sought after 5 93 and n. 4, popular assembly 157

Megarians, cultivated physical prowess 3 261, derided 5 291

Melancomas the Elder, from Caria 2 367, Olympic victor 377

Melancomas the Younger, athlete 2 363 f., 375, victorious without hitting or being hit 383 f., self-control 385, Discourses on: 357-371, 373-393

Meleager, mythical hero from Calydon, commends sister to Heracles 4 451 n. 1, cousin of Castor and Polydeuces 5 13 and n. 4, son of Althaea and Oeneus 125 and n. 1

Meles, father of Homer 5 411

Meles, king of Sardis, carried lion around ramparts 5 65 f.

Meletus, Athenian tragic poet, accused Socrates 4 183

Memnon, death not narrated by Homer 1 471, son of Tithonus and cousin of Paris, ruled Ethiopians 483, aid neglected by Homer 531, brought aid to Troy 533, slew Antilochus 535, death *ibid.*, 2 289, died young 371, 391, colossal statue in Egypt 3 97

Memphis, in Egypt, seat of Apis oracle 3 185, visited by tyrant of Syria 271

Menander, late rhetorician, linked Dio with Plato, Xenophon, Nicostratus, and Philostratus 5 365

Menelaüs, palace described by Homer 1 75, depicted as faint-hearted *ibid.*, palace Asiatic 77, related to Tantalus and Pelops *ibid.*, 481, effeminate in Euripides *ibid.*, gave gifts to Telemachus 339, entertained Paris *ibid.*, struggle to recover Helen *ibid.*, told Egyptians about Trojan War 475, Phrygian from Mt. Sipylus 485, brooded over failure to wed Helen 493, 503, duel with Paris 509, almost captured Paris 527, depicted by Homer as weakling *ibid.*, remained in Egypt and married king's daughter 549, 2 199, 263, 267, 289, actors in rôle of Menelaüs 4 85, attacked by Pandarus 393, behaviour toward Helen 5 13 and n. 5, wounded by Pandarus 223, hospitality abused by Paris 229, palace 305, blonde 341

Menander, poet of New Comedy, good preparation for orators 2 219, surpassed writers of Old Comedy in portraying character *ibid.*, statue at Athens 3 121, quoted 187

Meno, Thessalian general, used by Socrates as type 4 389, typified lovers and boy friends 399

Meriones, Homeric hero from Crete, skilled in enhoplic dance 1 89, among best of Achaeans *ibid.*

Messenia, district in Peloponnese 2 401, Aristomenes of 3 393

Messenians, freed after Leuctra 2 169, settled Messenê with aid of Thebes *ibid.*, once .called helots *ibid.*

Mestor, son of Priam, slain 1 505

Metapontum, in Magna Graecia, desolate 3 297

Methymnê, in Lesbos, home of Arion 4 5

Midas, mythical king of Phrygia, epitaph 4 37, tomb vanished *ibid.*, prayer 5 47 and n. 2

Miletus, city in Ionia, its Didymeium 4 115

Miltiades, victor at Marathon, mistreated 5 201 and notes 2 and 3

Mimes, actors of 1 353, means of courting popularity 5 97 and n. 1

Minos, king of Crete, famed for righteousness and association with Zeus 1 21, 187, 3 373, 4 367, 5 167 n. 3, 169 n. 1

Minotaur, offspring of Pasiphaë and bull 3 247 and n. 4

Miser, term of reproach 5 109

Mistletoe, traps birds 5 189

Mithranes, governor of Sardis 5 197 and n. 1

Mithridates Eupator, king of Pontus, repulsed by Rhodes 3 117, nicknamed Dionysus 4 9

Moira, a phase of Fortune 5 51

Molionidae (Eurytus and Cteatus), ambushed Heracles 5 335 f.

Molossians, people in Epirus, ruled by Helenus 1 551

Molus, a Cretan, father of Meriones 1 89

Monarchy, defined 1 125

Money, precautions attendant upon lending 5 235

Monster, Libyan 1 239

Moon, relations with sun 4 143

Mossynoecians, Thracian tribe, keep king in tower 2 139 and n. 1

Mother of the Gods, Cybelê, connected with divination and agriculture 1 29

Muleteers, uninterested in horses 2 273, 3 395

Mummius, Roman general, desecrated Greek statues 4 41

Museion, at Alexandria 3 269

Muses, invoked by Dio 1 7, spoke to Linus on Helicon

31, festival at Dium 51, composed song of victory 87, loved Hesiod 2 25, " maidens " 3 227 f., 233, Archilochus a " servant of the Muses " 285, instruct bards 451, their prophets plausible 459, 475, inspire poets 4 363, inspired Hesiod 381, 5 277, honoured by Dio with song and dance 359

Music, of limited value for kings 1 67, syncopated 87, moral value 3 191, 327, invented as remedy for emotions 227 f., prevalence at Alexandria 239, modes 313, does not monopolize artist's attention 5 157

Musician, tûnes instrument 3 385 f., 5 153, 157, 171

Musonius Rufus, Stoic philosopher, in high repute 3 127 and n. 3, rebuked Athenians for impiety *ibid.*, 5 353, coupled by Lucian with Dio and Epictetus 363

Myconos, island near Delos 3 155

Myndians, people in Ionia, held in scorn 3 131

Myrmidons, troops of Achilles, few in comparison with Trojan forces 1 515

Myrtilus, charioteer of Oenomaüs 3 247

Myrtle, used for crowns 5 91 and n. 1

Mysians, Homer's name for Getae 2 21, women despised by Paris 263, commonly held in contempt 3 163 and n. 2, tributary to Croesus 5 289

Mystagogoi, officials at Eleusinian Mysteries, assist initiates 4 217

Mysteries, instruction in 2 191, attendants 451 f., sham battle 4 85

Myths, Libyan 1 203, 237, composed for a purpose *ibid.*, in tragedy 451, of the Magi 3 455-475

Mytilenê, pays court to Romans 3 109, home of Pittacus 4 9, extended its sway 221

Naples, holds athletic contests 2 363, possible connexion with Athens 5 43, first settled from Cumae *ibid.*, Greek in origin and prosperous 61

Nasamonians, African people, wear feathers 5 179 and n. 3, seen in Rome *ibid.*, do not arouse distrust 181

Native City, Discourse in 4 165-171, Political Address in 172-187

Naucratis, Greek settlement in Egypt, city of shopkeepers 2 103

Nauplius, king of Euboea 1 305 and n. 2, father of Palamedes 4 447

Navigators, occupied with seasons, winds, and stars 1 117

INDEX

Naxos, Aegean island, attacked by Persians 1 559

Necklaces, used for recognition of foundlings 1 179

Neleus, father of Nestor, victor at Isthmian Games 4 17

Nemesis, invoked 4 103, images of 121, a phase of Fortune 5 51

Neoptolemus, son of Achilles, joins Trojan expedition 1 533, 535, exiled 549, in Sophocles' *Philoctetes* 4 351 f.

Nereid, Thetis 1 61

Nero, devoted to music and acting 1 163 and n. 1, 3 231, relations with Sporus 2 277 and n. 1, wanton conduct 281, suicide *ibid.*, despoiled Olympia, Delphi, Athens, Pergamum but not Rhodes 3 151 f., precinct at Pergamum *ibid.*, golden house 4 259, a singer 5 87, ruined by tongue 95 and n. 4, 161, ambitions 171 f., falsely connected with Dio's exile 415

Nerva, thanked for honouring Dio 4 197 and n. 1, praised 209

Nessus, Centaur, Discourse entitled Nessus or Deïaneira 4 451-461, story treated by Archilochus and Sophocles 451, plied a ferry 453 n. 2, only Centaur to escape from cave of Pholus 455 and n. 2,

shot by Heracles while carrying Deïaneira over river 457

Nestor, sage and persuasive 1 63, helped Odysseus 65, 503, 507, withstood Hector 513, helped by Diomede *ibid.*, brought Antilochus' bones from Troy 525, 531, name falsely inscribed by Mummius 4 41, Agamemnon's chief advisor 297, used by Homer to typify prudence and tact 395, controlled Agamemnon 409 f., upbraided Agamemnon concerning Briseïs 413, Discourse entitled 417-429, advice to Agamemnon and Achilles 419, invited to Thessaly 421, former influence *ibid.*, eloquence 425, given shield by Fortune 5 71, methods compared with Dio's 409 f., 413

Nicaea, in Bithynia, noble and worthy of renown 4 97, founded by heroes and gods *ibid.*, progressive 257, Pliny holds court 419

Nicaeans, 4 57, relations with Nicomedia 69 f., 89, agree in costume and language 99

Nicanor, native of Stageira, statue at Athens 3 121 and n. 4

Niceratus, father of Nicias 5 203

Nicias, guiding spirit of Athens 2 329, died in Sicily 5 203

475

Nicomedia, in Bithynia, gave Dio citizenship **4** 51, relations with Nicaea 69 f., 89, metropolis 77, 85, maritime influence 79, witnesses plays almost daily 85, progressive 257, building operations 261

Nicostratus, rhetorician, wrote simple, artless prose **5** 365

Nightingale, once human **1** 413, sings at early dawn **2** 7, mourns for Itys in spring 305, **3** 233, name given to Dio **4** 261, gift of paederasts **5** 99

Nile, unusual in nature and utility **3** 205 f., 209, 211, 295, 297, **5** 415

Nineveh, bedecked by Sardanapallus **1** 73, not a true city **3** 439, ruled by Sardanapallus **5** 29, fall of 31 n. 1, sacked with help of Cyaxares 311 n. 2

Ninus, founder of Babylon **2** 13 and n. 3

Ninyas, son of Ninus **2** 289 and n. 10

Niobê, sorrows of **1** 355

Nireus, handsome Homeric Greek **2** 289

Nisaean Horses, famous **1** 161, maintained for Zeus by Magi **3** 457

Nisus, mythical king of Megara, had purple tress **5** 71 and n. 4

North Wind, impregnated Trojan mares **2** 267

Numa, legendary king of Rome, guiding spirit of Romans **2** 331, author of Rome's prosperity 333 f., **4** 299, acquainted with Pythagorean philosophy *ibid.*, ruled Romans 407, laws **5** 317 and n. 2

Nurses, tell children stories **1** 203, **4** 389, **5** 187, use honey in administering bitter medicines **3** 283

Nymphs, compared with Dionysus **2** 349, **3** 229, part owners of Poseidon's horse 465

Oak, used for crowns **5** 91

Occupations, analysed **1** 347-373, some falsely derided 351

Ocean, traversed by Rhodian warships **3** 107, 117

Oceanus, father of Tychê in Hesiod **5** 33

Octavia, wife of Nero, imprisoned **2** 279 and n. 2

Oculists, **1** 381

Odd and Even, game of **2** 341, 345

Odysseus, eloquent **1** 63, checks army with help of Nestor 65, 507, 511, 531, 537, dwelling described by Homer 77, had one purple cloak 81, comrades fed cornel berries by Circê 283, entertained by Eumaeus 333, **2** 157, upbraids Antinoüs **1** 333, converses with Penelopê *ibid.*, received by Phaeacians 337, companions drugged by

INDEX

Circê 389, mocked by suitors 407, told many lies 457, learned from Calypso debates of gods 461, visits Hades 473, 5 227, 235, narrates adventures to Alcinoüs 1 473, delayed return 549, abandoned by friends *ibid.*, received Hecuba as prize 563, longed for home 2 93, 4 253, took advice of Teiresias 2 97, a beggar 139, 147, 3 287, sacked Troy 257, came from barren island 291, caused capture of Troy *ibid.*, 311, domestic affairs declined 4 219, fought Irus 305, behaviour toward Philoctetes 339, 345, 443, disguised by Athena 343, 349, 443, used by Homer to typify prudence and tact 395, scorned by Antinoüs 395 f., philosophizes 441, restored Chryseïs to father 5 17, raft 53, 161, versatile 165 f., son of experienced farmer 165, challenged Eurymachus to compete in reaping and ploughing 167, undaunted by misconduct of maidservants 337, hair praised by Homer 341

Oechalia, in Aetolia, *The Taking of*, a cyclic epic 4 451, taken by Heracles 459

Oedipus, exposed by Laïus 1 437, slew Laïus *ibid.*, did not consult Apollo but

Teiresias 439, sad fate 441, solved riddle of Sphinx *ibid.*, myth 451, hero in tragedy 2 107, fortunate in blindness 5 49 f.

Oeneus, bastard son of Pandion 2 151, slave girl of *ibid.*, father of Meleager 5 125

Oenomaüs, father of Hippodameia 1 481, skilful driver 3 247

Officials, complete term even though unworthy 4 29

Old Comedy, less useful than Menander for orators 2 219

Oligarchy, characterized 1 127

Olive, marvellous growth of Athena's 1 229, wild olive crown 385, 5 91, 245 f., used for crowns 91, 247 n. 1, olive branch connected with vote in Assembly 91 and n. 2, wild olive inedible 93

Olympia, herald proclaims victor 1 61, 2 00, Heracum held chest of Cypselus 1 479, statue of Zeus 2 55 f., 59, ancient statues 273, 367, despoiled by Nero 3 151, altar to Poseidon Taraxippus 247

Olympian, title conferred at Athens 3 121, title conferred at Prusa 4 283

Olympias, mother of Alexander, praised 1 61, denied Alexander was Philip's son 177, 181, died after mourning death of grandson Heracles 5 67

Olympic Discourse, 2 1-87

Olympic Games, attractions of 2 9, re-established by Iphitus and Lycurgus 59 and notes 2 and 3, most renowned festival of all 87, victory commemorated with inscription 3 25, olive crown highly prized 115, Nero contestant 115 and n. 1, Dorieus and Leonidas of Rhodes victors 133, Hippias at 5 163

Olympic Victor, receives huge retainer 5 99

Olympieum, temple at Athens, cost more than 10,000 talents 1 75

Olympus, legendary musician 1 3

Olympus, mountain in Greece, no less famous than Pelion 1 59, shaken by Zeus' nod 2 29, 67, 81

Olympus, mountain near Prusa 5 415, 419

Olynthus, town in Thrace, had Stageira in its domain 1 101, 4 255, captured by Philip ibid.

Omens, interrupt fighting 4 67, never give signal for war ibid.

Onchestus, town in Boeotia, sacred to Poseidon 4 15

Onuphis, town in Egypt, priest denies tale of Trojan War 1 475, priest's own version of Trojan War 479-487

Ophthalmia, victims should not touch eyes 2 191

Opinion, a poor guide 5 119 f., likened to man's shadow 121 ff., Discourse on Popular Opinion 117-125, Discourse on Opinion 127-135

Opuntian, inhabitant of Locris, showed lack of feeling 2 401 f.

Oracles, obscure 1 435, 3 103, of Serapis 183 n. 3, of Apis 185, ambiguous 5 243

Orators, at Olympic Games 2 9, power of 213 f., should study Menander and Euripides 219, do not need lyric and elegiac poetry or iambics and dithyrambs 221, history essential ibid., later orators worth study 223 f., dictation better than composition 229, school compositions inferior to Xenophon's speeches 229 f., compared with actors and singers 241, speak ex tempore ibid., have much in common with philosophers 293, discriminated ibid., contrasted with philosophers 297, 5 141, not indispensable 143

Oratory, has practical utility 2 319 f.

Orchomenos, town in Boeotia, impoverished 4 35

Orestes, son of Agamemnon and Clytemnestra, inveighs against Apollo 1 439, murdered mother 451, **5** 95, plotted against Helen **1** 551, colloquy with Electra **2** 93 f., mad **5** 47 and n. 4, behaviour disturbed Electra 215, famous for friendship with Pylades 237

Orgas, river in Celaenae **3** 405

Orichalc, mountain copper **5** 323 and n. 2

Orion, mythical huntsman, taller and more beautiful than Otus and Ephialtes **2** 391

Ormenus, father of Ctesias and grandfather of Eumaeus **2** 157

Oroetes, Persian satrap, impaled Polycrates **2** 201

Orphans, have state-appointed guardians **3** 79

Orpheus, legendary musician, lived in Thrace **1** 31, **2** 239, tamed beasts **3** 233, Phrygian version 235 f., son of Calliopê 235, 399, **5** 153, victor at Isthmian Games **4** 15, 17, surpassed by Homer 363 f., **5** 153, had magic power 277 f.

Otus, son of Poseidon, inferior to Orion in beauty and stature **2** 391

Owl, attracts other birds **2** 5, beloved of Athena 9, honoured by Pheidias *ibid.*, in Aesop's fable 11 f., **5** 174, useful as decoy **2** 17, now differs from other birds only in appearance **5** 191

Pactolus, river in Lydia, gold-bearing **3** 295, **5** 289

Paean, sung by Achaeans over body of Hector **1** 87

Paederasty, **1** 373, **5** 95, lures of 99

Paeonians, people in Macedonia, employed by Alexander **1** 171

Pain, Discourse on **2** 175-185, a symptom of recovery **3** 39

Painted Porch, colonnade at Athens **4** 263

Painters, helped more by criticism than by formal instruction **2** 231, **5** 171, unintelligent criticism 281

Palamedes, inventor of many arts, stoned to death **2** 107 f. and n. 1, son of Nauplius **4** 447

Palibothra, city of ancient India **2** 15 and n. 1

Pamphylia, district in Asia Minor, scene of Cimon's victory **5** 201

Pamphylians, market in Celaenae **3** 405

Pan, in love with Echo **1** 261, son of Hermes *ibid.*, invented masturbation *ibid.*, shepherds' name for Fortune **5** 51

Pancratiasts, **1** 387, **2** 367, a bait for popularity **5** 97 and n. 2

Pancration, Nero a contender **5** 171

Pandarus, used by Homer to typify impiety **4** 393, smitten through tongue

479

397, wounded Menelaüs 5 223 and n. 2

Panders, garb and nature 1 213

Pandion, father of Oeneus 2 151

Pandora, created by all the gods, bane to mortals 5 283 and n. 1

Pantheia, wife of Abradatas of Susa, blames Fortune 5 45 and n. 1

Parabasis, feature of Old Comedy, reproved audience 3 179

Parades, behaviour of participants 3 371

Parian, Archilochus, famous poet 1 53

Paris, entertained by Menelaüs 1 339, 455, caused Trojan War 467, 475, 483, sued for Helen and accepted by Tyndareüs 483-487, kingdom reached as far as Ethiopia 483, brought country folk into city 505, upbraided by Hector 507, interview with Helen 507 f., duel with Menelaüs 509, slew Achilles 527, almost captured by Menelaüs *ibid.*, 531, slain by Philoctetes 535, 543, reared by slave woman 2 153 f., story summarized 261 ff., 289, lured from Greece most beautiful woman 3 293, 4 393, ships 5 169, caused ruin of Priam 221, abused Menelaüs' hospitality 229

Parmenion, Macedonian general, slain by Alexander 5 63 and n. 8

Parsley, used as wreath 1 385, 5 247 and n. 1

Parthenians, class of youths at Sparta 1 371 and n. 2

Parthenon, 4 115, 287

Parthians, wear turbans and trousers 5 179, seen in Rome *ibid.*

Partridges, lured with food 5 227

Parysatis, Persian queen, favoured Cyrus because of beauty 5 335 and n. 3

Pasicrates, father of Dio 5 387, 417

Pasiphaë, Cretan queen, enamoured of bull, bore Minotaur 3 247 and n. 4, abetted by Daedalus 5 167 f. and n. 1

Passengers, behaviour of 1 135, 167, 3 367

Pataecion, stock character typifying rascality 4 345

Patroclus, substituted by Homer for Achilles 1 521 f., buried with Achilles 525, funeral games ridiculous 529, 543, funeral pyre 2 121, 289, died young 371, 391, friendship with Achilles proverbial 5 237

Pausanias, Spartan king, son of Cleombrotus, victor at Plataea, descendant of Heracleidae, slain by ephors 4 407

Peace, promoted by preparedness for war 1 17,

INDEX

Discourse on **2** 291-299, compared with war **4** 65 f., proclaimed by heralds 67, any peace better than war 133

Peacock, appearance and behaviour **2** 5 f., 9

Pegasus, winged horse, made fountain at Corinth **3** 463, **5** 57

Peiraeus, harbour of Athens **1** 251, joined to Athens by walls 253, fortified by Themistocles **2** 329, extent of walls *ibid.*, **4** 287, walls destroyed **5** 59 and n. 4

Peirithoüs, comrade of Theseus **1** 501, encounter with Centaur **2** 351, superior to Agamemnon and Achilles **4** 419, abducted Helen **5** 13 n. 3, friendship with Theseus proverbial 237

Peisistratus, tyrant of Athens, scattered Athenians through Attica **1** 345 f., once an orator in best sense **2** 293, reforms 327, destroyed democracy **4** 7

Peleus, father of Achilles, not superior to Philip **1** 59, **4** 423, athletic **1** 393, victor at Isthmian Games **4** 15, gods sang at wedding 437, received sword from Hephaestus **5** 71 and n. 1

Pelion, mountain in Thessaly, not more famous than Olympus **1** 59

Pella, Philip's capital, taken from Macedonians by Alexander **2** 333, in ruins **3** 299

Pelopia, lay with father Thyestes and bore Aegisthus **5** 95 and n. 2

Pelopidae, descendants of Pelops, extinct **1** 549

Pelopidas, Theban statesman, associated with Philip **4** 298

Peloponnesian War, Persian intervention in **2** 113 and n. 1

Peloponnesians, **2** 55, 297

Peloponnesus, visited by Dio **1** 27, topography 251, 539, Achaeans expelled 549, **5** 13, 411

Pelops, connected with Menelaüs **1** 77, 481, had ivory shoulder 393, house 451, married Hippodameia 481, came from Asia *ibid.*, sons 483, became master of Peloponnese through connexion with Oenomaüs 499, 539, **2** 289, skilful driver **3** 247, **4** 403, ancestor of Atreidae and native of Phrygia **5** 11, winged car 57 and n. 1, house overthrown by golden lamb 93 f. and n. 1

Penelopê, behaviour toward Odysseus **1** 333 f., daughter of Icarius 335, courted by Cephallenians 549, chaste **2** 147, **4** 349, 397

Peneüs, river in Thessaly **3** 297

Perfume, **5** 113, 115

Pergamum, despoiled by Nero **3** 151

481

Periander, tyrant of Corinth, son of Cypselus, received Arion **4** 5 f., inherited throne 7 f., both tyrant and sage 9, entertained Solon *ibid.*

Pericles, likeness on Athena's shield 2 9 f., friend of Pheidias 61, orator in best sense 293, guiding spirit of Athens 329, disciple of Anaxagoras and benefactor of Athens **4** 299, not continuously in office 333, convicted of embezzlement **5** 199 and n. 1, funeral oration 373

Peripatos, Aristotle's school **5** 369

Persaeus, pupil of Zeno, explained Homer's inconsistencies **4** 361, in charge of Acrocorinth **5** 197 and n. 2

Perseus, legendary hero, a "harmost from the gods" **2** 423, **3** 199, honoured in Tarsus 275, 315, 317, 373, statue by Pythagoras **4** 13, used Gorgon's head against foes **5** 109

Persian King, extent of empire **1** 121, 281, ruined by luxury 171, spent much time going from capital to capital 253, wretched existence 269 f., wore tiara erect and sat on golden throne **2** 111, 141, drove troops with lash *ibid.*, carried off statues of Harmodius and Aristogeiton 4 39 and n. 6, punishment of peers 45, dispatched "Ears" in all directions 429 and n. 2

Persian War, divergent views **1** 557, two invasions **2** 109 f.

Persians, luxurious **1** 75, 81 f., huntsmen 163 f., wealthy 173, literature of 181, invade Greece 189, Sacian Feast 199, do not object to incest 441, their version of war with Greece 559 f., trained to shoot, ride, and hunt **2** 111, shunned exposure of body and spitting in public *ibid.*, driven with lash *ibid.*, intervene in Peloponnesian War 113 and n. 1, regard for beauty 275, treatment of boys 277, freed by Cyrus 329, at Thermopylae **3** 23, in Alexandria 211, horsemen 213, called Zoroaster's followers Magi 457, plane tree **4** 259, Porch at Sparta 263, appointed Magi supervisors of religion 301, ruled by Cyrus 405, **5** 49, 61, failed to overcome Alexander 65, wear turbans and trousers 179, seen in Rome *ibid.*, do not arouse distrust 181, defeated by Miltiades 201, despoiled by Macedonians 311, hurled criminals into ash-filled room 323 f. and n. 1

Personal Appearance, Discourse on **5** 174–191

Persuasion, a deity **1** 7

INDEX

Phaeacians, palace beautified **1** 77, entertained Odysseus 337

Phaedra, wife of Theseus, falsely accused stepson **5** 47 and n. 3, 221 and n. 3

Phaenaretê, mother of Socrates **5** 411

Phaenomena, didactic poem of Aratus, quoted **5** 225 and n. 2

Phaëthon, feeble charioteer **1** 25, caused destruction of universe **3** 465, victor at Isthmian Games **4** 17

Phalaris, Sicilian tyrant **1** 99

Phalerum, Demetrius of, statues destroyed by Athenians **4** 39

Phaon, famed for beauty **2** 389

Pharmakoi, purificatory scapegoats **1** 383 and n. 2

Pheidias, Athenian sculptor, included owl in Athena's statue **2** 9, depicted Pericles and himself on Athena's shield 9 f., inspired by *Iliad* (1 528-530) 29, 49, divinely inspired 55, statue of Zeus praised 55 f., 59, friend of Pericles 61, supreme artist 85, pupil of Hegias **4** 381

Pheneüs, in Arcadia, statues renamed Nestor and Priam by Mummius **4** 41

Phereclus, builder of Paris' ships **5** 169 and n. 2

Pherecydes, philosopher, taught Pythagoras **4** 381, death **5** 61

Philammon, legendary musician, contemporary with Orpheus **5** 279

Philip of Macedon, reluctantly took Alexander on campaign **1** 51, discusses poets with Alexander 53 ff., not inferior to Peleus 59, studied oratory at Thebes 67, let Aristotle rebuild Stageira 101, said by Olympias not to have been Alexander's father 177, made peace with Athens **2** 163, 247, 297, became master of nearly all Europe 331, **3** 135, statue defiled by Athenians **4** 39, harshness toward Athens *ibid.* and n. 9, deified by Athens 39 f., son of Amyntas 41, statue at Thespiae labelled Zeus by Mummius *ibid.*, acquainted with Aristotle 255, captured Olynthus *ibid.*, made Aristotle Alexander's tutor 297, extent of empire *ibid.*, while in Thebes as hostage associated with Pelopidas and Epaminondas 299, fatherhood denied by Alexander **5** 63 and n. 7, relied on perjury and bribery 223

Philip the Jester, **5** 113 and n. 3

Philistus, Sicilian soldierpolitician **5** 195 and n. 2

Philoctetes, aided Achaeans **1** 533, slew Paris 535, story used by Aeschylus, Sophocles, and Euripides

483

4 339, treatment by Odysseus *ibid.*, 345 f., 443, did not recognize Odysseus 343, in *Philoctetes* of Aeschylus and Euripides chorus consists of Lemnians *ibid.*, acquainted with Lemnian named Actor 345, offered throne of Troy 349, Discourse entitled 438-449, son of Poeas 443, bitten by serpent 447 and n. 2

Philosophers, interpreters of divinity 2 53, defined 115, Socrates rarely used name *ibid.*, require seclusion 255, have much in common with orators 293, their concerns 299 ff., contrasted with orators 297 f., useful advisors 299, criticized 3 179 f., likened to physicians 189 f., bad influence 385, nude sect 393, praise concord 4 59, inconsistent conduct 247 f., study how to rule well 297, rarely held office, yet conferred great benefits 299 f., supervisors to kings 301, self-controlled 301 f., not to be judged by appearance 303 f., equipped to rule 305 f., function, equipment and activity 5 155 f., likened to coroplasts 4 461, generally superior in truth and wisdom 5 119, essential characteristics 159, Discourse on 161-173, limitations 163, points of superiority to craftsmen 167, need not compete in technique 171, appearance occasions insult 177 f., numerous in Rome 179, resemble Roman statues of gods and generals 181, held to be supercilious 181 ff., likened to tutors 185, attract crowds by appearance alone 191, court the wealthy 293, pseudophilosophers submit to haircut 295, Discourse on 5 161-173

Philosophy, likened to medical treatment 2 353 f., Discourse on 5 149-159

Philostratus, author of *Heroïca* and *Imagines*, wrote simple and artless prose 5 365

Philostratus, famous sophist, testifies regarding Dio 5 362 f., linked Dio with philosophers commonly classed as sophists through beauty of style 367, defines sophist 371, perplexed as to Dio's classification *ibid.*, thought Dio's *Encomium on the Parrot* and *Euboean Discourse* belonged to same school 375

Philotas, Macedonian general, slain by Alexander 5 63 and n. 8

Phocians, war with Thebes 2 297

Phocion, famous Athenian general, mistreated 5 201 and n. 6

INDEX

Phocylides, gnomic poet, linked with Theognis 1 53, compared with Homer 3 431 ff., unknown in Borysthenes 431, poems brief 433, mentioned name in poems *ibid.*, quoted *ibid.*, 435

Phoenicia, abandoned for Libya by Carthaginians 2 333

Phoenicians, literature of 1 181, effeminate 3 121, licentious 311, airs and rhythm 313, sculpture differs from Greek and Roman 5 181

Phoenix, son of Amyntor, taught Achilles 1 59, 63, 503, 523

Pholus, Centaur, attacked while entertaining Heracles 4 455 and n. 2

Photius, Patriarch of Constantinople, deals with Dio's life and writings 5 386-407

Phrygia, in Asia Minor, its women scorned by Paris 2 263, 3 117, protected by Celaenae 405, Pelops' fatherland 5 11, 289, ancient sarcophagi of variegated stone 307

Phrygians, ruled by Priam 1 261, slave woman reared Paris 2 153, despised 3 161, sons may wear earrings 175, kinsman of Aesop tells tale of Orpheus 235 f., musical mode 313, clever at divination 341, ruled

by Dardanus 4 407, Helenus the ablest prophet 443, sent embassy to Philoctetes *ibid.*, reaction to pain 5 129 f., wars with Lydians 317

Phrynê, famous beauty of Thespiae, has statue at Delphi 4 29

Phrynichus, tragic poet, fined for presenting *Capture of Miletus* 5 325 n. 4

Phthia, home of Achilles, not more powerful than Macedonia 1 59, 539, seat of Peleus' court 4 435

Physicians, used as illustrations by Socrates 1 115, called *hygieinoi* and *iatrikoi* 117, 179, use drugs and dieting 2 105, treatment 129, repeat orders 189, 311 f., likened to philosophers 353 f., 3 181, 189 f., true and false types 279, give learned lectures *ibid.*, 315, control patients 4 57, 277, 287, use cautery and surgery 315, 335, use self-praise 423, 5 141, not indispensable 143, 171, huge profits possible 269, Egyptian physicians 271, 275, not moved by false pity 299

Pieria, Dium in, scene of Olympic festival founded by Archelaüs 1 51 and n. 2

Pilots, used as illustrations by Socrates 1 115, responsibilities and conduct 135, 179, 2 39, recover course 43, 105, repeat orders 189,

485

must not be moved by nervous passengers 3 367, 4 289, association with courtesans 5 159, 171, attitude toward one another 267, loss of sleep *ibid.*, 275

Pindar, Theban poet, praised 1 67, 71, house spared by Alexander *ibid.*, told story of Deïaneira and Heracles 4 452 n. 1, fed by bees 5 67 and n. 4, quoted 1 71, 2 85, 3 277

Pine, crowns of 1 385, 409, Isthmian 5 247 and n. 1

Pipers, at funerals not flautists 4 305, 385

Pipes, not heard in city at dawn 3 307, played by Nero 5 173, bagpipe played by Nero *ibid.* n. 1

Pirates, exact ransom 2 131, 3 259

Pisa, city in Elis, visited by Dio 1 29

Pisidians, people of Asia Minor, market in Celaenae 3 405

Pittacus, tyrant of Mytilenê, lost tyranny 4 9

Pittheus, father of Aethra 1 493

Plane-tree, golden 1 271, 4 429 and n. 3

Planets, 3 461 and n. 2, orderly behaviour 4 145

Plataea, battle of, held by some to antedate battle of Salamis 1 557, won by Pausanias 4 407

Plataeans, at battle of Marathon 5 201 n. 2

Plato, comic poet, enjoyed licence at Athens 3 281

Plato, philosopher, reminiscences : 1 9 and n. 2, 2 215 and n. 2, notes epic heroes do not eat fish 1 81, 377, cherished at Borysthenes 445, most Greek *ibid.*, compared with Homer 447, slandered 4 31, charmed by Homer but barred him from ideal state because of treatment of gods 357 f., admired Homer 361 f., his prose compared to Dio's 5 365, resented term sophist 369, his funeral oration of Aspasia 373 and n. 2, his solemnity 417

Pliny the Younger, correspondence with Trajan about Dio 5 416-423, holds court at Nicaea 419 f., called Secundus by Trajan 421

Plution, teacher of rhetoric, worth reading 2 223 f.

Podargus, horse of Hippaemon 4 37

Poeas, father of Philoctetes 4 443

Poets, embody opinions of average man 1 341, encourage falsehood 479, inspire belief in gods 2 45 ff., influence popular belief 63, power of expression 67 f., have advantage over artists 73 f., tragic poets trusted 153, praised orators 215, inspired by

Muses 3 451 f., "attendants of Muses" *ibid.*, early and later compared 453, responsible for concept of Zeus as King and Father *ibid.*, praise concord 4 59

Pollux, see Polydeuces

Polus, famous tragic actor 5 99 and n. 6

Polus, pupil of Gorgias, vain 2 19, won fame and wealth as sophist 4 373, used as type by Socrates 389

Polycleitus, famous sculptor 2 49, 85

Polycles, late sculptor, made statue of Alcibiades 4 39

Polycrates, tyrant of Samos, slain by Oroetes 2 201, blamed Fortune for capture 5 45 and n. 4

Polydamas, Trojan hero, used by Homer to typify prudence and generalship 4 395

Polydeuces, did not join Trojan expedition 1 501, brother of Helen 2 263, won in boxing at Isthmian Games 4 15, family connexions 5 13, reputed son of Zeus and worshipped as god 13 and n. 2, overwhelmed Athens 13

Polydora, daughter of Peleus, mother of Eudorus 1 371

Polygnotus, famous painter 2 51, pupil of Aglaophon 4 381

Polyneices, son of Oedipus, relied on priority of birth 5 69 and n. 3, quarrelled with Eteocles 221 and n. 2

Polyperchon, successor to Antipater of Macedon, murdered Alexander's son Heracles 5 67 n. 9

Polypoetes, Homeric hero 4 393 n. 7

Polyxena, daughter of Priam, slain at Achilles' tomb 1 261, 563

Pontus, kingdom south of Black Sea 1 385, honey 405, home of Amazons 533, 3 425, home of Heracleides 4 357

Poor People, country *versus* city 1 345

Poppaea Sabina, wife of Nero 2 279 and n. 1

Porch (The), colonnade in Athens identified with Stoic school 5 375

Porus, Indian prince, failed to overcome Alexander 5 65

Poseidon, in Homer rides chariot 1 119, has temple at the Isthmus 381, 2 155, Taraxippus at Olympia 3 247, honoured at Tarsus 275, helped fortify Troy 293, his horse identified by poets with Pegasus 463, horse drowns universe in sweat 465, vied with Helius for possession of Corinth 4 13, patron of Onchestus 15, receives Argo as dedication 17, 31, raises storm with trident 5 53, cursed Pasiphaë 169 n. 1, statues

487

in Rome wear only cloak 181, father of Theseus 221

Potters, used as illustration by Socrates 1 115, rivalry in Hesiod 5 261, 263, 273

Priam, slain at altar of Zeus 1 261, 563, ruled most of Asia 483, brother of Tithonus *ibid.*, hears Helen lament 507, ransoms Hector's body 529, entertained by Achilles 563, son Paris reared by slave woman 2 153, name falsely inscribed by Mummius 4 41, well known in India 363, father of Helenus 443, made wretched by Paris 5 221

Prices, of purple mantle 5 91, of ribbons *ibid.*

Priests, " of purification " 1 209 and n. 2, exorcists 263, had special seats in theatre at Athens 3 127, advisors to royalty 4 301

Primacy, source of strife 4 73, 75 f.

Prisoners, chained together 2 413

Proconnesus, island in Propontis 4 45

Prodicus, sophist from Ceos, won fame and wealth 4 373, used as type by Socrates 389

Prometheus, punished for discovery of fire and bestowal on mankind 1 263, 265 f., " a sort of sophist " 395, rescued by Heracles 395 f., made mankind of clay 4 43, 5 323 n. 3

Prophesying, manner of 1 31

Propriety, questions of 2 295

Propylaea, gateway to Acropolis 1 75, admired 253, 4 115, 287

Protagoras, philosopher from Abdera, lost property 4 373 and n. 4

Protesilaüs, Thessalian hero, slaughtered 1 503, buried on Chersonese *ibid.*, 531

Proteus, mythical character of epic 3 329

Proverbs, 1 15, 2 225 and n. 1, 4 285

Provincial Governors, in Bithynia 4 79, take advantage of local strife 81 f.

Proxenies, unite Nicaea and Nicomedia 4 71

Prusa, city in Bithynia, outstripped by neighbours in public works 4 113, relations with Apameia 123 ff., 131 ff., 137 f., 151, 155 ff., aided by Dio 175, honoured Dio's family 193, had good reputation in comparison with size and antiquity 199, ambitions 201, won concessions from Trajan 209 f., beguiled by promises 211 f., financial problems 213, 263, 283 f., new Council organized 217, public works fostered by Dio 221 ff., food shortage 235 f., founder Prusias 261, Zeus' temple burnt 263, inhabited by pure

Hellenes 281, has "supervisor of public morals" 331, generous with honours 335, near Mysian Olympus 5 415, 417, 419 f., Discourses dealing with Prusa: Defence of Relations with 4 204-225, Mistreatment in 226-241, Efforts to Beautify 243-271, Political Address in Assembly at 272-291, On Declining Office at 292-309, Dio's Record at 310-323

Prusias, mythical founder of Prusa, tomb and statue removed 4 261

Pterelas, mythical personage, had golden locks 5 71 and n. 3

Ptolemy XI (Auletes), 1 163 and n. 2, restored to power at Alexandria by Romans 3 241 and n. 3

Public Speaking, Discourse on 2 209-233

Pugilists, aid to popularity 5 97

Pulydamas, famous Thessalian wrestler 5 279 and n. 2

Pylades, friendship with Orestes proverbial 5 237

Pylians, in Agamemnon's army 4 409

Pylus, in Peloponnese, Spartan shields taken 1 73, home of Nestor 4 409, 421

Pythagoras, philosopher, slandered 4 31, 251, taught Lysis 299, pupil of Pherecydes 381, taught Empedocles ibid.

Pythagoras, sculptor, made statue of Perseus 4 13

Pythagoreans, benefited Italian Greeks 4 299 f.

Pythian Games, 2 367, victory commemorated by inscription 3 25

Pythian Priestess, prophecies 3 103, 5 187, contrasted with Seven Sages ibid.

Pythius, Lydian who gave golden plane-tree to Darius 4 429 n. 3

Quails, used as lure by paederasts 5 99, 153

Rainbow, dark blue, sign of war 2 81

Rams, engines of war 3 299

Ravens, cries of 5 109

Red Sea, controlled by Alexandria 3 207

Remus, mythical founder of Rome, rescued by shepherds 5 67 and n. 5

Reputation, Discourse on 5 86-115, pursuit leads to beggary 91

Retirement, Discourse on 2 245-269, defined 247 ff.

Rhea, mother of Zeus 1 365

Rhesus, Thracian king in Iliad, betrayed by Dolon 4 391

Rhodes, has altars of all the gods 3 17, most prosperous 45, 111, owned Caria 51, kept official list of statues 53, plundered by Cassius

71 f. and n. 1, resisted bankruptcy 73, got revenue from Caria and Lycia 105, depository for many 107, naval operations *ibid.*, had uninterrupted peace 107 f., had statues of Roman emperors *ibid.*, loyal to Rome 117, military power *ibid.*, captured *ibid.*, grounds for pride 149 f., many statues 151, belongs to Helius 4 13 f.

Rhodian Discourse, 3 1-169

Rhodians, deliberate daily 3 11, mistreat benefactors 13 f., valiant 23, wealthy 61, 105, have law barring executioner from city 129 f., personal characteristics 165 f., decorous 223

Rhodogunê, daughter of Mithradates I 2 279 and n. 3, 5 47 and n. 5

Ribbons, lure seekers of reputation 5 89 and n. 2

Roman Citizenship, 4 159

Romans, addressed by Dio 2 117, guided by Numa 331, 4 299, 407, statues at Rhodes inviolate 3 47, waged long civil war 71, granted provinces remission of debts 73, did not molest Rhodian statues 151, helped Ptolemy Auletes regain power 241 and n. 3, practised shaving 437, 4 25, duped by Mummius 41, disdain Greeks 83, 500 cities sacked by Libyan king 5 67, finger rings of slain fill tunic of Libyan conqueror *ibid.*

Rome, founded by Aeneas 1 553 and n. 1, visited by Dio 2 115, choice of emperor 279 f., almost taken by Carthaginians 333, ruled harshly by Romulus *ibid.*, courted by Greeks 3 109, 4 33, generous toward aliens 159, has golden colonnades 263, 5 67, exotic costumes in evidence 179, statues of gods and generals resemble philosophers 181, statues same as in Greece *ibid.*

Romulus, harsh ruler 2 333, rescued by shepherds 5 67 and n. 5

Runners, used to court popularity 5 97

Sabinianus, unidentified correspondent of Dio 5 357 f.

Sabinus (T. Flavius), friend of Dio 2 91 and n. 1

Sacae, Scythian tribe, in Persian army 1 189

Sacian Feast, held by Persians 1 199

Sacred Band, Theban troop organized by Epaminondas 2 295, defeated Spartans at Leuctra *ibid.*

Sacrifice, ritual of 3 15 f.

Sacrilege, includes even changed position of temple treasure 3 93

Sailors, attentive to duty in storm though reckless in fair weather 3 167, wear only tunic 5 177, do not arouse distrust 181 f.

Salamis, traversed *en route* to Athens 1 255, battle of, held by some later than that of Plataea 557, ransomed by means of statue 3 121, had statue of Solon 4 9 and n. 7, 11, Corinthians responsible for victory 19, Leon of 183

Salt, gives flavour to meat 2 237

Samos, ruled by Polycrates 2 201, its Heraeum 4 115, 5 213

Sappho, her poetry not suitable for kings 1 67, quoted 4 45 f., 5 47

Sarambus, shopkeeper at Athens 1 215

Sardanapallus, depraved 1 3, 5 29 and n. 1, 31 n. 1, 49, 287, bedecked Nineveh with jasper, carnelian, and onyx 1 73, 139, " Syrian king " 221 and n. 1, quoted 231, extent of empire 5 29

Sardis, capital of Lydia, kings descended from slave woman 2 149, Agesilaüs victorious near 4 407, overcome by a Mardian 5 67, under Mithranes '197 and n. 1, traversed by Pactolus 289

Sardonian Plant, caused grim laughter 3 269

Sarpedon, Lycian king and reputed son of Zeus, slain 1 517, died young 2 371, 391, statue 3 97

Satraps, Persian viceroys, flattered 3 287, 5 101

Satyrs, crazed by song 3 229

Sauromatians, Iranian tribe, king of 3 423 and n. 5, 429

Scamander, river in Troad, endowed with speech 1 207, called Xanthus by gods 435, 463, battled with Hephaestus 471

Scamandrius, son of Hector, heir to kingdom 1 541

Scamandrius, Trojan huntsman, censured by Homer 5 169 and n. 3

Schoolboys, write original compositions 2 229, memorize whole treatises 231

Schoolmasters, derided 1 351, disliked by boys 5 185

Scirite Company, Spartan band, held non-existent by Thucydides 1 557

Scorpions, sting of 5 229

Scriveners, 1 357

Sculptors, helped more by criticism than by formal instruction 2 231

Scylla, story told by Odysseus 1 471 f.

Scyros, Aegean island, temporary home of youthful Achilles 4 431

Scythians, king ruined by luxury 1 171, bury cupbearers, cooks, and concubines with kings 2 91, attacked by Darius 331, in Alexandria 3 211, *en route* to Getae 421, could not equip rpoper trading centre 425, costume 427, attack Borysthenes 435, subjugated by Heracles 4 249, do not farm 5 57, good citizens though nomads 143

Sea, does not disturb neighbours 2 257, in a storm 4 283, safer than coast 5 231 f.

Seasons, governed by sun 1 139 ff., act as waiters at life's banquet 2 425, 433

Selenê, goddess, coursing of 3 459

Sema Myrines, divine name for Batieia 1 435, 463

Semelê, mother of Dionysus, birth pangs piped 5 291 and n. 2, mother of Heracles 411

Semiramis, Assyrian queen, had luxurious palace 1 75, 271, founded Babylon 2 13 and n. 3, lustful 4 269 f., 5 47 and n. 6, leader of Asia 63 n. 4, a builder 65

Serapis, god of oracles and dreams 3 183 and n. 3, epiphany of 211 and n. 1

Seriphos, island near Athens, colonized by Athens 2 421

Servants, Discourse on 1 417-443

Sesostris, legendary king of Egypt 2 289

Seven Sages, their maxims at Delphi 5 187 and n. 1

Sexual Relations, pleasurable 5 131

Shadow, in simile of popular opinion 5 121 f.

Shaving, practised by Romans 3 437

Sheep, mingle peacefully with goats 4 145, resent bad masters 295, get wool matted 5 337 f.

Shepherds, considerate toward sheep 1 11, suffer loss when neglectful of dogs 17, functions 123, contrasted with butchers 189, garb 5 177, do not arouse distrust 181, 183

Ship-captains, indulge crew and neglect passengers and ship 1 17, 131, order passengers to help 2 127, jettison cargo 3 113

Ships, lured to destruction 1 305, in a storm 3 167, require concord on board 351 f., 4 63, 101, 287, simile of 5 31, 49, 135, helpless without pilot 37

Ship-wright, 4 289

Shoe, simile of 4 119

Shoemakers, not indispensable 5 143, 179

Shooting Stars, evil omen to sailors and soldiers 2 81

Sibyl, 2 121, 3 391, 4 15

Sicily, represented at Isthmian Games 1 405, coveted by Athens 2 203, a hill in Attica *ibid.*, freed from Carthage by Corinth 4 21, Nicias in 5 203, enslaved Athenians 323 and n. 4

Sicyon, city near Corinth, ruled by Cleisthenes 1 123 and n. 1

Sidon, city in Phoenicia 3 121

Siege-towers, 3 299

Silver, genuineness of coins tested 5 113 and n. 4, inferior to gold 115, adorned palaces of Alcinoüs and Menelaüs 305

Simaristoi, turbulent faction at Alexander 3 241

Simoïs, river in Troad 3 293

Simon, name denoting ordinary man 5 235 and n. 2

Simonides, poet from Ceos, composed epitaph for Corinthians slain at Salamis 4 19, composed epitaph for Adeimantus 21

Singers, compared with orators 2 241

Singing, voluptuous kind decried by Alexander 1 85, of Ares 87, of Muses *ibid.*, Spartan 89, of Attic symposia 91

Sinopê, Black Sea city, exiled Diogenes 1 169, 251, 377

Sipylus, mountain in Lydia, ancestral home of Agamemnon and Menelaüs 1 485

Sirens, song of 2 39, 3 217, 307, 313, surpassed by Homer 4 363

Slavery and Freedom, Discourses on 2 123-141, 143-173

Slaves, purchase of 3 47, not trusted to make agreements 5 217

Smithy, at Prusa 4 115 f., 257

Smyrna, reputed birthplace of Homer 1 355, quarrels with Ephesus 3 383, cited as example 4 119, enriched by Emperor 121 f.

Snakes, bite of 5 229

Sneezing, betrays a catamite 3 325

Snorting, a practice attributed to Tarsians 3 273, 301 ff., 5 395 n. 1

Socrates, questioned about Persian king 1 105, encounters Hippias of Elis 115, had friends surviving in time of Diogenes 377, professed ignorance 2 19, urged cultivation of philosophy 101 ff., rarely used name philosopher 115, " wisest of men " *ibid.*, 4 387, invited to Macedonia 2 115, punished for obeying Apollo 3 281 f., victim of slander 4 31, defied the Thirty 183, accused by Meletus *ibid.*, composed hymn to Apollo and Artemis 185, reproved wickedness *ibid.*, received hearing in court 187, obeyed laws 253, death a disaster to Athens *ibid.*, put to death by Athens 333, personality, family, and behaviour 375, left no writings 375 f., 387, understood by few 377, admired by Dio 381, studied father's calling 383, pupil of Homer, not Archelaüs *ibid.*, resembled Homer 385 ff., effective in similes 387 f., used actual persons as types 389 f., purposeful

397 f., based virtue on
reason 421 n. 2, repeated
in Academy words spoken
in Lyceum and *vice versa*
427 and n. 1, dealt with
men of all callings 461,
condemnation 5 61, 113,
wisdom 71, followed motto
Know Thyself 117, 185,
189, 191, sometimes at-
tacked by Dio with coarse
jests 375, son of Sophro-
niscus and Phaenaretê 411,
Discourse on 4 371-377

Socratics, appraised 2 225 ff.,
indispensable as training
for orators *ibid.*

Sodom, near a community of
Essenes 5 379

Soldiers, owe prompt obedience 2 127, 5 141, mer-
cenaries arrogant and
cowardly 285

Soli, city in Cilicia, hostile to
Tarsus 3 349

Solon, encounter with Croesus 1 439, 5 49, saying of
2 213 n. 1, philosopher in
politics 293, cancelled debts
of Athenians 3 75, visited
Periander 4 7 f., fled from
Peisistratus *ibid.*, had
statue on Salamis 9 and
n. 7, benefited Athens 299,
did not envy Alcmaeon
289, legislation 317 and
n. 3, 321

Sons, subject to fathers 2 161

Sophists, scorned by Dio-
genes 1 181, 183, attract
simpletons 185, compared
to eunuchs *ibid.*, 187,

mercenary 231, misguided
443, likened to peacocks
2 9, 3 397 f., not all bad
401, won fame and wealth
but speeches lack sense
4 373

Sophocles, regarding wealth
1 343 and n. 3, compared
with Aeschylus and Euri-
pides 4 349 ff., competed
with both Aeschylus and
Euripides 341, his *Philoctetes* compared with
Aeschylus' and Euripides'
351 f., praised by Aris-
tophanes 353, his *Achilles'
Lovers* 431, dealt with
Nessus story in *Trachiniae*
451, criticized by some for
treatment of Nessus story
453, praised 5 95

Sophroniscus, father of Socrates 5 411

Soul, contrasted with body
1 137, 4 43

Sown Men, mythical pro-
genitors of Theban no-
bility, bore mark of spear
1 179, 2 287

Spako, woman who rescued
Cyrus 5 67 and n. 7

Sparta, had disastrous earthquake 1 281 f., home of
Menelaüs 339, Parthenians
371 and n. 2, home of
Tyndareüs 479, had ships
493, its dogs 2 171,
263, 267, founded Cythera
421, courts Romans 3
109, scrupulous regarding
statues 129, rival of Athens
383 f., caps 403, inspired

troops with Tyrtaeus' songs 431, object of Helot plots 455, foiled by Corinth in attempt to play tyrant 4 19, its king Agesilaüs 41, sought primacy 73, 83, one of three foremost Greek cities 195, Persian Porch 263, kings, ephors, and elders contrasted with commons 313, meagre living 5 57, kings 157

Spartans, sang Tyrtaeus' songs 1 69, 89, lost shields at Pylos 73, perhaps derived common mess from Homer 79, defeated at Leuctra 2 169, 295, forced to cede Messenia *ibid.*, consulted Apollo about Arcadia 201, defeated at Tegea *ibid.*, 247, appearance 287, advised by Apollo against fortification 295, owed hardships to Lycurgus 327, heroism at Thermopylae 3 23, 4 19, 5 297 and n. 2, 339, fallen on evil days 3 161, made war to accompaniment of pipe 231, cut away strings of harp 239, 327, contrasted with Alexandrians 241, valiant 261, had trouble with Aristomenes 393, foiled by coalition of Elis, Thebes, and Corinth 4 19, owed ancient prestige to civic morals 201, 315, 5 71, their reactions to pleasure and pain 129 f., once wore felt caps 179, lost

leadership to Themistocles 199 f., cautious 219, punished for murder of Persian heralds 257 and n. 1

Spear-polishers, 5 273

Sphinx, winged 1 241, endowed with speech *ibid.*, riddle 441, devoured Theban children 451, sent by Hera *ibid.*, invented by poets and artists 3 199

Spleen, diseases of 1 381

Sporus, favourite of Nero 2 279 and n. 1

Squill, used for purification 4 291

Stadium, noisy 4 135

Stageira, town near Olynthus, birthplace of Aristotle, rebuilt with permission of Philip 1 101, 4 255, uninhabited in Dio' day 257

Stags, come to close quarters when exhausted 2 385

Starlings, a plague to farmers 5 91

Stars, behave in orderly fashion 4 143

Statesman, influential through eloquence 2 213 f., proper training for 219 ff.

Statues, varieties and production 2 49, materials and cost of chryselephantine 55, abundant at Rhodes 3 13 f., 151, voted by Rhodes 15, Macedonian and Spartan molested 47, identified by inscription 53, 59, listed officially at Rhodes *ibid.*, desecrated

87 f., 145, relabelled 93, some unlabelled 95 f., Heracles' *ibid.*, seized by Nero 151, honorary variety not of clay 155, repeatedly re-used 157 f., fraud in dedication easily detected 159, Arion's 4 7, Solon's 9, Favorinus' 11, made by Daedalus 11 f., equestrian 13, Pythagoras' Perseus *ibid.*, tyrants' at Syracuse 21 f., sanctity 27, Gorgias *ibid.*, Phrynê 29, ruined by lapse of time 37, falsely labelled 39, statues of Demetrius of Phalerum destroyed *ibid.*, Philip's insulted *ibid.*, mistreated by Mummius 41, none of Agesilaüs *ibid.*, Euphranor's Hephaestus *ibid.*, of beaten gold 191, Roman statues of gods and generals resemble philosophers 5 181, Egyptian and Phoenician differ from Greek and Roman *ibid.*

Stays, worn by effeminate Phoenician 3 121

Stentor, Homeric hero, had throat of bronze 3 331

Stesichorus, native of Himera, punished by Helen 1 59, odes suitable for kings 67, imitated Homer 71, 4 385, his *Capture of Troy* creditable 1 71, his palinode 477, 5 319 n. 1

Stheneboea, type of lustful woman 5 223 and n. 1

Sthenelus, son of Capaneus,

boasted superiority over father 5 59 and n. 7

Stoics, define " city " 3 449, base virtue on reason 4 421 n. 2

Storks, migrate 1 267

Story-tellers, ply their vocation in Hippodrome 2 255

Straight-edge, compared with opinion 5 119 f.

Streamers, tell direction of wind 5 217

Stymphalus, district in Arcadia, birds of 4 249

Suidas, lexicographer, regarding Dio 5 416 f.

Suitors (of Penelopê), do not eat fish 1 81

Sun, function and behaviour 1 139 ff., relations with other heavenly bodies 4 143 f.

Sunium, cape of Attica 1 251

Supposititious Children, 3 157

Surgery, practice of 2 129, 4 315, 423

Surveyors, see more clearly with one eye 3 319, 5 147, may associate with courtesans or flute-girls 159, 171

Susa, capital of ancient Persia 1 189, 193, 215, 251, 2 13, taken by Alexander 331, golden plane-tree 4 429 n. 3, park 5 311 and n. 3

Swans, sing 2 7, 3 233, make music with wings 313

Swellings, reduced by pricking or squeezing 4 425

Sybaris, city of Magna

Trie
4 40

INDEX

cities would have been captured early 5 7

Trust, Discourse on 5 193-205

Trustees, varieties 5 197, worries of 197 f.

Tunic, when worn alone does not arouse suspicion 5 177, garb of sailors *ibid.*, a variety of *ibid.*, worn by tavern-keepers belted high *ibid.*

Turban, worn by many barbarians 5 179

Tutors, disliked by boys 5 185

Tychê, child of Tethys and Oceanus, rarely personified by later Greeks 5 33

Tyndareüs, born in Sparta 1 479, father of Helen, Clytemnestra, and Dioscuri *ibid.*, did not join Trojan expedition 503, not older than Nestor and Phoenix *ibid.*, king of Sparta 5 11, bound Helen's suitors to lend aid 13 and n. 1

Typhon, monster of primitive world 1 35

Typhoons, visit the universe 2 409

Tyranny, Discourse on Kingship and 5 23 ff.

Tyrants, contrasted with kings 1 123, friendless 157, sad plight of 273 ff., licentious 2 261, Syrian tyrants visited Memphis 3 271, conduct 4 269, jealous and suspicious 5 203

Tyrians, removed to Carthage 2 333

Tyrtaeus, sung by Spartans 1 69, 3 431, quoted 1 89

Ulcers, 3 147

Universe, administration of 1 23, an evil prison 2 409, beautiful house 423, constitution 449, " home of Zeus " 453 f., invisible movement 459, consumed by fire 463 f., 467, preserved by concord 4 143

Uranus, early god, mutilated by Cronus 1 559

Varenus Rufus, proconsul of Bithynia, benevolent toward Prusa 4 275 f.

Vertigo, afflicts the body 2 411

Vespasian, benefited from Dio's speeches *On Kingship* 5 409, connexion with Dio 415

Virtue, Discourses on 1 375-399, 5 137-147

Walking, an index to character 3 225

Wall-builders, 5 273

War, avoided by preparedness 1 17, stirs even meaner souls 3 109, announced by raising standard 435, folly 4 65, unheralded 67, foe liberty 75, worse than a peace 133

Warfare, compared with athletics 2 381, 387 5 303-

Wealth, Discourse on

502

mostly confined to "ancient" plays with lyrics omitted 241, **4** 427 and n. 2, not favoured by Dio **1** 283, scorned current events *ibid.*, recited by Nero **5** 171

Tragic Poets, seldom competed with plays on same theme **4** 341, not free from inconsistencies 343 f., Discourse on Aeschylus and Sophocles and Éuripides 336-353

Trainers (athletic), **5** 141 f.

Traitors, denied burial **3** 89 f.

Trajan, .addressed **1** 21, 31 and n. 1, 105, character described 105 f., devoted to reason **3** 231 and n. 4, plans to visit Alexandria 265, congratulated by Prusa **4** 121 and n. 2, munificent 121 f., made concessions to Prusa 209 f., benevolent toward Dio *ibid.*, greatness foretold by Asiatic god 211 and n. 2, authorized improvements at Prusa 259 and n. 1, 279 and n. 1, addressed by Dio 417, **5** 23, 25 n. 2, showed preference for Dio 365, 417, correspondence with Pliny regarding Dio 416-423, statue at Prusa 419 f., calls Dio Cocceianus 423

Triballians, Thracian tribe, once served by Macedonians **1** 55

Trierarch, commands trireme **4** 405

Tripod, of Pythian priestess **5** 187

Trireme, commanded by trierarch **4** 405

Troad, not controlled by Achaeans **1** 507, made subject to Mytilenê **4** 221

Troïlus, Trojan prince, slain in boyhood **1** 505, 507, 515, **2** 289

Trojan, Discourse **1** 445-565, mares impregnated by North Wind **2** 267

Trojans, contrasted with Achaeans by Homer **1** 85, routed by Achilles' voice 87, **3** 433, **4** 349, repulsed from Achaean camp **1** 517, looted Achaean camp 533, had no fleet *ibid.*, aided by Memnon and Amazons *ibid.*, connected with Atreidae by marriage and kinship with Pelops 539, licentious **3** 257, disheartened by Pandarus' perfidy 393, a Trojan builder **5** 169, suffered for Helen's sake 319

Trousers, worn by many barbarians **5** 179

Troy, capture **1** 261, 531, **3** 257, 291, **5** 67, activity of its rivers **1** 505, became more prosperous after the war 551, **2** 267, **3** 251, its initial advantages 291 f., walled by Poseidon and Apollo 293, its disasters known everywhere 295, throne offered to Philoctetes **4** 349, neighbouring

87 f., 145, relabelled 93, some unlabelled 95 f., Heracles' *ibid.*, seized by Nero 151, honorary variety not of clay 155, repeatedly re-used 157 f., fraud in dedication easily detected 159, Arion's 4 7, Solon's 9, Favorinus' 11, made by Daedalus 11 f., equestrian 13, Pythagoras' Perseus *ibid.*, tyrants' at Syracuse 21 f., sanctity 27, Gorgias *ibid.*, Phrynê 29, ruined by lapse of time 37, falsely labelled 39, statues of Demetrius of Phalerum destroyed *ibid.*, Philip's insulted *ibid.*, mistreated by Mummius 41, none of Agesilaüs *ibid.*, Euphranor's Hephaestus *ibid.*, of beaten gold 191, Roman statues of gods and generals resemble philosophers 5 181, Egyptian and Phoenician differ from Greek and Roman *ibid.*

Stays, worn by effeminate Phoenician 3 121

Stentor, Homeric hero, had throat of bronze 3 331

Stesichorus, native of Himera, punished by Helen 1 59, odes suitable for kings 67, imitated Homer 71, 4 385, his *Capture of Troy* creditable 1 71, his palinode 477, 5 319 n. 1

Stheneboea, type of lustful woman 5 223 and n. 1

Sthenelus, son of Capaneus,

boasted superiority over father 5 59 and n. 7

Stoics, define " city " 3 449, base virtue on reason 4 421 n. 2

Storks, migrate 1 267

Story-tellers, ply their vocation in Hippodrome 2 255

Straight-edge, compared with opinion 5 119 f.

Streamers, tell direction of wind 5 217

Stymphalus, district in Arcadia, birds of 4 249

Suidas, lexicographer, regarding Dio 5 416 f.

Suitors (of Penelopê), do not eat fish 1 81

Sun, function and behaviour 1 139 ff., relations with other heavenly bodies 4 143 f.

Sunium, cape of Attica 1 251

Supposititious Children, 3 157

Surgery, practice of 2 129, 4 315, 423

Surveyors, see more clearly with one eye 3 319, 5 147, may associate with courtesans or flute-girls 159, 171

Susa, capital of ancient Persia 1 189, 193, 215, 251, 2 13, taken by Alexander 331, golden plane-tree 4 429 n. 3, park 5 311 and n. 3

Swans, sing 2 7, 3 233, make music with wings 313

Swellings, reduced by pricking or squeezing 4 425

Sybaris, city of Magna

troops with Tyrtaeus' songs 431, object of Helot plots 455, foiled by Corinth in attempt to play tyrant 4 19, its king Agesilaüs 41, sought primacy 73, 83, one of three foremost Greek cities 195, Persian Porch 263, kings, ephors, and elders contrasted with commons 313, meagre living 5 57, kings 157

Spartans, sang Tyrtaeus' songs 1 69, 89, lost shields at Pylos 73, perhaps derived common mess from Homer 79, defeated at Leuctra 2 169, 295, forced to cede Messenia *ibid.*, consulted Apollo about Arcadia 201, defeated at Tegea *ibid.*, 247, appearance 287, advised by Apollo against fortification 295, owed hardships to Lycurgus 327, heroism at Thermopylae 3 23, 4 19, 5 297 and n. 2, 339, fallen on evil days 3 161, made war to accompaniment of pipe 231, cut away strings of harp 239, 327, contrasted with Alexandrians 241, valiant 261, had trouble with Aristomenes 393, foiled by coalition of Elis, Thebes, and Corinth 4 19, owed ancient prestige to civic morals 201, 315, 5 71, their reactions to pleasure and pain 129 f., once wore felt caps 179, lost

leadership to Themistocles 199 f., cautious 219, punished for murder of Persian heralds 257 and n. 1

Spear-polishers, 5 273

Sphinx, winged 1 241, endowed with speech *ibid.*, riddle 441, devoured Theban children 451, sent by Hera *ibid.*, invented by poets and artists 3 199

Spleen, diseases of 1 381

Sporus, favourite of Nero 2 279 and n. 1

Squill, used for purification 4 291

Stadium, noisy 4 135

Stageira, town near Olynthus, birthplace of Aristotle, rebuilt with permission of Philip 1 101, 4 255, uninhabited in Dio' day 257

Stags, come to close quarters when exhausted 2 385

Starlings, a plague to farmers 5 91

Stars, behave in orderly fashion 4 143

Statesman, influential through eloquence 2 213 f., proper training for 219 ff.

Statues, varieties and production 2 49, materials and cost of chryselephantine 55, abundant at Rhodes 3 13 f., 151, voted by Rhodes 15, Macedonian and Spartan molested 47, identified by inscription 53, 59, listed officially at Rhodes *ibid.*, desecrated

Graecia, destroyed **3** 297, indolent **5** 57

Symposia, reveal character **2** 349 f., leaders **4** 405, Discourse on **2** 347-355

Syncretism, in religion **3** 17

Synesius, Neoplatonist, preserved Dio's *Encomium on Hair* **5** 331-343, appraised Dio's literary qualities 364-387, would label Dio's compositions pre-exilic and post-exilic 375

Syracuse, freed from tyrants by Corinth **4** 21, colony of Corinth *ibid.*, broke up bronze statues when short of funds *ibid.*, rewarded Lucanian for speaking Doric 23 f., under command of Leptines and Philistus **5** 195

Syrians, luxurious **1** 81, literature of 181, king of 221, contrasted with Greeks **3** 167, in Alexandria 211, tyrant of 271, progressive **4** 257, fabrics of **5** 305, despoiled by Medes 311 and n. 2, confused with Assyrians *ibid.*

Syrtis, district in Africa, described **1** 239, 243

Taenarum, promontory of Peloponnese, landing place of Arion **4** 7, had image of Arion and dolphin *ibid.*

Taker-of-cities, title applied to Demetrius **5** 65 and n. 3

Talaüs, father of Adrastus **4** 403

Tantalus, related to Menelaüs **1** 77, punished 279, **4** 403, **5** 51 and n. 7

Tarentum, city in Magna Graecia, desolate **3** 297, prized Arion **4** 5

Tarsians, even Argives **3** 275, 311, addicted to " snorting " **3** 273, 301 ff., **5** 395 n. 1, called Cercopes **3** 309, of mixed origin 311, honour Heracles, Perseus, Apollo, and Athena 315, have pyre in honour of Heracles 317, have grievance against certain philosophers 339

Tarsic Discourses, **3** 273-333, 335-387

Tarsus, founded by heroes **3** 275 and n. 1, advantages 289, capital of Cilicia *ibid.*, founded by Heracles 317, women veiled and corrupt 319 f., episode of character expert from 323 f., befriended by Augustus 343 f., greatest city in Cilicia *ibid.*, captured by Cassius 345 and n. 2, quarrels with neighbours 347 f., 381, Elders 351 and n. 2, factional strife 355 f., Youth and Elders 357, linen-workers 357 f., cost of citizenship 359, respects most trades *ibid.*, relations with Emperor 361, office-holding 369 f., an example **4** 119, busied with construction 261 f.

Tattooing, practised in Thrace **2** 137 f.

Tavern-keepers, wear tunic belted high 5 177

Taxes, collection disreputable business 2 133, personal taxes unusual at Rhodes 3 51

Teachers, flog pupils 2 161, hold school in streets 255

Teeth, resist fire 1 183

Tegea, scene of Spartan defeat 2 201, strength of *ibid.*

Teiresias, Theban seer, misunderstood by Oedipus 1 439 f., advised Odysseus to roam 2 97

Telamon, father of Ajax, won with discus at Isthmian Games 4 15 f.

Telemachus, son of Odysseus, inhospitable 1 335, received gifts from Helen and Menelaüs 339, parentage 2 147, set up axes for trial of bow 4 397

Telephus, son of Augê and Heracles 2 153, reared by a woman, not a hind *ibid.*, received deer from Fortune 5 67 and n. 6

Tellus, Athenian, blessed in his children 5 49 f.

Tenedos, island near Troad, makes fragile pottery 4 171

Teos, in Asia Minor, celebrated for variegated marble 5 307

Tethys, mother of Tychê in Hesiod 5 33

Thamyris (Thamyras), punished by Muses for arrogance 2 107, 5 153

Thasos, Aegean island, famous for wine 1 259, 5 95, 113, neglected statue of Theagenes 3 101 f.

Theagenes, Thasian athlete, tale of 3 101 f.

Theatre, in Euboea 1 299, a public meeting-place *ibid.*, 4 113 f., statues 1 309, 3 127, scene of gladiatorial shows *ibid.*, the " ear " of a people 175, in Alexandria *ibid.*, 225 f., shouting in 4 135, place where honours are conferred 5 93 and n. 1

Thebans, pre-eminent in flute-playing 1 355, restored Hermes' statue because of laudatory inscription *ibid.*, cherish their myths 451, victorious at Leuctra 2 169, aided Messenians *ibid.*, fallen on evil days 3 161, did not aid Heracles 4 251, helped by Epaminondas 299, stupid 5 55 and n. 4, failed to overcome Alexander 65

Thebê, town in Mysia, plundered by Achilles 1 69

Thebes, boyhood home of Heracles 1 35, sacked by Alexander 71, founded by Amphion 453, 2 253, 3 233, had statue of Alcaeus 97, together with Elis and Corinth foiled Sparta 4 19, exalted by Epaminondas 177, under dictator 179, made head of Boeotia by Epaminondas 221, held

INDEX

Philip as hostage 299, flautist in **5** 277

Thebes in Egypt, **5** 57

Themis, a phase of Fortune **5** 51

Themistius, late sophist, testifies to Trajan's regard for Dio " of the golden tongue " **5** 363 f.

Themistocles, Athenian statesman, orator in the best sense **2** 293, guiding spirit of Athens 329, exiled *ibid.*, **5** 199, promoted interests of Athens *ibid.*

Theodorus, late rhetorician of Gadara, worth reading **2** 223 f.

Theognis, gnomic poet, quoted **1** 7, linked with Phocylides 53

Theophilus, unidentified person, visited Alexandria but refrained from speaking **3** 267

Theopompus, historian, second to Thucydides **2** 221, style analysed 221 f.

Theopompus, Spartan king, established ephorate **4** 407

Thermodon, river of Pontus, home of Amazon **1** 481

Thermopylae, battle of **1** 559, involved 400 Corinthians and 300 Spartans **4** 19, congress of **5** 265 and n. 1

Thersites, agitator in *Iliad* **1** 65 and n. 1, jester **3** 269, treated badly by Homer 283, warning to upstarts **5** 109

Theseus, abducted Helen **1** 479, **2** 389, **5** 13 n. 3, 139, defeated by Dioscuri **1** 479, mother captured *ibid.*, married Antiopê 481 and n. 2, comrade of Heracles and Peirithoüs 501, aided by Thessalians and Boeotians 501 f., beautiful and brave **2** 389, laboured for the sake of virtue **3** 21, statues 97, victor at Isthmian Games **4** 17, united Attica 221, reign **5** 13, son of Poseidon, caused death of Hippolytus 221 and n. 3, friendship with Peirithoüs proverbial 237, saved by Ariadnê 325 and n. 3

Thespiae, town in Boeotia, home of Phrynê **4** 29, had statue of Philip 41

Thessaly, famed for horses and cavalry **1** 161, 171, **2** 171, topography 251, its assembly 385, allied with Theseus 501, desolate **3** 297, noted for witchcraft **4** 253 f., 435 n. 2, **5** 105, visited by Nestor **4** 421, failed to overcome Alexander **5** 65, sensuous 131

Thetis, mother of Achilles, compared with Olympias **1** 61, warned Achilles in connexion with Patroclus 523, brought armour to Achilles 527, entreated Zeus **2** 67, mother of Achilles **4** 423, " silver-footed " **5** 343

INDEX

Thief, term deserved by one who refrains from thieving through fear 5 147

Thirty (The), 2 275, defied by Socrates 4 183

Thrace, home of Orpheus 1 31, subject to Persia 121, practised tattooing 2 137, 157, 3 317

Thracians, employed by Alexander 1 171, despised 3 161, fought Macedonians 299, subjugated by Heracles 4 249, ruled by Philip 297, failed to overcome Alexander 5 65, include Getae 179

Thrasylus, admired by Tiberius 5 365

Thrasymachus, sophist, used as type by Socrates 4 389

Thucydides, Athenian historian, denied existence of Scirite company 1 557, first among historians 2 221, recorded his own name in connexion with account of each winter and summer 4 365 f., funeral oration of Pericles 5 373

Thucydides, Athenian politician, opposed Pericles 2 293

Thunderbolt, title applied to son of Ptolemy Soter and also to Seleucus III 5 65 and n. 3

Thurii, Athenian colony in Magna Graecia, desolate 3 297

Thyestes, sorrows of 1 355, defiled wife of Atreus 451, 2 149, ate his own children 1 451, 5 95, 221 and n. 1, disloyal to Atreus 1 485, committed incest with Pelopia 5 95

Tiberius, Roman Emperor 4 271 and n. 1, admired Thrasylus 5 365

Timandra, Corinthian hetaera, mistress of Alcibiades 5 47 and n. 7

Timarchus, father of Charidemus 2 401

Timotheüs, Athenian general, affronted Fortune 5 63 and n. 1

Timotheüs, flute - player, played for Alexander 1 3 f., 3 231, mistreated at Sparta 327

Tissaphernes, Persian satrap, treacherous toward Clearchus 5 223

Titans, progenitors of mankind 2 409, fought the gods *ibid.*, not progenitors of mankind 421, founded Tarsus 3 275

Tithonus, brother of Priam and father of Memnon 1 483

Tlepolemus, son of Heracles, statue 3 97

Toil, more blessed than ease 1 143, 159

Tomyris, nomad queen, slew Cyrus 5 45 and n. 5

Traders, 5 141, 155 f.

Tradesmen, punished for false measures 3 41

Tragedy, typical heroes 2 107, supposititious children 151, in Dio's day

INDEX

311, men of wealth desire attention of philosophers 293

Weather, unsettled at solstice 1 203

Weddings, suitable days for 1 325, preliminaries of 331

Wet-nurses, derided 1 351

Wind, direction indicated by streamers 5 217

Wind-eggs, not impregnated by male seed 2 267

Wine, from Thasos 5 95, 113, 115, used in pursuit of popularity 97

Wise Man, Discourse on 2 301-315

Witches, Thessalian 4 253 f., 435 and n. 2, 5 105

Women, compared with men 1 137 f., of low repute 3 203, fight at close quarters 4 433, delight to hear other women disparaged 5 15, limited in business dealings 217 f.

Wooden Horse, brought within Ilium 1 541

Words, invented by Homer 2 71

Wrestlers, toy with weaker opponents 2 231, used in pursuit of popularity 5 97

Wrestling, practised by Nero 5 171

Writers, attend Olympic Games 2 9

Xanthus, divine name for Scamander 1 435, 463, 3 293

Xenophon, Athenian writer, quoted 1 115, exiled because of campaign with Cyrus 377, 5 61, satisfies needs of men in public life 2 225 ff., moved Dio to tears 227, has simple and artless style 5 365

Xerxes, dug canal across Athos 1 119, bridged Hellespont *ibid.*, had motley army 189, exploits in Greece 559 f., led hosts of Asia against Greece 2 111, obeyed ship captain 129, ruined through greed 199 f., his army not brilliant 3 257, 5 377

Zaleucus, Locrian lawgiver 5 317 and n. 2

Zeno, founder of Stoic school, inconsistent with professions 4 249 f., wrote on Homeric poems 359, considered *Margites* a youthful work of Homer 359 f., explained Homer's inconsistencies 361, teacher of Persaeus *ibid.*, attacked by Dio with coarse jests 5 375

Zetes, son of Boreas, athletic 1 391

Zethus, son of Antiopê and Zeus, exposed 2 153 and n. 1, 155, criticized brother for devotion to music 5 205 and n. 1

Zeus, fosters good kings, humbles bad 1 9, 25, 99 f., 187, ideal king 21, 99, 177, 4 367 f., relations with Minos 1 21, 187, titles 21,

INDEX

2 45, 77 ff., 4 103, father of
Heracles 31, 245, father of
men and gods 99, 177 f.,
punished Prometheus 263,
god of family life 365,
relations with Hera 459 f.,
3 471, 4 31, partial toward
Ilium 1 509, 3 293, de-
stroyed Ilium *ibid.*, reputed father of Sarpedon
1 517, responsible for
Hector's ransom 525, mutilated Cronus 559, had
altar at Troy 563, statue
at Olympia 2 15 and n. 3,
27 f., 55 f., protected by
mist 39, attributes 77 ff.,
appointed Paris judge of
beauty contest 265, praised
421, statue at Rhodes 3
117, turned animals into
men at request of Calliopê
235, made Ganymede cup-
bearer 293 f., wisest and
eldest lawgiver 451, his
chariot hymned by Zoro-
aster and Magi 457, had
Nisaean horses 457 f.,
his heavenly horse 461,
credited with statues of
Poseidon and Philip 4 41,
his temple at Olympia 419
n. 1, compared with Aga
memnon 5 9, his weapon
53 and n. 2, maligned by
Alexander 63 and n. 7, his
storage jars 69, statues at
Rome wear only cloak 181,
laws inviolable 321, hair
praised by Homer 343

Zeuxis, famous painter 2 51

Zopyrus, son of Megabyzus,
conquered Babylon 5 67
and n. 2

Zoroaster, founder of Persian
religion, had miraculous
career 3 457, sang of Zeus'
chariot *ibid.*

Printed by CLARK CONSTABLE, *Edinburgh, London, Melbourne*

THE LOEB CLASSICAL LIBRARY

VOLUMES ALREADY PUBLISHED

LATIN AUTHORS

AMMIANUS MARCELLINUS. J. C. Rolfe. 3 Vols.

APULEIUS: THE GOLDEN ASS (METAMORPHOSES). W. Adlington (1566). Revised by S. Gaselee.

ST. AUGUSTINE: CITY OF GOD. 7 Vols. Vol. I. G. E. McCracken. Vol. II. W. M. Green. Vol. III. D. Wiesen. Vol. IV. P. Levine. Vol. V. E. M. Sanford and W. M. Green. Vol. VI. W. C. Greene. Vol. VII. W. M. Green.

ST. AUGUSTINE, CONFESSIONS OF. W. Watts (1631). 2 Vols.

ST. AUGUSTINE: SELECT LETTERS. J. H. Baxter.

AUSONIUS. H. G. Evelyn White. 2 Vols.

BEDE. J. E. King. 2 Vols.

BOETHIUS: TRACTS AND DE CONSOLATIONE PHILOSOPHIAE. Rev. H. F. Stewart and E. K. Rand. Revised by S. J. Tester.

CAESAR: ALEXANDRIAN, AFRICAN AND SPANISH WARS. A. G. Way.

CAESAR: CIVIL WARS. A. G. Peskett.

CAESAR: GALLIC WAR. H. J. Edwards.

CATO AND VARRO: DE RE RUSTICA. H. B. Ash and W. D. Hooper.

CATULLUS. F. W. Cornish; TIBULLUS. J. B. Postgate; and PERVIGILIUM VENERIS. J. W. Mackail.

CELSUS: DE MEDICINA. W. G. Spencer. 3 Vols.

CICERO: BRUTUS AND ORATOR. G. L. Hendrickson and H. M. Hubbell.

CICERO: DE FINIBUS. H. Rackham.

CICERO: DE INVENTIONE, etc. H. M. Hubbell.

CICERO: DE NATURA DEORUM AND ACADEMICA. H. Rackham.

CICERO: DE OFFICIIS. Walter Miller.

CICERO: DE ORATORE, etc. 2 Vols. Vol. I: DE ORATORE, Books I and II. E. W. Sutton and H. Rackham. Vol. II: DE ORATORE, Book III; DE FATO; PARADOXA STOICORUM; DE PARTITIONE ORATORIA. H. Rackham.

CICERO: DE REPUBLICA, DE LEGIBUS. Clinton W. Keyes.

CICERO: DE SENECTUTE, DE AMICITIA, DE DIVINATIONE. W. A. Falconer.

1

THE LOEB CLASSICAL LIBRARY

CICERO: IN CATILINAM, PRO MURENA, PRO SULLA, PRO FLACCO. New version by C. Macdonald.

CICERO: LETTERS TO ATTICUS. E. O. Winstedt. 3 Vols.

CICERO: LETTERS TO HIS FRIENDS. W. Glynn Williams, M. Cary, M. Henderson. 4 Vols.

CICERO: PHILIPPICS. W. C. A. Ker.

CICERO: PRO ARCHIA, POST REDITUM, DE DOMO, DE HARUSPICUM RESPONSIS, PRO PLANCIO. N. H. Watts.

CICERO: PRO CAECINA, PRO LEGE MANILIA, PRO CLUENTIO, PRO RABIRIO. H. Grose Hodge.

CICERO: PRO CAELIO, DE PROVINCIIS CONSULARIBUS, PRO BALBO. R. Gardner.

CICERO: PRO MILONE, IN PISONEM, PRO SCAURO, PRO FONTEIO, PRO RABIRIO POSTUMO, PRO MARCELLO, PRO LIGARIO, PRO REGE DEIOTARO. N. H. Watts.

CICERO: PRO QUINCTIO, PRO ROSCIO AMERINO, PRO ROSCIO COMOEDO, CONTRA RULLUM. J. H. Freese.

CICERO: PRO SESTIO, IN VATINIUM. R. Gardner.

[CICERO]: RHETORICA AD HERENNIUM. H. Caplan.

CICERO: TUSCULAN DISPUTATIONS. J. E. King.

CICERO: VERRINE ORATIONS. L. H. G. Greenwood. 2 Vols.

CLAUDIAN. M. Platnauer. 2 Vols.

COLUMELLA: DE RE RUSTICA, DE ARBORIBUS. H. B. Ash, E. S. Forster, E. Heffner. 3 Vols.

CURTIUS, Q.: HISTORY OF ALEXANDER. J. C. Rolfe. 2 Vols.

FLORUS. E. S. Forster.

FRONTINUS: STRATAGEMS AND AQUEDUCTS. C. E. Bennett and M. B. McElwain.

FRONTO: CORRESPONDENCE. C. R. Haines. 2 Vols.

GELLIUS. J. C. Rolfe. 3 Vols.

HORACE: ODES AND EPODES. C. E. Bennett.

HORACE: SATIRES, EPISTLES, ARS POETICA. H. R. Fairclough.

JEROME: SELECT LETTERS. F. A. Wright.

JUVENAL AND PERSIUS. G. G. Ramsay.

LIVY. B. O. Foster, F. G. Moore, Evan T. Sage, A. C. Schlesinger and R. M. Geer (General Index). 14 Vols.

LUCAN. J. D. Duff.

LUCRETIUS. W. H. D. Rouse. Revised by M. F. Smith.

MANILIUS. G. P. Goold.

MARTIAL. W. C. A. Ker. 2 Vols. Revised by E. H. Warmington.

MINOR LATIN POETS: from PUBLILIUS SYRUS to RUTILIUS NAMATIANUS, including GRATTIUS, CALPURNIUS, SICULUS NEMESIANUS, AVIANUS, with "Aetna," "Phoenix" and other poems. J. Wight Duff and Arnold M. Duff. 2 Vols.

THE LOEB CLASSICAL LIBRARY

NEPOS CORNELIUS. J. C. Rolfe.

OVID: THE ART OF LOVE AND OTHER POEMS. J. H. Mozley. Revised by G. P. Goold.

OVID: FASTI. Sir James G. Frazer.

OVID: HEROIDES AND AMORES. Grant Showerman. Revised by G. P. Goold.

OVID: METAMORPHOSES. F. J. Miller. 2 Vols. Revised by G. P. Goold.

OVID: TRISTIA AND EX PONTO. A. L. Wheeler.

PETRONIUS. M. Heseltine; SENECA: APOCOLOCYNTOSIS. W. H. D. Rouse. Revised by E. H. Warmington.

PHAEDRUS AND BABRIUS (Greek). B. E. Perry.

PLAUTUS. Paul Nixon. 5 Vols.

PLINY: LETTERS, PANEGYRICUS. B. Radice. 2 Vols.

PLINY: NATURAL HISTORY. 10 Vols. Vols. I-V. H. Rackham. Vols. VI-VIII. W. H. S. Jones. Vol. IX. H. Rackham. Vol. X. D. E. Eichholz.

PROPERTIUS. H. E. Butler.

PRUDENTIUS. H. J. Thomson. 2 Vols.

QUINTILIAN. H. E. Butler. 4 Vols.

REMAINS OF OLD LATIN. E. H. Warmington. 4 Vols. Vol. I (Ennius and Caecilius). Vol. II (Livius, Naevius, Pacuvius, Accius). Vol. III (Lucilius, Laws of the XII Tables). Vol. IV (Archaic Inscriptions).

SALLUST. J. C. Rolfe.

SCRIPTORES HISTORIAE AUGUSTAE. D. Magie. 3 Vols.

SENECA: APOCOLOCYNTOSIS. Cf. PETRONIUS.

SENECA: EPISTULAE MORALES. R. M. Gummere. 3 Vols.

SENECA: MORAL ESSAYS. J. W. Basore. 3 Vols.

SENECA: NATURALES QUAESTIONES. T. H. Corcoran. 2 Vols.

SENECA: TRAGEDIES. F. J. Miller. 2 Vols.

SENECA THE ELDER: CONTROVERSIAE SUASORIAE. M. Winterbottom. 2 Vols.

SIDONIUS: POEMS AND LETTERS. W. B. Anderson. 2 Vols.

SILIUS ITALICUS. J. D. Duff. 2 Vols.

STATIUS. J. H. Mozley. 2 Vols.

SUETONIUS. J. C. Rolfe. 2 Vols.

TACITUS: AGRICOLA AND GERMANIA. M. Hutton; DIALOGUS, Sir Wm. Peterson. Revised by R. M. Ogilvie, E. H. Warmington, M. Winterbottom.

TACITUS: HISTORIES AND ANNALS. C. H. Moore and J. Jackson. 4 Vols.

TERENCE. John Sargeaunt. 2 Vols.

TERTULLIAN: APOLOGIA AND DE SPECTACULIS. T. R. Glover; MINUCIUS FELIX. G. H. Rendall.

THE LOEB CLASSICAL LIBRARY

VALERIUS FLACCUS. J. H. Mozley.
VARRO: DE LINGUA LATINA. R. G. Kent. 2 Vols.
VELLEIUS PATERCULUS AND RES GESTAE DIVI AUGUSTI.
F. W. Shipley.
VIRGIL. H. R. Fairclough. 2 Vols.
VITRUVIUS: DE ARCHITECTURA. F. Granger. 2 Vols.

GREEK AUTHORS

ACHILLES TATIUS. S. Gaselee.
AELIAN: ON THE NATURE OF ANIMALS. A. F. Scholfield.
3 Vols.
AENEAS TACTICUS, ASCLEPIODOTUS AND ONASANDER. The
Illinois Greek Club.
AESCHINES. C. D. Adams.
AESCHYLUS. H. Weir Smyth. 2 Vols.
ALICIPHRON, AELIAN AND PHILOSTRATUS: LETTERS. A. R.
Benner and F. H. Fobes.
APOLLODORUS. Sir James G. Frazer. 2 Vols.
APOLLONIUS RHODIUS. R. C. Seaton.
THE APOSTOLIC FATHERS. Kirsopp Lake. 2 Vols.
APPIAN'S ROMAN HISTORY. Horace White. 4 Vols.
ARATUS. *Cf.* CALLIMACHUS: HYMNS AND EPIGRAMS.
ARISTIDES. C. A. Behr. 4 Vols. Vol. I.
ARISTOPHANES. Benjamin Bickley Rogers. 3 Vols. Verse trans.
ARISTOTLE: ART OF RHETORIC. J. H. Freese.
ARISTOTLE: ATHENIAN CONSTITUTION, EUDEMIAN ETHICS,
VIRTUES AND VICES. H. Rackham.
ARISTOTLE: THE CATEGORIES. ON INTERPRETATION. H. P.
Cooke; PRIOR ANALYTICS. H. Tredennick.
ARISTOTLE: GENERATION OF ANIMALS. A. L. Peck.
ARISTOTLE: HISTORIA ANIMALIUM. A. L. Peck. 3 Vols.
Vols. I and II.
ARISTOTLE: METAPHYSICS. H. Tredennick. 2 Vols.
ARISTOTLE: METEOROLOGICA. H. D. P. Lee.
ARISTOTLE: MINOR WORKS. W. S. Hett. " On Colours,"
" On Things Heard," " Physiognomics," " On Plants,"
" On Marvellous Things Heard," " Mechanical Prob-
lems," " On Invisible Lines," " Situations and Names of
Winds," " On Melissus, Xenophanes, and Gorgias."
ARISTOTLE: NICOMACHEAN ETHICS. H. Rackham.
ARISTOTLE: OECONOMICA AND MAGNA MORALIA. G. C.
Armstrong. (With METAPHYSICS, Vol. II.)

4

THE LOEB CLASSICAL LIBRARY

ARISTOTLE: ON THE HEAVENS. W. K. C. Guthrie.

ARISTOTLE: ON THE SOUL, PARVA NATURALIA, ON BREATH. W. S. Hett.

ARISTOTLE: PARTS OF ANIMALS. A. L. Peck; MOVEMENT AND PROGRESSION OF ANIMALS. E. S. Forster.

ARISTOTLE: PHYSICS. Rev. P. Wicksteed and F. M. Cornford. 2 Vols.

ARISTOTLE: POETICS; LONGINUS ON THE SUBLIME. W. Hamilton Fyfe; DEMETRIUS ON STYLE. W. Rhys Roberts.

ARISTOTLE: POLITICS. H. Rackham.

ARISTOTLE: POSTERIOR ANALYTICS. H. Tredennick; TOPICS. E. S. Forster.

ARISTOTLE: PROBLEMS. W. S. Hett. 2 Vols.

ARISTOTLE: RHETORICA AD ALEXANDRUM. H. Rackham. (With PROBLEMS, Vol. II.)

ARISTOTLE: SOPHISTICAL REFUTATIONS. COMING-TO-BE AND PASSING-AWAY. E. S. Forster; ON THE COSMOS. D. J. Furley.

ARRIAN: HISTORY OF ALEXANDER AND INDICA. 2 Vols. New version. P. Brunt.

ATHENAEUS: DEIPNOSOPHISTAE. C. B. Gulick. 7 Vols.

BABRIUS AND PHAEDRUS (Latin). B. E. Perry.

ST. BASIL: LETTERS. R. J. Deferrari. 4 Vols.

CALLIMACHUS: FRAGMENTS. C. A. Trypanis; MUSAEUS: HERO AND LEANDER. T. Gelzer and C. Whitman.

CALLIMACHUS: HYMNS AND EPIGRAMS, AND LYCOPHRON. A. W. Mair; ARATUS. G. R. Mair.

CLEMENT OF ALEXANDRIA. Rev. G. W. Butterworth.

COLLUTHUS. *Cf.* OPPIAN.

DAPHNIS AND CHLOE. *Cf.* LONGUS.

DEMOSTHENES I: OLYNTHIACS, PHILIPPICS AND MINOR ORATIONS: I-XVII AND XX. J. H. Vince.

DEMOSTHENES II: DE CORONA AND DE FALSA LEGATIONE. C. A. Vince and J. H. Vince.

DEMOSTHENES III: MEIDIAS, ANDROTION, ARISTOCRATES, TIMOCRATES, ARISTOGEITON. J. H. Vince.

DEMOSTHENES IV-VI: PRIVATE ORATIONS AND IN NEAERAM. A. T. Murray.

DEMOSTHENES VII: FUNERAL SPEECH, EROTIC ESSAY, EXORDIA AND LETTERS. N. W. and N. J. DeWitt.

DIO CASSIUS: ROMAN HISTORY. E. Cary. 9 Vols.

DIO CHRYSOSTOM. 5 Vols. Vols. I and II. J. W. Cohoon. Vol. III. J. W. Cohoon and H. Lamar Crosby. Vols. IV and V. H. Lamar Crosby.

THE LOEB CLASSICAL LIBRARY

DIODORUS SICULUS. 12 Vols. Vols. I–VI. C. H. Oldfather. Vol. VII. C. L. Sherman. Vol. VIII. C. B. Welles. Vols. IX and X. Russel M. Geer. Vols. XI and XII. F. R. Walton. General Index. Russel M. Geer.

DIOGENES LAERTIUS. R. D. Hicks. 2 Vols. New Introduction by H. S. Long.

DIONYSIUS OF HALICARNASSUS: CRITICAL ESSAYS. S. Usher. 2 Vols.

DIONYSIUS OF HALICARNASSUS: ROMAN ANTIQUITIES. Spelman's translation revised by E. Cary. 7 Vols.

EPICTETUS. W. A. Oldfather. 2 Vols.

EURIPIDES. A. S. Way. 4 Vols. Verse trans.

EUSEBIUS: ECCLESIASTICAL HISTORY. Kirsopp Lake and J. E. L. Oulton. 2 Vols.

GALEN: ON THE NATURAL FACULTIES. A. J. Brock.

THE GREEK ANTHOLOGY. W. R. Paton. 5 Vols.

THE GREEK BUCOLIC POETS (THEOCRITUS, BION, MOSCHUS). J. M. Edmonds.

GREEK ELEGY AND IAMBUS WITH THE ANACREONTEA. J. M. Edmonds. 2 Vols.

GREEK LYRIC. D. A. Campbell. 4 Vols. Vol. I.

GREEK MATHEMATICAL WORKS. Ivor Thomas. 2 Vols.

HERODES. Cf. THEOPHRASTUS: CHARACTERS.

HERODIAN. C. R. Whittaker. 2 Vols.

HERODOTUS. A. D. Godley. 4 Vols.

HESIOD AND THE HOMERIC HYMNS. H. G. Evelyn White.

HIPPOCRATES AND THE FRAGMENTS OF HERACLEITUS. W. H. S. Jones and E. T. Withington. 4 Vols.

HOMER: ILIAD. A. T. Murray. 2 Vols.

HOMER: ODYSSEY. A. T. Murray. 2 Vols.

ISAEUS. E. S. Forster.

ISOCRATES. George Norlin and LaRue Van Hook. 3 Vols.

[ST. JOHN DAMASCENE]: BARLAAM AND IOASAPH. Rev. G. R. Woodward, Harold Mattingly and D. M. Lang.

JOSEPHUS. 10 Vols. Vols. I–IV. H. St. J. Thackeray. Vol. V. H. St. J. Thackeray and Ralph Marcus. Vols. VI and VII. Ralph Marcus. Vol. VIII. Ralph Marcus and Allen Wikgren. Vols. IX–X. L. H. Feldman.

JULIAN. Wilmer Cave Wright. 3 Vols.

LIBANIUS: SELECTED WORKS. A. F. Norman. 3 Vols. Vols. I and II.

LONGUS: DAPHNIS AND CHLOE. Thornley's translation revised by J. M. Edmonds; and PARTHENIUS. S. Gaselee.

LUCIAN. 8 Vols. Vols. I–V. A. M. Harmon. Vol. VI. K. Kilburn. Vols. VII and VIII. M. D. Macleod.

THE LOEB CLASSICAL LIBRARY

Lycophron. *Cf.* Callimachus: Hymns and Epigrams.

Lyra Graeca. J. M. Edmonds. 2 Vols.

Lysias. W. R. M. Lamb.

Manetho. W. G. Waddell.

Marcus Aurelius. C. R. Haines.

Menander. New edition by W. G. Arnott.

Minor Attic Orators. 2 Vols. K. J. Maidment and J. O. Burtt.

Musaeus: Hero and Leander. *Cf.* Callimachus: Fragments.

Nonnos: Dionysiaca. W. H. D. Rouse. 3 Vols.

Oppian, Colluthus, Tryphiodorus. A. W. Mair.

Papyri. Non-Literary Selections. A. S. Hunt and C. C. Edgar. 2 Vols. Literary Selections (Poetry). D. L. Page.

Parthenius. *Cf.* Longus.

Pausanias: Description of Greece. W. H. S. Jones. 4 Vols. and Companion Vol. arranged by R. E. Wycherley.

Philo. 10 Vols. Vols. I.-V. F. H. Colson and Rev. G. H. Whitaker. Vols. VI-X. F. H. Colson. General Index. Rev. J. W. Earp.

Two Supplementary Vols. Translation only from an Armenian Text. Ralph Marcus.

Philostratus: The Life of Apollonius of Tyana. F. C. Conybeare. 2 Vols.

Philostratus: Imagines; Callistratus: Descriptions. A. Fairbanks.

Philostratus and Eunapius: Lives of the Sophists. Wilmer Cave Wright.

Pindar: Sir J. E. Sandys.

Plato: Charmides, Alcibiades, Hipparchus, The Lovers, Theages, Minos and Epinomis. W. R. M. Lamb.

Plato: Cratylus, Parmenides, Greater Hippias, Lesser Hippias. H. N. Fowler.

Plato: Euthyphro, Apology, Crito, Phaedo, Phaedrus. H. N. Fowler.

Plato: Laches, Protagoras, Meno, Euthydemus. W. R. M. Lamb.

Plato: Laws. Rev. R. G. Bury. 2 Vols.

Plato: Lysis, Symposium, Gorgias. W. R. M. Lamb.

Plato: Republic. Paul Shorey. 2 Vols.

Plato: Statesman, Philebus. H. N. Fowler; Ion. W. R. M. Lamb.

Plato: Theaetetus and Sophist. H. N. Fowler.

Plato: Timaeus, Critias, Clitopho, Menexenus, Epistulae. Rev. R. G. Bury.

THE LOEB CLASSICAL LIBRARY

Plotinus. A. H. Armstrong. 7 Vols. Vols. I-V.

Plutarch: Moralia. 16 Vols. Vols. I-V. F. C. Babbitt. Vol. VI. W. C. Helmbold. Vol. VII. P. H. De Lacy and B. Einarson. Vol. VIII. P. A. Clement, H. B. Hoffleit. Vol. IX. E. L. Minar, Jr., F. H. Sandbach, W. C. Helmbold. Vol. X. H. N. Fowler. Vol. XI. L. Pearson, F. H. Sandbach. Vol. XII. H. Cherniss, W. C. Helmbold. Vol. XIII, Parts 1 and 2. H. Cherniss. Vol. XIV. P. H. De Lacy and B. Einarson. Vol. XV. F. H. Sandbach.

Plutarch: The Parallel Lives. B. Perrin. 11 Vols.

Polybius. W. R. Paton. 6 Vols.

Procopius: History of the Wars. H. B. Dewing. 7 Vols.

Ptolemy: Tetrabiblos. F. E. Robbins.

Quintus Smyrnaeus. A. S. Way. Verse trans.

Sextus Empiricus. Rev. R. G. Bury. 4 Vols.

Sophocles. F. Storr. 2 Vols. Verse trans.

Strabo: Geography. Horace L. Jones. 8 Vols.

Theophrastus: Characters. J. M. Edmonds; Herodes, etc. A. D. Knox.

Theophrastus: De Causis Plantarum. G. K. K. Link and B. Einarson. 3 Vols. Vol. I.

Theophrastus: Enquiry into Plants. Sir Arthur Hort. 2 Vols.

Thucydides. C. F. Smith. 4 Vols.

Tryphiodorus. Cf. Oppian.

Xenophon: Anabasis. C. L. Brownson.

Xenophon: Cyropaedia. Walter Miller. 2 Vols.

Xenophon: Hellenica. C. L. Brownson.

Xenophon: Memorabilia and Oeconomicus. E. C. Marchant; Symposium and Apology. O. J. Todd.

Xenophon: Scripta Minora. E. C. Marchant and G. W. Bowersock.

DESCRIPTIVE PROSPECTUS ON APPLICATION

CAMBRIDGE, MASS.   LONDON

HARVARD UNIV. PRESS   WILLIAM HEINEMANN LTD.

HOW TO
WRITE A LETTER

HOW TO WRITE A LETTER

BY PATRICIA DRAGISIC

A SPEAK OUT, WRITE ON! BOOK
Franklin Watts
A Division of Grolier Publishing
New York / London / Hong Kong / Sydney
Danbury, Connecticut

For permissions for quoted materials see page 122.

Library of Congress Cataloging-in-Publication Data

Dragisic, Patricia.
How to write a letter / by Patricia Dragisic.
p. cm.—(A Speak out, write on! book)
Includes bibliographical references and index.
Summary: Describes the basic parts of many types of business
and personal letters, offers examples of each kind, and suggests ways to
write effectively for particular situations.
ISBN 0-531-11391-4 (lib. bgd.)   0-531-15931-0 (pbk.)
1. Letter writing—Juvenile literature. [1. Letter writing.]
I. Title. II. Series.
PE 1483.D73 1998
808.6—dc21   97-35265
                                                   CIP
                                                   AC

To George Kruto, Gail Papke, and
Linda J. Stepanich, for their encouragement and
support, and to "all my children" (nieces and
nephews, biological and honorary): Jason Brown,
Kelly Brown, Nick Joseph Dragisic,
Michelle Dubrovin, Dr. Craig Iwamoto,
Eric Iwamoto, Neal Iwamoto, Kenneth Kucinski,
Lauren Kucinski, Alexandria Ollman,
Kathryn Ollman, Haley R. Retterer, Scott Retterer

CONTENTS

Introduction
11

Chapter One
What Goes in Your Letter?
15

Chapter Two
Personal Letters: "Dear World"
31

Chapter Three
Business Letters—Getting a Foot in the Door
46

Chapter Four
More Business Letters—Getting the Job Done
58

Chapter Five
Electronic Mail
71

Chapter Six
Write It Right: Grammar and Word Usage
83

Chapter Seven
Sources To Use at the Library
91

Chapter Eight
Famous Writers, Famous Letters
98

Appendix
Titles and Salutations: A Quick Reference
114

For More Information
119

Acknowledgments
122

Index
123

HOW TO
WRITE A LETTER

INTRODUCTION

Letter writing is a basic part of life. Being able to write a good letter is a very useful skill, no matter what your age. True, many people don't write to friends anymore—it's so easy just to pick up the telephone and call your friends. But many times, letter writing is important. When you want to look for a job, for example, often the first step is writing a letter to send with your résumé. Also, many good office jobs require that you know how to write letters as part of your work.

If you plan to go to college, you will write a number of letters to various schools to request catalogs, application materials, information, and appointments. As part of the application process, you may need to write to teachers, coaches, employers, and others to request references.

Many finance problems can only be straightened out by letter, not by phone, according to federal law. Even a routine problem such as returning an item and confirming that you've received credit for it requires a letter.

You may keep in touch with your own friends by phone, but you may also have a parent, grandparent, or friend who cannot afford to phone friends around the country (or around the world) very often. If you are asked to write a letter, can you do it and do a good job? Adults may need to write a letter of reference for a friend seeking a job, or for a relative trying to enter the United States. They may turn to you as the one who has a computer at home or at school, or they may turn to you as the one with better writing skills. Can you help them with the important letter they need to write?

One kind of letter that will never go out of style is the love letter. You may be saying to yourself, "I'm not going to use a book to help me write a love letter!" Of course, your personal dreams, feelings, and emotions are just that—very personal. But if you want to put pen to paper to tell that special person just how you feel, you'll be happy that you have put some time into using this book to help you organize your thoughts on paper.

But *is* letter writing going out of style? Some say, "It's the computer age! I send e-mail, not some old-fashioned letter." This book will give you valuable hints on communicating better via electronic messages. Business writers have noticed that e-mail messages are usually shorter and more informal than a letter written on a typewriter or computer. We must learn a whole new set of skills for writing and organizing effective e-mail, and this book teaches those skills.

When you send a letter to anyone, the letter is your personal representative. When you're writing to someone you don't know, as usually happens when you apply for a job, your letter is the only thing the recipient has by which to form an opinion about you—so you'll want to make a good impression, no matter why you're writing. You may be smart and hard-working *and* have great training for a job. If your letter or friend who cannot afford to phone friends around the country (or around the world) very often. If you are asked to write a letter, can you do it and do a good job? Adults may need to write a letter of reference for a friend seeking a job, or for a relative trying to enter the United States. They may turn to you as the one who has a computer at home or at school, or they may turn to you as the one with better writing skills. Can you help them with the important letter they need to write?

One kind of letter that will never go out of style is the love letter. You may be saying to yourself, "I'm not going to use a book to help me write a love letter!" Of course, your personal dreams, feelings, and emotions are just that—very personal. But if you want to put pen to paper to tell that special person just how you feel, you'll be happy that you have put some time into using this book to help you organize your thoughts on paper.

But *is* letter writing going out of style? Some say, "It's the computer age! I send e-mail, not some old-fashioned letter." This book will give you valuable hints on communicating better via electronic messages. Business writers have noticed that e-mail messages are usually shorter and more informal than a letter written on a typewriter or computer. We must learn a whole new set of skills for writing and organizing effective e-mail, and this book teaches those skills.

When you send a letter to anyone, the letter is your personal representative. When you're writing to someone you don't know, as usually happens when you apply for a job, your letter is the only thing the recipient has by which to form an opinion about you—so you'll want to make a good impression, no matter why you're writing. You may be smart and hard-working *and* have great training for a job. If your letter

$\mathcal{I}$NTRODUCTION

Letter writing is a basic part of life. Being able to write a good letter is a very useful skill, no matter what your age. True, many people don't write to friends anymore—it's so easy just to pick up the telephone and call your friends. But many times, letter writing is important. When you want to look for a job, for example, often the first step is writing a letter to send with your résumé. Also, many good office jobs require that you know how to write letters as part of your work.

If you plan to go to college, you will write a number of letters to various schools to request catalogs, application materials, information, and appointments. As part of the application process, you may need to write to teachers, coaches, employers, and others to request references.

Many finance problems can only be straightened out by letter, not by phone, according to federal law. Even a routine problem such as returning an item and confirming that you've received credit for it requires a letter.

You may keep in touch with your own friends by phone, but you may also have a parent, grandparent,

ONE

WHAT GOES IN YOUR LETTER?

Generations of journalism students have learned to ask and answer a series of questions to write a newspaper article. Writers and reporters do not ask the questions just because "it's always been done that way," but because answering the queries helps them do a good job communicating with their readers. These same questions should be in your mind as you write a letter:

- Who?
- What?
- When?
- Where?
- Why?
- How?
- How much?

Not every question applies to every situation. And it is important to note that you don't need to answer them in any particular order. But if you ask yourself those questions first, and answer them for the reader, chances are good that you have touched on the basic information that people need to know. Look at how confusing it is when a letter writer omits the answer to one of these questions:

Dear All-America Soccer Coaches:

Please come to a meeting of all coaches on Wednesday, January 7, at 7 p.m. We need to plan the championship series for this fall. Coach Esteban Suarez has proposed that we cut down on the number of elimination rounds, to help shorten the season and save money for all the schools.

If you cannot attend, please call Spring Taylor at 555-1234 and let her know. Also, if you will not be at the meeting, please tell Spring whether you are in favor of reducing the number of elimination rounds. Thank you!

Sincerely,
Macho T. Mann

This letter certainly covers anyone's questions about who, what, when, why, and how. But *where* is the meeting?

To help save time for everyone, put all the facts in your letter. In this example, all sixteen coaches in the All-America league may have to call just to find out where the meeting is. Worse yet, many of the coaches may toss the letter aside, intending to call about the place but just not get around to finding out. There goes the meeting and the chance to organize next year's soccer season.

In answering basic questions in your letter, use simple, direct language whenever possible. A letter is not a vocabulary test or a chance to show off those new ten-dollar words you learned last week. Some people think that they need to sound formal or use technical words to convey a message. The best letter—that is, the one that gets results—is easy to read and well written. To review tips that may help you with your letter, see Chapter Six, "Write It Right: Grammar and Word Usage."

PARTS OF A LETTER

Every business letter, and many personal letters, should be set up in a style that answers the reader's questions about you. See the sample on page 19 for details. Begin with your return address and the date. Next comes the address, including the postal ZIP code, of the person you are writing to.

Then you fill in the salutation, or the line that says "Dear So-and-so." When you are writing a letter looking for a job, or any business letter to someone you don't know yet, it's best to be businesslike and address them as "Dear Mr. Smith" or "Dear Dr. Curezit." Let's say you get that great job at the senior center and write letters regularly to Ms. Betty Bureaucrat at the state's office of aging. The first time you write to her, it's polite to address her as "Dear Ms. Bureaucrat" in the salutation. After you write to her a couple of times and talk to her on the phone, it might be perfectly acceptable and normal then to begin your letters "Dear Betty."

The body of your letter contains as many paragraphs as it needs to say what you need to say. This is the information, the heart of the matter—why you are writing the letter.

Then there is a complimentary close, such as "Sincerely," "Very truly yours," or "Cordially." Most people use "Sincerely" or "Very truly yours" for a business letter to someone they haven't met yet or don't know well. For example, "Sincerely" is always a good way to end a letter applying for a job. "Cordially" is an upbeat and positive complimentary close to use on letters to those people you like and work well with. (It means "warmly," or, more literally, from the heart.)

Then you leave four lines of space for your written signature, and type your name below that. Just in case your handwriting is not the clearest on the planet, the person will still know how to spell your name when he or she writes back to you.

For business letters, and some kinds of personal letters, you may also add a "cc" list, or copies' list, after you type your name. Originally "cc" stood for "carbon copies." People no longer use carbon paper to make a copy of a letter or other document; instead, they photocopy the letter or print an extra copy on the computer. But you'll still want to send copies of some letters to other people, and you designate those after the letters "cc:" (with a colon and then a space or two before the first name listed).

A FORMAT FOR YOUR LETTER

Anyone who has used WordPerfect or Microsoft Word software for a computer is familiar with the term "format." It refers to the way you set up your document to look, including margins on the top, bottom, and sides; amount of space between lines (single-spacing or double-spacing); the typeface you use; and the use of page numbers and other features. Whether you are using a typewriter or computer software to write your letter, you still need to think about and set up a format as you start.

PARTS OF A LETTER:

123 Ida B. Wells Drive
Bronx, NY 00000
January 7, 1999

Harry Arms
Director of Admissions
Delta Business College
123 Michael Jordan Drive
Raleigh, NC 00000

Dear Mr. Arms:

Enclosed is my application for the hospitality management program
at your college. I really want to go to Delta to help my brother with
his catering business. He already makes the world's best enchiladas,
tacos, guacamole, and other food. But he and I both think the business
needs the type of background I could get from your program.

When we talked recently, you asked that I include the name of a reference, someone who knows me well from school or work. Please write
to Velvet Voice, Assistant Principal, Joe's High School, 456 Joe
Boulevard, Bronx, NY 00000. Ms. Voice is our faculty adviser at
the candy sale at school.

I look forward to hearing from you soon.

Sincerely,

Marianna Islands

cc: Velvet Voice

Most teachers and employers today are flexible about margins at the top, bottom, left, and right of your document. If you write on a typewriter, it's important to remember that you shouldn't type too close to the bottom of the paper; this is sloppy and difficult to photocopy. Also, if your letter is extremely short (one or two short paragraphs) it will look better if you add some additional space at the top above or below your return address, so that the letter does not look crowded onto the top part of the page. You might also be able to use a document layout feature to center the text vertically, that is, with equal space above and below the letter on the page.

The samples here are single-spaced. If your employer asks you to draft a letter for him or her to edit, it's usually a good idea to make the lines double-spaced, so that the boss has room to make corrections or add comments. To emphasize that it's a draft, stamp or write in red "draft" at the top of the first page.

The sample letter also shows double-spacing between paragraphs; this makes your letter easier to read. Most businesses today use block style or modified block style. In block style, you do not indent the first line of each paragraph. You position all the major elements of your letter (date, name and address, text, complimentary close, and typed signature) flush left, as shown in the letter on page 21. In modified block style, the date, your return address (if you are not writing on letterhead stationery) and complimentary close and typed signature may be indented to the center of your paper. For a sample of modified block style, see the letter on page 22.

BLOCK STYLE:

October 16, 1998

Evelyn Chang Lee
111 Prairie Drive
Iowa City, Iowa 00000
(515) 563-0749

China Seas Fortune Cookies, Ltd.
111 Harvey Milk Drive
San Francisco, California 90000

Dear China Seas:

Thank you for your letter notifying us that there will be a delay in shipping our order of 750 fortune cookies (series 2C: adult themes) that we need by November 5. If we pay extra for express shipping, is there a possibility that you can still meet the date of our class reunion, November 5?

Please call me at the above number to let us know about express shipping and what it costs for an order of this amount.

Sincerely,

Evelyn Chang Lee

MODIFIED BLOCK STYLE:

CHINA SEAS FORTUNE COOKIES, LTD.
111 HARVEY MILK DRIVE,
SAN FRANCISCO, CALIFORNIA 90000

November 12, 1998

Ms. Evelyn Chow Lee
111 Prairie Drive
Iowa City, Iowa 00000

Dear Ms. Lee:

Thank you for your recent letter to my supervisor, complimenting me for expediting the shipment of your rush order of fortune cookies. You and several other people were thoughtful enough to return the postcard providing feedback on service with positive comments about me. As a result, I received a bonus check.

We are sorry that your minister was offended by the adult themes in the fortune cookies. We offer adult themes for showers, bachelor parties, "roasts," and reunions. If you still have our catalog on hand, you'll note that we give several examples of adult-type messages to help our customers avoid embarrassing surprises. We hope you will still be a customer in the future; perhaps you'll want to consider an order of series 3A: Positive Inspiration messages, for your next church event.

Yours very truly,

John Doe

HOW TO PICK A TYPEFACE

Part of your message when you communicate is how your letter looks. The typeface you use is an important part of how the reader sees your letter. Sometimes you don't have a choice of type. Most electric typewriters use one typeface only, although there is one popular brand that uses a rotating metal ball which contains all the letters. The rotating metal ball can be switched to change the typeface. Some electronic word processors, which are halfway between a typewriter and a computer, offer only one kind of type. With most computers, however, there is a range of typefaces available to you.

Often the choice of type is a personal matter, and many of the faces that are available on a computer are appropriate for you to use. Consider some special typefaces that you have probably noticed, whether you think you are aware of type styles or not. For example, gothic type is often used for invitations to Halloween events and for some kinds of music shows; note these examples:

World's Coolest Halloween Party!

Concert by Nightshade Nail Twisters

If you or a family member has ever ordered personalized stationery through a catalog or department store mailing, you may have noticed that a few type styles seem especially popular. A graceful, flowing script designed to look like handwriting may seem suitable for a party invitation. A bolder style might seem right for a memo pad. A fanciful or childlike style might be appropriate for a humorous newsletter.

The point is that you can exercise creativity in choosing type to use on posters, invitations, and many types of personal letters. But it's good to stick with the tried-and-true when you are writing a business letter, especially a cover letter with a résumé when you are looking for a job. Some people, aware that there are usually many applicants for every job, think that they need to make their letters stand out or look visibly different to get the attention of the person hiring. Usually, however, the employer is looking for someone who can fit into his or her organization, rather than someone who has simply found an offbeat typeface.

TYPE WITH OR WITHOUT SERIFS

There are two broad groups of type, and within these two broad groups are many individual typefaces. The first group is made up of types with serifs, which are the small extenders on letters such as "r," "t," and "y." The sample letters in this book are set in Times Roman, a type with serifs. Many people believe that those extenders on the letters make it easier for our eyes to read easily across a line, so this fairly traditional style of type remains common.

The other broad group of typefaces are considered more contemporary. This is the sans-serif group, which eliminates those extenders on the letters. ("Sans" is French for "without.") This book uses Helvetica Light, a sans-serif type. Here's another example of sans-serif type:

Anxiety today: any progress?

Many students like sans-serif type, when they have access to it, for their homework and personal correspondence. They think it is cleaner or crisper looking and gives an up-to-date impression. In business, however, it is smart to ask the employer his or her preference or consult the company's style sheet (which lists the standard format for many kinds of documents), if there is one.

THE SIZE OF YOUR TYPE

Again, you don't always have a choice. But if you're working on a computer, you can change the size of the type when formatting your document. A good rule of thumb is to save larger sizes of type for display materials such as posters, ads, and invitations.

Most businesses use 10-point, 11-point, or 12-point type for the text of letters. The point system of measuring type was developed by printers before computers were invented; a point is 1/72 of an inch. A capital letter in 12-point type, then, is 1/6 of an inch (4.25 mm) tall. On a computer, it is easy to view the letter in different type sizes and decide what size is best before printing the document.

ADVANCED FORMAT: ONE LETTER TO MANY DIFFERENT PEOPLE

If you want to send the same letter to many people, you have a couple of options. One is to use a general salutation, such as "Greetings," and omit the individual's address from the letter itself. See, for example, the letter to the All-America Soccer Coaches on page 16. You can photocopy the more general letter for all sixteen people, and then you just need to type the names and addresses onto the envelopes. This is acceptable for many kinds of letters that you send or receive as a volunteer—for example, letters from school clubs, community centers, amateur sports groups, community religious groups, block clubs, and arts groups.

In business, however, it is considered too casual to send the same letter to sixteen people, addressing them all as "Dear Major Mogul." But you do not need to retype the same letter sixteen times if you are working on a computer. You can use a "mail merge" feature that enables you to use your body text as the first document, a list of names and addresses (including salutations) as a second document, and the mail-merge feature to create the sixteen letters that you need. See the manual for the word processing software that you use for instructions on how to use the mail-merge feature.

PICKING YOUR PAPER

For business, especially for résumés and cover letters applying for a job, it is best to stick with the proven favorite colors: white or off-white. Use standard-sized business paper (often labeled as typing paper), which is 8-1/2 by 11 inches. Odd sizes of paper may look interesting or pleasing to the eye but are difficult to stack for photocopying or filing.

When writing a cover letter to apply for a job, some people—once again, conscious of a large group of competing applicants—think that they might help their letter or résumé stand out by using lime-green or purple paper. This is an urge to resist! Colorful papers are fun but not businesslike.

LETTERHEAD AND LOOKING SHARP

Suppose you get that job you applied for, whether it is part-time while you are in school or full-time after doesn't reflect these points about you, however, the chances that you will get an interview, let alone the job, are very small. This book describes the basic parts of many types of business letters and personal letters and offers examples of each kind to help you decide which letter is best for you.

Investing some time in learning to write letters also brings a return in terms of other forms of communication. Trying to communicate in the form of a letter requires that you organize your thoughts and how you want to express them. That's also what you are doing when you write a book report, a news article for your neighborhood or school newspaper, or a speech. Once you can write a good letter, you have moved ahead in terms of improving your written communications skills for other purposes, too.

There are two ways to see every letter—how it looks and what it says. Let's say that you put together all the thoughts you want to tell someone, but your letter is messy or hard to read. Put yourself in the place of the person who gets that letter. You probably wouldn't be impressed by such a letter or take it seriously. Using this book, you can figure out the right way to write every time!

graduation. If your job involves letter writing, you will probably be expected to use the company's letterhead. This is stationery with the company's name, address, and phone numbers already printed on it.

Here are a few thoughts to keep in mind when you use letterhead:

- Do a draft of your letter on plain white paper first and proofread it, or present it to your supervisor for his or her approval as requested, before going to letterhead. This saves money: Letterhead is usually a heavier, more expensive grade of paper than the white paper normally used for printouts.

- Line up, or align, the left margin of your document to align with the letterhead. If your text is too far to the left or right of the type on your letterhead, the resulting letter looks unprofessional and sloppy. Note these examples:

Poor alignment, or lack of alignment at the left margin:

Jane Austen Memorabilia
234 Literature Lane
Anglophile, Pennsylvania 10400
Telephone: 213-555-1212

Professor Peter Piper
Chair, English Department
Earnest Community College
Earnest, Oklahoma 80888

Dear Professor Piper:

Good alignment (nice use of letterhead!):

Jane Austen Memorabilia
234 Literature Lane
Anglophile, Pennsylvania 10400
Telephone: 213-555-1212

Professor Peter Piper
Chair, English Department
Earnest Community College
Earnest, Oklahoma 80888

Dear Professor Piper:

Using letterhead stationery might sometimes affect the content of your letter slightly. As in the above example, if you want to ask Professor Piper to call you, you can include in your letter a line that says, "If you have any questions, or want to discuss any of the proposals I have outlined, please give me a call any morning at the above number." But, if you are writing a letter for a business that just got a new fax machine and there is no fax number on the letterhead stationery you are using, remember to include the fax number: "If you want to fax your order in the future, the number for our new fax machine is 213-555-2121."

Letterhead stationery is useful not only to convey a certain image about you or your organization, but it also provides information that the person or company you are writing to may need. As long as you keep in mind what information is and is not included in the letterhead, you are doing your best to communicate via letter.

THE ENVELOPE: PART OF A PACKAGE

Let's imagine that you have finished your letter and checked it over. You are satisfied with what it says and how it looks; this letter represents you well! Is anything missing? Yes, you also need to produce an envelope that will get the letter to its correct destination quickly and that also reflects how well you communicate.

A standard-sized envelope is a business envelope that measures about 4-1/4 by 9-1/2 inches (11 by 24 cm). It is best to use a white business envelope for your business correspondence and many types of personal letters, such as letters to the editor (see next chapter). For personal letters to friends and family, you can choose envelopes from a wide range of papers, colors, and sizes.

In the upper left corner of the envelope, write or type your return address, starting with your name. Always include your own 5-digit postal ZIP code. The "ZIP + 4" code pinpoints your address more closely for the US Postal Service. This information is then handy when the person decides to write back to you. Also, if the person you are writing to has moved, or if the address is incorrect, the Postal Service may return the letter to you, and that process will be delayed if you have omitted your ZIP code.

Just about in the middle of the envelope, write or type the name and address (again including ZIP code) of the person to whom you are writing. If one line of the address is exceptionally long, break that line at some logical point and indent the remainder of it two to five spaces on the next line. This helps avoid running the address off the right edge of the envelope. Here's an example:

Professor Luke Skywalker
Foundation for the Advancement of
    Science Fiction in Literature
1000 Asimov Boulevard
Bradbury, WA 90000

If you use a computer, consult your manuals to see if you can print address labels with the hardware and software available to you.

TWO

PERSONAL LETTERS: "DEAR WORLD"

Some people think of the personal letter, if they think of it at all, as extinct, like the dinosaur or the home without a color television set. Yet, despite the lure of the telephone, there are many times when a personal letter is your best choice for expressing yourself. A personal letter can be very informal and brief. For some types of personal letters, however, it is best to keep a few rules in mind to help you communicate effectively.

LETTERS TO THE EDITOR

You may feel strongly about an issue and decide to write a letter to the editor of your school newspaper or to the daily or weekly newspaper in your city or town. Or you may be involved in a club or community group that asks you to write a letter to the editor to get the group's opinion on record.

There are two simple tests of whether your letter to the editor is effective. The first is whether the editor of the newspaper selects it to appear in the paper, and the second is whether the readers of the news-paper understand your letter and are influenced by it.

Here are some guidelines that may help you get the editor's attention. Some of this advice is based on my experience in getting letters published, and a lot of it is based on common sense:

- Be brief. Space is limited in most letters to the editor sections or columns. The editor of the paper is looking for an offbeat subject or an unusual angle to a story that a lot of people are writing about. No one has time to wade through pages of your opinions, however interesting or informed they may be.

- Get to the point fast. Rather than going through a big buildup on an issue and then stating your main point as a conclusion, be sure to state the main point in your first sentence or paragraph. This keeps the casual reader from losing interest or getting confused.

- Be specific. If you are writing to a Los Angeles newspaper, but your letter is about the mayor of a suburb, be sure to specify that to avoid confusion: "Mayor Ralph Rabblerouser of Paradise Beach has been criticized for. . . ."

- Be polite and respectful. Even if you are writing to contradict another opinion published in the paper, or to challenge a statement by a public figure, you need to tame your intense feelings about the topic as part of the communication process. The editor will not need (and readers will not heed) opinions expressed in an insulting way. Always turn your thoughts around to ask yourself how you would feel if someone wrote about you, your family, or your community group in terms like those you want to use!

- Mention sources for your information. Don't just say that Mayor Rabblerouser's spending on his campaign exceeded normal limits. What are normal limits and who says so? For example: "According to a Government and Politics Foundation report published in *Newsguy*, a mayoral candidate for a city of this size spends $100,000 to $250,000 on his or her campaign; Mayor Rabblerouser spent ten times more."

Following is an example of a letter to the editor discussing whether taxes should be raised to increase funding for community libraries. Note that the writer is aware of the fact that many readers will not agree with him, but he does not adopt a defensive tone. Trying to change the perspectives in a debate or argument is a classic way to approach a controversial topic.

Letters to the Editor Section
Banana Bay Bugle
123 Peel Street
Banana Bay, AR 00000

To the Editor:

The junior English classes at Plantain High have gotten together to urge voters to support the 1.5-cent increase in property taxes (for each $10,000 of assessed value). The money raised by this tax increase will go to help the Banana Bay public library system. With the funds to be raised by the tax increase, the library system will be able to afford two new computers for each of the branch libraries. In addition, the main library can afford to stay open every weekday evening, not just two evenings.

As students, we use the library regularly for homework assignments. Some Banana Bay residents may say that they do not want to pay the tax because their children are out of school and do not use the libraries. Twenty students from our classes visited the main library regularly for three weeks to collect information on the type of activities there. We learned that about 20 percent of the programs were targeted to senior citizens, including Elderhostel classes and a series of lectures on "Arthritis and Joint Replacement: What Are the Facts?"

Also, the busiest section is the Business and Commerce library, and the average age of patrons in that section is well over 30. Librarians in Business and Commerce told us that most people who ask for reference help are looking for information on companies that will help them find new jobs, or they are looking for material that will help them improve their businesses or streamline their work. The entire community benefits from the library system, and we hope everyone will vote to continue the community support of libraries.

Sincerely,

LETTERS TO A PUBLIC OFFICIAL

Sometimes you feel strongly about an issue and decide to write to your congressional representative, senator, or other public official to express your opinion. It is your right as a voter, or future voter, to take a stand and to attempt to influence the way your representative will vote in a legislative session. There is no guarantee that your letter will influence your representative; he or she may reply that conscience is an important factor or that the community gave some discretion to the representative in the process of electing him or her. But if you don't even try to make your viewpoint known, how can you complain when your representative votes against what you want?

Many of the informal rules for letters to the editor also work well for this type of letter. Your letter is most likely to have an impact if it is brief and to the point, respectful in tone, and factual whenever that is appropriate. If you are writing in response to a speech that you heard on television, it is helpful to mention that as a source. It is also good common sense to mention that you live in the representative's district or perhaps that your family has been living and voting in the district for many years. Also, if your family has supported or worked for candidates in the senator's party, that's useful to mention.

You may or may not get a reply letter. Usually, when you write to a congressional representative in the US House, or to your US Senator, you get a form letter in reply. The form letter was written to anticipate the many letters your representative expects to receive. Sometimes this seems disappointing, but remember that your chances of establishing a personal correspondence with a busy public official are slim. Your real goal should be to influence a vote.

Where do you get the names and addresses of various public officials? Try your school library or your local public library. The librarian can tell you which officials represent which towns or communities and can look up the addresses for your state capitol or for the US Congress.

THANK-YOU NOTES

One of the biggest contradictions in the universe is that everyone likes to receive gifts, but most people hate to write thank-you notes! This is another type of letter writing in which it is most helpful to put yourself in the other person's position. You like the fact that Aunt Shirley sends you gifts on your birthday and for the holidays, but doesn't she understand that you're really too busy to write a thank-you note? No, she doesn't understand that, and if you don't write, eventually good old Aunt Shirley will figure you didn't care about her gift packages, and she'll stop sending them.

Etiquette writers usually advise a handwritten note on plain note paper. If you feel comfortable only with typing on a computer, then a computer-generated letter is better than no letter. Some people who are reminded to write letters think that it is OK to substitute a thank-you card and just sign their names, but again, put yourself in Aunt Shirley's shoes. Would she appreciate more than just your name on a card? Of course she would.

Your thank-you note should have at least two sentences in it. The first should be along the lines of "thanks very much for thinking of me with this gift." The second should mention something specific you liked about the gift. (A printed card that says "thank you for your gift" doesn't reveal if you even remember what the gift was.)

A personal thank-you letter is an informal note, so you don't need to put the person's name and address on the letter as you would for a letter to the editor or a letter to your representative. Also, for this type of personal letter, you use a comma after the salutation ("Dear So-and-so"), rather than a colon. This sample thank-you letter will give you an idea of how to let Aunt Shirley know you appreciate her thoughtfulness (and should help keep those gifts coming):

Dear Aunt Shirley,

Thank you very much for sending me a Chicago Bulls sweatshirt. As you know, I am really a fan of the Bulls and hope to be able to attend one of their games in person someday. Our biology class is planning a nature walk this fall, and it will be cool to wear a Bulls shirt to stay warm!

We all hope to see you soon.

Love,
Elvis, Jr.

SYMPATHY LETTERS

As with the thank-you letter, you can just go out and buy a printed sympathy card. A letter, though, is a more personal way to express your support for a friend or acquaintance who has suffered the death of a family member or close friend. If you knew the person who died, remember to include a sentence or two mentioning what you liked about him or her—or recalling some significant occasion that you spent together. If you did not feel close to the person who died, this is not the time to mention it; in such a case, you can mention the fact that you know how much your friend will miss the loved one.

To make sure that your letter helps or is a nice gesture, remember that the purpose is to express sympathy in a positive way for the living person who has lost someone from his or life. This is *not* a time to play medical reporter and say something like, "Everyone agreed the case was hopeless, and he was sick so long; it's all for the best." Imagine receiving a letter like this, and you can see that it's not comforting and does not speak to your feelings of loss or sadness!

This sample letter incorporates the above ideas of trying to make the survivor feel better while addressing your memories of the person who has died:

Dear Darius,

I was so sorry to hear that your father died, and at such a young age. We all remember how he showed up for all the Boy Scout hikes and outdoor expeditions and helped us find the trails. He always tried to be a leader and care about all the kids. See you soon at school.

> Your friend,
> Dion

NOTES OF APOLOGY

A brief note with a couple of sentences can help you smooth over some awkward situations. When you need to say you're sorry, and it's difficult to call the person to talk about it, consider a letter of apology. As in a sympathy note, be honest, but not critical or negative. You don't need to "crawl" or grovel, but neither do you want to keep an argument going. Try to be positive and say what you need to, no more and no less.

Consider this example:

Dear Mr. Soldes,

I'm sorry that we broke the window in your store on Monday. It was nice of your nephew Hector to say that he did it, but I was the one batting. Here is a check for $30 to help replace the window. My mom suggested that if that's not enough money, maybe I could work for you after school a couple of days to make up the difference. Please let me know. You can call her or me at 321-5555.

Sincerely,
Joe Castro

LETTERS OF INVITATION

You can buy printed cards for many occasions at a card store or drugstore, but it's nice to be able to write a personalized letter or note inviting people to a party or reception. Be sure to include answers to all the basic questions mentioned in Chapter One—*who, what, when, where,* and *why.* (*How* and *how much* may not always need to be included.) You can write your invitation out in sentence form, like any other note, or you can center each of the lines in an artistic fashion; see the following example:

Please come to a reception
in honor of Coach Susan Washington
and the Girls' Basketball Team
Saturday, June 20,
4 p.m. at the North Fieldhouse

(shh! it's a surprise for the coach)

FAN LETTERS

You may have the urge to write a letter to your favorite musician or actor to tell him or her how much you like his or her work, and how much a favorite song, film, or TV series means to you. All stars love to get fan mail, but to keep your letter positive for you and for the person you're writing to, here are some informal rules to keep in mind:

- Keep your letter short—one page at the most.

- Don't enclose a gift; Sammie Z. Star will probably never see it or be able to appreciate it.

- Don't ask for a phone call or an appointment to visit. Exception: if the person is an actor on a TV series performed before a studio audience, you can ask for information on how to get tickets for a certain date (at least a month in advance).

If you are writing to request a photo, state that clearly. Some recording companies and TV or film production companies send out free pictures of their stars as part of their normal publicity program. In other cases, a secretary will send you a form to order a photo or other memorabilia such as T-shirts, and payment will be required. Or you may be sent the name and address of a fan club for that star, and the club will charge a membership fee or ask for a separate payment for a photo.

How do you get the address of your favorite star? For a recording star, read the information on the label for the audiocassette or compact disc (CD). Sometimes there will be a separate address provided for the singer, musician, or group. If not, write to Sammie Z. Star "c/o Starflight Music" at the address provided on the cassette or CD. You might find an Internet address for the home page of the performer or the record company; go to that web site to find a mailing address. For a television or film star, write down the name of the production company at the end of a show, and go to your local library to get the address of the production company.

REQUESTS FOR INFORMATION

At the end of a newspaper or magazine article, you may find a notice indicating that you can get more information on the subject you've been reading about by writing to XYZ agency or association. You may be writing a report on environmental issues, for example, and could use authoritative information from or about an environmental organization.

Remember to keep your letter brief and as specific as possible. For example, if you are writing to an environmental organization, don't ask for "any information about the environment." That's too general and too broad. Are you Interested in air pollution, water quality, on saving some endangered animal species? Mention your particular concern if you have one.

Many organizations are committed to outreach programs and prepared to supply information. But many government agencies and nonprofit organizations have been through budget-cutting crises and may not have the staff or resources to answer your queries in detail. So don't just assume that by writing a letter you can get someone you don't know to do your homework for you! The *Encyclopedia of Associations* is a reference work that you may find at your school library or public library; it lists addresses for many types of organizations and often notes whether the group provides information to the public.

Wherever you find the address, make a point of noticing if the organization asks for a self-addressed stamped envelope ("SASE") to save on its postage costs. If so, put your name and address on a full-sized business envelope as the addressee, and don't forget the stamp.

LETTER TO TOURIST AGENCY

Most countries and all the fifty states in the United States operate tourist offices or agencies and provide information to encourage you to visit and spend your travel dollars there. Often these tourist agencies have a lot of good free information available, including calendars of events, maps, and other information geared to your interests. In the travel section of your newspaper (usually a Sunday feature in most cities), you'll see ads from nearby states or from countries that have some hopes of attracting people from your area.

Often you can call for information, but what if you're busy during the day when the office is open, or if the line is always busy when you do have a chance to call? Assuming that you have plenty of time (six weeks or two months) before a possible trip, write a brief letter explaining specifically what you're interested in. You'll probably get more useful information if you say, for example, that you're interested in visiting Michigan in the fall and you're particularly interested in cross-country skiing and downhill skiing.

To find the address of a tourist agency "cold"—without an ad right in front of you—ask your local library for assistance.

COMPLAINING TO A MANUFACTURER

Let's say you buy a new portable radio with headphones, and it comes with a thirty-day warranty or guarantee. A week or two after the warranty expires, you notice that the stations are "drifting," that you do not get clear reception anywhere. Chances are that the store where you purchased the item will say you're out of luck because the warranty is expired. Another option then is to write to the manufacturer and ask that the item be replaced.

State the facts clearly and simply, and again, keep your letter short. Be careful not to be abusive or use insulting language. Picture yourself or one of your family members reading a letter filled with sarcastic insults—you would not be inclined to help a person who sent such a letter.

Anything positive that you can say as part of your presentation is probably a good idea to help get your request taken seriously. Review this sample letter with an eye towards adapting it to your situation, noting the first sentence especially:

June 26, 1998

Happy Electronics, Ltd.
777 Stereo Blvd.
Rahway, NJ 00000

Dear Happy Electronics:

My family has always been satisfied with radios and CD players made by your company, and we have owned several different models. Recently, however, I was disappointed by the Joggers' Jiggle-Free X99 model radio with headphones that I bought with my birthday money. I can't run or even walk while wearing this unit. Shortly after the warranty expired, I found that even sitting quietly in the park, I could not get clear reception on any stations.

I tried tuning in to all the big 50,000-watt stations in our town, thinking that a station with more broadcast power would work better. I did check the batteries and the connection from the radio to the headset, and that was all fine.

Because the radio is so new, and because I expect better quality from a Happy product, I ask that you provide me with a replacement unit. Please advise how I can get the replacement unit. Thank you.

Sincerely,
Joe Junior

HOLIDAY LETTERS

Many families do not have the time to send individual greetings at Christmas or Hannukah to all their friends, relatives, and neighbors, and they prefer to send a form letter prepared on the computer. This is another type of letter that your parents may be interested in writing, but they turn to you as a computer-friendly person to put it together for the family.

It's easy to make fun of these letters, and many good writers have done so! The writers often brag too much, or they include too much depressing personal information. "We're so pleased and proud that Keisha won the Nobel Prize and Harrington discovered a cure for cancer. But here's a tragic note: Grandma just keeps suffering with that new partial plate that doesn't fit; her dentist won't even help her!" This is exaggeration (I hope!) as an example of what no one expects to read.

Your letter can be warm, friendly, full of updates, and enjoyable to all those who get it. Again, as with so many other types of letters, don't write too much. If

contractions such as "isn't" or "we've," but that instead you spell out "is not" or "we have." You may personally believe that this is a minor point, because you are smart and have a lot to offer. Nevertheless, just as you expect people to behave in a certain way if they visit your school or home, the people to whom you are sending your letters have ideas about how you should communicate to meet their needs.

Neatness counts. A business letter with smudges, crossed-out or written-in information, or strikeovers in typing does not make a good impression. Again, you may think that a neat letter does not really matter because your thoughts are so profound. But with many people applying for the same job or to the same college, how do you make your letter look good? The answer is by making it neat and professional-looking.

APPLYING TO A COLLEGE OR VOCATIONAL SCHOOL

Most students are relieved to find that an application to a college or vocational school is a form for you to fill out, with questions such as the name of your high school or community college and names and addresses of people who will give you references. This is a "fill-in-the-blanks" process once you locate all the information, such as the complete address of Uncle Dan, your father's friend from military service who is now mayor of a nearby town. Often, however, you are asked to submit a letter or essay explaining why you want to attend a particular school, what you have learned at school so far besides the subject matter taught in the courses on your transcript, why the school should choose you over someone else, and what your goals for the future are.

If you are asked to supply this information, your best chance of making a good impression on the admitting officer is to write a letter on a computer or typewriter. Read the instructions carefully to see if the essay should be on a separate sheet of paper or must be typed into a space provided on the application form (or if you are specifically asked to write out your thoughts in your own handwriting). Address each question with specific examples of things you have done, rather than with adjectives ("excellent" or "really terrific," for example) to make the best impression. Here are a couple of examples of how to answer the question of why the school should choose you over someone else:

- For the past two years, I have learned responsibility and how to organize my time by working 20 hours a week for the park district while maintaining a B average.

- During the current school year, I am president of the career club and secretary of the Junior Achievement chapter; my guidance counselor calls that leadership in action.

COVER LETTER IN REPLY TO AN AD FOR A JOB

So the big day has arrived, and you are ready to look for a job. Like most people, you will probably start your search by looking at the help-wanted classified ads in the newspapers in your town, or in the town where you want to work. Often the ad will state something like "résumés to this address." So do you even need a cover letter? Yes, you need a cover letter, for at least a couple of reasons. The cover letter shows that you are willing to go that extra mile to make a good impression. Also, if your qualifications are light in some areas mentioned in the ad, you can use the cover letter to put a positive spin on that information, in a straightforward, nondefensive manner.

Begin your cover letter by mentioning the ad you are answering, and summarize or explain your qualifications as set out in the ad. Then, describe *how* the prospective employer can contact you to set up an interview. If you are currently employed and cannot receive calls where you work, ask the recruiter to call you at home and leave a message on your voice mail or answering machine. If you can receive calls at your current workplace, note that you can take calls at that number on a confidential basis during business hours.

See the letter below as a possible reply to an ad for an Editorial Assistant who types at least 50 words per minute, knows certain word processing programs, has used proofreading symbols, and is willing to do clerical work in addition to editorial tasks:

99 Lake Shore Drive
Chicago, IL 60600
October 28, 1998

Box 1234
New York Big Bugle
123 Hobnob Highway
Importantville, Long Island,
New York 10400

Dear *New York Big Bugle*:

In response to your recent ad in the *Chicago Gazette*, I would like to apply for the position of Editorial Assistant with your newspaper. For the past two years, I have worked as an editor on the sports section of our college newspaper, the *Student Standard*, where I learned to write and edit on a computer under deadline pressure, to proofread, and to love journalism.

Please see my enclosed résumé, which also mentions the 36 hours of English courses I have completed in college. It's hard to communicate enthusiasm on a résumé; however, I consider myself a team player and a hard worker ready to take on all the everyday jobs that will help your editorial team move forward.

I look forward to the opportunity of a personal interview, and I plan to be in New York visiting my sister the week of November 26. Please leave a message on my phone machine at the dorm, where my number is 773-555-0000. Thank you.

Sincerely,
Sammy Sidelines

COVER LETTER APPLYING FOR A JOB WHERE YOUR FRIEND WORKS

You may be in the fortunate position of knowing someone who works at a company or organization that might have a place for you. Also, you may then have the opportunity to hear about job openings from your friend or relative before they are advertised. If a friend tells you about a possible opening, make sure that the person feels comfortable about recommending you before you sit down to write your letter. That is, do not use the person's name without permission, as the personnel department or prospective supervisor may call the person directly to ask him or her about you. Here's a sample of the type of letter you might use; note that it's in your best interest to position yourself for many different types of job openings, not just the one in your friend's department.

555 Lane Boulevard
Reno, NV 89000
September 2, 1998

Mr. Henry Lee, Director of Personnel
Asian American Museum of the West
111 West Heritage Way
Reno, NV 89000

Dear Mr. Lee:

My friend Lucyann Iwamoto suggested that I write to you regarding the position available for a computer operator in the museum's systems department. I am in the last semester of the two-year program at Reno State College and expect to receive an Associate of Arts degree in computer studies in January. Please see the enclosed résumé for more details on the summer jobs I have held that are good background for your opening.

If the position in Lucyann's department has already been filled, please let me know if you have openings in other areas for someone with my qualifications. I have worked as a clerk-typist and would be interested in an administrative position with your computer area or another department.

Please call me at the phone number on my résumé to schedule an interview or for more information about my background. Thank you.

Sincerely,
Karen Ann Tangong

APPLYING FOR A JOB AT AN ORGANIZATION YOU LIKE

Many people like to start a job search by answering classified ads for job openings and getting listings of open positions from a vocational counselor at school. As mentioned above, hearing about jobs through friends is another good avenue for your search. It is also possible to broaden your search by writing to a company or other organization that you have heard of, admire, or think would be a good place to work. In such a situation, your letter should be positive and enthusiastic, but not to the point that the person reading it will question your sincerity.

Mention a specific reason that you thought of this organization. Note, for example, "I have often heard positive reports about your company, as it is Pine Valley's largest employer." Even better, do a little research to show a real interest in the company or organization; this is usually most feasible for large employers, especially those that are nationally known or are publicly held companies. For example, you can mention something like the following: "I was impressed when I read in *Momentum* news magazine that Bubbly Cola has made major increases in sales to customers formerly loyal to the big two brands of soda pop. I hope there are some good opportunities in a company with such a bright future."

APPLYING FOR INTERNSHIPS

Many organizations today offer full-time or part-time internships to students or older workers who are making career changes. An internship can be a good opportunity to learn from experienced people in your field or a field in which you are interested. For example, you may find a position as an intern in a library or archives, in a publishing operation, or at a school.

Many, but not all, of these internships are paying positions. If you hear about an internship, write for more information. Again, you may be thinking, "Why write a letter? I could call the company and find out all about it." You want to make sure you get the right information, and asking for it in writing helps to insure your request is clear. You might reach someone on the phone as well, but that person might not have all the information you need at hand.

Here are some important questions to ask about the internship:

- What are the qualifications in terms of education and previous jobs?

- Is this a paying position, and how much does it pay?

- Will there be an opportunity to do research (writing or editing, for example), in addition to administrative duties?

- Is there any college credit available upon completion of the internship? (This is most often applicable for an internship at a university.)

- Is there a set time period for this internship (six months or one year, for example), or is it open-ended?

- Will I be asked to sign a contract?

- Who will evaluate my work as an intern, and will the evaluation be in writing?

DO I NEED A RÉSUMÉ?

Many students wonder if they need résumés when they are just starting their careers. The answer from almost all career gurus is a definite "yes." You may think that you could just fill out an application for a job and list your experience there. With so many people applying for positions today, though, your first "job" when looking for a job is to get the attention of the hiring person and get that interview (and/or the opportunity to fill out an application, if that is linked to interviewing).

Even if you are looking for an entry-level position, there is still a lot of competition from other people graduating from high school, community college, or college. Many students have had summer jobs or part-time jobs that give them relevant experience for positions they want later, and their résumés should reflect that. Many students are active in school or community activities, and those activities show initiative, social skills, and possibly other skills relevant to job-hunting.

There are various ways to organize your résumé, but none is the absolute best for everyone. For students seeking entry-level jobs, many career counselors and business writers advise leading with your education in your résumé. For more experienced job candidates, the advice is to lead with job experience, and this approach may work for students with some appropriate experience already under their belts.

SAMPLE RÉSUMÉ EMPHASIZING EDUCATION

When you think that the school you went to, or the degree or certificate you earned, is a main selling point to employers, then start with that, as in this example:

·· note that you do not include the word "résumé"

David Weiner
1234 Success Lane
Winnerville, OH 41900
Telephone: 506-555-1212

Education

Bachelor of Science in Business, The Ohio State University,
June 1998
> Minor: Computer science
> Honors: Ohhh My honorary society

Graduate, Winnerville High School, 1994
> Honors: President of National Honor Society

Employment

Clerk, Office of Admissions, Business School, The Ohio
State University, September 1996 through June 1998; part-
time position answering phones, entering student data on
computers, and updating mailing lists.

Waiter, Joe's Yacht Club, Upper Winnerville, Ohio,
summers of 1996, 1997; temporary position in four-star
restaurant.

Skills

Computer programming, typing 60 wpm, fluency in
German

Software experience: Word, Word Perfect, Excel, and
Power Point

References

Available upon request.

SAMPLE RÉSUMÉ EMPHASIZING JOB EXPERIENCE

When you have worked at jobs that help qualify you for a position you want, even if you are a recent graduate, start with your work history. This approach also works well for those with several years of experience.

Davida Weiner
5678 Success Way
Winnerville, OR 90000
Telephone: 719-555-1212

optional

Career objective
To obtain a graphic design position in an advertising agency that enables me to use my technical and artistic skills.

Work experience
Associate designer, Bob's Cutting Edge Agency, 1995-1996, summer 1997; used page makeup software to design print ads for two major campaigns (please see sample portfolio).

Clerk, WMPCC (World's Most Powerful Computer Company), Summer 1994; performed beta testing of new scanner, working with laser and inkjet printers.

Education
Associate of Arts, Graphic Design, Brooding Buffalo Community College, Greater Winnerville, Oregon, January 1998
    Notable courses: Archiving Images Online; Multimedia and You
    Honors: Treasurer, Ad Club

Graduate, Rogers and Clark Academy, Winnerville, OR, 1995

Community activities
Volunteer designer, monthly newsletter of the Save Our Coastline Coalition, 1997 to the present (please see sample portfolio)

References
Available upon request.

Be aware that these are by no means the only possible approaches to writing a résumé or cover letter. Job hunting is an entire field of study in itself. No doubt your school library, local library, and bookstore have countless reference books available to help you hone these skills. See "For More Information" at the end of this book for a few recommendations to get started on such a project.

FOUR

MORE BUSINESS LETTERS—GETTING THE JOB DONE

So now you have that new job you were looking for, either full-time or part-time. Often you are asked to write a letter to a customer or client, or to set up a form letter for dealing with many similar situations. The same guidelines that you used in other chapters will work well in these situations: include all needed information, be brief, and organize your material logically.

CUSTOMER SERVICE LETTERS

Every business receives complaints about products, service, or both. It is just human nature to complain, and people want to feel they are getting their money's worth when they buy something. Moreover, although customers may occasionally express themselves too angrily or seem to be annoying, the first rule for dealing with the public is still, and always will be, "The customer is always right." Whether you are a part-time clerk or the owner of a new company, you need feedback from customers; if many customers are not satisfied, the business may not survive.

When you are writing a business letter to respond to a complaint, be professional in tone, period. It does not matter if Ms. X makes sarcastic remarks suggesting that your ancestors must have crawled out from under rocks. You are responding not as an individual involved in a snappy conversation, but as a representative of an organization that would like Ms. X to spend her money on its products again in the future.

Here is a sample form letter for responding to calls or letters of complaint from individual consumers:

Tuff Toaster Company
6 Breadcrumb Road
Raisin Toast, OK 80000

March 2, 1999

Ms. Notably Angry
22 Homeowner Road
Happyville, MO 50500

Dear Ms. Angry:

Thank you for your letter (call) of (date including month, day, year). We are sorry to hear that you are unhappy with your Tuff Toaster model # _____.

Because your original warranty has expired, we can offer repair service for a fee of $20 plus parts. Send your toaster in the original carton, if possible, to the following address:

_____

Please note that the Tuff Toaster repair alcove cannot accept packages that are mailed postage due or "COD."

To keep your toaster working well in the future, we suggest that (add any special information here that you learned from the complaint—for example: You persuade your grandson not to deposit crayons in the slots where the bread goes).

Tuff Toaster wants your business and thanks you again for letting us know about this problem.

Sincerely,
Robb Rye
Customer Service Assistant

CUSTOMER SERVICE, BUSINESS TO BUSINESS

Rather than corresponding with individual consumers, as in the above example, you may need to write to another business that your organization works with. Let's say, for example, that you work for Friendly Flour Company, and the largest restaurant chain in your area (Lunch Land) is complaining about receiving its deliveries of flour late. Be specific in your reply, and explain not only what the problem is, but also what Friendly Flour is doing to fix it. For example, if delivery problems were caused by breakdowns in your fleet of trucks, explain that breakdowns were too frequent, so Friendly Flower has purchased two new trucks and changed mechanics' services for the existing fleet. The person you are writing to at Lunch Land is not interested in the details of your problems, but rather in the details of how you can provide better service in the future.

If the complaint is a serious one, and Lunch Land

is threatening to stop ordering from your company, find out if you can offer a special incentive to keep them as a customer. Ask your supervisor or whoever is the main contact with Lunch Land what the special incentive might be, and be sure to explain the incentive positively and clearly. For example, you might say, "To thank you for your patience during our recent problems with delivery, we are happy to offer you a 10 percent discount on your next order."

In any customer service letter from one business to another, make a point of including a brief statement of thanks to the other business. For example, it is good to say, "Thank you for doing business with Friendly Flour! We value you as a customer and look forward to hearing from you."

CONTESTING CHARGES ON AN INVOICE OR BILL

If you are writing to another business or professional organization to contest a charge on a bill or invoice, follow the same guidelines as above. Even if you think that the shipping department at Augie's Auto Supply is a bit sloppy about checking its invoices, be professional in tone. As with any other type of letter, put yourself in the place of the person who will read the letter you send. If you write something heated or angry about a mistake, you are less likely to get prompt service to have the error corrected. Also, your job could be in danger if the company you are writing to does not like your tone—they might turn around and complain about you.

Always be specific. Refer to an invoice or bill by its number and date (rather than "your recent invoice"). Whenever possible, enclose a copy of the invoice or bill in question. Also, enclose a copy of any other information that will help you get the mistake fixed. For example, if you have a shipping ticket dated April 3 for ten cases of 10W-30 motor oil, and a bill for twenty cases shipped the same date, be sure to enclose a copy of the shipping ticket.

When you send a letter questioning a bill your company has received, make a note on your calendar to check back with the company in thirty days (or whatever interval your supervisor recommends) if you have not received an answer.

APPOINTMENT LETTERS

Say a new dentist has set up an office in your neighborhood, and you are lucky enough to get a job in her office just as you are graduating with your two-year associate's degree in business. She asks you to set up a form letter to remind patients of their appointments. You yourself are not Gaytrice Gum, DDS, but you are representing her, so your letter must make that clear.

Office of Gaytrice Gum, DDS
32 Adult Teeth Avenue
Flossing, NJ 20000
Telephone: 012-122-5555

November 9, 1998

Mr. Fearless Patient
415 Healthy Drive
Greater Flossing, NJ 20010

Dear Mr. Patient:

This is a friendly reminder that your next appointment for a regular checkup with Dr. Gum is as follows:

PEOPLE'S PUBLISHING COMPANY
• *Books for you and your community* •

To: Abdul Gupta

From: Mary Smith

Date: June 19, 1998

Re: China Sea proposal

As you requested, I reviewed the response from China Sea Community Center to our outline for a book to help Asian immigrants adapt to life in the southern United States. Although there are many points of difference between us, I think we can still make this project work.

Here are some points I think we can change to compromise with China Sea:
- broaden the target audience to include southeast Asian countries, as well as the original countries of China, Japan, Korea, and India;
- include 8 to 12 photos of men, women, and children of various ages from various countries to make the point that the advice is for everyone, not just for males;
- include a section on how to use the health care system, specifically targeted to women as the mothers of children and the ones who make health care arrangements for the family.

Rather than responding to these points by letter, however, I think we should propose a meeting between several of us from People's Publishing and the board of China Sea. That way, we can discuss in an atmosphere of good will what kinds of changes would make their board more comfortable with the book and even—we hope—eager to participate.

I hope that we can meet next week. Please let me know what day and time you prefer. Also, I would be happy to invite the China Sea leadership; let me know if you would prefer to do that from your office. Thank you.

For another example, you may be working as an editorial assistant at a publishing company and want to propose a new book on a favorite topic of yours. Rather than writing five or six pages to explain your idea, try composing a one-page cover memo suggesting the title, such as *Promoting Your Band or Other Music Act,* and mentioning the highlights of the book and the possible market. Then you can add an outline of several pages to develop your idea in detail, including types of promotion (press releases about forthcoming appearances of a band, advertising your compact disc in local newspapers, or distributing demonstration cassettes to radio stations). The cover memo should tempt the reader to want to know more about your idea.

FAX MANIA

Many people today send letters via fax. The word fax is a commonly used abbreviation for the term telefacsimile. The fax itself is a machine that is capable of scanning documents and transmitting, receiving, and printing them. You may choose to send a formal letter, nicely word-processed as usual on your organization's letterhead, via fax with or without a cover sheet. Or you may write or type a few lines on a fax cover sheet and just transmit that.

Faxes are an excellent way to introduce yourself to someone who is difficult to reach by phone. They also prove useful for transmitting detailed information. For example, you receive a phone message asking for the names of three contacts in your sales department; rather than spelling out the names in another phone message and listing their phone extensions, you can quickly and neatly fax the information.

Many organizations instruct you to fax a letter so that the recipient will get it immediately and then mail

Tuff Toaster Company
Raisin Toast, OK 80000
Fax number: 808-555-1211

FAX

To: [name]
_____

[company]
_____

[their fax number]
_____

From: [your name]
_____

[your department or title]
_____

[your phone number]
_____

Message:

[leave a blank space of several inches here for typing, or add ruled lines if you will be writing messages by hand]

Total pages including this sheet: _____

If you have problems reading any of the pages in this transmission, please phone Wanda Wheat at 1-800-637-1412.

the original letter to the same person. If you do this, stamp the letter or write neatly at the top, "sent via fax [date]." This will prevent the recipient from being confused about receiving two copies. Other organizations now choose not to mail the letter after they have faxed it. Ask what the policy is in your workplace.

You may be asked to set up a fax cover sheet, particularly if you are working for a new business or setting up a business yourself. Make sure to include your fax number in return and also a phone number the recipient can call in case there are any transmission problems, that is, difficulty reading the fax. Also important is a line or box for you to mark how many sheets you are faxing; this way the recipient knows if he or she has all the pages needed. A sample fax cover sheet incorporating all the points you need appears on page 69.

FIVE

Electronic Mail

In many ways, "e-mail" has changed the way people think about letters. You write a conventional letter ("snail mail" to e-mail enthusiasts) in a certain format, copy it for your files, mail it, and then wait for the recipient to receive it and open it. Even if you are in a hurry, the person may not get your letter for a couple of days. And it is probably smart, given the variables of mail service, to assume that it will take a week for someone to get your letter and open it. By contrast, using e-mail, you can send a message quickly—in minutes or seconds—across town, to another state, or another country. All you need is a computer with a modem, a device that attaches to a telephone line or some other communication path, and an e-mail software program.

In many ways, e-mail is similar to any business mail: Your best approach is to express yourself simply, briefly, and very clearly. As we have seen, the business letter in general needs to be brief or at least concise—that is, expressing all the necessary thoughts in the smallest number of words and sentences. This is even more true for an e-mail than for a business letter. Why? Time is at a premium online. For one thing, the recipient may pay a monthly fee to a company that provides the host computer (which allows you to connect to the Internet) and a monthly telephone bill for charges incurred while hooked up to "the Net." In that situation, time truly is money.

But aside from the financial factor, everyone is busy today. Even if your e-mail correspondent is writing from his or her workplace, and so does not have to pay for the privilege of using e-mail, that person is sure to be busy. He or she is working on other documents and/or e-mailing other people in and out of the workplace; your e-mail may be read while your correspondent is trying to complete an urgent project on another screen.

PARTS OF AN E-MAIL MESSAGE

To enjoy the convenience of sending and receiving e-mail, you need to master the first step of addressing your message. If you are using e-mail at your workplace, and there is an in-house computer network for reaching your colleagues and supervisors, follow the instructions for that system to type in the name or, often, to star it in an "address book" (often called a nickname list) or in-house list of personnel.

To access someone out in the world (that is, not in your workplace in an internal directory), generally you start by accessing the "to" space or window and typing in the following:

joe@companyname.org

The two basic parts of the address are the mailbox on the destination computer ("joe") and the host part following the "at" symbol ("companyname.org"), which identifies the Internet service provider.

Remember that the computer is "dumb" in the sense that it cannot guess what you meant to type into it. If you are off by one letter or one punctuation mark, the message will not go through. Note especially in the preceding example that there are no spaces between any of the elements of the address; even "companyname" is run together. If you have located the name "Rap Recording Hood," that name as part of an e-mail address must be typed as "raprecordinghood."

Some e-mail addresses may include an underline; again using the example above, substitute "joe_player@companyname.org." Any punctuation, just like regular characters, must be included as shown. If you misread the underline and use a hyphen instead, the message will not go through. So it's worth a brief amount of your time to double-check the address and proofread it on your screen before you send the message, especially if this is the first time you've written to the person.

If you are just starting to use e-mail, friends will give you their e-mail addresses. Where else do you get e-mail addresses for those you want to write to? Ask your school librarian or town librarian if the library has a hard-copy directory of e-mail addresses. Many newspapers and magazines now have pages or sections of interesting computer sites that include their addresses; if you see, for example, a listing of sites or newsgroups (usenet groups) for people who love horses, you can clip and save the article for future reference. Most search engines have online directories that you can access, but some charge a fee.

Other parts of an e-mail message, in addition to the address, are as follows:

- Message title—This may be called "subject," "re," or "topic" on your particular system.

Friends, especially students, often write very casual and/or supposedly humorous titles for their messages, such as "duh" or "huh" or "WHAT girl?" For business messages, however, it is good to use a straightforward descriptive title, and it helps the recipient if you don't use the same title each time. Instead of heading every message "Fox Network project," for example, use "Deadline for Fox Network project" on one, "Financial question re Fox" on another, and "Edits on Fox Network project" on another message. That way, if someone is storing your messages online to access later, he or she does not need to open every message of a dozen or more pertaining to the same project (and that same convenience will be available to you).

- Body of the message—This is usually called "message," "text," or "your words" on your system. This is the essence of your message, what you want to say and get across; see "Content of your message" below for more details on what to include.

- Lists for "cc" and "bcc"—Addresses for those to whom you want to send "carbon copies" or "blind carbon copies" are included here. On some systems, to send an e-mail to someone outside your home or workplace, you must repeat the person's address under "cc" or "bcc"; follow the instructions that come with your e-mail server. When sending e-mails at work, don't get into the habit of sending a "cc" of each message to your boss's boss. Think about the interests of the main recipient before cc-ing others; if the message contains confidential information just for the recipient, he or she will not want you to show that message to others.

- Attached computer file—This is one of the greatest conveniences of e-mail. You can send a document with your message for review by the recipient. For example, let's say you work for the county parks' department and are on the committee to increase recycling in each park. You have drafted a quick list of your suggestions, as you had a lot of ideas to share. Rather than printing and copying one document to distribute to the committee via interoffice mail or US mail, you can simply write a brief e-mail to each person on the committee and attach the document with your list of recycling ideas. See below for additional tips on forwarding your résumé via e-mail to apply for a job.

CONTENT OF YOUR MESSAGE

One of the most important e-mail tips is that each message should stand alone. That is, to understand and answer your message, the person receiving it should not have to access other messages from you or to you. Here's a simple example: You are in purchasing and send an e-mail to Letitia Jones in communications. You ask her if she wants red report covers or silver report covers for her new proposal. You are out of the office for several days and return to find a reply from Letitia that says, "Yes, the first one." So you have to go back to your own message and then send her another one saying, "By that do you mean red?" By this time, she might not remember the original question!

In some e-mail systems, you can attach the message you received to your reply, so remember to do that if it helps make your message clear. If you do not have that convenience on your e-mail, then you would want her to reply like this, "Silver report covers are good; the quantity is 250, yes?" This way you have confirmation of the color, plus, a useful reminder of the quantity, too.

Sometimes it is necessary to refer to another e-mail already on file. Perhaps the original message was a detailed budget or schedule that is too long and involved to retype. In such cases, you can refer to "my message Fox budget, April 23" and ask the person if he or she still has that on file. If not, you can resend or print out the April 23 message. On some systems, you can forward your old message or re-send. As you use any particular e-mail server, you will pick up other tips for saving time and sending messages more efficiently.

As important as it is to be concise in a conventional business letter, it is twice as important when writing e-mail. Sometimes students think it sounds businesslike or dignified to throw in a lot of long words or windy phrases; this is always boring and especially useless in e-mail.

How do you sign an e-mail message? You will naturally notice that your e-mail server has included your name in the "from" box or window. Most people still sign the text with their name or initials. That's not always enough, however. In many business messages, particularly the first or second time you are writing to someone online, it's advisable to include your full name, title, and telephone number; this helps the person place you and helps him or her reply. Also, if he or she needs to forward your message to someone else, that person will then also know who you are and how to get in touch with you.

This sample message incorporates a lot of the above information:

To: joe@companyname.com
cc: maria@companyname.com

From: jane@parkdistrict.org

Re: Meeting of the park district board

Message:
Hi Joe and Maria: Because you are the president and secretary of the board, please let me know if this time will work for the next board meeting—Tuesday, January 17, at 4 p.m.

Also, I've attached a draft agenda for the meeting. Please review and let me know if you want to add items or change the order of the agenda.—Thanks, Jane Electronic-Woman, Administrative Assistant, Friendlyville Park District, 630-555-1212

Sent: January 2, 1998, 9 a.m.

Attachment: WPfile: agenda1

APPLYING FOR JOBS VIA E-MAIL—YOUR RÉSUMÉ SPEEDS THROUGH CYBERSPACE

Many help-wanted classified ads are still written as they have been for years, directing any interested applicants to mail their résumés to the company or organization, or to mail the résumés to a box number at the newspaper where the ad is running. There are at least a couple of circumstances, however, in which you can send your résumé via e-mail. One is when you have located a job opening on an organization's home page on the web; normally, the list of positions open includes a brief list of qualifications needed and ends with the e-mail address for the recruiter responsible for screening candidates. In this case, your "cover letter" via e-mail is a message saying that you saw the listing for the position and want to apply for that job; you can send your résumé at the same time as an attached file. The classified ads in the newspaper, most often those for computer jobs, might simply ask you to reply or forward your résumé to an e-mail address.

If you are specifically interested in finding a job via the Internet, try accessing the following site, Monsterboard, which compiles and displays information from many sources on various types of occupations in various locations. You can reach Monsterboard at

http://www.monster.com/

When sending out your résumé to a variety of organizations, possibly around the country or around the world, you have no way of knowing which word-processing system is used at the receiving organization. It is useful, therefore, in the word-processing program that you use, to convert your résumé to a "text file," which can then be read by any word-processing program and converted to its format. That way, the organization to which you are applying does not have to spend time trying to figure out how to access or print the résumé you want everyone to read and appreciate.

SIX

WRITE IT RIGHT: GRAMMAR AND WORD USAGE

The word "grammar" often has a paralyzing effect on students, and this has been true for generations. Do not imagine that your grandparents loved to study grammar —unless they were writers or English teachers. But there is no reason to be afraid of grammar, which is the study of words and how they fit together, especially in sentences.

Your best approach is to think of grammar as an aide to helping you express yourself better. You have a lot of great ideas to put across in your community group, you want to get that special job at the Nature Conservancy, or you want to get a scholarship to study music in Asia. To achieve one or more of these goals, you need to write a good letter, craft a fine résumé, and compose a statement about your qualifications that will convince people to give you what you want. Writing clearly and effectively will help you reach these goals.

Many good books have been published to help you deal with questions about grammar, spelling, and word usage, including *How to Improve Your Grammar and Usage* in the Speak Out, Write On! series. Other books are listed in "For More Information" at the end of this book. If you can buy one or two of these books, that's great. Otherwise, locate them at your school library or public library.

TYPES OF SENTENCES

A *sentence* is usually defined as a complete thought. Here are some examples:

The dinosaur chased Ooogie through the valley.

Skydiving can be dangerous.

I am so happy that I feel like dancing.

Aliens do not live next door to you.

Each sentence has a subject (a noun or pronoun—for example, "dinosaur" in the first sentence above) and a predicate (a verb or verb-adverb combination—for example, "chased" in the first sentence above). Parts of speech, such as the noun and the verb, will be discussed below.

A phrase and a clause are also parts of sentences. A *phrase* is a group of words that modify, or describe, something. Example: *Born on a ranch* [phrase], Maria always loved horses. A clause is a group of words with a separate thought that does not stand alone as a sentence. Example: Sam accepted the job, *although he did not know if he would like the work* [clause].

Here are the three main types of sentences:

Simple sentence: Jose walked to the games arcade.

Compound sentence, which combines two thoughts in separate clauses: Jose walked to the games arcade, and he met Moses at three o'clock.

84

Complex sentence, which adds a qualifying clause to a basic sentence: Jose walked to the games arcade, even though it is three miles from his house.

In a business letter, memo, or any other type of business writing, it is best to write in complete sentences. An employer wants to know that you can write correctly, and this is true even if you want to be a computer operator or an electrician. You still have to write memos and reports as a computer operator or in other technical jobs.

In personal correspondence you may occasionally use a sentence *fragment*. This is a collection of words that is not a complete sentence by itself. Often an expression we use in everyday conversation is easily understood but does not constitute a sentence. For example, you might write or say "no problem" to a friend who asks a favor; your meaning is clear, but the words "no problem" do not make up a full sentence. You might say to a brother or sister, "What a nut!" This is a sentence fragment, almost a kind of shorthand for a complete sentence, which would be "What a nut you are!" As long as your meaning is clear, there is no problem using sentence fragments in personal writing.

Clear and simple writing wins the day most of the time. Don't pile a lot of useless ten-dollar words onto your sentence, as someone would pile furniture onto a pickup truck, because the sentence might be too overloaded to do its job! There's no prize for using long words or writing the longest sentence.

QUICK REVIEW OF PARTS OF SPEECH

We classify words as parts of speech to help determine how to use them best.

Noun

A person or thing. Examples: boy, girl, dog, computer, Freddie, Linda, White House.

As mentioned above, a noun is usually the subject of a sentence—the actor or the doer.

Pronoun

A shorthand way of referring to a person or thing. Examples: it, you, me, they.

Verb

An action word or a word that describes a condition. Examples: walk, run, scream, challenge, defy, is, are. As mentioned earlier, a verb or verb phrase ("is running") is the predicate of a sentence.

Adverb

A word that describes a verb. Examples: quickly, slowly, fast, deeply, loudly. Adverbs often end in "-ly," but not always.

Adjective

A word that describes a noun. Examples: blue, red, big, beautiful, hideous, thoughtful, brilliant. Beginning writers often use too many adjectives. Especially in letters, be careful not to overuse adjectives as a sign of your enthusiasm. That just looks like sloppy writing.

Preposition

A word that ties together a phrase with a noun or pronoun. Examples: in, into, on, above, over.

Conjunction

A word that links two clauses or phrases. Examples: and, but, or.

"WHAT IS THEY?"

Subject-verb agreement is another aspect of writing that sounds harder than it really is. Most readers have noticed the mistake in the subhead above. To be correct, the subhead should ask, "What are they?" The big question in subject-verb agreement usually comes down to this: Should the verb have an "s" on the end? Or, if the verb is a form of "to be," should it be "is" or "are"?

A plural subject normally takes a verb without the "s." For example, it is correct to say, "Rita and Latoya walk to the river." For a singular subject, we need the "s." For example, "Latoya walks to the river."

Again, if you have difficulty telling which form of the verb goes with the noun, it is best to consult a handbook of grammar, style, or writing. See "For More Information" later in this book.

GO, WENT, GONE

Verb tenses are easy to master, if you just take some time to think about it. Present tense is used to describe something happening now. Example: "I *work* at Joe's Tacqueria every week." Past tense describes something that is complete or finished. Example: "I *worked* at Joe's Tacqueria for six months, until they noticed that I was eating up all the profits." Past perfect tense is used to talk about something that was completed before something else. Example: "I *had worked* at the bank before I worked at Joe's." Present perfect tense describes something that started in the past but may still occur again in the future. Example, "I *have worked* at Joe's Tacqueria from time to time."

In the English language, many regular verbs change from past to present by adding a "d" or "ed."

Examples: talk/talked, walk/walked, move/moved, climb/climbed. For many irregular verbs, however, you need to memorize the past and past perfect tenses, as they are not so predictable. Some examples: go/went/have gone, do/did/have done, sing/sang/have sung.

Sometimes the verb in English depends on whether the noun or pronoun you are using with the verb is first person ("I" or "we), second person ("you," singular or plural), or third person ("he," "she," or "they"). Some of the most commonly used verbs are various forms of the infinitive "to be." Correct forms are "I am" for first person, "you are" for second person, and "she is" for third person. If you are still learning English, write down some of these common exceptions to the rules in a reminder list for yourself.

SPELLING

Now you're confident you have mastered sentences and parts of speech. How's your spelling? A misspelled word can stick out like a sore thumb. Think about your cover letter and résumé when you are applying for jobs: one misspelled word is often enough to deny you an interview. So it's worth your while to make sure every word is spelled correctly.

If you are writing on a computer, use a spell-checking program, if you have one. A spell-checking program commonly gives you alternatives to a word it identifies as spelled incorrectly. You must then approve the proper substitution. You still need to proofread your own work carefully, too, to make sure that you have not overlooked a problem. Be careful of homonyms (words that sound alike but that are different in meaning)—the spell-checking program will not alert you to the use of *hear* when you mean *here*.

Even with a spell-checking feature on a computer,

you need a good dictionary to verify definitions of words as well as the appropriate spelling. *Webster's New Collegiate Dictionary* or *American Heritage Dictionary* are popular choices among teachers and students.

WORD USAGE

Whether you are a beginning writer or an experienced one, you want to target your writing to your intended audience. If you are applying for a job or writing a letter to the editor of the *New York Times*, you probably should not use slang expressions such as "way excellent" or "then I go" (for "then I said"). Slang is fine in personal letters to friends and in e-mail that is not strictly business.

Be straightforward in your word choices. Do not refer to yourself in the third person, as former Senator Robert Dole often did in his unsuccessful campaign for the US presidency in 1996. (He frequently said, "Bob Dole thinks. . . .") This is confusing and pretentious, especially for students or young people.

Connotation is the meaning attached to words other than the straight dictionary definition. Consider the difference between "Hung Wha pondered the choices too long" and "Hung Wha considered his options carefully." Try to be nonemotional in your business letters, even if you are writing a letter of complaint about a product or service or if you are writing a letter to the editor with your political views. You might feel better momentarily if you write a letter that uses words as arrows to attack someone, but realistically, what are your chances of convincing the uncommitted when you write in that manner?

Use technical jargon sparingly in a letter or résumé. It may be that the first person screening your job application is a personnel recruiter or a personnel clerk. Even if you are applying for a job as a computer programmer or engineer, you need to communicate clearly with people who may not know technical terms. Your letter should be professional and should not depend on technical terms to get your points across.

Similarly, do not load your business correspondence with initials abbreviating terms or acronyms for names of organizations and so on. You may appear pompous if you give the impression you do not have the time to spell out a name or term. For example, do not use "ASAP" (as soon as possible) except in very informal notes or e-mails. Also, the acronym you may be familiar with may stand for something else to your listener; is "ADA" short for American Dental Association, American Dietetic Association, or Assistant District Attorney?

It is to your credit as a well-read person if you can quote from some of the classics of literature. Many people find themselves quoting, "To be or not to be," the famous line from Shakespeare's *Hamlet*, at one time or another. But basically you should reserve all literary quotations and flowery phrases for your creative writing, including poetry, or for your personal letters. Again, keeping your business letters straightforward is always a good goal.

At the same time, writing in a businesslike manner does not mean you have to be dull. I admit I was immediately captivated by a cover letter with a résumé from a prospective editorial assistant that began, "When I read the ad for your position, I was amazed at how closely I fit the qualifications you are looking for." This fresh, enthusiastic approach appealed to me, and I called to offer an appointment for a job interview.

SEVEN

*S*OURCES TO USE AT THE LIBRARY

For many letters that you write, you may already have all the information you need at your fingertips. If you are answering a "help wanted" classified ad in the newspaper, the ad will tell you where to send your letter. But for other letters, you will need to locate or develop information. Let's say you have always wanted to work at Compact Disc Corporate Paradise, but you don't have the address; also, you would like to do a little research to include some impressive fact about the company in your cover letter. You should certainly try to find the information you need for your letter at the library or on the World Wide Web.

To take another example, suppose you are secretary of your school's student council, and the council wants to involve other schools and some community groups in a recycling campaign. You may have the names of all the groups you want to write to, but not the addresses or the ZIP codes. It is vital to include postal ZIP codes on all your mail to help achieve timely delivery.

BASIC REFERENCE BOOKS

For almost any type of writing, you need to refer regularly to a dictionary to check spellings and to verify that you are using the word you want (not a homonym). Also, you should have handy, or know where to find at the library, a *thesaurus*, a reference book that offers synonyms—words similar in meaning to the one you have in mind. If you are writing a paper about Rodin's sculpture, "The Thinkers," you may notice you have used the word "thoughtful" five or six times. You could then look in a thesaurus to find other words to use, for example, "pensive" or "reflective."

A general encyclopedia is the best source to look up facts on a variety of topics. Authoritative and popular encyclopedias in most school or town libraries include *Grolier's Multimedia Encyclopedia*, *Compton's Encyclopedia* on CD-ROM, *Encyclopedia Americana*, *Encyclopaedia Britannica*, and *World Book*. You may need to look up "manatee" in an encyclopedia to find out more specific information about that animal before you write a letter to your US Senator on saving the manatee; the television show that got you interested in this topic may not have been very specific, or you may not have had time to write down the information you heard.

No doubt you've been told that it is not acceptable to use an encyclopedia as your only source (or even the main source) for a research paper. But encyclopedias include many useful facts that will help you understand more about nature, science, sports, history, geography, literature, and other subjects. Encyclopedias are also useful for job searches, because you may need to look up an unfamiliar term you see in an ad, and you'll want more background than you can find in a dictionary.

Dictionaries of quotations are useful for many types of writing, and these are also found in the general reference section of your library. *Bartlett's Familiar Quotations* is probably the most famous book of quotations, but many other books of quotations are now available. These include books of famous or notable sayings by women, African-Americans, business leaders, and so on.

Another good general reference source for all of your writing, including letters, is the *Reader's Guide to Periodical Literature*. This is an index published annually, with frequent updates during the year, of articles in general interest magazines such as *Time, Newsweek, US News and World Report, Smithsonian*, and the *New York Times Magazine*. You can look up possible subject headings, including the names of famous individuals or corporations, to locate articles about them.

Also in the general reference section or department of your library is a very handy directory, the *Encyclopedia of Associations*. This multi-volume reference book, updated annually, lists names, addresses, phone numbers, key contacts, and other useful information on associations and voluntary groups (as opposed to for-profit companies). Here you can access such information as the headquarters address and phone number for the March of Dimes or the American Bar Association. Or you can find answers to such questions as, "Is there a society for both stamp collecting and coin collecting?" (there is) and figure out how to get in touch with that group.

BUSINESS RESEARCH

It is very useful to get to know the business section of your library, whether you are starting a job search, changing jobs, or working in a job that involves sending out correspondence. A good basic source for information about corporations is *Standard & Poor's Register of Corporations, Directors, and Executives*, published each year by the Standard & Poor Corporation. (The name varies a little with the annual editions, but just make sure the book you are looking at is a Standard & Poor's directory.) This reference book includes the full name and address of the headquarters of corporations, useful information about their lines of business, and names and titles of key executives. Why do you need these names and titles? It is always best when applying for a job "cold"—that is, with no classified ad or recommendation—to address your letter to a specific person at the company; this improves the chances of having your letter read and answered.

The largest corporations in the United States are described in *Standard & Poor's 500 Guide*, published annually. This reference volume includes information on the five hundred largest and most successful corporations, by dollar volume of business. You may need to consult this book, for example, if you are looking for major corporations to support a campaign for healthier babies in the southern United States. There's no sense directing your appeals to the Struggling Guys and a Girlfriend Company down the street if they do not have a large operating budget for their new business; you need companies with major resources.

The business section of your library is also a good place to look if you are interested in material about careers. Often a school or town library has a career section or career corner within it, including vertical files of information about careers filed alphabetically by the name of the career. For example, under "G" for "geologist," you might find pamphlets from the American Association for the Advancement

Jonathan Swift

Author of the famous satire *Gulliver's Travels*, Swift is always remembered for his biting sense of humor, which he turns on himself in this excerpt:

Letter to Miss Vanbromrigh, August 1720:
"If Heaven had looked upon riches to be a valuable thing, it would not have given them to such a scoundrel."

Benjamin Franklin

The noted political figure, inventor, and writer was a key player in the American Revolution. Here are famous quotations from two of his letters:

Letter to Josiah Quincy, September 1773: "There never was a good war or a bad peace."

Letter to M. Leroy, 1789: "Our Constitution is in actual operation; everything appears to promise that it will last; but in this world nothing is certain but death and taxes."

Helen Maria Williams

Letters have long been important in politics and government, and sometimes the writing of letters has been a key part of revolutions. English writer Helen Williams lived in France during the French Revolution in the late eighteenth century. At first, she enthusiastically supported the French Revolution in her letters home to England. But then, as the revolutionary committee imprisoned and executed more and more people with guillotines—in the so-called Reign of Terror—Williams herself began to be suspected of treason, and her letters put her life in danger:

I had written to my friends in England, a few letters about the period of the Terror, and unfortunately, someone had the imprudence to insert extracts from them in the London journals. This indiscretion compromised my status in the eyes of the Committee of Public Safety, and this awful band began to direct its attention to me. . . . Thus I passed the winter at Paris, with the knife of the guillotine suspended over me by a frail thread.

Fortunately, Williams was not executed. She continued to write letters to England and to smuggle out of France letters from prisoners and from people trying to stop the Reign of Terror. For a time, she was exiled in Switzerland, where she still tried to help the French legislators fighting the Terror. How did the Committee on Public Safety try to stop the legislators?

The barriers of the city were shut, all communication cut off, the secrecy of letters violated, the hall of the convention blockaded by an armed force.

Jose Maria Morelos

Letters played a key role in the birth of the country of Mexico. The first president of Mexico and two of his aides wrote the following earnest and eloquent letter to US President James Madison in July 1815. Mexico had recently declared its independence from Spain and asked for support from the United States:

Puruaran, Mexico, July 14, 1815

To: James Madison, President of the United States

Most Excellent Sir:

The Mexican people, weary of the enormous weight of Spanish domination and having forever lost the hope of being happy under the rule of their conquerors, broke through the barriers of moderation and, facing difficulties and perils which seemed insuperable to the efforts of an enslaved colony, they raised the cry of freedom and heavily undertook the work of regeneration.

We relied on the protection of Heaven which could not withdraw it from the well-known justice of our cause nor ignore the rectitude and purity of our intentions exclusively bent on the good of mankind: we relied on the mettle and enthusiasm of our compatriots, who had decided to die rather than to again bear the shameful yoke of slavery: and finally we relied on the powerful aid of the United States, which as they widely guided us by their example would favor us with their generous assistance upon signing treaties of friendship and alliance in which good faith would preside and where the reciprocal interests of both nations would be remembered. . . .

Jose Maria Morelos, President of Mexico
Jose Maria Linaga
Remigio de Yarza, Secretary of Government

Frederick Douglass

Born a slave, Frederick Douglass ran away from his "master" and became a writer and leader of the antislavery movement. In 1848, he wrote this very powerful letter to Thomas Auld, his former owner, on the occasion of the tenth anniversary of his freedom. Although the letter was addressed to Auld, Douglass wrote it for publication in antislavery literature and in general newspapers. This letter explains in very human terms why one man or woman cannot and should not own another:

September 1848

Thomas Auld:

Sir—The long and intimate, though by no means friendly relation which unhappily subsisted between you and myself, leads me to hope that you will easily account for the great liberty which I now take in addressing you in this open and public manner. The same fact may possibly remove any disagreeable surprise which you may experience on again finding your name coupled with mine, in any other way than in an advertisement, accurately describing my person, and offering a large sum for my arrest. . . .

I have selected this day on which to address you, because it is the anniversary of my emancipation; and knowing of no better way, I am led to this as the best mode of celebrating that truly important event. Just ten years ago this beautiful September morning, yon bright sun beheld me a slave—a poor, degraded chattel—trembling at the sound of your voice, lamenting that I was a man, and wishing myself a brute. The hopes which I had treasured up for weeks of a safe and successful escape from your grasp, were powerfully confronted at this last hour by dark clouds of doubt and fear, making my person shake and my bosom to heave with the heavy contest between hope and fear. I have no words to describe to you the deep agony of soul which I experienced on that never to be forgotten morning— (for I left by daylight). I was making a leap in the dark. The probabilities, so far as I could by reason determine them, were stoutly against the undertaking. . . . One in whom I had confided, and who had promised me assistance, appalled by fear at the trial hour, deserted me, thus leaving the responsibility of success or failure solely with myself. . . .

When yet but a child about six years old, I imbibed the determination to run away. The very first mental effort that I now remember on my part, was an attempt to solve the mystery, why am I a slave, and with this question my youthful mind was troubled for many days, pressing upon me more heavily at times than others. When I saw the slave-driver whip a slave woman, cut the blood out of her neck, and heard her piteous cries, I went away into the corner fence, wept, and pondered over the mystery. I had, through some medium, I know not what, got some idea of God, the Creator of all mankind, the black and the white, and that he had made the blacks to serve the whites as slaves. How he could do this and be good, I could not tell. I was not satisfied with this theory, which made God responsible for slavery, for it pained me greatly, and I have wept over it long and often. At one time, your first wife, Mrs. Lucretia, heard me singing and saw me shedding tears, and asked of me the matter, but I was afraid to tell her. I was puzzled with this question, till one night, while sitting in the kitchen, heard some of the old slaves talking of their parents having been stolen from Africa by white man, and were sold here as slaves. The whole mystery was solved at once. Very soon after this my aunt Jinny and uncle Noah ran away, and the great noise made about it by your father-in-law, made me for the first time acquainted with the fact, that there were free States as well as slave States. From that time, I resolved that I would some day run away. The morality of the act, I dispose as follows: I am myself; you are yourself; we are two distinct persons, equal persons. What you are, I am. You are a man, and so am I. God created both, and made us separate beings. I am not by nature bound to you, or you to me. Nature does not make your existence depend upon me, or mine to depend upon yours. I cannot walk upon your legs, or you upon mine. I cannot breathe for you, or you for me; I must breathe for myself, and you for yourself. We are distinct persons, and are each equally provided with faculties necessary to our individual existence. In leaving you, I took nothing but what belong to me, and in no way lessened your means for obtaining an honest living. . . .

Frederick Douglass

F. Scott Fitzgerald

In a more personal (as opposed to universal) vein, great writers and great historical figures are also individuals (naturally!) with families and personal lives. Fitzgerald, a famous American novelist (*The Great Gatsby, Tender Is the Night*), in August 1933 wrote some reflections to his daughter, Frances, who was away at camp:

Dear Pie:

All I believe in in life is the rewards for virtue (according to your talents) and the punishments for not fulfilling your duties, which are doubly costly. If there is such a volume in the camp library, will you ask Mrs. Tyson to let you look up a sonnet of Shakespeare's in which the line occurs, 'Lilies that fester smell far worse than weeds.'

. . . I will arrange the camp bill.

Half wit, I will conclude.

Things to worry about:
    Worry about courage
    Worry about cleanliness
    Worry about efficiency
    Worry about horsemanship
    Worry about . . .

Things not to worry about:
    Don't worry about popular opinion
    Don't worry about dolls
    Don't worry about the past
    Don't worry about the future
    Don't worry about growing up
    Don't worry about anybody getting ahead of you
    Don't worry about triumph
    Don't worry about failure unless it comes through
    your own fault
    Don't worry about mosquitoes
    Don't worry about flies
    Don't worry about insects in general
    Don't worry about parents
    Don't worry about boys
    Don't worry about disappointments
    Don't worry about pleasures
    Don't worry about satisfactions

Things to think about:
    What am I really aiming at?
    How good am I really in comparison to my contem-
    poraries in regard to:
    (a) Scholarship
    (b) Do I really understand about people and am I
         able to get along with them?
    (c) Am I trying to make my body a useful instru-
         ment or am I neglecting it?

With dearest love,
Daddy

Winston Churchill
Prime Minister of England during World War II,
Churchill is remembered as a courageous leader. His
speeches inspired the people of his country to keep
up their morale in the face of massive bombing at-

tacks from German planes sent by Adolf Hitler to conquer England. In 1940, he wrote (in part) to President Franklin D. Roosevelt as part of a long campaign to secure American support for the European war effort:

May 15, 1940

[Dear Mr. President:]

. . . As you are no doubt aware, the scene has darkened swiftly. The enemy have a marked preponderance in the air, and their new technique is making a deep impression upon the French.

I think myself the battle on land has only just begun, and I should like to see the masses engage. Up to the present, Hitler is working with specialized units in tanks and air.

The small countries are simply smashed up, one by one, like matchwood. We must expect, though it is not yet certain, that Mussolini will hurry in to share the loot of civilisation. We expected to be attacked here ourselves, both from the air and by parachute and air-borne troops in the near future, and are getting ready for them.

If necessary, we shall continue the war alone, and we are not afraid of that. But I trust you realise, Mr. President, that the voice and force of the United States may count for nothing if they are withheld too long. You may have a completely subjugated Nazified Europe established with astonishing swiftness, and the weight may be more than we can bear.

Groucho Marx

While some letters represent politics, government, and history on very serious levels, others are fun and entertaining. Famed comedian Groucho Marx, one of the Marx Brothers who worked together in vaudeville and in Hollywood films such as *A Night at the Opera* and *Room Service*, was a delightful writer. Groucho (it would be unnatural somehow to refer to him as "Marx") corresponded with many other famous people of his time, including other comedians, writers, publishers, and actors. This 1951 letter to comedian Fred Allen reflects Groucho's tongue-in-cheek style:

August 30, 1951

Dear Fred:

It is very difficult to correspond regularly with one who is not a woman. This, in case you care, explains why my letters are so infrequent. If, for example, one is corresponding with an attractive female—preferably not too old—there's always the likelihood that, at some future date you might be able to get closer to her. Corresponding with a man—a man our age, at any rate—soon reduces itself to a mutual cataloging of aches and pains, and the constant trials they are both being subjected to by the tax department.

Please don't assume from this that your letters are not worth receiving. The joy they give me can only be compared to the happiness I experienced years ago when a wire would arrive saying that we had received a year's booking on the Pantages Circuit [steady job in vaudeville]. I cherish each letter as though it were 'a gem of purest ray serene.' This, in case you care, is lifted from Thomas Gray and can be found on page 262 of Bartlett's Quotations.

My friend Goody [Ace, comedy writer] tells me that you're London-bound with the rowdy and predictable Tallulah [Bankhead, actor]. As one who has journeyed on the high seas a number of times, I trust that you will beware of card sharks, pool sharks, and in case you should be lucky enough to fall overboard, just plain sharks.

I wish I were going with you. What high old times we could have—Goody, you, and I. Three old biddies swapping aches and pains, telling tall tales of romantic exploits and cursing television. Yes, Fred, we could make the ship rock with our laughter.

So have a good time and my best to the Duchess.

Groucho

NOVELS MADE UP OF LETTERS

Many writers have used the form of letters to and from various characters as the medium for a short story or novel. An *epistolary novel* is one made up of fictional letters. Using letters prompts the writer to express his or her thoughts in a conversational tone and to organize the material so as to fit into letters while keeping the plot moving along. Additionally, the reader enjoys the feeling of being privileged to peek into someone's private correspondence, even though the individuals involved are characters of the imagination.

Jane Austen

Jane Austen was a writer in the 1800s whose witty, finely detailed novels portrayed provincial English life. In recent years several popular films based on her novels have brought her work new attention. One of her lesser-known works is *Lady Susan,* an epistolary novella, or short novel, made up of letters to and from the title character. To appreciate Jane Austen's understanding of human passions, consider Lady Susan, a character who is a beautiful, hard-hearted, and manipulative woman. She would be a match for most of the scheming characters who are featured in "The Film of the Week" or the "real people" who appear on talk shows revealing how they have mistreated their families and friends. This is evident in a letter from Lady Susan (Mrs. Vernon) to her only friend, in which she discusses some communications between her own fiancé and her teenage daughter Frederica:

Mrs. Vernon to Mrs. Johnson

. . . I shall always detest them both. He can have no true regard for me, or he would not have listened to her; and she, with her little rebellious heart and indelicate feelings to throw herself into the protection of a young man with whom she had scarcely ever exchanged two words before. I am equally confounded at her impudence and his credulity. How dared he believe what she told him in my disfavour! Ought he not to have felt assured that I must have unanswerable motives for all that I had done! Where was his reliance on my sense or goodness then; where the resentment which true love would have dictated against the person defaming me, that person, too, a chit, a child, without talent or education, whom he had been always taught to despise?

I was calm for some time, but the greatest degree of forbearance may be overcome, and I hope I was afterwards sufficiently keen. He endeavoured, long endeavoured to soften my resentment, but that woman is a fool indeed who while insulted by accusation, can be worked on by compliments. At length he left me, as deeply provoked as myself, and he showed his anger more. I was quite cool, but he gave way to the most violent indignation. I may therefore expect it will sooner subside; and perhaps his may be vanished forever, while mine will be found still fresh and implacable.

He is now shut up in his apartment, whether I heard him go, on leaving mine. How unpleasant, one would think, must his reflections be! But some people's feelings are imcomprehensible. I have not yet tranquilized myself enough to see Frederica. She shall not soon forget the occurrences of this day. She shall find that she has poured forth her tender tale of love in vain, and exposed herself forever to the contempt of the whole world, and the severest resentment of her injured mother.

Yours affectionately,
S. Vernon

Gordon R. Dickson

Science fiction writer Gordon R. Dickson used the format of letters to tell a sinister tale in his 1965 short story "Computers Don't Argue." Some sci-fi writers love and embrace technology, and they use technological advances and their creative ideas about science, in their stories. Others, like Dickson in this story, paint a picture of technology out of control. Humans welcome and celebrate inventions that will make our lives easier, but then those devices can do things their inventors did not foresee, and machines end up ruling us.

Walter A. Child, the fictional main character, exchanges a series of letters with a book club that has been dunning him for money for a book he never received. Eventually, he gets a letter from an attorney and writes this reply in the hopes of ending the confusion:

437 Woodlawn Drive
Pandluk, Michigan
May 4, 1966

Mr. Hagthorpe M. Pruitt, Jr.
Maloney, Mahoney, MacNamara and Pruitt
89 Prince Street
Chicago, Illinois

Dear Mr. Pruitt:

You don't know what a pleasure it is to me in this matter to get a letter from a live human being to whom I can explain the situation.

This whole matter is silly. I explained it fully in my letters to the Treasure Book Company. But I might as well have been trying to explain to the computer that puts out their [bills], for all the good it seemed to do. Briefly, what happened was I ordered a copy of "Kim," by Rudyard Kipling for $4.98. When I opened the package they sent me, I found the book had only half its pages, but I'd previously mailed a check to pay them for the book.

I sent the book back to them, asking either for a whole copy or my money back. Instead, they sent me a copy of "Kidnapped," by Robert Louis Stevenson—which I had not ordered, and for which they have been trying to collect from me.

Meanwhile, I am still waiting for the money back that they owe me for the copy of "Kim" that I didn't get. That's the whole story. Maybe you can help me straighten them out.

Relievedly yours,
Walter A. Child

P.S. I also sent them back their copy of "Kidnapped," as soon as I got it, but it hasn't seemed to help. They have never even acknowledged getting it back.

Unfortunately, the law firm is not able to help, and the reference to Robert Louis Stevenson, famed author of *Kidnapped*, makes the situation worse. Computerized court records sent from Illinois to Michigan, where Child lives, are so garbled that he is accused and convicted of kidnapping and murdering Robert L. Stevenson! His lawyer understands that he is innocent and writes to the governor to try to get a pardon and forestall the death penalty. The governor responds appropriately, but bureaucracy—another common "enemy" in science fiction literature—and technology combine to stop the pardon. Presumably the execution goes forward, as the story ends with this chilling letter or memo (on the day of the planned execution):

Interdepartmental Routing Service

Failure to route Document properly.
To: Governor Hubert Daniel Willikens
Re: Pardon issued to Walter A. Child, July 1, 1966

Dear State Employee:

You have failed to attach your Routing Number.

PLEASE: Resubmit document with this card and form 876, explaining your authority for placing a TOP RUSH category on this document. Form 876 must be signed by your departmental supervisor.

RESUBMIT ON: Earliest possible date ROUTING SERVICE office is open. In this case, Tuesday, July 5, 1966.

WARNING: Failure to submit form 876 WITH THE SIGNATURE OF YOUR SUPERIOR may make you liable for prosecution for misusing a Service of the State Government. A warrant may be issued for your arrest.

There are NO exceptions. YOU have been WARNED.

Perhaps you can think of letters you have enjoyed reading, or have found memorable, either through history or literature. Letters are changing and evolving as are other types of communication, but letter writing is still a basic skill needed to "speak out and write on!"

APPENDIX

TITLES AND SALUTATIONS: A QUICK REFERENCE

Occasionally you may want to or need to write to a person who deserves as a mark of respect a special title and salutation, other than the usual "Mr.," "Mrs.," "Miss," or "Ms." These are generally people with religious titles, those in political offices, or those in military offices. The following selected list of special titles was adapted with permission from *Webster's New Collegiate Dictionary* (Merriam-Webster). When more than one salutation is given, the first one is the more formal; if you know the person, you can choose the second, or more informal, salutation.

THE PERSON	FORM OF ADDRESS	SALUTATION
Clerical and religious orders		
archbishop	The Most Reverend Archbishop of _____ OR The Most Reverend Joe Jones Archbishop of _____	Your Excellency: Dear Archbishop Jones:
bishop, Catholic	The Most Reverend Joe Jones Bishop of _____	Your Excellency: Dear Bishop Jones:

THE PERSON	FORM OF ADDRESS	SALUTATION
bishop, Episcopal	The Right Reverend Joe Jones Bishop of _____	Right Reverend Sir: Dear Bishop Jones:
bishop, Protestant other	The Reverend Joe Jones	Reverend Sir: Dear Bishop Jones:
brother, Catholic	Brother Joe, S.J. [initials of order]	Dear Brother Joe:
brotherhood, Catholic, superior of	Brother Nick, S.J., Superior	Dear Brother Nick:
clergyman, Protestant	The Reverend Joe Jones OR The Reverend Dr. Joe Jones (if the person has a doctor's degree)	Dear Sir: Dear Mr. Smith: Dear Dr. Smith:
nun	Sister Mary Angelica, S.C.	Dear Sister Mary Angelica: Dear Sister:
patriarch (of Eastern church)	His Beatitude the Patriarch of _____	Most Reverend Lord:
pope	His Holiness Pope _ _____ OR His Holiness the Pope	Your Holiness: OR Most Holy Father:
priest	The Reverend Joe Jones OR The Reverend Father Jones	Dear Father Jones: Dear Father:
rabbi	Rabbi Joe Jones OR Rabbi Joe Jones, DD (if having a doctor's degree)	Dear Rabbi Jones: Dear Dr. Jones:

Diplomats

ambassador to US	His Excellency Joe Jones Ambassador of _____	Sir: Dear Mr. Ambassador:
American ambassador	The Honorable Joe Jones American Ambassador	Sir: Dear Mr. Ambassador:
chargé d'affaires, foreign	Ms. Jo Jones Chargé d'Affaires of _____	Madame: Dear Ms. Jones:

THE PERSON	FORM OF ADDRESS	SALUTATION
consul	Joe Jones, Esq.	Dear Sir:
secretary-general, UN	His Excellency Joe Jones Secretary-General of the United Nations	Excellency: Dear Mr. Secretary-General:

Government officials

alderman	The Honorable Joan Jones	Dear Ms. Jones:
assemblyman	See "representative, state"	
associate justice, Supreme Court	Mr. Justice Jones The Supreme Court of the United States	Sir: Dear Justice Jones:
cabinet officers	The Honorable Joe Jones Secretary of State	Dear Sir:
chief justice, Supreme Court	The Chief Justice of the United States	Dear Mr. Chief Justice:
governor	The Honorable Joan Jones Governor of _____	Dear Governor Jones:
judge, federal	The Honorable Joe Jones	Dear Judge Jones:
judge, state or local	The Honorable Joe Jones Chief Judge of the Court of Appeals	Dear Judge Jones:
mayor	The Honorable Joe Jones Mayor of _____	Dear Mayor Jones:
president, US	The President The White House	Mr. President: Dear Mr. President:
representative, state	The Honorable Joe Jones House of Representatives State Capitol	Dear Mr. Jones:
representative, US	The Honorable Joe Jones The United States House of Representatives	Sir: Dear Mr. Jones:

THE PERSON	FORM OF ADDRESS	SALUTATION
senator, state	The Honorable Joe Jones The State Senate State Capitol	Dear Senator Jones:
senator, US	The Honorable Joe Jones United States Senator	Dear Senator Jones:
vice-president, US	The Vice-President United States Senate	Dear Mr. Vice-President:

military ranks (a selected list)

admiral	(full rank plus full name plus a comma plus abbreviation of branch of service; example: Rear Admiral Joe Jones, USN [United States Navy])	Sir: Dear Admiral Smith:
cadet	Cadet Joe Jones United States Military Academy	Dear Cadet Jones:
captain (air force, army, coast guard, marine corps, or navy)	(full rank plus full name plus a comma plus abbreviation of branch of service)	Dear Captain Jones:
colonel or lieutenant colonel	(same as above)	Dear Colonel Jones:
commander (coast guard or navy)	(same as above)	Dear Commander Jones:
corporal	(same as above)	Dear Corporal Jones:
first lieutenant, second lieutenant (air force, army, or marine corps)	(same as above)	Dear Lieutenant Jones:
general, lieutenant general, major general	(same as above)	Sir: Dear General Jones:

THE PERSON	FORM OF ADDRESS	SALUTATION
major (air force, army, or marine corps)	(same as above)	Dear Major Jones:
midshipman	Midshipman Joe Jones United States Naval Academy	Dear Midshipman Jones:
petty officer and chief petty officer	(full rank plus full name plus comma plus branch of service)	Dear Mr. Jones: OR Dear Chief Jones:
private	(same as above)	Dear Private Smith:
other ranks	(same as above)	Dear + rank + last name:

Miscellaneous professions

attorney	Mr. Joe Jones Attorney-at-law OR Joe Jones, Esq.	Dear Mr. Jones:
dentist	Joan Jones, DDS (office address) OR Dr. Joan Jones (home address)	Dear Dr. Jones:
physician	Joe Jones, MD (office address) OR Dr. Joe Jones (home address)	Dear Dr. Jones:
professor, associate professor, assistant professor	(rank plus full name)	Dear + rank + last name:
veterinarian	Joe Jones, DVM (office address) OR Dr. Joe Jones (home address)	Dear Dr. Jones:

$\mathcal{F}$OR MORE
INFORMATION

For Further Reading

Ahmad, Nyla. *Cybersurfer: the Owl Internet Guide for Kids*. Toronto, Ont.: Owl Books (distributed in United States by Firefly books), 1996. Book plus computer disk.

The Associated Press Stylebook and Libel Manual. 6th trade ed. Reading, Mass.: Addison-Wesley, 1996.

The Chicago Manual of Style. 14th ed. Chicago: University of Chicago Press, 1993.

Clark, David. *Student's Guide to the Internet.* 2nd ed. Indianapolis, Ind.: Que Corporation, 1996.

Collin, Simon. *E-mail: A Practical Guide.* Oxford: Butterworth-Heinemann, 1995.

Farr, J. Michael. *The Quick Résumé & Cover Letter Book.* Indianapolis, Ind.: JIST Works, Inc., 1994.

Fein, Richard. *Cover Letters! Cover Letters! Cover Letters!* Hawthorne, N.J.: Book-Mart Press, 1994.

Gonyea, James C., and Wayne M. Gonyea. *Electronic Resumes: A Complete Guide to Putting your Resume Online.* New York: McGraw-Hill, 1995.

Kennedy, Joyce Lain. *Cover Letters for Dummies, 2nd ed.* Foster City, Calif.: IDG Books Worldwide, 1998.

Li, Xia, and Nancy B. Crane. *Electronic Style: A Guide to Citing Electronic Information.* Westport, Conn.: Meckler, 1993.

Magid, Lawrence J. *Cruising Online: Larry Magid's Guide to the New Digital Highways.* New York: Random House Electronic Publishing, 1994.

Morris, Larry. *New Riders' Guide to E-mail and Messaging.* Indianapolis, Ind.: New Riders Publishing, 1994.

Occupational Outlook Handbook. Washington, D.C.: US Department of Labor, Bureau of Labor Statistics, US Government Printing Office, annual.

Standard & Poor's Register of Corporations, Directors, and Executives. New York: Standard & Poor's Corporation, annual.

Internet Sites

Due to the changeable nature of the Internet, sites appear and disappear very quickly. Internet addresses must be entered exactly as they appear.

The Yahoo directory of the World Wide Web is an excellent place to find Internet sites on any topic. The directory is located at: http://www.yahoo.com

Harnack, Andrew, and Gene Kleppinger. "Beyond the MLA Handbook: Documenting Electronic Sources on the Internet." http://falcon.eku.edu/honors/beyond-mla/

"Letter Writing." http://www.sasked.gov.sk.ca/docs/ela/ela_lett.html
An elementary introduction to letter writing as a way to communicate with others.

Lynch, Jack. "Grammar and Style Notes." http://www.english.upenn.edu/~jlynch/Grammar/

"Thank-You Letter Writing." http://www. american. edu/other.depts/career/thanku.htm
A guide to writing thank-letters after job interviews.

"Unforgettable Letters." http://www.usps.gov/letters/
An exploration of the power, humor, and drama of the written word.

"What is a Cover Letter?" http://www.american. edu/other.depts/career/coverlet.htm
Advice on writing cover letters to prospective employers.

"Writing a Complaint letter." http://www.pueblo.gsa. gov/1997crh/res_prt1.htm

"Writing Labs & Writing Centers on the Web." http://owl.english.purdue.edu/owls/writing
A website listing about 50 online writing sites offered by colleges and universities for all kinds of writing.

ACKNOWLEDGMENTS

The publishers listed here have generously given permission to use extended quotations from the following copyrighted works: From *Romantic Correspondence: Women, Politics, and the Fiction of Letters* by Mary A. Favret, copyright © 1993 by Cambridge University Press. Reprinted by permission of Cambridge University Press. From *The Mind of the Negro as Reflected in Letters Written During the Crisis: 1800-1860,* Carter G. Woodson, ed. Copyright © 1926 by The Association for the Study of Negro Life and History, Inc. Reprinted by permission of Reprint Services Corp. From *The Letters of F. Scott Fitzgerald.* Reprinted by permission of Scribner/ Simon and Schuster, Inc. From *Love Anyhow: Famous Fathers Write to their Children,* Reid Sherline, ed. Copyright © 1994 by Reid Sherline. Reprinted by permission of Harold Ober Associates, Inc. From *Winston S. Churchill,* vol. 3, Martin Gilbert, ed. Copyright © 1983 by C & T Publications Ltd. Reprinted by permission of Houghton Mifflin Co. From *The Groucho Letters* by Groucho Marx. Copyright © 1967 by Groucho Marx. Reprinted by permission of Simon and Schuster, Inc. From *Merriam-Webster's Collegiate® Dictionary,* 10th ed. Copyright © 1997 by Merriam-Webster, Inc. Reprinted by permission of Merriam-Webster, Inc.

ℐNDEX

Acronym, 90
Addresses, finding, 40–41
Address format, 17–18, 19
Address labels, 30
Adjective, 86
Advanced format, 26
Adverb, 86
Alignment with letter-head, 27–28
American Heritage Dictionary, 89
America's Top 300 Jobs, 95
Apology note, 38–39
Application letter, 47–53
Appointment letter, 62–63
Attached computer file, 75
Austen, Jane, 108–10

Bartlett's Familiar Quotations, 93
"bcc" list, 74–75
Billing disagreement, 61–62
Blind carbon copy, 74–75
Block style spacing, 20, 21
Body of letter, 17–18, 19
Business letter, 58–70
    and getting the job, 46–57
    and special incentives, 60–61
Business research, 93–94

Career information, 94–95
cc: format, 18, 19
Churchill, Winston, 105–106

Communication skill, 13
Complaint letter, 58–62
   to a manufacturer, 42–44
Complimentary close, 17–18, 19
Compton's Encyclopedia, 92
"Computers don't argue," 110–13
Confidential e-mail, 74–75
Confidential memo, 65–66
Conjunction, 86
Connotation, 89
Contraction, 46–47
Cover letter, 48–52
"Customer is always right" rule, 58
Customer service letter, 58–60

Dickson, Gordon R., 110–13
Douglass, Frederick, 101–104
Draft copy, 20

Electronic mail. See E-mail
E-mail, 71–82
   addresses, 72–73
   mailboxes, 72
   message titles in, 73–74
   online directories for, 73
   punctuation in, 73

Encyclopedia Americana, 92
Encyclopaedia Britannica, 92
Encyclopedia of Associations, 41, 93
Envelopes, 29–30
   self-addressed stamped, 42
Epistolary novel, 108–10
Essay, application, 47–48

Facsimile. *See* Fax
Fan letter, 40–41
   addresses for, 40–41
Fax, 68–70
   cover sheet example, 69
First draft, 27
Fitzgerald, F. Scott, 104–105
Format, 18–22
Form letter, 62–63
Forms of address, 114–18
Franklin, Benjamin, 99

Gothic typeface, 23–24
Grammar, 83–89
Grolier Multimedia Encyclopedia, 92

Helvetica Light type, 25
Holiday letter, 44–45
Homonym, 88, 92

Infinitive verb, 88

Information, completeness of, 16
Inquiry letter, 52–53
Internet, 71–82
  for addresses, 41
  manners, 81–82
  service providers, 72–73
  sex on the, 81
  and ZIP codes, 96
Internship application, 52–53
Interoffice memo, 64–68
  guidelines, 65–66
Invitation letter, 39
Invoices, 61–62

Jargon, 89–90
Job application, 11–12

Lady Susan, 109–110
Language, directness of, 16–17
Letter, 11–13
  of application, 47–48
  business, 46–57
  content, 15–30
  to the editor, 31–34
  parts of a, 17–18, 19
  personal, 31–45
  to public official, 34–35
Letterhead paper, 27–29
  and content, 28–29
Letters, famous, 98–113
Library research sources, 91–97

Love letter, 12, 45

Magazines, 93
Mailbox (e-mail), 72
Mail merge, 26
Manners, 81–82
Margins, 20
Marx, Groucho, 106–107
Memorandum, 64–66
Microsoft Bookshelf, 96
Modified block style, 20, 22
Morelos, Jose Maria, 100–107
Multiple addresses, 26

National Directory of Post Offices with ZIP Codes, 96
National ZIP Code Directory, 96
Neatness, 47
Networking, 50–51
Newspaper, letter to, 31–34
Noun, 86
Novel, epistolary, 108–10

Occupational Outlook Handbook, 95
Occupational Outlook Quarterly, 95

Paper choice, 26–27
Parts of speech, 85–86
Permission form, 63–64

Personal letters, 31–45
Point system, type measurement, 25–26
Preposition, 86
Product complaint, 42–44
Pronoun, 86
Proofreading, 88
Punctuation, 73

Qualifying clause, 85
Questions, seven essential, 15–17, 46, 65
Quotations, 92–93

Reader's Guide to Periodical Literature 93
Reference books, 92–93
Reference, letter of, 11–12
Reminder letter, 62–63
Request for information, 41–42
Research, 52, 91–97
Resumes, 54–57, 95–96
    emphasizing education, 54–55
    emphasizing job experience, 56–57
    sending via e-mail, 96

Salutations, 17–18, 19
    list of, 114–18
Sans-serif type, 24–25
SASE (self-addressed stamped envelope), 42
Sentence fragment, 85

Sentences, types of, 84–85
Serif type, 24–25
Seven essential questions, 15–17, 46, 65
"Snail mail," 71
Sources, reference to, 33, 95
Spacing, 20
Special incentives, 60–61
Spell-check, 88
Spelling, 88–89
Standard & Poor's 500 Guide, 94
Standard & Poor's Register of Corporations, Directors, and Executives, 93–94
Subject-verb agreement, 87
Swift, Jonathan, 99
Sympathy letter, 37–38
Synonym, 92

Technical jargon, 89–90
Telefacsimile. See Fax
Thank-you note, 36–37
Thesaurus, 92
Times Roman type, 24–25
Titles and salutations, 114–18
Tourism letter, 42
Travel plans, 42
Typeface choice, 23–25
Type size, 25–26

Valentine note, 45
Verb, 86–87

"Webmaster," 95
Web sites, 41
Webster's New Collegiate Dictionary, 89, 114–18
"Who, what, when, where, why, how, and how much" questions, 15–17, 46, 65
Williams, Helen Maria, 99–100
Word usage, 89–90
World Book Encyclopedia, 92

ZIP codes, 29–30, 91, 96

ABOUT THE AUTHOR

Patricia Dragisic has worked as an editor and writer for more than twenty-five years in reference book publishing in Chicago. She has also edited English textbooks for the high school and college levels. During her career, she has corresponded with numerous publishers, writers, editors, professors, artists, and others. A graduate of Northwestern University's Medill School of Journalism, she is a longtime volunteer at the Chicago Public Library. In her spare time she writes letters to the editor (she's had dozens published in various newspapers) and to her elected representatives.

MY SOUL IS A WITNESS

Bettye Collier-Thomas and V. P. Franklin

HENRY HOLT AND COMPANY   NEW YORK

MY SOUL IS A WITNESS

A Chronology of the Civil Rights Era

1954–1965

Henry Holt and Company, LLC
Publishers since 1866
115 West 18th Street
New York, New York 10011

Henry Holt® is a registered trademark of Henry Holt and Company, LLC.

Published in Canada by Fitzhenry & Whiteside Ltd.,
195 Allstate Parkway, Markham, Ontario L3R 4T8.

Library of Congress Cataloging-in-Publication Data
Collier-Thomas, Bettye.
My soul is a witness: a chronology of the civil rights era, 1954–1965 /
Bettye Collier-Thomas and V. P. Franklin.—1st ed.
p.   cm.
Includes bibliographical references and index.
ISBN 0-8050-4769-7
1. Afro-Americans—Civil rights—History—20th century Chronology.
2. Civil rights movements—United States—History—20th century Chronology.
I. Franklin, V. P. (Vincent P.), date.   II. Title.
E185.61.C697   2000
973'.0496073'00202—dc21   99-27987
                                                                    CIP

Henry Holt books are available for special promotions and
premiums. For details contact: Director, Special Markets.

First Edition 2000

Designed by Kate Nichols

Photograph on title page by Jack T. Franklin, 1963

Printed in the United States of America

1   3   5   7   9   10   8   6   4   2

IN MEMORY OF

THE VERY REVEREND WAYLAND EDWARD MELTON

(1949–1997)

CONTENTS

ACKNOWLEDGMENTS xi

INTRODUCTION xiii

ABBREVIATIONS xix

1954   "HIGHER GROUND" 3

Civil Rights Entries—January to December 1954

The Desegregation of U.S. Colleges and Universities 5

Brown v. Board of Education: Legal Segregation in Public Education Unconstitutional. 6

The Formation of the White Citizens Councils 8

Mob Violence over School Integration in Delaware 11

Ending of Racial Segregation in the U.S. Armed Forces 14

1955   "CLIMBING JACOB'S LADDER" 19

Civil Rights Entries—January to December 1955

White Students Enrolled in All-Black Colleges and Universities 23

Race Relations Survey—1955 25

Citing *Brown* Decision, Courts Prohibit Segregation in Public
Recreational Facilities 27

Southern Black Teachers Under Attack 31

Racial Violence and Attacks on NAACP Leaders 35

1956   "BETTER BE READY" 39

Civil Rights Entries—January to December 1956

The Montgomery Bus Boycott 42

Bus Boycotts Spread to Other Southern Cities 45

Legislative Attacks on the NAACP and Court-Ordered School Integration 48

White Citizens Councils Launch Attacks on Urban League Branches 52

Positive and Negative Responses of Organized Labor to Civil Rights Demands. 54

1957   "AMAZING GRACE" 57

Civil Rights Entries—January to December 1957

Organized Religion and Racial Segregation, 1956–57 59

Nonviolent Protests Spread to Other Southern Cities 63

State Bans on Interracial Sports Competition 66

Showdown at Central High School in Little Rock, Arkansas 69

Concerts, Movies, Television, and Civil Rights 73

1958   "A BALM IN GILEAD" 77

Civil Rights Entries—January to December 1958

"Crusade for Citizenship"—Voter Registration Campaigns 80

Problems of Discrimination in Housing 83

1958—The Year of the Bombings 87

Southern Politicians Respond to Federal Intervention in Public
School Integration 91

Congressman Adam Clayton Powell, Jr.: Political Independent 93

1959   "THE STORMS OF LIFE ARE RAGING" 97

Civil Rights Entries—January to December 1959

The U.S. Commission on Civil Rights Swings into Action 101

International Incidents Caused by Racial Discrimination in the United States 104

The Rabbit's Wedding: An Interracial Romance? 107

Little Rock Public Schools Reopen, But Violence and Massive Resistance Continue............. 110

The Failure of Massive Resistance in Virginia 113

1960 "GOIN' TO LAY DOWN MY SWORD AND SHIELD" 117

Civil Rights Entries—January to December 1960

Southern Students Launch the Sit-In Movement 118

Economic Reprisals Directed Against Black Voters in Fayette and Haywood
Counties, Tenn., 1960–61 122

Wade-Ins, Kneel-Ins, Read-Ins: Desegregation of Public Facilities 124

Confronting Discrimination in Employment and Labor Unions 128

Black Voters and the Presidential Election of 1960 131

1961 "I'VE BEEN 'BUKED AND I'VE BEEN SCORNED" 137

Civil Rights Entries—January to December 1961

The University of Georgia and the Desegregation of U.S. Colleges and Universities 139

"Jail, No Bail": Sit-Ins as Civil Disobedience 142

"Plans for Progress"—Campaigns to End Employment Discrimination 146

CORE Launches the Freedom Rides 150

"No Negroes Wanted": Housing as a Step Toward Equality 156

1962 "ON JORDAN'S STORMY BANKS" 159

Civil Rights Entries—January to December 1962

"Bury Jim Crow": CORE Campaigns for Integration 162

Opening the Floodgates: Public Accommodations Under Assault 165

Public School Desegregation in the South 169

The Albany Movement, 1961–62 172

James Meredith and the Integration of Ole Miss 176

1963 "WE SHALL OVERCOME" 181

Civil Rights Entries—January to December 1963

Campaigns Against Segregated Public Education in the North 185

Attacks on Discrimination in Government-Sponsored Employment 187

The Battle of Birmingham 190

SNCC Workers and Voter Registration Campaigns in the South 195

Civil Rights Protests Grip the Nation 198

1964   "FREE AT LAST?" 201

Civil Rights Entries—January to December 1964

Violence Erupts in St. Augustine, Fla. 203

The Killing Fields: Mississippi and the Freedom Summer Project 207

The Civil Rights Act of 1964 211

Voting Rights and the Mississippi Freedom Democratic Party's Challenge 213

Desegregating Public Accommodations in 1964 218

1965   "MARCHING TO ZION" 223

Civil Rights Entries—January to December 1965

Full Compliance: Federal Officials Move to Implement the Civil Rights
Act of 1964 226

The Selma to Montgomery March and the Voting Rights Act of 1965 229

"Reverse Freedom Rides": The SCLC and SNCC Join the NAACP and CORE
in Civil Rights Protests in the North 233

Church Burnings, Bombings, and Racial Violence Continue in the South 237

Deacons of Defense and Justice 241

THE AFTERMATH: The Emergence of the Student Rights, Anti-War,
Women's Liberation, and Black Power Movements. 243

SELECTED BIBLIOGRAPHY 247

INDEX 251

ACKNOWLEDGMENTS

My Soul Is a Witness has been many years in the making. It began in 1994 with our concern that, though there was a great deal of material on the Civil Rights Movement, there was no overview that captured the extent and interconnections of activities at the local, state, and national levels. Moreover, there was very little information on the movement in the North, Midwest, and West.

Our research and efforts to coordinate the voluminous data on the Civil Rights Movement were greatly aided by the students and staff at the Temple University Center for African American History and Culture. Michael Collins, Mitsuru Sono Walker, and Benjamin Hassing, undergraduate students in the History Department, followed up leads in Jet magazine, The New York Times, and the Southern School News, which were integrated into the chapters. Danielle Smallcomb, a research associate at the Center, performed an inestimable service in painstakingly codifying data found in Jet magazine during the period after 1960. Jerry Bjelopra, a doctoral student in the History Department, was most helpful in identifying sources for the bibliography. Richard Woodland, a research associate at the Center, used his excellent computer skills to separate the data by subject, and Joanne Hawes Speakes, Marie McCain, and Lorraine Harris at different times performed typing and organizational tasks. We thank Jack Franklin, Terri Rouse, and Aileen Rosenberg at the African American Museum of Philadelphia for granting permission to use several photographs. We owe a debt of gratitude to all of these people for the individual and collective contributions they made to this work. We also thank our agents, Charlotte Sheedy and Neeti Madan, and the editors at Henry Holt, Tracy Sherrod, Elise Proulx, and Elizabeth Stein.

On a personal level, the love and support of our families and friends have nurtured and sustained us: Charles Thomas, Katherine Collier, Joseph Collier, Thelma Polk Collier, Ida Mae Thomas, Christine Lee, Vincent F. Franklin, Ed Collins, Sandra B. Motz, John Hope Franklin, Mary Frances Berry, Sharon Harley, Cheryl Townsend Gilkes, Lillian S. Williams, Genna Rae McNeil, Gloria Harper Dickinson, James Turner, Simeon Booker, Rosalyn Terborg Penn, Kenneth Kusmer, Craig Eisendrath, Anise Ward, Julie Mostov, Eric D. Brose, the Rev. Elizabeth Colton, the Rev. William Shepard, and the Rev. Paula Lawrence Wehmiller.

At the end of every Sunday religious service at Philadelphia's Cathedral Church of the Savior, the Very Reverend Wayland E. Melton fervently sang out and asked, "Who'll be a witness for my Lord?" because he understood the song's power in evoking the spirit of struggle of past, present, and future generations.

INTRODUCTION

My soul is a witness
for my Lord,
My soul is a witness
for my Lord . . .

O, who'll be a witness
for my Lord?

O, who'll be a witness
for my Lord?
My soul is a witness
for my Lord,
My soul is a witness
for my Lord.

TRADITIONAL NEGRO SPIRITUAL

This is the first book to provide a comprehensive survey of the issues, events, and personalities that defined the civil rights era and to place them in proper sequence, locale, and perspective. It extends the examination of civil rights activities between 1954 and 1965 beyond the southern states to the rest of the country. Although Martin Luther King, Jr., was a towering figure in the civil rights era, this volume includes the thousands of people, places, and events that the Civil Rights Movement encompassed. While King was the center of so much that took place during that time, the Civil Rights Movement was much more than any one personality, and it engulfed all parts of the nation and touched most of the important sociocultural issues.

When we began this research we had no idea how extensive and rich the data were. We discovered that civil rights activity was not exclusive to any city, state, or region, but reached all levels of American society.

In order to include as much as possible in this study, we have supplemented the basic chronology with five features per chapter, allowing us to explore some larger topics in more depth. Features also permit us to highlight issues well known at the time but since forgotten.

Historical Overview

In the period from 1954 through 1965 Americans witnessed profound changes in the nature of race relations. At the beginning of 1954 black-white relations—not just in the South, but throughout the nation—were defined by legalized and de facto systems of segregation that most closely resembled the practice of apartheid or "separate development" that existed in the Republic of South Africa from the late 1940s until the 1990s. In southern law, and in northern and western practice, under "American apartheid" black and white citizens were forbidden to commingle publicly, and citizens of African descent were barred from restaurants, hotels, theaters, schools, railroad cars, and other public accommodations reserved for whites only. The system of legal or Jim Crow segregation was implemented to keep blacks and whites separated from cradle to grave.

As a result of the litigation carried out by Thurgood Marshall and the other lawyers for the National Association for the Advancement of Colored People (NAACP), the Supreme Court decision that upheld the separate but equal doctrine in *Plessy v. Ferguson* (1896) was declared unconstitutional not merely because the separate public facilities provided for citizens of African descent were rarely equal, but because legal segregation of the races was found to be in violation of the equal protection of the law clause of the Fourteenth Amendment. While the *Brown v. Board of Education* decision was directed at public education specifically, NAACP lawyers and others used the ruling to attack legal segregation in other areas of public life. Finally, with the passage of the Civil Rights Act of 1964, the U.S. Congress banned discrimination on the basis of race, creed, color, or nationality by any institution or facility open to the public.

With the launching of the Montgomery, Alabama, bus boycott in December 1955, the Civil Rights Movement entered a new phase of nonviolent direct action protest. While boycotts, picketing, sit-ins, and various other forms of nonviolent actions had been employed before 1955 to protest de jure and de facto segregation in various parts of the United States, the Montgomery bus boycott ushered in a new wave of activism that spread throughout the South and to other parts of the country. While historians continue to disagree about when the Civil Rights Movement began, or when the *first* nonviolent direct action protests were launched, there is little debate about the significance of the Montgomery protest to subsequent developments in the Civil Rights Movement.

The events cited in this chronology make it clear that the *Brown* decision in May 1954 ushered in a new era in U.S. history that witnessed the beginning of activities in the name of civil rights throughout the country, in the areas of public and private schooling, higher education, employment, public accommodations, housing, voting rights, sports, and organized religion.

Significance of This Chronology

This chronology cites articles on the significant events that received national and international attention, such as the Montgomery bus boycott, 1955–56, and the March on Washington, 28 August 1963, as well as extensive articles on civil rights activities at the local level. Oftentimes, local civil rights events established the patterns for subsequent incidents that achieved national and international attention. For example, it is well known that President Dwight D. Eisenhower sent soldiers and paratroopers from the 101st Airborne to assist in the integration of Central High School in Little Rock, Arkansas, in September 1957. Less well known is that many times before that date the governors of several border states had to call out the state National Guard to assist in carrying out the integration of local public school districts because of mob violence and intimidation by local whites. In other words, the precedent of sending the military to assist in carrying out court-ordered desegregation plans had already been set at the state level before the Little Rock incident. There it was necessary to send in federal troops because Gov. Orval Faubus had used the state National Guard to prevent, rather than implement, integration orders issued by the federal courts.

This chronology provides summaries of newspaper or magazine articles on civil rights activities outside the South during the period from 1954 through 1965. By including discussions of articles on civil rights activities in northern, midwestern, and western cities and states, we are able to demonstrate for the first time that the Supreme Court's *Brown* decision spurred challenges to de jure and de facto segregation in areas other than public education throughout the country. In the late 1950s and early 1960s, before the passage of the Civil Rights Act of 1964, when African Americans and others openly challenged segregatory practices in employment or public accommodations and took these matters to local and state courts, they often won their suits because the judges argued that the *Brown* decision banned segregation in all areas of public life, not just public education. While many city councils and state legislatures began passing laws during this period banning segregation in public accommodations and racial discrimination in employment, these statutes often came about because of civil rights protests and litigation by African Americans at the local and state levels and court decisions by state, local, and federal judges. These civil rights protests and court decisions are cited in this chronology.

Sources

Each entry in this chronology is based on information found in articles and reports published in three newspaper and periodical sources: *The New York Times*, *Jet* magazine, and the *Southern School News*.

The New York Times

As the most important and authoritative newspaper in the United States, *The New York Times* (NYT) provided detailed coverage of civil rights activities throughout the United States and regularly published articles and reports on race relations in various other parts of the world in the period from 1954 to 1965. While the NYT published ongoing accounts of major civil rights campaigns, such as the Montgomery and Tallahassee bus boycotts in the 1950s and the student sit-ins and Freedom Rides in the 1960s, significant events related to the struggle for civil rights at the state and local levels were also reported. Articles on the passage of civil rights measures by the state legislatures and city councils across the country, such as fair employment practices laws or legislation banning racial discrimination in housing, were regular features in the NYT, and these reports are cited in this chronology. Since it was often the case that the NYT article on the passage of a particular ordinance or state law was published days, and sometimes weeks, after it was enacted, the dates for the entries in this chronology refer only to the issue of the newspaper, magazine, or journal where the article appeared. In the case of *Jet* magazine and the *Southern School News*, the dates for entries refer to the issue of the periodical in which the article appeared.

Jet Magazine

Jet magazine (JM) began weekly publications on Thursday, 1 November 1951. Following the success of the *Negro Digest* and *Ebony* magazine, which began publication in 1942, John H. Johnson decided that he wanted to publish a "pocket-sized newsmagazine." In the first issue, Johnson declared that "each week we will bring you complete news coverage on happenings among Negroes all over the U.S.—in entertainment, politics, sports, social events as well as features on unusual personalities, places, and events." *Jet* was an immediate success, and within six months it was selling more than three hundred thousand copies each week.

From its first issue, JM published articles and features on civil rights issues. JM is one of the best sources for "black firsts," which came about as a result of civil rights protests and legislation in the areas of employment, housing, voting rights, public accommodations, and schooling in the period from 1954 to 1965. Regular columns were devoted to coverage of civil rights issues throughout the country, and many of these issues were not covered by the NYT or other white-oriented newspapers and periodicals. For example, it was only on a few occasions that attacks on black families moving into all-white neighborhoods in the North, Midwest, or West were reported in the NYT, but these stories were given full coverage in JM between 1954 and 1965. Racially motivated violence and murders were systematically reported in JM; however, some of these heinous crimes went unreported in the NYT. In 1956 in many southern cities, local branches of the National Urban League (NUL), which was not a civil rights organization but instead provided black workers with job training and placement, came under attack from the White Citizens Councils (WCC). Local administrators of the Community Chest dropped the Urban League from their list of community agencies receiving funds after WCC leaders accused the League of promoting integration and interracial relations. In many instances the loss of funding had a devastating impact on the ability of the local Urban League to continue functioning in those cities. JM began coverage of the WCC attacks on the southern Urban League branches in March 1956; the NYT first reported the issue as part of its coverage of the NUL annual convention in September 1956. In many areas of civil rights activity, JM not only complemented the information reported in the NYT, but it also covered important topics that were not found in the NYT or that were reported in the NYT at a much later date.

Articles on particular events usually appeared in JM two weeks or more after they occurred. Thus JM's coverage of responses to the Supreme Court's *Brown* decision began appearing with the 27 May 1954 issue. In locating additional information on civil rights issues found in this chronology based on information found in JM, the researcher should refer to local, daily, and weekly newspapers and magazines two weeks *before* the date of the JM article.

Southern School News

Our third source is the *Southern School News* (SSN), which began publishing in Nashville, Tennessee, on 3 September 1954. In April 1954 several southern members of the American Society of Newspaper Editors came together with representatives of the Fund for the Advancement of Education and agreed that there was a need for a news reporting service that would provide accurate information on southern education. In May 1954 the Southern Education Reporting Service (SERS) was formed with *Richmond Times-Dispatch* editor Virginius Dabney as chairman and *Charleston News & Courier* editor Thomas R. Waring as vice chairman. In June 1954 at the second SERS meeting, *Charlotte News* editor C. A. Knight was chosen executive director, and the George Peabody College of Education in Nashville, Tennessee, was chosen as the site and fiscal agent for the project. From the first issue C. A. Knight, the editor of the SERS official publication, the SSN, promised "to tell the story, factually and objectively, of what happens in education as a result of the Supreme Court's May 17 [1954] opinion that segregation in the public schools is unconstitutional."

In the period from 1954 to 1965, the SSN provided detailed information on a monthly basis on the school desegregation process in each of the southern and border states, and the District of Columbia, directly affected by the *Brown* decision. With reports from correspondents from each state, the SSN maintained an ongoing account of the activities of the NAACP, the local, state, and federal courts, the municipal, county, state, and federal governments, and the various groups formed to assist or oppose the implementation of public school desegregation. Because of the sheer volume of information from the SSN, we had to be selective. However, the sampling of SSN articles in this chronology complements the information on these topics and events cited from JM and the NYT.

From 3 September 1954 to 6 July 1955, the SSN included the day as well as month of publication. However, beginning in August 1955, the full date was not provided. Thus the authors have placed all citations from the SSN at the first of every month from August 1955 to June 1965, when the journal ceased publication. In that final issue, the editors explained that they believed they had "substantially accomplished their original purpose. That was to provide a reliable, central source of information on developments in education arising from the United States Supreme Court decision declaring compulsory racial segregation in the public schools unconstitutional." The SERS board of directors decided to issue a new publication, a magazine titled *Southern Education Report*, that "will be selective, rather than all-inclusive, in reporting developments in its field of interest."

For anyone interested in information on southern school desegregation in the period from 1954 to 1965, we believe that this chronology is an excellent place to start. At the same time, this chronology covers much more than southern education during this period, and thus it should be an excellent place to start for anyone interested in knowing more about civil rights activities in the areas of employment, public accommodations, housing, voting rights, organized religion, the military, entertainment, and sports in cities and towns throughout the United States.

ABBREVIATIONS

AFL	American Federation of Labor
AFL-CIO	American Federation of Labor/ Congress of Industrial Organizations
AME	African Methodist Episcopal
CORE	Congress of Racial Equality
FBI	Federal Bureau of Investigation
IRS	Internal Revenue Service
JM	*Jet* magazine
KKK	Ku Klux Klan
NAACP	National Association for the Advancement of Colored People
NYT	*The New York Times*
ROTC	Reserve Officer Training Corps
SCLC	Southern Christian Leadership Conference
SNCC	Student Nonviolent Coordinating Committee
SSN	*Southern School News*
UCLA	University of California at Los Angeles
UN	United Nations
YMCA	Young Men's Christian Association
YWCA	Young Women's Christian Association

MY SOUL IS A WITNESS

On 17 May 1954, in Washington, D.C., George E. C. Hayes, Thurgood Marshall, and James Nabrit, attorneys who argued the *Brown v. Board of Education* case, stand triumphantly in the front of the U.S. Supreme Court after the high tribunal ruled that legal segregation in public education was unconstitutional. (SOURCE: CORBIS BETTMANN)

1954

"HIGHER GROUND"

While *the United States government was well on the way to ending segregation in the armed services, a process begun during the Truman administration, very few Americans, especially southerners, believed that the U.S. Supreme Court would outlaw segregation in public education. Many whites were initially shocked by the* Brown v. Board of Education *decision; African Americans were joyous. When it became apparent what the decision could mean to the "southern way of life," many southern politicians declared, "Never!" While the Supreme Court's* Brown *decision clearly placed American society on "Higher Ground," with the coming of the massive resistance movement, the White Citizens Councils, and violent opposition to school integration in Delaware, it was unclear to many in 1954 how it would remain there.*

JANUARY 1954

1 In **New York City**, Democratic politician Hulan Jack was sworn in as Manhattan borough president. Jack became the first African American to serve in that position (NYT).

7 In **Louisville, Ky.**, physicians Orville Ballard and Grace M. James were appointed to the faculty of the University of Louisville Medical School. They became the first African Americans to serve as instructors at southern white medical schools (JM).

14 In **Washington, D.C.**, NAACP leader Clarence Mitchell asked Defense Department officials to investigate and take necessary action to halt acts of brutality leveled against black soldiers stationed in the South by white military personnel and civilians. Incidents were reported at Fort Belvoir, Va.; Camp Polk, La.; and Fort Jackson, S.C. (JM).

14 In **Los Angeles, Calif.**, Howard University Medical School graduate LeRoy S. Weekes, M.D., became the first black physician appointed to the surgical staff of Los Angeles County General Hospital (JM).

14 In **Memphis, Tenn.**, black residents threatened to boycott the Memphis Street Railway Company. Among the changes demanded were an end to segregated or "Jim Crow" seating practices, the general mistreatment of black passengers by white drivers, and the hiring of African Americans as bus drivers. Col. Roane Waring, president of the Memphis Street Railway Company, replied that the city was not ready to have black bus drivers (JM).

21 In **Washington, D.C.**, Jane Morrow Spaulding, the highest-ranking black woman in the federal government, resigned her position as assistant to Department of Health, Education, and Welfare (HEW) secretary Oveta Culp Hobby. NAACP officials claimed Spaulding was forced to resign because she criticized HEW's foot-dragging in desegregation of public schools on U.S. military bases (NYT).

21 In Washington, D.C., Defense Department officials announced the appointment of Col. Benjamin J. Davis, Jr., highest-ranking African American in the U.S. Air Force, as commander of the Fifty-first Fighter Interceptor Wing in Korea. During World War II Davis was highly decorated for flying more than sixty combat missions in Europe (JM).

22 In Florence, Ala., Dr. J. L. Hicks was admitted to the Alabama Medical Association. The Meharry Medical School graduate was the first black physician allowed membership in the statewide medical society (NYT).

28 In Charleston, S.C., in compliance with President Eisenhower's orders for desegregation on U.S. military bases in 1953, Jim Crow signs were removed from rest rooms at the Charleston Naval Shipyard. White workers, however, decided to boycott desegregated cafeterias on the base (JM).

28 In Pittsburgh, Pa., fire chief Stephen Adley issued an executive order desegregating the Pittsburgh Fire Department, and thirty-four members of two all-black stations were transferred to previously all-white fire units (JM).

28 In Cambridge, Mass., twenty-year-old Clifford L. Alexander was elected president of the Harvard University Student Council. He was the first African American to be elected to that position (JM).

FEBRUARY 1954

4 In New York City, Lt. Robert J. Mangum was appointed Deputy Police Commissioner to head the Department of Licenses and Inspections, with a staff of over 200. Mangum became the highest ranking black police official in the U.S. (NYT).

4 In Washington, D.C., J. A. Broadwater, president of the Capital Transit Company, announced that no African Americans would be hired in the transit system as bus or streetcar drivers as long as there was a threat of a wildcat strike by the transit workers unions in the District (JM).

5 In Philadelphia, Pa., Negro Baseball League third baseman Judy Johnson was hired as assistant coach by the Philadelphia Athletics and became the first black to receive a coaching position on a Major League Baseball team (NYT).

11 In Washington, D.C., Secy. of State John F. Dulles issued an order setting up a Fair Employment Practices Committee within the U.S. State Department. The order banned discrimination in hiring and promotion on the basis of race, creed, or color and named Walter Chapman to study race relations within the State Department (JM).

11 In Birmingham, Ala., the city commission repealed its ban on black and white athletes playing baseball and football together. This statute paved the way for African Americans to join the Southern Baseball Association (JM).

18 In Washington, D.C., the Presidential Railroad Emergency Board ordered "equal pay for equal work" for black and white workers for the Railway Express Agency in the South. The board ordered that both races receive at least the national minimum wage of $273.75 a month (NYT).

24 In Washington, D.C., in testimony before the U.S. Senate, labor secretary James P. Mitchell spoke out in support of federal fair employment practices legislation. President Eisenhower had publicly expressed his opposition to the measure (NYT).

25 In Chicago, Ill., rioting erupted in the Trumbull Park Homes, a federal housing project, when the family of Donald Howard (black) tried to move in. Four policemen were wounded and four whites were arrested (JM).

25 In Fayetteville, Ark., at midyear graduation ceremonies at the University of Arkansas, sixty-one African Americans received degrees. Since the first African American, Edith Irby, was admitted in 1948, the University of Arkansas had graduated 203 African Americans in a wide variety of fields (JM).

27 In Cleveland, Ohio, Catholic auxiliary bishop Floyd L. Begin denounced the Cleveland Council of the Knights of Columbus for denying membership to three African Americans. Bishop Begin

THE DESEGREGATION OF U.S. COLLEGES AND UNIVERSITIES

On 15 March 1954, *The New York Times* published a survey that revealed there were more than two thousand black students attending previously all-white colleges and universities in the South. The greatest increase took place in graduate and professional schools following the 1950 U.S. Supreme Court decision in *Sweatt v. Painter.* In that decision the court ruled that in states where public graduate and professional schools existed for white students but not for African Americans, black students must be admitted to the all-white institutions.

In April 1954 the federal district court in Shreveport, La., ordered Southwestern Louisiana Institute in Lafayette to admit four black students. The school was the only state-supported institution within eighty-nine miles of Shreveport but it had refused to enroll qualified black students. The Supreme Court's *Brown* decision in May 1954 accelerated the process of desegregation in southern colleges and universities, and by the end of the year black students were newly enrolled at previously all-white colleges and universities in the District of Columbia, West Virginia, Maryland, Missouri, Kentucky, and Texas.

also criticized the Knights for refusing to charter interracial branches of the fraternal group (NYT).

MARCH 1954

5 In Washington, D.C., attorney J. Ernest Wilkins was named by President Eisenhower as assistant secretary in the U.S. Department of Labor. The first African American in this position, Wilkins would serve directly under labor secretary James P. Mitchell. Wilkins became the highest-ranking African American in the executive branch of the U.S. government (NYT).

9 In Washington, D.C., the U.S. Supreme Court ruled that black craftsmen can sue the all-white American Federation of Labor (AFL) Latherers Union in Chicago for discrimination under the terms of the Sherman Anti-Trust Act. The court ruled that the union was involved in interstate commerce (NYT).

10 In Caracas, Venezuela, delegates to the tenth annual Inter-American Conference unanimously passed a resolution, introduced by Carita Ramon of Panama, calling for an end to racially discriminatory practices by governmental agencies. U.S. racial practices, such as the segregation of blacks and whites in the Panama Canal Zone, were cited as particularly egregious (NYT).

11 In Louisville, Ky., the local office of the Kentucky State Employment Service abolished its sepa-

rate black office and transferred the seven black employees to the main branch with full seniority rights. State officials claimed that the move was ordered to avoid duplication and "to provide more adequate service" (JM).

11 In St. Louis, Mo., U.S. Postal Service officials ordered a probe of anti-black and anti-Jewish literature sent to residents in Iowa, Missouri, and Illinois. Postal officials accused the Citizens Protective League of sending the offensive materials in violation of post office regulations (JM).

11 In Washington, D.C., President Eisenhower told two thousand delegates to the NAACP Freedom Conference that he would continue to work to end segregation in the U.S. military and in the nation's capital (NYT).

18 In Washington, D.C., Justice Department officials confirmed that they had sent investigators to Chicago to report on racial disturbances at the Trumbull Park Homes housing project. Chicago mayor Martin Kennelly was denounced by local NAACP officials for failing to act to reduce racial tensions (JM).

29 In New York City, actor-singer Harry Belafonte received a Tony Award for best supporting actor in a musical for his performance in *Almanac*. The first African American to receive a Tony Award was Juanita Hall, for her supporting role in the musical *South Pacific* in 1950 (NYT).

1 In West Point, N.Y., after bitterly criticizing school officials for their discriminatory treatment of black cadets, Rep. Adam Clayton Powell, Jr., was invited to visit the West Point Academy. Powell was assured that black cadets were no longer being used as waiters and cooks at the school (NYT).

8 In Baltimore, Md., hotel owners refused to lift a ban on African Americans, despite the recent acquisition of the Orioles baseball team with several black players. Although their position was denounced by Maryland governor Theodore McKeldin, the hotel owners insisted they would not "go ahead of public opinion" (NYT).

8 In Charleston, S.C., the managers of the Dock Street Theater announced the cancellation of the scheduled performance of the opera *Porgy and Bess*. Black performers refused to appear before segregated audiences (JM).

8 In Winter Garden, Fla., officials for the Washington Senators baseball team announced that throughout the spring training season, the eight black players would be housed inside the camp. A team manager was quoted as saying, "there was no point in provoking trouble" with whites in the surrounding areas (JM).

10 In San Antonio, Tex., Archbishop Robert E. Lucey issued an order ending segregation in the

---

BROWN V. BOARD OF EDUCATION:
LEGAL SEGREGATION IN PUBLIC EDUCATION UNCONSTITUTIONAL

On 17 May 1954, the U.S. Supreme Court delivered one of its most important decisions in the twentieth century, *Brown v. Board of Education*. The decision in effect reversed the court's ruling fifty-eight years earlier in *Plessy v. Ferguson* (1896), which declared that "separate but equal" public accommodations for the races was not a violation of the Fourteenth Amendment to the U.S. Constitution.

In school segregation cases coming from Kansas, South Carolina, Virginia, and Delaware, Supreme Court chief justice Earl Warren pointed out that "in each of the cases other than the Delaware case, a three-judge federal district court denied relief to the plaintiffs on the grounds of the so-called 'separate but equal' doctrine announced by this Court in *Plessy v. Ferguson*, 163 U.S. 537. Under that doctrine, equality of treatment is accorded when the races are provided substantially equal facilities, even though these be separate. In the Delaware case, the supreme court of Delaware adhered to that doctrine, but ordered that the plaintiffs be admitted to the white schools because of their superiority to the Negro schools. The plaintiffs contend that segregated public schools are not 'equal' and cannot be made 'equal,' and that hence they are deprived of the equal protection of the laws."

Chief Justice Warren noted that arguments were heard on both sides during the court's 1952 and 1954 terms. He then discussed the significance of education, "perhaps the most important function of state and local governments," and concluded that "in these days, it is doubtful any child may reasonably be expected to succeed in life if he is denied the opportunity of an education. Such an opportunity, where the state has undertaken to provide it, is a right which must be made available on equal terms.

"We come then to the question present: Does segregation of children in public schools solely on the basis of race, even though the physical facilities and other 'tangible' factors be equal, deprive the children of the minority group equal educational opportunities? We believe that it does. . . .

"We conclude that in the field of public education the doctrine of 'separate but equal' has no place. Separate educational facilities are inherently unequal. Therefore, we hold that the plaintiffs and others similarly situated for whom the actions have been brought are, by reason of the segregation complained of, deprived of the equal protection of the laws guaranteed by the Fourteenth Amendment. This disposition makes unnecessary any discussion whether such segregation also violates the Due Process Clause of the Fourteenth Amendment."

Roman Catholic school system. He is believed to be the first Deep South Catholic leader to order the desegregation of Catholic schools (NYT).

15 In Washington, D.C., the U.S. Supreme Court ruled that the practice in Fulton County, Ga., and other parts of the South of maintaining separate lists for black and white jurors was unconstitutional. From this point on, all potential jurors would be chosen from one list (JM).

15 In Detroit, Mich., University of Michigan basketball star John Codwell was barred from addressing the school's Detroit alumni chapter because the event was held at the exclusive University Club, which did not admit African Americans. Alumni officials offered no apology for the incident (JM).

22 In Washington, D.C., following protests by the NAACP's Clarence Mitchell, U.S. Marine brigadier general R. H. Ridgely, director of personnel, announced the suspension of the recruitment of blacks as marine stewards to serve as cooks and waiters in the homes of officers. No blacks were to be recruited as stewards until "more useful duties" were identified (JM).

27 In Washington, D.C., American Nursing Association president Elizabeth K. Porter denounced officials in the organization's Georgia branch for its continued refusal to allow membership to black nurses. By 1954 all other branches of the nursing association nationwide were integrated (NYT).

29 In Morrisville, Pa., after three years of negotiation, National Urban League officials announced that they were successful in gaining the employment of chemist Leon Fennoy at the U.S. Steel plant. Fennoy became the first African American hired as a research technician at the facility (JM).

MAY 1954

2 In Los Angeles, Calif., as a result of pressure from local NAACP officials, Mayor Norris Poulson called for the desegregation of the city's fire department. However, the Citizens Fire Commission and fire commissioner Howard J. Callahand rec-

ommended the continued segregation of black firemen in two of the city's ninety fire stations. Callahand claimed that he received seventeen hundred letters from white firemen who said they would resign if fire stations were integrated. The NAACP threatened to bring suit against the city (NYT).

6 In Chicago, Ill., despite the fact that housing authority officials asked for grand jury indictments against white residents arrested in the bombings and rioting at the Trumbull Park Homes housing project, Donald Howard and his family decided to move out of the housing project. Howard had been told that the reimbursement for the damage to his property would be forthcoming, but he received no financial support from the local NAACP or those who urged him "to stick it out to make it possible for Negroes to live in the project" (NYT).

12 In Boston, Mass., the Pullman Company, based in Chicago, Ill., agreed to end a ninety-year policy of prohibiting the hiring of African Americans as conductors on its railroad cars. Black porter George Greenidge, who sought a supervisory position held only by whites, made the complaint to the Massachusetts Commission Against Discrimination. The agreement also called for the opening up of Pullman porter positions to whites (NYT).

13 In Hartford, Conn., the state supreme court ordered the AFL's International Brotherhood of Electrical Workers, Local 35, to admit Mansfield Tilley and Warren Stewart to membership. After five years of litigation, the court rejected the union's claim that the two men were unqualified for admission. The suit was brought under the state's fair employment practices law (JM).

19 In Washington, D.C., in the wake of the Supreme Court's *Brown* decision, President Eisenhower urged school officials to end the practice of segregation in the public schools of the nation's capital by fall 1954 and "serve as a model for the rest of the country" (NYT).

22 In Savannah, Ga., in response to a suit filed by fourteen black residents, city housing officials argued that the desegregation of the Fred Wessels Homes would result in "great mental, psychological and physical distress" for whites in the project, as well as a violation of the whites' Fourteenth Amendment rights to equal protection of the law (NYT).

24 In Atlanta, Ga., NAACP officials issued the Atlanta Declaration, in which they pledged to fight any delay in implementation of public school integration. They also recommended that members of southern branches begin to petition local school officials to help speed the process of school desegregation (NYT).

24 In Chicago, Ill., in the wake of the Supreme Court's *Brown* decision, the National Council of YMCAs passed a resolution calling for "the elimination of segregation and other forms of discrimination" by all its branches. The council called on the local branches to deal frankly and move swiftly on exclusionary practices (NYT).

24 In Washington, D.C., Assistant Secretary of the Army Robert D. King announced that segregation in the public schools in the U.S. Panama Canal Zone would end in September 1954. NAACP officials had made several protests to President Eisenhower about the segregated schools in the Canal Zone (NYT).

25 In the United States, during the week following the Supreme Court's public school desegregation decision, governors of nine states (Delaware, Kansas, Kentucky, West Virginia, Maryland, Missouri, Tennessee, Texas, and Oklahoma) announced that they would comply with the court's ruling. Public officials in the Deep South states (Alabama, Arkansas, Mississippi, Louisiana, South Carolina, Florida, and Georgia), however, denounced the decision and threatened to close down public schools rather than integrate them (NYT).

26 In Washington, D.C., members of the district's school board, in response to urging by President Eisenhower, voted 6 to 2 to begin the desegregation of the capital's public schools in the fall. The board voted to outlaw pupil and teacher transfers on the basis of race and ended race labeling in school records (NYT).

26–31 In New York City, Ethiopian emperor Haile Selassie arrived for a six-week tour of the United States. The African leader, accompanied by twenty staff members, was greeted upon arrival by members of the U.S. State Department. Selassie traveled to Washington, D.C., and met with Vice President Nixon and on 28 May 1954 addressed a joint session of the U.S. Congress (NYT).

THE FORMATION OF THE WHITE CITIZENS COUNCILS

In the aftermath of the Supreme Court's *Brown* decision, numerous groups were formed in the southern states to thwart the implementation of public school desegregation, including the American States Rights Association, Southerners in Alabama, the National Association for the Advancement of White People, and others. The organization that became most closely associated with the campaigns of "massive resistance" was the White Citizens Council (WCC).

Formed in Indianola, Miss., in July 1954, within a matter of weeks the WCC spread throughout the state. Robert B. Patterson, one of the WCC's founders, claimed that by October 1954, there were eighty thousand council members in Mississippi alone. By the end of the year, WCCs had been organized in Alabama, Louisiana, Virginia, Texas, and Georgia and began to develop various legal and extra-legal strategies to prevent the integration of black and white children in local public schools. Although WCC leaders would try to distance themselves and their organization from the Ku Klux Klan (KKK) and other violent white supremacist groups, the memberships overlapped greatly. However, in trying to overthrow the *Brown* decision and thwart the implementation of public school integration, the WCC in many places would make common cause with groups considered much less "respectable."

3 In Birmingham, Ala., after a brief experiment with integration (January to June 1954), local citizens voted to end the practice of allowing professional baseball and track teams with black and white members to compete in the city-owned sports facilities. More than ten thousand residents had petitioned to put the measure on the ballot (NYT).

17 In New York City, NAACP official Henry Lee Moon announced the launching of a campaign to register an additional one million black voters in thirteen southern states. Moon pointed out that there were fourteen congressional districts where African Americans made up 40 percent or more of the total population. Moon predicted that "sooner or later, Negro congressmen will be elected from these districts" (JM).

17 In Baltimore, Md., school board members voted unanimously to end the practice of assigning pupils to public schools on the basis of race, beginning in September 1954 (JM).

22 In Nashville, Tenn., Mary E. Howard of Washington, D.C., received a master's degree in sociology from Fisk University and became the first white student to graduate from an all-black southern college since 1893. She later became the first white employee at the Urban League branch in Milwaukee (NYT).

24 In New York City, Bishop Henry K. Sherrill announced that the Protestant Episcopal Church had canceled its plans to hold its general convention in Houston, Tex., in 1956, in favor of Honolulu, Hawaii. Episcopalians in Philadelphia and New York City opposed holding the meeting in Texas because of its segregation laws (JM).

24 In Houston, Tex., the members of the First Unitarian Church voted to admit African Americans to membership. The Unitarian church became the first white denomination in Texas to end its policy of racial segregation (JM).

1–5 In Dallas, Tex., at the forty-fifth annual convention, NAACP officials urged members in branches in seventeen southern states to petition local school boards to end segregation. Several southern politicians had already started petition drives calling on school boards to ignore the *Brown* decision and continue the policy of public school segregation. NAACP legal counsel Thurgood Marshall also announced that legal segregation in municipal parks, transportation, and housing would be the next targets for litigation (NYT).

7 In Baton Rouge, La., members of the state house of representatives moved to place the public education system under the state's "police powers" to avoid desegregation. The measure gave local school superintendents the right to assign all pupils to public schools (NYT).

8 In Detroit, Mich., federal judge Arthur F. Lederle issued a permanent injunction against local housing officials for maintaining separate black and white lists for assignments to public housing units. Suit against the Detroit Housing Authority had been brought by twelve black residents in 1951 (JM).

8 In San Antonio, Tex., members of the city council passed an ordinance requiring segregation of black and white citizens in municipal swimming pools. The action was taken when black adults and children attempted to enter pools reserved for "whites only" (JM).

15 In Baltimore, Md., Public Housing Authority officials announced the end of the practice of segregating black and white tenants. Housing authority chairman Chester Carey stated that it would take three to four months to complete the changes in its practices (JM).

22 In San Francisco, Calif., the Public Housing Authority announced that it had completed the desegregation of seven public housing units in the city. The practice of assigning African Americans and Asians to separate housing units ended in May 1954 (JM).

28 In Washington, D.C., in testimony before the Interstate Commerce Commission, NAACP officials reported on the persistence of Jim Crow practices on eleven major railroads operating in the South and called on the commission to issue broad regulations banning segregation on all interstate trains (NYT).

29 In **Annapolis, Md.**, educator, suffragist, civil and women's rights activist Mary Church Terrell died. A founder and the first president of the National Association of Colored Women (1896), Terrell worked closely with the NAACP, the National Urban League, and a number of civil rights organizations. Engaging in picketing, boycotting, and sit-ins, from 1950 to 1953 Terrell led a movement to end segregation in public eating places in Washington, D.C. Terrell was one of three plaintiffs in *District of Columbia v. John Thompson,* the successful test case that led to the 8 June 1953 Supreme Court ruling that segregation in eating facilities in Washington, D.C., was unconstitutional. She was also active in the movement to end segregation in the District's theaters and hotels (NYT).

29 In **Washington, D.C.**, Veterans Administration (VA) official Harvey H. Higley announced that the practice of segregation within VA hospitals around the country would be ended in keeping with President Eisenhower's military desegregation plan (NYT).

AUGUST 1954

12 In **Nashville, Tenn.**, at the fifty-first annual meeting of the American Teachers Association (black), Fisk University educator Bonita Valien expressed her belief that black teachers need not fear unemployment as a result of the school desegregation process. Valien urged the members to prepare themselves to compete for fewer and fewer teaching positions (JM).

19 In **Dade County, Fla.**, B. O. Lott, principal of the Mount Dora Negro School, called it "a cowardly thing" when crosses were burned in front of his school and two other places in the surrounding black neighborhood. Lott believed the cross burnings were a response to the local NAACP's announcement that black pupils would be seeking admittance to white schools in their neighborhoods (NYT).

19 In **Daytona Beach, Fla.**, Paul Decker became the first white to graduate from the fifty-year-old Bethune Cookman College. Decker received a bachelor of science degree in psychology (JM).

19 In **Philipi, W.Va.**, members of the Barbour County school board withdrew plans to transfer twelve white pupils to a black school after a mob of two hundred people stormed the board's meeting to protest the move (NYT).

31 In **Hobbs, N.Mex.**, District Attorney Pat Hennegan warned Rev. Bill Carter, leader of the pro-segregation forces, that charges would be brought against him if any black student was injured during the integration of local public schools. Carter threatened violence if the school board went ahead with desegregation plans. It was later reported that black students enrolled in the previously all-white public schools without incident (NYT).

SEPTEMBER 1954

2 In **Evanston, Ill.**, at the World Council of Churches annual meeting, AME Zion church official Rev. J. Clinton Hoggard chastised the predominantly white Christian denominations for failing to appoint black clergy to policy-making positions. "The only full fledged Negro delegates here," Rev. Hoggard complained, were "from the Negro denominations." AME Bishop D. Ward Nichols and Rev. Joseph Jackson of the National Baptist Convention (black) were the only African Americans appointed to the ninety-member central committee for the World Council (JM).

3 In **Jackson, Miss.**, in the face of "voluntary segregation plans" put forward by the all-white Mississippi Education Association, 250 black leaders in the state issued a statement in support of the NAACP's public school desegregation activities (SSN).

3 In **Montgomery, Ala.**, twenty-three black students who attempted to enroll at an all-white school were denied admission by school principal R. T. Anderson. NAACP officials who accompanied the students vowed to take the issue up with school board officials (NYT).

3 In **Richmond, Va.**, the Virginia Synod of Presbyterians passed a resolution calling on local churches to admit members "without reference to race." The resolution was an endorsement of the position taken by the General Assembly of the Presbyterian Church in May 1954 (NYT).

3 In **Sulphur Springs, Tex.**, the home of NAACP official H. W. Ridge was blasted by shotguns and pistols following the delivery of a petition to the local school board calling for speedy desegregation of public schools. No one was hurt in the attack (SSN).

4 In **Washington, D.C.**, President Eisenhower issued an executive order clarifying and strengthening the ban on discrimination by employers receiving government contracts. The President's Committee on Government Contracts, headed by Vice President Nixon, issued a pamphlet stressing the need for skilled manpower to counter Communist propaganda (NYT).

4 In **Nashville, Tenn.**, the Southern Education Reporting Service published the first issue of *Southern School News* (SSN). This monthly publication, edited by C. A. Knight, would go on to provide information on the implementation of the Supreme Court's decision calling for public school integration in the southern and border states (NYT).

9 In **Bullock County, Ala.**, three members of the board of registrars resigned after four African Americans who were not allowed to register to vote filed suit in federal court. In a county with 11,815 blacks and 4,239 whites, only six African Americans were registered, compared to 2,500 whites (JM).

9 In **Tylertown, Miss.**, thirty members of the local NAACP branch were summoned before the Walthall County grand jury. Although no reason was given for the action, NAACP southern director Ruby Hurley claimed the move was meant to

MOB VIOLENCE OVER SCHOOL INTEGRATION IN DELAWARE

The greatest violence and organized protests against public school integration that took place in 1954 did not occur in the Deep South, where political leaders called for "massive resistance," but in the small town of Milford, Del. The local school board voted to begin public school desegregation in September with the transfer of ten black students to the all-white Milford High School. However, mobs of whites surrounded the school on opening day threatening violence and not only prevented the black students from enrolling but forced school officials to close down the entire public school system on 17 September.

The protests by white parents attracted the attention of Bryant Bowles, the president of the newly organized National Association for the Advancement of White People, who came to the town and urged white students to boycott the public schools. Bowles was later arrested and charged with two counts of conspiracy to violate the state's school laws. He was later released on six thousand dollars' bail.

Four school board members resigned on 22 September after receiving numerous death threats over their support of public school desegregation. State education officials came to Milford and took over the running of the schools, reopening them on 27 September, but 70 percent of the white students continued to boycott classes. In October, after several new members were appointed to the school board, the board decided to remove the ten black students from Milford High School and postpone any future attempts at public school desegregation. The local NAACP brought suit against the school board, but the Delaware chancery court and supreme court ruled that the Milford school officials did not get approval from the state board of education for their integration plan, and thus the black students had been illegally admitted to the all-white Milford High School.

intimidate those blacks who signed a petition calling for the integration of local public schools (JM).

9 In Washington, D.C., black educator Dr. Ambrose Caliver, assistant to U.S. commissioner of education Samuel Brownell, was among the government officials involved in the preparation of a manual on methods for achieving public school desegregation in the seventeen southern states affected by the *Brown* decision (JM).

10 In Washington, D.C., the all-white group, the Federation of Citizens Association, filed a suit in federal district court to halt the desegregation of the D.C. public schools until the U.S. Supreme Court issued its school desegregation "master plan" (NYT).

16 In Amitie, Miss., a meeting of the local NAACP was broken up by Sheriff Robert Jenkins and forty other whites, and branch records were confiscated. Ruby Hurley, director of the NAACP's southern division, called on the FBI to investigate the incident. This is the first reported attack on an NAACP branch in the South since the Supreme Court's *Brown* decision of May 1954 (JM).

16 In Washington, D.C., the Board of Commissioners ordered an end to racial segregation in the District's 1,075-man fire department. Despite a threatened strike by white firefighters, Fire Chief Millard Sutton was directed to assign men to station houses regardless of race or color (JM).

17 In Sacramento, Calif., state attorney general Edmund G. Brown ruled that segregated fire stations in cities throughout the state violated the state constitution. Fire chief John Alderson's plan for the "gradual integration" of Los Angeles fire stations was rejected by the state justice department (NYT).

17–18 Black students entered without incident previously all-white public schools in Lafayette, Ark.; Hillsboro, Ohio; Baltimore, Md.; and Sikeston, Mo. Black students were turned away when they tried to enroll in all-white public schools in Baton Rouge, La.; Hitchens, Tex.; and in numerous school districts in Mississippi (NYT).

19 In Greenbrier County, W.Va., after a week of protests and violence by mobs of whites, school officials ordered black students to return to the all-black schools. Similar demonstrations in Rupert, Crichton, and White Sulphur Springs, W. Va., forced the withdrawal of black students from white public schools (NYT).

23 In Washington, D.C., Adam Clayton Powell, Tennessee congressman Howard Baker, and Illinois congressman William Dawson issued statements calling for the admission of African Americans as cadets at the U.S. Air Force Academy to open in Colorado Springs, Colo., in September 1955. Baker was the first southern politician to recommend the admission of blacks to any U.S. military academy (JM).

23 In Dade County, Fla., fifteen black mechanics were admitted to the AFL's bricklayers, masons, and plasterers union as a result of a federal court order. They were the first African Americans to be admitted to AFL craft unions in the state. Black skilled workers had been barred from most AFL craft unions in the southern states (JM).

23 In Greensboro, N.C., members of the Mecklenburg County Medical Society voted to admit Dr. Emery L. Rann to membership in the organization. In May the members voted to remove the word *white* from its bylaws and constitution, and in September Dr. Rann became the first black physician admitted to a North Carolina medical society (JM).

25 In Philadelphia, Pa., city solicitor Abraham L. Freedman and the mothers of five black boys filed suits in orphans court to get the City Board of Trusts to lift the ban on black students attending Girard College, a private elementary and secondary school. Under the terms of the will of the founder, Stephen Girard, only "poor white orphan boys" were to be admitted to the school; however, the school's trustees were appointed by public officials and the school received substantial state aid (NYT).

28 In Mound Bayou, Miss., in the face of threats from members of the newly organized White Citizens Councils of economic sanctions against

African Americans who supported voting rights and school desegregation, members of the Regional Council of Negro Leadership, representing one hundred black organizations, agreed to withdraw funds from Mississippi banks and deposit them in black banks in Memphis, order supplies through out-of-state mail-order companies, and purchase other goods from black-owned businesses in the state (NYT).

28 In Los Angeles, Calif., at the annual AFL convention, a resolution was passed calling for the end of segregation in federal public housing. The resolution was introduced by A. Philip Randolph, Brotherhood of Sleeping Car Porters president and AFL vice president (NYT).

30 In Norfolk, Va., the home of a second black family who moved into the Coronado section was seriously damaged by a dynamite blast. This was the latest in a series of attacks upon black families who moved into the previously all-white neighborhood (JM).

30 In Zion, Ill., KKK members burned a cross near and painted three-foot letters on the newly purchased home of Hattie Wynn. Police were ordered in to guard Wynn and her family against further attacks (JM).

30 In Hillsboro, Ohio, NAACP attorney Thurgood Marshall filed a suit on behalf of black parents and against the Hillsboro school board for rezoning district lines so that black children could not attend all-white schools. Marshall argued that the school board's policies were aimed at getting around the Supreme Court's *Brown* decision (NYT).

OCTOBER 1954

I In Institute, W. Va., at West Virginia State College, Dean Harrison Ferrell reported that 166 white students were enrolled at the previously all-black institution. The total enrollment at the school was 983 (SSN).

I In Phoenix, Ariz., superior court judge Charles C. Bernstein outlawed segregation in public elementary schools in the state. Judge Bernstein declared that segregated public education fostered the maintenance of a "racially conscious society." In 1953 superior court judge Fred S. Sturckeyer had ruled that segregation in public colleges and secondary schools in the state was illegal (SSN).

I In Washington, D.C., Arthur D. Jewell became the first black administrator appointed to a formerly all-white high school. Appointed assistant principal at Eastern High School, Jewell had formerly served as assistant principal of Armstrong High School (black) in the District (SSN).

I In Washington, D.C., for the first time in its history, the national board of the Daughters of the American Revolution announced the award of college scholarships to black women. Jessie Irene Bell of Ashland, Ky., and Velma Lynne Smith and Doris Henderson of Washington, D.C., received four-year nursing scholarships (NYT).

I–2 In Washington, D.C., the Interstate Commerce Commission (ICC) dismissed a complaint brought by a black woman, Sarah Keyes, against a private bus company in North Carolina for racial discrimination. The ICC ruled that the Supreme Court's *Brown* decision "does not preclude segregation in a private business, such as a bus company" (NYT).

5–6 In Baltimore, Md., mobs of whites protested against the admittance of four black students to Southern High School. Bryant Bowles, leader of the National Association for the Advancement of White People, brought a suit to keep Baltimore public schools segregated and urged white parents to keep their children at home. The courts subsequently dismissed Bowles's suit (NYT).

14 In Ocilla, Ga., after filing petitions to become the first African American to run for the town council, building contractor Ernest Davis, and his brother Curtis, were kidnapped at gunpoint by an unidentified policeman. After firing a shot at the two men while detaining them in his squad car, the policeman warned the two that they had gone too far and would be killed. Davis later withdrew from the council race (NYT).

15–30 In New York City, Liberian president William Tubman arrived for his first official visit and witnessed firsthand U.S. Jim Crow practices. Tubman visited Lincoln University in Oxford, Pa., before going to Washington, D.C., for an official White House reception on 18 October. Tubman also traveled to Ohio and returned to New York City on 27 October to meet with financier Bernard Baruch and visit the United Nations. When Tubman and his ten-person party traveled to the South and visited Tuskegee Institute in Alabama, they were forced to stay in private accommodations. When Tubman arrived in Atlanta, although Gov. Herman Talmadge refused to greet him, Tubman was met by Atlanta mayor William Hartsfield. Tubman stayed at Atlanta University at the invitation of Rufus Clement, the school's president, because he was barred from most hotels in At-lanta. Tubman addressed an interracial student conference at Clark College before leaving for New Orleans, the final stop in his southern visit (NYT).

21 In New Orleans, La., in the first interracial football game held in the city, Xavier University defeated the Keesler Air Force team from Biloxi, Miss., by a score of 39 to 6 (JM).

28 In Washington, D.C., Pentagon officials announced that Col. Benjamin O. Davis, Jr., who was serving in Japan as the director of operations and training for the U.S. Air Forces in the Far East, was promoted to the rank of brigadier general. The son of army brigadier general Benjamin O. Davis, Sr., the younger Davis became the first black to achieve this rank in the U.S. Air Force (NYT).

ENDING OF RACIAL SEGREGATION IN THE U.S. ARMED FORCES

The desegregation of the U.S. armed services and military installations begun in 1949 under the executive order issued by President Harry S. Truman continued throughout 1954. The U.S. Department of the Navy announced early in February that the separate recruitment of blacks as stewards had ended. All men enlisted in the navy would enter as seamen and then would be assigned to the various branches. Despite this change in policy, in July National Urban League executive secretary Lester Granger resigned from his position as special consultant on race relations to the U.S. Navy because of the slow pace of racial change and the fact that there appeared to be "no serious recognition of the urgency in this matter" by navy officials.

Following protests by the NAACP's Clarence Mitchell, U.S. Marine Corps officials announced in April that they were suspending the recruitment of blacks as stewards to serve as cooks and waiters in homes of marine officers. In July, Veterans Administration official Harvey H. Higley announced that segregatory policies and practices at Veterans Administration hospitals around the country would be ended. And in December 1954 Secy. of the Air Force Harold Talbott announced that recreational areas and facilities in Europe that denied access to black soldiers were to be declared off-limits to all American soldiers. This was the first pronouncement calling for the enforcement of the U.S. military's nonsegregation regulations in Europe. The change in policy came about primarily because of the complaints registered by Harlem congressman Adam Clayton Powell.

In July 1954 Pentagon officials also announced the closing of separate black schools at Fort Myer and Fort Belvoir in Virginia and Craig Air Force Base in Alabama. These were the first closings of segregated schools on nineteen bases located in the South. However, when Defense Department officials informed members of the Norfolk, Va., school board that the all-white Benmoree School at the Norfolk Naval Yard must be desegregated by September 1955, local school officials voiced strong objections. Spokesmen for the Defense Department promised that if local school officials refused to provide staff for the desegregated school, it would be provided by the military.

NOVEMBER 1954

1 In Atlanta, Ga., T. M. Alexander, real estate broker, was appointed fee appraiser by the Federal Housing Administration and became the first African American in the South to hold such a position. Alexander would later oversee the processing of loan applications for the various federal housing programs (JM).

2 In Hot Springs, Ark., at a meeting of sixty-two leading black educators, a resolution was passed calling for immediate compliance with the Supreme Court's *Brown* decision. The resolution, drafted by Morehouse College president Benjamin Mays and Howard University professor Charles S. Thompson, declared that black educators as a group could not support any plan designed to impede the implementation of public school desegregation (NYT).

3, 4 In the 1954 elections, thirty-one-year-old Charles C. Diggs, an undertaker in Detroit, became the third African American elected to the U.S. Congress in the twentieth century. Bessie Buchanan was elected to the New York State Assembly representing Harlem. She became the first black woman to serve in the New York legislature. In Hot Springs, Ark., Fred W. Martin defeated two white candidates to become the first African American to serve on the city council since the Reconstruction era.

In referenda in Georgia, South Carolina, and Louisiana, voters passed by wide margins constitutional amendments upholding racial segregation in the public school systems in defiance of the Supreme Court's *Brown* decision. In Mississippi voters approved by a 9 to 1 margin a constitutional provision that would require that applicants to vote be able to read, write, and interpret the state constitution "to the satisfaction of the registrar." Many believed that the new measure would further reduce the number of black voters. In a state with more than 980,000 black residents, it was estimated that only 22,000 were registered to vote in 1954 (NYT).

4 In Richmond, Va., the leaders of the newly incorporated group Defenders of State Sovereignty and Individual Liberties vowed to fight public school integration "by any honorable and legal means." The organizers claimed to already have thirteen chapters and two thousand members (SSN).

4 In Sulphur Springs, Tex., Hardy and Eleanor Ridge were forced to flee after their home was bombed and their lives were threatened by local whites. Ridge, the president of the local NAACP branch, had led the campaign for the desegregation of the city's public schools (SSN).

17 In New York City, A. Philip Randolph, president of the Brotherhood of Sleeping Car Porters, announced that a lawsuit was to be brought by the AFL to end racially discriminatory practices in four "lily-white" railroad brotherhoods. Over two hundred thousand black railway workers had been denied membership by these four unions (NYT).

18 In Philadelphia, Pa., Lt. Thomas L. James, Meharry Medical School graduate, became the first African American to serve in the regular U.S. Navy as a dental officer. Dr. James enlisted in the navy in 1951 and served in Japan before being assigned to the Philadelphia Naval Shipyard (JM).

19 In Lafayette, Ind., Purdue University president Frank L. Houle announced that the executive council of the Association of Land Grant Colleges and Universities had voted to extend an invitation of membership to the seventeen black land grant colleges in the South. The state land grant colleges were opened to provide instruction in "agriculture and the mechanical arts" as a result of the 1862 Morrill Act, and the black land grant colleges were founded as a result of the Second Morrill Act of 1890 (NYT).

21 In Indianola, Miss., bank president Herman Moore, leader of the state White Citizens Council, announced a program of intimidation and boycotts against black businesspeople and professionals who agitated for school desegregation or the right to vote. Moore claimed that there were councils active in thirty-five counties, with twenty-five thousand members (NYT).

25 In Baton Rouge, La., the Louisiana Bar Association's Committee on Ethics announced the investigation of attorneys Alex Pitcher and Johnnie Jones. Pitcher and Jones had served as the lawyers for twenty-three black children who attempted to enroll in all-white public elementary schools in the city (JM).

25 In Washington, D.C., according to a survey published by *The Washington Star* newspaper, the enrollment of white students in district public schools had declined 8.7 percent since May 1954. Individual schools in the district had lost as much as 51 percent of the white student enrollment following the beginning of the desegregation program (JM).

25 In Fairfax County, Va., public school officials announced a plan for "voluntary" desegregation. The new policy would allow black students to choose to remain in all-black schools or transfer to previously all-white schools (JM).

25 In Washington, D.C., lawyers for seven southern states (Virginia, North Carolina, South Carolina, Arkansas, Texas, Maryland, and Delaware) filed briefs with the U.S. Supreme Court calling for a delay in the implementation of public school desegregation. At a conference of southern governors, only six refused to sign a resolution to preserve public school segregation (Maryland, West Virginia, Kentucky, Arkansas, Tennessee, and Alabama) (NYT).

28 In St. Louis, Mo., members of the board of aldermen voted down two bills that would have banned racial discrimination in theaters, restaurants, hotels, and other public accommodations (NYT).

DECEMBER 1954

1 In St. Louis, Mo., public school superintendent Philip J. Hickey announced a new plan for the desegregation of the city's high schools by 1 February 1955. All beginning high school students would be assigned to schools on the basis of residence, and no transfers would be allowed; other white high school students would remain in schools where they were enrolled. Public elementary schools would be integrated beginning September 1955 (SSN).

2 In Hillsboro, Ohio, Rev. Rita E. H. Lee, pastor of Wesleyan Methodist Church and president of the local NAACP branch, received several death threats because of her efforts to enroll black students in all-white public elementary schools in the city (JM).

2 In Washington, D.C., in a recent survey conducted by the National Council of Churches, one-third of the 13,597 ministers at predominantly white churches responded that they believed that nonwhites prefer to attend churches of their own group. Clergy from the United Lutheran Church in America, Congregational Christian Church, the Presbyterian Church of the USA, and others stated that nonwhites have little or no opportunity for leadership in racially mixed churches (NYT).

9 In Jackson, Miss., in the face of threats from the White Citizens Councils (WCC), NAACP members, meeting in a state conference in Jackson, called for an "all-out boycott of products and services of all companies whose top officials use threats and intimidation to halt the advance of civil rights." The resolution was a response to a WCC-organized boycott of black businessmen and professionals who participated in civil rights activities (JM).

9 In Washington, D.C., the board of commissioners warned owners of restaurants, hotels, theaters, and other public accommodations that beginning 1 January 1955 refusal to serve blacks as customers would result in prosecution under the terms of laws passed in the 1870s. The anti-discrimination measures had been on the books since Reconstruction but had not been enforced for over fifty years (NYT).

9 In Atlanta, Ga., the Georgia State Commission on Education recommended to the state legislature the adoption of specific measures to prevent public school integration. The commission called for the passage of laws to (1) make it a felony to provide state funds to racially mixed public schools; (2) grant local school officials complete jurisdiction in the assignment of pupils; and (3) give local school boards the authority to determine attendance districts (NYT).

16 In the United Kingdom, the huge influx of Jamaican immigrants, averaging one thousand per month, triggered racial conflicts in several British communities. Jamaican immigrants complained of racial discrimination in public accommodations and employment, and some British newspapers have exacerbated the situation by supporting calls to "Keep Britain White" (JM).

18 **In New York City,** NAACP officials announced the appointment of Dr. John W. Davis, former president of West Virginia State College and director of U.S. Foreign Operations Administration in Liberia, as director of a new department formed within the organization "to protect Negro teachers, principals, and administrative personnel against loss of jobs in the desegregation transition" (NYT).

22 **In the state of Mississippi,** voters by a 2 to 1 margin endorsed a constitutional amendment that authorized the state legislature to abolish the public schools and subsidize private schools in order to maintain segregated education. Gov. Hugh White planned to call a special session of the legislature to appropriate funds for upgrading black public schools to the level of those for whites (NYT).

22–24 **In Washington, D.C.,** Secretary of the Navy Charles Thomas issued an order stating that seating at the Sugar Bowl football game between Navy and the University of Mississippi would be on a nonsegregatory basis. NAACP official Clarence Mitchell declared that "apparently this means that the Navy will start the year right by spurning segregation and upholding the dignity of man without regard to race." Unfortunately, the NAACP had to file an official protest to navy officials once it was revealed that tickets sold for the game were still stamped "for whites only" (NYT).

25 **In Birmingham, Ala.,** NAACP state branch leaders urged reprisals against White Citizens Council (WCC) members who participated in the boycott launched against Selma insurance executive C. W. Boynton. Ruby Hurley, director of NAACP southern branches, told state leaders to apply similar measures against businesses owned by WCC members. Since black residents outnumbered whites 5 to 1 in many Black Belt counties, Hurley declared that the WCC leaders have "met their match" (JM).

25 **In Charleston, W. Va.,** state school superintendent W. W. Trent announced that 96 of 122 public schools in the state have both black and white pupils enrolled. The state official also noted that at least four black teachers in West Virginia were instructing in mixed classrooms (JM).

26 **In Los Angeles, Calif.,** delegates to the 167th General Assembly of the Presbyterian Church USA approved a report entitled "Operation Desegregation" that called for the end of all forms of segregation inside and outside the church. According to the report, the Supreme Court's *Brown* decision "points up the failure of the church to achieve full fellowship within its own lifetime" (NYT).

30 **In New York City,** NAACP officials announced plans to raise a $30 million war chest to support southern blacks active in civil rights campaigns who had been threatened with loss of home mortgages by southern banks. Regional Council of Negro Leadership president Dr. T. R. M. Howard revealed that at least nine black families in Mississippi faced cancellation of home mortgages by white bankers due to their anti-segregation activities (JM).

30 **In Washington, D.C.,** NAACP official Clarence Mitchell denounced Department of Health, Education, and Welfare (HEW) Secretary Oveta Culp Hobby's continued practice of providing federal funds to hospitals where black physicians and nurses were denied staff positions. Mitchell declared that HEW's practices aided the perpetuation of discrimination against black health professionals (NYT).

31 **In New York City,** Robert C. Weaver, former housing aide in the federal government and professor at Howard University, was named deputy commissioner of housing by New York's governor-elect Averell Harriman. Weaver became the highest-ranking African American in the New York state government (NYT).

On 2 September 1955, in Chicago, Illinois, Mrs. Mamie Bradley weeps as the body of her slain son, Emmett Louis Till, fourteen, arrives at the rail station. The youth was found dead in a Mississippi creek with a bullet hole behind his ear. Till was murdered for supposedly whistling at a white woman. (SOURCE: CORBIS BETTMANN)

1955

"CLIMBING JACOB'S LADDER"

For southerners who organized the massive resistance campaigns against the implementation of the Brown decision, the leaders of the local branches of the NAACP became obvious targets for attack. NAACP officials provided instructions to branch leaders on how to initiate the school integration process in their local communities. At the same time, when African Americans challenged in the courts the discriminatory practices at parks, beaches, swimming pools, or golf courses open to the public, the judges endorsed the plaintiffs' argument that the Supreme Court's ban on segregation in "public" education should be expanded to include "public" recreational facilities. In outlawing racial segregation in additional areas of American public life in 1955, it suggested that the courts were interested in "Climbing Jacob's Ladder," if only one rung at a time.

JANUARY 1955

1 In New York City, UN secretary-general Dag Hammarskjöld announced the appointment of Ralph Bunche as undersecretary in his cabinet. Nobel Prize–winner Bunche will carry out assignments throughout the world on behalf of the UN (NYT).

4 In Columbia, S.C., in a desperate effort to avert the implementation of the Supreme Court's public school desegregation decision, South Carolina's Educational Finance Commission recommended the spending of $65 million to bring black public schools up to the level of white schools. In a state with 229,000 black and 296,000 white pupils, this figure would allot $314 per black student compared with $147 per white pupil in the 1955–56 school year (NYT).

6 In Austin, Tex., in the face of continued attacks upon the NAACP coming from state officials, the 7,400-member Texas Teachers Association, composed of black teachers, refused to endorse a resolution calling for a donation of one dollar per member to the civil rights group "in faith and appreciation." The majority who opposed the resolution argued that the leadership should not attempt to tie the teachers organization too closely to the NAACP (SSN).

6 In the states of Georgia and Mississippi, education officials announced plans to raise millions of dollars in taxes for the equalization of public school facilities for black and white students. The Georgia School Building Authority planned to spend $200,000 on black public schools over the following five years (SSN).

8 In New York City, contralto Marian Anderson made her debut at the Metropolitan Opera Company in the role of Ulrica in Verdi's *Un Ballo in Maschera*. Miss Anderson became the first African American to sing at the Met (NYT).

12 In Oak Ridge, Tenn., officials at the Atomic Energy Commission announced that racial segregation in public schools would be ended in September 1955. School district lines, teacher and other personnel appointments, and student school assignments would no longer be made on the basis of race (NYT).

13 In Los Angeles, Calif., fire chief John Alderson brought about the "token integration" of the city's fire department when he assigned black firefighters John Rheta and George Winchester to the previously all-white station house in Studio City. Local black leaders complained about Alderson's less than modest actions (JM).

13 In Rosewood, Md., after a grand jury investigation, fifteen mentally retarded black children were ordered transferred from the Crownsville State Hospital, which investigators termed "a disgrace," to the all-white Rosewood Training School. This marked the first time in the state of Maryland that black and white mental patients were admitted to the same state hospital (JM).

13 In Washington, D.C., officials for the Capital Transit Company announced that African Americans were to be trained as bus drivers for the first time in the city's history. White House aide Maxwell Rabb was one of President Eisenhower's assistants who worked to convince company officials to change their policies. The announcement climaxed a fourteen-year push to open up drivers' positions to African Americans in the District (NYT).

14 In Philadelphia, Pa., NAACP attorney Thurgood Marshall filed two suits in federal court to end racial discrimination in private housing. On behalf of six black veterans, NAACP lawyers filed suit against Levitt and Sons Development Corp. for discriminating against African Americans seeking to purchase homes in the Levittown housing developments in New York and Pennsylvania. An-

other suit was filed in federal court to prevent Federal Housing Authority officials from discriminating against blacks seeking admission to federally funded rental housing units in the Philadelphia area (NYT).

19 In Washington, D.C., it was announced that Chicago alderman Archibald Carey and Assistant Secretary of Labor J. Ernest Wilkins were appointed to President Eisenhower's five-member Committee on Government Employment Policy, which would make recommendations for ending employment discrimination by agencies of the federal government. This board replaced the federal government's Fair Employment Board created by President Harry S. Truman (NYT).

20 In Washington, D.C., at the opening session of Congress, Adam Clayton Powell introduced twelve civil rights measures and charged that "the U.S. Congress has done absolutely nothing in civil rights." Hubert H. Humphrey and other liberal Democratic senators introduced twelve separate civil rights measures into the Senate, including legislation for the creation of a permanent fair employment practices commission (NYT).

27 In Baltimore, Md., liquor control board officials threatened to revoke the licenses of black clubs that served both black and white customers. In a recent ruling, the board stated that licenses were given to establishments to serve one race only. White club owners had complained to the liquor control board about the increasing number of whites frequenting black clubs in the city (JM).

27 In New York City, NAACP officials announced plans to raise a $1 million war chest to assist victims of boycotts and other forms of retaliation leveled against those blacks who participated in civil rights campaigns in the South. Pledges were sought from labor, religious, and civic groups throughout the country (JM).

27–28 In Washington, D.C., during an official visit to the U.S., Haitian president Paul E. Magloire praised President Eisenhower's civil rights record in an address to the joint session of Congress and noted that the Haitian people valued his efforts to "eliminate prejudices of all sort which constitute handicaps to the mutual understanding which is our common objective in this hemisphere." President Magloire became the third black leader to address the U.S. Congress. Liberian president Edwin Barclay in 1943 and Emperor Haile Selassie in 1954 preceded the Haitian leader (NYT).

30 In Cecil County, Md., despite President Eisenhower's order ending segregation in schools at government installations, the parents of seven black children charged that they were not allowed to enroll their children in the civilian-operated public school at the Bainbridge (Md.) Naval Training Center. The parents filed suit in federal court against Morris Rannells, superintendent of the Cecil County school district (NYT).

FEBRUARY 1955

1–3 In Miami, Fla., the executive council of the AFL announced that the union would support the "Powell amendment" to the federal aid to education bill. The amendment called for the termination of federal funds to local school districts that failed to move on public school desegregation (NYT).

3 In Mound Bayou, Miss., Dr. Theodore R. M. Howard, chairman of the Regional Council of Negro Leadership, was threatened by whites on the local Selective Service Board with reclassification of his draft status to 1-A. The NAACP viewed the action as part of a program of intimidation against civil rights activitsts and asked Selective Service officials in Washington, D.C., to investigate the matter (JM).

3 In St. Louis, Mo., the desegregation of the public high schools began and was accomplished without incident. Under the official desegregation actions the elementary schools and technical high schools were to become integrated in the fall semester, 1955 (SSN).

3 In Washington, D.C., the Metropolitan Police Boys Club, with fourteen thousand black and eight thousand white boys in segregated units, was banned by the Department of the Interior from facilities owned by the federal government because of its segregatory practices. The Police

Boys Club was earlier banned from facilities owned by the Unitarian Church because of its official policy of segregation (SSN).

3 In Washington, D.C., school board member Margaret Just Butcher asked school superintendent Hobart M. Corning to investigate charges of racial discrimination brought by twelve black students in the district. The students claimed that they were denied admission to the predominantly white Anacostia and Eastern high schools. Legal segregation ended in the district's public schools in September 1954 (SSN).

4 In Harpers Ferry, W. Va., Storer College, an all-black private institution, was denied its annual $20,000 grant by state legislators. Since all the state public colleges and universities were open to African Americans, the legislators decided to suspend state funding to the private black school (NYT).

6 In Washington, D.C., the President's Committee on Government Contracts (also referred to as the "Little FEPC"), headed by Vice President Nixon, announced that it had received 104 complaints of job discrimination by federal contractors, and thirteen contractors were found to be in violation of government regulations. The committee also noted that thirty-seven federal contractors ended discriminatory practices as a result of the committee's intervention (NYT).

6,8 In Washington, D.C., the National Press Club in a secret ballot voted to admit Louis R. Lautier of the *Atlanta Daily World* to membership. Lautier, a veteran journalist who was also a member of the White House Correspondents Association, became the first African American allowed admission to the National Press Club (NYT).

10 In Oakland, Calif., district court of appeals judge Maurice T. Dooling ruled that the Mountain View Cemetery had the right to refuse to entomb the bodies of African Americans. The judge argued that a cemetery was not a public accommodation and therefore was not subject to the state's anti-discrimination law (JM).

10 In St. Louis, Mo., after filing a complaint with the National Labor Relations Board (NLRB),

George Newsome became the first African American in the AFL Carpenters Union in this city. Newsome had previously been barred from the union, but with the assistance of the St. Louis Urban League took the matter to the NLRB, which ruled in his favor (JM).

13 In Hollywood, Calif., Dorothy Dandridge was nominated for an Academy Award for best actress for her performance in the film *Carmen Jones*. Miss Dandridge became the first African American ever nominated for an Oscar in the best actor or best actress categories (NYT).

13 Throughout the United States, Race Relations Sunday was celebrated in an estimated 147,000 congregations belonging to the National Council of Churches. In the official message issued for the 1955 programs, the council's executive committee declared that race prejudice is a sin and that it is "more than merely bad, unfortunate or unrighteous. He who wrongs his brother sins against God" (NYT).

14 In Miami, Fla., when the managers of the Urmey Hotel announced that they would not serve the twenty-four black guests attending the annual Abraham Lincoln Day dinner, sponsored by the state's Republican party, 150 of the 425 whites joined the blacks and left the event. Dinner co-chairperson Wesley Garrison upon leaving declared that "Abe Lincoln would turn over in his grave if he knew what was happening." Republican party officials later voted to take legal action against the hotel (NYT).

23 In Chicago, Ill., Rep. William Dawson took credit for the defeat of Mayor William Kennelly in his bid for renomination as Democratic candidate. Dawson and other black Democrats opposed Kennelly because he was "not right on the race question" and provided insufficient protection to blacks moving into the white Trumbull Park Homes housing project. Dawson supported the county Democratic chairman Richard J. Daley, who won the nomination (NYT).

24 In Atlanta, Ga., state representative C. C. Perkins introduced a bill into the legislature calling for a ban on interracial dancing and athletic competitions in the state. If passed, violators could face up to two thousand dollars in fines and eighteen months in prison (JM).

27 In New York City, NAACP officials announced that the "War Chest" being gathered to aid civil rights activists in the South under attack from opponents of integration had surpassed the $100,000 mark. Among the major contributors to the fund were the AME Church ($10,000), North Carolina Mutual Life Insurance Company ($10,000), Supreme Life Insurance Company ($6,000), and New York City radio station WLIB ($500) (NYT).

MARCH 1955

3 In Miami, Fla., the AFL Carpenters Union District Council voted to integrate work assignments and allow black and white carpenters to work together. Previously, the union officials called in the police to keep black and white workers separated at work sites (JM).

10 In Bismarck, N.D., Gov. Norman Brunsdale signed into law a bill that lifted the ban on interracial marriages in the state. The original ban had been passed in 1861 (JM).

10 In Washington, D.C., President Eisenhower's Committee on Government Contracts met and was ordered to conduct a survey of the hiring practices of federal departments and agencies. Government contractors who were asked to end discriminatory hiring practices charged that the federal government had "a disgraceful record" in hiring African Americans. It was reported that officials in many federal agencies, such as the Interstate Commerce Commission and the Federal Communications Commission, refuse to consider blacks for upper-level posts (JM).

17 In Philadelphia, Pa., the NAACP suit initiated in 1954 against the home builders in Levittown, Pa., was dismissed in federal court. Attorney Thurgood Marshall had argued that the builders discriminated against African Americans, but the court ruled that neither the Federal Housing Authority nor the Veterans Administration "has been charged by Congress with the duty of preventing

WHITE STUDENTS ENROLLED IN ALL-BLACK COLLEGES AND UNIVERSITIES

The number of white students enrolled in all-black colleges and universities increased substantially in 1955. In June 1954 Mary E. Howard received a master's degree in sociology from Fisk University in Nashville, Tenn., and became the first white graduate since 1893. In June 1955 Joan Arlene Wood became the first white student to receive a B.A. degree from Fisk and Willard A. L. Jarrett became the first white student to graduate from Simmons University in Louisville, Ky. Jarrett received a bachelor of theology degree. At Lincoln University in Jefferson City, Mo., 150 white students were enrolled during the 1954–55 school year, and in Institute, W. Va., there were 180 white students attending West Virginia State College, the black land-grant college for the state.

During the 1955–56 school year, even more white students were attending all-black colleges. It was estimated that in September 1955, one-third of the 1,450 students attending West Virginia State College were white. At the all-black Bluefield State College in Bluefield, W. Va., 10 white students were enrolled in the fall of 1955. At the same time, there were only 160 black students enrolled in all of the previously all-white colleges and universities in West Virginia.

In May 1956, *The New York Times* reported that in the private black colleges during the 1955–56 school year, there were 19 white students enrolled at Xavier University in New Orleans, La.; 18 at Lincoln University in Oxford, Pa.; 18 at Fisk University in Nashville, Tenn.; 6 at Hampton Institute in Hampton, Va.; 5 at Talladega College in Talladega, Ala.; and 5 at Bethune-Cookman College in Daytona Beach, Fla.

discrimination in the sale of housing project properties" (NYT).

22 In New York City, NAACP executive secretary Walter F. White died of a heart attack. White had joined the staff of the NAACP in 1920, become executive secretary in 1930, and spearheaded the organization's campaign for federal anti-lynching legislation in the 1930s and 1940s. In May 1954 the NAACP achieved its greatest victory, the Supreme Court's *Brown v. Board of Education* decision, and at the time of White's death the organization had more than 250,000 members. Thousands attended his funeral at St. Martin's Episcopal Church in Harlem (NYT).

24 In Montgomery, Ala., a fifteen-year-old girl named Claudette Colvin was arrested and charged with disorderly conduct after she refused to move to the rear of a city bus. The police were called when the girl refused to give up her seat to white passengers. Colvin was later convicted of violating the state's Jim Crow travel laws and was placed on probation (JM).

24 In Mound Bayou, Miss., Dr. Theodore R. M. Howard, president of the Regional Council of Negro Leadership, challenged the views presented by newspaper publisher Hodding Carter in a *Look* magazine article. Carter suggested that the White Citizens Councils had been successful in silencing those African Americans who supported integration campaigns in the state through threats of economic sanctions. Dr. Howard said that Carter's assessment was "absolutely untrue" and noted that African Americans had threatened economic sanctions against white businessmen in the state who participated in the Councils' activities. The Tri-State Bank in Memphis, Tennessee, had amassed over $180,000 to provide loans to any civil rights activists in Mississippi denied credit because of their support for integration (JM).

24 In St. Bernard, La., it was reported that eight interracial couples were indicted by the grand jury for violation of the state's anti-miscegenation laws. It was considered the first crackdown on interracial marriages in several years (JM).

31 In Washington, D.C., Rep. Charles Diggs called on Attorney General Herbert Brownell to investigate White Citizens Councils' activities. Diggs argued that the moves to prohibit so-called militants from speaking on college campuses throughout the South clearly violated constitutional guarantees of freedom of speech. Diggs called for an official investigation of reports of economic sanctions being leveled against southern blacks who supported the NAACP (JM).

APRIL 1955

7 In Atlanta, Ga., officials for the United Packinghouse Workers of America announced the launching of a $10 million drive to end segregation in public schools and transportation in the South. John H. Telfer, coordinator for the program, said the funds would be used to support test cases in the courts, to conduct research on segregatory practices in all areas of southern life, and to sponsor educational programs to change public opinion in favor of desegregation (SSN).

7 In North Carolina, South Carolina, and Mississippi, state legislators passed measures to thwart the implementation of public school desegregation. In North Carolina a bill was passed giving local school boards complete control over pupil assignments; in South Carolina, the state senate approved a bill denying state funds to mixed public schools; and the Mississippi house and senate passed a bill that called for a six-month jail sentence for any white person who attended a black school (SSN).

10 In Baton Rouge, La., manufacturer J. B. Easterly announced the formation of the Southern Gentlemen's Organization, whose purpose was to organize whites in the state to oppose school desegregation. The group was seeking members in six cities and was linked to the White Citizens Councils in Mississippi, but according to Easterly, "We're opposed to rough stuff and are not members of the KKK" (NYT).

12 In Kansas City, Mo., Roy Wilkins, formerly a journalist for *The Kansas City Call* who joined the NAACP's staff in 1931 and served as editor of *The Crisis* magazine, was named the new NAACP executive secretary. In 1949 and 1950 Wilkins had served as acting executive secretary when Walter White took a leave of absence. Between 1950 and 1955 Wilkins served as the NAACP's director of internal affairs (NYT).

12 In Washington, D.C., the U.S. Supreme Court began hearing oral arguments on how to carry out the implementation of public school desegregation. Attorneys from ten southern states, the District of Columbia, and the NAACP were scheduled to make oral presentations before the court (NYT).

14 In Jackson, Miss., as a result of the educational requirements for voting passed by the legislature in an effort to slow down the increase in the number of African Americans registering to vote, many whites in the state became ineligible to participate in the August Democratic primary. Under the new regulations, all citizens who registered to vote after 26 January 1955 were required to take new literacy tests. Those whites who refused to take the tests became ineligible to vote (JM).

16 In Albany, N.Y., members of the general assembly voted to ban discrimination on the basis of race in all housing financed by the Federal Housing Administration (FHA). The measure included both sale and rental units financed by FHA loans (NYT).

21 In Boston, Mass., students from seventy colleges and universities from around the country met at the Massachusetts Institute of Technology (MIT) to discuss ways of ending racial discrimination by fraternities and other student organizations. MIT undergraduates raised more than five thousand dollars to help pay transportation costs for many of the more than two hundred students and faculty members attending the conference (JM).

21 In Detroit, Mich., Judge Wade McCree, recently appointed to fill an unexpired term, was elected county judge, and Dr. Remus G. Robinson was elected to the city's school board. McCree and Robinson were the first African Americans elected to these positions. In Port Arthur, Tex., Congress of Industrial Organizations (CIO) union official Willie Hollier became the first African American elected to the city council (JM).

23 In Washington, D.C., representatives from twenty-one state and local fair employment practices commissions met at a conference sponsored by the President's Committee on Government Contracts. The purpose was to coordinate actions to end government job bias. The committee had already held meetings with civil rights groups and leaders of organized labor (NYT).

26 **In New York City,** when public hearings called by the New York State Commission Against Discrimination opened to review charges of discrimination by the Bottlers and Drivers Union, Local 1345, union officials agreed to drop the color bar. Subsequently, a consent decree was signed by union leaders with the Commission, and fourteen African Americans were admitted to the union. New York Urban League officials, who had worked for several years to change the practices of this union, called the settlement a landmark decision (NYT).

28 **In St. Paul, Minn.,** Gov. Orville Freeman signed into law a bill recently passed by the Minnesota legislature creating a state fair employment practices commission. The new nine-member commission was given power to issue contempt citations against employers found to be engaged in discriminatory hiring practices (JM).

MAY 1955

4 **In Mound Bayou, Miss.,** Detroit congressman Charles Diggs was the main speaker at a rally sponsored by the Regional Council of Negro Leadership. An estimated thirteen thousand representatives from Arkansas, Tennessee, Louisiana, and Mississippi came together in support of campaigns to end racial segregation and increase

---

RACE RELATIONS SURVEY—1955

On 29 May 1955 *The New York Times* published a survey of race relations in thirteen states in the Far West and reported that "marked progress is being made in the elimination of racial discrimination." The legislatures in eight states—Washington, California, Arizona, New Mexico, North Dakota, Montana, Colorado, and Wyoming—enacted measures over the previous year to combat discriminatory practices in public schools, employment, and public accommodations, reflecting the impact of the *Brown* decision of May 1954. Bills to repeal the bans on interracial marriage passed in Montana, but failed in Idaho and Colorado; measures to guarantee equality in public accommodations failed in Nevada and Arizona.

In other parts of the country, actions were taken to end racially discriminatory practices in employment and by labor unions. Officials for the Memphis, Tenn., fire department announced in April their intention to hire at least ten African Americans as firefighters. These would be the first blacks employed by the fire department in the city's history. Following the announcement more than 280 African Americans filled out applications for these positions. As a result of a campaign undertaken by the local Urban League, officials in the Tulsa, Okla., fire department announced in May that they would be hiring as many as six blacks as firemen.

At the annual meeting of the American Federation of Teachers (AFT), held in Fort Wayne, Ind., in August, the delegates voted to revoke the charter of any local union that practiced racial discrimination. AFT unions in the South were given until 1 June 1956 to end discrimination against black teachers. And in Sacramento, Calif., in August 1955 Gov. Goodwin Knight signed into law a bill that prohibited school boards in the state from refusing to hire a teacher on the basis of race, creed, or color.

In Daytona Beach, Fla., after George Ingram, an experienced electrician, had been denied membership to the AFL's International Brotherhood of Electrical Workers Local 756 because of his race, he filed suit against the union. In August, the U.S. circuit court ordered Ingram's admission to the union. State legislators in St. Paul, Minn., in April and in Harrisburg, Pa., in December passed legislation creating state fair employment practices commissions. In both instances the measures gave the governors the power to appoint the nine-member committees to carry out the law, which prohibited discrimination on the basis of race, creed, or color by state agencies and all employers doing business with the state government.

black voter registration. Diggs called on those present to support the NAACP war chest that provided financial support to those militant blacks denied credit and loans by white banking institutions (SSN).

5 In Detroit, Mich., in an integration order issued in July 1954, officials of the housing commission assigned three black families to the all-white Charles Terrace Project. Federal judge Arthur F. Lederle had ordered the desegregation of all public housing projects, and housing commission lawyers had requested more time "to carry out the decision in an orderly way" (JM).

12 In Springfield, Ill., a survey conducted by the Illinois Commission on Human Relations revealed that sixteen counties in the state had segregated public schools. It was also reported that of 217 hospitals surveyed in Illinois, 60 admitted African Americans to separate facilities only, and 22 of 28 cities with populations over ten thousand had no black firemen (JM).

15 In New York City, NAACP officials released results of a national survey and estimated that more than five hundred public schools had been peacefully integrated over the previous year. More than 250,000 black and white children who were previously enrolled in segregated elementary and high schools were attending school together by this date. The report criticized the news media's coverage of public school desegregation. "For every Milford [Del.] incident, there have been scores of unheralded instances of Negro children being welcomed by their white school mates and teachers" (NYT).

19, 20, 24 In Daytona Beach, Fla., educator, political leader, and government administrator Mary McLeod Bethune died of a heart attack in her home at the age of seventy-nine. Bethune was the founder of Bethune-Cookman College and the National Council of Negro Women and was considered the most influential member of Franklin Roosevelt's "Black Cabinet" during the New Deal era. Bethune also served as president of the National Association of Colored Women's Clubs and as president of the Association for the Study of Negro Life and History and was a recipient of the NAACP's Spingarn Medal. More than four thousand mourners attended funeral services in Daytona Beach (NYT).

JUNE 1955

1 In Washington, D.C., in response to requests from southern school districts for more time for the implementation of public school desegregation, the Supreme Court ruled that it should be carried out "with all deliberate speed." This purposefully vague language was interpreted by some school officials and politicians in the Deep South states to mean that they could move slowly on public school desegregation. School administrators in Amarillo, Tex.; Louisville, Ky.; and Asheville, N.C., announced that they would make an "honest effort" to desegregate the public schools in the 1955–56 school year (NYT).

5 In Atlanta, Ga., at a meeting at Atlanta's Wheat Street Baptist Church, NAACP officials announced that they would target two rural public school districts, Prince Edward County, Va., and Clarendon County, S.C., as well as ten cities for desegregation efforts for the fall of 1955. The ten cities were Atlanta, Ga.; Birmingham, Ala.; New Orleans, La.; Durham, N.C.; Richmond, Va.; Columbia, S.C.; Miami, Fla.; Dallas, Tex.; Memphis, Tenn.; and Jackson, Miss. (NYT).

7 In Harpers Ferry, W. Va., Rev. L. K. Terrell, acting president of the all-black Storer College, announced that the school would close at the end of the 1954–55 school year, after 87 years in operation. The college was virtually without operating funds following the decision of West Virginia legislators to end its $20,000 annual appropriation. There were over 150 students enrolled at the college in 1955 (NYT).

9–10 In Washington, D.C., legislative measures for public school construction, public housing, and military reserve units were held up in Congress by Adam Clayton Powell through the addition of an amendment that specified that federal funds should not be provided to segregated school districts or other public facilities. The "Powell amendment," as it is known, had previously been endorsed by the NAACP as a necessary element in the ongoing struggle to end legal segregation (NYT).

13 In **Washington**, D.C., despite protests, officials for the American Association for the Advancement of Science decided that the annual meeting would be held in Atlanta, Ga., in December. Dr. W. Montague Cobb, a vice president and head of the five-hundred-member anthropology section, announced that this section would hold no sessions in Atlanta because of hotel segregation (NYT).

21–27 In **Atlantic City**, N.J., at the NAACP annual convention, officials announced to the 850 delegates that fund-raising efforts were lagging and that a new campaign to raise $500,000 for legal suits in southern states would be launched. Additional legal staff was needed for individual suits in southern school districts, which could run up to $12,000 per case (NYT).

22–23 In **Wadley**, Ala., at Southern Union College, an interracial seminar on international relations was broken up when carloads of masked and unmasked men stormed the campus and threatened, "We'll give you thirty minutes to get these niggers out of here or we'll blow the place up." The whites paraded around the campus until the blacks left. Gov. James Folsom promised to investigate the incident (NYT).

23 In **Chicago**, Ill., after more than one thousand whites rioted and stoned a black family as they were moving into Chicago's Trumbull Park Homes housing project, black protesters marched on city hall and demanded that Mayor Richard J. Daley (1) end white rioting and bombings of black families; (2) integrate the housing project police force; and (3) take action against white groups fomenting racial violence (JM).

28 In **Washington**, D.C., NAACP official Clarence Mitchell in hearings before the House Armed Services Committee called for an end to racial discrimination by state units of the National Guard. Following the Spanish-American War, National

---

CITING *BROWN* DECISION, COURTS PROHIBIT SEGREGATION IN PUBLIC RECREATIONAL FACILITIES

The influence of the *Brown* decision could be seen in court decisions involving segregation in other areas of public life. In March 1955 as a result of a suit brought by African Americans who were segregated in Fort Smallwood Park and Sandy Point State Park in Maryland, the U.S. Fourth District Court of Appeals in Richmond, Va., ruled that the practice of segregation in public parks was unconstitutional. The federal court reversed an earlier ruling upholding segregation made by the U.S. district court in Baltimore. In July 1955 the Municipal Park Board in Kansas City, Mo., ordered the end of discrimination in all city-owned swimming pools and bathing facilities. The board specifically cited the Supreme Court's *Brown* decision as the reason for the change. However, when NAACP officials filed a suit in federal district court in Charleston, S.C., in August to open all twenty-one state parks and beaches to African Americans, charging that the ban in public recreational facilities was a violation of the Fourteenth Amendment, South Carolina governor George Bell Timmerman, Jr., declared that he would close down the state parks and beaches rather than integrate them.

In October 1955 in Beaumont, Tex., U.S. district judge Cecil Lamar ruled in a case brought by six African Americans that park officials could not exclude citizens from the public facilities because of race. Judge Lamar declared that black citizens had a constitutional right to free use of the public parks in the state. In November 1955, in cases brought by African Americans in Baltimore, Md., and Atlanta, Ga., the U.S. Supreme Court refused to review, and therefore upheld lower-court decisions that segregation in public parks, swimming pools, and golf courses was unconstitutional. And in December, the state court of appeals in Kentucky outlawed segregation in the public parks in that state. Appellate judge Porter Sims, ruling on a case from Louisville, declared that the action was "in keeping with the precedent set by U.S. Supreme Court in the *Brown* decision, striking down the 'separate but equal' doctrine."

Guard units throughout the South banned recruitment of African Americans and severely restricted black participation in national defense and other military programs (NYT).

30 In **Columbus, Ga.**, after closely examining the boy's hair, eyes, and skin, Judge T. Hicks Fort declared that the adopted son of an unidentified white army sergeant was "a Negro" and would have to be taken away. The judge ordered the boy to be taken to the Georgia State Welfare Department, where he would eventually be put up for adoption by a black family (JM).

30 In **Kansas City, Mo.**, within four days of adopting a policy allowing African Americans as customers, the owners of the Flamingo Club received an eviction notice. This was the first club in the downtown area to desegregate. Black and white lawyers in the city volunteered their services to try to prevent the closing of the club (JM).

30 In **Montgomery, Ala.**, U.S. district judge Hobart Grooms ruled that black students Polly Ann Myers and Autherine Lucy could not be barred from attending the University of Alabama (NYT).

JULY 1955

6 In **Oklahoma City, Okla.**, the State Board of Regents voted to admit any qualified black students to all state colleges and universities beginning in fall 1955. Board president W. D. Little stated that this came about only as a result of the Supreme Court's *Brown* decision (SSN).

9 In **Athens, Ga.**, state attorney general Eugene Cook announced that the state would fight any attempt at desegregation and promised that state officials would close the University of Georgia Law School rather than allow a black student to attend (NYT).

10, 12 In **Washington, D.C.**, Rutgers Law School graduate E. Frederic Morrow was appointed an administrative officer for the Special Projects Group at the White House and became the first African American ever appointed to a White House position. Morrow would coordinate internal management affairs for the group, which in-

cluded the Council on Foreign Economic Policy and the offices of special assistants to the president on disarmament and foreign policy (NYT).

14 In **Greenville, S.C.**, the NAACP membership drive led by white attorney John Bolt Culbertson was responsible for at least three thousand new members. As the only white member of the NAACP, Culbertson had been victimized by a boycott of his law practice and anonymous threats against his life. Culbertson declared that many whites in South Carolina knew their racist attitudes were wrong, but they "haven't the moral courage to do something. They're afraid of censure from neighbors and [of] losing their jobs" (JM).

14 In **Washington, D.C.**, after schoolteacher Dola Walker was beaten in Alabama for using a rest room for whites only at a Standard Oil Company station, Rep. Charles Diggs urged African Americans in Alabama, Georgia, Florida, Kentucky, and Mississippi to boycott the company. Diggs believed the company should be targeted because of its refusal to abolish Jim Crow facilities (JM).

15 In **Washington, D.C.**, Detroit congressman Charles Diggs testified before the House Subcommittee on Transportation, urging the passage of legislation to end the practice of racial segregation at federally assisted airports. Diggs had earlier complained to the Interstate Commerce Commission about "whites only" waiting rooms in southern airports, separate black and white toilet facilities, and taxi drivers at airports who refused to carry African American passengers (NYT).

19 In **Prince Edward County, Va.**, the U.S. district court ruled that school officials did not have to integrate public schools by September 1955, but would have to do so sometime in the 1955–56 school year. NAACP attorney Thurgood Marshall opposed school officials' request to operate for the entire school year on a segregated basis (NYT).

21 In **Washington, D.C.**, on the floor of the House of Representatives, Adam Clayton Powell was punched in the face by sixty-nine-year-old West Virginia congressman Cleveland M. Bailey when

Powell called Bailey "a liar." Bailey had accused Powell of wanting to "wreck the public education system" by calling for the withholding of federal funds to southern school districts that remained segregated (NYT).

23 In Montgomery, Ala., a bill was introduced in the state legislature by Senator Sam Engelhardt that would require the NAACP to reveal how much money the group had collected in the state and how it was spent. The bill would also impose a fee of $100 for a license for anyone soliciting money for the NAACP in Alabama (NYT).

23 In Princeton, N.J., Dr. Charles T. Davis was appointed an assistant professor in the English Department at Princeton University. Davis became the first African American appointed to Princeton's faculty (NYT).

28 In Williamsport, Pa., National Little League president Peter J. McGovern ruled that there would be no entry in the Little League championships from South Carolina in 1955, even though the Charleston, S.C., black community had raised nine hundred dollars to send the members of the Cannon Street YMCA team to the national tournament. When fifty-five white teams from South Carolina had refused to enter into integrated competition, Charleston's all-black Cannon Street YMCA team won the state championship by default. South Carolina Little League commissioner Danny Jones resigned, declaring that the boys' baseball teams were being used for "propaganda purposes." The all-white Little League teams in the state planned a Jim Crow tournament to be sponsored by the South Carolina Recreational Society (NYT).

AUGUST 1955

1 In Baton Rouge, La., the state legislature appropriated $100,000 to pay for lawyers' fees to fight suits brought by black parents to end segregation in the Louisiana public schools (SSN).

1 In Vicksburg, Miss., 140 black parents petitioned local school officials to end segregation in public schools. State leaders of the White Citizens Councils rushed to the city and began organizing a chapter. School officials later rejected the peti-

tion. Rev. H. H. Hume, president of Mississippi's National Baptist Convention, which was meeting in Vicksburg at the time, condemned the actions of the black parents. Hume called on black Baptists not to join the NAACP's attempts "to disturb race relations" (SSN).

4 In Richmond, Va., the Fourth U.S. Circuit Court of Appeals ruled that segregation on city buses was unconstitutional. In a case brought by Sarah Fleming against the Columbia, S.C., Municipal Bus Company after she was punched by a white bus driver when she refused to leave by the rear door, the appeals court ruled that for African Americans to be required to sit in the rear of buses was a violation of the Fourteenth Amendment. Bus company officials later declared that they would appeal the decision to the U.S. Supreme Court (JM).

4 In Washington, D.C., Rep. Adam Clayton Powell revealed a plan adopted by the U.S. State Department to increase the number of black employees in all its sections. Working with White House aide Maxwell Rabb, Powell's proposal called for the expanded recruitment of African Americans from black colleges and universities throughout the country (JM).

11 In Birmingham, Ala., NAACP Southern director Ruby Hurley declared that increased economic pressure was being applied by White Citizens Council (WCC) members against African Americans in Mississippi, Georgia, and Florida who sign petitions calling for the desegregation of local public schools. Threatened with the loss of jobs and credit, black residents were told to remove their names from school petitions. Hurley also noted that the WCC was "resorting to every kind of pressure" to block the NAACP's actions in those states (JM).

11 In New York City, National Urban League officials asked the federal government's Committee on Government Contracts to issue an order banning racial discrimination by all airlines with federal contracts. The move was aimed at increasing the number of African Americans employed as pilots, stewardesses, and engineers by the nation's airlines (JM).

11 In **Philadelphia, Pa.**, orphans court judge Robert V. Bolger upheld the ban on admission of two black orphan boys to Girard College, a private elementary and secondary school. School officials denied them admission on the basis of founder Stephen Girard's will, which stated that it should admit only poor white male orphans (JM).

13 In **Washington, D.C.**, the executive council of the AFL turned down the proposal of Brotherhood of Sleeping Car Porters president A. Philip Randolph to bar unions that practice racial discrimination from admission into the newly merged AFL-CIO. Council members believed that the problem of racial discrimination by labor unions "would take a long time to solve" (NYT).

17 In **Washington, D.C.**, after receiving more than fifteen affidavits from NAACP officials charging that threats and intimidation were made against black voters in Mississippi, Attorney General Herbert Brownell announced that the Justice Department was launching an investigation. Brownell promised to take "vigorous and immediate action" if black citizens' constitutional rights had been violated. Detroit congressman Charles Diggs charged that white politicians in Mississippi were behind the efforts to keep black voters from the polls (NYT).

18 In **Chicago, Ill.**, at the annual meeting of the Knights of St. Peter Claver, a black Roman Catholic fraternal organization, a resolution was passed calling on all Roman Catholic bishops to desegregate parochial schools and commending those bishops in St. Louis, Mo., Raleigh, N.C., and other cities who had already brought about parochial school desegregation (JM).

20 In **Fort Wayne, Ind.**, at the annual meeting of the American Federation of Teachers (AFT), the delegates voted to revoke the charter of any local union that practiced racial discrimination. Separate black and white AFT unions in cities in the South were given until 1 June 1956 to desegregate or merge (NYT).

23 In **Horry County, S.C.**, at a rally of fifteen hundred people, KKK imperial wizard E. L. Edwards declared that the group was "fighting for white supremacy" against groups such as the NAACP, the Catholic Knights of Columbus, and the Jewish Anti-Defamation League. Attorney generals in ten southern states, however, went on record condemning the resurgence of this terrorist organization (NYT).

25 In **Los Angeles, Calif.**, at the sixtieth annual meeting of the National Medical Association, militant civil rights leader and physician Dr. Theodore R. M. Howard was elected president. One official for the predominantly black organization stated that Dr. Howard was elected "to prove to the world that five thousand doctors in America are backing the fight Negroes are putting up in Mississippi" (JM).

25 In **Old Fort, N.C.**, five black children, escorted by Albert Joyner, were denied entrance to the Old Fort Elementary School as sheriff's deputies and state troopers kept order among five hundred whites who had come to see what would happen. McDowell County school superintendent Melvin Taylor met Albert Joyner and the five students at the door of the school and told them they were not to be admitted. Violence erupted and Joyner and another black man, William Brittain, were physically assaulted by groups of whites (NYT).

25 In **Washington, D.C.**, in an address before the National Press Club, evangelist Billy Graham argued that the churches in the United States must take the lead in ending racial segregation. Rev. Graham declared, "I believe that anything that makes a man a second class citizen is not only un-American, but un-Christian" (JM).

27 In **New Orleans, La.**, Archbishop Joseph Rummel announced that the desegregation of the city's Roman Catholic schools would be delayed until September 1956. Mounting opposition to the desegregation plans among Catholic parents and lay leaders forced the archbishop to delay the plan (NYT).

SEPTEMBER 1955

1 In **Austin, Tex.**, the U.S. district court set aside all Texas school segregation laws, and local school officials began to make plans for desegregation beginning in fall 1955. In Howard County, Tex., the recently formed Texas Citizens Council filed a suit in state court to block funds going to public schools undertaking desegregation. The school board members in Texarkana and Plainview, Tex., voted against proposals to desegregate the public schools; in Austin and San Marcos the school boards voted to desegregate the public schools, beginning with the high schools; and in Lubbock, all public schools were to be desegregated without residential restrictions (SSN).

In New York City, Thurgood Marshall announced that, despite the fund-raising efforts surrounding the NAACP "War Chest," the organization was "almost broke" and did not have sufficient cash "to meet the new challenges." In his first appeal for financial support, Marshall urged the group's supporters "to dig deep into their pockets" (JM).

SOUTHERN BLACK TEACHERS UNDER ATTACK

The problems facing black teachers in public school systems undergoing desegregation was a much-debated topic in the news media in 1955. In a special report in *Jet* magazine (5 May 1955) titled "Should Negro Teachers Fear Integration?" it was noted that over the previous year in Baltimore; Washington, D.C.; and parts of Arizona, New Mexico, Delaware, West Virginia, and Missouri, public school integration was carried out without any black teachers losing their positions. The few highly publicized cases, such as in Hannibal and Moberly, Mo., where black teachers lost jobs as a result of integration, had been used by white politicians to try to turn black opinion against public school integration. At the end of the 1954–55 school year, 80 black teachers had lost their jobs in Missouri and 127 in Oklahoma.

At the end of the same school year, black teachers who voted or were either members of the NAACP or supportive of school integration faced dismissal from their positions. In June 1955 Hodding Carter, editor of the *Delta Democrat-Times* in Greenville, Miss., reported that White Citizens Council members in the area were demanding that local school boards dismiss black teachers who were listed on the voting rolls. In July, Georgia attorney general Eugene Cook suggested that measures should be taken to obtain the names of public school teachers who belonged to the NAACP and then ban them from state jobs for life. In Clarendon County, S.C., after the federal district court ordered county officials to desegregate the public schools, they promised to "root out NAACP members in the teaching ranks." NAACP officials learned that teachers at the three black schools were asked if they were members of the organization, and if they answered in the affirmative, they were told that their contracts would not be renewed for the 1955–56 school year.

The Georgia state board of education adopted a resolution in August 1955 that barred teachers in the state from membership in the NAACP. Any teacher who refused to quit the organization faced revocation of his or her teaching license. The new regulation came as state NAACP officials began planning to petition for the desegregation of public schools in Atlanta, Valdosta, Savannah, and Macon. It was estimated that as many as eighty-four hundred black teachers in Georgia belonged to the NAACP. The state board was forced to rescind the measure two weeks later under the advice of counsel, but to demonstrate its opposition to public school desegregation, the state board ordered all school districts to require that teachers take an oath by 15 October to uphold the state constitution, which forbids racial integration in the public schools.

In September, the *Southern School News* issued a report, funded by the Ford Foundation, on the attitudes of black teachers toward public school integration. The report noted that although many felt insecure, they still fully supported the policy. The researchers estimated that, thus far, three hundred black teachers had lost their positions out of seventy-five thousand employed in the South. By the end of the year black teachers who had lost their positions in Missouri and Oklahoma had filed suits against school officials for breach of contract.

1 In Norfolk, Va., school officials came up with a plan for "voluntary desegregation" in which parents would be able to choose to send their children to black schools, white schools, or integrated schools, whereas in Raleigh, N.C., Gov. Luther Hodges urged African Americans in the state to accept a plan for voluntary desegregation and "take pride in attending your own schools" (SSN).

1 In Hoxie, Ark., school officials bowed to local pressure and ordered the closing of the recently desegregated public schools. White parents, led by Henry Brewer, organized a boycott of the public schools. In Mobile, Ala., board members rejected a black parents' petition favoring public school desegregation (SSN).

3 In Guilford, N.C., a group of thirty-four white parents petitioned school superintendent E. D. Idol to admit black students into white schools and avoid the bitterness created by extensive litigation. The petition stated that "it is both just and wise for our local school committee to admit Negro pupils from this district" (NYT).

4 In New York City, the NAACP reported that at the opening of the 1955–56 school year, eight of seventeen states with compulsory segregation laws had begun the process of desegregation in public schools. The states were Maryland, Missouri, Arkansas, Oklahoma, West Virginia, Delaware, Kentucky, and Texas. Of the remaining nine, only in Tennessee did school officials express a willingness to begin desegregation in 1955, while three more states formed commissions to study the issue (North Carolina, Virginia, and Florida). School officials in South Carolina, Georgia, Louisiana, Mississippi, and Alabama expressed outright defiance of the Supreme Court's decision (NYT).

7 In Nashville, Tenn., officials at Vanderbilt University Law School announced plans to begin publishing the *Race Relations Law Reporter,* a periodical on legal problems and court cases associated with the implementation of the Supreme Court's school desegregation decisions (NYT).

7 In Orleans Parish, La., Xavier University professor Asa H. Atkins and insurance executive Clifford

H. Denton were selected members of the grand jury. They became the first African Americans to serve on the New Orleans grand jury since the Reconstruction era (NYT).

8 In San Francisco, Calif., to address a conference on civil rights, NAACP leader Roy Wilkins joined the picket lines protesting employment discrimination by the Yellow Cab Company. Local NAACP leaders Franklin Williams and Jean Kimes had organized the protest against the taxi company because it refused to hire African Americans as drivers (JM).

10 In Milwaukee, Wis., at the annual meeting of the National Urban League, which traditionally focuses on employment issues, the delegates from sixty branches voted to make improvements in housing the primary goal for the organization in 1956. National Urban League president Robert W. Dowling announced that they would seek a conference with President Eisenhower to gain a commitment to nondiscrimination in all federal housing loan programs (NYT).

17 In Dallas, Tex., two black students were admitted to the Catholic Jesuit High School. However, in a case brought by twenty-eight black parents, federal judge William M. Atwell ruled that the Dallas Independent School District did not have to admit black students to the public schools until after school officials made a study of the desegregation process. NAACP lawyers promised to appeal the judge's ruling (NYT).

22 In Louisville, Miss., in a strike called by the CIO's International Woodworkers of America at the D. L. Fair Lumber Co., black and white workers walked the picket lines together. This was believed to be the first interracial picketing in Mississippi and was protested by nonunion whites. The strike was called to gain an increase in wages (JM).

22 In Washington, D.C., following Rep. Adam Clayton Powell's demand that the U.S. State Department use more African Americans in diplomatic missions, CIO executive George L. P. Weaver was assigned to make a thirty-thousand-mile tour of seven countries in the Far East to discuss labor issues and U.S. relations with prominent leaders. Weaver became the first African American given this type of diplomatic assignment by the State Department (JM).

25 In Hoxie, Ark., Attorney General Herbert Brownell sent FBI agents to investigate the school boycott launched by white parents. When twenty-five black students were admitted to all-white public schools, White Citizens Council leaders called for a boycott by white students that eventually led to the closing of the city's public schools. School superintendent K. E. Vance and school board members received telephone threats and protests from local whites who opposed the desegregation plan (NYT).

29 In Houston, Tex., the members of the Harris County Medical Society voted overwhelmingly to admit qualified black physicians to the organization. The society's president, Dr. James E. Pittman, stated he would accept applications from the twenty or twenty-five black physicians in the county (JM).

29 In Randolph County, Ga., twenty-two black voters brought a $110,000 civil rights suit against the members of the board of registrars charging that they had illegally removed the names of three hundred blacks from the voting rolls, using "literacy tests." However, many of the African Americans purged from the rolls were college graduates, while two officials on the board of registrars never finished high school (JM).

29 In Washington, D.C., the NAACP branch filed a suit in federal court against the Metropolitan Police Boys Club for practicing racial segregation. The suit alleged that the Boys Club was a "quasi-public" institution, using public facilities and city personnel, and therefore could not maintain separate black and white units (JM).

OCTOBER 1955

▌In Charleston, Mo., angry white citizens burned a six-foot cross on the lawn of the home of school board president T. J. Brown after the board refused to rescind their decision to allow twenty-seven black children to attend the city's all-white high school. Whites also held a series of mass protest meetings over the school board's decision (SSN).

▌In the state of Florida, although state officials defiantly denied all black petitions for public school desegregation in local cities and towns, black children were integrated into the formerly all-white schools at Elgin and Tyndall Air Force bases, in accordance with Defense Department orders to end segregation in schools on military installations (SSN).

▌In New Orleans, La., Rabbi Julian B. Feibelman led a delegation of citizens that met with school board members and presented a petition with 179 names calling for public school desegregation. Subsequently, White Citizens Council leaders in the city announced an expanded membership drive and petition campaign to gather 15,000 signatures opposing school desegregation (SSN).

▌In Oak Ridge, Tenn., members of the Tennessee Federation for Constitutional Government demanded the firing of school superintendent B. E. Capehart, who had authorized the integration of the public schools, and educator Fred Brown, the only black teacher in the city's high school. The federation claimed that public school integration violated the state constitution (SSN).

▌In Orangeburg, S.C., NAACP leader Rev. Matthew D. McCollum burned the list of names of NAACP members, after unidentified whites offered $10,000 for a copy. The list included the names of NAACP members among the faculty and students at South Carolina State College (all-black). State representative Jerry M. Hughes called for an investigation "to determine who are members and sympathizers of the NAACP among the faculty and student body" at South Carolina State. Hughes also accused students and faculty members of supporting a boycott of businesses owned by White Citizens Council members in the state (SSN).

6 In London, England, at a news conference, Rep. Adam Clayton Powell reported increasing complaints from black American soldiers in England of racial discrimination in public accommodations, including taverns, restaurants, and hotels. Powell called upon the British government to face up to the increasing color problem there and do something, or "the situation is liable to become explosive" (JM).

15 In Jesuit Bend, La., Archbishop Joseph F. Rummel suspended religious services at St. Cecelia Mission after five white men prevented Father Gerald Lewis from saying mass. Having recently arrived from St. Augustine Seminary in Bay St. Louis, Miss., Father Lewis was told by these men that a black priest would not be allowed to say mass for the predominantly white congregation (NYT).

17 In Dallas, Tex., members of the NAACP branch's Youth Council organized picketing outside the entrance to the Texas State Fair. The young people were protesting the policy of allowing African Americans to attend the fair only on "Negro Achievement Day" (NYT).

18 In Memphis, Tenn., in a suit filed by five black students seeking admission to Memphis State University, federal judge Marion Boyd ruled against the state's school segregation laws, but accepted a five-year "gradual integration" plan submitted by state education officials (NYT).

20 In Galveston County, Tex., three black physicians became the first African Americans admitted to the Galveston County Medical Society. But in Lynchburg, Va., the members of the Academy of Medicine voted not to admit black physicians to membership (JM).

24 In Harrisburg, Pa., state legislators passed a bill for the creation of a state fair employment practices commission. Gov. George M. Leader, a supporter of the measure, said he would move swiftly to appoint the nine-member commission to administer the law, which prohibited discrimination on the basis of race, creed, or color by state agencies and employers doing business with the state government (NYT).

26 In Washington, D.C., the White House sponsored the National Equal Economic Opportunity Conference, bringing executives from sixty-five businesses and labor unions together to discuss ways of ending employment discrimination. Labor Secy. James P. Mitchell addressed the group and emphasized that hiring, promotions, and underutilization of black and other minority workers were also serious problems that needed to be solved by the nation's economic leaders (NYT).

27 In Waco, Tex., more than nine hundred white workers staged a wildcat strike after Ben H. Danford, an African American, was promoted and transferred to an all-white department at the General Tire and Rubber Co. CIO Rubber Workers Union officials condemned the strike and called on their members to return to work (JM).

NOVEMBER 1955

1 In Fort Worth, Tex., black parents from Mansfield, Tex., filed suit in U.S. district court against members of their local school board. Black children in Mansfield were forced to travel forty miles to Fort Worth every day to attend school because they were not allowed in the city's all-white public schools (SSN).

7, 10 In New York City, the Public Education Association issued a report concluding that predominantly black and Puerto Rican schools in the city were inadequate and substandard. Subsequently, New York Urban League officials called on school officials to take measures "to correct the shocking inferiority in educational standards" and to institute an "emergency desegregation program" for black and Puerto Rican students (NYT).

8 In Richmond, Va., the state supreme court ruled that the proposal to shift state funds to support private white academies violated the state constitution and argued that those who would like to put this plan into effect would have to change the constitution first (NYT).

9 In the November 1955 elections, Grant W. Hawkins became the first African American elected to the Indianapolis, Ind., school board. In Hartford, Conn., John C. Clark, Jr., became the first African American elected to the nine-member city council, while A. C. Wallace became the first black on the Alexander, Ark., five-member city council. Dr. Hyland Reid became the first African American

RACIAL VIOLENCE AND ATTACKS ON NAACP LEADERS

In August 1955 the brutal murder of fourteen-year-old Emmett Till in Money, Miss., for allegedly whistling at a white woman was the act of racial violence that generated the most national attention. When Till's accused killers, John Milam and Roy Bryant, were acquitted by an all-white jury in October, mass rallies were held in New York City, Chicago, Detroit, and other cities to protest what A. Philip Randolph referred to as the "wave of terrorism against Negroes" in the South.

Many southern black victims of this wave of white terrorism were officers or members of the local NAACP. In Belzoni, Miss., in May 1955, NAACP leader Rev. George Lee was killed by three unknown assailants while driving his car into the black section of town. At a mass protest rally in Belzoni following the murder, the NAACP's Roy Wilkins decried the "return to violence" by southerners opposed to school desegregation and voting rights. Wilkins called on the Justice Department to investigate "the first racial murder in the South since the Supreme Court's edict" in May 1954. Soon afterward, reports circulated that seven additional black leaders in Mississippi had been targeted for death by local white supremacists, among them Gus Courts, NAACP leader in Belzoni, who was shot and wounded by an unknown assailant inside his grocery store in November 1955.

NAACP supporters in Clarendon and Orangeburg counties, S.C., who signed petitions for school integration were refused service by local stores as a direct result of a White Citizens Council–initiated boycott. WCC leaders not only denied the petitioners jobs and credit to buy food and clothing, but they interrupted the delivery of bread, milk, farm supplies, and other goods to stores owned or patronized by black customers. The squeeze placed upon these families was meant "to starve them into removing their names from the petitions." Appeals went out for food, clothing, and other supplies, and NAACP leader Modjeska Simkins coordinated the relief program. Goods arrived in Columbia, S.C., from thirty states and were distributed to the needy residents.

Early in October, St. James AME Church in Lake City, S.C., was engulfed in flames and burned to the ground in thirty minutes. The pastor, Rev. Joseph A. Delaine, had been the leader of the NAACP drive to end school segregation in Clarendon County, and before the church burning, his home had been pelted with bricks and bottles and he had received numerous death threats. A few days after the fire, Delaine was forced to "run for his life" after shooting and wounding two men who were part of a motorcade of whites firing shots into his home. Delaine fled to Brooklyn, N.Y., but was later charged with assault and battery and attempted murder. South Carolina state officials sought Delaine's extradition, but New York State officials refused to return him upon hearing accounts of the threats and violence leveled against blacks in Clarendon County. In December 1955, South Carolina governor George Bell Timmerman, Jr., decided that it would not be in the state's interest to further pursue Delaine's extradition from New York.

elected as councilman-at-large in Plainfield, N.J. Carson C. Baker was elected municipal judge in Brooklyn, N.Y., and Theodore O. Spaulding, who was appointed municipal judge in Philadelphia, Pa., in 1953, was elected to a full ten-year term. In New York City, special sessions judge Harold Stevens, who had been appointed by Gov. Averell Harriman to the New York Supreme Court to fill the unexpired term of the late Judge Thomas J. Corcoran, was elected to a full fourteen-year term (NYT).

12 In **Randolph County, Ga.**, the federal district court awarded $880 in damages to twenty-two African Americans who brought suit against three white registrars whom they charged deprived them of their right to vote. The three registrars resigned in protest, stating that the acts charged against them "were done in good faith" (NYT).

13 In **Richmond, Va.**, the state department of education cut off financial aid to 128 black students attending graduate and professional schools outside the state. The state courts had ruled that public funds could not be used to support private schools. Subsequently, Governor Thomas B. Stanley called a special session of the legislature, which approved a bill to amend the constitution to permit public funds to be used to support segregated private schools (NYT).

13 In Washington, D.C., CIO executive Willard Townsend, who was also president of the United Transport Service Employees Union, and A. Philip Randolph, president of the Brotherhood of Sleeping Car Porters, called for stronger constitutional guarantees for nondiscrimination in the newly merged AFL-CIO. Townsend charged that there was no penalty clause for violations in the present constitution (NYT).

15 In Oklahoma City, Okla., after the U.S. Supreme Court banned racial labels on election ballots, attorney A. B. McDonald filed a $200,000 suit against the local election board. McDonald charged that in the 1952 Democratic primary, he was listed as "Negro" on the ballot for candidates seeking the nomination to the U.S. Senate (NYT).

18 In Washington, D.C., Attorney General Herbert Brownell announced that FBI agents had been sent to Mississippi to gather evidence on voting rights violations. Several members of Congress, including Rep. Charles Diggs, Rep. James Roosevelt, and Sen. Herbert Lehman, planned to introduce legislation to reduce the number of representatives from Mississippi because state officials were refusing to allow African Americans to vote. Under the Fourteenth Amendment, Congress has the power to reduce the representation of any state that denies its citizens the right to vote (NYT).

18 In Washington, D.C., Rep. Adam Clayton Powell announced that, as a result of an arrangement he worked out with the U.S. State Department, jazz musicians Louis Armstrong, Dizzy Gillespie, and Count Basie were signed for cultural programs and tours in Communist Eastern Europe, Asia, and Africa (NYT).

22 In Baton Rouge, La., circuit court judge Coleman Lindsey ordered the continuation of an injunction suit filed by eight blacks against the recent authorization by the state legislature of a $100,000 grant to fight public school desegregation (NYT).

26 In Washington, D.C., the Interstate Commerce Commission issued a ruling banning racial segregation of interstate passengers on buses, trains, and in railroad waiting rooms. The order was to become effective on 10 January 1956, but officials in Georgia, Alabama, South Carolina, and Louisiana vowed to resist it. They argued that there would be problems enforcing the order because local laws for those traveling within the state required segregation of black and white passengers (NYT).

28 In Erath, La., Bishop Jules B. Jeanmard excommunicated three white women who attacked the white teacher of an integrated catechism class. Although the ban was lifted once the women made clear their repentance, Bishop Jeanmard made it clear that integrated churches, schools, and classes would continue in the diocese, which contained more than seventy-five thousand black Catholics (NYT).

29–30 In Washington, D.C., NAACP officials were among the two thousand delegates attending the White House Conference on Education. During the conference NAACP official Clarence Mitchell asked Department of Health, Education and Welfare (HEW) officials to disallow the travel expenses for South Carolina delegates because of the state educational officials' outspoken opposition to the implementation of the *Brown* school desegregation decision. HEW secretary Oveta Hobby responded that the issue had no relationship to the financing of the conference (NYT).

DECEMBER 1955

1 In Knoxville, Tenn., federal district judge Robert L. Taylor ordered the desegregation of public high schools in Anderson County by September 1956. Desegregation had already begun at Tennessee colleges and universities, where black students had been admitted to the graduate schools (SSN).

2 In Jackson, Miss., at a White Citizens Council rally, Sen. James Eastland declared that as a result of the desegregation of the Washington, D.C., public schools, "white students are being pulled down to the intelligence levels of the Negroes," and pledged his full support for the movement to use tax money to finance the struggles against the Supreme Court's school desegregation decisions (NYT).

3 In **Atlanta, Ga.**, after Gov. Marvin Griffin demanded that the Georgia Institute of Technology break its contract and not play in the Sugar Bowl in New Orleans because its opponent, the University of Pittsburgh, had one black player, he was burned in effigy at a protest rally organized by Tech's white students. Griffin also asked the Georgia State Board of Regents to bar all Georgia athletic teams from playing opponents with racially integrated teams (NYT).

6 In **Montgomery, Ala.**, Rosa Parks, a seamstress and NAACP officer, was arrested after she refused to give up her seat on a city bus to a white passenger when ordered to do so by the driver. News of Parks's arrest led to several meetings organized by NAACP leader E. D. Nixon to protest racial segregation in the city transportation system. African Americans announced a citywide boycott of public transportation to protest the practice of segregation. Dr. Martin Luther King, Jr., pastor of Dexter Avenue Baptist Church, agreed to serve as spokesperson for the bus boycott, and at a mass meeting, King was elected president of the newly formed Montgomery Improvement Association (NYT).

6 In **New York City**, at a meeting of the newly merged AFL-CIO, A. Philip Randolph, president of the Brotherhood of Sleeping Car Porters, and Willard Townsend, president of the United Transport Services Union, were two of the twenty-seven national labor leaders elected vice presidents of the fifteen-million-member federation. Randolph and Townsend, both African Americans, were also appointed to the AFL-CIO's Civil Rights Department, which would work to end racial discrimination by unions within the federation (NYT).

8 In **New York City**, despite intimidation and threats of economic reprisals from southern whites, NAACP officials announced that membership increased 13 percent in the South during the first ten months of 1955. Increases were reported in Alabama, Florida, Georgia, North Carolina, South Carolina, and Mississippi (JM).

9, 10 In **Montgomery, Ala.**, the bus boycott continued with more than 90 percent of the black riders participating. Martin Luther King conferred with Jack Crenshaw, lawyer for the bus company, and called for seating on a first-come, first-served basis and the hiring of black bus drivers for black routes, but Crenshaw said it was state law that prevented these changes and suggested there was a need for changes in that law. At a mass rally during the second week of the boycott, more than five thousand people pledged to stay off city buses (NYT).

15 In **San Francisco, Calif.**, NAACP regional official Franklin Williams issued an official protest and charged military officers at the Sixth Army Headquarters with racial discrimination in foreign assignments. Williams received a copy of a memorandum issued by army officials that stated that "Caucasians only" were eligible for overseas assignments (JM).

16 In **Los Angeles, Calif.**, fire chief John H. Alderson was suspended from his position by the city's fire commissioner after he rescinded his earlier order to transfer black firefighters to bring about the integration of the city's fire stations. Alderson had made the original transfers of a few black firefighters only under protest. Subsequently, charges of insubordination were dropped by city officials and Alderson was allowed to retire (NYT).

22 In **Washington, D.C.**, George L. P. Weaver, former secretary of the CIO's Anti-Discrimination Committee, was appointed executive secretary of the AFL-CIO Civil Rights Committee. Weaver became the first African American to serve on the administrative staff of the newly merged national union (NYT).

On 31 August 1956, in Mansfield, Texas, swinging grotesquely above the entrance of Mansfield High School was the effigy of a black person, which greeted schoolchildren on the second day of registration following a confrontation by a mob of more than four hundred people who had gathered around the building vowing that no black students would be allowed to register. (SOURCE: CORBIS BETTMANN)

1956

"BETTER BE READY"

The NAACP branches in the southern states were not the only black-controlled institutions that came under attack as part of the massive resistance campaigns. Many branches of the National Urban League, which primarily addressed black employment problems, lost funding from the local Community Chests and other philanthropic agencies in the southern states. With the launching of the Montgomery bus boycott, in addition to litigation, civil rights campaigns moved into nonviolent direct action protests, and more and more organizations, especially labor unions, were forced to take sides. With the Montgomery protest in 1956, Dr. Martin Luther King, Jr., was thrust upon the national and international scene, and he often explained to his parishioners and the entire black community that when the opportunity comes to take a stand for freedom and justice, they "Better Be Ready."

l In Hoxie, Ark., where an injunction had to be issued to allow admission of black students in September 1955, school superintendent Robert Williams declared that things were going smoothly in the 1956–57 school year with "ten or twelve Negro students and about nine hundred whites attending the same school." Initially, several white supremacist groups attempted to block the implementation of school integration (SSN).

l In Knoxville, Tenn., federal district judge Robert L. Taylor ordered the desegregation of public high schools in Anderson County by September 1956. Desegregation had already begun at Tennessee colleges and universities, where black students had been admitted to the graduate schools (SSN).

l In New York City, several Wall Street investment houses decided that bonds issued by school officials in Norfolk and Hopewell, Va., to pay for the construction of segregated schools were "too risky." The bonds were to be used to finance segregated public schools, rather than allow the integration of existing schools (SSN).

5 In Chicago, Ill., insurance broker Walter L. Lowe proposed to NAACP officials that they take out insurance policies on the lives of NAACP presidents and secretaries working in branches in the South. Lowe claimed that "greater security should be provided for NAACP officials in these areas of tension because they are carrying the burden to fight for those of us who only look on from afar" (JM).

5 In New York City, NAACP officials announced that they would open an office in Mound Bayou,

Miss., to coordinate civil rights activities in the Delta region. With the absence from the state of Dr. Theodore R. M. Howard, founder and president of the Mississippi Council on Negro Leadership, for long periods of time, it was necessary for the organization to have an ongoing presence. One objective was to launch a program to assist more than one thousand black farmers who were denied credit and access to farm materials because of their support for civil rights activities in the area (JM).

6 In **Washington, D.C.**, following President Eisenhower's speech to Congress calling on members to form a bipartisan committee to investigate charges that African Americans were being deprived of the right to vote and subjected to "economic pressures," a 201-person bipartisan "civil rights bloc" was formed to seek legislation to expand the Justice Department's authority to investigate racial violence. The proposed bill would also abolish the poll tax (NYT).

10 In the state of **Virginia**, voters endorsed the call for a constitutional convention to amend that state's constitution to allow public funds to be used for the support of segregated private schools. The so-called Gray Plan was passed by a 2 to 1 margin (NYT).

11 In the states of **Mississippi, Alabama, and Louisiana**, in defiance of the Interstate Commerce Commission's (ICC) ban on segregation in interstate transportation, police officials put up new signs for "White" and "Colored" passengers in railway stations and bus terminals. NAACP leader Roy Wilkins announced that the continued segregation in southern railroads and bus stations would be taken up with ICC officials, but only suits filed by passengers against the transportation authorities were likely to bring about any changes at the local level (NYT).

12 In **Springfield, Ill.**, following the order issued by the ICC banning segregation on public transportation, officials for the Illinois Commerce Commission took steps to end the practice on all railroads and bus companies operating within the state (JM).

15 In **Arlington County, Va.**, school board members became the first in the state to vote to begin integration in the fall of 1956 with the public elementary schools. Junior high schools would be integrated in 1957 and high schools in 1958. No student would be required to attend an integrated school, but those parents who wanted their children in "unmixed" schools would have to pay the transportation costs (NYT).

17 In **Adair County, Ky.**, seventeen black students began attending the local high school without incident. Although black students had been admitted to other all-white high schools in the state, this was the first desegregation that was brought about by court order. Adair County High School principal Joe Jones stated that "integration was just another day's work" for which he made no special preparations (NYT).

20 In **Columbia, S.C.**, a shotgun blast was fired into the home of NAACP president Rev. James M. Hinton, but no one was injured. The perpetrators were not identified, but police chief Lyle J. Campbell suggested that "it might have had something to do with him [Hinton] being president of the NAACP" (NYT).

20 In **New York City**, NAACP officials supported the Powell amendment, which would deny federal funds for school construction to segregated districts. According to the NAACP, five states—Louisiana, Mississippi, Alabama, Georgia, and South Carolina—still practiced school segregation and should be denied federal school aid. Should the measure reach the Senate, southern Democrats promised to filibuster (NYT).

24 In **Little Rock, Ark.**, school superintendent Virgil Blossom told NAACP official Daisy Bates that applications by black students for admission to all-white public schools were denied under the school board's policy of postponing school integration. Bates responded that they would appeal the policy in federal court (NYT).

26 In **Nashville, Tenn.**, a federal judge ordered city officials to open municipal golf courses to black players, as had occurred earlier in Atlanta and Baltimore (NYT).

2 In Jackson, Tenn., when it was announced that soft drink bottler M. C. Jolly, owner of Dr Pepper, was backing a suit to keep state funds from going to public colleges and universities that desegregate, a dozen black merchants in the city immediately launched a boycott of the soda (NYT).

4 In Oklahoma City, Okla., public officials decided to open all municipal facilities, including parks and swimming pools, to all citizens, including African Americans (NYT).

5 In Baton Rouge, La., after debating for seven hours, the Louisiana State University Board of Supervisors voted overwhelmingly in favor of a proposal to prohibit the university's athletic teams from playing home games with teams that have African Americans on their rosters (NYT).

5–7 In Tuscaloosa, Ala., as a result of a court order, Autherine Lucy was admitted to classes at the University of Alabama. Some white students shouted and hurled rocks and eggs at her car, but Lucy entered the campus escorted by campus and highway police. The following day white students rioted over Lucy's admission and were successful in their attempts at having her removed from campus. University officials decided to suspend Lucy because of the disruptions (NYT).

8 In Los Angeles, Calif., Democratic presidential candidate Adlai Stevenson, when asked whether he would use the FBI and army to end school segregation, replied that the process should "proceed gradually, not upsetting habits and traditions that are older than the Republic." NAACP and other local black leaders present expressed their disappointment with Stevenson's position (NYT).

9 In Houston, Tex., black parents trying to enroll their children in all-white public schools were turned away, and NAACP leader Francis L. Williams promised to take the matter to court (JM).

9 In East Baton Rouge, La., public parks and recreational officials declared that they would close the facilities rather than admit African Americans. A suit brought by black plaintiffs in the city was pending before the courts (JM).

9 In Philadelphia, Pa., Willie Sharper and his wife and five children arrived penniless and hungry at the Emmanuel Baptist Church after fleeing their farm in Orangeburg, S.C. Sharper lost his job and had several crosses burned in front of his home by Klan members because he signed a petition calling for the desegregation of the town's public schools (JM).

10 In Columbia, S.C., faced with a court order to desegregate the facility, officials for the South Carolina Commission on Forestry decided to close Edisto Beach State Park (NYT).

15 In Brooklyn, N.Y., Dr. John Hope Franklin received the unanimous approval of the Brooklyn College Personnel Committee for appointment as chair of the Department of History. The Fisk and Harvard University graduate will be the first African American to head a department at the college (JM).

15 In New York City, officials for the Brooklyn Dodgers canceled a scheduled baseball exhibition game in Birmingham, Ala., with the Milwaukee Braves because of the state law that barred white players from participating in athletic competitions with black players (NYT).

16 In Washington, D.C., New Jersey congressman Peter Frelinghuysen introduced legislation for the creation of a federal civil rights commission that would investigate claims by citizens who felt that their constitutional rights have been violated. The commission could then forward its findings to the U.S. attorney general for action (JM).

23 In Montgomery, Ala., state judge George Wallace threatened to jail FBI officials who attempted to investigate charges that African Americans had been barred from serving on grand juries in Cobbs County. The probe was ordered after the Supreme Court reversed the conviction of a black man for rape on the basis of the absence of African Americans on the Cobbs County grand jury. Judge Wallace claimed that the federal investigation was "a direct insult to the people of the state" (JM).

23 In Los Angeles, Calif., at the University of California, twenty-two sororities withdrew from the Student Legislative Council rather than submit their constitutions for review for any racial restrictions. UCLA's fraternities were expected to follow suit (JM).

24 In Washington, D.C., Justice Department officials announced that they would assist school board members in Hoxie, Ark., in dealing with suits filed against them for implementing the desegregation of the public schools (NYT).

29 In Florence, S.C., the case against NAACP official Clarence Mitchell and Rev. Horace P. Sharper of Sumter, S.C., was dropped. The men had been arrested for entering the city's train station through the front ("White") entrance, rather than the one for "Colored" in the back. In court, Mitchell noted that segregation of interstate passengers was illegal. After the case was dismissed, Mitchell, Sharper, and about fifty other African Americans headed straight for the train station and entered through the front entrance (NYT).

MARCH 1956

1 In Columbia, Miss., local NAACP president Dr. Thomas H. Brewer was shot seven times by white store owner Lucio Flowers, who claimed that the physician was reaching into his pocket after the two argued over the earlier beating and arrest of a black customer. Brewer's family believed the killing was related to his civil rights activities (JM).

2 In Tuscaloosa, Ala., officials at the University of Alabama permanently expelled Autherine Lucy from the university, accusing her of suggesting that they conspired with rioters to drive her from the campus. Lucy, who was upset and suffering from exhaustion, was resting in New York City, while NAACP officials there were planning their next move (NYT).

THE MONTGOMERY BUS BOYCOTT

The major event of the emerging Civil Rights Movement reported in 1956 was the Montgomery bus boycott, which began in December 1955. The city's black community mobilized its resources and provided alternative means of transportation for all who needed it. The response of elements of the white community to the Montgomery Improvement Association's boycott made headlines in January and February 1956, when bomb blasts shattered windows in the homes of Martin Luther King and E. D. Nixon, leaders of the protest. No one was hurt in the explosions.

Despite persistent threats, black citizens vowed to continue the boycott, which had cost the transit system an estimated $250,000 in two months. By the end of January 1956, Mayor W. A. Gayle instituted a "get-tough policy," and many African Americans participating in the bus boycott were arrested on minor traffic violations. However, the mayor denied charges that the city commission had been encouraged to fire black workers participating in the boycott. On 21 February, under the terms of an old state law, local sheriff's deputies arrested ninety leaders and participants, including twenty ministers, in the Montgomery bus protest and charged them with "encouraging a boycott." At King's trial in March, he was convicted of conspiracy to boycott city buses and was sentenced to 386 days at hard labor. King's attorney, Fred Gray, announced that they would appeal the court's decision. King was released on bail pending appeal, while eighty-nine others still awaited trials.

Throughout the year rallies were held in churches in Montgomery; Baltimore, Md.; Columbus, Ohio; New York City; Chicago, Ill.; and other cities around the country to raise funds to help sustain the protest. In June 1956, when a three-judge federal court ruled that segregation in public transportation in Montgomery was unconstitutional, there was no change in the local bus company's seating practices. State officials soon announced that they would appeal the federal court's ruling all the way to the U.S. Supreme Court.

6 In Washington, D.C., the Supreme Court upheld the decision of the U.S. district court in Greensboro ordering the admission of three black students to the University of North Carolina at Chapel Hill. In this case, the Supreme Court extended its ban on segregation in public elementary and secondary schools to include tax-supported institutions of higher education (NYT).

12 In Washington, D.C., ninety-six congressmen from eleven southern states agreed to join forces to thwart the implementation of the U.S. Supreme Court's *Brown* decision and issued the "Southern Manifesto," which stated that movement toward integration would replace the present "friendship and understanding" between blacks and whites with "hatred and suspicion" (NYT).

13 In New York City, *The New York Times* published its "Report on the South: The Integration Issue" and examined the effects of the Supreme Court's *Brown* decision upon southern communities. The report also discussed the impact of the opposition to public school integration on United States prestige abroad, particularly in Africa and Latin America (NYT).

13 In Washington, D.C., the U.S. Supreme Court ruled that there was no reason to delay the enrollment of Bethune-Cookman College graduate Virgil D. Hawkins at the University of Florida Law School. Hawkins had filed suit in 1950 to be admitted to the school, and university officials' latest appeal for delay had been denied. Florida governor LeRoy Collins later vowed to resist the court order through every lawful means (NYT).

15 In Lake City, S.C., for the second time in two weeks, shotgun blasts were fired from a car into the home of Walter Scott, president of the Lake City NAACP, but no one was injured. Scott was unable to identify any assailants, and the police said there were no clues (JM).

15 In Los Angeles, University of California officials announced that the school would offer a course in "Negro Literature" in its evening division, taught by UCLA faculty member Edward Hagemann. UCLA was one of the first predominantly white universities in the country to offer a course on this topic (JM).

22 In Capahosic, Va., reports circulated from a secret meeting that UN leader Ralph Bunche, Fisk president Charles S. Johnson, Phelps-Stokes Fund director Frederick Patterson, and several black college presidents asked NAACP official Roy Wilkins to "go slow" on public school integration efforts in the Deep South. When questioned by reporters, Wilkins stated that some southern NAACP leaders believed that the organization was already moving too slowly, "especially in areas where whites flatly declare they will entertain no integration." However, Wilkins said he disagreed with Mississippi leader Dr. Theodore R. M. Howard's suggestion that federal troops be brought in to desegregate the public schools (JM).

22 In Columbia, S.C., the motel owned by Modjeska Simkins received several blasts from shotguns fired by unknown assailants. Simkins, the NAACP official who headed up the relief campaign for the black families being boycotted in Clarendon County, was the second victim of an attack in Columbia in several weeks. The home of NAACP leader James Hinton was fired upon in January, and police claimed they had no clues about the perpetrators of either incident (JM).

22 In Hillsboro, Ohio, school officials continued to refuse to allow black students to enroll in the all-white Webster School, claiming that they should attend the ninety-six-year-old all-black Lincoln School. Black parents of twenty-two children decided to boycott the Lincoln School and teach their children at home. School officials claimed that a new elementary school for black and white students would be opened in September 1956 (JM).

23 In San Antonio, Tex., city councilmen voted unanimously to repeal ordinances calling for racial segregation in the city's swimming pools and other public facilities, including tennis courts, golf courses, and rest rooms. Desegregation of the city's public schools began in the fall of 1954 (NYT).

30 In Birmingham, Ala., local White Citizens Council leader Arthur Carter charged that the NAACP propaganda infiltrated the minds of white youth through "rock and roll music." Carter called for the removal of records by black performers from jukeboxes in the Birmingham and Anniston areas (NYT).

APRIL 1956

1 In Florence County, S.C., NAACP leader Walter Scott reported his home fired upon by unknown assailants. Less than two weeks earlier, shotgun blasts, fired from a passing car, ripped through the Simkins Motel, owned by NAACP leader Modjeska Simkins. Police said they had no clues about perpetrators (SSN).

1 In Wilmington, Del., NAACP officials filed eight separate suits for the desegregation of public schools in the state. NAACP lawyer Louis Redding noted that the suits included seventy-five separate cases of segregation in the public schools (SSN).

4 In Milwaukee, Wis., attorney Vel R. Phillips was elected alderman representing Milwaukee's Second Ward. A graduate of Howard University and the University of Wisconsin Law School, Phillips was the first woman and African American elected to the city council. Socialist mayor Frank Zeidler was elected to a third term despite a vicious campaign in which he was denounced as a "Nigger-lover" by bigoted white residents (NYT).

5 In Boulder, Colo., the University of Colorado Board of Regents voted that all campus fraternities and sororities must remove from their constitutions and admission requirements all restrictions based on race, color, or religion by 1 September 1956 or be placed on probation (JM).

8 In Washington, D.C., Postmaster General Arthur E. Summerfield issued a directive to southern postmasters to end discrimination against black postal workers. In the South, the tradition in the post office was for "whites to work inside, and Negroes work outside." Summerfield assigned Joseph A. Clarke (black) to investigate complaints of racial discrimination from postal workers (NYT).

11 In Birmingham, Ala., at the Municipal Auditorium, singer Nat King Cole was attacked while performing onstage before an all-white audience of thirty-five hundred. Four white men rushed the stage and grabbed the singer's feet and pulled him to the floor. Immediately, police swarmed the stage and began fighting the men, who were finally subdued and hauled away. A total of six men were arrested. Later their car was discovered to contain rifles, blackjacks, and brass knuckles (NYT).

12 In Chicago, Ill., Martin Luther King and wife Coretta Scott King appeared on the cover of *Jet* magazine; the article inside suggested that he was "Alabama's Modern Moses." The story presented a discussion of his family and educational background, highlighting the fact that the twenty-seven-year-old minister's "youthful humility gives the boycotters new spirit" (JM).

17 In Capetown, South Africa, black and some white Africans began a Montgomery-type bus boycott to protest new segregation orders, which stated that black Africans must ride only on the upper decks of double-decker buses. The National Transport Company had yet to rule on single-deck buses (NYT).

19 In Chicago, Ill., in an article on "Oklahoma's Jobless Negro Teachers," *Jet* magazine profiled several of the estimated 175 black teachers who lost their positions as a result of school desegregation. Gov. Raymond Gary and state school superintendent Oliver Hodge threatened to withhold state funds from school districts that refused to integrate; however, local school officials decided to "drop Negro teachers in the bargain." Many black educators have taken up the situation with NAACP officials, who threatened to take the issue to court (JM).

19 In Liberty County, Fla., after eleven black residents registered to vote for the first time in the county's history, they were terrorized by white mobs that burned crosses and fired shots in front of their homes. Subsequently, ten of the eleven remaining in the county asked that their names be removed from the voting lists (JM).

24 In Washington, D.C., the U.S. Supreme Court left standing the lower-court ruling that declared segregation in intrastate bus travel unconstitutional. The decision, in a case brought by a black woman, Sara Mae Flemming, against the Columbia, S.C., Municipal Bus Company and the South Carolina Gas and Electric Company, which operated the system, was the first ruling prohibiting segregation on transit systems within a city or state (NYT).

25 In Washington, D.C., A. Philip Randolph and NAACP officials organized a meeting of black leaders from seventy-three organizations to respond to the Southern Manifesto. The group agreed (1) to seek a meeting with President Eisenhower, (2) to raise $2 million for the NAACP, (3) to urge black voters to remain uncommitted to either political party until their civil rights planks were forthcoming, (4) to start voter registration drives in local communities, and (5) to seek unity among black leadership in opposing "gradualism" on civil rights demands (NYT).

26 In Philadelphia, Pa., more than eight hundred black and white citizens, including Democratic mayor Richardson Dilworth, signed the "declaration of intention" designed to help end racial discrimination. Those who made the pledge agreed not to join churches or clubs that discriminated or buy or rent homes in racially restricted neighborhoods (JM).

26 In Washington, D.C., Ross Clinchy, director of the federal government's Committee on Employ-

---

BUS BOYCOTTS SPREAD TO OTHER SOUTHERN CITIES

Beginning in May 1956, Montgomery-style bus boycotts were launched by black citizens in several other southern cities. In Tallahassee, Fla., after two Florida A&M University students, Wilhelmina Jakes and Carrie Patterson, were arrested for refusing to move to the rear of a bus, Rev. C. K. Steele, president of the Tallahassee NAACP, took the lead in the formation of the Inter-Civic Council to coordinate a bus boycott. By the end of June 1956, although city and bus officials agreed to some of the demands of the Inter-Civic Council, the bus boycott continued. The bus officials' offers to hire black drivers for routes in black neighborhoods and to allow seating on a first-come, first-served basis were viewed by boycott leaders as unsatisfactory.

In August 1956 as many as eighty-four leaders and participants in the Tallahassee bus boycott were arrested by local police. Among those charged with operating a commercial vehicle without a license and fined $150 were Steele, AME minister Rev. King S. Dupont, and Florida A&M black faculty members Edward and Bessie Irons. In October Florida state legislators voted funds to investigate the activities of the state's NAACP and the Inter-Civic Council, and officials of those organizations moved records out of state for fear of public disclosure by state officials similar to that which had occurred in Texas. Subsequently, the records of the Inter-Civic Council were subpoenaed and turned over to the court. At the trial of twenty-one leaders of the bus boycott, each was given a five-hundred-dollar fine, a sixty-day suspended jail sentence, and one year's probation for operating motor vehicles for hire without a license. Their attorneys called the fines excessive and promised to appeal the convictions.

Similar bus boycotts began in Miami, Fla., in June, led by Rev. Theodore Gibson; and Birmingham, Ala., in July, led by Rev. Fred Shuttlesworth. On 13 November 1956 the U.S. Supreme Court affirmed the federal district court's ruling that segregation in city public transit systems was unconstitutional. In Montgomery, Ala., Martin Luther King and other boycott leaders decided to wait until the decision was transmitted to the local circuit court before ending the bus boycott. Segregation ended on public transportation in Montgomery on 20 December 1956 and later that month in Tallahassee, Fla. Protests continued in Miami and Birmingham, however, when local officials refused to implement the Supreme Court's order. In Birmingham on Christmas Day 1956, the home of Rev. Fred Shuttlesworth was bombed, and more than forty people were subsequently arrested for attempting to ride local buses on a nonsegregated basis.

ment Policy, announced that a survey was to be conducted of black government workers. Information would be collected in Chicago, Milwaukee, St. Louis, Los Angeles, and other cities on where African Americans were employed and at what ranks and salaries. The survey would be used to develop programs to broaden black employment in government agencies (JM).

28 In Washington, D.C., retired U.S. army general Mark Clark, president of The Citadel, the South Carolina military college, told a group of southern legislators that he opposed the integration of black and white troops in 1950. Clark also claimed that during World War II, when he commanded the U.S. Fifth Army, the worst unit was the all-black Ninety-second Division. The statement touched off a controversial reexamination of the Ninety-second's performance in combat in Europe (NYT).

29 In San Antonio, Tex., following the opening of all municipal public swimming pools to African Americans, that city became the first in the South to order the complete desegregation of all public recreation facilities (NYT).

MAY 1956

3 In Baltimore, Md., Mayor Thomas D'Alessandro, Jr., signed a bill creating a fair employment practices commission for the city. The city council voted 14 to 6 in favor of the measure, which was the first passed by a city below the Mason-Dixon line (JM).

3 In New York City, singer Nat Cole's decision to sing before a segregated white audience in Birmingham, where he was attacked onstage by four white men, stirred a debate among black entertainers over the practice. Dinah Washington, Louis Jourdan, Roy Hamilton, and Cab Calloway made statements condemning Cole for having made the appearance in Birmingham (JM).

6 In New York City, Frederick D. Patterson, president of the United Negro College Fund, announced that more than six hundred white students were enrolled at nine of the thirty-one member institutions (NYT).

10 In Chicago, Ill., singer Mahalia Jackson's home and the homes of three other black families in the Chatham Village area were attacked by arsonists. Bomb blasts destroyed rooms in the homes of two black policemen, while Miss Jackson's residence was peppered with gunshots. These were the latest attacks on the homes of blacks who moved into the previously all-white neighborhood (JM).

10 In New York City, after Wendell Jeanpierre filed suit against Pan American Airlines for discriminatory hiring practices, the New York Commission Against Discrimination announced an investigation into the hiring practices of Pan American, TWA, United, and American Airlines. Jeanpierre was a pilot in World War II, but was denied a position as steward by Pan Am (NYT).

21 In Washington, D.C., Rep. Adam Clayton Powell, Jr., produced evidence for Pentagon officials demonstrating continued practices of segregation and discrimination at U.S. military bases in Texas, North Carolina, Maryland, Virginia, New Jersey, and Louisiana. The evidence included signed orders from commanding officers authorizing racially discriminatory practices (NYT).

24 In Delray, Fla., following a clash between 150 blacks and whites on the beach, the city council adopted an ordinance calling for the segregation of blacks and whites in bathing facilities. Black citizens led by Ozie Youngblood filed suit in federal court to open beaches to all residents regardless of race (NYT).

24 In Homer, La., former governor James A. Noe joined in protests against the purge of five thousand blacks from the voting rolls. White Citizens Council leader Billye Adams accused blacks of "bloc voting" in previous elections and bringing about the defeat of WCC candidates (JM).

24 In Washington, D.C., the six-hundred-member District of Columbia Bar Association ended its ban on qualified blacks as members. Among the first African Americans to apply was D.C. city commissioner George E. C. Hayes (JM).

28 In Washington, D.C., James C. Evans, assistant to the secretary of the army, and Columbia University professor Eli Ginzburg challenged General

Mark Clark's views decrying the effects of the integrated armed forces. Evans argued that "the use of integrated manpower was the greatest victory we had in Korea." Professor Ginzburg conducted a study of black troops in World War II and in Korea and found that the integration policy was very effective in the Korean War (NYT).

JUNE 1956

4 In Knoxville, Tenn., it was estimated that more than fifteen hundred blacks and whites were involved in a bloody conflict over occupation of Alexander Park, a local recreation area. During the incident the home of a black resident was blasted by a shotgun, and eighteen police officers were needed to quell the violence (NYT).

7 In Memphis, Tenn., a cross was burned on the lawn of the home of O. Z. Evers, a U.S. postal worker, after he filed suit in local courts against the Memphis Street Railway to end the practice of segregation by the public transit company (NYT).

12 In Louisville, Ky., twelve black students were enrolled in the summer session of the Manual High School, beginning the desegregation process in the city's public schools. Full desegregation would begin throughout the school system in the fall of 1956 (NYT).

14 In Accra, Gold Coast (West Africa), despite State Department warnings that she would be "insulted and humiliated," Mabel Dove, the first woman elected to the congress in the Gold Coast, West Africa, declared that during her three-month U.S. tour she would visit Montgomery, Ala.; Atlanta, Ga.; and other black population centers in the South (JM).

14 In Fort Smallwood and Sandy Point, Md., as a result of a suit filed by the Maryland NAACP, two publicly owned beaches in the two state parks were opened on a nonsegregated basis (JM).

24 In Washington, D.C., after a thirteen-month campaign by the local NAACP branch, two black women were hired as switchboard operators by the Chesapeake & Potomac Telephone Co. Before action was taken, the NAACP had to file complaints of discrimination with the federal government's Committee on Contract Compliance (NYT).

25 In Baltimore, Md., Walter T. Dixon, the first African American to serve on the city council in fifty years, launched a campaign to end the racially discriminatory practices of hotels in the city. Dixon called on the members of the city council to conduct an investigation into hotel practices. Public swimming pools were recently integrated in the city, and 35 percent of the guards and attendants were black (NYT).

JULY 1956

1 In Arlington, Va., the two white families who filed suit to force the desegregation of the public schools were victimized by telephone threats from white supremacist groups. As a result, Jack G. Orndoff decided to withdraw from the suit, while Barbara Marx vowed to continue. NAACP officials expressed their belief that as many as ten other white families would join Ms. Marx in the suit against the Arlington school board (SSN).

1 In Atlanta, Ga., the Georgia State Board of Education changed its plans to allow seven hundred black children to attend a newly constructed public school in Laurens County. Local school officials claimed they could not guarantee the safety of the children after receiving anonymous threats to dynamite the building, which was located in a white neighborhood (SSN).

1 In Raleigh, N.C., Edward Carson and Manuel Houston Crockett became the first African Americans enrolled as undergraduates at North Carolina State College. Enrolled in the summer term, they planned to major in electrical engineering. A third black student, Walter Van Buren, was admitted to the mechanical engineering program for the fall semester (SSN).

1–2 In San Francisco, Calif. the NAACP's forty-seventh convention was attended by more than four thousand delegates. Among the speakers were Brotherhood of Sleeping Car Porters leader A. Philip Randolph and Martin Luther King. NAACP executive secretary Roy Wilkins accused the Eisenhower administration of assuming a

LEGISLATIVE ATTACKS ON THE NAACP
AND COURT-ORDERED SCHOOL INTEGRATION

In 1956 the massive resistance campaign moved into a new stage when southern legislators in Louisiana, South Carolina, Alabama, Texas, and Florida entered the fray, passing laws aimed at banning the NAACP from operating in the states and prohibiting membership in the organization by public employees. These measures led to the firing of twenty-four black teachers in Elloree, S.C., in April for refusing to sign affidavits declaring their nonmembership in the NAACP; a student strike at all-black South Carolina State College in Orangeburg after state officials denounced NAACP influence on the campus; and a fine of ten thousand dollars being levied against NAACP officials in Alabama who refused in August to turn over membership records to circuit court judge Walter Jones.

In July 1956, Louisiana legislators not only passed a law to ban the NAACP from the state but also enacted a series of anti-integration measures that required segregation in recreational areas, parks, and rest rooms for intrastate travelers, abolished compulsory attendance in areas where public school desegregation had been ordered by the courts, and mandated the firing of any public school teacher who worked for or contributed to the NAACP.

A "freedom of choice" law, which would give parents the right to send their children to segregated or integrated public schools, was passed in Alabama in April 1956, and the Virginia, Texas, and Florida legislatures enacted various measures to assist financially those local school districts facing lawsuits aimed at bringing about desegregation.

At the beginning of the 1956–57 school year, the state National Guard had to be called out to implement court-ordered integration in several cities. *The New York Times* reported on 27 August 1956 that after a mob of two hundred whites shouted and jeered as fifteen black pupils were escorted by police into the Clinton (Tenn.) High School, the National Guard was called out to protect the black students. For two weeks mobs of angry whites continued to surround the school, but more than six hundred Guardsmen under Gen. Joe Henry were able to prevent any violent actions. Following a boycott of classes by white students, Clinton High School principal D. J. Brittain decided to close the school in December 1956. National Guardsmen were also used to protect black students integrating public schools in Clay, Tenn., and Sturgis, Ky.

When Texas governor Allen Shivers refused to provide protection for ten black students attempting to enter Mansfield (Texas) High School in the face of hundreds of jeering whites, NAACP attorney L. Clifford Davis refused to take the children onto school grounds. Despite Supreme Court justice Hugo Black's refusal to issue an order to stay the implementation of the integration plan, no police or National Guard protection was provided, and the black students were subsequently forced to register at the all-black I. M. Terrell High School in Ft. Worth, Tex.

"passive attitude" toward those state officials acting in defiance of the Supreme Court's *Brown* decision. The NAACP's annual report revealed that their income in 1955 was more than $600,000, with memberships as its largest source of funds. After the payment of expenditures, the organization ended the year $149,758 in the black. The total number of members was 284,089 in 1,080 branches (NYT).

5 In Davenport, Iowa, Charles Toney, local NAACP official, in testimony before a state com-

mission investigating discrimination in employment, claimed that no African Americans were employed as skilled workers in the city. Although there were many skilled black workers in the area, Toney believed that they had to go to Illinois to find employment (JM).

6 In Baton Rouge, La., members of the Education Committee of the state senate passed a measure prohibiting interracial sports events in public schools, colleges, and universities. According to the sponsor of the bill, Lawrence Gibbs, the measure was aimed at "northern schools fielding Negro players or demanding nonsegregated seating" at sports events (NYT).

9 In Washington, D.C., C. A. Moore, race relations adviser for the Federal Housing Administration, resigned from her position because she disagreed with the housing policies pursued by the administration. She believed that the home building programs supported by the agency would increase racial segregation in U.S. communities (NYT).

12 In Durham, N.C., Joseph S. Parker, Jr., a science teacher from Hillsboro, N.C., became the first African American to enroll at Duke University. Despite support for integration expressed by students, the school's trustees declared that it would remain all white. However, Parker was admitted to Duke as part of a program supported by the Atomic Energy Commission for the retraining of high school science teachers (JM).

15–16 In Charlottesville, Va., University of Virginia student Roland Rowley was arrested by the FBI for burning fiery crosses in front of the Washington, D.C., homes of Chief Justice Earl Warren and Solicitor General Simon E. Sobeloff in anger over the Supreme Court's *Brown* decision. The FBI also investigated similar burnings at the homes of Associate Justice Felix Frankfurter, New York senator Herbert Lehman, and Mrs. Douglass King, president of the Beltsville County, Md., NAACP (NYT).

22 In Baltimore, Md., public school superintendent John Fischer declared that after more than one year, integration was "working well" in city schools, and teachers and parents were quite pleased with the results (NYT).

22 In Chicago, Ill., sixty black Democrats submitted a civil rights plank to be presented to the party's Platform Committee. It called for (1) federal support for civil rights of all citizens; (2) federal support for the right to vote; (3) enactment and enforcement of laws for equal employment opportunity; (4) positive action toward the implementation of the Supreme Court's *Brown* decision; (5) federal action to ensure nondiscrimi-

nation in government-assisted housing programs; (6) revision of U.S. Senate rules to assure that the will of the majority was not thwarted by a minority. The plank was later submitted to the convention delegates (NYT).

24 In Lakeland, Fla., Paul Seiderman, a spokesman for the Florida B'nai B'rith's Anti-Defamation League, asked Gov. LeRoy Collins to investigate KKK activities in Lakeland. The league's officials reported that the Klan group had recently issued threatening statements against African Americans and Jews (NYT).

26 In Jackson, Miss., Everett Page, national vice commander of the American Legion, stated that he would not serve as a delegate from Texas to the Democratic convention in Chicago because of the inclusion of three blacks in the state's delegation. Page stated that he would not attend the convention because he "did not want to sit with them." Page later apologized for his statement and "serious error in judgment" to Detroit congressman Charles Diggs (NYT).

26 In Washington, D.C., National Council of Negro Women president Vivian Carter Mason announced the formation of a group to meet with Democratic and Republican leaders at the party conventions to demand the appointment of more black women to senior positions in the federal government. Mason stated that the group was compiling a list of at least one hundred outstanding black women professionals who had been bypassed for government positions in the past (JM).

AUGUST 1956

1 In Arlington, Va., federal judge Albert V. Bryan ordered public school officials to desegregate the elementary schools by January 1957 and the high schools by September 1957 (NYT).

1 In Camden, S.C., an interracial group of Methodist teenagers who came to Camden, S.C., to work on repairs at Mather Academy, a church school for blacks, were forced to flee following threats from local whites to burn down their work camp. Camden mayor Henry Savage promised to seek police protection for the youths, but they decided to leave the town and went to work at a Methodist school in Olive Hill, Ky. (SSN).

1 In Dallas, Tex., White Citizens Council (WCC) leaders petitioned the city council to reinstate segregation in the city's public transit system. The Dallas Transit Company ended segregated seating earlier in the year, but WCC leaders believed that transit officials had no authority to make the changes (SSN).

1 In Milford, Del., more than one thousand people attended a WCC mass meeting to protest the local school board's decision to enroll two black children in all-white elementary schools. The WCC leaders called for the ouster of all school board members who supported public school integration (SSN).

5 In New York City, *The New York Times* published the results of an extensive survey of public school integration in the southern and border states and reported that in the 1955–56 school year 540 school districts were desegregated. The *Southern School News* reported that some 4,000 school districts remained segregated and that fifty pieces of pro-segregation legislation were passed in 1956 (NYT).

14 In Greensboro, N.C., Acting Chancellor W. W. Pierson announced that two black women, Betty Tillman and Elizabeth Jo Ann Smart, would enroll at the Woman's College at the University of North Carolina. They became the first black women admitted to the Greensboro branch of the state university (NYT).

16–17 In Chicago, Ill., when the Democratic convention opened, there were 105 African Americans attending as delegates and alternates. Houston rancher Hobart Taylor was the first African American to serve as a full delegate from a southern state. Attorney W. J. Durham served as an alternate from Dallas, Tex. State representative Truly Hatchett and lawyer Robert Watts were the first black alternates from Maryland. Martin Luther King, Jr., spoke before the convention, urging strong support for voting rights, and Detroit, Mich., congressman Charles Diggs led an unsuccessful attempt to get a strong civil rights plank

placed in the platform. Southern delegates threatened to walk out of the convention if strong support for the implementation of the Supreme Court's *Brown* decision was included in the platform (NYT).

19, 24 In Montgomery, Ala., twelve whites announced the formation of the Segregation party, under the leadership of architect John Frederick Duggar. The segregationists planned to put forward their own slate of candidates in the fall elections because they felt that neither the Democratic nor Republican candidates represented their interests (NYT).

21–24 In San Francisco, Calif., at the Republican National Convention, there were seventy black delegates and alternates representing twenty-seven states. Historian Helen Edmonds from North Carolina gave the seconding speech for Dwight Eisenhower's nomination for president, and attorney Perry Howard and eight members of his "Black and Tan" delegation from Mississippi were named delegates. The seven white Mississippi delegates refused to sit with the blacks and had to sit in the balcony. The Republicans pledged to uphold the *Brown* decision (NYT).

23 In Pittsburgh, Pa., officials for the American Federation of Teachers gave eight southern locals until 1 March 1957 to integrate their membership or face ouster from the union. The order applied to both all-black and all-white locals (JM).

23 In Baltimore, Md., during an official visit by Nashville, Tenn., city officials to survey housing projects, two black city councilmen, Z. Alexander Looby and Robert Lillard, were refused service in a restaurant. The white officials were served. Councilman Looby left the city after the incident (JM).

23 In Braddock, Pa., after the NAACP filed suit against the local school board for racial discrimination, Alice Teal became the first black teacher in the local public school system. When Teal and another black first applied for positions earlier in the year, school officials refused to hire them (JM).

23 In Mound Bayou, Miss., Dr. Theodore R. M. Howard, who led the campaigns in 1955 to bring the killers of Emmett Till to justice, announced that he was being forced to leave the state and move to Chicago because of continued threats against his life from local whites. Dr. Howard declared that "I feel I can do more in the battle for Negro rights alive anywhere in the North than dead in a weed-grown grave in Dixie." Dr. Howard had learned that the White Citizens Council had offered a bounty of one thousand dollars to anyone who killed him (JM).

30 In Buenos Aires, **Argentina**, trumpeter Dizzy Gillespie and his orchestra, on a goodwill tour of South America for the U.S. State Department, were denied accommodations at the Hotel de la Ciudad. Hotel spokespersons said that because they were black, allowing them to stay there would hurt the hotel's business (JM).

30 In Columbus, Ohio, after several attacks on her family and home, Mrs. George Lawson declared that she would remain in her all-white neighborhood. White mobs burned crosses on her lawn and made numerous threats against the black family (JM).

30 In Houston, Tex., a Fats Domino dance concert was abruptly halted by police when thousands of whites began dancing on the floor with blacks. Blacks received refunds for what was advertised as an all-black affair, and whites left the City Auditorium singing "Let the Good Times Roll" (JM).

30 In New Orleans, La., Archbishop Joseph Rummel announced that the proposed desegregation of Roman Catholic schools would be postponed until September 1957. This was the second postponement due to protests by white Catholics (JM).

30 In Montgomery, Ala., lawyers for Autherine Lucy Foster (she had married that year) failed in their attempt to have her readmitted as a student at the University of Alabama. Lucy Foster was expelled after she accused school officials of conspiring with others to cause the riots on campus earlier in the year. U.S. district judge Hobart Grooms ruled that the trustees had the right to expel students for just cause (NYT).

SEPTEMBER 1956

❙ In Baton Rouge, La., in light of the new state law prohibiting integrated sports activities and social meetings, Louisiana State University officials announced that black students would remain in the graduate school but would have to sit separately at the school's athletic events. Officials for the Sugar Bowl, which was played in New Orleans, were denied an exemption to the new law and Sugar Bowl officials stated that as of 1 January 1957 no interracial sporting events would be scheduled. This would mean a huge loss in revenue for the city (NYT).

❙ In Charlottesville, Va., the Virginia Council for Human Rights was formed, under the leadership of author Sarah Patton Boyle, for the purpose of supporting the state's implementation of public school desegregation. The group wanted to serve as "a rallying point for those who wish to uphold the law" (SSN).

❙ In Dallas, Tex., public school officials decided to appeal to the U.S. Supreme Court after the federal district courts ordered the admission in September 1956 of black pupils to all-white elementary schools (SSN).

❙ In the state of Kentucky, public school officials in three towns announced desegregation plans. In Hopkinsville, public school integration was confined to the first grade, while in Ashland, the first and second grades were desegregated. In Newport, the separate black school was closed and black students and three teachers were integrated into previously all-white schools (SSN).

❙ In Tuscaloosa, Ala., despite the presence of police, black bystanders were attacked during a Klan rally and cross-burning. Klan leaders claimed that the blacks hurled curses at them. The Klan claimed to have three thousand members in the city (SSN).

❙ In Washington, D.C., NAACP leaders Eugene Davidson and Clarence Mitchell denounced the hearings on the District's school desegregation efforts held by the Special House District Subcommittee, chaired by Georgia congressman James C. Davis. Mitchell claimed that the hearings were

WHITE CITIZENS COUNCILS LAUNCH ATTACKS ON URBAN LEAGUE BRANCHES

The National Urban League was founded in New York City in 1911 by black and white social workers and philanthropists to address the social and economic needs of African Americans in U.S. cities. Whereas the NAACP was engaged in activities to protect the legal rights of African Americans, the Urban League was committed to improving employment opportunities and by the 1950s had numerous branches throughout the North and the South. At the league's annual convention in September 1956, held in Cincinnati, Ohio, Lester Granger, the executive secretary, announced that several branches of the organization were under attack in various southern and border cities.

In April 1956 the White Citizens Council, the National Citizens Protective Association, and other groups in St. Louis were vilifying the organization for its "interracial activities" and demanding that financial support through the Community Chest be dropped. In September, the league's branch in Tallahassee, Fla., was dropped from the local Community Chest, and WCC and KKK attacks had spread to eight other cities. The WCC in these cities spearheaded a letter-writing and phone campaign in an effort to curtail Community Chest funding. By the end of 1956, Urban League branches in Richmond, Va., New Orleans, La., Jacksonville, Fla., and Norfolk, Va., had also lost funding totaling nearly ninety thousand dollars as a direct result of the WCC's charges that they were controlled by "trouble-making integrationists."

called to generate anti-desegregation propaganda by focusing on the potentially negative consequences of public school integration (SSN).

3 In **Fort Worth, Tex.**, unidentified people threatened to bomb the home of Mr. and Mrs. Lloyd G. Austin after the couple moved into an all-white neighborhood. Mrs. Austin was fired from her job in a local department store once her white employers learned where she had moved (NYT).

6 In **Placentia, Calif.**, a bomb was thrown into the home of Gerald Harris. Although two Harris children were in the room where the bomb exploded, they were not injured. The Harrises were the first blacks to move into the all-white neighborhood, and they vowed to stay (JM).

8 In **Pritchard, Ala.**, after Rev. Joshua A. Barney became the first black in recent decades to announce his candidacy for public office, an unidentified man fired shots into his home. Barney, the first black to run for the city council in the town, was unhurt and promised to remain in the race (NYT).

27 In **Washington, D.C.**, following increasing reports in several European publications that black soldiers stationed there were "rapists," the Pentagon announced the appointment of army chaplain Col. John A. DeVeaux to headquarters staff in Heidelburg, Germany, to investigate these charges. Colonel DeVeaux became the highest-ranking black officer in the European Command (JM).

OCTOBER 1956

1 In **Baton Rouge, La.**, the Louisiana State Board of Education issued a ruling that all students seeking admission to state colleges and universities needed "certificates of eligibility and moral character." The measure is intended to keep black students out of state colleges because issuance of a certificate to a black student would be interpreted as support for integration. The state legislature had already passed a law forbidding state employees from advocating integration, or else face loss of their positions (SSN).

1 In **Nashville, Tenn.**, the Southern Education Reporting Service estimated that since 1954, 650 southern school districts out of 3,711 had been desegregated. There were forty-six new prosegregation groups organized and eighty-four anti-integration laws passed in eight states. No desegregation had occurred in Mississippi, Alabama,

Florida, Georgia, and South Carolina; three districts in Arkansas, one high school in Tennessee, and state colleges in North Carolina, Louisiana, and Virginia had been integrated. Substantial school desegregation had occurred in West Virginia, Oklahoma, and Missouri, while one hundred school districts in Texas and thirty-three in Kentucky were integrated (SSN).

1 In Nashville, Tenn., Tennessee A & I graduate Edward M. Porter and Fisk graduate Frederick T. Work became the first African Americans admitted to Vanderbilt University Law School (SSN).

2 In Albany, N.Y., after four months of negotiations, Charles Abrams, chair of the New York State Commission Against Discrimination, announced an agreement with eighteen airline companies to hire qualified African Americans as pilots and other flight personnel. The complaint was brought by the National Urban League after the companies failed to liberalize their hiring practices (NYT).

3 In Beaumont, Tex., five black students were admitted to Lamar College of Technology's freshman class after a court order was issued by federal judge Cecil Lamar. At least twenty-five whites set up pickets outside the school to protest their admission (NYT).

4 In Madison, Wis., state supreme court chief justice Edward T. Fairchild denied the appeal to rescind the earlier order for the integration of the Wisconsin Bar Association. The order called for all attorneys in the state to belong to one bar association (JM).

4 In Washington, D.C., Democratic party officials announced the appointment of Washington lawyer Elmer Henderson as special adviser to presidential candidate Adlai Stevenson. Henderson became the first African American to serve in that position. Others chosen to work for the campaign included Charles Wartman, Andrew Hacker, Christine Davis, and Venice Spraggs (JM).

11 In Washington, D.C., Rep. Adam Clayton Powell and several liberal congressmen joined NAACP officials Eugene Davidson, Clarence Mitchell, and Roy Wilkins in denouncing the hearings held by the Special House District Subcommittee to investigate public school desegregation. In light of the negative information presented during the hearings, Howard University professor Ellis O. Knox announced plans to conduct a survey of five hundred D.C. teachers to obtain their views on the success or failure of school desegregation (JM).

11 In Wichita Falls, Tex., students at Midwestern University voted 155 to 95 to keep the dormitories "lily-white" after a black student applied for residency (JM).

12 In Washington, D.C., at a news conference, Rep. Adam Clayton Powell announced that he would actively campaign for President Eisenhower's reelection and dropped his earlier endorsement of Democratic candidate Adlai Stevenson. Powell declared that he would speak throughout the country in support of the president. Democratic leaders predicted that this would be "political suicide" for the Harlem congressman (NYT).

18 In Washington, D.C., the U.S. Department of Justice decided not to pursue the case brought against Bruce Biffkin, a Florence, S.C., police officer who arrested NAACP official Clarence Mitchell for using the "white" entrance to the train station. Justice Department spokespersons said they would have difficulty gaining a conviction in the "emotion-charged" South Carolina area (JM).

NOVEMBER 1956

1 In Arlington, Va., Barbara Marx became the first white person elected to the board of directors of the Virginia NAACP. Marx had earlier joined with white parents in a suit to integrate the Arlington public school system (SSN).

1 In Birmingham, Ala., George Johnson and Clyde Jones filed a $25,000 suit against the city's personnel board for its refusal to allow African Americans to take civil service examinations for police patrolman positions. The personnel director, Ray Mullins, was not sure if this was the law but knew it was "a matter of policy" (JM).

1 In Richmond, Va., U.S. district judge Walter Hoffman threatened to rescind the legal restrictions placed on the implementation of school integration in Norfolk and Newport News. Judge Hoffman agreed to allow Virginia state and NAACP attorneys to file arguments before making a final ruling on the desegregation issue (SSN).

I In Nashville, Tenn., the *Southern School News* reported that most of the 462 black teachers in the border states dismissed from their positions due to school integration had been placed in other positions with the exception of those in Oklahoma. In Elloree, S.C., it was reported that school officials received 290 applications for the positions formerly held by the twenty-four black teachers fired for their refusal to sign affidavits denying membership in the NAACP (SSN).

POSITIVE AND NEGATIVE RESPONSES OF ORGANIZED LABOR TO CIVIL RIGHTS DEMANDS

By the end of 1955, the leaders of the newly merged AFL-CIO had taken steps to eradicate racial discrimination practiced by member unions. The AFL-CIO Civil Rights Committee was established within the federation, and George L. P. Weaver, former secretary of the CIO's Anti-Discrimination Committee, was appointed executive secretary. In February 1956, however, ninety-four members of the United Steelworkers Union in Tuscaloosa, Ala., signed a letter addressed to AFL-CIO president George Meany stating that they would quit and form a new union if they were forced to admit African Americans as members. The following month spokespersons for the newly organized Southern Aircraft Workers Union announced that they would appeal to the National Labor Relations Board for a new election to become the new bargaining agent for machine workers because the United Auto Workers, the current union, was trying to break down southern traditions in the workplace.

AFL-CIO president and chairman of the Civil Rights Committee George Meany announced in May 1956 the formation of a committee to raise $2 million to support civil rights issues. Brotherhood of Sleeping Car Porters (BSCP) president A. Philip Randolph stated that the twelve thousand members of the BSCP would tax themselves one and a half dollars each to contribute to the civil rights fund. However, within a month in Nashville, Tenn., A. A. Canada, president of the Society to Maintain Segregation, called for the formation of the Southern States Conference of Union People. Canada made the announcement to protest the AFL-CIO's decision to contribute money to civil rights causes.

In August in Birmingham, Ala., Elmer Brock, an official in the AFL-CIO–affiliated Painters Local 432, was instrumental in the formation of the Southern Federation of Labor. Brock was subsequently expelled from the AFL-CIO for "fostering an independent labor union and taking steps toward secession" through the creation of an all-white labor federation. Brock later declared that he would not appeal the ruling, but would continue to fight "all attempts to destroy our southern traditions."

At a September 1956 labor meeting in Forest Park, Pa., AFL-CIO president George Meany announced the launching of a "mammoth educational campaign" to change southerners' views about labor unions and civil rights. Meany argued that opposition in these areas stemmed from "misguided southern traditions." However, in 1956 black workers also filed complaints with state fair employment practices commissions charging racial discrimination by AFL-CIO–affiliated unions in New York, New Jersey, and Ohio. In Norfolk, Va., three black brakemen employed by the Norfolk and Western Railway won their lawsuit in appeals court claiming discrimination in promotion practices by the company and the Brotherhood of Railroad Trainmen. As a result, in November Meany approved plans to step up anti-discrimination efforts within unions belonging to the federation. Negotiations had begun with unions in Cleveland, St. Louis, Chicago, and other cities to end long-term discrimination in railroad and building-trades unions, including carpenters, electricians, and plumbers.

4 In New York City, *The Nat King Cole Show* premiered on NBC television and became the first network-sponsored television program starring an African American entertainer. The fifteen-minute program also featured the Nelson Riddle Orchestra and a choral group (NYT).

7 In the 1956 presidential elections, Dwight Eisenhower defeated Adlai Stevenson in forty-one of forty-eight states and received higher percentages from black voters in all regions of the country than in 1952. Democrats regained control of both houses of Congress, but promised to take up civil rights issues seriously in the upcoming session (NYT).

13 In Harrisburg, Pa., the state supreme court refused to lift a ban on the enrollment of black orphan boys in Philadelphia's Girard College. In the suit brought by Robert Felder and William Ash Fost, the court upheld the will of merchant Stephen Girard, who provided the $6 million endowment for the institution for poor white male orphans. Attorney Raymond Pace Alexander said he would take the matter to the U.S. Supreme Court (NYT).

14 In Washington, D.C., the return of the Democrats to power in Congress led to demands that Rep. Adam Clayton Powell, Jr., be removed from his positions on the House Committees on Education and Labor and Insular Affairs because of his support of President Eisenhower in the presidential election. Rep. Emmanuel Celler, chair of the New York delegation, announced that House Speaker Joseph Martin would lay the groundwork for Powell's removal from these committees (NYT).

15 In Washington, D.C., U.S. Army officials issued a ban on segregation in schools and courses offered on army bases. Black soldiers complained that they were excluded from courses offered at Fort Benning and Fort Gordon in Georgia and Fort Jackson in South Carolina because of segregation laws in those states (JM).

1 In Little Rock, Ark., a five-foot cross was burned on the lawn of the home of Daisy and L. C. Bates on 27 October. Daisy Bates was state director of the NAACP and L. C. Bates was editor and publisher of the *Arkansas State Press*. Both were spearheading efforts to integrate the Little Rock public schools (SSN).

6 In Baltimore, Md., acting fire chief Charles H. Theiss announced the end of all segregatory regulations in the city's 101 firehouses. This directive ended the remaining restrictions on the 120 black firemen serving in the city's fire department (JM).

7 In Montgomery, Ala., a southern Institute on Nonviolence and Social Change was held with the theme "Freedom Through Love." Among the civil rights leaders present were Martin Luther King, Baton Rouge's Rev. T. J. Jemison, and Tallahassee's Rev. C. K. Steele (NYT).

13 In Atlanta, Ga., NAACP official Clarence Mitchell, in a letter to Commerce Secy. Sinclair Weeks, requested that those states receiving federal funds to build new highways guarantee a policy of nondiscrimination for all travelers on those roadways. Mitchell said the policy would be in keeping with similar bans on discrimination in bus, railroad, and other interstate transportation (JM).

27 In Oklahoma City, Okla., following the desegregation of the public transit system earlier in the year, the Oklahoma City Bus Company announced that Robert Harris had been hired as the first black bus driver for the city (JM).

27 In Tallahassee, Fla., state officials decided to halt bus service in the city after violence erupted when black citizens attempted to ride buses on a nonsegregated basis. Among other violent incidents, a cross was burned in front of the home of Rev. C. K. Steele and rocks were thrown through the window, injuring his young son. As a result, bus service was ended in the city (NYT).

On 9 October 1957, in Little Rock, Arkansas, nine black students attending Central High School are shown leaving the school under the protection of federalized Arkansas National Guardsmen. The students, in their third week of classes, were confronted daily with mass protests from local whites who challenged their right to attend the school. (SOURCE: CORBIS BETTMANN)

1957

"AMAZING GRACE"

Following the example of Montgomery, Ala., other southern black communities organized boycotts against local transit companies and other public institutions practicing segregation. Martin Luther King and other civil rights leaders organized the Southern Christian Leadership Conference (SCLC) to disseminate information about effective nonviolent strategies for social change. As public institutions were forced to desegregate, increasing pressure was brought to bear on Christian religious denominations to end the practices of separating the races in the houses of God. As racial barriers tumbled in movie theaters, concert halls, and at religious gatherings, violent conflicts sometimes erupted. In Little Rock, Ark., the nine black children who agreed to be the first to integrate Central High School demonstrated "Amazing Grace" as they faced violent mobs opposed to any changes in the southern way of life.

JANUARY 1957

In New Orleans, La., NAACP attorney A. P. Tureaud took steps to allow the organization to begin operating in the state again by turning over its three-hundred-name membership list to the state attorney. Five other NAACP branches in the state promised to turn over membership lists in the near future (NYT).

In Washington, D.C., school superintendent Hobart M. Corning rejected the findings of a congressional subcommittee that concluded that integration of the public schools was "too hasty" and denied the report's suggestion that "sex problems" were causing white parents to remove their children from the public schools (SSN).

In Washington, D.C., a group of black leaders from Mississippi turned over to Attorney General Herbert Brownell documents relating to attacks on black citizens in the state involved in school integration efforts. The leaders, who asked that their names not be used for fear of reprisals, called on the Justice Department to investigate the terrorist incidents (SSN).

4 In Washington, D.C., at the opening session of the U.S. Congress, Minnesota senator Hubert Humphrey called for the adoption of a strong civil rights program, including support for a civil rights bill that guaranteed federal protection for voting rights. Rep. Adam Clayton Powell also promised to reintroduce legislation that would prohibit federal aid to segregated public school systems (NYT).

8 In New York City, NAACP executive director Roy Wilkins announced that the organization received more than $1 million in receipts in 1956 and had more than 350,000 members. Despite attacks on the organization in Louisiana, Alabama,

Texas, Georgia, and Virginia, there were 40,000 new members added (NYT).

10 In Oklahoma City, Okla., the Oklahoma State Planning and Resources Board voted to end segregation in all state parks, opening them to black citizens on a nondiscriminatory basis, following a threatened lawsuit by J. J. Simmons and members of the state NAACP. Simmons promised that the NAACP would seek cancellation of leases to any lodges in state parks that practiced discrimination (JM).

12 In Atlanta, Ga., at the Southern Leadership Conference on Transportation and Nonviolent Integration, the sixty delegates called on President Eisenhower and the Department of Justice to intervene to end the bombing and other acts of violence leveled against black citizens. Martin Luther King and the other leaders called upon Eisenhower to make a tour of the South and put the weight of his office behind integration efforts. White House officials later announced that Eisenhower had no plans for touring the South (NYT).

16 In Atlanta, Ga., six ministers led by William Holmes Borders were arrested after sitting in the white section of a bus. Released after paying thousand-dollar bonds, the ministers, who were members of the "Love, Law, and Liberation Movement," declared that this would set the stage for a court case to test Georgia's segregation laws (NYT).

17 In New Bedford, Mass., the local NAACP asked school officials to end blackface minstrel shows in the public schools. The NAACP officials claimed that the shows and certain books used in classrooms ridiculed black citizens (JM).

21 In Washington, D.C., at President Eisenhower's second inauguration, concert singer Marian Anderson became the first African American to sing the national anthem at this event, and other black Republicans participated in festivities. Mississippi governor J. P. Coleman snubbed the inauguration in protest over Eisenhower's stand on civil rights (NYT).

27 In Tallahassee, Fla., John Boardman, a white student at Florida State University, was not allowed to register for the spring semester because of his active support for efforts of black citizens to desegregate the transit system. NAACP member Boardman promised to file a court suit if his petition for readmission was rejected (NYT).

28 In Montgomery, Ala., a bomb exploded at the home of a black resident, injuring three people, while another on the porch of the home of Martin Luther King failed to detonate. King told those who gathered, "Don't get your guns. Don't shoot back—but fear no one. We won't stop our fight for justice. They'll have to blow up God Himself" (NYT).

31 In Los Angeles, Calif., a three-judge appellate court declared that "a dentist's office is not a place of public accommodation" and upheld a lower court's dismissal of a suit brought by Ada Coleman against a dentist who refused her service (JM).

31 In Washington, D.C., as a result of a letter to President Eisenhower sent by Rep. Adam Clayton Powell charging that the army still used racial designations in official records, U.S. Army officials announced that, beginning 1 February 1957, they would end the practice of using racial identification in the assignment of orders for soldiers (NYT).

FEBRUARY 1957

1 In Baton Rouge, La., a black graduate student, Arnease Ludley, was granted a court injunction to be admitted to Louisiana State University without a "certificate of eligibility." Ludley claimed that her high school principal refused to issue it because of fear of loss of his job. Signing a certificate would be interpreted by state officials as support for integration (SSN).

1 In New Orleans, La., federal judges issued orders to admit black students after suits were filed by attorney A. P. Tureaud against Southwestern State Institute, Southwestern State College, and McNeese State College. The suits were aimed at testing the constitutionality of a law requiring "certificates of eligibility" for admission to state colleges (SSN).

1 In Rocky Mount, N.C., Dr. Joseph W. Parker, Jr., was unanimously elected to the school board

ORGANIZED RELIGION AND RACIAL SEGREGATION, 1956–57

After the U.S. Supreme Court declared segregation in public education unconstitutional, the leaders of the major religious denominations came under increasing pressure to end official practices of racial segregation within their churches. In April 1956 at a meeting of the Southern Baptist Convention in Nashville, Tenn., twenty-eight leading ministers issued a statement deploring prejudice and discrimination and urging a "Christian solution" to racial tensions in the country. In May 1956 Roman Catholic archbishop Joseph F. Rummel in New Orleans threatened to excommunicate Catholics who formed a White Citizens Council branch. The members of the Association of Catholic Laymen, a group opposed to the desegregation of New Orleans Catholic schools, said they would appeal to Pope Pius XII for support of their pro-segregation views.

Officials of the United Presbyterian church meeting in Philadelphia in May 1956 issued a report condemning the continued practice of racial discrimination in housing, voting, and employment. The report concluded that "nowhere in our land can Negroes and, to a lesser extent, other minority persons escape the indignity of segregation or discrimination in one form or another." At the Lutheran Church World Conclave, held in Minneapolis, Minn., in August 1957, Edgar M. Carlson, president of Gustavus Adolphus College, told the seven hundred delegates that racial segregation in all its "ugly forms" must be battled throughout the world.

Despite these statements, racial incidents involving religious congregations were regularly reported in the newspapers in 1956 and 1957. For example, in September 1956 at the annual convention held by the Jehovah Witnesses in Augusta, Ga., it was reported that while the religious services were interracial, the baptisms were conducted on a segregated basis—blacks at one pool, whites at another. In Philadelphia in November 1956, Rev. David E. Gregory resigned as pastor of New Berean Baptist Church after the church's deacon board voted to bar African Americans from membership. Deacon board chair Thomas Cox said, "Negroes are welcome to attend our services, but we do not feel that they should be actual members." In Los Angeles, Calif., in August 1957, when Methodist bishop A. P. Shaw assigned a black minister to an all-white congregation, the parishioners organized a boycott of religious services. The incident spurred church officials to sponsor a series of twenty-four public meetings around the country to address the issue of segregation in the Methodist Church.

by the Board of Aldermen, becoming the first African American member. An estimated forty percent of the public school students in the city were African American (SSN).

14 In Chicago, Ill., in an article in the March issue of *Ebony* magazine, former University of Alabama economics professor Harry Schaffer revealed that as many as twenty-five faculty members resigned their positions at the school following the campus riots and expulsion of Autherine Lucy in 1956. Most left because they believed the "principles of democracy" had been violated by university officials (JM).

14 In Memphis, Tenn., Birmingham, Ala., and New Orleans, La., black citizens filed suits in federal courts against city and bus transit officials who had failed to begin the desegregation of local transportation services. The Supreme Court had affirmed the lower court's decision in *Browder v. Gayle* that declared segregation in intrastate public transit unconstitutional (JM).

21 In New York City, three Columbia University faculty members resigned from Theta Tau, the national engineering fraternity, for its refusal to change its rules barring African Americans from membership. Associate Dean Wesley Hennessy and Professors Mario Salvidori and Frank Maggio said they took the action to dramatize the attempts of the Columbia chapter to amend the fraternity's national charter (NYT).

24 In Miami, Fla., a plot was discovered to kill five NAACP officials, and members of the Seaboard White Citizens Council (WCC) were arrested by police as they were planting a cross in front of the home of Frank Legree, a black man who had moved into a white neighborhood. The informant, Hampton Earl Shaver, warned NAACP officials of the plot organized by Fred Hockett and David Hawthorne, leaders of the local WCC and the Dade County Property Owners Association. The projected dynamite attacks on black homes and housing projects in Miami were planned to start a "race war" in the city (NYT).

27 In Little Rock, Ark., Gov. Orval Faubus signed two anti-integration bills into law. One established the Arkansas State Sovereignty Commission, which could demand registration by certain organizations with outside connections, and another provided that no parents were to be forced to send their children to an integrated school. The *Southern School News* estimated that, since 1954, southern legislators had passed 120 segregation laws (NYT).

28 In New York City, members of the predominantly black Longshoremen's Union Local 968 filed a petition with 122 names with the State Commission Against Discrimination complaining of employment discrimination by companies and unions operating on New York City's waterfront (JM).

MARCH 1957

1 In Atlanta, Ga., when a group of Spelman College students were spotted in the gallery of the state house of representatives assigned to whites, speaker Marvin Moate asked that they be removed. "We have segregation in this place, Mr. Sheriff," he shouted. "Will you please go up to the gallery and see that it is maintained" (JM).

7–9 In Accra, Ghana (West Africa), among the Americans attending the celebration of the independence of Ghana were Vice Pres. Richard Nixon, A. Philip Randolph, UN official Ralph Bunche, Martin Luther King, the NAACP's Thurgood Marshall and Roy Wilkins, Rep. Charles Diggs, and *Ebony* and *Jet* magazine publisher John H. Johnson. Ghana became the first former European colony in Africa to achieve its independence. Martin and Coretta King planned to make a seven-nation tour after their stay in Ghana (NYT).

7, 10–12 In Lorman, Miss., after Alcorn A&T College history professor Clennon King wrote an article for the (white) *Jackson State Times* criticizing the activities of the NAACP and supporting racial segregation, the students launched a campus boycott. When white trustees came to campus and found that the students refused to return to classes, they ordered the closing of the college. College president J. R. Otis, who wanted to fire King, was threatened by the trustees and later resigned. John D. Boyd was brought in by the trustees as the new president, but students packed their belongings and left the campus. Some students decided to return to campus the following week (NYT).

21 In Birmingham, Ala., the car of the white supporter of the anti-segregation campaign was attacked by a mob of whites while Rev. Frank Shuttlesworth sat in at a "white" waiting room in the railroad terminal. When police prevented the attackers from reaching Rev. Shuttlesworth, the mob then turned on Lamar Weaver, who was waiting in his car (JM).

28 In University, Ala., seventy hooded Klansmen disrupted a forum on race relations being held at the University of Alabama Methodist Students Center. Their spokesman read a statement that said, "The University of Alabama is a white man's school. It has always been that way and we intend for it to stay that way." After the Klansmen left, Dr. Paul Ramsey, who organized the forum, went on with the program (JM).

APRIL 1957

1 In Durham, N.C., law students at Duke University voted in favor of a resolution calling for the university to end discriminatory practices in all its schools and colleges, and to omit all references to race and religion on application forms. A similar resolution was passed by Duke's Women's College and the Divinity School (SSN).

I In Little Rock, Ark., two candidates who endorsed the gradual integration of the city's public schools were elected to the school board. Henry V. Rath and Wayne Upton won their seats opposing two staunch segregationists, Robert Ewing Brown and George Branscum (SSN).

I In Purcellville, Va., after interior designer Samuel C. Murray threatened to sue the trustees of the city library for not allowing him to use the facilities because he was an African American, the trustees voted 7 to 5 to desegregate all library facilities. Following announcement of the decision, white segregationists vowed to seek private support for the library rather than allow integration (SSN).

4 In Santa Barbara, Calif., the Interfraternity Council at Santa Barbara College passed a resolution calling on all eight fraternities to end racial discrimination in membership. Most allow "Christians of the Caucasian race only" to join the fraternities (JM).

6 In Washington, D.C., plans were announced for a "prayer pilgrimage" and march on Washington on 17 May 1957 in support of public school integration and to protest increasing racial violence in the South. The chairpersons—Martin Luther King, Roy Wilkins, and A. Philip Randolph—invited sixty religious, fraternal, educational, civic, and labor leaders to a meeting in Washington to plan the event (NYT).

10 In Madison, Wis., the state supreme court ruled that two black bricklayers, Randolph Ross and James Harris, could be barred from membership in a Milwaukee, Wis., bricklayers union. Officials for the state's fair employment practices commission announced that they would appeal the decision to the U.S. Supreme Court (NYT).

II In Little Rock, Ark., two candidates who endorsed the gradual integration of the city's public schools were elected to the school board. Henry V. Rath and Wayne Upton won their seats opposing two staunch segregationists, Robert Ewing Brown and George Branscum (JM).

12 In the Bronx, N.Y., a public bathing club, The Castle Hill Beach Club, was ordered by the state court of appeals to open its facilities to African Americans after a complaint was filed with the New York State Commission on Discrimination by Anita Brown, a black woman who was denied admission. The state court of appeals upheld a lower court's ruling that the club must admit African Americans (NYT).

12 In Richmond, Va., state courts began preliminary hearings on cases designed to test the constitutionality of the four "anti-NAACP laws" passed by the state legislature. Among other things, these laws required the NAACP and other organizations advocating racial integration to register and provide membership information to the state attorney general (NYT).

14 In New Brunswick, N.J., officials at Rutgers University ordered an end to discriminatory clauses in the constitutions of fraternities by 1 September 1959. At Stanford University, Palo Alto, Calif., presidents of twenty-four fraternities went on record opposing membership restrictions based on race and religion. Thirteen of the fraternities have restrictive clauses in their national constitutions (NYT).

17 In New Orleans, La., a federal court declared unconstitutional the state law requiring certificates of eligibility for admission to state colleges and universities. The measure was introduced to limit the enrollment of black students, and the courts ordered that more than one hundred black students, who had been kept from enrolling because they did not have the certificates, be admitted to several colleges in the state (NYT).

18 In Oklahoma City, Okla., for the first time in the state's history, Gov. Raymond Gary declared 26 and 27 April "NAACP Days" in conjunction with an NAACP youth conference taking place in Oklahoma City. In the proclamation issued by the governor, he stated the importance of developing "a climate of tolerance to help eliminate prejudices in the minds of people of all races" (JM).

18 In Terrell County, Ga., Rev. Gerald Kersey (white) was dismissed from his pastorate at New Bethel Baptist Church because he expressed his belief that "segregation is un-Christian" (JM).

19 In Tallahassee, Fla., Gov. LeRoy Collins vowed to veto bills passed by the state legislature condemning the Supreme Court's school desegregation decision and preventing the implementation of school integration in the state. Subsequently, the Education Committee of the state senate voted 26 to 16 against the bill that would have allowed local districts to close public schools rather than integrate (NYT).

20 In Washington, D.C., AFL-CIO president George Meany announced that a Cleveland local of the International Brotherhood of Electrical Workers (IBEW) was given until 1 July 1957 to revoke its discriminatory policies or face expulsion from the federation. The measure was taken after Theodore Pinkston, a black electrician, was refused a city job because he did not belong to the union. Meany's decision led to the resignation of James R. Carey, IBEW president, from the AFL-CIO's Civil Rights Committee (NYT).

24 In Atlanta, Ga., the state board of education passed a resolution banning participation by any public school students, teachers, and administrators in interracial activities sponsored by outside organizations such as the 4-H Clubs, the YMCA or YWCA (NYT).

25 In Chicago, Ill., a series of racially motivated murders shocked residents. Three white teenagers had been accused of murdering Curtis Bevins, the latest victim of racial attacks that began in July 1956. Mayor Richard J. Daley promised that the police department would take prompt action against those involved in racial violence in the city (NYT).

25 In Richmond, Va., Gov. Thomas Stanley was embarrassed when he learned that invitations to an all-white dinner sponsored by the state's Chamber of Commerce to honor "distinguished" Virginians also were sent to black NAACP members, including Dr. Cillian Powell, publisher of the *Amsterdam News*; Ella P. Stewart, past president of the National Association of Colored Women; and New York judge Edward R. Dudley. Gov. Stanley said, "It was an awful mistake" (JM).

25 In Washington, D.C., Rep. Adam Clayton Powell called upon the secretaries of the army, navy, and air force to investigate complaints he received from black soldiers stationed in Japan who claimed that they had been discriminated against in clubs, cabarets, and other public places. Two years earlier, Powell called for a probe of complaints coming from black soldiers in France. The investigation led to an end of discriminatory treatment (JM).

27 In Greensboro, N.C., federal judge Johnson J. Hayes ordered officials at a city-owned, though privately operated, golf course to admit African Americans by 5 June 1957. Even though the lease was held privately, Judge Hayes ruled that publicly owned facilities could not deny entrance to black residents (NYT).

30 In Albany, N.Y., Gov. Averell Harriman signed into law a bill banning discrimination in the hiring of apprentices in the state building trades. The bill also allowed the New York State Labor Relations Board to investigate and determine bargaining agents selected by employees. Sponsored by the New York State Commission Against Discrimination, this was believed to be the first state law banning discrimination against minority group members seeking apprenticeships (NYT).

30 In Greensboro, N.C., after Rev. Melvin Swann was ordered to the Jim Crow balcony of a local movie theater showing *The Ten Commandments*, a mass meeting was held and local NAACP president Dr. Edson Edmonds called for a boycott of the city's movie houses (NYT).

30 In Washington, D.C., the U.S. Supreme Court ruled unanimously that Girard College officials in Philadelphia may not exclude African American orphans from the school, despite Stephen Girard's will, which limited students to white orphan boys. The court declared that since the school was administered by the City Board of Trusts, a state agency, failure to admit African Americans was in effect "state discrimination" (NYT).

MAY 1957

1 In Fairfax County, Va., when Mrs. Theo De-Febio (white) refused to sign pupil placement applications, a device to keep public schools seg-

NONVIOLENT PROTESTS SPREAD TO OTHER SOUTHERN CITIES

The successful bus boycott in Montgomery, Ala., that led to the Supreme Court upholding the lower court's ruling in *Browder v. Gayle* not only triggered violent responses by southern whites opposed to desegregation, but also nonviolent direct action protest campaigns by African Americans in other southern communities. In January 1957 in Montgomery, after the bombing of Ralph Abernathy's First Baptist Church and several other black churches and homes, city officials decided to halt all bus service temporarily. The following month Montgomery's new police chief George J. Ruppenthal arrested five Klan members and charged them with the seven bombings and six attacks on black bus passengers. At their trials in May and June, the five were found not guilty by an all-white jury. In Tallahassee, Fla., the state committee set up to investigate the NAACP's role in the seven-month bus boycott in 1956 uncovered a cache of one hundred sticks of dynamite that an unidentified informant claimed were to be used to blow up a black housing project in the city.

In June 1957 Alabama state senator Samuel Engelhardt introduced legislation to change the boundaries of the city of Tuskegee to remove the black neighborhoods from the city limits in order to maintain white control in the predominantly black area. In response, the Tuskegee Civic Association (TCA) was formed and launched a boycott of forty white-owned stores in the city, following the merchants' outspoken support for the legislation.

Within a month white businesses began to feel the effects of the boycott (black residents outnumbered whites 4 to 1 in the city and surrounding Macon County), and in July, state officials launched a raid on the TCA's offices to locate "incriminating evidence." In August, circuit court judge Will O. Walton issued an injunction against the TCA's leaders, Rev. K. L. Buford and Charles G. Gomillion, ordering them to end the seven-week boycott of white merchants. Buford declared that there was "no injunction, no threat that can make us spend our money where we don't want to." Meanwhile, the Klan stepped up its activities in the area, riding into the nearby town of Maplesville and firing shots at six black men. The local police investigated the incident but made no arrests.

Despite regular threats and intimidation, and a fire of suspicious origin that destroyed the city's largest black grocery store, owned by Emmanuel Miller, at the end of the year the TCA and black residents vowed to continue the boycott until black neighborhoods were brought back within the city limits.

Black citizens in Rock Hill, S.C., in August 1957 launched a boycott of the local bus company that continued to force black passengers to give up their seats to whites. Under the leadership of Rev. Cecil Ivory, chair of the local NAACP, black residents organized the Committee for the Protection of Human Rights, which coordinated the boycott. The protest was so effective that within two months the Star Bus Company in Rock Hill went out of business.

In Birmingham, Ala., when twenty-two of the forty black citizens arrested in December 1956 for violating bus segregation laws were convicted in March 1957 and fined fifty dollars each by Judge Ralph E. Parker, they subsequently filed a countersuit against the Birmingham Transit Company for violating their civil rights. In September, violence erupted when Rev. Fred Shuttlesworth attempted to enroll four black children at an all-white school. This was the third time in less than a year that Shuttlesworth had been attacked by white mobs opposed to any attempts to desegregate public accommodations in Birmingham.

regated, for her two children, they were not allowed to enroll. Mrs. DeFebio refused legal assistance from the NAACP and other groups but planned to keep her children out of segregated public schools (SSN).

1–3 In Chicago, Ill., at a two-day conference of the President's Committee on Government Contracts, Vice Pres. Richard Nixon declared that there was "a real pattern of discrimination" by employers in the Chicago region who held government contracts. Nixon called for the enforcement of the federal government's nondiscrimination policies, which would help end job discrimination (NYT).

2 In Baltimore, Md., Howard University professor M. Wharton Young, who was scheduled to deliver a paper at the American Association of Anatomists annual meeting, boycotted the conference because of hotel discrimination. The members took no action on a resolution to hold future meetings only in cities that would provide hotel accommodations on a nondiscriminatory basis (JM).

2 In Ann Arbor, Mich., at the twenty-sixth annual meeting of the American Association of Physical Anthropologists, Dr. W. Montague Cobb, chairman of Howard University Medical School's Department of Anatomy in Washington, D.C., was unanimously elected president of the 450-member organization. Dr. Cobb became the first African American to head the national scientific society (JM).

2 In London, England, it was reported that the National Council Against Racial Discrimination was organized for the purpose of promoting racial equality in housing, hotels and restaurants, employment, and education. It was believed to be the first group of its type formed in Britain. In recent months leaflets had been distributed in London and other cities asking Britons to become members of the Ku Klux Klan (JM).

2 In Southwest Chicago, Ill., a white mob of 250 fired shotgun blasts into the building of Harry Gaynor, breaking out thirteen windows, after he rented a second-floor apartment to C. Joseph Clem, a black rehabilitation counselor, and his family. Although both families sent the young children away, the Gaynors and Clems decided to stay in the building after receiving moral support from the NAACP and the Mayor's Commission on Human Relations (JM).

9 In Tyler, Tex., district court judge Otis Dunagan issued a permanent injunction requiring the NAACP to pay back taxes to the state and pay litigation costs for the nine-month trial. Duna-

gan also issued a permanent injunction barring NAACP operation in Texas except under "certain conditions." NAACP officials said they would appeal the ruling (NYT).

15 In Springfield, Ill., a measure guaranteeing equal employment opportunities to minority group members failed to be passed by a state senate committee. Attempts to override the committee's action failed on the senate floor because of opposition from Republican politicians (NYT).

16 In Montgomery, Ala., the 22 March 1956 conviction of Martin Luther King for his role in the bus boycott was overturned on a technicality by the Alabama Court of Appeals. The court reporter's failure to file the case within sixty days triggered the dismissal (JM).

16 In New Orleans, La., federal district court judge J. Skelly Wright ruled that state laws requiring segregation on city buses, streetcars, and public parks were unconstitutional, and permanent injunctions would be issued to end enforcement of the laws (NYT).

18 In Washington, D.C., an estimated twenty-five thousand people from thirty states attended the Prayer Pilgrimage for Freedom and heard addresses by Revs. C. K. Steele, Fred Shuttlesworth, Martin Luther King, Rep. Adam Clayton Powell, and others. Among the chants heard was "Give us the ballot" and calls for putting more pressure on elected officials to implement public school integration and to pass civil rights legislation (NYT).

23 In New York City, officials for the New York Public Library announced that the board of trustees accepted a bust of Dr. W. E. B. Du Bois by sculptor William Zorach for the Schomberg Collection on Negro Literature and History, located in Harlem. Although Dr. Du Bois had been criticized by government officials for his "leftist sympathies," the library accepted the bust because he is considered "a great Negro historian" (JM).

24 In Philadelphia, Pa., Edward W. Oescher, president of the Girard College Alumni Board of Governors, announced plans by the group to fight the implementation of the Supreme Court's decision allowing black orphan boys to attend the school. The Philadelphia City Board of Trusts asked the Supreme Court to reconsider its decision (NYT).

25 In Clinton, Tenn., where white mobs attempted to prevent public school integration in September 1956, Bobby Cain became the first African American to graduate from the Clinton High School. Commencement exercises were integrated (NYT).

30 In Harrisburg, Pa., following an investigation of practices in the state's twenty-four hundred school districts authorized by Gov. George Leader, it was reported that three still maintained segregated public schools, even though they were illegal. Coatesville, Kennett Square, and Steelton-Highspire continued the practice of segregating black and white students in public elementary schools (JM).

30 In Fort Worth, Tex., the Urban League branch lost $9,500 in funding from the United Fund following accusations from a White Citizens Council group in St. Louis that the organization was "antiwhite." This was the latest withdrawal of funding from branches in the South, but Urban League president Lester Granger said loss of United Fund and Community Chest funds was made up by increases in individual contributions (JM).

30 In Prince Georges County, Md., school superintendent William Schmidt, responding to inquiries from the local NAACP, stated that there were no plans to have "mixed" faculties in the public schools. The Supreme Court's *Brown* decision, according to Schmidt, did not deal with integration of teachers (JM).

JUNE 1957

1 In Loram, Miss., although controversial history professor Clennon King had earlier declined an invitation to return to Alcorn A&M College because of death threats, renewed unrest was reported on the campus following King's return. King's pro-segregation article touched off a campus boycott by students and resignation of the college president. NAACP officials and the Regional Council of Negro Leadership began fund-raising campaigns to provide financial assistance to the twelve students who were expelled over the boycott and were forced to enroll in new schools. Three expelled students were already enrolled at Central State University in Ohio (SSN).

1 In Charlottesville, Va., NAACP officials were subpoenaed by the state's Committee on Offenses Against the Administration of Justice and must produce financial and other records. Membership lists were requested earlier in the year, and the organization planned to take that issue to the state court of appeals in September (SSN).

1 In New Orleans, La., bowing to pressure from white segregationists, officials for the Community Chest voted to drop the local Urban League from its membership. The executive director J. Harvey Kearns revealed that the league's receipts from that fund averaged sixteen thousand dollars annually (SSN).

5 In Cleveland, Ohio, fourteen black railroad firemen filed suit in U.S. district court to strike down the Brotherhood of Locomotive Firemen and Enginemen's rules that limit membership to whites. The suit was brought because black firemen had no say in the labor negotiations with employers that determine wages and working conditions (NYT).

6 In New York City, at the forty-third annual meeting of the American Association of University Professors, a resolution was passed upholding the right of any professor to belong to any organization opposed to legal segregation. The resolution also opposed any legislation that would "deny or inhibit" this right (JM).

10 In New York City, the New York State Commission Against Discrimination announced that public hearings would be held to investigate charges of discriminatory hiring practices by Trans World Airlines. Scheduled to testify was Dorothy Franklin, who filed a complaint against the airline after she was denied employment as a stewardess (NYT).

13 In Detroit, Mich., the NAACP leveled five complaints of excessive brutality against city police officers. NAACP executive secretary Arthur Johnson claimed that police violence against black citizens was on the increase in the city (JM).

13 In London, England, Ian Shaw, the grand dragon of the British branch of the Klan, went on television to report that the group was all but dead in that country. Scotland Yard, working with the FBI, planned on halting the flow of Klan literature into England (JM).

14 In Washington, D.C., Martin Luther King and Ralph David Abernathy met with Vice Pres. Richard Nixon and Labor Secretary James P. Mitchell for two hours and discussed the state of race relations in the country. King emphasized the need for strong voting rights legislation to restore black civil rights in the southern states and urged Nixon to come to the South and speak out on the civil rights issue (NYT).

15 In Washington, D.C., the proposed amendment offered by southern Democrats to the civil rights bill was defeated in the House of Representatives by a vote of 199 to 167. The amendment sought to allow jury trials for those indicted for civil rights violations (NYT).

19 In Greensboro, N.C., Martha S. Brisbane filed suit in federal court challenging the legality of segregated eating facilities at the Greensboro–High Point Airport. The black New York native was refused service in the airport restaurant earlier in the year (NYT).

20 In Memphis, Tenn., although the federal courts ordered Memphis State College to admit black students, school officials still continued to reject African Americans who applied for admission. Maxine Smith, who had a master's degree from Middlebury College, and Miriam Sugerman, who was a graduate of Wellesley College, were both denied admission to the graduate school at Memphis State on "technicalities" (JM).

STATE BANS ON INTERRACIAL SPORTS COMPETITION

In the year that tennis star Althea Gibson became the first African American to win both the women's singles title at the Wimbledon Tennis Tournament in England and the U.S. Open women's title at Forest Hills, N.Y., laws passed in Louisiana, Georgia, and Alabama banning interracial sports competitions continued to plague team owners, players, and fans. In Shreveport, La., Bonneau Peters, owner of the Pelicans baseball team, announced in August that the team would be sold because of low attendance at games. Black baseball fans launched a boycott of the team because of the law that prohibited interracial sports teams from playing in the state. In September in Birmingham, Ala., when the Detroit Lions played an exhibition game with the Washington Redskins, fullback John Henry Johnson, the only African American on the Lions team, was not allowed to play because of the state law barring interracial athletic competitions.

In New Orleans, La., in August 1957, lightweight boxer Ralph Dupas was barred from fighting white opponents by the state athletic commission after Christopher Duplessis, a black man, claimed that Dupas was his nephew. Dupas disputed the claim before the state commission in September, presenting various documents that stated he was white. The commission agreed to allow Dupas to fight white boxers pending a formal court ruling on his racial status.

When the officials of the National Boxing Association met in Denver, Colo., in October, they failed to pass a resolution opposing southern state laws prohibiting interracial athletic competitions. Several boxing officials stated that they took no action because they believed these laws would soon be repealed. New Orleans district court judge Rene Viosca finally ordered the issuing of a birth certificate to boxer Ralph Dupas at the end of October, stating he was white and thus allowing him to participate in matches in the state with white contenders. Unfortunately, Dupas would not be able to fight for the title in his home state because the world lightweight boxing champion in 1957 was Joe Brown, a black man.

22 In Atlanta, Ga., the state revenue department ordered the NAACP to pay $17,459 in back taxes after the group's tax-exempt status was revoked. State NAACP president John H. Calhoun was sent to jail for refusing to open the organization's books to state agents, but through a court order the records were examined by Georgia revenue agents in the New York headquarters. Roy Wilkins later declared that the NAACP would not pay the tax assessment and planned to appeal the court order to open its books (NYT).

27 In Atlanta, Ga., Rev. Samuel W. Williams and Rev. John T. Porter filed a suit in federal court against the Atlanta Transit System and other state agencies and officials after they were forced to move to the rear of a city bus. The ministers were seeking an injunction to prevent further segregation (JM).

27 In Detroit, Mich., at the NAACP's forty-eighth annual convention, greetings were received from President Eisenhower, but Herbert Hill, the organization's labor secretary, declared the President's Committee on Government Contracts was failing to enforce the anti-discrimination clauses in federal contracts. Americans for Democratic Action (ADA) vice chair Joseph Rauh, Jr., called on Attorney General Herbert Brownell to bring a test case to determine whether the laws passed by the southern states to ban the NAACP violated federal civil rights statutes (NYT).

27 In Shreveport, La., although three black ministers, T. B. Simpson, L. B. Sims, and J. R. Rutledge, were not arrested for sitting in the white section of a trolley, police officials warned that others attempting to ride on a nonsegregated basis would be jailed (JM).

29 In Detroit, Mich., Dr. Martin Luther King, Jr., received the prestigious Spingarn Medal at the NAACP's annual meeting. Awarded annually to the individual who made the most important contribution to the improvement of race relations, King at age twenty-eight was the youngest of the medal's forty-two recipients (NYT).

JULY 1957

1 In Atlanta, Ga., officials for the Community Chest announced that the charges brought against the local Urban League by the States Rights Council of Georgia were "baseless" and the organization would continue to receive funding. The white supremacist group claimed that the Urban League engaged in "civil disobedience and violence throughout the nation" (SSN).

4 In Baltimore, Md., as a result of a court order to admit African Americans to the local typographical union, three black workers were able to get positions as linotype operators on daily newspapers. Henry Wedley and Emerson L. Coleman were admitted to the union and were hired by the *Sun* newspaper, and Leslie L. Bell obtained a position on the *News-Post* (JM).

9 In Detroit, Mich., a riot almost erupted when police officers tried to arrest Elijah Walker, a member of the Nation of Islam, who was addressing a crowd of three hundred. Eight policemen and eleven civilians were injured in the ensuing conflict, and nine black men were arrested. Police commissioner Edward Piggins claimed that Walker was making a "deliberate attempt to incite violence" (NYT).

11 In Los Angeles, Calif., schoolteachers Evangeline Johnson and Ella Redmond were harassed by whites who hurled rocks through their windows and burned a cross on their lawn after they moved into an all-white neighborhood. The two sisters complained that the local police failed to act to prevent the attacks (JM).

14 In Richmond, Va., the U.S. circuit court of appeals ruled that the pupil-placement law passed by the Virginia legislature to avoid public school integration was unconstitutional. State officials promised to appeal the measure to the U.S. Supreme Court (NYT).

17 In Wilmington, Del., U.S. district court judge Paul Leahy ordered state board of education officials to submit a plan by September 1957 for the integration of public schools in that state. Black parents had filed the petition after their children were denied admission to seven all-white public schools in the state (NYT).

18 In **Charlottesville, Va.**, after University of Virginia graduate student James L. Williams and his family moved into the all-white campus housing project, a protest demonstration was held by the local White Citizens Council. Residents of the university housing project asked for police protection following the demonstration (JM).

18 In **Durham, N.C.**, Rev. Douglas E. Moore and six others were arrested when they refused to leave an ice-cream parlor's "white" section. Moore declared that "there is no state law saying we should be discriminated against," but the seven were arrested, charged with trespassing, found guilty by a jury, and fined ten dollars each (NYT).

25 In **Detroit, Mich.**, five black ministers filed a $50,000 federal lawsuit against the Statler-Hilton Hotel chain after they allegedly were refused service by hotel managers in Dallas, Tex. The ministers claimed that their reservations were not honored when they arrived to attend the National Baptist Sunday School Convention (JM).

25 In **Gulfport, Miss.**, despite threats from Gov. J. P. Coleman that "imported agitators" would be arrested, executive secretary Roy Wilkins spoke at the annual meeting of the state's NAACP branches (JM).

31 In **San Francisco, Calif.**, the recently passed fair employment practices ordinance went into effect, and Yellow Cab Company officials announced that they would begin to hire African Americans as drivers. Black residents in the city had refused for years to patronize Yellow Cabs because of its discriminatory hiring practices (NYT).

AUGUST 1957

1 In **Chapel Hill, N.C.**, Bennett College graduate Carolyn Ingram was admitted to the School of Social Work and became the first black woman admitted to the University of North Carolina (JM).

1 In **Chicago, Ill.**, the city council's Health Committee, headed by Alderman William Harvey, passed a resolution calling for the end of alleged discrimination at city hospitals against black physicians. A recent survey revealed that in the city's forty-six hospitals there were no African American doctors with staff appointments (JM).

1 In **Greenville, Miss.**, according to a report to the *Delta Democrat-Times* as many as thirty-one professors have resigned their positions at the University of Mississippi because of the lack of academic freedom on the segregation issue. Low salaries was given as a secondary cause for the resignations (SSN).

6 In **Washington, D.C.**, President Eisenhower named Chicago clergyman and former alderman Archibald J. Carey, Jr., chair of the seven-member Committee on Government Employment Policy. Carey became the first African American to head a White House committee (NYT).

10 In **Cleveland, Ohio**, the U.S. Sixth Circuit Court of Appeals threw out the desegregation plan submitted by Tennessee's state board of education, which called for the desegregation of the six state colleges and universities at the undergraduate level over a four-year period. Black students had already been admitted to the graduate programs at the Tennessee state universities in 1955 (NYT).

15 In **Lansing, Mich.**, state attorney general Thomas J. Kavanagh declared that the refusal by privately owned Haven Hill Nursing Home in Benzie County to admit African Americans as patients was not in violation of the state's civil rights laws (JM).

15–20 In **Levittown, Pa.**, four days of violence by white mobs forced World War II veteran William J. Meyers and his family to flee their newly purchased home in the all-white planned community. Following the mob action, Gov. George Leader dispatched state troopers to the area to prevent further violence (NYT).

22 In **Dutchtown, La.**, Archbishop Clarence C. Addison, head of the African Universal Church, denounced the integrationist activities of the NAACP and condemned the organization's interference in race relations in the South. Addison denied sug-

SHOWDOWN AT CENTRAL HIGH SCHOOL
IN LITTLE ROCK, ARKANSAS

Daisy Bates, president of the Arkansas NAACP, had been working on the integration plans with superintendent Virgil Blossom and other school officials for more than a year. After much delay and litigation in the federal courts, nine black students were scheduled to be enrolled in Little Rock's Central High School on 4 September 1957. However, when mobs of angry whites threatened violence, police chief Marvin Potts was not sure he would be able to protect the students. Daisy Bates reached eight of the youths to tell them to assemble at her home rather than attempt to enter the school, but Elizabeth Eckford's parents had no phone. When she showed up in front of Central High that morning, Elizabeth Eckford was jeered at and taunted by scores of whites, but her grace under pressure was captured by news photographers on the scene from around the world. Later that day, Gov. Orval Faubus, who had opposed the integration plans from the beginning, decided to call out the Arkansas National Guard to prevent the students from entering the school.

In Clinton, Tenn., and Milford, Del., in 1955 and 1956, when confronted by federal court orders to allow black children to enroll in all-white schools, the governors called out the states' National Guards to enforce the courts' rulings. In Little Rock, Governor Faubus was using the state troops to *prevent* the carrying out of federal court orders. After hearing Justice Department attorneys argue that Governor Faubus's actions were obstructing the implementation of federal court orders, Judge John Davies issued an injunction on 20 September against the governor, forcing him to remove the National Guardsmen from Central High School.

On 22 September 1957, with National Guardsmen removed, Daisy Bates escorted the nine black students through a back entrance into Central High School. Violence and mob action soon erupted in Little Rock's entire downtown area. By 2:00 P.M. Chief Potts realized that he could not protect the children given this reign of terror, and Daisy Bates had to take the nine out of the school through the back entrance. The children remained at home the next day, but news was soon released that President Eisenhower had federalized the Arkansas National Guard and Defense Secretary Charles Wilson had ordered one thousand paratroopers from the 101st Airborne "Screaming Eagle" Division of the 327th Infantry to Little Rock. That evening Eisenhower went on national television and declared that "disorderly mobs" would not prevent "the carrying out of proper orders from the federal court."

The following morning, 24 September, the paratroopers, under the leadership of Major General Edwin Walker, escorted Daisy Bates and the children into Central High School. The paratroopers remained there until 30 September, when they were moved to nearby Camp Robinson. They were replaced by members of the federalized Arkansas National Guard. Although the Little Rock Nine were victimized by harassment and insults through the end of the school year, the presence of National Guardsmen on patrol at the school prevented any further violence.

gestions that his church received funds from the White Citizens Councils (JM).

22 In Chicago, Ill., *Ebony* magazine (September 1957) began publishing a regular column authored by Martin Luther King entitled "Advice on Living." The column would be devoted to answering queries on life and religion (JM).

25 In the southern states, at the beginning of the 1957–58 school year, public school systems in Virginia, Alabama, Louisiana, South Carolina, Florida, and Georgia remained segregated. In Oklahoma, it was reported that 210 of its 261 school districts had begun the desegregation process (NYT).

28 In New York City, officials for Trans World Airlines announced the appointment of James Plinton as executive assistant to the vice president for personnel. TWA was under investigation by the New York State Commission Against Discrimination because of its unfair hiring practices (NYT).

29 In Washington, D.C., following complaints made by Rev. B. Reaves Britt, the President's Committee on Government Contracts made a recommendation to the Lockheed Corporation that it end Jim Crow practices at its Marietta, Ga., plant. Britt revealed that the company was in violation of Executive Order 10590 because segregation was in effect in the company cafeteria, rest rooms, and work areas. The Lockheed Corporation had several government contracts (JM).

30 In Washington, D.C., through the efforts of Democratic leader Lyndon B. Johnson, the first civil rights bill in eighty-two years was passed in the Senate by a vote of 60 to 15. The compromise measure called for the creation of a civil rights division within the Justice Department; interference with an individual's voting rights was made a federal offense; the attorney general was authorized to prosecute voting rights abuses; and the president was to appoint a bipartisan commission on civil rights that would investigate complaints of discrimination in voting and make recommendations to the Justice Department for action (NYT).

31 In Clinton, Tenn., where violence marked the attempts to enroll black children in all-white public schools at the beginning of the 1956–57 school year, there were no incidents on the first day of school and a larger number of black students were enrolled in previously all-white public schools (NYT).

SEPTEMBER 1957

1 In the state of Alabama, a law went into effect without the signature of Gov. James Folsom that gave local school boards greater power over pupil placement and made school board members "judicial officers" not subject to prosecution and damage suits (SSN).

5 In Chicago, Ill., at the annual convention of the American Federation of Teachers, the executive council refused to reconsider its 1 January 1958 deadline for the end of segregated teachers locals in the South. The southern delegates in attendance claimed they needed more time to merge the black

and white locals. After the ultimatum was issued in August 1956, the 1,855-member Atlanta local withdrew from the federation (JM).

12 In Monroe, N.C., Dr. Albert J. Perry and NAACP president Robert F. Williams asked the board of aldermen to integrate public recreational facilities in the city following the death of a black boy in an unsupervised swimming hole. Despite threats on his life, Dr. Perry testified before the city aldermen, who decided to take his request under advisement (JM).

12 In Nashville, Tenn., a federal court issued an order enjoining white groups from preventing the integration of public elementary schools. Police guarded the schools around the clock and mob agitation had ceased by the second week of classes. National Association for the Advancement of White People leader John Kasper, who had been leading the white protests, was arrested and fined two hundred dollars by a Nashville judge (NYT).

12 In Washington, D.C., the president's newly formed Committee on Government Employment Policy, chaired by Archibald Carey, announced that the members would make a nationwide inspection tour of government installations to determine the hiring and promotion practices regarding minority workers (JM).

12, 13, 19 In Charlotte, N.C., Dorothy Counts, the first black student, faced screaming white mobs as she entered Harding High School. White Citizens Council members attempted to block her enrollment, and the police eventually arrested two white students for disorderly conduct. The violence and harassment by white students forced Dorothy Counts eventually to withdraw from the school. In Ozark, Ark., death threats leveled at Rayford and Inola West (black) led to the removal of their two children from the local public school by police (NYT).

19 In Chicago, Ill., Mayor Richard J. Daley issued a press release disputing the critical statements made by the Urban League's executive secretary Edwin Berry in a speech in Detroit at the group's annual convention. Berry charged that the reason there was so much racial violence and housing segregation in the city was because "Chicago accepts it." Following Daley's press release, the local Urban League president, Dr. N. O. Calloway, issued a conciliatory statement praising the mayor's record in the field of race relations (JM).

19 In Levittown, Pa., four "Molotov cocktail–type bombs" were found near the home of William J. Meyers, who was the victim the previous month of white mob action when he moved into his new home. Police were called and removed the bombs and promised to make an investigation (JM).

19 In Washington, D.C., White House aides announced that President Eisenhower would hold private meetings with several black leaders, including Rep. Adam Clayton Powell, AME bishop D. Ward Nichols, Baptist leader William Jernagin, and several others, to discuss civil rights issues. The White House failed to comment on possible meetings with Roy Wilkins and other NAACP leaders (NYT).

26 In Amherst, Mass., two University of Massachusetts fraternities, Theta Xi and Phi Gamma Delta, that pledged black students were suspended by their national bodies. Both planned to operate as independent fraternities until their appeals of the action were taken up at the national conventions (NYT).

26 In Jackson, Miss., state representative Upton Sisson suggested that in light of the new civil rights law guaranteeing voting rights, it was possible that African Americans would be elected to political office in the thirty-two predominantly black counties. Sisson called on state legislators to revise the state constitution and reapportion legislative districts to prevent the election of African Americans to public offices (JM).

26 In Washington, D.C., officials for Radio Free Europe announced the appointment of National Council of Negro Women president Vivian Carter Mason to a fifty-one-member mission to Europe to inspect installations and to determine the effectiveness of programs aimed at the residents of Eastern Europe (JM).

1 In Columbia, S.C., after Hungarian exchange student Andre Toth was admitted to AME-sponsored Allen University, the state board of education sent a notice to university president Frank R. Veal that graduates from the school would be denied certificates to teach in the state. Despite the state action, Veal declared that he would allow the Hungarian student to remain at the college (SSN).

2 In Colp, Ill., following the decision of the local school board to integrate public schools, a bomb damaged the nightclub owned by board president William Hatchet. The FBI was called in by the local police to investigate the incident (NYT).

3 In Chicago, Ill., in an address before the annual meeting of the United Packinghouse Workers Union, Martin Luther King declared that the road to equal rights for African Americans was through the voting booth. With regard to the crisis in Little Rock, Ark., King suggested that, "if he [President Eisenhower] had taken a stronger stand earlier in the Little Rock situation, he might not have had to send troops" (NYT).

3 In Chicago, Ill., in the October 1957 issue of *Ebony* magazine, singer and actor Paul Robeson denounced the U.S. State Department, which denied him a passport because of his favorable statements about the Soviet Union. Robeson also criticized black leaders who did not support him in his battles with the government (JM).

3 In Fort Lauderdale, Fla., when the publicly owned Golf and Country Club was ordered by the circuit court to open its doors to black players, city officials sold the club to a private golf association rather than integrate (NYT).

3 In Washington, D.C., it was announced that Chicago attorney and former United Nations U.S. alternate delegate Edith Sampson was named to the Democratic National Committee's Advisory Committee on Foreign Policy. Sampson, who also served as a member-at-large of the U.S. Commission for UNESCO, was the only African American appointed to the advisory committee (JM).

5 In Philadelphia, Pa., after refusing to allow the admission of two black boys, the orphans court paved the way for the appointment of thirteen new trustees for Girard College to replace the City Board of Trusts that had previously administered the school. Ordered by the U.S. Supreme Court to admit black boys, the new trustees were expected to sidestep the court's ruling. City officials promised to appeal the orphans court's decision to the Pennsylvania Supreme Court (NYT).

12 In Baton Rouge, La., twelve-year-old Barbara Ann Remo was barred from playing in a concert with the New Orleans Symphony Orchestra because of the state law prohibiting interracial activities. Remo was chosen after a statewide competition to appear in a concert to be broadcast by radio throughout the state (NYT).

16 In Houston, Tex., after a suit was filed by black parents, federal judge Ben Connally ordered the desegregation of the local public schools but gave school officials no specific date by which to comply (NYT).

17 In San Francisco, Calif., Vice Pres. Richard Nixon declared that integration was even more necessary given the Soviet Union's launching of the *Sputnik* satellite. "We can't afford having substantial numbers of our citizens having a second-class education. We need more George Washington Carvers and people of that caliber" (NYT).

22 In Washington, D.C., the U.S. Supreme Court refused to review a lower court's order to integrate the Norfolk and Newport News, Va., public schools. Federal circuit court judge Walter Hoffman had declared unconstitutional the state's new pupil placement law, which authorized a board appointed by the governor to make all student placements in public schools (NYT).

24 In Chicago, Ill., the city council passed by a vote of 43 to 0 its first civil rights law. The measure banned discrimination on the basis of race, creed, color, or national origin in all public accommodations (JM).

24 In Little Rock, Ark., Urban League president Edwin Dunaway announced that the group would voluntarily withdraw from the local Community Chest. Pressure from the White Citizens Council led to decreased contributions to the Chest last year; as a result, Urban League officials decided to withdraw and seek private donations instead (JM).

24 In Union County, S.C., local white residents purchased riot guns "to prevent a lawful and unlawful military or civilian invasion." State legislator John D. Long defended the purchase and claimed that the guns were considered a defense against federal troops forcing school integration, even though the possibility was still quite remote (JM).

27 In Pleasanton, Tex., the citizens voted 343 to 88 to integrate thirty-six black students into all-white schools, and Pleasanton became the first locality to approve integrated public schools under a new state law. According to the new law, any school district that implemented school desegregation without a majority vote of the residents would be denied state aid. There were 1,476 children in the Pleasanton public schools (NYT).

31 In Washington, D.C., the President's Committee on Government Contracts canceled scheduled public hearings in Atlanta. Committee members agreed that the climate in the South would make it impossible to do an acceptable job of investigating conditions for black workers among federal contractors (JM).

NOVEMBER 1957

1 In Deale, Md., when prominent black physician Harry N. Jones enrolled his adopted son in an all-white public school, bricks were showered on his home, crosses were burned on his lawn, and he received telephone threats. Dr. Jones decided to withdraw his son from the school. Local black residents were disappointed, but Dr. Jones said, "I'm no crusader." The school integration issue was considered dead in Deale (SSN).

1 In Monroe, N.C., NAACP leader Dr. Albert E. Perry, after receiving numerous death threats, was arrested and accused of performing an abortion on a twenty-five-year-old white woman. On hearing of the arrest, black residents went to the jail to make sure Dr. Perry was well and to pay his bail. Following the death of a black boy in a local swimming hole in July, Dr. Perry, Robert Williams, and other NAACP officers demanded that public swimming pools in the city be integrated, but city officials refused (SSN).

1 In Montgomery, Ala., the recent interview of Martin Luther King on NBC-TV with Martin Agron-sky was blacked out due to a power failure caused by a chain wrapped around the transmitter for station WSPA-TV (SSN).

1, 8 In Birmingham, Ala., six white men accused of castrating a black man, J. E. Aaron, were convicted by an all-white jury and given sentences of twenty years maximum. The six were members of the local Klan chapter (NYT).

CONCERTS, MOVIES, TELEVISION, AND CIVIL RIGHTS

After singer Nat King Cole was attacked by four white men during a concert before an all-white audience in Birmingham in April 1956, more and more black entertainers refused to perform before segregated audiences in the South. In Nashville, Tenn., at Fisk University, students organized the Social Action Committee that picketed Louis Armstrong's concert in March 1957 at the Municipal Auditorium before a segregated audience.

In April, when Hollywood producer Darryl Zanuck began publicizing his film *Island in the Sun*, which featured romantic relationships between the characters portrayed by Harry Belafonte and Joan Fontaine and John Justin and Dorothy Dandridge, southern politicians went into an uproar. In Columbia, S.C., the following month, legislators began debating a bill that provided a five-thousand-dollar fine for any movie theater in the state that showed *Island in the Sun*. Politicians in other southern states called for a boycott of the film.

When *Island in the Sun* opened in July 1957, Twentieth Century Fox announced that in its first two weeks, the controversial film grossed over $1.5 million and set box office records in some parts of the country. The threatened boycott by southerners because of the interracial romances depicted failed to affect the movie's early profits. However, in some southern cities picket lines appeared around theaters showing the film. In October in Atlanta, for example, state solicitor general Richard Bell used a court injunction to close a movie theater showing *Island in the Sun*, which was being picketed by more than five hundred people. In December at the annual meeting in Hollywood of the Motion Picture Association of America, however, a resolution was approved that revised the production codes to eliminate terms that tended "to incite bigotry or hatred among peoples of different racial, religious, or national backgrounds." The new provision called for an end of the use of "derogatory racial terms" in motion pictures.

Nat King Cole's weekly television show began airing in November 1956. Despite high ratings, executives for NBC-TV revealed in August 1957 that they were having difficulty finding sponsors. Spokespersons for Madison Avenue advertising agencies said there was fear that there would be resentment in the South against any company that sponsored the program. The show was broadcast by seventy-seven stations nationally, eighteen located in the South. After attempts to find a national sponsor failed, the show was able to pick up six sponsors at the local level in New York, California, Washington, and Pennsylvania, and others were sought. In October, however, claiming that there had been "a dispute over the time slot," NBC-TV officials announced that *The Nat King Cole Show* would be canceled and its last airing would be on 17 December 1957.

During the crisis in Little Rock, it was reported that Louis Armstrong, who had toured Europe several times as a U.S. "ambassador of goodwill," blasted government officials for their failure to act to protect the children integrating Central High School. The generally conservative Armstrong denounced President Eisenhower as "two-faced," claiming that "it's getting so a colored man hasn't got any country." When asked about future government-sponsored trips abroad, Armstrong responded, "The government can go to hell." After Eisenhower ordered U.S. paratroopers to Little Rock, Armstrong changed his tune, applauded the president's action, and said he would probably go to the Soviet Union for the U.S. government after all.

2 In Pleasanton, Tex., after citizens voted overwhelmingly to integrate local public schools, nine black students were welcomed into the high school and twenty-six black students were integrated into the elementary schools. High school principal Duard C. Baldee, who sent nine whites to escort the black students around during their first day of classes, said, "It was swell" (NYT).

3 In the 1957 elections, six of seven candidates who remained neutral on the public school integration issue were elected to serve in the newly formed city manager government in Little Rock, Ark., with overwhelming support from black voters. In Virginia, pro-segregationist J. Lindsay Almond, Jr., was elected governor. In Atlanta, Ga., despite charges by his opponent Lester Maddox that he was "catering to the Negro vote," Mayor William B. Hartsfield was reelected by a landslide and received overwhelming support from black voters. Atlanta University president Rufus Clement (black) was reelected to the school board (JM).

7 In New York City, according to a report in *The Wall Street Journal*, businesses with plants in the South had no intention "to hire Negroes for anything but janitorial work." An unnamed General Motors executive was quoted as stating, "When we moved into the South, we agreed to abide by local custom and not hire Negroes for production work. This is no time for social reforming in that area, and we're not about to try it." NAACP labor secretary Herbert Hill suggested that in order to change these practices, particularly among defense contractors, black employees would have to file complaints with the government in instances of discrimination and make sure that black youths enroll in industrial courses to prepare them for jobs in industry (JM).

7 In West Berlin, Germany, in light of the Texas law banning interracial marriages, thirty black soldiers married to German women were told by U.S. Army officials that they would have to leave their wives in Germany or transfer out of the Second Armored Division, which was being sent to Fort Hood, Tex. All of the soldiers applied for reassignments rather than leave their wives and families in Germany (NYT).

8 In Washington, D.C., President Eisenhower named those to be appointed to the newly created U.S. Commission on Civil Rights. They were Assistant Labor Secy. J. Ernest Wilkins, former Supreme Court justice Stanley F. Reed, former Virginia governor John S. Battle, Michigan State University president John Hannah, Notre Dame president Theodore Hesburgh, and Southern Methodist University Law School dean Robert G. Story (NYT).

9 In Nashville, Tenn., the state board of education lifted its ban on racial integration at state-supported colleges and called on administrators to admit "all qualified students." However, individual schools were given permission to limit enrollments when necessary. The Nashville school board also voted to comply with a recent court order and submit plans before 31 December 1957 for the integration of the public schools (NYT).

18 In New York City, National Urban League executive director Lester Granger announced that the organization was experiencing a serious financial crisis, forcing it to close regional offices in Atlanta and Los Angeles and branches in several cities. Granger said a major factor causing this situation was the pressure brought by the White Citizens Councils, forcing many branches out of local Community Chests and other fund-raising organizations (NYT).

20 In Washington, D.C., in the fourth annual report issued by the President's Committee on Government Contracts, the members noted that discrimination against black workers in industries with government contracts was greater in white-collar positions than in production and skilled positions. Black workers held white-collar positions primarily in the larger cities, such as Chicago, Philadelphia, and New York (NYT).

21 In Gaffney, S.C., the home of Claudia Thomas Sanders was bombed by unknown assailants. Sanders was the author of the book *South Carolinians Speak,* in which she advocated a moderate approach to race relations and the gradual abolition of the dual public school systems (NYT).

24 In Atlanta, Ga., a state house committee proposed an amendment to the state's constitution to add more restrictions on the right to vote. The proposed measure called for the withholding of voting privileges to anyone convicted of selling or possessing non-tax-paid liquor, child abandonment, adultery, common-law marriage, failure to register for military service, dishonorable discharge from the military service, or being the father of an illegitimate child (NYT).

28 In Colp, Ill., after three white members resigned from the local school board following a vote to merge the black and white public schools, the four remaining black members retained control of the system. White students refused to attend the consolidated public schools and enrolled in public schools in Carterville, Ill. (JM).

DECEMBER 1957

3 In Washington, D.C., AFL-CIO official Franz Daniel stated that increasing racial tensions were hurting the union movement in the South. Although eighty union organizers were active in the region, unions were defeated in recent elections in Madison and Ore Knob, N.C., because employers sent out letters claiming that the union would give white workers' jobs to blacks and that union dues would be used to finance campaigns for integration (NYT).

5 In Nashville, Tenn., under court order to come up with an integration plan by 31 December 1957, school board officials announced plans for opening schools for "whites only, Negroes only, and for parents who prefer integration." Attorney Coy Ennix, the only black school board member, said he thought the plan was unconstitutional (NYT).

6 In New York City, the city council passed a controversial housing law banning racial or religious discrimination in houses or apartment buildings of three or more units. The city's real estate agencies vigorously opposed the measure (NYT).

8 In Birmingham, Ala., the home of Robert Greer was bombed before he and his family were able to move in. Located in the predominantly white Fountain Heights section, this was the latest in a series of bombings aimed at black residents in the city (NYT).

12 In Montgomery, Ala., city officials promised to fight the proposed filming of the movie *The Montgomery Story* with Harry Belafonte as Martin Luther King, scheduled to begin filming in spring 1958. An unidentified city commissioner was quoted as saying they would fight the project because it merely sought "to praise and glorify Martin Luther King" (JM).

13 Throughout the southern states, anti-discrimination posters began to be displayed in post offices and on postal vehicles. The posters showed blacks and whites working together. The poster campaign was recommended by the President's Committee on Government Contracts as part of its efforts to improve race relations and increase minority employment in the federal government (NYT).

19 In Clarksdale, Miss., members of the Mississippi Council of Negro Leadership noted that no African Americans were registered to vote in thirty-one of the state's eighty-two counties. Council members pledged to use the new civil rights law to register between twenty-two thousand and one hundred thousand black voters (NYT).

22 In Atlanta, Ga., after the American Federation of Teachers announced that it would allow no segregated locals in the South, the officials in the Atlanta local decided to surrender their charter rather than integrate. Separate black and white teachers unions would be organized in the city (NYT).

On 10 November 1958, in Osage, West Virginia, a state trooper picked up the American flag from amid the debris in a classroom of the recently integrated junior high school. Earlier that day a dynamite charge placed in the front hall tore out a section of a wall, bowed a reinforced concrete ceiling, and shattered every window in the school's seventeen rooms. (SOURCE: CORBIS BETTMANN)

1958

"A BALM IN GILEAD"

The passage of the Civil Rights Act of 1957 focused attention on the need to restore voting rights to the southern black population. While the black vote in the North was becoming a decisive factor, particularly in close elections, and black voters elected to office effective and independent politicians, such as Harlem's Rev. Adam Clayton Powell, Jr., there was violent opposition in 1958 to any attempts to register African Americans to vote in the southern states. The Southern Christian Leadership Conference's Crusade for Citizenship met with only limited success, and NAACP leaders could provide little assistance because they were in the courts fighting to maintain the group's existence in the South. With the huge increase in the number of white southerners resorting to bombings and other acts of terrorism, many Americans, including southern politicians opposed to black civil rights, began to wonder whether "there is a balm in Gilead to heal the sin-sick soul."

JANUARY 1958

1 In New Orleans, La., the federal court of appeals overruled the lower court's decision that school integration in Dallas, Tex., must begin by January 1958. Although the suit was brought against the Dallas school board in 1955, the federal appeals judges decided to give school officials additional time to come up with an acceptable desegregation plan (SSN).

1 In Birmingham, Ala., Rev. Fred Shuttlesworth and other black parents filed suit in Federal District Court to obtain a ruling on the constitutionality of the state's Pupil Placement Law. They also sought to obtain a declaratory decree on the rights of black students to attend the school closest to their homes on a non-segregated basis (SSN).

3 In Washington, D.C., Dr. Robert Carr, general secretary of the American Association of University Professors, pointed out that South Carolina governor George Bell Timmerman's recent revocation of the accreditation of the teacher training program at Allen University was an attempt to force the resignation of three professors at the school. Dr. Carr requested, but did not receive, information from the governor as to why the teacher training program had been suspended (NYT).

7 In New York City, NAACP leader Roy Wilkins reported that although the organization had its best financial year ever, taking in more than $964,000, it ended the year with a deficit of $52,734 due to court costs and campaigns in the southern states. Total membership was placed at 302,403, down from 350,000 in 1956. The membership loss was greatest in Florida, Georgia,

South Carolina, Mississippi, and Tennessee, where, according to southern NAACP director Ruby Hurley, the branches were "under the hammer of fear from the White Citizens Councils" (NYT).

9 In New York City, an article in *The Wall Street Journal* reported that northern and southern businessmen were beginning to complain about "the high costs of segregation." The recent racial incidents had discouraged many manufacturers from locating plants in the region, and the old and new laws calling for separate facilities for blacks and whites meant doubling the costs for providing rest rooms, cafeterias, locker rooms, and other accommodations (JM).

12 In Washington, D.C., Althea Gibson, Wimbledon and U.S. Women's tennis champion, was named "Athlete of the Year" by the Associated Press. Gibson, along with Arkansas NAACP president Daisy Bates, had earlier been included in the list of ten "Women of the Year" named by the Associated Press (NYT).

16 In Columbia, S.C., after eleven students at Allen University (black) attempted to apply for admission to the University of South Carolina, bomb threats were made against the school. Although the students were denied applications by university counselors, they announced they would continue to attempt to enroll (NYT).

16 In Sacramento, Calif., the state appellate court overturned the earlier Los Angeles municipal court ruling that merchants in shoe stores can refuse to sell merchandise to black customers. In a suit brought by Virginia Lambert, the appellate court ruled that "retail stores are places of public accommodation" and could not discriminate against customers (JM).

19 In Maxton, N.C., Klansmen who were threatening members of the local Lumbee Indian tribe were routed after a shootout on Indian land. The rally called by Klan leader James Cole included a cross burning, and the Indians decided to dislodge the heavily armed Klansmen. The Klansmen fled and four people were injured. Those arrested were fined sixty dollars after trials in Indian courts (NYT).

22 In Richmond, Va., a three-judge federal panel in a 2 to 1 decision declared unconstitutional three state laws aimed at the NAACP. The judges upheld the right of an organization to refuse to make public its membership and financial records and struck down the law that prohibited organizations from engaging in certain types of litigation. Similar legislation in Alabama, Arkansas, and Texas was also being challenged in the federal courts (NYT).

25 In Harrisburg, Pa., the state supreme court upheld a lower court's decision to remove the administration of Girard College from Philadelphia's City Board of Trusts. In 1957 the U.S. Supreme Court had ruled that as long as it was administered by a public agency, it could not deny admission to black orphan boys. The new ruling allows the private trustees to continue to limit enrollment to white orphan boys only (NYT).

30 In Albany, N.Y., the state supreme court ruled that apartment owners in New Rochelle violated the state's anti-bias laws when they refused to rent an apartment to black advertising executive Norris G. Shervington. Since the owners accepted Federal Housing Administration loans, they were subject to laws governing housing available to the public (JM).

FEBRUARY 1958

1 In Hartford County, Md., NAACP attorneys charged the local school board with deliberately delaying the implementation of school integration. The board's plan called for the integration of the local high school by 1963. In Nashville, Tenn., parents of twenty-one black students filed suit in federal court against the school board to end segregation. The current plan called for all-black, all-white, and mixed schools, an approach that was rejected by federal courts earlier (SSN).

1 In Jackson, Miss., the state legislature appropriated funds for three black schools to ensure that their accreditation was maintained. Alcorn State, Jackson State, and Mississippi Vocational Institute received construction funds in order to decrease the likelihood that attempts would be made to integrate all-white colleges and universities in the state (SSN).

1 In Tallahassee, Fla., National Association for the Advancement of White People leader John Kasper was sentenced to one year in prison for his role in the Clinton, Tenn., mob violence opposing school integration. Kasper was assigned to the integrated federal correctional institution, where he shared a cellblock with black inmates (SSN).

3 In Los Angeles, Calif., at a meeting of the President's Committee on Government Contracts, Vice Pres. Richard Nixon declared that job discrimination and racial prejudice were too costly for the country. Nixon stated that nothing hurt the U.S. position abroad more than "to practice one philosophy at home and preach another abroad." International Brotherhood of Electrical Workers president James R. Carey remarked that Nixon seemed sympathetic to the union's call for government action against employers using race-hate literature to hinder organizing drives (NYT).

12 In Little Rock, Ark., state circuit court judge William Kirby upheld the state law requiring organizations to file membership and fiscal data with state officials. However, Kirby reduced the fine on NAACP official Daisy Bates to twenty-five dollars for failing to produce membership and financial records. NAACP attorney Robert L. Carter promised to appeal the conviction to the state supreme court (NYT).

13 In New York City, Arkansas governor Orval Faubus announced the revocation of franchises of three hundred domestic and out-of-state corporations operating in the state for their failure to pay the 1957 state franchise tax. Faubus's move was seen as an attempt at dissolving the state branch of the NAACP (NYT).

14 In New Orleans, La., the U.S. Fifth Circuit Court of Appeals upheld three orders issued by lower courts to end segregation in the New Orleans public schools, city parks, and public transportation, and at Louisiana State University. The court injunction against the New Orleans school board ordered it to refrain from requiring or permitting segregation in any school under its supervision.

Segregation in public accommodations continued, however, pending an appeal of the decision to the U.S. Supreme Court (NYT).

18 In Little Rock, Ark., Minnie Jean Brown, one of the nine black students enrolled in Central High School, was expelled after she responded physically to white students' harassment. Put on probation after she was suspended for two earlier incidents, Brown was expelled after the third incident. The three white students involved were also suspended. Shortly after the expulsion, Brown accepted a $1,050 scholarship to attend the New Lincoln School in New York City (NYT).

20 In Detroit, Mich., the federal court refused to grant the petition for the extradition of Rev. Caldwell Caver to Lomax, Ala., where he was charged with shooting a deputy sheriff during a Klan raid in a black neighborhood. The Klansmen killed Willie Dunnigan, a black church deacon, in the raid, but Caver denied that he was one of the people shooting at Klansmen as they attacked the homes of black residents (JM).

20 In Flint, Mich., Katherine Thompson filed a suit for breach of contract against the Bentley School District in the city. Thompson had negotiated a contract by mail, but when she arrived for employment was told by school superintendent F. E. Barnhitte that school policy prohibited the hiring of African Americans as teachers (JM).

27 In Miami, Fla., at a meeting of the AFL-CIO executive council a resolution was passed requiring all unions to include clauses in labor contracts barring racial discrimination in hiring, wages, and promotions. The council also directed all unions to establish committees and procedures to ensure "a meaningful civil rights program" (JM).

MARCH 1958

1 In Washington, D.C., singer and actor Paul Robeson filed a suit in federal court charging that the U.S. State Department violated his constitutional rights by denying him a passport. Robeson was continually denied a passport because of his refusal to state whether or not he was a member of the Communist party (NYT).

"CRUSADE FOR CITIZENSHIP"—VOTER REGISTRATION CAMPAIGNS

The passage of the Civil Rights Act of 1957, guaranteeing federal protection for voting rights, spurred Martin Luther King to focus the newly organized Southern Christian Leadership Conference (SCLC) on voter registration, and on 12 February 1958, the Crusade for Citizenship was launched in twenty-two southern cities. The objective was to register one million new black voters by the November 1960 election. Unfortunately, this new voter registration campaign spawned great opposition from southern Democratic politicians. Within weeks of the launching of the Crusade for Citizenship, Georgia governor Marvin Griffin announced his support for the reintroduction of a one-dollar poll tax as a means of halting mass voter registration by blacks in the state.

Under the provisions of the Civil Rights Act, Rev. H. D. Darby of Prentiss, Miss., filed a suit in federal court in March 1958, charging that he and thirteen hundred black citizens were being kept off the voting rolls in Jefferson County. In response to the suit, Gov. J. P. Coleman issued a call for a state constitutional convention to erect new barriers to prevent a "Negro onslaught" at the polls in upcoming elections. When Darby's suit was brought before federal appeals judges in Jackson, Miss., in July, Jefferson County clerk James Daniels denied charges of voter discrimination, and the federal panel subsequently dismissed Darby's suit.

Throughout 1958 in Tuskegee, Ala., black citizens, led by the Tuskegee Civic Association (TCA), continued to boycott white merchants following the removal of black voters from the election rolls in Macon County to diminish black political power. Although state officials attempted to get a court order to restrain the activities of the TCA, they were rebuffed in the federal courts. In a state referendum in December, however, Alabama voters approved by a wide margin a constitutional amendment calling for the abolition of the current boundaries of Macon County in order to limit black voting strength.

Complaints of voter discrimination were filed with the U.S. Commission on Civil Rights by black citizens from Georgia, Louisiana, Tennessee, and other southern states throughout 1958. But there was little increase in the number of black southerners registered to vote. In November, the Southern Regional Council reported that the number of black voters increased only slightly between 1956 and 1958, from an estimated 1,238,100 to 1,266,488 in eleven southern states. The council also reported that there were twenty-eight counties in the southern states in 1958 where the black population ranged up to 82 percent of the total population and there was not one African American registered to vote.

1 In Washington, D.C., NAACP official Clarence Mitchell announced agreements made with federal officials to prohibit racial discrimination in parks, playgrounds, and recreational areas owned by the federal government and leased to private operators. The Departments of the Interior and Agriculture and the Army Corps of Engineers agreed to enforce nondiscrimination clauses in leases to private operators on public lands (SSN).

3 In New York City, more than one thousand people attended the ninetieth birthday celebration for the scholar and civil rights leader W. E. B. Du Bois. Presented with a check for five thousand dollars, he said he would use some of the money to support the publication of a three-volume novel he was completing depicting African American history since the Reconstruction era (NYT).

6 In Little Rock, Ark., Gov. Orval Faubus announced that he would seek a third term in office. This was not a surprise to many, but black voters who supported him in his last campaign vowed to oppose him in the July primary. Rev. Oliver W. Gibson, president of the Little Rock Improvement League, said, "Governor Faubus is an evil which Arkansas cannot afford" (NYT).

6 In St. Louis, Mo., despite support from Mayor Raymond R. Tucker, the board of aldermen failed by a vote of 15 to 13 to pass a city ordinance prohibiting discrimination in hotels, restaurants, theaters, and stores in the city. This was the third time the measure was voted down by the aldermen (JM).

6 In Rock Hill, S.C., Rev. Cecil Ivory, chairman of the Committee for the Promotion of Human Rights, announced that the volunteer bus service begun during a boycott of the Star Bus Company, which went out of business, would expand operation and collect daily, rather than weekly, fares from riders. The city council refused to give Walter Craig, a local businessman, a franchise for commercial bus service because Craig had promised to "abide by the law of the land, not of the state" and provide service on a nonsegregated basis (JM).

6 In Memphis, Tenn., Theodore Webber, director of the University of Tennessee extension program, announced that African Americans would not be able to receive credit for the course in child psychology presented by Memphis TV station WKNO. The TV station director Keith Neighbert recommended that the course be open to all, since the only direct contact with the university would be to take the final examination, but school officials denied the request (JM).

8 In Oklahoma City, Okla., Gov. Raymond Gary signed an order authorizing the admission of African Americans to the state National Guard. The request was made by local National Guard units that were having trouble recruiting members (NYT).

11–12 In Mobile, Ala., a cross was burned in front of the home of Rev. J. T. Parker, a white minister who had signed a statement in support of a petition of thirty-six black ministers calling on city officials to desegregate public transit in the city. The next day, crosses were burned in front of the churches of three white clergymen who had also supported the black ministers' petition (NYT).

13 In Philadelphia, Pa., it was revealed that pianist Natalie Hinderas's solo appearance with the Dallas Symphony Orchestra was abruptly canceled when the directors learned that she was African American. They later claimed that they chose her for the engagement from a brochure and had assumed she was white (JM).

17 In Washington, D.C., Rev. E. Franklin Jackson called for a one-day boycott (March 24) of four downtown department stores that have no black clerks or salespeople. Three District commissioners, working with White House officials, proposed the formation of a nine-member council on human relations to investigate employment discrimination in the District as an alternative to the boycott (NYT).

21 In Los Angeles, Calif., fifteen black musicians, including Nat King Cole, issued a public appeal to AFL-CIO president George Meany to abolish racial restrictions on membership in the American Federation of Musicians (AFM). The group claimed that AFM president James Petrillo failed to respond to three letters calling for the integration of black and white musicians locals (NYT).

27 In Jackson, Miss., NAACP field secretary Medgar Evers was attacked while riding a Trailways bus from Meridian. Questioned by police in Meridian, Evers sat in the front of the bus and was attacked by a white cab driver who stopped the bus. Evers refused to change his seat, but the white man left the bus at the urging of the driver (JM).

27 In Washington, D.C., a bill sponsored by Arkansas senator John L. McClellan was passed by the Senate by a voice vote. The bill would return to state authorities jurisdiction over federal properties. Denounced by NAACP leaders, the bill, if passed by the House, would allow state officials to reimpose segregation in schools on federal military installations in southern states. The bill quietly passed the Senate, but the NAACP leaders said they would lobby to amend it in the House and change the provisions that would undermine recent policies outlawing racial discrimination on federal properties (JM).

28 In Washington, D.C., the one-day boycott of five downtown department stores was reported to have been 90 percent successful. Boycott leader Rev. E. Franklin Jackson declared that few black shoppers entered stores, while two hundred ministers picketed outside. Twenty-two prayer meetings were held in churches throughout the city, and boycott leaders scheduled meetings with store executives about the hiring of African Americans as clerks and salespeople (NYT).

APRIL 1958

1 In Nashville, Tenn., the school board voted 7 to 1 to integrate the public schools one grade a year. The first grade was integrated in the 1957–58 school year, and this pattern would continue for twelve years. Coyness Ennix, the only black school board member, voted against the plan and reminded the other board members that the federal courts in Kentucky already ruled that desegregation one grade at a time was too slow (NYT).

1 In Sussex County, Del., the all-black Sussex County Teachers Association voted to dissolve and merge with the all-white Sussex County Education Association. The 141 black teachers followed the lead of black teachers who earlier voted to merge with white teachers' groups in Kent, Wilmington, and New Castle, Del. (SSN).

7 In Montgomery, Ala., despite open threats from the Klan, Martin Luther King addressed a rally of twenty-five hundred people protesting the electrocution of twenty-two-year-old Jeremiah Reeves for the rape of a white woman, with whom Reeves was known to have been having an affair. During the same week of Reeves's execution, a white man who allegedly raped a black girl went unpunished. King declared that "we are here to repent for the constant miscarriage of justice that we confront every day in our courts" (NYT).

10 In Seattle, Wash., the family of Leroy Collins, the long-missing witness in the Emmett Till case, arrived from Mississippi after receiving numerous death threats. Seattle NAACP leaders voiced strong objections to the local welfare office's attempts to force the family to return to the South and initiated a campaign to ensure that the Collins family remained in the city (JM).

10 In Washington, D.C., the U.S. Senate made an unprecedented move to reconsider a bill passed earlier that would have allowed the resegregation of federal facilities in the South. Minnesota senator Hubert Humphrey, who led the fight for the passage of the original bill, called for its reconsideration after objections were raised by NAACP officials and others. The new bill would have anti-segregation features added (JM).

17 In Washington, D.C., reports circulated that government officials in Bucharest, Romania, were infuriated over the appointment of Clifton Wharton (black) as the U.S. minister in Romania. A veteran diplomat, Wharton formerly served in diplomatic posts in Liberia, the Canary Islands, and as consul general in Marseilles, France. Claiming not to be racially prejudiced, the Romanian officials voiced their resentment over being the first European country to have an African American as the highest official from the U.S. (JM).

18 In Harriman, N.Y., the findings of a secret interracial conference held in January 1958 at Freedom House were made public. Among those present were UN secretary Ralph Bunche, Tuskegee University president Luther F. Foster, and New York Intergroup Relations commissioner Frank Horne. The northern and southern leaders called for "moderation" in the school integration disputes, "firmer leadership" from Washington, and the rebuilding of communications between the races (NYT).

24 In Chicago, Ill., although leaders of the separate black and white waiters unions claimed that the city is "ahead of any other U.S. city in the hiring of Negro hotel workers," most hotels in the downtown area had no black waiters. The state commission against discrimination reported that of 2,601 waiters in 33 hotels in New York City, only 58 were black, half of whom worked in one hotel (JM).

24 In Littleton, Colo., the local school board was ordered to end its discriminatory hiring practices by the state's new fair employment practices commission (FEPC). Ora D. Martin and Beatrice Beatty were denied positions as teaching aides by school officials because there were "only a few Negro students" in the district. State FEPC officials said this was discriminatory and ordered them to reconsider the black women's applications (JM).

24 In State College, Miss., L. E. Miller, editor of the Mississippi State College student newspaper, was voted out of his position by the student council because he refused to "drop the race issue" in editorials and features. Miller believed that both sides of the race issue should be presented in the college newspaper. The vote against him was 29 to 2 (JM).

26 In Alexandria, Va., attorney Charles E. Williams filed a suit against the Howard Johnson restaurant that denied him service. Although the restaurant's owners had to apologize to a Ghanaian minister for denying him service in one of its restaurants in 1957, the new suit claimed that the restaurant chain continued its discriminatory practices (NYT).

28 In Philadelphia, Pa., the Commission on Human Relations declared that the clause in the constitution of the International Brotherhood of Locomotive Engineers stating that membership was limited to white men was illegal. It gave the union sixty days to change the discriminatory rule (NYT).

MAY 1958

1 In Los Angeles, Calif., Joanne Ransome filed a suit against Vic Tanny Gym after she was given a life membership but was told she would have to hide the fact that she was a Negro. After leaving

---

PROBLEMS OF DISCRIMINATION IN HOUSING

While the arson and bombings aimed at African Americans and other people of color attempting to move into all-white residential neighborhoods filled the newspapers in 1958, other forms of housing discrimination also were regularly reported. In many communities the new federally funded "slum clearance" and "urban renewal" programs were turning into what the NAACP's housing official Madison Jones referred to as "Negro removal." When urban renewal projects were initiated in Gadsden, Ala., in March and Eufala, Ala., in September 1958, black homeowners filed suits in the federal courts to restrain the local housing authorities from removing black families from areas scheduled for redevelopment as housing and recreational areas for whites only. The complaint asked that black families not be forced into public housing projects, but be allowed to purchase homes in the redeveloped neighborhoods.

In New York and New Jersey, discriminatory housing practices were prohibited by state law. The New York State Commission Against Discrimination (SCAD) received numerous complaints of housing bias from African Americans, Puerto Ricans, and other minorities who were not allowed to rent apartments or purchase homes in various parts of the state. In Albany, N.Y., in August, SCAD chairman Charles Abrams reported that housing bias in upstate communities prevented black professionals and skilled technicians from working in those areas and thus limited New York's industrial productivity.

Under New Jersey law, no housing development that received Federal Housing Authority (FHA) or other public funds could discriminate on the basis of race. As a result, in June 1958 when real estate developer William Levitt presented his plan to build a Levittown near Burlington, N.J., state representatives warned him that they would not tolerate the type of discrimination and violence leveled against black families who attempted to purchase homes in Levittown, Pa., in 1957.

In an important decision in June 1958, superior court judge James H. Oakley in Sacramento, Calif., ruled that racial bias in the sale of homes funded by the FHA or GI loans was illegal. This became the FHA's official policy and within a month officials in the Veterans Administration agreed to withhold approval of GI loans involving home builders who discriminated on the basis of race, creed, or color.

However, discrimination in housing remained a serious problem. In November 1958, the Commission on Race and Housing, a nongovernmental group, reported on its three-year study of housing problems. The commission recommended the formation of a presidential committee that would provide advice to federal, state, and local governments about ways to eliminate discrimination in the distribution of federal housing benefits. This study revealed that Puerto Ricans, Mexicans, Jews, and African Americans faced severe restrictions in their choice of neighborhoods for purchase or rental of homes and apartments.

for several months, she tried to return to classes but was refused admission four times. Ransome and other African Americans filed a suit for $280,000 (JM).

1 In Miami, Fla., after a federal appeals court ruled that segregation on city buses was unconstitutional, local NAACP president Rev. Theodore R. Gibson rode in the front of a bus without incident. Police reported no complaints from whites about changes in bus seating practices (JM).

6 In New York City, it was announced that *The Arkansas Gazette* had been awarded two Pulitzer Prizes for its coverage of the integration of Little Rock's Central High School in September 1957. A third prize was given to Associated Press reporter Reiman Morin for his coverage of the school integration story. *The Arkansas Gazette* editor, Harry Ashmore, had been condemned by the White Citizens Council for his editorials and features calling for "law and order" in school desegregation (NYT).

13 In Washington, D.C., President Eisenhower's speech at the annual meeting of the National Newspaper Publishers Association caused an uproar when in his first appearance before a black audience he called for "patience and forbearance" in the quest for equal rights. Among those who objected to the president's endorsement of "gradualism" in the campaign for civil rights were NAACP officials Thurgood Marshall, Roy Wilkins, and Clarence Mitchell (NYT).

15 In Columbia, S.C., despite earlier claims that he would not give in to white state officials who wanted the dismissal of three controversial professors, Allen University president Frank R. Veal announced the firing of Dr. John G. Rideout, Dr. Edwin Hoffman (both white), and Dr. Forrest O. Wiggins (black). Dean A. D. Green claimed that the three were dismissed for "acts of insubordination and lack of production." The firings could pave the way for the recertification of the school's teacher training program by the South Carolina Board of Education, chaired by Gov. George Bell Timmerman (JM).

15 In Detroit, Mich., Rev. George Hill, head of the Briggs Stadium Boycott Committee, promised that

unless black players were added to the Tigers roster, the boycott would begin on 1 June 1958. Tigers president Harvey Hansen said there were seventeen black players in their farm system, but "we refuse to make a definite commitment in spite of the threat of boycott" (JM).

23 In Little Rock, Ark., Ernest Green became the first African American to graduate from Central High School. Carlotta Walls, a sophomore, became the first black student to make the school's honor roll, and sophomore Gloria Ray placed a prize-winning exhibit in the state's science fair. The eight remaining black Central High School students planned to make their first national speaking tour, with engagements in New York City, Chicago, and Washington, D.C. It was announced that the Little Rock students would receive the NAACP's coveted Spingarn Medal at the NAACP's annual convention. As the 1957–58 school year ended, President Eisenhower ordered the removal of troops from Central High School (NYT).

27 In New Orleans, La., despite the U.S. Supreme Court's refusal to review a lower court's decisions granting injunctions against the enforcement of state laws mandating segregation on the city's buses and in the public schools, local officials said segregation would continue while they examined possible new legal maneuvers. A cross was later burned in front of the home of federal judge J. Skelly Wright, who had signed the original orders ending segregation on the city's public transit (NYT).

30 In Birmingham, Ala., Edwin H. Estes (white), owner of WEDR, a black radio station, reported that vandals had overturned the broadcast tower, painted "KKK" and various epithets on the walls of the building, and left three dogs with their throats slashed near the station's transmitter. Estes said he believed the radio station was attacked because the broadcasters had been encouraging black citizens to vote (NYT).

JUNE 1958

5 In Birmingham, Ala., Rev. Fred Shuttlesworth marched on city hall leading a group of African

Americans who were interested in taking the civil service examination for policeman. However, the county personnel director Ray Mullins claimed that "they don't meet the qualifications" (meaning they had to be white). Mullins suggested that the group take up the issue with the County Civil Service Personnel Board (JM).

6 In Detroit, Mich., one week after black citizens agreed to postpone their boycott of the Tigers baseball team, a club spokesperson announced that Ossie Virgil, a black player in the Tigers' Charlestown, W. Va., farm team, was promoted and would become a regular member of the team. The only remaining Major League Baseball team never to have a black player was the Boston Red Sox (NYT).

6 In New York City, the NAACP's Spingarn Medal Committee reconvened and added Daisy Bates's name to the list of award recipients for 1958. Ellis Thomas, chair of the Parents Committee for the Little Rock Nine, had informed the award committee that "the children will not accept the Spingarn Medal unless Mrs. Bates is included" (NYT).

19 In Chicago, Ill., in an article published in *Jet* magazine, Central High School graduate Ernest Green provided a personal account of his experiences over the school year. Green said that he had been asked many times how they survived the year. "So many people today talk about young people going to the dogs and I think our example has shown adults just what this coming Negro kid is made of and what he can do under pressure" (JM).

19 In Detroit, Mich., following the passage in April 1958 of a resolution allowing black churches to join their local Methodist Conference, Grace Methodist Church in Detroit and John Wesley Methodist Church in River Rouge, Mich., became the first to be admitted to the Michigan Methodist Conference. In Pittsburgh, the Johnstown Methodist Church became the first and only black church admitted to the Pittsburgh Methodist Conference, which included more than 463 white churches. Black Methodist churches in Indiana were also to be allowed to join the Northern Indiana Methodist Conference (JM).

19 In New York City, the Jewish Labor Committee officially requested that the Automobile Association of America (AAA) withhold its endorsement of any motel, hotel, or restaurant that practices racial or religious discrimination. An AAA official responded that they would study the request (JM).

19 In Tallahassee, Fla., federal district court judge Dozier Devane ruled that the state-imposed ban on the enrollment of black students at the University of Florida must be lifted. Virgil Hawkins, who had been trying to enroll in the University of Florida Law School since 1949, said that he would reapply for admission, along with fifteen to twenty other African Americans (NYT).

23, 24 In Washington, D.C., President Eisenhower met at the White House with Martin Luther King, Roy Wilkins, A. Philip Randolph, and Lester Granger to discuss civil rights issues. They found Eisenhower "less informed" about civil rights issues than his predecessors and refused to issue a statement of "glowing praise" about the outcome of the meeting. The four leaders asked that the Justice Department file a brief in Little Rock, Ark., to stay the recent court order issued by federal judge Harry J. Lemley suspending for two and one-half years the integration of the Little Rock public schools. The ruling could prohibit the return of black students to Central High School in September 1958 (NYT).

26 In Fort Hood, Tex., black soldiers and their families complained about the lack of suitable housing in the area. Housing on the base for the members of the Second Armored Division recently transferred from Germany was overcrowded, and while white soldiers were provided temporary housing in nearby Killeen, Tex., the town maintained a ban on African Americans residing there. One black army wife complained that "only in Germany did we live like all Americans should" (JM).

26 In Washington, D.C., for the sixth time in eight years the District of Columbia Bar Association voted not to admit black lawyers to membership. While a majority voted to admit African American attorneys, two-thirds of the membership had to agree to the change (JM).

26–27 In Washington, D.C., the State Department finally issued a passport to singer and activist Paul Robeson to travel anywhere in the world where the U.S. had diplomatic relations. In April the ban was partially lifted, allowing him to travel anywhere within the Western Hemisphere. Robeson immediately announced plans to travel to England to perform in a Stratford-upon-Avon production of Shakespeare's *Othello* (NYT).

27 In Dallas, Tex., despite several federal court orders, public schools would remain segregated during the 1958–59 school year because of the failure of the federal district court in New Orleans to make a ruling on a Texas law barring school integration. According to state law, any school district that desegregated without the approval of the voters would lose all state funding (NYT).

JULY 1958

1 In Columbia, S.C., certification was restored to Allen University's teacher training program. Certification had been withdrawn in September 1957 because several professors were alleged to be Communists. The school's president, Frank R. Veal, fired the three accused professors earlier in the year (SSN).

1 In North Little Rock, Ark., Lois Patillo, mother of Melba Patillo, one of the Little Rock Nine, finally had her teaching contract renewed for the 1958–59 school year. *The New York Times* had reported earlier (6–7 May) that she was fired from her teaching position in the North Little Rock public schools. School officials declined to explain the long delay in making the decision on her reappointment (SSN).

1 In Philadelphia, Pa., the U.S. Supreme Court's refusal to review a state court's decision means that Girard College will enroll only white orphan boys. The state courts had ruled that the shift of control from public to private trustees was legal, and the new private trustees decided the school would not be racially integrated (NYT).

1 In Washington, D.C., the U.S. Supreme Court set aside the $100,000 fine imposed by the Alabama state courts on the NAACP for refusing to surrender its membership lists because the action violated the Fourteenth Amendment. The court said a separate hearing was needed to set aside the restraining order that keeps the group from operating in the state (NYT).

10 In Kansas City, Mo., the merging of General Hospital No. One (white) and No. Two (black) was completed. The staffs of the two institutions were integrated and black nursing and medical staff were teaching black and white students (JM).

10 In Washington, D.C., the President's Committee on Government Contracts reported that it received 341 complaints of job discrimination between May 1956 and January 1958. Ninety percent of the complaints came from African Americans and 3.2 percent came from Jewish Americans. The remainder came primarily from other religious minorities. The NAACP charged that there were flagrant and widespread violations of anti-discrimination clauses in government contracts throughout the year (NYT).

17 In Boston, Mass., the front office for the Boston Red Sox announced that the club had signed its first black player, Larry Plenty, a recent graduate of Boston College. Plenty was sent to a farm club in Iowa for "seasoning." The Red Sox had been the only Major League Baseball team without a black player (JM).

17 In Washington, D.C., plans were announced for the picketing of the downtown branch of the YMCA, which remained segregated. Dr. Edward Mazique, the head of a citizens group organizing the protest, said that YMCA officials have been asked numerous times to integrate the facility, but still refused (JM).

24 In Cleveland, Ohio, at the NAACP's forty-ninth annual meeting, Daisy Bates and the Little Rock Nine received the coveted Spingarn Medal. Unfortunately, during the convention former baseball player Jackie Robinson criticized the organization's leaders for "not reaching the little man" and "not doing a good selling job." Robinson's comments played well in the southern white press, but many NAACP supporters said that Robinson's statements were ill-informed and inaccurate (JM).

1958—THE YEAR OF THE BOMBINGS

The huge increase in the number of arson fires and bombings in 1958 caused grave alarm among elected officials and uncompromising demands from the public for concerted action. In February 1958, when fire destroyed the gymnasium at Arkansas Baptist College (black) in Little Rock, an anonymous white segregationist claimed credit for the arson. In March, Jewish community centers in Nashville, Tenn., and Miami, Fla., were blasted by dynamite; and in Atlanta, Ga., a house in an all-white neighborhood that had been sold to a black family was wrecked by a dynamite blast. In Memphis, the home of Rev. Charles H. Mason, Jr., in a predominantly white neighborhood caught fire mysteriously, and the Church of God in Christ he pastored, valued at $150,000, was set ablaze and completely destroyed. In April, after the James Weldon Johnson Elementary School and the Jewish community center in Jacksonville, Fla., were bombed, twenty-eight southern mayors went to the city to discuss how to deal with the most recent rash of bombings. They called for legislation mandating the death penalty for people found guilty of bombing churches, homes, or schools.

Racially motivated bombings were a regular feature in Birmingham, Ala., in 1956 and 1957 and continued in 1958. In May, after the bombing of a Jewish community center in the city and the homes of Ernest Coppins and Dora Maudlin in nearby Bessemer, black and white citizens contributed money toward a fifteen-thousand-dollar reward for information leading to the conviction of the person responsible for the bombings. In July, following the bombing of the recently purchased home of Essie Mae Ellison located near a white neighborhood in Columbus, Ga., the Justice Department issued a report that documented forty-four racially or religiously motivated bombings in eight southern states over the previous eighteen months.

Arson and bombings were reported outside the South as well. In June in Rutledge, Pa., the home of Chester, Pa., NAACP president George T. Raymond was burned down the day before he was to move into the all-white suburb. In August, vandals set fire to the newly purchased home of Lillie Cooper in an all-white neighborhood in the southwest section of Chicago, and in October, in one of the worst explosions in recent years, the homes of John and Thelma Daniels and James and Mary Branch were bombed in Chicago's Englewood section, which had been plagued by anti-black demonstrations.

In Clinton, Tenn., the scene of racial violence over school integration in 1956, the local high school was bombed in October, destroying sixteen classrooms and causing $300,000 worth of damage. Tennessee governor Frank G. Clement offered a five-thousand-dollar reward for information leading to the conviction of the dynamiters. The Jewish Reform Temple in Atlanta was also bombed in October, as was the grocery store of James Turner (black) in Lowndes County, Ala. In November, a dynamite explosion seriously damaged the Osage (W. Va.) Junior High School, forcing 423 white and black students into temporary quarters while police investigated the incident.

By the end of 1958, New York congressmen Emmanuel Celler and Kenneth Keating had introduced a bill in Congress that would give the FBI authority to intervene in school and church bombings, make it a federal crime to possess or transport dynamite used to damage religious, educational, or charitable buildings, and provide for a one-year maximum jail sentence and thousand-dollar fine for those found guilty of such attacks.

---

24 In Detroit, Mich., Dr. Remus Robinson, the first African American to head the local school board, declared that black teachers were not allowed to teach in predominantly white schools. Dr. Robinson said the practice of assigning black teachers to majority black schools was only increasing racial isolation in the school system (JM).

AUGUST 1958

1 In Charleston, W. Va., the state board of education approved the appointment of Rev. Robert H. Firth to the faculty of Bluefield State College. Firth became the first white professor at the previously all-black institution (SSN).

I In Little Rock, Ark., after Daisy and L. C. Bates announced that they might have to stop publishing the *Arkansas State Press* because of loss of revenue due to a boycott sponsored by segregationists, contributions came in from all over the country to make up the loss in advertising revenue. Among those who sent in contributions was former first lady Eleanor Roosevelt (SSN).

I In Mecklenburg County, N.C., the school board denied the applications of ten black children for admission to all-white public schools. The board had made the same decision last year and declared that it was still studying the issue of integrating the public schools. The black parents appealed the decision and requested new hearings (SSN).

I In Nashville, Tenn., the *Southern School News* reported that while 777 southern and border-state school districts had been desegregated, 2,122 remained segregated. Southern states had passed 196 laws to maintain school segregation since 1954 (SSN).

2 In Clarendon County, S.C., one of the school districts included in the *Brown* decision in 1954, eight black parents again petitioned the school authorities to admit their children into all-white schools. As was the case earlier, school officials said they would take the petitions "under advisement" (NYT).

5 In Richmond, Va., while U.S. district judge Sterling Hutcheson issued an order delaying school integration in Prince Georges County, Va., public school systems in Arlington, Norfolk, and Charlottesville were ordered to integrate in September 1958. In defiance, one week after the court order, school officials in Norfolk rejected the applications of 151 black students for admission to all-white public schools (NYT).

7 In Toledo, Ohio, in the first hearing under the city's 1955 fair employment practices law, the Grace E. Smith Co., a restaurant and cafeteria firm, was ordered to end its discriminatory hiring practices by the Toledo Board of Commissioners. A complaint was filed by Mary Ann Simpkins after she was denied a position by the company.

Local NAACP president Dr. Samantha Adams also asked state officials to bar apprenticeship programs in the Toledo public schools that excluded applicants on the basis of race, creed, or color (JM).

17 In Perry County, Ala., Jimmy Wilson, who was convicted in October 1957 of stealing $1.95 from an elderly white woman, was sentenced to death in the electric chair on 5 September 1958. During the trial before an all-white jury, the woman, Estelle Barker, also blurted out during her testimony that "he tried to rape me." Wilson was not charged with attempted rape but was given the death sentence for the robbery. Wilson claimed that he never robbed the woman but merely tried to get advance payment for some yard work he was going to do, and she became angry. News of the conviction and death sentence led to condemnations of the Alabama court system from around the country and the world (NYT).

21 In Birmingham, Ala., after the Jefferson County Personnel Department dropped its "whites only" regulation, four African Americans took civil service examinations, three for policeman and one for a clerical position. They were the first African Americans allowed to take the examination (JM).

21 In Stephenville, Newfoundland, Canada, at the Ernest Harmon Air Base, black airmen complained of discriminatory practices on and off the base. There were problems with discrimination in dining and recreation areas on the base, and white airmen threatened to boycott local merchants who served black airmen. Women who socialized with the black airmen had lost their jobs. Base commander Col. Leon Bell issued a warning against discrimination and promised to investigate the charges (JM).

21 In Fairbanks, Alaska, black and white members of the Fairbanks Civic League picketed the Thrifty Supermarket, owned by city councilman Joe Franich, after the managers reneged on their pledge to hire African Americans as cashiers. The store managers claimed that they decided not to hire black cashiers after reading "inflammatory statements" in reports at a recent jobs conference (JM).

21 In Montgomery, Ala., Rev. Robert S. Graetz, one of the few white supporters of the successful bus boycott, announced that he was becoming pastor of the St. Philip Lutheran Church in Columbus, Ohio. Graetz had been targeted for violence over the previous three years because of his civil rights activities (JM).

22–24 In Washington, D.C., Department of Health, Education, and Welfare officials announced that the $900 million in new funds appropriated by Congress to aid science and mathematics education would be distributed by state officials. Black educators voiced their fears that black institutions would not receive a fair share of the funds because of discriminatory practices by southern state agencies (NYT).

23–24, 26, 28 In Oklahoma City, Okla., thirty-five members of the NAACP Youth Council, under the leadership of Clara Luper, occupied all the seats in a local lunchconette, but were refused service. When they returned and remained the second day, they were served. The same sit-in tactic was attempted unsuccessfully at the lunch counter of the Brown Company department store. The Kress store acquiesced in desegregating its fountain service (NYT).

27 In Milwaukee, Wis., at the American Federation of Teachers' (AFT) annual meeting, delegates voted to expel the Chattanooga–Hamilton County Local 246 for failing to progress on integration. This was the first local to be expelled; five others withdrew from the union after they were told to integrate. The AFT also decided to readmit three suspended African American locals that had been ousted because they were segregated (NYT).

27 In the southern states, with the opening of the 1958–59 school year, black students were admitted to previously all-white elementary schools in Preston, Okla., Winston-Salem, N.C., and Nashville, Tenn. Twenty-three black students were enrolled in the all-white high school in Fulton, Ky. In Okmulgee, Okla., school officials refused to enroll black students and the NAACP filed suit (NYT).

27 In Gainesville, Fla., officials at the University of Florida Law School said the only black student who passed entrance exams, Morehouse graduate George H. Starke, would be admitted in the fall semester (NYT).

28 In Detroit, Mich., on the recommendation of the Community Relations Commission, Mayor Louis C. Miriani named a thirteen-member interracial committee to advise the local police department on race relations. Among those appointed to the committee were Rev. Malcolm Dade, Lillian Hatcher, Dr. Lloyd E. Lawson, and Dr. Alfred Thomas (JM).

28 In Washington, D.C., the Senate Judiciary Committee, headed by James Eastland, decided it would not consider the nomination of former Virgin Islands governor Walter Gordon (black) as U.S. federal district judge. White House officials announced that Gordon would be appointed to the position on an interim basis (JM).

28 In Washington, D.C., President Eisenhower's statement at a press conference that he believed school integration efforts should proceed at a "slower pace" drew praise from Arkansas governor Orval Faubus and condemnation from NAACP leader Roy Wilkins, who pointed out that seven states had not yet begun to integrate their public school systems (NYT).

SEPTEMBER 1958

1 In Montgomery, Ala., NAACP attorney Fred Gray filed suit in U.S. circuit court to test the injunction preventing the organization from operating in the state. While the Supreme Court overturned the $100,000 fine, the NAACP still must go to court to have the state injunction lifted (SSN).

1–5 In Nottingham and London, England, six days of the worst racial rioting in British history erupted. Among the causes were increasing competition for housing and jobs between poor whites and colored immigrants. People of color were attacked by mobs of whites on the streets, in restaurants, and in their homes. U.S. soldiers were told that London's Notting Hill district, scene of the worst violence, was off-limits. The rioting led to calls for limiting the number of colored immigrants entering the country (NYT).

3 In **Stillwater, Okla.,** six black youths staged a sit-in demonstration at several restaurants, similar to those that took place earlier in Oklahoma City. They were eventually served in Smith's Restaurant, but not in Skeen's Cafeteria (NYT).

4 In **Jackson, Miss.,** R. Jess Brown, attorney for Rev. Philip Coleman, who was arrested for "conspiracy to overthrow the state segregation laws," said they planned to appeal the conviction. Coleman was fined fifty dollars and sentenced to thirty days in jail for allowing Rev. J. W. Vaughn and his wife, both white, to stay in his home while attending a revival service at his church (JM).

4 In **Wichita, Kans.,** the NAACP Youth Council conducted a sit-in at the lunch counter of the Dockum Drug Store. After four days, the managers decided to serve them (JM).

4–6 In **Montgomery, Ala.,** Martin Luther King was choked and arrested by two white policemen, O. M. Strickland and J. V. Johnson, who said he was loitering outside the city courthouse. Reporters on hand photographed the incident as King was booked and thrown into jail. At the trial the next day, the police changed the charge to resisting arrest, and King was fined ten dollars plus four dollars in court costs. When King said he would not pay the fine because he had done nothing wrong, police commissioner Clyde Sellers paid the fine and King was released (NYT).

5 In **Columbus, Ga.,** in the first suit brought under the 1957 Civil Rights Act, the Justice Department's civil rights division asked for an injunction against white registrars accused of keeping black citizens from voting. Among those rejected by the white registrars were four black teachers. In 1956 only 48 out of 5,036 African Americans in the city eligible to vote were registered (NYT).

5 In **Montgomery, Ala.,** when the state supreme court failed to rule on his appeal for a new trial, the execution of Jimmy Wilson, convicted in Perry County, Ala., of stealing $1.95, was postponed. Letters from Secretary of State John Foster Dulles and others from around the world were pouring into the office of Gov. James Folsom asking him to commute Wilson's death sentence (NYT).

5, 6, 9 In the **southern states,** massive resistance to public school integration continued. Black students were turned away from white schools in Memphis, Tenn., and Raleigh, N.C. White students boycotted the Van Buren, Ark., high school because thirteen black students were enrolled. Although their parents forced fifty-five students to return to school, the black students decided not to attend. In Ardmore, Okla., white parents were charged with rioting at a school board meeting when the board members voted to integrate the local public schools (NYT).

8 In **New York City,** after winning the Wimbledon and U.S. Open women's tennis titles for the second time in a row, Althea Gibson announced that she would retire from professional tennis competition to concentrate on her singing career (NYT).

9, 10, 13, 14 In **New Orleans, La.,** after ten black students filed suit to be admitted to Louisiana State University at New Orleans (LSUNO), U.S. district court judge Herbert Christianberry issued a preliminary injunction against LSUNO's biased admissions policy. When Judge Christianberry's injunction was upheld by the U.S. First Circuit Court of Appeals four days later, fifty-nine black students were admitted to LSUNO (NYT).

11 In **New Auburn, Wisc.,** an eight-foot cross was burned on the lawn after a black couple stayed at a local summer resort. The owner, John Gordon, was disturbed by the incident and pointed out that under state law, hotels must not discriminate against any customers (JM).

16 In **Memphis, Tenn.,** although four black students had passed all entrance examinations, they were not allowed to enroll at Memphis State University. The university's president, Jack M. Smith, made the argument in federal court that allowing the black students to enroll "would lead to violence" (NYT).

18 In **Memphis, Tenn.,** six African Americans were ejected from Overton Park Zoo by police because it was not "Colored Day." The incident led to a legal suit by NAACP attorney H. T. Lockart, and the Civic League's O. Z. Evers called for the "complete desegregation" of all public facilities in the city (JM).

18 In Montgomery, Ala., the city commissioners refused to discuss a petition submitted by 120 black citizens to open the city's public parks to all citizens. In a written response the commissioners said there was no need for a hearing because the city "will not operate integrated parks" (NYT).

21 In New York City, civil rights leader Martin Luther King was stabbed by a mentally disturbed black woman, Isola Curry, while he was autographing copies of his new book *Stride Toward Freedom* in a Harlem department store. Although King narrowly escaped death in the incident and said he would not file charges against the deranged woman, the Manhattan grand jury subsequently indicted Curry for attempted murder, and she faced a twenty-five-year jail sentence (NYT).

25 In Buffalo, N.Y., sixty mothers, black and white, marched in support of black students fighting segregation in Little Rock. The women went to city hall to ask for a one-day suspension of classes to show solidarity with desegregation efforts. No action was taken by city officials (JM).

SOUTHERN POLITICIANS RESPOND TO FEDERAL INTERVENTION IN PUBLIC SCHOOL INTEGRATION

The use of federal courts and the military to bring about public school integration in Little Rock, Ark., in September 1957 sparked a wide range of responses by southern legislators. In October 1957, state legislators in Florida and Texas passed laws authorizing the governor to close public schools in the state when they were occupied by federal troops to enforce court orders calling for integration. A similar law was passed in Mississippi in May 1958 and in Louisiana in June. When federal judge John Paul, Jr., issued an order in May 1958 to integrate the Charlottesville, Va., public schools, Gov. J. Lindsay Almond threatened to close the city's public schools rather than integrate them.

In June 1958 school officials in Little Rock asked federal judge Harry J. Lemley to halt the further integration of the public schools for two and a half years, and Gov. Orval Faubus filed a suit against the federal government for sending troops to Central High School. After winning a landslide victory in the Democratic gubernatorial primary in July, Governor Faubus claimed that this was the voters' way of condemning the president's decision to send troops to Little Rock in 1957.

After Judge Lemley granted the request to halt school desegregation, the NAACP challenged the decision in the U.S. Supreme Court. On 12 September 1958 in *Cooper v. Aaron*, the justices not only overruled Judge Lemley's decision, but also declared that public funds could not be used to support private schools. The following day, Gov. Faubus ordered the closing of the Little Rock public schools indefinitely rather than allow integration to continue into the second year. In a referendum on public school integration held on 27 September 1958, Arkansas voters overwhelmingly endorsed the governor's decision.

In September, in the face of federal court orders to integrate, Governor Almond ordered the closing of the all-white public schools in Charlottesville, Front Royal, and Norfolk, Va. Private white academies were soon set up, and parents held classes for students in their homes, sometimes taught by regular public school teachers. However, in early October 1958, Judge John Paul ruled that "private academies" in Virginia could not use "publicly-paid teachers" unless black students were allowed to attend these schools. Private schools that began operating in Little Rock in October used the teachers and facilities of the University of Arkansas and Ouachita Baptist College.

By the middle of October, however, serious opposition to the school closings had arisen in Norfolk, and white parents filed suit against Governor Almond, charging that closing the public schools deprived their children of their constitutional rights. In Little Rock, Mrs. Byron House, Jr., organized the Women's Emergency Committee to Open the Schools, and she claimed in December 1958 that the group had more than 750 members.

30 In Montgomery, Ala., Gov. James Folsom commuted the death sentence given to Jimmy Wilson, for stealing $1.95, to life imprisonment. He will be eligible for parole in fifteen years. Folsom took the action after letters and petitions came in from all over the world calling for clemency (NYT).

OCTOBER 1958

7 In Washington, D.C., the Supreme Court's 1958–59 term opened with Justice Felix Frankfurter denouncing as "profoundly subversive" southern officials' "obstructive measures" taken to avoid public school desegregation. The court refused to review (1) the lower-court decision that prohibited Ark. Governor Orval Faubus from using National Guardsmen to keep black students out of Little Rock's Central High School, (2) the Delaware Board of Education's attempt to delay the integration of seven school districts, and (3) lower courts' decisions invalidating two Louisiana laws barring black students from state-supported colleges. The court was also planning to rule on Virginia's anti-NAACP laws (NYT).

8 In Washington, D.C., federal judge Potter Stewart, nominated for the Supreme Court to replace retiring justice Harold M. Burton, wrote pro-integration opinions while on the Sixth Circuit Court of Appeals. In ordering the integration of the Hillsboro, Ohio, public schools in 1956, Judge Stewart condemned the local school board's attempts to delay implementation of desegregation orders (NYT).

9 In Laurel, Del., elementary school principal Alonzo H. Shockley, Jr., claimed that he was dismissed from his position when school superintendent Leon B. Elder learned that Shockley's daughter had applied for admission to the all-white Milford (Del.) High School. Elder claimed that Shockley was fired for refusing to teach additional courses (JM).

9 In Washington, D.C., former baseball star Jackie Robinson was called to the White House to discuss the proposed Children's March scheduled for 25 October 1958. Government officials asked him to reconsider the march to protest continued school segregation because of infiltration by "subversive" elements. Robinson did not accede to the request (JM).

9 In Winston-Salem, N.C., two black students who applied for admission to Wake Forest College, a private Baptist school, were turned down. Director of admissions A. L. Aycock said he was not authorized to admit Negroes to the school (JM).

16 In Little Rock, Ark., despite warnings from the guard who was posted following several incidents of harassment, three white men returned and hurled bricks and stones into the home of Daisy and L. C. Bates. After the third incident, Daisy Bates fired a shot at the men, who then fled. The police had refused to protect the Bates home (JM).

16 In Washington, D.C., members of the District of Columbia Bar Association finally voted to strike the word *white* from membership requirements by a vote of 583 to 224. Earlier voting for the change failed to get the two-thirds majority needed for passage of the resolution (NYT).

17 In Harrisburg, Pa., at the Thirty-ninth General Conference of the Evangelical United Brethren Church (five thousand churches nationally), the delegates voted to prohibit use of the churches' facilities for private segregated classes used to avoid integration. "We unalterably oppose all practices of segregation" (NYT).

20 In Washington, D.C., Democratic party chairman Paul M. Butler declared that in 1960 the party would take a "positive and forthright stand on civil rights." Those southern Democrats who opposed this position should just "go their own way" because they "do not represent the position of the Democratic party" (NYT).

26 In Washington, D.C., the Children's March against segregated schools attracted more than twenty thousand people to the Lincoln Memorial. Among the speakers at the march were Jackie Robinson, Harry Belafonte, Coretta Scott King, and A. Philip Randolph. At the White House, guards prevented a delegation of ten black and white students led by Belafonte from meeting with President Eisenhower (NYT).

28 **In Birmingham, Ala.,** Revs. Fred Shuttlesworth and J. S. Phifer were given ninety- and sixty-day jail sentences respectively and fined one hundred dollars each for violating the city's new "bus passenger placement" law. Twelve others were given warnings and 180-day suspended sentences. The ministers planned to appeal the convictions, and twenty-two black citizens filed a federal suit to determine the constitutionality of a law that allowed drivers to tell bus passengers where to sit. At a mass rally, one thousand black citizens supported calls for a bus boycott to protest the ordinance (NYT).

31 **In Ozark, Ark.,** three black girls enrolled in the local high school left after they were threatened by white students. They eventually transferred to the all-black high school in Clarksdale, twenty-five miles away. They said they were willing to commute daily and pay $150 in tuition rather than return to Ozark High School (NYT).

CONGRESSMAN ADAM CLAYTON POWELL, JR.: POLITICAL INDEPENDENT

In the November 1958 elections, the reelection of Harlem congressman Adam Clayton Powell, Jr., was a foregone conclusion, despite the earlier opposition from the powerful Tammany Hall Democratic political machine in New York City. When Powell, the pastor of Harlem's Abyssinian Baptist Church, ran for Congress the first time, in 1944, he campaigned as an independent, but had won the nomination as the candidate for the Democratic, Republican, and American Labor parties. In Congress Powell maintained his political independence throughout the 1950s as he attempted to gain the passage of a measure that would deny federal funding to educational and other institutions that remained segregated. While the Powell amendment was added to federal appropriation bills passed in the House on several occasions, southern Democrats made sure the amendment was removed before these measures were voted on in the Senate.

Powell demonstrated his political independence in the 1956 presidential election when he decided to endorse and work for the reelection of Dwight Eisenhower. Powell had supported the Democratic nominee, Illinois governor Adlai Stevenson, in the 1952 election, but in 1956 Stevenson's civil rights record remained weak, and in October of that year after Eisenhower personally agreed to support the passage of a new civil rights law, Powell endorsed his reelection.

Powell was fiercely criticized by both Republican and Democratic leaders for his political independence. In December 1956, after the Internal Revenue Service began investigating Powell's tax returns for the years 1950–55, he received no assistance from White House officials in response to his complaints of IRS "harassment." Finally, in May 1958, Powell was indicted by a New York grand jury on three counts of income tax evasion.

In the House of Representatives, Democratic leaders stripped Powell of his seniority on the House Interior Committee in January 1957, thus denying him the chairmanship of the Subcommittee on Mines and Metals. Early in 1958 New York City's Democratic leaders announced they would not support Powell's bid for reelection to Congress that year. Although they were able to convince city councilman Earl Brown to challenge Powell in the Democratic primary, Powell won overwhelmingly both the Democratic and Republican nominations for Harlem's Second Congressional District. After the primary victory, Powell agreed to endorse the Democratic candidate for governor, Averell Harriman, and the Tammany Hall leadership reciprocated by agreeing to assist Powell in regaining his seniority rights in Congress.

In the November 1958 election, four black politicians were elected to the U.S. Congress—Detroit's Charles Diggs, Chicago's William Dawson, Philadelphia's Robert Nix, and Powell. Despite (or because of) his political independence, Representative Powell remained the most powerful black elected official in the United States.

1 In Atlanta, Ga., U.S. district judges Boyd Sloan and Frank Hooper said that attempts to delay hearings on the school integration suit brought by ten black parents in Atlanta on behalf of twenty-eight black children would not be tolerated. Hearings were scheduled to begin in January 1959. Governor-elect Ernest Vandiver warned black leaders to abandon school integration efforts unless they wanted public education for black and white students in the state to be destroyed (SSN).

1 In Moberly, Mo., eight black teachers who lost their jobs when the public schools were integrated promised to appeal the decision of Judge Roy W. Harper, who ruled against them. Judge Harper said white teachers also lost their jobs; the dismissals were not racial (SSN).

6 In Washington, D.C., NAACP official Clarence Mitchell charged Pentagon officials with sending children of black personnel to a segregated school near Redstone Arsenal, a missile base, in Huntsville, Ala. This was the second charge of racial discrimination on federal bases leveled against military officials. In August the NAACP protested against the sending of black children to segregated schools near Little Rock Air Force Base in Pulaski County, Ark. (JM).

13 In Washington, D.C., Pentagon officials announced that the Air Force Academy's football team did not accept the invitation to play in the Sugar Bowl on New Year's Day, 1959, because Louisiana law required segregated seating of spectators. The Air Force Falcons had an undefeated record, and there were no black players on the team. However, in the past army and navy teams had also refused to play teams in Louisiana (NYT).

14 In Washington, D.C., at a meeting of 220 Roman Catholic bishops a statement was released entitled "Discrimination and the Christian Conscience" in which the church leaders declared that any form of legal or compulsory racial segregation was wrong and did not conform with "the Christian view of man's nature and rights" (NYT).

25 In Washington, D.C., the Supreme Court refused to review a lower court's decision uphold-ing the Alabama pupil placement law. The law gave the local school boards broad discretion in pupil assignment, but Birmingham's Rev. Fred Shuttlesworth, one of the plaintiffs in the case, said that discriminatory actions by local school boards in student placements would continue to be challenged in the courts (NYT).

27 In Ann Arbor, Mich., the student council at the University of Michigan voted to ban from the campus the Sigma Kappa sorority. The move came after officers in the national headquarters suspended the chapters at Tufts and Cornell universities when they pledged black women students (JM).

29, 30 In New Orleans, La., the U.S. district court struck down the Louisiana law banning competition between black and white athletes. While the decision paved the way for black and white players to meet in the Sugar Bowl, it did not affect the state law mandating segregated seating at public events (NYT).

1 In Little Rock, Ark., state attorney general Blue Bennett filed a suit against the NAACP claiming that it had not registered as a corporation doing business in the state. Any "foreign" corporation failing to register was subject to a fine of five thousand dollars (SSN).

7 In Washington, D.C., the Democratic National Committee by a vote of 84 to 18 endorsed the strong pro–civil rights positions taken by the chairman, Paul M. Butler. Protests by southerners on the committee against the resolution were overwhelmingly defeated. Also defeated was Louisiana members' attempt to unseat Camille Gravel as the state's national committeeman because of his support for the party's civil rights program (NYT).

8 In New York City, in a speech before B'nai B'rith's Anti-Defamation League, Attorney General William P. Rogers warned southern leaders that the federal government and private industry would be reluctant to expand or establish plants and other facilities where schools and other public conveniences were not open to all people. As far as Rogers was concerned, the school integration issue was settled and the Justice Department would enforce all federal decrees (NYT).

11 In Boston, Mass., Celtics player Bill Russell complained to officials of the National Basketball Association (NBA) after he and six other black players were not allowed into the same hotel with their white teammates during a visit to Charlotte, N.C. NBA league president Maurice Podoloff said the issue of possibly banning games in the South would be discussed at the upcoming NBA meeting in January 1959 (JM).

11 In Monroe, N.C., Dr. A. P. Perry, the militant leader of the local NAACP branch, was convicted in a second trial by an all-white jury of performing an abortion on a white woman and was sentenced to two to three years in prison. Perry, who fired on a KKK motorcade in 1957, planned to appeal the verdict (JM).

18 In Burlington, Vt., Phillip H. Hoff, chair of the Community Relations Committee, announced that the group had found a great deal of housing and employment discrimination in the city. The Committee was formed the previous year after black personnel at Ethan Allen Air Force Base complained about being denied housing in several neighborhoods. Hoff said, "many people sincerely believe there is no discrimination here" (JM).

19 In Jackson, Miss., the charter of the separate black American Legion post was revoked by state commander Fred Metcalfe because of statements made by post commander Albert Powell calling for the hiring of black policemen and firemen. Black Legion posts had been warned that they would be expelled if the membership included "radical agitators." Post commander Powell promised to appeal the state commander's action (NYT).

20 In Chicago, Ill., William R. Ming, Jr., president of the American Veterans Committee, offered a charter with his organization to the American Legion post in Jackson, Miss., ousted from the state organization because of the leaders' support for civil rights. Ming announced that if the Jackson post made it clear that membership was also available to whites, it could be given a charter (NYT).

25 In Houston, Tex., the harassment of Mrs. Charles White, the first African American elected to the school board and only black public official in the state, continued. In November, a gasoline-soaked cross was burned on the lawn of her home. Subsequently, unidentified persons sprayed her car with air-rifle pellets (JM).

25 In Little Rock, Ark., after Attorney General Blue Bennett filed charges against the NAACP claiming that it had not registered as a corporation doing business in the state, ten black ministers filed a suit in federal court challenging the constitutionality of the law that created the Arkansas State Sovereignty Commission. The new law required groups, such as the NAACP, to submit their financial and membership records to the new commission or be subject to a fine of five thousand dollars. The ministers' suit charged that this legislation was passed "to circumvent the supreme law of the land" (JM).

25 In Oberlin, Ohio, Oberlin College president William Stevenson canceled a scheduled student exchange program in Washington, D.C., after being informed by American University president Hurst Anderson that black women students from Oberlin would not be allowed to live in the dorms with white students (JM).

25 In Tallahassee, Fla., an interracial research team sponsored by twelve major civic organizations reported that segregation was decreasing in accommodations in Dade County, except in the public schools. In Miami, Coral Gables, and Miami Beach, bus segregation had practically disappeared, black guests were provided accommodations at most hotels, and an increasing number of restaurants served black customers (JM).

On 18 April 1959, in Washington, D.C., more than 15,000 people, white and black, participated in the Youth March in support of school integration and civil rights legislation. In this photo, part of the group is shown marching down Madison Drive in the mall leading to the Washington Monument. They then moved to the Sylvan Theater to participate in a rally sponsored by the NAACP. (SOURCE: CORBIS BETTMANN)

1959

"THE STORMS OF LIFE
ARE RAGING"

The U.S. Commission on Civil Rights came into existence under the provisions of the Civil Rights Act of 1957. Through public hearings held throughout the country, and the investigations sponsored by the commission's state advisory committees, civil rights abuses were exposed and recommendations for legislation and other legal action were offered. The commission focused attention on growing southern opposition to massive resistance campaigns that deprived black and white children of public education. Moreover, instances of racial discrimination moved from domestic affairs to international incidents in 1959 when they involved diplomats from the independent black nations emerging on the African continent, and thus served to embarrass the United States on the world stage. Also embarrassing were the bizarre objections raised by segregationists to the children's books found in southern public libraries. As "the storms of life" were raging, white extremists provided comic relief from the deadly serious business of bringing true democracy to the United States.

JANUARY 1959

❙ In **Jackson, Miss.**, the state supreme court struck down the 1956 law providing a ten-year maximum prison sentence for "interracial cohabitation" on a technicality. The suit was brought by an elderly black woman, Daisy Ratcliff, who was given a ten-year sentence for living with a white man, E. L. Arrington. The court found that the law was "ambiguously worded," and the decision paved the way for overturning other felony convictions for interracial cohabitation (JM).

❙ In **Montgomery, Ala.**, all thirteen public parks were closed by the city commission after a suit was filed in federal court by eight black residents. In August 1958 Martin Luther King and others asked the commissioners to open the parks to all residents, and they responded that they would never allow integration. The suit sought to end the ban on African Americans entering all-white city parks (SSN).

3 In **Monroe, N.C.**, when two black boys, aged nine and ten, were sent to a state reformatory for allegedly forcing a young white girl to kiss one of them, protests were sent from around the country. State education commissioner Blaine M. Madison announced the two boys would be returned to their parents after a minimum time at the Morrison State Training School, but NAACP lawyers planned to appeal the boys' convictions (NYT).

3 In **Sacramento, Calif.**, in his last opinion as state attorney general, Edmund G. Brown, the California governor-elect, wrote to eight state legislators who requested his views that state-supported colleges could not subsidize fraternities that restricted membership on racial or religious grounds (NYT).

8 In New Orleans, La., as a result of a U.S. Supreme Court order, the board of commissioners for the city parks decided that all citizens could use these facilities. Ellis Laborde, city parks' general manager, stated that this decision means "that Negroes are now permitted to use all park facilities—the tennis courts, baseball fields, the golf courses, the amusement rides—all facilities" (JM).

8 In New York City, Thurgood Marshall, director of the NAACP Legal Defense Fund, said that under pressure from southern congressmen the Internal Revenue Service (IRS) was again investigating the NAACP's tax-exempt status. Marshall stated that they were fully complying with IRS regulations. The organization had been subjected to an IRS investigation in October 1954 (JM).

8 In Kansas City, Mo., Rev. Arthur Marshall, Jr., and other ministers led the picketing and boycott of five downtown department stores whose cafeterias did not serve black customers. Marshall said the protest would continue until the store managers changed the discriminatory practices (JM).

8 In Denver, Colo., the Colorado Anti-Discrimination Commission ordered Continental Airlines officials to hire Marlon D. Green as a pilot. Green complained to the state agency that he had been turned down for employment because of his race, while the company hired white pilots who were less qualified (JM).

10 In Atlanta, Ga., federal judge Frank Hooper ruled segregation on the city's public transportation system unconstitutional. The suit was brought by Rev. Samuel Williams and John Porter, who led a group of black residents who challenged bus seating practices by sitting in the "white" section. Mayor William B. Hartsfield was pleased with the smooth transition to desegregated seating on the city's buses and trolleys. He believed the lack of incidents or problems proved wrong "the clowns and demagogues who predicted riots, bloodshed, and intermarriage" (NYT).

11 In Atlanta, Ga., federal judge Boyd Sloan ruled that Georgia State College could not deny students admission on the basis of race. In a case brought by Barbara Hunt, Myra E. D. Holland, and Iris M. Welch, the judge argued that the requirement that three alumni sign students' applications for admission discriminated against black applicants because Georgia State had no black alumni (NYT).

11 In Washington, D.C., U.S. commissioner of education Lawrence G. Derthick revealed that more than $250,000 in funding for vocational education under the National Defense Education Act went to segregated vocational schools in Alabama, Mississippi, and Florida. Justice Department officials proposed a ban on federal funding to states that maintained segregated public schools (NYT).

15 In Des Moines, Iowa, a ten-foot cross made of bales of hay was burned on the lawn of the home of Rev. Ian J. McCrae after he agreed to sell it to Mr. and Mrs. Harold Carr. The black couple was offered one thousand dollars not to move into the all-white neighborhood, but refused it because they were in immediate need of housing, having been displaced by freeway construction (JM).

15 In Lansing, Mich., Charles Brown, aide to Gov. G. Mennen Williams, blamed racial discrimination for his failure to find housing in the state capital for over a year. Brown said his situation was not unique, and he recommended that Governor Williams support "forceful legislation" to end housing bias in the state (JM).

15 In Pasadena, Calif., after Joan R. Williams was chosen queen of the Tournament of Roses, she found that because she was African American, she was not invited to events associated with the celebration, did not ride on a float during the Rose Bowl Parade (Pasadena city officials decided not to include one in their own parade), and was not given a special place of honor at the Rose Bowl Football Game (JM).

20 In Montgomery, Ala., for the first time in many years, no bands from Tuskegee Institute and other black state schools were asked to participate in inaugural parades. Ed Azar, chair of the inaugural ceremonies, said that governor-elect John Patterson vowed to use every legal means to block public school integration in the state and felt it would be embarrassing to ask the black bands to participate in the parade. Patterson later fired Winston Craig (black), who served as chauffeur for the last four Alabama governors, and replaced him with a state highway patrolman (NYT).

21 In Atlanta, Ga., the state house and senate moved quickly on a series of anti-integration bills. Among the measures being considered were laws giving the governor power to close individual public schools that were integrated and to close the school from which the black student(s) had transferred and to close any unit in the state university system in order to maintain public order (NYT).

23 In Detroit, Mich., at a meeting of National Basketball Association club owners, it was decided that in order to spare black players any embarrassment, all teams must receive assurances of nondiscrimination in housing and dining facilities before signing for a game. NBA president Maurice Podoloff said discrimination complaints by Bill Russell and Elgin Baylor required these changes (NYT).

23 In Detroit, Mich., the second Governor's Conference on Civil Rights was held, sponsored by Gov. G. Mennen Williams, and the discussions revolved around proposals for gaining the passage of fair employment practices legislation by the U.S. Congress (NYT).

29 In New Haven, Conn., before Martin Luther King gave a lecture at Yale University on the topic "The Future of Integration," an anonymous bomb threat was made against Woolsey Hall, where the speech was to take place. Police searched the premises but found no bomb, and King was able to address the more than eighteen hundred people in attendance (JM).

29 In Washington, D.C., in an open letter, the President's Committee on Government Contracts demanded that the construction trades unions working on the Southwest Washington Redevelopment Project accept a nondiscrimination agreement and begin to admit black workers into their apprenticeship programs. John Roosevelt, a committee member, said that the companies holding the contracts wanted to hire black workers, but the construction trades unions, especially the electricians and plumbers, refused to admit them (JM).

29 In Nashville, Tenn., the Southern Regional Council issued a report noting that thirty-three southern cities in nine states had desegregated their transit systems without incident. The action was voluntary in all locations, except New Orleans, La., Montgomery, Ala., Atlanta, Ga., and Columbia, S.C. (JM).

29 In Washington, D.C., fourteen-year-old James A. Johnson from Chicago, who came to the District to become the first black page on Capitol Hill, was told there was no opening in the Capitol Page School. However, five congressmen assigned him to their office staffs, making him eligible to enter the school in March 1959 (NYT).

FEBRUARY 1959

1 In Tampa, Fla., when Gov. LeRoy Collins revealed that it cost $62,000 to train each black student in the law school at Florida A & M University, rather than allow them to attend the University of Florida Law School, where the cost was $800 per student, the pro-segregation *Tampa Tribune* reversed its earlier position and opposed state legislator Tom Beasley, who said, "Segregation at any cost." The *Tribune* editors said integration was more "realistic" (SSN).

5 In Bessemer, Ala., Asbury Howard, Sr., vice president of the International Mine, Mill, and Smelter Workers Union, was summoned to recorders court for putting up a billboard asking black citizens to register and vote. Howard was convicted of "breach of the peace" for putting up the billboard and given a six-month jail sentence and $105 fine. Howard and his son were attacked by a white mob outside the courtroom. Police finally interceded and arrested Howard for disorderly conduct and resisting arrest. Howard's home had been bombed in April 1957 (JM).

5 In Boston, Mass., the Massachusetts State Commission Against Discrimination announced a plan to distribute an official poster to hotels, restaurants, resorts, and other public accommodations stating that these facilities were open to all orderly persons, regardless of race, creed, or color, in keeping with the state anti-discrimination laws (JM).

5 In Washington, D.C., officials for the Democratic National Committee said that although Miami had better facilities, their convention would be held in Los Angeles. Increasing racial tensions in Miami were cited as a reason for bypassing the southern city (JM).

9 In New York City, in response to information reported in Chet Huntley's NBC-TV program *The Second Agony of Atlanta*, NAACP official Roy Wilkins pointed out that the NAACP was not an "extremist" group. Wilkins made it clear that the extremists were those in the South who were determined to deny black citizens their equal rights (NYT).

11 In New Delhi, India, Martin Luther King, his wife, Coretta, and Dr. Lawrence Reddick began a month-long study tour of India, sponsored by the American Friends Committee. Dr. King wanted to study the Gandhian nonviolent resistance movement to determine its appropriateness as a strategy for the civil rights struggle in the United States (NYT).

11 In Snow Hill, N.C., twenty-eight hundred black students staged a boycott of the all-black high school and elementary schools because of inadequate facilities. The high school had no gym, inadequate cafeteria and library facilities, and overcrowded classrooms. Jasper E. Williams, one of the student leaders, said, "If it takes integration to get us a decent school, let's have it." School officials promised to request more funds for black schools (NYT).

14 In Monroe, N.C., the two black boys, James H. Thompson, ten, and David Simpson, nine, who were sent to reform school for being convicted of kissing a white girl were finally released after great protest and the efforts of the NAACP. When they had been sent away, they were not allowed to meet with their parents. After release, they were reunited with their mothers in Charlotte, N.C. (NYT).

19 In Chicago, Ill., in a special article in *Jet* magazine titled "How Negro Kids Prepared for Virginia Integration," the students' tutoring programs and church meetings were described. The students recognized that they would be pioneers and were determined to be prepared (JM).

22 In Hollywood, Calif., after winning the award for the best performance by an actor at the Berlin Film Festival, Sidney Poitier was nominated for an Academy Award in the best actor category for his role in *The Defiant Ones*. Poitier was the first African American nominated for an Oscar in this category (NYT).

22 In Scottsdale, Ariz., Jerry "Pumpsey" Greene, the only black player on the Boston Red Sox baseball team, was denied accommodations at the Safari Hotel, where the team members were staying during spring training. Team officials said they would make arrangements for Greene to stay at a hotel in Phoenix (NYT).

22 In Washington, D.C., southern Democrats made plans to oppose appropriations for the continued activities of the President's Committee on Government Contracts. Established by an executive order, the committee received $200,000 annually to investigate charges of discrimination by federal contractors. President Eisenhower had expressed his desire that the committee become a permanent government agency (NYT).

26 In Little Rock, Ark., after state senator Morrell Gathright warned legislators that Arkansas A&M College (black) in College Heights might lose its accreditation, leading to a "mass" of black students applying to white state colleges, the lawmakers raised their annual appropriation from $700,000 to $800,000. The threat to the college's accreditation came from earlier moves by legislators to reduce the school's annual budget (JM).

MARCH 1959

1 In Macon County, Ala., when a Justice Department suit against two white registrars, Grady

THE U.S. COMMISSION ON CIVIL RIGHTS
SWINGS INTO ACTION

The U.S. Commission on Civil Rights (USCCR) conducted hearings and investigations into discriminatory policies and practices in the areas of voting rights and housing throughout the country in 1959. Through the commission's state advisory committees, information was gathered and arrangements were made for hearings to investigate charges of discrimination and make recommendations to the Department of Justice and the U.S. Congress for action. The Utah State Advisory Committee conducted an investigation into civil rights abuses in that state and reported in April 1959 that although there were only about four thousand African Americans in the state, they were the most victimized minority group. The committee reported that there was also significant discrimination leveled at Mexican-Americans and Native Americans in Utah.

The Missouri State Advisory Committee reported in June 1959 that although 95 percent of the black students in the state were assigned to desegregated public school districts, the individual schools remained segregated due to discriminatory housing practices. Housing patterns served to perpetuate de facto segregation in public schools.

Former baseball star Jackie Robinson testified in February at USCCR hearings held in New York City to investigate housing discrimination. Robinson said that when he and several associates tried to launch a housing development project in Brooklyn, they were not allowed to purchase property that was later sold to white developers. In May 1959 at commission hearings held in Chicago, NAACP leader Rev. Carl Fuqua called for an executive order banning the use of federal funds to build all-white communities and rejected the suggestion that racial quotas be established for the number of black families allowed to move into all-white neighborhoods.

After gathering information on voting practices in eight southern states, and just days before it would have gone out of existence, the USCCR recommended the passage of a constitutional amendment outlawing literacy tests for voting, and the appointment of federal registrars to cities and counties where voter discrimination was prevalent. The registrars would receive complaints from citizens and report them to the Justice Department. While a version of this proposal was passed by the House Judiciary Committee in July 1959, it was blocked in the Senate by southern Democrats. However, on the last day of the Senate session, 16 September 1959, an amendment was added to an appropriations bill that extended the life of the USCCR for two years, and the bill passed the Senate.

In 1959 the USCCR also recommended that the federal government withdraw funds from colleges and universities with racially discriminatory admissions policies and called for the adoption of a policy of nondiscrimination in federally funded housing. These recommendations would be taken up by the U.S. Congress in the early 1960s.

Rogers and E. P. Livingston, was dropped after they resigned their positions, U.S. district court judge Frank M. Johnson warned other county registrars not to try the same tactic. Judge Johnson said he would support a suit to compel state officials to appoint registrars in that area (SSN).

1 In State College, Miss., despite a vote by the student body of 973 to 162 in favor of having its high-ranking basketball team play in the racially integrated NCAA Tournament, Mississippi State

University president Ben Hilbun said students could not determine school policy. Athletic teams from the state adhered to an unwritten rule that they could not play out-of-state contests with integrated teams. Students later burned President Hilbun in effigy on campus after their basketball team was forced to forgo participation in the NCAA playoffs (NYT).

2 In Marrero, La., when two black high school students, Carroll Pierre and John Mitchell, decided to sit in the front pews at St. Joseph the Worker Catholic Church, bypassing the Jim Crow section, fifty white parishioners walked out. New Orleans archbishop Joseph Rummel expressed despair and disapproval at the incident. The following week the students were joined in the front pews by black adults, and Father Anthony Rousseau ordered whites not to interfere. Father Rousseau promised to maintain the changes because the New Orleans diocese had officially ended segregated seating in 1953 (NYT).

2 In **Wilmington, Del.,** in the suburb of Collins Park mobs of more than three hundred white people had been protesting against the move of a black family into the neighborhood. Within days of the protests, a boycott was called against all merchants who served George Rayfield and his family. Rayfield was subsequently forced out of his home because of the negative impact the protest was having on his garbage removal business (NYT).

3 In **Detroit, Mich.,** the strike by 4,232 white policemen against the order for squad-car integration with 133 black policemen eased after police commissioner Herbert W. Hart declared that white policemen must follow the order or resign from the force. Hart said the white policemen must understand that "integration is here to stay" (NYT).

5–6 In **Washington, D.C.,** hearings were held in the Senate and House on numerous civil rights bills. The most important measure was the Douglas-Javits-Celler bill, which called for recognition of the Supreme Court's school desegregation decision, authorized the Justice Department to intervene in civil rights cases, and provided funds for public schools faced with a cutoff of state support due to integration (NYT).

12 In **New York City,** Urban League officials announced that eleven black musicians had been hired by several orchestras and Broadway productions in recent months. The hiring came about after charges of discrimination were leveled against managers. Among those charged were the New York Philharmonic, the Radio City Orchestra, and several Broadway shows, including *The Music Man* (JM).

12–13 In **New York City,** after a successful tour, Lorraine Hansberry's *A Raisin in the Sun* opened on Broadway to rave reviews. Starring Sidney Poitier, Ruby Dee, and Claudia McNeil and directed by Lloyd Richards, the play dealt with the trials of a black family about to move into an all-white neighborhood (NYT).

13 In **Rutledge, Pa.,** after the newly purchased home of Chester NAACP president George T. Raymond was damaged by a fire of suspicious origins in the all-white suburb, the borough council decided he could not rebuild it, but must sell the land to the council to construct a municipal office building. If Raymond refused to sell it, the council promised to take the issue to the local common pleas court (NYT).

19 In **New York City,** following his month-long tour of India, Martin Luther King said he was often asked about the problem of segregation in this country. King found that "India is integrating its 'untouchables' faster than the United States is integrating its Negro minority" (NYT).

21 In **Washington, D.C.,** at a meeting between AFL-CIO president George Meany and the NAACP's Roy Wilkins, Herbert Hill, and Labor leader A. Philip Randolph, Meany promised to intervene personally to end discrimination by unions and give the federation's Civil Rights Committee more power to crack down on unions that refused to allow black workers to join (NYT).

21–22 In **Lakeland, Fla.,** three black players on the Detroit Tigers baseball team were denied accommodations at the New Florida Hotel with the team's white players during spring training. Club managers offered Ossie Virgil, Maury Wills, and Ossie Alvarez the option of staying in the Tigers' nearby training camp or finding apartments in the local black community (NYT).

APRIL 1959

1 In **Atlanta, Ga.,** education officials revealed more evidence that the state law designed to keep black students out of white colleges had completely backfired and was keeping white students from enrolling. At the University of Georgia, Georgia State College, and other white schools enrollments since the spring semester were 50 percent or more lower than in the fall of 1958. The law requires that undergraduates be under twenty-one and graduate students under twenty-five to be admitted to the state university system. At Armstrong Junior College in Savannah, president Foreman Hawes complained that efforts to avoid integration had resulted in a 90 percent drop in the number of white students (SSN).

2 In Topeka, Kans., the state legislature passed a civil rights bill that prohibited racial discrimination in hotels, restaurants, and other public accommodations. The bill provided for fines up to one thousand dollars for violations. The measure was later signed by Gov. George Docking (JM).

4 In Washington, D.C., the second Youth March for Public School Desegregation took place at the Washington Monument with more than thirty thousand people in attendance. Among the speakers were Jackie Robinson, Martin Luther King, Roy Wilkins, and Kenyan labor leader Tom Mboya. Four student organizers of the march presented a petition to White House aide E. Frederic Morrow calling for faster action by the federal government in bringing about school integration (NYT).

12 In Boston, Mass., protests were mounted at Fenway Park following the sending down of Jerry "Pumpsie" Green, the only black player on the Boston Red Sox baseball team, to their minor league club in Minneapolis. Protesters carried signs saying "We want a pennant, not a white team." The NAACP and the Ministerial Alliance of Boston asked the Massachusetts State Commission Against Discrimination to probe the hiring policy of the team (NYT).

17 In Washington, D.C., Democratic party chairman Paul Butler in a speech before the American Society of Newspaper Editors predicted that the 1960 platform would support the Supreme Court's school desegregation decisions and oppose the massive resistance campaigns. Butler suggested that those southern Democrats who could not support these positions should consider leaving the party (NYT).

19 In Sacramento, Calif., Gov. Edmund G. Brown signed the fair employment practices bill and directed the heads of all state agencies to make sure that they followed through on all its provisions. Brown said it would be tragic for the state government to fail to carry out policies and practices mandated for private enterprises (NYT).

22 In Boston, Mass., the Massachusetts State Commission Against Discrimination launched an investigation into charges that the Boston Red Sox baseball team practiced discrimination. The charges were brought after the only black player, Jerry "Pumpsie" Green, was sent to the minor leagues. According to Joe Cronin, American League president, Red Sox owner Tom Yawkey was not prejudiced and had "colored help on his South Carolina plantation and takes excellent care of them, pays good salaries, and they are all very happy" (NYT).

23 In Atlanta, Ga., given the negative impact on white enrollments, the state board of regents was given the power to make exceptions to the regulation that no undergraduates over twenty-one or graduates students over twenty-five be admitted. The regents were allowed to require academic tests and any other standards for university admission they deemed necessary (NYT).

23 In Sacramento, Calif., the state senate passed and sent to the governor for signature a bill that repealed the state's prohibition against interracial marriages and eliminated all references to race on marriage licenses (JM).

23 In Little Rock, Ark., a black woman, Hazel Payne, with rare type A negative blood almost died during surgery because of the new state law requiring labeling of all blood by race. There were not enough African Americans with her rare blood type, and despite city-wide appeals whites failed to come forward because they thought she would not be able to receive whites' blood. While the law allowed mixing of blood with the patient's consent, protests against the new law came from white and black physicians and others who pointed out that the law added unnecessary confusion about donating blood (JM).

30 In Los Angeles, Calif., the state superior court dismissed a suit brought by A. Palmer Reed, whose daughter was denied admission to the Hollywood Professional School because of her race. The appeals court ruled that "state anti-discrimination statutes were never designed for the purpose of regulating what strictly private groups do" (JM).

MAY 1959

1 In Birmingham, Ala., the state court of appeals dismissed the appeals and left standing the fines and jail terms given to Rev. Fred Shuttlesworth and twelve others for protests against bus segregation carried out in 1958 (SSN).

INTERNATIONAL INCIDENTS CAUSED BY RACIAL DISCRIMINATION IN THE UNITED STATES

The racist practices in the United States toward people of African descent created international incidents when African dignitaries and diplomats became the victims of racial discrimination. In October 1957 when K. A. Gbedemah, the finance minister of Ghana, was traveling from Washington, D.C., to New York City, he was refused service at a Howard Johnson restaurant in Dover, Del. Radio stations broadcast news of the incident worldwide, and State Department and Howard Johnson executives issued public apologies. The minister accepted an invitation to dine at the White House with both President Eisenhower and Vice President Nixon, but government officials publicly expressed fears of future incidents as more African diplomats came to the United States.

The West Indian Federation, made up of British territories of the Caribbean, was formed in January 1958, and Princess Margaret inaugurated its parliament in April. Iris Winnifred King, the mayor of Kingston, Jamaica, made an official visit to the United States in November 1958. *The New York Times* reported that while traveling through Louisville, Ky., Mayor King was refused a cup of coffee by a clerk in a local drugstore, who told her, "We don't serve colored people." Mayor King made an official complaint to the British ambassador Sir Harold Caccia, and afterward she received an official apology from Louisville's acting mayor, R. C. Bing. However, Mayor King said she had "no desire to travel in the South ever again." In June 1959, the *Times* reported that the U.S. circuit court of appeals in New Orleans awarded a Jamaican couple, Mr. and Mrs. Grover C. Bullock, $500,000 in damages after they were assaulted by whites while riding in Louisiana on a bus owned by the Tamiami Trails Bus Company.

The incident that received the most attention in 1959, however, took place in October during a state visit by Sekou Toure, president of the newly independent Republic of Guinea in West Africa. When State Department officials announced that President Toure would visit Durham and Chapel Hill, N.C., where Gov. Luther Hodges would host an official dinner for him at the University of North Carolina, white segregationists protested vehemently and threatened to disrupt the event. While the dinner did take place, fifty policemen and Secret Service agents had to provide a network of security for President Toure throughout his visit.

Because Asian and African visitors were regularly victimized by racial discrimination in Washington, D.C., and the surrounding suburbs, administrators for the International Cooperation Administration (ICA), which brought hundreds of foreign technicians to the United States for training sessions, ordered its instructors not to assign trainees to facilities that practiced racial discrimination. In September 1959, the ICA compiled and distributed to trainees a list of hotels and restaurants to be avoided.

After the successful revolution in Cuba in early 1959, Fidel Castro announced that the practice of segregating Afro-Cubans would be outlawed and government officials in Havana would take steps to end all forms of racial discrimination. In a widely reported speech in April 1959, Castro praised the contribution of Afro-Cubans to the revolution and pointed out that there were "no pure Caucasians" in Cuba; "all of us have African blood."

1 In **Nashville, Tenn.**, eleven leaders of the National Council of Churches protested against what had become a "southern version of McCarthyism." While initially it was members of the NAACP who were attacked as "subversive," attempts were more recently made "to silence those who do not accept the extremist position of segregation" (SSN).

4 In **Tallahassee, Fla.**, twenty-seven hundred Florida A&M University students staged a protest calling for "equal justice" in the case of four white men who were arrested for abducting and raping at gunpoint a black woman student. The four men were captured by local police and indicted for the crime. Although the trial was set to begin on 26 May 1959, not one white man had ever been convicted of raping a black woman in the Florida courts (NYT).

4–5 In **Tallahassee, Fla.**, Rev. C. K. Steele called for the abolition of the death penalty in rape cases as the only way to gain equal treatment for African Americans accused of interracial crimes. Steele pointed out that the four whites convicted of raping a black woman student were not likely to be sentenced to death, while four blacks were awaiting execution in the state for the same crime (NYT).

5 In **Poplarville, Miss.**, the disfigured body of Mack Charles Parker, who was accused of raping a white woman, was found in the Pearl River one week after he was kidnapped from the local jail by masked men. FBI and local police were investigating the murder, and his mother, Eliza Parker, fled the state after she received death threats warning her not to appear at a rally to protest the killing (NYT).

7 In **Washington, D.C.**, legislation was reintroduced by Arkansas senator John McClellan to authorize the federal government to surrender jurisdiction of property located in the various states. Withdrawn after black protests in the previous session, the bill would allow state and local segregation laws to be in effect on military bases throughout the South (JM).

7 In **Oklahoma City, Okla.**, thirteen black firemen were assigned to two previously all-white stations in a move to integrate the city's fire stations. Fire chief Haskel Graves said that in the future black firemen would be assigned regularly to all-white stations to complete the integration process (JM).

7 In **Kansas City, Mo.**, the managers of the Jones and Emery Bird Thayer stores joined those at Macy's, Peck, and Kline stores and agreed to end discrimination against black customers in their cafeterias. The Committee for Social Action had been picketing and organized a boycott against the five department stores to end racially discriminatory practices (JM).

12 In **Albany, N.Y.**, in the first jail sentence upheld for violation of the state's anti-discrimination law, the state supreme court upheld the conviction of Henry G. Finn, the manager of the Mid-City Swimming Pools in Menards, N.Y., for discriminating against Barbara Ann Sharpe because of her race. Finn was given a five-day jail sentence (NYT).

14 In **Miami, Fla.**, a group of black and white customers, led by Dr. John O. Brown, were refused service when they conducted a sit-in at a lunch counter at the W. T. Grant department store. Dr. Brown said he would attempt to meet with store managers to gain service for black customers (JM).

14 In **Camden County, N.J.**, Judge Edward V. Martino issued a cease and desist order against the Holly House Restaurant in Pennsauken. The restaurant owners were accused of discriminating against black customers. This was the first such action taken against a public establishment accused of racial discrimination in New Jersey (JM).

21 In **Springfield, Mass.**, Lindsey B. Johnson, a black decorated war veteran and businessman, complained to police about harassment and phone threats warning him not to move into the home he had under construction in an all-white neighborhood. Johnson said his family had been saving all their lives for the home and had no intention of being forced out by whites (JM).

21 In **Charlotte, N.C.**, because the only black senior, Gus Roberts, was interested in attending the junior-senior prom, principal Edward Sanders canceled the dance and invited 1,000 eligible white students and 250 guests to his home for a private party. Gus Roberts was not invited (JM).

26 In Washington, D.C., the U.S. Supreme Court upheld a lower court's decision declaring the Louisiana law barring interracial athletic competition unconstitutional. The court also upheld the lower court's decision that segregated seating at public sporting and other events was unconstitutional (NYT).

JUNE 1959

4 In Detroit, Mich., after receiving numerous threats and violent attacks, Ethel Watkins decided to sell the home she had purchased in an all-white neighborhood. Watkins was victimized by almost nightly protests by 100 to 150 whites ever since she moved into her home in 1957 (JM).

6 In Atlanta, Ga., the U.S. district court declared segregation in the local public schools unconstitutional and ordered school officials to desegregate "within a reasonable time." Judge Frank A. Hooper ordered school officials to present a complete integration plan by 1 December 1959. Attorney Constance Baker Motley led the NAACP team in this important victory (NYT).

9 In Little Rock, Ark., in a suit brought by black teacher B. T. Shelton, a three-judge federal court declared unconstitutional a state law forbidding the hiring of NAACP members by any state or local governmental agency. However, the court ruled that it was legal for the state to require teachers in public schools to file affidavits listing all organizations to which they belonged or contributed (NYT).

9 In Washington, D.C., the U.S. Supreme Court for the second time voided the $100,000 fine leveled against the Alabama NAACP for failing to turn over membership and financial records to state officials. The earlier decision was challenged by the Alabama Supreme Court. The justices also upheld the constitutionality of a North Carolina law requiring prospective voters to be able to read and interpret any section of the state constitution (NYT).

10 In Houston, Tex., the only black member of the school board, Mrs. Charles White, voted against the majority's decision to order a public referendum on public school integration in response to NAACP action. White pointed out that a referendum was unnecessary, but the board needed to come up with an acceptable integration plan (NYT).

18 In New York City, the all-white International Longshoremen's Union admitted its first black members, Albert Miller and James Caldwell. Miller had filed a complaint against the union's discriminatory membership practices with the New York State Commission Against Discrimination (JM).

23 In New York City, the announcement that composer-musician Duke Ellington won the 1959 Spingarn Medal was praised and criticized by the organization's membership. While most admitted Ellington's great contributions to music, others questioned his record in the field of civil rights. Most recently, Ellington had written the score for the MGM movie *Anatomy of a Murder*, starring James Stewart (NYT).

25 In Washington, D.C., southern congressmen tried to gain the passage of a bill that would give the state laws priority over federal legislation and allow the states to enforce their own "sedition" laws. Sponsored by Virginia representative Howard Smith and Mississippi senator James Eastland, if enacted the law would allow the states to determine what groups were considered "subversive" or involved in conspiracies against its laws. The NAACP launched an all-out campaign to prevent the measure's passage (NYT).

JULY 1959

2 In Los Angeles, Calif., Herbert A. Greenwood, the only black member of the city's police commission, resigned, charging that police chief Frank Parker bullied the commission into uselessness and failed to provide records on black police personnel. Greenwood came under attack from the black community as the number of black arrests and incidents of police brutality increased (JM).

THE RABBIT'S WEDDING: AN INTERRACIAL ROMANCE?

As part of the demands for an end to racial segregation in public accommodations, African Americans petitioned numerous city councils to be allowed to use the main public libraries. After the city councils and library boards in cities in North Carolina, Arkansas, Florida, Louisiana, and Virginia decided to allow African Americans to use the main libraries, Atlanta's main library was integrated without incident in May 1959. Library board chairman Hix Green noted that there had been many requests for service by black residents and "we could find no law prohibiting it." However, in Savannah, Ga., in November, when black residents requested use of the main library, the library board refused. Board chairman Clarence Reinschmidt declared that any books they wanted from the main library would be made available at the separate black branch.

In Portsmouth, Va., two black dentists, Dr. Hugo Owens and Dr. James W. Holley, filed a suit in federal court in December 1959 to enjoin city officials from appropriating funds for the public library because it was still "for whites only." Library officials had promised in March 1959 that they would pursue "voluntary desegregation," but had failed to live up to their commitment.

In 1959, however, the children's books found in southern public libraries caused more controversy than demands by African Americans for access. In Montgomery, Ala., in May, Emily W. Reed, director of the Alabama Public Library's Service Division, reported that the children's book *The Rabbit's Wedding* had to be removed from the open shelves and placed on reserve following numerous protests from segregationists that the book condoned "intermarriage," because the black rabbit marries the white rabbit. The author, Garth Williams, commented, "I was completely unaware that animals with white fur were considered blood relations to white human beings." Harper Brothers, the publisher, later reported that the controversy created a huge increase in the demand for the book.

In June 1959 state legislators in Tallahassee, Fla., denied the request by Miami segregationist David Hawthorne to remove from public libraries in the state the children's book *The Three Little Pigs* because of its "pro-integration stance." The lawmakers dismissed Hawthorne's contention that the "big bad wolf" blew down the home of the "white pig" and the "mulatto pig" but was unable to blow down the home of the "black pig."

In July 1959, George Shannon, editor of the *Shreveport* (La.) *Journal,* called for the removal of the children's book *Black and White* from the shelves of the local public library because he believed it advocated integration. Chief librarian Inez Boone removed the book, which told the story of the marriage of a "grumpy black man and a white lady" because it was worn out, "not because of being objectionable." Boone protested against the "witch hunt" taking place in the South against children's books and said that most books contain material objectionable to some people, "even the Bible."

2 In Washington, D.C., FBI director J. Edgar Hoover made public a letter he sent to military policeman Henry B. Charleston at Redstone Arsenal (Ala.). Charleston had accused the FBI of withdrawing from the investigation of the recent kidnap and murder of Mack Charles Parker and thus "making it more dangerous" for black citizens in Mississippi. Hoover claimed that the FBI investigated the murder and turned over to the Justice Department all information. It was the Justice officials who decided not to enter the prosecution of the case (JM).

9 In Washington, D.C., President Eisenhower publicly stated that he believed that segregation was "morally wrong." The president finally made the statement after he had been criticized on numerous occasions by Martin Luther King for not taking a public position. King said that Eisenhower's statement was "encouraging" (NYT).

10 In Forest Hills, N.Y., after UN diplomat Ralph Bunche and his son were denied membership in the West Side Tennis Club because of their race, six U.S. senators called for moving the Davis Cup matches from Forest Hills, and the New York Commission on Intergroup Relations launched a probe to determine if the club was violating state law (NYT).

15 In **Craven County, N.C.**, school officials announced that some black children of military personnel at Cherry Point Air Marine Air Station would be allowed to attend all-white public schools near the base. The decision was made because of the difficulty of transporting the students twenty miles to the nearest all-black school (NYT).

15 In **Forest Hills, N.Y.**, after waves of protest were made over the denial of membership to UN diplomat Ralph Bunche and his son, Wilfred Burglund resigned as president of the West Side Tennis Club. The board of governors claimed that Burglund had no right to turn down the Bunches and that they would welcome their application. Dr. Bunche said he had no intention of reapplying, but his son could decide what he wanted to do (NYT).

16 In **Springfield, Ill.**, despite nine days of filibustering by black and white Democratic representatives to prevent any bill from passing the state house until the state senate passed the bill creating a state fair employment practices commission, the legislation was defeated in the senate by Republican senators (JM).

19 In **Sacramento, Calif.**, the state board of regents ordered all student groups that exclude people on the basis of race or religion to end their discriminatory policies within five years or face loss of official recognition. The order affected seven fraternities and sororities at the state universities and colleges (NYT).

23 In **Newport, R.I.**, the fourth annual Jazz Festival, which included performances by Erroll Garner and Duke Ellington's Orchestra, attracted more than sixteen thousand people. However, despite assurances to African Americans that their hotel reservations would be honored, there were numerous reports of hotel discrimination. Festival officials promised that the nondiscrimination policy in housing accommodations would be enforced in 1960 (JM).

23 In **New York City**, celebrating its fiftieth anniversary at its annual convention, the NAACP listed its achievements. These included the revival of black voting in the South, the enactment of fair employment practices laws in 12 states and 30 cities, the passage of the Civil Rights Act of 1957, the enrollment of more than 2,000 African American students in previously all-white southern state universities, the affirmation of the right of blacks to serve on juries, the improvement of the African American image in the mass media—especially the diminution of the use of anti-black stereotypes—the abolition of segregation in the armed services, and the invalidation of state laws requiring racial segregation in public education, transportation, housing, and recreational facilities. At the same time, NAACP leaders set 1963 as its target for "the complete elimination of all vestiges of second-class citizenship under which Negro Americans still suffer" (JM).

26 In **Atlanta, Ga.**, the Southern Regional Council reported that despite new federal regulations, many southern bus and train terminals continued to practice racial segregation. The council found that only airline terminals appeared to have begun the desegregation process (NYT).

30 In **Gary, Ind.**, a local civil rights group, Fair Share Organization, Inc., gained the employment of two black women as clerks in the Kroger grocery store in the Village Shopping Center. When picketing of the store began eight months earlier, Kroger's managers obtained a court order barring demonstrations. The leaders of Fair Share were challenging the court order and had already gained the employment of other black workers in local stores (JM).

30 In **Memphis, Tenn.**, a city where no African American had been elected to public office, five black candidates were on the ballot for the August 1959 election. Among those seeking election were Harvard Law School graduate Russell B. Sugarmon, running for commissioner of public works, and attorney Benjamin L. Hooks, who was seeking a judgeship on the municipal court (JM).

AUGUST 1959

1 In **Little Rock, Ark.**, the home of L. C. and Daisy Bates was damaged for the fourth time by a homemade bomb. Daisy Bates, president of the Arkansas NAACP, and L. C. Bates, publisher of the newspaper the *Arkansas State Press*, were not injured in what was the fiftieth incident of vandalism launched against the home of the civil rights activists (JM).

2 In Monteagle, Tenn., police conducted a raid on the Highlander Folk School following a banquet and movie and arrested several people. Among those arrested was Septima Clark, the school's director of education, on charges of illegal possession of whiskey. The school had been conducting workshops on voter registration. Police said that they would attempt to have the school closed (NYT).

6 In Levittown, N.J., after a suit was filed against developer William J. Levitt, the New Jersey state courts ruled that he could not discriminate against African Americans in the sale of homes in his housing development (NYT).

6 In Nashville, Tenn., the school board's decision to integrate only students in the third grade as part of its "gradual integration plan" was denounced by the local NAACP as "token integration." In Wilmington, Del., black parents appealed the court-approved plan to integrate the public schools over a twelve-year period (NYT).

11 In St. Louis, Mo., Alderman William L. Clay and two others were arrested on charges of disturbing the peace when they refused to leave a Howard Johnson restaurant that denied them service. The hostess, Dorothy Congleton, was also arrested, and all four were later released on five hundred dollars' bond. Alderman Clay filed a countersuit against the restaurant manager. Charges were later dropped against the three men, one of whom was white (NYT).

13 In Denver, Colo., at a concert by singer Fats Domino, a race riot erupted at the Rainbow Ballroom when a white man objected to the presence of an interracial couple on the dance floor. Fighting broke out and spread into the streets. Eighteen police cars were called to the scene to quell the disturbance (JM).

13 In Monteagle, Tenn., district attorney A. F. Sloan filed a petition in state court to close the Highlander Folk School because it was a "public nuisance," or at least to withdraw its tax-exempt status. Education director Septima P. Clark charged that the earlier raid and arrests of staff were carried out because the school had always been integrated (NYT).

15 In Washington, D.C., the Senate Internal Security Subcommittee made known plans to investigate Elijah Muhammad and the Nation of Islam after the group was accused of conducting a "hate program against whites." The Nation had been active in nineteen cities, including Philadelphia, New York, and Chicago (NYT).

16 In Dade County, Fla., white residents were moving out of the neighborhood and taking their children out of Orchard Villa Elementary School, scheduled to be integrated in September 1959. White enrollment dropped from 420 in 1956 to only 130 in June 1959 (NYT).

22 In Memphis, Tenn., following the record turnout by white voters and the defeat of all five black candidates for public office, black leaders promised an all-out voter registration campaign in the black community. In the primary election some twenty thousand additional white voters went to the polls to ensure the victory of white candidates. One of the black candidates defeated in the election, Russell Sugarmon, said although thirty-eight thousand black citizens voted, he believed that there were as many as ninety-eight thousand potential black voters in the city (NYT).

27 In Washington, D.C., Senate liberals led by Michigan Democrat Philip Hart blocked the appropriation of $1 million for Arkansas's segregated Hot Springs Army Hospital. Southern Democrats vowed to restore the funding and argued that African Americans did not object to the segregated facilities (JM).

29 In Washington, D.C., after American Legion members at the annual meeting in Minneapolis, Minn., voted down a proposal for the voluntary integration of its 40 and 8 Society, Detroit congressman Charles Diggs sent his letter of resignation to the group. Diggs said, "This shocking demonstration of intolerance makes a mockery of the democratic ideals to which your organization is committed" (NYT).

29 In Havelock, N.C., seventeen children of black military personnel entered previously all-white elementary schools without incident. This was the largest number of black students to enter all-white schools in the state. Small numbers of black students were attending white schools in Greensboro, Charlotte, and Winston-Salem (NYT).

SEPTEMBER 1959

3 In Chicago, Ill., in an article in *Jet* magazine entitled "The Truth about the Muslims," Marc Crawford provided a detailed account of the controversial group that openly preached that "the white man is a devil." The Nation of Islam received national attention when two Senate subcommittees began investigations into the activities of the religious group. Rep. Adam Clayton Powell, in a television interview, said he found the New York minister Malcolm X to be "brilliant" (JM).

9 In Montgomery, Ala., federal judge Frank M. Johnson ruled that segregation in city parks and playgrounds was unconstitutional. When the suit was originally filed by local black residents, the city commissioners closed the city parks (NYT).

10 In Lafayette, Ind., the National Student Methodist Commission, an organization of state and re-

---

LITTLE ROCK PUBLIC SCHOOLS REOPEN, BUT VIOLENCE AND MASSIVE RESISTANCE CONTINUE

The closing of the Little Rock public schools in September 1959 by order of Gov. Orval Faubus and the leasing of public school facilities to "private schools" was challenged in federal court by the NAACP. In January 1959, federal judge John E. Miller gave the school board thirty days to come up with an integration plan and forbade the leasing of school property to open segregated private schools. In March the federal district court ordered the state department of education to end tuition payments for white students attending private schools, and the federal appeals court in June 1959 declared the laws authorizing these actions unconstitutional. Within days Little Rock school officials announced that the schools would open on an integrated basis in September 1959. Upon learning of the school officials' decision, Governor Faubus stated that a "federal force and live ammunition" would be needed to integrate the Little Rock public schools.

In September 1959, twenty-seven black students registered to attend three previously all-white high schools, with twenty-three at Central High School, including five of the original Little Rock Nine. At the same time, however, the "buyers strike" or boycott of downtown merchants who favored school integration called by the Capital Citizens Council was a complete failure as hundreds of shoppers flocked to the stores. In response, the leader, Amos Gutheridge, said the group would target for economic reprisals African Americans whose children were enrolled in the white schools.

Then on Labor Day, 6 September 1959, three bombs exploded in Little Rock. One exploded in the school administration building, another in the private offices of Mayor Werner C. Knoop, and the third in a city-owned car parked in the driveway of the home of fire chief Gann L. Nalley. Within seventy-two hours police and FBI agents arrested trucker and Klan member J. D. Simms and held him on $50,000 bond. Simms later confessed and implicated four others in the bombings. Simms claimed that he set the explosions because "I don't want my daughter to go to school with Negroes."

In October 1959 the U.S. district court reversed a lower court's ruling that the Dollarway School District in Pine Bluff, Ark., had to desegregate. Black students who wanted to transfer to all-white public schools there were told to follow the procedures set up by the Arkansas Pupil Placement Board before they took the matter to court. And in Pulaski County, Ark., air force officials threatened to seek the withdrawal of all federal aid to the school district because of its failure to allow the enrollment of the children of black military personnel from Little Rock Air Force Base. School officials decided in October to lease one school building to military officials in order to enroll ten black students.

gional Methodist students, meeting at Purdue University, issued a statement calling for an "all-out" war against racial discrimination. The students called for faster progress on incorporating black Methodist congregations into the general Methodist church body (JM).

10 In **Washington, D.C.**, at the annual convention of the National Urban League, among the speakers were Vice President Nixon and HEW secretary Arthur Flemming. League director Lester Granger announced the launching of the Tomorrow's Scientists and Technicians program to encourage black youths to prepare for careers in engineering and science. The program was aimed at thirty-two cities in twenty-one states (NYT).

15 In **Queens, N.Y.**, white parents picketed and boycotted five previously all-white public schools because of the transfer of black students from overcrowded schools in Brooklyn. The white parents who began protesting the transfers in June 1959 claimed that the transfers disrupted the traditional concept of neighborhood schools. Black parents complained about the split shifts and overcrowding in Brooklyn schools. The white students began returning to schools after a week of boycotting (NYT).

17 In **Smyrna, Tenn.**, twenty-four hours after federal judge William E. Miller issued an integration order, sixteen black students, children of military personnel at Stewart Air Force Base, were enrolled in the all-white Coleman Elementary School without incident. Children of black military personnel were integrated into all-white public schools near Homestead Air Force Base in Florida as well (NYT).

20 In **San Francisco, Calif.**, at the AFL-CIO annual convention, union vice president A. Philip Randolph got into a shouting match with union president George Meany over the advisability of segregated unions. Randolph called for the end of all segregated locals, and Meany claimed that he was "for the democratic rights of Negro members to maintain a union if they want to." Afterward, Randolph said he maintained his position and would work to end segregated unions (NYT).

24 In **Baltimore, Md.**, three members of the Congress of Racial Equality (CORE) were attacked and beaten by a white mob for picketing the All Nations Day celebration at Gwyn Oak Park. The three were protesting the exclusion of African Americans from the private park. The three protesters were later arrested by the police and charged with disorderly conduct (JM).

OCTOBER 1959

1 In **North Tampa, Fla.**, black parents kept seventy-seven children out of portable classrooms in North Tampa, refused to send them to school in Tampa, and demanded that they be enrolled in nearby all-white schools. NAACP attorney Francisco Rodriguez filed suit in the U.S. court of appeals for admission to schools closest to their homes (SSN).

8 In **Jacksonville, Fla.**, the NAACP branch received the support of the local Interdenominational Ministerial Alliance in its picketing of the new Sears, Roebuck department store. NAACP officials launched a "trade freeze" against Sears for alleged discriminatory hiring practices (JM).

8 In **St. Louis, Mo.**, picketing of the local Howard Johnson restaurant, led by Alderman William Clay, continued into its second month. In August 1959 Clay and two others were refused service and were later arrested by police for disturbing the peace. Although the charges were eventually dropped, Clay launched pickets around the restaurant (JM).

9 In **Indianapolis, Ind.**, the national executive committee of the American Legion passed a resolution ordering Commander Martin McKneally to take all necessary steps to "eliminate the word 'white' from the national constitution of the 40 and 8 Society." Detroit congressman Charles Diggs earlier resigned from the American Legion because of the society's membership restrictions (NYT).

12 In **Bradenton, Fla.**, police suspected arson in the fire that damaged the home of Margaret Jenkins under construction in an all-white neighborhood. When Jenkins moved into the area forty-three years earlier, there were no whites or other blacks there.

However, whites bought up all the land nearby and attempted to purchase her property, but Jenkins refused. Sheriff's deputies found a half-empty can of kerosene near the burned-out structure (NYT).

13 In Washington, D.C., the U.S. Supreme Court refused to review the decision of the U.S. appeals court that granted a new trial for Robert Lee Goldsby, who was sentenced to death for killing a white woman. The lower court ruled that because there were no African Americans on the jury, Goldsby should get a new trial. Unfortunately, jurors in Mississippi were chosen from the voter registration lists, and in Carroll County, where the crime occurred, there were no black registered voters (NYT).

15 In Bay City, Mich., twenty-four black women filed charges of discriminatory employment practices with the state fair employment practices commission against the Autolite Company and the Michigan Employment Security Commission. The women charged that the referral system used by the state employment agency was being used to discriminate against black workers (JM).

15 In Mobile, Ala., Rev. Joseph Lowery, president of the Alabama Civic Affairs Association, and J. L. LaFlore, director of the local Citizens Committee, filed a complaint with the Federal Communications Commission against the "race hate" being spread by white supremacists on local radio and TV stations. The two leaders claimed that the racist appeals have contributed to the dangerous increase in local racial tension (JM).

22 In Tampa, Fla., NAACP state chairman Rev. A. Leon Lowry denounced the opinion issued by Florida attorney general Richard Ervin that restaurant owners had the right to eject anyone from their premises, even if they were not engaging in disruptive behavior. Lowry declared that for law-abiding black customers that was "an open invitation to mayhem" (JM).

26 In New York City, NAACP officials announced that they would file a suit against Eastern Airlines and Greenville (S.C.) Airport on behalf of baseball great Jackie Robinson. Robinson was not allowed in the "white" waiting room and was told that if he sat anywhere other than the "colored" lounge, he would be taken to jail. Segregation on interstate public transportation was illegal (NYT).

29 In Miami, Fla., the city commission voted unanimously to reverse city manager Ira Willard's decision to allow black residents into all city recreational areas and swimming pools. The commissioners claimed that Willard had acted without authorization or consultation (NYT).

NOVEMBER 1959

1 In Baton Rouge, La., the NAACP was again banned from operating in the state by order of Judge John Dixon, Jr., because the organization had failed to turn its membership lists over to the Louisiana attorney general (SSN).

1 In Houston, Tex., the controversial decision by school officials to attempt to hold a referendum on school integration failed to get the needed number of signatures on election petitions. Only 5,900 of the necessary 46,991 signatures were obtained (SSN).

5 In Birmingham, Ala., sixteen black residents, led by Rev. Fred Shuttlesworth, filed a class-action suit in federal court seeking an injunction to restrain the city from segregating parks, swimming pools, golf courses, playgrounds, and other public recreational facilities (JM).

5 In Monroe, N.C., Dr. Albert Perry, the militant vice president of the local NAACP, was sentenced to two and a half years in prison for giving a white woman an abortion. The U.S. Supreme Court refused to review the conviction (JM).

5 In Charleston, W.Va., G. William Dunn, a delegate to the West Virginia Federation AFL-CIO constitutional convention, became the first African American to register in a downtown hotel. Labor leader Miles C. Stanley called it a "signal victory" in local race relations (JM).

6 In Washington, D.C., Justice Department officials said they would again enter the Mack Charles Parker case after the local grand jury in Poplarville, Miss., failed to indict those arrested for the brutal lynching. Earlier, Attorney General William Rogers said no federal statute had been violated

THE FAILURE OF MASSIVE RESISTANCE IN VIRGINIA

In September 1958 in response to court-ordered integration, the Virginia General Assembly passed several "freedom of choice" laws calling for the closing of public schools facing desegregation orders and state funding for students wishing to attend private schools. As a result, Gov. J. Lindsay Almond closed public schools in Norfolk, Charlottesville, and Front Royal. However, before the end of the year NAACP lawyers and white parents filed suits in federal courts to have the schools reopened.

In January 1959 a three-judge federal panel ruled that the anti-integration law that led to the closing of nine public schools in those three cities was unconstitutional. In February, Norfolk school superintendent J. J. Brewbaker reopened the public schools and allowed seventeen black students to enroll in junior and senior high schools in the city. In Front Royal, however, when the federal court ordered the admission of twenty-two black students to the Warren County High School, white parents launched a boycott of the school and white students began attending a private white academy opened by the Textile Workers Union.

In April, feeling the pressure of white parents opposed to his action, Governor Almond endorsed the proposal that local school boards should determine whether to implement desegregation orders, and by the end of the month school officials in Charlottesville submitted an integration plan to federal judge John Paul, Jr., that called for the enrollment of twelve black students in two white schools in September 1959.

When white parents' attempts to buy the Warren County High School under the terms of the "freedom of choice" law failed, they decided to end the school boycott and in September 1959 a small number of black students were integrated into the previously all-white school. This also occurred in Floyd County, Va., in October. However, in Prince Edward County, Va., school board members voted in August 1959 to close down the public school system altogether rather than integrate. In September, while fifteen hundred white students enrolled in private white academies, more than seventeen hundred black students were left without public schools for the remainder of the year. NAACP lawyers filed suits in federal court to reopen the Prince Edward County schools.

In Newport News, Va., in December 1959, federal judge Walter Hoffman denounced as "nothing short of contemptuous" the one-paragraph desegregation plan submitted by the city's school board. Judge Hoffman gave school officials until 15 March 1960 to come up with an acceptable plan or "face the consequences."

By the end of 1959, many white segregationists blamed the failure of the massive resistance campaign in Virginia on the indecisive policies of Gov. J. Lindsay Almond. They vowed to oppose Almond's reelection in 1962.

and the Justice Department withdrew from the case. However, numerous protests were launched over the decision, and the officials decided to reopen the investigation (NYT).

7 In Chicago, Ill., Dr. John Scudder, at a meeting of the American Association of Blood Banks, said that mixing Negro and white blood was perilous and at times fatal, especially when "white" blood was given to "Negro" patients. The statement caused a storm of controversy around the world, with most experts arguing that the statement was incorrect and served no useful purpose other than to reinforce race prejudice (NYT).

12 In Vaiden, Miss., after the U.S. Supreme Court ordered a new trial for Robert Lee Goldsby in the murder of a white woman because there were no black jurors in the original trial, six African Americans were hastily registered in Vaiden, Miss., to serve on the jury. However, when Goldsby's lawyer George Leighton challenged the procedure, the trial was moved to Jackson (NYT).

12 In Toronto, Canada, Barbara Arrington of St. Albans, N.Y., was barred from pledging the Kappa Kappa Gamma sorority at the University of Toronto because of her race. Arrington found that the application form asked for the race of the applicant, similar to practices among sororities in the United States. Arrington was later asked to join another white sorority, Beta Sigma Phi (JM).

14 In Montgomery, Ala., the state legislature passed and sent to Gov. John Patterson a series of bills that gave voter registrars broad leeway in performing their duties and provided state funding for private schools. The school bill would allow the state to appropriate funds for private schools if public schools were closed because of integration orders (NYT).

19 In Washington, D.C., National Urban League officials met with representatives of the Census Bureau and Committee on Government Employment Policy to recommend that every effort be made to employ black workers at all levels in the upcoming U.S. census to increase the likelihood of an accurate count. Up to 170,000 people would be needed for canvassing and compiling the census statistics (JM).

19 In Washington, D.C., Illinois senator Everett Dirksen refused to attend the Illinois State Society dance because the invitation said that only white graduates from Illinois colleges and universities were to be honored at the affair (JM).

22 In Atlanta, Ga., the Southern Regional Council reported that the number of public schools that had voluntarily desegregated far exceeded the number integrated by court orders. The council reported that of the 269 desegregated school districts in Arkansas, Florida, Kentucky, North Carolina, Tennessee, and Texas, only 11 came about due to court orders (NYT).

26 In Warren, Ohio, the Lionel Hampton Band canceled a scheduled appearance at the Trumball Memorial Hospital Guild's annual ball. Hampton backed out of the engagement when he learned from local black musicians that African Americans were not allowed to attend. Ball chairperson Mrs. James Cole said that "if Negroes were admitted to the ball some of the best people in town might not attend." Hampton later announced that it would be a blow to his reputation to perform at the event (JM).

26 In New York City, Louis Armstrong declared, "I don't care if I never go to New Orleans again." Louisiana state law prohibited bands with black and white musicians from performing, and Armstrong had several white players in his group. When asked to comment on the situation, Louisiana attorney general Jack Gremillion said as far

as he was concerned, "As long as the law is still there, I'm going to enforce it" (JM).

DECEMBER 1959

1 In Little Rock, Ark., despite the support they received from around the country, L. C. and Daisy Bates regretfully announced they would cease publication of the *Arkansas State Press*, primarily due to the decline in advertising revenues and loss of their lease on the State Press Building. NAACP state president Daisy Bates had been subject to bombing attacks and economic reprisals since the 1957 school integration crisis (SSN).

3 In Phoenix, Ariz., a Japanese man and white woman agreed to go to the state supreme court to challenge the state law prohibiting interracial marriages. Henry Oyama and Mary Ann Jordon had been refused a marriage license in Tucson (JM).

6 In Nashville, Tenn., the *Southern School News* reported that desegregation in colleges was occurring more rapidly than in elementary and secondary schools in thirteen of seventeen southern and border states. However, all state colleges and universities remained segregated in Georgia, South Carolina, Mississippi, and Alabama (SSN).

6 In Washington, D.C., a report issued by the National Association of Intergroup Relations concluded that between 1949 and 1959, the nation's capital had moved from complete segregation to full desegregation in schools, recreational facilities, and public accommodations. The report noted that a community could move from segregation to desegregation peaceably and "with more speed than most people believe" (NYT).

10 In Memphis, Tenn., O. Z. Evers, NAACP leader and postal worker, was fired from his position for violating the Hatch Act, which prohibits government workers from participating in political activities. Evers, who ran for city commissioner of police and fire in August 1959 and lost, planned to fight the charges (JM).

10 In Minneapolis, Minn., officials for the Minneapolis Lakers announced the cancellation of a game with the Cincinnati Royals, scheduled to take place in Charleston, W.Va., because of racial discrimination practiced by local hotels. Other National Basketball Association teams had also refused to play in Charleston because of racial discrimination (JM).

10 In **San Francisco, Calif.**, after receiving a warning from state attorney general Stanley Mosk that they were in violation of the state's new anti-discrimination law, leaders of the American Federation of Musicians Local 6 (white) and Local 669 (black) began negotiations for a merger of the two unions (JM).

14 In **Forest Hills, N.Y.**, an investigation by the New York Commission on Intergroup Relations of the West Side Tennis Club found that although the owners claimed to have Jewish members, they could not name one. The club had no black members. The investigation was spurred by the club's denial of membership to UN diplomat Ralph Bunche and his son (NYT).

16 In **Squaw Valley, Nev.**, where the 1960 Winter Olympics were to begin in February 1960, Gov. Grant Sawyer claimed that there would be no racial discrimination in public accommodations. Sawyer said he spoke with hotel and restaurant owners and they promised to relax their discriminatory practices during the eleven-day period of the Olympics (NYT).

17 In **Chicago, Ill.**, in a lengthy article in *Jet* magazine, Martin Luther King explained why he decided to leave Montgomery in February 1960 to return to Atlanta. King mentioned that the previous four years had been exhausting physically and mentally because he had taken on too many responsibilities. The move to co-pastor Ebenezer Baptist Church, pastored by his father, Rev. Martin Luther King, Sr., would give him more time to devote to the Southern Christian Leadership Conference (SCLC) and civil rights activities. "Actually, I will be involved in it on a larger scale. I can't stop now. History has thrust something upon me from which I cannot turn away" (JM).

17 In **Baton Rouge, La.**, NAACP attorney A. P. Tureaud filed suit in the U.S. district court on behalf of fourteen black parents for a summary judgment on the integration of public schools. School board members in East Baton Rouge had voted unanimously that they were "unequivocally opposed to school integration" (JM).

17 In **Washington, D.C.**, Rep. Charles Diggs held a press conference and denounced the Little Rock, Ark., police for their failure to protect L. C. and Daisy Bates's home and accused them of not pursuing whites who attacked the couple. Diggs, who visited the Bateses in Little Rock, also found that black students at Central High School had been kicked and beaten by white students and the police had done nothing. Diggs called on President Eisenhower to visit the city and oppose these practices (NYT).

20 In **Sacramento, Calif.**, Gov. Edmund G. Brown issued a directive calling for the end of racial discrimination in all National Guard units in the state. The 119th Military Police Battalion, stationed in Los Angeles, with twelve officers and sixty enlisted men, the last segregated unit in the state, was dissolved by the governor's directive (NYT).

24 In **Birmingham, Ala.**, members of the school board rejected the petition signed by 135 black parents to have their children enrolled in all-white public schools. School officials claimed that the petition was an inappropriate form for application for school transfers (JM).

24 In **Washington, D.C.**, even after city officials ruled that policemen could not solicit funds for the segregated programs offered by the Metropolitan Police Boys Clubs, and seven of the nine programs had to be closed down as a result, the club members failed to pass a resolution calling for desegregation of its activities (JM).

31 In **Fresno, Calif.**, state attorney general Stanley Mosk launched an investigation into a shotgun blast into the home of black air force veteran Ward Mosley, who had recently moved with his family into an all-white neighborhood. Mosley had received anonymous telephone threats earlier telling him to leave the area (JM).

On 2 February 1960, in Greensboro, North Carolina, Joseph McNeil, Franklin McCain, Billy Smith, and Clarence Henderson—North Carolina A&T College students—went to the Woolworth store, sat down at the lunch counter, as shown here, and continued the sit-in movement launched the day before. (SOURCE: CORBIS BETTMANN)

1960

"GOIN' TO LAY DOWN MY SWORD AND SHIELD"

The launching of the sit-ins by black and white students in North Carolina in 1960 opened a new phase in the Civil Rights Movement. While student activists agreed to "lay down their swords and shields," this did not prevent them from battling segregation through wade-ins, kneel-ins, read-ins, and other nonviolent direct action protests that landed them in jails throughout the country. The Student Nonviolent Coordinating Committee (SNCC) sponsored voter registration drives and opened "Freedom Schools" to prepare black southerners to take on new duties and responsibilities. In Fayette and Howard counties, Tenn., black residents who attempted to register were victimized by economic reprisals, while federal authorities failed to intervene. With the election of John F. Kennedy through massive support from northern and midwestern black voters, many Americans hoped that the moral horizons of the "New Frontier" would not be darkened by the sinister shadows of racial conflict and discrimination.

JANUARY 1960

1 In Prince Edward County, Va., sales declined by 20 percent among some businesses. They blamed the decline on the closing of nearby schools to prevent integration (SSN).

4 In Washington D.C., despite receiving death threats, Rep. Adam Clayton Powell gave a speech from the House floor about discrimination in racketeering arrest patterns. He charged that the police arrested only African American gamblers, ignoring the whites involved (NYT).

7 In Atlanta, Ga., federal court judge Boyd Sloan ordered the end of segregation practices at Dobbs House Restaurant at the Atlanta airport. The suit was brought by Birmingham insurance executive H. D. Coke (NYT).

7 In Pacoima, Calif., the Holmes family refused to leave their home in an all-white, middle-class neighborhood, despite ongoing harassment, which included phone calls in the middle of the night, the mysterious death of their cats, and verbal abuse from white teenagers (JM).

7 In Phoenix, Ariz., black substitute teacher Louis Pete charged that the school district of Phoenix discriminated against black teachers. Only one African American out of 175 was hired by the district during a two-year period (JM).

7 In Washington, D.C., Dorothy Height, president of the National Council of Negro Women, invited top black women leaders to a meeting in order to push for the opening of public schools in Prince Edward County, Va. The schools were closed by officials to prevent integration (JM).

7 In Wichita, Kans., following a complaint by local NAACP president Chester Lewis, city manager Frank Backstrom agreed to integrate the city's fire stations (JM).

13 In Dover, Del., the state supreme court ruled that privately operated restaurants were not required by law to serve African Americans (NYT).

15 In New York City, NAACP leader Roy Wilkins called on the FBI to release its report on the Mack Charles Parker lynching. His remarks followed the failure of a federal grand jury in Biloxi to return a true bill in the abduction and lynching of Parker (NYT).

17 In Prince Edward County, Va., an NAACP-promoted boycott scuttled an all-white group's plan to provide segregated classes for black children. NAACP leaders urged black parents to await court action to force reopening of the public schools on an integrated basis (NYT).

21 In Athens, Ohio, three southern delegations (Alabama, North Carolina, and Texas) attending the National Student Christian Federation Conference vowed to help bring about desegregation in all areas once they returned home (JM).

21 In Baton Rouge, La., state senator John Petre criticized a state law designed to limit the number of black voters. He argued that the requirement that people state their age in years, months, and days was excluding too many whites (JM).

21 In Cleveland, Ohio, Ralph Findley became the president of the Board of Education and Paul White became the chief assistant police prosecu-

---

SOUTHERN STUDENTS LAUNCH THE SIT-IN MOVEMENT

On 1 February 1960, four black college students defied the southern ban on interracial dining by sitting down and placing an order at the "white" lunch counter at the F. W. Woolworth store in Greensboro, N.C. Refused service, Ezell Blair, Jr., Joseph McNeil, David Richmond, and Franklin McCain sat quietly, reading their books until, after an hour, the store closed. This carefully planned and orchestrated action by freshmen students from North Carolina A&T College launched a direct action nonviolent movement aimed ostensibly at desegregating lunch counters, but specifically at all public accommodations.

Garnering support from the NAACP, CORE, and SCLC, the movement launched by the Greensboro students spread quickly to other campuses in North Carolina and then across the South. In Greensboro, white students from Guilford and Greensboro colleges and the Women's College of the University of North Carolina joined black students from North Carolina A&T and Bennett College in sit-in protests against Woolworth and S. H. Kress stores. Spurred by reports of the sit-ins disseminated by television, radio, newspapers, and word of mouth, by mid-February 1960 black and white students were engaged in sit-in protests against segregated lunch counters in Raleigh, High Point, Winston-Salem, and Fayetteville, N.C.; Columbia and Rock Hill, S.C.; Nashville, Tenn.; and Hampton, Va. They suffered physical and verbal abuse at the hands of average white citizens as well as KKK members. By June 1960 reports of student arrests, use of tear gas and billy clubs, and police brutality were daily topics in the national and international media.

In April 1960, through the initiation of Ella Baker, the interim director of SCLC, 142 southern student leaders met in Raleigh, N.C., where they founded the Student Nonviolent Coordinating Committee (SNCC) to guide their anti-segregation activities. In cities and towns throughout the South, sit-in protests continued at lunch counters, leading to a decrease in business for the establishments. One Charlotte, N.C., eatery removed counter seats to thwart the protesters. A street fight occurred between black and white teenagers in Portsmouth, Va. In Baltimore, Md., orchestra leader and composer Duke Ellington joined students in a sit-in demonstration at a local restaurant. By April the movement had expanded to boycotts of local businesses and marches on state capitals and downtown areas in Louisiana, Alabama, Georgia, and South Carolina. Initially, many store managers chose to ignore the sit-ins; however, as the movement grew, they opted to close rather than serve protesters.

tor. They were the first African Americans to serve in these positions in the city (JM).

21 In New Haven, Conn., Mayor Richard Lee filed a report with the Connecticut State Commission on Human Relations when a black member of his Human Relations Committee was denied housing in exclusive Ivy Manor. Owners of Ivy Manor returned Richard Dowdy's rent deposit when they discovered he was an African American (JM).

21 In Park Forest, Ill., the Park Forest Residents Association, a white citizens group designed to keep African Americans out of the neighborhood, filed papers of incorporation. They planned a "social boycott" of the family of Charles Wilson, the only African Americans in the neighborhood (NYT).

21 In Washington, D.C., a seventy-member interracial commission recommended in a report that the Methodist church retain its all-black Central Jurisdiction. Some Methodists have criticized the jurisdiction as a symbol of racial segregation. Theologians at Drew University condemned the decision of the church (JM).

24 In Washington, D.C., officials of the Veterans Administration agreed to sell 46,500 homes throughout the United States without discriminating on the basis of race. In response to this initiative, Federal Housing Administration official Norman Mason notified local developers of "their obligation to comply" fully with laws forbidding bias in housing (NYT).

28 In Atlanta, Ga., Carolyn Becknell refused to attend a community planning program at Georgia Tech because no African Americans were invited. Becknell (white), a founder of the Atlanta Arts Festival and the winner of the 1959 "Woman of the Year in the Arts" award, stated that she did not believe that "you can plan for part of the community and ignore the rest" (JM).

28 In Muncie, Ind., a letter to President Eisenhower from black minister Rev. A. J. Oliver prompted the hiring of the first black employees at the Warner Gear Division of Borg-Warner Corp. Oliver, pastor of the Shaffer Chapel AME Church, protested to Eisenhower that he had received complaints of discrimination from six people (JM).

28 In San Francisco, Calif., state officials warned all bar owners that they faced suspension or revocation of their licenses if they refused to serve African Americans, Mexican-Americans, or other minorities (JM).

FEBRUARY 1960

1 In Atlanta, Ga., former governor Ellis Arnall vowed to run again for governor if public schools were closed by the state's integration crisis. Arnall, a liberal, favored school integration (SSN).

3 In Atlanta, Ga., Dr. Ovid Futch, a white professor from Morehouse College, was ejected from the chambers of the Georgia House of Representatives for sitting too close to his black students. Members of the house later admitted that there was no law segregating the house gallery. Another recent incident involved two white children who sat in the black section because the white section was full (NYT).

4 In Miami, Fla., the city commissioner ordered racial integration of the city's police training school. This ended the practice of sending armed black patrolmen out to police neighborhoods without having received the extensive training provided white policemen (JM).

6, 8, 9 In New York City, Rep. Adam Clayton Powell called for the resignation of New York police commissioner Stephen Kennedy because he refused to appoint a black deputy police commissioner. Kennedy stated that he would not appoint anyone on the basis of race (NYT).

8 In Montgomery, Ala., Martin Luther King turned over leadership of the Montgomery Improvement Association to Ralph David Abernathy. King left for permanent residence in Atlanta, Ga., headquarters of SCLC (NYT).

9 In Little Rock, Ark., the state supreme court ruled that public school teachers still had to submit lists of organizations to which they belonged, but those lists could not be used in a discriminatory fashion. White Citizens Council leaders called for the dismissal of teachers belonging to the NAACP and Urban League (NYT).

10, 20, 21 In Little Rock, Ark., a bomb exploded in the home of Carlotta Walls, one of the original Little Rock Nine. Two black men, Maceo Binns, Jr., and Herbert Monts, were charged with the bombing. Despite the abuse that she and the other black students faced at Central High School, they had no plans to quit (NYT).

11 In Washington, D.C., Mrs. Aretha McKinley, the only black woman lobbyist, started a "Write for Rights" campaign. She contacted black leaders and organizations and urged them to write to members of Congress regarding the passage of civil rights legislation (JM).

17 In Altamont, Tenn., Judge C. C. Chattin ordered the interracial Highlander Folk School, founded by Myles Horton, closed. Chattin claimed that the school's administrators violated its charter as a nonprofit institution and Tennessee's segregation laws (NYT).

17 In Baltimore, Md., Sara Slack, who sued a White Tower Restaurant when she was refused service, lost her case when federal judge Roszel Thomas ruled that restaurants could segregate customers (NYT).

18 In Atlanta, Ga., Martin Luther King was arrested and charged with failing to report $31,000 on his income tax return. He stated that he would like to gather a group of distinguished citizens to go over his books. He believed that the arrest was another attempt by state officials to harass him (NYT).

24 In Albany, N.Y., Gov. Nelson Rockefeller proposed an anti-bias measure that would prevent real estate brokers from discriminating in the sale and lease of housing and commercial space (NYT).

25 In Washington, D.C., for the first time in history, African Americans were employed in skilled jobs on Capitol Hill building projects. It marked a breakthrough in a long campaign to end the color bar in craft unions (JM).

26 In Montgomery, Ala., NAACP leaders and others pledged their support to Martin Luther King,

who was facing a ten-year prison term on two counts of perjury on charges of filing false income tax returns. An emergency defense committee was formed to raise money to defray his court costs (NYT).

MARCH 1960

1 In Baton Rouge, La., Gov. Earl Long voiced his support for the Supreme Court's decision that returned 1,377 African Americans to the voting rolls in Washington Parish, La. He stated that there were probably more than fourteen hundred African Americans educated and intelligent enough to vote in Washington Parish (NYT).

1 In Louisville, Ky., the proposal by black alderman William Beckett to integrate theaters, restaurants, hotels, and motels by force was rejected by the other members of the aldermanic board. Beckett argued that integration would not work voluntarily (SSN).

1 In Prince Edward County, Va., NAACP leaders opened two training centers to teach black children. They announced plans to open eight more. Public schools in the county were closed to prevent integration (SSN).

3 In Washington, D.C., Labor Secretary James Mitchell blocked the appointment of Cora Brown as the first black to hold the position of executive director of the Committee on Government Contracts. He requested that the committee abolish the position (JM).

3, 4 In Washington, D.C., Rep. Adam Clayton Powell defended his use of franking privileges to organize an anti-segregation demonstration in New York City. He pointed out that Mississippi senator James Eastland used his frank to support the White Citizens Councils (NYT).

8 In Houston, Tex., four white youths, with masks on their faces and holding guns, abducted twenty-seven-year-old Felton Turner, a black man. The youths tied Turner to a tree, beat him with chains, and carved six K's an inch deep into his chest and stomach. The white youths told Turner that they had been hired to beat African Americans because of the publicity Texas Southern University black students received for conducting sit-ins at a Houston lunch counter (NYT).

9 In Madison, Wis., University of Wisconsin officials gave Sigma Chi, a white fraternity, eleven months to remove discriminatory provisions from its constitution (NYT).

10 In Albany, N.Y., the State Commission Against Discrimination (SCAD) ordered Capital Airlines to hire African Americans as pilots, copilots, flight officers, and stewardesses. SCAD made the announcement after considering the complaint of Patricia Banks, an applicant for a stewardess job, who charged she was rejected because of her race (NYT).

10 In Norfolk, Va., the Tidewater Federal Employees Association filed a complaint with the President's Committee on Government Employment Policy. The employees charged Norfolk's Naval Supply Center with racial discrimination in the areas of job assignments, promotions, and in the creation of segregated units (JM).

12 In Austin, Tex., white and black students picketed the University of Texas. They protested against discriminatory policies in housing, athletics, and dramatic productions (NYT).

13 In St. Petersburg, Fla., a bomb threat failed to stop an address given by Mrs. Eleanor Roosevelt to an integrated audience at Gibbs Junior College. She stated that "if it blew up, it wouldn't change one bit of what is going to happen inevitably" (NYT).

17 In Atlanta, Ga., the Fulton County Republican party elected nine African Americans to its executive committee, apportioned thirty-five of seventy-six delegate seats on the district and state level for African Americans, and selected thirty-five African American alternates (JM).

17 In Chicago, Ill., attorney Theophilus Mann was named to the newly created Chicago Police Board. NAACP and Urban League officials had asked Mayor Richard Daley to appoint an African American to the five-man commission (JM).

17 In Chicago, Ill., representatives to the Illinois Committee on Discrimination in Higher Education announced that colleges throughout the state were having a difficult time finding off-campus housing for black students and faculty members (JM).

17 In Washington, D.C., President Eisenhower said that southern communities should form local interracial groups to work out their problems. He stated that he deplored the use of violence either to assure or prevent the enjoyment of constitutional rights (NYT).

24 In Gary, Ind., the city council passed a motion asking the mayor, the police chief, and members of the Civil Service Commission to investigate complaints that black policemen were restricted to working in black areas (JM).

24 In Philadelphia, Pa., the Commission on Human Relations used a pamphlet to urge African Americans to move into white neighborhoods in order to break the pattern of segregated housing. This followed the publication of a similar booklet by the American Jewish Congress attacking the misconceptions about the effects of African Americans moving into white neighborhoods (JM).

24 In Portsmouth, Va., Andrew Lassmore filed suit against segregated public housing facilities. He argued that many white projects had vacancies into which African Americans should be allowed to move (JM).

30 In Houston, Tex., four African Americans were arrested when they refused to pay the prices on the special, high-priced cafe menu at the Tasita Drive-In. Eugene Martinez, the cafe owner, stated that "Negroes can eat here all they want, but they're going to have to pay heavy for it" (NYT).

31 In Lansing, Mich., Gov. G. Mennen Williams pledged his support to an NAACP delegation whose members demanded the passage of a fair housing act by the Republican legislature. Williams had already urged real estate agents to help end housing bias (JM).

31 In Minneapolis, Minn., Professor Thomas Manger (black), formerly of the University of Minnesota, received threats and his car was sprayed with acid after he was shown a home in an all-white neighborhood (JM).

ECONOMIC REPRISALS DIRECTED AGAINST BLACK VOTERS IN FAYETTE AND HAYWOOD COUNTIES, TENN., 1960–61

Under the terms of the 1957 Civil Rights Act, the Department of Justice instituted voting rights suits in Alabama, Georgia, and Louisiana between 1957 and 1960. These cases were upheld by the Supreme Court; however, registrars continued to evade the law. In January 1960 in Washington Parish, La., Justice Department officials ordered the names of 1,377 black voters restored to the voting lists. Adopting a typical pattern of discrimination, used to eliminate black voters, the city had dropped blacks from the rolls for such things as misspellings and other mistakes or discrepancies that also existed in the applications of retained white voters. In a few cases, such as in Tuskegee, Ala., district boundaries were changed to eliminate from the city all but four or five of its four hundred black voters.

NAACP bureau chief Clarence Mitchell rejected President Eisenhower's proposal for a study of a bill providing federal registrars to protect black voting rights. Mitchell and other black leaders pressured Congress and the president for more stringent legislation and enforcement of existing legislation. These measures, along with escalating black protest, such as the sit-ins, led to the passage of the 1960 Civil Rights Act (6 May), which called for the preservation of records in federal elections and the use of referees to facilitate voting.

In 1960 and 1961, Fayette and Haywood Counties, Tenn., became a focal point of the voting rights struggle. In March 1960 several white Fayette County election aides resigned in protest of what they called unwarranted FBI probes of black voter registration complaints. Two weeks later the Civic and Welfare League recruited seventy blacks who registered to vote, despite a federal court suit still pending against barring black voters. White merchants retaliated, launching a campaign to "starve out" ten thousand black farmers by not selling them gasoline to operate their farm machinery. The NAACP responded by urging its 350,000 members to boycott Texaco, Amoco, and Esso–Standard Oil companies. The NAACP sent food and clothing to local blacks, while the FBI began to probe the situation. Fearing a boycott, Gulf Oil's president, W. K. Whiteford, ordered an investigation of the local squeeze on black voters.

In August 1960, black residents in Fayette and Haywood Counties, voting for the first time, helped to elect liberal Senator Estes Kefauver, who defeated segregationist Judge Andrew Taylor. Following the election and negotiation of a deal with the oil companies, the NAACP ended the boycott; however, white merchants through wholesale firings and mass evictions continued to inflict economic reprisals upon black voters. In September the Justice Department filed civil rights suits against twenty-seven white merchants and banks in Haywood County. In December a delegation of Haywood and Fayette County leaders appealed to President Eisenhower to rush emergency food and gasoline to three hundred black farm families evicted from the land they worked as sharecroppers. The evicted farmers moved into Freedom Village, a tent city. In response to pleas from the Emergency Relief Committee of Fayette County, beginning in 1960 and continuing through 1961, black and white organizations and individuals, such as the Chicago Greater Harvest Baptist Church, the AFL-CIO Executive Council, the directors of the United Packinghouse Workers of America, the NAACP, the SCLC, and others, sent thousands of pounds of food and clothing to the evicted farm families.

APRIL 1960

1 In New York City, Capital Airlines announced that it accepted the application of complainant Patricia Banks for training as a flight hostess. This followed an order by the New York State Commission Against Discrimination to hire blacks as pilots, flight officers, and stewardesses (SSN).

7 In Anniston, Ala., eight black members of the Citizens Committee of the Alabama Voters League asked the city commission for protection from threats of violence and cross burnings. Mayor George Morris told the group that the city would make every effort to curb racial conflicts (JM).

7 In Jackson, Miss., NAACP field organizer Medgar Evers gave three reasons why Mississippi students had not initiated lunch counter demonstrations. According to Evers there was (1) a shortage of black lawyers in the state, (2) the intimidation of students by public school administrators, and (3) a lack of communication—the state had only one black newspaper (JM).

9 In Jackson, Miss., black students visited the homes of 7,000 African American families and urged them to consider wearing old clothing on Easter Sunday and to avoid patronizing merchants who operated segregated facilities and discriminated in any manner against African Americans. This was the first major protest led by Mississippi students (NYT).

14 In Las Vegas, Nev., after a threat of protest by the NAACP, casino and club owners dropped their unwritten ban against African Americans. The ban had long been a source of irritation for African Americans, for the clubs freely hired blacks as entertainers (JM).

14 In Washington, D.C., Rev. Archibald Carey, chairman of the President's Committee on Government Employment Policy, reported to President Eisenhower and his cabinet that black employment in the U.S. government increased by 14 percent since 1952. Carey became the first African American to address the full cabinet (JM).

19, 20, 21 In Chicago, Ill., *Jet* associate editor Alex Poinsette questioned former president Harry Truman regarding his criticism of student protesters. Truman reiterated his views and stated that the only way to overcome racism was through "goodwill and common sense." Truman also contended that the sit-ins were engineered by Communists, a statement he later denied. When confronted with a tape of his original statement, Truman admitted that he had been accurately quoted (NYT).

20 In Nashville, Tenn., members of the city council offered a ten-thousand-dollar reward for the arrest of the assailants responsible for bombing the home of Alexander Looby. Looby, an NAACP attorney, was responsible for defending student sit-in protesters (NYT).

21 In Detroit, Mich., Damon Keith, president and the only black member of the Detroit Housing Commission, stated that any employee found guilty of discriminating in renting public housing would be fired. A committee to probe bias charges in public housing was set up in the fall of 1959 by Mayor Louis Miriani (JM).

21 In Washington, D.C., Defense Department officials negotiated with representatives from Iceland to end their country's ban, which prevented black soldiers from the United States from serving with NATO forces in Iceland (JM).

28 In Atlanta, Ga., Mayor William Hartsfield used a speech at the YMCA Hungry Club forum to urge African Americans to educate white people about civil rights. Hartsfield said that African Americans should demand space from newspapers and airtime from television and radio stations to speak about civil rights (JM).

28 In Birmingham, Ala., the FBI investigated the case of Rev. C. Herbert Oliver, who was dragged from his home and thrown in jail overnight without charges being filed. He stated that his only "crime" was speaking with student demonstrators (NYT).

28 In Jackson, Miss., white merchants admitted that their businesses had fallen off by up to 75 percent as a result of NAACP boycotts. Antisegregation boycotts continued in cities and towns in Mississippi, Florida, Georgia, South Carolina, Tennessee, and Virginia (JM).

MAY 1960

5 In Harrisburg, Pa., union leader Charles Robinson filed suit in the state supreme court against the University of Pennsylvania and Temple University. The suit charged that the medical schools discriminated against African Americans, Jews, and Italians in admissions (JM).

5 In Kansas City, Mo., officials at the public transit company hired five blacks as bus drivers. The decision followed negotiations involving the company, the Urban League, and the Community Committee for Social Action (JM).

8 In New York City, NAACP leader Roy Wilkins announced that only 6 percent of the South's black students had been integrated into white schools since the *Brown* case six years earlier. About 2.5 million African Americans remained in segregated schools (NYT).

10 In Atlanta, Ga., U.S. district judge Frank Hooper ordered the desegregation of the city's public schools by 1 May 1961. The desegregation was ordered regardless of whether state laws forbidding integration were changed (NYT).

10 In Washington, D.C., Attorney General William Rogers announced that he would inspect voter registration records in select counties in South Carolina, Louisiana, Georgia, and Alabama. This was the first application of the 1960 Civil Rights Act (NYT).

12 In Atlanta, Ga., Martin Luther King removed a cross from his lawn. Unidentified persons burned the cross on his lawn to mark "Confederate Memorial Day" (JM).

12 In New Orleans, La., the U.S. Fifth Circuit Court of Appeals upheld a lower-court ruling outlawing segregation in city parks in Montgomery, Ala. Montgomery's parks had been closed since 1 January 1959 (JM).

WADE-INS, KNEEL-INS, READ-INS: DESEGREGATION OF PUBLIC FACILITIES

At the beginning of the lunch counter sit-ins, student leaders announced their goals, including full and free access to public facilities, enforcement of the Fifteenth Amendment, and access to all publicly supported schools and colleges. Thus the sit-ins opened the door for protest against segregation in all public facilities, including beaches, swimming pools, golf courses, theaters, libraries, hotels, motels, restaurants, museums, art galleries, nightclubs, casinos, bars, parks, and other recreational areas. As the movement advanced, boycotts of white businesses were employed to force major chains to desegregate their facilities and to hire African Americans. Black students and organizational leaders carefully selected the targets of their protests. This was particularly true where supportive legislation existed and where the courts had ordered the integration of city-, state-, or federally owned facilities. And protest was initiated where it was felt that major media attention could be garnered. For example, in Augusta, Ga., sixty African Americans picketed the Augusta National Golf Club while President Eisenhower played golf. Utilizing the segregated golf course as a backdrop, blacks protested Eisenhower's inaction on civil rights.

Early in 1960 NAACP leader Roy Wilkins announced a "wade-in" campaign to desegregate public beaches from New Jersey to Texas. Wade-in protests occurred in Mississippi, Tennessee, Florida, Georgia, and other states. White response to black protests varied from race rioting in Biloxi, Miss., and arrests of African Americans in Savannah, Ga., to the successful integration of a public beach in Miami, Fla., by fifty black and white members of CORE.

One of the most sensitive areas of protest was religious institutions. In 1960 protesters in Atlanta, Ga., Sumter, S.C., and other places continued to highlight white Christian ambivalence toward integration at all-white church services. In Atlanta, Ga., Martin Luther King was sued by a white politician for leading "from a distance" individuals staging kneel-ins in all-white churches.

Throughout the South, African Americans were excluded from most public libraries. In Norfolk, Va., federal judge Walter Hoffman ordered the Portsmouth, Va., library to integrate. In Danville, Va., a committee of local whites asked that the library be reopened under a "vertical integration" plan, where all chairs and tables would be removed and all patrons would stand. In Greenville, S.C., the public library closed in the wake of an integration suit but later reopened on an integrated basis. In Memphis, the city's zoo and art gallery were quietly desegregated. This action followed the desegregation of the city's library system.

12 In Washington, D.C., the U.S. Commission on Civil Rights released a report that documented racial discrimination in every state against African Americans, Mexicans, Indians, and other racial and religious minorities (JM).

17 In New Orleans, La., federal district judge J. Skelly Wright ordered the school boards in East Baton Rouge and St. Helena parishes to desegregate. He also ordered six all-white trade schools to desegregate. The orders followed an earlier ruling by Wright in which he ordered the desegregation of schools under the New Orleans Parish School Board (NYT).

18 In Atlanta, Ga., two thousand students staged a silent march to commemorate the sixth anniversary of the Supreme Court's school desegregation decision. The march was part of demonstrations taking place across the nation (NYT).

19 In Watertown, N.Y., R. C. Kirkwood, F. W. Woolworth Co. president, announced to shareholders attending the corporation's annual meeting that Woolworth would continue its policy of segregation in its stores located in southern cities. This announcement was made in response to the sit-in demonstrations, and despite the growing pleas of government officials and leaders of the civil rights organizations for Woolworth to desegregate its lunch counters (NYT).

26 In Washington, D.C., after returning from a Far East military inspection trip, Representative Charles Diggs blasted the Defense Department for not doing enough to end discrimination in the armed forces. However, he noted that the military was further along than the rest of the country when it came to ending discrimination (JM).

27 In Philadelphia, Pa., administrators of the University of Pennsylvania ordered white fraternities Sigma Chi, Sigma Nu, and Alpha Tau Omega to end racial and religious discrimination in their selection of members (NYT).

29 In Detroit, Mich., the State Corporation and Securities Commission drafted a ruling permitting the commission to revoke the licenses of real estate brokers or salesmen who discriminated against home buyers (NYT).

1 In Houston, Tex., the board of education voted to implement integration in only 3 of its 177 schools. The only African American on the board, Mrs. Charles White, voted against the plan and called it "insulting" (NYT).

5 In Dallas, Tex., U.S. district court judge T. Whitfield Davidson ordered the local school board to designate certain schools for integration. However, neither whites nor African Americans would be forced to attend the integrated schools (NYT).

9 In Nashville, Tenn., Diane Nash, a Fisk University student, served as a negotiator between Nashville merchants and student sit-in protesters. Nash made headlines in February for being in a group of students who were arrested and jailed for a lunch counter sit-in. She announced that she planned to continue the fight against Jim Crow laws (JM).

9 In New York City, UN undersecretary Ralph Bunche announced increasing job opportunities for African Americans in the State Department. Bunche also noted that there was no concerted effort to enroll qualified African Americans in diplomatic schools (JM).

14, 16 In New York City, thirty-six professors from Union Theological Seminary sent a letter to Vanderbilt University's chancellor criticizing the expulsion of Rev. James Lawson for his participation in sit-ins. Meanwhile, in Nashville, nine of the eleven Vanderbilt University professsors who had resigned withdrew their resignations when university officials agreed to award Rev. Lawson the divinity degree if he passed his examinations. Rev. Lawson refused to return to the university (NYT).

14 In Richmond, Va., the state supreme court upheld a circuit court ruling that the NAACP branches in the state would have to disclose their membership lists. In a similar case in February, the U.S. Supreme Court reversed a decision from Arkansas, ruling in favor of the NAACP (NYT).

16 In Madison, Wis., NAACP leader Odell Taliaferro urged support of legislation recently proposed by the Wisconsin Governor's Conference on Civil Rights. The legislation would require resort owners to display the Wisconsin statute prohibiting racial discrimination in public accommodations (JM).

16 In Pontiac, Mich., a white mob stormed the office of real estate agent Charles Tucker, Jr., after he sold a home to an African American in an all-white neighborhood. Police protection was assigned to Tucker's home and office (JM).

16 In Washington, D.C., Clarence Mitchell and other NAACP officials demanded that the Justice Department take action to curb the increasing number of cases of police brutality in southern cities and towns. Mitchell criticized local police for ignoring voting rights laws (JM).

23, 24 In St. Paul, Minn., confronted with the criticism from student sit-in leaders that the organization was "going too slow on integration," the NAACP fifty-first annual convention opened with a two-day secret meeting with their lawyers who discussed strategies for moving the civil rights agenda forward more quickly. Thurgood Marshall admitted that the organization had moved forward at a "snail's pace." He also pointed out that although the NAACP knew that legal victories were not enough to win the war against "Jim Crow," it took the student demonstrations to make the rank and file more aware of the problems (NYT).

24 In St. Paul, Minn., at the fifty-first annual NAACP convention, young delegates openly challenged the arbitrary restrictions on Youth Councils in implementing the organization's policies. Despite NAACP leaders' rejection of SCLC's "Gandhi-like civil disobedience approach" and CORE's militant "jail, no bail" technique, the young delegates called for more young people on the staff, larger budgets for them, and greater representation on the National Board as well as aggressive local protests against segregation (NYT).

JULY 1960

5 In Portland, Or., Rowan Wiley's house in an all-white neighborhood was burned down by an arsonist. He vowed to rebuild. Recently, the Wileys won a discrimination case in which the Rich-mond County Water District sought to condemn the land on which they were building (NYT).

7 In Tucson, Ariz., the Civil Liberties Committee of the National Council of Jewish Women released a survey on restaurant integration. Committee members found that African Americans were served only in 71 percent of the city's restaurants (JM).

9 In Chicago, Ill., president of the AFL-CIO George Meany told the GOP Platform Committee that civil rights was the "number one moral issue of our time." He emphasized the importance of legislation to achieve equal treatment for all U.S. citizens (NYT).

14 In Atlanta, Ga., Lonnie King, Jr., chairman of the Committee on Appeal for Human Rights, launched a campaign to persuade 1,000 customers to turn in their charge account plates from Rich's Department Store. The store refused to integrate its lunch counters. Meanwhile, in Knoxville, Tenn., more than 100 whites cancelled their accounts at Rich's Department Store there. Several whites also joined the picket lines in front of the Knoxville store (JM).

19 In Montgomery, Ala., city officials confirmed that Martin Luther King would not be tried on a second count of perjury. King was acquitted on a first count of perjury regarding his state income tax returns (NYT).

20 In Washington, D.C., U.S. Supreme Court justice Hugo Black refused to stay an order by a lower-court judge that called on New Orleans officials to begin the desegregation of the public schools in September 1960 (NYT).

21 In Washington, D.C., police broke up a small demonstration of students outside of the Capitol. The students called on Congress to forbid discrimination and segregation of black servicemen and veterans in the South (JM).

23 In Columbus, Ohio, officials at Ohio State University announced plans to remove from its approved student housing lists rooming houses that discriminated against students because of race, religion, or color. This ended the university's practice of trying to eliminate discrimination through negotiations with the individual owners of rooming houses (NYT).

27 In Arlington, Va., members of Virginia's Pupil Placement Board assigned twelve black students, involved in court cases seeking admission to all-white public schools, to previously all-white schools. There had been some school integration for more than a year in Arlington (NYT).

30 In Atlanta, Ga., SNCC officials called former president Harry S. Truman's recent statements, that the student sit-ins were under the influence of the Communists, irresponsible and unfounded. Eleanor Roosevelt also criticized Truman's utterances (JM).

AUGUST 1960

1 In Atlanta, Ga., a Fulton County grand jury condemned picketing and nonviolent marches. Yet the jury also called for action toward improving race relations by upgrading black housing, hospitals, and recreational facilities and increasing the ratio of black to white police officers (SSN)

1 In Atlanta, Ga., college students from the Committee on Appeal for Human Rights placed three wreaths with inscriptions from the Declaration of Independence on the state capitol steps in order to protest segregation of public facilities. State officials confiscated the wreaths (SSN).

2 In Chicago, Ill., leaders of the local NAACP chapter and church and labor leaders sent telegrams to Martin Luther King, Roy Wilkins, and A. Philip Randolph urging them to organize a movement for a march on Washington or a mass lobby for civil rights legislation during the reconvened session of Congress (NYT).

4 In Miami, Fla., members of the National Federation for the Blind amended their constitution to permit African Americans to hold memberships and offices. When representatives from Louisiana, Maryland, Georgia, and North Carolina objected to the measure, federation officials expelled them from the organization (JM).

4 In Springfield, Mass., superior court judge Reuben Lurie ruled that free speech included the right to picket Woolworth stores. The case applied to local protests against the company's racial segregation policies in the South (JM).

11 In Cleveland, Ohio, the James Lyons family found their house splattered with paint and tar when they moved into an all-white neighborhood. Lyons insisted that most of the people in the neighborhood were friendly (JM).

11 In St. Louis, Mo., officials for the American Life and Accident Co., which generally charged higher premiums to black clients, decided to delete the requirement that prospective customers indicate their "color" on the application (JM).

11 In Washington, D.C., U.S. attorney general William Rogers announced that a group of chain store executives had agreed to desegregate their lunch counters, which were located in sixty-nine southern cities. Between June and August 1960, Rogers had met with officials representing F. W. Woolworth, S. H. Kress, and several other southern chain stores for "informal" talks that concluded with this agreement (NYT).

13 In Washington, D.C., A. Philip Randolph and Roy Wilkins protested the tabling of civil rights legislation by the Senate. They strongly criticized Senators John F. Kennedy and Lyndon B. Johnson for agreeing with the tabling of the measure (NYT).

14, 22 In Chattanooga, Tenn., the homes of two black residents were damaged in the third and fourth racially motivated house bombings to occur in the city since mid-July. Attorney General William Rogers announced that FBI agents would investigate the bombings. The Chattanooga police commissioner had requested the intervention of the FBI (NYT).

16 In Raleigh, N.C., Bryce Wagoner, president of Bus Terminal Restaurants, Inc., announced that his company would no longer refuse service on the basis of race. The change in practice would affect restaurants in Trailways bus terminals in Virginia, North Carolina, Tennessee, Florida, Texas, and Maryland (NYT).

16 In Union, Miss., about two hundred whites warned James Stewart, the black secretary of the

CONFRONTING DISCRIMINATION IN EMPLOYMENT
AND LABOR UNIONS

Ongoing civil rights issues in the area of employment are well documented in the national and international news publications for the years 1954 to 1960. Despite efforts of fair employment practices commissions, courts, and protests by black organizations, as well as executive orders banning discrimination by employers receiving government contracts, employment discrimination against African Americans continued. There was no substantial change in the employment and apprenticeship training opportunities available for African Americans, and discrimination in most labor unions persisted.

In 1960, as African Americans continued to confront these kinds of problems, they focused upon enforcement of nondiscrimination laws and organized sit-ins and boycotts to desegregate businesses and unions. The NAACP reported findings of a five-year investigation that demonstrated that labor unions excluded African Americans from apprenticeship programs in virtually all craft unions. In the construction trades, where trainees were selected and endorsed by union members, black workers were unable to gain apprenticeships.

In January, Rep. Adam Clayton Powell charged that New York mayor Robert Wagner was not enforcing laws against racial discrimination. In April in Washington, D.C., NAACP leaders appealed to Vice President Nixon, chairman of the President's Committee on Government Contracts, to ensure compliance by government contractors. They presented reports that showed discrimination on all levels against black workers. In October in Washington, D.C., the president's committee instituted a probe of the alleged denial of jobs to African Americans at the Ingalls Shipbuilding Corp. of Pascagoula, Miss. The Alabama Dry Dock and Shipbuilding Co. of Mobile, Ala., was told to end its job discrimination. At the end of December, Nixon endorsed new proposals for ending job and housing discrimination where federal funds were involved. Some companies refused to comply with federal directives. In September in Washington, D.C., the Howard Foley Co. rejected the government's ultimatum to hire black electricians. The company held a $2 million contract for the new federal office building in the capital.

In March in Detroit, Mich., black labor leaders formed the Negro American Labor Council (NALC), whose goals were to end employment discrimination and work for the inclusion of African Americans in all labor unions. In September NALC officials disclosed plans to hold national hearings spotlighting employment inequities in the building trades and apprenticeship programs. In December in Chicago, Ill., a group of black construction workers filed suit for damages and sought a court order to restrain three International Hod Carriers, Building, and Common Laborers Union locals from discriminatory practices. The laborers charged that they were banned from higher-paying jobs because of their race.

In 1960 in addition to the organized protest of major civil rights organizations, numerous local groups challenged the employment bias practiced by local businesses. In March in Atlanta, Ga., students picketed A&P stores, protesting discrimination in hiring policies for clerk and cashier jobs. In October Harold Fleming, director of the Atlanta-based Southern Regional Council, announced that the next target in the fight against race bias would be department stores and chain supermarkets that did not hire black sales personnel. Meanwhile, in New Orleans, La., members of the all-black Consumer's League led a boycott against merchants on Dryades Street to protest their refusal to hire African Americans. The boycott forced the merchants to hire twenty-seven employees. In October police arrested six members of the Consumer's League after they participated in a protest march against the Claiborne Shopping Center. The shopping center only employed African Americans in menial jobs. In June in Detroit, Mich., Dr. Lawrence Lackey charged three Detroit hospitals—Grace, Harper, and Woman's—with continuing discriminatory policies against hiring black doctors. The hospitals had signed a nondiscrimination pledge in February 1960.

newly formed Bay Ridge Christian College, to get out of town. The instructors and the black students vowed to stay. However, following the beating of J. H. Germany, the white president, by a white mob, the Church of God abandoned plans to build the college (NYT).

18 In **Greensboro, N.C.**, Vice President Nixon declared that any American allowed to patronize a store should be entitled to use all its facilities. Nixon also stated that he expected his audiences to be nonsegregated during his southern campaign tours (NYT).

18 In **New York City**, NAACP leader Roy Wilkins blasted the kidnapping and flogging of Henry Jones, a black service station attendant in Harpersville, Ala. Jones's unknown assailants objected to his working at the service station (JM).

18 In **Washington, D.C.**, Postmaster General Arthur Summerfield threatened to crack down on postal officials who refused to enforce nondiscrimination orders in Virginia, Texas, and Alabama. The officials refused to promote African Americans and end rest room and locker room discrimination (JM).

21 In **Grosse Pointe, Mich.**, real estate agents in the all-white suburb dropped the controversial point system for screening home buyers. Buyers were given points according to their appearance, occupation, education, and economic and social status. Jews and southern European immigrants needed more points than white Anglo-Saxon Protestants. African Americans and Asians had been barred entirely (NYT).

25 In **Chattanooga, Tenn.**, two white men ambushed a carload of African Americans and wounded Ezell Tibbs and Rosalyn Reed. In another incident, twenty whites attacked and wounded Gilbert Baldwin, David Franklin, Perry Williams, and Thomas Quarles. The identities of the white assailants were unknown (JM).

25 In **Chicago, Ill.**, white University of Illinois freshman Dolores Romero and black Roosevelt University senior Ralph Wright were arrested for passing out leaflets in front of a Woolworth store. The leaflets urged patrons to boycott the store be-

cause of its southern segregation policy. Romero and Wright were members of the Chicago Youth Committee for Civil Rights (JM).

25 In **Chicago, Ill.**, a spokesperson for the Elks announced that student sit-in movement leaders would receive thousand-dollar scholarships during the Grand Lodge Convention of Elks. The Elks awarded the scholarships to ten leaders: Ezell Blair, Joseph McNeil, Fred Jones, Bernard Lee, Edgar Young, Marion Barry, Jr., Kenneth Frazier, Virginia Thornton, Lonnie King, and Mary Smith (JM).

25 In **Hollywood, Fla.**, Beatrice Brown and Gloria Thomas announced plans to file a suit against the city. After they were arrested on disorderly conduct charges, Sgt. John Bianco forced them to undress in his presence and refused to allow them to call a lawyer, in violation of their civil rights (JM).

25 In **Philadelphia, Pa.**, four hundred black ministers called off a boycott against the Tastykake Baking Co. after company administrators hired black driver-salesmen and plant and office personnel. The ministers had accused the company of discriminating against black job applicants (JM).

30, 31 In **New Orleans, La.**, despite protests by the NAACP, U.S. judge J. Skelly Wright postponed for two months the integration of seven thousand African American and four thousand white first graders. He stated that he was impressed with the arguments of four school board members who pleaded for the postponement of integration (NYT).

SEPTEMBER 1960

1 In **Houston, Tex.**, only three black students registered to attend white schools at the start of registration for kindergarten and first grade. City schools were under a federal court order to integrate. School superintendent John McFarland said he expected the majority of between forty-eight hundred and five thousand black students to enroll in all-black schools (NYT).

7, 8 In **New York City**, during the annual convention of the National Urban League, nationally known figures pleaded with members to wage all-out campaigns for integration in labor unions and employment and the eradication of institutionalized practices of racial discrimination in all aspects of public life. Martin Luther King and Gov. Nelson Rockefeller were among those who addressed the convention (NYT).

8 In Jefferson County, Ark., when six-year-old Delores York was enrolled in Pine Bluff's Dollarway School, she shattered a 141-year tradition of segregation in Jefferson County. Many feared a repetition of the violence that erupted at the school in the spring when a black man was beaten while attempting to register his grandchild (NYT).

8 In Washington, D.C., officers of Alpha Phi Alpha, a black fraternity, threatened to end its conference prematurely and leave the Sheraton Park Hotel unless delegates were allowed to swim in the pool. Hotel officials relented and allowed them to use the pool (JM).

15 In Atlanta, Ga., members of the Atlanta Medical Association (black) picketed two A&P stores. They wanted the store to hire African Americans as cashiers, butchers, and stock clerks. The store had been regularly picketed by members of the student Committee on Appeal for Human Rights since May 1960. Atlanta's black dentists joined the doctors one week later (JM).

15 In East Chicago, Ind., a group led by attorney Henry Walker began sit-ins on the porches of African Americans in the state who had not registered to vote. The group announced sit-ins in South Bend, Fort Wayne, Indianapolis, and Gary, Ind. Walker estimated that two-thirds of the one hundred thousand qualified black voters in the state were not registered. Sit-ins on the doorsteps of unregistered voters in East Chicago, Ind., had boosted the number of African Americans registered by 90 percent (JM).

15 In Washington, D.C., both John F. Kennedy and Richard Nixon vowed not to tolerate discrimination against black staffers or newspeople traveling with the candidates in the South. This marked the first time such a policy had been adopted by both presidential candidates (JM).

22 In Chicago, Ill., James Southard was sentenced to four months in jail for carrying a homemade bomb to an NAACP wade-in. Another white youth, Adrian Jones, was sentenced to a week in jail when he admitted that he made the bomb for Southard (JM).

22 In Levittown, N.J., William J. Levitt notified New Jersey that he had abandoned his "no Negroes" policy in the sale of homes in his housing development. In 1959 the New Jersey state courts had ruled that he could not discriminate against African Americans in the sale of homes in Levittown. One black family had already moved into the development (JM).

29 In Atlanta, Ga., after several cabs refused to pick them up at the airport, attorney Len Holt and SCLC director Wyatt Walker filed a federal court suit seeking desegregation of the city's taxicabs (JM).

29 In Brooklyn, N.Y., black parents and children called off a boycott after members of the board of education agreed to transfer African American and Puerto Rican children from overcrowded schools and permit voluntary transfers from schools in nonwhite areas. The agreement was reached during a meeting between parents and board members (JM).

29 In New Rochelle, N.Y., after administrators at the new all-white William Ward Elementary School refused to enroll twelve black students, stating that students had to attend schools in the districts where they lived, twenty-three African Americans participated in a sit-down strike. Police charged eight protesters with disorderly conduct (JM).

29 In Tallahassee, Fla., the justices on the state supreme court granted Rev. Theodore Gibson an additional month of freedom before ruling on a lower court's sentence for contempt. Gibson, president of the Miami NAACP, was convicted and sentenced to jail for refusing to turn over to a state investigative committee the branch's membership rolls and other records (JM).

BLACK VOTERS AND THE PRESIDENTIAL ELECTION OF 1960

The year 1960 was memorialized by the student-led sit-ins. The expansion of activities bolstered by mass demonstrations and rallies in the South and by picketing and demonstrations outside the South attracted attention as the media focused the nation on the mass, nonviolent protests, wholesale arrests, brutal treatment of demonstrators, and bombings of homes and churches. Martin Luther King vowed to work with other leaders and use sit-in techniques to pressure whites for the right to vote in southern states. Confronted with these activities, the nation demanded that the federal government take action. The passage of the 1960 Voting Rights Act, federal intervention in southern elections, the U.S. Civil Rights Commission's hearings on voting irregularities, and a nonpartisan crusade by black organizations to register one million black voters led by the NAACP, organized labor, and the SCLC contributed to the November election of John F. Kennedy as president.

President Eisenhower, Richard Nixon, and John F. Kennedy were not interested in embracing any idea or strategy for eliminating segregation or discrimination if it meant alienating the southern vote. However, Nixon, the Republican presidential candidate, very early in the year made statements supportive of civil rights. Rep. Adam Clayton Powell strongly criticized Eisenhower for lacking the courage to stand up for African Americans. Kennedy felt that moral persuasion by the president could be more effective than force in ending race bias. The naming of Lyndon Johnson as the vice presidential candidate to run on the ticket with Kennedy led to a rash of protests from black Democrats, who viewed Johnson's commitment to civil rights as questionable.

Following the Democratic and Republican conventions, A. Philip Randolph urged African Americans not to be "in the vest pocket" of Democrats or Republicans. He stated that neither Nixon nor Kennedy was a crusader for civil rights. Mrs. Vel Phillips, the first African American to serve on the national committee of a major political party, urged enactment of a strong civil rights plank and almost precipitated a Dixie walkout at the Democratic National Convention. In Chicago, Ill., NAACP officials Roy Wilkins and Clarence Mitchell and Martin Luther King, A. Philip Randolph, and other black leaders led a "Freedom Now" demonstration and urged the Platform Committee of the Republican convention to devise a civil rights plank that was stronger than that of the Democrats. The Republican plank called for nondiscrimination in employment and housing and broader opportunities in voting.

By September the national prominence of the civil rights agenda persuaded both candidates to make carefully studied comments about the movement. In October, following King's arrest and subsequent imprisonment at the Reidsville Penitentiary, a maximum security prison, Kennedy telephoned Coretta Scott King to express concern and offer assistance. Robert Kennedy intervened, and King was later released on bond. This action had a dramatic effect on the black community, which turned out in large numbers to vote for Kennedy. Kennedy's narrow margin of victory was attributed to the large black voter turnout in northern and midwestern states.

29 In Washington, D.C., Sen. Vance Hartke urged the State Department and the District Commissioner's Council on Human Relations to take steps to end discrimination against black diplomats serving in the United States. Hartke added that, because of racial segregation, Washington was a "hardship post" for black diplomats (JM).

OCTOBER 1960

1 In Dade County, Fla., seven black students were admitted to Dade County Community College. It became the first integrated junior college in the state (SSN).

1 In St. Marys County, Md., an unidentified fifth-grade black girl was admitted to an all-white school. Public schools in fifteen of Maryland's twenty-three counties had been integrated (SSN).

7 In Long Island, N.Y., Mrs. Nilda Flott filed a complaint with the State Commission Against Discrimination against barber Angelo Mustachio. Flott accused Mustachio of violating New York's anti-bias statute when he overcharged her son five dollars because he had "kinky" hair (NYT).

13 In Dayton, Ohio, Dr. M. R. Clarke told the Ohio Civil Rights Commission that the three hospitals in the city discriminated against black patients. He pointed out that St. Elizabeth's had two segregated wards (JM).

20 In Greenville, Miss., segregationist senator James Eastland announced his support of the Democratic ticket because he did not want to lose his chairmanship of the Senate Judiciary Committee. As chair of the committee, Eastland continued to block civil rights legislation (NYT).

27 In Detroit, Mich., a group of two thousand white parents planned to keep their children out of school for two days to protest a decision by members of the local school board to transfer 314 black students to white schools. Board members sought to reduce overcrowding at all-black schools (NYT).

27 In Los Angeles, Calif., NAACP official Frank Barnes charged that a black army officer at a southern California Nike base was excluded from government-leased housing because of his race. He made the charges before the Housing Division of the California Advisory Committee on Civil Rights (JM).

27 In Louisville, Ky., the Disciples of Christ apologized in a resolution to black delegates who were denied service at six hotels and restaurants. Rev. King Allen stated that the resolution was initiated by white friends of the black delegates (NYT).

28 In De Kalb County, Ga., Martin Luther King was freed on a two-thousand-dollar bond to appeal a four-month prison term for violating an earlier sentence of twelve months on probation. The earlier sentence was for driving with an Alabama rather than a Georgia driver's license. At the urg-

ing of Robert F. Kennedy, Judge J. Oscar Mitchell allowed King's release from Reidsville Penitentiary pending the ruling on his appeal (NYT).

31 In Chicago, Ill., the four youths from A&T College in Greensboro, N.C., who sparked the sit-in demonstration movement received the Thomas J. Crowe Award from the Catholic Interracial Council of Chicago. Recipients were: Joseph McNeil, Ezell Blair, Jr., David Richmond, and Franklin McCain (NYT).

NOVEMBER 1960

1 In Athens, Ga., Hamilton Holmes, recently denied admission to the University of Georgia, revealed that his interview included inappropriate questions, like whether he had ever visited a house of prostitution and whether he participated in sit-ins. The other black applicant, Charlayne Hunter, was admitted to the university and stated that her interview had been cordial (SSN).

1 In Burnsville, N.C., members of the Yancy County Board of Education bowed to a federal court order to integrate. They assigned ten black high school students to previously all-white schools (SSN).

1 In Prince Edward County, Va., Rev. L. Francis Griffin, president of the all-black Prince Edward County Christian Association, announced plans to raise twenty thousand dollars to open sixteen training centers to educate black students. County school officials closed the public schools in 1959 in order to avoid integration (SSN).

3 In Greensboro, N.C., NAACP official Herbert Hill charged public schools with teaching African Americans obsolete skills. He stated that while white students learned physics and chemistry, black students were often placed in home economics and industrial arts classes (JM).

3 In Jackson, Tenn., Lane College students picketed buses to protest the arrest of nine black students who refused to move to the back of the bus. Three white youths picketed the black students and carried signs that read "If you don't want to ride our buses, then walk" (JM).

3 In Philadelphia, Pa., seventeen white and black teenagers under the leadership of Temple University student Joyce Barrett, staged a "roll-in" against the Chez Vous skating rink. After owner Mrs. Elizabeth Kelly allowed them to skate, white hecklers punched and spit on the protesters (JM).

3 In Syracuse, N.Y., air force major Eldridge Williams published a story in the *Syracuse Herald-Journal* that stated that no one would sell or rent him a house because he was black. After the article appeared, he received more than one hundred offers to sell him a house (JM).

4 In New Rochelle, N.Y., members of the school board voted against allowing African Americans to register their children outside of their home districts. Black parents had been fighting to have their children moved from the all-black Lincoln School to other schools. Meanwhile, a city court judge dismissed disorderly conduct charges against eight black parents who tried to enroll their children in all-white schools (NYT).

9 In Washington, D.C., twenty-four white and black students picketed the White House, demanding immediate action by President Eisenhower on civil rights. Similar demonstrations occurred in Philadelphia, Boston, Pittsburgh, Atlanta, and at the University of Michigan (NYT).

11 In New Orleans, La., federal district judge J. Skelly Wright issued a court order that banned new segregation laws and prohibited state interference with New Orleans's public schools. The order came after the state legislature named an eight-man committee to run the city's schools. Meanwhile, members of the Orleans parish board voted to integrate schools by placing five black girls into two of the city's all-white schools (NYT).

11 In Washington, D.C., John F. Kennedy named Andrew Hatcher as an associate press aide. Hatcher became the first African American to be named as a White House press aide (NYT).

15 In New Orleans, La., U.S. Marshals escorted four black first graders into two white schools. Abron Bridges, the father of one of the students, was fired from his job as a gasoline station attendant because he refused to back down on inte-

gration. The integration of the schools sparked citywide rioting (NYT).

22 In Macon County, Ala., registration board chairman Wheeler Dyson obeyed a court order and handed over the county's voter records to two representatives of the U.S. attorney general's office. He refused to register anyone while the federal agents were present (NYT).

24 In Washington, D.C., Labor Secretary James Mitchell ruled that the United Auto Workers headquarters could take over UAW Memphis Local 988 and hold it under trusteeship. The local had separate washrooms and drinking fountains for its black members (JM).

27 In Atlanta, Ga., African Americans picketed Rich's department store while KKK members paraded on the opposite side of the street. Klan leaflets called for immediate action to ensure the maintenance of segregation in public accommodations (NYT).

29 In New York City, a spokesperson for the FBI announced an intensive probe of racist hate notes sent to five nonwhite UN delegations in New York. The notes attacked Africans, Asians, Catholics, and Jews. The FBI tried to determine whether the letters were written by an American (NYT).

DECEMBER 1960

1 In Atlanta, Ga., Rev. Fred Shuttlesworth of Birmingham filed a $9 million suit in federal court against Southeastern Greyhound Lines, charging that the arrest of his daughter Patricia Ann violated her constitutional rights. She refused to move to the rear of the bus (JM).

1 In Birmingham, Ala., members of the Alabama Christian Movement for Human Rights were denied a temporary injunction seeking to prevent police commissioner Eugene Connor and police chief Jamie Moore from attending their weekly meetings. Revs. Fred Shuttlesworth and Charles Billups charged that police presence at meetings intimidated and discouraged blacks from attending (SSN).

I In **Memphis, Tenn.**, a spokesperson for the Tennessee State Revenue Department announced that it would hire Benjamin Blakey, a black man, as a tax inspector for its Memphis office. Spokesperson Frank Murphy stated that Blakey would deal only with African Americans (JM).

I In **New Rochelle, N.Y.**, the suit filed by African Americans in order to integrate all-white schools was suspended for two weeks. Mrs. Barbara Mason, black principal of the all-white Roosevelt Elementary School, stated she did not favor the integration of the schools because it would give African Americans special treatment (NYT).

I In **New York City**, Mrs. Irene Willins vowed to stay in her home in a predominantly white South Brooklyn neighborhood, despite eight days of harassment by her neighbors. Whites hurled rocks through windows, directed insults and profanity at the family, and started a fire in an adjacent lot (JM).

I In **Prince Edward County, Va.**, Rev. L. Francis Griffin of the Prince Edward County Christian Association announced the opening of sixteen morale-building centers for black children. The centers were formed to provide math and remedial reading sessions for more than six hundred students. Public schools were closed in order to prevent integration (SSN).

I In **Taylor Township, Mich.**, officials of the Michigan Fair Employment Practices Commission ordered the Taylor Township school board to hire Mrs. Mary Ross and Mrs. Jessie Simmons and pay them back wages. The board had earlier refused to hire the two teachers on the basis of race (JM).

I In **Terrell County, Ga.**, the white chairman of the board of registers, James Raines, resigned his post. He charged that segregated polling places were set up in the courthouse, which violated the spirit of a federal court order that required the end of discrimination in voting (JM).

3 In **Hattiesburg, Miss.**, NAACP field secretary Medgar Evers was fined one hundred dollars and given a thirty-day jail sentence by circuit judge Stanton Hall. Hall cited Evers for contempt for criticizing the conviction of Clyde Kennard. Evers had

called Kennard's trial "the greatest mockery of social justice" after Kennard (black) received a seven-year prison sentence on burglary charges (NYT).

6 In **New Orleans, La.**, several reports stated that the school integration crisis had caused the hotel and restaurant trade to fall off by about 20 percent. Hotel cancellations averaged about 25 percent and sales plummeted as much as 40 percent in some major department stores (NYT).

6 In **Richmond, Va.**, judges of the U.S. Fourth Circuit Court of Appeals issued a temporary injunction giving African Americans the right to use white waiting rooms at the Greenville, S.C., airport. The complaint was filed by Richard Henry, who charged that in November 1958 he was forced into a segregated waiting room while waiting for a plane at the Greenville Airport (NYT).

6 In **Washington, D.C.**, the Supreme Court ruled that restaurants in interstate bus terminals could not refuse to serve African Americans making journeys across state lines. The action resulted from an appeal filed by former Howard University student Bruce Boynton, who was fined ten dollars for refusing to leave a "white" restaurant in the Richmond, Va., Trailways bus terminal (NYT).

8, 9 In **Wilberforce, Ohio**, Arkansas NAACP president Daisy Bates praised Daisy Gabrielle (white), who had been escorting her daughter to her recently integrated New Orleans school despite threats. Bates spoke before an audience at Central State College. However, despite money and telegrams of praise sent by supporters, Mrs. Gabrielle and her family decided to move to Rhode Island (NYT).

13 In **Atlanta, Ga.**, the English Avenue Elementary School was bombed one day after two thousand African Americans held a prayer service there and marched downtown. Several civic leaders, including *Atlanta Constitution* editor Ralph McGill, condemned the bombing (NYT).

13 In **Washington, D.C.**, the Supreme Court justices ruled a 1958 Arkansas law that required public school teachers to list the organizations to which they have belonged or contributed in the previous five years unconstitutional. Black leaders viewed the law as a way to discriminate against civil rights organizations (NYT).

15 In Macon, Ga., U.S. district judge W. A. Bootle ordered the University of Georgia registrar to make available to Hamilton Holmes and Charlayne Hunter all records pertaining to the admission of undergraduates currently enrolled at the school. The black students requested the information because they were applying for admission (NYT).

17, 19, 28 In Washington, D.C., President Eisenhower praised the James Gabrielles, a white family forced to move from New Orleans to Rhode Island after attempting to break a white boycott of an integrated school. The black fraternity Omega Psi Phi sent $250 to the family for their "contribution to democracy" (NYT).

18, 22 In New Orleans, La., judges of the New Orleans federal courts ordered Lt. Gov. C. C. Aycock, Louisiana house speaker Thomas Jewell, and school superintendent Shelby Jackson to release the funds necessary to pay the salaries to teachers in newly integrated Frantz and McDonogh Elementary Schools. Before the court order, St. Louis heiress Ellen Steinberg offered $500,000 to the New Orleans school board to help keep its schools open (NYT).

22 In Batesville, Miss., farmer Willie Kuykendall fled with his family to Gary, Ind. His daughter was beaten and his family harassed and threatened because he attempted to vote (JM).

22 In Chicago, Ill., Harry Belafonte refused to appear as a guest star at a tribute dinner for former president Harry Truman. Belafonte turned down the invitation because of Truman's statements denouncing sit-ins (JM).

26 In Washington, D.C., new proposals by the President's Committee on Government Contracts were endorsed by Vice President Richard Nixon, the committee's chairman. The proposals concerned ending job and housing discrimination where federal funds were involved (NYT).

27 In New York City, Health Commissioner Leona Baumgartner announced that all birth certificates issued after 1 January 1961 would not contain references to race or color. The New York City Board of Health would keep color or race information only in confidential medical records (NYT).

29 In Atlanta, Ga., officials at the Federal Reserve Bank released statistics that revealed that city department stores reported a major decline in business during the first big week of Christmas shopping. The decline was attributed to resumed boycotts and sit-in demonstrations at segregated stores (JM).

29 In Chicago, Ill., members of the local NAACP, led by Charles Fuqua, picketed Chicago's city hall, demanding action to end hospital discrimination. The protest occurred after two African Americans were transferred from a white hospital to Cook County Hospital, where they died shortly thereafter (JM).

30 In Fayette County, Tenn., Early Williams, a resident of Freedom Village, the tent city established for sharecroppers evicted from their homes, was shot in the arm by a person in a passing car while attending a meeting of the Civic and Welfare League. It was the first violent incident since the league began to register African Americans in the spring of 1960 (NYT).

31 In Washington, D.C., John F. Kennedy appointed Robert Weaver administrator of the Federal Housing and Home Administration. Weaver, a recognized expert on black labor and racial issues, had been a key figure in the Roosevelt administration's Black Cabinet (NYT).

On 14 May 1961, in Anniston, Alabama, members of the "Freedom Riders," a group sponsored by the Congress of Racial Equality (CORE), sit on the ground after their bus was set afire by a mob of whites who had met the bus at the terminal, stoned it, slashed the tires, and then followed it from town. When the tires went flat, the mob set the bus on fire and attacked the passengers as they disembarked. (SOURCE: CORBIS BETTMANN)

1961

"I'VE BEEN 'BUKED AND I'VE BEEN SCORNED"

The momentum created by the student sit-ins inspired the Congress of Racial Equality (CORE) to launch the Freedom Rides in 1961. Americans were shocked by the deadly violence that erupted when the Freedom Riders reached Alabama and Mississippi. "I've been 'buked and I've been scorned" was as much the lament for the black home buyer attempting to move into an all-white neighborhood in 1961 as it was for the Freedom Rider trying to desegregate a southern bus terminal. "Jail, No Bail" became the slogan for social activists whose civil disobedience presented a formidable challenge to unjust laws. While business leaders promised to address employment discrimination through the Plans for Progress campaigns, legal suits were used to end segregation at the University of Georgia and other state-supported institutions of higher education. The new administration had to move quickly to develop strategies to keep track of a social movement that was rapidly moving beyond its control.

JANUARY 1961

1 In Columbia, S.C., Robert Kennedy, the new U.S. attorney general designate, told a conference of U.S. district attorneys that the federal government was going to move ahead in civil rights. He stated, "We will use as much power as the federal government possesses to see that court orders are followed" (SSN).

6 In Anniston, Ala., a demonstration of 350 African Americans in front of police headquarters turned into a racial brawl. Police arrested one white man and two black men. The black college students were at the headquarters to protest the earlier beating of two African Americans who entered a white waiting room at the local train station (NYT).

6 In Fayette County, Tenn., a second Freedom Village was opened for African Americans who at-

tempted to register to vote, but the location remained secret to ensure privacy for its inhabitants. Meanwhile, U.S. district judge Marion Boyd extended a temporary restraining order that prevented further evictions of black sharecroppers (NYT).

8 In Jackson, Miss., Robert Smith and three other African Americans filed a lawsuit in federal court seeking an injunction against payments of public funds by the State Sovereignty Commission to White Citizens Councils. Gov. Ross Barnett recently admitted that the commission was making monthly payments of five thousand dollars to the WCCs from an appropriation for the purpose of advertising segregation (NYT).

8 In New York City, NAACP treasurer Alfred Baker Lewis revealed that it received $985,731 in contributions in 1960. This marked a 15 percent increase over 1959 figures (NYT).

12 In Austin, Tex., more than two thousand University of Texas students signed a petition protesting segregation, while other students began picketing theaters in Austin. Students complained that African Americans often could not complete film assignments because of segregated theaters (JM).

12 In Detroit, Mich., Mayor Louis Miriani ordered a probe of the police department after two ex-policemen alleged police brutality. William Patrick, Jr., the city's only black councilman, called the probe a "token" action (JM).

13 In Washington, D.C., former secretary of state Christian Herter sent a note of apology to the Nigerian government for the refusal of a restaurant in Charlottesville, Va., to provide service to Nigerian diplomat C. C. Uchuno. The restaurant gave him a bag of food and told him to eat outside (NYT).

19 In New York City, a group of black newspaper publishers met with John F. Kennedy to offer suggestions for his first term. They discussed the appointment of more African Americans to federal courts, housing, and better employment opportunities for minorities. Thomas Young, Dr. Carlton Goodlett, Mrs. Nannie Mitchell Turner, E. Washington Rhodes, Dr. C. B. Powell, and Carl Murphy represented the National Newspaper Publishers Association (JM).

19 In San Francisco, Calif., members of the National Council of Churches passed a resolution urging an intensified effort to break down discriminatory barriers still existing in employment practices. The resolution also urged churches to examine their own practices and possible employment discrimination (JM).

20 In Shreveport, La., officials of the Justice Department's civil rights division accused Sheriff John Gilbert and ten businessmen of using serious economic coercion against Francis Atlas, a black farmer who tried to vote. The sheriff told Atlas that businessmen would no longer process cotton for him after he tried to vote in Carroll Parish. There were no black voters in the parish, although 5,330 African Americans were eligible (NYT).

21 In Washington, D.C., President Kennedy's inauguration attracted the largest number of African Americans and was the most integrated in history. One of his first acts in office was to sign an executive order that supplied food to displaced families in Fayette and Haywood counties, Tenn. (NYT).

24, 28 In Atlanta, Ga., members of the Georgia Senate passed a bill wiping out all previous public school segregation laws. The bill set up a program of tuition grants for pupils who chose not to attend integrated schools (NYT).

25 In New Rochelle, N.Y., federal judge Irving Kaufman stated that the school board deliberately gerrymandered school district lines to establish the all-black Lincoln School. He ordered the board to present a desegregation plan by 14 April 1961 (NYT).

26 In Dallas, Tex., a group of sixty white Southern Methodist University students were sprayed with an insecticide at a sit-in held at a drugstore counter. The sit-in occurred after two African Americans were refused service (JM).

26 In Shelby County, Tenn., officials of the Memphis Transit Co., which voluntarily integrated bus seating, were indicted by a grand jury on charges of violating a state law requiring segregated seating on buses. Bus company official Frank Ragsdale stated that the company would continue to ignore the segregation law (JM).

29 In Chicago, Ill., Cardinal Albert Gregory Meyer ordered the complete integration of African Americans into the local Catholic schools, hospitals, and fraternal and parish organizations. He stated that priests "have the responsibility of forming public opinion rather than following it" (NYT).

30 In Washington, D.C., Rep. Adam Clayton Powell demanded that his proposal to bar federal funds to schools discriminating against African Americans be adopted immediately. He stated that it could be done either through legislation or executive order (NYT).

I In Montgomery, Ala., an all-white jury awarded Mayor Earl James a $500,000 libel judgment against *The New York Times* and four black ministers: Revs. Ralph Abernathy, S. S. Seay, Fred Shuttlesworth, and Joseph Lowery. The mayor claimed that an advertisement in *The New York Times* on behalf of Martin Luther King had damaged his reputation. Meanwhile, garnishment orders were issued against the financial assets of the ministers as a result of a previous $500,000 libel judgment awarded to police commissioner L. B. Sullivan (NYT).

I In Washington, D.C., President Kennedy ordered the Coast Guard's officer school in New London, Conn., to admit African Americans. He had noticed that no African Americans marched with Coast Guard units in the inauguration parade (NYT).

16 In Chicago, Ill., members of the American Library Association adopted a resolution calling for the integration of the nation's libraries. This action followed a recommendation made by Rice Estes, a librarian at Brooklyn's Pratt Institute, that the organization should make a public statement in

THE UNIVERSITY OF GEORGIA AND THE DESEGREGATION OF U.S. COLLEGES AND UNIVERSITIES

On 6 January 1961 in Atlanta, Ga., district court judge W. A. Bootle ordered the University of Georgia to admit Charlayne Hunter and Hamilton Holmes immediately. He stated that the black students were qualified and would already have been admitted had it not been for their race. Meanwhile, in Washington, D.C., U.S. Commission on Civil Rights members accused the federal government of using its own funds to perpetuate segregated colleges in six southern states. The commission urged that all federal funds be cut off from any publicly supported college that discriminated. The court order and the possibility of losing federal funds forced Georgia governor Ernest Vandiver to renege on his pledge to preserve segregation at all state schools. He endorsed a program of limited integration to keep the state schools open. The governor's new program included a guarantee that no child be required to attend an integrated school and provided private school grants.

Within days of their arrival on the University of Georgia's campus in Athens, Ga., Hunter and Holmes were confronted with massive student violence. After police used tear gas to break up student rioting, administration officials decided to suspend the black students for their "personal safety." Following their departure, three hundred faculty members issued a petition demanding their return with full protection. Reporting on her return to the University of Georgia after a one-week "suspension," Hunter stated that crowds had dispersed and she felt part of the community. Fifty University of Georgia student leaders drafted a handbill urging their colleagues to treat Hunter and Holmes with kindness. In March, Judge Bootle ordered the dining room, swimming pool, and all other facilities at the University of Georgia opened to the black students. The ruling followed a request from the students' attorney, Donald Hollowell.

Federal intervention and the successful admission of Hunter and Holmes to the University of Georgia paved the way for the desegregation of other southern white institutions of higher learning and set the stage for the elimination of blatant racist practices at northern and western universities. By October the list of desegregated institutions included Georgia Tech in Atlanta, Ga.; the University of Miami in Coral Gables, Fla.; Wake Forest College in Winston-Salem, N.C.; Duke University in Durham, N.C.; The University of the South in Sewanee, Tenn.; Texas Technological University in Lubbock, Tex.; and the Guilford College in Greensboro, N.C. Meanwhile, in Biloxi, Miss., a federal district court hearing was scheduled on James Meredith's suit seeking to enter the University of Mississippi. NAACP counsel Constance Baker Motley also sought a temporary restraining order and a preliminary injunction to permit Meredith's enrollment.

support of integrated libraries. The resolution was later added to the Library Bill of Rights (JM).

17 In Washington, D.C., Rep. Adam Clayton Powell appointed five African Americans as assistants to the House Labor and Education Committee. Those appointed were Maxienne Dargans, Odell Clark, Livingston Wingate, John Harkless, and Mary Pinkard. It was the largest number of African Americans to be employed by a congressional committee (NYT).

21 In Washington, D.C., the Supreme Court justices ruled that Chicagoan James Monroe could sue city police in federal court. Police had forced his family out of bed naked and used words like "black boy" and "nigger" (NYT).

22 In New York City, school board members granted 2,795 students permission to attend schools outside their immediate areas in order to counter charges of segregation resulting from its neighborhood school policy. The action followed a successful integration experiment involving the transfer of black and Puerto Rican students to schools in white areas (NYT).

23 In Atlanta, Ga., it was announced that the SCLC had joined forces with the Highlander Folk School in Monteagle, Tenn., to train black leaders for the civil rights struggle. Martin Luther King served as head of the SCLC, and Myles Horton was the director of the Highlander Folk School (NYT).

24 In Washington, D.C., President Kennedy named Sen. Joseph Clark and Rep. Emmanuel Celler to draw up a six-part program of legislation to carry out the civil rights promises of the Democratic platform. They planned to introduce the program during the current congressional session (NYT).

28 In New York City, members of the Committee of Religious Leaders of New York urged the real estate board to introduce a nondiscriminatory policy in making available housing for delegates from the seventeen new African nations in the UN. The committee stated that it wanted to avoid international incidents (NYT).

28 In Montgomery, Ala., federal judge Frank Johnson ruled that a 1957 law that redrew Tuskegee's boundaries and left only five blacks inside the city limits was unconstitutional. Charles G. Gomillion, president of the Tuskegee Civic Association, and twelve other African Americans had filed the suit against gerrymandering and organized a fourteen-month boycott of white merchants in Tuskegee who had supported the measure (NYT).

MARCH 1961

1 In Albany, N.Y., two hundred black and white demonstrators staged an orderly protest march and picketed the state legislature, demanding stronger laws to combat racial discrimination in private housing. Meanwhile, Gov. Nelson Rockefeller told a delegation of fifty NAACP leaders that he shared their objective, and that during his administration he would endeavor to end discrimination in all aspects of life in New York State (NYT).

2 In Chicago, Ill., members of the Chicago Federation of Labor declared that the group would not contribute support to or cooperate with any agency whose funds were allocated to any hospital or institution that practiced discrimination or segregation. The action was taken after ten black doctors filed an antitrust suit charging that fifty-six hospitals had carried out a boycott against black physicians since 1938 (JM).

2 In New Rochelle, N.Y., attorney Paul Zuber asked President Kennedy and Governor Nelson Rockefeller to investigate threats of violence against black parents who won a recent desegregation case against the New Rochelle school board. Zuber stated that the parents had been besieged with threatening letters since they won their suit (JM).

2 In Tampa, Fla., the FBI investigated a cross-burning and threats against Nathaniel Cannon. Cannon sought a seat on the city council and was one of four litigants in a suit to desegregate schools in Hillsborough County, Fla. (JM).

4 In New Orleans, La., a three-judge federal panel placed state school superintendent Shelby Jackson on three weeks' probation and ordered that he refrain from interfering with actions of the Orleans Parish school board. He had been charged with withholding salaries and lunch funds and refusing to furnish textbooks and certify new teachers (NYT).

16 In Flint, Mich., J. Merrill Spenser, a black mortician, won the right to have an eight-grave lot in all-white Flint Memorial Cemetery. Circuit judge John Baker ordered a mandatory injunction against the Flint Memorial Cemetery Association, which had a clause in its purchase agreement prohibiting the burial of nonwhites in the cemetery (JM).

18 In Montgomery, Ala., federal judge Frank Johnson dismissed conspiracy charges filed against Gov. John Patterson and three city commissioners by Revs. Ralph Abernathy, S. S. Seay, Fred Shuttlesworth, and Joseph Lowery. The suit charged Patterson and the commissioners with conspiracy to sue the ministers for libel. The suit was an effort to keep authorities from attaching the ministers' personal property to help pay for the libel damages assessed against them (NYT).

19 In New York City, members of the NAACP and the Negro American Labor Council picketed Broadway theaters where shows had touring companies playing the South. The action was part of a new campaign aimed at boycotting Jim Crow theaters in the South (NYT).

21 In Washington, D.C., Rep. Adam Clayton Powell warned the annual conference of the AFL-CIO that he would kill legislation sought by building and trade unions unless they integrated their membership. Labor Secy. Arthur Goldberg and AFL-CIO president George Meany also urged integration of labor unions (NYT).

23 In Washington, D.C., novelist Lillian Smith blasted a racial sex-fear play, *This Is Integration,* produced by the White Citizens Councils. The play portrayed integrated school life and ended with erotic lovemaking between white and black students. Smith dubbed the play "racial gangsterism" (JM).

24 In Washington, D.C., Walter Reuther, president of the United Auto Workers (UAW), ordered a crackdown on any UAW union that discriminated against African Americans (NYT).

APRIL 1961

1 In Jackson, Miss., Gov. Ross Barnett announced that he would oppose Mississippi State University entering the NCAA playoffs if the team had to face an opposing team with black players. He argued that integrated athletics might lead to social integration (SSN).

6 In Savannah, Ga., twenty-five hundred high school students boycotted their classrooms to protest the firing of black principal Al Cheatham, who was considered "too progressive." At least twenty-three students were arrested for picketing the Chatham County school board. Cheatham had been active with the Crusade for Voters, which encouraged black voter registration (JM).

6 In Washington, D.C., the Kennedy administration quietly removed the name of Dr. Benjamin Mays from consideration as an appointee to the U.S. Commission on Civil Rights after protests from Georgia senators Herman Talmadge and Richard Russell. The senators opposed him because of his outspoken racial views. Mays served as president of Atlanta's Morehouse College (JM).

8 In De Kalb County, Ga., Judge J. Oscar Mitchell gave Martin Luther King a six-month suspended sentence for driving without a license. The Georgia Court of Appeals had overruled Mitchell's original twelve-month sentence and ordered Mitchell to resentence King (NYT).

8 In New York City, NAACP official Roy Wilkins announced "Operation Mississippi," a drive to increase registered black voters, to desegregate schools, and survey the hiring practices of firms with government contracts (NYT).

13 In Durham, N.C., NAACP regional official Ruby Hurley announced that four more department stores hired black personnel in order to encourage black patronage. Earlier, five department stores agreed to integrate, but five others refused to hire black employees (JM).

"JAIL, NO BAIL": SIT-INS AS CIVIL DISOBEDIENCE

The year following the launching of sit-ins in 1960 was another peak year for student activism. Viewed by some civil rights leaders as one of the most successful tactics for forcing change in segregation practices, the sit-ins demonstrated the importance of nonviolent direct action protest.

On 31 January 1961 in Rock Hill, S.C., students sitting in at McCrory's lunch counter were arrested, taken to jail, convicted of trespassing, and sentenced to thirty days of hard labor or a one-hundred-dollar fine. Nine students chose jail instead of bail. This was the beginning of the highly publicized "jail, no bail" tactic. Among those arrested was Diane Nash, one of SNCC's four regional leaders. Two weeks after their imprisonment, eight of the nine students were placed in solitary confinement and put on bread and water after charging they had been overworked and were going on a sit-down strike. In Rock Hill, S.C., Diane Nash, Ruby Doris Smith, Charles Sherrod, and Charles Jones completed their thirty-day jail sentences and were released. In the following months whites and African Americans were also arrested for sit-ins in Lynchburg, Va.; Atlanta, Ga.; Montgomery, Ala,; and Jackson, Miss.

Between 7 and 16 February in Atlanta, Ga., thirty-one students were imprisoned for participating in sit-ins. Following the imprisonment of an additional eighty-two protesters, Martin Luther King urged African Americans to continue violating unjust segregation laws and going to jail. In early March, King was jailed as a probation violator when he participated in a sit-in protest. Fifty-four of the Atlanta students from the "jail, no bail" movement were released after spending fourteen days in jail for participating in a sit-in. This marked a temporary shift from demonstration to negotiation with downtown merchants. King persuaded the city's sit-in demonstrators to accept an agreement negotiated between downtown merchants and black leaders. Under the agreement, movement leaders halted demonstrations, and merchants agreed to desegregate lunch counters in September 1962 if the public schools were desegregated.

As a strategy, the "jail, no bail" movement placed additional pressure on local governmental authorities to desegregate eating facilities. Recognizing the huge economic costs associated with segregation of hotels, restaurants, and other public facilities, a few mayors and governors began to argue for desegregation. For example, in January Mayor William Hartsfield stated that the practice "hurts Atlanta's development as a convention city," and in Columbus, Ohio, Gov. Michael DiSalle asked the state legislature to enact stronger laws banning bias in hotels, restaurants, and motels. The federal government, particularly the State Department, was concerned about the international implications of discrimination against African and other "Colored" diplomats.

The "jail, no bail" movement also led to sit-in cases that reached the U.S. Supreme Court. Between October and December, the Supreme Court heard twenty civil rights cases, ten of which dealt with suits growing out of lunch counter demonstrations in Virginia and North Carolina. The first sit-in cases scheduled for hearing were three appeals filed by the NAACP, representing sixteen Southern University students convicted of disturbing the peace at the Greyhound bus station, Kress's department store, and Sitman's Drug Store in Baton Rouge, La. In December the justices overturned the students' convictions, stating that the police had "nothing to support their actions except their own opinions."

13 In Washington, D.C., after President Kennedy asked officials of the White House News Photographers Association to admit African Americans, Maurice Sorrell became its first black member. This action climaxed a three-year effort by black newspaper and magazine photographers to join the organization (NYT).

18 In Washington, D.C., the U.S. Supreme Court ruled that African Americans must be served in a Wilmington, Del., restaurant that leased space from a local government agency. William Burton, who was refused service in the Eagle Coffee Shoppe, sued on behalf of all African Americans (NYT).

20 In Atlanta, Ga., city aldermen voted to equalize the salaries of fourteen hundred black city workers with those of whites doing similar work. The act followed Mayor William Hartsfield's announcement that the time had come to equalize wages for black and white city workers (JM).

20 In Washington, D.C., President Kennedy named Erwin Griswold and NAACP lawyer Spottswood Robinson III to the U.S. Commission on Civil Rights. The appointments were expected to create a majority on the commission favoring the advancement of black civil rights. Robinson also served as dean of the Howard University Law School (NYT).

21 In Washington, D.C., President Kennedy issued a strict order that no executive department or agency would permit its name, sponsorship, facility, or activity to be used in conjunction with any employees' recreational group practicing discrimination. The order followed reports that the U.S. Patent Office had withdrawn from the Federal Golf Association after two African Americans were refused membership (NYT).

27 In Chicago, Ill., NAACP official Roy Wilkins said city governments in the U.S. were swamped with tax difficulties, housing, and industrial growth problems because they chose to segregate and thus inhibited economically viable housing development (JM).

27 In Chicago, Ill., members of the Chicago City Council passed a resolution asking that the Illinois General Assembly pass a state fair housing practices law. The measure would outlaw racial and religious discrimination in the purchase of homes (JM).

27 In Richmond, Va., the Justice Department filed a motion in federal district court to become part of the suit seeking the integration of Prince Edward County schools. The school suit was originally filed on 23 May 1951 by 118 pupils and 68 parents. The public schools in Prince Edward County had been closed since September 1959 (NYT).

29 In East Carroll Parish, La., Justice Department lawyers filed a second civil rights suit charging election officials of East Carroll Parish with barring more than four thousand African Americans from voter registration (NYT).

30 In Nashville, Tenn., several downtown theaters began admitting small groups of blacks in an experimental integration program. The action followed negotiations between theater managers and black leaders (NYT).

MAY 1961

6 In New Orleans, La., testifying before the U.S. Commission on Civil Rights, voter registrar Mary Ethel Fox failed the test she used to determine if African Americans were qualified to vote. The test involved stating one's age in years, months, and days (NYT).

6–7 In Syracuse, N.Y., Marjorie Smith, Syracuse University's dean of women, advised two white female students to inform their parents they were dating across racial lines. Syracuse students reacted to the advice by staging campus demonstrations (NYT).

7 In Washington, D.C., Attorney General Robert F. Kennedy asked prospective U.S. marshals to consider naming qualified African Americans as deputies. Kennedy made the request after learning that only 10 out of 950 deputy U.S. marshals were African Americans (NYT).

9 In Montgomery, Ala., Martin Luther King announced plans to raise between $75,000 and $100,000 for legal defense in the libel suits against Revs. Ralph Abernathy, S. S. Seay, Fred Shuttlesworth, and Joseph Lowery. King also revealed the formation of an eighteen-member national council of attorneys to help defend the ministers and others (NYT).

11 In Washington, D.C., members of the Kennedy administration submitted a school desegregation program for congressional approval. Schools would be required to adopt a desegregation plan within six months and file it with the Department of Health, Education, and Welfare (NYT).

14 In Washington, D.C., administration officials ended the State Department practice of barring African and Asian guests from traveling in certain areas of the South. Officials also urged southern governors to monitor potential discrimination against foreign visitors (NYT).

18 In Atlanta, Ga., members of the aldermanic board announced that taxicabs and cars for hire in Atlanta could carry both white and black passengers. The board's attorney, Henry Bowden, stated that the law segregating the cabs had no legal ground under existing court rulings (JM).

18 In Hampton, Va., Dr. Benjamin Mays, the president of Morehouse College, stated that black colleges and universities should practice their belief in desegregation by seeking out qualified white applicants. Mays also served as the president of the United Negro College Fund, Inc. (JM).

25 In Huntsville, Ala., Bob Cutrell, white, shot and killed Richard Lee Barnes, a black man, after he allegedly said "Hey baby" to Cutrell's wife. No charges were brought against Cutrell for the murder (JM).

JUNE 1961

1 In Atlanta, Ga., school superintendent John Leston announced that a series of briefing sessions on the nature of desegregation would take place for all parents. The sessions would prepare the parents for school integration in the fall (SSN).

1 In Atlanta, Ga., operators of the Dobbs House Restaurant at the airport dismissed twenty-five African Americans because they did not "fit the decor." Ten of the twenty-five were later employed as kitchen help or bartenders. All of the waitresses who replaced the black waiters were white (JM).

1 In Chicago, Ill., Edwin Berry, director of Chicago's Urban League, announced that African Americans paid a high cost for housing discrimination. In its latest survey, the League found that the city's African Americans paid $12,515,890 in extra rent for apartments, and $157,611,244 more than whites for the rent and purchase of homes (JM).

1 In New York City, Robert Williams, a former NAACP branch president, helped break up an NAACP rally in Harlem and announced that he

was going to "meet violence with violence." He and thirty black nationalists managed to shout down the speaker, NAACP leader Roy Wilkins (JM).

2 In Montgomery, Ala., Greyhound manager W. L. Russell removed "White Only" and "Colored Only" signs from waiting rooms in the bus terminal after the public relations department in Chicago ordered him to do so (NYT).

4 In Washington, D.C., three black employees of Consolidated Edison Co. testified in hearings held by the House Committee on Education and Labor. They stated that Local 12 of the Utility Workers Union barred African Americans from job advancement and policy-making positions (NYT).

5 In New Orleans, La., Justice Department officials asserted that states cannot arbitrarily close public schools to avoid integration. In a brief filed in a case from St. Helena Parish, officials argued against a Louisiana law authorizing school boards to close schools if a majority of the local electorate approved (NYT).

8 In Baltimore, Md., officials of the Baltimore Classified Municipal Employees Association opened its doors to black city workers. Their action complied with an agreement the group had reached with the President's Committee on Equal Employment Opportunity (JM).

8 In Houston, Tex., more than five hundred African Americans marched on city hall to protest continuing police harassment. Longshoremen and members of the National Bar Association and Progressive Youth Association stated that they were protesting brutal police tactics in breaking up a union gathering (NYT).

8 In Washington, D.C., Walter Washington was appointed the head of the National Capital Housing Authority, an agency that was created to help African Americans who were living in substandard housing. Washington was the first African American to serve in that position (JM).

15 In Indianapolis, Ind., owners of motels that excluded African Americans temporarily agreed to drop their bans and house the one thousand delegates attending the African Methodist Episcopal General Conference. Only one motel had agreed to house the delegates the previous week (NYT).

21 In Albany, Ga., five African Americans filed the first federal court suit against segregated polling places. The district court suit requested voter registration lists and asked for permanent injunctions against segregated polling places in Albany and Dougherty County and for voting lists (NYT).

27 In Montgomery, Ala., district judge Frank Johnson ruled that city and state officials fraudulently joined Revs. Ralph Abernathy, S. S. Seay, Fred Shuttlesworth, and Joseph Lowery to $3 million worth of libel suits against *The New York Times* to keep the suits out of federal court. Judge Johnson stated that officials had no legal basis for naming the ministers as defendants and ordered the three pending suits held in federal court instead of an Alabama circuit court (NYT).

28 In Chicago, Ill., NAACP officials declared their opposition to the reelection of Benjamin Willis as a school superintendent. They charged that public schools under his administration remained overcrowded and segregated and few African Americans were placed in administrative positions (NYT).

JULY 1961

1 In Springfield, Ill., Gov. Otto Kerner announced that he would sign a bill establishing the state's first fair employment practices commission, designed to eliminate discrimination in employment on the basis of race, color, or creed (NYT).

7, 9, 11 In Washington, D.C., several real estate owners offered to open large luxury apartment buildings to black diplomats in response to an appeal from President Kennedy. The announcement came after Harris Wofford, special assistant to the president, conveyed Kennedy's views to a meeting of real estate leaders called by the State Department (NYT).

8 In Cleveland, Ohio, delegates of the American Library Association (ALA) proposed the expulsion of ALA chapters in cities with segregated libraries. They also proposed an investigation of southern chapters violating an ALA rule requiring integration of the chapters themselves (NYT).

9, 10, 16, 17, 22 In Chicago, Ill., one hundred African Americans conducted a wade-in on the all-white Rainbow Beach. An interracial task force of five hundred police officers protected the swimmers from any violence. Alderman Nicholas Bohling and twelve whites later filed complaints against the Chicago police. They accused the officers of violating the civil rights of white beachgoers and giving "preferred treatment" to African Americans during wade-in demonstrations (NYT).

11 In Philadelphia, Pa., the NAACP held its fifty-second annual convention. Meanwhile, 1,250 NAACP members took a Freedom Train to Washington to pressure their congressmen on civil rights legislation. A sixty-person delegation met with President Kennedy in Washington, D.C. (NYT).

13 In Baltimore, Md., Barbers Union Locals 795 (black) and 241 (white) merged following criticism of the segregated units by Francis Filby, the president of the Baltimore Council of the AFL-CIO. Meanwhile, members of the AFL-CIO Executive Council rejected A. Philip Randolph's demand that the Virginia AFL-CIO be ousted because it scheduled a convention in segregated Norfolk (JM).

13 In Chicago, Ill., Home Opportunities Made Equal (HOME) sought Chicago-area property owners willing to sell to blacks who wanted to move into integrated areas. HOME was a voluntary interracial group dedicated to encouraging integration in housing (JM).

13 In Portsmouth, N.H., the state house and senate passed a law banning racial and religious discrimination in hotels, motels, restaurants, and private housing (JM).

15 In Washington, D.C., the House Committee on Labor and Education, headed by Rep. Adam Clayton Powell, began hearings on legislation designed to attack racial discrimination in labor unions. AFL-CIO president George Meany served as the first witness (NYT).

19 In Washington, D.C., State Department protocol chief Angier Biddle Duke revealed that he had

"PLANS FOR PROGRESS"—CAMPAIGNS TO END EMPLOYMENT DISCRIMINATION

During the Eisenhower administration, federal, state, and local committees and commissions, including the President's Committee on Government Contracts and the Committee on Employment Policy, were established to investigate job discrimination and to monitor and implement federal labor legislation. The activities of these and other governmental agencies would be expanded in the Kennedy administration.

In February 1961 in Washington, D.C., Rep. Adam Clayton Powell, A. Philip Randolph, Martin Luther King, and other black leaders called on President Kennedy and heads of unions and industry to take immediate steps to end employment discrimination. In a speech to the Negro American Labor Council, A. Philip Randolph stated that the federal government was the nation's chief offender in discriminating against black job seekers. He argued that every government department had "lily-white" bureaus and many discriminated in promotions of African Americans. In March in Columbus, Ohio, National Urban League official Julius Thomas declared that it was easier for an African American to get a medical degree than to become a licensed electrician, plumber, or technician. He stated that African Americans were not being trained for the jobs needed in the coming years. Thomas cited a survey that showed that African Americans in fifty U.S. cities made up one third to one half of the total unemployed.

In March 1961 President Kennedy issued an executive order to end employment discrimination. The functions of the Government Contracts and Employment Policy committees were merged, and the Labor Department was authorized to implement the order. In April Kennedy pledged to cancel contracts with any firm refusing to comply with the order. The announcement followed NAACP criticism of a government award of a $1 billion contract to Lockheed Aircraft Corp. in Marietta, Ga. Prior to signing the contract, Kennedy ordered a probe of NAACP charges of discrimination. The investigation revealed that African Americans were barred from the apprenticeship training program and that one black employee was fired for using a "Whites only" time clock. In July officials at Lockheed Aircraft Corp. announced their "Plans for Progress," which involved hiring more African Americans, allowing black employees access to high-level jobs, and eliminating segregation within their plant. The owners of seven other major corporations met with Vice President Johnson and agreed to sign a similar plan. The corporations were Western Electric, Boeing, Douglas Aircraft, General Electric, Martin Aircraft Co., North American Aviation, Radio Corp. of America, and United Aircraft.

In May, Vice President Johnson, chairman of the President's Committee on Equal Employment Opportunity (PCEEO), announced that an anti-discrimination clause would be included in "virtually every domestic government contract." During that month the PCEEO met with presidents of the forty-eight largest defense contracting firms and labor and railroad officials for a full review of the administration's anti-discrimination order.

The Kennedy administration required that all cabinet officers develop plans for identifying, recruiting, and hiring qualified minorities in every government agency. Secy. of Labor Arthur Goldberg ordered a tour of twenty southern black colleges to interview students approaching graduation. In April, Kennedy ordered a breakdown on the number of African Americans holding federal jobs and the salary grades they occupied. The survey was needed to provide information for the PCEEO. Johnson urged government officials to take steps to eliminate racial and other discrimination in apprenticeship training programs.

In August, Kennedy ordered heads of departments and agencies to hire more qualified African Americans in key positions and to file regular progress reports on the trends. A government survey showed that less than 1 percent of jobs at grades 12 and above were held by African Americans. In October, a House subcommittee scheduled hearings in Chicago, Los Angeles, Atlanta, and New York City, which would provide a basis for congressional consideration of fair employment legislation in the following year. Meanwhile, the U.S. Commission on Civil Rights recommended a set of sweeping congressional and executive remedies to end job discrimination, as a result of a nine-city survey of black employment. In December, Labor Department official Arthur Chapin announced a nationwide drive to recruit African Americans for its apprenticeship programs. The Bureau of Apprenticeship and Training named African Americans to key posts in four regional offices to coordinate the plans.

Following through on Kennedy's pledge to erase racial bars in government hiring, the administration appointed a number of well-known African Americans. These and other appointments, as well as the placement of African Americans in many other lesser posts, were in large part a response to the aggressive organized civil rights campaigns in progress throughout the nation.

resigned from Washington's exclusive Metropolitan Club because it refused to admit African Americans. After the resignation, club officials permitted assistant labor secretary George Weaver, an African American, to visit as a luncheon guest of Henry Cabot Lodge; however, the club continued to exclude African Americans as members and as guests (NYT).

20 In Atlanta, Ga., NAACP officials launched a full-scale investigation into police brutality. NAACP president Rev. Samuel Williams also announced an investigation into complaints that black policemen were not allowed to arrest white offenders (JM).

20 In Wilmington, Del., members of the city council passed an ordinance banning segregation in the city's restaurants. Mayor E. Barbiarz called for the ordinance after three visiting black Methodist dignitaries were refused service in a local restaurant (JM).

24 In Alameda, Calif., NAACP president Charles Woods required eleven stitches after being cut during racial violence. The fight started after Woods investigated alleged discrimination against the Ink Spots, a celebrated singing group, who were refused service by a suburban restaurant (NYT).

27 In Baltimore, Md., members of the Jackie Robinson Youth Council picketed the Baltimore Gas and Electric Co. and the C&P Telephone Co. The pickets aided the local NAACP's push for one thousand jobs for qualified African Americans (JM).

27 In Mound City, Ill., former schoolteachers L. L. Owens and his wife Gertrude filed a federal suit charging they were fired because of racial discrimination. After an all-white and an all-black school merged, all of the black teachers were fired while all of the white teachers were retained (NYT).

27 In Richmond, Va., attorney Edward Dawley was denied a room in the John Marshall Hotel while attending the GOP convention. After he held a sleep-in in the hotel lobby, administrators woke him up and gave him a room "on the house" (JM).

28 In Washington, D.C., NAACP labor secretary Herbert Hill filed charges of discrimination against GE and Shell Oil with the President's Committee on Equal Employment Opportunity. He charged the companies with discriminating against African Americans in hiring and promotion policies (NYT).

AUGUST 1961

3 In Chicago, Ill., a major Chicago department store beauty salon began servicing African Americans on a regular basis after a woman complained to the Chicago Commission on Human Relations. The woman stated that she was refused service because the operators said they were not trained to work on "her type of hair" (JM).

3 In Tuskegee, Ala., registered African Americans came within one hundred votes of the white majority. The increased registration resulted from a U.S. district court order to the board of registrars to cease discrimination (JM).

4 In Washington, D.C., federal officials filed three suits against several southern counties for denying African Americans the right to vote. The counties named were Montgomery, Ala., and Walthall and Jefferson Davis, Miss. (NYT).

7 In Nashville, Tenn., a group of white youths threw punches, eggs, and tomatoes at forty black and white pickets protesting a supermarket chain store's refusal to hire black clerks. Police arrested fifteen African Americans and whites. Student leader Diane Nash was among those arrested. The next day, twenty-three people were arrested at the police station, where they were protesting the arrests of the day before (NYT).

15 In Los Angeles, Calif., NAACP members voted to boycott a Redskins-Rams game sponsored by the *Los Angeles Times* because of discrimination practiced by the *Times* and the Redskins. They stated that the *Times* practiced discriminatory hiring practices and Redskins owner George Marshall refused to hire African Americans for his team (NYT).

15 In Washington, D.C., NAACP officials urged the Supreme Court for the third time to review the legal methods that Alabama officials have used for five years to bar the NAACP from operating in the state. NAACP counsel Robert Carver charged that Alabama courts failed to determine the validity of an injunction banning NAACP activity, despite the Supreme Court's request to do so (NYT).

17 In Claiborne Parish, La., school superintendent F. C. Haley warned state public school teachers to quit the National Education Association, which endorsed school integration, or lose their jobs. He cited a 1956 law that forbade teachers from belonging to groups advocating integration (JM).

17 In Meridian, Miss., lawyers for James Meredith won the first round of their case when district judge Sidney Mize ordered University of Mississippi officials to produce records of summer term transfer students. His lawyers wanted to prove Meredith was denied the right to transfer into the school because of his race (JM).

24 In Atlanta, Ga., Dr. R. C. Bell announced plans to seek a court order to desegregate the city's $26 million municipal hospital and other southern hospitals, which were "rigidly segregated." He argued that the all-black pavilion of Grady Memorial Hospital did not provide adequate care for its patients (JM).

24 In Atlanta, Ga., a spokesperson for the Committee on Appeal for Human Rights (COAHR) reported that 150 new voters per day were recruited during their Atlanta vote drive. COAHR was a student organization that sponsored sit-ins and voting rights campaigns (JM).

24 In Cleveland, Ohio, NAACP officials demanded that the state revoke the license of the Allstate Insurance Co. Local president Clarence Holmes argued that the company refused to grant insurance to African Americans on the basis of race (JM).

24 In McComb, Miss., SNCC members, led by Bob Moses, opened the first voter education school. The purpose of this pioneering school was to teach black citizens how to deal with the maze of registration procedures used to prevent them from registering to vote (JM).

24 In Washington, D.C., local CORE leaders announced the completion of successful negotiations with the William Hahn Shoe Store chain on hiring African American as salespersons. CORE also stated that leaders would negotiate with Mann Potato Chip Co., Wilkins Coffee Co., and Warner Theaters to end job discrimination at their facilities (JM).

25 In Detroit, Mich., Catholics held the first nationwide mass to dramatize the need for the improvement of civil rights. Bishop Victor Reed called for increased church and national leadership on the racial problem (NYT).

25 In Richmond, Va., federal judge Oren Lewis ruled that Prince Edward County would have to stop allowing the use of public funds for private schools as long as its public schools were closed. He stated that the funds were being used to thwart a federal desegregation order (NYT).

29 In Madison, Wis., Gov. Gaylord Nelson greeted and addressed the nearly two hundred persons who staged a protest march on the state capital. He spoke out in favor of an anti-discrimination housing bill. Nelson also proposed that all civil rights work in the state be coordinated by the Governor's Commission on Human Rights (JM).

29 In Memphis, Tenn., fifty black children applied to enter all-white first-grade classrooms and were rejected. Mayor Henry Loeb cautioned school board members that if some blacks were not admitted to the first grade, a court order might force them to integrate all twelve grades (NYT).

31 In Atlanta, Ga., nine black students were admitted to four of the city's previously all-white schools. Mayor William Hartsfield, chief of police Herbert Jenkins, and NAACP members were credited with creating a favorable climate for integration (NYT).

31 In Adams County, Wis., black state legislator Isaac Coggs charged that he was refused accommodations in five motels when he went there to fish. The state NAACP asked the Wisconsin attorney general's office to investigate the complaint (JM).

31 In Chicago Ill., James Parsons was nominated as a federal court judge and testified before a Senate Judiciary subcommittee. He served as a superior court judge. Parsons became the first African American nominated to a federal judgeship (NYT).

31 In Montgomery, Ala., Rev. Ralph David Abernathy left his church to accept an appointment as pastor of Atlanta's West Hunter St. Baptist Church. He denied he was leaving because of the racial tension in Montgomery; he said he wanted to be located in the city with the SCLC headquarters (JM).

31 In New Orleans, La., a three-judge federal court struck down Louisiana's school-closing law. The law permitted school districts to vote in favor of abandonment of public schools faced with desegregation orders (NYT).

31 In St. Louis, Mo., while attending the annual American Sociological Association conference, Dr. Charles Willie was refused permission to swim in the pool at the St. Louis Chase-Park Plaza Hotel, and he registered a complaint with the St. Louis Council on Human Relations. His complaint resulted in the integration of the pool (NYT).

SEPTEMBER 1961

1 In Montgomery, Ala., former Tuskegee Institute trustee John Pinson urged the state legislature to find sufficient funds to upgrade the school. He warned that federal judges would force the integration of Auburn and the University of Alabama if Tuskegee lost its accreditation (SSN).

1 In New York City, Asian and African delegations to the UN filed a complaint with Secretary General Dag Hammarskjöld in regard to recent incidents involving racial discrimination against African and Asian diplomats. Their decision followed a police assault on Michel Collet of Guinea while he was on a visit to Harlem (NYT).

7 In Chicago, Ill., in response to African American demands for improved housing for low-income families, the city decided to build a concentration of public housing on Chicago's South Side. Attorney Theophilus Mann, the Chicago Housing Authority's only black commissioner, voiced his objections to the city's decision to create racially segregated public housing (JM).

7 In Dayton, Ohio, at the fifty-first annual convention of the National Urban League, Whitney M. Young, Jr., who was scheduled to replace Lester Granger as executive director in October 1961, in an address before the seven hundred delegates predicted that after African Americans had won their fight for civil rights, they would "face a battle against 'hidden' prejudice and discrimination." Young declared that it would be necessary "to prevent society from forgetting that the Negro still bears the scars of generations of prejudice and is not yet starting out on an equal footing" (NYT).

7 In Montgomery, Ala., Attorney General Robert Kennedy sought court orders in U.S. district court to speed up procedures for the registering of black voters in Macon and Bullock counties, Ala. The government previously brought suits to assure eligible African Americans a chance to vote in the May 1962 primary election (JM).

7 In Nashville, Tenn., six black employees walked off their jobs at a white dining room in the Eighty-niner Inn. Bud Cutter, the inn's owner and manager, had ordered them to spray insecticide on an interracial group that sought service (JM).

7 In Ruston, La., Gloria Duncan was beaten by an unidentified white man for standing too close to a "white" drinking fountain in city hall. She had been standing in line for a driver's license (JM).

7 In Washington, D.C., Pentagon officials announced the appointment of three black military aides to U.S. embassies in Africa, the first of their race to serve at African diplomatic posts. Lieutenant Colonel Luther Evans, Jr., was assigned to Ghana and Lieutenant Colonel Gorham Black, Jr., was assigned to the Congo. A third, unidentified military officer was assigned to Liberia. The appointments marked a major breakthrough in U.S. diplomatic policy (JM).

CORE LAUNCHES THE FREEDOM RIDES

On 4 May 1961 in Washington, D.C., fifteen white and black members of CORE left on Project Freedom Ride: 1961, a tour of seven southern states: Virginia, North Carolina, South Carolina, Alabama, Georgia, Florida, and Mississippi. James Farmer, CORE's newly appointed national director, introduced the Freedom Rides as a nonviolent direct action test of a Supreme Court decision, *Boynton v. Virginia* (1960), which declared segregation laws and practices in interstate transportation unconstitutional. The carefully planned Freedom Ride route included rallies and overnight housing. CORE received immediate support from local branches of the NAACP, SNCC, SCLC, and the Nashville Student Movement. The Freedom Riders challenged segregation on buses and in terminal eating facilities, waiting rooms, and rest stops. In Anniston, Ala., racists attacked members of CORE's Freedom Ride. They set fire to one bus, seized a second bus, and the police beat the Freedom Riders. In Birmingham, Ala., businessmen expressed concern over the effect racial violence had on attracting new industry to the area. Charles Stant, director of Birmingham's Committee of 100, conveyed the businessmen's concern after a mob attacked and beat a bus full of Freedom Riders.

President Kennedy dispatched U.S. Marshals and National Guardsmen with fixed bayonets to surround the First Baptist Church of Montgomery, Ala., to protect a black mass meeting from a howling mob. Inside, Martin Luther King called upon African Americans to launch a massive campaign to end segregation in Alabama. Leaving the city, the Freedom Ride bus required a heavy police escort. However, the "hate bus" of the American Nazi party required no escort.

In Jackson, Miss., police arrested the Freedom Riders when they entered a white waiting room at the bus station. The riders were fined two hundred dollars and given sixty-day jail sentences (suspended). Because of attacks in Anniston, Birmingham, and Montgomery, few of the original group made it to Jackson. National Guard members accompanied the riders. By the end of May, officials of the U.S. Justice Department moved to place police in Montgomery and Birmingham under a federal court injunction prohibiting any interference with interstate travel. The injunction would prohibit police from failing or refusing to provide police protection for people, such as the Freedom Riders, traveling through their cities on interstate buses. Attorney General Robert Kennedy petitioned the Interstate Commerce Commission (ICC) to issue regulations banning segregation in interstate bus transportation. He requested that the regulations also include waiting rooms, rest rooms, and terminal restaurants.

In June, King announced that the Freedom Riders would continue their drive for integrated travel facilities in the South. This announcement followed federal judge Frank Johnson's order restraining CORE, the SCLC, and five African American ministers from sponsoring Freedom Riders. The order also restrained the KKK and Montgomery police from interfering with interstate travel. Meanwhile, a Greyhound spokesman in Chicago announced that racial segregation on buses or in company terminals was banned. Few southern bus stations abided by the company's directive.

In June, July, and August, Freedom Riders continued to pour into Mississippi, where they frequently met with violence and were arrested. By mid-August, Mississippi reportedly was spending $100,000 per month in order to keep Freedom Riders in jail. This amount was in addition to the millions in business and tourist trade the state had lost because of demonstrations.

By mid-July, Robert Kennedy suggested that Freedom Riders discontinue their crusade in the South until the ICC and the courts acted to end discrimination in interstate travel. In September in Jackson, Miss., police arrested fourteen Episcopal ministers (including three African Americans) when the group attempted to enter a segregated restaurant at a bus station and refused to leave. They were part of a twenty-eight-member Freedom Rider group that arrived in Jackson from New Orleans on a "prayer pilgrimage" to protest segregation. The priests received four-month jail sentences and two-hundred-dollar fines for attempting to integrate a restaurant. In September, the ICC voted to bar racial segregation in interstate bus transportation, prohibiting bus companies from segregating buses or utilizing segregated bus terminals. Drivers were ordered to enforce the new law. Calling the order "the most far-reaching administrative action ever taken by the federal government," Robert Kennedy promised full enforcement. In November in Jackson, Miss., Rev. Charles Jones was arrested as he entered the white waiting room of a Trailways bus station. It was the first test of new federal regulations banning discrimination. The ICC began investigating complaints from Freedom Riders in the seven states as the Deep South continued to defy new federal regulations desegregating bus and railroad stations. In December in Shreveport, La., Justice Department officials filed suit in federal district court seeking the removal of racial segregation signs in the Trailways bus terminal in Ruston, La.

9 In Dover, Del., an unidentified fifteen-year-old white student enrolled in the all-black William Henry High School without incident. Principal James Hardcastle stated that he hoped more white students would follow suit (NYT).

13 In Washington, D.C., representatives of thirty governors, meeting with protocol chief Angier Biddle Duke and other federal officials, gave support to State Department plans to prevent discrimination against foreign diplomats. The representatives agreed to help the diplomats plan travel and determine which public accommodations would be open. Governors of Mississippi, Alabama, and South Carolina did not participate (NYT).

17 In Chicago, Ill., members of the school board, under the direction of its only black member, Mrs. Wendell Green, directed Superintendent Benjamin Willis to prepare a plan for utilizing vacant classrooms to take 24,800 children, mostly African American, off a half-day schedule. The statement resulted from a threat of an NAACP-backed lawsuit, which followed an unsuccessful attempt to transfer 225 African Americans into underutilized public schools (NYT).

24 In Washington, D.C., President Kennedy announced the nomination of Thurgood Marshall to a circuit court judgeship. Marshall, the general counsel and director of the NAACP's Legal Defense and Educational Fund from 1939 to 1961, was the principal architect of the legal strategy for ending de jure racial segregation. *Brown v. Board of Education* (1954)—which invalidated *Plessy v. Ferguson* (1896), the constitutional basis for segregation—was the most famous of the thirty-two cases he argued before the U.S. Supreme Court (NYT).

25 In Washington, D.C., because of the slow pace of school integration, the members of the U.S. Commission on Civil Rights made the following recommendations: (1) that the Congress pass legislation requiring counties to file integration plans within six months; (2) that the U.S. attorney general be given the power to enforce a speed-up in school desegregation; and (3) that Congress withhold up to 50 percent of federal education grants from states where schools operated on a discriminatory basis. The members also criticized racial discrimination in public schools outside the South (NYT).

28 In Philadelphia, Pa., members of the 400 Ministers of Philadelphia launched a selective patronage campaign against Breyers Ice Cream Co. The preachers protested alleged discriminatory employment practices by the company (JM).

28 In Talladega, Ala., an all-white jury convicted KKK leader Thomas Graham of assault with intent to murder for the flogging of a white couple. Mr. and Mrs. Marlin White were beaten for associating with African Americans and for allowing their son to be disciplined by an African American (JM).

OCTOBER 1961

1 In Chicago, Ill., school superintendent Benjamin Willis proposed adjustment of school boundaries and announced plans to take ten thousand pupils off double shifts. The proposal came after attorney Paul Zuber filed a school integration suit in Chicago on behalf of thirty-two black pupils (NYT).

1 In Lake Forest, Ill., all five white sororities at exclusive Lake Forest College lost their national charters in a dispute over the right of local chapters to determine membership free of racial and religious restrictions. Lake Forest College administrators stated that sororities had the right to include members without racial and religious restrictions. The national officers of Alpha Delta Phi, Alpha Phi Alpha, Xi Delta, Chi Omega, and Gamma Phi Beta disagreed and rescinded the charters of their Lake Forest chapters (NYT).

1 In Washington, D.C., a three-man U.S. Postal Service review board cleared Savannah NAACP president W. W. Law of charges brought by his postmaster that resulted in his dismissal. Law had been accused of inefficiency in carrying out his postal carrier duties. NAACP lawyers Robert Carter and Frank Reeves successfully argued that Law was singled out for his militant efforts to end segregation and discrimination (NYT).

2 In Albany, N.Y., state education commissioner Dr. James Allen, Jr., announced that a racial census of every public school would be taken as the first step of a planned attack on segregation. The New York Department of Education would then intervene and place black students in school districts that had been gerrymandered or rigged for the purpose of excluding African Americans from the all-white public schools (NYT).

4 In Memphis, Tenn., the school board was able to peacefully integrate four public schools because the board chose not to inform the public until after the integration had been carried out (NYT).

4 In Washington, D.C., officials of the Federal Home Loan Bank Board passed a resolution opposing racial discrimination in mortgage lending by any savings and loan associations (NYT).

5 In Los Angeles, Calif., attorney Arnett Hartsfield, a retired fireman, testified before the Civil Service Commission that the fire department planned and encouraged discrimination and segregation. He reported that fire officers prohibited blacks from eating in the common mess and maintained a "Negro bed" at the station for the use of black firemen (JM).

5 In McComb, Miss., 114 students were arrested for participating in a march on city hall. The students were beaten by a white mob and the police officers who arrested them. They were protesting the expulsion of Brenda Travis and Isaac Lewis from Burgland High School after the two participated in a sit-in. After the mass protest, school officials agreed to readmit Travis and Lewis. Instead, they placed the students in reform school (NYT).

5 In New York City, attorney Jack Greenberg succeeded Thurgood Marshall as general counsel of the NAACP Legal Defense Fund. The white lawyer had worked for the NAACP for twelve years (NYT).

5 In Sacramento, Calif., damages totaling $6,100 were awarded by an all-white jury to five African Americans who charged they were discriminated against in a local tavern. Bartender Anthony

Cabrielli served the African Americans two drinks each, but refused to serve them a third (JM).

5 In Washington, D.C., NAACP leader Clarence Mitchell announced that the organization investigated complaints by African Americans in the U.S. Air Force. The African Americans charged that they were barred from flying with flight crews to Australia because of the country's new racial policy. Defense Department spokesmen said they would investigate the situation (JM).

7 In New Haven, Conn., one hundred people participated in a "sit-out" demonstration sponsored by CORE. The demonstrators, including many residents, sat on the sidewalk in front of the Elm Haven public housing project to protest alleged housing discrimination (NYT).

9 In New York City, members of the Actors Equity and the League of New York Theaters pledged that Equity members would refuse to appear in any theater permitting segregation in front of or behind the footlights. The agreement included out-of-town theaters (NYT).

11 In Prince Edward County, Va., the school board initiated a countywide survey to determine the number of parents willing to send their children to integrated public schools. The survey was in preparation for a school desegregation report ordered by federal district judge Oren Lewis. Of the 1,400 white families polled, 487 replied, and only one family supported integration (NYT).

12 In Knoxville, Tenn., fifty-one students from Knoxville College were arrested for attempting to integrate an all-white movie theater. Protests continued nightly after the arrests. Theater owners eventually agreed to meet with demonstration leaders (NYT).

16, 24 In New York City, Attorney General Robert Kennedy agreed to serve as a board member of the new, integrated Federal Club. The club was formed after Kennedy, one-time New York governor and U.S. senator Herbert Lehman, and others resigned from the all-white Washington, D.C., Metropolitan Club (NYT).

17 In New Orleans, La., Justice Department officials asked the federal district courts to end discrimination against African Americans seeking to register to vote in Plaquemine Parish, La. Department officials also asked the court in Oxford, Miss., to end discrimination against black voters in Panola County, Miss. (NYT).

18 In Lexington, Ky., the Phoenix Hotel coffee shop refused to serve coffee to two black members of the Boston Celtics. In protest of this action, black team members from the Celtics and the St. Louis Hawks boycotted their exhibition game (NYT).

18 In Tallahassee, Fla., district court judge G. Harold Carswell gave city officials three days to tear down "White" and "Colored" signs at all Municipal Airport facilities. The order came after Revs. David Brooks, A. Joseph Reddick, and Theodore Gibson filed a suit (NYT).

19 In Atlanta, Ga., the Atlanta Medical Association (white) issued a declaration asking for immediate and complete integration of all facilities and services of Grady Memorial Hospital. Although African Americans constituted 75 percent of the hospital's patients, black doctors and dentists could not practice there (JM).

24 In Wilson County, Tenn., district judge William Miller ordered the county to integrate its public schools. It became the state's first school system ordered to integrate both faculties and student bodies (NYT).

26 In Centreville, Ill., state NAACP officials charged in federal court that Chenot Elementary School was segregated. Attorney Raymond Harth argued that the school segregated its African American and white students internally—in separate classes, play, and lunchtimes (JM).

26 In McComb, Miss., signs segregating waiting rooms at the bus station were painted over in compliance with an Interstate Commerce Commission ruling against segregation. However, city officials erected new signs on the sidewalk (NYT).

26 In Tallahassee, Fla., Gov. Farris Bryant urged African Americans not to enlist in the state's Na-

tional Guard, stating that it might bring about disharmony, which could hurt national defense goals. He issued the statement after state NAACP president Rev. A. Leon Lowry urged him to drop the color bar in the guard units (JM).

29 In Washington, D.C., local CORE chairman Julius Hobson announced plans for a hundred-car motorcade to test restaurant segregation along Highway 40. Plans were made despite the call of Maryland's state restaurant association for a special session of the state assembly to end segregation (NYT).

NOVEMBER 1961

2 In Chicago, Ill., two hundred Temporary Woodlawn Organization (TWO) members picketed the school administration building, calling for the integration of public schools. The board listened to eight hours of complaints on the topic of school segregation (JM).

2 In Chicago, Ill., school superintendent Benjamin Willis suspended elementary school teacher Mrs. Ernest Baker after she joined a picket line protesting double-shift classes at her children's school. Willis asked the school board to consider firing Mrs. Baker (JM).

2 In Peoria, Ill., members of the state AFL-CIO adopted a resolution offered by black labor leaders to set up an interracial committee to combat discrimination in the apprenticeship trade programs. The resolution was adopted at the annual state conference (JM).

2 In Rutland, Vt., Mr. and Mrs. Frederick Miller planned an appeal of a court order by Judge George Jones denying them adoption of a black child they had raised since she was twenty-two months old. He stated that he was unable to bring himself "to complete the adoption by people of one color and a child of another" (JM).

4 In Birmingham, Ala., Greyhound bus cafe manager Ralph Sizemore appealed his conviction on two counts of serving African Americans in the cafe. Police arrested Sizemore after he complied with the new Interstate Commerce Commission order against discrimination in interstate travel facilities. City officials ordered Sizemore to show why the cafe's operating license should not be revoked (NYT).

4 In Washington, D.C., Justice Department attorneys charged Louisiana officials with violating the new Interstate Commerce Commission rules barring segregation in bus terminals. State officials had ordered Continental Southern Lines to restore racial signs in its terminals (NYT).

9 In Moline, Ill., delegates to the Illinois NAACP convention announced that stores that refused to hire African Americans during the Christmas shopping period would be picketed. State NAACP president Dr. L. H. Holman stated that "unless it wakes up to the facts, the North will be more segregated than the South" (JM).

9 In Shreveport, La., CORE director James Farmer asked Attorney General Robert Kennedy to investigate the firebombing of the St. Rest Baptist Church. The church had been bombed while CORE members held a meeting there to plan the boycott of the Louisiana State Fair (JM).

16 In Miami, Fla., members of the United Church Women's Assembly launched a three-year crusade to enlist twelve million Protestant and Orthodox churchwomen in a "holy war" against racial discrimination. Miss Carrie Meares would direct the project through a series of annual workshops in eight areas of the country (JM).

16 In New York City, author-director Louis Lomax censured black leadership for dragging its feet in accepting a $250,000 grant from the Taconic Foundation for an eighteen-state voter registration drive to be launched by the NAACP, SCLC, CORE, and two student groups. NAACP official Roy Wilkins criticized Lomax for not knowing the facts. Wilkins stated that the black leadership was still working out the details of the administrative structure for the drive (JM).

16 In Washington, D.C., Agriculture Secretary Orville Freeman canceled the yearly 4-H Club meeting in Washington, D.C. White youngsters attended a yearly meeting at their club's Washington, D.C., center while the uninvited black youngsters held their own meeting at Howard University. Freeman ordered the 4-H Club to include African Americans in the official encampment of the group (JM).

17 In Washington, D.C., the U.S. Commission on Civil Rights reported that African Americans in the South lived in fear and were disproportionately the victims of police brutality. The commission urged Congress to pass a legislative program that would include the granting of funds to state and local governments to improve police forces; amendment of federal law to include prosecution of police brutality cases; and the granting of power to the Justice Department to seek injunctions against the exclusion of African Americans from jury service (NYT).

19 In Atlanta, Ga., Arizona senator Barry Goldwater announced his opposition to the federal government forcing public school integration and voiced his support for a constitutional amendment "to return control of schools to the states." He made the statements before a twelve-state Republican conference (NYT).

19 In Los Angeles, Calif., CORE officials announced a "Freedom Dweller" campaign. The campaign was aimed at areas where African Americans were barred from either home ownership or apartment rentals (NYT).

23 In Chicago, Ill., eight hundred people attended a rally to protest deplorable conditions in many all-black public schools. Fearing reprisals, two teachers testified to the poor conditions while covered in sheets (JM).

23 In Madison County, Ind., the local NAACP announced a boycott against the United Fund. The fund contributed money to the Anderson YMCA, which refused membership to African Americans (JM).

23 In New Orleans, La., black leaders, citizens, and high school students pooled their resources to initiate a registration drive for 100,000 qualified voters. Dr. Daniel Thompson headed the coordinating council for the campaign (JM).

29 In San Diego, Calif., all new contracts for black members of the San Diego Chargers contained a notice that the players would not be required to play before segregated audiences. Sid Gillman, head coach and general manager, made the announcement after the NAACP petitioned the nine African Americans on the team to boycott a segregated game against the Houston Oilers (NYT).

30 In Greenwood, Miss., White Citizens Council official Robert Patterson announced that groups of white "Minute Men" were organized in many southern communities. The groups were founded to rush to the scene of integration attempts and lend moral support to local officials preventing integration (NYT).

DECEMBER 1961

1 In Durham, N.C., members of the local NAACP youth chapter—Quinton Baker, Ralph Luke, La Fayette McDonald, and Walter Riley—attended a meeting of the city council and demanded across-the-board desegregation in public facilities and local employment. Mayor E. J. Evans asked the council to give their petition serious consideration (SSN).

1 In Greensboro, N.C., a committee of the North Carolina Baptist Convention prepared a resolution asking delegates to the state convention to urge trustees of the state's Baptist colleges to move quickly toward a policy of admitting all qualified students regardless of race (SSN).

1 In Savannah, Ga., the local branch of the NAACP filed suit in federal court against the local school board to bring about the integration of the entire school system. NAACP counsel Constance Baker Motley handled the suit (SSN).

1 In Washington, D.C., President Kennedy asked the U.S. Commission on Civil Rights to prepare a report on progress made in wiping out racial discrimination in the last one hundred years. The report would be released in conjunction with the anniversary of the Emancipation Proclamation (SSN).

3, 6 In Grand Forks, N.D., Sgt. Joseph McClendon accused a bartender of discrimination after the officer was charged five dollars for a soft drink when he visited a bar with another African American. It was the first complaint filed under a state law guaranteeing equal treatment in public establishments (NYT).

4 In McComb, Miss., J. Oliver Emmerich, editor of the *Jackson State Times* and *McComb Enterprise Journal,* was beaten by unidentified whites for allowing northern newsmen in his office. Emmerich had recently urged the state to end police brutality and the double standard of justice and give African Americans job opportunities and the right to vote (NYT).

5 In Washington, D.C., the Supreme Court justices upheld a lower court's ruling that students expelled for misconduct from a tax-support college were entitled to a hearing. The case involved several African American students who had attended the all-black Alabama State College in Montgomery. St. John Dixon, Bernard Lee, Marzette Watts, Edward Jones, Joseph Peterson, and Elroy Embry were expelled for taking part in the sit-ins (NYT).

7 In Norfolk, Va., eleven African Americans filed suit in district court to desegregate three Portsmouth, Va., cemeteries. The suit charged that the cemeteries were sold to a private corporation to preserve segregation (JM).

7 In Washington, D.C., Rep. Charles Diggs reported that discrimination was a way of life in all of the U.S. armed services. He stated that black soldiers suffered discrimination in housing and segregation in off-duty activities in southern bases and in bases located outside of the U.S. Diggs's findings supported a recent survey completed by the U.S. Commission on Civil Rights. Meanwhile, members of the Senate's Constitutional Rights Subcommittee began probing complaints that a number of black servicemen had been denied their constitutional rights (JM).

8 In Clarksdale, Miss., seven NAACP officials were arrested and charged with conspiracy to

"NO NEGROES WANTED": HOUSING AS A
STEP TOWARD EQUALITY

In June 1961 in Chicago, Ill., Eleanor Roosevelt told the American Freedom of Residence Fund that integration in housing was the first step toward equality. The fund raised money to finance integration litigation. African Americans had struggled for many years to obtain "equality" through decent housing.

In February 1961 the U.S. Senate voted to confirm Dr. Robert Weaver as administrator of the Federal Housing and Home Finance Agency, the highest federal position ever held by an African American. From 1930 to 1961 Weaver's public and professional career had focused on issues of black housing, employment, and urban conditions. Although President Kennedy's campaign promises included the launching of a comprehensive program to assist cities, embracing racially integrated housing as well as other housing initiatives that addressed the problems faced by low- and moderate-income families, little was achieved in 1961. Some members of Congress rebuffed Kennedy's plan and opposed Weaver because of his race and his emphasis on integration. In March in Philadelphia, Weaver charged that housing for minorities had been shunted aside in favor of the mass market for the upper middle class. He stated that the supply of good housing for minority families was not available in proportion to their ability to pay.

In 1961 housing discrimination in areas outside of the South dominated the news media and emphasized the problems faced by upwardly mobile African Americans seeking better housing in suburbia and in upscale apartment developments. For example, in January in Hamden, Conn., a state tribunal ordered white real estate developer Albert Swanson to sell a house within thirty days to DeWitt Jones. Jones had been turned down in his attempts to buy a house because of his race. In Boston, Mass., members of the Massachusetts Commission Against Discrimination ordered A. J. Colangelo, owner of the Glenmeadow Apartments, and real estate agent John Nahigan to find an apartment for Maurice Fowler. They had denied Fowler an apartment on the basis of race. In March in San Francisco, Calif., lawyer and local NAACP head Terry Francois charged that he was prevented from buying a home in the exclusive St. Francis Woods development because of his race. In May in Los Angeles, Calif., former Harlem Globetrotter Jackie White filed a suit against K & T Construction, Joseph Cordia, and Jack Barro. He charged that they refused to sell him a home because of race. In San Francisco, Calif., attorney Willie Brown, his family, and friends staged a sit-in protest outside of a Forest Knolls model home. The family had tried three times to inspect the model home but were not allowed to do so. In June in Long Island, N.Y., Dr. David Pickney became the first African American to buy a home in the exclusive Great Neck area. The Great Neck Committee for Human Rights had met the integration problem "head-on" by listing thirty homes available for black buyers.

In July in Santa Anna, Calif., Dr. Vincent Mark filed a damage suit against Craig Development Corp. and the Santa Anna Board of Realtors. He charged that salesman Esau Smith refused to sell his family a home in a certain area because of his race. In August in Glencoe, Ill., the Sadler and Hultman Real Estate Co. was charged with refusing to sell a home located in an all-white neighborhood to Mr. and Mrs. William Walker (black).

In September in New York City, housing administrator Robert Weaver, responding to questions raised as to why African Americans move into white neighborhoods, stated that it is because they want to live in nice homes, not because they have a burning desire to live next to whites. He argued that African Americans were willing to endure potential trouble with their neighbors in order to have better homes. In December in Honolulu, Hawaii, local NAACP president Mrs. Marva Garrett stated that many African Americans in Honolulu encountered difficulty finding homes.

African Americans seeking homes in white suburbs frequently were met with vandalism and violence, including bombings. In 1961 Cleveland, Ohio; Indianapolis, Ind.; Lima, Pa.; Chicago and Skokie, Ill.; and Los Angeles, Oceanside, Westlake, and Palmdale, Calif., were among the many places such violence occurred.

withhold trade from downtown merchants. The boycott began when two local black schools were banned from the annual Christmas parade. The arrests came after the boycott became 85 percent effective (NYT).

28 In Berkeley, Calif., Hink's department store ended its fifty-seven-year-old discriminatory hiring policy and hired two African Americans as salesclerks. The store's action followed picketing and protests by CORE (JM).

28 In High Point, N.C., NAACP officials canceled a threatened statewide boycott of A&P supermarkets after the promotion of an African American to cashier. The NAACP had earlier warned store managers that African Americans would boycott A&P if African Americans were not hired in higher-level positions (JM).

28 In St. Louis, Mo., pupils from overcrowded black schools were sent to underpopulated white schools, but were segregated within the school, or "resegregated." The school system had been one of the first to implement a desegregation plan after the 1954 *Brown* Supreme Court case. Black parents made complaints to school officials about the practice (JM).

29 In Birmingham, Ala., district judge Seybourne Lynne gave the city ten days to decide to amend or nullify the city ordinance requiring segregation at restaurants located in interstate facilities; otherwise, Lynne said he would ban use of the law. Justice Department officials had already obtained an order prohibiting the Birmingham City Commission from revoking the license of the Greyhound Post House Restaurants, Inc. at the local terminal (NYT).

On 11 July 1962, in Albany, Georgia, a small group of blacks are being escorted to jail following their arrest for participating in a march protesting the earlier arrest of Dr. Martin Luther King, Jr. (SOURCE: CORBIS BETTMANN)

1962

"ON JORDAN'S STORMY BANKS"

The rioting at Ole Miss in Oxford, Miss., on the day that federal marshals escorted James Meredith to the campus demonstrated that public school integration was not going to be accomplished with any less violence in 1962 than it had in 1954. After being tossed and turned on a sea of troubles, Martin Luther King, SCLC, SNCC, and local civil rights activists in Albany, Ga., managed to land "on Jordan's stormy banks," only to be arrested and taken nonviolently to nearby jails and prisons. The failure of SCLC and SNCC in Albany contrasted sharply with the success of CORE in desegregating public accommodations in northern, midwestern, and western cities as well as in the South in 1962. Nonviolent direct action protests were taking place in all parts of the country, and this dynamic social movement was beginning to have a significant influence on the minds and hearts of the vast majority of American citizens.

JANUARY 1962

3 In Nashville, Tenn., officials from the state attorney general's office submitted a proposal to federal court ordering the readmission of eight student Freedom Riders to Tennessee A&I University. The students had been expelled from the university the previous spring under a Tennessee Department of Education rule. The court ordered the eight students readmitted (NYT).

4 In McComb, Miss., *Jackson State Times* and *McComb Enterprise Journal* editor J. Oliver Emmerich stated that racial violence hurt Mississippi's efforts to attract new industry. He had been beaten by a white mob in McComb (JM).

4 In Montgomery, Ala., hearings began on an action requesting that the Montgomery County Board of Registrars be enjoined from engaging in any act that would delay, prevent, hinder, or discourage black citizens from registering and voting. The action was based on a Justice Department charge that registrars discriminated against black voters (NYT).

4 In Washington, D.C., officials of the President's Committee on Equal Employment Opportunity announced a coast-to-coast network of reporting by companies that held U.S. contracts. The reports included information regarding policies on recruitment, job assignment, promotion, and layoff. The reports were utilized to better understand the conditions for black workers (JM).

5 In Montgomery, Ala., two federal judges refused to delay implementation on an order ending segregation at Dannelly Municipal Airport. City attorney Calvin Whitesell stated that seats would be removed from the waiting rooms, toilets would be locked, and water fountains plugged in order to prevent desegregation (NYT).

10 In **Birmingham, Ala.,** Rev. Fred Shuttlesworth surrendered himself to police to begin serving a ninety-day sentence growing out of a violation of a bus segregation law that had since been declared unconstitutional. Martin Luther King asked Attorney Gen. Robert Kennedy to monitor how Shuttlesworth was treated by Birmingham police (NYT).

11 In **Jackson, Miss.,** members of SNCC began publishing the weekly newspaper the *Mississippi Free Press.* Editor Paul Brooks stated that the *Free Press* was dedicated to maintaining "the freedoms of speech, worship, and movement" (JM).

11 In **Jackson, Miss.,** two leaders of the Freedom Riders, Diane Nash and Rev. James Bevel, were married after settling in the state to continue the protest movement against segregation. Both were appealing two-year jail sentences as a result of their conducting civil rights demonstrations in the state (JM).

11 In **Jackson, Miss.,** NAACP attorney Derrick Bell was arrested when he refused to leave a white waiting room at the Illinois Central Railroad Terminal. The state later dropped its case against Bell (NYT).

12 In **Montgomery, Ala.,** the board of directors of the local YWCA voted to withdraw from the national organization and form the Young Women's Christian Organization of Montgomery. A spokesperson said that the board members did not agree with the national YWCA board's endorsement of sit-in demonstrations and desegregation activities (NYT).

12 In **Washington, D.C.,** President Kennedy used his State of the Union address to urge Congress to abolish literacy tests and poll taxes as requirements for voting. The message created major dissension among southern Democratic politicians (NYT).

16 In **Washington, D.C.,** Rep. Herbert Zelenko introduced a bill to close private Washington clubs that discriminated. The action followed the rejec-

tion of Deputy Assistant Secretary of State Carl Rowan for membership in the Cosmos Club (JM).

18 In **Jackson, Miss.,** Mrs. Hazel Brannon Smith, editor of the *Lexington Weekly Advertiser,* charged that the State Sovereignty Commission and the White Citizens Council had engaged in a criminal conspiracy to put her out of business since she began printing the *Mississippi Free Press.* Local businessmen refused to provide goods and services to Smith. She stated that if businessmen declined to do business with African Americans, the businessmen would shortly go broke (JM).

18 In **Montgomery, Ala.,** Gov. John Patterson posted a five-hundred-dollar reward for information leading to the conviction of the murderer of Alfred Crishon (black), president of the Mobile Non-Partisan Voters League. Crishon was found beaten to death in his car (JM).

18 In **Providence, R.I.,** Ellen Tarry, a black inter-group relations specialist, was snubbed by members of the local Catholic Women's Club when only twenty-five of its eight hundred members attended the meeting at which she spoke. Margaret Walker, president of the club, criticized her own organization in a letter to the local Catholic weekly (JM).

19 In **Baton Rouge, La.,** President Felton Clark announced the closing of Southern University, the nation's largest black university. Students had to leave campus and reapply for admission. The decision was made in order to weed out students regarded as troublemakers. Two thousand students had demonstrated against lunch counter segregation and job bias in local stores. More than one hundred faculty members signed a petition protesting Clark's action (NYT).

20 In **Jackson, Miss.,** Dr. Robert Marston, director of the University of Mississippi Hospital, appealed to state legislators for suggestions on how to enforce segregation rules and prevent young white and black patients from playing together. He stated that it was "hard to keep little children from playing with other children of another race" (NYT).

21 In **Washington, D.C.,** Justice Department officials investigated charges that Deputy Assistant

Secretary of State Carl Rowan was refused service at a Memphis airport restaurant because of his race (NYT).

21 In **Brownsville, Tenn.**, members of the Haywood County Civic and Welfare League began erecting a new tent city for black tenant farmers evicted from their land because they registered and voted. It was modeled after a tent city in Fayette County, Tenn. (NYT).

21 In **Tallahatchie County, Miss.**, civil rights attorney John Doar charged Sheriff Ewlet Dogan in a Justice Department suit with refusing to accept two-dollar poll tax fees from African Americans. Doar asked for a quick ruling because poll taxes were due 1 February. A federal judge rejected the Justice Department's request (NYT).

21 In **New York City**, NAACP defense fund director Jack Greenberg announced that the fund planned to concentrate much of its efforts on Mississippi. He also reaffirmed the fund's commitment to defend all Freedom Riders who sought the help of the NAACP (NYT).

25 In **Atlanta, Ga.**, NAACP officials filed a complaint with the President's Committee on Equal Employment Opportunity accusing the president of the Federal Reserve Bank in Atlanta of refusing to carry out the administration's directives ordering desegregation of federal buildings. President Malcolm Bryan notified employees that their new building would have a desegregated cafeteria, but segregated rest rooms and shower facilities (JM).

25 In **Champaign County, Ill.**, the Illinois Public Aid Commission voted to reprimand the County Advisory Committee for denying employment to Mrs. Anna Scott because she was married to a white man. Scott had scored the highest in an employment placement test (JM).

25 In **Lynchburg, Va.**, local NAACP members protested the exclusion of black children from the city's National Spelling Bee. The *Lynchburg News*, local sponsor of the contest, published a statement declaring that the paper would not change the whites-only contest because of pressure by the NAACP. James Wagner, national contest director, stated that his headquarters did not know about or determine local contest rules (NYT).

25 In **Toledo, Ohio**, Sealtest Foods, a subsidiary of National Dairy Products, announced a nondiscriminatory hiring policy and immediately hired two African Americans. The announcement resulted from a successful selective buying campaign conducted by the local NAACP and the Interdenominational Ministerial Alliance (JM).

26, 31 In **Washington, D.C.**, the Senate Judiciary Committee received President Kennedy's proposal to bar unreasonable literacy tests for voters in federal elections. Senate leaders promised to offer the proposal to the entire Senate if it was not cleared by the committee in sixty to ninety days (NYT).

FEBRUARY 1962

1 In **Charleston, W. Va.**, Gov. William Barron issued an executive order banning job discrimination against African Americans in state government. He pledged to cooperate with the West Virginia Human Rights Commission (SSN).

1 In **Roanoke, Va.**, Mrs. R. G. Colbert received numerous threats and her home was damaged after her white neighbors learned she had sold her home to NAACP attorney Reuben Lawson. The nearest African Americans lived two blocks away (JM).

4 In **Atlanta, Ga.**, a spokesperson for Grady Memorial Hospital announced that Alvin Johnson would be the first black intern to begin training at the hospital, which had a segregated section. Meanwhile, Dr. Frank Mitchell was appointed to the staff of Sarah Morris Children's Hospital in Chicago, the first black pediatrician ever appointed to the institution (NYT).

7 In **Washington, D.C.**, Vice President Johnson praised Lockheed Aircraft Corp. for substantial progress in ending discriminatory hiring practices. Since the start of Lockheed's Plans for Progress, the company had shown a 26 percent increase in black employment at its Georgia, California, and New Jersey facilities (NYT).

"BURY JIM CROW": CORE CAMPAIGNS FOR INTEGRATION

CORE, founded in 1942 as a northern interracial direct action protest group, expanded its protest activity to include the South and the West with the launching of the Freedom Rides in 1961. At the beginning of 1962 CORE joined Southern University students in Baton Rouge, La., in sit-in demonstrations against segregation in the state capital. In February CORE leader Rev. B. Elton Cox was sentenced to a year and nine months in jail and fined $7,500 for his role in the Louisiana protest. In Huntsville, Ala., CORE members joined students in the Woolworth lunch counter protest. CORE member Henry Thomas was extensively burned by mustard gas poured or sprayed in his car and was then beaten by unknown assailants for his participation in the sit-in. Meanwhile, in Hinds County, Miss., CORE director James Farmer received a four-month jail sentence and a $200 fine after he was convicted of violating segregation laws by refusing to leave a "white" waiting room in a bus station. He was released on $1,500 bond. In February in Baltimore, Md., David Klitenic, manager of the Jewish-operated Mandell and Ballow's restaurant, refused to admit a group of Jewish sailors from Yemen because their dark skin led him to believe they were African Americans. A group of CORE members, African Americans, and members of the Zionist youth group Habonim picketed the restaurant to protest the incident. In San Francisco, Calif., members of the board of education voted to have Supt. Harold Spears report how many schools were segregated. The vote followed complaints leveled by members of CORE and the Council for Civic Unity.

In June 1962 in Covington, Ky., CORE director James Farmer announced that Freedom Rides would begin anew in the summer in a continuing attack on segregated interstate transportation. He stated that Freedom Rides would take place from Washington to Miami and from Chicago through St. Louis and into the South and Southwest. At the same time, CORE activities between June and December 1962 included restaurant sit-ins in St. Louis, Mo.; pickets against residential segregation in Los Angeles, Calif.; sit-ins in Attorney General Robert Kennedy's office to protest the administration's slowness in the area of civil rights; and, in Kansas City, Mo., protests against Kansas City Research Hospital's rejection of African Americans for its practical nursing classes, which led to the acceptance of African Americans in classes the following year.

Through picketing, boycotts, sit-ins, direct negotiations, and simple threats to initiate protest activities, CORE succeeded in having fifty-five blacks hired as transit workers in Washington, D.C.; as bakery employees in New York City; as sales clerks, manager trainees, and in other positions throughout the Kroger Co. grocery store chain; and as clerks at the Denver Dry Goods Co. in Colorado. In San Francisco and Wilmington, Calif., CORE targeted housing discrimination in the renting of apartments and selling of homes to African Americans. Following two years of direct action protest, CORE succeeded in desegregating sixty restaurants and lunch counters in New Orleans, La., including facilities at Woolworth, Walgreens, Katz and Bestoff, Maison Blanche, and Holmes. The year ended with CORE bearing a coffin that read "Bury Jim Crow" while marching at the White House in protest of church burnings in Georgia and whites' defiance of Supreme Court edicts. The diverse initiatives begun in 1961 continued in 1962, with a special emphasis on protesting the policies and activities of highly visible white leaders, such as Gov. Ross Barnett, picketing their speeches outside of the South, and by protesting their actions to officials in the Kennedy administration. A central goal of CORE, as well as the other civil rights organizations, was to pressure Kennedy to take stronger civil rights action.

8 In **Brandon, Miss.,** FBI agents launched a probe of police brutality charges filed by the local NAACP following an interracial fight during which eight persons were arrested. The fight was touched off when a car driven by two white men collided with one driven by Ed Jenkins, a black man (JM).

8 In **Bradenton, Fla.,** Mississippi governor Ross Barnett announced that his state had committed $350,000 every two years to fight desegregation since 1954 and urged other southern states to follow suit. He made the statement during an address to the segregationist Manatee County White Citizens Council (JM).

8 In Chicago, Ill., state representatives William Robinson, Cecil Partee, and Abner Mikva and state senator Fred Smith agreed that the future of civil rights legislation in Illinois depended on vigorous and continuous public pressure, such as pickets, boycotts, and demonstrations. They addressed a meeting of the National Urban League's Council of Religious Leaders (JM).

8 In Washington, D.C., Rep. Charles Diggs received a letter from a group of black WACs, asking him to investigate segregation at the Women's Army Corps Training Center at Fort McClellan, Ala. The WACs charged that they were segregated in the assignment of duties, barred from joining the army band and performing motor pool duties, and that they had received specific instruction not to fraternize with white WACs off the post (JM).

8 In Washington, D.C., officials of the President's Committee on Equal Employment Opportunity directed major manufacturing firms holding federal contracts to tell the government by 1 April how many African Americans they employed. The reports would help measure progress achieved under a nondiscrimination clause that was part of every federal contract (NYT).

14 In Montgomery, Ala., members of the state board of education fired Dr. Joseph Drake, president of the all-black Alabama A&M College. They were following Gov. John Patterson's instructions to find a president who would "make the students behave." The firing followed the arrest of more than thirty A&M students at a Huntsville sit-in (NYT).

14 In New York City, federal housing administrator Robert Weaver called for efforts to effect open occupancy in housing by permitting interested and able nonwhites to buy into suburban areas and by attracting whites back into the central cities. The National Urban League's Edwin Berry agreed, stating that white flight to the suburbs would further divide the races (NYT).

15 In Atlanta, Ga., members of the Greater Atlanta Council on Human Relations insisted that the Fulton-DeKalb Hospital Authority desegregate Grady Hospital. The council cited examples of ten other southern hospitals that had desegregated (JM).

15 In Clinton, Okla., airman John Muse, his wife, Ann, and friend Norma Gotten fled to Chicago after several weeks of harassment. They had rented a house in an all-white neighborhood and feared for their lives after vandals broke into the home (JM).

15 In Sarasota, Fla., real estate broker Mrs. Elizabeth Moore filed a $100,000 damage suit in circuit court. She claimed that she was expelled from the Sarasota County Board of Realtors because she sold a home to Dr. John Chenault, an African American (JM).

15 In St. Louis, Mo., John Gregory was dismissed from his job with the worldwide Army Engineer Supply Control Office. He blamed his firing on his practice of filing grievances against the office on behalf of black employees. Most grievances concerned the inability of African Americans to receive promotions (JM).

18 In Washington, D.C., President Kennedy ordered a review of all federal government hiring and promotion policies to determine the extent of racial discrimination. The government was to examine first civil service, then non–civil service employees. Each cabinet member was instructed to supervise personally the review of hiring and promotion policies and priorities (NYT).

22 In New York City, Mayor Robert Wagner resigned from the New York Athletic Club after charges that the club discriminated against African Americans and Jews were made public (JM).

26 In Jackson, Miss., Jackie Robinson, Floyd Patterson, and other athletes urged NAACP supporters to keep fighting for human dignity and first-class citizenship. The all-star rally climaxed a three-day southern regional NAACP conference attended by two hundred delegates from seven states (NYT).

27 In Washington, D.C., the Supreme Court justices urged the lawyers for Rev. Fred Shuttlesworth, serving a ninety-day sentence in Birmingham for sitting in the white section of a bus, to try again for a hearing and bail. The justices advised the lawyers to return with an appeal if they were unsuccessful (NYT).

MARCH 1962

1 In Chicago, Ill., Judge Harry Comerford kept his pledge to nine CORE sit-in protesters and dismissed trespassing charges against them. He had promised to dismiss charges against them for protesting the University of Chicago's policy of limited desegregation in 125 school-owned apartment buildings if they discontinued their activities (NYT).

1 In Dallas, Tex., local NAACP president Rev. H. Rhett James announced that the Dallas Transit Co. agreed to hire African Americans as bus drivers. The announcement resulted from conferences between the local NAACP officials and Leon Tate, the transit company president (JM).

1 In Washington, D.C., the NAACP's Clarence Mitchell accused the Justice Department of failing to send the FBI to investigate the hate bombings of three black churches in Birmingham, Ala. Mitchell stated that the Justice Department failed to perform adequately its duties as prescribed by the Civil Rights Act of 1960 (JM).

2 In Birmingham, Ala., Rev. Fred Shuttlesworth was released from jail after serving thirty-five days at hard labor for violation of a bus-seating segregation law. A federal court ruling had freed him during the appeal process (NYT).

8 In Atlanta, Ga., Martin Luther King and the SCLC prepared to take their Freedom Corps into Virginia and Alabama. The organization had recently undertaken a voter registration drive for African Americans in Mississippi (JM).

8 In Washington, D.C., President Kennedy urged a United Negro College Fund delegation to continue efforts to desegregate their schools in enrollment and faculties. He expressed concern about the financial plight of the black institutions and promised to help them raise money from private sources (JM).

12 In Washington, D.C., Rep. Adam Clayton Powell ordered the chief of his House Education and Labor Committee's investigative staff to look into charges that no African Americans were employed on the executive staff of the New York World's Fair (NYT).

14 In Chicago, Ill., a faculty committee from the University of Chicago recommended a change in the administration of off-campus housing to combat racial discrimination. The committee was ordered to investigate after several students were arrested for protesting the university's housing desegregation policy at a local rental agency (NYT).

22 In Washington, D.C., Philippine ambassador Carlos Romulo warned members of the National Press Club that the United States would fail as a world leader if racial discrimination continued. He reminded the audience that the democratic creed of the United States differentiated the country from totalitarian nations (JM).

22 In Washington, D.C., NAACP officials protested to the Defense Department and Memphis school officials about the lack of ROTC units in local black schools. Defense Department officials announced that they would not expand the ROTC program in Memphis until black schools applied (JM).

26 In Augusta, Ga., local NAACP leader C. S. Hamilton urged African Americans to boycott local newspapers. He charged that newspapers were giving African Americans poor coverage and slanting the news against them (NYT).

29 In Atlanta, Ga., Grady Hospital administrators announced the addition of all-black Spaulding Pavilion to the municipal hospital. They also appointed Dr. Asa Yancey to the hospital staff. Both actions were viewed as steps toward desegregation (JM).

29 In Birmingham, Ala., eleven African Americans were rejected as candidates for the Jefferson County Democratic Executive Committee because it was viewed as inappropriate for the party of "white supremacy" in the South. Attorney Orzell Billingsley announced legal action to have their applications reinstated. The group also requested the court to remove the white rooster, a symbol of white supremacy, from voting ballots. Later, a federal judge ordered the Democratic party to allow the names of ten African Americans on the ballot (JM).

29 In Los Angeles, Calif., UCLA students staged a two-day sit-in at the office of Chancellor Franklin Murphy. They were protesting refusal of school officials to approve a five-thousand-dollar loan for bail for five Freedom Riders. UCLA officials believed that a loan might be considered an endorsement of the Freedom Ride movement (JM).

<hr>

APRIL 1962

❚ In Little Rock, Ark. attorney Wiley Branton filed a suit in federal court on behalf of twenty-two African Americans to desegregate all city-owned facilities. Branton also announced planned litigation to desegregate North Little Rock and Pulaski County schools and the Fort Smith Airport restaurant (SSN).

❚ In Atlanta, Ga., officials at Emory University asked a local court to rule that the school's acceptance of Aaron Rucker (black) would not cause it to lose its tax-exempt status. As a private institution, it was exempt from state laws requiring public institutions to maintain segregation, which was in violation of the U.S. Constitution (SSN).

OPENING THE FLOODGATES:
PUBLIC ACCOMMODATIONS UNDER ASSAULT

In 1962 public accommodations issues surged to the fore with nonviolent direct action protests occurring in cities throughout the nation, particularly in the South. The actions included the adjudication of a number of federal court cases dealing primarily with enforcement of Interstate Commerce Commission rulings barring segregation in interstate commerce, as well as state laws upholding segregation. The Civil Rights Movement had moved into a new phase during the two years since the launching of the student sit-in campaigns. The impact of the campaigns could be measured at the local as well as national level. In October 1961 in Atlanta, Ga., members of the Southern Regional Council announced that an estimated seventy thousand African Americans and whites had participated in sit-in demonstrations during the previous eighteen months, resulting in the integration of eating establishments in more than one hundred southern cities. About thirty-six hundred of the demonstrators had been arrested.

In 1962, as a result of several long-standing sit-in campaigns, the majority of lunch counters and restaurants in a number of southern cities—Nashville and Memphis, Tenn.; Oklahoma City, Okla.; Pensacola, Fla.; Augusta, Ga.; and Mobile, Ala.—were desegregated. Moreover, in addition to the lunch counters, demonstrators also targeted public recreational facilities, libraries, museums, beaches, courtrooms, hospitals, and churches. In the South, the cities that witnessed significant protests included Atlanta, Macon, Augusta, Albany, Marietta, and Savannah, Ga.; Edenton, Lexington, Raleigh, and Greensboro, N.C.; Talladega, Birmingham, and Montgomery, Ala.; Jackson, Clarksdale, and Greenville, Miss.; Houston and Fort Worth, Tex.; Springfield, Charleston, and St. Louis, Mo.; Baltimore, Md.; New Orleans, La.; and Tallahassee, Fla. Among the northern and western cities where protests took place were Evanston, Cairo, and Peoria, Ill.; Waukesha and Beloit, Wis.; Indianapolis and Bloomington, Ind.; and Toledo, Ohio. As students increasingly became involved in grassroots political organizing, they also targeted employment discrimination and began voter registration drives.

Racial conflict increased with the expanded civil rights activity. In 1962 Huntsville, Ala., a community that had boasted of progress in race relations, was representative of the kind of hostility that could develop when white moderates, especially merchants and politicians, became angered over protests. In Huntsville, public transportation, the city library, bus and airport terminals, and the municipal golf courses had been desegregated without protest. However, the students held out for total desegregation, including the Woolworth and Walgreens lunch counters. This stance elicited anger and violence from whites. Huntsville had its first major protests beginning on 4 January 1962.

5 In Baton Rouge, La., a three-judge federal panel ordered an end to bus terminal segregation. The court was carrying out an earlier ruling by the Supreme Court that no state could require segregation of interstate or intrastate transportation facilities (JM).

5 In Little Rock, Ark., Nancy Hall, the state secretary, stated that she would rather cancel Easter services on the capitol steps than permit two black school choirs to participate. She feared that desegregation might lead to an incident. The sponsor of the services considered moving the program to another location (JM).

5 In Washington, D.C., an administration official announced that major hotels in Houston, Tex., would admit black guests and open facilities to all people regardless of race. The announcement came after talks between administration officials and hotel owners. Previously, Assistant Labor Secretary George Weaver had been refused accommodations at Houston's Shamrock Hilton Hotel (JM).

6 In New York City, NAACP official Herbert Hill stated that the Plans for Progress project advanced by the President's Committee on Equal Employment Opportunity had made little progress. The plans were designed to increase the number of African Americans hired by firms holding government contracts. He stated that most firms had made no changes in hiring practices after agreeing to the plans (NYT).

10 In Jackson, Miss., Judge Russell Moore reversed his decision to let charges against fifteen Freedom Ride ministers be dropped. He stated that they would have to stand trial "to uphold the integrity of this court" (NYT).

10 In Washington, D.C., Martin Luther King accused President Kennedy of not providing the level of leadership that civil rights problems demand. King criticized the president for not issuing a housing nondiscrimination order and for his reluctance to enforce civil rights legislation (NYT).

12 In Tuskegee, Ala., following an extensive black voter registration drive, Tuskegee had a black voting majority of 150. A federal court nondiscrimination order had been issued to halt attempts by city officials to split Tuskegee into five sections to prevent the formation of a black voting majority (JM).

13 In Washington, D.C., the U.S. Commission on Civil Rights held hearings on housing discrimination in the district. African diplomats and African Americans testified that "dark-skinned people" were confined to the city limits and had little or no chance of living in the suburbs due to discriminatory practices of real estate agencies (NYT).

17 In New Orleans, La., Archbishop Joseph Rummel excommunicated Leander Perez, Mrs. B. J. Gaillot, and J. G. Ricau, head of the state White Citizens Council. All three opposed his desegregation of Catholic schools. The excommunication followed Pope John XXIII's statement that "there is no color bar in the Catholic church" (NYT).

19 In Homerville, Ga., for the first time during a major election, city officials discontinued separate registration and voting places for whites and African Americans. Their action followed receipt of directives from the Justice Department (NYT).

19 In Portsmouth, Va., Anthony Gist and his family vowed to move into their home once it was repaired. The home, in an all-white neighborhood, had been bombed. However, when the family began to rebuild, the home was set on fire (JM).

19 In St. Louis, Mo., Taylor Fuller was selected to begin the Carpenters Union Joint Apprenticeship Training Program. He became the first African American to participate in the program. The selection followed months of talks between the National Urban League's Frank Campbell and union leaders (JM).

20–30 In New Orleans, La., members of the White Citizens Council sent the destitute Lewis Boyd family, African Americans, on a one-way bus ride to New York City in an avowed test of tolerance in the North. The family was met by members of the National Urban League, NAACP, and civic and welfare organizations. They provided the family with clothing and shelter and offered Mr. Boyd a choice of several jobs. NAACP official Roy Wilkins blasted the White Citizens Council for using the family as a pawn and called the stunt "a pretense to maintain segregation" (NYT).

21 In New York City, managers of the New York World's Fair announced the hiring of Dr. George Bennett to an administrative post. The action came after protests by the National Urban League and Rep. Adam Clayton Powell, who threatened to withhold federal funds unless African Americans were hired at the top administrative level (NYT).

22 In Jackson, Miss., Rev. Robert Smith, the first black candidate for Congress from Mississippi since 1875, was granted a half hour to campaign on Jackson's only television station. In order to get the time, he had appealed to the Federal Communications Commission, the Democratic National Committee, and President Kennedy (NYT).

26 In Montgomery, Ala., a black group asked the city commission to issue an ordinance requiring ambulances to serve all races without discrimination. Their request followed an incident involving a critically injured black girl forced to wait fifteen minutes for a black ambulance, even though a white ambulance had already arrived on the scene (JM).

28 In Bossier, La., white businessmen and civic leaders offered to replace a Masonic lodge hall that had been bombed, along with a black-owned fishing lodge and recreation building. Edward Jackson stated that "we want to show the world we don't condone this type of thing" (NYT).

28 In Winston-Salem, N.C., the trustees of Wake Forest College voted to admit African Americans in September 1962. They had been directed by the Baptist Convention of North Carolina to desegregate the denomination's college (NYT).

30 In Washington, D.C., Senator Kenneth Keating accused Senator James Eastland and the staff of the Senate Judiciary Committee of preparing a report that assailed Judge Thurgood Marshall. The report could be used by southern senators who opposed the confirmation of Marshall as a federal circuit court judge. Keating stated that there was no precedent for a committee to prepare such a critical report prior to confirmation hearings. Also, Keating, a committee member, had been denied access to the report (NYT).

MAY 1962

1 In Hattiesburg, Miss., the district court ordered Forest County registrar Theron Lynd to show cause as to why he should not be cited for contempt of court. The court stated that Lynd disobeyed an order by the circuit court of appeals to stop discriminating against African Americans attempting to register to vote (NYT).

3 In Birmingham, Ala., representatives of the Alabama Christian Movement for Human Rights, SNCC, and the Southern Conference Educational Fund met to discuss ways to end segregation in the Deep South. It was the first time white and black leaders met in Birmingham in a major, public conference (JM).

3 In Washington, D.C., officials of the President's Committee on Equal Employment Opportunity cited seven firms doing business with the U.S. government for promoting equal employment opportunities for African Americans. Those named were Continental Oil, Westinghouse Electric, Douglas Aircraft, Chesapeake and Potomac Telephone, Shell Oil, Sangamo Electric, and International Harvester (JM).

3 In Washington, D.C., Comet Rice Mills agreed to submit a plan to comply with federal employment anti-discrimination procedures. Because of their agreement, the President's Committee on Equal Employment Opportunity lifted the ban on the company selling rice to the government (NYT).

10 In Chicago, Ill., *Chicago American* columnist Jack Mabley denounced the city's fire department as one of the last bastions of segregation in the city. He pointed out that there were no African Americans assigned to white companies. He also claimed that the black companies servicing slum areas were the busiest and faced the greatest danger (JM).

10 In Jackson, Miss., SNCC leader Diane Nash began serving a ten-day sentence for contempt of court for not moving to a segregated section of a courtroom. After she completed her sentence, she began a sit-in at the jail, refusing to leave until all charges against her were dropped. She was previously charged with conspiracy and contributing to the delinquency of minors (JM).

10 In Talladega, Ala., professor Herman Eisman assumed guardianship of Brenda Travis. Travis had been placed in a reform school after she participated in a McComb, Miss., demonstration against segregation. Eisman was moved by her plight and convinced authorities to release her to him. She could not be released in Mississippi because she was considered an "enemy of the state" (JM).

10 In Washington, D.C., the AFL-CIO Executive Council stated that it could not endorse a standard approach for eliminating discriminatory practices in its ranks. Council members instructed each local to work out their own arrangements with the President's Committee on Equal Employment Opportunity (JM).

17 In Atlanta, Ga., police chief Herbert Jenkins announced that black policemen could arrest white offenders. Previously, black officers were restricted to black neighborhoods and could only arrest African Americans (JM).

17 In Birmingham and Talladega, Ala., attorney Orzell Billingsley led court attacks in these two cities on the Alabama jury system. He charged that the state practice of excluding African Americans from jury panels was unconstitutional (JM).

18 In Washington, D.C., civil rights leaders met to discuss new directions for the movement. Martin Luther King urged President Kennedy to issue a second Emancipation Proclamation. Vice President Johnson urged the leaders to make sure schools did not omit vocational training for African Americans (NYT).

20 In New York City, the Commission on Human Rights announced a strong drive against racial and religious discrimination in employment practices by contractors doing business with the city. Chairman Stanley Lowell announced that a discrimination ban would be included in all city contracts (NYT).

26 In Washington, D.C., Mrs. Eleanor Roosevelt presided over a public hearing on southern civil rights violations held by the private Committee of Inquiry into the Administration of Justice in the Freedom Struggle. More than twenty black and white witnesses were called to testify. Data compiled from the hearings were later turned over to the Justice Department and to the U.S. Commission on Civil Rights (NYT).

27 In Baltimore, Md., symphony conductor Leonard Bernstein and his party walked out of a restaurant after the manager refused to serve black violinist Sanford Allen. They were served meals at a nearby hotel (NYT).

29 In New London, Conn., Merle Smith, Julian Earls, Richard Tolbert, and Ronald Cox were offered appointments to the U.S. Coast Guard Academy. The school had never graduated a black cadet. White House aides had pressed the Academy to desegregate after President Kennedy noticed during the inauguration parade that there were no African Americans in the Coast Guard's marching delegation (NYT).

31 In Jackson, Miss., Judge Russell Moore freed fifteen Episcopal ministers on charges stemming from their participation in the Freedom Rides. He also took under advisement a motion to forfeit the ten-thousand-dollar bond of Diane Nash and commit her to prison for two years (JM).

31 In St. Louis, Mo., local NAACP officials charged the city's police board with engaging in Jim Crow practices. They stated that board members refused to meet with the NAACP and that unfair practices in recruitment, assignments, and promotions kept qualified African Americans from applying for police jobs (JM).

JUNE 1962

1 In Jackson, Miss., federal judge Sidney Mize ruled that the airport must remove the "White" and "Colored" signs that had been substituted for "White only" and "Colored only." He also ordered Cicero Carr, owner of the airport restaurant, to be prepared in ten days to testify about his policy on serving African Americans. Carr later desegregated his restaurant (NYT).

1 In Washington, D.C., NAACP official Herbert Hill criticized the AFL-CIO for not moving faster to support President Kennedy's drive against racial discrimination in hiring by government contractors and in labor unions. Hill also criticized the decision of the AFL-CIO Executive Council to ask each individual international union to sign an anti-discrimination pledge (NYT).

3 In Bibb County, Ga., federal judge W. A. Bootle ordered all voting places in the county desegregated within one year. The decision resulted from

PUBLIC SCHOOL DESEGREGATION IN THE SOUTH

In the South local and state laws were enacted that often conflicted with the Supreme Court's ruling in *Brown v. Board of Education*. For example, Louisiana's Local Option Law permitted the closing of public schools to avoid desegregation. In February the U.S. Supreme Court ruled the law unconstitutional. In 1962 a number of public school districts in the South remained segregated. Some federal judges continued to undermine school desegregation, thus supporting the continued campaign of massive resistance. In some cases judges overturned decisions made by their predecessors. For example, in May 1962 federal district judge Frank Ellis ruled that public schools in New Orleans would be required to desegregate the first grade by the fall. This struck down the ruling by his predecessor, Judge J. Skelly Wright, who ordered the desegregation of the first six grades by September 1960. Local black leaders believed that the 1962 ruling turned back the clock on school desegregation.

Perhaps one of the most egregious examples of evasion of the law occurred in Prince Edward County, Va. The original suit to desegregate the Prince Edward County public schools was one of the cases ruled on by the U.S. Supreme Court in the 1954 *Brown* decision. However, the Prince Edward County school board resisted implementation of the decision and in 1959 decided to close all public schools rather than desegregate.

State funds were funneled into a private academy open only to white students, and African Americans raised funds to set up training centers for black children. Embroiled in litigation for many years, in March 1962 the Virginia Supreme Court refused to order Prince Edward County officials to reopen their public schools, arguing that under the state constitution, a county was not obligated to operate a school system. In April the NAACP responded by asking a federal court to make permanent a temporary order blocking the use of public funds for the private school system. In June 1962 in an effort to end the eleven-year struggle over school desegregation, the NAACP asked a federal court to rule that the closing of public schools three years earlier was unconstitutional. In October federal judge Oren Lewis issued an order stating that Virginia could not operate other public schools while those of Prince Edward County remained closed.

Prince Edward County and New Orleans mirror the struggle for public school desegregation that occurred in 1962 in other southern cities, including Baton Rouge, La.; Chattanooga and Memphis, Tenn.; Jackson, Miss.; Savannah, Ga.; Houston and Waco, Tex.; Cleveland and Xenia, Ohio; North Little Rock, Gosnell, and Pulaski County, Ark.; Fredericksburg, Ft. Lee, Stafford, Hopewell, and Powhatan County, Va.; Durham and Greensboro, N.C.; and Pensacola, Escambia, and Duval, Volusia, and Hillsborough Counties, Fla.

To speed up public school desegregation, in February Rep. Adam Clayton Powell, chair of the House Education and Labor Committee, ordered a four-month investigation into the use of millions of dollars in federal funds to support school segregation. He charged that many schools from the lowest grades through college did not adhere to the federal nondiscriminatory standard. In April in Washington, D.C., *Afro-American* editor Chuck Stone testified before a House subcommittee considering bills to withhold funds from segregated schools. He stated that black teachers in Washington, D.C., schools felt there was an effort to keep top jobs white and that less competent white teachers were promoted over African Americans. In December 1962, Department of Health, Education and Welfare officials reminded school administrators that federal funds to schools enrolling children of federal employees would be cut off unless the schools were desegregated.

the first suit of its nature filed by the Justice Department (NYT).

5 In Washington, D.C., the U.S. Supreme Court set aside the conviction of six Freedom Riders who entered the white waiting room of a Shreveport, La., bus terminal. The case was remanded to the lower courts, requiring that the defendants appeal to the Louisiana state circuit court and supreme court (NYT).

7 In Washington, D.C., Rep. Charles Diggs charged that the National Employment System Act contained no guarantee of equal opportunity for job training. In a letter to Labor Secretary Arthur Goldberg, he complained that the law did not include an "anti-discrimination provision" (JM).

14 In Los Angeles, Calif., John Buggs, an official of the County Commission on Human Relations, stated that Los Angeles was one of the most segregated cities in the country. He made the statement after the Robert Liley family became the first African Americans to buy a home directly in an all-white suburban development. African Americans had conducted a thirty-five-day sit-in at the real estate office before the Lileys were allowed to buy the home (JM).

14 In Lowndes County, Miss., African Americans were included on the list of prospective jurors for the first time. The action resulted from a U.S. Supreme Court decision that ordered a new trial for George Gordon, who had been convicted by an all-white jury of raping a pregnant white woman (JM).

14 In Montgomery, Ala., district judge Frank Johnson reversed his earlier decision and ruled that the expulsion of nine Alabama State College students for sit-in activity was unconstitutional. He ruled that the all-black college must process applications of any who applied for readmission. Johnson had been overruled in his earlier decision by the Fifth Circuit Court of Appeals (JM).

14 In Washington, D.C., the U.S. Commission on Civil Rights announced that there were thirteen Mississippi counties where no African Americans were registered to vote. In forty-two other counties, less than 10 percent of the black voting-age population was registered (JM).

17 In Jackson, Miss., Justice Department officials filed suit against the Greene County school board. They charged that Mrs. Ernestine Denham Talbert was not rehired in an effort to intimidate her because she registered to vote (NYT).

21 In Philadelphia, Pa., local members of the NAACP filed a complaint against the Philadelphia branch of the U.S. Mint. NAACP official Philip Savage charged that the mint had virtually no African Americans in supervisory positions (JM).

21 In Washington, D.C., Attorney General Robert Kennedy met with Clarence Mitchell III, who was recently nominated to the Democratic ticket for the Maryland House of Delegates. Kennedy advised Mitchell on the importance of voter registration and getting his message to the people (JM).

23 In Washington, D.C., Robert Troutman, President Kennedy's aide for the Plans for Progress, told officials of thirty-three national companies with government contracts to seek out qualified black workers. All of the officials signed nondiscrimination agreements (NYT).

24 In Washington, D.C., President Kennedy appointed a civilian committee to study racial discrimination in the armed services. The action was taken as a result of continual protests by Rep. Charles Diggs. Gerhard Gesell was named chairman of the advisory committee (NYT).

28 In Atlanta, Ga., members of the newly formed Southern Democratic Conference launched a South-wide program to end the barring of African Americans from Democratic state and county organizations and to scrap racial labels used on some party emblems. The group would also stress the importance of black voter registration (JM).

28 In Glen Burnie, Md., unidentified assailants shattered the picture window of a home belonging to the Benjamin Wallace family. It was the seventh time the window had been broken since the family moved into the all-white Sun Valley housing development (JM).

5 In Heflin, Ala., eight hooded men chased black construction workers from a school construction site and warned the contractor to get rid of them. All of the African Americans were fired the next day (JM).

5 In Washington, D.C., NAACP leaders accused Labor Department official Arthur Chapin of "whitewashing" reports of discriminatory conditions in the Arizona and Mississippi state employment offices. Chapin stated that Arizona's offices did not discriminate, but private companies refused to hire African Americans. He also said he had not yet investigated Mississippi (JM).

9 In Washington, D.C., Thurgood Marshall endured hours of questioning on NAACP activities in Texas during his second Senate confirmation hearing for his federal judgeship. Sen. Olin Johnson expressed the need for a third hearing, but refused to schedule one. Sen. Kenneth Keating called the hearings "a complete waste of time" and announced a floor drive to end the stalling on the nomination (NYT).

12 In Baltimore, Md., Attorney General Robert Kennedy announced that fourteen southern airports had voluntarily abolished racial segregation over the previous six months. Kennedy predicted that all airports in the country would soon comply (JM).

12 In Greenville, Miss., members of the NAACP Youth Council requested that the city council allow African Americans to use the Percy Memorial Library. The NAACP members complained that the facilities at the Miller Memorial Library (black) were inadequate. The city council denied their request (JM).

12 In Memphis, Tenn., the U.S. Commission on Civil Rights praised city officials for their stated intention to follow the law without violence. The praise came despite the testimony of black witnesses that the city maintained segregated housing, was moving at a snail's pace toward school desegregation, and condoned widespread employment discrimination (JM).

13 In Monroe, La., twenty-eight African Americans passed the test and became eligible to vote in East Carroll Parish after district judge Edwin Hunter supervised voter qualification tests. Applicants took the tests in Monroe after the discovery of a 1960 Civil Rights Act provision calling for federal jurists to take such action where a pattern of discrimination had been found (NYT).

19 In Atlanta, Ga., on the opening day of the fifty-third annual convention of the NAACP, an emergency resolution authorizing the peaceful picketing of the major hotels of Atlanta by NAACP delegates was passed. The following day an estimated four hundred delegates armed with placards demonstrated outside ten hotels and six major downtown restaurants, protesting their refusal to accept African American customers. This action was taken in response to the denial of hotel accommodations to UN undersecretary Ralph Bunche and other delegates during the convention (JM).

19 In Atlanta, Ga., at the NAACP's fifty-third annual convention, officials announced no new programs, but indicated that the organization would continue to "challenge all racial bias." AME Bishop Stephen Gill Spottswood, chairman of the NAACP board of directors, in his keynote address to the 1,500 delegates stated that "if the U.S. completely desegregates and truly integrates all the people of this country, as far as basic civil rights and economic opportunities are concerned, democracy will spread across the world and Communism will perish by the sheer force of an egalitarian civilization!" (JM).

20 In Washington, D.C., Martin Luther King became the first African American to address the National Press Club. He described the nonviolent movement and its success in undermining segregation and discrimination in the South. King also called on Justice Department officials to act in the thousands of communities that barred African Americans from voting (NYT).

26 In Birmingham, Ala., Rev. Fred Shuttlesworth filed a $75,000 suit against the driver of a city bus. He stated that the driver verbally assaulted him and threatened physical violence if he did not move to the back of the bus. The action violated Judge H. H. Grooms's injunction prohibiting the bus company from attempting to seat passengers or enforce segregation on buses (JM).

26 In Washington, D.C., the U.S. Commission on Civil Rights reported that complaints in the fields of law enforcement, education, employment, housing, and transportation increased from 242 to 354 between June 1961 and March 1962 (JM).

THE ALBANY MOVEMENT, 1961–62

In 1962 national attention focused on Albany, Ga., the site of the first large-scale community mobilization since the Montgomery boycott. The protest's goals included complete desegregation of public accommodations in the city and tests of the compliance of bus companies with the Supreme Court's *Boynton v. Virginia* (1960) decision, which extended the prohibition against segregation in interstate travel to cover privately operated eating facilities in bus terminals, and with the November 1961 Interstate Commerce Commission (ICC) ruling (the result of the Freedom Rides) that racial segregation in interstate bus terminals was illegal. Following the arrest of five SNCC workers, a march was held in October 1961 and the "Albany Movement" was formed, led by Dr. William Anderson, a local physician. The movement included the Baptist Minister's Alliance, the Albany Federation of Colored Women's Clubs, SNCC, and the NAACP Youth Council. On Thanksgiving weekend the arrest and imprisonment of Bertha Gober and Carol Reagon, two SNCC students who attempted to sit in the white section of the Trailways bus station, galvanized the black community. The ICC ruling was tested again on 10 December by a group of black and white SNCC workers, who were arrested. Subsequently, rallies and protest marches by high school and college students led to mass arrests.

In mid-December, Martin Luther King and Ralph David Abernathy arrived in Albany and with Dr. Anderson led a silent march to city hall. They were among seven hundred demonstrators arrested and imprisoned for a week. Protests continued when the city failed to return cash bonds to black demonstrators, who had signed property or signature bonds for their release. In February 1962 Walter Sweeting, superintendent of the Albany Bus Co., announced that the bus line would halt operations. Black activists had conducted a boycott of the buses for eight weeks, eliminating 90 percent of the ridership. Protests continued from March to July. Although there was serious organizational factionalism and persistent questions about the legitimacy of King's role in the Albany Movement, in July King and Abernathy attempted to dramatize the mistreatment of blacks in Albany by going to jail. However, they were soon freed against their wishes when an unidentified benefactor paid their fines. Police chief Laurie Pritchett agreed to drop charges against the seven hundred people arrested with the leaders if the movement agreed to halt demonstrations. King refused.

At the end of July the seven-month struggle to desegregate public facilities came to a head when black residents defied a federal injunction by marching toward city hall. In August, demonstrations continued despite the jailing of King and Abernathy. Of the twelve hundred people who had voluntarily gone to jail since December 1961, some four hundred remained in custody. SCLC officials stated that although protests would continue, they planned more emphasis on voter registration. After King and Abernathy were released, city authorities went back on their promise and continued to harass and arrest demonstrators. Attorney Gen. Robert Kennedy spoke personally with King in jail and with Mayor Asa Kelley in an effort to stop the spread of demonstrations. The attorney general warned the mayor that the incidents were having international repercussions.

By October, by most accounts the Albany Movement had failed to achieve its purpose. In December, similar to their protest in July, student members of the Albany Movement picketed and marched outside the Justice Department. They were protesting President Kennedy's inaction and the failure of the Justice Department to protect African Americans in Albany.

27 In New York City, members of the New York County Democratic Committee filed suit to demand the redrawing of congressional district lines on the grounds that Puerto Rican and black voters were unfairly segregated by race. The suit charged that the Republican-controlled legislature had deliberately used gerrymandering to exclude African Americans and Puerto Ricans from the Seventeenth District (NYT).

27 In Terrell County, Ga., civil rights leaders continued their voter registration campaign among African Americans despite threats from Sheriff Z. T. Matthews. Matthews told SNCC leader Charles Sherrod, "We don't need no outside agitators in here" (NYT).

AUGUST 1962

2 In Bessemer, Ala., district judge H. H. Grooms ruled that black citizens were legally entitled to use all public facilities in the city. At the same time, he denied pleas from African Americans for an injunction against the Bessemer Housing Authority. African Americans charged that they were being displaced by the building of a new housing project (JM).

2 In Greensboro, N.C., Justice Department officials asked a federal court to declare the separate-but-equal provision of the Hill-Burton Act unconstitutional. The act provided federal aid for hospital construction, channeled through state agencies. The officials filed the motion in support of a desegregation suit filed by eleven African Americans against Greensboro city hospitals (JM).

2 In Montgomery, Ala., city solicitor William Thetford urged the state bar association to make sure African Americans were included in the jury pool in large numbers. He stated that sooner or later, prosecutors would realize that if African Americans were not included on jury rolls, the cases would be lost on appeal (JM).

5, 7 In New York City, after being repeatedly picketed by CORE members, the Ebinger Baking Company announced that it would hire qualified employees regardless of racial, religious, or ethnic background. The announcement followed negoti-

ations between company officials and leaders of CORE's Brooklyn chapter (NYT).

9 In Chicago, Ill., real estate broker James Lynch urged Mayor Richard Daly to halt "blockbusting" techniques of selling African Americans housing in white neighborhoods. He advocated setting up a mortgage pool to provide financing to any home buyer who could not get money from regular channels because of housing discrimination practiced by lending institutions (JM).

13 In New York City, Rev. Dan Potter, executive director of the Protestant Council of the City of New York, urged the member churches of the council to promote neighborhood desegregation through the council's Open-Occupancy Housing Program. He declared that churches "have a special Christian obligation and opportunity to help desegregation" (NYT).

16 In Atlanta, Ga., members of the Fulton County Medical Society voted to drop racial bars and allow African Americans to become members (JM).

18, 19, 21 In Cairo, Ill., attorney Raymond Harth charged the state police with standing by while four hundred whites attacked SNCC demonstrators who were picketing a for-Whites-only roller skating rink. Harth announced that he would ask Governor Otto Kerner to discipline the officers. Six persons were hospitalized with injuries (NYT).

24 In Washington, D.C., attorney Robert Troutman resigned as Plans for Progress director. He stated that unless permanent steps were taken, black unemployment was likely to worsen in the next twenty-five to thirty years (NYT).

26 In New York City, attorneys for the NAACP announced plans for formal legal action against the Hilton Hotel chain because representatives refused to honor reservations made by NAACP delegates for Atlanta's Hilton Inn. The NAACP called on all state branches to boycott the chain (NYT).

28 In Mobile, Ala., Justice Department officials asked a federal court to order officials of Perry County to halt discrimination against African Americans in voter registration. It was the thirty-second voting rights suit filed under the 1960 Civil

Rights Act and the sixth case brought in Alabama (NYT).

30 In Chicago, Ill., Cook County Department of Public Aid director Raymond Hillard announced that segregated housing patterns cost the department $3 million a year. He stated that African Americans receiving Aid to Families with Dependent Children (AFDC) were forced to live in overpriced housing, while better and cheaper accommodations were available in white areas (JM).

SEPTEMBER 1962

1 In New Orleans, La., a three-judge panel in the Fifth U.S. Circuit Court of Appeals dismissed a suit by Wilmer Reed to enroll his son in Reeds Chapel School in Alabama. The community of Reeds Chapel was composed of mulattos. His son was expelled after mothers complained that he was "too dark." The judges dismissed Reed's complaint, calling the complaint a "squabble among the Negroes of mixed blood" (SSN).

3 In the state of Louisiana, the KKK burned crosses in at least fourteen towns to protest the desegregation of Catholic schools in the Archdiocese of New Orleans. The FBI investigated threats of violence that closed the desegregated school in Buras, La. (NYT).

5 In New Orleans, La., Catholic schools were desegregated for the first time in fifty years with no major violence. One hundred ninety black students entered thirty-six Catholic schools. Under the leadership of excommunicated politician Leander Perez, whites conducted a total boycott of Our Lady of the Good Harbor School in suburban Buras (NYT).

6 In Lake Providence, La., former NAACP president Rev. John Henry Scott was shot and seriously injured while returning from a federal court hearing on contempt actions against Cecil Manning, a white registrar who had quit his job rather than register African Americans to vote as ordered by a federal court (JM).

6 In Liberty, Miss., black news photographer Dewey Green had his camera seized by an unidentified racist constable as he shot pictures of African Americans waiting at the Amite County Courthouse to register to vote. The constable then ordered Green to "get the hell out of town" (JM).

6 In Meridian, Miss., twenty-five African Americans appeared before the State Advisory Committee to the U.S. Commission on Civil Rights to protest alleged police brutality and discrimination in voting and employment. They charged that a new state law requiring publication of the names of all applicants for voter registration was designed to intimidate African Americans and prevent them from registering (JM).

6 In Orleans Parish, La., FBI agents began photographing voter records to determine whether there was race bias in registering. This action followed the Justice Department's winning a six-month legal battle (JM).

8 In Washington, D.C., members of the Senate Judiciary Committee approved the nomination of Thurgood Marshall to the Second U.S. Circuit Court of Appeals, almost one year after President Kennedy first nominated him. Southern senators planned a filibuster to block his nomination once it reached the Senate floor. However, Marshall was eventually confirmed by the Senate (NYT).

10 In Sasser, Ga., Virgil Puckett, white, was jailed for assaulting a federal officer after he struck an FBI agent investigating the burning of two black churches where voter registration rallies had been held. The assault followed the burning of another church and incidents of gunfire directed at African Americans. SNCC leaders Charles McDew and James Forman urged both President Kennedy and Attorney Gen. Robert Kennedy to intervene in the area (NYT).

10, 11 In Valdosta, Ga., Justice Department officials sent FBI agents to investigate the discovery of burned-out Molotov cocktails found in two black churches, Payton AME Church and the Church of Christ. Sheriff Jewell Futch said that little damage was done to the churches (NYT).

12 In Kansas City, Mo., NAACP official Leonard Carter filed an official complaint with the President's Committee on Equal Employment Opportunity against General Motors. He charged that the Kansas City plant continued discriminatory hiring practices despite the parent company's Plans for Progress pledge (NYT).

13 In **Indianola, Greenwood, and Clarksdale, Miss.**, civil rights leaders appealed to President Kennedy and Attorney General Robert Kennedy for federal protection after reports of intimidation of voter registration instructors. The intimidating tactics coincided with the campaign to increase black voter registration (JM).

13 In **Shreveport, La.**, NAACP leader Dr. C. O. Simpkins decided to move himself and his family to Chicago. His decision resulted from the bombing of his two houses, the canceling of his insurance policies, and constant harassment and threats from the KKK (JM).

13 In **Shreveport, La.**, civil rights supporter John Downes, Jr. (white), offered a five-thousand-dollar reward for information about five racially motivated bombings in the city. The latest bomb destroyed the home and car of Jacob Heller (white). Other targets of bombings included two homes owned by Dr. C. O. Simpkins, the recreation building at Lake Bistineau, and St. James Masonic Lodge (JM).

18, 19, 21 In **Washington, D.C.**, ceremonies were held at the Lincoln Memorial to commemorate the signing of the Emancipation Proclamation. Threatened with a boycott by African Americans, at the last minute sponsors booked Thurgood Marshall and other prominent African Americans to sit on the platform. Ceremonies were also held in Chicago and Springfield, Ill. (NYT).

20 In **Tulsa, Okla.**, entertainer Ray Charles's orchestra was refused service at the Pines Drive-In Restaurant and was forced to stop in Kansas City in order to eat. The band had played to a desegregated audience at Tulsa University (JM).

26 In **Atlanta, Ga.**, *The Atlanta Constitution* received three thousand dollars in contributions from white Georgians to help rebuild three black churches in Terrell County that were burned during a voter registration drive. Jackie Robinson, SNCC, and the Albany Movement also launched campaigns for funds to rebuild the churches (NYT).

26 In **Birmingham, Ala.**, Martin Luther King led the annual SCLC conference. The delegates explored new nonviolent ways to deal with the terror sweeping the South. They also reported signs of race relations progress in Birmingham. Meanwhile, police commissioner Eugene "Bull" Connor canceled all press passes in the city (NYT).

28 In **Washington, D.C.**, the U.S. Commission on Civil Rights prodded President Kennedy to use the "stroke of a pen" to end housing discrimination nationally in federally assisted projects. The commission also urged the creation of specific laws "with teeth" to prohibit housing discrimination in Washington, D.C. (NYT).

29 In **Birmingham, Ala.**, Roy James, a member of the American Nazi party, attacked Martin Luther King, who was attending the annual SCLC conference. King did not fight back and refused to press charges against James. James was fined twenty-five dollars and sentenced to thirty days in jail (NYT).

OCTOBER 1962

4 In **Birmingham, Ala.**, Jimmy Louis Warren was severely beaten by approximately one hundred whites when he attempted to desegregate a Georgia-Alabama football game. A second African American, Wilson Brown, fled to safety before whites could turn on him (JM).

4 In **Forrest County, Miss.**, circuit court clerk Theron Lynd was charged with contempt of court after he declined to assist African Americans and refused to tell them why they did not qualify for voting. Several whites testified that Lynd helped them with their voting applications (JM).

4 In **Macon, Ga.**, seven African Americans were routed from a house in a white neighborhood by fire. Joseph Dowling, the renter of the house, had been warned to move out. One week before this incident a church sponsoring voter registration classes for African Americans was also burned down (JM).

JAMES MEREDITH AND THE INTEGRATION OF OLE MISS

Of all the efforts to integrate U.S. colleges and universities, the events preceding and following the 1962 Supreme Court order to admit James Meredith to the University of Mississippi were among the most dramatic and violent. Meredith's struggle to enter Ole Miss began in January 1961 when he applied to transfer from the all-black Jackson State College. Ole Miss rejected his application. In late March 1961 in Biloxi, Miss., NAACP counsel Constance Baker Motley sought a temporary restraining order and a preliminary injunction to permit Meredith's enrollment. In August 1961, Meridian, Miss., lawyers for James Meredith won the first round of their case when district judge Sidney Mize ordered university officials to produce records of summer-term transfer students. His lawyers wanted to prove Meredith was denied the right to transfer into the school because of his race. In March 1962 James Meredith charged that the U.S. district court was moving too slowly in his case and asked the court of appeals in New Orleans for immediate action. In June in Oxford, Miss., Fifth Circuit Court of Appeals judge John Wisdom ordered the University of Mississippi to admit James Meredith. State attorney general Joe Patterson announced he would appeal the order and "exhaust every legal means and resource at our command" to keep Meredith out. The case was appealed to the U.S. Supreme Court.

In September in Jackson, Miss., Gov. Ross Barnett vowed to defy a direct Supreme Court order to admit James Meredith to the University of Mississippi. Arriving in Oxford, Miss., on 30 September, Meredith was escorted to the University of Mississippi by U.S. Marshals and a U.S. attorney. Attorney General Robert Kennedy, unable to gain assurances from Gov. Barnett that Meredith would be protected, dispatched five hundred federal marshals to the campus. Ole Miss students and other whites, many from outside the state and armed with lethal weapons, started rioting. Under orders not to shoot and to deter rioters with tear gas, the outnumbered marshals were assaulted with bottles, bricks, acid, flaming gas, and buckshot. On 1 October in the midst of rioting, Meredith registered and began classes while five thousand army and National Guard troops and deputy marshals battled more than two thousand rioters. Two people, including a French newsman, were killed, and many others were injured in a riot that lasted for fifteen hours. In Oxford, Miss., the Fifth Circuit Court of Appeals issued a sweeping injunction barring the state of Mississippi and all of its officials from interfering with James Meredith's attendance at the University of Mississippi. The injunction followed a university trustee's disclosure of Governor Barnett's plan to expel Meredith.

The events at Ole Miss made national and international headlines. In Washington, D.C., aides to President Kennedy reaffirmed his desire to preserve law and order. The federal troops remained in the city to prevent violence and ensure James Meredith's continued enrollment. Unable to get at Meredith, segregationists attacked the homes of civil rights leaders in Biloxi, Carthage, and Columbus. NAACP leader Medgar Evers predicted that the next battle in the state would be the desegregation of local public school systems.

4 In Sarasota, Fla., realtor Mrs. Elizabeth Moore was aided by the Florida Civil Liberties Union in an unethical conduct hearing before the state real estate commission. She had been ordered out of the Sarasota County Realtors' Board after she sold a house in 1961 in a white neighborhood to a black family (JM).

4 In Washington, D.C., attorney Burke Marshall, head of the Justice Department's Civil Rights Division, admitted that his agency could not protect African Americans who attempted to vote in the South. Marshall stated that his department had no authority to interfere unless there was an outbreak of violence (JM).

7 In New Orleans, La., Catholic officials stated that the segregationist boycott of newly desegregated Catholic schools was a failure. They reported that classroom attendance rose to 97 percent of the previous year's figure (NYT).

7 In Washington, D.C., the President's Committee on Equal Employment Opportunity launched a fight against discrimination in the construction industry, the nation's last stronghold of biased employment practices. The committee planned to survey contractors across the United States on their hiring practices. The information from the surveys would be used to interpret the discriminatory situation and take action against biased contractors (NYT).

9 In Atlanta, Ga., Allie Saxon and Mrs. Verdell Bellamy were accepted at Emory University. Their acceptances came ten days after the state supreme court confirmed its decision that the school could desegregate and retain its tax-exempt status (NYT).

11 In Hasbrouck Heights, N.J., John Joseph, president of Brrr Products Co., announced that he would no longer fill toy orders in Mississippi while the people of the state "continue to defy the laws of the United States." He urged other companies to boycott the state in order to place economic pressure on state officials (JM).

17 In Atlanta, Ga., a $100,000 damage suit was filed in federal court by five black railroad employees who claimed they were dismissed from their jobs on the basis of race. They filed suit against the Southern Railway Co. and the International Association of Machinists for failure to even hear their appeal (NYT).

17 In New York City, NAACP officials announced a new legal strategy to break the backs of all-white unions. They planned to file actions against racially segregated unions, asking that those unions lose their certification as exclusive bargaining agents (NYT).

18 In Chicago, Ill., Mrs. William Thurman withdrew her son Barry from a Catholic kindergarten after harassment from white mothers. He had attended school quietly for a month until the story was printed in local newspapers (JM).

18 In Detroit, Mich., an angry crowd of whites stoned the home of Mr. and Mrs. Leroy Church and broke several windows. The Church family had recently moved in a house on an all-white

block. Four policemen were injured when they attempted to restore order. They arrested Warren McCarter, Mrs. Bonnie Racine, and five juveniles (JM).

18 In San Francisco, Calif., NAACP leader Herbert Hill filed complaints with the President's Committee on Equal Employment Opportunity against the Army Quartermaster's clothing sales store at the Presidio. NAACP official Terry Francois charged the store operators with refusing to hire qualified African Americans and telling offensive black jokes (JM).

23 In Washington, D.C., the U.S. Supreme Court upheld a lower-court ruling that federal judges could order state voter registrars to place names of specific African Americans on voting lists. The case sprang from Macon County, Ala., where eligible black voters once outnumbered whites twelve thousand to three thousand (NYT).

25 In Springfield, Ill., members of the Illinois State Federation of Labor adopted resolutions urging nondiscrimination by race in apprentice training programs. The federation also endorsed the parent AFL-CIO civil rights program aimed at inserting a nondiscrimination clause in every contract negotiated (JM).

NOVEMBER 1962

1 In Washington, D.C., a White House source revealed that governors of most southern states refused to cooperate in next year's celebration of the Emancipation Proclamation centennial. Because more than half of the nation's African Americans live in the South, their refusal could severely limit the national celebration (JM).

1, 14 In Charleston, S.C., a federal court heard the case of Harvey Gantt, who was attempting to desegregate Clemson College. Meanwhile, Henri Monteith filed suit to enter the University of South Carolina (NYT).

6 In Washington, D.C., NAACP attorney Constance Baker Motley, appearing before the U.S. Supreme Court, appealed the 1960 convictions of Rev. Fred Shuttlesworth and Charles Billups, who received jail sentences for inciting ten college students to sit-in at Birmingham. The appeal was the first of seven crucial appeals cases emerging from student sit-ins in six states (NYT).

7 In **Baton Rouge, La.**, the state supreme court reversed the conviction of five former Southern University students for picketing restaurants that engaged in racial segregation. Jerome Smith, David Dennis, Doris Castle, Julia Aaron, and Constance Bradford were freed by the court (NYT).

10, 14 In **Washington, D.C.**, AFL-CIO official George Meany rammed through the executive council a resolution condemning the NAACP as anti-labor and banishing further money gifts to the group. The action was a response to the NAACP's court fights to eliminate the union seniority system, which the NAACP attorneys viewed as discriminatory (NYT).

11 In **Atlanta, Ga.**, city postmaster B. F. Sanders was stripped of his promotional powers. The action resulted from the local NAACP's drive against local post office segregation. Sanders became the second postmaster to be stripped of his power to promote because of his lack of action on postal desegregation (NYT).

15 In **Clarksdale, Miss.**, Mrs. Noelle Henry, wife of Aaron Henry, the state's NAACP president, was fired from the teaching position she had held for eleven years. She filed suit against the school board in the district court's Delta Division (JM).

15 In **Miami Beach, Fla.**, Dr. R. C. Bell led picketing at the American Dental Association (ADA) convention, protesting the fact that twelve southern states denied membership to black dentists. The ADA's board of trustees proposed suspension of state dental societies that barred African Americans from membership (JM).

17 In **Washington, D.C.**, President Kennedy signed an executive order banning discrimination in government-sponsored housing. The order established the President's Committee on Equal Opportunity in Housing and detailed a program of enforcement for federally assisted housing projects (NYT).

20 In **Washington, D.C.**, Justice Department officials appointed attorney William Mason as an assistant U.S. attorney in Norfolk, Va. He became the first African American in Virginia named to the position since Reconstruction (NYT).

22 In **Anderson, Ind.**, local YMCA officials agreed to accept African Americans as members after several months of study and negotiations. One year earlier, the local NAACP boycotted the United Fund campaign because it donated money to the segregated YMCA (JM).

22 In **Detroit, Mich.**, the city council passed an ordinance making it illegal for real estate salesmen to use unscrupulous blockbusting scare tactics in trying to push a sale. The Detroit Real Estate Brokers Association fought hard against the passage of the measure (NYT).

24 In **Tuscaloosa, Ala.**, the University of Alabama's student newspaper, the *Crimson White*, urged school officials to learn from the mistakes of Mississippi in handling desegregation. Their statements anticipated the possible admittance of a black student who had applied for entry (NYT).

29 In **Springfield, Ill.**, the state legislature voted to ratify a proposed amendment to the U.S. Constitution that would outlaw poll taxes in federal elections. Illinois became the first state to ratify the amendment (JM).

29 In **Washington, D.C.**, a Pentagon spokesperson stated that the President's Committee on Equal Opportunity in the Armed Forces, set up to study discrimination in the services, was ineffective. The spokesperson pointed out that the committee had inadequate staff, no program for members to actually visit bases, and some of the civilian committee members lacked essential knowledge about military life. The committee had been formed to respond to complaints of discrimination from black soldiers (JM).

DECEMBER 1962

6 In **New Orleans, La.**, federal judge J. Skelly Wright ruled unconstitutional that section of the state law creating Tulane University that required the school to be segregated. The state law was written in accordance with the white-only provisions in the wills of Paul Tulane and Sophie Newcombe. The decision paved the way for black enrollment at the university (NYT).

6 In New York City, Mayor Robert Wagner directed New York's Commission on Human Rights to compile an ethnic census of civil service personnel. The census would provide data for the city to upgrade the skills of African Americans and Puerto Ricans and implement the city's program of equality of opportunity in employment (NYT).

13 In Macon, Ga., a boycott of merchants ended after only three days when merchants agreed to hire African Americans as clerks, cashiers, and office workers. Local NAACP leaders stated that the boycott was 97 percent effective among African Americans and 50 percent effective among whites (JM).

13 In New Orleans, La., in response to an order issued by federal judge J. Skelly Wright, Tulane University officials accepted Mrs. Pearlie Hardin Elloie and Barbara Marie Guillory as graduate students. They had previously been refused admission to the school. School officials stated that they had rejected the women because of restrictions in donations (NYT).

18 In Birmingham, Ala., the Bethel Baptist Church, formerly the church of civil rights leader Rev. Fred Shuttlesworth, was bombed. Although once the hub of anti-segregation campaigning, the church had remained relatively quiet since his departure. The blast also damaged two nearby houses (NYT).

20 In Chicago, Ill., Dr. N. O. Calloway confirmed that the AFL-CIO had donated five thousand dollars to the Chicago Committee to End Hospital Discrimination. Dr. Calloway said that the suit filed by the committee sought to allow black doctors to practice at all hospitals (JM).

20 In Richmond, Va., the state supreme court agreed to review the order of Judge W. Moscoe

Huntley that the NAACP would have to submit a list of its donors to the State Committee on Offenses Against the Administration of Justice. The NAACP contended that a published list would subject its donors to abuse and intimidation (JM).

25 In Washington, D.C., President Kennedy conducted a two-hour meeting with prominent black leaders. Those present were Roy Wilkins, Martin Luther King, A. Philip Randolph, Dorothy Height, James Farmer, Whitney Young, and Theodore Brown. Kennedy promised to appoint more black ambassadors and increase the presence of African Americans in key diplomatic positions (JM).

27 In Chicago, Ill., according to a survey made by University of Chicago sociologist Karl Taeuber and funded by the Urban League, housing discrimination in Chicago was at its highest point in fifty years. Taeuber concluded that African Americans were more segregated than any of the European immigrant groups past or present (JM).

27 In Oklahoma City, Okla., plumber Chester Arterberry asked for a restraining order in federal court against Health, Education, and Welfare Secretary Anthony Celebrezze. Arterberry filed the request to bar further use of federal funds in apprentice training programs in the city's building, construction, and manufacturing trades because of their alleged racial discrimination (JM).

27 In Washington, D.C., Roland Barnes became the first person in the United States to place a written complaint under the president's order barring discrimination in housing. He charged Abraham Sind, Israel Cohen, and Sind Associates with refusing to sell him a house, even after he offered more than the asking price (JM).

27 In Washington, D.C., managers of the ultra-elite Cosmos Club admitted historian John Hope Franklin for membership. He became the first African American accepted into the club. After the club turned down Carl Rowan, the black deputy assistant secretary of state, President Kennedy, Edward R. Murrow, John Kenneth Galbraith, Jr., Howard Smith, Raymond Swing, and Bruce Catton resigned their memberships (JM).

On 28 August 1963, over 250,000 people marched on Washington, D.C., in support of the civil rights bill sent to Congress by President John F. Kennedy in June 1963. Initially called by A. Philip Randolph, president of the Brotherhood of Sleeping Car Porters, the march was planned by leaders of the major civil rights organizations and coordinated by activist Bayard Rustin. (SOURCE: JACK FRANKLIN COLLECTION, AFRICAN AMERICAN MUSEUM IN PHILADELPHIA)

1963

"WE SHALL OVERCOME"

*T**he Civil Rights Movement reached new heights in 1963 with the weeks of demonstrations in Birmingham, Ala., and the March on Washington on 28 August 1963, where Martin Luther King, Jr., delivered his famous "I Have a Dream" speech and predicted that "we shall overcome." At the same time, civil rights protests took place throughout the country, encompassing more and more issues and generating greater and greater support. While the "Battle of Birmingham" galvanized the Kennedy administration into introducing the civil rights bill in Congress, the murder of Medgar Evers in Jackson, Miss., and four black girls preparing for Sunday school at Birmingham's Sixteenth Street Baptist Church sadly demonstrated that many people would have to make the ultimate sacrifice in pursuit of the "Beloved Community" and equal rights for all American citizens.*

JANUARY 1963

1 In **Oxford, Miss.**, provost Dr. Charles Haywood resigned from the University of Mississippi. He reportedly was disgusted over the light punishment given to students who rioted when James Meredith was enrolled in September 1962 (SSN).

3 In **Atlanta, Ga.**, Mayor Ivan Allen and the board of aldermen approved a measure to erect an artificial barrier or "buffer zone" by closing down two streets that linked an exclusive white neighborhood to an equally exclusive and expanding black residential area. Attorney David Hollowell undertook a fight to secure a restraining order barring the street closures (JM).

3 In **Berkeley, Calif.**, the Berkeley Realty Board agreed that racial discrimination in residential housing should be abolished in the city. However, they urged the city council to go slow in ordering violators to be jailed and to pay fines (JM).

3 In **Edgewater, N.J.**, CORE members conducted sit-ins at the private homes of three apartment house owners. The owners had refused to rent an apartment to Charles David and his family, although white CORE members secured the same apartment easily (JM).

3 In **New Orleans, La.**, CORE leader James McCain filed suit in federal court challenging Louisiana's law enforcing racial segregation in hotels and rented housing. He had been refused accommodations at the Royal Orleans Hotel (JM).

7 In **Washington, D.C.**, Mississippi civil rights leaders filed a federal suit to force Attorney Gen. Robert Kennedy and FBI director J. Edgar Hoover to prevent harassment of African Americans fighting for equality in Mississippi. They hoped that the suit would force government officials into taking action. Kennedy announced the postponement of the U.S. Commission on Civil Rights hearing in Mississippi. He stated that the Justice Department could not protect witnesses scheduled to testify (NYT).

8 In Oakland, Calif., at a rally celebrating the one hundredth anniversary of the Emancipation Proclamation, Martin Luther King announced his support for a nationwide selective-buying campaign organized against the products of firms that discriminated against African Americans. SCLC's Operation Breadbasket was launched in October 1962 to organize boycotts of local businesses that discriminated against African Americans (NYT).

8 In Oxford, Miss., James Meredith announced he would not continue at the University of Mississippi unless conditions at the school changed. His statements caused an increase in campus demonstrations as students protested his "publicity stunt" (NYT).

9 In Greenville, S.C., federal judge C. C. Wyche agreed with Clemson College's claim that Harvey Gantt did not complete an application and thus did not deserve admission. The school's claim centered around a portfolio from Gantt that they requested but then refused to review because Gantt had filed suit against the school. He planned to appeal the decision to the Fourth Circuit Court of Appeals (NYT).

10 In Milwaukee, Wis., Alderman Vel Phillips charged the police department with employment discrimination against its black officers. She stated that African Americans were promoted slower, were not permitted on the vice squad, and were prevented from teaming with whites in detective duos. Police chief Howard Johnson denied the charges but promised to investigate (JM).

10 In New York City, five CORE members were arrested after they staged a sit-in at the West Side Federal Savings and Loan Co. The sit-in was a response to the bank's insistence on prohibiting the Molo Construction Co. from renting one of its Midwood homes to a black family (JM).

10 In Washington, D.C., CORE leader Dave Dennis protested the actions of Mississippi officials to Attorney General Robert Kennedy and Secretary of Agriculture Orville Freeman. He charged local officials with dropping twenty thousand African Americans active in voter registration campaigns from lists of those eligible for surplus food and other commodities (JM).

15 In Washington, D.C., Attorney General Robert Kennedy submitted his civil rights report to President Kennedy. The attorney general claimed that segregation in interstate transportation had ceased to exist. Although many southern African Americans had begun to vote, he cited the need for additional legislation to guarantee the right to vote (NYT).

15 In Washington, D.C., the Supreme Court ruled unconstitutional the Virginia law set up to curb the civil rights activities of the NAACP in the state. Under the terms of the law, any lawyer who accepted an NAACP case was considered to be illegally soliciting business (NYT).

15–18 In Chicago, Ill., Catholic, Protestant, and Jewish delegates met for the National Conference on Religion and Race. They chose ten cities to launch tri-faith projects against racial discrimination. The delegates also voted to oppose the segregationist views of Alabama governor George Wallace (NYT).

16 In Columbia, S.C., African Americans attended the inaugural ceremonies for Gov. Donald Russell. For the first time in the history of the state, African Americans were invited to lunch at the governor's mansion (NYT).

17 In Atlanta, Ga., Emory University accepted Mrs. Verdell Bellamy and Allie Saxon as the first full-time black students in the school's history. The university had successfully defeated a state law denying tax exemptions to integrated schools (JM).

19 In Washington, D.C., Justice Department officials filed suits to desegregate schools near military installations in Alabama, Mississippi, and Louisiana. The schools received federal aid because parents who worked at military and federal installations sent their children to the local public schools (NYT).

29 In Clemson, S.C., Harvey Gantt was enrolled at Clemson College without incident. This was the first school desegregation in South Carolina on any level since Reconstruction. State police were stationed at every town within thirty miles of the school in order to prevent outbreaks of racial violence (NYT).

FEBRUARY 1963

1 In Pine Bluff, Ark., George Howard, Jr., the NAACP state president, withdrew his daughter Sarah from Dollarway High School after she suffered beatings and verbal abuse. He refused to send her back until she received adequate protection. She had integrated the high school after a fifteen-month court battle (SSN).

7 In Dougherty County, Ga., school board members defied an order to integrate twenty-seven children of military personnel into all-white public schools. Justice Department officials indicated that they would sue to compel integration or cut off federal aid (JM).

7 In Albany, Ga., sixteen hundred white citizens, led by Dr. Frank McKemie, petitioned the city commission to reopen the library. The library, along with public parks and swimming pools, had been closed in August 1962 to avoid integration (JM).

7 In Cleveland, Ohio, the National Urban League's Whitney Young, Jr., announced that Cleveland was the city with the highest percentage of residential segregation in the nation. He stated that of the 250,000 African Americans in the city, only 1 in 40 lived outside the central city, though more than half of the white population lived in the suburbs (JM).

7 In New Haven, Conn., CORE members picketed the United Illuminating Co., protesting unfair hiring practices. They charged that of the fourteen hundred employees of the firm, only twenty were nonwhites, almost all in custodial positions (JM).

7 In Jackson, Miss., Gov. Ross Barnett agreed to allow the transfer of Clyde Kennard from Parchman Prison to the University of Mississippi Hospital, following an appeal to the state supreme court by Kennard's mother and sister. Kennard was suffering from cancer. He was serving a seven-year sentence on a trumped-up charge of stealing twenty-five dollars' worth of chicken feed after he attempted to enroll at the Mississippi Southern College in 1958 (JM).

12 In Nashville, Tenn., NAACP attorneys filed a class-action suit against Holiday Inns of America, Inc., seeking a permanent injunction barring the motel from refusing to serve African Americans. The suit alleged that Dr. Vasco Smith was refused accommodations by the hotel, even though he had a reservation and there were rooms available (NYT).

14 In Montgomery County, Ala., SCLC leaders charged county voting officials with discrimination. SCLC reported to the Justice Department that although seven hundred African Americans attempted to register, only two hundred were added to the rolls (JM).

14 In Pierre, S.D., state legislators passed by a huge margin a bill prohibiting discrimination in public places on the basis of race, creed, color, or national origin. Black servicemen stationed in the state had long complained about discrimination in hotels, bars, and restaurants (JM).

14 In Washington, D.C., Vice President Johnson refused to cast the deciding vote that would have ended filibusters on civil rights legislation in the Senate. NAACP leader Clarence Mitchell accused Johnson of acting on his true beliefs and showing that he would not push the South too hard (JM).

21 In Washington, D.C., black members of the President's Committee on Equal Opportunity in the Armed Forces proposed putting southern towns that discriminated against black soldiers off-limits to all troops. Despite the fact that southern cities received billions of dollars from the military bases in their areas, local officials refused to integrate public schools, make housing available to African Americans, or allow black soldiers to use public facilities (JM).

21 In **Whitewater, Wis.**, local NAACP members picketed a minstrel show at Whitewater State College. They argued that the show portrayed derogatory racial stereotypes (JM).

25 In **New York City**, A. Philip Randolph announced plans to march on Washington to protest continuing black unemployment. He expressed the belief that President Kennedy had no conception of the enormity or seriousness of the situation. He made the announcement at a board meeting of the Negro American Labor Council (NYT).

26 In **Washington, D.C.**, the Supreme Court reversed the conviction of 187 South Carolina youths on charges of common law breach of the peace. The students had paraded around the state house in Columbia carrying signs calling for an end to racial segregation in public accommodations (NYT).

28 In **Leflore County, Miss.**, comedian Dick Gregory announced he was seeking to raise $37,000 to pay for distribution of federal surplus food. He had offered to give local officials $5,000 to distribute food to families, but officials later upped the price to $37,000 (JM).

28 In **Tupelo, Miss.**, twenty-eight black reservists from the 689th Army Engineer Company were quietly moved into drills with the 323rd Army Engineer Company, a previously all-white unit. The original integration order came from Defense Department officials in Washington, D.C. (JM).

MARCH 1963

1 In **Mobile, Ala.**, four black high school students who asked for a transfer to a white school were rejected by school officials. They would have become the city's first pupils to integrate a public school. Black leader J. L. LaFlore announced plans to file a federal suit for public school desegregation (SSN).

1 In **Prince Edward County, Va.**, Justice Department officials asked the Fourth Circuit Court of Appeals to order public education resumed. Department officials pointed out that following the 1959 closing of the schools most white children had received state and local tuition grants to attend private schools, while nearly fifteen hundred black children had received little formal education (SSN).

1 In **Washington, D.C.**, President Kennedy called for new laws in the spheres of voter education and civil rights. He supported the appointment of federal voting referees while voting rights cases were pending in court. He also asked for a technical and financial assistance program to aid school districts in the process of desegregation (NYT).

5 In **Jackson, Miss.**, African Americans filed suit in federal court seeking desegregation of all public schools in Leake County, Miss. They stated that their request for integration was met with threats and violence from school board members and white segregationists. This was one of the first public school desegregation suits filed in Mississippi (NYT).

7 In **Columbus, Ohio**, fair housing legislation was introduced in the Ohio General Assembly that would ban discrimination in the sale, rental, building, and financing of real estate. The legislation had been recommended by the Ohio Civil Rights Commission and endorsed by Gov. James Rhodes (JM).

7 In **Jackson, Miss.**, Robert Smith, friend and landlord of James Meredith, had his grocery store riddled with gunfire during the previous two weekends. He had placed a picture of Meredith in a showcase display (JM).

7 In **Little Rock, Ark.**, a federal court order ended racial segregation at the city auditorium, tennis courts, golf courses, and playgrounds. However, two city-owned swimming pools remained segregated (JM).

7 In **Springfield, Ill.**, members of the education committee of the state house of representatives voted in favor of a bill to forbid school boards from building schools or drawing school districts to promote racial segregation. The bill would outlaw

CAMPAIGNS AGAINST SEGREGATED PUBLIC EDUCATION IN THE NORTH

While the NAACP and other groups attempted to bring about the desegregation of public school systems in the southern states, segregated public schools in cities and towns outside the South increasingly came under attack in 1962 and 1963. Lawsuits were filed against the school districts in Detroit, Mich.; Englewood and Orange, N.J.; Long Island and West Point, N.Y.; Gary, Ind.; and Chicago, Ill., in 1962, and nonviolent protests took place at school board meetings in San Francisco, Calif.; Syracuse, N.Y.; Xenia, Ohio; and Eloy, Ariz., over segregation in local public schools.

In November 1962 black parents organized a boycott of the Northwestern High School in Detroit because of poor conditions and overcrowding. In Englewood, N.J., after several years of petitioning officials to end de facto segregation and to improve the quality of education at the school, black parents staged a boycott of the all-black Lincoln Elementary School in March 1963. Volunteers set up makeshift schools for the black students until April 1963, when twenty parents were arrested for not sending the children to school. In June 1963 the Supreme Court ruled that African Americans seeking the integration of high schools in East St. Louis, Ill., need not exhaust state remedies before going into federal court. Black parents in Englewood, N.J., and Chicago, Ill., filed similar suits in federal courts.

Black parents organized picket lines to protest the "mobile classrooms" being installed at all-black public schools in Chicago's Jackson Park section in June 1962 because they believed the temporary structures would perpetuate segregation. Throughout 1963 civil rights groups protested the policies of school superintendent Benjamin Willis, and in August 1963, comedian Dick Gregory charged Chicago police with excessive brutality when he was arrested with other demonstrators attempting to block the construction of mobile classrooms at another school in Jackson Park.

Superintendent Willis thwarted the school board's attempt to implement a more liberal transfer policy in September 1963, and black leaders united to stage the massive "Freedom Day Boycott" of segregated schools on 22 October 1963. Approximately 225,000 pupils took part in the boycott and 20,000 people participated in a protest march. Leaders set up Freedom Centers where students could go to receive instruction during the boycott. In November 1963, a school board report revealed that although the majority of elementary public school students were African American, they attended one hundred fewer schools than whites. Although Illinois superintendent of public instruction Ray Page admitted that there were inequalities in the city's school system, he considered them unrelated to race, and in November 1963 federal judge Abraham Marovitz upheld Chicago's policy of assigning students only to their neighborhood school.

After several years of protest over public school segregation and overcrowding, the New York Citywide Committee for Integrated Schools was formed in June 1963 and included representatives of the NAACP, CORE, the National Urban League, and several parents' groups. While school superintendent Calvin Gross agreed to "open enrollment" and to allow Puerto Rican and black children to attend schools outside their neighborhoods, he opposed the "involuntary transfer" of white children to predominantly black schools. In December 1963, when Gross promised to present a plan for citywide integration, he instead called for more "open enrollment," and the Citywide Committee set up pickets in front of the school administration building and began making plans for a massive school boycott in February 1964.

Chicago's practice of drawing school district boundaries to conform with established patterns of segregated housing (JM).

7 In Washington, D.C., Detroit congressman Charles Diggs urged the Agriculture Department to move against officials who cut off surplus food allotments to Mississippi African Americans because they tried to register to vote. Diggs stated that there was ample evidence of discrimination against African Americans in Mississippi in other Agriculture Department programs as well (JM).

14 In Atlanta, Ga., Mayor Ivan Allen confirmed reports that C. C. Thornton purchased a home from a white owner on the "white side" of the barrier between the white and black residential areas. In a separate action, a Fulton County superior court judge ruled that the barrier must come down (JM).

14 In Huntsville, Ala., after meeting with local black leaders, city officials quietly integrated public facilities in order to ensure that the federal government kept its space research facilities in the city (JM).

21 In Washington, D.C., Defense Department officials announced plans to open integrated schools on six military bases in South Carolina, Georgia, and Alabama, where local schools resisted integration. The local segregated schools were scheduled to lose federal aid (JM).

26 In Washington, D.C., the Supreme Court overturned the contempt conviction against Rev. Theodore Gibson, head of the Miami NAACP. Gibson had refused to turn over NAACP membership rolls to a Florida legislative committee (NYT).

28 In Atlanta, Ga., the Episcopal church–sponsored Lovett School rejected the admission of five-year-old Martin Luther King III. School officials stated that they were in no position to accept an application from an African American because they had never received one before (JM).

28 In Grand Forks, N.D., the North Dakota Committee on Civil Rights held hearings to gather complaints from African Americans who testified that they were forced to pay exorbitant rents in the city. Black servicemen were told by local police, "Get out of town and stay out. The people don't want you here" (JM).

28 In Kingstree, S.C., local registration officials took one hour to register one black applicant while 124 African Americans waited on line to register to vote. CORE leader Frank Robinson pointed out that the registration slowdown was the latest technique in discouraging black citizens from voting (JM).

28 In Washington, D.C., Justice Department officials admitted that they received a report that Martin Luther King had barely escaped attack when he spoke in Chicago. They recommended that sponsors of future King addresses advise local police of his appearance and work out some kind of protection for him (JM).

29 In Washington, D.C., Republican lawmakers in Congress, led by Sen. Jacob Javits, introduced legislation to outlaw discrimination in hotels, motels, and public facilities. They also asked for new legislation in the fields of voting, education, employment, housing, and administration of justice. Additionally, they also urged Congress to make the U.S. Commission on Civil Rights permanent (NYT).

APRIL 1963

1 In Washington, D.C., Rep. Adam Clayton Powell called for civil rights organizations to be more independent and totally controlled and maintained by African Americans. He criticized the NAACP, SNCC, CORE, the National Urban League, and SCLC for becoming too dependent on funds from philanthropic foundations and other institutions outside the African American community (NYT).

1, 2 In Washington, D.C., air force officials named Capt. Edward Dwight, Jr., as the first black astronaut trainee. He was among sixteen new candidates chosen for the aerospace research pilot program at Edwards Air Force Base in California (NYT).

3, 4 In Berkeley, Calif., the electorate voted down an ordinance that would have banned racial

ATTACKS ON DISCRIMINATION
IN GOVERNMENT-SPONSORED EMPLOYMENT

The attempts of the President's Committee on Equal Employment Opportunity (PCEEO) and state and local fair employment practices commissions to end the discriminatory practices of governmental agencies and contractors continued to make news in 1963. In February black workers in Pascagoula, Miss., filed fifty-three complaints of discrimination with the PCEEO against the Ingalls Shipbuilding Company, which built atomic submarines. In May NAACP official Clarence Mitchell charged that funds from the federal government's Manpower Development and Retraining Program were being used in Alabama, Georgia, Mississippi, South Carolina, and Florida to train African Americans in menial tasks and called for an investigation. While whites were being trained for industrial skills, African Americans were being trained as waiters, waitresses, and chambermaids.

In Chicago, Ill., federal judge James Parsons sparked a controversy when he reported in June that there were no black workers at the construction site for the new federal office building; and in Cincinnati, Ohio, NAACP officials threatened mass picketing at a federally funded construction site because the Teamsters and other unions discriminated against black workers. At the recommendation of the PCEEO, the president issued an executive order in June 1963 giving government agencies authority to cut off federal funds at any construction project where discrimination was practiced. He also instructed Defense Secy. Robert McNamara to recommend action on the proposal to close military installations in areas where there was discrimination in housing, military jobs, and public accommodations.

In Philadelphia, New York City, and Cleveland, protests and pickets were mounted at construction projects funded by the local municipal governments, but where no minority workers were employed. In Philadelphia, following a sit-in by CORE members at the office of Mayor James Tate in May 1963, work was halted on construction of a new municipal services building pending an investigation of charges of discrimination by construction trades unions. Later that month violence erupted when NAACP pickets clashed with police guarding workers at a construction site for a new junior high school. After several days of demonstrations and negotiations, an agreement was reached with the construction trades unions that led to the hiring of several black workers.

In New York City in July 1963 Mayor Robert Wagner ordered the suspension of work on the Harlem Hospital Annex following nine days of demonstrations by CORE, the NAACP, and other civil rights groups over discriminatory hiring practices. The work was suspended until an inquiry into the discrimination charges against construction trades unions was completed. In Cleveland, Ohio, following picketing by the United Freedom Movement, a local civil rights group, two black plumbers were hired at the construction site for the new public hall. Mayor Ralph Locher participated in the negotiations with local unions, contractors, and representatives of the United Freedom Movement that led to the hiring of the black workers.

In East St. Louis, Ill., after the NAACP staged a week-long series of protests and demonstrations in August 1963, eight banks and loan firms promised to hire African Americans in noncustodial positions, and the NAACP launched a campaign against employment discrimination by public utilities in the city.

or religious discrimination in the city's housing sales or rentals. Wallace Johnson, who campaigned against the ordinance, was also elected mayor (NYT).

4 In Chicago, Ill., Veterans Administration chief John Gleason announced that all real estate agents renting or selling homes must sign non-

discrimination agreements. Some white real estate agents had refused to show homes in white areas to black families (NYT).

4 In Defiance, Ohio, the national Delta Zeta Sorority dropped the Defiance College chapter a few days after two black women had been accepted. Mrs. Robert Whitfield, president of the national sorority, denied racial bias and claimed that the reason for the action was that the black pledges had been rude to their regional director (JM).

11 In Albany, Ga., because city officials refused to reopen Albany's recreational facilities on an integrated basis, city swimming pools, recreational centers, and tennis courts were put up for sale to private individuals. The facilities had been closed since the summer of 1962 to thwart desegregation efforts (JM).

11 In Nashville, Tenn., executive director of the black YWCA Mrs. Robert Outlaw was fired by the board of directors of the Nashville YWCA. Mrs. Outlaw was dismissed after she wrote a signed newspaper article condemning the segregation policy of the Nashville YWCA. The YWCA had refused to house ten black Memphis student nurses (JM).

18 In New Orleans, La., cafeteria workers at the local branch of Louisiana State University refused to serve a visiting black medical student. Black cafeteria employees walked out, and white Tulane and Loyola students began picketing the establishment. Unable to get any more workers, the cafeteria closed (JM).

20 In Washington, D.C., President Kennedy opposed the U.S. Commission on Civil Rights' recommendation that federal funds be cut off in Mississippi because of racially discriminatory policies and practices of state officials. Kennedy said he did not approve of using federal spending programs merely to reward or punish local government officials (NYT).

25 In Atlanta, Ga., sixteen African Americans were hired as firemen for a fire station located in the heart of a black neighborhood. They became the first African Americans hired as firemen in the city's history (JM).

25 In Bowling Green, Ky., federal judge Mac Swinford ordered the integration of the city's public schools by September 1963 and threatened to bring in federal troops if necessary. He rejected a three-year plan offered by the school board (JM).

25 In Charleston, Mo., federal judge James Meredith rejected a gradual integration plan and ordered school officials to outline a complete integration plan by September 1963. The city operated two white and two black elementary and high schools (JM).

25 In Oxford, Miss., in an interview that appeared in *Jet* magazine, James Meredith revealed that he was trying to help Dewey Greene, Jr., get into the University of Mississippi as the second black student. He also disclosed plans to establish a national foundation after he graduated in August 1963 to help finance underprivileged students in college (JM).

26 In Montgomery, Ala., Attorney General Robert Kennedy met with Gov. George Wallace to discuss the state's volatile racial climate. Kennedy had also hoped to head off an impending integration showdown over the admission of African Americans to the University of Alabama. Although they stated they had a "pleasant, courteous visit," both men refused to compromise (NYT).

30 In Washington, D.C., the U.S. Supreme Court ruled racial segregation in courtrooms unconstitutional. The court thus threw out a ten-dollar contempt of court fine against Ford Johnson, who refused to move from the white to the black section of a Richmond, Va., courtroom (NYT).

MAY 1963

2 In Fredericksburg, Va., attorneys S. W. Tucker and Henry Marsh asked a federal judge to reject the grade-a-year integration plan offered by school officials. They contended that the plan might not accomplish integration because of a pupil-transfer clause and failure to spell out district lines. They also noted that the plan contained no provision for teacher integration (JM).

2 In Tuscaloosa, Ala., Vivian Malone, Sandy English, and Jimmy Hood filed suit to enter the University of Alabama. The suit was filed by NAACP attorney Fred Gray on behalf of the students (JM).

9, 10 In Washington, D.C., both Republican and Democratic lawmakers called for the passage of part three of President Eisenhower's original civil rights bill, which would give the attorney general the power to enter civil rights cases. The action resulted from President Kennedy's statement that he had no federal statute to use to intervene in the Birmingham crisis or the violence precipitated by the suit filed by Vivian Malone, Sandy English, and Jimmy Hood for admission to the University of Alabama (NYT).

26 In New York City, CORE official Jerome Smith, novelist James Baldwin, and eight other prominent African Americans met with Attorney General Robert Kennedy and had a heated discussion on methods of solving the problem of segregation and discrimination in the North as well as the South. Smith stressed the frustration felt by many northern black youths. The black leaders who attended the meeting expressed disappointment and felt that Kennedy did not grasp the urgency of the situation (NYT).

27, 30 In Louisville, Ky., Martin Luther King and SCLC leaders finished a six-city cross-country tour, which raised $145,000 to help pay expenses arising from civil rights demonstrations, especially bail money. The rally in Los Angeles was the largest, raising $75,000 and attracting fifty thousand people (NYT).

30 In Louisville, Ky., the board of aldermen enacted an ordinance outlawing all racial discrimination in public business establishments. The ordinance applied to restaurants, theaters, taverns, and amusement facilities (JM).

30 In Washington, D.C., Justice Department officials revealed that U.S. Marshal Luke Moore (black), who had been assigned to protect James Meredith during his stay at the University of Mississippi, played a crucial role in convincing Meredith to remain at the school when he considered quitting (JM).

JUNE 1963

1 In Putnam County, Tenn., the school board members in Cookeville, Tenn., assigned five black teachers to teach in predominantly white schools. It was the first such action in the state (SSN).

2 In Dallas, Tex., integrated International Hospital, a private institution, recently opened. It was considered the first integrated hospital to operate in the state, serving patients on a "first come, first served" basis (NYT).

11 In Honolulu, Hawaii, several of the nation's most powerful mayors attending the National Mayors' Conference pledged battles in their home cities to combat racism. President Kennedy had asked each local government to erase segregation ordinances from the books, set up biracial committees to reduce tensions, abolish city job discrimination, enact public accommodations ordinances, and organize special campaigns to encourage youths of both races to stay in school (NYT).

12 In Tuscaloosa, Ala., Gov. George Wallace attempted to block the registration of Jimmy Hood and Vivian Malone at the University of Alabama. After federal troops arrived, he stepped aside. Hood and Malone became the first black students to enroll since Autherine Lucy attempted to attend the school in 1956. Robert Muckel became the first white student to enter the all-black Alabama A & M College in Normal (NYT).

13 In Franklin Parish, La., E. J. Blount was beaten by five KKK members who warned him to leave the area. Blount and his family were unable to identify his assailants and no charges were filed. Blount stated he would not leave the area, although he did resign his position as principal of Waverly High School (JM).

13 In Washington, D.C., NAACP officials confirmed the assassination of NAACP leader Medgar Evers in Jackson, Miss. Evers was shot in the back by an unidentified assailant when he arrived at his home. President Kennedy urged the enactment of new civil rights legislation, but also called for localities and states to take the lead in eliminating discrimination and segregation. Several black leaders threatened wide-scale civil disobedience and a protest march on Washington (NYT).

15 In New York City, the NAACP established the NAACP–Medgar Evers Scholarship Fund to raise $30,000 for the education of the Everses' three

THE BATTLE OF BIRMINGHAM

The ongoing civil rights protests in the South received even greater attention nationally and internationally in 1963 when Dr. Martin Luther King and the SCLC targeted Birmingham, Ala. (also known as "Bombingham"), for a major campaign. Working with Alabama Christian Movement for Human Rights (ACMHR) leader Rev. Fred Shuttlesworth, SCLC's James Bevel, Andrew Young, and others held a series of meetings in the black community early in 1963 to prepare for direct confrontations with the police force led by Sheriff Eugene "Bull" Connor. Workshops were held in black churches to train protesters in nonviolent strategies for protecting themselves during the demonstrations.

On 3 April 1963, King issued the Birmingham Manifesto, which called for the desegregation of all lunch counters, department stores, rest rooms, and drinking fountains in downtown department stores; the hiring of black workers in business and industry; and formation of a biracial committee to develop a schedule for the desegregation of all other areas of public life. The campaign began that day when sixty-five protesters staged a sit-in at five downtown department stores.

On Good Friday, 12 April 1963, King decided that he would violate the court injunction and march on city hall. King led a group of fifty downtown and right up to the police barricades where Sheriff Connor was waiting. After King and Ralph David Abernathy knelt and said a prayer, the police grabbed them by their belts and pushed them and all the marchers into paddy wagons. When local white ministers published a letter in *The Birmingham News* condemning the demonstrations as "ill-timed" and King and SCLC as "outside agitators," King decided to respond, and his "Letter from a Birmingham Jail" is considered one of the most important statements on nonviolent protest ever written. King made it clear that he had never participated in a protest that the oppressors considered well timed and that they were in Birmingham "because injustice is here."

On 2 May 1963 James Bevel led more than one thousand children from the Sixteenth Street Baptist Church to the downtown area, where they were met by the police and were loaded into paddy wagons and taken to jail. The next day hundreds of students again assembled at Sixteenth Street Baptist Church, but this time as they attempted to leave, they were attacked by police dogs, and the police fired on them with water hoses. The force of the water was so strong that it knocked the children to the ground. Photographers and cameramen captured the vicious and unrelenting attacks on film, and within days the images had been transmitted around the world. When President Kennedy viewed the police outrages on television, he said it made him "sick."

The president sent Burke Marshall to the city to help negotiate a settlement, and local businessmen and newly elected mayor Albert Boutwell came to an agreement on 10 May that brought a halt to the demonstrations and called for the eventual desegregation of all public facilities. King, SCLC, and ACMHR had every reason to be proud of the agreement; however, segregationists in Birmingham continued their reign of terror, and on 15 September, four black girls were killed when a bomb exploded at the Sixteenth Street Baptist Church. Other bombings occurred in black neighborhoods and at the homes of civil rights activists in September and October, and strong opposition to the desegregation continued to the end of the year. It became clear that it would only be through the passage of the civil rights bill that the president sent to Congress in July 1963 that apartheid would end in Birmingham.

children. Mrs. Evers voiced her preference for the NAACP fund over one established by the Gandhi Society for Human Rights (NYT).

16 In Arlington, Va., Medgar Evers was buried in Arlington National Cemetery. More than twenty-five thousand mourners in two days streamed past his casket at the John Wesley AME Church (NYT).

18 In New York City, National Council of Churches officials called on its thirty-one member denominations to stage nationwide demonstrations against racial discrimination and to join others engaged in nonviolent protests. Officials set up a commission instructed to encourage negotiations, demonstrations, and direct action in places of particular crisis (NYT).

20 In Washington, D.C., President Kennedy sent to Congress a comprehensive bill to guarantee equal rights in public accommodations. The measure would also give the attorney general power to enter cases of voting rights violations, forbid discrimination in state programs receiving federal aid, and outlaw discrimination by labor unions and employment agencies. Kennedy also called for a moratorium on civil rights demonstrations for several months while Congress considered his proposal (NYT).

23 In Dearborn, Mich., three hundred people staged a demonstration rally on the steps of city hall, protesting rigid housing segregation. Although ten thousand African Americans worked in the city, none was allowed to live there (NYT).

23 In Greenwood, Miss., FBI agents arrested Byron de la Beckwith for the murder of Medgar Evers. A former marine and member of the White Citizens Council, he was linked to the murder weapon by a fingerprint left on the rifle scope. (NYT).

23, 28 In Washington, D.C., members of the President's Committee on Equal Opportunity in the Armed Forces in their first report ignored racial discrimination practiced in the National Guard and reserves. African Americans with military service had been excluded from the units in all the southern states. Committee members indicated that they would deal with that problem in a later study (NYT).

24 In Detroit, Mich., Martin Luther King led a Walk for Freedom that protested continued housing segregation. An estimated 125,000 people, mostly African American, participated in the march (NYT).

27 In Chicago, Ill., slain NAACP leader Medgar Evers was posthumously awarded the Spingarn Medal at the annual NAACP convention. Mrs. Myrlie Evers accepted the medal for her slain husband (NYT).

27 In Cleveland, Ohio, a secret summit meeting of thirty-four organizations working on civil rights was held to launch a concerted effort on all forms of racial discrimination in the region. Participating organizations included ministerial groups, labor unions, fraternal clubs, neighborhood councils, the NAACP, and CORE (JM).

28 In Washington, D.C., a Defense Department report revealed that the armed forces had achieved complete integration down to and throughout the reserve units in all parts of the country. However, Alabama, Arkansas, Florida, Georgia, Louisiana, North Carolina, South Carolina, Mississippi, Tennessee, and Virginia had no black National Guardsmen (NYT).

JULY 1963

2 In Powhatan, Va., a U.S. appeals court enjoined school officials from closing schools to avoid integration. The court also ruled that southern localities fighting integration must pay the lawyers hired by black plaintiffs (NYT).

3 In Washington, D.C., air force officials announced that they would discontinue questioning mixed-marriage couples returning from overseas about their racial status. The announcement came after a black airman complained in a letter to Sen. Jacob Javits that he believed the practice was designed to deny privileges to the servicemen (NYT).

4 In Chicago, Ill., Mayor Richard Daley and the National Baptist leader Rev. Joseph Jackson were barred from speaking at the NAACP convention's Freedom Rally. Delegates objected to Daley participating in a program aimed at protesting the housing policies pursued by his administration and objected to Jackson's invitation because of his outspoken opposition to nonviolent civil rights demonstrations (NYT).

5 In Hattiesburg, Miss., Clyde Kennard died. Kennard had been convicted of stealing five sacks of chicken feed after he tried to enroll at Mississippi Southern University. He had been serving a seven-year jail sentence when it was revealed that he had been denied treatment for cancer. He had been released from prison earlier in the year through the appeals of his mother and sister (NYT).

11 In Cleveland, Ohio, the United Freedom Movement announced plans for a peaceful freedom march in the downtown area in support of the civil rights bill. More than thirty civil rights groups, including the NAACP, belonged to the movement (JM).

11 In Columbus, Ohio, Gov. James Rhodes issued a sweeping executive order forbidding any form of racial discrimination by state governmental agencies. Rhodes had just returned from a civil rights conference with President Kennedy (JM).

11 In Columbia, S.C., University of South Carolina officials admitted that they excluded Henri Monteith on the basis of race. Attorney Matthew Perry stated that the school's admission of racial discrimination would help their case for integrating the university (JM).

12, 25 In Durham, N.C., federal judge Edwin Stanley ordered immediate desegregation of the city's elementary and junior high schools. He gave students the opportunity to apply for transfer to any school in the city (NYT).

13 In Baltimore, Md., officials at Johns Hopkins Medical School announced that Robert Gamble was accepted into the program, becoming its first African American student. Duke University Medical School in Durham, N.C., and Emory University Medical School in Atlanta, Ga., also announced that they would be admitting African Americans for the first time (NYT).

13, 18 In Washington, D.C., President Kennedy endorsed the nation's biggest civil rights demonstration, scheduled for 28 August in Washington. Recruitment of participants began in the previous week as pamphlets explaining the march were distributed from the New York City headquarters (NYT).

15 In Chicago, Ill., members of the American Library Association reported that only 24 percent of the library systems in the South were free from racial discrimination. They suggested that many public libraries remained segregated because they had not been targeted by civil rights activists (NYT).

17 In Jackson, Miss., Charles Evers replaced his brother Medgar as NAACP field secretary. He began touring the country to raise money for people arrested in the Mississippi Freedom Movement.

Evers announced plans to ask black entertainers to hold a benefit concert in Mississippi (NYT).

18 In Columbus, Ohio, Gov. James Rhodes signed legislation outlawing segregation in public places licensed by the state. Kentucky governor Bert Combs approved a similar order. Earlier in 1963 Minnesota governor Karl Rolvaag and Indiana governor Matthew Welsh banned employment discrimination by all state agencies (JM).

18 In New York City, six major civil rights organizations formed a temporary coalition called United Civil Rights Leadership. UCRL was formed to better coordinate overlapping civil rights programs and demonstrations. The organizations included were the NAACP, CORE, SCLC, SNCC, the National Council of Negro Women, and the National Urban League (NYT).

24 In Oxford, Miss., the last of five thousand soldiers guarding James Meredith withdrew from their position at the University of Mississippi (NYT).

25 In Chicago, Ill., at the fifty-fourth annual convention of the NAACP, James Meredith was criticized by NAACP youth leader John Davis for making unfounded verbal attacks on the organization's youth leadership. Meredith said that a small percentage of the younger leadership was of "bad quality." Praising Meredith's courage for speaking his mind, NAACP executive director Roy Wilkins defended Meredith's right to criticize youthful leaders (JM).

25 In Washington, D.C., President Kennedy appealed to three hundred women, fifty of them African Americans, to help with the civil rights crisis. It was the largest meeting in a series appealing to groups to help pass civil rights legislation. The group formed a continuing committee, headed by Mildred Horton and Patricia Roberts Harris (JM).

30 In Los Angeles, Calif., National Urban League director Whitney Young, Jr., proposed a "Marshall Plan" to eliminate the economic gaps between black and white citizens. The plan called for the giving of compensatory consideration and preference in employment, education, and housing to African Americans and the poor (NYT).

AUGUST 1963

1 In **Toledo, Ohio,** Judge Arthur Tudor ruled that the city's fair housing ordinance was constitutional. He dismissed a suit seeking to bar enforcement of the ordinance on the grounds that it would interfere with property rights (JM).

1–4 In **Chicago, Ill.,** violence flared up when the family of Reginald Williams rented an apartment in the all-white West Englewood district. Crowds of as many as fifteen hundred pelted the apartment with rocks and broken bottles. Police arrested 227 people during week-long demonstrations (NYT).

5 In **Cleveland, Ohio,** black Baptist leader Rev. Joseph H. Jackson declared his belief that kneel-ins by black demonstrators in southern white churches were un-Christian acts. He stated that demonstrators became anti-religious when they called upon the state to force the integration of churches and other religious institutions (NYT).

7–9 In **Washington, D.C.,** more than six hundred delegates attended the NAACP Legislative Strategy Conference. Those attending had meetings with congressmen and discussed methods to be used in their local areas to support the passage of President Kennedy's civil rights bill (NYT).

8 In **Atlanta, Ga.,** Spelman College officials fired white history professor Dr. Howard Zinn for no stated reason. Zinn believed that the action was based on his active support of civil rights groups, especially SNCC. The American Association of University Professors announced plans to investigate the incident (JM).

8 In **Chicago, Ill.,** speaking before the Coordinating Council of Community Organizations, Dick Gregory urged African Americans to write their congressmen and tell them to vote for the civil rights bill. CORE leader James Farmer and Martin Luther King also spoke out about the importance of African Americans contacting members of Congress (JM).

8 In **Cincinnati, Ohio,** members of the local NAACP launched a campaign to register seventy thousand African Americans by the November elections. Only 40 percent of eligible African

Americans in Hamilton County had been registered to vote (JM).

15 In **Prince Edward County, Va.,** African Americans agreed to a system of private schooling for their children. The program was announced after a U.S. appeals court overruled a decision that Prince Edward's public schools must remain open as long as others in the state operated. The county's black students had been without classes since public schools were closed in 1959 to avoid integration (NYT).

19 In **Oxford, Miss.,** James Meredith graduated from the University of Mississippi. He announced plans to work for the James Meredith Education Fund for underprivileged children before entering graduate school. Meanwhile, James Hood dropped out of the University of Alabama, suffering from mental and physical exhaustion (NYT).

20 In **Plaquemine, La.,** groups of black adults and children, including CORE director James Farmer, were arrested and jailed for participating in anti-segregation demonstrations. A federal judge signed an injunction prohibiting further demonstrations (NYT).

28 In **Accra, Ghana,** scholar and pioneer civil rights activist W. E. B. Du Bois died on the eve of the March on Washington. Du Bois was a founder of the NAACP and the first African American elected to the National Institute of Arts and Letters. At the march both Martin Luther King and A. Philip Randolph paid tribute to Du Bois and mourned his passing (NYT).

29 In **Chicago, Ill.,** the Andrew Thomas family charged that a clerk at the Chicago Beach Hotel refused to accommodate them solely because of their race. They filed suit under the state's new public accommodations law, which forbids racial discrimination in hotels (JM).

29 In **Seattle, Wash.,** demonstrators protesting alleged racial bias in the city staged a week-long sit-in at the city council chamber. Angry councilmen had the group of protesters arrested (JM).

29 In **Washington, D.C.,** more than two hundred thousand people participated in the March on

Washington for Jobs and Freedom. One of the major objectives of the march was to lobby Congress for the passage of President Kennedy's civil rights bill. Throughout the day prominent black leaders delivered speeches at the Lincoln Memorial. One of the highlights of this event was King's "I Have a Dream" speech. Although army troops, marines, and local police were mobilized in anticipation of violence resulting from the march, the event was peaceful (NYT).

31 In Washington, D.C., federal housing officials announced the withdrawal of all federal mortgage guarantees from House and Home Ltd. An Orlando, Fla., company operated by Norman A. Rossman had refused to sell a home to a black customer, David Johnson. The action marked the first time federal agencies invoked President Kennedy's order that prohibited federal assistance to segregated housing developments (NYT).

SEPTEMBER 1963

1 In Memphis, Tenn., members of the board of education proceeded with plans to extend the school day at three black schools to ease overcrowding. Local NAACP members protested the move, stating that the only answer to overcrowding was public school desegregation. NAACP leaders later led a protest march of four hundred people opposed to the board's plan (NYT).

1, 3, 4, 8 In Folcroft, Pa., a white mob rioted after Mr. and Mrs. Horace Baker moved into an all-white housing development. The mob smashed the windows of the home and attacked black police officers who arrived to keep the peace (NYT).

4 In Savannah, Ga., nineteen demonstrators, who had been in jail for fifty-five days for lack of $1,200 bonds, were released after they signed statements repudiating violence for social change. Hosea Williams, president of the Chatham County Crusade for Voters, later said he regretted advising the demonstrators to sign the statements (NYT).

5 In Little Rock, Ark., six-year-old Steven Fitts (white) enrolled at the all-black McAlmont Elementary School. His mother Yvonne Fitts announced he would continue attending the school,

despite smashed windows and threats against her life (NYT).

5 In Washington, D.C., a special group appointed by President Kennedy and headed by attorney Gerhard Gesell documented the many problems still facing black servicemen on southern military bases and in nearby communities. The Gesell Report recommended placing off-limits those communities that persisted in discriminating, and advocated closing and transferring many of the bases from the rigidly segregated areas (JM).

6 In Birmingham, Tuskegee, Huntsville, and Mobile, Ala., Gov. George Wallace attempted to prevent integration of public schools. Federalized National Guardsmen replaced Wallace's state troopers and ensured that integration would take place. Many white citizens accepted integration and turned against Wallace when he closed public schools for a week (NYT).

10, 11 In Northport, Ala., three Ghanaian youths, Emmanuel Bansa, Roland Glover, and Stephen Goli, were dragged from their car and flogged by a band of white men. Rev. Walter Trost and white student James Glover were accompanying the youths. State Department officials hurriedly apologized to Ghana's ambassador to the United States (NYT).

12 In Chicago, Ill., members of the city council approved a revised fair housing ordinance while four thousand white demonstrators marched around city hall in protest. The bill provided for the suspension of licenses of real estate brokers who discriminated in the sale, rental, or lease of private homes (NYT).

13 In Chicago, Ill., two thousand people picketed the office of Illinois senator Everett Dirksen. The demonstration, organized by SNCC, was meant to protest Dirksen's opposition to the Title II (public accommodations) section of President Kennedy's civil rights bill (NYT).

16 In Anniston, Ala., Rev. William McClain was beaten when he tried to enter the public library. The following day, McClain returned with another minister, a city commissioner, two library board

SNCC WORKERS AND VOTER REGISTRATION CAMPAIGNS IN THE SOUTH

At the March on Washington on 28 August 1963, Roy Wilkins, A. Philip Randolph, and Whitney Young prevented SNCC chairman John Lewis from denouncing in his speech the federal government's failure to protect civil rights workers in the South. In October 1962 as a result of the SNCC, NAACP, and Council of Federated Organizations (COFO) voter registration campaign in Leflore County, Miss., local officials decided not to distribute the federal government's surplus food or welfare assistance to those in need as the winter approached. SNCC and COFO workers sent out a call for food and other commodities, and a food airlift was organized with the help of the "Friends of SNCC" around the country.

In January 1963 Michigan State students Ivanhoe Donaldson and Benjamin Taylor were arrested in Clarksdale, Miss., after they arrived with a truckload of food, clothing, and medicine for black families. Local police claimed that the shipment included narcotics donated by doctors. Charges against the students were later dropped when a local grand jury refused to indict them. By the end of February, SNCC and COFO had distributed food and supplies to more than twenty-two thousand African Americans across the state.

In March in Greenwood, Miss., racial violence erupted throughout the city. Incidents included the burning of the SNCC office and several other houses, the jailing of student leader Samuel Block, and the midnight shooting of voter education workers Jimmy Travis and two others. The NAACP, SNCC, SCLC, and other groups appealed to the Justice Department for protection, but nothing was done.

In March 1963 SNCC director James Forman announced the beginning of Operation MOM, an all-out "Move on Mississippi," and asked for federal protection for the campaign. In Meridian, Miss., local NAACP leader C. R. Darden requested federal marshals to protect black citizens attempting to vote and wired Attorney General Robert Kennedy that "all decent Americans who believe in law and order are shocked by these brutal attacks of shootings, with intent to kill." It was only after Rev. D. L. Tucker was bitten by a police dog after he attempted to register and eight voter registration workers were jailed that the Justice Department filed suit in federal court to stop city and county officials from interfering with African Americans' right to register to vote.

Rep. Charles Diggs narrowly escaped injury from a Molotov cocktail thrown through the window of NAACP leader Aaron Henry's home during a fact-finding visit in Leflore County in May 1963. Diggs echoed the earlier calls for federal intervention. However, the violence continued in June 1963 with the bombing of a black church and the arrest of fifty-eight African Americans attending a SNCC voter registration clinic in Itta Bena, Miss. Later that month in Canton, Miss., five black residents were fired upon by a white man as they stood in a voter registration line. And the entire nation was shocked by the murder of NAACP leader Medgar Evers on 21 June 1963 in front of his home in Jackson, Miss. SNCC's Bob Moses believed a "racial murder ring" was operating in the state and pointed out that in addition to Medgar Evers, four other African Americans had been murdered, and five had been shot that year. Before the end of 1963, SNCC workers in Albany and Americus, Ga.; Selma and Attalla, Ala.; as well as Leflore and Sunflower Counties, Miss., were victims of violent attacks because of their voter registration activities. They had received little or no protection from the federal government.

---

members, and the chairman of the local human relations council. He and the other black minister checked out two books while policemen stood guard (NYT).

17, 26 In **Misawa Air Force Base, Japan,** four hundred airmen conducted a mass sit-in to protest segregation at bars around the base. Following the demonstration, military authorities threatened to place off-limits all businesses refusing to serve African Americans (NYT).

20 In **St. Francisville, La.,** Rev. Joseph Carter filed a $100,000 suit under the Civil Rights Act of 1960 against Sheriff William Percy and Fletcher Harvey, registrar of voters. Rev. Carter charged that he was arrested for disturbing the peace when he and Rev. Rudolph Davis went to the voter registration office to register (NYT).

24 In Oxford, Miss., NAACP official Charles Evers blamed the Justice Department for the expulsion of law school student Cleve McDowell from the University of Mississippi. He was expelled for carrying a gun on campus. Evers argued that the government refused to provide one marshal for McDowell's protection off campus (NYT).

26 In Chicago, Ill., National Urban League and NAACP leaders charged the housing authority with segregating homes for the aged. They claimed that public institutions accepted only applicants living nearby and that none of the public housing for the aged was located in black neighborhoods (JM).

26 In Plaquemine, La., 68 of the 230 jailed anti-segregation demonstrators were released because of the shortage of jail facilities. CORE official James Farmer was released on $300 bond after he surrendered to authorities on charges of disorderly conduct (JM).

OCTOBER 1963

2 In Orangeburg, S.C., more than one thousand demonstrators were arrested while protesting discrimination and segregation in the city. They marched through the business district and gathered in front of establishments that segregated African Americans (NYT).

3 In Lansing, Mich., Gov. George Romney appointed Damon Keith and John Feikens to chair a new civil rights commission. The commission was organized to deal with employment problems normally tackled by the state fair employment practices commission. It was also created to operate in the fields of housing, education, public accommodation, and other areas (JM).

9 In Orangeburg, S.C., NAACP pickets ringed all seven black schools, and teachers turned students away. Students later marched downtown to protest the firing of third-grade teacher Gloria Rackley, who was dismissed for participating in anti-segregation demonstrations (NYT).

10 In Greenville, S.C., after a vote by the board of trustees, Furman University became the first white college in South Carolina to agree to integrate its student body voluntarily. Clemson and the University of South Carolina admitted African Americans under court orders (NYT).

14 In Washington, D.C., Attorney General Robert Kennedy urged the House Judiciary Committee working on the civil rights bill to curtail the scope of the accommodations section, knock out protections for African Americans voting in state and local elections, and restrict the power of the Justice Department to probe only cases dealing with school desegregation. Although criticized by NAACP leader Clarence Mitchell, Kennedy believed that these compromises were needed in order to get the bill moving again (NYT).

15, 30 In Jackson, Miss., state NAACP president Aaron Henry announced he would run for governor in a mock election designed to dramatize the fact that unregistered African Americans would vote if they were allowed. He said he hoped to mobilize at least 150,000 African Americans at the mock polls (NYT).

17 In Atlanta, Ga., seven African Americans filed suit in district court contending that they were denied use of state-owned facilities at Jekyll Island. Gov. Carl Sanders stated that he did not understand "what all the ruckus is about," because part of the island was specifically set aside for African Americans (JM).

17 In Huntsville, Ala., seven major motels and the largest hotel agreed to accept African American guests. Previously, golf courses, elementary schools, and the University of Alabama extension center had desegregated (JM).

17 In Maplesville, Ala., Thelton Henderson (black) was arrested for speeding and was rapped on the knuckles with a nightstick when he refused to call the arresting officer "sir." He was released only after he showed credentials identifying himself as an attorney in the Civil Rights Section of the Justice Department (JM).

17 In **Savannah, Ga.**, although African Americans successfully integrated hotels after four months of protests, trials continued to go on for the eight hundred people arrested. Convictions brought hundred-dollar fines and two-month sentences for each arrest (JM).

18 In **West Feliciana Parish, La.**, CORE members led a voter registration drive. African Americans who attempted to vote were beaten and threatened with death. As Joe Brown waited to take his voter registration test, his house was burned down. After Justice Department officials received 750 complaints from the area, they asked the federal court to restrain registrar Fletcher Harvey from making "unnecessary complications" for black applicants to register to vote (NYT).

19 In **Atlanta, Ga.**, CORE officials appeared before the U.S. appeals court to overturn a Louisiana court order barring the group from staging civil rights demonstrations anywhere in the state. If the Louisiana court decision was upheld, other states could use the same technique to restrict the activities of civil rights organizations (NYT).

24 In **Augusta, Ga.**, city officials operated the polls on an integrated basis during city elections for the first time in the city's history. Two of the five mayoral candidates also had black poll workers on hand (JM).

24 In **Dade County, Fla.**, a recent voter registration campaign registered 5,549 African Americans in two weeks. Churches, civic groups, schools, and fraternal organizations assisted in the registration campaign (JM).

NOVEMBER 1963

2 In **Richmond, Va.**, the U.S. Fourth Court of Appeals ruled that two hospitals in Greensboro, N.C., receiving federal aid must admit patients and employ staff physicians without regard to race. The ruling struck down the "separate but equal" clause of the Hill-Burton Hospital Act (NYT).

7 In **Chicago, Ill.**, the wives of black Chicago Bears players were not invited to a luncheon and fashion show hosted by Mrs. George Halas, wife of the team's owner. All of the wives of the white players were invited, but the eight black wives did not find out about the affair until they read about it in the newspaper. Halas denied making up the invitation list (JM).

14 In **Detroit, Mich.**, Rev. C. L. Franklin called the first meeting of the Northern Negro Leadership Conference, which included most of the leading names in the nationwide civil rights struggle. Franklin announced plans to eventually merge the conference with the SCLC and create a national civil rights organization (JM).

14 In **Washington, D.C.**, Rep. Adam Clayton Powell met with representatives of forty-five national black organizations. He urged that heads of the National Association of Colored Women's Clubs and the National Council of Negro Women be included in the civil rights leadership elite. Powell argued that the NAACP, SCLC, SNCC, CORE, National Urban League, and the Negro American Labor Council needed the women's organizations in order to reach more people (JM).

14 In **White Castle, La.**, Joan Bunche, daughter of UN undersecretary Ralph Bunche, volunteered her services to CORE. She planned to remain with the organization in Louisiana until the voter registration drive was completed (JM).

14, 15, 18 In **Chester, Pa.**, members of the Committee for Freedom Now picketed the all-black Franklin Elementary School and caused it to close. The school was planned for five hundred pupils, but served twelve hundred pupils and was falling into disrepair (NYT).

16, 18 In **Williamston, N.C.**, fifteen white ministers from Massachusetts were among sixty-one people arrested during a civil rights march. The clergymen stated that they had come to the South to participate in civil rights protests at the request of Martin Luther King (NYT).

19 In **Gadsden, Ala.**, twelve African Americans filed a federal court suit to desegregate the city's

CIVIL RIGHTS PROTESTS GRIP THE NATION

While the "Battle of Birmingham" received the greatest amount of news media attention nationally and internationally in 1963, sit-ins, marches, and other demonstrations to protest racial segregation continued throughout the United States. Beginning in February 1963 black students from Arkansas A&M College launched sit-ins in nearby Pine Bluff at lunch counters in Woolworth and Walgreens stores to protest discriminatory practices. Even though many students were expelled, the boycotts and protests spread to other stores, movie theaters, hotels, and other public accommodations in the city, and in May 1963 store owners finally agreed to end segregation and other discriminatory practices.

Sit-ins and other demonstrations organized by students at Hampton Institute in Hampton, Va., Antioch College in Yellow Springs, Ohio, and Morehouse College in Atlanta, Ga., in May 1963, and Prairie View College in Hempstead, Tex., in November resulted in the end of discriminatory practices in local public accommodations.

In Knoxville and Clarksville, Tenn.; Lexington, N.C.; St. Louis, Mo.; and New Orleans, La., black and white students participated in ongoing protest campaigns organized by local civil rights organizations. In Sacramento, Calif., student CORE members, who conducted a sit-in at the state capitol to protest the delay in enacting a state fair housing bill, were joined on the picket lines by several celebrities, including Marlon Brando, Paul Newman, and Joanne Woodward. In Gary, Ind., after a proposed ordinance banning hospital segregation failed in city council, the NAACP Youth Council launched picket lines around Methodist Hospital, while NAACP officials entered into negotiations with hospital administrators. As a result of the protests, hospital officials agreed to end the practice of identifying patients and assigning hospital beds on the basis of race.

In May 1963 the mass arrests of Gloria Richardson and members of the Cambridge (Md.) Nonviolent Action Committee (CNAC) trying to integrate the Dizzyland Restaurant triggered a series of marches, demonstrations, and violent confrontations that culminated in the calling out of the Maryland National Guard and imposition of martial law on 13 June 1963. On the day the National Guard left Cambridge, 8 July 1963, another violent confrontation occurred at Dizzyland Restaurant, and within days the National Guard returned. Through the intervention of Attorney General Robert Kennedy negotiations between CNAC and city officials were conducted and an agreement was reached on 22 July 1963 calling for the desegregation of public schools and hospitals. The provision calling for desegregation of all public accommodations in Cambridge was later overturned by a citywide referendum. In September 1963, the local public schools and hospitals were desegregated, and the U.S. Commission on Civil Rights subsequently issued a report vindicating black protesters and criticizing state and local officials and private industry for the depressed economic conditions of African Americans on Maryland's Eastern Shore.

public schools. In September, schools in Birmingham, Mobile, and Tuskegee were integrated under court orders (NYT).

21 In New Orleans, La., the U.S. Fifth Circuit Court of Appeals ordered a district court to hear Sybil Morial's suit challenging the state law prohibiting educators from joining groups advocating integration. She was a public school teacher and the wife of the city NAACP leader Ernest Morial (JM).

21 In St. Augustine, Fla., members of the Florida Advisory Committee to the U.S. Commission on Civil Rights named the city as having the worst racial conditions in the state. Despite increasing racial tensions and violence, white city officials refused to meet with civil rights leaders to discuss the situation (JM).

22 In Dallas, Tex., President Kennedy was assassinated while riding in a motorcade with his wife Jackie and two others. Texas governor John Connally was wounded by the assassin's bullets. Vice President Lyndon Johnson was given the oath of office and pledged to follow through on the programs of the martyred president (NYT).

23 In Atlanta, Ga., members of the aldermanic board adopted a resolution urging that immediate consideration be given to voluntary desegregation of public accommodations in the city. However, the resolution was a suggestion and did not have the force of a law (NYT).

28 In Atlanta, Ga., Martin Luther King questioned the city's "liberal" reputation toward integration and race relations. He stated that the majority of hotels still refused to admit African Americans and that half of the restaurants that desegregated the previous summer no longer served black customers (JM).

28 In Atlanta, Ga., Ralph David Abernathy announced that SCLC used 35 percent of its 1963 budget for bail bonds in Alabama, Georgia, and Mississippi. Over the year, the group took in $735,534, the largest portion coming from letters of appeal and freedom rallies (JM).

28 In Pine Bluff, Ark., civil rights leader William Hansen (white), who married Ruth Buffington (black), announced that they planned to remain in the state despite possible harassment. Arkansas attorney general Bruce Bennett had condemned the marriage as a "deliberate insult and disservice" to the people of the state (JM).

28 In Washington, D.C., the nation's top civil rights leaders issued a public statement pledging their support to President Johnson and said they were ready to work with the president to achieve President Kennedy's goal of equality for all. Those leaders who signed the pledge were Roy Wilkins, Whitney Young, James Forman, James Farmer, Martin Luther King, Dorothy Height, and Jack Greenberg. Johnson had personally called several civil rights leaders to ask their support in the coming months (NYT).

DECEMBER 1963

2 In Folcroft, Pa., Horace Baker, who moved his family into a previously all-white area, was committed to a mental institution. A spokesperson attributed his mental condition to a "conspiracy of harassment and terrorism" by his white neighbors (NYT).

2, 3 In Washington, D.C., President Johnson called civil rights leaders to the White House for a private meeting. Those in attendance included Martin Luther King, Roy Wilkins, John Lewis, James Forman, and A. Philip Randolph. Johnson invited them to send memos back to the White House to fully explain their more important projects and how he could assist them (NYT).

3 In Richmond, Va., the state supreme court outlawed attempts by a legislative investigating committee to secure the lists of donors to the Virginia NAACP (NYT).

5 In Atlanta, Ga., Sierra Leone political leader Abu Magba Kamara, a State Department escort, and two black companions were cursed and ejected from a restaurant that refused to serve them because of their race. Kamara had made the trip South to see firsthand how African Americans were treated (JM).

5 In Savannah, Ga., NAACP officials vowed to appeal a court decision awarding $85,793 to a white grocer boycotted by African American customers. The NAACP boycott of Buck's Tropical Market began when the owner allegedly beat a fourteen-year-old black employee (JM).

11 In St. Joseph, Mo., a public accommodations ordinance barring racial discrimination in hotels, motels, restaurants, and places of entertainment was approved in a special election. Members of the city council had passed the measure the previous summer (NYT).

26 In Washington, D.C., Dr. Rosa Gragg and Dorothy Height met with President Johnson and asked him to include black women in administrative and policy-making posts. They promised to work through the National Association of Colored Women's Clubs and the National Council of Negro Women to increase black voter registration and to send petitions to Congress urging the passage of the civil rights bill (JM).

On 31 August 1964, rioting erupted in Philadelphia, Pa., after the police arrested a black woman at a traffic intersection. Stores in black neighborhoods owned by whites were looted, and the police were ordered not to shoot looters. As a result, there were no riot deaths in Philadelphia during three days of violence, although hundreds were injured. Investigators later revealed that the major cause of the rioting was police brutality. (SOURCE: JACK FRANKLIN COLLECTION, AFRICAN AMERICAN MUSEUM IN PHILADELPHIA)

1964

"FREE AT LAST?"

This was a year of contrasts. The low points included the disappearance and murder of the three civil rights workers in Philadelphia, Miss., the violent attacks on civil rights protesters in St. Augustine, Fla., and the rioting and destruction that occurred in several American cities during the summer of 1964. The high points included the passage of the Civil Rights Act, which brought about the end of legal segregation in public accommodations; the awarding of the Nobel Peace Prize to Martin Luther King, Jr., and the smashing defeat of Sen. Barry Goldwater in the presidential election. In 1964 there was good reason for African Americans to sing, "Free at Last, Free at Last!" but conspicuous in its absence from the civil rights legislation was any guarantee of nondiscrimination in voting rights. The testimony of Fannie Lou Hamer and other Mississippi Freedom Democratic Party delegates before the Platform Committee at the Democratic convention made it undeniably clear to all who watched and listened that there was still much unfinished business on the civil rights agenda in 1964.

1 In Auburn, Ala., the Fifth Circuit Court of Appeals upheld a lower-court ruling that Auburn University must enroll black student Harold Franklin in its graduate school. The school had rejected his application because he graduated from Alabama State College, an unaccredited college (SSN).

2 In Berkeley, Calif., city officials opened public debate on a plan for reducing racial segregation in city schools. The plan resulted from a thirty-three-member citizens committee appointed to study de facto segregation and offer recommendations. Recommendations in the plan included education programs to bring black schools up to citywide standards and redrawing school boundaries to promote integration (JM).

2 In New York City, NAACP counsel Constance Baker Motley announced that the NAACP Legal Defense Fund handled more than 90 percent of the nation's civil rights cases. During 1963, the organization gave legal and financial assistance to 10,485 people arrested for participation in anti-segregation demonstrations. In addition, the Legal Defense Fund aided an undetermined number of people in school, hospital, and other public accommodations cases (JM).

3 In Folcroft, Pa., the state human relations commission filed suit against fifteen residents, charging them with "unlawful, and malicious, and evil conspiracy" against the Horace Bakers. The Bakers had moved into a previously all-white suburb. The suit charged the accused people with urging a boycott among businesses against the Bakers, starting a campaign of telephone calls and threatening letters, distributing leaflets about the family, instituting a "freedom march," and blocking the Baker driveway (NYT).

4, 5 In Philadelphia, Pa., Mayor Richardson Dilworth declared that the recent controversy that resulted in the banning of blackface from the city's traditional Mummer's Parade set the black community back ten years. He called black leaders "demagogues" and stated that the time had come for the African American to stop feeling sorry for himself. He made the remarks while addressing a Chamber of Commerce seminar. Black city registration commissioner Harvey Schmidt countered by stating that African Americans intended to enhance and advance "creative comprehension" within every area of community life (NYT).

7 In New York City, NAACP officials announced that membership in the organization increased by 100,000 in 1963. The total membership in the NAACP was 515,396 (NYT).

9 In Washington, D.C., President Johnson delivered his State of the Union address. In it, he called for the abolition of racial discrimination and increased opportunities in employment, education, and housing for all races. He also urged Congress to pass the pending civil rights bill (NYT).

16 In Washington, D.C., CORE officials launched a test of a new fair housing law approved by the board of commissioners. The new regulations prohibited racial discrimination in the sale or rental of most private housing. CORE sent black house hunters and renters to make the first bids, and then sent whites after them to see if both were treated in the same fashion (JM).

17, 26 In Atlanta, Ga., comedian Dick Gregory and SNCC officials led demonstrations through the downtown area to protest segregation in restaurants, hotels, and other public facilities, and to pressure the City Council to pass a public accommodations ordinance. Gregory and the SNCC

officials organized the event to coincide with the visit of the United Nations Commission on Prevention of Discrimination and Protection of Minorities, which chose Atlanta as the site for assessing the treatment of minorities in southern cities. Members of the commission were impressed with the demonstrations (NYT).

22, 23 In Washington, D.C., President Johnson appointed Carl Rowan, an African American, director of the U.S. Information Agency, replacing Edward Murrow. Rowan had previously served as deputy assistant secretary of state under President Kennedy (NYT).

23 In Jennings, Mo., the David Thompson family tentatively returned to their home in an all-white residential area. Whites had thrown bricks through their windows and made threatening telephone calls to the family. Local NAACP leader Morris Henderson accused the police of tolerating teenage "hooliganism" (JM).

23 In Washington, D.C., managers of the A&P supermarket chain announced that they would place black employees in all fifteen Seattle-area stores. The announcement followed negotiations between management and CORE officials (JM).

28–31 In Jackson, Miss., Byron de la Beckwith went on trial before an all-white jury for the murder of Medgar Evers. District Attorney Bill Waller sought the death penalty for Beckwith. However, within days a mistrial was declared (NYT).

30 In Baltimore, Md., officials of the city's four Catholic hospitals—St. Agnes, St. Joseph, Bon Secours, and Mercy—announced they would admit all patients regardless of race. Their decision followed a directive from Archbishop Lawrence J. Shehan banning racial discrimination in all Catholic institutions (JM).

30 In Cleveland, Ohio, one hundred people from CORE, the local United Freedom Movement, and a local parents' association picketed the Hazeldell Elementary School. They called for the transfer of black pupils from overcrowded schools to white schools. At least one minister involved in the protest was attacked and a newspaper photographer was thrown to the ground (NYT).

VIOLENCE ERUPTS IN ST. AUGUSTINE, FLA.

Following the 1963 March on Washington, the SCLC evaluated a number of cities before choosing St. Augustine, Fla., as the next site for anti-segregation protests. In November 1963 members of the Florida Advisory Committee to the U.S. Commission on Civil Rights cited the city as having the worst racial conditions in the state. Despite increasing racial tensions and limited rioting, white officials refused to meet with civil rights leaders to discuss the situation. The committee report was in part a response to an all-white jury's acquittal of four KKK members who were accused of viciously beating NAACP members Dr. Robert Hayling, James Hauser, Clyde Jenkins, and James Jenkins, four blacks who were dragged from their car by Klansmen and beaten with chains, lug wrenches, and ax handles. Days after the release of the Klansmen, Dr. Hayling was convicted and fined on assault charges. Hayling was later forced to move his family out of the city after his home was riddled with gunfire.

In late March 1964, SCLC leader Rev. Wyatt T. Walker arrived to determine if more resources from SCLC were needed to break the segregationist stronghold. More than three hundred people had been arrested during demonstrations and attempts to integrate restaurants. Meanwhile, Dr. Hayling went to Washington to confer with Justice Department official Burke Marshall about the violence in the city.

In June, in Jacksonville, Fla., the U.S. district court was asked to prohibit segregation at Flagler Hospital in St. Augustine. Dr. Hayling argued that the hospital came under the court's jurisdiction because it received $629,546 in federal funds under the Hill-Burton Act. At the beginning of the second week in June, Martin Luther King and Ralph David Abernathy were jailed. Abernathy stated that they came to the city because demonstrations were getting out of hand and people had begun to use violence. King appealed to President Johnson to send U.S. Marshals and U.S. attorneys into the area. Johnson responded that the White House was giving special attention to the conflict. Florida governor Farris Bryant took command of troops in the area, and local merchants pledged to obey federal civil rights laws. King said talks were blocked because of city officials' insistence that Dr. Hayling not be a member of the biracial negotiating team.

In late June 1964, state police brought weapons allegedly collected during racial strife in St. Augustine to a Jacksonville federal court. Governor Bryant claimed that the weapons backed his decision to ban nighttime protests and argued that he should not be held in contempt of court for disobeying a judge's order lifting such a ban. Surrounded by angry mobs of white segregationists, protesters continued the daily demonstrations. King called for federal intervention to end the violence. In August, federal district judge Bryan Simpson ordered seventeen restaurants and motels to desegregate. He also forbade a group of militant racists, including Holstead Manucy and the Ancient City Gun Club, from molesting, threatening, intimidating, or coercing African Americans or the business owners. African Americans had charged the business owners with resegregating after pressure was exerted by racists. In October 1964 Judge Bryan Simpson jailed Manucy and a Mr. Goodwin when they refused to submit the names of club members. The club was enjoined from further interference in peaceful integration in the city. Manucy and Goodwin produced 174 names after they were jailed.

30 In Washington, D.C., NAACP attorney Norman Amaker asked the Supreme Court to accept the appeal of CORE member Mary Hamilton, who had been found in contempt of court when she refused to answer questions put to her by a Gadsden, Ala., trial solicitor who insisted on calling her "Mary" rather than "Miss Hamilton" (NYT).

31 In Washington, D.C., members of the House Rules Committee cleared the civil rights bill for debate. Roy Wilkins, chairman of the Leadership Conference on Civil Rights, called on hundreds of representatives from organizations, unions, and religious groups to travel to Washington. The representatives were assigned to individual congressmen and were responsible for contacting them every day until the bill was passed. The House committee passed the bill two weeks later (NYT).

FEBRUARY 1964

1 In New Orleans, La., the U.S. Fifth Circuit Court ordered U.S. district court judge Sidney Mize to hear school integration suits filed by Mrs. Myrlie Evers and other parents in Leske County, Biloxi, and Jackson, Miss. The district court had refused to hear the cases on the grounds that the parents had not exhausted all of their administrative remedies (SSN).

1 In Tuskegee, Ala., school board members closed Tuskegee High School, where only twelve black students remained after all white students transferred following desegregation. The decision was reached after the board met with Gov. George Wallace, who opposed the desegregation (SSN).

1 In New Orleans, La., white schoolteacher Virginia Cox Welch filed suit in federal district court seeking permission to enroll in a course at the all-black local branch of Southern University. The action also sought to enjoin state school officials in New Orleans from preparing legislation that would limit attendance at the school to African Americans (SSN).

2 In Gloster, Miss., civil rights worker Lewis Allen was shot outside his home. Allen was a key witness in the earlier slaying of NAACP voter registration worker Herbert Lee (NYT).

4 In New York City, African Americans and Puerto Ricans kept their children out of school in a one-day protest against racial imbalance in public schools. More than five thousand students and adults marched on Gov. Nelson Rockefeller's Manhattan office, city hall, and the board of education building (NYT).

5 In Cleveland, Ohio, after protests by African Americans, members of the school board announced complete integration in city schools. Previously, black children were transferred from overcrowded schools to white schools, but were kept in separate classrooms (NYT).

6 In Asheville, N.C., an anonymous caller warned of a bomb planted on Martin Luther King's plane. Authorities searched the plane and found nothing. It was the latest in a series of threats against the civil rights leader (JM).

6 In Clarksdale, Miss., NAACP official Aaron Henry voiced his opposition to plans for a recreational center for African Americans. He stated that since African Americans were fighting for integration not segregation, they did not want separate facilities from whites (NYT).

6 In Clinton, La., officials of the Civil Service Commission ordered the Villa Feliciana Geriatrics Hospital to reinstate Currie Collins. He had been fired from his job as a food service worker after he was arrested for picketing segregated cafes (JM).

6 In Hot Springs, Ark., president of the National Baptist Convention Rev. James H. Jackson told church delegates that African Americans should keep their struggle for civil rights within the framework of law and order or anarchy would result. SNCC officials John Lewis and James Forman responded to his comments by stating that unjust laws had to be destroyed before African Americans could become full citizens. They also said that "creative chaos" was necessary to bring about a new order (JM).

6 In Washington, D.C., Justice Department officials announced that at least 633 racial protests had occurred in southern and border states during the previous four years. They also quoted the Southern Regional Council as reporting that 20,083 people had been arrested in the South for demonstrating for civil rights (JM).

6 In Washington, D.C., Commerce Secretary Luther Hodges created a task force to improve employment opportunities, including recruitment, training, and promotion for members of minority groups in the Commerce Department and in industry. The task force was also urged to improve prospects for businesses owned and operated by members of minority groups (JM).

12 In Cincinnati, Ohio, students boycotted thirty-five public schools to protest racial discrimination. "Freedom Schools" were set up for the day to educate the children (NYT).

13 In Cincinnati, Ohio, Richard Nixon delivered a Lincoln Day speech. In the speech, he criticized the "irresponsible tactics" of some civil rights leaders. He also stated that the encouragement of disrespect for law through mass demonstrations, boycotts, and violations of property rights hurt civil rights in the long run (NYT).

16 In Warren, Ohio, two firebombs were hurled through the window of the W. Robert Smalls home. The local Urban League official and his family escaped injury. They had been living in an all-white neighborhood for one month (NYT).

20 In Lansing, Mich., members of the state civil rights commission ordered the Farm Bureau Mutual Insurance Company to cease its discriminatory practices and offer employment to Mrs. Candis Lindsey. Lindsey had charged that her employment application was rejected while less qualified white clerk-typists were hired by the company (JM).

20 In Lawtey, Fla., city council member Robert Scott resigned from office after only three weeks. Scott stated that he feared for his life after receiving numerous telephone threats. He was the first African American to be elected to a two-year term on the city council (JM).

20 In Washington, D.C., Rep. Charles Diggs launched an investigation into alleged discrimination in housing, recreational facilities, and promotional opportunities at Patuxent River Naval Air Station. He had received twelve complaints of racially discriminatory practices at the station in one month (JM).

23–25, 27–29 In Princess Anne, Md., state troopers used snarling dogs to disperse civil rights protesters. Most of the demonstrators were Maryland State College students protesting segregation in public accommodations. Student protestors called on Cambridge, Md., civil rights leader Gloria Richardson to assist in the demonstrations (NYT).

26 In Chicago, Ill., 172,350 students boycotted public schools in order to protest de facto segregation. The protest was organized by members of the Coordinating Council of Community Organizations. Black councilmen Kenneth Campbell and Claude Holman attempted to organize a strong anti-boycott campaign, but failed to get student participation. In Boston, more than 100,000 students boycotted schools to protest segregation. Some of the students attended Freedom Schools and learned black history and citizenship (NYT).

26 In Pine Bluff, Ark., comedian Dick Gregory was sentenced to six months in jail and fined five hundred dollars for entering an all-white restaurant. Gregory stated that he had thought it was a black establishment and did not intend to integrate it. He appealed the sentence (NYT).

27 In Detroit, Mich., Rep. Charles Diggs and state senate candidate James Del Rio joined NAACP pickets outside of the First Federal Savings and Loan Association. They decided to participate after the Cotillion Club of business and professional men voted to join the demonstrations protesting discriminatory loan practices (JM).

27 In San Francisco, Calif., Haspina and Kostas Paxinos, owners of an apartment house, were found guilty of discriminating against Doris Thomas because of her race. She was refused rental of an apartment five minutes after a white CORE member had been told it was available (JM).

27 In St. Louis, Mo., Alderman William Clay was sentenced to nine months in jail for defying a contempt of court order by leading pickets against the Jefferson Bank and Trust Co. He was among demonstrators protesting discriminatory hiring practices at the bank (JM).

MARCH 1964

3 In St. Louis, Mo., following their release from jail, five of fifteen anti-segregation demonstrators returned to a six-month-old picket line in front of the Jefferson Bank and Trust Co. Alderman William Clay continued to protest the bank's employment policy from jail (NYT).

3 In Washington, D.C., the U.S. Supreme Court refused to overrule an anti-segregation order against two hospitals in Greensboro, N.C. It upheld a lower-court ruling barring hospitals that discriminated in physician hiring or patient registration from receiving construction funds under the Hill-Burton Act (NYT).

5 In Jackson, Miss., a self-styled black vigilante force was formed to protect Mrs. Medgar Evers and her children. The group was assembled after four carloads of whites were seen circling the Evers home. Police chief M. B. Pierce assured black leaders that patrol protection would be provided for the Evers family and the other seventeen plaintiffs in a statewide school integration suit (JM).

5 In Jackson, Miss., NAACP attorneys won a preliminary injunction from a judge calling for school desegregation in Jackson, Biloxi, and Leake County. Mississippi was the only remaining state with total public school segregation (NYT).

5 In Nashville, Tenn., NAACP official Charles Evers stated that he feared the day was near when Mississippi African Americans would have to abandon nonviolence as a tactic and resort to force to gain equal rights. He addressed his remarks to a local NAACP chapter (JM).

10 In Houston, Tex., district judge William Holland ruled that the trustees of Rice University could integrate the school. The founder of the school had stipulated that the school remain all white (NYT).

10 In Washington, D.C., the U.S. Supreme Court overruled a $500,000 libel judgment against the Revs. Fred Shuttlesworth, Ralph Abernathy, J. E. Lowery, and S. S. Seay. Montgomery police commissioner L. B. Sullivan had charged the ministers with making "defamatory falsehoods" about his official conduct in a *New York Times* advertisement. The court ruled that Sullivan neglected to prove "actual malice" and "reckless disregard" (NYT).

12 In Pittsburgh, Pa., members of the school board announced that they would pursue a policy of "conscious preferment" in hiring black employees, including teachers. They stated that the measure was initiated to make amends for past racial discrimination (JM).

12 In San Francisco, Calif., five rifle shots were fired into the home of Wilbur Gary. The Gary family had been greeted by a hostile crowd of one hundred fifty rock-throwing whites when they moved into the all-white neighborhood in 1952. Over the years, they were confronted with other harassments, including a cross-burning on their front lawn (JM).

13 In New York City, fifteen thousand African Americans and whites picketed city hall to protest the school board's plan to transfer pupils from neighborhood schools to others nearby to achieve a greater racial balance. The protesters felt that the measure did not go far enough (NYT).

18 In Birmingham, Ala., members of the city council rejected demands by local segregationists that a planned integrated Easter service be stopped. A citizens group had protested that the service would be "provocative." The service attracted thirty-five thousand people and no violence was reported (NYT).

19 In Chicago, Ill., Mrs. Clara Katitus, a white employee of the Illinois State Employment Service, charged she was dismissed after she complained that the agency was violating state and federal regulations by accepting white-only job orders from firms. The Illinois Fair Employment Practices Commission began investigating her charges (JM).

19 In Chicago, Ill., members of the executive council of the American Federation of Teachers issued a statement supporting the aims and objectives of "mass action protests for public school integration." The statement also defended the rights of teachers themselves to participate in such demonstrations (JM).

19 In Chicago, Ill., A. J. Glawson, spokesperson for the Western Electric Co., invited other major firms in the area to join with his company in a program to train African Americans for skills in

THE KILLING FIELDS: MISSISSIPPI
AND THE FREEDOM SUMMER PROJECT

During the summer of 1964, SNCC and CORE members, Council of Federated Organizations workers, and black and white supporters in Mississippi were subject to at least one thousand arrests, over forty shooting incidents, numerous beatings, and six known murders. Between June and September, eleven churches were burned to the ground in McComb, Miss., alone. Additionally, the homes, businesses, and Freedom Schools were targeted for tear gas grenades, firebombing, dynamiting, shotgun blasts, and Molotov cocktails; and civil rights workers and their supporters regularly received terroristic threats in McComb, Gloster, Natchez, Canton, Columbus, Meadville, Batesville, Meridian, Vicksburg, and Jackson, Miss.

Nonviolent direct action protests were being met with violence in many places; however, in 1964 Mississippi was undoubtedly the most deadly place a black person could be. In terms of racial violence, Mississippi had a reputation for being one of the most vicious states in the union. In July the Mississippi Advisory Committee to the U.S. Commission on Civil Rights stated that African Americans in the state "fear the police more than they fear criminals." The committee documented numerous instances of police brutality and the wholesale arrests of black citizens. Between June 1963 and June 1964 its rating on the violence scale surpassed that of any other state. Anchoring the two dates were the assassination of Medgar Evers in Jackson, Miss., and the murder of three SNCC workers, James Earl Chaney, Andrew Goodman, and Michael Schwerner, near Philadelphia, Miss.

In 1961 SNCC leaders had chosen Mississippi as a target area for their organizing. In contrast to the other civil rights organizations, SNCC decided to work with rural blacks in areas untouched by the NAACP, SCLC, and CORE. In 1964 Bob Moses launched the Freedom Summer Project, which brought a large number of affluent northern white students to Mississippi to work in community centers, teach in Freedom Schools, and encourage voter registration and support for the Mississippi Freedom Democratic party. Mississippi governor Paul Johnson, with the approval of the state legislature, doubled the number of highway patrolmen and police officers in Jackson. Northern volunteers attended a training center, funded by the National Council of Churches, at Western College for Women in Oxford, Ohio.

In June CORE workers James Chaney and Michael Schwerner, with recently arrived volunteer Andrew Goodman, went to Philadelphia, Miss., to investigate a black church burning. Their disappearance became national news. On 4 August, their bodies were found buried in an earthen dam in Philadelphia, Miss. The Medical Committee for Human Rights confirmed that the interracial trio disappeared after Chaney was beaten in jail and Goodman and Schwerner refused to leave him. Mississippi officials blocked plans for a combined funeral service and burial in the black Rest Haven Cemetery. FBI officials announced in December that they had identified the killers of the three civil rights workers, but no arrests were made.

demand by local business and industry. He delivered his remarks during the Chicago Urban League's annual banquet (JM).

20, 22, 24 In Atlanta, Ga., U.S. district court judge Boyd Sloan ordered the case for the sit-in arrest of SNCC worker Prathia Hall transferred to the federal courts. However, Fulton County judge Durwood Pye issued a counter-order and instructed county deputies to refuse to relinquish custody of Hall when U.S. Marshals came to get her (NYT).

24, 25 In Jacksonville, Fla., Mayor Haydon Burns, gearing up for a run for governor, threatened to crush peaceful anti-segregation demonstrations and deputized the all-white, 496-man fire department. When 2,000 black students marched downtown, police led an aggressive counterattack, beating some of the demonstrators and sparking a race riot. By the end of the week more than 400 African Americans were arrested as compared to only a few whites (NYT).

26 In San Francisco, Calif., the management of the Sheraton-Palace Hotel agreed to a two-year pact calling for a policy of hiring in all job categories without regard to race. The agreement followed a series of lie-ins, sleep-ins, sit-ins, and picket lines led by eighteen-year-old Tracy Sims (JM).

26 In Washington, D.C., Rep. Adam Clayton Powell urged a federal probe of the exclusion of certain racial and religious groups in school textbooks. He announced plans to introduce legislation to authorize the U.S. Office of Education to survey curriculum materials used in public schools (JM).

31 In Washington, D.C., the U.S. Supreme Court reversed the Gadsden, Ala., contempt conviction imposed without a hearing on Miss Mary Hamilton when she refused to respond in court when she was addressed as "Mary." Six justices ruled that liberties taken with the names of black defendants in southern courtrooms were key elements in the South's racial caste system (NYT).

APRIL 1964

1 In Chapel Hill, N.C., the University of North Carolina chapter of the American Association of University Professors urged universities not to take punitive action against students and professors who participated in peaceful demonstrations for civil rights (SSN).

1 In Washington, D.C., CORE leader Julius Hobson called off plans for a boycott of public schools due to their "poor quality," stating that it had been a scare tactic to force the school board to make changes. He stated that the strategy had prompted some improvements (SSN).

2 In Chester, Pa., Lawrence Landry was named chairman of a new civil rights organization called ACT. The group was set up as an ad hoc committee to coordinate and support school boycotts and demonstrations in all areas. The idea for the orga-

nization came out of the Grass Roots Negro Leadership Conference held in Detroit in the fall of 1963 (JM).

2 In Los Angeles, Calif., members of the executive committee of the United Civil Rights Committee (UCRC) launched a boycott of all chickens coming from Mississippi, Texas, Alabama, Arkansas, and Georgia. UCRC official Wendell Green stated that the organization was determined not to be guilty of economically supporting the racist power structure of southern states (JM).

2 In Richmond, Va., a federal appeals court ruled that the James Walker Memorial Hospital in Wilmington must drop its racial bars prohibiting black doctors from staff membership. Even though it was established as a private hospital, the hospital operated with public funds and was built on land donated by the city and county (NYT).

5 In Washington, D.C., President Johnson named Hobart Taylor, Jr., as White House special counsel. He became the first African American to serve in the position and the top African American in Johnson's anti-poverty program. Taylor had previously served as executive vice chairman of the President's Committee on Equal Employment Opportunity, and private counsel to Johnson (NYT).

7 In Albany, Ga., black students began registering to attend classes at previously all-white elementary schools. The peaceful registration came about under a federal court order (NYT).

7–18 In Jackson, Miss., circuit court judge Leon Hendricks called a mistrial in the second trial of Byron de la Beckwith. The jury had deadlocked after ten hours trying to determine if Beckwith was responsible for the murder of NAACP leader Medgar Evers. Beckwith was released on bond pending a decision on whether he would have to stand trial for murder a third time (NYT).

9 In Atlanta, Ga., SCLC leader Rev. Wyatt T. Walker protested Jeremiah X's ban on whites' attendance at a Black Unity meeting. Walker walked out of the meeting when SNCC members were turned away because their group was integrated. Meanwhile, Jeremiah X and an integrated group of SNCC workers did join together to invade a KKK rally (JM).

9 In **Detroit, Mich.**, managers of Food Fair stores agreed to hire 112 African Americans within ninety days. City ministers had led a selective buying campaign against Food Fair since October 1963 (JM).

9 In **Toledo, Ohio**, the owners of forty-one firms, employing forty thousand people, signed a pledge of equal opportunity in employment and upgrading, regardless of race, creed, or color. The pledge resulted from five months of conferences between black leaders and officials of industry, commerce, and government (JM).

9 In **Washington**, D.C., NAACP counsel Francis Polhous asked Health, Education, and Welfare Secretary Anthony Celebrezze to cut off funds to Huntsville Memorial Hospital in Texas. Polhous charged the hospital with treating African Americans in hallways while empty beds were available in the white section of the hospital (JM).

10–15 In **New York City**, the militant civil rights organization ACT announced plans to conduct a "stall-in" in order to block roads to the World's Fair. Representatives of CORE, NAACP, SNCC, the National Urban League, and the National Council of Negro Women went on record in Washington as opposing the demonstration. The national leadership of CORE suspended its Brooklyn chapter for its support of the stall-in to gain jobs for blacks at the fair (NYT).

11 In **Baltimore, Md.**, Verda Welcome was wounded outside her home in a barrage of gunfire. Welcome was the first black woman elected to serve in the state senate. She also helped organize support for Maryland governor J. Millard Tawes's efforts to enact new civil rights laws in the state (NYT).

13 In **New York City**, NAACP leader Dr. Eugene Reed announced plans for a statewide boycott of public schools to protest de facto segregation. Two boycotts of schools had been effective in New York City (NYT).

15 In **White Plains, N.Y.**, the school board adopted a policy of student busing to achieve integration in the schools. Nineteen percent of the city's elementary school population was black (NYT).

17, 19 In **Washington, D.C.**, the new civil rights militant group ACT held a second organizational meeting. The group criticized national black leadership for "paralyzing" the black revolution in order to save the civil rights bill. Members of ACT included Malcolm X, Gloria Richardson, and Lawrence Landry (NYT).

23 In **Chicago, Ill.**, a taxpayers' suit was leveled against school superintendent Benjamin Willis seeking to immediately utilize some twenty-five thousand empty classroom seats in public schools. Willis and school board members had been accused of allowing space and facilities in white schools to go empty rather than allowing black students to use them (JM).

23 In **Little Rock, Ark.**, three black homeowners appealed the dismissal of their suit to block a federal housing project because it would be segregated. Fiza Graves, Joe Reasoner, and Orance Talley told the court that taking their homes by eminent domain and then barring them from living in the area would be a violation of the Fourteenth Amendment (JM).

23 In **San Francisco, Calif.**, officials of the state fair employment practices commission ordered John and Antonette Ciufo to rent an apartment to Mr. and Mrs. David Wells, a black couple. The commission ruled that the Ciufos had violated the Rumford Housing Act when they refused to rent an apartment to the Wells family (JM).

23–29 In **Flushing, N.Y.**, thousands of CORE demonstrators picketed the World's Fair. One CORE member stated that because the fair pointed to what people can expect in the future, demonstrations had a place at the event "until the problems of race are solved." The stall-in called for by ACT was not carried out, and traffic flowed smoothly (NYT).

24, 26 In **Chester, Pa.**, black demonstrators protesting de facto school segregation were attacked by policemen swinging billy clubs. When black bystanders began throwing bricks, rocks, and bottles at the police, the mayor called in state troopers. The troopers joined in the beating of the protesters (NYT).

28 In Nashville, Tenn., police attacked protesters with billy clubs during three days of anti-segregation demonstrations. SNCC leaders met with Mayor Beverly Briley and asked for total school desegregation, a public accommodation ordinance, and fair employment commitments. The mayor refused to agree to any SNCC demands (NYT).

MAY 1964

1 In New York City, all the plumbers on a New York City Terminal Market project walked off the job after three Puerto Ricans and one African American reported for work. The New York City Commission on Human Rights immediately ordered the city to take steps toward canceling the contract (NYT).

8 In Detroit, Mich., officials at Ford and Chrysler agreed to meet after NAACP leaders threatened to carry out a nationwide selective buying campaign to protest discrimination in the auto industry. General Motors, the target of the first demonstration, acknowledged receipt of the NAACP threat, but refused to comment (NYT).

11 In Chester, Pa., Father Clayton Hewett was moved from jail to the hospital as he continued fasting to protest police brutality in the city's school demonstrations. He vowed to continue fasting until Gov. William Scranton talked to the protesters beaten by the Chester police (NYT).

11–15 In Cambridge, Md., African Americans attended a SNCC meeting to hear speeches delivered by John Lewis and Gloria Richardson. After the speeches, the crowd marched toward the building where Alabama governor George Wallace was campaigning in the Democratic primary. State troopers and National Guardsmen moved through the crowd and used tear gas to try to disperse them (NYT).

14 In Washington, D.C., the NAACP finally acquired their non-profit status tax deductible rating from the IRS. The organization was allowed to set up a special contributions fund, and people making contributions to the fund would be able to declare donations for income tax purposes (JM).

15 In New York City, members of the New York State Advisory Committee to the U.S. Commission on Civil Rights charged that black doctors were being discriminated against in New York City. Their report stated that black physicians' most critical problem was getting an appointment to a hospital staff, which carries with it admitting privileges for patients (NYT).

21 In Albany, N.Y., the state supreme court ruled that racial factors could be used in drawing public school district lines to achieve integration. The case arose when a white parent protested the New York City school board's plan to draw boundary lines to make a school one-third white, one-third African American, and one-third Puerto Rican (JM).

21 In Chicago, Ill., boycott leader Lawrence Landry delivered a speech before the city council. He warned that unless superintendent Benjamin Willis was fired and the school board reconstituted to include at least five members who had the complete support of the civil rights groups, African Americans would boycott the Democratic ticket (JM).

21 In Milwaukee, Wis., school officials warned that teachers who missed work to teach in freedom schools during a public school boycott would be docked one day's pay. The Milwaukee Teachers' Union protested the announced plans (JM).

21 In Washington, D.C., the U.S. Supreme Court set aside the death sentence against John Coleman, an African American. The justices stated that African Americans had been systematically excluded from the grand and trial juries that heard the case that convicted Coleman of the slaying of John Johnson, a white mechanic (JM).

25 In New York City, seven civil rights groups formed the Lawyers Constitutional Defense Committee. The sixty lawyers in the committee agreed to spend two weeks or more in Mississippi, Ala-

THE CIVIL RIGHTS ACT OF 1964

In January 1964 in Washington, D.C., members of the House Rules Committee cleared the 1964 civil rights bill for debate. Roy Wilkins, as chair of the Leadership Conference on Civil Rights, called on hundreds of representatives from organizations, unions, and religious groups to travel to Washington to lobby Congress for passage of the legislation. On 2 July, in Washington, D.C., President Johnson signed into law the 1964 Civil Rights Act, which brought an end to legal racial segregation in the United States. Martin Luther King and NAACP officials Roy Wilkins and Clarence Mitchell were among the civil rights leaders who attended the signing.

The act consisted of ten titles. Title I prohibited the use of literacy tests as a qualification for voting in federal elections. Title II declared that all people are entitled to "full and equal enjoyment of the goods, services, facilities, privileges, and advantages . . . of any place of public accommodation without discrimination or segregation." In instances of discrimination, under Title III the U.S. attorney general rather than the victim of the discrimination was authorized to bring suit against offending individuals or agencies. Under the terms of Title IV, the attorney general was also authorized to bring suits to enforce public school desegregation.

Title V extended the term of the U.S. Commission on Civil Rights to 1968. One of the act's most controversial provisions was Title VI, which directed all federal agencies to adopt regulations banning discrimination and called for the withholding of federal funds to any public or private agency that refused to comply.

Title VII prohibited employment discrimination by employers and labor unions with more than twenty-five members as well as employment agencies and authorized the creation of the Equal Employment Opportunity Commission (EEOC), whose five members were to investigate complaints of employment discrimination, hold hearings, and make recommendations for action to the attorney general and to Congress for future legislation.

Title VIII authorized the secretary of commerce to conduct a survey to determine the extent of voter registration and participation in state and national elections. Title IX authorized the attorney general to enter into any court cases dealing with discrimination, where the issues involved are deemed to be of "general public importance." And Title X established the Community Relations Service within the Department of Commerce to assist local communities "in resolving disputes, disagreements, or difficulties relating to discriminatory practices . . . wherever the peaceful relations among citizens of the community involved are threatened."

bama, Georgia, Louisiana, and Florida during the summer to protect the legal rights of demonstrators (NYT).

26 In **Evanston, Ill.**, the Newman Council of the Knights of Columbus became the first Chicago-area council to admit an African American when Virgil Hagedorn was accepted. In November 1963, six officials of a downtown Chicago council quit in protest of the unit's rejection of black candidate Joseph Bertrand (JM).

26 In **New Rochelle, N.Y.**, school officials disclosed that integration saved the school system $93,000 per year. The all-black Lincoln School had cost $100,000 a year to operate, while transporting black students to white schools cost only $7,000 (JM).

JUNE 1964

3, 4 In **New York City**, Max Wolf, a consultant to the Commission on Human Rights, charged that the school board's building program created segregated schools faster than the board could end racial imbalance under its integration plans. He stated that the millions of dollars spent on new buildings represented an "additional investment in segregation" (NYT).

4 In **Des Moines, Iowa**, in his first executive order, Gov. Harold Hughes prohibited racial and religious discrimination in all state agencies under his supervision (JM).

4 In **Gainesville, Fla.**, members of the city commission suspended social dancing activities at both the white and black recreational centers, following attempts to integrate the white dances. Several African Americans had attended a white recreation center dance without incident (JM).

9 In Washington, D.C., President Johnson summoned seventy-five labor leaders to the White House for a day-long conference. AFL-CIO president George Meany urged the leaders to respond to Johnson's urgent and repeated request and see that African Americans got full equality in apprenticeship training programs (NYT).

11 In Champaign, Ill., while NAACP official Gerald Weiss (white) was talking with NAACP leaders Raymond Harth and Rev. Blaine Ramsey, both African American, at a reception for Gov. Otto Kerner, Champaign mayor Emerson Dexter approached and said, "This is not a civil rights meeting." He then struck Weiss in the face (JM).

11 In Newtonville, N.J., Margaret Chamberlain admitted that a three-week boycott by the NAACP was ruining her grocery store business. The boycott was to protest discriminatory hiring practices (JM).

11 In New York City, license commissioner Joseph DiCarlo suspended the licenses of two Manhattan employment agencies for sixty days after finding them guilty of practicing racial and ethnic discrimination. The Mahoney Employment Agency Inc. and the Republic Employment Agency had permitted the use of codes in making employment evaluations of Puerto Rican, foreign, and black job seekers (JM).

11–15 In Los Angeles, Calif., Father William DuBay sent a letter to Pope Paul VI charging Cardinal James Francis McIntyre with failing to exercise moral leadership among the white Catholics of his diocese on the issue of racial discrimination. He also charged McIntyre with conducting a vicious program of intimidation and repression against priests, seminarians, and laity who had tried to reach the consciences of white Catholics. A few days after publicly revealing the content of his letter to the pope, DuBay was relieved of his duties at St. Albert the Great Church (NYT).

18 In Chicago, Ill., members of the Mayor's Commission on Human Relations ordered entrance examinations for two African Americans to gain admittance to Plumbers Local 27. The commission found that John Anderson and Dudley Brumfield had been prevented from joining the union on the basis of race (JM).

20 In Washington, D.C., Rep. William Ryan led the drive of a bipartisan group of legislators seeking federal protection for some five hundred to eight hundred civil rights workers who would be helping the Council of Federated Organizations conduct voter registration and education projects in Mississippi. Thirteen white parents representing parents of eight hundred students in the Mississippi Freedom Summer Project asked Attorney General Robert Kennedy to send "preventive police" to the state. They urged Kennedy to "show the courage" his brother had discussed in *Profiles in Courage* (NYT).

22 In Chicago, Ill., seventy-five thousand people attended the biggest civil rights rally in the city's history at Soldiers Field. At least half of those attending the rally signed pledges to implement the goals of human rights. Martin Luther King, James Farmer, James Forman, and Father Theodore Hesburgh were among those who addressed the rally (NYT).

23–24 In Washington, D.C., at the NAACP annual convention, the board passed a special resolution urging President Johnson to take over complete administration of the state of Mississippi. Board chairman Stephen Spottswood urged the organization to take more extreme action in the area of civil rights. The Spingarn Medal was presented to NAACP leader Roy Wilkins (NYT).

24 In Atlanta, Ga., Rev. Wyatt T. Walker announced that he was leaving his position in SCLC for an executive job with Educational Heritage, Inc. He stated that he would maintain a connection with Martin Luther King as director of SCLC's New York office (NYT).

24 In Prince Edward County, Va., county officials answered a court order to reopen public schools by appropriating only $189,000, less than half of the amount the school board said was needed to

VOTING RIGHTS AND THE MISSISSIPPI FREEDOM DEMOCRATIC PARTY'S CHALLENGE

Voter registration campaigns, first introduced in 1958 with the Crusade for Citizenship, became a major focus by 1961. Between 1961 and 1964 a massive three-year voter registration drive by the Democratic National Committee had added an estimated million and a quarter new black voters in the North and South. In September 1964, in its final weeks before the presidential election, the drive received assistance from the NAACP, SCLC, AFL-CIO, CORE, and SNCC. Specific successes could be cited in places such as Macon County, Ala., where the black electorate had a clear majority of registered voters. Once denied the right to register and vote in the county, black registered voters numbered 3,634 against the white voters' total of 3,499. And the passage of the 1964 Civil Rights Act, the most comprehensive civil rights measure ever to be passed by Congress, was an encouraging sign.

Despite the passage of civil rights legislation, thousands of citizens were being denied the right to vote. Although the sit-ins, boycotts, and Freedom Rides had succeeded in the Upper South, they had met massive and violent resistance in the Deep South, where African Americans were almost totally disenfranchised. And many states still required a poll tax. In February 1964 in Pierre, S.D., the state legislature ratified the Twenty-fourth Amendment to the Constitution, which banned the payment of poll taxes as a requirement for voting in federal elections. It was the thirty-eighth state to approve the amendment, thus making it part of the Constitution. In Louisiana, Mississippi, Alabama, and Georgia, literacy tests for prospective voters were challenged. In October in Jackson, Miss., a three-judge federal panel threw out Mississippi's poll tax requirements for voting, but the ruling applied only to federal elections. Victoria Gray, an unsuccessful Senate candidate, and Cedia Wallace filed the suit.

During the summer and fall of 1964 the Council of Federated Organizations (COFO) and the National Council of Churches launched the Mississippi Freedom Summer Project. In 1962 COFO, with SNCC's Bob Moses as program director, had formally launched the Voter Education Project, which registered more than five hundred thousand blacks by 1964, fewer than four thousand of whom were in Mississippi. In 1964 Moses launched the Freedom Summer Project, which received extensive financial support from fund-raising events held in Detroit, Mich., Chicago, Ill., and other cities. Freedom Summer brought many northern students to Mississippi, to work on voter registration and to develop support for the Mississippi Freedom Democratic Party (MFDP). In June in Washington, D.C., SNCC and COFO held a public hearing to dramatize their plan to register four hundred thousand African Americans in Mississippi during the summer. Witnesses like Fannie Lou Hamer told stories of harassment and abuse at the hands of whites, including police officers.

The MFDP held its convention in Jackson, Miss., in August. NAACP and COFO official Aaron Henry was elected chairman of the sixty-eight member, interracial delegation to be sent to the Democratic National Convention. Later that month in Washington, D.C., and in Atlantic City, N.J., MFDP delegates testified at hearings before the Democratic National Convention's Platform Committee in an unsuccessful attempt to unseat the regular (all-white) Mississippi delegation. At the hearings Fannie Lou Hamer again told of the abuse and harassment she received after she registered to vote in Mississippi. Others who testified in support of the MFDP's challenge included Martin Luther King, Adam Clayton Powell, NAACP's Roy Wilkins, and CORE's James Farmer. Fearing a loss of support among southern Democrats, President Johnson arranged for the Platform Committee to allow the MFDP delegation two at-large seats at the convention. On 26 August, the MFDP rejected this offer and left Atlantic City, disillusioned about the possibility of meaningful social change through electoral politics.

educate its sixteen hundred African Americans. The action virtually assured the inadequacy of the public school system (NYT).

25 In Chicago, Ill., CORE officials announced that they would mobilize the unemployed of the city to fight racial discrimination in employment, housing, education, and recreation. They appealed for money, materials, contributions, and workers in their effort to develop organizations in the city's black neighborhoods (JM).

25 In Montgomery, Ala., six African Americans filed a class-action suit in district court to force the inclusion of more African Americans on Macon County juries. They charged that African Americans were rarely chosen for jury duty, even though there were 6,234 black males of voting age as compared to 1,365 white males (JM).

28 In Washington, D.C., former intelligence chief Allen Dulles recommended to President Johnson a three-point program for halting terrorist activities in Mississippi. The program involved increasing the FBI force in the state, maintaining contacts between President Johnson and Gov. Paul Johnson, and establishing contact with the National Council of Churches and CORE, which were sending unprotected groups into the area (NYT).

28 In Washington, D.C., National Urban League officials announced that since 1954, the D.C. public schools had become "resegregated." The city schools had become 12.4 percent white and 87.6 percent African American. Before the 1954 Supreme Court decision, only 47 percent of the pupils were African American (NYT).

JULY 1964

2 In Warner Robins, Ga., airmen of Robins Air Force Base were denied federal tuition assistance for attending the Warner Robins Center of the University of Georgia. A recent Defense Department directive stated that federal funds would no longer be used to assist active duty personnel attending segregated institutions (JM).

2 In Washington, D.C., more than 2,000 delegates and 5,000 visitors attended the NAACP's fifty-fifth annual convention. Celebrating a decade of successful civil rights activity since the *Brown* decision, they marveled over the transformation that had occurred in the nation's capital. NAACP leader Henry Lee Moon recalled that when the convention was held after World War II (1947), the more than 700 delegates were forced to stay in private homes and government facilities, and to meet in churches and dine only in black restaurants on U Street. Formerly known as the "capital of Jim Crow," Moon commented that the District of Columbia was now trying to live up to its title as the capital of democracy (JM).

3 In Houston, Tex., the National Labor Relations Board (NLRB) declared that the all-white Independent Metal Workers Union Local 1 was guilty of unfair labor practices under federal law in practicing racial discrimination against a black member of the all-black Local 2 of the Metal Workers. The NLRB stripped Local 1 of its certification and required the union to sign an anti-discrimination pledge (NYT).

8 In San Francisco, Calif., Martin Luther King, Roy Wilkins, Dick Gregory, and Norman Hill appeared before a panel of Republican preconvention platform members. They requested special measures to aid both black and white poor families and called for full support and implementation of the Civil Rights Act (NYT).

9 In New York City, Rev. Wyatt T. Walker, formerly executive secretary of the SCLC, filed two formal complaints with the State Commission Against Discrimination. He charged two real estate companies with refusing to show him houses because he was African American (JM).

10, 13 In Washington, D.C., NAACP official Roy Wilkins, National Medical Association president Dr. Kenneth Clement, and D. Alonzo Yerby, president of the New York City Public Health Association, asked President Johnson to open clinics in Mississippi. They expressed fear that civil rights workers in the state might suffer for want of adequate and prompt medical care (NYT).

11 In Jackson, Miss., J. Edgar Hoover opened a new FBI office in the city. The office was created to serve as the "civil rights office" staffed by the FBI's experts in tracking murder suspects and uncovering murder victims. Former CIA chief Allen Dulles had recommended a beefed-up FBI force in the state to prosecute terrorist activities (NYT).

14 In Washington, D.C., Defense Secy. Robert McNamara ordered the armed forces to quickly develop programs and policies that would give full effect to the Civil Rights Act. Although a 1963 directive advocated the removal of racial designations from most personnel forms, many military installations continued to list race on most forms (NYT).

16 In Birmingham, Ala., attorney Orzell Billingsley resigned from the Adult Re-Education and Job Training Subcommittee of the Community Affairs Committee. He charged that the subcommittee had failed to meet in the seven months of its existence. The subcommittee had been charged with working out the problem of equal job opportunities for African Americans (JM).

16 In Denver, Colo., a district court ordered Continental Airlines to hire Marlon Green, an African American. The court's ruling backed up similar orders from the Colorado Anti-Discrimination Commission in 1959 and the U.S. Supreme Court in 1963 (NYT).

16 In Pittsburgh, Pa., the all-white Plumbers Local No. 27 charged that the Pittsburgh fair employment practices ordinance was unconstitutional. The union had been fined four hundred dollars and costs for discriminating against two black applicants for membership. The union also filed an appeal in county court (JM).

16 In San Francisco, Calif., Sen. Barry Goldwater was named the Republican candidate for the presidency. The forty-three black delegates refused to endorse the party platform and Barry Goldwater and vowed not to support the candidate when they returned home. Martin Luther King called the nomination "disastrous," and CORE leader James Farmer stated that Goldwater's selection was a mistake for the party. Their comments were among many condemnations issued by black leaders across the country (NYT).

16 In Washington, D.C., Defense Department officials ordered racial designations removed from most of its personnel forms. It was the latest action by the Pentagon to eradicate racial discrimination within the military (JM).

17–24 In New York City, rioting erupted in Harlem and Brooklyn after a fifteen-year-old boy was shot and killed by a white policeman. Violence and looting occurred, and one person was killed, 140 injured, 489 arrested, and more than 625 businesses were damaged during the more than three days of rioting (NYT).

20 In Fayette County, Tenn., thirty-six white student volunteers from Cornell University helped increase black voter registration from about fifty to forty-seven hundred, a slim countywide majority. For the first time in the county's history, local candidates went after the newly powerful black vote. In 1960, the county had become famous for its tent city, consisting of black sharecroppers evicted for registering to vote (NYT).

23 In Washington, D.C., the President's Committee on Equal Employment Opportunity sponsored the first Plans for Progress conference. Four hundred delegates from black colleges, major firms, and government agencies attended the conference. Dr. Clarence Hilberry reported that African Americans were incapable of taking advantage of industry's changing attitudes because black colleges had been steering African Americans away from business training (NYT).

25–31 In Rochester, N.Y., racial violence erupted and scores were injured when rioters looted stores and battled police. After two days of rioting, Gov. Nelson Rockefeller sent one thousand National Guardsmen to the city to restore order (NYT).

30 In Indianapolis, Ind., a cross was burned on the lawn of the Henry Atkins family who lived in an integrated neighborhood. It was the second cross-burning to occur at the Atkins home in one year, and the second cross-burning in the city within one week (JM).

30 In **San Francisco, Calif.**, Judge David French sentenced militant civil rights leader Dr. Thomas Burbridge to nine months in jail. He had been arrested for participating in a sit-in demonstration protesting discriminatory hiring policies in a Cadillac showroom (JM).

AUGUST 1964

1 In **Raleigh, N.C.**, Willa Johnson filed suit in federal court charging that her teaching contract was not renewed because of her civil rights activity. She stated that she was active in voter registration in Halifax County and that her dismissal was designed to punish her and intimidate other African Americans (SSN).

1 In **Montgomery, Ala.**, Arthur Worthy became the second African American appointed as a deputy U.S. Marshal in the state. White deputy U.S. Marshal William Parker resigned in protest and was quickly given a job with the state police (NYT).

1 In **Hattiesburg, Miss.**, U.S. district judge Sidney Mize approved a plan for desegregating the first grade in public schools in Jackson, Biloxi, and Leake County. The integration would be the first in a public school in Mississippi below the college level (SSN).

1 In **New Orleans, La.**, the Fifth U.S. Circuit Court of Appeals reversed a decision by Judge Clarence Allgood and ordered the Birmingham, Ala., school board not to expel a student for participating in civil rights activities. Linda Cal Woods had been expelled after she was arrested for participating in a demonstration (SSN).

3–4 Jersey City, N.J., racial violence and rioting broke out in African American and Puerto Rican neighborhoods. Stores were looted and rioters battled police for two nights. Two people were seriously injured, and hundreds were arrested (NYT).

6 In **Prince Edward County, Va.**, white parents traveled at night to the county recorder's office to pick up tuition grants. The grants enabled the parents to send their children to private schools and thus avoid public school integration. Attorney Samuel Tucker called the after-dark scheme a "midnight raid on the county treasury" (NYT).

6, 7 In **Honolulu, Hawaii**, comedian Dick Gregory accused the FBI of knowing the identity of the killers of the three Mississippi civil rights workers "for a long time." He also stated that his offer of a $25,000 reward to anyone giving information leading to the arrest and conviction of the murderers still stood (NYT).

7 In **Louisville, Ky.**, at the fifty-fourth annual convention of the National Urban League, the delegates passed a resolution pledging the organization's resources to a large-scale voter registration campaign. To be conducted in the sixty-six cities where the Urban League had branches, the campaign was to be headed by Sterling Tucker, director of the Washington, D.C., branch. Urban League executive director Whitney M. Young announced that the organization would raise $300,000 to finance the voter registration drive (NYT).

12–14 In **Elizabeth and Paterson, N.J.**, racial disorder erupted and violence and looting occurred. Molotov cocktails, rocks, and bottles were thrown at police by rioters. Order was restored with the assistance of the state police. More than fifty people were arrested over the two days of rioting (NYT).

13 In **Berkeley, Calif.**, Mrs. Virginia Burton and other CORE members sent a coffin to President Johnson to dramatize their anger over alleged federal inaction in protecting civil rights workers in Mississippi (JM).

13 In **Philadelphia, Pa.**, NAACP leader Cecil B. Moore threatened the state's top Republican politicians with a voter boycott if they did not disassociate themselves from Sen. Barry Goldwater. He issued the threat to Gov. William Scranton, Sen. Hugh Scott, and behind-the-scenes leader William Meehan (JM).

17 In **Chicago, Ill.**, rioting erupted on 15 August in the suburb of Dixmoor after the arrest of Belinda Woods (black) of Chicago on charges of attempting to steal a bottle of liquor from a store. African Americans began breaking and smashing store windows and setting fire to several buildings. Rioters battled the police who threw tear gas grenades at the protesters. Fifty people were injured in the riot, most of whom were white. The violence lasted for two days (NYT).

19 In Washington, D.C., members of the National Citizens Committee for Community Relations met for the first time. Delegates, consisting of whites and African Americans from all walks of life, discussed ways of solving racial problems in their areas. The meeting was sponsored by the new Community Relations Service headed by former Florida governor LeRoy Collins (NYT).

20 In Durham, N.C., Local 208 and its president Walter Daye filed a petition in U.S. district court, charging that the International Union of Tobacco Workers attempted to destroy the local because it sought equal opportunities for its black members (JM).

20 In Tampa, Fla., a burning cross with firecrackers was planted on the lawn of Mr. and Mrs. Joe Hunter. The Hunters were unable to use their telephone to call the police because the white family on their party line had the receiver off the hook. The family also had endured egg throwing and other forms of harassment at their home after they moved into the all-white neighborhood (JM).

29, 30, 31 In Philadelphia, Pa., rioting erupted after a white and black police officer attempted to move a black couple's stalled auto, which was blocking traffic. The woman was arrested by the officers, and a crowd of African Americans came to her defense. Black leaders blamed black nationalist activities for the outbreak, claiming that the riots were planned. Militant NAACP leaders Stanley Branche and Cecil B. Moore addressed the rioters and attempted to stop the violence (NYT).

SEPTEMBER 1964

1 In Jackson, Miss., forty-three black students enrolled in eight previously white schools. No incidents resulted from the integration. Peace-

ful school integration also took place in Biloxi, Clarksdale, and Leake County, Miss. (SSN).

3 In Baltimore, Md., attorney Edward Toles pointed to the lack of black lawyers on the Federal Power, Federal Communications, Federal Aviation, Civil Aeronautics, and the U.S. Civil Service Commissions. Although he reported some gains in other government agencies and departments, he deplored the scarcity of black judges and bankruptcy referees. He addressed his comments to the National Bar Association (JM).

3 In Washington, D.C., AFL-CIO president George Meany outlined a stepped-up civil rights program designed to help labor fight the white backlash in its ranks while at the same time encouraging labor support for the new Civil Rights Act. He outlined the plan during a meeting with 250 national, state, and local labor leaders (NYT).

7 In Chicago, Ill., NAACP leader Roy Wilkins compared Sen. Barry Goldwater to the late racist senator Theodore Bilbo. Wilkins argued that Goldwater couched his racism in softer language than Bilbo used. He addressed his remarks to a meeting of the American Political Science Association (NYT).

10 In Sacramento, Calif., members of the California State Commission on Equal Opportunities in Education reported continued discrimination in the hiring of black teachers in California schools. A commission report showed that while African Americans accounted for 5.6 percent of the state's population, black teachers made up only 2.5 percent of the public school teaching force (JM).

17 In Jackson, Miss., NAACP official Charles Evers announced the launching of a fund-raising drive for the family of Debra Lewis, who integrated an all-white school. Her father was fired the day after he enrolled his daughter. Other black parents decided not to enroll their children after they were intimidated by whites (JM).

20, 25 In New York City, the fifty-six United Nations Afro-Asian delegations caucused to discuss what steps they could take to curb the rising number of racist incidents involving their members. The delegates claimed that they and their staffs

DESEGREGATING PUBLIC ACCOMMODATIONS IN 1964

Title II of the 1964 Civil Rights Act forbade discrimination in public accommodations. Some cities and states had passed ordinances requiring complete desegregation of public accommodations prior to the enactment of federal legislation. Others had laws ordering desegregation of specific facilities or were considering the adoption of similar measures.

Sit-ins, boycotts, pickets, selective buying campaigns, and other nonviolent direct action protests continued in 1964 in Jackson and Indianola, Miss.; Atlanta, Ga.; Little Rock, Ark.; Memphis, Tenn.; Chapel Hill, N.C.; Birmingham, Montgomery, and Tuscaloosa, Ala.; Frankfort, Ky.; Lakeland, Tallahassee, and St. Augustine, Fla.; New Orleans and Clinton, La.; Princess Anne and Annapolis, Md.; Phoenix, Ariz.; and New York City. Court cases and U.S. Commission on Civil Rights (USCCR) complaints alleging discrimination were adjudicated in Gary, Ind.; Petersburg, Va.; Washington, D.C.; and Atlanta, Ga.

In January 1964 in Kansas City, Kans., city commissioners passed a public accommodations law that ordered the desegregation of 225 taverns and bowling alleys. It was the first such law to be enacted in Kansas. In Atlanta, Ga., state senator Leroy Johnson announced plans to seek legislation allowing Atlanta to enact a public accommodations ordinance. In Mobile, Ala., district judge Daniel Thomas declared that segregation of the races on city buses was unconstitutional. The decision ended a five-year legal fight to desegregate the buses.

In April in Kansas City, Mo., a citywide referendum approved a public accommodations ordinance that prohibited discrimination by virtually all businesses serving the public. Backers of the ordinance celebrated around a hearse marking the death of Jim Crow. In May in Fort Wayne, Ind., Lawrence Burwell filed suit in circuit court against the American Heritage Restaurant and its former employee Robert Call. Burwell stated that he and three other African Americans were denied service at the restaurant based on race, a violation of the state's public accommodations law. In October in Milwaukee, Wis., Judge William Brandel fined tavern owner Richard Prisk $115 for violating the state public accommodations statute. Prisk had refused to serve Charles Wilson, an African American.

In June 1964 in Washington, D.C., Sen. Hubert Humphrey recommended that after the passage of the 1964 Civil Rights Act, President Johnson, governors, and mayors set up local and national conferences. The conferences would lay the groundwork for community action and support by American citizens to end legal segregation in public accommodations.

In July, immediately after President Johnson signed the new legislation, testing of local compliance occurred in a number of places, including Raleigh, N.C.; Richmond, Va.; Atlanta, Ga.; and Little Rock, Ark. In New York City, NAACP officials announced that groups were headed for Clarksdale, Canton, Meridian, Philadelphia, and Moss Point, Miss., in order to test the new civil rights law. Although the groups successfully desegregated restaurants and hotels along the way, they faced a hostile white mob in Philadelphia, Miss. The trip ended when Gov. Paul Johnson refused to meet the delegation and NAACP members called on the USCCR for immediate hearings in the state. Since most were not residents of those states, James Forman asked them to continue their voter registration projects and leave the testing of the laws to local citizens.

In November 1964 in McComb, Miss., restaurant and theater owners served eight out-of-town African Americans and twelve local residents who were accompanied by forty state patrolmen, twenty FBI agents, local police, and newsmen. The last time civil rights activists attempted to integrate public accommodations was in 1961, when Freedom Riders were severely beaten while conducting a sit-in at the bus station lunchroom.

In Washington, D.C., in December 1964, the Supreme Court upheld the public accommodations section of the 1964 Civil Rights Act and decided that the act's provisions should be retroactive. The ruling voided the prosecutions and convictions of at least three thousand sit-in demonstrators arrested all over the South.

were subjected to hostility from some residents, shopkeepers, and local businessmen (NYT).

24 In San Francisco, Calif., after the Emporium and the Roos/Atkins stores ignored subpoenas to produce personnel records at a state fair employment practices commission hearing, the state agency filed complaints with the superior court seeking to compel the firms to comply. The hearing was called after two African Americans filed racial discrimination charges against the two stores (JM).

30 In Savannah, Ga., delegates attended SCLC's annual convention. Martin Luther King altered his policy of not endorsing any presidential candidate and publicly called on African Americans to vote for President Johnson. Rev. Fred Shuttlesworth, A. Philip Randolph, James Farmer, Aaron Henry, Rev. Ralph Abernathy, and Harry Golden also gave their endorsements to Johnson during the convention (NYT).

OCTOBER 1964

1 In Mobile, Ala., the Raymond Young family endured two firebombings, three smoke bombings, constant threats, harassment, and an unending stream of hostility from their white neighbors during the previous year. Despite damage to their home, the family announced that they were determined to remain in the all-white neighborhood (JM).

1 In New York City, George Fowler, chairman of the New York State Commission on Human Rights, and National Urban League official Adolph Holmes warned businessmen that selective buying would be used to obtain equal employment opportunities under the new Civil Rights Act. The remarks were made during a National Association of Manufacturers' seminar (JM).

5 In Washington, D.C., eighteen Democratic congressmen, in an open letter to President Johnson, urged the federal government to "take all necessary steps to prevent further violence and bloodshed" in Mississippi. The congressmen outlined minimum recommendations to keep peace, like opening FBI offices throughout the state and preparing an FBI report on violence during the summer (NYT).

8 In Atlanta, Ga., Dr. Aaron Henry was given the Rosa Parks Award, the highest honor given by SCLC. Henry served as president of the Mississippi NAACP, an SCLC board member, and led the Mississippi Freedom Democratic party delegation to the Democratic convention (JM).

8 In Bethesda, Md., Republican vice presidential nominee William Miller admitted that his home had been covered by an anti-black restrictive covenant. He argued that the covenant had been inserted in 1946, long before he purchased the home (JM).

8 In Chicago, Ill., white members of the Stony Island Heights Civic Association registered their protests against block-busting tactics with more than three hundred signs reading "This is our house. It is not for sale." The signs were placed on the homes of white families who refused to be made to panic and sell when African Americans moved into their neighborhood (JM).

10 In New Orleans, La., President Johnson stated that he had signed the civil rights bill and planned on enforcing it. He also chided southern politicians for trying to win elections by ranting about African Americans. The speech was part of a southern campaign swing made by Johnson and his wife, Lady Bird (NYT).

15 In Stockholm, Sweden, it was announced that Martin Luther King was selected as the winner of the 1964 Nobel Peace Prize. He immediately made it clear that he would donate the $54,600 prize money to the Civil Rights Movement, with a large amount going to SCLC. King declared, "I don't want anyone to believe that I engage in civil rights protests for the money" (NYT).

15 In New York City, CORE demonstrators chained themselves to the columns outside the federal courthouse and blocked exits to protest the unpunished murders of African Americans in Mississippi. Officials avoided the exits and ignored the protesters (NYT).

21, 24, 25 In McComb, Miss., police jailed thirteen civil rights workers on charges of operating a food-handling establishment without obtaining a health certificate. The thirteen had been merely cooking food for themselves in their Freedom House. Meanwhile, a judge freed nine white men even after some of them pled guilty to bombing the homes of African Americans (NYT).

22 In New York City, CORE leader Val Coleman stated that Dick Gregory raised $50,000 for the organization during a month-long string of benefit performances (JM).

NOVEMBER 1964

4, 6 In Washington, D.C., officials of the U.S. Housing and Home Finance Agency halted the flow of federal funds to all California urban renewal projects. The stoppage resulted from the voters' approval of Proposition 14, a constitutional amendment banning anti-discrimination housing laws (NYT).

5 In Birmingham, Ala., SCLC officials met at the A. G. Gaston Hotel to plan for the future. They dispatched field staff to the Dorchester citizenship headquarters for new assignments in sixty southern counties where voter registration drives would be intensified. Other staff members began talks with black leaders in several southern communities that showed resistance to the Civil Rights Act (NYT).

5 In Jefferson Barracks, Mo., for the fourth time in two years, black employees of the Veterans Administration Hospital launched a boycott of the canteen because of alleged hiring discrimination. Boycotters stated that the canteen refused to hire African Americans for counter jobs, although most of the canteen's customers were African Americans (JM).

12 In Chicago, Ill., Rep. Adam Clayton Powell voiced his support for a boycott of classes held in the Robert Taylor and Washington Park homes. Powell also vowed to investigate if school officials violated federal policy by conducting classes in the high-rise housing projects (JM).

12 In Kansas City, Mo., black airman John Warner requested and received a transfer from Richards-Gebaur Air Force Base when he was unable to find quarters for his wife. He stated that he had

similar difficulties when assigned to Chanute Air Force Base near Rantoul, Ill., in 1961 (JM).

12 In Memphis, Tenn., the all-white membership of the Shelby County Bar Association voted to admit black attorneys to membership. The seven-hundred-member organization voted to delete the word *white* in reference to qualification and eligibility for membership (JM).

13 In Washington, D.C., NAACP leader Roy Wilkins revealed that President Johnson thanked black leaders for their support in his overwhelming election victory. Johnson met with and thanked Wilkins, A. Philip Randolph, Whitney Young, Dorothy Height, and Jack Greenberg. He also asked their help in suggesting candidates for posts on the Equal Employment Opportunity Commission and the staff directorship of the U.S. Commission on Civil Rights (NYT).

18 In Washington, D.C., Lawrence Guyot, chairman of the Mississippi Freedom Democratic party (MFDP), announced plans to block the seating of all of Mississippi's Democratic congressmen and senators. He stated that the MFDP also appealed to the Democratic National Committee for help in unseating the congressmen. More than four hundred thousand African Americans in Mississippi had been prevented from voting in the recent election (NYT).

19 In Washington, D.C., FBI director J. Edgar Hoover called Martin Luther King "the most notorious liar in the country." He made the statement after King advised African Americans not to report any civil rights violations to the Albany, Ga., FBI office because the staff members were all white southerners (NYT).

20 In Springfield, Ill., members of the state fair employment practices commission ordered Motorola to pay Leon Myart one thousand dollars and told the company to cease and desist from future unfair employment practices. They found that the company refused to hire Myart because of his race (NYT).

24 In Washington, D.C., Coretta and Martin Luther King met with President Johnson for a forty-five-minute conversation. King told Johnson that southern federal judges "abuse and misuse" their power in the area of black rights (NYT).

27 In Louisville, Ky., Republican committeeman John Thomas was fired from his city job for attempting to distribute racist handbills to fellow employees before the election. Howard Poteet and Albert Lynn were suspended from their jobs for attempting to distribute the handbills on Thomas's orders (NYT).

27 In Philadelphia, Pa., members of the Philadelphia Bar Association recommended the enactment of a city ordinance banning the use of blackface makeup in the annual Mummer's Parade. Blackface was barred from the 1 January 1964 parade by a court injunction obtained by the NAACP, which contended that the practice was offensive to African Americans (JM).

DECEMBER 1964

2, 5 In Washington, D.C., Martin Luther King visited FBI director J. Edgar Hoover and warned him of possible black violence if the government failed to protect African Americans. A few days later, FBI agents arrested twenty-one people in northern Mississippi on charges growing out of the slaying of James Chaney, Michael Schwerner, and Andrew Goodman, three civil rights workers in Mississippi. Among those arrested were Neshoba County sheriff Lawrence Rainey, Deputy Sheriff Cecil Price, and Patrolman Otha Neal Burkes (NYT).

3 In New York City, NAACP official Edward Odum urged the more than six hundred local members and their churches to participate in a massive "community self-help" program, designed to help African Americans implement the provisions of the 1964 Civil Rights Act. Odum emphasized the need for African Americans to take advantage of the benefits offered under the federal government's anti-poverty programs and outlined the NAACP's program for assisting disad-

vantaged black youths, which included recruitment of volunteers for tutorials, organizing community campaigns to deter school dropouts, and development of adult and youth counseling and literacy programs (JM).

10 In Birmingham, Ala., Rev. C. H. Oliver, executive secretary of the Inter-Citizens Committee, protested the reactivation of the K-9 Corps. He stated that it was a disgrace that dogs could be hired on the police force while African Americans could not. Police dogs were temporarily retired in December 1963 following their use against civil rights protesters (JM).

11 In Washington, D.C., President Johnson delivered a twenty-five-minute civil rights declaration before the National Urban League's Community Action Assembly. He urged the complete assimilation of African Americans into American life. He also announced that Vice President elect Hubert Humphrey would coordinate the various civil rights programs of his administration (NYT).

15 In San Francisco, Calif., NAACP counsel Robert Carter announced a $55,000 budget to fight the state's anti–fair housing amendment, Proposition 14. He also stated that the organization would challenge the law in the courts (NYT).

15 In St. Louis, Mo., Teamsters official Harold Gibbons telegraphed Martin Luther King that the organization promised to support the boycott of Mississippi goods during the present civil rights struggle. He stated that no material or services from Mississippi would be used in the construction of the new Teamsters' Council Plaza in St. Louis (NYT).

31 In Houston, Tex., Gloria and Rosella Harmon filed suit in federal court to enroll at the all-white San Jacinto High School in order to participate in the school's vocational courses. Under the current grade-a-year desegregation plan, high school desegregation would not begin until 1969 (JM).

On 21 March 1965, civil rights activists and others from all over the country converged to participate in the march from Selma to Montgomery, Alabama. The earlier attack on unarmed civil rights activists on the Pettus Bridge on "Bloody Sunday" spurred people from around the country to come to Selma to participate in the march led by Rev. Martin Luther King, Jr., and SNCC's John Lewis. Among the marchers were Philadelphia attorney C. Dolores Tucker and UN Deputy Secretary-General Dr. Ralph Bunche. (SOURCE: JACK FRANKLIN COLLECTION, AFRICAN AMERICAN MUSEUM IN PHILADELPHIA)

1965

"MARCHING TO ZION"

*T*he *Selma to Montgomery March in 1965 expressed the outrage of many over the deaths of Jimmie Lee Jackson, Rev. James Reeb, and the violence leveled against unarmed civil rights activists seeking equal rights for all Americans, and dramatized the need for legislation mandating federal intervention when voting rights were denied. People from all over the country came "Marching to Zion" to demonstrate their unequivocal support for nonviolent protests in the face of the increasing threats from more militant activists calling for "an eye for an eye." The acceptance by civil rights workers in southern Louisiana and Alabama of offers of armed protection from the Deacons of Defense and Justice, and the violent uprising in the Watts section of Los Angeles, signaled the beginning of the end of the Civil Rights Movement. With the advent of the anti-war protests, the student rights campaigns, women's liberation, and eventually Black Power, the civil rights era came to an end. Numerous social protests and demonstrations took place in the United States after 1965, but the participants were marching to many different drummers.*

1 In Washington, D.C., J. Edgar Hoover reiterated his view that the FBI had no authority under the 1964 Civil Rights Act to make arrests for civil rights violations, nor could it guarantee the protection of nonviolent demonstrators (NYT).

5, 6 In New York City, the NAACP's Roy Wilkins voiced his concern over the Council of Federated Organizations (COFO), suggesting that it had become a SNCC-controlled vehicle operating in Mississippi and other states. There appeared to be a growing split between younger and older civil rights group members, as reflected in an NAACP internal memo urging the group to withdraw from COFO. A complicating factor was the election of COFO head Aaron Henry to the NAACP board of directors. One issue in dispute was the advisability of launching a third-party movement in Mississippi (NYT).

7 In Washington, D.C., U.S. Civil Service chairman John Macy announced that only charitable agencies that operated under nondiscriminatory rules would be allowed to solicit donations on federal property. Soliciting charities would not be allowed to discriminate because of race in giving service, hiring, or naming governing boards and they would not be allowed to segregate those served on the basis of race (JM).

7 In Washington, D.C., Office of Economic Opportunity director Sargent Shriver advised NAACP leader Roy Wilkins in a letter that people arrested for participating in peaceful civil rights demonstrations would not automatically be barred from the Job Corps or other anti-poverty programs (JM).

7 In **Sacramento, Calif.**, NAACP official Nathaniel Colley filed a suit in the state superior court seeking the invalidation of Proposition 14, which repealed all laws mandating nondiscrimination in housing. The action was filed on behalf of Clifton Hill, who was evicted from his apartment because of his race (JM).

7 In **Cleveland, Ohio**, NAACP official Herbert Hill warned that if racial discrimination continued in the construction of the new federal building, mass demonstrations would ensue. Union officials denied discrimination, but only five African Americans were accepted as journeymen or apprentices by the five unions working on the building (JM).

7 In **Ripley, Miss.**, students and faculty from Oberlin College, Yankton College, and the University of Massachusetts spent their holiday rebuilding a church that had been burned down by white racists during the previous summer. Meanwhile, the interracial, interfaith Committee of Concern raised $36,430 to help rebuild the more than twenty churches burned during the summer (JM).

7 In **Philadelphia, Pa.**, Eugene Miller filed suit against Radnor Valley Builders, accusing them of refusing to sell him a home in the Rosemont suburb. A spokesperson from General Electric, Miller's employer, publicly insisted that Miller had a right to expect housing suitable for his income (JM).

7 In **Annapolis, Md.**, a survey by the state department of education revealed that all counties with black students in their school population achieved some measure of desegregation. State superintendent James Sensenbaugh called this a "milestone" in the state's progress toward complete school desegregation (JM).

14 In **New York City**, officials of the city's Commission on Human Relations warned the city's taxi drivers to cease refusing service to Puerto Rican and black citizens. Commission chair Stanley Lowell warned that refusal of service to people because of race or color was illegal and that a driver could lose his license if found guilty (JM).

20 In **New York City**, 136 pupils (90 percent of the student body) were absent from P.S. 617, Brooklyn, in a boycott called by Rev. Milton Galamison, chairman of the Citywide Committee on Integrated Schools. Plans were made to extend the boycott to fourteen other schools to protest alleged inferior education. These schools enrolled more than two thousand mainly black and Puerto Rican students (NYT).

20 In **New York City**, the New York Supreme Court temporarily enjoined the boycott called by Rev. Milton Galamison, school board member and chairman of the Citywide Committee on Integrated Schools, and ordered a public hearing. School board president James Donovan criticized the boycott and called for Galamison's resignation from the school board for violating the state compulsory attendance law (NYT).

21 In **Montgomery, Ala.**, Gov. George Wallace ordered constant protection for Martin Luther King as he returned to the state. Wallace was responding to death threats against King and feared the implications if King was harmed in the state (JM).

21 In **Jackson, Miss.**, an estimated ten thousand dollars was raised to send to the Mississippi Freedom Democratic party lobbyists in Washington, D.C. Annie Devine, Fannie Lou Hamer, and Victoria Gray challenged the right of five Mississippi congressmen-elect to sit in the House chambers while Congress investigated charges of voting discrimination in the state. The three were prevented from entering the House by capital police chief Carl Schamp (JM).

28 In **Akron, Ohio**, thirty-three black ministers and leaders of the Committee for Justice and Equality in Housing urged African Americans to join in a boycott against the city businesses and the Akron Area Board of Realtors. The boycott was called after a fair housing ordinance was defeated in November 1964 (JM).

28 In **Liberty County, Fla.**, eighty-six African Americans, all over fifty years old, registered to vote at the courthouse. They became the first black voters in the county since Reconstruction. CORE workers then turned their efforts to Lafayette County, the last of the state's sixty-seven counties to register African Americans (JM).

28 In Topeka, Kans., state attorney general William Ferguson announced that only beauty shops located in hotels, motels, and cosmetology schools were covered by the Civil Rights Act of 1964 and the state anti-bias law. All other beauty shops were not required to serve African Americans (JM).

28 In Clarksdale, Miss., school officials legally desegregated the second grade of local public schools. However, NAACP leader Aaron Henry charged that the intent was thwarted by a school zoning plan. No African Americans lived within the zones of nine white schools targeted for desegregation by federal court orders (JM).

FEBRUARY 1965

1 In Boston, Mass., the Massachusetts Advisory Committee to the U.S. Commission on Civil Rights called for federal, technical, and financial aid to help school districts correct racial imbalance in public schools. The commission also urged federal housing officials to recognize that "racial discrimination in public housing contributes to segregation in Boston public schools" (SSN).

1 In Montgomery and Bullock Counties, Ala., county officials submitted plans to federal judge Frank Johnson for the total desegregation of their public school systems over a five-year period. In fall 1964, grades one and ten through twelve were desegregated in Montgomery County, and grades nine through twelve in Bullock County (SSN).

4 In Chicago, Ill., attorney John Houston urged fifty members of the National Lawyers Guild to aid in the fight to unseat the white Mississippi delegation in the House of Representatives. Twelve members immediately joined a task force of more than one hundred lawyers whose job was to secure depositions from African Americans who were prevented from voting (JM).

4 In St. Louis, Mo., officials of the Greater St. Louis Committee for Freedom of Residence revealed that African Americans had moved into fifty-one suburban neighborhoods that had been rigidly segregated three years earlier (JM).

4 In Trenton, N.J., Gov. Richard Hughes directed the New Jersey Division on Civil Rights to investigate charges of racial discrimination in two Newark unions. Civil rights groups charged the Ironworkers Local 11 and Plumbers Local 24 with discriminating against African Americans in their apprenticeship programs (JM).

7 In Washington, D.C., President Johnson issued an executive order creating the cabinet-level Council on Equal Opportunity, with Vice Pres. Hubert Humphrey as chairman, to coordinate civil rights activities of all federal agencies (NYT).

10 In Washington, D.C., Martin Luther King and Roy Wilkins met with President Johnson in separate meetings. They discussed a new civil rights measure providing federal registrars and eliminating literacy tests for voting. King said that Johnson assured him of the administration's intent to remove all barriers to the vote. King's proposals included enforcement of new voting legislation by federal registrars appointed by and responsible to the president (NYT).

11 In Washington, D.C., Hubert Humphrey urged five hundred of the nation's top business firms to use ingenuity in developing programs to guarantee equal opportunities for African Americans. He addressed his comments to the third annual Plans for Progress conference, sponsored by the President's Committee on Equal Employment Opportunity (JM).

11 In Atlanta, Ga., Martin Luther King was honored at a testimonial dinner organized by Rev. Paul Hallinan, Rabbi Jacob Rothschild, Dr. Benjamin Mays, Ralph McGill, and others. The celebration took place in the face of strong objections from many white Atlantans (JM).

17 In New York City, three African Americans and a white woman, members of the Black Liberation Front, were arrested by police and FBI after the four had plotted to blow up the Statue of Liberty,

FULL COMPLIANCE: FEDERAL OFFICIALS MOVE
TO IMPLEMENT THE CIVIL RIGHTS ACT OF 1964

Throughout 1965 officials for the federal government moved ahead to implement the provisions of the Civil Rights Act of 1964. Under the terms of Title III, the U.S. attorney general was to bring suits for discriminatory practices in public accommodations, and by the end of 1964, the Supreme Court ruled against restaurant owners from Birmingham, Atlanta, and other southern cities who had suits brought against them by the Justice Department for refusing to serve black customers.

Under the terms of Title VII, all employers and labor unions with twenty-five or more members were to end discriminatory practices by 2 July 1965. In February officials of the AFL-CIO announced the scheduling of a series of meetings to quicken the pace for achievement of voluntary compliance with the 1964 law. And in April 1965, AFL-CIO leader George Meany declared that labor unions should be prepared to use strikes or boycotts if necessary to force employer compliance with the new federal ban on job discrimination.

What caused the greatest amount of controversy in 1965, however, were the provisions of Title VI, which called for an end of federal funding to any public or private agencies found to be engaging in racial discrimination. Department of Health, Education and Welfare (HEW) officials sent out notices to hospitals and state and local educational agencies receiving federal funds informing them that they would have to pledge in writing that they would not discriminate. By September 1965, HEW assistant secretary James Quigley made it clear that hospitals must be completely integrated to remain eligible for federal money. Quigley defined hospital integration as black and white patients "sharing the same rooms, wings, floors, and sections."

The U.S. Office of Education had begun to review thousands of letters of compliance filed by southern and border school districts and state education agencies in March 1965. Educational agencies and districts that refused to comply could lose federal school funds. In March 1965 education commissioner Francis Keppel announced that North Carolina was the first southern state in full compliance with Title VI regulations and was thus entitled to federal funds, but Keppel sent a warning to Alabama state officials that they would have to act immediately to comply or face the loss of millions of dollars in federal aid.

In April 1965 HEW officials announced that public school systems would have to eliminate all racial segregation by September 1967 and would have to make a "substantial good faith start" toward desegregation by September 1965 to continue to receive federal financial assistance. As a result, school board members in Bessemer, Ala., voted in June 1965 to refuse federal funds rather than desegregate. Justice Department officials immediately filed a suit in federal court against the Bessemer school board. Faced with both lawsuits and potential loss of federal funding, Alabama governor George Wallace met with state school administrators in September 1965 and urged them to admit no more African Americans "than law and courts require."

In July 1965 the House Committee on Education and Labor, chaired by Rep. Adam Clayton Powell, launched an investigation of the de facto school segregation found in most northern public school districts. School superintendent Benjamin Willis testified before the committee and claimed that segregation was part of a historical housing pattern in Chicago, but admitted that his staff had not worked on the problem. Ninety percent of black and white students in Chicago attended segregated schools in 1965. Powell made it clear that public school systems in the North faced loss of federal funding if they continued to maintain segregated schools.

Washington Monument, and the Liberty Bell. Robert S. Collier, the group's leader, said they planned the action to dramatize the plight of African Americans (NYT).

18 **In Detroit, Mich.**, to illustrate the difficulty of passing the Alabama voter registration test, reporters from the *Detroit News* excerpted three of the three hundred questions on the U.S. Constitution and asked the federal judges in the area to answer them. None of the eight judges answered all three questions correctly (JM).

22 **In New York City**, Malcolm X, black nationalist leader and president of the Organization for Afro-American Unity, was assassinated while addressing a rally of followers at Harlem's Audubon Ballroom on West 166th Street. Several black leaders voiced their belief in a larger conspiracy behind the murder (NYT).

MARCH 1965

1 **In Mobile, Ala.**, NAACP official Roy Wilkins announced that following the Supreme Court's invalidation of the 1956 injunction banning the NAACP from operating in Alabama, the organization was back in business. The original injunction issued by circuit court judge Walter B. Jones claimed that the NAACP had not registered as an out-of-state corporation (SSN).

1 **In Chattanooga, Tenn.**, school officials launched their in-service training program to prepare teachers of both races to work in desegregated schools. About 175 teachers were to participate in the program, which was the first of its kind in the South. The program was financed by a federal grant (SSN).

1 **In Washington, D.C.**, in a letter to President Johnson and the Congress, U.S. Commission on Civil Rights officials described the discrimination practiced against southern black farmers by four agencies of the Agriculture Department. The commission noted that few basic economic problems could be solved in the South until this situation was corrected and urged Johnson to direct these agencies to reform their practices (NYT).

5 **In Elizabeth, N.J.**, attorney Alvin Bronstein (white), head of the Lawyers Constitutional Defense Committee, charged that he was beaten and jailed in Magnolia, Miss. Bronstein was there to check on eighty-nine civil rights workers arrested for violation of a court injunction against picketing the local courthouse (NYT).

11 **In Cleveland, Ohio**, NAACP official Herbert Hill threatened mass demonstrations if there was no change in the discriminatory hiring practices in Pipefitters Local 120 and the Mechanical Contractors Association. He called for demonstrations at all federal office buildings (JM).

16 **In Washington, D.C.**, in an address before a joint session of Congress, President Johnson called for the passage of voting legislation that would protect the constitutional rights of black citizens (NYT).

17 **In New York City**, about one thousand students and faculty members of Fordham University held a rally protesting conditions in Selma, Ala., and the death of Rev. James Reeb. More than two hundred faculty and students at the New York University School of Social Work also held a memorial rally for Reeb (NYT).

18 **In Atlanta, Ga.**, the Southern Regional Council reported that in 1964 almost two million African Americans were registered to vote in eleven southern states. The figure marked an increase of 724,644 voters since 1956 (JM).

23 **In Albany, N.Y.**, Gov. Nelson Rockefeller signed a bill giving the New York State Commission Against Discrimination (SCAD) power to initiate probes into alleged racial discrimination. Previously, SCAD could only investigate the complaints it received from citizens of the state (NYT).

26 **In New York City**, the Jewish Rabbinical Council of America formed the Task Force of Civil Rights to spur the involvement of Orthodox leaders in the fight for equal rights (NYT).

27 **In Atlanta, Ga.**, Martin Luther King called for an economic boycott of Alabama products and the withdrawal of federal funds from the state.

The major objective of the boycott was to force voting officials to register at least 50 percent of eligible black citizens in the state and to end police brutality (NYT).

APRIL 1965

1 In Richmond, Va., in *Griffin v. State Board of Education,* a special three-judge federal panel held that Virginia's tuition grant laws were not unconstitutional on their face, but that grants could not be used to provide the whole or greater part of the cost of operation of a segregated private school (SSN).

1 In New Orleans, La., seven new school segregation suits were filed in federal district courts. Five sought the desegregation of public schools in Rapides, Pointe Coupee, St. Landry, Lafayette, and Jefferson Davis parishes; one sought the desegregation of a trade school in Avoyelles Parish; and one by a white woman sought the desegregation of Grambling College, an all-black institution (SSN).

1 In Detroit, Mich., attorney Ernest Goodman, president of the National Lawyers Guild, offered to provide volunteer lawyers for Martin Luther King's voter registration drive in Alabama. The guild already maintained a permanent regional office in Jackson, Miss. (JM).

1 In Selma, Ala., after the march to Montgomery, officials of SNCC and SCLC agreed to stop fighting among themselves and continue working together. According to their agreement, SCLC was to continue to mobilize a mass following and generate finances, while SNCC would continue to serve as "shock troops" by performing advance legwork and organizing local leadership (JM).

4 In New York City, Dr. Kenneth B. Clark wrote about the ambivalent role of white liberals toward African Americans. Clark declared that liberals faced conflicting desires to maintain the democratic image of themselves as well as good relations with those who did not share their views. Clark believed this tendency increased blacks' misconceptions about liberals' willingness to act on their behalf (NYT).

12 In New York City, James Farmer announced that CORE's summer drive was set for Louisiana and would focus on voting rights, improvement of police-community relations, and desegregation of public accommodations. Farmer said that South Carolina would be a secondary target, with a major voter registration drive aimed at ousting Sen. Strom Thurmond (NYT).

14 In New York City, an NAACP spokesperson announced that the organization was withdrawing from the Council of Federated Organizations (COFO). The spokesperson cited the NAACP's policy of avoiding permanent alliances and its inability to wrest control of COFO from SNCC as the reasons for the break. The split reflected the growing disagreements among civil rights groups over protest strategies (NYT).

15 In Baltimore, Md., Martin Luther King reemphasized the call for a two-pronged, three-stage, escalated withdrawal of economic support from Alabama. He called upon industry to suspend plant expansion and location in Alabama and the federal government to step up enforcement of Title VI of the Civil Rights Act of 1964. King also called upon private institutions, churches, and labor unions to withhold investments in the area (JM).

15 In Lansing, Mich., state attorney general Frank Kelley ordered his staff of lawyers to prepare a suit against the state of Alabama, charging the state with violation of the Fourteenth Amendment. The suit was intended to reduce Alabama's congressional representation if the arguments were upheld in federal court (JM).

15 In Wilmington, N.C., Dr. Hubert Eaton charged that black patients at James Walker Memorial Hospital were still segregated within the facility and asked a federal court to find the managers in contempt. In 1964, a U.S. district court had ordered the hospital staff not to assign patients on the basis of race and to admit black doctors to the staff (JM).

15 In Camden, Ala., police officers used smoke bombs to stop several hundred civil rights marchers from protesting at a local black high school. Marchers were stopped at the city limits when they could not produce a parade permit.

THE SELMA TO MONTGOMERY MARCH
AND THE VOTING RIGHTS ACT OF 1965

The vicious attack on unarmed civil rights marchers on the Pettus Bridge by Alabama state troopers and local police in Selma on Sunday, 7 March 1965 demonstrated the determination of southern elected officials to prevent at any cost the political advancement of black citizens. Martin Luther King and SCLC targeted Dallas and Perry counties for a major voter registration drive before the end of 1964. In January and February 1965, SCLC's Hosea Williams and SNCC's John Lewis had been leading registration drives, but on 17 February Jimmie Lee Jackson was killed trying to protect his mother when a small group of civil rights marchers was attacked by state troopers. In response to Lee's murder, SCLC and SNCC workers organized a march from Selma to Montgomery, the state capital, but were attacked by police and forced to flee. More than fifty people had to be hospitalized.

Martin Luther King and Ralph David Abernathy, who were in Atlanta, rushed to Selma. Plans were being made for another march on Tuesday, 9 March, but Attorney Gen. Nicholas Katzenbach urged King to postpone the march until the federal courts lifted the state injunction and protection could be guaranteed for the protesters. Because hundreds of ministers and others had already come to Selma to participate in the march, King led the protesters out of the Brown Baptist Church to the bridge. When state troopers told them they could not continue, King knelt in prayer, then turned and led the columns of people back to the church, believing that another bloody confrontation had to be avoided. That night, Rev. James Reeb, a Boston clergyman who had come to Selma to participate in the march, was attacked and beaten by local whites and died two days later. On Monday, 15 March, President Johnson addressed a joint session of Congress, announcing new voting rights legislation.

People came to Selma from all over the country to participate in the Selma to Montgomery march, which began with federal approval and police protection on Sunday, 21 March, and culminated three days later on the steps of the state capitol, where King and other leaders addressed the more than twenty-five thousand people assembled. The violence that plagued the voting rights campaigns throughout the year continued with the shooting of Viola Liuzzo from Detroit as she transported marchers between Selma and Montgomery. As in the case of the accused murderers of Rev. James Reeb, the three indicted for the Liuzzo murder were acquitted by an Alabama jury. However, federal indictments were brought against Klansmen Collie Wilkins, Eugene Thomas, and William Eaton for Liuzzo's murder, and in December 1965, they were convicted of manslaughter and sentenced to ten years in prison.

Between May and August 1965, civil rights groups lobbied hard for the passage of the Voting Rights Act, which passed Congress and was signed by the president on 6 August 1965. The measure provided for suspension of literacy tests as a requirement to vote and federal registration of potential voters in states and counties where less than 50 percent of the voting-age population was registered or voted in November 1964. The law also called upon the attorney general to challenge the constitutionality of state poll taxes as a requirement to vote.

Immediately after the law took effect, federal registrars were dispatched to Alabama, Mississippi, and Louisiana. Despite the attempts by Alabama governor George Wallace and others to thwart the registrars' activities, it was estimated that by September 1965 more than fifty thousand new voters were added to the rolls in those three states alone.

Mayor F. R. Albritton warned marchers that they were jeopardizing the town's chance of getting a $65 million industrial facility (JM).

15 In **Jonesboro, La.**, pupils completed a three-week boycott of classes to protest classroom conditions. Gov. John McKeithen negotiated with white and black students and promised to provide more and better books, additional water fountains, and landscaping of the playground (JM).

21 In **New York City**, NAACP leader Roy Wilkins announced the group was seeking twelve hundred volunteers for summer voter registration drives in Alabama, Mississippi, and South Carolina. Local branches were asked to contribute $500,000 to cover costs. Wilkins believed that the new voting drives would not conflict with programs of other civil rights groups (NYT).

22 In **Carson City, Nev.**, Gov. Grant Sawyers signed into law the state's new civil rights law, which banned discrimination in public accommodations and in employment. Under the new law, a person had the right to file a criminal misdemeanor complaint and sue for civil damages or appeal to the state equal rights commission when victimized by discrimination (JM).

22 In **Nashville, Tenn.**, the recently organized Southern Student Organizing Committee sent letters to supporters asking for donations of one dollar each. The organization, composed of southern white students, was formed by SNCC members and sought to bolster civil rights activity in the southern states (JM).

29 In **Washington, D.C.**, Department of Health, Education and Welfare officials directed six hospitals in Alabama to desegregate facilities or lose funds from the Hill-Burton Act. The hospitals were Tuscaloosa, Fayette, Decatur, Dothan, Wetumpka, and Oneonta (JM).

29 In **New York City**, Donald Barnes of the Childs Securities Corp. announced that the company would no longer buy or sell bonds issued by the state of Alabama or any of its political subdivisions. Barnes said that the company took the step because of the failure of the Wallace administra-

tion "to protect citizens of Alabama in the exercise of their constitutional rights" (JM).

29 In **Selma, Ala.**, a grand jury indicted three out of four white men arrested in connection with the murder of Rev. James Reeb, a (white) Unitarian minister killed during the Selma march. Indicted were O'Neal Hoggles, William Hoggles, and Elmer Cook (JM).

MAY 1965

1 In **Baton Rouge, La.**, federal judge E. Gordon West issued a permanent injunction ordering all eighteen of the state-operated trade and vocational schools in Louisiana to integrate. Ten of the schools were already under court orders to do so (SSN).

1 In **Austin, Tex.**, it was revealed that while some black teachers were being assigned to teach racially mixed classes, others were losing their jobs. In West Columbia, Tex., for example, the black high school of the Columbia-Brazoria School District was to be consolidated with Columbia High School (white). Only five black teachers were being retained in the merger, while eight were losing their positions (SSN).

6 In **Washington, D.C.**, southern congressmen moved to block appropriations for the Agriculture Department to protest the implementation of nondiscrimination orders. They geared up for the fight after Agriculture Department officials prepared to hire black agents for the first time. Although the department's budget was initially slashed, Rep. Charles Diggs intervened, threatened a floor fight, and got the money restored (JM).

12 In **Washington, D.C.**, American Civil Liberties Union (ACLU) executive director John de J. Pemberton announced a "total commitment program" to aid civil rights workers in the South, using the Lawyers Constitutional Defense Committee as the ACLU's legal arm. Pemberton said the committee would still get its direction from civil rights organizations, but the ACLU would seek $75,000 for its operations (NYT).

13 In Washington, D.C., federal welfare administrator Dr. Ellen Winston warned Alabama governor George Wallace to integrate the state's welfare agencies within thirty days. She warned Wallace that if integration did not occur, the government would withdraw $30 million in federal funds from the state (JM).

13 In Tuscaloosa, Ala., the Tuscaloosa Transit Co. obtained a city franchise, put three buses into operation, and hired a black driver. The company replaced the old bus line, which went out of business as a result of a boycott by black riders (JM).

13 In Chicago, Ill., Sargent Shriver, director of the Peace Corps and the Office of Economic Opportunity (OEO), announced that 8.8 percent of all top jobs in the Peace Corps and the OEO were held by African Americans. He also pointed out that African Americans directed the anti-poverty efforts in seven of the nation's ten largest cities (JM).

20 In Washington, D.C., Hammermill Paper Co. stockholder John Silvera announced plans to take the floor at the next stockholders meeting to protest the company's decision to locate a plant in Selma, Alabama. Silvera served as the president of the Negro and Allied Shareholders of America, an organization formed to improve the hiring practices and racial policies of leading corporations (JM).

25 In Milwaukee, Wis., black state representative Lloyd Barbee and ten others were arrested at the Brown Street School after blocking school buses transferring black youths to another less crowded school. They were protesting the fact that black students were bused to white schools but were kept in segregated classrooms within the schools (NYT).

27 In Greenville, Miss., a group of white community leaders called on businessmen to offer employment opportunities to all qualified job seekers regardless of race. Leaders of the Washington County NAACP and twenty-nine other organizations praised the declaration as providing "a gateway to a new era for human relationships" (JM).

JUNE 1965

1 In New York City, NAACP Legal Defense Fund director Jack Greenberg, in a telegram to U.S. commissioner of education Francis Keppel, expressed concern that a trend toward "wholesale dismissal of Negro public school teachers was emerging throughout the South." Greenberg said that at least five hundred black teachers in North Carolina would lose their jobs this year because of desegregation. He reported receiving protests of dismissals from Florida, Georgia, Texas, and Virginia (SSN).

1 In Aiken County, S.C., federal officials rejected a desegregation plan by local school officials and withheld $350,000 in federal funds from the school district. The money was withheld under Department of Health, Education, and Welfare nondiscrimination rules (SSN).

1 In New Orleans, La., two of Louisiana's three remaining "one race" institutions of higher learning were to be desegregated. The Louisiana State University Medical School at New Orleans accepted a black student for enrollment in September. Grambling College, a black institution, was ordered by a federal district court to accept white students. Of the fourteen state-operated campuses, only Louisiana State University at Alexandria had not desegregated (SSN).

1 In Tuscaloosa, Ala., Vivian Malone became the first African American to graduate from the University of Alabama. James Hood, a black student who enrolled with Malone, dropped out before graduation. In Clemson, S.C., Harvey Gantt became the first black to graduate from Clemson University. He was an honors graduate in architecture (SSN).

3 In Birmingham, Ala., the Alabama Christian Movement for Human Rights published a twelve-page pamphlet called *See How We Die*. The pamphlet dealt with the murder of Robert McKinley, who was shot by a policeman. Although the policeman claimed self-defense, pamphlet photos revealed that McKinley was shot in the back (JM).

10 In Gary, Ind., the city council passed a fair housing bill banning discrimination on the basis of race. It was one of the strongest municipal ordinances of its kind in the nation. The bill carried a penalty clause allowing fines of up to three hundred dollars or six months in jail for those convicted of racial discrimination (JM).

10 In Natchez, Miss., Mayor John Nosser asked both African Americans and whites to end boycotts of his three supermarkets and one variety store. Whites started a boycott because they felt the mayor was doing too much for civil rights. African Americans, under the guidance of the Council of Federated Organizations, also started boycotting the stores because they felt the mayor was not doing enough (JM).

10 In Washington, D.C., President Johnson appointed attorney Patricia Roberts Harris, a Howard University professor, as ambassador to Luxembourg. She became the first African American woman to serve as a U.S. ambassador (JM).

10 In Honolulu, Hawaii, members of the International Longshoremen's and Warehousemen's Union (ILWU) temporarily halted unloading of the *Steel Advocate,* which carried Alabama-made water pipe, fittings, and paper. They finished only after ILWU Local 142 president Carl Damaso received assurances from most of the consignees that they would not order any more products from Alabama (JM).

24 In Washington, D.C., President Johnson announced a White House conference on the conditions of African Americans to be held in the fall. The meeting was called to explore new legislation, new programs, and new ideas. He made the announcement in a commencement speech delivered at Howard University (JM).

24 In Washington County, Miss., a group of twelve black tractor drivers and seventy cotton workers walked off their jobs on the plantation of A. L. Andrews to press for higher wages. Their strike was backed by the Delta Ministry, the Council of Federated Organizations, SNCC, the Missis-sippi Freedom Democratic party, and other civil rights groups (JM).

24 In Atlanta, Ga., SCLC officials announced a new program called VISION, under the leadership of Rev. C. T. Vivian. Under the program, one hundred tutors would be sent to ten cities in Alabama to instruct fifteen hundred youngsters in college preparatory classes (JM).

25 In the state of Ala., 84 of 118 Alabama school boards had submitted desegregation plans to the Department of Health, Education, and Welfare in defiance of Gov. George Wallace's plan for resisting compliance with the Civil Rights Act of 1964. Most plans called for desegregation of all twelve grades by September 1965 rather than the required minimum of four (NYT).

26, 27 In Philadelphia, Pa., 350 policemen patrolled the area around Girard College after violence flared as the NAACP maintained a picketing vigil. Two policemen were hurt and nineteen demonstrators were arrested in an outbreak of violence when the pickets stormed police barricades. The school had been picketed nightly since 1 May because of its racially discriminatory admission policy (NYT).

JULY 1965

1 In Detroit, Mich., General Motors (GM) official Louis Seaton ordered factory managers to permit an NAACP delegation to view the company's personnel records. The NAACP sought to survey the progress made by GM in improving its hiring of black salaried personnel (JM).

1 In Huntsville, Ala., Dr. Werner Von Braun, director of the U.S. Space Center, warned a meeting of the Alabama Chamber of Commerce that the federal government might close the space center unless racial relations were improved in the state. He urged local residents to mobilize to defeat segregation in the state (JM).

1 In Augusta, Ga., University Hospital administrators announced the desegregation of all of its wards. It became the second major hospital in the

"REVERSE FREEDOM RIDES":
THE SCLC AND SNCC JOIN THE NAACP AND CORE
IN CIVIL RIGHTS PROTESTS IN THE NORTH

The SCLC's decision in April 1965 to expand its activities into northern cities reflected the growing awareness that racial discrimination, violence, and the denial of black civil rights was not limited to the southern states. The NAACP and CORE branches had been actively involved in civil rights struggles in many northern and western cities and often welcomed the additional support from SCLC and SNCC. Early in 1965 CORE officials organized a six-state boycott of Trailways Bus Company after the company refused to hire African Americans as drivers. CORE branches in Philadelphia, Baltimore, Chicago, and other cities targeted Trailways bus terminals for protests against employment discrimination. Despite disclosures of increasing debts by some CORE branches, members of CORE and SNCC in May 1965 launched the "Reverse Freedom Rides" to expose "northern hypocrisy." Both groups went to Syracuse, N.Y., and launched a series of demonstrations against the Niagara Mohawk Power Corporation because of its discriminatory hiring practices. The protests, which included sit-ins, stall-ins, and jail-ins and lasted for over two months, resulted in the tripling of the number of black workers at the company.

In addition to employment discrimination, another important issue addressed by CORE and SNCC members as they expanded their activities in northern cities was police brutality. In New York City, CORE members organized demonstrations at city hall in July 1965 demanding the creation of a civilian police review board that would oversee police activities and investigate charges of police brutality and misconduct. In July 1965 in Newark, N.J., ten white and black demonstrators from the Newark-Essex CORE chapter were arrested outside Mayor Hugh J. Addonizio's office while protesting alleged police brutality and demanding establishment of a civilian police review board.

It was in Chicago, beginning in June 1965, that SNCC and SCLC came together to support the ongoing protests, demonstrations, and boycotts protesting public school segregation organized by the Coordinating Council of Community Organizations (CCCO), which included the local branches of CORE and the NAACP. The school board's announcement in May 1965 that it was renewing the contract of school superintendent Benjamin Willis, whose policies fostering racial segregation had triggered a massive school boycott in 1963, led to CCCO calls for a second boycott. After a court injunction against the proposed school boycott was issued, CCCO, SNCC, SCLC, and CORE launched a week of "massive disruption" (9–16 June). SNCC, SCLC, and CORE demonstrators created massive traffic jams for several days by staging sit-down protests at intersections in the downtown area. About five hundred people were arrested, including many Catholic priests and nuns, in a march on city hall and the school board headquarters. As a result of the week-long protests, Willis agreed to remain as superintendent for only one more year, and plans were announced for finding his successor.

In June 1965 Martin Luther King officially announced that Chicago would be the target of SCLC's first full-scale civil rights drive in the North. On 26 July 1965 King led a march on Chicago's city hall accompanied by CCCO's Albert Raby, Dick Gregory, and local SNCC, CORE, and NAACP leaders and pledged to work as strenuously for an end to housing and public school segregation in Chicago and other northern cities as he had in the South.

state to desegregate, following the lead of Atlanta's Grady Memorial Hospital (JM).

1 In Cincinnati, Ohio, the one African American on the school board, Calvin Conliffe, joined other members in denying that they maintained segregated schools and discriminated against black educators. The NAACP filed a suit in federal court charging that school officials practiced discrimination and segregation in the hiring and assignment of black teachers, in the appointment of black principals, in the failure to promote African Americans to supervisory positions, and in the location of new schools (JM).

8 In Atlanta, Ga., eight hundred white and black volunteers attended a six-day orientation for a SCLC project called SCOPE, the Summer Community Organization and Political Education. After the orientation, the volunteers fanned out over sixty counties in six southern states to attempt to boost black voter registration over a three-month period (JM).

8 In Philadelphia, Miss., fifty people marched to commemorate the deaths of James Chaney, Andrew Goodman, and Michael Schwerner. The march ended at the burned-out Mt. Zion Methodist Church, the destination of the workers the day they were killed. At the march it was also revealed that Fannie Lou Chaney, mother of James Chaney, was still being terrorized by KKK youth groups and was refused employment by local whites (JM).

8 In Jackson, Miss., civil rights militants and their supporters complained of "concentration camp–type" brutality exerted against jailed demonstrators. Clergymen, nurses, and physicians reported finding bruises, miscarriages, and evidence of torture inflicted on prisoners. The medics complained that police refused them permission to administer first aid to prisoners (JM).

13 In Philadelphia, Pa., two policemen and three NAACP pickets were hurt in a clash outside the State Office Building as Gov. William Scranton, Mayor James H. Tate, and U.S. Community Relations director LeRoy Collins met with Girard College officials. An accord was reached to seek court action to desegregate the college without breaking the founder's will (NYT).

14 In Washington, D.C., Thurgood Marshall left his federal judgeship in order to serve as U.S. solicitor general. Three previous solicitor generals—William Howard Taft, Stanley Reed, and Robert Jackson—had been appointed to the U.S. Supreme Court (NYT).

15 In Camden, Ala., city police and Wilcox County sheriff's officers arrested eighteen people on charges of violating a city anti-boycott ordinance. Merchants had begun to feel the pinch of a boycott organized by SCLC workers (JM).

15 In Denver, Colo., at its fifty-sixth annual convention NAACP officials utilized clinics, mass meetings, and briefings to provide delegates with information on the key areas covered by the 1964 Civil Rights Act, especially the newly created Equal Employment Opportunity Commission. Leaders from 1,845 NAACP branches in forty-eight states studied action plans for the implementation of public school and housing desegregation, reactivating the President's Committee on Housing, increasing the number of southern black voters, and changing the voting practices of northern blacks. Executive secretary Roy Wilkins stated that the theme was "more results than headlines" (JM).

22 In Milwaukee, Wis., state representative Lloyd Barbee asked Department of Health, Education and Welfare secretary Anthony Celebrezze to cut off all federal funds to city schools because the school board was practicing segregation. Barbee described several areas where the school board was practicing segregation through the location of schools and in the assignment of students and teachers (JM).

26 In Seattle, Wash., the Central Area Committee on Civil Rights launched Freedom Patrols to follow police while they patrolled the black community. The patrols were organized following the 20 June 1965 fatal shooting of Robert Reese, a black man, by white off-duty patrolman Harold Larsen (NYT).

29 In Birmingham, Ala., Mayor Albert Boutwell appointed an interracial six-member panel of local educators to "examine and evaluate all applications and tests for the position of policeman in the past few years." His order came after black community leaders insisted on the hiring of black policemen for the city (JM).

29 In Chicago, Ill., the SNCC Freedom Center issued a bulletin containing information about civil and property rights for black residents. The bulletin also gave readers practical advice on police brutality, evictions, current legislation, and the war on poverty (JM).

29 In Atlanta, Ga., SNCC and other student civil rights groups began publication of the *Southern Courier*. They planned to distribute copies of the paper throughout Georgia, Alabama, and Mississippi (JM).

29 In San Francisco, Calif., members of the housing authority enacted two measures to counteract charges of discrimination and to improve its public image. Housing commissioners approved a new set of hiring rules that would give minorities greater employment opportunities in the agency and eliminated references to race in the agency's rental applications (JM)

31 In South Africa, the civil rights song "We Shall Overcome" was almost entirely suppressed, without having been officially banned. White South African authorities were afraid of the impact the song might have on the black African majority. Folksinger Pete Seeger, the song's arranger, donated profits from the song's copyright to civil rights organizations (NYT).

AUGUST 1965

1 In Atlanta, Ga., SCLC, SNCC, and CORE announced that they were expanding the number of full-time workers in the South, particularly in North Carolina and South Carolina. Black leaders warned against increasing violence and identified areas where nonviolent campaigns were met by anti-black violence and little success. Some voter registration gains were noted, mainly in Delta counties of Arkansas, through efforts of students and community workers (NYT).

2 In Greensboro, Ala., and other areas, Freedom Schools were flourishing. The schools were established as a means of ensuring SNCC, SCLC, and CORE of a "vast reservoir of grass roots workers" for the future. The NAACP decided to concentrate its efforts on voter registration drives (NYT).

3, 4 In Philadelphia, Pa., Martin Luther King arrived in the city and applauded NAACP protests around Girard College. An earlier controversy over King's visit was resolved, and he and the NAACP's Cecil B. Moore led five thousand people in a protest rally near the college. Gov. William Scranton had urged an end to picketing pending legal efforts to integrate the school (NYT).

5 In Hot Springs, Ark., National Education Association (NEA) officials proposed that all certified teachers in dual systems be retained for at least one year after the separate public school systems were united. The NEA announcement followed pressure from civil rights organizations to save teachers' jobs affected by desegregation, especially those of black teachers (JM).

5 In Houston, Tex., Jacqueline McCauley and Edward Freeman enrolled at Rice University and marked the successful completion of the school's voluntary desegregation. Trustees had to get court permission to break the will of William Marsh Rice, who stipulated that the school was to admit only whites (JM).

7, 21 In Washington, D.C., Department of Health, Education, and Welfare officials reported that 3,455 school districts in seventeen southern and border states had complied with nondiscrimination guidelines. HEW set a deadline for 181 school districts, mainly in the Deep South, to comply with the regulations or risk loss of federal aid (NYT).

12 In Washington, D.C., officials of the Equal Employment Opportunity Commission (EEOC) announced that they had received more than 170 job complaints based on discrimination because of sex, race, or religion. They announced that the EEOC would begin processing the forms pending the establishment of regional offices and the hiring of a staff of 190 investigators (JM).

12 In Birmingham, Ala., officials of the Sixteenth Street Baptist Church rejected SCLC's request to use the building during its August meeting. Church members later had a change of heart and offered their church to the organization. In 1963, the church had been destroyed by a bomb, which killed four black girls (JM).

12–14 In Los Angeles, Calif., rioting erupted in the Watts section of the city. The riot was sparked after a state trooper arrested a black man on suspicion of drunk driving. Thirty-seven people were killed and 3,934 were arrested. More than two thousand National Guardsmen were brought in to quell the rioting and looting. During the riot, comedian Dick Gregory was shot in the leg when he urged rioters to return to their homes. President Johnson's top black aide, Louis Martin, flew to Los Angeles and met with black political leaders (NYT).

14 In Chicago, Ill., 150 police battled rioters in the Fillmore district. Twenty-four people were arrested and seventy-five injured, including eighteen policemen. Gov. Otto Kerner placed two thousand National Guardsmen on alert at the request of Chicago police officials. The riot occurred after a rally protesting the death of a black woman struck by a fire engine. Protest leaders demanded the immediate desegregation of the fire company involved (NYT).

19 In Los Angeles, Calif., Martin Luther King toured the Watts neighborhood in the wake of the riot. Although he faced a hostile crowd of black youths, he eventually won them over. Later in the day, King met with Gov. Edmund Brown, who had urged him to stay out of Los Angeles and rejected King's request for a civilian police review board. Brown did announce that $1.77 million in federal funds would be applied toward a "work experience program" involving sixteen hundred people to rehabilitate the riot area (NYT).

21 In Washington, D.C., President Johnson signed a $3.5 billion public works economic development bill. He also announced a ten-point program for rebuilding Los Angeles after the riots. The project included a stepped-up youth training program, establishment of a small business development center, a back-to-school program, and more low-income housing (NYT).

23 In Washington, D.C., SNCC field secretary Stokely Carmichael reported efforts to get votes for black candidates seeking positions on the Lowndes County (Ala.) Agriculture Stabilization and Conservation Service Committee. Carmichael noted that no African American had served on the farmer-elected committee that shaped local farm policy (NYT).

26 In Birmingham, Ala., SCLC held its ninth annual convention. Although he acknowledged that Birmingham had come a long way since 1963, Martin Luther King stated that demonstrations were planned for the city to rid it of all remaining racial discrimination (JM).

26 In Prince Edward County, Va., federal funds helped launch "Operation Catch-Up." The program was designed to raise the reading level of county students, where public schools had been closed for five years to avoid integration (JM).

28 In Natchez, Miss., NAACP leader George Metcalfe was seriously injured when a bomb destroyed his car as he was leaving the Armstrong Tire and Rubber Company plant. Metcalfe's secretary said that he had been receiving telephone threats for weeks, because whites resented Armstrong's efforts to integrate the plant's cafeteria. Civil rights workers reported that hundreds of armed black residents swarmed into the city's streets threatening revenge for the bombing. Police instituted a curfew and black leaders met with the mayor and a biracial committee to discuss the demands of the black community (NYT).

29 In Los Angeles, Calif., various government, private, and religious organizations seeking to improve the plight of African Americans in the Watts area cited feelings of isolation and rejection by residents, even among the middle class, as keys to the rioting. Some Watts residents rejected recommendations from outside civil rights groups about ways to solve the area's problems (NYT).

CHURCH BURNINGS, BOMBINGS, AND RACIAL VIOLENCE
CONTINUE IN THE SOUTH

According to *The New York Times,* by the beginning of 1965 there had been at least thirty-five church burnings or bombings in the state of Mississippi alone over the previous three years. In February 1965 in Jackson, Miss., civil rights activist Ollie Shelby was killed while in the custody of sheriff's deputies. In Indianola, Miss., in May 1965 firebombs destroyed two African American homes and a store and damaged the local "freedom house." In Laurel, Miss., in July, thirteen buildings owned by black residents, including one containing the Council of Federated Organizations headquarters, were damaged or destroyed by gasoline firebombs. After several additional shootings and arson attacks, Laurel mayor Henry Bucklew went on television in November 1965 and criticized the Klan and offered a thousand-dollar reward for information leading to the conviction of any persons for church burnings and other arson attacks or firing shots into homes. In Vicksburg, Miss., that same month, a black-owned grocery store was heavily damaged by an explosion, which shattered the windows of surrounding homes and injured three people. The bombing followed local black leaders' announcement of a boycott of several white merchants over discriminatory hiring practices.

Unfortunately, there was even greater racial violence in Alabama in 1965 than in Mississippi. Unarmed civil rights marchers were attacked by white mobs in Marion, Ala., in February. In Birmingham, Ala., in March 1965, a bomb damaged the home of T. L. Crowell, slightly injuring his son. In addition, six undetonated bombs were discovered by police in black areas, including the home of Rev. A. D. King, brother of Martin Luther King, and at all-black Western High School. Two army demolition experts found that the bombs failed to explode because of faulty assembly. African Americans in Lowndes County, Ala., who participated in the Selma to Montgomery march were fired on by Klan night riders in May 1965. That same month black churches in Oxford and Friendship, Miss., known for sponsoring civil rights activities, were bombed.

In Hayneville, Ala., white seminarian Jonathan M. Daniels was killed and Richard F. Morrisroe, a white Catholic priest, was critically injured by shotgun blasts in August 1965. The clergymen were shot in front of a store patronized by local black residents; according to witnesses, they were shielding a black girl accompanying them. Deputy Sheriff Tom L. Coleman was charged with murder and assault; although no weapons were found, he pleaded self-defense and in October was acquitted of all charges by an all-white jury.

Bombings, church burnings, and other forms of violence occurred in other parts of the South as well. In Baton Rouge, La., an explosion ripped the roof off a black nightclub in August 1965. This was the third explosion involving a black business in the city that year. In Greensboro, N.C., that same month, the burning of two black churches heavily involved in civil rights activities sparked a massive march on city hall that was broken up by police using tear gas. In Charlotte, N.C., in November, night riders bombed the homes of four black civil rights leaders, including NAACP leader Kelly Alexander and city councilman Fred Alexander. North Carolina governor Daniel K. Moore promised swift action, and Mayor Stan R. Brookshire urged all residents to contribute to a fund to aid in rebuilding the homes. Alabama attorney general Richmond Flowers issued a report in October 1965 on Klan activity and noted that the terrorist group was linked to forty of forty-five racial bombings in Birmingham since 1961, as well as twelve of seventeen murders in various parts of the South since 1963.

SEPTEMBER 1965

2 In Los Angeles, Calif., NAACP leader Ike Adams offered six proposals to bring peace to the city and prevent another riot. Suggestions included keeping an Office of Economic Opportunity representative in the city, offering job training, improving community-police relations, providing an ample supply of teachers and classrooms, keeping National Guardsmen in the area, and seeking input from all segments of the community in decision making (JM).

2 In Washington, D.C., at the White House Conference on Equal Employment, "To Fulfill These Rights," Vice President Hubert Humphrey warned four hundred delegates that African Americans were on the verge of a major economic crisis. Humphrey told the representatives from business, government, and labor that the gap was widening between the amount of training received by black youths and the requirements of the labor market (JM).

3 In Natchez, Miss., Gov. Paul Johnson sent 650 National Guard troops to quell racial violence. NAACP state leader Charles Evers called off a black march, saying the guard came not to protect black residents, but to "beat and kill" them if they tried to demonstrate (NYT).

8 In Bridgeport, Conn., the Bridgeport-Stratford NAACP branch planned a protest against segregated school conditions and the refusal of school officials to correct them. The NAACP planned three days of demonstrations in front of school board headquarters (NYT).

10, 11, 12 In Boston, Mass., several hundred black parents transported their children to predominantly white schools in a move labeled "Operation Exodus." The parents vowed not to enroll their children in overcrowded schools in Roxbury and North Dorchester. The Boston School Committee opposed busing the children to the white schools (NYT).

16 In East Caroll Parish, La., black citizens moved into the majority of the registered voters. The parish became the first in the state where black voters outnumbered whites (JM).

25 In Washington, D.C., the President's Committee on Equal Employment Opportunity was phased out of business. President Johnson replaced the committee with the new Office of Federal Contract Compliance and named Edward Sylvester, Jr., as director (NYT).

30 In Washington, D.C., the House of Representatives voted to dismiss the voting challenge brought against five Democratic congressmen from Mississippi by members of the Mississippi Freedom Democratic party. A huge liberal lobby composed of national black organizations, the National Council of Churches, the Leadership Conference on Civil Rights, and labor groups had attempted to unseat the Mississippi congressmen (JM).

OCTOBER 1965

4 In Natchez, Miss., policemen jailed NAACP leader Charles Evers for parading without a permit. When violence almost erupted between marchers and Klansmen, police brought Evers from jail to attempt to control "his" people. After the crowds dispersed, police took Evers back to jail. Evers later declared that demonstrations and the boycott of downtown merchants by black customers would continue until city officials satisfied black demands for desegregation of public accommodations (NYT).

7 In Laurel, Miss., Judge Lunsford Casey ordered a grand jury to "leave no stone unturned in seeking evidence to bring those responsible [for night riders' crimes] to justice." Casey made the remarks following the third shooting into the home of local NAACP leader Dr. B. E. Murph (JM).

7 In Washington, D.C., NAACP leaders Aaron Henry and Robert Smith and the United Church of Christ appealed to the U.S. court of appeals after the Federal Communications Commission rejected their request to withdraw a Mississippi television station's license. They argued that station WLBT discriminated against African Americans in the presentation of news and announcements and in selection of program material (JM).

14 In Birmingham, Ala., Mayor Albert Boutwell announced plans to establish an auxiliary police force for the city. Members of the Alabama Democratic Conference, a black organization, urged him to name at least half of the body from the black community. There were no black policemen in Birmingham (JM).

14 In Kansas City, Mo., real estate agent Betty Hennessey became the first person convicted and fined for violating the anti–block busting law. Ray Colvin, a white homeowner, testified that the agent tried to get him to sell his house because an

African American bought the house next door (JM).

14 In Crawfordville, Ga., as part of white residents' economic reprisals against civil rights activists, several black women were fired from their jobs. SCLC began an "aid the maids" campaign afterward. Demonstrations continued as black students attempted to ride buses with white pupils to schools in nearby counties (JM).

17 In Washington, D.C., attorney Wiley Branton was named special assistant to Attorney Gen. Nicholas Katzenbach, as a result of a shift in civil rights enforcement from Vice President Hubert Humphrey to Katzenbach. Branton favored stronger Justice Department action in black voter registration than Katzenbach, who had been criticized by civil rights groups for not appointing enough federal registrars (NYT).

17, 18, 20, 27 In Milwaukee, Wis., CORE leaders called a halt to a school boycott after four days. Black students had been boycotting segregated public schools. Before the boycott, Auxiliary Bishop Roman Atkilski forbade his clergymen and nuns from taking part and barred the use of church property for "freedom schools." A group of priests and nuns ignored his order and participated in the boycott (NYT).

21 In Los Angeles, Calif., NAACP attorney Leroy Clarke filed suit in the state supreme court asking that the prosecution of the forty-three hundred people arrested in connection with the Los Angeles riot be suspended until the people were adequately represented by legal counsel. The suit resulted from a letter the NAACP received from a man who said he had been held in jail since August without a lawyer (JM).

21 In New Orleans, La., NAACP official Arthur Chapital asked the Justice Department to investigate charges that African Americans in Plaquemine Parish were forced at gunpoint to clean up debris left by Hurricane Betsy. Clarence Marchand and Fred Patterson charged that they were forcibly taken by school official Leander Perez to clean up a damaged white school (JM).

21 In Birmingham, Ala., Joe Bruce died after a white ambulance driver, Owen Collett, refused to take him to the hospital. The ambulance driver arrived minutes after Bruce was hit by a car, but then drove away. Collett was later fired over the incident (JM).

26 In Lowndes County, Ala., the Justice Department intervened in a suit filed by five African Americans charging systematic exclusion from jury duty. This was the first time that the department intervened in a private suit brought under the 1964 Civil Rights Act (NYT).

28 In Washington, D.C., the U.S. Supreme Court heard another of Alabama's many suits against Rev. Fred Shuttlesworth. Shuttlesworth had been convicted of loitering and refusing to comply with a police order when he participated in a protest demonstration (JM).

28 In the state of Missouri, the first civil rights law went into effect. All businesses except neighborhood barber- and beauty shops were barred from discriminating because of race, religion, or national origin (JM).

28 In Crawfordville, Ga., city officials promised to make concessions to the black community, such as ending police brutality, if civil rights leaders ended demonstrations. SCLC leader Hosea Williams ended the demonstrations only after a federal court order was issued closing the black public school and ordering school officials to place the eighty-seven black pupils in desegregated schools (JM).

NOVEMBER 1965

11 In Washington, D.C., Clarence Mitchell disclosed that the NAACP and the Leadership Conference of Civil Rights lawyers were drafting legislation making it a federal crime to attack or kill a civil rights worker. The legislation would allow families of victims to sue the perpetrators or the government for damages (JM).

11 In Atlanta, Ga., Martin Luther King met with SCLC personnel to develop plans to put pressure on Congress to adopt legislation that would forbid exclusion of African Americans from southern juries and make the murder of civil rights workers a federal crime (JM).

11 In **Los Angeles, Calif.**, the district court of appeals refused to halt the trials and order more legal counsel for the forty-three hundred people arrested during the Watts riot. NAACP Legal Defense Fund lawyers then appealed to the U.S. Supreme Court to halt the prosecutions. The petition stated that the state, by not allowing adequate representation, was "perpetuating the same injustices which gave rise to the disturbances" (JM).

17 In **Washington, D.C.**, two hundred black and white leaders attended the White House Conference on Civil Rights. President Johnson revealed that he had asked Attorney Gen. Nicholas Katzenbach to prepare legislation to prevent injustices to African Americans at the hands of all-white juries. He also stated that he had asked the U.S. Commission on Civil Rights to turn its careful attention to problems of race and education in all parts of the country (JM).

18 In **Springfield, Ohio**, Robert Henry was elected as the first black mayor of a major city since Reconstruction. In Dayton, Ohio, Don Crawford lost his bid for mayor, as did Carl Stokes in Cleveland (JM).

18 In **Jefferson City, Mo.**, the state commission on human relations heard charges from five black teachers in Dunklin County who lost their positions when the public schools were desegregated. The teachers charged the firings were in violation of the state's fair employment law (JM).

25 In **Washington, D.C.**, U.S. Office of Education officials announced that all of Florida's school districts qualified for federal funds under the non-discrimination provisions of Title VI of the Civil Rights Act of 1964. It was the first state from the lower South to qualify (JM).

28 In **Wilmington, Del.**, the state legislature passed a fair housing bill drawn up by Gov. Charles L. Terry. The bill was developed under pressure from the state human rights commission, the NAACP, and other civil rights groups. Real estate interests in the state headed the opposition to the measure (NYT).

DECEMBER 1965

2 In **Cleveland, Ohio**, the NAACP, representing parents of thirty-four black and nine white pupils in Dayton, Ohio, asked a federal court to invalidate the neighborhood school plan. The suit charged that Dayton's public schools were racially segregated (JM).

2 In **Greenville, Ala.**, police turned back two civil rights marches involving more than one hundred African Americans when city officials decided a previous demonstration at a local school had pushed racial tensions to the boiling point. State troopers were called in to help restore order and seal off the black section of town when violence broke out after the first march (JM).

2 In **Washington, D.C.**, Rep. Adam Clayton Powell called on President Johnson to appoint an interracial committee to investigate the Civil Service Commission, which Powell claimed denied promotion opportunities to black federal employees. Powell argued that black employees had remained in the lower classifications of federal employment for decades (JM).

2 In **Washington, D.C.**, for the fifth time, the U.S. Supreme Court threw out a lower-court conviction against Rev. Fred Shuttlesworth. The case thrown out was a conviction for loitering that grew out of civil rights activities in Birmingham in 1962 (JM).

2 In **Oxford, Miss.**, Republican House minority leader Gerald Ford canceled a speech to a group of Mississippi Republicans in Natchez because the audience would be segregated. He made the announcement before an integrated audience at the University of Mississippi. He also used the opportunity to criticize KKK activities (JM).

2 In **Little Rock, Ark.**, eight black teachers who lost their jobs when the all-black school was closed appealed to the federal court to be reinstated. A lower court had ruled that school officials did not have to guarantee positions to teachers displaced because of school desegregation (JM).

2 In **Nairobi, Kenya**, government officials ordered the withdrawal of Kenyan students from

DEACONS OF DEFENSE AND JUSTICE

While many black southerners were willing to participate in nonviolent direct action protests to obtain equal rights, others believed that they should carry arms to protect themselves during "peaceful" demonstrations. After civil rights activists and black schoolchildren were attacked by the KKK during civil rights marches in Jonesboro and Bogalusa, La., in December 1964, local black residents formed the Deacons of Defense and Justice. According to one of the founders, Charles Sims, the group consisted of heavily armed African Americans who vowed to defend themselves from marauding whites. Sims stated that it was police brutality and the failure of law enforcement officials to protect African Americans that led to the founding of the group.

In April 1965 in Bogalusa, La., CORE members staying in the local Freedom House came under attack from bricks and Klan gunfire. Twelve members of the Deacons of Defense, armed with shotguns, rushed to defend the civil rights workers and fired back at the attackers. In May 1965 after a dozen firebomb attacks on homes, automobiles, and churches of civil rights activists, Bogalusa mayor Jesse Cutrer agreed to negotiate a peaceful settlement of the town's racial crisis with the Bogalusa Civic and Voters League, the local civil rights group. Among the demands Mayor Cutrer agreed to were the repeal of all segregation ordinances and the employment of African Americans on the police force and in other city departments. Unfortunately, O'Neil Moore was shot to death and his partner Creed Rodgers was seriously wounded even before the two black deputies began to patrol the black neighborhoods. The attacks in June 1965 were viewed as a tactic by hostile whites to discourage African Americans from joining the police force.

In July 1965 during a civil rights march in Bogalusa, Alton D. Crowe, Jr., white, was shot by Henry Austin when he tried to enter a car to attack a young black girl. Austin, a member of the Deacons for Defense, had to be taken to an unidentified town for protection. When violence erupted, Louisiana governor John McKeithen sent state troopers to the city at Mayor Cutrer's request. CORE leader James Farmer said the Deacons were merely protecting the unarmed marchers from attack. Governor McKeithen called for a cooling-off period of thirty days for civil rights demonstrations and ordered state troopers to seize all guns they saw at demonstrations.

By July 1965 the Deacons for Defense had received national attention and had expanded into several nearby southern states. Because of the group's emphasis on armed self-defense, Martin Luther King felt that he must address this new development. In a speech in Los Angeles in July, King expressed his disapproval of the "defense violence" advocated by the Deacons and warned that their methods would shift the civil rights movement toward aggressive violence. However, problems persisted in Bogalusa through the end of 1965, including the failure of city officials to desegregate schools, movies, hotels, and other public facilities. Civil rights protests continued, led by CORE members and protected by the Deacons of Defense, who were gaining more and more supporters. In December 1965, Deacons of Defense leader Ernest Thomas reported that the group had sixty-four branches in various parts of the South and chapters were being organized in Detroit, Chicago, and other northern cities.

schools in Nashville, Tenn. The order followed the beating of Ralph Oduor, a student at Fisk University, by police. The beating of two other African students at Fisk earlier in the year, one of them Kenyan, contributed to the decision to withdraw (JM).

3 In Anniston, Ala., an all-white jury in a federal court convicted Hubert Strange of murdering Willie Brewster. This was the first time in recent Alabama history that an all-white jury convicted a white man for killing a black man (NYT).

4 In Natchez, Miss., a three-month boycott of white merchants ended after city officials agreed to a list of civil rights demands, which included hiring African Americans in sales positions in downtown stores, requiring city employees to use courtesy titles when dealing with African Americans, and desegregating public facilities. NAACP leader Charles Evers announced that a boycott would continue against stores that had not hired African Americans for sales positions (NYT).

9 In Oklahoma City, Okla., the state supreme court ruled that it would not void the state's law prohibiting interracial marriages unless the U.S. Supreme Court declared the law unconstitutional. Jesse Marquez, Mexican, and Frances Jones, African American, requested the ruling (JM).

9 In Carthage, Miss., for the second time in one week, a white mob of one hundred kept a biracial group of twenty-seven from desegregating the Fox Theater. Local and state police intervened to prevent an outbreak of violence (JM).

16 In Boston, Mass., black leaders in Roxbury threatened to circulate petitions to create a separate municipality. The impetus for the secession stemmed from the Boston School Committee election, which placed into office people opposed to black demands for busing to alleviate the racial imbalance in public schools (JM).

19–23 In Fayette, Miss., about five hundred African Americans marched to the courthouse as the "Black Christmas" boycott, called by the NAACP's Charles Evers, against white stores began. Black demands included the appointment of African Americans to the police force and desegregation of public facilities (NYT).

20 In New York City, the city received a $135,000 federal grant for Operation Reclaim to train five hundred teachers displaced by public school desegregation in southern states. A National Education Association report estimated that 452 black teachers in seventeen southern and border states lost their jobs (NYT).

23 In Sacramento, Calif., CIA chief John McCone delivered a report to Governor Edmund Brown on the Watts riot titled "Violence in the City—An End or a Beginning?" The report recommended improving law enforcement, education, and employment opportunities for African Americans (JM).

30 In Milwaukee, Wis., a white ex-nun was charged with disorderly conduct and sentenced to thirty days in jail for her part in demonstrations at the construction site of a new, potentially segregated school. Marilyn Morheuser stated that she preferred the jail term to paying a fine or probation (JM).

30 In Bismarck, N.D., Mayor Evans Lips finally agreed to the establishment of a federal Job Corps camp after Gov. William Guy signed a contract approving establishment of the conservation work camp. Lips stated that he was concerned because all-white Bismarck did not have any black families with whom black corpsmen could associate (JM).

30 In Atlanta, Ga., police chief Herbert Jenkins instituted a weekly forum where he and six other policemen listened to citizens' complaints about police misbehavior. The forum resulted from the increased militancy of the black community regarding alleged police brutality (JM).

THE AFTERMATH:

The Emergence of the Student Rights, Anti-War, Women's Liberation, and Black Power Movements

With the passage of the Civil Rights Act of 1964 and the Voting Rights Act of 1965, the Civil Rights Movement most closely associated with the leadership of Dr. Martin Luther King, Jr., had achieved its most significant objectives—the end of legal racial segregation and second-class citizenship for African Americans and other nonwhite minorities in the United States. Through nonviolent direct action protests—marches, demonstrations, boycotts, sit-ins, and other forms of civil disobedience—supporters of the Civil Rights Movement convinced lawmakers and judicial authorities to change both the letter of the law and legal practices to promote rather than discourage the full participation of all citizens in a truly democratic society.

Moreover, the Civil Rights Movement, which dominated domestic social issues in the first half of the 1960s, also greatly influenced the more important social movements in the second half of the decade. Indeed, we can point to direct connections between civil rights campaigns and the emergence of the student rights, anti-war, women's liberation, and black power movements.

Civil Rights and the Student Rights Movement

Mario Savio, philosophy student at the University of California at Berkeley, had been one of the students who worked on the SNCC voter registration campaigns in Mississippi during the summer of 1964. When Savio returned to the university campus in the fall of 1964, he became involved in activities to recruit more students to work on civil rights projects. In October 1964, however, university chancellor Clark Kerr placed a ban on further political activity in front of campus buildings. When the university police tried to remove the SNCC recruiters, the students reacted and several hundred decided to stage a sit-in at the spot to protest the order. Within hours they were joined by thousands of other chanting students, and when police reinforcements arrived, the students refused to leave. After a tense standoff, the university administration relented. Following the confrontation the students formed the Free Speech Movement (FSM) to demand greater student rights on campus.

In 1960, Tom Hayden and Al Haber, students at the University of Michigan, had formed

Students for a Democratic Society (SDS), and two years later they issued the Port Huron Statement, in which they declared that students should oppose the actions of the large corporate and bureaucratic structures that dominated their lives. The statement proclaimed that students had the power to restore "participatory democracy" to American life and they should move to seize "control of the educational process from the administrative bureaucracy." SDS spread to numerous campuses around the country, and when the FSM was formed at Berkeley, the two groups became the focal points for the new student rights movement.

Between 1965 and 1970 students began to demand an end to the parietal regulations that defined how they were to behave and what they were to learn and do on campus. On college campuses across the country students launched massive protests against university participation in military research and investments in South Africa and other repressive regimes. With the escalation of U.S. involvement in Vietnam and the huge increase in the military draft, the student rights movement merged with anti-war protests, and hundreds of thousands of students became activists in the widespread campaigns to end U.S. military intervention in Vietnam.

Civil Rights and the Anti-War Movement

On 28 July 1965, just days before the signing of the Voting Rights Act, President Johnson announced that he was increasing the number of U.S. troops in Vietnam from 50,000 to 125,000. Although at this time Martin Luther King still considered Johnson a good friend of the Civil Rights Movement, the escalating U.S. military involvement in Vietnam threatened that friendship. King continued to call for peaceful negotiations between the South Vietnamese Communist guerrilla movement, the Vietcong, who were being supported by the North Vietnamese; and the South Vietnamese government led by Nguyen Van Thieu.

Following Johnson's announcement of an increase in U.S. troop strength in Vietnam, King stated that he would send letters to Johnson and the leaders of North and South Vietnam, the Vietcong, China, and the Soviet Union to urge them to enter into peace negotiations. "I held back until it got to the point that I felt I had to speak out," King told reporters, but he sought no role in peace negotiations or anti-war protests at that time. King did urge others to follow his letter-writing initiative in opposition to the war.

Upon receiving a flood of criticism for his statement from both supporters and opponents of the Civil Rights Movement, King made few public statements on the war in 1965. However, throughout 1966 King supported the rights of SNCC leaders, such as Julian Bond, and others to dissent publicly against the administration's military policies. In April 1966 the SCLC board of directors passed a resolution calling on the administration to "seriously examine the wisdom of a prompt withdrawal from Vietnam." Finally, at the beginning of 1967, King came to the conclusion that it was "time to break the silence." And on 4 April 1967, in his famous speech at Riverside Church in New York City, King declared, "We must continue to raise our voices if our nation persists in its perverse ways in Vietnam. We must be prepared to match actions with words by seeking out every creative means of protest possible." In March 1968, when Lyndon Johnson shocked the entire nation and announced that he would not be a candidate for the presidency in November 1968, congratulations flowed into King's SCLC office from all over the country. Many believed that it was King's forthright opposition to the war in Vietnam that laid the groundwork for the abdication of a powerful leader whose military ambitions and personal hubris had proven so deadly to the nation.

Civil Rights and the Women's Liberation Movement

As was the case with the women's rights movement that emerged in the U.S. in the 1850s among women who had been activists in the anti-slavery campaigns, the seeds for the women's liberation movement were planted by women who assumed important roles in the civil rights campaigns of the early 1960s. Casey Hayden, Mary King, and Betty Carmen, who had been SNCC activists in the South during the early 1960s, raised the issue of the treatment of women by men in the organization in a position paper presented at a retreat in 1964. As SNCC moved further and further in the direction of black power, these white women activists became involved in SDS, and in 1967 they tried to get its male leaders to place the fight for equal rights for women on its agenda.

The leaders of SDS, however, were even less sympathetic to feminist issues than were the black men in SNCC. Betty Carmen, who belonged to both groups, recalled that "as a woman I was allowed to develop and had, and was given, more responsibility in SNCC than I ever was in SDS. It would have been tougher for me to develop at all in SDS."

As a result, many white women who had been activists in the Civil Rights Movement shifted their energies to the National Organization for Women (NOW), formed in 1966 under the leadership of Betty Friedan, author of *The Feminine Mystique* (1963), and Pauli Murray, Episcopal priest and lawyer. The goals pursued by NOW can be traced to President John Kennedy's Commission on the Status of Women, formed in 1961 and chaired by Eleanor Roosevelt. The commission's report, released in 1963, called for "equal pay for equal work" for women workers and led to the passage that year of the Equal Pay Act, the first federal legislation that prohibited employment discrimination on the basis of sex. The Civil Rights Act of 1964 had a direct and significant impact on working women by banning discrimination on the basis of sex by public and private employers and labor unions.

There were many African American women who were among the organizers of NOW, including Pauli Murray, civil rights leader Fannie Lou Hamer, Democratic congresswoman Shirley Chisholm, and Aileen Hernandez, a former union official and member of the Equal Employment Opportunity Commission. However, as NOW evolved in the late 1960s and early 1970s, black women, especially those who were active in civil rights, became alienated from the group because of its middle-class concerns. While black women activists recognized the significance of the attainment of equal employment opportunities, they also understood that they were oppressed by the racist beliefs and practices of white men *and* women. Black women developed their own organizations, such as the Third World Women's Alliance (1969), the National Black Feminist Organization (1973), and the National Alliance of Black Feminists (1976), which addressed the dual problems of racism and sexism that continued to plague American society.

From Civil Rights to Black Power

When civil rights activists rushed to Greenwood, Miss., in June 1966 to complete the march across the South started by James Meredith, the first African American to enroll in the University of Mississippi, the African American objective of "civil rights" was almost overnight replaced by the demand for "Black Power." The objective of Meredith's Memphis to Mississippi March was to encourage intimidated black southerners to overcome their fears and to register and vote. Unfortunately, on the second day of Meredith's march, he was ambushed and received two shotgun blasts in the back. Meredith survived the attack, and within days

Martin Luther King announced that the SCLC would take up Meredith's march; subsequently Floyd McKissick, who became CORE's national chairman in January 1966, Stokely Carmichael, SNCC's new chairman, and other civil rights leaders agreed to join.

The Lowndes County Freedom Organization (LCFO), whose symbol became the black panther, was formed in March 1966 and ran black candidates in the Alabama primary in May and in the November elections. Armed members of the Deacons of Defense and Justice provided protection for LCFO officials in Alabama, and the Deacons offered to protect the participants in the Meredith March. Stokely Carmichael had often worked with the Deacons and convinced King to accept their offer. Carmichael was arrested by police in Greenwood, Miss., for pitching a tent in the yard of a black school, and he used the incident to publicize his new objective for the Civil Rights Movement.

"This is the twenty-seventh time I've been arrested," Carmichael told the crowd on the evening of 16 June. "I ain't gonna be arrested no more. . . . [Police chief] Buff Hammond has to go. I'm gonna tell you, baby, that the only way we're gonna get justice is when we have a black sheriff. . . . Every courthouse in Mississippi should be burnt down tomorrow so we can get rid of the dirt." The following day, Carmichael exhorted the marchers, "What do we want?" The loud rejoinder was "Black Power!" "When do we want it?" "Now!"

For many the call for black power was initially interpreted as black self-defense against violent attack, but even in this limited context the new rallying cry signaled the end of the types of nonviolent protest associated with Martin Luther King. While King, Roy Wilkins, James Farmer, and other civil rights leaders publicly denounced "black power" because of its anti-white overtones, just as they had earlier opposed the militant black nationalism of Malcolm X, the slogan was taken up by the black students in SNCC because nonviolent protests had not brought about the social changes for which they had been struggling. As the word was spread by newspapers, radio, television, and magazines, black activists, intellectuals, and artists across the country began to spell out what they thought the black power slogan meant.

Regardless of the particular definition, however, the coming of Black Power created divisions within the Civil Rights Movement between those who continued to support nonviolent protest and those who emphasized black self-defense and the need for African Americans to gain power and control over the institutions within their communities. As civil rights marches and demonstrations attracted more and more militant black youths in 1967 and 1968, the protests often degenerated into violence and rioting.

The campaigns to destroy the "herrenvolk" democracy, in which first-class citizenship rights were restricted to the white population, represented the most significant and far-reaching social reform movement in the United States in the twentieth century. The civil rights era was truly a watershed period that would have a profound impact on American life and society for the next forty years.

SELECTED BIBLIOGRAPHY

Abernathy, Ralph David. *And the Walls Came Tumbling Down: An Autobiography.* New York: Harper & Row, 1989.

Anderson, Alan B., and George W. Pickering. *Confronting the Color Line: The Broken Promise of the Civil Rights Movement in Chicago.* Athens: University of Georgia Press, 1986.

Anderson, Jervis. *A. Philip Randolph: A Biographical Portrait.* New York: HarperCollins, 1987.

————. *Bayard Rustin: Troubles I've Seen, A Biography.* New York: HarperCollins, 1997.

Ashe, Arthur R. *A Hard Road to Glory: A History of the African American Athlete since 1946.* New York: Warner Books, 1988.

Barnes, Catherine A. *Journey from Jim Crow: The Desegregation of Southern Transit.* New York: Columbia University Press, 1983.

Bates, Daisy. *The Long Shadow of Little Rock: A Memoir.* New York: David McKay, 1962.

Belknap, Michael R. *Federal Law and Southern Order: Racial Violence and Constitutional Conflict in the Post-Brown South.* Athens: University of Georgia Press, 1987.

Bennett, Lerone, Jr. *Confrontation: Black and White.* Baltimore: Penguin Books, 1965.

————. *What Manner of Man: A Biography of Martin Luther King, Jr.* Chicago: Johnson Publishing Co., 1964.

Berry, Mary Frances. *Black Resistance, White Law: A History of Constitutional Racism in America.* New York: Penguin Press, 1994.

Berry, Mary Frances, and John W. Blassingame. *Long Memory: The Black Experience in America.* New York: Oxford University Press, 1982.

Blaustein, Albert, and Robert Zangrando. *Civil Rights and the American Negro.* New York: Washington Press, 1968.

Bloom, Jack. *Class, Race, and the Civil Rights Movement: The Political Economy of Southern Racism.* Bloomington: Indiana University Press, 1987.

Blumberg, Rhoda Lois. *Civil Rights: The 1960's Freedom Struggle.* 2d. ed. Boston: Twayne Publishers, 1991.

Branch, Taylor. *Parting the Waters: America in the King Years, 1954–1963.* New York: Simon & Schuster, 1988.

————. *Pillar of Fire: America in the King Years, 1963–65.* New York: Simon & Schuster, 1998.

Brauer, Carl M. *John F. Kennedy and the Second Reconstruction.* New York: Columbia University Press, 1977.

Brisbane, Robert. *Black Activism: Racial Revolution in the United States, 1954–1970.* Valley Forge, Pa.: Judson Press, 1971.

Brooks, Thomas R. *Walls Come Tumbling Down: A History of the Civil Rights Movement, 1940–1970.* Englewood Cliffs, N.J.: Prentice-Hall, 1974.

Burk, Robert F. *The Eisenhower Administration and Black Civil Rights.* Knoxville: University of Tennessee Press, 1984.

Carson, Clayborne. *In Struggle: SNCC and the Black Awakening of the 1960s.* Cambridge, Mass.: Harvard University Press, 1981.

————, ed. *The Papers of Martin Luther King, Jr.* Vols. I–3. Berkeley: University of California Press, 1992–1996.

Chafe, William. *Civilities and Civil Rights: Greensboro, North Carolina, and the Black Struggle for Freedom.* New York: Oxford University Press, 1980.

Colburn, David R. *Racial Change and Community Crisis: St. Augustine, Florida, 1877–1980.* New York: Columbia University Press, 1985.

Collier-Thomas, Bettye. *Daughters of Thunder: Black Women Preachers and Their Sermons, 1850–1979.* San Francisco, Calif.: Jossey-Bass, 1998.

Cone, James H. *Martin and Malcolm and America: A Dream or a Nightmare.* Maryknoll, N.Y.: Orbis Books, 1991.

Crawford, Vicki L., et al., eds. *Women in the Civil Rights Movement: Trailblazers and Torchbearers.* Brooklyn, N.Y.: Carlson Publishing, 1990.

Dickerson, Dennis C. *Militant Mediator: Whitney M. Young, Jr.* Lexington: University Press of Kentucky, 1998.

Evans, Sara M. *Personal Politics: The Roots of Women's Liberation in the Civil Rights Movement and the New Left.* New York: Vintage Books, 1980.

Fairclough, Adam. *"To Redeem the Soul of America": The Southern Christian Leadership Conference and Martin Luther King, Jr.* Athens: University of Georgia Press, 1987.

———. *Race and Democracy: The Civil Rights Struggle in Louisiana, 1915–1972.* Athens: University of Georgia Press, 1995.

Farmer, James. *Lay Bare the Heart: An Autobiography of the Civil Rights Movement.* New York: Arbor House, 1986.

Findley, James F. *Church People in the Struggle: The National Council of Churches and the Black Freedom Movement, 1950–1970.* New York: Oxford University Press, 1993.

Fleming, Cynthia Griggs. *Soon We Will Not Cry: The Liberation of Ruby Doris Smith Robinson.* Lanham, Md.: Rowman & Littlefield, 1998.

Franklin, John Hope, and Alfred A. Moss, Jr. *From Slavery to Freedom: A History of Negro Americans.* 7th ed. New York: Alfred A. Knopf, 1994.

Franklin, V. P. *Black Self-Determination: A Cultural History of African-American Resistance.* Brooklyn, N.Y.: Lawrence Hill Books, 1992.

———. *Living Our Stories, Telling Our Truths: Autobiography and the Making of the African-American Intellectual Tradition.* New York: Oxford University Press, 1996.

———. *Martin Luther King, Jr.: A Biography.* New York: Park Lane Press, 1998.

Garrow, David J. *Protest at Selma: Martin Luther King, Jr., and the Voting Rights Act of 1965.* New Haven, Conn.: Yale University Press, 1978.

———. *Bearing the Cross: Martin Luther King, Jr., and the Southern Christian Leadership Conference.* New York: William Morrow, 1986.

Gault, Charlayne Hunter. *In My Place: Charlayne Hunter-Gault.* New York: Vintage Books, 1993.

Graham, Hugh Davis. *The Civil Rights Era: Origins and Development of National Policy, 1960–1965.* New York: Oxford University Press, 1990.

Grant, Joanne. *Ella Baker: Freedom Bound.* New York: John Wiley, 1998.

Hamilton, Charles. *Adam Clayton Powell, Jr.: The Political Biography of an American Dilemma.* New York: Collier Books, 1991.

Hampton, Henry, et al., eds. *Voices of Freedom: An Oral History of the Civil Rights Movement from the 1950s through the 1980s.* New York: Bantam Books, 1990.

Harding, Vincent. *The Other American Revolution.* Los Angeles: UCLA Center for Afro-American Studies, 1980.

———. *Hope and History: Why We Must Share the Story of the Movement.* Maryknoll, N.Y.: Orbis Books, 1990.

Harvey, James C. *Civil Rights During the Kennedy Administration.* Hattiesburg: University and College Press of Mississippi, 1971.

———. *Black Civil Rights During the Johnson Administration.* Jackson: University and College Press of Mississippi, 1973.

Haygood, Wil. *King of the Cats: The Life and Times of Adam Clayton Powell, Jr.* New York: Houghton Mifflin, 1993.

Hilty, James W. *Robert Kennedy: Brother Protector.* Philadelphia, Pa.: Temple University Press, 1997.

Kapur, Sudarshan. *Raising up a Prophet: The African-American Encounter with Gandhi.* Boston: Beacon Press, 1992.

King, Martin Luther, Jr. *Stride Toward Freedom: The Montgomery Story.* New York: Harper, 1958.

———. *Why We Can't Wait.* New York: Harper & Row, 1963.

———. *Where Do We Go From Here? Chaos or Community.* Boston: Beacon Press, 1968.

Kluger, Richard. *Simple Justice: The History of* Brown v. Board of Education *and Black America's Struggle for Equality.* New York: Alfred Knopf, 1976.

Lewis, John, with Michael D'Orso. *Walking with the Wind: A Memoir of the Movement.* New York: Simon & Schuster, 1998.

Lowery, Charles D., and John S. Marzolek, eds. *Encyclo-*

pedia of African-American Civil Rights: From Emancipation to the Present. Westport, Conn.: Greenwood Press, 1992.

Marable, Manning. Race, Reform and Rebellion: The Second Reconstruction in Black America, 1945–1982. 2d ed. Jackson: University Press of Mississippi, 1991.

McAdam, Doug. Political Process and the Development of Black Insurgency, 1930–1970. Chicago: University of Chicago Press, 1982.

———. Freedom Summer. New York: Oxford University Press, 1988.

Meier, August, and Elliott Rudwick. CORE: A Study in the Civil Rights Movement, 1942–1968. New York: Oxford University Press, 1975.

Mershon, Sherie, and Steven Schlossman. Foxholes and Color Lines: Desegregating the U.S. Armed Services. Baltimore: Johns Hopkins University Press, 1998.

Moreno, Paul D. From Direct Action to Affirmative Action: Fair Employment Law and Policy in America, 1933–1972. Baton Rouge: Louisiana State University Press, 1997.

Morris, Aldon D. The Origins of the Civil Rights Movement: Black Communities Organizing for Change. New York: The Free Press, 1984.

Norrell, Robert J. Reaping the Whirlwind: The Civil Rights Movement in Tuskegee. New York: Alfred Knopf, 1985.

Oates, Stephen B. Let the Trumpet Sound: The Life of Martin Luther King, Jr. New York: Harper & Row, 1982.

O'Reilly, Kenneth. "Racial Matters": The FBI's Secret File on Black America, 1960–1972. New York: The Free Press, 1989.

Parks, Rosa, and Jim Haskins. Rosa Parks: My Story. New York: Dial Books, 1992.

Payne, Charles M. "I've Got the Light of Freedom": The Organizing Tradition and the Mississippi Freedom Struggle. Berkeley: University of California Press, 1995.

Powledge, Fred. Free at Last? The Civil Rights Movement and the People Who Made It. Boston: Little, Brown, 1991.

Ralph, James. Northern Protest: Martin Luther King, Jr., Chicago, and the Civil Rights Movement. Cambridge, Mass.: Harvard University Press, 1993.

Robinson, Jo Ann Gibson. The Montgomery Bus Boycott and the Women Who Started It: The Memoir of Jo Ann Gibson Robinson. Knoxville: University of Tennessee Press, 1987.

Robnett, Belinda. How Long? How Long?: African-American Women in the Struggle for Civil Rights. New York: Oxford University Press, 1997.

Schlesinger, Arthur M., Jr. Robert Kennedy and His Times. New York: Ballantine, 1978.

Shapiro, Herbert. White Violence and Black Response: From Reconstruction to Montgomery. Amherst: University of Massachusetts Press, 1988.

Sitkoff, Harvard. The Struggle for Black Equality, 1954–1992. Rev. ed. New York: Hill and Wang, 1993.

Taylor, Clarence. Knocking at Our Own Door: Milton A. Galamison and the Struggle for School Integration in New York City. New York: Columbia University Press, 1997.

Tushnet, Mark V. The NAACP's Legal Strategy Against Segregated Education, 1925–1950. Chapel Hill: The University of North Carolina Press, 1987.

———. Making Civil Rights Law: Thurgood Marshall and the Supreme Court, 1936–1961. New York: Oxford University Press, 1994.

VanDeMark, Brian. Into the Quagmire: Lyndon Johnson and the Escalation of the Vietnam War. New York: Oxford University Press, 1991.

Washington, James M. A Testament of Hope: The Essential Writings of Martin Luther King, Jr. New York: Harper & Row, 1986.

Weisbrot, Robert. Freedom Bound: A History of America's Civil Rights Movement. New York: Norton, 1990.

Weiss, Nancy J. Whitney Young, Jr., and the Struggle for Civil Rights. Princeton, N.J.: Princeton University Press, 1989.

Whalen, Charles, and Barbara Whalen. The Long Debate: A Legislative History of the 1964 Civil Rights Act. New York: New American Library, 1985.

Wilkins, Roy, with Tom Mathews. Standing Fast: The Autobiography of Roy Wilkins. New York: Penguin Books, 1984.

Williams, Juan. Eyes on the Prize: America's Civil Rights Years, 1954–1965. New York: Viking Press, 1987.

———. Thurgood Marshall: American Revolutionary. New York: Times Books, 1998.

Young, Andrew. An Easy Burden: The Civil Rights Movement and the Transformation of America. New York: HarperCollins, 1996.

Zaroulis, Nancy, and Gerald Sullivan. Who Spoke Up?: American Protest against the War in Vietnam, 1963–1975. New York: Doubleday, 1984.

INDEX

Aaron, J. E., 73
Aaron, Julia, 178
Abernathy, Ralph, 63, 66, 119, 139, 141, 143, 145, 149, 172, 190, 199, 203, 206, 219, 229
Abrams, Charles, 53, 83
Accra, Gold Coast/Ghana (West Africa), 47, 60, 193
ACT, 208, 209
Adair County, Ky., 40
Adams, Billye, 46
Adams, Ike, 237
Adams, Dr. Samantha, 88
Adams County, Wis., 148
Addison, Archbishop Clarence C., 68, 69
Addonizio, Mayor Hugh J., 233
Adley, Stephen, 4
AFL, 30. *See also* AFL–CIO; annual convention in 1954 of, 13; Carpenters Union of, 22; craft unions of, 12; International Brotherhood of Electrical Workers of, 7, 25; Latherers Union of, 5; "Powell amendment" support by, 21; suit against railroads by, 15
AFL–CIO, 37, 54, 62, 126, 153, 169, 177, 179; 1959 annual meeting of, 111; 1961 annual meeting of, 141; American Federation of Musicians (AFM) in, 81; Barbers Union of, 145; Civil Rights Act of 1964 and, 226; civil rights demands and responses by, 54, 102; discrimination in ranks of, 168; executive council meeting (1958) of, 79; NAACP and, 178; union movements in south of, 75
aftermath, 243–246; civil rights and anti-war movement, 244; civil rights and student rights movement, 243–244;

civil rights and women's liberation movement, 245; civil rights to black power, 245–246
Agronsky, Martin, 73
Aiken County, S.C., 231
Akron, Ohio, 224
Alameda, Calif., 147
Albany, Ga., 172, 183, 188, 208
Albany, N.Y., 24, 53, 62, 78, 105, 120, 121, 140, 145, 152, 210, 227
Albany Movement (1961–62), 172
Albritton, Mayor F. R., 230
Alderson, John H., 12, 20, 37
Alexander, Clifford L., 4
Alexander, Fred, 237
Alexander, Kelly, 237
Alexander, Raymond Pace, 55
Alexander, T. M., 15
Alexandria, Va., 83
all-black colleges and universities and white students enrollment, 23
Allen, Mayor Ivan, 181, 186
Allen, Dr. James, Jr., 152
Allen, Rev. King, 132
Allen, Lewis, 204
Allen, Sanford, 168
Allgood, Clarence, 216
Almond, Gov. J. Lindsay, Jr., 74, 91, 113, 135
Altamont, Tenn., 120
Alvarez, Ossie, 102
Amaker, Norman, 203
American Association of Physical Anthropologists, election of Dr. W. Montague Cobb as president, 64
American Federation of Labor. *See* AFL
American Federation of Teachers (AFT), 25, 30, 206

American Nazi party, 150
American States Rights Association, 8
American Teachers Association, 10
Amherst, Mass., 71
Amitie, Miss., 12
Anderson, Hurst, 95
Anderson, John, 212
Anderson, Marian, 20, 58
Anderson, R. T., 10
Anderson, William, 172
Anderson, Ind., 178
Andrews, A. L., 232
Ann Arbor, Mich., 64, 94
Annapolis, Md., 10, 224
Anniston, Ala., 122, 136, 137, 150, 194, 241
anti-war movement and civil rights, 244
Arlington, Va., 40, 47, 49, 53, 127, 190
Armstrong, Louis, 73, 114
Arnall, Ellis, 119
Arrington, Barbara, 113
Arrington, E. L., 97
Arterberry, Chester, 179
Asheville, N.C., 204
Ashmore, Harry, 84
astronaut trainee, first black, 186
Athens, Ga., 28, 132
Athens, Ohio, 118
Atkilski, Bishop Roman, 239
Atkins, Asa H., 32
Atkins, Henry, 215–216
Atlanta, Ga., 8, 15, 16, 24, 26, 47, 55, 58, 60, 62, 67, 74–75, 94, 98, 99, 102, 103, 106, 114, 117, 119, 121, 123, 126, 127, 133, 135, 137, 140, 144, 154, 164, 165, 170, 173, 175, 177, 178, 182, 186, 193, 196, 197, 199, 202, 207, 208, 212, 219, 225, 227, 232, 234, 235, 239–240; A&P

Atlanta, Ga. (cont'd)
stores in, 130; ban on interracial dancing and athletic competitions bill, 22;
bombing in school in, 134; buffer zone
barriers in, 181, 186; city workers
salary in, 143; cross burning on lawn
of Martin Luther King, Jr., in, 124; department stores business decline in,
135; economic boycott called by Martin Luther King, Jr. of, 227-228; Federal Reserve Bank of, 161; firemen in,
188; Grady Memorial Hospital in, 153,
161, 163, 164, 234; hospitals in, 148;
hotel segregation in, 27; King, Martin
Luther, Jr., arrest in, 120; King, Martin
Luther, Jr., on (1963), 199; Ku Klux
Klan in, 133; march (1960) in, 125;
NAACP annual meeting of 1962 in,
171; police in, 147, 168, 242; public
transportation integration in, 98, 108;
school integration in, 124, 138, 144,
148; Sierra Leone leader in, 199; sports
team integration and, 37; taxicabs in,
130, 144; teachers unions in, 75; Urban
League branch in, 67; voter registra-
tion drive (1961) in, 148
Atlanta Declaration by NAACP, 8
Atlantic City, N.J., 27
Atlas, Francis, 138
attacks on discrimination in government-
sponsored employment (1963), 187
Atwell, William A., 32
Auburn, Ala., 201
Augusta, Ga., 164, 197, 232, 234
Austin, Henry, 104
Austin, Mr. and Mrs. Lloyd G., 52
Austin, Tex., 19, 30, 121, 138, 230
Aycock, A. L., 92
Aycock, C. C., 135
Azar, Ed, 98-99

Backstrom, Frank, 118
Bailey, Rep. Cleveland M., 28-29
Baker, Carson C., 35
Baker, Ella, 118
Baker, Mrs. Ernest, 153
Baker, Mr. and Mrs. Horace, 194, 199
Baker, Rep. Howard, 12
Baker, John, 141
Baker, Quinton, 155
Baldee, Duard C., 74
Baldwin, Gilbert, 129
Baldwin, James, 189
Ballard, Orville, 3
Baltimore, Md., 6, 9, 13, 20, 46, 49, 50, 64,
111, 120, 144, 147, 168, 171, 192, 209,
217, 228; barbers union in, 55;
Catholic hospitals in, 202; firemen in,
55; hotels and racially discriminatory
practices in, 47; Public Housing Au-
thority and end of segregation in, 9; ty-
pographical union in, 67

banking discrimination, 204, 205
Banks, Patricia, 121, 122
Bansa, Emmanuel, 194
Barbee, Lloyd, 231, 234
Barbiarz, Mayor E., 147
Barclay, Liberian president Edwin, 21
Barker, Estelle, 88
Barnes, Donald, 230
Barnes, Frank, 132
Barnes, Richard Lee, 144
Barnes, Roland, 179
Barnett, Gov. Ross, 137, 141, 162, 176, 183
Barney, Rev. Josuha A., 52
Barnhitte, F. E., 79
Barrett, Joyce, 133
Barro, Jack, 156
Barron, Gov. William, 161
Barry, Marion, Jr., 129
Baruch, Bernard, 14
baseball, 9; Baltimore Orioles team, 6;
Boston Red Sox as last team without
black player, 85, 86, 103; Brooklyn
Dodgers game in Birmingham, Ala., 41;
Detroit Tigers team, 84, 85, 102; Lake-
land, Fla., and lack of hotel accommo-
dations for black players, 102; National
Little League, 29; Negro Baseball
League, 4; Philadelphia Athletics team,
4; Scottsdale, Ariz., and lack of hotel
accommodations for black players,
100; Washington Senators team, 6
Bates, Daisy, 40, 55, 69, 77, 78, 79, 85, 86,
88, 92, 108-109, 114, 115, 134
Bates, L. C., 55, 88, 92, 108-109, 114, 115
Batesville, Miss., 135
Baton Rouge, La., 9, 16, 24, 166, 178, 230
Battle, Gov. John S., 74
Bay City, Mich., 112
Baylor, Elgin, 99
Beasley, Tom, 99
Beatty, Beatrice, 82
Beaumont, Tex., 53
Beckett, William, 120
Becknell, Carolyn, 119
Begin, Floyd L., 4, 5
Belafonte, Harry, 5, 73, 75, 92-93, 135
Bell, Derrick, 160
Bell, Jessie Irene, 13
Bell, Col. Leon, 88
Bell, Leslie L., 67
Bell, Dr. R. C., 148, 178
Bell, Richard, 73
Bellamy, Mrs. Verdell, 177, 182
Bennett, Blue, 94, 95
Bennett, Bruce, 199
Bennett, Dr. George, 167
Berkeley, Calif., 157, 181, 186, 187, 201,
216
Bernstein, Charles C., 13
Bernstein, Leonard, 168
Berry, Edwin, 70-71, 144, 163
Bertrand, Joseph, 211

Bessemer, Ala., 99, 173, 226
Bethesda, Md., 219
Bethune, Mary McLeod, 26
Bethune Cookman College and first
white graduate, 10
Bevel, Rev. James, 160, 190
Bevins, Curtis, 62
Bianco, John, 129
Bibb County, Ga., 169, 170
Biffkin, Bruce, 53
Bilbo, Sen. Theodore, 217
Billingsley, Orzell, 164, 168, 215
Billups, Charles, 133, 177
Bing, R. C., 104
Binns, Maceo, Jr., 120
Birmingham, Ala., 4, 9, 17, 29, 44, 59, 60,
63, 104, 115, 123, 133, 153, 157, 160,
164, 167, 168, 206, 215, 220, 221, 231,
239; attack on Nat King Cole in, 44;
Battle of, 190, 198; beating at Georgia–Alabama football game in, 175; bus
passenger placement law in, 93, 172;
church bombing in, 179; Ku Klux Klan
bombings in, 237; Ku Klux Klan castra-
tion of black man in, 73; police positions in, 53, 84-85, 88, 235, 238; public
recreational facilities lawsuit in, 112;
residential bombings in, 75; SCLC annual meeting (1962) in, 175; SCLC annual meeting (1965) in, 236; WEDR
radio station attacked in, 84
Bismarck, N.D., 22, 242
Black, Lt. Col. Gorham, Jr., 149
Black, Hugo, 48, 126
black firsts, 3, 4, 7, 10, 13, 14, 15, 20, 21,
22, 24, 28, 29, 32-33, 41, 44, 50, 53, 55,
58-59, 64, 65, 68, 84, 106, 118-119,
120, 123, 131, 133, 142, 144, 149, 157,
161, 166, 168, 171, 178, 186, 188, 205,
208, 211, 224-225, 232, 240
Black Liberation Front, 225, 227
black militants, 208-209, 225-227
black power from civil rights, 245-246
black students turned away and accepted, 12
black teachers, 10, 15, 17, 19, 31, 33, 44,
50, 54, 64, 68, 72, 79, 82, 85, 86, 91, 94,
106, 117, 119-120, 134, 141, 147, 148,
153, 170, 178, 189, 196, 198, 205, 216,
217, 227, 230, 231, 234, 235, 240, 242
black voters and presidential election of
1960, 131
black women, 3, 4, 5, 7, 9, 10, 11, 12, 13,
15, 16, 17, 18, 20, 21, 22, 23, 26, 28, 29,
35, 40, 41, 42, 43, 44, 45, 46, 47, 49, 50,
51, 52, 53, 55, 58, 59, 60, 61, 62, 63, 65,
66, 67, 68, 69, 70, 71, 72, 74, 77, 78, 79,
81, 82, 83, 84, 85, 86, 87, 88, 89, 90, 91,
92, 94, 95, 97, 98, 100, 101, 102, 104,
105, 106, 107, 108, 109, 113, 114, 115,
117, 118, 119, 120, 121, 122, 125, 129,
130, 131, 132, 133, 134, 135, 138, 139,

140, 141, 142, 143, 147, 149, 151, 152,
153, 154, 155, 156, 160, 161, 163,
166, 167, 168, 170, 172, 174, 176, 177,
178, 179, 182, 188, 189, 191, 192,
194, 196, 197, 198, 199, 201, 203, 204,
205, 206, 207, 208, 209, 210, 212,
213, 216, 217, 220, 221, 222, 224, 231,
232, 234, 235, 242, 245
Blair, Ezell, 129
Blair, Ezell, Jr., 118, 132
Blakey, Benjamin, 134
Block, Samuel, 195
Blossom, Virgil, 40, 69
Blount, E. J., 189
Boardman, John, 58
Bogalusa, La., 241
Bohling, Nicholas, 145
Bolger, Robert V., 30
bombings in 1958, 87
Bond, Julian, 244
book banning, 107
Boone, Inez, 107
Bootle, W. A., 135, 139, 169
Borders, William Holmes, 58
Bossier, La., 167
Boston, Mass., 24, 95, 100, 103, 225; "Operation Exodus" in, 238; Pullman Company in, 7; Red Sox baseball team in, 85, 86, 103; Roxbury section threatening secession from, 242
Boulder, Colo., 44
Boutwell, Mayor Albert, 190, 235, 238
Bowden, Henry, 144
Bowles, Bryant, 11, 13
Bowling Green, Ky., 188
Boyd, John D., 60
Boyd, Lewis, 166
Boyd, Marion, 34, 137
Boyle, Sarah Patton, 51
Boynton, Bruce, 134
Boynton, C. W., 17
Boynton v. Virginia, 150, 172
Braddock, Pa., 50
Bradenton, Fla., 111–112, 162
Bradford, Constance, 178
Bradley, Mamie, 18
Branch, James and Mary, 87
Branche, Stanley, 217
Brandel, William, 218
Brando, Marlon, 198
Brandon, Miss., 162
Branscum, George, 61
Branton, Wiley, 165, 239
Brewbaker, J. J., 113
Brewer, Henry, 32
Brewer, Thomas H., 42
Brewster, Willie, 241
Bridgeport, Conn., 238
Bridges, Abron, 133
Briley, Mayor Beverly, 210
Brisbane, Martha S., 66
Britt, Rev. B. Reaves, 70

Brittain, D. J., 48
Brittain, William, 30
Broadwater, J. A., 4
Brock, Elmer, 54
Bronstein, Alvin, 227
Bronx, The, N.Y., 61
Brooklyn, N.Y., 41, 130
Brooks, Rev. David, 153
Brooks, Paul, 160
Brookshire, Mayor Stan R., 237
Browder v. Gayle, 59, 63
Brown, Anita, 61
Brown, Beatrice, 129
Brown, Charles, 98
Brown, Cora, 120
Brown, Earl, 93
Brown, Gov. Edmund G., 12, 97–98, 103, 115, 236, 242
Brown, Fred, 33
Brown, Joe, 66, 197
Brown, Dr. John O., 105
Brown, Minnie Jean, 79
Brown, R. Jess, 90
Brown, Robert Ewing, 61
Brown, T. J., 33
Brown, Theodore, 179
Brown, Willie, 156
Brown, Wilson, 175
Brown v. Board of Education, xvi, xvii, 2, 3, 6, 12, 15, 23, 25, 28, 36; Clarendon County, S.C., as part of, 88; Democratic national convention of 1956 and, 50; Eisenhower, President Dwight David, and, 7; General Assembly of the Presbyterian Church USA and, 17; groups formed in aftermath of, 8; Hillsboro, Ohio, and, 13; laws conflicting with, 169; Marshall, Thurgood, and, 151; 1954 elections and, 15; Prince Georges County, Md., teachers and, 65; private business and, 13; public recreational facilities and ruling of, 27; Republican national convention of 1956 and, 50; Southern Manifesto and, 43
Brownell, Herbert, 23, 30, 33, 36, 57, 67
Brownell, Samuel, 11
Brownsville, Tenn., 161
Bruce, Joe, 239
Brumfield, Dudley, 212
Brunsdale, Gov. Norman, 22
Bryan, Albert V., 49
Bryan, Malcolm, 161
Bryant, Gov. Farris, 153, 203
Bryant, Roy, 35
Buchanan, Bessie, 15
Bucklew, Mayor Henry, 237
Buenos Aires, Argentina, 51
Buffalo, N.Y., 91
Buffington, Ruth, 199
Buford, Rev. K. L., 63
Buggs, John, 170
Bullock, Mr. and Mrs. Grover C., 104

Bullock County, Ala., 11, 225
Bunche, Joan, 197
Bunche, Ralph, 19, 43, 60, 82, 107, 108, 115, 125, 171, 197, 222
Burbridge, Dr. Thomas, 216
Burglund, Wilfred, 108
Burke, Otha Neal, 221
Burlington, Vt., 95
Burns, Mayor Haydon, 207
Burnsville, N.C., 132
Burnwell, Lawrence, 218
Burton, Harold M., 92
Burton, Virginia, 216
Burton, William, 142
bus boycotts and protests, 3, 22, 34, 35–36, 37, 42, 44, 45, 47, 50, 63, 64, 80, 81, 92, 137, 231
bus boycotts spread in southern cities, 45
Butcher, Margaret Just, 21
Butler, Paul M., 92, 94, 103

Cabrielli, Anthony, 152
Caccia, Sir Harold, 104
Cain, Bobby, 65
Cairo, Ill., 173
Caldwell, James, 106
Calhoun, John H., 67
Caliver, Dr. Ambrose, 12
Call, Robert, 218
Callahand, Howard J., 7
Calloway, Dr. N. O., 179
Cambridge, Mass., 4
Cambridge, Md., 210
Camden, Ala., 228, 230, 234
Camden, S.C., 49–50
Camden County, N.J., 105
campaigns against segregated public education in North (1963), 185
Campbell, Frank, 166
Campbell, Kenneth, 205
Campbell, Lyle J., 40
Canada, A. A., 54
Cannon, Nathaniel, 140
Capahosica, Va., 43
Capehart, B. E., 33
Capetown, South Africa, 44
Capital Transit Company, 4
Caracas, Venezuela, 5
Carey, Archibald J., Jr., 20, 68, 70, 123
Carey, Chester, 9
Carey, James R., 62, 79
Carlson, Edgar M., 59
Carmen, Betty, 245
Carmichael, Stokely, 236, 246
Carr, Cicero, 168
Carr, Mrs. Harold, 98
Carr, Dr. Robert, 77
Carson, Edward, 47
Carson City, Nev., 230
Carswell, G. Harold, 153
Carter, Rev. Bill, 10

Carter, Hodding, 23, 31
Carter, Rev. Joseph, 195-196
Carter, Leonard, 174-175
Carter, Robert L., 79, 151, 221
Carthage, Miss., 242
Carver, Robert, 148
Casey, Lunsford, 238
Castle, Doris, 178
Castro, Fidel, 104
Catholic schools, 6, 7, 30, 51, 138, 166,
  173, 174, 175, 176, 177
Catton, Bruce, 179
Caver, Rev. Caldwell, 79
Cecil County, Md., 21
Celebrezze, Anthony, 179, 209, 234
Celler, Rep. Emmanuel, 55, 87, 140
Centreville, Ill., 153
Chamberlain, Margaret, 212
Champaign County, Ill., 161, 212
Chaney, Fannie Lou, 234
Chaney, James Earl, 207, 221, 234
Chapel Hill, N.C., 68, 208
Chapin, Arthur, 146, 171
Chapital, Arthur, 239
Chapman, Walter, 4
Charles, Ray, 175
Charleston, Henry B., 107
Charleston, Mo., 33, 188
Charleston, S.C., 4, 6, 177
Charleston, W.Va., 17, 87, 112, 114-115,
  161
Charlotte, N.C., 70, 105-106
Charlottesville, Va., 49, 51, 65, 68
Chattanooga, Tenn., 127, 129, 227
Chattin, C. C., 120
Cheatham, Al, 141
Chenault, Dr. John, 163
Chester, Pa., 197, 208, 209, 210
Chicago, Ill., 4, 7, 8, 22, 27, 30, 39, 44, 46,
  49, 50, 59, 62, 63-64, 68, 69, 70, 71, 72,
  82, 85, 95, 100, 110, 113, 115, 121,
  123, 126, 127, 129, 130, 132, 135, 138,
  139, 140, 143, 144, 145, 147, 149, 151,
  153, 154, 163, 164, 167, 173, 174, 177,
  179, 181, 187, 191, 192, 193, 194, 196,
  197, 205, 206, 207, 209, 210, 212,
  214, 216, 217, 219, 220, 225, 231, 235,
  236
Children's March of 1958 in D.C., 92-
  93
Chisholm, Shirley, 245
Christianberry, Herbert, 90
Church, Mr. and Mrs. Leroy, 177
church burnings, 154, 164, 174, 175, 224,
  237
church burnings, bombings, and racial violence continue in the South (1965),
  237
Cincinnati, Ohio, 193, 205, 234
CIO. See Congress of Industrial Organizations
Citizens Protective League, 5

Ciufo, John and Antonette, 209
civil rights; and anti-war movement, 244;
  to black power, 245-246; demands
  and responses of organized labor and,
  54; movies, television, concerts and,
  73; and student rights movement,
  243-244; and women's liberation
  movement, 245
Civil Rights Act of 1957, 70, 77, 80, 90,
  97, 108, 122
Civil Rights Act of 1960, 122, 124, 164,
  171, 173-174, 195
Civil Rights Act of 1964, xvi, xvii, 211,
  213, 215, 218, 221, 223, 226, 239, 240,
  243, 245
civil rights bill, 1963-1964, 68, 191, 192,
  193, 194, 196, 202, 203
Civil Rights Movement end, 223
civil rights protests grip the nation
  (1963), 198
Claiborne Parish, La., 148
Clarendon County, S.C., 35, 43, 88
Clark, Felton, 160
Clark, John C., Jr., 34
Clark, Sen. Joseph, 140
Clark, Dr. Kenneth B., 228
Clark, General Mark, 46, 47
Clark, O'Dell, 140
Clark, Septima, 109
Clarke, Joseph A., 44
Clarke, Leroy, 239
Clarke, Dr. M. R., 132
Clarksdale, Miss., 75, 155, 157, 175, 178,
  204, 225
Clay, William L., 109, 111, 205
Clem, C. Joseph, 64
Clement, Gov. Frank G., 87
Clement, Dr. Kenneth, 214
Clement, Rufus, 14, 74
Clemson, S.C., 183
Cleveland, Ohio, 4, 5, 65, 68, 86, 118,
  127, 145, 148, 183, 191, 193, 202, 204,
  224, 227, 240
Cleveland Council of the Knights of
  Columbus, 4, 5
Clinchy, Ross, 45, 46
Clinton, La., 204
Clinton, Okla., 163
Clinton, Tenn., 65, 70, 87
Cobb, Dr. W. Montague, 64
Codwell, John, 7
Coggs, Isaac, 148
Cohen, Israel, 179
Coke, H. D., 117
Colangelo, A. J., 156
Colbert, Mrs. R. G., 161
Cole, James, 78
Cole, Mrs. James, 114
Cole, Nat King, 44, 46, 55, 73, 81
Coleman, Ada, 58
Coleman, Emerson L., 67
Coleman, Gov. J. P., 58, 68, 80

Coleman, John, 210
Coleman, Rev. Philip, 90
Coleman, Tom L., 237
Coleman, Val, 220
colleges and universities, problem of seg-
  regation/desegregation, 4, 5, 8, 9, 10,
  12, 15, 17, 21, 23, 24, 26, 27, 34, 35-36,
  37, 41, 42, 43, 44, 46, 47, 49, 50, 51, 53,
  58, 59, 60, 61, 64, 65, 66, 68, 71, 74, 77,
  78, 79, 81, 82-83, 84, 85, 86, 87, 89, 90,
  92, 94, 95, 97, 98, 99, 100, 101, 102,
  103, 105, 108, 113, 114, 116, 118, 119,
  120, 121, 123, 125, 126-127, 129, 131,
  132, 135, 138, 139, 142, 143, 144, 148,
  149, 151, 152, 155, 159, 160, 162, 163,
  164, 165, 166, 167, 168, 170, 176, 177,
  178, 179, 181, 182, 183, 184, 187, 188,
  189, 191, 192, 193, 196, 198, 201, 204,
  205, 206, 208, 212, 214, 215, 224, 227,
  228, 231, 235, 240-241
Collet, Michel, 149
Collett, Owen, 239
Colley, Nathaniel, 224
Collier, Robert S., 227
Collins, Currie, 204
Collins, LeRoy, 43, 49, 62, 99, 217, 234
Colp, Ill., 71, 75
Columbia, Miss., 42
Columbia, S.C., 19, 40, 41, 43, 45, 71, 78,
  84, 86, 137, 182, 192
Columbus, Ga., 28, 90
Columbus, Ohio, 51, 126-127, 184, 192
Colvin, Claudette, 23
Colvin, Ray, 238-239
Combs, Gov. Bert, 192
Comerford, Harry, 164
Congleton, Dorothy, 109
Congress of Industrial Organizations, 24,
  32, 36
Congress of Racial Equality (CORE), 136,
  137, 148, 150, 152, 154, 159, 164, 173,
  182, 183, 186; campaigns for integra-
  tion by, 162; Chicago campaign of,
  214; Edgewater, N.J., sit-in by, 181; ef-
  forts in North of, 233; fair housing law
  tests by, 202; Louisiana campaign of,
  228; UCRL formation and, 192
Conliffe, Calvin, 234
Connally, Ben, 72
Connor, Eugene (Bull), 133, 175, 190
Cook, Elmer, 230
Cook, Eugene, 28, 31
Cooper, Lillie, 87
Cooper v. Aaron, 91
Coppins, Ernest, 87
Corcoran, Thomas, J., 35
Cordia, Joseph, 156
CORE. See Congress of Racial Equality
Corning, Hobart M., 21, 57
Counts, Dorothy, 70
Courts, Gus, 35
Cox, Rev. B. Elton, 162

Cox, Ronald, 168
Cox, Thomas, 59
Craig, Winston, 99
Craven County, N.C., 108
Crawford, Don, 240
Crawford, Marc, 110
Crawfordville, Ga., 239
Crenshaw, Jack, 37
Crishon, Alfred, 160
Crockett, Manuel Houston, 47
Cronin, Joe, 103
Crowe, Alton, D., Jr., 241
Crowell, T. L., 237
Culbertson, John Bolt, 28
Curry, Isola, stabs Martin Luther King.,
  Jr., 91
Cutrell, Bob, 144
Cutrer, Mayor Jesse, 241
Cutter, Bud, 149

Dade County, Fla., 10, 12, 109, 131, 197
Daley, Mayor Richard J., 22, 62, 70-71,
  121, 173, 191
Dallas, Tex., 9, 32, 34, 50, 51, 86, 125,
  138, 164, 189, 198
Damaso, Carl, 232
Dandridge, Dorothy, 22
Danford, Ben H., 34
Daniel, Franz, 75
Daniels, James, 80
Daniels, John and Thelma, 87
Daniels, Jonathan M., 237
Darby, Rev. H. D., 80
Darden, C. R., 195
Dargans, Maxienne, 140
Daughters of the American Revolution's
  college scholarships, 13
Davenport, Iowa, 48
David, Charles, 181
Davidson, Eugene, 51, 53
Davidson, T. Whitfield, 125
Davies, Christine, 53
Davis, Col. Benjamin O., Jr., 4, 14
Davis, Dr. Charles T., 29
Davis, Curtis and Ernest, 13
Davis, James, 51
Davis, John, 192
Davis, Dr. John W., 17
Davis, L. Clifford, 48
Davis, Rev. Rudolph, 196
Dawley, Edward, 147
Dawson, Rep. William, 12, 22, 93
Daye, Walter, 217
Dayton, Ohio, 132, 149
Daytona Beach, Fla., 10, 26
de la Beckwith, Bryon, 191, 202, 208
Deacons of Defense and Justice, 241,
  246
Deale, Md., 72
Dearborn, Mich., 191
Decker, Paul, 10
DeFabio, Mrs. Theo, 62, 63

Defenders of State Sovereignty and
  Individual Liberties, 15
Defiance, Ohio, 187-188
DeKalb County, Ga., 132, 141
Del Rio, James, 205
Delaine, Rev. Joseph A., 35
Delaware and mob violence over school
  integration, 11
Delray, Fla., 46
Democratic National Convention of
  1956, 49, 50
Dennis, Dave, 182
Dennis, David, 178
Denton, Clifford H., 32
Denver, Colo., 98, 109, 215, 234
Derthick, Lawrence G., 98
Des Moines, Iowa, 98, 211
Detroit, Mich., 7, 9, 24, 25, 66, 67, 68, 79,
  84, 85, 86, 89, 99, 102, 106, 123, 125,
  132, 138, 148, 17, 178, 191, 197, 205,
  209, 210, 227, 228, 232
Detroit Housing Authority, 9
Devane, Dozier, 85
DeVeaux, Col. John A., 52
Devine, Annie, 224
Dexter, Mayor Emerson, 212
DiCarlo, Joseph, 212
Diggs, Rep. Charles C., 15, 23, 24, 25, 28,
  30, 36, 49, 50, 60, 93, 109, 111, 115,
  125, 155, 163, 170, 186, 195, 205, 230
Dilworth, Mayor Richardson, 45, 202
Dirksen, Sen. Everett, 114, 194
DiSalle, Gov. Michael, 142
discrimination in housing problems, 83
District of Columbia v. John Thompson,
  10
Dixon, John, Jr., 112
Dixon, St. John, 155
Dixon, Walter T., 47
Doar, John, 161
Dock Street Theater, 6
Docking, Gov. George, 103
Dogan, Ewlet, 161
Domino, Fats, 51, 109
Donovan, James, 224
Dooling, Maurice T., 21
Dougherty County, Ga., 183
Dove, Mabel, 47
Dover, Del., 118, 151
Dowdy, Richard, 119
Dowling, Joseph, 175
Dowling, Robert W., 32
Downes, John, Jr., 175
Drake, Dr. John, 163
DuBay, Father William, 212
DuBois, W. E. B., 80, 193
Dudley, Edward R., 62
Duggar, John Frederick, 50
Duke, Angier Biddle, 145, 147, 151
Dulles, Allen, 214, 215
Dulles, John Foster, 4, 90
Dunagan, Otis, 64

Dunaway, Edwin, 72
Duncan, Gloria, 149
Dunn, G. William, 112
Dunnigan, Willie, 79
Dupas, Ralph, 66
Duplessis, Christopher, 66
Dupont, Rev. King S., 45
Durham, W. J., 50
Durham, N.C., 49, 60, 68, 141, 155, 192,
  217
Dutchtown, La., 68, 69
Dwight, Capt. Edward, Jr., 186
Dyson, Wheeler, 133

Earls, Julian, 168
East Carroll Parish, La., 143, 238
East Chicago, Ind., 130
Easterly, J. B., 24
Eastland, Sen. James, 36-37, 89, 106, 120,
  132, 167
Eaton, Dr. Hubert, 228
Eaton, William, 229
Ebony magazine, 59, 60, 69, 71
Eckford, Elizabeth, 69
economic boycotts, 16, 17, 20, 23, 33,
  81-82, 98, 102, 105, 123, 126, 129,
  140, 151, 154, 156, 160, 161, 164, 173,
  177, 179, 182, 199, 206, 208, 209, 210,
  212, 219, 221, 224, 227-228, 232, 233,
  234, 237, 238, 241, 243
economic reprisals directed against
  black voters in Fayette and Haywood
  Counties, Tenn. (1960-61), 122
Edgewater, N.J., 181
Edisto Beach State Park, 41
Edmunds, Dr. Edison, 62
Edmunds, Helen, 30
Edwards, E. L., 30
Eisenhower, President Dwight David, xvi,
  4, 5, 10, 20, 21, 45, 50, 55, 58, 67, 68,
  71, 84, 85, 89, 104, 107, 115, 119, 122,
  131, 135, 189; black voting rights and,
  40, 122; *Brown v. Board of Education*
  decision and, 7, 8; Capital Transit
  Company and, 20; Children's March in
  1958 and, 92-93; desegregation on U.S.
  military bases orders by, 4; government
  contracts offerings and desegregation
  and, 11; Little Rock, Ark., school incident and, 69; National Urban League
  and, 32; picketing against, 133; picketing at golf course played at by, 124;
  President's Committee on Government
  Contracts and, 100; reelection of, 55;
  speech at NAACP Freedom Conference
  by, 5; support of Rep. Adam Clayton
  Powell for, 53, 93; on violence, 121;
  Wilkins, J. Ernest, appointment by, 5
Eisman, Herman, 168
Elder, Leon B., 92
elections, 15, 24, 33-34, 55, 74, 93, 131,
  197, 220

Elizabeth, N.J., 216, 227
Ellington, Duke, 106, 108, 118
Ellis, Frank, 169
Ellison, Essie Mae, 87
Elloie, Pearlie Hardin, 179
Embry, Elroy, 155
Emmerich, J. Oliver, 155, 159
employment and labor unions, confronting discrimination in, 128
employment discrimination, 4, 5, 6, 7, 11, 12, 20, 21, 22, 24, 25, 29, 32, 34, 37, 44, 45-46, 47, 48, 49, 53, 54, 55, 62, 63-64, 65, 66, 67, 68, 69, 70, 72, 74, 75, 81, 82, 84, 86, 88, 89, 98, 99, 102, 105, 108, 111, 112, 114, 117, 118, 119, 120, 121, 122, 123, 125, 126, 127, 128, 129, 130, 138, 141, 143, 144, 145, 146, 147, 148, 151, 154, 155, 157, 159, 161, 162, 163, 164, 165, 166, 167, 168, 170, 171, 173, 174, 175, 176, 177, 178, 179, 182, 183, 184, 186, 188, 192, 196, 202, 204, 205, 206, 208, 209, 210, 211, 212, 214, 215, 216, 217, 219, 220, 224, 225, 227, 230, 231, 232, 233, 235, 236, 237, 240, 241
Engelhardt, Samuel, 29, 63
English, Sandy, 188, 189
Ennix, Coyness, 75, 82
entertainment, 5, 6, 20, 22, 36, 44, 46, 51, 55, 73, 74, 81, 100, 102, 106, 108, 109, 114, 134, 135, 141, 145, 192
Erath, La., 36
Ervin, Richard, 112
Estes, Edwin H., 84
Estes, Rice, 139
Evans, Mayor E. J., 155
Evans, James C., 46-47, 134
Evans, Lt. Col. Luther, Jr., 149
Evanston, Ill., 10, 211
Evers, Charles, 192, 206, 217, 238, 242
Evers, Medgar, 123, 176; arrest of murderer of, 191; assassination of, 181, 189, 190, 195, 207; bus riding attack of, 81; scholarship fund for children of, 189-190; Spingarn Medal for, 191; trial for murder of, 202, 208
Evers, Myrlie, 191, 204, 206
Evers, O. Z., 47, 90, 114

fair employment practice commissions (FEPCs), 4, 20, 25, 34, 46, 54, 61, 64, 68, 82, 88, 99, 103, 108, 112, 134, 145, 187, 190, 206, 209, 215, 216, 220, 240
Fair Employment Practices Committee, 4
Fairbanks, Alaska, 88
Fairchild, Edward T., 53
Fairfax County, Va., 16, 62-63
Farmer, James, 150, 154, 162, 179, 193, 196, 199, 212, 213, 215, 219, 228, 241, 246
Faubus, Gov. Orval, xvi, 60, 69, 79, 80, 89, 91, 92, 110

Fayette, Miss., 242
Fayette County, Tenn., 122, 135, 137, 138, 215
Fayetteville, Ark., 4
Federation of Citizens Association, 12
Feibelman, Rabbi Julian B., 33
Feikens, John, 196
Felder, Robert, 55
Fennoy, Leon, 7
Ferguson, William, 225
Ferrell, Dean Harrison, 13
Filby, Francis, 145
Findley, Ralph, 118
Finn, Henry G., 105
firemen, 7, 12, 20, 25, 26, 37, 55, 65, 105, 118, 167, 188
Firth, Rev. Robert H., 87
Fischer, John, 49
Fisk University, 9, 23, 41, 125, 241
Fitts, Steven, 194
Fitts, Yvonne, 194
Fleming, Arthur, 111
Fleming, Harold, 128
Fleming, Sara Mae, 45
Fleming, Sarah, 29
Flint, Mich., 79, 141
Florence, Ala., 4
Florence, S.C., 42, 44
Flott, Nilda, 132
Flowers, Richmond, 237
Flushing, N.Y., 209
Folcroft, Pa., 194, 199, 201
Folsom, Gov. James, 27, 70, 90, 92
football, 14; Chicago Bears players' wives luncheon, 197; exhibition game in Birmingham, Alabama, 66; Georgia-Alabama 1962 game, beatings at, 175; NAACP boycott of Redskins-Rams game, 147; Rose Bowl game of 1959, 98; San Diego Chargers 1961 contracts, 155; Sugar Bowl games, 17, 37, 51, 94
Ford, Gerald, 240
Forest Hills, N.Y., 107, 108, 115
Forman, James, 174, 195, 199, 204, 212, 218
Forrest County, Miss., 175
Fort, T. Hicks, 28
Fort Hood, Tex., 85
Fort Lauderdale, Fla., 71
Fort Smallwood, Md., 47
Fort Wayne, Ind., 30
Fort Worth, Tex., 34, 52, 65
Fost, William Ash, 55
Foster, Autherine Lucy. See Lucy (Foster), Autherine
Foster, Luther F., 82
Fowler, George, 219
Fowler, Maurice, 156
Fox, Mary Ethel, 143
Francois, Terry, 156, 177
Franich, Joe, 88

Frankfurter, Felix, 49, 92
Franklin, Rev. C. L. 197
Franklin, David, 129
Franklin, Dorothy, 65
Franklin, Harold, 201
Franklin, Dr. John Hope, 41, 179
Franklin Parish, La., 189
Frazier, Kenneth, 129
Fredericksburg, Va., 188
Freedman, Abraham L., 12
Freedom Riders/Rides, xvii, 136, 137, 165, 168, 170, 172, 213, 218, 233; expulsion of students who went on, 159; launching of, 150, 162; NAACP and, 161
Freedom Summer, 211, 212, 213, 214
Freeman, Edward, 235
Freeman, Gov. Orville, 25
Freeman, Orville, 154, 182
Frelinghuysen, Rep. Peter, 41
French, David, 216
Fresno, Calif., 115
Friedan, Betty, 245
full compliance: federal officials move to implement Civil Rights Act of 1964, 226
Fuller, Taylor, 166
Fulton County, Ga., 7
Fuqua, Rev. Carl, 101
Fuqua, Charles, 135
Futch, Jewell, 174
Futch, Dr. Ovid, 119

Gabrielle, Daisy, 134
Gabrielle, James, 135
Gadsden, Ala., 197, 198
Gaffney, S.C., 74
Gaillot, Mrs. B. J., 166
Gainesville, Fla., 89, 211-212
Galamison, Rev. Milton, 224
Galbraith, John Kenneth, Jr., 179
Galveston County, Tex., 34
Gamble, Robert, 192
Gantt, Harvey, 177, 182, 183, 231
Garrett, Marva, 156
Garrison, Wesley, 22
Gary, Gov. Raymond, 44, 61, 81
Gary, Wilbur, 206
Gary, Ind., 108, 121, 232
Gathright, Morrell, 100
Gayle, Mayor W. A., 42
Gaynor, Harry, 64
Gbedemah, K. A., 104
General Assembly of the Presbyterian Church USA, 17
Germany, J. H., 129
Gesell, Gerhard, 170, 194
Gibbons, Harold, 221
Gibson, Althea, 66, 78, 90
Gibson, Rev. Oliver W., 80
Gibson, Rev. Theodore, 45, 84, 130, 153, 186
Gilbert, John, 138
Gillespie, Dizzy, 51

Gillman, Sid, 155
Ginzburg, Eli, 46–47
Girard College, 12, 30, 55, 62, 64–65, 72, 78, 86, 232, 234, 235
Gist, Anthony, 166
Glawson, A. J., 206
Gleason, John, 187
Glen Burnie, Md., 170
Gloster, Miss., 204
Glover, James, 194
Glover, Roland, 194
Gober, Bertha, 172
Goldberg, Arthur, 141, 146, 170
Golden, Harry, 219
Goldsby, Robert Lee, 112, 113
Goldwater, Sen. Barry, 154, 201, 215, 216, 217
Goli, Stephen, 194
Gomillion, Charles G., 63, 140
Goodlett, Dr. Carlton, 138
Goodman, Andrew, 207, 221, 234
Goodman, Ernest, 228
Gordon, George, 170
Gordon, John, 90
Gordon, Walter, 89
Gotten, Norma, 163
government-sponsored employment and attacks of discrimination (1963), 187
Graetz, Rev. Robert S., 89
Gragg, Dr. Rosa, 199
Graham, Billy, 30
Graham, Thomas, 151
Grand Forks, N.D., 155, 186
Granger, Lester, 14, 52, 65, 74, 85, 111, 149
Gravel, Camille, 94
Graver, Fiza, 209
Graves, Haskel, 105
Gray, Fred, 42, 89, 188
Gray, Victoria, 213, 224
Green, A. D., 84
Green, Dewey, 174
Green, Ernest, 84, 85
Green, Hix, 107
Green, Marlon D., 98, 215
Green, Wendell, 208
Green, Mrs. Wendell, 151
Greenberg, Jack, 152, 161, 199, 220, 231
Greenbrier County, W. Va., 12
Greene, Dewey, Jr., 188
Greene, Jerry "Pumpsey," 100, 103
Greenidge, George, 7
Greensboro, Ala., 235
Greensboro, N.C., 12, 50, 62, 66, 116, 118, 129, 132, 155, 173
Greenville, Ala., 240
Greenville, Miss., 68, 132, 231
Greenville, S.C., 28
Greenwood, Herbert A., 106
Greenwood, Miss., 155, 175, 191
Greer, Robert, 75
Gregory, Rev. David E., 59

Gregory, Dick, 184, 185, 193, 202, 205, 214, 216, 220, 233, 236
Gregory, John, 163
Gremillion, Jack, 114
Griffin, Rev. L. Francis, 132, 134
Griffin, Gov. Marvin, 80
Griffin v. State Board of Education, 228
Griswold, Erwin, 143
Grooms, H. H., 172, 173
Grooms, Hobart, 28, 51
Gross, Calvin, 185
Grosse Pointe, Mich., 129
Guilford, N.C., 32
Guillory, Barbara Marie, 179
Gulfport, Miss., 68
Gutheridge, Amos, 110
Guy, Gov. William, 242
Guyot, Laurence, 220

Haber, Al, 243–244
Hacker, Andrew, 53
Hagedorn, Virgil, 211
Hagemann, Edward, 43
Halas, Mrs. George, 197
Haley, F. C., 148
Hall, Juanita, 5
Hall, Nancy, 166
Hall, Prathia, 207
Hallinan, Rev. Paul, 225
Hamer, Fannie Lou, 201, 213, 224, 245
Hamilton, C. S., 164
Hamilton, Mary, 203, 208
Hammarskjöld, Dag, 19, 149
Hammond, Buff, 246
Hampton, Lionel, 114
Hampton, Va., 144
Hannah, John, 74
Hannibal, Mo., 31
Hansberry, Lorraine, 102
Hansen, Harvey, 84
Hansen, William, 199
Hardcastle, James, 151
Harkless, John, 140
Harmon, Gloria and Rosella, 221
Harper, Roy W., 94
Harpers Ferry. W.Va., 21, 26
Harpersville, Ala., 129
Harriman, Averell, 17, 35, 62, 93
Harriman, N.Y., 82
Harris, Gerald, 52
Harris, James, 61
Harris, Patricia Roberts, 192, 232
Harris, Robert, 55
Harrisburg, Pa., 34, 55, 65, 78, 92, 123
Hart, Herbert W., 102
Hart, Sen. Philip, 109
Hartford, Conn., 7
Hartford County, Md., 78
Harth, Raymond, 153, 173, 212
Hartke, Sen. Vance, 131
Hartsfield, Arnett, 152

Hartsfield, Mayor William B., 14, 74, 98, 123, 142, 143, 148
Harvey, Fletcher, 196, 197
Harvey, William, 68
Hasbrouck Heights, N.J., 177
Hatcher, Andrew, 133
Hatcher, Lillian, 89
Hatchet, William, 71
Hatchett, Truly, 50
Hattiesburg, Miss., 134, 167, 191, 216
Hauser, James, 203
Havelock, N.C., 110
Hawes, Foreman, 103
Hawkins, Grant W., 34
Hawkins, Virgil D., 43, 85
Hawthorne, David, 60, 107
Hayden, Casey, 245
Hayden, Tom, 243–244
Hayes, George E. C., 2, 46
Hayes, Johnson J., 62
Hayling, Dr. Robert, 203
Haywood, Dr. Charles, 181
Haywood County, Tenn., 122, 138
Heflin, Ala., 171
Height, Dorothy, 117, 179, 199, 220
Heller, Jacob, 175
Henderson, Clarence, 116
Henderson, Doris, 13
Henderson, Elmer, 53
Henderson, Morris, 202
Henderson, Thelton, 196–197
Hendricks, Leon, 208
Hennegan, District Attorney Pat, 10
Hennessey, Betty, 238–239
Hennessy, Wesley, 59
Henry, Dr. Aaron, 178, 195, 196, 204, 213, 219, 223, 225, 238
Henry, Gov. Joe, 48
Henry, Noelle, 178
Henry, Richard, 134
Henry, Robert, 240
Hernandez, Aileen, 245
Herter, Christian, 138
Hesburgh, Theodore, 74, 212
Hewett, Father Clayton, 210
Hickey, Philip J., 16
Hicks, Dr. J. L., 4
High Point, N.C., 157
Higley, Harvey H., 10, 14
Hilberry, Dr. Clarence, 215
Hilbun, Ben, 101
Hill, Clifton, 224
Hill, Rev. George, 84
Hill, Herbert, 67, 74, 102, 132, 147, 166, 169, 177, 224, 227
Hill, Norman, 214
Hillard, Raymond, 174
Hillsboro, Ohio, 13, 16, 43
Hinderas, Natalie, 81
Hinton, Rev. James M., 40, 43
historical overview, xv–xvi
Hobbs, N.Mex., 10

Hobby, HEW Secretary Oveta Culp, 17, 36
Hobson, Julius, 153, 208
Hockett, Fred, 60
Hodge, Oliver, 44
Hodges, Gov. Luther, 32, 104, 204
Hoff, Phillip H., 95
Hoffman, Dr. Edwin, 84
Hoffman, Walter, 53–54, 72, 113, 124
Hoggard, Rev. J. Clinton, 10
Hoggles, O'Neal, 230
Hoggles, William, 230
Holland, Myra E. D., 98
Holland, William, 206
Holley, Dr. James W., 107
Hollier, Willie, 24
Hollings, Gov. 135
Hollowell, David, 181
Hollowell, Donald, 139
Hollywood, Calif., 22, 100
Hollywood, Fla., 129
Holman, Claude, 205
Holman, Dr. L. H., 154
Holmes, Adolph, 219
Holmes, Clarence, 148
Holmes, Hamilton, 132, 135, 139
Holt, Len, 130
Homer, La., 46
Homerville, Ga., 166
Honolulu, Hawaii, 189, 216, 232
Hood, James, 188, 189, 193, 231
Hooks, Benjamin L., 108
Hooper, Frank, 94, 98, 106, 124
Hoover, J. Edgar, 107, 181, 215, 220, 221, 223
Horne, Frank, 82
Horry County, S.C., 30
Horton, Mildred, 192
Horton, Myles, 120, 140
hospitals and medical staff, problem of segregation/desegregation, 3, 4, 7, 10, 17, 20, 24, 33, 34, 68, 86, 109, 132, 133, 135, 140, 148, 153, 160, 161, 163, 164, 167, 173, 178, 179, 189, 197, 198, 202, 203, 204, 206, 208, 210, 226, 228, 230, 232–234
Hot Springs, Ark., 15, 204, 235
Houle, Frank L., 15
House, Mrs. Byron, Jr., 91
housing and problems of discrimination, 4, 5, 7, 9, 13, 15, 17, 20, 22, 26, 27, 32, 46, 49, 59, 62–63, 68, 70, 74, 78, 83, 85, 98, 101, 102, 105, 106, 108, 109, 111–112, 119, 120, 121, 123, 125, 126, 129, 130, 132, 133, 135, 138, 140, 143, 144, 145, 148, 149, 152, 154, 156, 161, 162, 163, 166, 170, 171, 173, 175, 176, 178, 179, 181, 182, 183, 184, 186, 187, 191, 192, 193, 194, 196, 198, 199, 201, 202, 205, 209, 214, 217, 219, 224, 225, 228, 232, 235, 238, 240
housing as step toward equality, 156

Houston, John, 225
Houston, Tex., 9, 33, 41, 51, 72, 95, 106, 112, 120, 121, 125, 129, 144, 206, 214, 221, 235
Howard, Asbury, 99
Howard, Donald, 4, 7
Howard, George, Jr., 183
Howard, Mary E., 9, 23
Howard, Perry, 50
Howard, Dr. Theodore R. M., 17, 21, 23, 30, 40, 43, 50–51
Hoxie, Ark., 32, 33, 39, 42
Hughes, Gov. Harold, 211
Hughes, Jerry M., 33
Hughes, Gov. Richard, 225
Hume, Rev. H. H., 29
Humphrey, Vice President Hubert H., 20, 57, 82, 218, 221, 225, 238, 239
Hunt, Barbara, 98
Hunter, Charlayne, 132, 135, 139
Hunter, Edwin, 171
Hunter, Mr. and Mrs. Joe, 21
Huntley, Chet, 100
Huntley, W. Moscoe, 179
Huntsville, Ala., 144, 165, 186, 196, 232
Hurley, Ruby, 11, 12, 17, 29, 141
Hutcheson, Sterling, 88

Idol, E. D., 32
Indianapolis, Ind., 111, 144–145, 215–216
Indianola, Miss., 15, 75; White Citizens Council formation in, 8
Ingram, Carolyn, 68
Ingram, George, 25
Ink Spots incident, 147
Institute, W.Va., 13
international incidents caused by racial discrimination in United States, 104
international relations, problem of discrimination in the United States, 5, 8, 14, 20–21, 33–34, 47, 51, 60, 64, 66, 71, 82, 85, 88, 89, 100, 104, 123, 129, 138, 140, 143, 145, 148, 149, 164, 194, 199, 202, 216, 240–241
interracial cohabitation, 97
Interracial dancing, 109
interracial marriages, 22, 23, 25, 74, 97, 103, 114, 161, 191, 199, 242
interstate transportation, problem of discrimination, 9, 12, 34, 40, 42, 55, 112, 126, 133, 150, 152, 153, 155, 162, 165, 166
Irby, Edith, 4
Irons, Edward and Bessie, 45
Island in the Sun (movie), 73
Ivory, Rev. Cecil, 63, 81

Jack, Hulan, 3
Jackson, Edward, 167
Jackson, Rev., Franklin, 81
Jackson, Rev. James H., 204

Jackson, Jimmie Lee, 223, 229
Jackson, Rev. Joseph, 10, 191, 193
Jackson, Mahalia, 46
Jackson, Robert, 234
Jackson, Shelby, 135, 140–141
Jackson, Miss., 10, 16, 24, 36–37, 49, 71, 78, 81, 90, 95, 97, 123, 137, 141, 160, 166, 167, 168, 170, 183, 184, 192, 196, 202, 206, 208, 215, 217, 224, 234
Jackson, Tenn., 41, 132
Jacksonville, Fla., 111, 207–208
"jail, no bail" strategy, 142
Jakes, Wilhelmina, 45
James, Grace M., 3
James, Rev. H. Rhett, 164
James, Roy, 175
James, Lt. Thomas L., 15
Jarrett, Willard A. L., 23
Javits, Sen. Jacob, 186, 191
Jeanmard, Bishop Jules B., 36
Jeanpierre, Wendell, 46
Jefferson Barracks, Mo., 220
Jefferson City, Mo., 240
Jefferson County, Ark., 130
Jemison, Rev. T. J., 55
Jenkins, Clyde, 203
Jenkins, Ed, 162
Jenkins, Herbert, 148, 168, 242
Jenkins, James, 203
Jenkins, Robert, 12
Jennings, Mo., 202
Jeremiah X, 208–209
Jernagin, William, 71
Jersey City, N.J., 216
Jesuit Bend, La., 34
Jet magazine, xvii–xviii, 44, 60; article by Ernest Green in, 85; article on James Meredith in, 188; article on children preparing for Virginia integration in, 100; article on Martin Luther King, Jr., in, 44, 115; article on Nation of Islam group in, 110
Jewell, Arthur D., 13
Jewell, Thomas, 135
Jim Crow signs removal, 4
Jim Crow travel laws, 23
Johnson, Alvin, 161
Johnson, Arthur, 66
Johnson, Charles, S., 43
Johnson, David, 194
Johnson, Evangeline, 67
Johnson, Ford, 188
Johnson, Frank M., 101, 110, 140, 141, 145, 150, 170, 225
Johnson, George, 53
Johnson, J. V., 90
Johnson, James A., 99
Johnson, John H., 60, 66, 210
Johnson, Judy, 4
Johnson, Howard, 182
Johnson, Leroy, 218
Johnson, Lindsey B., 105

Johnson, President Lyndon Baines, 70, 127, 131, 146, 161, 168, 183, 198, 199, 202, 203, 208, 210, 212, 213, 216, 218, 219, 220, 221, 225, 227, 229, 232, 236, 238, 240, 244
Johnson, Olin, 171
Johnson, Gov. Paul, 207, 214, 218, 238
Johnson, Mayor Wallace, 187
Johnson, Willa, 216
Jolly, M.C., and Dr Pepper boycott, 41
Jones, Adrian, 130
Jones, Charles, 142
Jones, Rev. Charles, 150
Jones, Clyde, 53
Jones, Danny, 29
Jones, DeWitt, 156
Jones, Edward, 155
Jones, Frances, 242
Jones, George, 153
Jones, Dr. Harry N., 72
Jones, Henry, 129
Jones, Joe, 40
Jones, Johnnie, 16
Jones, Madison, 83
Jones, Walter B., 48, 227
Jonesboro, La., 230
Jordon, Mary Ann, 114
Joseph, John, 177
Joyner, Albert, 30
jury duty/jurors, 7, 32, 41, 112, 113, 154, 168, 170, 173, 210, 214, 239, 240

Kamara, Abu Magba, 199
Kansas City, Mo., 24, 28, 86, 98, 105, 123, 174–175, 220, 238–239
Kasper, John, 70, 79
Katitus, Clara, 206
Katzenbach, Nicholas, 229, 239, 240
Kaufman, Irving, 138
Kavanagh, Thomas J., 68
Kearns, J. Harvey, 65
Keating, Sen. Kenneth, 87, 167, 171
Kefauver, Sen. Estes, 122
Keith, Damon, 123, 196
Kelley, Asa, 172
Kelley, Frank, 228
Kennard, Clyde, 134, 183, 191
Kennedy, President John F., 117, 127, 130, 131, 133, 135, 138, 140, 142, 143, 145, 146, 150, 151, 155, 156, 163, 168, 174, 175, 182, 184, 189, 190, 192, 198, 245; black newspaper publishers meeting with, 138; civil rights bill by, 180, 191, 193, 194; Coast Guard officer school and, 139, 168; Cosmos Club and, 179; diplomatic corps and, 179; endorsement of D.C. civil rights march (1963) by, 192; on federal funds to Mississippi, 188; housing discrimination order signed by, 178; inauguration speech (1962) of, 160; King, Martin Luther, Jr., speaking about (1962),

166; literacy tests and, 161; NAACP 1961 meeting with, 145; racial discrimination in armed services study and, 170; United Negro College Fund delegation and, 164; U.S. Commission on Civil Rights appointees by, 143
Kennedy, Robert F., 131, 132, 137, 143, 149, 150, 152, 154, 160, 170, 171, 174, 175, 181, 182, 189, 196, 198, 212; Albany Movement of 1961–62 and, 172; meeting with Gov. George Wallace and, 188; Meredith, James, enrollment into Ole Miss and, 176; sit-in in office of, 162
Kennedy, Stephen, 119
Kennelly, Martin, 5
Kennelly, Mayor William, 22
Keppel, Francis, 226, 231
Kerner, Gov. Otto, 145, 173, 212, 236
Kerr, Clark, 243
Kersey, Rev. Gerald, 61
Keyes, Sarah, 13
Kimes, Jean, 32
King, Rev. A. D., 237
King, Clennon, 60, 65
King, Coretta Scott, 44, 60, 92, 100, 131, 220
King, Mrs. Douglass, 49
King, Mayor Iris Winnifred, 104
King, Lonnie, Jr., 126, 129
King, Martin Luther, III, 186
King, Martin Luther, Jr., xv, 37, 39, 47, 55, 58, 73, 75, 80, 97, 102, 107, 127, 131, 139, 146, 150, 160, 168, 182, 186, 189, 193, 197, 212, 213, 214, 221, 225, 239–240, 243, 246; Alabama boycott called for by, 227, 228; Albany Movement of 1961–62 and, 172; arrest of, 90, 120, 159; on Atlanta, Ga. (1963), 199; attack (1962) of, 175; Birmingham, Ala., as target by, 190; bomb at home of, 58; Chicago as target and, 233; at Civil Rights Act of 1964 signing, 211; cross burning on lawn of, 124; Crusade for Citizenship, 80; Detroit Walk for Freedom by, 191; *Ebony* magazine column by, 69; endorsement of Lyndon Baines Johnson for president (1964) by, 219; Freedom Corps and, 164; fund-raising for legal defense of reverends by, 143; Ghana independence and, 60; on Goldwater nomination for president, 215; Hoover, J. Edgar, on, 220; "I Have a Dream" speech of, 181, 194; in India, 100; *Jet* magazine article on, 44; kneel-ins led by, 124; lecture at Yale by, 99; on Little Rock incident, 71; march on D.C. plan announced and, 61; meeting with J. Edgar Hoover (1964) by, 221; meeting with President Eisenhower by, 85;

meeting with President Johnson (1964) by, 220–221, 225; meeting with President Kennedy (1962) by, 179; meeting with Richard Nixon by, 66; Montgomery bus boycott and, 42, 45, 64; move from Montgomery to Atlanta of, 115, 119; NAACP convention of 1956 and, 47; National Urban League annual meeting of 1960 and, 130; National Press Club address by, 171; Nobel Peace Prize for, 201, 219; perjury charges against, 126; in Philadelphia (1965), 235; Prayer Pilgrimage for Freedom and, 64; on President Kennedy (1962), 166; protest march for arrest of, 158; rally for Jeremiah Reeves and speech by, 82; release from prison of, 132; St. Augustine, Fla., protest (1964) and, 203; Selma to Montgomery, Ala., march (1965) and, 222, 229; sentencing of, 141; sit-ins and, 142; Southern Christian Leadership Conference (SCLC) formation by, 57; Southern Christian Leadership Conference annual meetings and, 115, 119, 140, 175, 236; Spingarn Medal awarded to, 67; stabbing in New York of, 91; support for Lyndon Baines Johnson by, 199; threats against, 204, 224; on Vietnam, 244; Watts area tour by, 236; Youth March for Public School Desegregation of 1959 in D.C., 103
King, Mary, 245
King, Robert D., 8
Kingstree, S.C., 186
Kirby, William, 79
Kirkwood, R. C., 125
Klitenic, David, 162
Knight, C. A., 11
Knight, Gov. Goodwin, 25
Knoop, Mayor Werner C., 110
Knox, Ellis O., 53
Knoxville, Tenn., 36, 39, 47, 152
Ku Klux Klan (KKK), 8, 13, 24, 30, 49, 51, 52, 60, 63, 64, 66, 73, 78, 79, 82, 84, 95, 110, 118, 120, 133, 150, 151, 174, 175, 189, 203, 209, 229, 234, 237, 240, 241
Kuykendall, Willie, 135

labor unions and discrimination, 4, 7, 12, 15, 21, 22, 23, 24, 25, 30, 31, 32–33, 36, 37, 50, 54, 60, 61, 62, 65, 67, 70, 71, 75, 79, 81, 82, 83, 89, 99, 102, 106, 111, 112, 115, 120, 125, 127–130, 133, 140, 141, 144, 145, 146, 151, 153, 166–168, 169, 170, 177, 178, 179, 187, 191, 206, 210, 211, 212, 214, 215, 216, 217, 221, 224, 225, 226, 227, 228, 232
Laborde, Ellis, 98
Lackey, Dr. Lawrence, 128
Lafayette, Ind., 15, 110, 111

LaFlore, J. L., 112, 184
Lake City, S.C., 43
Lake Forest, Ill., 151
Lake Providence, La., 174
Lakeland, Fla., 49, 102
Lamar, Cecil, 27, 53
Lambert, Virginia, 78
Landry, Lawrence, 208, 209, 210
Lansing, Mich., 68, 98, 121, 196, 205, 228
Larsen, Harold, 234
Las Vegas, Nev., 123
Lassmore, Andrew, 121
Laurel, Del., 92
Laurel, Miss., 238
Lautier, Louis R., 21
Law, W. W., 151
Lawson, Mrs. George, 51
Lawson, Rev. James, 125
Lawson, Dr. Lloyd E., 89
Lawson, Reuben, 161
Lawtey, Fla., 205
Leader, Gov. George M., 34, 65, 68
Leahy, Paul, 67
Lederle, Arthur F., 9, 26
Lee, Bernard, 129, 155
Lee, Rev. George, 35
Lee, Herbert, 204
Lee, Mayor Richard, 119
Lee, Rev. Rita E., 16
Leflore County, Miss., 184
Legree, Frank, 60
Lehman, Sen. Herbert, 36, 49, 152
Leighton, George, 113
Lemley, Harry J., 85, 91
Leston, John, 144
Levitt, William, 83, 109, 130
Levittown, N.J., 109, 130
Levittown, Pa., 68, 71, 83
Lewis, Alfred Baker, 137–138
Lewis, Chester, 118
Lewis, Debra, 217
Lewis, Father Gerald, 34
Lewis, Isaac, 152
Lewis, John, 195, 199, 204, 210, 222, 229
Lewis, Oren, 148, 152, 169
Lexington, Ky., 153
Liberty, Miss., 174
Liberty County, Fla., 44, 224–225
libraries and integration, 107, 145, 183, 192, 194, 195
Liley, Robert, 170
Lillard, Robert, 50
Lindsey, Candis, 205
Lindsey, Coleman, 36
Lips, Mayor Evans, 242
literacy tests for voting rights, 24, 33, 101, 106, 160, 161, 210, 225, 229
Little, W. D., 28
Little Rock, Ark., 40, 55, 56, 57, 60, 61, 72, 79, 80, 85, 86, 88, 91, 94, 95, 100, 106, 114, 119, 165, 166, 194, 209, 240;

Bates home and lack of protection in, 92, 108–109; blood donation by race in, 103; bombings in, 110, 120; 1959 reopening of schools in, 110; showdown at Central High School in, 69; troops removal at Central High School in, 84
Littleton, Colo., 82
Liuzzo, Viola, 229
Livingston, E. P., 101
Locher, Mayor Ralph, 187
Lockart, H. T., 90
Lodge, Henry Cabot, 147
Loeb, Mayor Henry, 148
Lomax, Louis, 154
Lomax, Ala., 79
London, England, 33–34, 64, 66, 89
Long, Gov. Earl, 120
Long, John D., 72
Looby, Z. Alexander, 50, 123
Lorman, Miss., 60, 65
Los Angeles, Calif., 3, 13, 17, 30, 41, 42, 43, 67, 79, 81, 83, 84, 104, 106, 132, 154, 165, 170, 192, 208, 239, 240; Catholic leadership in, 212; dentists in, 58; firemen in, 7, 20, 37, 152; football game boycott by NAACP in, 147; riot prevention proposals for, 237; Watts riots in, 236, 242
Lott, B. O., 10
Louisville, Ky., 3, 5, 47, 120, 132, 189, 216, 221
Louisville, Miss., 32
Lowe, Walter L., 39
Lowell, Stanley, 168, 224
Lowery, Rev. Joseph, 112, 139, 141, 143, 145, 206
Lowndes County, Ala., 239
Lowndes County, Miss., 170
Lowry, Rev. A. Leon, 112, 153
Lucey, Archbishop Robert E., 6, 7
Lucy (Foster), Autherine, 28, 41, 42, 51, 59, 189
Ludley, Arnease, 58
Luke, Ralph, 155
Luper, Clara, 89
Lurie, Reuben, 127
Lynch, James, 173
Lynchburg, Va., 34, 161
Lynd, Theron, 167, 175
Lynn, Albert, 221
Lynne, Seybourne, 157
Lyons, James, 127

Mabley, Jack, 167
Macon, Ga., 135, 175, 179
Macon County, Ala., 100, 101, 133
Macy, John, 223
Maddox, Lester, 74
Madison, Blaine M., 97
Madison, Wis., 53, 61, 121, 125–126, 148
Madison County, Ind., 154

Maggio, Frank, 59
Magloire, Haitian president Paul E., 20–21
Major League Baseball, 4
Malcolm X, 110, 209, 227, 246
Malone, Vivian, 188, 189, 231
Manger, Thomas, 121
Mangum, Lt. Robert J., 4
Mann, Theophilus, 121, 149
Manning, Cecil, 174
Mansfield, Tex., 34, 38
Manucy, Holstead, 203
Maplesville, Ala., 196–197
March on Washington (August 28, 1963), 180, 184, 192, 194
Marchand, Clarence, 239
Mark, Dr. Vincent, 156
Marovitz, Abraham, 185
Marquez, Jesse, 242
Marrero, La., 101–102
marriages, interracial, 22, 23, 25, 74, 103, 114, 161, 191, 199, 242
Marsh, Henry, 188
Marshall, Rev. Arthur, Jr., 98
Marshall, Burke, 176, 190, 203
Marshall, George, 147
Marshall, Thurgood, xvi, 2, 9, 13, 20, 22, 28, 31, 60, 84, 98, 126, 151, 152, 167, 171, 174, 175, 234
Marston, Dr. Robert, 160
Martin, Fred W., 15
Martin, Joseph, 55
Martin, Louis, 236
Martin, Ora D., 82
Martinez, Eugene, 121
Martino, Edward V., 105
Marx, Barbara, 47, 53
Mason, Barbara, 134
Mason, Rev. Charles H., 87
Mason, Norman, 119
Mason, Vivian Carter, 49, 71
Mason, William, 178
Matthews, Z. T., 173
Maudlin, Dora, 87
Maxton, N.C., 78
Mays, Dr. Benjamin, 15, 141, 144, 225
Mazique, Dr. Edward, 86
Mboya, Tom, 103
McCain, Franklin, 116, 118, 132
McCain, James, 181
McCarter, Warren, 177
McCauley, Jacqueline, 235
McClain, Rev. William, 194
McClellan, Sen. John L., 81, 105
McClendon, Joseph, 155
McCollum, Rev. Matthew D., 33
McComb, Miss., 148, 152, 153, 155, 159, 207, 219–220
McCone, John, 242
McCrae, Rev. Ian J., 98
McCree, Judge Wade, 24
McDew, Charles, 174

McDonald, A. B., 36
McDonald, La Fayette, 155
McDowell, Cleve, 196
McFarland, John, 129
McGill, Ralph, 134, 225
McGovern, Peter J., 29
McIntyre, Cardinal James Francis, 212
McKeithen, Gov. John, 230, 241
McKeldin, Gov. Theodore, 6
McKemie, Dr. Frank, 183
McKinley, Aretha, 120
McKinley, Robert, 231
McKissick, Floyd, 246
McKneally, Martin, 111
McNamara, Robert, 187, 215
McNeil, Joseph, 116, 118, 129, 132
Meany, George, 54, 62, 81, 102, 111, 126,
    141, 145, 178, 212, 217, 226
Meares, Carrie, 154
Mecklenburg, N.C., 88
Meehan, William, 216
Memphis, Tenn., 3, 34, 47, 59, 66, 81,
    90–91, 108, 109, 114, 134, 148, 152,
    171, 194, 220
Meredith, James (federal judge), 188
Meredith, James, 139, 148, 159, 181, 182,
    184, 188, 189, 245–246; graduation of,
    193; integration of Ole Miss and, 176;
    at NAACP annual convention of 1963,
    192; withdrawal of soldiers guarding,
    192
Meridian, Miss., 148, 174
Metcalfe, Fred, 95
Metcalfe, George, 236
Meyer, Cardinal Albert Gregory, 138
Meyers, William J., 68, 71
Miami, Fla., 21, 22, 59–60, 79, 84, 105,
    112, 119, 127, 154
Miami Beach, Fla., 178
Mikva, Abner, 163
Milam, John, 35
Milford, Del., 11, 50
military and problem of segregation/
    desegregation, 3, 4, 5, 6, 7, 10, 12, 13, 14,
    15, 27–28, 33, 34, 37, 46, 47, 52, 55, 58,
    62, 74, 81, 85, 88, 94, 95, 105, 110, 123,
    125, 139, 152, 153, 155, 163, 164, 168,
    170, 178, 182, 183, 184, 186, 187, 191,
    194, 195, 205, 212, 214, 215, 219, 220
Miller, Albert, 106
Miller, Emmanuel, 63
Miller, Eugene, 224
Miller, Mr. and Mrs. Frederick, 153
Miller, John E., 110
Miller, L. E., 82–83
Miller, William E., 111, 153, 219
Milwaukee, Wis., 32, 44, 89, 182, 210,
    231, 234, 239, 242
Ming, William R., Jr., 95
Minneapolis, Minn., 114–115, 121
minstrel show, 184
Miriani, Mayor Louis C., 89, 123, 138

Misawa Air Force Base, Japan, 195
Mississippi and the freedom summer
    project (1964), 207
Mitchell, Clarence, 3, 7, 14, 17, 27, 36, 42,
    51, 53, 55, 80, 84, 94, 122, 126, 131,
    152, 164, 183, 187, 196, 210, 239
Mitchell, Clarence, III, 170
Mitchell, J. Oscar, 132, 141
Mitchell, James P., 4, 5, 34, 66, 120, 133
Mitchell, John, 101–102
Mize, Sidney, 148, 168, 176, 204, 216
Moate, Marvin, 60
Moberly, Mo., 31, 94
Moline, Ill., 154
Money, Miss., 35
Monroe, James, 140
Monroe, La., 171
Monroe, N.C., 70, 72–73, 95, 97, 100, 112
Monteagle, Tenn., 109
Monteith, Henri, 177, 192
Montgomery, Ala., 10, 23, 28, 29, 37, 41,
    50, 51, 52, 55, 58, 73, 89, 90, 92, 98–99,
    113–114, 120, 126, 140, 141, 145, 149,
    157, 163, 170, 188, 224; Abernathy,
    Rev. Ralph David, leaves, 149; airport
    in, 159; ambulances in, 167; bus boy-
    cott in, xvi, xvii, 39, 42, 45, 63, 64; city
    public parks in, 91, 97, 110, 124, 143;
    death of Alfred Crishon in, 160; filming
    of The Montgomery Story and, 75;
    Greyhound terminal in, 144; juries in,
    173, 214; King, Martin, Luther, Jr.,
    leaves, 119; marshal's office in, 216;
    protest of electrocution of Jeremiah
    Reeves in, 82; school desegregation
    plan of 1965 in, 225; YMCA in, 160
Montgomery County, Ala., 183
Monts, Herbert, 120
Moon, Gov. Daniel K., 237
Moon, Henry Lee, 9, 214
Moon, O'Neil, 241
Moore, C. A., 49
Moore, Cecil B., 216, 217, 235
Moore, Rev. Douglas E., 68
Moore, Elizabeth, 163, 176
Moore, Herman, 15
Moore, Jamie, 133
Moore, Luke, 189
Moore, Russell, 166, 168
Morheuser, Marilyn, 242
Morial, Ernest, 198
Morial, Sybil, 198
Morin, Reiman, 84
Morris, Mayor George, 122
Morrisroe, Richard F., 237
Morrisville, Pa., 7
Morrow, E. Frederic, 28, 103
Moses, Bob, 148, 195, 207, 213
Mosk, Stanley, 115
Mosley, Ward, 115
Motley, Constance Baker, 106, 139, 155,
    176, 177–178, 201

Mound Bayou, Miss., 12–13, 21, 23, 25,
    26, 39–40, 50–51
Mound City, Ill., 147
movies, television, concerts, and civil
    rights, 73
Muckel, Robert, 189
Muhammad, Elijah, 109
Mullins, Ray, 53, 85
Muncie, Ind., 119
Murph, Dr. B. E., 238
Murphy, Carl, 138
Murphy, Frank, 134
Murphy, Franklin, 165
Murray, Pauli, 245
Murray, Samuel C., 61
Murrow, Edward R., 179, 202
Muse, John and Ann, 163
Mustachio, Angelo, 132
Myart, Leon, 220
Myers, Polly Ann, 28

NAACP, xvi, 5, 7, 10, 11, 15, 16, 17, 21, 23,
    24, 26, 27, 29, 30, 32, 33, 40, 41, 44, 57,
    61, 65, 78, 79, 81, 82, 90, 94, 112, 118,
    121, 122, 135; AFL–CIO and, 178;
    Alabama banning of, 89, 147–148, 227;
    annual conventions of, 9, 27, 47, 48,
    67, 86, 108, 126, 145, 171, 191, 192,
    212, 214, 234; athletes requesting sup-
    port from, 163; Atlanta Declaration
    issued by, 8; attack on, 39; brutality
    complaints filed by, 66; complaint
    against U.S. Mint in Philadelphia by,
    170; contributors to war chest of, 22;
    court rulings on release of member-
    ship and financial records of, 78, 79,
    86, 95, 106, 112, 125, 130, 179; Eisen-
    hower, President, speech at confer-
    ence of, 5; Federal Reserve Bank of
    Atlanta and, 161; financial status of
    (1958), 77–78; Freedom Riders and
    support of, 161; fund raising for, 45;
    funding of, 186; government contracts
    and discrimination alleged by, 161;
    Hilton Hotel chain and lawsuit against,
    173; homes for the aged and, 196;
    housing suits by, 20, 22; Illinois state
    convention (1961) of, 154; insurance
    policies for officials of, 39; IRS investi-
    gation of, 98; Las Vegas casinos and,
    123; labor unions study by, 128; legal
    defense fund of, 201; legislative attacks
    on, 48; Lynchburg, Va.'s National
    Spelling Bee and, 161; membership in-
    crease (1955) in, 37; membership in-
    crease (1964) in, 202; membership list
    burning and, 33; minstrel shows and,
    58; Mound Bayou, Miss., and, 39–40;
    NBC-TV character assassination of,
    100; New Orleans school integration
    and, 129; nonprofit status granted to,
    210; Panama Canal Zone and, 8; Parks,

NAACP (*cont.*)
Rosa, and, 37; plot to kill members of, 59–60; police brutality investigation by, 147; "Powell amendment" and, 26–27 Prince Edward County, Va., training centers and, 120; racial violence and attacks on leaders of, 35; raid of Amitie, Miss., meeting of, 12; Savannah, Ga., lawsuit of, 155; school survey by, 26; Sears, Roebuck department store and, 111; Spaulding, Jane Morrow, resignation and, 3–4; Spingarn Medal of, 26, 67, 84, 85, 86, 106, 191, 212; Sugar Bowl football game of 1954 and, 17; support for Martin Luther King, Jr., after his arrest and, 120; taxation in Georgia of, 67; teachers as members of, 31; Texas and barring of, 64; Texas State Fair and, 34; Texas Teachers Association and, 19; trains and segregation on and, 9–10; Trumbull Park Homes and, 7; turning over of membership list, 57; Tylertown, Miss., and, 11; UCRL formation and, 192; unions and, 177; Virginia's laws against, 61; voter registration and, 9; war chest of, 17, 20, 22, 26, 31; White Citizens Council and, 17, 78; White House Conference on Education and, 36; Willis, Benjamin, opposition by, 145
Nabrit, James, 2
Nahigan, John, 156
Nairobi, Kenya, 240, 241
Nalley, Gann L., 110
Nash, Diane, 125, 142, 147, 160, 167, 168
Nashville, Tenn., 9, 10, 11, 32, 40, 52, 53, 54, 70, 74, 75, 82, 88, 99, 105, 109, 114, 123, 125, 143, 147, 149, 159, 183, 188, 206, 210, 230
Natchez, Miss., 232, 236, 238, 241–242
Nation of Islam group, 109, 110
National Association for the Advancement of Colored People. *See* NAACP
National Association for the Advancement of White People, 8, 11; Baltimore, Md., and, 13; jailing of leader of, 99
National Association of Colored Women, 10, 26, 62, 197, 199
National Council of Negro Women, 26, 49, 71, 117, 192, 197, 199
National Organization of Women (NOW), 245
National Urban League (NUL), xviii, 7, 14, 22, 25, 29, 39, 65, 70–71, 121, 163, 186, 214; airline hiring and, 53; annual meeting of, 32, 111, 129–130, 149, 216; Atlanta, Ga., branch of, 67; branch closings of, 74; bus drivers hired in Kansas City and, 123; first white employee of, 9; Fort Worth, Tex., branch

of, 65; homes for aged and, 196; Little Rock, Ark., branch of, 72; musicians hiring and, 102; New York branch of, 25, 34; U.S. census and, 114; White Citizens Councils attacks on, 52, 74
Negro American Labor Council (NALC), 128, 146, 184
Negro Baseball League, 4
Neighbert, Keith, 81
Nelson, Gov. Gaylord, 148
New Auburn, Wis., and cross burning, 90
New Bedford, Mass., 58
New Brunswick, N.J., 61
New Delhi, India, 100
New Haven, Conn., 99, 119, 152, 183
New London, Conn., 168
New Orleans, La., 14, 30, 33, 51, 57, 58, 59, 61, 64, 65, 77, 79, 84, 90, 94, 98, 124, 125, 129, 133, 134, 135, 140–141, 143, 144, 149, 153, 154, 166, 174, 176, 178, 179, 181, 188, 198, 204, 216, 219, 228, 231, 239
New Rochelle, N.Y., 130, 133, 134, 138, 140, 211
New York City, 3, 4, 5, 8, 9, 14, 15, 17, 19, 20, 22, 23, 25, 26, 29, 31, 32, 34, 37, 39, 40, 41, 43, 46, 50, 55, 57–58, 59, 60, 64, 65, 69, 74, 75, 77, 78, 79, 80, 84, 85, 90, 91, 94–95, 98, 100, 102, 106, 108, 112, 114, 118, 119, 122, 124, 125, 129, 133, 134, 137, 138, 140, 141, 149, 152, 154, 161, 163, 166, 167, 168, 173, 177, 179, 181, 184, 189, 190, 192, 201, 202, 204, 206, 209, 210, 211, 212, 214, 215, 217, 219, 220, 221, 223, 224, 225, 227, 228, 230, 231, 242
New York Times, xvii, 43, 48, 50; libel judgment against, 139, 145; on Mississippi church bombings over the years, 237
Newcombe, Sophie, 179
Newman, Paul, 198
Newport, R.I., 108
Newsome, George, 22
Newtonville, N.J., 212
Nichols, Bishop D. Ward, 10
Nix, Robert, 93
Nixon, E. D., 37, 42, 66
Nixon, Vice President Richard, 11, 21, 60, 63–64, 72, 79, 104, 111, 128, 129, 130, 131, 135, 205
Nobel Peace Prize of 1964 to Martin Luther King, Jr., 201, 219
Noe, Gov. James A., 46
nonviolent protests spreading in southern cities (1957), 63
Norfolk, Va., 13, 32, 121, 155
Northport, Ala., 194
Nosser, Mayor John, 232
Nottingham, England, 89

Oak Ridge, Tenn., 20, 33
Oakland, Calif., 21, 182

Oakley, James H., 83
Oberlin, Ohio, 95
Ocilla, Ga., 13
Odum, Edward, 221
Oduor, Ralph, 241
Oescher, Edward W., 64
Oklahoma City, Okla., 28, 36, 41, 55, 58, 61, 81, 89, 105, 179, 242
Old Fort, N.C., 30
Oliver, Rev. A. J., 119
Oliver, Rev. C. Herbert, 123, 221
Orangeburg, S.C., 33, 196
organized labor responses to civil rights demands, 54
organized religion and racial segregation (1956–57), 59
Orioles baseball team, 6
Orleans Parish, La., 32, 174
Orndof, Jack G., 47
Osage, W.Va., 76
Otis, J. R., 60
Outlaw, Mrs. Robert, 188
Owens, Dr. Hugo, 107
Owens, L. L. and Gertrude, 147
Oxford, Miss., 159, 181, 182, 188, 192, 193, 196, 240
Oyama, Henry, 114
Ozark, Ark., 93

Pacoima, Calif., 117
Page, Everett, 49
Page, Ray, 185
Palo Alto, Calif., 61
Park Forest, Ill., 119
Parker, Eliza, 105
Parker, Frank, 106
Parker, Rev. J. T., 81
Parker, Joseph S., Jr., 49
Parker, Joseph W., Jr., 58
Parker, Mack Charles, 105, 107, 112, 113, 118
Parker, Ralph E., 63
Parker, William, 216
Parks, Rosa, 37
Parsons, James, 149, 187
Partee, Cecil, 163
Pasadena, Calif., 98
Paterson, N.J., 216
Patillo, Lois, 86
Patrick, William, Jr., 138
Patterson, Carrie, 45
Patterson, Floyd, 163
Patterson, Fred, 239
Patterson, Frederick, 43, 46
Patterson, Joe, 176
Patterson, Gov. John, 99, 141, 160, 163
Patterson, Robert B., 8, 155
Paul, John, Jr., 91, 113
Paxinos, Haspina and Kostas, 205
Payne, Hazel, 103
Pemberton, John de J., 230

Peoria, Ill., 153
Percy, William, 196
Perez, Leander, 166, 174, 239
Perkins, C. C., 22
Perry, Dr. A. P., 95
Perry, Dr. Albert J., 70, 72-73, 112
Perry, Matthew, 192
Perry County, Ala., 88
Pete, Louis, 117
Peters, Bonneau, 66
Peterson, Joseph, 155
Petre, John, 118
Petrillo, James, 81
Phifer, J. S., 93
Philadelphia, Miss., 201, 207, 234
Philadelphia, Pa., 5, 15, 20, 22-23, 30, 41,
    45, 81, 83, 121, 125, 129, 133, 170,
    216; Breyers Ice Cream Company in,
    151; Girard College in, 12, 30, 55, 62,
    64-65, 72, 78, 86, 232, 234, 235; hous-
    ing discrimination in, 224; Mummer's
    Parade in, 202, 221; NAACP 1961
    annual convention in, 145; rioting in
    (1964), 200, 217
Philadelphia Athletics, 4
Philipi, W.Va., 10
Phillips, Mrs. Vel R., 44, 131, 182
Phoenix, Ariz., 13, 114, 117
Pickney, Dr. David, 156
Pierce, M. B., 206
Pierre, Carroll, 101-102
Pierre, S.D., 183
Pierson, W. W., 50
Piggins, Edward, 67
Pine Bluff, Ark., 183, 199, 205
Pinkard, Mary, 140
Pinkston, Theodore, 62
Pinson, John, 149
Pitcher, Alex, 16
Pittman, Dr. James E., 33
Pittsburgh, Pa., 4, 50, 206, 215
Placentia, Calif., 52
Plaquemine, La., 193, 196
Pleasanton, Tex., 72, 74
Plessy v. Ferguson, xvi, 6, 151
Plinton, James, 69
Podoloff, Maurice, 95, 99
Poinsette, Alex, 123
Poitier, Sidney, 100, 102
Polhous, Francis, 209
police brutality, 66, 106, 118, 126, 129,
    138, 140, 144, 147, 149, 154, 162, 174,
    207, 210, 214, 218, 227-228, 231, 233,
    234, 235, 239, 241, 242
politics, 3, 12, 22, 44, 49, 50, 52, 53,
    79-80, 92, 93, 94, 100, 103, 121, 126,
    130, 153, 170, 173, 214, 216, 219, 238
poll tax, 160, 161, 178, 213, 229
Pontiac, Mich., 126
Pope John XXIII, 166
Pope Paul VI, 212
Poplarville, Miss., 105

Porgy and Bess (opera), 6
Porter, Edward M., 53
Porter, Elizabeth K., 7
Porter, Rev. John T., 67, 98
Portland, Ore., 126
Portsmouth, N.H., 145
Portsmouth, Va., 121, 166
postal workers, 44, 75, 129, 151, 178
Poteet, Howard, 221
Potter, Rev. Dan, 173
Potts, Marvin, 69
Poulson, Mayor Norris, 7
Powell, Rep. Adam Clayton, Jr., 6, 12, 14,
    20, 26, 28-29, 32, 33-34, 36, 40, 46,
    53, 55, 57, 58, 62, 64, 71, 77, 93, 110,
    117, 119, 120, 128, 131, 138, 140, 141,
    145, 146, 164, 167, 169, 186, 197, 208,
    213, 220, 226, 240
Powell, Albert, 95
Powell, Dr. Cillian B., 62, 138
Powell amendment, 26-27
Powhatan, Va., 191
Prayer Pilgrimage for Freedom in D.C., 64
presidential election of 1960 and black
    voters, 131
Presidential Railroad Emergency Board, 4
President's Committee on Employment
    Policies, 20, 67, 69, 114, 120, 122,
    144
President's Committee on Equal Employ-
    ment Opportunity, 146, 147, 159, 161,
    163, 166, 167, 168, 174, 175, 177, 214,
    225, 238
President's Committee on Government
    Contracts, 9, 20, 22, 62, 65, 68, 71, 72,
    74, 78, 86, 99, 100, 120, 128, 134
Price, Cecil, 221
Prince Edward County, Va., 28, 117, 118,
    120, 132, 134, 143, 148, 152, 169, 184,
    193, 212, 214, 216, 236
Prince Georges County, Md., 65
Princess Anne, Md., 205
Princeton, N.J., 29
Prisk, Richard, 218
Pritchard, Ala., 52
Pritchett, Laurie, 172
private schools, 104, 109, 113, 114,
    119-120, 186
Providence, R.I., 160
public accommodations and problem of
    segregation/desegregation, 9, 10, 13, 15,
    16, 20, 21, 22, 23, 25, 26, 27, 28, 29, 34,
    36, 40, 41, 43, 46, 47, 50, 55, 58, 59, 60,
    61, 62, 63, 64, 65, 66, 67, 68-69, 70, 71,
    72, 78, 79, 80-81, 82, 83, 84, 85, 88, 89,
    90, 91, 93, 95, 97, 98, 100, 103, 104,
    105, 107, 108, 109, 110, 111, 112, 114,
    115, 117, 118, 119, 120, 121, 123, 124,
    125, 126, 127, 129, 130, 131, 132, 133,
    134, 138, 139, 140, 141, 142, 143, 144,
    145, 147, 148, 149, 150, 151, 152, 153,
    154, 155, 157, 159, 160, 161, 162, 163,

165, 166, 168, 169, 170, 171, 172, 173,
    175, 178, 179, 181, 183, 184, 186, 188,
    189, 190, 191, 192, 193, 194, 195, 196,
    197, 198, 199, 202, 203, 204, 205, 207,
    208, 209, 210, 211-212, 218, 225, 226,
    228, 230, 232, 233, 239, 240, 241,
    242
public accommodations under assault
    (1962), 165
public facilities desegregation by wade-
    ins, kneel-ins, and read-ins, 124
public school desegregation, 3, 6, 7, 8, 9,
    10, 11, 12, 13, 14, 15, 16, 17, 19, 20, 21,
    24, 25, 26, 27, 28, 29, 30, 31, 32, 33, 34,
    35, 36, 38, 39, 40, 41, 42, 43, 44, 47, 48,
    49, 50, 51, 52, 53-54, 55, 57, 58, 60, 61,
    62-63, 64, 65, 67, 68, 69, 70, 71, 72, 74,
    75, 76, 77, 78, 79, 82, 84, 85, 86, 87, 88,
    89, 90, 91, 92, 93, 94, 95, 96, 98, 99,
    100, 101, 102, 103, 105, 106, 108, 109,
    110, 111, 112, 113, 114, 115, 117, 118,
    119, 120, 123, 124, 125, 126, 127, 129,
    130, 131, 132, 133, 134, 135, 138, 140,
    141, 143, 144, 145, 147, 148, 149, 151,
    152, 153, 154, 155, 162, 169, 170, 171,
    182, 183, 184, 185, 186, 188, 191, 192,
    193, 194, 196, 197, 198, 201, 202, 203,
    204, 205, 206, 208, 209, 210, 211, 212,
    214, 215, 216, 217, 219, 220, 221,
    224, 225, 226, 227, 228, 230, 231,
    232, 233, 234, 235, 236, 238, 239, 240,
    242
public school integration and southern
    politicians respond to federal interven-
    tion (1958), 91
Puckett, Virgil, 174
Pullman Company, 7
Purcellville, Va., 61
Putnam County, Tenn., 189
Pye, Durwood, 207

Quarles, Thomas, 129
Queens, N.Y., 111
Quigley, James, 226

Rabb, Maxwell, 20, 29
Rabbit's Wedding, The (book), 107
Raby, Albert, 233
Race Relations Law Reporter (periodi-
    cal), 32
Race Relations Sunday in 1955, 22
racial segregation and organized religion
    (1956-57), 59
Racine, Bonnie, 177
Rackley, Gloria, 196
Ragsdale, Frank, 138
Raines, James, 134
Rainey, Lawrence, 221
Raisin in the Sun, A (play), 102
Raleigh, N.C., 47, 127, 216
Ramon, Carita, 5
Ramsey, Rev. Blaine, 212

Ramsey, Paul, 60
Randolph, A. Philip, 13, 15, 35, 36, 37, 45,
    47, 54, 60, 61, 85, 92, 102, 111, 127,
    131, 145, 146, 179, 180, 184, 193, 195,
    199, 219, 220
Randolph County, Ga., 33, 35
Rann, Emery L., 12
Rannells, Morris, 21
Ransome, Joanne, 83, 84
Ratcliff, Daisy, 97
Rath, Henry V., 61
Raugh, Joseph, Jr., 67
Ray, Gloria, 84
Rayfield, George, 102
Raymond, George T., 87, 102
Reagon, Carol, 172
Reasoner, Joe, 209
Reddick, Rev. A. Joseph, 153
Reddick, Dr. Lawrence, 100
Redding, Louis, 44
Redmond, Ella, 67
Reeb, Rev. James, 223, 227, 229, 230
Reed, A. Palmer, 104
Reed, Emily W., 197
Reed, Dr. Eugene, 209
Reed, Rosalyn, 129
Reed, Stanley F., 74, 234
Reed, Bishop Victor, 148
Reed, Wilmer, 174
Reese, Robert, 234
Reeves, Frank, 151
Reeves, Jeremiah, 82
Reid, Dr. Hyland, 34
Reinschmidt, Clarence, 107
religious institutions and problem of seg-
    regation/desegregation, 4, 10, 11, 16,
    17, 21, 36, 59, 68–69, 85, 92, 93, 94,
    101–102, 105, 109, 110, 118, 119, 125,
    126, 132, 138, 148, 154, 166, 173, 182,
    190, 191, 202, 204, 206, 212, 213, 220,
    239
Remo, Barbara Ann, 72
Republican national convention of 1956,
    50
Reuther, Walter, 141
Reverse Freedom Rides (1965), 233
Rheta, John, 20
Rhodes, E. Washington, 138
Rhodes, Gov. James, 184, 192
Ricau, J. G., 166
Rice, William Marsha, 235
Richardson, Gloria, 198, 205, 209, 210
Richmond, David, 118, 132
Richmond, Va., 11, 15, 29, 34, 35–36,
    53–54, 61, 62, 67, 78, 88, 125, 134,
    143, 147, 148, 179, 197, 199, 208, 228
Rideout, Dr. John G., 84
Ridge, H. W., 11
Ridge, Hardy and Eleanor, 15
Ridgely, R. H., 7
Riley, Walter, 155
Ripley, Miss., 224

Roanoke, Va., 161
Roberts, Gus, 105–106
Robeson, Paul, 71, 79, 86
Robinson, Charles, 123
Robinson, Frank, 186
Robinson, Jackie; airline lawsuit by, 112;
    Children's March of 1958 in D.C. and,
    92; church rebuilding funds and, 175;
    at NAACP 1958 annual meeting, 86; re-
    questing NAACP support, 163; USCCR
    testimony of, 101; Youth March for
    Public School Desegregation of 1959
    in D.C. and, 103
Robinson, Dr. Remus G., 24, 87
Robinson, Spottswood, III, 143
Robinson, William, 163
Rochester, N.Y., 215
Rock Hill, S.C., 63, 81
Rockefeller, Gov. Nelson, 120, 130, 140,
    204, 215, 227
Rocky Mount, N.C., 58, 59
Rodgers, Creed, 241
Rodriguez, Francisco, 111
Rogers, Grady, 100, 101
Rogers, William P., 94–95, 112, 113, 124,
    127
Rolvaag, Gov. Karl, 192
Romero, Dolores, 129
Romney, Gov. George, 196
Romulo, Carlos, 164
Roosevelt, Eleanor, 88, 121, 127, 156,
    168, 245
Roosevelt, President Franklin D., 26
Roosevelt, Rep. James, 36
Roosevelt, John, 99
Rosewood, Md., 20
Ross, Mary, 134
Ross, Randolph, 61
Rossman, Norman A., 194
ROTC units, 164
Rothschild, Rabbi Jacob, 225
Rousseau, Anthony, 102
Rowan, Carl, 160, 161, 179, 202
Rowley, Roland, 49
Rucker, Aaron, 165
Rummel, Archbishop Joseph F., 30, 34,
    51, 59, 102, 166
Ruppenthal, George J., 63
Russell, Bill, 95, 99
Russell, Gov. Donald, 182
Russell, Sen. Richard, 141
Russell, W. L., 144
Rustin, Bayard, 180
Ruston, La., 149, 150
Rutland, Vt., 153
Rutledge, J. R., 67
Rutledge, Pa., 102
Ryan, Rep. William, 212

Sacramento, Calif., 12, 78, 97, 103, 108,
    115, 152, 217, 224, 242
Salvidori, Mario, 59

Sampson, Edith, 71
San Antonio, Tex., 6, 7, 9, 43, 46
San Diego, Calif, 155
San Francisco, Calif., 32, 37, 72, 115, 119,
    138, 174, 205, 206, 209, 219, 221, 233;
    AFL–CIO annual (1959) convention in,
    111; NAACP convention of 1956 in,
    47, 48; Public Housing Authority and
    end of segregation in, 9; Republican
    National Convention of 1956 in, 50;
    Republican National Convention of
    1964 in, 215; Sheraton-Palace Hotel in,
    208; Yellow Cab Company in, 68
Sanders, B. F., 178
Sanders, Gov. Carl, 196
Sanders, Claudia Thomas, 74
Sanders, Edward, 105–106
Sandy Point, Md., 47
Santa Barbara, Calif., 61
Sarasota, Fla., 163, 176
Sasser, Ga., 174
Savage, Henry, 49
Savage, Philip, 170
Savannah, Ga., 7, 141, 155, 194, 197, 199,
    219
Savio, Mario, 243
Sawyers, Gov. Grant, 115, 230
Saxon, Allie, 177, 182
Schaffer, Harry, 59
Schamp, Carl, 224
Schmidt, William, 65
school boycotts, 185, 204, 205, 208, 209,
    210, 220, 224, 230, 239
school integration and mob violence in
    Delaware, 11
Schwerner, Michael, 207, 234
SCLC. See Southern Christian Leadership
    Conference
Scott, Anna, 161
Scott, Sen. Hugh, 216
Scott, Rev. John Henry, 174
Scott, Robert, 205
Scott, Walter, 43, 44
Scottsdale, Ariz., 100
Scranton, Gov. William, 210, 216, 234,
    235
Scudder, Dr. John, on the mixing of
    "white" and "Negro" blood, 113
Seaton, Louis, 232
Seattle, Wash., 82, 193, 234
Seay, Rev. S. S., 139, 141, 413, 145, 206
Seeger, Pete, 235
segregated public education in North
    and campaigns against (1963), 185
Seiderman, Paul, 49
Selassie, Emperor Haile, 8, 21
Sellers, Clyde, 90
Selma, Ala., 227, 228, 230
Selma to Montgomery, Ala., march
    (1965), 222, 223, 237; Voting Rights
    Act of 1965 and, 229
Sensenbaugh, James, 224

Shannon, George, 107
Sharpe, Barbara Ann, 105
Sharper, Rev. Horace P., 42
Sharper, Willie, 41
Shaver, Hampton Earl, 60
Shaw, A. P., 59
Shaw, Ian, 66
Shehan, Archbishop Lawrence J., 202
Shelby, Ollie, 237
Shelby County, Tenn., 138
Shelton, B. T., 106
Sherrill, Bishop Henry K., 9
Sherrod, Charles, 142, 173
Shervington, Norris G., 78
Shivers, Gov. Allen, 48
Shockley, Alonzo H., Jr., 92
Shreveport, La., 67, 138, 154, 175
Shriver, Sargent, 223–224, 231
Shuttlesworth, Rev. Fred, 45, 60, 63, 64,
    77, 84–85, 93, 94, 104, 112, 133, 139,
    141, 143, 145, 160, 163, 164, 171–172,
    177–178, 179, 190, 206, 219, 239, 240
Silvera, John, 231
Simkins, Mary Ann, 88
Simkins, Modjeska, 35, 43, 44
Simmons, J. J., 58
Simmons, Jessie, 134
Simpkins, Dr. C. O., 175
Simpson, Bryan, 203
Simpson, David, 100
Simpson, T. B., 67
Sims, Charles, 241
Sims, J. D., 110
Sims, L. B., 67
Sims, Porter, 27
Sims, Tracy, 208
Sind, Abraham, 179
Sisson, Upton, 71
sit-in movement launch by southern
    students, 118
sit-ins, 89, 90, 105, 116, 118, 123, 124,
    125, 126, 127, 129, 130, 134, 135, 138,
    142, 150, 152, 156, 157, 162, 163, 164,
    165, 167–168, 170, 172, 177–178, 182,
    187, 193, 194, 198, 207, 208, 209, 213,
    215, 218, 233
Sizemore, Ralph, 153
Slack, Sara, 120
Sloan, A. F., 109
Sloan, Boyd, 94, 98, 117, 207
Smalls, W. Robert, 205
Smart, Elizabeth Jo Ann, 50
Smart, Jack M., 90
Smart, Maxine, 66
Smith, Billy, 116
Smith, Esau, 156
Smith, Fred, 163
Smith, Hazel Brannon, 160
Smith, Howard, 179
Smith, Rep. Howard, 106
Smith, Jerome, 178, 189
Smith, Lillian, 141

Smith, Marjorie, 143
Smith, Mary, 129
Smith, Merle, 168
Smith, Robert, 137, 184, 238
Smith, Rev. Robert, 167
Smith, Ruby Doris, 142
Smith, Dr. Vasco, 183
Smith, Velma Lynne, 13
Smyrna, Tenn., 111
SNCC. See Student Nonviolent Coordi-
    nating Committee
SNCC workers and voter registration
    campaigns in the South (1963), 195
Snow Hill, N.C., 100
Sobeloff, Simon E., 49
Sorrell, Maurice, 142
South Africa, 235
Southard, James, 130
Southern Baseball Association, 4
southern black teachers under attack
    (1955), 31
Southern Christian Leadership Confer-
    ence (SCLC), 122, 126, 159, 164, 212;
    Albany Movement (1961–62) and, 172;
    Birmingham, Ala., as target by, 190;
    Chicago as target for, 233; formation
    of, 57; King, Martin Luther, Jr., and,
    115, 119, 140, 236; 1963 budget usage
    of, 199; 1964 planning meeting of,
    220; 1965 annual meeting of, 236; Op-
    eration Breadbasket of, 182; Selma to
    Montgomery march (1965) and, 229;
    UCRL formation and, 192; on Vietnam,
    244; VISION program of, 232; voter
    registration and, 80, 183
Southern Education Report, xix, 52–53
Southern Gentlemen's Organization, 24
Southern Manifesto, 43, 45
southern politicians respond to federal
    intervention in public school integra-
    tion (1958), 91
Southern School News, xviii–xix, 50, 54;
    first publication of, 11; on school de-
    segregation in 1958, 88; on school
    desegregation in 1959, 114
Southerners in Alabama, 8
Spaulding, Jane Morrow, 3
Spaulding, Theodore O., 34
Spears, Harold, 162
Spenser, J. Merrill, 141
sports. See also individual sports, 4, 5, 6,
    9, 14, 17, 22, 29, 34, 41, 48–49, 51, 66,
    71, 85, 86, 90, 94, 95, 98, 99, 100,
    101, 102, 103, 106, 107, 108, 114–115,
    124, 141, 143, 147, 153, 155, 163, 175,
    184, 188, 197
Spottswood, Bishop Stephen Gill, 171, 212
Spraggs, Venice, 53
Springfield, Ill., 26, 40, 64, 108, 145, 177,
    178, 184, 220
Springfield, Mass., 105, 127
Springfield, Ohio, 240

Squaw Valley, Nev., 115
St. Augustine, Fla., 198, 203
St. Bernard, La., and interracial mar-
    riages, 23
St. Francisville, La., 195–196
St. Joseph, Mo., 199
St. Louis, Mo., 5, 21–22, 127, 149, 157,
    163, 166, 168, 205, 221, 225; desegre-
    gation of public schools start in, 21;
    desegregation of schools plan in, 16;
    Howard Johnson restaurant incident
    in, 109, 111; public accommodations
    and bills to ban racial discrimination
    in, 16, 80–81
St. Marys County, Md., 131–132
St. Paul, Minn., 25, 126
St. Petersburg, Fla., 121
Stanley, Edwin, 192
Stanley, Miles C., 112
Stanley, Gov. Thomas B., 36, 62
Stant, Charles, 150
Starke, George H., 89
Steele, Rev. C. K., 45, 55, 64, 105
Steinberg, Ellen, 135
Stephenville, Newfoundland, Canada, 88
Stevens, Harold, 35
Stevenson, Adlai, 41, 53, 55, 93
Stevenson, William, 95
Stewart, Ella P., 62
Stewart, James, 127
Stewart, Potter, 92
Stewart, Warren, 7
Stillwater, Okla., 90
Stockholm, Sweden, 219
Stokes, Carl, 240
Stone, Chuck, 169
Storer College, 21, 26
Story, Robert G., 74
Strange, Hubert, 241
Strickland, O. M., 90
Student Nonviolent Coordinating Com-
    mittee (SNCC), 173, 186, 193, 194,
    197, 207, 208, 209, 210, 228, 232, 243,
    244, 245; Albany Movement (1961–62)
    and, 159, 172; Carmichael, Stokely,
    and, 236, 246; Freedom Center of, 235;
    Freedom Rides formation of, 118; and,
    150; Freedom Schools of, 117, 235;
    Freedom Summer Project and, 207,
    213; Lewis, John, and, 222, 229; Nash,
    Diane, and, 142, 167; Selma to Mont-
    gomery march (1965) and, 222, 229;
    sit-in movement and, 117, 118, 127,
    135, 142, 243; United Civil Rights
    Leadership (UCRL) formation and,
    192; voter education school, opening
    of first, by, 148; voter registration and,
    117, 173, 195, 213, 243
student rights movement and civil rights,
    243–244
Students for a Democratic Society (SDS),
    244, 245

Sturckeyer, Fred S., 13
Sugarmon, Russell B., 108, 109
Sugerman, Miriam, 66
Sulphur Springs, Tex., 11, 15
Sullivan, L. B., 139, 206
Summerfield, Arthur E., 44, 129
Sussex County, Del., 82
Sutton, Fire Chief Millard, 12
Swann, Rev. Melvin, 62
Swanson, Albert, 156
Sweeting, Walter, 172
Swinford, Mac, 188
Swing, Raymond, 179
Sylvester, Edward, Jr., 238
Syracuse, N.Y., 133, 143

Taeuber, Karl, 179
Taft, William Howard, 234
Talbert, Ernestine Denham, 170
Talbott, Harold, 14
Taliaferro, Odell, 125
Talladega, Ala., 151, 168
Tallahassee, Fla., 55, 58, 62, 79, 85, 95, 105, 130, 153
Tallahatchie County, Miss., 161
Talley, Orance, 209
Talmadge, Gov. Herman, 14, 141
Tampa, Fla., 99, 111, 112, 140, 217
Tarry, Ellen, 160
Tate, Mayor James, 187, 234
Tate, Leon, 164
Tawes, Gov. J. Millard, 209
Taylor, Andrew, 122
Taylor, Benjamin, 195
Taylor, Hobart, Jr., 50, 208
Taylor, Melvin, 30
Taylor, Robert L., 36, 39
Taylor Township, Mich., 134
Teal, Alice, 50
television, movies, concerts, and civil rights, 73
Telfer, John H., 24
Terrell, Rev. L. K., 26
Terrell, Mary Church, 10
Terrell County, Ga., 61, 134, 173
Terry, Gov. Charles L., 240
Thetford, William, 173
Thomas, Dr. Alfred, 89
Thomas, Andrew, 193
Thomas, Secretary of the Navy Charles, 17
Thomas, Daniel, 218
Thomas, Doris, 205
Thomas, Ernest, 241
Thomas, Eugene, 229
Thomas, Henry, 162
Thomas, John, 221
Thomas, Julius, 146
Thompson, Charles, S., 15
Thompson, Dr. Daniel, 154
Thompson, David, 202
Thompson, James H., 100

Thompson, Katherine, 79
Thomsen, Roszel, 120
Thornton, C. C., 186
Thornton, Virginia, 129
Thurman, Mrs. William, 177
Thurmond, Sen. Strom, 228
Tibbs, Ezell, 129
Till, Emmett Louis, 18, 35, 51, 82
Tilley, Mansfield, 7
Tillman, Betty, 50
Timmerman, George Bell, Jr., 27, 35, 77, 84
Tolbert, Richard, 168
Toledo, Ohio, 88, 161, 193, 209
Toles, Edward, 217
Toney, Charles, 48
Tony Award, 5
Topeka, Kans., 103, 225
Toronto, Canada, 113
Toth, Andre, 71
Toure, Sekou, 104
Townsend, Willard, 36, 37
Travis, Brenda, 152, 168
Travis, Jimmy, 195
Trent, W. W., 17
Trenton, N.J., 225
Troutman, Robert, 170, 173
Truman, President Harry S., 14, 20, 123, 127, 135
Trumbull Park Homes, 4, 5, 7, 22, 27
Tubman, Liberian president William, 14
Tucker, C. Dolores, 222
Tucker, Charles, Jr., 126
Tucker, Rev. D. L., 195
Tucker, Mayor Raymond R., 80
Tucker, S. W., 188
Tucker, Samuel, 216
Tucker, Sterling, 216
Tucson, Ariz., 126
Tudor, Arthur, 193
Tulane, Paul, 179
Tulsa, Okla., 175
Tupelo, Miss., 184
Tureaud, A. P., 57, 58, 115
Turner, Felton, 120-121
Turner, James, 87
Turner, Mrs. Nannie Mitchell, 138
Tuscaloosa, Ala., 41, 42, 51, 63, 178, 188, 189, 231
Tuskegee, Ala., 147, 166, 204
Tyler, Tex., 64
Tylertown, Miss., 11

Uchund, C. C., 138
Union, Miss., 127, 129
Union County, S.C., 72
United Civil Rights Leadership (UCRL) formation, 192
United Kingdom and Jamaican immigrants in 1954, 16-17
University, Ala., 60

University of Georgia and the desegregation of U.S. colleges and universities, 139
Upton, Wayne, 61
Urban League. See National Urban League (NUL)
urban rioting, 200, 215, 216, 236, 239, 242
U.S. Air Force Academy and call for integration of, 12
U.S. Armed Forces ending of racial segregation, 14; first dental officer in U.S. Navy, 15
U.S. Commission on Civil Rights, 155, 171, 175, 186, 240; 1959 swinging into action of, 101; appointees to, 143; Boston, Mass., and, 225; Civil Rights Act of 1964 and, 211; on farmers, 227; formation of, 74; Fox, Mary Ethel, and, 143; Mays, Dr. Benjamin, removal as appointee to, 141; Meridan, Miss., and, 174; Mississippi and voter registration and, 170; report (1961) of, 154; on school integration (1961), 151; U.S. armed forces survey by, 155

VA (Veterans Administration) hospitals integration, 10, 14
Vaiden, Miss., 113
Valdosta, Ga., 174
Valien, Bonita, 10
Van Buren, Walter, 47
Vance, K. E., 33
Vandiver, Gov. Ernest, 94, 139
Vaughn, Rev. J. W., 90
Veal, Frank R., 71, 84, 86
Vicksburg, Miss., 29
violence, 4, 10, 11, 12, 13, 15, 16-17, 18, 27, 29, 35, 40, 41, 42, 43, 44, 46, 47, 49, 50-51, 52, 55, 57, 58, 59, 60, 61, 62, 63, 67, 68, 69, 70, 71, 74, 75, 78, 79, 81, 84, 87, 90, 102, 122, 123, 126, 127, 129, 132, 133, 134, 135, 136, 137, 139, 140, 144, 147, 149, 152, 154, 155, 156, 157, 159, 160, 162, 163, 164, 165, 166, 167, 170, 171, 174, 175, 176, 177, 179, 184, 189, 190, 193, 194, 195, 198, 199, 200, 202, 203, 204, 206, 207, 208, 209, 210, 215, 216, 217, 219-220, 221, 224, 225, 229, 231, 232, 234, 235, 236, 237, 238, 240, 241, 242
Viosca, Rene, 66
Virgil, Ossie, 85, 102
Virginia and failure of massive resistance, 113
Vivian, Rev. C. T., 232
Von Braun, Dr. Werner, 232
voter registration, 109, 153, 170, 173, 174, 216, 218, 220; Alabama test for, 227; Albany Movement of 1961-62 and, 172; Atlanta, Ga., drive (1961) for, 148; Baton Rouge, La., and, 120; Bul-

CAESAR

II

LCL 39

CAESAR

CIVIL WAR

EDITED AND TRANSLATED BY

CYNTHIA DAMON

HARVARD UNIVERSITY PRESS

CAMBRIDGE, MASSACHUSETTS

LONDON, ENGLAND

2016

Library of Congress Control Number 2015953137
CIP data available from the Library of Congress

ISBN 978-0-674-99703-5

*Composed in ZephGreek and ZephText by
Technologies 'N Typography, Merrimac, Massachusetts.
Printed on acid-free paper and bound by
The Maple-Vail Book Manufacturing Group*

CONTENTS

PREFACE   vii

INTRODUCTION   xi

GENERAL BIBLIOGRAPHY   xlix

CIVIL WAR

    BOOK I   2

    BOOK II   124

    BOOK III   192

INDEX   356

MAPS   375

PREFACE

This edition replaces A. G. Peskett's 1914 Loeb edition of the *Civil Wars,* which is now outdated in both text and translation. Peskett's text was based largely on the 1847 edition of Nipperdey and the 1906 edition of Kraner-Hofmann-Meusel. The century since its publication has seen new critical editions in the Teubner and Budé series, and my Oxford Classical Text, which is based on a new collation and stemma, appeared in 2015 along with a volume of studies on the text. The text presented in the present Loeb edition differs from Peskett's in more than four hundred places. The new Loeb *Civil War* also has a different editorial philosophy, one that encourages readers to acknowledge the nature of the text they are reading, which is not Caesar's text exactly, but rather a text resulting from the mediation—copying, preserving, emending, printing, studying—of many agents over the course of two millennia. Where that mediation has resulted in readings whose discrepancies significantly affect the meaning, I provide both textual notes *and* help for the reader who wants to use them: the competing readings are translated in the notes to the translation.

The translation, too, is new, and not just where the texts diverge. Our understanding of the collapse of the Republic and of Caesar's style and rhetoric has advanced considerably since 1914, as can be seen in the General Bibliography provided below. While far from comprehensive, the bibliography does indicate the range of work done over the course of the twentieth and now twenty-first centuries on subjects as diverse as Roman history, Latin prose style, propaganda, narrative technique, and intertextuality, to mention only a few. All of this work makes Peskett's very readable translation look rather too smooth; it is the story of Caesar's triumph over yet another "foe," and we are told that the narrative "may be regarded as in the main trustworthy" (vii). Although he acknowledges in a general way that Caesar seems to have engaged in some misrepresentation (vii–viii), the places where Caesar gives an uncomplicated account of a complicated or different reality are almost never indicated in Peskett's translation. I have tried to give the reader a fuller appreciation of the way Caesar makes words work for him. I refrained from following Peskett in using the historical present, which, although wonderfully effective in Latin, is more distracting than vivid in English, or so it seems to me. But to restore some of the lost vividness, I converted many speeches from Caesar's paraphrase form into direct utterances, thereby improving the precision of the rendering, as well, since English lacks some features necessary for the grammatical construction used in the Latin ("indirect statement"). Like its predecessor, this Loeb edition has a generous index that simultaneously functions as a glossary identifying historical individuals and supplying modern place names. Place names marked with an asterisk (*) in the index can be found on the maps at the end of the volume. English place-names on the maps identify some geographical features not mentioned by Caesar. A timeline of events concludes the introduction.

To the gratitude I expressed in the OCT preface to the many scholars and friends who have helped and influenced my work on Caesar over the years, I am pleased to add here an acknowledgment of new debts accrued while preparing the Loeb edition, to Philip Schwartzberg for the maps, to Cheryl Lincoln for the production of the volume, and to Michael Sullivan, Richard Thomas, and above all Jeffrey Henderson for welcoming a new edition of Caesar's *Civil War* into the Loeb Classical Library.

INTRODUCTION

The civil war fought in 49–48 BC involved much of the Roman world, as the armies of Caesar and Pompey clashed in Italy, Gaul, Spain, Africa, and Greece. Rome's prodigious military strength and the expertise so long honed against external enemies turned inward, with results made more dreadful by the tumultuous political and social context of the Late Republic and the personal antipathies fueled by that turmoil. In the *Civil War* Caesar tells the story—his version of the story, that is—to an audience for whom the history surveyed in sections I–III of this Introduction would have been only too familiar. All dates are BC, and references are to the *Civil War* unless otherwise specified.

I. THE COLLAPSE OF THE REPUBLIC

A. *Rome Dominant*

In the middle of the second century the Greek historian Polybius, looking back at Rome's conquest of the Mediterranean world over the previous half century or so, felt that the achievement—"a thing unique in history," he says—called for explanation. "How did the Romans do this?" he asked in the opening paragraph of his *History*, and, strikingly, "With what sort of political system?" This politically canny writer, who knew both the Greek states over which Rome had achieved hegemony and the Roman state itself, drew particular attention to the role of Rome's (unwritten) constitution in her startling military and political success.

The distinctive feature of Rome's constitution as Polybius saw it was its stability, a result of the system's combination of monarchic, aristocratic, and democratic elements, and the way these were balanced and controlled.

Balance was provided by the distribution of responsibilities: monarchic functions such as the enlistment and command of soldiers and the presidency of political assemblies and courts were exercised by magistrates; aristocratic functions such as deliberation about wars, finances, and legislation were exercised by the senate; and democratic functions such as elections and the ratification of laws were exercised by a variety of popular assemblies. No group ran the state alone.

Control came from effective curbs on each group's actions. Magistracies from the highest to the lowest were collegial (meaning that there was more than one magistrate at each level), and each colleague had veto power over his peers. Furthermore, a magistrate's term of office was limited to a year, and there were significant barriers to reelection to the most senior magistracy, the consulship. The senate, made up of former magistrates with lifetime membership, could allocate money and commands but could not execute its will directly. The people, as mustered in its various assemblies, could bestow office and pass laws but could not put candidates on the slate or draft the laws it wanted. A further check on the group possessed of power at its most untrammeled, the magistrates, came from the judicial system in which, after their year in office, they could be tried for abuses of power.

This mixed and balanced constitution, impressive as it was, was not the only source of Rome's stability. Practical and cultural factors also contributed.

Chief among the practical factors was of course wealth. Wealthy men held Rome's magistracies and served in her senate. There was no property qualification for office at this period, but government service was unremunerated, and bringing oneself to the attention of the electorate was expensive. Since wealth in this period mostly took the form of land, two of the three branches of government were manned by wealthy landowners, a traditionally conservative group. And in the third branch, the popular assemblies, particularly in the assembly that elected the senior magistrates (two annual consuls and six annual praetors at this period), the votes of wealthy citizens counted for more than the votes of poor ones.

An important segment of these wealthy voters was a group called the *equites*. (The term, which means "horsemen," derives from an early phase of military organization at Rome in which the *equites* equipped themselves for military service with a cavalry mount and the appropriate paraphernalia, whereas of the ordinary citizen, on whom see below, only body armor and weapons were required.) Instead of holding public office, these men provided the financing and corporate organization that enabled the state to accomplish major undertakings such as road-building, aqueducts, temples, military supplies, and tax collection—for a price, of course. Their interests were long aligned with those of their social peers, the office-holding elite.

Below the elite were two economically distinct types of citizen, those with property and those without. The former, peasant farmers for the most part, manned the legions; the latter, which dominated the urban populace, were ineligible for legionary posts. The interests of citizen soldiers were guaranteed some protection by their crucial service to the state, those of the populace by their potentially disruptive presence in the city of Rome.

The political, social, and economic divisions between social groups—senators, *equites*, propertied, landless—were to some extent blurred by patronage, or *clientela*, which facilitated the creation of mutually beneficial vertical links between individuals at different levels and (not coincidentally) discouraged the formation of broad interest groups within any given level. And the profits of Rome's expanding empire made it seem possible to attend to the interests of all groups; there was ever more wealth in the "commonwealth" (*res publica*). Successful military campaigns yielded immediate booty—in the form of goods and slaves—which was distributed in varying proportions among commander, army, and commonwealth coffers. Longer-term gains were public land for distribution to individuals or to new towns called "colonies," as well as tax revenues for the state and its collection agents.

The fact that this influx of wealth long contributed to Rome's stability was due, at least as the Romans saw it, to their civic virtue, which privileged the collective good over the individual (*res publica* over *res privata*) and activity over leisure (*negotium* over *otium*). These fundamental values were enshrined in "ancestral custom" (*mos maiorum*) and transmitted by stories about meritorious men and women who provided models for all citizens. Among the upper echelons of society these values motivated both the pursuit of personal prestige (*dignitas*) and the preservation of oligarchic consensus (*concordia*). The former

accrued from military and political achievements, the latter from a kind of senatorial self-policing that kept levels
of individual wealth and prestige reasonably equal; in-
fringement was deemed "aspiring to kingship" (*regnum*).

Such was the system that, according to Polybius, enabled Rome with its vast resources of manpower in peninsular Italy and its rigorously militaristic ethos to over-
whelm its opponents around the Mediterranean in the late
third and early second centuries. At the time Polybius
wrote (mid-second century), this system had been fairly
stable for about two centuries, a period traditionally referred to as the Middle Republic. But the stability he admired in Rome required that many powerful forces be
kept in balance, a balance needing constant adjustment as
real-world conditions changed; stability and the preservation of the status quo were not synonymous. Polybius in
fact saw trouble coming, and he modified his work's original plan—a history of the crucial fifty-three years of
Rome's rise to power (220–167)—to include a treatment
of the period after 167, when Rome showed how it would
run its empire. Some of the problems descried by the well
informed historian in the immediate post-167 period were
blazingly evident by the time Caesar was born in 100.

B. Problems

At the beginning of the first century the task of preserving
and extending the empire was putting terrible pressure
on the political system and creating dangerous tensions
within Roman society. With ever more provinces to administer and ever more territory to defend, there were
ever more opportunities for the exercise of power and

the winning of personal glory; could parity be preserved?
More legions were needed, and they were employed on
longer campaigns; could soldiers remain farmers? Profits
multiplied, too, but the additional resources were not an
unmixed boon; one troubling byproduct was heightened
tension over their distribution.

The expansion of the empire was not matched by expansion in Rome's political system. The traditional structure of magistrates, senate, and popular assemblies remained in place. But the thirty or so officeholders elected
by the people each year did not nearly suffice to staff all
of the posts needed to run the government at home and
abroad, even after the modest increase in the number of
junior magistrates in the revised constitution established
by Sulla in the 80s (more on this below). Workarounds
were devised such as extending ("proroguing") the power
of senior magistrates beyond their year in office so that
they could be sent off to army commands and provincial
governorships as proconsuls and propraetors. Another expedient was to contract out some of the necessary tasks.
Eventually provincial defense and administration were
almost entirely in the hands of ex-magistrates commanding the legions and presiding over the local courts, and of
corporations holding contracts to collect the taxes owed to
Rome (the tax-farmers, or *publicani*). Moreover, the institutions that traditionally curbed the exercise of power at
Rome—strict term limits and veto power—were largely
irrelevant in the provinces, which functioned under something akin to martial law. More men wielding power, fewer
constraints: in the provinces, at least, the constitution's
balance and control were under threat.

But if the pressure caused by the empire's needs was

bad, the tensions arising from its opportunities were worse. Rome was still the center of her political world in 100, and the beneficiaries of the new opportunities for the exercise of power still focused their ambition on the offices in Rome, particularly, of course, on the two annual consulships. Competition for these offices grew increasingly fierce over the course of the first century, and so, accordingly, did the cost (construed broadly) of political ambition: a candidate needed both greater achievements and more cash than his ancestors had needed, and the consequences of his needs were more deleterious.

Provincial commands were the best and nearly the only venues in which members of the Roman political elite could enrich themselves quickly; agriculture was too slow, manufacturing too low, and trade and banking were technically off limits for senators (the *equites* occupied themselves with these). Rome's military victories had always profited her commanders, but the scale of both campaigns and profit grew drastically in this period. Furthermore, a prospective candidate's need for cash, coupled with the political influence of his class, altered in the elite's favor the distribution of the wealth accruing from campaigns. These factors also fostered a culture of corruption that led to widespread abuses: extortionate governors secured acquittal by bribing their juries, for example. The first century saw rapid growth in the wealth of the powerful few along with growing alienation on the part of those who, for a variety of reasons, did not benefit to the same extent or who suffered: the urban populace, military veterans, allies, provincials, and of course unsuccessful politicians.

The need for achievements, together with Roman militarism, encouraged ever larger wars, and as the empire

grew these wars were fought further and further from
the Italian homeland of Rome's soldiers. Agricultural production could be accomplished with slave labor (itself a
newly problematic element of the Roman world in the
second and first centuries), and the food supply could be
supplemented by in-kind taxation of the provinces, but
the soldier-farmers themselves lost out and their numbers
dwindled. Like the distribution of wealth, the patterns of
landownership shifted in this period, again in favor of the
wealthy. The reduction in the number of smallholders,
however, left Rome's ambitious generals with manpower
problems. And the newly landless inevitably swelled the
ranks of the urban populace, where they needed support
in both the short term (food subsidies) and the long (land
distribution). Neither measure was palatable to the senate, although the latter at least would have remedied
the manpower shortage. Equally unpalatable was another
possible remedy, namely, the extension of citizenship to
Rome's Italian allies, who had been supplying auxiliaries
to the army for centuries and had helped acquire the empire: the allies felt entitled to a greater share of the empire's rewards, but as new citizens they would inevitably
alter the balance of power in Rome.

In the first century, then, the military task of governing
the provinces and the political task of preserving the social
order were bigger jobs than ever before. So, of course, was
the prestige attendant upon success. But as we have seen,
success brought its own problems for senatorial *concordia*.
In fact, the system was seriously out of kilter, lurching
toward the future. For the trends described in the preceding paragraphs were experienced not as trends but as a
series of crises in which dichotomies presented them-

selves: tradition versus innovation, collective versus individual, urban versus rural, senate versus people, wealthy versus poor, Rome versus Italy, and so on. The following example illustrates the point. A dangerous string of defeats in Numidia in the late second century discredited the traditional military leadership and threatened the empire's stability: if Numidia's wily king Jugurtha could defy Rome, so too could other powers, it was felt. In this crisis a political newcomer, one Gaius Marius, a proven commander of undistinguished antecedents (a "new man," *novus homo*), was put in charge of the war, replacing an aristocrat from a family long involved in running Rome. Not only that, but Marius' appointment was made by a popular assembly rather than, as was traditional, by the senate. His eventual victory over Jugurtha—and with it the victories of new man over aristocrat, people over senate—represented a powerful challenge to the republican status quo.

A particularly influential dichotomy in the first century concerned the location of political authority. Sovereignty, unquestionably, belonged to the people, which acted through its electoral and legislative assemblies. But for at least two centuries the senate had been the dominant authority in the polity referred to as "the senate and people of Rome" (*senatus populusque Romanus*, SPQR). At every crisis, appeals were made to each group, and at some point those who leveraged popular sovereignty and senatorial authority into political power took or acquired labels that are now used as a convenient shorthand in the analysis of first-century politics. The *optimates*, or "supporters of the best men," asserted the authority (and interests) of the senate, the *populares*, or "supporters of the people," the sovereignty (and interests) of the *populus*

Romanus. So dominant was this dichotomy in the century's political struggles that other divisions clustered around it, such that "optimate" could also signify "traditional" and "aristocratic," while "popular" could signify "egalitarian" and "possessing personal merit." *Optimates* and *populares* were neither interest groups nor political parties, and a man might describe himself as an optimate in one context and a *popularis* in another; Cicero certainly did. But the labels are a convenient and now traditional device for highlighting a powerful and ultimately destructive tension in Roman political life during the Late Republic.

While any public figure could claim that he or the policy he advocated was in the popular interest, there was a particularly strong connection between the officials known as "plebeian tribunes" or "tribunes of the people" and *popularis* proposals. Early in the history of the Republic the office of tribune was created to give citizens protection against abuses of power by magistrates. Ten were elected each year, and they were eventually a force to be reckoned with: they could summon (or dismiss) assemblies and veto the actions of any magistrate, plus their persons were sacrosanct, meaning that physical harm to them would be avenged by the Roman populace. The political struggles of the Late Republic often saw one or more tribunes pitted against the authority of the senate and the executive power of the consuls; the aforementioned appointment of Marius, which was proposed and put to a vote by a tribune, is a case in point. When a still sharper crisis in the 80s prompted modifications to the constitution, some of the most important changes served to curb tribunician action. But the interests to which tribunes traditionally gave expression found other supporters, and the tribunes themselves had recovered their full powers by 55 (1.7.3–4).

The response of senate and optimates to tribunician activism sometimes took the form of a declaration of emergency. Known as "the senate's final decree," or SCU (*senatus consultum ultimum*), this measure entreated magistrates and military commanders "to take care that the republic suffer no harm" (1.5.3, 1.7.5–6). Its passage signaled the failure of political processes and the necessity of military action. The first SCU was passed in 121; thereafter they came at ever shorter intervals.

C. Solution?

As crisis followed crisis in the provinces and at Rome in the last century of the Republic, the precedent set by Marius' command was followed again and again. The causes of any individual crisis are difficult to disentangle, but recourse was repeatedly had to solutions—extraordinary military commands and dictatorships superseding the power of ordinary magistrates, including tribunes—that by their very nature undermined the constitution they were meant to rescue.

Rome's armies made a poor showing against a number of challenging enemies besides Jugurtha in this period. Correctly or not, blame was laid at the door of the commanders, and it seemed that the traditional political processes for selecting magistrates and allocating commands were no longer yielding commanders competent to preserve and extend the empire. Although the traditional processes continued to operate, the more spectacular failures were followed by ad hoc measures whereby the people (often through their tribunes) rather than the senate appointed men to marshal and lead their forces.

After his triumph over Jugurtha, for example, Marius received two unusual kinds of authority to head the resistance to tribes invading Italy from the north: the populace elected him to an unprecedented string of consulships (107, 104–100, 86), and it allowed him to enlist landless citizens in the legions, a first for Rome. All such soldiers—and the precedent set by Marius quickly became the norm—eventually depended on their general's political clout for the land grants upon discharge that would support them in retirement.

An even more drastic solution was attempted a decade later, after the republic was torn by successive wars against allies (the "Social War," from *socii*, "allies") and between citizens (the "Civil War" of the 80s), when the requisite rebuilding was entrusted to one Lucius Cornelius Sulla as "dictator for establishing the constitution of the republic." The dictatorship was a traditional emergency office, but no dictatorships had been needed for the past century, and Sulla held onto power for nearly three years, far longer than the standard six-month term. As dictator, Sulla was beyond the reach of the veto and above the law itself (he could, for example, kill and confiscate with impunity).

Then a decade after Sulla, in the early 60s, the stability of the empire was threatened again, this time by disruptions to trade and communication caused by piratical activity in the Mediterranean. A popular assembly proceeded to give Pompey the Great, who had proven himself in earlier extraordinary commands, unprecedented powers to deal with the problem: a three-year command with authority superior to that of all provincial governors, plus an army more than one hundred thousand strong and the money to pay it.

Marius turned back the Northern tribes in 100, Sulla shored up the authority of the senate with his new constitution in the late 80s, and Pompey swept the Mediterranean free of pirates in 67. The success of these and other ad hoc appointments seemed to justify toleration of their dangerous byproducts, which included armies more loyal to their commanders than to the state, and vast wealth and influence for the leaders. Not to mention the example these leaders set of using (or threatening to use) military force in Rome to achieve their own ends: Marius and Sulla to secure command of the war against Mithridates in the 80s, Pompey to be honored with a triumph in the 80s and to satisfy the needs of his soldiers in the 70s and 60s. But the creation of one "strongman" after another failed to avert the collapse.

D. Collapse

By the 50s the chronic problems plaguing Rome had become acute. The "strongman" precedent exacerbated political competition by setting the stakes of success ever higher, and the profits of empire, well- or ill-gotten, fueled the competition. Social tensions gave political rivals issues around which to build support: *popularis* candidates lobbied for the distribution of public lands to the poor and to veterans, or for subsidized grain, or for extensions of citizenship, while optimate candidates resisted all of these, and indeed any change to traditional practices undergirding senatorial hegemony and aristocratic privilege. Corruption, too, became more prevalent in the political and judicial processes, rendering the results of elections and trials suspect or even void. Meanwhile street violence covering the spectrum from intimidation to assassination became an appallingly effective political tactic. Indeed in the 50s the electoral process was so compromised that a number of years began with no magistrates in office: either elections could not be held because of the violence or those elected were disqualified for corruption. Furthermore, Pompey and Caesar were now in control of powerful armies—Rome's armies, in theory—that they could (and would) use for their own ends (1.7.7–8).

Full-scale civil war broke out between them in 49, when Caesar crossed the Rubicon (more on this below). Civil war continued after Pompey's death in 48 until Caesar's final victory over the Pompeian faction in 45, and it resumed upon his assassination in 44. During a brief period of political supremacy marked by his string of consulships and dictatorships from 48 to 44, Caesar, like Marius, Sulla, and Pompey before him, failed to restore the republic as a functioning system. His legacy was more political turmoil, more ad hoc solutions, and more civil war. Not until his heir, Octavian, defeated the last of his rivals at the battle of Actium in 31 did Rome have a stable government again. A republic it was not.

II. CAESAR'S CAREER TO 49

One of the last extraordinary commands under the republican system was Caesar's proconsulship in Gaul, which began in March of 58. Over the next nine years Caesar transformed the territory's political organization and solidified his control of the army with which he would later transform Rome. Caesar was forty-one when he took up his provincial command, fifty-five when he died. In order to understand what he achieved (and failed to achieve) in power, we need to look briefly at his route to the top.

Caesar was born at the beginning of the first century into a noble family, the Iulii Caesares, whose political record in recent generations was mixed. His father's and grandfather's careers had been undistinguished, but another branch of the family had done rather better (1.8.2). His mother's relatives were more prominent still and enjoyed particular favor under Sulla. But Caesar's most important connection by far was his aunt Julia's husband, who had triumphed over Jugurtha, saved Italy from invasion, and held the consulship seven times: Gaius Marius. (Marius also led one faction in a bloody civil war against Sulla and his supporters, but Caesar never evokes that aspect of his career, at least not deliberately.) The influence of Marius, who was consul for the last time in 86, was presumably responsible for his young nephew's first mark of political distinction, a priesthood for which Caesar was selected that year. (Priesthoods in the state religion were political offices as much as religious ones and were regularly combined with magistracies and military commands.) But Marius died early in his consulship, and his faction was driven from power by Sulla later in the decade. When Sulla required a show of allegiance from Caesar thereafter—Caesar was to divorce his wife, who had Marian connections of her own—Caesar refused. His nascent political career suffered accordingly: stripped of his priesthood, he went overseas on military service. Here, however, he eventually distinguished himself by earning a "civic crown" for saving the life of a fellow citizen.

Sulla's death in 78 cued Caesar's return to Rome. High-profile prosecutions of extortionate provincial governors from Sulla's faction followed, with Caesar losing his cases but showing himself willing to challenge powerful men on behalf of their victims. In 72 he started up the *cursus honorum*, the career ladder of a Roman politician, which led to a decade in which he alternated between political offices and military commands of ever-increasing authority. In 62 he held the penultimate office in the *cursus*, the praetorship, and moved then into a provincial governorship in Spain. Also acquired in this period were lifetime memberships in the senate (from 69) and the priestly order of pontiffs (from 73; he was chief pontiff, or *pontifex maximus*, from 63 until his death).

While the shape of Caesar's career thus far was fairly typical for men of his background, the political actions in which he distinguished himself had a decidedly *popularis* character. They also involved him in political alliances with far-reaching consequences. For example, as the only senator speaking in favor of a tribunician proposal to give Pompey his extraordinary command against the pirates in 67, Caesar gratified both Pompey and the popular assembly that passed the proposal and associated himself with Pompey's resounding success. As a junior magistrate he also sponsored several lavish entertainments for the populace, expensive undertakings that were now all but required for electoral success at the next level. The timing of such shows was always a problem: a candidate had to provide games *before* holding the office(s) in which he might hope for profits on a scale sufficient to pay for the games. In Caesar's case the pressing debts he incurred by his generosity and showmanship prompted him to seek financing from Rome's wealthiest man, Marcus Crassus.

Caesar returned to Rome from Spain in 60 after a term as governor in which he earned military distinction and remedied his financial situation. In the normal course of events he could reasonably expect a triumph and election to the top post on the political career ladder, the consulship. The political situation in 60, however, was at a stalemate. A number of issues required action, including measures proposed by Pompey and Crassus, but the more pressing the need for an action, the greater the political credit to someone for spearheading it, and some senators opposed all substantive measures lest any one senator profit. Thwarting Caesar's bid for a triumph was of relatively little consequence, but thwarting Pompey and Crassus, who represented large and powerful interest groups, prompted a response. Caesar, Pompey, and Crassus joined forces to accomplish their various priorities; the informal political alliance they forged in 60 is known as the First Triumvirate, and among its first results was the election of Caesar to the consulship of 59.

In a stormy year as consul, Caesar forced through his new allies' measures against concerted opposition. Traditional procedures and principles were flouted, and political deliberation was interrupted by violence as Caesar overrode all resistance. Even contemporaries who found the opposition to the Triumvirate obviously and frustratingly shortsighted were shocked by Caesar's actions. Compensation for the political risks he took that year and the reward for his success in getting necessary political business done took the form of an extraordinary five-year command, proposed to and passed by a popular assembly.

Gaul was not his original destination. Caesar's initial proconsular appointment was to five-year commands in the Balkan peninsula and Italy north of the Po. The provinces of Illyricum and Cisalpine Gaul, as these areas were called, were contiguous to one another and, more importantly, to Italy, over whose politics Caesar intended to keep a watchful eye. The five-year term was unusually long but not unprecedented, and the posts provided him with immunity from prosecution for their duration. (Some of his actions as consul had been of dubious legality at best and had earned him many powerful enemies.) Later in 59, when news reached Rome of threats to her transalpine province in Gaul—a strip along the southern coast of France (modern Provence) that secured the route to the two Spanish provinces and extended up the Rhone valley to Lake Geneva—this area was added to Caesar's charge. By March of 58 the news was sufficiently alarming to draw him directly to Gaul.

Rome had been intermittently involved in southern Gaul for centuries, particularly in connection with the affairs of Marseilles, a free Greek city allied to Rome. Marseilles itself remained independent, but the rest of Provence was organized as a Roman province some time in the sixty-year period before Caesar's arrival; the precise date is a matter of scholarly debate. The governor's responsibility for his province's security required attention to and sometimes military involvement in events at a distance from Provence itself. At some point in the early first century, for example, a relationship was established with the Aedui of central France, who became "friends of the Roman people." And in the late 60s a war was fought to pacify a tribe based east of the Rhône, the Allobroges. Most recently (in the year of Caesar's consulship, in fact) the senate had recognized Ariovistus, a powerful German leader who had taken possession of lands southwest of the Rhine, as another "friend of the Roman people" (*BG* 1.40.2, 1.42.3). In short, Rome's sphere of influence in Gaul was extensive. So in 58 when Caesar heard from the Aedui that the Helvetii (from the area of modern Switzerland) were planning a mass migration west through Aeduan territory, he deemed it a matter requiring his attention (*BG* 1.11.6, where Caesar refrains from mentioning the complication presented by a Sullan law that prohibited a governor from leaving his province without authorization from the senate).

After his arrival in March of 58, Caesar and his legions (four at first, ten by 50) fought a series of wars ever farther from Provence: north to Belgium, northwest to Brittany, west to Aquitaine. His forces eventually crossed the Rhine into Germany and the Channel into Britain. These are the campaigns whose achievements he records in the *Gallic War*, achievements that rivaled Pompey's and dismayed his peers.

In 56, the third year of Caesar's command, the question of what would happen after the end of his original five-year term became acute. The senate, which decided such matters, had been kept apprised of Caesar's achievements and had given him unprecedented recognition for them (*BG* 2.35.4). Caesar wanted more time, however, while his political opponents wanted to replace him. In support of Caesar's position Cicero delivered a speech, *On the Con-*

sular Provinces, in which he assessed Caesar's achievements; the rhetorical challenge was to communicate the magnitude of what Caesar had done without suggesting that the job itself was done. Cicero made his case, and Caesar's command was renewed for another five-year term in 55, with the support of the year's consuls—Pompey and Crassus, for the second time (the Triumvirate had been renewed in 56). Thereafter Caesar occupied himself with the conquest of Gaul until he crossed the Rubicon into Italy in 49 to fight his own countrymen.

III. CAESAR'S CIVIL WARS

The careers of both Pompey and Caesar represented an obvious danger for the constitution that Polybius so admired. In 56 Caesar was perhaps the more pressing challenge to the aforementioned ideal of consensus (*concordia*), and Cicero urged the senate that year to put Caesar in their debt by prolonging his command (*On the Consular Provinces* 38). By so doing, he argued, the senate would both assert its role as the primary purveyor of prestige and deflect Caesar from his *popularis* path. But in the end it was Pompey, not Caesar, who turned to the senate for the affirmation of his *dignitas*.

Throughout the 50s Pompey remained in Italy, the most eminent figure of his day; Crassus was a distant second, at least in military glory. Pompey's politics were rather inscrutable, however, while Crassus was more active in the public sphere. In 57 Pompey received another extraordinary commission, this time to organize Rome's food supply for five years. As consuls in 55 he and Crassus acted forcefully in the interests of the Triumvirate, securing five-year proconsular appointments for themselves to match Caesar's; Pompey was to have Spain, Crassus Syria. But political conditions in Rome continued to deteriorate, and Pompey postponed his departure for Spain. (Crassus went to Syria and died campaigning against the Parthians in 53.) By 52 the situation was so unmanageable—no magistrates had been elected for the year, and widespread rioting in January prompted the senate's emergency decree, the SCU—that contrary to all republican precedent Pompey became consul without a colleague. Rome's regular magistracies had been collegial for nearly five hundred years, but for three years running regular elections had been compromised and delayed by corruption and violence. Pompey, backed by a military garrison and protected by a bodyguard, wielded his power energetically, expediting trials and passing legislation that revised procedures for elections and provincial appointments (3.1.4, 1.85.9). Some measures threatened Caesar, others worked in his favor (1.8.2 3, 1.32.3); the marriage connection uniting the two men since 59 had vanished with the death of Caesar's daughter Julia in 54 (1.4.4). When Pompey made his subsequent father-in-law, Metellus Scipio, his consular colleague for the second half of 52, the immediate political crisis had been weathered. The threat represented by Caesar, however, remained.

In 51, the year after his victory over the vast coalition of Gallic tribes assembled by Vercingetorix, Caesar began winding up his provincial command. Hirtius' narrative of the years 51–50 shows Caesar settling affairs in Transalpine Gaul and basking in his popularity in Cisalpine Gaul

(*BG* 8). Caesar's political future required him to return to Rome, but every aspect of the timing and terms of that return required careful calculation.

The details of the process whereby the Roman world lurched toward civil war in 50 are now difficult to discern. Negotiating positions shifted considerably as months passed and parameters changed, and everything was reformulated again after Caesar's victory. The supply of contemporary evidence for this period is unusually rich thanks to Caesar himself, Cicero and his correspondents, and Asinius Pollio, among others, but historians disagree about which of the many factors in play were decisive in bringing the two sides into armed conflict. Was Caesar motivated by fear of prosecution, as his former legate Asinius Pollio, writing after Pharsalus, has him assert (Suet. *Jul.* 30)? Or was he trying to avoid undeserved and unprecedented humiliation, as he himself asserts repeatedly (1.9.2, 1.22.5, 1.32.4, 1.85.10)? Or did he foresee meeting the same fate as Clodius, a recent favorite of the Roman People and "justly murdered," according to Cicero (*Mil.* 30)? So Caelius suggests in the fall of 50 (Cic. *Fam.* 8.14.2; cf. *BC* 1.9.4; *BG* 1.44.12). Is it even possible to identify a rational motivation for Caesar's actions? Cicero could find none (*Att.* 7.4.3 etc.). The decisive factors on the other side are harder to discern, since the actors are more numerous and less well represented in the surviving sources. That Pompey and his adherents viewed Caesar as an intolerable threat to the status quo is clear. But the urgency of the threat was assessed variously, and many people, including Cicero, seem to have felt that civil war was worse than any compromise, even if the compromise represented an impermanent solution. Only the main events can be mentioned here. A peculiar feature of the period is that both Caesar and Pompey had to use proxies in politics because their respective military commands kept them from entering Rome. So they are largely absent from the following sketch.

One of the consuls of 50, Gaius Claudius Marcellus, was an outspoken opponent of Caesar. According to an arrangement reached in 51, the issue of appointing a successor to Caesar—and thereby terminating his command— was to come before the senate in March of 50. In 52 Pompey had fundamentally changed the process of selecting provincial governors, with the result that a successor, once appointed, would be able to relieve Caesar of his command immediately; previously, when provinces were allocated before the election of the praetors and consuls who would eventually govern them, more than a year elapsed between allocation and succession (1.85.9). In 50 discussion was hampered and in the end halted by the actions of Curio, a tribune of the people who parried attacks on Caesar's interests that year. (Curio's aims are explained variously, but Caesar favors him with a notably positive portrayal in the *Civil War* [2.23–44] despite his poor military showing.) A more modest attempt to weaken Caesar was more successful: the senate reassigned two legions from Gaul to Syria in order, ostensibly, to counter the Parthians threatening Rome's eastern borders. Caesar complied, sending two legions to Italy for the purpose (1.2.3, 1.3.2, 1.4.5, 1.9.4, 1.32.6). But he had preempted the senate's various attempts to regain control of the men serving under him by, among other favors, doubling legionary pay. At the end of the campaigning season he quartered eight legions in Transalpine Gaul, maintaining another on garrison duty in Cisalpine Gaul. Pompey had seven legions in Spain and, once the reassigned legions were transferred to his command in December, two in Italy. In the consular elections for 49 Caesar's candidate was defeated; his legate Mark Antony, however, was elected to a tribunate. At this point the outlook for Caesar's political future was no better than it had been in 51, and the military justification for retaining his command in Gaul was increasingly unconvincing. Late in 50 Cicero returned from a stint as provincial governor in Cilicia. His correspondents, especially Caelius, had kept him well informed about developments at Rome, and he now dedicated himself to finding a peaceful settlement, both before and after the outbreak of hostilities.

By December of 50 Caesar had established himself at Ravenna, a town in his province of Cisalpine Gaul but close to the Italian border. At the beginning of the month the senate revived the discussion of provincial appointments, and Curio's proposal that Caesar and Pompey resign their commands *simultaneously* won the approval of a large majority: 370 to 22, according to Appian (*BC* 2.118–21). The presiding consul, Marcellus, ignored the vote. Curio later conveyed a new set of Caesar's proposals to the senate: these were "menacing and harsh" according to Cicero, "extremely mild" according to Caesar (Cic. *Fam.* 16.11.2; Caes. *BC* 1.5.5). When presented on January 1, they precipitated the first phase of the civil war (1.1.1). Caesar was declared a public enemy, the tribunes acting on his behalf were themselves threatened with reprisals, and a public emergency was declared on January 7 (1.5.2–4). Caesar responded by invading Italy with the one legion he had with him in Ravenna, transforming himself, in Cicero's eyes, from a Roman proconsul into a Hannibal-like figure (*Att.* 7.11.1). And not only Cicero's: shortly after crossing the Rubicon, Caesar was deserted by his long-standing political associate Labienus, who had served him ably throughout the years in Gaul (3.87). There would be no compromise.

The main events of the war between Caesar and Pompey are listed below. The battle of Pharsalus with which the war concluded in 48 was a decisive military victory for Caesar. Pompey survived the battle and began to assemble new forces in the East but was killed soon thereafter in Alexandria. Some of Pompey's adherents treated Pharsalus as decisive politically, as well, accepting Caesar's pardon and returning to (some form of) political engagement. Many, however, did not. The opposition to Caesar reformed under leaders who belonged to Pompey's party or took advantage of Rome's preoccupation (Scipio, Cato, Pompey's sons, Pharnaces), drawing Caesar and his legions to Asia Minor in 47, to Africa in 46, and to Spain in 45. Each phase of the ongoing war ended with a victory: at Zela in 47, at Thapsus in 46, at Munda in 45. The whole Roman world was convulsed, and the political consequences were as transformative as the military campaigns were murderous. Caesar's accumulation of political offices for these years tells the tale in brief: in 48 he was consul for the second time, in 46 for the third, in 45 for the fourth, in 44 for the fifth; in 48, prior to his consulship, he was dictator for the first time (for eleven days; 3.2.1); after Pharsalus he was made dictator for a year; after Thapsus, dictator for ten years; after Munda, dictator for life. As dictator he could (and did) fill Rome's "elective" offices by appointment and for years to come. A monopoly of office like this, and even more, his control of the path to office, made nonsense of traditional Republican competitive (if elite) officeholding. More broadly, Rome's affairs were in Caesar's hands now; nothing could be done without his favor. The motives of the senators who conspired to assassinate him on March 15, 44, were no doubt various, but there were plenty to go around.

IV. CAESAR'S *CIVIL WAR*

Caesar's *Civil War* recounts his conflict with Pompey and the beginning of the war he fought on Rome's behalf in Egypt, approximately two years of action in three books. In form and style the three books of the *Civil War* have much in common with his seven books on the campaigns fought in Gaul. The content naturally puts pressure on both form and style, but Caesar creates a clear continuity between Rome's proconsul and Pompey's opponent.

The narrative starts in January of 49, with Caesar and one legion in Cisalpine Gaul. Pompey and Caesar's other political enemies are in Rome with two legions nearby in Italy. When a political solution to the standoff caused by Caesar's demands and his enemies' refusal to meet them proves impossible, Caesar moves into Italy near Rimini and advances down the Adriatic coast, apparently unstoppable. (He does not mention the Rubicon; the story of the crossing is transmitted by other sources.) After turning inland he wins a key victory at the city of Corfinium, where he forces the surrender of a sizable Pompeian force. He enrolls these soldiers in his own army and releases their officers unharmed. His opponents withdraw from Rome southward, and eventually leave Italy for Greece. Without ships, Caesar cannot follow, so he turns his attention to Spain. The rest of Book 1 focuses on the fight in Spain, with a brief digression on Caesar's efforts, eventually successful, to overcome the resistance shown by Marseilles. The Spanish campaign and Book 1 end in the fall of 49 with Caesar's victory.

Book 2 wraps up the story of the siege of Marseilles and some loose ends pertaining to Spain, but most of it concerns the expeditionary force sent by Caesar to gain control of the province of North Africa, an important source of grain for the always-hungry capital city. Caesar did not go to Africa himself, sending Curio instead. Curio lost his whole army there and himself died in the final battle. Book 2 ends with this failure.

The focus of Book 3 is the contest between Caesar and Pompey in Greece. It begins with Caesar's bold winter crossing of the Adriatic in January of 48 and contains a long account of his encirclement of Pompey near a place on the west coast called Dyrrachium In this effort Caesar overreaches and suffers a damaging defeat. He withdraws to the interior of the country, changes tactics, and finally meets Pompey's forces in pitched battle near the town of Pharsalus. Here he wins a decisive victory in August of 48. The narrative then follows Pompey to Alexandria, where he is treacherously assassinated in September. Caesar himself arrives in Alexandria in October, and the narrative comes to an abrupt halt in the early phases of a war fought to impose a Roman settlement on the Egyptian kingdom of the Ptolemies.

The *Civil War* is unfinished and seems to have been

written shortly after the end of the war in Egypt in 47. It was apparently abandoned by its author, who of course lived on until 44 (more on this below).

One might expect the *Civil War* to be structured around the contest for primacy between Pompey and Caesar. It begins with Pompey's political opposition to Caesar in early 49 and builds through two books to their military confrontation in Greece. But neither Pompey's defeat at Pharsalus nor his death at Alexandria is the end of the work. Pompey's defeat was, Caesar hoped, the end of the civil war, but he carried the narrative on into a foreign war. And Pompey's death was not part of Caesar's plan at all: it was a badly miscalculated favor from Egypt's ruler. Thus the very structure of the *Civil War* indicates that for its author the contest with Pompey was not the whole story.

Caesar's pursuit of more than victory can be seen in a letter he wrote soon after the fighting began. Addressed to two of his most loyal supporters, it was also distributed to a wider public, including Cicero, in whose collection of correspondence it is preserved (*Att.* 9.7C). Cicero describes it as "a sanely-written letter, considering the prevailing insanity."

> It makes me happy indeed that you say in your letter how much you approve of the things that were done at Corfinium. I shall follow your advice willingly— the more willingly since I had of my own accord decided to behave as mildly as possible and to make an effort to win Pompey over. Let us see whether in this fashion we can recover everyone's support and experience a lasting victory.

INTRODUCTION

In this letter of March, 49, written less than three months
into a civil war that would last five years, Caesar is already
pondering the foundations of future stability. "There are
many possibilities," he says as the letter continues; the
Civil War was one of them.

V. THE TEXT

When Caesar was assassinated in 44, the *Civil War* seems
to have been in an unfinished state. For example, it contains references to an episode that belongs in Book 2 but
is not present in our text, namely, the defeat of Caesar's
legate Gaius Antonius in Illyricum (3.4.2, 3.10.5, 3.67.5);
other sources supply the details. The fact that Caesar
launched but did not complete the narrative of the war in
Alexandria also suggests that the project was overtaken by
events. In the conflict-filled months that followed the assassination, members of Caesar's inner circle and officer
corps, specifically Hirtius and Balbus but presumably others as well, initiated the publication of narratives of Caesar's campaigns as a corpus (see Hirtius' prefatory letter to
Balbus in *BG* 8). Suetonius knows of a corpus of Caesarian
texts that includes narratives of the Gallic war and the
"Pompeian civil war" by Caesar himself, and narratives of
the Alexandrian, African, and Spanish Wars by other variously identified authors (*Jul.* 56.1). This corpus bears only
a general resemblance to the one that Hirtius describes,
which does not demarcate by military theater the campaigns of 48–45 and carries the story to the end of Caesar's
life. But it matches the extant collection of five Caesarian
narratives, the *corpus Caesarianum*, in both its content

and in the anonymity of the authors of the Alexandrian, African, and Spanish Wars. At least one copy of the collection survived from antiquity into the Middle Ages. This was copied at least twice some time early in the Carolingian period, and all of the roughly two hundred extant manuscripts of the *Civil War* descend from one of the copies. So while the series of copies made between antiquity and the present is unbroken, it cannot be traced back beyond that one Carolingian exemplar, which is called the archetype of the tradition.

The derivation of the extant manuscripts from a single copy—and a copy that was not Caesar's original—is shown by the fact that they share readings that cannot be authentic and could not have arisen independently. The most striking are errors such as lacunose syntax and nonsensical expressions, which must have been present in the common source. Inauthentic readings, or innovations, accumulated as the text was copied in the course of the centuries after the publication of the Caesarian corpus. For the *Civil War*, a work of some thirty-three thousand words, the perceptible innovations (that is, those that produce textual problems) number in the hundreds. (Some innovations will be invisible.) Most of them have been removed by conjecture over more than a millennium; at present the spots where the text is lost or uncertain number in the dozens, not hundreds. The significant problem spots are marked in this edition with notes to the Latin text. Repairs that are noted but not adopted in the text are translated in the notes on the facing page.

The text of this edition is based on the oldest and most independent descendants of the archetype. These are referred to by the initial letters of (some part of) their names, and the names themselves reflect (some part of) their history (more on this below): **S** and **M** from the tenth century, **T** and **U** from the eleventh, and **V** from the twelfth. Their relationships to the archetype and to one another are summarized in the following diagram, or stemma:

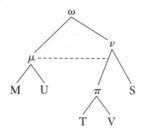

The innovations present in the archetype (ω) were transmitted to its descendants μ, and ν, each of which added innovations of its own as its scribe strove to produce a new and (perhaps) improved copy of the text. Similar branching structures emanate from each of these copies, and so on from generation to generation. (The solid lines in the stemma indicate the movement of text from source to copy but do not imply that the copy was taken directly from the source. So "generation" has to be understood loosely.)

This stemma shows that the extant manuscripts M and U descend from the archetype ω via an intermediary called μ, which is the source of innovations they share with one another but not with S, T, and V. Similarly, S descends from the archetype via the lost intermediary ν. T and V are (at least) a generation further removed, since π intervenes between them and ν. The dashed line represents a moment of contact between the two families and indicates that some (but by no means all) of μ's readings turn up in π, which for the most part reproduces the text of ν. Some of ν's readings may have traveled the other direction, into the tradition of μ, which for the most part reproduces the text of ω.

For the purpose of reconstructing the text of the copy closest to Caesar's original, ω, all other extant manuscripts can be disregarded, since they can be shown to be descended from one of the five on the stemma, M, U, S, T, or V. The full names of the manuscripts used to constitute the text are as follows:

M Florence, Biblioteca Medicea Laurenziana, Plut. lat. 68.8 ("codex Mediceus")

U Vatican, Biblioteca Apostolica Vaticana, Vaticanus lat. 3324 ("codex Ursinianus")

S Florence, Biblioteca Medicea Laurenziana, Ashburnhamensis 33 ("codex sancti Petri Beluacensis")

T Paris, Bibliothèque Nationale, Lat. 5764 ("codex Thuaneus")

V Vienna, Österreichische Nationalbibliothek, 95 ("codex Vindobonensis")

This edition is largely based on my Oxford Classical Text edition of the *Civil War* and its companion volume *Studies on the text of Caesar's Bellum civile*. The two Latin texts are not, however, identical, since I print more emendations here than I accepted in the OCT, where the critical apparatus allows readers to make these mostly trivial emendations for themselves, if they so choose. I also print here repairs to some of the more difficult problems that were left unresolved and daggered in the OCT; these repairs are not perfect, but they are better than nothing. In such spots I report and translate other possible repairs in the notes. All of these differences are listed below. (The list does not include differences of punctuation or orthography. For a fuller overview of textual differences among modern editions, see the Conspectus editionum in the preface of the OCT.)

Civil War	LCL	OCT
1.2.3	ereptis	correptis
1.3.3	ipsum	†ius†
1.10.1	L. Caesar	Caesar
1.18.2	tertiaedecimae	†VIII†
1.22.3	agit orat	orat
1.39.2	huc	huic
1.39.2	aliquos addidit quod	. . .
1.43.3	instructa	structa
1.46.2	nonnullam partem	-ulla -te
1.47.4	praesidiumque	praesidium
1.52.3	ita	tam
1.60.1	[cum] Oscensibus	cum Oscensibus
1.64.1	sustineri	sustinere
1.64.6	ablati flumine	arma in fl- . . .
1.71.3	decederent	recederent
1.74.2	Dein de	Deinde
1.74.2	fide	fidem
1.75.1	Afranius	Afranio
1.76.2	Postulat	Postulant
1.80.4	expeditis	†relictis†
1.82.1	educunt	ducunt
1.86.4	sacramentum	sacramento

Civil War	LCL	OCT
2.2.6	etiam	tamen
2.5.4	in eius	eius
2.6.3	Albici	Albicis
2.14.1	erumpunt	rumpunt
2.18.4	modium	modios
2.20.6	praemisisset	promisisset
2.21.3	populis publicis	populis
2.23.1	et iam	etiam
2.29.1	At	Atque
2.31.7	At	Aut
2.31.8	uti spe	ut ipse
2.34.3	armaturae	armatura
2.37.5	loci et	et loci
3.9.8	acceptis	receptis
3.9.8	recepit	recipit
3.11.1	ideo	idem
3.11.1	oppidis	†copiis†
3.17.4	illi	illis
3.22.1	se ea	ea
3.23.1	omnia	omnium
3.29.1	recepit	recipit
3.29.1	ex oppido	oppido
3.30.1	eas terras	eas terras
3.32.6	illas ex	ex illo
3.36.1	rem fama	fama rem
3.37.1	instruit	struit
3.49.3	ut specus	†ad specus†
3.49.5	succedere	†subte(r)rere†

Civil War	LCL	OCT
3.50.1	noctu	nocte
3.55.4	Caesari	Caesaris
3.57.1	A. Clodium	Clodium
3.58.4	quodque	quoque
3.58.5	frons	frus
3.67.5	fortissime	fortissimeque
3.68.2	pertinere	pertingere
3.69.4	[dimissis equis]	dimissis †equis†
3.73.5	aliquis	aliqui
3.84.2	primum	primus
3.101.1	C. Cassius	Cassius
3.105.5	templi	templis
3.106.1	in Aegyptum	Aegyptum
3.108.2	consilii sui	conscios
3.111.3	quadriremes	triremes

TIMELINE OF THE *CIVIL WAR*

Calendar dates are those given at the time, when the political calendar was roughly a month ahead of the seasonal calendar. *Civil War* references are provided; bold font indicates a discrepancy between narrative order and actual order, where the latter is known from Cicero's correspondence. For a more detailed timeline and Julian dates, see Kraner-Hofmann-Meusel (1959 [1906]) 367–74.

49 BC

Jan.–Dec.	The consuls are L. Lentulus Crus and C. Claudius Marcellus (1.1.2, 1.6.4)

Jan. 1–10	Caesar is in Cisalpine Gaul (1.5.5)
Jan. 1	Caesar's letter is delivered to the consuls (1.1.1)
Jan. 1–7	Senatorial debates about public affairs, esp. Caesar (1.1–2, 5–6)
Jan. 7	State of emergency declared; Caesarean tribunes flee Rome (1.5.3–5)
Jan. 8–9	The senate meets with Pompey, makes war preparations (1.6)
Jan. 10 or 11	Caesar invades Italy with one legion, reaches Ariminum (1.8.1)
mid-Jan.	Caesar takes Arretium, Pisaurum, Fanum, Ancona (**1.11.4**)
mid- to late Jan.	Negotiations are attempted but fail (**1.8.2–11.3**)
mid-Jan.	Pompey and the consuls leave Rome for Brundisium (**1.14.2–3**)
late Jan.	Caesar takes Iguvium and Auximum (**1.12–13**)
late Jan.–Feb.	Caesar takes Picenum (1.15–16.1)
Feb. 15–21	Siege of Corfinium; after victory Caesar heads to Brundisium (1.16.2–23.5)
early Mar.	Blockade of Pompey at Brundisium; the consuls are in Greece (1.25–28)
mid-Mar.	Pompey leaves for Greece (1.28.3)
Apr. 1–7	Caesar meets the senate in Rome, leaves for Gaul (1.32–33)
early April	Caesar sends L. Fabius to Spain (**1.37.1**)
mid-Apr.	Caesar prepares for siege of Marseilles, orders ships built at Arles (1.34–36)

late Apr.	Curio leaves for Sicily (**1.30.2**)
mid-May	Fabius reaches Ilerda (**1.39.2**)
early June	Caesar leaves Marseilles for Spain (1.36.5)
Jun.–Aug.	Caesar is in Nearer Spain; defeats Pompeian forces there (1.41–87)
early Aug.	Curio leaves Sicily for N. Africa (2.23.1)
late summer	Defeat of Curio in N. Africa (2.41–42)
Sept.–Oct.	Caesar is in Further Spain and Marseilles; both capitulate (**2.1–22**)
late Oct.	Caesar leaves Marseilles for Rome (2.22.6)
Dec.	Caesar is dictator in Rome; holds elections, conducts state business (3.1)
mid–Dec.	Caesar resigns dictatorship, leaves for Brundisium (3.2.1)

48 BC

Jan.–Dec.	Caesar is consul for the second time, with P. Servilius (3.1.1)
Jan.	Pompey is in Greece (3.3–5); Scipio, presumably, in Asia (**3.31–33**)
Jan. 4	Caesar crosses to Greece with part of his army (3.6.1)
Jan.	Scipio leaves for Greece (**3.33.2**)
Jan.–Aug.	Caesar is in Greece
Jan.–Mar.	Caesar establishes garrisons along the Adriatic coast (3.7–19)

? spring	Caelius' failed political and later military rebellion in Italy (3.20–22)
Mar.	Antony and more of the army cross to Greece, join Caesar (3.26–30)
spring	Caesar secures more territory in Greece (3.34–39); Scipio arrives (3.36.1)
Apr.–Jul.	Caesar besieges Pompey near Dyrrachium, is defeated (3.41–71)
early July	Caesar moves his forces inland (3.75.1); Pompey follows (3.75.3)
Aug. 9	Caesar defeats Pompey at Pharsalus (3.97.5); Pompey flees (**3.96.3**)
Aug.–Sept.	Pompey goes to Asia Minor and Egypt with Caesar following (3.102–4)
late Sept.	Pompey is murdered in Alexandria by agents of King Ptolemy (3.104.3)
Oct.–Dec.	Caesar is in Alexandria, settling a dynastic dispute, under attack (3.106–12)

SIGLA

ω   common source of μ and ν
  μ common source of **M** and **U**
    M   Florence, BML Plut. lat. 68.8 (s. X/XI and XII, lacks 1.1.1–1.33.3)
    U   Vatican, BAV Vat. lat. 3324 (s. XI^4 or XII^1)
  ν common source of **S** and π
    S   Florence, BML Ashburnham 33 (s. X^{2-3})
    π common source of **T** and **V**
      T   Paris, BNF lat. 5764 (s. XI^{3-4})
      V   Vienna, ÖN 95 (s. XII)

GENERAL BIBLIOGRAPHY

References to ancient authors and works cited in the Introduction and the notes follow the *Oxford Classical Dictionary*.

PRINT EDITIONS OF THE *CIVIL WAR*

Those listed here contribute emendations mentioned in the apparatus.

First edition, printed May 12, 1469: Bussi, G., ed. Rome: In domo Petri de Maximis [= Sweynheym and Pannartz].

Beroaldo: Beroaldus, P., ed. *Commentarii Caesaris recogniti per Philippum Beroaldum*. Bologna, 1504.

Aldus: Giocondo, G., ed. Venice, 1513.

Vascosan: Vascosanus, M., ed. Paris, 1543.

Estienne: Estienne, R., ed. Paris, 1544.

Manutius: Manutius, Aldus, ed. *C. Iulii Caesaris commentarii ab Aldo Manutio Paulli filio Aldi nepote emendati et scholiis illustrati*. Venice, 1597. (First ed., 1571.)

Hotoman: Hotoman, F., ed. *C. Julii Caesaris commentarii . . . cum scholiis . . . Hotomani . . . Vrsini . . . Manutii*. Lyon, 1574.

Lipsius: Lipsius, J., ed. *C. Iulii Caesaris commentarii . . . eiusdem . . . fragmenta*. Antwerp, 1586.

Orsini: Orsini, F., ed. *C. Iulii Caesaris Commentarii novis emendationibus illustrati . . . ejusdem fragmenta . . . ex bibliotheca Fulvii Vrsini.* Antwerp, 1595.

Jungermann: Jungermann, G., ed. *C. Iulii Caesaris quae exstant . . . praeterea . . . notae, adnotationes, commentarii Rhellicani, Glareani, Glandorpii, Camerarii, Bruti, Manutii, Sambuci, Vrsini, Ciacconii, Hotmani, Brantii.* Frankfurt, 1606.

Scaliger: Scaliger, J., ed. *C. Iulii Caesaris quae extant.* Amsterdam, 1661. (First ed., 1635.)

Cellarius: Cellarius, C. ed. *C. Iulii Caesaris Commentarii de bello gallico et civili. Cum utriusque supplementis ab A. Hirtio vel Oppio adiectis.* Leipzig, 1705.

Davies: Davies, J., ed. *C. Julii Caesaris quae exstant omnia . . . cum eiusdem animadversionibus ac notis Pet. Ciacconii, Fr. Hotomanni, Joan. Brantii, Dionys. Vossii et aliorum.* Cambridge, 1706.

Clarke: S. Clarke, ed. *C. Julii Caesaris et A. Hirtii De rebus a Caesare gestis commentarii . . . cum fragmentis ex recensione Samuelis Clarke fideliter expressi.* Glasgow. 1750. (First ed., 1712.)

Davies[2]: Davies, J., ed. *C. Julii Caesaris et Auli Hirti quae extant omnia.* Cambridge, 1727.

Oudendorp: Oudendorp, F., ed. *C. Julii Caesaris De bellis gallico et civili pompejano: nec non A. Hirtii aliorumque De bellis alexandrino, africano et hispaniensi commentarii ad MSStorum fidem expressi, cum integris notis Dionysii Vossii, Joannis Davisii et Samuelis Clarkii cura et studio Francisci Oudendorpii qui suas animadversiones ac varias lectiones adjecit.* Leiden, 1737.

Bentley: Bentley, T., ed. *Caii Julii Caesaris de bello gallico et civili nec non A. Hirtii aliorumque de bellis Alexan-*

drino, Africano, et Hispaniensi commentarii. Notas et animadversiones addidit Tho. Bentleius. Accessere conjecturae et emendationes Jacobi Jurini. London, 1742.

Morus: Morus, S. F. N., ed. *C. Iulii Caesaris commentari de bello Gallico et civili. Accedunt libri de bello Alexandrino, Africano, et Hispaniensi, e recensione Francisci Oudendorpii.* Leipzig, 1780.

Held: Held, J. C., ed. *Caii Iulii Caesaris commentarii de bello civili.* 4th ed. Sulzbach: J. E. von Seidel, 1856. (First ed., 1822.)

Herzog: Herzog, M. C. G., ed. *C. Julii Caesaris commentariorum de bello civili libri III.* Leipzig: K. F. Kohler, 1834.

Apitz: Apitz, J., ed. *Caii Iulii Caesaris commentarii de bello civili.* Berlin: C. F. Plahn, 1837.

Nipperdey: Nipperdey, K., ed. *C. Iulii Caesaris commentarii.* Leipzig: Breitkopfius et Haertelius, 1847.

Oehler: Oehler, F., ed. *C. Iulii Caesaris commentarii cum supplementis A. Hirtii et aliorum.* Leipzig: Teubner, 1852.

Dübner: Dübner, F., ed. *C. Julii Caesaris commentarii de bellis gallico et civili. Tomus secundus.* Paris: Imprimerie impériale, 1867.

Dinter: Dinter, B., ed. *C. Iuli Caesaris commentarii cum A. Hirti aliorumque supplementis. Vol. II: Commentarii de bello civili.* Leipzig: Teubner, 1870.

Paul: Paul, W. T., ed. *C. Iulii Caesaris commentarii de bello civili.* Editio maior. Vienna: F. Tempsky, 1889.

Hoffmann: Hoffmann, E., ed. *C. Iulii Caesaris commentarii cum supplementis A. Hirtii et aliorum. Vol. II: Commentarii de bello civili. Accedunt commentarii de bello Alexandrino, Africano, Hispaniensi.* New ed. Vienna: Gerold. 1890.

GENERAL BIBLIOGRAPHY

Kübler: Kübler, B., ed. *C. Iulii Caesaris commentarii. Vol. II: Commentarii de bello civili*. Editio maior. Leipzig: Teubner, 1894.

Paul[2]: Paul, W. T., ed. *C. Iulii Caesaris commentarii de bello civili*. 2nd ed. Leipzig: Freytag, 1898.

Holder: Holder, A., ed. *C. Iuli Caesaris Belli civilis libri III*. Leipzig: Teubner, 1898.

du Pontet: du Pontet, R., ed. *C. Iuli Caesaris commentariorum pars posterior*. Oxford: Clarendon Press, [1900].

Klotz: Klotz, A., ed. *C. Iulii Caesaris commentarii. Vol. II: Commentarii belli civilis*. Editio maior. Leipzig: Teubner, 1926. (Second ed. 1950.)

Fabre: Fabre, P., ed. *César, Guerre civile*. 2 vols. Paris: Les belles lettres, 1936. (Rev. ed., Balland ed. 2006.)

Damon: Damon, C., ed. *C. Iuli Caesaris commentariorum libri III de bello civili*. Oxford: Clarendon Press, 2015.

OTHER SOURCES OF EMENDATIONS

For a fuller list, see Meusel [1893], listed below.

Bähr: Bähr, C. "Review of von Göler." *Heidelberger Jahrbücher für Literatur* (1854): 401–11.

R. Bentley: Bentley, R. (see Davies).

Brutus: Brutus, J. M. (see Jungermann).

Bücheler: Bücheler, Franz (see Holder).

Carter: Carter, J. M., ed. *Julius Caesar, The Civil War, Books I & II*. Warminster: Aris & Phillips, 1991.

———. *Julius Caesar, The Civil War, Book III*. Warminster: Aris & Phillips, 1993.

Castiglioni: Castiglioni, L. "Intorno a Cesare ed ai suoi continuatori (*Bellum Civile, Africanum, Alexandrinum*)." *Athenaeum* n.s. 11 (1924): 229–40.

Chacon: See Jungermann; Davies; Oudendorp.

Constans: Constans, L.-A. (see Fabre).

Cornelissen: Cornelissen, J. J. "Adversaria critica." *Mnemosyne* n.s. 17 (1889): 44–55.

Cujas: See Oudendorp; Madvig.

Dederich: Dederich, A. "Kritische und exegetische Bemerkungen zu Cäsars *Bellum Civile*." *Zeitschrift für die Alterthumswissenschaft* 3 (1836): 204–32, 462–80.

Deiter: Deiter, H. "Miscellen." *Philologus* 44 (1884): 368.

Elberling: Elberling, Carl Wilhelm. *Observationes criticae ad Caii Iulii Caesaris commentarios de bello civili.* Copenhagen: P. T. Brünnich, 1828.

Eussner: Eussner, Adam. "Adversarien." *Blätter für das bayerische Gymnasialschulwesen* 20 (1884): 261–70.

Faerno: See Orsini; Jungermann; Davies; Oudendorp; Meusel.

Forchhammer: Forchhammer, J. N. G. *Quaestiones criticae de vera commentarios de Bellis Civili, Alexandrino, Africano, Hispaniensi emendandi ratione.* Copenhagen: B. Luno, 1852.

Frese: Frese, Richard. *Beiträge zur Beurteilung der Sprache Caesars, mit besonderer Berücksichtigung des Bellum civile.* Munich: J. B. Lindl, 1900.

Freudenberg: Freudenberg, J. "Zur Kritik von Cäsars Büchern de bello civili." *Neue Jahrbücher für Philologie und Pädagogik* 85 (1851): 224–28.

Fröhlich: Fröhlich, Franz. *Das Kriegswesen Cäsars.* Zürich: F. Schulthess, 1889.

GENERAL BIBLIOGRAPHY

Fuchs: Fuchs, Harald (reported by Kurt Raaflaub).

Glandorp: See Jungermann; Meusel.

Glarean: See Jungermann.

Gruter: See Oudendorp; Kraner-Hofmann-Meusel.

Hartz, H. "Adnotationum ad Caesaris de Bello Civili libros fasciculus." *Jahresbericht der Steinbart'sche Erziehungs- und Unterrichtsanstalten* (1864).

Haupt: Haupt, M. "Zu Caesar und Tacitus." *Philologus* 1 (1846): 586–87.

Heller: Heller, Heinrich Justus. "Die commentarien des C. Iulius Caesar." *Philologus* 13 (1858): 358–572.

Hotoman. For some items not in his 1574 edition, see Jungermann.

Hug: Hug, Arnold. "Über einige Stellen aus Cäsars Bellum civile." *Philologus* 11 (1856): 664–71.

Jurin: See T. Bentley.

Kayser: See Holder.

Kindscher: Kindscher, Franciscus. *Emendationes Caesarianae.* Zerbst: Römer & Sitzenstock, 1860.

Koch: Koch, H. "Zu Cäsars bellum civile." *Rheinisches Museum* 18 (1863): 320–22.

Köchly: Köchly, H., trans. *Memoiren über den Bürgerkrieg.* Berlin: Langenscheidt, 1868.

Kohl: Kohl, F. T. *Commentationes criticae in difficiliora scriptorum classicorum . . . loca vel dilucidata vel explicata.* Hamburg: J. Korte, 1727.

Kraffert: Kraffert, Hermann. *Beiträge zur Kritik und Erklärung lateinischer Autoren.* Aurich: Tapper & Sohn, 1882.

Kraner-Hofmann-Meusel: Kraner, F., and F. Hofmann. *C. Iulii Caesaris commentarii de bello civili.* Edited by Heinrich Meusel. 12th ed. Nachwort und bibliographische Nachträge by H. Oppermann. Berlin: Weid-mann, 1959.

Kruse: Kruse, K. "Review of Hartz." *Neue Jahrbücher für Philologie und Pädagogik* 94 (1866): 604–6.

La Penna: La Penna, A. "Marginalia: De lacuna apud Caes. *B.C.* 1.6, 7 statuenda et supplenda." *Maia* 7–8 (1955): 128–30.

Latino Latini: See Chacon; Davies.

Madvig: Madvig, J. N. Notes on the *Bellum Civile*. In *Adversaria critica ad scriptores graecos et latinos. Vol. 2: Emendationes latinae*, 261–80. Copenhagen: Gylden-dal, 1873.

Markland: Markland, Jeremiah. "Explicationes veterum aliquot auctorum." In *Euripidis Supplices Mulieres*, 310–23. Leipzig: C. H. F. Hartmann, 1822.

Menge: Menge, Rudolf, ed. *C. Iulii Caesaris commentarii de bello civili für den Schulgebrauch*. Gotha: F. A. Perthes, 1893.

Meusel: See Kraner-Hofmann-Meusel.

Mommsen: Mommsen, Theodor. "Zu Caesar." *Hermes* 2 (1867): 145–46.

Nicasius: Nicasius Ellebodius (see Oudendorp).

Nitsche: Nitsche, W. Review of Kraner-Hofmann-Meusel (1906). *Jahresberichte des philologischen Vereins zu Berlin* (1907): 19–48.

Novák: Novák, R. (See Kraner-Hofmann-Meusel; Meusel [1893])

Peskett: Peskett, A. G. *Caesar, The Civil Wars*. Cam-bridge, MA: Harvard University Press, 1914.

Roscher: Roscher, W. H. "Zu Caesar de bello civili." *Neue Jahrbücher für Philologie und Pädagogik* 115 (1871): 559–62.

Rubenius: Rubenius, P. *Electorum libri II*. Antwerp: ex officina Plantiniana, 1608.

Schiller: Schiller, Heinrich. "Zu Cäsars Bellum civile." *Berliner philologische Wochenschrift* 25 (1905): 238–39.

Schnelle: Schnelle, Karl. "Zu Caesar de bello civili." *Neue Jahrbücher für Philologie und Pädagogik* 115 (1877): 562–65.

Stoffel: Stoffel, Eugène Georges Henri Céleste, baron. *Histoire de Jules César: Guerre civile*. 2 vols. Paris: Imprimerie nationale, 1887.

Sydow, Rudolf. "Kritische Beiträge zu Caesar." *Hermes* 60 (1925): 261–79.

Terpstra: Terpstra, D. *Observationes criticae in Caesaris commentarium de bello civili*. 36–75. Utrecht: Kemink, 1854.

van Veen: van Veen, Jacobus Simon. "Ad Caesaris commentarios." *Neue Jahrbücher für Philologie und Pädagogik* 141 (1890): 595–96.

Veith: Veith, Georg. *Der Feldzug von Dyrrhachium zwischen Caesar und Pompejus*. Vienna: L. W. Seidel, 1920.

Vittori: See Oudendorp.

Vielhaber: Vielhaber, Leopold. Review of Kraner 1860 edition. *Zeitschrift für die österreichischen Gymnasien* 12 (1861): 474–83.

von Göler: See Bähr.

Vossius: Vossius, Dionysius (see Davies; Oudendorp).

I. Vossius: Vossius, Isaac (see Meusel [1893] on *BC* 2.1.2).

Weber: Weber, Hugo. "Zu Caesar de bello civili." *Neue Jahrbücher für Philologie und Pädagogik* 103 (1871): 336–38.

Weissenborn: Weissenborn, W. Review of Nipperdey edition. *Neue Jahrbücher für Philologie und Pädagogik* 56 (1849): 375–401.

Wilkes: Wilkes, J. J. *Dalmatia.* Cambridge, MA: Harvard, 1969.

Wölffel: Wölffel, Henricus. *Emendationes ad Caesaris libros de bello civili.* 2 vols. Nürnberg: F. Campe und Sohn, 1865–66.

PUBLICATIONS

Adcock, F. E. *Caesar as Man of Letters.* Cambridge: Cambridge University Press, 1956.

Avery, Harry C. "A Lost Episode in Caesar's *Civil War.*" *Hermes* 121 (1993): 452–69.

Barwick, Karl. *Caesars* Bellum civile*: Tendenz, Abfassungszeit, und Stil.* Berlin: Akademie-Verlag, 1951.

Batstone, W. W. "*Etsi*: A Tendentious Hypotaxis in Caesar's Plain Style." *American Journal of Philology* 111 (1990): 348–60.

———. "A Narrative Gestalt and the Force of Caesar's Style." *Mnemosyne* 44 (1991): 126–36.

Batstone, W. W., and C. Damon. *Caesar's Civil War.* New York: Oxford University Press, 2006.

Boatwright, M. T. "Caesar's Second Consulship and the Completion and Date of the *Bellum civile.*" *Classical Journal* 84 (1988): 31–40.

Breed, Brian W. et al., eds. *Citizens of Discord: Rome and Its Civil Wars.* New York: Oxford University Press, 2010.

Brown, R. D. "Two Caesarian Battle-Descriptions: A Study in Contrast." *Classical Journal* 94 (1999): 329–57.

Brown, Virginia. *The Textual Transmission of Caesar's Civil War*. Leiden: Brill, 1972.

———. "Caesar, Gaius Julius." In *Catalogus translationum et commentariorum*, vol. 3, edited by F. E. Cranz, 87–139. Washington: Catholic University of America Press, 1976.

Bruhns, Hinnerk. *Caesar und die römische Oberschicht in den Jahren 49–44 v. Chr*. Göttingen: Vandenhoeck und Rupprecht, 1978.

Cairns, Francis, and Elaine Fantham, eds. *Caesar Against Liberty? Perpectives on His Autocracy. Papers of the Langford Latin Seminar*, 11. Cambridge: Francis Cairns Publications, 2003.

Canfora, L. *The Life and Times of the People's Dictator*. Translated by H. Hill and K. Windle. Berkeley: University of California Press, 2007 [1999].

Carter, J. M. *Julius Caesar. The Civil War, Books I & II*. Warminster, 1991.

———. *Julius Caesar. The Civil War, Book III*. Warminster, 1993.

———, trans. *Julius Caesar, The Civil War: With the Anonymous Alexandrian, African, and Spanish Wars*. Oxford: Oxford University Press, 1997.

Charles, Michael B. "Caesar and Maritime Troop Transport in the Civil War (49–45 av. J.-C.)." *Studies in Latin Literature and Roman History* 15 (2010): 130–52.

Ciaffi, Raffaele, and Ludovico Griffa, eds. *Gaio Giulio Cesare, Opere*. Turin: UTET, 2008 [1952, 1973].

Cipriani, G. "Il galateo del commandante: Modelli comportamentali in Sallustio (*Cat.* 60–61) e Cesare (*civ.* 3.94–96)." *Aufidus* 11–12 (1990): 101–25.

Collins, J. H. "On the Date and Interpretation of the *Bel-*

lum Civile." American Journal of Philology 80 (1959): 113–32.

———. "Caesar as Political Propagandist." *Aufstieg und Niedergang der römischen Welt* I.1 (1972): 922–66.

Damon, Cynthia. "Caesar's Practical Prose." *Classical Journal* 89 (1994): 183–95.

Dernoscheck, Oskar. *De elegantia Caesaris sive de commentariis de B.G. et de B.C. differentiis animadversiones.* Leipzig: Grimme & Trömel, 1903.

Deroux, Carl. "Au sujet des rumeurs en provenance d'Ilerda (César, *B.C.* 1,53,1)." *Latomus* 70 (2011): 513–15.

Eckstein, A. M. "Review-Discussion: Two Interpretations of Caesar." *American Journal of Ancient History* 9 (1984): 135–52.

Eden, P. T. "Caesar's Style: Inheritance versus Intelligence." *Glotta* 90 (1962): 74–117.

Gärtner, H. A. "Die Periochae der Bücher 109 bis 112 des Livius im Vergleich mit Caesars *Bellum civile.*" In *Livius: Werk und Rezeption, Festschr. E. Burck,* edited by E. Lefèvre and E. Olshausen, 163–73. Munich: Beck, 1983.

Gaertner, Jan Felix, and Bianca C. Hausburg. *Caesar and the Bellum Alexandrinum.* Göttingen: Vandenhoeck & Ruprecht, 2013.

Garcea, Alessandro. *Caesar's De analogia.* Oxford: Oxford University Press, 2012.

Gelzer, M. *Caesar: Politician and Statesman.* Translated by P. Needham. Cambridge, MA: Harvard University Press, 1968 [1921].

Goldsworthy, Adrian. "'Instinctive Genius': The Depiction of Caesar the General." In Welch and Powell, *Julius Caesar,* 193–219.

―――. *Caesar's Civil War, 49–44 BC*. Oxford: Osprey Publishing, 2002.

―――. *Caesar: Life of a Colossus*. New Haven, CT: Yale University Press, 2006.

Gotoff, H. C. "Towards a Practical Criticism of Caesar's Prose Style." *Illinois Classical Studies* 9 (1984): 1–18.

Green, P. "Caesar and Alexander: *Aemulatio, Imitatio, Comparatio*." *American Journal of Ancient History* 3 (1978): 1–26.

Griffin, Miriam, ed. *A Companion to Julius Caesar*. Chichester: Wiley-Blackwell, 2009.

Grillo, Luca. "*Scribam ipse de me*: The Personality of the Narrator in Caesar's *Bellum Civile*." *American Journal of Philology* 132 (2011): 243–71.

―――. *The Art of Caesar's* Bellum Civile: *Literature, Ideology, and Community*. Cambridge: Cambridge University Press, 2012.

Gruen, E. S. *The Last Generation of the Roman Republic*. Berkeley: University of California Press, 1974.

Hering, Wolfgang. *Die Recensio der Caesarhandschriften*. Berlin: Akademie-Verlag, 1963.

Henderson, John. "XPDNC/Writing Caesar (*Bellum Civile*)." *Classical Antiquity* 15 (1996): 261–88.

Hillman, T. P. "Strategic Reality and the Movements of Caesar, January 49 B.C." *Historia* 37 (1988): 248–52.

Jal, P. *La guerre civile à Rome: Étude littéraire et morale*. Paris: Presses universitaires de France, 1963.

Jehne, Martin. "Caesars Bemühungen um die Reintegration der Pompeianer." *Chiron* 17 (1987): 313–41.

―――. *Der Staat des Diktators Caesar*. Cologne: Böhlau, 1987.

―――. *Caesar*. Munich: Beck, 1997.

————. *Der grosse Trend, der kleine Sachzwang und das handelnde Individuum: Caesars Entscheidungen*. Munich: Deutscher Taschenbuch Verlag, 2009.

Kraner-Hofmann-Meusel: Kraner F., and F. Hofmann. *C. Iulii Caesaris commentarii de bello civili*. Edited by Heinrich Meusel. 12th ed. Nachwort und bibliographische Nachträge by H. Oppermann. Berlin: Weidmann, 1959.

Kraus, C. S. "Hair, Hegemony, and Historiography: Caesar's Style and Its Earliest Critics." In *Aspects of the Language of Latin Prose*, edited by T. Reinhardt et al., 97–115. Oxford: Oxford University Press, 2005.

————. "Caesar's Account of the Battle of Massilia (*BC* 1.34–2.22): Some Historiographical and Narratological Approaches." In *Companion to Greek and Roman Historiography*, edited by John Marincola, 371–78. Malden, MA: Blackwell, 2007.

La Penna, Antonio. "Tendenze e arte del *Bellum Civile* di Cesare." *Maia* 51 (1952): 191–233.

————. "La campagna di Curione in Africa: La narrazione e l'interpretazione di Cesare." In *L'ultimo Cesare: Scritti, riforme, progetti, congiure*, edited by G. Urso. 175–210. Rome: L'Erma di Bretschneider, 2000.

Lendon, J. E. "The Rhetoric of Combat: Greek Military Theory and Roman Culture in Julius' Caesar's Battle Descriptions." *Classical Antiquity* 18 (1999): 273–329.

Lovano, Michael. *All Things Julius Caesar: An Encyclopedia of Caesar's World and Legacy*. 2 vols. Santa Barbara, CA: Greenwood, 2015.

MacFarlane, R. T. "*Ab inimicis incitatus*: On Dating the Composition of Caesar's *Bellum Civile*." *Syllecta Classica* 7 (1996): 107–32.

Mackay, Christopher S. *The Breakdown of the Roman Republic: From Oligarchy to Empire.* Cambridge: Cambridge University Press, 2009.

Mader, Gottfried. "Myth-Making and Myth-Breaking: Cicero, Caesar, and the Deconstruction of Pompey in *Bellum Civile* 3." In *Bezugsfelder: Festschrift für Gerhard Petersmann zum 65. Geburtstag,* 70–81. Horn: F. Berger & Söhne, 2007.

McDonnell, M. "Borrowing to Bribe Soldiers: Caesar's *De bello civili* 1.39." *Hermes* 118 (1990): 55–66.

Meier, Christian. *Caesar.* Translated by D. McLintock. New York: Basic Books, 1995 [1982].

Mariner Bigorra, S., ed. *G. Julio César, Memorias de la guerra civil.* 2 vols. Barcelona: Ediciones Alma Mater, 1959–61.

Meusel, Heinrich. *Lexicon Caesarianum.* 2 vols. in 3. Berlin: W. Weber, 1887–93.

———. *Coniecturae Caesarianae.* Berlin: W. Weber, 1893.

Meyer, Eduard. *Caesars Monarchie und das Principat des Pompeius.* Berlin: Cotta, 1918.

Montanari, Lorenzo, trans. *Cesare, La guerra civile.* Siena: Lorenzo Barbera Editore, 2008.

Morgan, Llewelyn. "*Levi quidem de re . . .*: Julius Caesar as Tyrant and Pedant." *Journal of Roman Studies* 87 (1997): 23–40.

Morstein-Marx, Robert. "Caesar's Alleged Fear of Prosecution and His *ratio absentis* in the Approach to the Civil War." *Historia* 56 (2007): 159–78.

———. "*Dignitas* and *res publica*: Caesar and Republican Legitimacy." In *Eine politische Kultur (in) der Krise?,* edited by Karl-Joachim Hölkeskamp, 115–40. Munich: Oldenbourg, 2009.

Nordling, John G. "Caesar's Pre-Battle Speech at Pharsalus (*B.C.* 3.85.4): *Ridiculum Acri Fortius . . . Secat Res.*" *Classical Journal* 101 (2005–2006): 183–89.

Offermann, H. "Curio—Miles Caesaris? (Caesars Urteil über Curio in *BC* 2, 42)." *Hermes* 105 (1977): 351–68.

Oldsjö, Fredrik. *Tense and Aspect in Caesar's Narrative.* Uppsala: Uppsala University Library, 2001.

Osgood, Josiah. *Caesar's Legacy: Civil War and the Emergence of the Roman Empire.* Cambridge: Cambridge University Press, 2006.

Pecere, Oronzo. "Genesi e trasmissione antica del *Corpus Caesarianum.*" *Segno e testo* 1 (2003): 183–227.

Pelling, Christopher. "Pharsalus." *Historia* 22 (1973): 249–59.

———. *Plutarch,* Caesar. Oxford: Oxford University Press, 2011.

Peskett, A. G. *Gai Iuli Caesaris Commentariorum de Bello civili liber primus.* Cambridge: Cambridge University Press, 1890.

Potz, E. "*Ficta, non facta dicere.* Und trotzdem die Wahrheit berichten: Caesar, *Bellum civile* 1, 43–87 und Appian, *Emphylia* 2, 42f." *Grazer Beiträge* 21 (1995): 85–94.

Raaflaub, Kurt A. Dignitatis contentio: *Studien zur Motivation und politischen Taktik im Bürgerkrieg zwischen Caesar und Pompeius.* Munich: Beck, 1974.

———. "Caesar the Liberator? Factional Politics, Civil War, and Ideology." In Cairns and Fantham, *Caesar Against Liberty*, 35–67.

———. "*Bellum civile.*" In Griffin, *A Companion*, 175–91.

———. "Creating a Grand Coalition of True Roman Citizens: On Caesar's Political Strategy in the *Civil War.*" In Breed et al., *Citizens of Discord*, 159–70.

Raditsa, L. "Julius Caesar and His Writings." *Aufstieg und Niedergang der römischen Welt* I.3 (1973): 417–56.

Rambaud, Michel, ed. *César, De bello civili. La guerre civile, Livre 1.* 2nd ed. Paris: Presses universitaires de France, 1970 [1962].

———. "Le camp de Fabius près d'Ilerda. Un problème césarien (*Bellum civile* I,40)." *Les études classiques* 44 (1976): 25–34.

———. "Le point de vue de César dans le livre 3 du *Bellum civile*." *Vita Latina* 89 (1983): 25–32.

Ramsey, J. T. "The Senate, Mark Antony, and Caesar's Legislative Legacy." *Classical Quarterly* 44 (1994): 130–45.

Rawson, E. "Caesar's Heritage: Hellenistic Kings and their Roman Equals." *Journal of Roman Studies* 65 (1975): 148–59.

———. "Caesar, Etruria and the *Disciplina Etrusca*." *Journal of Roman Studies* 68 (1978): 132–52.

———. "Caesar: Civil War and Dictatorship." In *The Last Age of the Roman Republic, 146–43 BC, Cambridge Ancient History IX,* edited by J. A. Crook et al., 424–67. Cambridge: Cambridge University Press, 1992.

Reggi, G. "Cesare e il racconto delle battaglie navali sotto Marsiglia." *Rendiconti dell'Istituto Lombardo* 136 (2002): 71–108.

Richter, Will. *Caesar als Darsteller seiner Taten: Eine Einführung.* Heidelberg: Carl Winter, 1977.

Ridley, Ronald T. "The Dictator's Mistake: Caesar's Escape from Sulla." *Historia* 49 (2000): 211–29.

———. "Attacking the World with Five Cohorts: Caesar in January 49." *Ancient Society* 34 (2004): 127–52.

Riggsby, Andrew M. *Caesar in Gaul and Rome: War in Words.* Austin: University of Texas Press, 2006.

Rossi, A. F. "The Camp of Pompey: Strategy of Representation in Caesar's *Bellum Civile*." *Classical Journal* 95 (2000): 239–56.

Ruebel, James S. "Caesar's *Dignitas* and the Outbreak of Civil War." *Syllecta Classica* 7 (1996): 133–42.

Rüpke, J. "Wer las Caesar's *bella* als *Commentarii?*" *Gymnasium* 99 (1992): 201–26.

Scholz, Udo W. "Der *commentarius* und Caesars *Commentarii*." In *Musen und Medien*, edited by Peter Neukam, 82–97. Munich: Bayerischer Schulbuch Verlag, 1999.

Schönberger, Otto, ed. *C. Iulius Caesar, Der Bürgerkrieg*. Munich: Artemis, 1984.

Stadter, P. A. "Caesarian Tactics and Caesarian Style: *Bell. Civ.* 1.66–70." *Classical Journal* 88 (1993): 217–21.

Steel, Catherine. *The End of the Roman Republic: 146–44 BC: Conquest and Crisis*. Edinburgh: Edinburgh University Press, 2014.

Stevenson, Tom. *Julius Caesar and the Transformation of the Roman Republic*. Abingdon: Routledge, 2015.

Strasburger, H. *Caesar im Urteil seiner Zeitgenossen*. 2nd ed. Darmstadt: Wissenschaftliche Buchgesellschaft, 1969 [1968].

Strauss, Barry S. *The Death of Caesar: The Story of History's Most Famous Assassination*. New York: Simon and Schuster, 2015.

Stucchi, S. "Su alcune accezioni dell'ironia nel *De bello civili*." *Aufidus* 17 (2003): 151–72.

Sumner, G. V. "The *Lex annalis* under Caesar." *Phoenix* 25 (1971): 246–71.

Syme, R. "The Allegiance of Labienus." *Journal of Roman Studies* 28 (1938): 113–25.

———. "Caesar's Designs on Dacia and Parthia." In *The*

Provincial at Rome, edited by A. Birley, 174–92. Exeter: University of Exeter Press, 1999.

Tatum, W. Jeffrey. *Always I Am Caesar*. Malden, MA: Blackwell, 2008.

Tronson, A. "Pompey the Barbarian: Caesar's Presentation of 'The Other' in *Bellum civile* 3." In *In Altum: Seventy-five Years of Classical Studies in Newfoundland*, edited by M. Joyal, 73–104. St. Johns: Memorial University of Newfoundland, 2001.

Tschiedel, H. J. *Caesars Anticato. Eine Untersuchung der Testimonien und Fragmente.* Darmstadt: Wissenschaftliche Buchgesellschaft, 1981.

Veith, Georg. *Der Feldzug von Dyrrhachium zwischen Caesar und Pompejus*. Vienna: L. W. Seidel, 1920.

Weinstock, Stefan. *Divus Julius*. Oxford: Clarendon Press, 1971.

Welch, Kathryn. "Caesar and His Officers in the Gallic War Commentaries." In Welch and Powell, *Julius Caesar*, 85–110.

Welch, Kathryn, and Anton Powell, eds. *Julius Caesar as Artful Reporter: The War Commentaries as Political Instruments*. Swansea: Classical Press of Wales, 1998.

White, P. "Tactics in Caesar's Correspondence with Cicero." In Cairns and Fantham, *Caesar Against Liberty*, 68–95.

Winterbottom, Michael. "Caesar." In *Texts and Transmission: A Survey of the Latin Classics*, edited by L. D. Reynolds et al., 35–36. Oxford: Clarendon Press, 1983.

Wiseman, T. P. "Caesar, Pompey and Rome 59–50 BC." In *The Last Age of the Roman Republic, 146–43 BC, Cambridge Ancient History IX,* edited by J. A. Crook et al., 368–423. Cambridge: Cambridge University Press, 1992.

Wistrand, E. *Caesar and Contemporary Roman Society*. Göteborg: Vetenskaps- och Vitterhets-samhället, 1979.

Wyke, Maria. *Caesar: A Life in Western Culture*. London: Granta, 2007.

———, ed. *Julius Caesar in Western Culture*. Malden, MA: Blackwell, 2006.

Yates, David. "The Role of Cato the Younger in Caesar's *Bellum Civile*." *Classical World* 104 (2011): 161–74.

Yavetz, Z. *Julius Caesar and His Public Image*. Ithaca: Cornell University Press, 1983.

CIVIL WAR

LIBER I

1. . . . Litteris[1] [a Fabio] C. Caesaris consulibus redditis aegre ab his impetratum est summa tribunorum plebis contentione ut in senatu recitarentur. Vt vero ex litteris ad
2 senatum referretur impetrari non potuit. Referunt consules de re publica infinite.[2] L. Lentulus consul senatui rei publicae se non defuturum pollicetur si audacter ac forti-
3 ter sententias dicere velint; sin Caesarem respiciant atque eius gratiam sequantur, ut superioribus fecerint temporibus, se sibi consilium capturum neque senatus auctoritati obtemperaturum; habere se quoque ad Caesaris gratiam
4 atque amicitiam receptum. In eandem sententiam loquitur Scipio: Pompeio esse in animo rei publicae non deesse si senatus sequatur; si cunctetur atque agat lenius, nequiquam eius auxilium si postea velit senatum imploraturum.

2. Haec Scipionis oratio, quod senatus in urbe habebatur Pompeiusque aderat, ex ipsius ore Pompei mitti vide-

[1] *Some text is missing at the junction of the* BG *and the* BC.
[2] infinite *Hotoman* (*cf. Gel. 14.7.9*): in civitate ω: [in civitate] *Faerno*

BOOK I

1. . . . When Caesar's letter was delivered to the consuls, their consent for it to be read out in the senate was obtained with difficulty, indeed after a huge struggle by some tribunes. But consent could not be obtained for a motion on the letter's contents. The consuls' motion initiated a 2 general debate about public affairs. One consul, Lucius Lentulus, promised that he would not fail the republic if senators were willing to announce bold and forceful proposals. "But if you look to Caesar and chase after his 3 gratitude, as you have done on previous occasions, I will consult my own interests, not comply with the senate's authority; I too can take refuge in Caesar's gratitude and friendship." Scipio made the same point, that Pompey did 4 not intend to fail the republic if he had the senate behind him. "But if you hesitate, and are too mild when you do act, the senate will call for his help—if you want it later—in vain."

2. These words were Scipio's but, because the senate was meeting in the city and Pompey was nearby, they seemed to issue from the mouth of Pompey himself.[1] Some speakers had made milder proposals. For example, 2

[1] Pompey's military office (proconsul) kept him outside Rome's civic domain.

2 batur. Dixerat aliquis leniorem sententiam, ut primo M.
Marcellus ingressus in eam orationem: non oportere ante
de ea re ad senatum referri quam dilectus tota Italia habiti
et exercitus conscripti essent, quo praesidio tuto et libere
3 senatus quae vellet decernere auderet. Vt M. Calidius, qui
censebat ut Pompeius in suas provincias proficisceretur ne
quae esset armorum causa; timere Caesarem ereptis[3] ab
eo duabus legionibus ne ad eius periculum reservare et
retinere eas ad urbem Pompeius videretur. Vt M. Rufus,
qui sententiam Calidi paucis fere mutatis rebus sequeba-
4 tur. Hi omnes convicio L. Lentuli consulis correpti exagi-
5 tabantur. Lentulus sententiam Calidi pronuntiaturum se
omnino negavit. Marcellus perterritus conviciis a sua sen-
6 tentia discessit. Sic vocibus consulis, terrore praesentis
exercitus, minis amicorum Pompei plerique compulsi in-
viti et coacti Scipionis sententiam sequuntur: uti ante cer-
tam diem Caesar exercitum dimittat; si non faciat, eum
7 adversus rem publicam facturum videri. Intercedit M.
Antonius Q. Cassius, tribuni plebis. Refertur confestim de
8 intercessione tribunorum. Dicuntur sententiae graves. Vt
quisque acerbissime crudelissimeque dixit ita quam maxime ab inimicis Caesaris collaudatur.

3. Misso ad vesperum senatu omnes[4] qui sunt eius ordinis a Pompeio evocantur. Laudat ⟨audaces⟩[5] Pompeius
atque in posterum confirmat, segniores castigat atque inci-

---

3 ereptis *Nipperdey* (*see 1.32.6*): correptis ω
4 omnes ⟨sui⟩ Markland (*see 1.3.4*)   5 ⟨audaces⟩ *Paul*

---

2 Spain, that is, which proxies held for him (1.38.1).
3 In 50, by order of the senate, Caesar relinquished two legions for a possible war against the Parthians (*BG* 8.54).

first, Marcus Marcellus, who opened with these words: that it was not right for the matter to be referred to the senate before troops were recruited throughout Italy and armies enlisted, so that under their protection the senate could be safe and free in venturing to make the decisions it wanted. Or Marcus Calidius, who recommended that Pompey leave for his provincial command to remove any cause for war.[2] "Caesar is afraid, now that two of his legions have been snatched away, that Pompey will be thought to be holding them in reserve and keeping them near Rome as a threat against himself."[3] Or Marcus Rufus, who supported Calidius' proposal with a few amendments. All of these men, derisively rebuked by the consul Lentulus, were shaken. Lentulus refused outright to ask for a vote on Calidius' proposal. Marcellus, thoroughly alarmed by the derision, himself abandoned his proposal. Thus, what with the consul's language, fear of the nearby army, and threats from Pompey's friends, the majority —under compulsion, unwilling, and coerced—backed Scipio's proposal that Caesar must dismiss his army by a set date. "If he does not, it is evident that his actions will be hostile to the republic." This was vetoed by the tribunes Mark Antony and Quintus Cassius. The issue of the tribunes' veto was raised immediately. Proposals were urged, and the harshest and cruelest speakers got the most praise from Caesar's enemies.

3. After the senate's dismissal at sunset, all[4] members of the order were summoned by Pompey. He praised the bold and gave them heart for the future while scolding and

[4] For "all," Markland proposed "all his friends who were."

2 tat. Multi undique ex veteribus Pompei exercitibus spe
praemiorum atque ordinum evocantur, multi ex duabus
3 legionibus quae sunt traditae a Caesare arcessuntur. Com-
pletur urbs et ipsum[6] comitium tribunis [plebis] centurio-
4 nibus evocatis. Omnes amici consulum, necessarii Pompei
atque eorum qui veteres inimicitias cum Caesare gere-
5 bant in senatum coguntur. Quorum vocibus et concursu
terrentur infirmiores, dubii confirmantur. Plerisque vero
6 libere decernendi potestas eripitur. Pollicetur L. Piso censor sese iturum ad Caesarem, item L. Roscius praetor, qui
de his rebus eum doceant. VI dies ad eam rem conficien-
7 dam spati postulant. Dicuntur etiam ab nonnullis sententiae ut legati ad Caesarem mittantur qui voluntatem senatus ei proponant.

4. Omnibus his resistitur omnibusque oratio consulis,
Scipionis, Catonis opponitur. Catonem veteres inimicitiae
2 Caesaris incitant et dolor repulsae. Lentulus aeris alieni
magnitudine et spe exercitus ac provinciarum et regum
appellandorum largitionibus movetur seque alterum fore
Sullam inter suos gloriatur, ad quem summa imperi re-
3 deat. Scipionem eadem spes provinciae atque exercituum
impellit, quos se pro necessitudine partiturum cum Pompeio arbitratur, simul iudiciorum metus [adulatio][7] atque

---

[6] et ipsum *Hug*: et ius ω: militibus *Nipperdey*: forum *Köchly*

[7] [adulatio] *Madvig*: *Vielhaber moved* adulatio *to before* potentium. *Perhaps* adulatioque?

---

[5] The text is very uncertain here; the most significant emendations are Nipperdey's, which adds "soldiers" to the list of groups
filling the city, and Köchly's, which adds the Forum to the list of
places filled.

prodding the slack. In large numbers and from all direc- 2
tions men from Pompey's previous armies were summoned with rewards and rank in prospect; in large numbers men from the two legions surrendered by Caesar
were ordered to Rome. The city and the assembly place 3
itself[5] were full of staff officers, centurions, reenlisted
men. All of the consuls' friends as well as adherents of 4
Pompey and of men with a long-standing enmity toward
Caesar were collected for the senate meeting. Their lan- 5
guage and convergence generated terror in the insecure,
security in the undecided. But the majority were stripped
of their capacity for free decision. The censor Lucius Piso 6
and likewise the praetor Lucius Roscius volunteered to go
to Caesar to inform him about these matters; they requested a six-day period to accomplish the business. A few 7
senators even proposed that a delegation be sent to Caesar
to lay out for him the senate's decision.

4. Every proposal was resisted, encountering vocal opposition from the consul, Scipio, and Cato. Motivating
Cato were his long-standing enmity with Caesar and the
sting of electoral defeat.[6] Lentulus was prompted by the 2
size of his debts, the prospect of an army and provincial
commands, and bribes from kings awaiting confirmation.
Among friends he boasted that he would be a second Sulla
and that supreme power would be his. Scipio was driven 3
by the same prospect of a province and armies, which he
thought, in view of the family connection, he would share
with Pompey.[7] Also relevant were fear of prosecution and

[6] Cato made an unsuccessful bid for the consulship of 51.
[7] Scipio's daughter Cornelia was Pompey's wife in 49.

7

ostentatio sui et potentium, qui in re publica iudiciisque
4 tum plurimum pollebant. Ipse Pompeius ab inimicis Caesaris incitatus—et quod neminem dignitate secum exae-
quari volebat—totum se ab eius amicitia averterat et cum
communibus inimicis in gratiam redierat, quorum ipse
maximam partem illo adfinitatis tempore iniunxerat Cae-
5 sari. Simul infamia duarum legionum permotus quas ab
itinere Asiae Syriaeque ad suam potentiam dominatumque
converterat rem ad arma deduci studebat.

5. His de causis aguntur omnia raptim atque turbate.
Nec docendi Caesaris propinquis eius spatium datur, nec
tribunis plebis sui periculi deprecandi neque etiam extremi iuris intercessione[8] retinendi, quod L. Sulla relique-
2 rat, facultas tribuitur, sed de sua salute septimo die cogitare coguntur, quod illi turbulentissimi superioribus
temporibus tribuni plebis ⟨post⟩ VIII denique menses
3 variarum[9] actionum respicere ac timere consuerant. De-
curritur ad illud extremum atque ultimum senatus consultum, quo nisi paene in ipso urbis incendio atque in
desperatione omnium salutis †latorum†[10] audacia numquam ante descensum[11] est: dent operam consules, prae-

---

[8] intercessione] intercessionis *Chacon* (*see 1.7.2-3*): [inter-
cessione] *Manutius*   [9] ⟨post⟩ . . . variarum] *Dinter added*
⟨post⟩, *a minimal repair for this corrupt stretch of text.*
[10] latorum] *defended by Carter 1991, emended by others*: latronum *Manutius*: paucorum *Nipperdey*: et malorum *Weissenborn*   [11] descensum *Kohl*: discessum ω

---

[8] Vielhaber's transposition adds "flattery by" before "the powerful men." Another possibility is putting "flattery and" before
"promotion."

promotion of himself and the powerful men[8] who were at that time particularly influential in the government and courts. As for Pompey, spurred on by Caesar's enemies— and because he did not want anyone to match him in status—he had entirely turned away from Caesar's friendship and become reconciled with their common enemies, the majority of whom he himself had saddled Caesar with when they were relations by marriage.[9] At the same time, upset at being vilified over the two legions en route to Asia and Syria, which he had diverted to his own power and domination, he was eager for matters to be brought to a fight.

5. For these reasons everything was done in haste and confusion. Caesar's relatives were given no time to inform him, and the tribunes were granted no opportunity to protest their danger or even to hold onto their fundamental right by means of the veto,[10] a right that Lucius Sulla let them keep. Instead, seven days into January they were forced to think about their own safety, something that the most tumultuous tribunes of the past were generally attentive to and worried about only after eight months of all kinds of action.[11] Recourse was had to that last and final decree of the senate, to which—unless the city was all but aflame and everyone despaired of safety in view of the temerity of . . .[12]—the senate never before descended:

---

[9] The connection lapsed at the death of Julia, Caesar's daughter and Pompey's wife, in 54.   [10] Chacon proposed removing "by means of," Manutius "by means of the veto."

[11] For some names and historical details, see 1.7.2–6.

[12] Different kinds of troublemakers have been suggested here: men proposing subversive laws, criminals, scoundrels, a small cabal, and the like.

tores, tribuni plebis—quique ⟨pro⟩ consulibus sunt ad
4 urbem—ne quid res publica detrimenti capiat. Haec senatus consulto perscribuntur ante diem septimum Idus Ianuarias. Itaque V primis diebus quibus haberi senatus
potuit qua ex die consulatum iniit Lentulus, biduo excepto
comitiali, et de imperio Caesaris et de amplissimis viris,
tribunis plebis, gravissime acerbissimeque decernitur.
5 Profugiunt statim ex urbe tribuni plebis seseque ad Caesarem conferunt. Is eo tempore erat Ravennae expectabat-
que suis lenissimis[12] postulatis responsa, si qua hominum
aequitate res ad otium deduci posset.

6. Proximis diebus habetur extra urbem senatus. Pompeius eadem illa quae per Scipionem ostenderat agit.
Senatus virtutem constantiamque collaudat. Copias suas
2 exponit: legiones habere sese paratas X; praeterea cognitum compertumque sibi alieno esse animo in Caesarem
milites, neque iis posse persuaderi uti eum defendant aut
3 sequantur saltem. De reliquis rebus ad senatum refertur:
tota Italia dilectus habeatur; Faustus Sulla pro praetore[13]
in Mauretaniam mittatur; pecunia uti ex aerario Pompeio
detur. Refertur etiam de rege Iuba: ut socius sit atque
4 amicus. Marcellus consul[14] passurum in praesentia negat.
5 De Fausto impedit Philippus, tribunus plebis. De reliquis
rebus senatus consulta perscribuntur. Provinciae privatis
decernuntur, duae consulares, reliquae praetoriae. Sci-

---

[12] lenissimis *m*: levissimis *USTV*
[13] pro praetore *Manutius*: propere ω
[14] consul (*sc*. se) *Madvig* (*see 1.14.2*): non ω: hoc *Herzog*

---

[13] For prior occasions, see the Index under "SCU."
[14] The bulk of Pompey's forces are in Spain (1.38.1).

"Consuls, praetors, tribunes, and proconsuls near Rome must take care that the republic suffer no harm."[13] These words were recorded in a decree of the senate on January 7. Accordingly, within five days from the day Lentulus entered the consulship (not counting the two days reserved for assemblies) Caesar's governorship and some very consequential men, the tribunes, were the subject of extremely urgent and harsh decrees. The tribunes left Rome in flight immediately and made their way to Caesar. At the time, he was at Ravenna, awaiting response to his extremely mild demands, in case by some humane sense of equity the situation could be steered toward peace.

6. On the following days the senate met outside the city. Pompey made the points he had indicated through Scipio. He praised the senate for courageously standing firm, then stated his troop strength. "I have ten legions ready.[14] Furthermore, I know on good evidence that the soldiers are estranged from Caesar and cannot be convinced to defend or even follow him." The remaining issues were referred to the senate: recruitment should be undertaken throughout Italy, Faustus Sulla sent as propraetor to Mauretania, public funds provided to Pompey. There was also a motion about King Juba, that he should be an ally and friend. The consul Marcellus[15] declared that he would not permit this at that time. The Faustus proposal was blocked by the tribune Philippus. On the remaining issues senatorial decrees were recorded. Provincial commands were assigned to men in private life, two

[15] For Madvig's "the consul Marcellus," Herzog proposed "this action Marcellus."

pioni obvenit Syria, L. Domitio Gallia. Philippus et Cotta
privato[15] consilio praetereuntur, neque eorum sortes de-
6 iciuntur. In reliquas provincias praetores mittuntur. Neque exspectant—quod superioribus annis acciderat—ut
de eorum imperio ad populum feratur, paludatique votis
7 nuncupatis exeunt. Consules—quod ante id tempus accidit numquam[16]—ex urbe proficiscuntur ⟨inauspicato⟩[17]
lictoresque habent in urbe et Capitolio privatim contra
8 omnia vetustatis exempla. Tota Italia dilectus habentur,
arma imperantur, pecuniae a municipiis exiguntur e fanis
tolluntur. Omnia divina humanaque iura permiscentur.

7. Quibus rebus cognitis Caesar apud milites contiona-
tur. Omnium temporum iniurias inimicorum in se commemorat. A quibus deductum ac depravatum Pompeium
queritur invidia atque obtrectatione laudis suae, cuius ipse
2 honori et dignitati semper faverit adiutorque fuerit. Novum in re publica introductum exemplum queritur, ut
tribunicia intercessio armis notaretur atque opprimeretur

---

15 privato] *Perhaps* privati?
16 quod . . . numquam] *deleted by Vossius, rendering* ⟨inaus-
picato⟩ *unnecessary*: Kindscher *added* ⟨clam⟩ *after* numquam
17 ⟨inauspicato⟩ *Damon*: La Penna *added* ⟨ne auspicato qui-
dem⟩ *before* ex urbe

---

16 Under the system introduced by Pompey in 52, consuls and
praetors became eligible for provincial commands five years after
holding office. Commands were distributed to these now "private
individuals" by lot annually and ratified by popular vote.
17 Domitius is thus Caesar's replacement.
18 A tiny emendation would alter the meaning substantially:
"Philippus and Cotta, men in private life, were bypassed on pur-

at the consular level, the rest praetorian.[16] Scipio got Syria, Lucius Domitius Gaul.[17] The reason Philippus and Cotta were bypassed was not disclosed;[18] their lots were not even cast. Ex-praetors were sent to the remaining prov-   6 inces. These men did not wait—as had happened in prior years—for the bill ratifying their commands to be put to the assembly; they departed in uniform after announcing their vows.[19] The consuls left Rome without taking the   7 auspices, another thing that never happened before that occasion, and used lictors in Rome in a private capac- ity, contrary to every precedent.[20] Troops were recruited   8 throughout Italy, weapons were requisitioned, money was extorted from towns and taken from temples. All rights, divine and human, were thrown into confusion.

7. After learning of these matters Caesar addressed the soldiers. He mentioned the perpetual series of injuries inflicted by his enemies. It was by these men, he protested, that Pompey had been steered astray, jealous and critical of Caesar's renown, although he himself had always fa- vored and promoted Pompey's prestige and dignity. He   2 protested that an unprecedented practice had been intro- duced into the republic, such that the tribunes' veto was

pose." These men, consuls in 56 and 65, respectively, were senior in standing to Scipio (*cos.* 52) and Domitius (*cos.* 54).

[19] For example, a general might vow to build a temple after the successful completion of the upcoming campaign. In this sen- tence and the next, the text is very uncertain.

[20] "In a private capacity" seems to allude to a constitutional irregularity (e.g., that the formalities pertaining to the consuls' installation were incomplete), but the text may be corrupt.

3 [quae superioribus annis armis esset restituta]:[18] Sullam nudata omnibus rebus tribunicia potestate tamen inter-
4 cessionem liberam reliquisse; Pompeium, qui amissa restituisse videatur omnia,[19] etiam quae ante habuerint
5 ademisse; quotienscumque sit decretum darent operam magistratus ne quid res publica detrimenti caperet, qua voce et quo senatus consulto populus Romanus ad arma sit vocatus, factum in perniciosis legibus, in vi tribunicia, in secessione populi, templis locisque editioribus occupa-
6 tis. Atque haec superioris aetatis exempla expiata Saturnini atque Gracchorum casibus docet. (Quarum rerum illo tempore nihil factum, ne cogitatum quidem. Nulla lex promulgata, non cum populo agi coeptum, nulla secessio
7 facta.) Hortatur, cuius imperatoris ductu VIIII annis rem publicam felicissime gesserint plurimaque proelia secunda fecerint, omnem Galliam Germaniamque pacaverint, ut eius existimationem dignitatemque ab inimicis
8 defendant. Conclamant legionis tertiae decimae, quae aderat, milites—hanc enim initio tumultus evocaverat, reliquae nondum convenerant—sese paratos esse imperatoris sui tribunorumque plebis iniurias defendere.

8. Cognita militum voluntate Ariminum cum ea legione proficiscitur. Ibique tribunos plebis qui ad eum confuge-

18 [quae . . . restituta] *Nipperdey*
19 omnia *Markland* (*see 1.7.3*): dona ω: bona *Vittori*: [dona] *Terpstra*

---

21 Nipperdey excised a contradiction from the text: "although it was recently restored by force."
22 In place of Markland's "everything they lost," editors often accept Vittori's "their lost 'property.'" Terpstra's excision leaves "what they lost."

censured and suppressed by force.[21] "Sulla, although he 3
completely stripped the tribunes of power, nevertheless
left their veto unencumbered. Pompey, who is known for 4
having restored everything they lost,[22] has taken away
even what they had before. Whenever the senatorial de- 5
cree exhorting officials to take care that the republic suffer
no harm has been issued—and the decree thus worded is
the Roman people's call to arms—it has been done in situations involving subversive legislation, violent tribunes, or
the people's secession to occupied temples and heights."
These past instances, he explained, had come at the cost 6
of disaster to Saturninus and the Gracchi. (On that occasion none of these actions had been taken or even contemplated. No law had been proposed, no popular assembly
convened, and no secession had taken place.) He urged 7
the men to protect from his enemies the reputation and
prestige of a man under whose leadership they had done
the republic's business with outstanding good fortune for
nine years while fighting a huge number of successful
battles and pacifying the whole of Gaul and Germany. A 8
shout went up from the soldiers of the thirteenth legion—
it was at hand, since he had summoned this one at the start
of the emergency; the rest had not yet arrived[23]—that they
were ready to protect their commander and the tribunes
from injury.

8. Apprised of the soldiers' goodwill he set out with the
thirteenth legion for Ariminum, where he met the tribunes who had taken refuge with him.[24] He summoned

---

[23] Two others arrived by mid-February (1.15.3, 1.18.5); the
majority were still in Gaul (*BG* 8.54.3–4).   [24] At Ariminum,
mod. Rimini, Caesar is in Italy proper. He does not mention
crossing the Rubicon, which lies between Ravenna and Rimini.

rant convenit. Reliquas legiones ex hibernis evocat et sub-
2 sequi iubet. Eo L. Caesar adulescens venit, cuius pater
Caesaris erat legatus. Is reliquo sermone confecto cuius
rei causa venerat habere se a Pompeio ad eum privati offici
3 mandata demonstrat: velle Pompeium se Caesari purga-
tum; ne ea quae rei publicae causa egerit in suam contumeliam vertat; semper se rei publicae commoda privatis
necessitudinibus habuisse potiora; Caesarem quoque pro
sua dignitate debere et studium et iracundiam suam rei
publicae dimittere neque adeo graviter irasci inimicis ⟨ut⟩
4 cum illis nocere se speret rei publicae noceat. Pauca eiusdem generis addit cum excusatione Pompei coniuncta.
Eadem fere atque isdem ⟨de⟩[20] rebus praetor Roscius agit
cum Caesare sibique Pompeium commemorasse demonstrat.

9. Quae res etsi nihil ad levandas iniurias pertinere
videbantur tamen idoneos nactus homines per quos ea
quae vellet ad eum perferrentur petit ab utroque, quoniam Pompei mandata ad se detulerint, ne graventur sua
quoque ad eum postulata deferre, si parvo labore magnas
controversias tollere atque omnem Italiam metu liberare
2 possint: sibi semper primam fuisse dignitatem vitaque
potiorem; doluisse se quod populi Romani beneficium sibi
per contumeliam ab inimicis extorqueretur, ereptoque
semenstri imperio in urbem retraheretur cuius absentis

---

[20] ⟨de⟩ rebus *Aldus*: verbis *Clarke*

---

[25] For Aldus' emendation "on the same subjects," Clarke substituted "in the same words."

the rest of his legions from winter quarters and ordered them to follow immediately. Lucius Caesar came to Arimi- 2 num; his father was one of Caesar's officers. After finishing the conversation that was the official reason for his journey, he indicated that he had a message of a personal nature from Pompey for Caesar. "Pompey wants to clear 3 himself in your eyes, Caesar. You should not twist the things he did on behalf of the republic into disrespect for yourself. He has always considered the republic's advantage more important than personal relationships. You, too, given your standing, ought to dismiss partisan acrimony for the republic's sake, and you should not be in such a rage at your enemies that in the hope of harming them you harm the republic." He added a few things of the same 4 sort relevant to excusing Pompey. The praetor Roscius made nearly the same points on the same subjects[25] with Caesar and indicated that the arguments were Pompey's.

9. Although these points were plainly not directed at alleviating the damage done to him, nevertheless, having found men suitable for conveying his wishes to Pompey, Caesar appealed to each: "Since you carried Pompey's message to me, you should not object to carrying my demands to him. Perhaps with this small effort you will be able to remove serious disputes and free all Italy from fear. Dignity has always been my primary objective, dearer 2 than life itself. I resented the insult in having a favor granted by the Roman people torn from my grasp by personal enemies, and being dragged back to Rome stripped of six months of my command even though the people ordered that I be a valid candidate in absentia at the last

3   rationem haberi proximis comitiis populus iussisset; tamen hanc iacturam honoris sui rei publicae causa aequo animo tulisse; cum litteras ad senatum miserit ut omnes ab exercitibus discederent, ne id quidem impetravisse;

4   tota Italia dilectus haberi, retineri legiones duas quae ab se simulatione Parthici belli sint abductae, civitatem esse in armis; quonam haec omnia nisi ad suam perniciem pertinere?

5   sed tamen ad omnia se descendere paratum atque omnia pati rei publicae causa; proficiscatur Pompeius in suas provincias, ipsi exercitus dimittant, discedant in Italia omnes ab armis, metus e civitate tollatur, libera comitia[21] atque omnis res publica senatui populoque Romano permittatur;

6   haec quo facilius certisque conditionibus fiant et iureiurando sanciantur, aut ipse propius accedat aut se patiatur accedere; fore uti per colloquia omnes controversiae componantur.

10. Acceptis mandatis Roscius cum ⟨L.⟩[22] Caesare Capuam pervenit ibique consules Pompeiumque invenit.

2   Postulata Caesaris renuntiat. Illi ⟨re⟩ deliberata respondent scriptaque ad eum mandata per eos remittunt.

3   Quorum haec erat summa: Caesar in Galliam reverteretur, Arimino excederet, exercitus dimitteret; quae si fecisset

4   Pompeium in Hispanias iturum; interea quoad fides esset data Caesarem facturum quae polliceretur non intermissuros consules Pompeiumque dilectus.

11. Erat iniqua conditio postulare ut Caesar Arimino

[21] comitia ⟨habeantur⟩ *Fuchs*
[22] ⟨L.⟩ *Peskett*

---

[26] Caesar's apparent grievance is this: if he had returned to

elections.[26] Nevertheless, I accepted the loss of prestige   3
with equanimity for the sake of the republic. When I sent
a letter to the senate proposing that everyone leave their
armies, I did not get consent even for this. Troops are be-   4
ing recruited throughout Italy, two legions taken from me
on the pretense of a Parthian war are being held back, the
state is in arms—to what end are all these things directed
except destroying me? But I am nevertheless prepared to   5
lower myself and accept all of them, to tolerate all of them
for the sake of the republic. Here is what I propose: Pompey goes to his provinces, both of us dismiss our armies,
everyone in Italy lays arms aside, the state is relieved of
fear, free elections and the whole government are entrusted to the senate and people. To bring this about eas-   6
ily and on set terms, and to get it ratified by oath, he should
either come my way or let me come his. With negotiation
all our disputes will be settled."

10. With this message in hand Roscius, along with Lucius Caesar, arrived in Capua. There he found the consuls
and Pompey and presented Caesar's demands. After de-   2
liberation they replied in writing and sent the message to
Caesar through Roscius and Lucius Caesar. The gist was
this: Caesar was to return to Gaul, leave Ariminum, dis-   3
miss his army. "If you do this, Pompey will go to Spain.
Meanwhile, until we get some guarantee that you will do   4
what you promise, we will not discontinue recruiting."

11. The terms were unfair: to demand that Caesar leave

Rome for elections held in the summer of 50 for the magistrates
of 49, he would have given up half a year of his military command
(roughly July–Dec.). For some other considerations, see the Introduction, section III.

excederet atque in provinciam reverteretur, ipsum et provincias et legiones alienas[23] tenere, exercitum Caesaris
2 velle dimitti, dilectus habere, polliceri se in provinciam
iturum neque ante quem diem iturus sit definire, ut, si
peracto consulatu Caesaris nondum[24] profectus esset,
3 nulla tamen mendacii religione obstrictus videretur. Tempus vero colloquio non dare neque accessurum polliceri
4 magnam pacis desperationem adferebat. Itaque ab Arimino M. Antonium cum cohortibus V Arretium mittit.
Ipse Arimini cum duabus [legionibus] subsistit ibique dilectum habere instituit. Pisaurum, Fanum, Anconam singulis cohortibus occupat.

12. Interea certior factus Iguvium Thermum prae-
torem cohortibus V tenere, oppidum munire, omniumque
esse Iguvinorum optimam erga se voluntatem, Curionem
cum tribus cohortibus quas Pisauri et Arimini habebat
2 mittit. Cuius adventu cognito diffisus municipi voluntati
Thermus cohortes ex urbe reducit et profugit. Milites in
3 itinere ab eo discedunt ac domum revertuntur. Curio
summa omnium voluntate Iguvium recipit. Quibus rebus
cognitis confisus municipiorum voluntatibus Caesar cohortes legionis tertiae decimae ex praesidiis deducit Auxi-
mumque proficiscitur. Quod oppidum Attius cohortibus

---

23 alienas] absentem *Paul*
24 nondum *Damon*: cons [cs V] ω

---

27 For "he had no right to," Paul proposed "in absentia."
28 The text is uncertain here.
29 From "bound . . . lie" the Latin is terse and the meaning
uncertain, but cf. 3.28.4.

Ariminum and return to his province while Pompey controlled provinces and legions he had no right to,[27] to want
Caesar's army to be disbanded while Pompey recruited
troops, to promise that he would go to his province with- 2
out specifying a date by which he would go, so that if after
Caesar's consulship Pompey had not yet left[28] he would
nevertheless not be thought to be bound by the sanctity of
a lie.[29] The fact that Pompey was not making time for 3
negotiation and not promising to meet made peace seem
quite hopeless. Caesar therefore sent Marcus Antonius 4
from Ariminum to Arretium with five cohorts.[30] He himself stayed at Ariminum with two and began to recruit
troops there. He occupied Pisaurum, Fanum, Ancona with
one cohort each.

12. Meanwhile, having been informed that at Iguvium—a town the praetor Thermus was holding with five
cohorts, and fortifying—the attitude of all the inhabitants
toward him was strongly positive, Caesar sent Curio with
the three cohorts he had at Pisaurum and Ariminum. At 2
news of his approach Thermus, distrusting the community's attitude, withdrew his cohorts from the city and fled;
his soldiers abandoned him on the march and returned
home. Curio recovered Iguvium with great and universal 3
goodwill. Learning of this, and confident of goodwill in the
towns, Caesar withdrew the cohorts of the thirteenth legion from garrison duty and set out for Auximum, a town
that Attius held with cohorts he had brought in. Attius

---

[30] Caesar's "therefore" falsifies the chronology and overstates
his willingness to negotiate; the towns mentioned in this sentence
and the next were in Caesar's hands before the negotiations described in 1.10–11 (Cic. *Fam.* 16.12.2 and *Att.* 7.14.1).

introductis tenebat, dilectumque toto Piceno circummissis senatoribus habebat.

13. Adventu Caesaris cognito decuriones Auximi ad Attium Varum frequentes conveniunt. Docent sui iudici rem non esse; neque se neque reliquos municipes pati posse C. Caesarem imperatorem bene de re publica meritum tantis rebus gestis oppido moenibusque prohiberi; 2 proinde habeat rationem posteritatis et periculi sui. Quorum oratione permotus Varus praesidium quod introdux- 3 erat ex oppido educit ac profugit. Hunc ex primo ordine pauci Caesaris consecuti milites consistere coegerunt. 4 Commisso proelio deseritur a suis Varus. Nonnulla pars militum domum discedit, reliqui ad Caesarem perveniunt. Atque una cum iis deprensus L. Pupius, primi pili centurio, adducitur, qui hunc eundem ordinem in exercitu Cn. 5 Pompei antea duxerat. At Caesar milites Attianos collaudat, Pupium dimittit, Auximatibus agit gratias seque eorum facti memorem fore pollicetur.

14. Quibus rebus Romam nuntiatis tantus repente terror invasit ut, cum Lentulus consul ad aperiendum aerarium venisset ad pecuniamque Pompeio ex senatus consulto proferendam, protinus aperto[25] sanctiore aerario ex urbe profugeret. Caesar enim adventare iam iamque et 2 adesse eius equites falso nuntiabantur. Hunc Marcellus 3 collega et plerique magistratus consecuti sunt. Cn. Pompeius pridie eius diei ex urbe profectus iter ad legiones habebat quas a Caesare acceptas in Apulia hibernorum

---

25 ‹non› aperto *Rubenius*

---

31 The "treasury reserve" was an emergency fund supported by a manumission tax (Livy 27.10.11). Other sources deny that

was also recruiting troops throughout Picenum by sending senators from town to town.

13. Learning of Caesar's approach the town councilors at Auximum met as a body with Attius Varus. They told him that the affair was not something for them to decide. "Neither we nor the rest of our townspeople can tolerate that Gaius Caesar, a commander who has such important public achievements to his credit, be barred from the town and its fortifications. Furthermore, you should consider the future and your danger." Disturbed by their words 2 Varus led out the garrison he had installed, and fled. A few 3 of Caesar's advance-guard soldiers caught up and forced him to stop. A fight began, but Varus was deserted by his 4 men. A portion of the soldiers went home, the rest reached Caesar, bringing the chief centurion Lucius Pupius along as a prisoner. (He had earlier held that same rank in one of Pompey's armies.) Caesar for his part praised Attius' sol- 5 diers, dismissed Pupius, and thanked the people of Auximum, promising to remember their action.

14. When this news reached Rome the panic that suddenly hit was so great that, although the consul Lentulus had come to open the treasury to provide money for Pompey as per the senate's decree, he fled the city directly after opening the treasury reserve.[31] For—so went the false report—Caesar was already approaching, indeed his cavalry was already at hand. Lentulus was followed by his 2 colleague Marcellus and most of the magistrates. Pompey, 3 having left Rome the day before, was en route to the legions he had received from Caesar and distributed in win-

the treasury was left open: Cic. *Att.* 7.12.2; Luc. 3.117; App. *BC* 2.41.164; D.C. 41.17.2; Plut. *Caes.* 35.9.

4   causa disposuerat. Dilectus circa urbem intermittuntur. Nihil citra Capuam tutum esse omnibus videtur. Capuae primum sese confirmant et colligunt dilectumque colonorum qui lege Iulia Capuam deducti erant habere instituunt. Gladiatoresque quos ibi Caesar in ludo habebat ad forum productos Lentulus ‹spe› libertatis confirmat. At-
5   que iis equos attribuit et se sequi iussit. Quos postea, monitus ab suis quod ea res omnium iudicio reprehendebatur, circum familiae patres[26] conventus Campaniae custodiae causa distribuit.

    15. Auximo Caesar progressus[27] omnem agrum Picenum percurrit. Cunctae earum regionum praefecturae libentissimis animis eum recipiunt exercitumque eius
2   omnibus rebus iuvant. Etiam Cingulo, quod oppidum Labienus constituerat suaque pecunia exaedificaverat, ad eum legati veniunt quaeque imperaverit se cupidissime
3   facturos pollicentur. Milites imperat. Mittunt. Interea legio duodecima Caesarem consequitur. Cum his duabus Asculum Picenum proficiscitur. Id oppidum Lentulus Spinther X cohortibus tenebat, qui Caesaris adventu cognito profugit ex oppido cohortesque secum abducere
4   conatus magna parte militum deseritur. Relictus in itinere cum paucis incidit in Vibullium Rufum missum a Pompeio in agrum Picenum confirmandorum hominum causa. A quo factus Vibullius certior quae res in Piceno gererentur

---

26 familiae patres *Chacon*: familiares ω
27 auximo . . . progressus *S*: maximo . . . progressu *MUTV*

---

32 The "Julian law" proposed by Caesar as consul in 59 provided land grants in Campania to Pompey's veterans.

ter quarters around Apulia. Recruitment in the city's vi-   4
cinity was put on hold; nothing above Capua felt safe to
anyone. Capua was the first place they took heart and
rallied, instituting recruitment among the settlers brought
to Capua by the *lex Julia*.[32] As for the gladiators-in-training
that Caesar maintained there, Lentulus brought them
into the forum and encouraged them with the prospect of
freedom, giving them horses and ordering them to follow
him. Afterwards, advised by his supporters that this deci-   5
sion was universally criticized, he distributed them for
safekeeping to heads of household[33] in the Campanian
assembly.

15. Advancing from Auximum Caesar overran the entire territory of Picenum. All of the districts' communities
received him with the utmost enthusiasm and assisted his
army with everything. Even Cingulum, a town that Labi-   2
enus established and developed at his own expense, sent
representatives to him and promised to do his bidding
with great eagerness. He requisitioned soldiers; they sent   3
them. Meanwhile the twelfth legion reached Caesar. With
his two legions he set out for Asculum in Picenum, a town
held by Lentulus Spinther with ten cohorts. Informed of
Caesar's approach Spinther fled the town. He attempted
to bring his cohorts away but was deserted by a substantial
portion of the soldiers. Abandoned on the march, he had   4
few men with him when he happened upon Vibullius Rufus, who was sent by Pompey to Picenum to encourage
the population. From Spinther Vibullius learned what was
happening in Picenum. He took over Spinther's soldiers

[33] Cicero gives a slightly different version of this episode in a
letter to his friend Atticus (*Att.* 7.14.2).

5 milites ab eo accipit, ipsum dimittit. Item ex finitimis regionibus quas potest contrahit cohortes ex dilectibus Pompeianis. In his Camerino fugientem Lucilium Hirrum cum VI cohortibus quas ibi in praesidio habuerat excipit. Qui-
6 bus coactis XIII efficit. Cum his ad Domitium Ahenobarbum Corfinium magnis itineribus pervenit. Caesaremque
7 adesse cum legionibus duabus nuntiat. Domitius per se circiter XX cohortes Alba, ex Marsis et Paelignis, finitimis ab regionibus coegerat.

16. Recepto Firmo expulsoque Lentulo Caesar conquiri milites qui ab eo discesserant dilectumque institui iubet. Ipse unum diem ibi rei frumentariae causa moratus Cor-
2 finium contendit. Eo cum venisset cohortes V praemissae a Domitio ex oppido pontem fluminis interrumpebant, qui
3 erat ab oppido milia passuum circiter tria. Ibi cum antecursoribus Caesaris proelio commisso celeriter Domitiani
4 a ponte repulsi se in oppidum receperunt. Caesar legionibus transductis ad oppidum constitit iuxtaque murum castra posuit.

17. Re cognita Domitius ad Pompeium in Apuliam peritos regionum magno proposito praemio cum litteris mittit qui petant atque orent ut sibi subveniat: Caesarem duobus exercitibus et locorum angustiis facile intercludi
2 posse frumentoque prohiberi; quod nisi fecerit se cohortesque amplius XXX magnumque numerum senatorum atque equitum Romanorum in periculum esse venturum.
3 Interim suos cohortatus tormenta in muris disponit cer-
4 tasque cuique partes ad custodiam urbis attribuit. Militi-

---

34 Firmum is situated between Auximum and Asculum.
35 From Asculum (1.15.3).

26

and dismissed Spinther himself. He likewise assembled 5
whatever he could from nearby districts, cohorts from
Pompeian recruiting. Among these he took in Lucilius
Hirrus fleeing from Camerinum along with the six cohorts
he had kept there as a garrison. Putting them together
Vibullius made thirteen in total. With these he reached 6
Domitius Ahenobarbus at Corfinium after forced marches
and announced that Caesar was at hand with two legions.
Domitius for his part had collected about twenty cohorts 7
from Alba, from the Marsi and Paeligni of nearby districts.

16. After recovering Firmum[34] and expelling Lentulus,[35] Caesar ordered that the soldiers who deserted Lentulus be found and recruitment begun. After spending
a day at Asculum to arrange for provisions, he hastened
toward Corfinium. When he got there, five cohorts sent 2
forward from Corfinium by Domitius were in the process
of breaking up a river bridge about three miles distant
from town. Domitius' men, engaging Caesar's advance 3
guard in a fight there, were quickly driven away from the
bridge; they retreated to Corfinium. Caesar, once his le- 4
gions were across, halted near the town and made camp
up against its wall.

17. In view of this, Domitius sent men to Pompey in
Apulia with a letter, men who knew the country and had
been offered a substantial reward, to request and plead for
assistance: "With two armies and the narrow passes—Caesar can easily be trapped and cut off from his food supply.
But if you do not do this we will be in danger, I myself, 2
more than thirty cohorts, and a large number of senators
and men of equestrian rank." Meanwhile, encouraging his 3
men, he placed catapults along the walls and allocated to
each man a particular section of the city to guard. In an 4

bus in contione agros ex suis possessionibus pollicetur,
XL[28] in singulos iugera et pro rata parte centurionibus
evocatisque.

18. Interim Caesari nuntiatur Sulmonenses (quod oppidum a Corfinio VII milium intervallo abest) cupere ea
facere quae vellet sed a Q. Lucretio senatore et Attio Pae-
ligno prohiberi, qui id oppidum VII cohortium praesidio
2 tenebant. Mittit eo M. Antonium cum legionis tertiaede-
cimae[29] cohortibus V. Sulmonenses simul atque signa nostra viderunt portas aperuerunt universique—et oppidani
3 et milites—obviam gratulantes Antonio exierunt. Lucretius et Attius de muro se deiecerunt. Attius ad Antonium
deductus petit ut ad Caesarem mitteretur. Antonius cum
cohortibus et Attio eodem die quo profectus erat reverti-
4 tur. Caesar eas cohortes cum exercitu suo coniunxit At-
tiumque incolumem dimisit.

Caesar primis diebus castra magnis operibus munire et
ex finitimis municipiis frumentum comportare reliquasque
5 copias expectare instituit. Eo triduo legio octava ad eum
venit cohortesque ex novis Galliae dilectibus XXII equitesque ab rege Norico circiter CCC. Quorum adventu
altera castra ad alteram oppidi partem ponit. His castris
6 Curionem praefecit. Reliquis diebus oppidum vallo castellisque circumvenire instituit. Cuius operis maxima
parte effecta eodem fere tempore missi ad Pompeium
revertuntur.

19 Litteris perlectis Domitius dissimulans in consilio

---

[28] XL] quaterna *Glarean*
[29] tertiaedecimae] XIII. (*or* XII.) *Vossius*: VIII ω

assembly he promised the troops land from his own estates, twenty-four[36] acres each and proportionally more for centurions and reenlisted men.

18. Meanwhile Caesar got word that the people of Sulmo, a town seven miles from Corfinium, desired to follow his wishes but were prevented by Quintus Lucretius, a senator, and Attius, a man from Paelignum, who were holding the town with a garrison of seven cohorts. He sent Marcus Antonius to Sulmo with five cohorts of the thirteenth legion. As soon as the inhabitants saw our standards they opened the gates and everyone—townspeople and soldiers alike—came out to meet and congratulate Antonius. Lucretius and Attius jumped from the wall. Attius, brought to Antonius, asked to be sent to Caesar. Antonius returned with Attius and his cohorts the same day that he started. Caesar added those cohorts to his army and sent Attius away unharmed.

During his first days at Corfinium, Caesar decided, he would fortify his camp with substantial earthworks, collect provisions from nearby towns, and wait for the rest of his troops. Within three days the eighth legion reached him, along with twenty-two cohorts from the recent recruiting in Gaul and about three hundred cavalry from the king of Noricum. After their arrival he established a second camp on the other side of the city and put Curio in charge of it. For the rest of his time at Corfinium the plan was to surround the city with a rampart and outposts. The majority of this task was complete when the messengers sent to Pompey returned.

19. After reading the letter through, Domitius, con-

---

[36] The number is suspect.

pronuntiat Pompeium celeriter subsidio venturum horta-
turque eos ne animo deficiant quaeque usui ad defen-
2 dendum oppidum sint parent. Ipse arcano cum paucis
familiaribus suis colloquitur consiliumque fugae capere
3 constituit. Cum vultus Domiti cum oratione non consen-
tiret atque omnia trepidantius timidiusque ageret quam
superioribus diebus consuesset multumque cum suis con-
siliandi causa secreto praeter consuetudinem colloqueretur, concilia conventusque hominum fugeret, res diutius
4 tegi dissimularique non potuit. Pompeius enim rescripse-
rat: sese rem in summum periculum deducturum non
esse, neque suo consilio aut voluntate Domitium se in
oppidum Corfinium contulisse; proinde, si qua fuisset fa-
5 cultas, ad se cum omnibus copiis veniret. Id ne fieri posset
obsidione atque oppidi circummunitione fiebat.

20. Divulgato Domiti consilio milites qui erant Corfini
prima vespera secessionem faciunt atque ita inter se per
tribunos militum centurionesque atque honestissimos sui
2 generis colloquuntur: obsideri se a Caesare; opera muni-
tionesque prope esse perfectas; ducem suum Domitium,
cuius spe atque fiducia permanserint, proiectis omnibus
fugae consilium capere; debere se suae salutis rationem
3 habere. Ab his primo Marsi dissentire incipiunt eamque
oppidi partem quae munitissima videretur occupant. Tantaque inter eos dissensio existit ut manum conserere atque
4 armis dimicare conentur. Post paulo tamen internuntiis
ultro citroque missis, quae ignorabant de L. Domiti fuga
5 cognoscunt. Itaque omnes uno consilio Domitium pro-
ductum in publicum circumsistunt et custodiunt lega-

---

[37] Pompey's letters to Domitius are preserved in Cicero's correspondence (*Att.* 8.12B–12D).

cealing its content, announced to his war council that Pompey would come quickly to their support. He urged them not to lose heart, and to prepare whatever would be useful for the city's defense. He himself spoke secretly with a few 2 friends and decided to plan an escape. But Domitius' face 3 did not fit his words and his whole behavior was more fearful and timid than had been his habit in days past. Plus, his advice-taking conversations with friends were held in secret, contrary to custom, and he avoided meetings and crowds. So the matter could not be covered up and concealed any longer. For Pompey had written back: "I am 4 not going to put our cause into extreme danger. You went to Corfinium without my advice or intention. So if there is any way you can, join me with all of your troops."[37] This 5 could not be done because of the blockade and the town's encirclement.

20. After Domitius' plan was divulged the soldiers at Corfinium became mutinous early in the evening and they conferred as follows, using the most highly regarded staff officers and centurions as intermediaries: "We are block- 2 aded by Caesar, and his fortification works are nearly complete. Hope and confidence in our leader Domitius kept us here, but he has forsaken us all and planned his escape. We ought to consider our own welfare." The Marsi ini- 3 tially dissented from these views and occupied what they thought was the best fortified position in Corfinium. Indeed so strong was the difference of opinion that they tried to engage and fight it out. A little later, however, after 4 messengers were sent back and forth, the Marsi learned about Domitius' escape plan, of which they had been ignorant. So everyone was of one mind when Domitius was 5 brought into the open, surrounded, and placed under

tosque ex suo numero ad Caesarem mittunt: sese paratos
esse portas aperire quaeque imperaverit facere et L. Domitium vivum in eius potestatem tradere.

21. Quibus rebus cognitis Caesar, etsi magni interesse
arbitrabatur quam primum oppido potiri cohortesque ad
se in castra traducere ne qua aut largitionibus aut animi
confirmatione aut falsis nuntiis commutatio fieret voluntatis, quod saepe in bello parvis momentis magni casus
2 intercederent, tamen veritus ne militum introitu et noc-
turni temporis licentia oppidum diriperetur eos qui venerant collaudat atque in oppidum dimittit, portas murosque
3 asservari iubet. Ipse iis operibus quae facere instituerat
milites disponit non certis spatiis intermissis, ut erat
superiorum dierum consuetudo, sed perpetuis vigiliis
stationibusque ut contingant inter se atque omnem muni-
4 tionem expleant. Tribunos militum et praefectos circum-
mittit atque hortatur non solum ab eruptionibus caveant
sed etiam singulorum hominum occultos exitus asservent.
5 Neque vero tam remisso ac languido animo quisquam
6 omnium fuit qui ea nocte conquieverit. [tanta] Erat
summa rerum[30] expectatio, ut alius in aliam partem mente
atque animo traheretur: quid ipsis Corfiniensibus, quid
Domitio, quid Lentulo, quid reliquis accideret; qui quosque eventus exciperent.

22. Quarta vigilia circiter Lentulus Spinther de muro
cum vigiliis custodibusque nostris colloquitur: velle, si sibi
2 fiat potestas, Caesarem convenire. Facta potestate ex oppido mittitur. Neque ab eo prius Domitiani milites disce-

---

[30] tanta . . . rerum] *The text is uncertain here. Apitz excised*
tanta.

guard. They sent representatives from their number to Caesar saying that they were ready to open the gates and do Caesar's bidding, and that they would deliver Domitius alive into his power.

21. When this came to his attention Caesar reasoned as follows. He judged it to be crucially important to take possession of the town as soon as possible and transfer the cohorts into his own camp, since he was worried that they might have a change of heart owing to bribes or encouragement or misinformation, seeing that in warfare small causes often produce great effects. But he was also afraid 2 that his soldiers, entering the town under nighttime's lax discipline, would pillage Corfinium. So he praised the men who had come and sent them back into the town with orders to keep watch on the gates and walls. He himself 3 posted soldiers on the earthworks he had begun, not at fixed intervals according to his practice on previous days but so that they were in contact with one another in a continuous line of lookouts and pickets all along the fortification. He sent out staff officers and unit commanders, 4 exhorting them not only to beware of sallies but also to keep watch for covert individual departures. No soldier, 5 not even the slackest and laziest, slept that night. Spec- 6 ulation reigned supreme, with some men's thoughts and feelings pulled in one direction, others' in another. What would happen to the people of Corfinium? What to Domitius? To Lentulus? To the rest? What would be the fate of each?

22. Some hours before dawn Lentulus Spinther communicated from the wall with our lookouts and guards: he wanted to meet with Caesar if he could. Permission 2 granted, he was released from Corfinium; Domitius' sol-

3 dunt quam in conspectum Caesaris deducatur. Cum eo
de salute sua ⟨agit⟩,[31] orat atque obsecrat ut sibi parcat
veteremque amicitiam commemorat Caesarisque in se
4 beneficia exponit, quae erant maxima quod per eum in
collegium pontificum venerat, quod provinciam Hispaniam ex praetura habuerat, quod in petitione consulatus
5 erat sublevatus. Cuius orationem Caesar interpellat: se
non malefici causa ex provincia egressum sed uti se a
contumeliis inimicorum defenderet, ut tribunos plebis in
ea re[32] ex civitate expulsos in suam dignitatem restitueret,
ut se et populum Romanum factione paucorum oppres-
6 sum in libertatem vindicaret. Cuius oratione confirmatus
Lentulus ut in oppidum reverti liceat petit: quod de sua
salute impetraverit fore etiam reliquis ad suam spem sola-
tio; adeo esse perterritos nonnullos ut suae vitae durius
consulere cogantur. Facta potestate discedit.

23. Caesar ubi luxit omnes senatores senatorumque
liberos, tribunos militum equitesque Romanos ad se pro-
2 duci iubet. Erant [quinquaginta] ⟨senatorii⟩[33] ordinis L.
Domitius, P. Lentulus Spinther, L. Caecilius [Spinther]
Rufus, Sex. Quintilius Varus quaestor, L. Rubrius, praeterea filius Domiti aliique complures adulescentes et

---

31 ⟨agit⟩ *Bentley*   32 in ea re] iniuria *Faerno*
33 [quinquaginta] ⟨senatorii⟩ *ed. pr.*: V ⟨s-⟩ *Davies*

---

38 Caesar presided over the pontifical board from his election
as pontifex maximus in 63 until his death; when Lentulus became
a member is unknown. Lentulus governed Further Spain in 59.
His bid for the consulship of 57 was successful.

39 For "in connection with this business," Faerno proposed
"wrongfully."

diers did not leave his side until he was escorted into
Caesar's presence. He discussed his own welfare with him, 3
begged and pleaded that Caesar spare him. He reminded
Caesar about their long-standing friendship and listed the
favors Caesar had done him, which were substantial. (Cae- 4
sar was responsible for Lentulus' membership in the pontifical board, for his governorship in Spain after his praetorship, and for the assistance he received in his bid for
the consulship.[38]) Caesar interrupted him midspeech. "I 5
did not leave my province with harmful intent but to defend myself from the insults of my enemies, to restore
the tribunes—who have been expelled from Rome in connection with this business[39]—to their proper dignity, and
to liberate myself and the Roman people from oppression
by a small faction." Encouraged by his words Lentulus 6
requested permission to return to Corfinium. "The fact
that I have your consent for my preservation will com-
fort others, too, as they look ahead. Some people are
so thoroughly alarmed as to feel under compulsion to
make rather harsh plans for their own lives."[40] Permission
granted, he departed.

23. When the sun came up, Caesar ordered all senators, sons of senators, staff officers, and men of equestrian rank to be brought before him. From the senatorial 2
order there were these: Lucius Domitius, Publius Lentulus Spinther, Lucius Caecilius Rufus, the quaestor Sextus
Quintilius Varus, and Lucius Rubrius. In addition, Domitius' son and several other young men and a large number

[40] For example, Plutarch reports that Domitius attempted
suicide (*Caes.* 34.6–8).

35

magnus numerus equitum Romanorum et decurionum,
3 quos ex municipiis Domitius evocaverat. Hos omnes productos a contumeliis militum conviciisque prohibet. Pauca
apud eos loquitur quod sibi a parte eorum gratia relata non
sit pro suis in eos maximis beneficiis. Dimittit omnes inco-
4 lumes. Sestertium LX,'quod advexerat Domitius atque in
publico deposuerat, allatum ad se ab IIIIviris Corfiniensibus Domitio reddit ne continentior in vita hominum
quam in pecunia fuisse videatur. Etsi eam pecuniam publicam esse constabat datamque a Pompeio in stipendium.
5 Milites Domitianos sacramentum apud se dicere iubet
atque eo die castra movet iustumque iter conficit, VII
omnino dies ad Corfinium commoratus. Et per fines Mar-
rucinorum Frentanorum Larinatium in Apuliam pervenit.
    24. Pompeius iis rebus cognitis quae erant ad Corfi-
nium gestae Luceria proficiscitur Canusium atque inde
2 Brundisium. Copias undique omnes ex novis dilectibus ad
se cogi iubet. Servos pastores armat atque iis equos attri-
3 buit. Ex his circiter CCC equites conficit. L. Manlius praetor Alba[34] cum cohortibus VI profugit, Rutilius Lupus
praetor Tarracina cum tribus. Procul equitatum Caesaris
conspicatae, cui praeerat Vibius Curius, relicto praetore
signa ad Curium transferunt atque ad eum transeunt.
4 Item reliquis itineribus nonnullae cohortes in agmen Caesaris, aliae in equites incidunt. Reducitur ad eum depren-

[34] alba S: -am MUTV

---

[41] Roughly equivalent to a year's pay for one legion.

of men of equestrian rank and council members whom Domitius had summoned from the towns. When they 3 stood before him he protected them from insults and derision by his soldiers. He spoke briefly about the failure of some of them to show gratitude for the great favors he had conferred, then dismissed all of them unharmed. As for 4 the six million sesterces that Domitius had brought to Corfinium and deposited in the public treasury, although they were delivered to Caesar by the town's magistrates, he returned them to Domitius so that he would not be thought to have shown less self-control with respect to money than with respect to human lives.[41] And yet everyone knew that that this was public money and had been given by Pompey for paying the troops. He ordered Domitius' soldiers to 5 swear fidelity to himself. That same day he struck camp and traveled a full day's march. Altogether he had spent seven days at Corfinium. Traveling through the territory of the Marrucini, the Frentani, and the Larinates he came to Apulia.

24. After learning what had happened at Corfinium, Pompey set out from Luceria for Canusium and from there for Brundisium. He ordered all of the troops from 2 the recent recruiting, wherever they were, to be concentrated near him. He armed the slave herdsmen and gave them horses, creating thereby about three hundred cavalrymen. The praetor Lucius Manlius fled from Alba with 3 six cohorts, the praetor Rutilius Lupus from Tarracina with three; after a distant glimpse of Caesar's cavalry with Vibius Curius in command these cohorts abandoned their praetor, transferred their standards to Curius, and went over to him. The same thing happened on subsequent 4 marches: some cohorts fell in with Caesar's column, others

sus ex itinere N. Magius Cremona, praefectus fabrum Cn.
5 Pompei. Quem Caesar ad eum remittit cum mandatis:
quoniam ad id tempus facultas colloquendi non fuerit atque ipse Brundisium sit venturus interesse rei publicae et
communis salutis se cum Pompeio colloqui; neque vero
idem profici longo itineris spatio cum per alios conditiones
ferantur ac si coram de omnibus conditionibus discepte-
tur.

25. His datis mandatis Brundisium cum legionibus VI
pervenit, veteranis tribus, at reliquis quas ex novo dilectu
confecerat atque in itinere compleverat. Domitianas enim
2 cohortes protinus a Corfinio in Siciliam miserat. Repperit
consules Dyrrachium profectos cum magna parte exercitus, Pompeium remanere Brundisi cum cohortibus XX.
3 Neque certum inveniri poterat obtinendine Brundisi
causa ibi remansisset quo facilius omne Hadriaticum mare
<cum> extremis[35] Italiae partibus regionibusque Graeciae
in potestate haberet atque ex utraque parte bellum admi-
4 nistrare posset, an inopia navium ibi restitisset. Veritusque
ne ille Italiam dimittendam non[36] existimaret exitus
administrationesque Brundisini portus impedire instituit.
5 Quorum operum haec erat ratio. Qua fauces erant
angustissimae portus, moles atque aggerem ab utraque
parte litoris iaciebat quod iis locis erat vadosum mare.

---

35 <cum> extremis *Morus*: extremis *MUTV*: ex ultimis *S*
36 non] [non] *Paul*

---

42 For "along with the coastline," editors often adopt the reading of S, "from the furthest parts."

43 See 1.27.2 for more uncertainty about Pompey's plans. It is

with his cavalry. Numerius Magius of Cremona, Pompey's chief engineer, was captured on the road and brought to him. Caesar sent Magius back to Pompey with a message: 5 "Since hitherto there has not been an opportunity for direct talks and I myself am about to arrive in Brundisium, it is in the interest of the republic and the general welfare that I speak with you directly. When negotiating points are carried by intermediaries, and there is a long interval for traveling, the results are not as good as if the whole negotiation takes place in face-to-face debate."

25. After sending off this message he reached Brundisium with six legions. Three were veteran legions but the rest he had created from fresh recruits and brought up to strength along the way, for he had sent Domitius' cohorts directly from Corfinium to Sicily. He found that the 2 consuls had left for Dyrrachium with a large part of the army, but that Pompey was still in Brundisium with twenty cohorts. It could not be determined whether Pom- 3 pey had remained there in order to hold Brundisium, hoping thereby to retain control of the entire Adriatic along with the coastline[42] of Italy and territory in Greece and be able to wage war from both directions, or whether he had stayed because of a shortage of ships. Caesar worried 4 that Pompey would not think that Italy had to be abandoned, so he began to block his escape from and use of the harbor.[43]

The plan of Caesar's works was as follows. Where the 5 harbor entrance was narrowest he extended jetties of stone and fill from the shore on both sides, since the water was

unclear whether Caesar wanted to trap Pompey in Italy (Cic. *Att.* 9.13.1) or force him out of it (Cic. *Att.* 9.14.1).

6 Longius progressus cum agger altiore aqua contineri non
posset rates duplices quoquo versus pedum XXX[37] e re-
7 gione molis collocabat. Has quaternis ancoris ex IIII angu-
8 lis destinabat ne fluctibus moverentur. His perfectis collo-
catisque alias deinceps pari magnitudine rates iungebat.
9 Has terra atque aggere integebat <ne> aditus atque incursus ad defendendum impediretur, a fronte atque ab utro-
10 que latere cratibus ac pluteis protegebat. In quarta quaque
earum turres binorum tabulatorum excitabat quo commo-
dius ab impetu navium incendiisque defenderet.

26. Contra haec Pompeius naves magnas onerarias
quas in portu Brundisino deprehenderat adornabat. Ibi
turres cum ternis tabulatis erigebat easque multis tormentis et omni genere telorum completas ad opera Caesaris
appellebat ut rates perrumperet atque opera disturbaret.
Sic cotidie utrimque eminus fundis sagittis reliquisque
telis pugnabatur.

2 Atque haec Caesar ita administrabat ut conditiones
pacis dimittendas non existimaret. Ac tametsi magnopere
admirabatur Magium, quem ad Pompeium cum mandatis
miserat, ad se non remitti atque ea res saepe temptata etsi
impetus eius consiliaque tardabat tamen omnibus rebus in
3 eo perseverandum putabat. Itaque Caninium Rebilum
legatum, familiarem <et>[38] necessarium Scriboni Libonis,

[37] XXX] LXXX *or* XXXX *von Göler*   [38] <et> *Damon*

---

[44] For Magius as an intermediary between Caesar and Pompey, see 1.24.4. According to a letter by Caesar preserved in Cicero's correspondence, Pompey did in fact send Magius back with
terms around the time of Caesar's arrival at Brundisium (*Att.*
9.13A). Caesar replied "as he saw fit," perhaps through Magius.

shallow there. Further out, where the deeper water pre-   6
vented the fill from holding together, he placed double
pontoons thirty feet square near each jetty. These he fixed   7
in place with anchors from the four corners so they would
not shift in the waves. When the pontoons were finished   8
and in position he joined to them others of the same size,
one by one. He covered them with earth and fill so that   9
there would be no impediment to those running out onto
them for defense, and protected them from the front and
both sides with brushwood bundles and screens. On every   10
fourth pontoon he erected two-story towers to facilitate
their defense against attack by ship and fire.

26. In response Pompey outfitted the large cargo vessels he had seized in the port of Brundisium. He erected
three-story towers on each, and after filling these with
a multitude of catapults and all sorts of projectiles he
brought them to bear on Caesar's works, aiming to break
up the pontoons and disrupt his efforts. The fighting went
on thus for days with a long-distance exchange of sling-
shot, arrows, and other projectiles.

Caesar for his part conducted these operations still   2
thinking that peace negotiations should not be abandoned.
Although he was very surprised that Magius, whom he had
sent to Pompey with a message, was not sent back to him,
and although the repeated attempts at negotiation delayed
his progress and plans, nevertheless he felt that he ought
to persevere at it by every means possible.[44] Therefore he   3
sent his officer Caninius Rebilus, a close friend of Scribo-

His assertion about Pompey here is either false (if it refers to
Magius' first mission) or inadequately contextualized (if it refers
to a second mission).

mittit ad eum colloqui causa. Mandat ut Libonem de concilianda pace hortetur. In primis ut ipse cum Pompeio
4 colloqueretur postulat. Magnopere sese confidere demonstrat si eius rei sit potestas facta fore ut aequis conditionibus ab armis discedatur; cuius rei magnam partem laudis
atque existimationis ad Libonem perventuram si illo auc-
5 tore atque agente ab armis sit discessum. Libo a colloquio
Canini digressus ad Pompeium proficiscitur. Paulo post
renuntiat: quod consules absint sine illis non posse agi de
6 compositione. Ita saepius rem frustra temptatam Caesar
aliquando dimittendam sibi iudicat et de bello agendum.

27. Prope dimidia parte operis a Caesare effecta di-
ebusque in ea re consumptis VIIII, naves a consulibus
Dyrrachio remissae, quae priorem partem exercitus eo
2 deportaverant, Brundisium revertuntur. Pompeius sive
operibus Caesaris permotus sive etiam quod ab initio Italia excedere constituerat adventu navium profectionem
3 parare incipit. Et quo facilius impetum Caesaris tardaret,
ne sub ipsa profectione milites oppidum irrumperent portas obstruit vicos plateasque inaedificat ac fossas transversas viis praeducit atque ibi sudes stipitesque praeacutos
4 defigit. Haec levibus cratibus terraque inaequat. Aditus
autem atque itinera duo quae extra murum ad portum
ferebant maximis defixis trabibus atque iis praeacutis
5 praesaepit. His paratis rebus milites silentio naves con-

nius Libo's, to Libo for talks. Rebilus' task was to encourage Libo to mediate a peaceful settlement. Caesar's particular request was that he himself speak directly with
Pompey. He put it this way: "I am quite confident that if 4
there is an opportunity for direct talks equitable terms will
make it possible to stop fighting. And a large part of the
credit and renown for this will attach to Libo if it is with
his initiative and effort that the fighting stops." Libo left 5
his meeting with Caninius and went to Pompey. Shortly
thereafter he reported that without the consuls—since
they were absent—it was impossible to discuss a settlement. So Caesar decided that the objective attempted so 6
often in vain finally had to be abandoned and that he had
a war to fight.

27. Nearly half of Caesar's barrier was complete, and
nine days had been spent on it, when Pompey's ships were
sent back from Dyrrachium by the consuls. These had
transported the first part of the army and now returned to
Brundisium. Pompey, either prompted by Caesar's works 2
or because he had decided from the outset to leave Italy,
began preparing his departure after the ships' arrival. The 3
better to slow down Caesar's attack, in case his troops tried
to break into Brundisium at the very moment of his own
departure, Pompey blocked the gates, constructed obsta-
cles in streets and squares, and dug trenches across the
main roads; in the trenches he planted stakes and tree
trunks sharpened to a point, using lightweight brush and 4
a layer of dirt to make a level surface. As for the approach
routes and the two roads outside the walls that led to the
port, he barricaded them with a plantation of huge beams
likewise sharpened to point. After these preparations he 5
ordered his soldiers to embark in silence. Here and there

scendere iubet. Expeditos autem ex evocatis sagittariis
6   funditoribusque raros in muro turribusque disponit. Hos
certo signo revocare constituit cum omnes milites naves
conscendissent. Atque iis expedito loco actuaria navigia
relinquit.

28. Brundisini Pompeianorum militum iniuriis atque
ipsius Pompei contumeliis permoti Caesaris rebus fave-
2   bant. Itaque cognita Pompei profectione concursantibus
illis atque in ea re occupatis vulgo ex tectis significabant.
Per quos re cognita Caesar scalas parari militesque armari
3   iubet ne quam rei gerendae facultatem dimittat. Pompeius sub noctem naves solvit. Qui erant in muro custodiae causa collocati eo signo quod convenerat revocantur
4   notisque itineribus ad naves decurrunt. Milites positis
scalis muros ascendunt. Sed moniti a Brundisinis ut vallum caecum fossasque caveant subsistunt et longo itinere
ab his circumducti ad portum perveniunt duasque naves
cum militibus, quae ad moles Caesaris adhaeserant, scaphis lintribusque reprehendunt. Reprehensas excipiunt.

29. Caesar etsi ad spem conficiendi negoti maxime pro-
babat coactis navibus mare transire et Pompeium sequi
priusquam ille sese transmarinis auxiliis confirmaret, tamen eius rei moram temporisque longinquitatem timebat
quod omnibus coactis navibus Pompeius praesentem fa-
2   cultatem insequendi sui ademerat. Relinquebatur ut ex
longinquioribus regionibus Galliae Picenique et a freto

on the wall and towers he placed light-armed troops from
among his reenlisted men, archers, and slingers. He ar-   6
ranged to summon them with a set signal when the soldiers had all embarked, and left them some fast boats in
an accessible spot.

28. The people of Brundisium, provoked by injuries
suffered at the hands of Pompey's soldiers and insults from
Pompey himself, favored Caesar's side. Therefore when   2
they recognized that Pompey was leaving—his men were
rushing about busy with the departure—they signaled the
fact from every rooftop. Thanks to them, Caesar recognized what was happening. He ordered ladders to be made
ready and soldiers to be armed, aiming not to let any opportunity for action slip. Pompey set sail just before night-   3
fall. The men he had placed on guard duty on the wall,
summoned by the prearranged signal, ran along familiar paths to the boats. Caesar's soldiers raised their lad-   4
ders and climbed the walls. Warned by the Brundisians to
avoid the camouflaged barrier and trenches, they made
an abrupt halt; they reached the port by following the
Brundisians on a long circuitous route. Two ships full of
soldiers had run aground on Caesar's jetties, and they captured these using small craft and rowboats. They took possession of the captured vessels.

29. Caesar's best plan, in the hope of bringing matters
to a conclusion, was to collect ships and cross the Adriatic
on Pompey's heels before Pompey could strengthen himself with overseas auxiliaries. Nevertheless he was afraid
of the delay this would involve and the time cost, since
Pompey had removed the immediate possibility of pursuit
by collecting all the ships himself. This left Caesar having   2
to wait for ships from more distant areas, from Gaul and

naves essent expectandae. Id propter anni tempus longum
3 atque impeditum videbatur. Interea veterem exercitum
duas Hispanias confirmari, quarum erat altera maximis
beneficiis Pompei devincta, auxilia equitatum parari, Galliam Italiamque temptari se absente nolebat.

30. Itaque in praesentia Pompei sequendi rationem
omittit, in Hispaniam proficisci constituit, duumviris municipiorum omnium imperat ut naves conquirant Brundi-
2 siumque deducendas curent. Mittit in Sardiniam cum legione una Valerium legatum, in Siciliam Curionem pro
praetore cum legionibus tribus. Eundem, cum Siciliam
recepisset, protinus in Africam traducere exercitum iubet.

Sardiniam obtinebat M. Cotta, Siciliam M. Cato. Afri-
3 cam sorte Tubero obtinere debebat. Caralitani simul ad se
Valerium mitti audierunt, nondum profecto ex Italia sua
sponte Cottam ex oppido eiciunt. Ille perterritus quod
omnem provinciam consentire intellegebat ex Sardinia in
4 Africam profugit. Cato in Sicilia naves longas veteres refi-
ciebat, novas civitatibus imperabat. Haec magno studio
agebat. In Lucanis Bruttiisque per legatos suos civium
Romanorum dilectus habebat, equitum peditumque cer-
5 tum numerum a civitatibus Siciliae exigebat. Quibus rebus
paene perfectis adventu Curionis cognito queritur in
contione sese proiectum ac proditum a Cn. Pompeio, qui
omnibus rebus imparatissimis non necessarium bellum

---

45 For the situation in Spain, see 1.38–39.
46 The number here conflicts with that given at 2.23.1.

Picenum and the Sicilian strait. Given the time of year, this seemed likely to be a long and difficult matter, and he did 3 not want his absence to allow Pompey's veteran army and the two Spanish provinces to take heart in the meantime (one of the two provinces was obligated to Pompey by some very generous favors), or auxiliary troops and cavalry to be acquired, or Gaul and Italy to be disturbed.[45]

30. For the moment, therefore, he dropped the plan of following Pompey, decided to set out for Spain, and ordered magistrates in every town to find ships and see that they were conveyed to Brundisium. To Sardinia he sent 2 his officer Valerius with a single legion, to Sicily Curio as propraetor with three.[46] Curio's orders, after he regained control of Sicily, were to transport his army immediately to Africa.

Sardinia was held by Marcus Cotta, Sicily by Marcus Cato; Africa was supposed to be in Tubero's hands, according to the provincial allotment. As soon as the people 3 of Caralis heard that Valerius was being sent to them, and before he had even set out from Italy, of their own accord they ejected Cotta from the town. Terrified because he knew the whole province felt this way, Cotta fled from Sardinia to Africa. Cato was repairing old warships 4 in Sicily and requisitioning new ones from the province's cities; he went about these things with great determination. In Lucania and Bruttium he recruited Roman citizens through representatives, from Sicily's cities he demanded a fixed number of infantry and cavalry. These 5 measures were nearly complete when he learned of Curio's approach. At a public meeting he spoke with great bitterness: "I have been forsaken and betrayed by Pompey, who undertook an unnecessary war without any prepara-

suscepisset et ab se reliquisque in senatu interrogatus omnia sibi esse ad bellum apta ac parata confirmavisset. Haec in contione questus ex provincia fugit.

31. Nacti vacuas ab imperiis Sardiniam Valerius, Curio
2 Siciliam, cum exercitibus eo perveniunt. Tubero cum in Africam venisset invenit in provincia cum imperio Attium Varum, qui ad Auximum, ut supra demonstravimus, amissis cohortibus protinus ex fuga in Africam pervenerat atque eam sua sponte vacuam occupaverat dilectuque habito duas legiones effecerat, hominum et locorum notitia et usu eius provinciae nactus aditus ad ea conanda quod paucis ante annis ex praetura eam provinciam obtinuerat.
3 Hic venientem Vticam navibus Tuberonem portu atque oppido prohibet neque adfectum valetudine filium exponere in terra patitur sed sublatis ancoris excedere eo loco cogit.

32. His rebus confectis Caesar ut reliquum tempus a labore intermitteretur milites in proxima municipia deducit.
2 Ipse ad urbem proficiscitur. Coacto senatu iniurias inimicorum commemorat. Docet se nullum extraordinarium honorem appetisse sed expectato legitimo tempore consulatus eo fuisse contentum quod omnibus civibus
3 pateret; latum ab X tribunis plebis—contradicentibus inimicis, Catone vero acerrime repugnante et pristina con-

---

47 See Pompey's brief assertion at 1.6.1.

48 See 1.13.

49 Cicero, who reports the presence of legions at Tarentum and Sipontum, thought their locations betrayed rather Caesar's intention of blocking the exits from Italy (*Att.* 9.15.1).

50 On April 1, 49 (D.C. 41.15.2).

tions at all. Yet when I and others questioned him in the senate, he assured us that he had everything fit and ready for war."[47] After his bitter words at the meeting, he left the province in flight.

31. Valerius and Curio found Sardinia and Sicily vacant of military control when they arrived there with their armies. When Tubero got to Africa he discovered Attius 2 Varus exercising command in the province. (After losing his cohorts at Auximum, as I indicated above, Varus fled and went directly to Africa.[48]) He had seized the vacant province on his own initiative and recruited troops for two new legions. His knowledge of people and places and his past experience of the province created openings for these attempts, since a few years earlier, after his praetorship, he been the provincial governor. When Tubero arrived at 3 Utica with his ships, Varus barred him from the harbor and the town. He did not even permit Tubero to put his ailing son ashore, but forced him to weigh anchor and leave the area.

32. After finishing this business Caesar withdrew his men to towns in the immediate vicinity to give them a temporary break from exertion.[49] He himself set out for Rome. At a meeting of the senate[50] he recounted the in- 2 juries done by his enemies, explaining that his candidacy for office had not been anomalous; rather, he had waited until the legal time for a consulship, content with what was open to any citizen.[51] "A law proposed by the ten tribunes 3 — in the face of my enemies' opposition and Cato resisting with the utmost vehemence and using his old filibuster

[51] The legal interval between consulships was ten years, but an exception was made for Pompey (*cos.* 70, 55, 52).

suetudine dicendi mora dies extrahente—ut sui ratio absentis haberetur ipso consule Pompeio; qui si improbasset
cur ferri passus esset? si probasset cur se uti populi bene-
4 ficio prohibuisset? Patientiam proponit suam cum de exercitibus dimittendis ultro postulavisset, in quo iacturam
5 dignitatis atque honoris ipse facturus esset. Acerbitatem
inimicorum docet, qui quod ab altero postularent in se
recusarent atque omnia permisceri mallent quam impe-
6 rium exercitusque dimittere. Iniuriam in eripiendis legionibus praedicat, crudelitatem et insolentiam in circum-
scribendis tribunis plebis. Conditiones a se latas, expetita
7 colloquia et denegata commemorat. Pro quibus rebus
hortatur ac postulat ut rem publicam suscipiant atque una
secum administrent; sin timore defugiant illis se oneri non
8 futurum et per se rem publicam administraturum; legatos
ad Pompeium de compositione mitti oportere; neque se
reformidare quod in senatu Pompeius paulo ante dixisset:
ad quos legati mitterentur his auctoritatem attribui timo-
9 remque eorum qui mitterent significari; tenuis atque infirmi haec animi videri; se vero ut opibus[39] anteire studue-
rit sic iustitia et aequitate velle superare.

33. Probat rem senatus de mittendis legatis. Sed qui

---

[39] opibus] operibus V^{ac}

---

52 Ordinarily, candidates were required to declare their candidacy in Rome. Caesar and Cato had clashed over this requirement a decade earlier, when a filibuster by Cato forced Caesar to
forego a possible triumph in order to declare his candidacy for
the consulship of 59 (Plut. *Caes*. 13.1–2; App. *BC* 2.30). Caesar's
subsequent exemption from the requirement was passed during
Pompey's consulship in 52 (D.C. 40.51.2).

tactic to drag the time out with delay — ruled that my candidacy in absentia should be considered valid.[52] Pompey himself was consul at the time. If he disapproved, why did he allow it to be proposed? If he approved, why has he prevented me from using a favor granted by the Roman people?" Caesar brought up his own forbearance in initiating a request that both armies be dismissed, a matter in which he stood to lose dignity and prestige, and showed the harshness of his enemies, who were refusing to do what they asked him to do and preferred utter confusion to giving up power and armies. He emphasized the injury they did in depriving him of his legions, and their brutality and highhandedness in obstructing the tribunes. He recounted the terms he had proposed, the negotiations requested and refused. For all these reasons he exhorted the senators and asked them to take charge of the state and administer it with him. "But if fear makes you shirk the task, I will not be a burden to you but will administer the state myself."[53] He said that representatives ought to be sent to Pompey for a settlement, that he did not feel the anxiety expressed by Pompey in the senate a short while before, namely, that sending representatives increased the authority of those to whom they were sent and showed the fear of those who sent them. "This bears the stamp of a petty and feeble character. As for me, just as I have worked to get ahead in resources,[54] so I desire to outdo others in justice and equity."

33. The senate approved the sending of representa-

[53] Pompey had done so as sole consul for much of 52.

[54] For "in resources," editors often print "in achievements."

mitterentur non reperiebantur, maximeque timoris causa
2 pro se quisque id munus legationis recusabat. Pompeius
enim discedens ab urbe in senatu dixerat: eodem se habiturum loco qui Romae remansissent et qui in castris Cae-
3 saris fuissent. Sic triduum disputationibus excusationibus-
que extrahitur. Subicitur etiam L. Metellus tribunus plebis
ab inimicis Caesaris qui hanc rem distrahat reliquasque
4 res quascumque agere instituerit impediat. Cuius cognito
consilio Caesar frustra diebus aliquot consumptis, ne reliquum tempus dimittat infectis iis quae agere destina-
verat ab urbe proficiscitur atque in ulteriorem Galliam
pervenit.

34. Quo cum venisset cognoscit: missum ‹in Hispaniam› a Pompeio Vibullium Rufum, quem paucis ante
2 diebus Corfinio captum ipse dimiserat; profectum item
Domitium ad occupandam Massiliam navibus actuariis
VII, quas Igili et in Cosano a privatis coactas servis libertis
3 colonis suis compleverat; praemissos etiam legatos Massilienses domum, nobiles adulescentes, quos ab urbe discedens Pompeius erat adhortatus ne nova Caesaris officia
veterum suorum beneficiorum in eos memoriam expel-
4 lerent. Quibus mandatis acceptis Massilienses portas Caesari clauserant, Albicos, barbaros homines qui in eorum
fide antiquitus erant montesque supra Massiliam incole-
5 bant, ad se vocaverant, frumentum ex finitimis regionibus
atque [in] omnibus castellis in urbem convexerant, armorum officinas in urbe instituerant, muros portas classem
reficiebant.

---

55 That is, in the transalpine province of Gaul, roughly modern France. Italy north of the Po was also called Gaul from the
Gallic tribes that had settled in that fertile area centuries earlier.

tives. But no one could be found to send; it was mostly out of fear that everyone turned down their appointments as representative. (As Pompey was leaving Rome he had 2 said in the senate that he would treat those who stayed in Rome like those who were in Caesar's camp.) So three 3 days dragged out in arguments and excuses. Plus, Lucius Metellus, a plebeian tribune, was deputized by Caesar's enemies to sidetrack this business and obstruct anything else Caesar set in motion. When he recognized Metellus' 4 intent, and a few days had been spent to no purpose, to avoid wasting the rest of his time there Caesar left Rome without having accomplished what he had intended and went to Further Gaul.[55]

34. Upon arrival there he learned that Vibullius Rufus had been sent by Pompey to Spain; Caesar had taken him captive and dismissed him from Corfinium a few days earlier. Also that Domitius had set out to seize Marseilles with 2 seven fast ships requisitioned from private owners at Igilium and near Cosa and manned with his own slaves, freedmen, and tenants. And that Marseilles' representatives, 3 men of distinction, had been sent home ahead of him; Pompey at his departure from Rome had urged them not to let Caesar's recent services drive out the memory of the benefits he had conferred on them in the past. Upon re- 4 ceiving this message the people of Marseilles had closed the gates to Caesar and summoned the Albici to their side. (These natives had long been under their protection; they inhabited the hills above the city.) They had also brought 5 into the city provisions from nearby districts and all their strongholds, and established weapon-making workshops there. Repairs to the walls, gates, and fleet were in progress.

35. Evocat ad se Caesar Massilia XV primos. Cum iis
agit: ne initium inferendi belli ab Massiliensibus oriatur;
debere eos Italiae totius auctoritatem sequi potius quam
2 unius hominis voluntati obtemperare. Reliqua quae ad
eorum sanandas mentes pertinere arbitrabatur comme-
3 morat. Cuius orationem legati domum referunt atque ex
auctoritate haec[40] Caesari renuntiant: intellegere se divi-
sum esse populum ⟨Romanum⟩ in partes duas; neque sui
iudici neque suarum esse virium discernere utra pars ius-
4 tiorem habeat causam; principes vero esse earum partium
Cn. Pompeium et C. Caesarem, patronos civitatis, quorum alter agros Volcarum Arecomicorum et Helviorum
publice his concesserit, alter bello victas †gallias† attri-
5 buerit[41] vectigaliaque auxerit; quare paribus eorum beneficiis parem se quoque voluntatem tribuere debere et
neutrum eorum contra alterum iuvare aut urbe aut portibus recipere.

36. Haec dum inter eos aguntur Domitius navibus
Massiliam pervenit atque ab his receptus urbi praeficitur.
2 Summa ei belli administrandi permittitur. Eius imperio
classem quoquo versus dimittunt. Onerarias naves quas
ubique possunt deprehendunt atque in portum deducunt.
Parum clavis aut materia atque armamentis instructis ad

[40] haec] DC *Chacon*
[41] victas gallias attribuerit *MUS*: victas galliae a- *TV*: victos
Sallyas a- *Glandorp*: victa Gallia alia tribuerit *Paul*

[56] For "this official response," Chacon proposed "the response
of the six hundred (*sc.* town councilors)." The name "the six hundred" is known from other sources (V. Max 2.6.7; Str. 4.1.5).

35. Caesar summoned from Marseilles "The Fifteen," the city's leaders, and met with them. "The first move in the war should not come from the people of Marseilles. You ought to follow the authority of the whole of Italy, not comply with the wishes of a single man." He mentioned 2 everything else that he thought would bring them to their senses. The delegation took his words home and gave him 3 this official response:[56] "We understand that the Roman people is split in two. It is not within our discretion or strength to decide which side has the juster cause. But 4 the leaders of the two parties, Gnaeus Pompey and Gaius Caesar, are patrons of Marseilles: one of them granted Marseilles public ownership of the territory of the Volcae Arecomici and the Helvii, the other allocated some of[57] his military conquests and increased the city's revenue. We 5 are obliged, therefore, to accord equal goodwill to equivalent benefits. We must not help either man against the other or admit him into our city or harbors."

36. During these negotiations Domitius reached Marseilles with his ships. He was admitted by the inhabitants and put in charge of the city; the whole control of the war was placed in his hands. On his order they sent their fleet 2 in every direction. They seized merchant ships wherever they could and brought them to the port; ships with too little in the way of hardware or timber and tackle they used

[57] The uncertainty of the text here deprives us of the details underlying "some" and prevents us from saying which benefaction came from which patron. For "awarded some of his military conquests," the emendations of Glandorp and of Paul substitute "assigned the defeated Sallyes" and "awarded other benefits after the conquest of Gaul," respectively.

3 reliquas armandas reficiendasque utuntur. Frumenti quod inventum est in publicum conferunt. Reliquas merces commeatusque ad obsidionem urbis, ‹si› accidat,[42] reservant.

4 Quibus iniuriis permotus Caesar legiones tres Massiliam adducit. Turres vineasque ad oppugnationem urbis agere, naves longas Arelate numero XII facere instituit.

5 Quibus effectis armatisque diebus XXX a qua die materia caesa est adductisque Massiliam, iis D. Brutum praeficit. C. Trebonium legatum ad oppugnationem Massiliae relinquit.

37. Dum haec parat atque administrat C. Fabium legatum cum legionibus tribus quas Narbone circumque ea loca hiemandi causa disposuerat in Hispaniam praemittit. Celeriterque saltus Pyrenaeos occupari iubet, qui eo tem-

2 pore ab L. Afranio legato praesidiis tenebantur. Reliquas

3 legiones, quae longius hiemabant, subsequi iubet. Fabius, ut erat imperatum, adhibita celeritate praesidium ex saltu deiecit magnisque itineribus ad exercitum Afrani contendit.

38. Adventu L.Vibulli Rufi, quem a Pompeio missum in Hispaniam demonstratum est, Afranius et Petreius et Varro, legati Pompei, quorum unus Hispaniam citeriorem ‹tribus legionibus, alter ulteriorem› a saltu Castulonensi ad Anam duabus legionibus, tertius ab Ana Vettonum

---

[42] si accidat S: accidant *MUTV*. *The text is uncertain here.*

---

[58] For Fabius' original winter quarters assignment further north, see Hirt. 8.54.5. At Narbo he was better placed to block the route of Pompey's Spanish legions to Italy and, of course, to attack them in Spain.

to equip and repair the rest. Any provisions they found 3
were added to the public supply. They stockpiled other
goods and supplies for a siege, in case one occurred.

At the prompting of these provocations Caesar led 4
three legions to Marseilles. He began to move up siege
towers and screens for an attack on the city, and to build
warships at Arles, a total of twelve. These were finished 5
and equipped within thirty days from when the trees were
cut down, then brought to Marseilles. He put Decimus
Brutus in charge of the ships and left his officer Gaius
Trebonius for the assault on Marseilles.

37. While making these preparations and arrangements he sent his officer Gaius Fabius ahead to Spain with
the three legions he had stationed for the winter at Narbo
and nearby.[58] He ordered the immediate occupation of the
Pyrenees passes, which at that time were garrisoned by
Pompey's officer Lucius Afranius. Caesar ordered the rest 2
of the legions, whose winter quarters were further away,
to follow. Fabius, as ordered, acted swiftly to dislodge the 3
garrison from the pass[59] and hastened toward Afranius'
army by forced marches.

38. After the arrival of Lucius Vibullius Rufus, whose
mission from Pompey to Spain has been mentioned,[60]
Pompey's officers Afranius, Petreius, and Varro divided up
the tasks among themselves. (One of them held Nearer
Spain with three legions, another held Further Spain from
the pass at Castulo to the Anas River with two legions, and

[59] The pass that leads most directly to Fabius' immediate destination, Ilerda (1.38.4), is the Col de la Perche.
[60] At 1.34.1.

agrum Lusitaniamque pari numero legionum obtinebat,
2 officia inter se partiuntur, uti Petreius ex Lusitania per
Vettones cum omnibus copiis ad Afranium proficiscatur,
Varro cum iis quas habebat legionibus omnem ulteriorem
3 Hispaniam tueatur. His rebus constitutis equites auxiliaque toti Lusitaniae a Petreio, Celtiberiae Cantabris barbarisque omnibus qui ad Oceanum pertinent ab Afranio
4 imperantur. Quibus coactis celeriter Petreius per Vettones
ad Afranium pervenit constituuntque communi consilio
bellum ad Ilerdam propter ipsius loci opportunitatem ge-
rere.

39. Erant, ut supra demonstratum est, legiones Afrani
tres Petrei duae, praeterea scutatae citerioris provinciae
et caetratae ulterioris Hispaniae[43] cohortes circiter LXXX[44]
2 equitumque utriusque provinciae circiter V milia. Caesar
legiones in Hispaniam praemiserat [ad] VI [milia],[45] auxilia peditum nulla,[46] equitum tria milia ⟨quae⟩ omnibus
superioribus bellis habuerat et parem ex Gallia numerum
quam ipse pacaverat, nominatim ex omnibus civitatibus
nobilissimo quoque evocato. Huc[47] optimi generis hominum ex Aquitanis montanisque qui Galliam provinciam
3 attingunt ⟨aliquos addidit quod⟩[48] audierat Pompeium

43 [ulterioris Hispaniae] *Madvig* (*see 1.48.7*)

44 LXXX] XXX *Stoffel I.265* (*see 1.83.1*)

45 [ad] VI [milia] *Chacon* (*see 1.42.1–2*). *Fabre substituted* ad
VI milia *for* nulla *after* peditum.

46 nulla] V milia *Nipperdey* (*see Cic.* Att. *9.13.4*): [nulla] *ed.
pr., Fabre*

47 huc ς: huic (*sc.* numero) ω: II milia *Fabre*

48 ⟨aliquos addidit quod⟩ *Damon*

with the same number the third held the territory of the
Vettones starting at the Anas, as well as Lusitania.[61]) Pe- 2
treius was to make his way to Afranius, marching from
Lusitania through the Vettones with all of his forces, Varro
was to guard all of Further Spain with the legions he had.
After these decisions had been made, cavalry and auxiliary 3
troops were requisitioned by Petreius from all of Lusitania, by Afranius from Celtiberia, the Cantabrians, and all
of the natives as far as the Atlantic coast. After these mus- 4
tered, Petreius marched rapidly through the Vettones to
Afranius and they decided to prosecute the war jointly
near Ilerda because of the advantages of that location.

39. As was indicated earlier, there were three legions
belonging to Afranius and two to Petreius, plus about
eighty infantry cohorts (those from Nearer Spain equipped
with large shields, those from Further Spain with small
shields) and about five thousand cavalry from both provinces.[62] Caesar had sent ahead to Spain a force containing 2
six legions, no auxiliary infantry, three thousand cavalry
that had been with him in all previous campaigns, and an
equal number from Gaul, which he had recently pacified—he had summoned by name the most notable men
from every community. To this ⟨he added some⟩ of the
best sort of men from Aquitania and the mountain peoples
who border the province of Gaul, ⟨because⟩ he had heard 3

---

[61] The order of the two lists is different: before the outbreak
of hostilities Petreius held Lusitania, Varro Further Spain.

[62] Textual problems make this chapter's troop numbers somewhat uncertain, but the general picture is borne out by the narrative of the Ilerda campaign: the Pompeians were superior in
infantry, Caesar in cavalry.

per Mauretaniam cum legionibus iter in Hispaniam facere
confestimque esse venturum. Simul a tribunis militum
centurionibusque mutuas pecunias sumpsit. Has exercitui
4   distribuit. Quo facto duas res consecutus est, quod pignore
animos centurionum devinxit et largitione militum volun-
tates redemit.

40. Fabius finitimarum civitatum animos litteris nuntiisque temptabat. In Sicori flumine pontes effecerat duos
distantes inter se milia passuum IIII. His pontibus pabulatum mittebat quod ea quae citra flumen fuerant superi-
2   oribus ⟨diebus⟩ consumpserat. Hoc idem fere atque
eadem de causa Pompeiani exercitus duces faciebant.
Crebroque inter se equestribus proeliis contendebant.
3   Huc cum cotidiana consuetudine egressae pabulatoribus
praesidio propiore ⟨ponte⟩ legiones Fabianae duae flumen transissent impedimentaque[49] et omnis equitatus
sequeretur, subito vi ventorum et aquae magnitudine pons
est interruptus et reliqua multitudo equitum interclusa.
4   Quo cognito a Petreio et Afranio ex aggere atque cratibus
quae flumine ferebantur, celeriter suo ponte Afranius,
quem oppido castrisque coniunctum habebat, legiones
IIII equitatumque omnem traiecit duabusque Fabianis
5   occurrit legionibus. Cuius adventu nuntiato L. Plancus,
qui legionibus praeerat, necessaria re coactus locum capit
superiorem diversamque aciem in duas partes constituit
6   ne ab equitatu circumveniri posset. Ita congressus impari

[49] impedimentaque] iumentaque *Paul*

---

[63] The text is lacunose and the supplement is plausible but not
inevitable.

that Pompey was marching through Mauretania to Spain with his legions and would arrive very soon.[63] Caesar also borrowed money from his staff officers and centurions; this he distributed to his legions. By so doing he gained 4 two results: he secured the centurions' support by means of the loan, and he purchased the soldiers' goodwill by means of the largesse.

40. Fabius began rallying the support of nearby communities with letters and messengers. He had made two bridges over the Sicoris River about four miles apart. He started sending the cavalry across these bridges to graze, since he had consumed everything on his side of the river in the preceding days. The leaders of the Pompeian army 2 were doing practically the same thing for the same reason, and the two sides frequently clashed in cavalry battles. When Fabius' legions had gone out to this area to protect 3 the grazers, as they did every day, crossing the river by the nearer bridge, and the baggage train[64] and the entire cavalry was following them, all of a sudden the bridge broke up owing to a violent windstorm and flood. The mass of cavalry that remained behind was cut off. When Petreius 4 and Afranius understood the situation from the debris and brushwood carried by the current, Afranius quickly sent four legions and the entire cavalry across his own bridge, which was adjacent to Ilerda and his camp, and went to meet Fabius' two legions. At news of his approach Lucius 5 Plancus, who was in command of the legions, seized high ground, as the situation required him to do, and drew up a divided battle line facing two directions so that he could not be surrounded by the cavalry. In this manner, although 6

[64] For "baggage train," Paul proposed "pack animals."

numero magnos impetus legionum equitatusque sustinet.
7 Commisso ab equitibus proelio signa legionum duarum
procul ab utrisque conspiciuntur quas C. Fabius ulteriore
ponte subsidio nostris miserat suspicatus fore—id quod
accidit—ut duces adversariorum occasione et beneficio
8 Fortunae ad nostros opprimendos uterentur. Quarum adventu proelium dirimitur, ac suas uterque legiones reducit
in castra.

41. Eo biduo Caesar cum equitibus DCCCC quos sibi
praesidio reliquerat in castra pervenit. Pons qui fuerat
tempestate interruptus paene erat refectus. Hunc noctu
2 perfici iussit. Ipse cognita locorum natura ponti castrisque
praesidio VI cohortes relinquit atque omnia impedimenta,
et postero die omnibus copiis triplici instructa acie ad Ilerdam proficiscitur et sub castris Afrani consistit[50] et ibi
paulisper sub armis moratus facit aequo loco pugnandi
potestatem. Potestate facta Afranius copias educit et in
3 medio colle sub castris constituit. Caesar ubi cognovit
⟨per⟩ Afranium stare quo minus proelio dimicaretur, ab
infimis radicibus montis intermissis circiter passibus
4 CCCC castra facere constituit. Et ne in opere faciendo
milites repentino hostium incursu exterrerentur atque
opere prohiberentur vallo muniri vetuit, quod eminere et
procul videri necesse erat, sed a fronte castrorum[51] contra
5 hostem pedum XV fossam fieri iussit. Prima et secunda
acies in armis, ut ab initio constituta erat, permanebat.

---

[50] consistit *ed. pr.*: constitit ω
[51] castrorum *Beroaldo*: castra *MUTV*: *omitted by* S

---

[65] Editors often follow S and excise "of the camp."

fighting outnumbered, he withstood heavy attacks by the legions and cavalry. When the cavalry battle was under 7 way both sides saw the standards of two legions in the distance. Gaius Fabius had sent these across the further bridge in support of our men, suspecting the very thing that happened, namely, that the enemy leaders would try to use the occasion and Fortune's gift to crush our men. At their approach the battle broke up and each com- 8 mander led his legions back to camp.

41. Within two days Caesar reached Fabius' camp with nine hundred cavalry that he had reserved as protection for himself. The bridge that had been broken up by the storm was nearly rebuilt; he ordered it to be finished during the night. He himself, when he perceived the nature 2 of the location, left six cohorts and the whole baggage train as protection for the bridge and the camp and set out for Ilerda the following day with all of his forces formed up into three lines. He halted below Afranius' camp and by waiting there briefly under arms created an opportunity for Afranius to fight on level ground. With this opportunity before him Afranius led out his troops and stationed them halfway down the hill below his camp. When Caesar real- 3 ized that Afranius' move meant that no battle would be fought he decided to make camp at an interval of about four hundred paces from the hill's lowest slopes. Worried 4 that a sudden incursion would alarm the soldiers engaged in fortification and keep them from their work, he forbade the construction of a rampart, which would necessarily stand out and be visible from a distance. Instead, he ordered them to make a fifteen-foot trench on the side of the camp facing the enemy.[65] The first and second battle 5 lines remained battle ready in their initial positions; be-

Post hos opus in occulto a tertia acie fiebat. Sic omne prius est perfectum quam intellegeretur ab Afranio castra muniri. Sub vesperum Caesar intra hanc fossam legiones reducit atque ibi sub armis proxima nocte conquiescit.

42. Postero die omnem exercitum intra fossam continet et, quod longius erat agger petendus, in praesentia similem rationem operis instituit singulaque latera castrorum singulis attribuit legionibus munienda fossasque ad eandem magnitudinem perfici iubet. Reliquas legiones in armis expeditas contra hostem constituit. Afranius Petreiusque terrendi causa atque operis impediendi copias suas ad infimas montis radices producunt et proelio lacessunt. Neque idcirco Caesar opus intermittit confisus praesidio legionum trium et munitione fossae. Illi non diu commorati nec longius ab infimo colle progressi copias in castra reducunt. Tertio die Caesar vallo castra communit. Reliquas cohortes, quas in superioribus castris reliquerat, impedimentaque ad se traduci iubet.

43. Erat inter oppidum Ilerdam et proximum collem, ubi castra Petreius atque Afranius habebant, planities circiter passuum CCC. Atque in hoc fere medio spatio tumulus erat paulo editior. Quem si occupavisset Caesar et communivisset, ab oppido et ponte et commeatu omni quem in oppidum contulerant se interclusurum adversarios confidebat. Hoc sperans legiones tres ex castris educit acieque in locis idoneis instructa unius legionis antesignanos procurrere atque eum tumulum occupare iubet.

hind these men, and out of sight, the third line fortified the camp. In this way everything was done before Afranius understood that a camp was being fortified. Towards eve- 6 ning Caesar withdrew his legions behind the trench and rested there under arms that night.

42. On the following day he kept his whole army behind the trench. Because the fill for earthworks could only be procured at a distance, he adopted a similar fortification plan for the present: he assigned each side of the camp to one legion for fortifying and ordered trenches of the same size to be completed. He placed the remaining legions, unencumbered and battle ready, facing the enemy. Afra- 2 nius and Petreius led their troops out to the hill's lowest slopes in order to cause panic and hinder the fortification work, making feinting attacks. But this did not make Cae- sar interrupt his work; the protection of three legions and a fortification trench gave him confidence. They did not 3 stay long or advance beyond the bottom of the hill, but withdrew their troops to camp. On the third day Caesar 4 fortified his camp with a rampart. He ordered the remain- ing cohorts, which he had left in his previous camp, and the baggage train to be led to his present location.

43. Between the town of Ilerda and the hill closest to it, where Petreius and Afranius had their camp, there was level ground for about three hundred paces, and in roughly the middle of this space was a position a little higher than the rest. Caesar was confident that if he seized and forti- 2 fied it he would cut off his opponents from the town and the bridge and all of the supplies they had brought into the town. With this hope in mind he led three legions out 3 of camp. After drawing up his line in suitable positions, he ordered the elite guard of one legion to run forward and

4 Qua re cognita celeriter quae in statione pro castris erant
Afrani cohortes breviore itinere ad eundem occupandum
5 locum mittuntur. Contenditur proelio, et quod prius in
tumulum Afraniani venerant nostri repelluntur atque aliis
submissis subsidiis terga vertere seque ad signa legionum
recipere coguntur.

44. Genus erat pugnae militum illorum ut magno impetu primo procurrerent, audacter locum caperent, ordines suos non magnopere servarent, rari dispersique
2 pugnarent, si premerentur pedem referre et loco excedere
non turpe existimarent, cum Lusitanis reliquisque barbaris genere quodam pugnae assuefacti. (Quod fere fit, quibus quisque in locis miles inveteraverit, ut multum earum
3 regionum consuetudine moveatur.) Haec tum ratio nostros perturbavit insuetos huius generis pugnae. Circumiri
enim sese ab aperto latere procurrentibus singulis arbitrabantur. Ipsi autem suos ordines servare neque ab signis
discedere neque sine gravi causa eum locum quem cepe-
4 rant dimitti censuerant oportere. Itaque perturbatis antesignanis legio quae in eo cornu constiterat locum non tenuit atque in proximum collem sese recepit.

45. Caesar paene omni acie perterrita, quod praeter
opinionem consuetudinemque acciderat, cohortatus suos
legionem nonam subsidio ducit. Hostem insolenter atque
acriter nostros insequentem supprimit rursusque terga
vertere seque ad oppidum Ilerdam recipere et sub muro
2 consistere cogit. Sed nonae legionis milites elati studio

---

[66] This elite guard, the *antesignani*, normally marched and
fought "in front of the standards."   [67] The "open side" was
the side on which a soldier wielded his sword, usually the right,
which was unprotected by the shield in his other hand.

seize the higher ground.[66] When this was recognized, the 4
cohorts stationed in front of Afranius' camp were quickly
sent a shorter distance to seize the same position. A fight 5
ensued and, because Afranius' men had reached the
higher ground first, ours were pushed back, and when
Afranius sent other troops in support, ours were forced to
turn back and retreat to the legionary standards.

44. The enemy's combat style was this. The soldiers
would run forward at first with great urgency and boldly
seize a position. They did not really preserve their formations, tending to fight singly and scattered. They did not 2
think it shameful to withdraw and leave a position if hard
pressed, having become accustomed to a certain style of
combat with the Lusitanians and the rest of the natives. (It
generally happens that a soldier is greatly affected by the
local customs of the places in which he has spent his career.) On that occasion this method threw our men into 3
confusion, unaccustomed as they were to this style of combat. For they thought they were being outflanked on their
open side[67] by individuals advancing at a run, whereas
their opinion had been that the right thing to do was preserve their formations, not put a distance between themselves and the standards, or leave a position they had taken
except for some compelling reason. Therefore, given the 4
disarray of the elite troops, the legion stationed on that
wing did not hold its position, retreating to the closest hill.

45. With nearly his whole line terrified—an occurrence
contrary to expectation and habit—Caesar rallied his men
and brought up the ninth legion in support. He checked
the enemy's insolently aggressive pursuit of our men and
forced them to turn back, retreat to Ilerda, and take a
position in front of its wall. But the soldiers of the ninth 2

dum sarcire acceptum detrimentum volunt temere inse-
cuti longius fugientes in locum iniquum progrediuntur et
sub montem in quo erat oppidum positum Ilerda succe-
3 dunt. Hinc se recipere cum vellent, rursus illi ex loco su-
4 periore nostros premebant. Praeruptus locus erat utraque
ex parte derectus ac tantum in latitudinem patebat ut tres
instructae cohortes eum locum explerent, ut neque subsidia ab lateribus submitti neque equites laborantibus usui
5 esse possent. Ab oppido autem declivis locus tenui fastigio
6 vergebat in longitudinem passus circiter CCCC. Hac nostris erat receptus quod eo incitati studio inconsultius processerant. Hoc pugnabatur loco et propter angustias iniquo et quod sub ipsis radicibus montis constiterant, ut
nullum frustra telum in eos mitteretur. Tamen virtute et
patientia nitebantur atque omnia vulnera sustinebant.
7 Augebantur illis copiae, atque ex castris cohortes per oppidum crebro submittebantur ut integri defessis succe-
8 derent. Hoc idem Caesar facere cogebatur ut submissis in
eundem locum cohortibus defessos reciperet.

46. Hoc cum esset modo pugnatum continenter horis
V nostrique gravius a multitudine premerentur consumptis omnibus telis gladiis destrictis impetum adversus
montem in cohortes faciunt paucisque deiectis reliquos
2 sese convertere cogunt. Submotis sub murum cohortibus
ac nonnullam partem[52] propter terrorem in oppidum com-

---

[52] nonnullam partem *Paul*: nonnulla parte ω

legion were carried away by enthusiasm in their desire to repair the damage incurred. In their rash pursuit of the fleeing enemy they advanced onto unfavorable ground, coming all the way up to the hill on which Ilerda was situated. When our men wanted to withdraw from this 3 position, the enemy put pressure on them from above. The place was cliff-like, sheer on both sides and just wide 4 enough that three cohorts in formation filled the space, with the result that reinforcements could not be sent from the flanks and the cavalry could not be of any use if the men were in difficulties. In front of Ilerda stretched a 5 slope with an slight gradient about four hundred paces long. Our men's retreat lay along this, since spurred by 6 enthusiasm they had rather recklessly pressed on so far. The fighting took place here, in a location unfavorable because of its narrowness and because the men had halted at the very bottom of a hill, which meant that every weapon hurled at them hit something. Nevertheless, they exerted themselves with courageous endurance and held out against every sort of wound. The enemy forces kept 7 growing, as cohorts from their camp were sent through the town into battle one after another, so that fresh men could take the place of exhausted ones. Caesar was compelled to 8 do the same, to get exhausted troops out by sending up cohorts to take their place.

46. After the battle had gone on in this manner for five straight hours, our men, pressed ever harder by the enemy numbers and having used up all of their projectiles, drew their swords and attacked uphill against enemy cohorts. After dislodging a few they forced the rest to turn around. With the cohorts shifted to a position in front of the wall, 2 and some driven by terror into the town, an easy retreat

3 pulsis facilis est nostris receptus datus. Equitatus autem noster ab utroque latere etsi devexis[53] atque inferioribus locis constiterat tamen summum[54] ⟨in⟩ iugum virtute conititur atque inter duas acies perequitans commodio-
4 rem ac tutiorem nostris receptum dat. Ita vario certamine pugnatum est. Nostri in primo congressu circiter LXX ceciderunt, in his Q. Fulginius ex primo hastato legionis quartae decimae, qui propter eximiam virtutem ex inferi-oribus ordinibus in eum locum pervenerat. Vulnerantur
5 amplius DC. Ex Afranianis interficiuntur T. Caecilius, primi pili centurio, et praeter eum centuriones IIII, mi-lites amplius CC.

47. Sed haec eius diei praefertur opinio ut se utrique
2 superiores discessisse existimarent, Afraniani quod cum esse omnium iudicio inferiores viderentur comminus tam-diu stetissent et nostrorum impetum sustinuissent et ini-tio[55] locum tumulumque tenuissent quae causa pugnandi fuerat et nostros primo congressu terga vertere coegissent,
3 nostri autem quod iniquo loco atque impari congressi numero V horis proelium sustinuissent, quod montem gla-diis destrictis ascendissent, quod ex loco superiore terga vertere adversarios coegissent atque in oppidum compu-
4 lissent. Illi eum tumulum pro quo pugnatum est magnis operibus muniverunt praesidiumque ibi posuerunt.

53 devexis *Damon*: deiectis *M*: disiectis *U*: dilectis *TV*. *The manuscript S is missing here.*
54 summum] summa *Forchhammer*   55 ⟨ab⟩ initio *Paul*

68 For "valiantly struggled to the top of," Forchhammer pro-posed "with supreme valor struggled onto."
69 The first cohort of each legion was bigger than the other nine, and its centurions accordingly commanded more men.

was available to our men. Moreover, our cavalry, although 3
originally positioned lower on the slope, valiantly struggled to the top of[68] the ridge and by riding between the
two lines gave our men a more comfortable and safer retreat. The contest in this battle had mixed results. About 4
seventy of our men fell in the initial encounter, among
them Quintus Fulginius, formerly a first-cohort centurion[69] of the fourteenth legion, who had reached that position from lower ranks because of his conspicuous courage;
more than six hundred were wounded. Of Afranius' men 5
the casualties included Titus Castricius, chief centurion,
and besides him four centurions and more than two hundred soldiers.

47. But the prevailing opinion about the day is that
each side thought it had come off ahead. For Afranius' 2
men this was because, although they were generally viewed
as inferior, they had faced the enemy so long in close
combat, and had withstood the attack of our men, and had
held their position initially[70] as well as the high ground
that was the cause of the battle, and had forced our men
to turn and run at the first encounter. For our men, 3
however, it was because, despite fighting on unfavorable
ground and at a numerical disadvantage, they had sustained the battle for five hours, because they had advanced
uphill with drawn swords, because they had forced their
adversaries to turn and run from a position of superiority
and had driven them into the town. As for the high ground 4
over which the battle had been fought, the other side fortified it with substantial earthworks and stationed a garrison there.

[70] For "initially," Paul proposed "from the beginning."

48. Accidit etiam repentinum incommodum biduo quo haec gesta sunt. Tanta enim tempestas cooritur ut num-
2 quam illis locis maiores aquas fuisse constaret. Tum autem ex omnibus montibus nives proluit ac summas ripas flumi-nis superavit pontesque ambo quos C. Fabius fecerat uno
3 die interrupit. Quae res magnas difficultates exercitui Caesaris attulit. Castra enim, ut supra demonstratum est, cum essent inter flumina duo, Sicorim et Cingam—spatio milium XXX neutrum horum transiri poterat necessa-
4 rioque omnes his angustiis continebantur. Neque civitates quae ad Caesaris amicitiam accesserant frumentum sup-portare neque ii qui pabulatum longius progressi erant interclusi fluminibus reverti neque maximi commeatus[56] qui ex Italia Galliaque veniebant in castra pervenire pote-
5 rant. Tempus autem erat difficillimum, quo neque fru-menta in hibernis[57] erant—neque multum a maturitate aberant—ac civitates exinanitae quod Afranius paene omne frumentum ante Caesaris adventum Ilerdam con-vexerat. Reliqui si quid fuerat Caesar superioribus diebus
6 consumpserat. Pecora, quod secundum poterat esse in-opiae subsidium, propter bellum finitimae civitates lon-
7 gius removerant. Qui erant pabulandi aut frumentandi causa progressi hos levis armaturae Lusitani peritique earum regionum caetrati citerioris Hispaniae consecta-bantur, quibus erat proclive tranare flumen quod consue-tudo eorum omnium est ut sine utribus ad exercitum non eant.

[56] commeatus *Beroaldo* (*see 1.54.5*): comitatus ω
[57] hibernis] *The text is uncertain here.*

---

[71] The Latin, like the English, is awkward. It may be corrupt.

48. An unexpected setback occurred two days after these events, for so powerful a storm arose that everyone agreed that the flooding in the area had never been more extensive. On that occasion the storm washed snow down 2 from every mountain and overflowed the riverbanks and in a single day broke both of the bridges Gaius Fabius had made. These developments caused serious difficulties to 3 Caesar's army, for with his camp, as was indicated above, being between two rivers, the Sicoris and the Cinca—neither of these could be crossed for a stretch of thirty miles and of necessity everyone was confined within this narrow space.[71] The communities that had come over to Cae- 4 sar could not supply him with provisions, nor could those who gone some distance to forage return, cut off as they were by the rivers, nor could the extensive supplies coming from Italy and Gaul reach Caesar's camp. For the sea- 5 son was a very difficult one, such that there was no standing grain in the winter camps—and yet it was not far from maturity—and the local communities had been emptied out, since Afranius had taken practically all provisions to Ilerda before Caesar's arrival. Whatever was left Caesar had consumed on the preceding days. As for livestock, 6 which could have given additional support against scarcity, the nearby communities had moved it quite far away because of the war. Anyone who left camp to forage or collect 7 provisions was pursued by Lusitanians, part of Afranius' light-armed force, and by men knowledgeable about the area, native troops from Nearer Spain. It was a simple matter for these to swim across the river because all of them were customarily equipped with inflatable skins when they began a campaign.

49. At exercitus Afrani omnium rerum abundabat copia. Multum erat frumentum provisum et convectum superioribus temporibus, multum ex omni provincia com-
2 portabatur. Magna copia pabuli suppetebat. Harum omnium rerum facultates sine ullo periculo pons Ilerdae praebebat et loca trans flumen integra, quo omnino Caesar adire non poterat.

50. Hae permanserunt aquae dies complures. Conatus est Caesar reficere pontes, sed nec magnitudo fluminis permittebat neque ad ripam dispositae cohortes adversa-
2 riorum perfici patiebantur. Quod illis prohibere erat facile cum ipsius fluminis natura atque aquae magnitudine tum quod ex totis ripis in unum atque angustum locum tela
3 iaciebantur. Atque erat difficile eodem tempore rapidissimo flumine opera perficere et tela vitare.

51. Nuntiatur Afranio magnos comitatus,[58] qui iter habebant ad Caesarem, ad flumen constitisse. Venerant eo sagittarii ex Rutenis, equites ex Gallia cum multis carris magnisque impedimentis, ut fert Gallica consuetudo.
2 Erant praeterea cuiusque generis hominum milia circiter VI cum servis liberisque,[59] sed nullus ordo, nullum imperium certum cum suo quisque consilio uteretur atque omnes sine timore iter facerent usi superiorum temporum
3 atque itinerum licentia. Erant complures honesti adulescentes, senatorum filii et ordinis equestris, erant legationes civitatum, erant legati Caesaris. Hos omnes flumina

[58] comitatus] commeatus *Nipperdey* (*see 1.48.4*)
[59] liberisque] libertisque *Hotoman*

49. Afranius' army, however, had an abundance of everything. A great deal of grain had been arranged for and collected earlier, and a great deal was being transported from his entire province. A large supply of fodder was available. Access to all of these things was provided by the 2 bridge at Ilerda and the untouched districts across the river, which Caesar had no way at all of reaching.

50. These floodwaters stayed for several days. Caesar tried to rebuild the bridges, but the height of the river did not permit it, nor did the enemy cohorts stationed on the bank allow their completion. It was easy for them to stop 2 him, both because of the height of the water and because weapons were being thrown from the whole riverbank into a single narrow spot. And it was difficult to complete a 3 construction project in a rapidly rushing river while simultaneously dodging weapons.

51. Afranius received word that large convoys[72] on their way to Caesar had halted beside the river. The new arrivals were archers from the Ruteni and cavalry from Gaul with a multitude of wagons and a great deal of baggage, as is the Gallic custom. There were also about six 2 thousand men of all sorts with their slaves and children.[73] But there was no organization, no fixed command structure, since each man was acting according to his own plan and everyone was traveling fearless, with the lax discipline appropriate to earlier times and journeys. There were a 3 number of highly regarded young men, senators' sons and men of equestrian standing, plus delegations from communities, and Caesar's own envoys, all of them hemmed

[72] For "large convoys," Nipperdey substituted "abundant supplies." [73] For "children," Hotoman substituted "freedman."

4 continebant. Ad hos opprimendos cum omni equitatu tribusque legionibus Afranius de nocte proficiscitur imprudentesque ante missis equitibus aggreditur. Celeriter sese tamen Galli equites expediunt proeliumque commit-

5 tunt. Hi dum pari certamine res geri potuit magnum hostium numerum pauci sustinuere. Sed ubi signa legionum appropinquare coeperunt paucis amissis sese in proximos

6 montes conferunt. Hoc pugnae tempus magnum attulit nostris ad salutem momentum. Nacti enim spatium se in loca superiora receperunt. Desiderati sunt eo die sagittarii circiter CC, equites pauci, calonum atque impedimentorum[60] non magnus numerus.

52. His tamen omnibus annona crevit. Quae fere res non solum inopia praesentis sed etiam futuri temporis ti-

2 more ingravescere consuevit. Iamque ad ⟨HS⟩[61] XL in singulos modios annona pervenerat, et militum vires inopia frumenti deminuerat. Atque incommoda in dies au-

3 gebantur. Et ita[62] paucis diebus magna erat rerum facta commutatio ac se Fortuna inclinaverat ut nostri magna inopia necessariarum rerum conflictarentur, illi omnibus

4 abundarent rebus superioresque haberentur. Caesar iis civitatibus quae ad eius amicitiam accesserant, quo minor erat frumenti copia, pecus imperabat, calones ad longinquiores civitates dimittebat, ipse praesentem inopiam quibus poterat subsidiis tutabatur.

---

60 impedimentorum] iumentorum *Eussner*
61 ⟨HS⟩ *Carter*   62 et ita *Peskett*: et tam ω

---

74 For "baggage," Eussner proposed "pack animals."
75 The exact price is uncertain since the text is corrupt here, but the fact that it was unusually high is clear enough. A "measure" contained roughly fifteen pounds of grain.

in by the river. Afranius set out by night with his whole   4
cavalry and three legions to crush them. Sending ahead
his cavalry he attacked them unawares. The cavalry from
Gaul nevertheless prepared themselves quickly and joined
battle. So long as the situation could be kept to an equal   5
contest, a few of them withstood a large number of the
enemy. But when the legionary standards began to approach, the cavalry, having suffered a few losses, removed
themselves to the nearest hills. The time they spent fight-   6
ing was of great consequence for the safety of our people,
for in the interval thus gained they withdrew onto higher
ground. The losses that day were about two hundred archers, a few cavalry, and no great quantity of camp followers and baggage.[74]

52. Nevertheless, with all this the price of grain went
up. (The grain price generally appreciates not only with a
shortage of the moment but also with fear about the future.) It had already reached forty sesterces per measure,   2
and the soldiers' strength had diminished because of the
scarcity of provisions.[75] And their troubles were increasing
daily. Such was the huge change of circumstances pro-   3
duced within a few days—and Fortune had so tipped her
scales—that our men were contending with a serious
shortage of necessities, while the other side had plenty of
everything and was thought to have the advantage. Cae-   4
sar requisitioned livestock from the communities that had
come over to him, insofar as their grain supplies were
inadequate. He sent the camp followers to communities
some distance away. He himself devised defenses against
the present shortage from every possible source of help.

53. Haec Afranius Petreiusque et eorum amici pleniora etiam atque uberiora Romam ad suos perscribebant. Multa rumores adfingebant,[63] ut paene bellum confectum
2 videretur. Quibus litteris nuntiisque Romam perlatis magni ‹in› forum[64] concursus [ad Afranium][65] magnaeque gratulationes fiebant. Multi ex Italia ad Cn. Pompeium proficiscebantur, alii ut principes talem nuntium attulisse, alii ne eventum belli expectasse aut ex omnibus novissimi venisse viderentur.

54. Cum in his angustiis res esset atque omnes viae ab Afranianis militibus equitibusque obsiderentur nec pontes perfici possent imperat militibus Caesar ut naves faciant cuius generis eum superioribus annis usus Britanniae
2 docuerat. Carinae primum ac[66] statumina ex levi materia fiebant. Reliquum corpus navium viminibus contextum
3 coriis integebatur. Has perfectas carris iunctis devehit noctu milia passuum a castris XXII militesque his navibus flumen transportat continentemque ripae collem impro-
4 viso occupat. Hunc celeriter priusquam ab adversariis sentiatur communit. Huc legionem postea traiecit. Atque
5 ex utraque parte pontem institutum biduo perficit. Ita

---

63 multa rumores adfingebant *Oehler. The manuscripts are variously corrupt here.*

64 in forum *Damon*: domum ω

65 [ad Afranium] *Damon*: hominum *Vossius*: ad domum Afranii *Hotoman, transposing* domum

66 primum ac *Aldus*: ac primum ω: ac prima *Nipperdey*

53. Afranius and Petreius and their friends sent amplified and exaggerated accounts of these events to their partisans at Rome. Rumors added many fictions,[76] with the result that the war seemed practically over. After these 2 letters and announcements were brought to Rome, people rushed in great numbers[77] ⟨into⟩ the Forum and there were extensive congratulations. Many men started making their way from Italy to Gnaeus Pompey, some to be seen as the first with news like this, others to avoid being seen to have waited for the war's result or to have arrived last of all.

54. Since the situation had come to such a pass and every road was blocked by Afranius' soldiers and cavalry, and it was impossible to complete the bridges, Caesar ordered his men to make boats of a type that he had learned about in his past experience of Britain. First, the 2 keels and ribs[78] were made from a light wood; the rest of the boat's hull was woven from canes, then covered with hides. The finished boats were carried twenty-two miles 3 from the camp at night on coupled wagons. Caesar put his men across the river on these boats and without warning occupied a hill that touched the riverbank. He fortified the 4 hill quickly before his opponents could find out; he later brought a legion over to this spot. Within two days he finished the bridge, which he began from both banks at once.

[76] The text is uncertain.

[77] For "people rushed in great numbers," Vossius and Hotoman substituted "a great crowd of people rushed" and "people rushed in great numbers to Afranius' house," respectively.

[78] For "first the keels and ribs," Nipperdey substituted "the keels and the principal ribs."

commeatus[67] et qui frumenti causa processerant tuto ad
se recipit et rem frumentariam expedire incipit.

55. Eodem die equitum magnam partem flumen traiecit, qui inopinantes pabulatores et sine ullo dissipatos
timore aggressi quam magnum numerum iumentorum
atque hominum intercipiunt, cohortibusque caetratis subsidio missis scienter in duas partes sese distribuunt, alii ut
praedae praesidio sint, alii ut venientibus resistant atque
2 eos propellant, unamque cohortem quae temere ante ceteras extra aciem procurrerat seclusam ab reliquis cir-
cumveniunt atque interficiunt incolumesque cum magna
praeda eodem ponte in castra revertuntur.

56. Dum haec ad Ilerdam geruntur Massilienses usi L.
Domiti consilio naves longas expediunt numero XVII,
2 quarum erant XI tectae. Multa huc minora navigia addunt
ut ipsa multitudine nostra classis terreatur. Magnum numerum sagittariorum, magnum Albicorum—de quibus
supra demonstratum est—imponunt atque hos praemiis
3 pollicitationibusque incitant. Certas[68] sibi deposcit naves
Domitius atque has colonis pastoribusque quos secum
4 adduxerat complet. Sic omnibus rebus instructa classe
magna fiducia ad nostras naves procedunt, quibus praeerat D. Brutus. Hae ad insulam quae est contra Massiliam
stationes obtinebant.

57. Erat multo inferior numero navium Brutus. Sed
electos ex omnibus legionibus fortissimos viros ante-

---

[67] commeatus ω (*see 1.48.4*): comitatus *Manutius*
[68] certas] ceteras *van Veen*: tectas *Cornelissen*

---

[79] For "specific," van Veen and Cornelissen proposed "the
remaining" and "decked," respectively.   [80] See 1.34.2.

In this way he brought the supplies and those who had   5
gone out after provisions safely into camp and made it
easier to feed his army.

55. That same day he put a large part of his cavalry
across the river. In their attack on foragers who were
unsuspecting and carelessly dispersed they intercepted a
very large number of pack animals and men. When native
cohorts were sent in support, the cavalry split expertly into
two groups so that some could provide protection for the
booty while others resisted and repelled the newcomers.
One enemy cohort ran rashly ahead of the others and left   2
the line; cut off from the rest it was surrounded and killed.
The cavalry returned to camp by the same bridge, unscathed and with a lot of booty.

56. While this was going on at Ilerda, the Massilians,
acting on the plan of Lucius Domitius, got seventeen warships ready, eleven of them with decks. To these they   2
added many smaller vessels so that our fleet would be terrified by numbers alone. They embarked a large number
of archers and Albici—information about these was given
above—and excited their enthusiasm with the promise of
rewards. Domitius demanded specific[79] ships for himself   3
and filled them with the tenants and herdsmen he had
brought with him.[80] In this fashion, once the equipment   4
of their fleet was complete, they headed for our ships with
great confidence. Decimus Brutus was in charge of these,
and they were stationed near the island that lies opposite
Marseilles.

57. Brutus was greatly outnumbered in ships. But
Caesar had allocated to this fleet picked men from all of

signanos centuriones Caesar ei classi attribuerat qui sibi
2 id muneris depoposcerant. Hi manus ferreas atque harpa-
gones paraverant magnoque numero pilorum tragularum
reliquorumque telorum se instruxerant. Ita cognito hostium adventu suas naves ex portu educunt, cum Massi-
3 liensibus confligunt. Pugnatum est utrimque fortissime
atque acerrime. Neque multum Albici nostris virtute cedebant, homines asperi et montani et exercitati in armis.
4 Atque hi modo digressi ⟨a⟩ Massiliensibus recentem
eorum pollicitationem animis continebant, pastoresque
Domiti spe libertatis excitati sub oculis domini suam pro-
bare operam studebant.

58. Ipsi Massilienses et celeritate navium et scientia
gubernatorum confisi nostros eludebant impetusque eorum excipiebant ⟨cedendo⟩.[69] Et quoad licebat latiore uti
spatio producta longius acie circumvenire nostros aut pluribus navibus adoriri singulas aut remos transcurrentes
2 detergere, si possent, contendebant. Cum propius erat
necessario ventum ab scientia gubernatorum atque artifi-
3 ciis ad virtutem montanorum confugiebant. Qui[70] minus
exercitatis remigibus minusque peritis gubernatoribus
utebantur—qui repente ex onerariis navibus erant producti—⟨hi⟩[71] nequedum etiam vocabulis armamentorum
cognitis tum etiam tarditate et gravitate navium impedie-

---

[69] excipiebant ⟨cedendo⟩ *Damon* (*see Lucan* 3.555): ⟨non⟩
excipiebant *Kraner-Hofmann-Meusel*: decipiebant *Nipperdey*:
effugiebant *Terpstra*   [70] qui *MU*: quo *STV*: ⟨Nostri⟩ quom
Elberling   [71] ⟨hi⟩ *Damon*

---

[81] For "received their attacks by giving way," Kraner-Hofmann-
Meusel, Nipperdey, and Terpstra substituted "did not wait for

his legions—the bravest, the elite, the centurions—men
who had demanded this assignment for themselves. These   2
had prepared "iron hands"—grappling hooks—and had
equipped themselves with a large number of pikes and
spears and other projectiles. Thus at news of the enemy's
approach they moved their ships out of the harbor and
fought the Massilians. Both sides fought with the utmost   3
courage and vehemence, and the Albici were not much
inferior to our men in prowess, being hardy mountaineers
with experience in warfare; having just left Marseilles,   4
they had the people's recent promises firmly in mind.
Domitius' herdsmen, stimulated by the prospect of freedom, were eager to prove their effectiveness under their
master's eye.

58. For their part the Massilians, relying on both the
speed of their ships and the skill of the pilots, eluded our
men and received their attacks by giving way.[81] And as
long as they had ample space at their disposal, they kept
extending their line and strove to surround our men if they
could, or to attack single ships in groups, or to pass alongside and strip away the oars. When they were forced to   2
come closer, they turned for protection from the pilots'
skill and tactics to the mountaineers' prowess. As for the   3
side with[82] less experienced rowers and less knowledgeable pilots—these had been taken on short notice from the
transport ships—they did not even know the terms for the
ships' tackle and were also hindered by their slow and

their attacks," "frustrated their attacks," and "evaded their attacks," respectively.

[82] For "as for the side with," Elberling proposed "since our
men had."

bantur. Factae enim subito ex umida materia non eundem
4 usum celeritatis habuerant. Itaque dum locus comminus
pugnandi daretur aequo animo singulas binis navibus obiciebant atque iniecta manu ferrea et retenta utraque nave
diversi pugnabant atque in hostium naves transcendebant.
Et magno numero Albicorum et pastorum interfecto partem navium deprimunt, nonnullas cum hominibus capi-
5 unt, reliquas in portum compellunt. Eo die naves Massiliensium cum his quae sunt captae intereunt VIIII.

59. Hoc primum[72] Caesari ad Ilerdam nuntiatur, simul
2 perfecto ponte celeriter fortuna mutatur. Illi perterriti virtute equitum minus libere minus audacter vagabantur.
Alias non longo a castris progressi spatio ut celerem receptum haberent angustius pabulabantur, alias longiore circuitu custodias stationesque equitum vitabant aut aliquo
accepto detrimento aut procul equitatu viso ex medio iti-
3 nere proiectis sarcinis fugiebant. Postremo et plures inter-
mittere dies et praeter consuetudinem omnium noctu
constituerant pabulari.

60. Interim Oscenses et Calagurritani, qui erant [cum]
Oscensibus contributi, mittunt ad eum legatos seseque
2 imperata facturos pollicentur. Hos Tarraconenses et Iacetani et Ausetani et paucis post diebus Illurgavonenses, qui
3 flumen Hiberum attingunt, insequuntur. Petit ab his omnibus ut se frumento iuvent. Pollicentur atque omnibus

---

[72] primum *MUTV*: primum cum *S*: proelium *Davies*: [pri-
mum] *Chacon*

heavy ships; built in a hurry out of green wood, they had not acquired the same capacity for speed. Thus, so long 4 as our men had a chance for close combat, they did not mind sending one ship against two: after throwing an "iron hand" and securing each ship they would fight facing in two directions and board the enemy vessels. After killing a large number of the Albici and herdsmen they sank a proportion of the ships, captured some still manned, and drove the rest into the harbor. The Massilians lost nine 5 ships, including those that were captured.

59. This news reached Caesar first[83] at Ilerda, and at once, now that the bridge was complete, his fortune changed quickly. The enemy, thoroughly cowed by the 2 cavalry's prowess, began to roam less freely and less boldly. Sometimes they avoided going a long way from camp, in order to have a rapid retreat, and foraged in a rather restricted area. Sometimes they took quite a long detour and avoided the cavalry patrols and outposts, or else after taking some damage or seeing the cavalry in the distance they abandoned their loads midjourney and fled. Eventually 3 their decision was to skip several days at a time and to forage by night, contrary to all custom.

60. Meanwhile the people of Osca and those of Calagurris, which paid tribute to Osca, sent delegations to him and promised to do his bidding. The Tarronconenses, 2 Iacetani, and Ausetani followed them, and a few days later the Illurgavonenses, who border the Ebro River. He asked 3 all of them to help him with provisions. They promised to

---

[83] For "this news reached Caesar first," Davies and Chacon substituted "news of this battle reached Caesar" and "this news reached Caesar," respectively.

4 undique conquisitis iumentis in castra deportant. Transit
etiam cohors Illurgavonensis ad eum cognito civitatis con-
5 silio et signa ex statione transfert. Magna celeriter commutatio rerum. Perfecto ponte, magnis V civitatibus ad
amicitiam adiunctis, expedita re frumentaria, extinctis
rumoribus de auxiliis legionum, quae cum Pompeio per
Mauretaniam venire dicebantur, multae longinquiores
civitates ab Afranio desciscunt et Caesaris amicitiam
sequuntur.

61. Quibus rebus perterritis animis adversariorum
Caesar, ne semper magno circuitu per pontem equitatus
esset mittendus, nactus idoneum locum fossas pedum
XXX in latitudinem complures facere instituit quibus partem aliquam Sicoris averteret vadumque in eo flumine
2 efficeret. His paene effectis magnum in timorem Afranius
Petreiusque perveniunt ne omnino frumento pabuloque
intercluderentur, quod multum Caesar equitatu valebat.
Itaque constituunt ipsi locis excedere et in Celtiberiam
3 bellum transferre. (Huic consilio suffragabatur etiam illa
res, quod ex duobus contrariis generibus, quae superiore
bello cum [L.] Sertorio steterant civitates victae nomen
atque imperium absentis timebant, quae in amicitia manserant Pompei magnis adfectae beneficiis eum diligebant.
4 Caesaris autem erat in barbaris nomen obscurius.) Hic
magnos equitatus magnaque auxilia expectabant et suis
5 locis bellum in hiemem ducere cogitabant. Hoc inito consilio toto flumine Hibero naves conquiri et Otogesam ad-

do so. After rounding up pack animals from all over, they delivered food to his camp. Moreover, a cohort of Illurga- 4 vonenses left their post and came over to Caesar after learning of their community's decision. There was quickly 5 a great change in Caesar's situation. With the bridge complete, five substantial communities allied in friendship, supplies facilitated, and the rumors about legionary reinforcements silenced—legions were said to be coming with Pompey via Mauretania—many of the more distant communities defected from Afranius and fell in behind Caesar as friends.

61. With his opponents' spirits thoroughly cowed by these developments, and to avoid always having to send the cavalry on a huge detour by the bridge, Caesar found a suitable spot and began to dig several trenches thirty feet wide to divert some portion of the Sicoris and create a ford in the river. When the project was nearly finished Afranius 2 and Petreius became very worried that they would be entirely cut off from their food supply and fodder, since Caesar was the stronger in cavalry. So they themselves made the decision to leave the area and transfer the war to Celtiberia. (In favor of their plan was also the fact that, of the 3 two different types of community, those that had sided with Sertorius in the earlier war, and had been defeated, feared the name and power of the absent Pompey, while those that were on Pompey's side, and had received substantial benefits, were well disposed to him. For Caesar's name was comparatively unfamiliar to the natives.) They 4 anticipated finding large cavalry and auxiliary contingents there and contemplated extending the war into the winter season in an area they controlled. After adopting this plan 5 they ordered men to find boats anywhere on the Ebro and

duci iubent. Id erat oppidum positum ad Hiberum mi-
6 liaque passuum a castris aberat XX.[73] Ad eum locum
fluminis navibus iunctis pontem imperant fieri. Legionesque duas flumen Sicorim transducunt, castraque mu-
niuntur vallo pedum XII.

62. Qua re per exploratores cognita summo labore
militum Caesar continuato diem noctemque opere in flumine avertendo huc iam reduxerat rem ut equites, etsi
difficulter atque aegre fiebat, possent tamen atque au-
2 derent flumen transire, pedites vero tantummodo umeris
ac summo pectore extarent et cum altitudine aquae tum
etiam rapiditate fluminis ad transeundum [non] impe-
3 direntur. Sed tamen eodem fere tempore pons in Hibero
prope effectus nuntiabatur et in Sicori vadum reperiebatur.

63. Iam vero eo magis illi maturandum iter existimabant. Itaque duabus auxiliaribus cohortibus Ilerdae praesidio relictis omnibus copiis Sicorim transeunt et cum
duabus legionibus quas superioribus diebus traduxerunt
2 castra coniungunt. Relinquebatur Caesari nihil nisi uti
equitatu agmen adversariorum male haberet et carperet.
Pons enim ipsius magnum circuitum habebat, ut multo
3 breviore itinere illi ad Hiberum pervenire possent. Equites
ab eo missi flumen transeunt et, cum de tertia vigilia Petreius atque Afranius castra movissent, repente sese ad
novissimum agmen ostendunt et magna multitudine cir-
cumfusa morari atque iter impedire incipiunt.

64. Prima luce ex superioribus locis quae Caesaris castris erant coniuncta cernebatur equitatus nostri proelio
novissimos illorum premi vehementer, ac nonnumquam

[73] XX] XXX *von Göler*

bring them to Otogesa. This was a town on the Ebro about twenty miles from their camp. There they ordered that the boats be strung together to make a bridge, took two legions across the Sicoris, and fortified a camp with a twelve-foot high rampart. 6

62. Caesar learned of this from the scouts. With a huge effort by his soldiers, and by continuing the work of diverting the river day and night, Caesar had brought the project to the point that the cavalry could cross the river—although it was difficult and only just possible—and dared to do so. For the infantry, however, the water was up to their shoulders and the top of their chests, and they were hindered in crossing by both the depth of the water and the strength of the current. But just about when they had a ford across the Sicoris, word came that the bridge on the Ebro was nearly ready. 2 3

63. The enemy's immediate thought was that this was more reason to hasten their march. So leaving two auxiliary cohorts on guard at Ilerda they crossed the Sicoris with their whole force and camped with the two legions that had crossed previously. Caesar's only option was to harm and harass the enemy column with his cavalry, for his own bridge involved a long detour, so the enemy could reach the Ebro with a much shorter route. After Caesar sent his cavalry across the river, they immediately made their presence known to the enemy rearguard, even though Petreius and Afranius struck camp around midnight, and began to delay and hinder their march by encircling them in large numbers. 2 3

64. At daybreak people could see from the high ground adjoining Caesar's camp that the enemy rearguard was hard pressed when our cavalry attacked, and sometimes

sustineri extremum agmen atque interrumpi, alias ferri
signa, et universarum cohortium impetu nostros propelli
2 dein rursus conversos insequi. Totis vero castris milites
circulari et dolere—hostem ex manibus dimitti, bellum
necessario longius duci—centurionesque tribunosque militum adire atque obsecrare ut per eos Caesar certior fieret: ne labori suo neu periculo parceret; paratos esse
sese, posse et audere ea transire flumen qua traductus
3 esset equitatus. Quorum studio et vocibus excitatus Caesar etsi timebat tantae magnitudini fluminis exercitum
4 obicere conandum tamen atque experiendum iudicat. Itaque infirmiores milites ex omnibus centuriis deligi iubet,
quorum aut animus aut vires videbantur sustinere non
5 posse. Hos cum legione una praesidio castris relinquit.
Reliquas legiones expeditas educit magnoque numero
iumentorum in flumine supra atque infra constituto tra-
6 ducit exercitum. Pauci ex his militibus ablati flumine[74] ab
equitatu excipiuntur ac sublevantur. Interit tamen nemo.
Traducto incolumi exercitu copias instruit triplicemque
7 aciem ducere incipit. Ac tantum fuit in militibus studi ut
milium VI ad iter addito ad vadum circuitu magnaque
fluminis mora interposita eos qui de tertia vigilia exissent
ante horam diei nonam consequerentur.

65. Quos ubi Afranius procul visos cum Petreio conspexit nova re perterritus locis superioribus constitit.
2 Aciemque instruit. Caesar in campis exercitum reficit ne

[74] ablati flumine *Dübner*: arma in flumine *MUTV*: arma in
flumine arrepta *S. The text is variously emended, but the sense is
clear enough.*

the end of their column was held up and disrupted, at
other times that it took the offensive, while our men were
pushed back when the enemy cohorts made a concerted
charge, then pursued them again when the men turned
around. Throughout the camp soldiers clustered unhap- 2
pily—the enemy was slipping away, they thought, and the
war was necessarily going to be further prolonged—and
approached the centurions and staff officers, pleading that
they inform Caesar that he should not spare them effort
or danger, that they were ready, able, and willing to cross
the river where the cavalry had crossed. Caesar was en- 3
couraged by the determination they expressed. Despite
worries about exposing the army to so powerful a river
current, he nevertheless thought that he should try and
make the experiment. So he ordered a muster of every 4
unit's less robust soldiers, those whose spirit or physique
seemed incapable of holding out; these he left with one 5
legion to guard the camp. He led out the remaining legions unencumbered. With numerous pack animals positioned in the river upstream and downstream, he took his
army across. A few of these soldiers, swept away by the 6
river, were caught and assisted by the cavalry, but no one
was lost. Once the army was safely across he put his forces
into formation and began moving them forward in three
lines, and so great was the determination among the sol- 7
diers that despite the detour to the ford, which made their
march six miles longer than the enemy's, and the significant delay interjected by the river, they caught up with
those who had left around midnight before midafternoon.

65. Afranius saw them in the distance, as did Petreius.
Dismayed by the new development he halted on higher
ground and drew up his line. Caesar let his army recover 2

defessum proelio obiciat. Rursus conantes progredi inse-
3 quitur et moratur. Illi necessario maturius quam constituerant castra ponunt. Suberant enim montes, atque a
milibus passuum V itinera difficilia atque angusta excipie-
4 bant. Hos intra montes se recipiebant[75] ut equitatum effu-
gerent Caesaris praesidiisque in angustiis collocatis exercitum itinere prohiberent, ipsi sine periculo ac timore
5 Hiberum copias traducerent. Quod fuit illis conandum
atque omni ratione efficiendum, et[76] totius diei pugna atque itineris labore defessi rem in posterum diem distule-
runt. Caesar quoque in proximo colle castra ponit.

 66. Media circiter nocte iis qui aquandi causa longius
a castris processerant ab equitibus correptis fit ab his certior Caesar duces adversariorum silentio copias castris
educere. Quo cognito signum dari iubet et vasa militari
2 more conclamari. Illi exaudito clamore veriti ne noctu
impediti sub onere confligere cogerentur, aut ne ab equitatu Caesaris in angustiis tenerentur, iter supprimunt co-
3 piasque in castris continent. Postero die Petreius cum
paucis equitibus occulte ad exploranda loca proficiscitur.
Hoc idem fit ex castris Caesaris. Mittitur L. Decidius Saxa
4 cum paucis qui loci naturam perspiciat. Vterque idem suis
renuntiat: V milia passuum proxima intercedere itineris
campestris; inde excipere loca aspera et montuosa; qui

---

[75] intra montes se recipiebant *Aldus*: montes intra se recipiebant ω: montes intrare cupiebant *Nipperdey*
 [76] et] sed *Estienne. Perhaps* at?

---

[84] For "they were trying to retreat beyond," Nipperdey substituted "they wanted to get into." [85] For "and," Estienne
substituted "but"; a stronger adversative might be preferable.

on level terrain so as not to expose them to battle exhausted. When the enemy made another attempt to advance, he pursued, delaying them. They necessarily made 3 camp sooner than they had intended, for the mountains were coming close, and difficult and narrow paths awaited them five miles away. They were trying to retreat beyond[84] 4 these mountains in order to get clear of Caesar's cavalry, prevent the passage of his army by placing garrisons in the narrows, and take their own forces across the Ebro without danger or fear. They needed to try and accomplish this 5 whatever the cost, and[85] they put the matter off until the following day, tired from the day-long fight as they were, and weary from the exertion of the march. Caesar too made camp, on the next hill.

66. Around midnight the cavalry caught some men who had gone too far from their camp for water. The prisoners informed Caesar that the enemy commanders were moving their troops out of camp in silence. When he learned this he ordered men to give a signal and call out "pack up!" military fashion. When the enemy heard the shouting, worried that they would have to fight by night and 2 encumbered with baggage, or would be trapped by Caesar's cavalry in the narrows, they stopped the march and kept their troops in camp. On the next day Petreius set out 3 undercover with a few cavalry to explore the region. The same was done from Caesar's camp: Lucius Decidius Saxa was sent with a few men to reconnoiter the character of the terrain. Each announced the same thing to his side: 4 the first five miles of the route to the mountains were level, then rugged and mountainous terrain took over. It would

prior has angustias occupaverit, ab hoc hostem prohiberi nihil esse negoti.

67. Disputatur in consilio ab Petreio atque Afranio et tempus profectionis quaeritur. Plerique censebant ut noctu iter facerent: posse prius ad angustias veniri quam

2 sentiretur. Alii quod pridie noctu conclamatum esset Caesaris castris argumenti sumebant loco non posse clam

3 exiri; circumfundi noctu equitatum Caesaris atque omnia loca atque itinera obsidere; nocturnaque proelia esse vitanda quod perterritus miles in civili dissensione timori

4 magis quam religioni consulere consuerit; at lucem multum per se pudorem omnium oculis, multum[77] etiam tribunorum militum et centurionum praesentiam adferre, quibus rebus coerceri milites et in officio contineri so-

5 leant; quare omni ratione esse interdiu perrumpendum; etsi aliquo accepto detrimento tamen summa exercitus

6 salva locum quem petant capi posse. Haec evincit in consilio sententia, et prima luce postridie constituunt proficisci.

68. Caesar exploratis regionibus albente caelo omnes copias castris educit. Magnoque circuitu nullo certo itinere exercitum ducit. Nam quae itinera ad Hiberum atque Otogesam pertinebant castris hostium oppositis tenebant-

2 tur. Ipsi erant transcendendae valles maximae ac difficillimae. Saxa multis locis praerupta iter impediebant, ‹ut› arma per manus necessario traderentur militesque inermes sublevatique alii ab aliis magnam partem itineris

---

[77] multum] metum *Paul*

---

[86] For "as does," Paul proposed "fear is brought by."

be no trouble, they said, for an enemy to be blocked by whoever first seized the narrows.

67. Petreius and Afranius discussed the situation with their officers and asked about the timing of their departure. Most recommended marching by night: they could be at the narrows before anyone noticed. Others took the 2 previous night's outcry in Caesar's camp as proof that leaving secretly was impossible. "During the night, Caesar's 3 cavalry are deployed all around us and occupy every position and road. And nighttime battles should be avoided, since in a civil war context terrified soldiers usually attend to fear rather than obligation. But daylight brings a great 4 sense of shame automatically, with everyone watching, as does[86] the presence of officers and centurions. And it is by these things that soldiers are generally kept in line and held to their duty. Therefore we must break out by day, 5 whatever the cost. Even if we take some losses, we will nevertheless be able to reach our objective with most of our army safe." This opinion prevailed in the meeting, and 6 they decided to set out the following day at first light.

68. After exploring the district, Caesar moved his troops out of camp as the sky was turning white.[87] Making a huge detour he took his army on a cross-country route, for the roads leading to the Ebro and Otogesa were controlled by the intervening enemy camp. The ravines they had 2 to cross were deep and exceedingly difficult. In many places sheer cliffs held them up, such that weapons had to be passed hand to hand and the soldiers had to travel much of the route unarmed and giving one another a hand.

[87] The temporal expression is rare and has been taken as a reference to both morning and evening twilight.

3   conficerent. Sed hunc laborem recusabat nemo quod eum omnium laborum finem fore existimabant si hostem Hibero intercludere et frumento prohibere potuissent.

    69. Ac primo Afraniani milites visendi causa laeti ex castris procurrebant contumeliosisque vocibus prosequebantur nos:[78] necessari victus inopia coactos fugere atque ad Ilerdam reverti. Erat enim iter a proposito diversum,
2   contrariamque in partem iri videbatur. Duces vero eorum consilium suum laudibus ferebant quod se castris tenuissent. Multumque eorum opinionem adiuvabat quod sine iumentis impedimentisque ad iter profectos videbant, ut non posse inopiam diutius sustinere confiderent.
3   Sed ubi paulatim retorqueri agmen ad dextram conspexerunt iamque primos superare regionem castrorum animadverterunt nemo erat adeo tardus aut fugiens laboris quin statim castris exeundum atque occurrendum putaret.
4   Conclamatur ad arma atque omnes copiae paucis praesidio relictis cohortibus exeunt rectoque ad Hiberum itinere contendunt.

    70. Erat in celeritate omne positum certamen, utri prius angustias montesque occuparent. Sed exercitum Caesaris viarum difficultates tardabant, Afrani copias
2   equitatus Caesaris insequens morabatur. Res tamen ab Afranianis huc erat necessario deducta ut, si priores montes quos petebant attigissent, ipsi periculum vitarent, impedimenta totius exercitus cohortesque in castris relic-

---

[78] nos *M*: nos nec *U*: nec *TV*: *omitted by* *S*: nostros *Morus*

---

[88] For Caesar's vivid "us," Morus substituted "our men," which entails the conversion of subsequent first-person expressions ("we

But nobody balked at the exertion, because they thought 3
that it would be end of all their exertions if they were able
to get between the enemy and the Ebro and keep them
from their food supply.

69. Afranius' men at first ran out of their camp happily
to watch, and sent jeering words after us.[88] We were running away, they said, forced to do so by the scarcity of
necessary food, and were on our way back to Ilerda. (Our
route was different from the original one, and we seemed
to be going in the opposite direction.) The enemy leaders 2
extolled their own decision to stay in camp, and their opinion was greatly strengthened by seeing that we had started
our march without the baggage train, so that they were
confident that we could no longer endure privation. But 3
when they observed that the column was turning gradually
to the right and the vanguard already moving past the line
of their camp, even the slowest and laziest felt that immediate departure and countermeasures were necessary.
The call to arms was given and the whole force departed, 4
leaving a few cohorts to guard the camp. They took the
direct route toward the Ebro in a hurry.

70. The whole contest turned on speed: which of the
two would seize the narrows and the mountains first? Caesar's army was slowed by the difficulties of their route,
while Afranius' troops were delayed by Caesar's pursuing
cavalry. Still, the actions of Afranius' side had inevitably 2
brought matters to this: if they reached their mountain
objective first, they would be out of danger themselves but
unable to save the entire army's baggage or the cohorts left

were running away," "our route," etc.) into third-person forms
("they were running away," "their route," etc.).

tas servare non possent, quibus interclusis exercitu Caesa-
3 ris auxilium ferri nulla ratione poterat. Confecit prior iter
Caesar atque ex magnis rupibus nactus planitiem in hac
contra hostem aciem instruit. Afranius, cum ab equitatu
novissimum agmen premeretur, ante se hostem videret,
4 collem quendam nactus ibi constitit. Ex eo loco IIII caetratorum cohortes in montem qui erat in conspectu omnium excelsissimus mittit. Hunc magno cursu concitatos
iubet occupare, eo consilio uti ipse eodem omnibus copiis
contenderet et mutato itinere iugis Otogesam perveniret.
5 Hunc cum obliquo itinere caetrati peterent conspicatus
equitatus Caesaris in cohortes impetum facit. Nec mini-
mam partem temporis equitum vim caetrati sustinere
potuerunt omnesque ab his circumventi in conspectu
utriusque exercitus interficiuntur.

71. Erat occasio bene gerendae rei. Neque vero id Caesarem fugiebat tanto sub oculis accepto detrimento perterritum exercitum sustinere non posse, praesertim cir-
cumdatum undique equitatu cum in loco aequo atque
aperto confligeretur. Idque ex omnibus partibus ab eo
2 flagitabatur. Concurrebant legati centuriones tribunique
militum: ne dubitaret proelium committere; omnium esse
3 militum paratissimos animos; Afranianos contra multis
rebus sui timoris signa misisse, quod suis non subve-
nissent, quod de colle non decederent, quod vix equitum
incursus sustinerent collatisque in unum locum signis con-
4 ferti neque ordines neque signa servarent; quod si iniquitatem loci timeret datum iri tamen aliquo loco pugnandi
facultatem, quod certe inde decedendum esset Afranio
nec sine aqua permanere posset.

---

[89] Infantry units equipped with small round shields (1.39.1).

in camp; there was no way to get help to them, cut off as
they were by Caesar's army. Caesar completed the dis- 3
tance first. Emerging from the rocky heights, he came to
a flat area and drew up his line there facing the enemy.
Afranius, with his rearguard under pressure from the cavalry and the enemy visible ahead, halted when he came to
a hill. From there he sent four native cohorts to the high- 4
est mountain in sight.[89] He ordered them to move at a fast
run and seize this, thinking that he would head there with
his entire force and so reach Otogesa by a new route along
the ridges. When the native troops deviated toward this 5
objective they were observed and attacked by Caesar's
cavalry. Unable to withstand the charge even for a moment, they were all surrounded by the cavalry and killed
with both armies watching.

71. This was an opportunity for decisive action. It did
not escape Caesar that after taking—and watching—such
damage the terrified army could not hold out, particularly when surrounded on all sides by cavalry, since the
battlefield was level and open. From every direction he
heard demands for an engagement. Legionary command- 2
ers, centurions, and staff officers quickly gathered: "Do
not hesitate to engage. The morale of all of our soldiers is
at its peak. Afranius' men, by contrast, have signaled their 3
alarm in many matters: in not sending help to their own
men, not coming down from the hill, barely withstanding
the cavalry attacks, and not preserving their formations or
units, given that they have collected their standards in a
single spot and are crowded together. But if you are wor- 4
ried about the location's drawbacks, there will be an opportunity to fight somewhere, because Afranius certainly
has to withdraw from this area; he cannot stay long without
water."

72. Caesar in eam spem venerat se sine pugna et sine vulnere suorum rem conficere posse quod re frumentaria 2 adversarios interclusisset: cur etiam secundo proelio aliquos ex suis amitteret? cur vulnerari pateretur optime meritos de se milites? cur denique fortunam periclitaretur? praesertim cum non minus esset imperatoris consilio 3 superare quam gladio. Movebatur etiam misericordia civium quos interficiendos videbat, quibus salvis atque inco- 4 lumibus rem obtinere malebat. Hoc consilium Caesaris plerisque non probabatur. Milites vero palam inter se loquebantur: quoniam talis occasio victoriae dimitteretur, etiam cum vellet Caesar sese non esse pugnaturos. Ille in sua sententia perseverat. Et paulum ex eo loco digreditur 5 ut timorem adversariis minuat. Petreius atque Afranius oblata facultate in castra sese referunt. Caesar praesidiis <in> montibus dispositis, omni ad Hiberum intercluso itinere, quam proxime potest hostium castris castra communit.

73. Postero die duces adversariorum perturbati quod omnem rei frumentariae fluminisque Hiberi spem dimi- 2 serant de reliquis rebus consultabant. Erat unum iter Ilerdam si reverti vellent, alterum si Tarraconem peterent. Haec consiliantibus iis nuntiantur aquatores ab equitatu 3 premi nostro. Qua re cognita crebras stationes disponunt equitum et cohortium alariarum legionariasque interici- unt cohortes vallumque ex castris ad aquam ducere inci-

72. Caesar had conceived the hope that he would be able to finish the business without fighting or shedding his men's blood, since he had cut off the enemy from their food supply. "Even if the battle goes well, why should I 2 lose any of my men? Why should I allow soldiers who have given me excellent service to be wounded? Finally, why should I tempt fortune? Especially since a strategic victory is as appropriate to a general as a military victory." He 3 was also moved by pity for the fellow citizens who he saw would inevitably be killed; he wanted instead to accomplish his goal with them safe and sound. Most people did 4 not approve of Caesar's strategy. Indeed the soldiers said openly among themselves that they would not fight, not even when Caesar wanted them to, since he was throwing away such an occasion for victory. He held firm to his position, even moving a small distance off in order to give his opponents less cause for alarm. Petreius and Afranius 5 went back to their camp when offered the opportunity. Caesar stationed garrisons in the mountains and cut off every route to the Ebro. He then fortified his camp as close as possible to the enemy's.

73. On the next day the enemy leaders, perturbed now that they had given up the prospect of a food supply and the Ebro River, held a discussion about what remained. There was one road if they wanted to return to Ilerda, 2 another if Tarraco was their objective. They were still discussing these matters when they got word that the water detail was under pressure from our cavalry. Upon learn- 3 ing this they deployed numerous outposts of cavalry and auxiliary cohorts, with legionary cohorts in between, and began to extend an earthwork from the camp to a water source, so that they would be able to get water within

piunt ut intra munitionem et sine timore et sine statio-
4 nibus aquari possent. Id opus inter se Petreius atque
Afranius partiuntur ipsique perficiendi operis causa longius progrediuntur.

74. Quorum discessu liberam nacti milites colloquio-
rum facultatem vulgo procedunt, et quem quisque in
castris notum aut municipem habebat conquirit atque
2 evocat. Primum agunt gratias omnes omnibus quod sibi
perterritis pridie pepercissent: eorum se beneficio vivere.
Dein de imperatoris fide quaerunt rectene se illi sint com-
missuri, et quod non ab initio fecerint armaque quod cum
hominibus necessariis et consanguineis contulerint que-
3 runtur. His provocati sermonibus fidem ab imperatore de
Petrei atque Afrani vita petunt ne quod in se scelus con-
cepisse neu suos prodidisse videantur. Quibus confirmatis
rebus se statim signa translaturos confirmant legatosque
de pace primorum ordinum centuriones ad Caesarem
4 mittunt. Interim alii suos in castra invitandi causa addu-
cunt, alii ab suis abducuntur, adeo ut una castra iam facta
ex binis viderentur. Compluresque tribuni militum <et>
centuriones ad Caesarem veniunt seque ei commendant.
5 Idem hoc fit a principibus Hispaniae, quos illi evocaverant
et secum in castris habebant obsidum loco. Hi suos notos
hospitesque quaerebant per quem quisque eorum aditum
6 commendationis haberet ad Caesarem. Afrani etiam filius
adulescens de sua ac parentis sui salute cum Caesare per

their own defenses without fear and without outposts. Pe- 4
treius and Afranius divided the job between them and
went some distance from camp in order to bring it to
completion.

74. With their departure, the soldiers had a clear opportunity for negotiations, and they came out in a body,
each man looking and calling for his acquaintances and
townsmen in Caesar's camp. First they gave collective 2
thanks to everyone for having spared them the previous
day, when they were terrified. "Your kindness kept us
alive." Then they asked about the general's reliability, and
whether it would be a good move to entrust themselves
to him, lamenting the fact that they had not done so
from the beginning and had fought against men who were
their friends and relatives. Encouraged by this discussion 3
they asked for the general's promise concerning the future
of Petreius and Afranius, so that people would not think
that they had incurred guilt or betrayed their own side.
Once these matters were settled the men guaranteed that
they would transfer their standards immediately, and sent
to Caesar a peace delegation of chief centurions. Mean- 4
while, some led friends into their own camp to entertain
them, and others were led off by friends, with the result
that the two camps seemed to have become one. Several
staff officers and centurions went and commended themselves to Caesar. Spain's leading men did the same. (The 5
enemy had summoned these men and kept them in camp
with them as hostages.) These sought out their acquaintances and guests, hoping to get from them the opening
of a recommendation to Caesar. Even Afranius' adolescent 6
son began negotiations with Caesar, through Caesar's officer Sulpicius, about his own welfare and that of his father.

7 Sulpicium legatum agebat. Erant plena laetitia et gratula-
tione omnia, eorum qui tanta pericula vitasse et eorum qui
sine vulnere tantas res confecisse videbantur. Magnumque
fructum suae pristinae lenitatis omnium iudicio Caesar
ferebat, consiliumque eius a cunctis probabatur.

75. Quibus rebus nuntiatis Afranius ab instituto opere
discedit seque in castra recipit sic paratus, ut videbatur, ut
quicumque accidisset casus hunc quieto et aequo animo
2 ferret. Petreius vero non deserit sese. Armat familiam.
Cum hac et praetoria cohorte caetratorum barbarisque
equitibus paucis, beneficiariis suis quos suae custodiae
causa habere consuerat, improviso ad vallum advolat, colloquia militum interrumpit, nostros repellit a castris. Quos
3 deprendit interficit. Reliqui coeunt inter se et repentino
periculo exterriti sinistras sagis involvunt gladiosque de-
stringunt atque ita se a caetratis equitibusque defendunt
castrorum propinquitate confisi seque in castra recipiunt
et ab iis cohortibus quae erant in statione ad portas de-
fenduntur.

76. Quibus rebus confectis flens Petreius manipulos
circumit militesque appellat, neu se neu Pompeium absentem imperatorem suum adversariis ad supplicium tra-
2 dant obsecrat. Fit celeriter concursus in praetorium.
Postulat ut iurent omnes se exercitum ducesque non de-
serturos neque prodituros neque sibi separatim a reliquis
3 consilium capturos. Princeps in haec verba iurat ipse.
Idem ius iurandum adigit Afranium. Subsequuntur tribuni militum centurionesque. Centuriatim producti mi-

Everything was full of joy and thanksgiving on both sides: 7
the one saw themselves as having escaped great danger,
the other as having achieved a great success without
bloodshed. In everyone's opinion Caesar was winning
great credit for his former clemency, and his strategy had
everyone's approval.

75. When this news arrived Afranius left the work he
had begun and returned to camp, apparently prepared
to accept the situation quietly and steadily however it
turned out. Petreius, however, remained himself, arming   2
his household. With this and the Spanish cohort that was
his official escort, and a few native cavalry on special assignment whom he customarily used as a bodyguard, he
raced unexpectedly to the fortification, broke off the soldiers' discussions, and ejected our men from his camp.
Whoever he caught he killed. The rest came together and,   3
alarmed by the sudden danger, wrapped cloaks around
their left arms and drew their swords. In this way they
defended themselves against the Spanish infantry and cavalry, counting on the proximity of the two camps, and returned to their own camp under the protection of the
cohorts stationed near the gates.

76. When he had accomplished this Petreius went
weeping from one unit to the next and appealed to the
soldiers; he pleaded with them not to deliver either him
or their absent commander Pompey to the enemy for punishment. A crowd assembled quickly at headquarters. He   2
demanded that everyone swear that they would neither
desert nor betray the army or their leaders, nor take
thought for themselves separately from the rest. He was   3
the first to take this oath. He forced the same on Afranius.
Staff officers and centurions followed; the soldiers came

4 lites idem iurant. Edicunt penes quem quisque sit Caesaris miles ut producat. Productos palam in praetorio
interficiunt. Sed plerosque ii qui receperant celant noc-
5 tuque per vallum emittunt. Sic terrore oblato a ducibus
crudelitas in supplicio nova religio iuris iurandi spem
praesentis deditionis sustulit mentesque militum convertit
et rem ad pristinam belli rationem redegit.

77. Caesar milites adversariorum qui in castra per tempus colloqui venerant summa diligentia conquiri et remitti
2 iubet. Sed ex numero tribunorum militum centurionum-
que nonnulli sua voluntate apud eum remanserunt. Quos
ille postea magno in honore habuit. Centuriones in priores
ordines, equites Romanos in tribunicium restituit honorem.

78. Premebantur Afraniani pabulatione, aquabantur
aegre. Frumenti copiam legionarii nonnullam habebant
quod dierum XXII ab Ilerda frumentum iussi erant ef-
ferre, caetrati auxiliaresque nullam, quorum erant et facultates ad parandum exiguae et corpora insueta ad onera
2 portanda. Itaque magnus eorum cotidie numerus ad Caesarem perfugiebat. In his erat angustiis res. Sed ex propo-
sitis consiliis duobus explicitius videbatur Ilerdam reverti,
quod ibi paulum frumenti reliquerant. Ibi se reliquum
3 consilium explicaturos confidebant. Tarraco aberat longius, quo spatio plures rem posse casus recipere intellege-

---

90 The number seems too high.
91 Their departure from Ilerda was four days behind them.

forward by centuries and swore the same thing. Petreius 4
and Afranius issued an edict that anyone who had a Caesarian soldier with him had to bring him forward. Those
brought forward were openly killed at headquarters. But
most of the men who had taken someone in concealed
them and sent them out over the fortification during
the night. In view of the terror thus disseminated by the 5
commanders, the cruelty of the executions and the fresh
scruples of an oath removed the hope of an immediate
surrender and changed the men's minds, returning the
situation to the previous plan of campaign.

77. Caesar ordered that the enemy soldiers who had
come into his camp during the discussions be sought with
the utmost diligence and sent back. But some of the staff 2
officers and centurions remained with him of their own
volition. Afterward he treated them with high honor, re-
storing the centurions to their former ranks and the Romans of equestrian status to their officer positions.

78. Afranius' army was pressed for fodder, and obtained water with difficulty. The legionaries had some reserves of grain because they had been ordered to carry
twenty-two[90] days' worth of grain from Ilerda.[91] But the
native infantry and auxiliary troops had none, since they
had few opportunities to acquire grain and their bodies
were not used to carrying loads. So every day a large num- 2
ber of them deserted to Caesar. Such were the difficulties
of the situation. But of the two plans before them it
seemed simpler to return to Ilerda because they had left
a little grain there; they were confident about working out
the rest of the plan at Ilerda. (Tarraco was further away, 3
and they realized that in that distance a number of misfortunes could befall the maneuver.) After this plan was ap-

4 bant. Hoc probato consilio ex castris proficiscuntur. Caesar equitatu praemisso qui novissimum agmen carperet atque impediret ipse cum legionibus subsequitur. Nullum intercedebat tempus quin extremi cum equitibus proeliarentur.

79. Genus erat hoc pugnae. Expeditae cohortes novissimum agmen claudebant pluresque in locis campestribus

2 subsistebant. Si mons erat ascendendus facile ipsa loci natura periculum repellebat quod ex locis superioribus

3 qui antecesserant suos ascendentes protegebant. Cum vallis aut locus declivis suberat neque ii qui antecesserant morantibus opem ferre poterant, equites vero ex loco superiore in aversos tela coiciebant, tum magno erat in

4 periculo res. Relinquebatur ut cum eiusmodi locis esset appropinquatum legionum signa consistere iuberent magnoque impetu equitatum repellerent, eo submoto repente incitati cursu sese in valles universi demitterent atque ita

5 transgressi rursus in locis superioribus consisterent. Nam tantum ab equitum suorum auxiliis aberant, quorum numerum habebant magnum, ut eos superioribus perterritos proeliis in medium reciperent agmen ultroque eos tuerentur. Quorum nulli ex itinere excedere licebat quin ab equitatu Caesaris exciperetur.

80. Tali dum pugnatur modo lente atque paulatim proceditur, crebroque ut sint auxilio suis subsistunt, ut tum

2 accidit. Milia enim progressi IIII vehementiusque peragitati ab equitatu montem excelsum capiunt ibique una fronte contra hostem castra muniunt neque iumentis

---

92 Or, "there were no intervals in which the rearmost were not engaged with the cavalry" (cf. *BG* 5.53.5).

proved they set out from camp. Caesar sent his cavalry   4
ahead to harass and delay the rearguard; he himself followed with the legions. In no time the rearmost were engaged with the cavalry.[92]

79. The nature of the fighting was as follows. Unencumbered cohorts brought up the rear of Afranius' column. The majority would make a stand where the ground
was flat. If a hill had to be climbed, the nature of the ter-   2
rain itself warded off danger, in that those who had gone
ahead would protect their own from higher ground as they
came up. When they came to a ravine or descent, and   3
those who had gone ahead were unable to assist those
behind, and Caesar's cavalry was hurling weapons from
higher ground at their backs, then their situation was very
dangerous. The only thing to do when they approached   4
locations of this sort was to order the legions to make a
stand, push the cavalry back with a concerted charge, descend into the ravines at a run and all together as soon as
the cavalry was out of the way, and make a stand again on
higher ground after crossing in this fashion. (Their cavalry,   5
of which they had a great number, was of so little assistance that Afranius and Petreius took these men, thoroughly cowed as they were by earlier battles, into the
middle of their column and themselves provided cover for
them; none of them could deviate from the line of march
without being captured by Caesar's cavalry.)

80. When men fight in this manner, their advance is
slow and incremental, and they stop frequently to help
their own, as happened then. When Afranius and Petreius   2
had gone four miles and were being harassed quite vigorously by the cavalry, they seized a high hill and fortified
a camp there on the one side facing the enemy. They

3   onera deponunt. Vbi Caesaris castra posita tabernacu-
laque constituta et dimissos equites pabulandi causa animadverterunt sese subito proripiunt hora circiter sexta
eiusdem diei. Et spem nacti morae discessu nostrorum

4   equitum iter facere incipiunt. Qua re animadversa Caesar
expeditis[79] legionibus subsequitur. Praesidio impedimentis paucas cohortes relinquit. ⟨Relictas⟩[80] hora decima
subsequi, pabulatores equitesque revocari iubet. Celeriter
equitatus ad cotidianum itineris officium revertitur.

5   Pugnatur acriter ad novissimum agmen, adeo ut paene
terga convertant, compluresque milites—etiam nonnulli
centuriones—interficiuntur. Instabat agmen Caesaris atque universum imminebat.

     81. Tum vero neque ad explorandum idoneum locum
castris neque ad progrediendum data facultate consistunt
necessario et procul ab aqua et natura iniquo loco castra

2   ponunt. Sed isdem de causis Caesar quae supra sunt de-
monstratae proelio non lacessit. Et eo die tabernacula
statui passus non est quo paratiores essent ad insequen-

3   dum omnes sive noctu sive interdiu erumperent. Illi animadverso vitio castrorum tota nocte munitiones proferunt
castraque castris convertunt. Hoc idem postero die a
prima luce faciunt totumque in ea re diem consumunt.

4   Sed quantum opere processerant et castra protulerant
tanto aberant ab aqua longius, et praesenti malo aliis ma-

5   lis remedia dabantur. Prima nocte aquandi causa nemo

---

[79] expeditis *Nipperdey*: relictis [-tas T^{ac}] ω: refectis *Deiter*:
relictis ⟨munitionibus cum⟩ *Köchly*   [80] ⟨relictas⟩ *Kruse*

---

[93] Among the many alternatives to Nipperdey's emendation
"followed with unencumbered legions," are those proposed by

did not unload the pack animals. When they saw Caesar's 3
camp established, his tents pitched, and his cavalry released for foraging, they suddenly launched themselves
onward around noon that same day. They began their
march in the hope that our cavalry's departure would
cause delay. Upon seeing this, Caesar followed with unen- 4
cumbered[93] legions, leaving a few cohorts to guard the
baggage. He ordered those left behind to follow in the late
afternoon and the cavalry to be recalled. The cavalry re- 5
turned quickly to their regular role on the march. At the
enemy's rearguard the combat was intense, such that they
nearly ran away, and a number of soldiers, indeed some
centurions, were killed. Caesar's whole column began to
press and threaten.

81. At that point, with no chance of looking for a suitable spot for camp or advancing, they were forced to halt
and make camp far from water in a spot that was by its
nature disadvantageous. For the aforementioned reasons, 2
however, Caesar did not provoke a fight. That day he did
not permit the men to pitch their tents, so that everyone
would be quite ready to follow whether the enemy broke
out by night or by day. Aware of their camp's faults Afra- 3
nius and Petreius pushed their defenses forward all night
long and gradually shifted their campsite. They did the
same thing the next day starting at dawn and spent the
whole day on it. But the further they went with their earth- 4
work, and the more they pushed their camp forward, the
further they were from water, and the remedies for the
present problem were other problems. The first night no 5

Deiter and Köchly: "followed with refreshed legions" and "left
the fortifications and followed with his legions," respectively.

egreditur ex castris. Proximo die praesidio in castris relicto
universas ad aquam copias educunt. Pabulatum emittitur
6 nemo. His eos suppliciis male haberi Caesar et necessa-
riam subire deditionem quam proelio decertare malebat.
Conatur tamen eos vallo fossaque circummunire ut quam
maxime repentinas eorum eruptiones demoretur. Quo
7 necessario descensuros existimabat. Illi et inopia pabuli
adducti et quo essent ad id[81] expeditiores omnia sarcinaria
iumenta interfici iubent.

82. In his operibus consiliisque biduum consumitur.
Tertio die magna iam pars operis Caesaris processerat. Illi
impediendae rei [quae munitionis fiebat][82] causa hora circiter nona signo dato legiones educunt aciemque sub ca-
2 stris instruunt. Caesar ab opere legiones revocat, equitatum omnem convenire iubet, aciem instruit. Contra
opinionem enim militum famamque omnium videri proe-
3 lium defugisse magnum detrimentum adferebat. Sed isdem de causis quae sunt cognitae quominus dimicare
vellet movebatur atque hoc etiam magis, quod spati bre-
vitas etiam in fugam coniectis adversariis non multum ad
4 summam victoriae iuvare poterat. Non enim amplius pedum milibus duobus a castris castra distabant. Hinc duas
partes acies occupabant duae. Tertia vacabat ad incursum
5 atque impetum militum relicta. Si proelium committere-

[81] id] iter *Faerno*

[82] rei [quae munitionis fiebat] causa *Faerno*: reliquae munitionis causa [fiebat] *Forchhammer. The manuscripts offer three
unacceptable variants for the words between* rei *and* causa.

94 For "when sallying," Faerno proposed "for the march."

one left the camp to get water. The following day they left a guard in the camp and led out their whole force to the water source; no one was sent out to forage. It was better 6 that they suffer this sort of torture and submit to a necessary surrender, Caesar felt, than that he decide matters with a battle. He nevertheless tried to enclose them with an earthwork and a trench in order to maximize the delay for sudden sallies; he thought they would necessarily have recourse to this tactic. They ordered all the pack animals 7 to be killed, induced by the shortage of fodder, and in order to reduce their encumbrances when sallying.[94]

82. Two days were spent fortifying and planning. On the third day a large part of Caesar's earthwork was already complete. With a signal at around midafternoon Afranius and Petreius led out their legions in order to hinder his work,[95] and drew up their line near his camp. Caesar recalled his legions from their work, ordered his entire cavalry to assemble, and drew up his line, for the appearance of having avoided a battle—in opposition to what the soldiers' thought and everyone said[96]—was very damaging. But he was inclined to want to avoid fighting for the familiar reasons, and even more because the limited space could do little to facilitate a decisive victory even if the enemy was routed. (For the two camps were no more than two thousand feet apart. The two lines occupied two thirds of this space; one third was left clear for the soldiers' running charge.) If an engagement were to begin, the proxim-

[95] For "his work," Forchhammer proposed "the rest of his fortification."

[96] The phrase "what everyone said" (cf. 3.36.1) could also be rendered "his reputation in everyone's eyes" (cf. 3.56.2).

tur propinquitas castrorum celerem superatis ex fuga receptum dabat. Hac de causa constituerat signa inferenti-
bus resistere, prior proelio non lacessere.

83. Acies erat Afraniana duplex legionum V, tertium in
2 subsidiis locum alariae cohortes obtinebant, Caesaris tri-
plex, sed primam aciem quaternae cohortes ex V legionibus tenebant. Has subsidiariae ternae et rursus aliae toti-
dem suae cuiusque legionis subsequebantur. Sagittarii
funditoresque media continebantur acie. Equitatus latera
3 cingebat. Toli instructa acie tenere uterque propositum
videbatur, Caesar nisi coactus proelium non committere,[83]
ille ut opera Caesaris impediret. Producitur tamen res,
aciesque ad solis occasum continentur. Inde utrique in
castra discedunt.

4   Postero die munitiones institutas Caesar parat perficere, illi vadum fluminis Sicoris temptare si transire pos-
5 sent. Qua re animadversa Caesar Germanos levis armaturae equitumque partem flumen traicit crebrasque in ripis
custodias disponit.

84. Tandem omnibus rebus obsessi, quartum iam diem
sine pabulo retentis iumentis, aquae lignorum frumenti
inopia, colloquium petunt et id si fieri possit semoto a
2 militibus loco. Vbi id a Caesare negatum et palam si colloqui vellent concessum est datur obsidis loco Caesari fi-
3 lius Afrani. Venitur in eum locum quem Caesar delegit.
Audiente utroque exercitu loquitur Afranius: non esse aut
ipsis aut militibus suscensendum quod fidem erga impe-

---

[83] non committere *MU* (*see 1.82.5*): committere *STV*

---

[97] The text is uncertain but the sense is clear from context.

ity of the camp gave the defeated a quick refuge after they fled. For this reason he had decided to resist an attack by the enemy, but not to initiate a fight.

83. Afranius' battle formation had two lines made up of five legions; auxiliary cohorts held the third position as reserves. Caesar's had three lines, the first of them occu- 2 pied by four cohorts each from five legions. Behind and supporting these were three cohorts from the respective legions, and then the same number again. Archers and slingers were kept in the middle of the formation. Cavalry secured the flanks. With their armies drawn up thus, each 3 commander seemed to be achieving his purpose, Caesar not to engage unless compelled,[97] Afranius to hinder Caesar's works. The business dragged on, however, and they maintained their formations until sunset. Then they both went back to camp.

The following day Caesar prepared to complete the 4 fortifications he had begun, Afranius and Petreius to test the ford on the Sicoris River, to see whether they could cross. When this came to his attention Caesar sent the 5 Germans from his light-armed force and a portion of his cavalry across the river and posted numerous patrols on the banks.

84. At last, thwarted in everything, with animals deprived of fodder for the fourth straight day and a shortage of water, firewood, and food supplies, Afranius and Petreius asked for talks, if possible somewhere away from the soldiers. When that was refused by Caesar, and he agreed 2 to talks if they were willing to hold them in public, Afranius' son was given to Caesar as a hostage. They came to 3 a place Caesar had chosen. Each army listened as Afranius spoke. "You should not be angry with us or our soldiers be-

115

4 ratorem suum Cn. Pompeium conservare voluerint; sed
satis iam fecisse officio satisque supplici tulisse perpessos
omnium rerum inopiam; nunc vero paene ut feras[84] cir-
cummunitos prohiberi aqua, prohiberi ingressu, neque
corpore dolorem neque animo ignominiam ferre posse;
5 itaque se victos confiteri; orare atque obsecrare si qui locus misericordiae relinquatur ne ad ultimum supplicium
progredi necesse habeat. Haec quam potest demississime
et subiectissime exponit.

85. Ad ea Caesar respondit: nulli omnium has partes
2 vel querimoniae vel miserationis minus convenisse; reliquos enim omnes officium suum praestitisse, ⟨se,⟩ qui
etiam bona conditione et loco et tempore aequo confligere
noluerit ut quam integerrima essent ad pacem omnia,
exercitum suum, qui iniuria etiam accepta suisque interfectis quos in sua potestate habuerit conservarit et texerit,
illius denique exercitus milites, qui per se de concilianda
pace egerint, qua in re omnium suorum vitae consulendum
3 putarint; sic omnium ordinum partes in misericordia
constitisse, ipsos duces a pace abhorruisse; eos neque colloqui neque indutiarum iura servasse et homines imperi-
tos[85] et per colloquium deceptos crudelissime interfecisse;
4 accidisse igitur his quod plerumque hominum nimia pertinacia atque arrogantia accidere soleat, uti eo recurrant
et id cupidissime petant quod paulo ante contempserint;

---

[84] feras *Vossius* (*see Lucan 4.313*): feminas ω
[85] imperitos] imparatos *R. Bentley*

---

[98] For negotiations ensuring the safety of Afranius and Petreius in particular, see 1.74.3.   [99] For "inexperienced
men," Richard Bentley proposed "men caught off guard."

cause we chose to keep faith with our commander, Gnaeus Pompey. But we have now satisfied our duty and suffered 4 enough punishment in every sort of privation. At present, in fact, we are being kept from water, walled in almost like wild animals, kept from moving, and our bodies cannot take the pain or our spirits the humiliation. Therefore we 5 confess ourselves beaten. We beg and plead—if there is any room left for compassion—that you not consider it necessary to proceed to the ultimate punishment." He laid out this case as humbly and submissively as possible.

85. To this Caesar replied: "Anyone would be more suitable than you to deliver either reproaches or appeals for pity, for everyone else has done what he should: I 2 myself, who chose not to fight, even when the conditions were good and the location and occasion favorable, in order to keep the whole situation as open as possible to peace; my army, which preserved and protected those whom it had in its power, even though it had been mistreated and its men had been killed; and finally the soldiers of your army, who took the initiative in arranging a truce, a matter in which they felt they ought to consider the safety of everyone on their side.[98] Thus the actions of 3 every rank involved compassion, but you leaders shied away from peace. You did not uphold the rules pertaining to talks and truces, and with extreme cruelty you killed inexperienced men[99] duped by the talks. You are therefore 4 in the situation that generally tends to arise from human obstinacy and arrogance, when excessive: you are reverting to something you scorned a little while ago, and now seek it with the utmost eagerness. I am not now going 5

5   neque nunc se illorum humilitate neque aliqua temporis
opportunitate postulare quibus rebus opes augeantur
suae, sed eos exercitus quos contra se multos iam annos

6   aluerint velle dimitti; neque enim VI legiones alia de causa
missas in Hispaniam septimamque ibi conscriptam, neque
tot tantasque classes[86] paratas neque submissos duces rei

7   militaris peritos; nihil horum ad pacandas Hispanias, nihil
ad usum provinciae provisum, quae propter diuturnitatem

8   pacis nullum auxilium desiderarit; omnia haec iam pridem
contra se parari; in se novi generis imperia constitui, ut
idem ad portas urbanis praesideat rebus et duas bellicosis-

9   simas provincias absens tot annos obtineat; in se iura magistratuum commutari, ne ex praetura et consulatu, ut
semper, sed per paucos probati et electi in provincias mittantur; in se aetatis excusationem nihil valere, quod superioribus bellis probati[87] ad obtinendos exercitus vincen-

10   tur; in se uno non servari quod sit omnibus datum semper
imperatoribus, ut rebus feliciter gestis aut cum honore
aliquo aut certe sine ignominia domum revertantur exer-

11   citumque dimittant; quae tamen omnia et se tulisse patienter et esse laturum; neque nunc id agere ut ab illis
abductum exercitum teneat ipse, quod tamen sibi difficile

12   non sit, sed ne illi habeant quo contra se uti possint; proinde, ut esset dictum, provinciis excederent exercitumque
dimitterent; sed si id sit factum se nociturum nemini; hanc
unam atque extremam esse pacis conditionem.

[86] tot tantasque classes] cohortes alasque *Madvig (see 1.39.1)*
[87] probati[2]] fracti *Heller*

---

[100] For "so many large fleets," Madvig proposed "auxiliary
infantry and cavalry."
[101] For "tested," Heller proposed "worn out."

to use your prostration or any temporary advantage to make demands that will increase my resources. But I want the armies that you have maintained against me for many years now to be dismissed. It was for this reason alone that 6 six legions were sent to Spain and a seventh was raised there, and that so many large fleets[100] were prepared, and generals with military expertise dispatched. None of this 7 was intended for the pacification of Spain, none for the benefit of a province that, given the longstanding peace, needed no support. All of these preparations have long 8 since been aimed at me. It is with reference to me that a new type of military command is now in place, such that one man presides over Rome's affairs just outside the city and controls two very warlike provinces in absentia for years at a time. It is with reference to me that magistrates' 9 rights are being altered, such that men are not sent to govern provinces after serving as praetor or consul, as always, but after being approved and selected by a few men. It is with reference to me that the excuse of age is rendered invalid, such that men tested[101] in earlier wars are being recalled to command armies. It is with reference to 10 me alone that a benefit always accorded to every victorious general has fallen into abeyance, namely, that after successful campaigns they return home and dismiss their armies with a degree of honor and certainly without humiliation. And yet I have borne everything patiently and 11 will continue to do so. My present aim is not to take an army from you and keep it for myself, although this would not be difficult for me, but to prevent you from having an army to use against me. Accordingly, as I said, you must 12 leave your provinces and dismiss your army. But if this happens, I will not harm anyone. This is the single and final condition for peace."

86. Id vero militibus fuit pergratum et iucundum—ut ex ipsa significatione cognosci potuit—ut qui victi[88] aliquid incommodi expectavissent ultro praemium missionis
2 ferrent. Nam cum de loco et de tempore eius rei controversia inferretur, et voce et manibus universi ex vallo ubi constiterant significare coeperunt ut statim dimitterentur: neque omni interposita fide firmum esse posse si in aliud
3 tempus differretur. Paucis cum esset in utramque partem verbis disputatum res huc deducitur ut ii qui habeant domicilium aut possessionem in Hispania statim, reliqui
4 ad Varum flumen dimittantur. Ne quid iis noceatur neu quis invitus sacramentum dicere cogatur a Caesare cavetur.

87. Caesar ex eo tempore dum ad flumen Varum veniatur se frumentum daturum pollicetur. Addit etiam ut quod quisque eorum in bello amiserit, quae sint penes milites suos, iis qui amiserant restituatur. Militibus aequa facta
2 aestimatione pecuniam pro his rebus dissoluit. Quascumque postea controversias inter se milites habuerunt sua
3 sponte ad Caesarem in ius adierunt. Petreius atque Afranius cum stipendium ab legionibus paene seditione facta flagitaretur, cuius illi diem nondum venisse dicerent, Caesar ut cognosceret postulatum est eoque utrique quod
4 statuit contenti fuerunt. Parte circiter tertia exercitus eo biduo dimissa duas legiones suas antecedere, reliquas subsequi iussit, ut non longo inter se spatio castra facerent.

---

[88] victi aliquid *Damon*: aliqui victi *MUS*: aliqui iusti *TV*

---

[102] In place of "being the defeated party," editors usually print *iusti*, "justified," which modifies hardship.

[103] That is, the eastern boundary of Transalpine Gaul.

86. This pleased and gladdened the soldiers, as could be understood simply from their demonstrations, inasmuch as those who, being the defeated party,[102] had expected some hardship, were being given, without having asked for it, the reward of discharge. For when its location 2 and timing came under discussion, they all began shouting and gesticulating from the rampart where they stood to signify that they should be discharged immediately. No pledge given in the meantime, they said, could make their discharge a sure thing if it was deferred to another time. After a brief statement on each side of the question, the 3 matter ended thus: those who had a home or property in Spain would be dismissed immediately, the rest at the Var River.[103] Caesar guaranteed that they would not be 4 harmed and that no one would be forced to enlist unwillingly.

87. Caesar promised to supply food from then until they reached the Var. He also added that whatever items any of them had lost in the war, if they were in his soldiers' possession, would be returned to those who had lost them. To his soldiers he gave monetary compensation for these items after a fair appraisal. Thereafter the soldiers of their 2 own accord approached Caesar for adjudication of whatever internal disputes they had. As for Petreius and Afra- 3 nius, when the legions demanded—in what nearly became a mutiny—their pay, and they claimed that it was not yet due, people requested that Caesar hear the case, and both sides were content with his settlement. After dismissing 4 about a third of the army within two days, he ordered two of his legions to go ahead and the rest to follow; they were to make camp at no great distance from one another. He

5   Eique negotio Q. Fufium Calenum legatum praeficit. Hoc
eius praescripto ex Hispania ad Varum flumen est iter
factum atque ibi reliqua pars exercitus dimissa est.

put Quintus Fufius Calenus in charge of this operation. The march to the Var proceeded in accordance with his instructions, and there the remainder of the army was discharged. 5

LIBER II

1. Dum haec in Hispania geruntur C. Trebonius legatus,
qui ad oppugnationem Massiliae relictus erat, duabus ex
partibus aggerem vineas turresque ad oppidum agere in-
2 stituit. Vna erat proxima portui navalibusque, altera ad
partem[1] qua est aditus ex Gallia atque Hispania,[2] ad id
3 mare quod vergit ad[3] ostium Rhodani. Massilia enim fere
tribus ex oppidi partibus mari alluitur. Reliqua quarta est
quae aditum habeat ab terra. Huius quoque spati pars ea
quae ad arcem pertinet, loci natura et valle altissima mu-
4 nita, longam et difficilem habet oppugnationem. Ad ea
perficienda opera C. Trebonius magnam iumentorum atque hominum multitudinem ex omni provincia vocat, vi-
mina materiamque comportari iubet. Quibus comparatis
rebus aggerem in altitudinem pedum LXXX extruit.

2. Sed tanti erant antiquitus in oppido omnium rerum
ad bellum apparatus tantaque multitudo[4] tormentorum ut

---

[1] altera (*sc.* oppugnatio) ad partem *ω*: al- (*sc.* pars) ad p- *Nip-*
perdey: al- [ad p-] *Oudendorp*: al- ad portam *Jurin*

[2] [ex . . . Hispania] *Chacon*

[3] vergit ad *Chacon*: adigit [agit T^{ac}] ad *ω*: adigitur ad *Madvig*:
attingit [ad] *I. Vossius*

[4] multitudo] magnitudo *Jurin*

BOOK II

1. While this was going on in Spain, Caesar's officer Gaius Trebonius, who had been left behind for the assault on Marseilles, began to deploy a siege ramp, screens, and towers against the city from two sides. One was very close 2 to the harbor and dockyards, the other on the side[1] where there is an approach from Gaul and Spain, near the sea that faces[2] the Rhone mouth. For the sea washes against 3 Marseilles for practically three-quarters of the city's circumference, leaving one quarter that permits a land approach. Here too, in the part that lies near the citadel, protected as it is by the nature of the terrain and a very deep ravine, an assault is a long and difficult operation. To 4 complete his works Trebonius requisitioned a large quantity of pack animals and men from the whole province, and ordered wicker canes and timber to be delivered. After procuring these he built a siege ramp eighty feet high.

2. But from long past the city contained a great store of military supplies of every kind; so great was the quan-

---

[1] For "the other (*sc.* assault) on the side," scholars have proposed "the other (*sc.* side) on the side," "the other (*sc.* side)," and "the other (*sc.* side) near the gate."

[2] For "faces," Madvig and I. Vossius proposed "is driven against" and "touches," respectively.

eorum vim nullae contextae viminibus vineae sustinere
2 possent. Asseres enim pedum XII cuspidibus praefixi atque ii maximis ballistis missi per IIII ordines cratium in
3 terram defigebantur. Itaque pedalibus lignis coniunctis
inter se porticus integebantur atque hac agger inter manus
4 proferebatur. Antecedebat testudo pedum LX aequandi
loci causa, facta item ex fortissimis lignis, convoluta omnibus rebus quibus ignis iactus et lapides defendi possent.
5 Sed magnitudo operum, altitudo muri atque turrium,
multitudo tormentorum omnem administrationem tarda-
6 bat. Crebrae etiam per Albicos eruptiones fiebant ex oppido, ignesque aggeri et turribus inferebantur, quae facile
nostri milites repellebant magnisque ultro illatis detrimentis eos qui eruptionem fecerant in oppidum reiciebant.

3. Interim L. Nasidius, ab Cn. Pompeio cum classe
navium XVI, in quibus paucae erant aeratae, L. Domitio
Massiliensibusque subsidio missus, freto Siciliae impru-
2 dente atque inopinante Curione pervehitur. Appulsisque
Messanam navibus atque inde propter repentinum terrorem principum ac senatus fuga facta ⟨navem⟩ ex nava-
3 libus eorum deducit. Hac adiuncta ad reliquas naves cursum Massiliam versus perficit. Praemissaque clam navicula
Domitium Massiliensesque de suo adventu certiores facit
eosque magnopere hortatur ut rursus cum Bruti classe
additis suis auxiliis confligant.

4. Massilienses post superius incommodum veteres ad

---

3 For "quantity," Jurin proposed "size," which entails rendering *vim* with "their power" rather than "their number."

4 Curio held Sicily for Caesar (1.30.2).

5 See 1.58.5. Marseilles lost nine ships on that occasion.

tity[3] of catapults that no screens woven from wicker canes could withstand their number. Twelve-foot long shafts fit- 2 ted with points and hurled by huge engines would go through four layers of brushwood bundles and fix them- selves in the earth. Therefore covered galleries were made 3 from foot-square beams joined one to another, and the material for the ramp was passed hand to hand down these. At the front end, for leveling the ground, was a 4 "tortoise" sixty feet wide. This too was made from the strongest timbers and covered with every kind of defense against incendiary shot and stones. But the whole opera- 5 tion was hindered by the size of the works, the height of Marseilles' wall and towers, and the quantity of catapults. There were also frequent sorties by the Albici, and at- 6 tempts to set fire to the ramp and siege towers; our sol- diers repulsed these with ease and forced those who had made the sortie back into the town after themselves in- flicting significant losses.

3. Meanwhile Lucius Nasidius, who had been sent by Gnaeus Pompey as support for Lucius Domitius and Mar- seilles with a fleet of sixteen ships, a few equipped with rams, sailed through the Sicilian strait without Curio being aware of or anticipating the fact.[4] When he had put in at 2 Messana, and the town's leaders and councilors had evac- uated the place because of the sudden panic, he took a ship from their dockyards. After adding this to the rest he 3 finished his course toward Marseilles. Sending ahead a boat in secret he informed Domitius and the people of Marseilles about his approach and urged them strongly to add his forces to their own and engage with Brutus' fleet again.

4. After the earlier setback[5] Marseilles had brought

127

eundem numerum ex navalibus productas naves refece-
rant summaque industria armaverant. Remigum guberna-
2 torum magna copia suppetebat. Piscatoriasque adiecerant
atque contexerant ut essent ab ictu telorum remiges tuti.
3 Has sagittariis tormentisque compleverunt. Tali modo instructa classe omnium seniorum matrum familiae virgi-
num precibus et fletu excitati—extremo tempore civitati
subvenirent—non minore animo ac fiducia quam ante
4 dimicaverant naves conscendunt. Communi enim fit vitio
naturae ut invisis [latitatis] atque incognitis rebus magis
confidamus [vehementiusque exterreamur],⁵ ut tum accidit. Adventus enim L. Nasidi summa spe et voluntate civi-
5 tatem compleverat. Nacti idoneum ventum ex portu exeunt et Tauroenta, quod est castellum Massiliensium, ad
Nasidium perveniunt. Ibique naves expediunt rursusque
se ad confligendum animo confirmant et consilia com-
municant. Dextra pars attribuitur Massiliensibus, sinistra
Nasidio.

5. Eodem Brutus contendit aucto navium numero.
Nam ad eas quae factae erant Arelate per Caesarem cap-
tivae Massiliensium accesserant VI. Has superioribus die-
2 bus refecerat atque omnibus rebus instruxerat. Itaque
suos cohortatus—quos integros superavissent ut victos
contemnerent—plenus spei bonae atque animi adversus
eas proficiscitur.

---

⁵ [vehementiusque exterreamur] *Fabre*: vehementiusque ef-
feramur *Bentley*

---

⁶ After "unknown things," Fabre excised the nonsensical "and
become more intensely terrified," while Bentley proposed replacing it with "and become more intensely enthusiastic."

an equal number of old ships out of the dockyards, repaired them, and equipped them with the utmost effort. A large supply of rowers and pilots was available. Plus, 2 fishing boats had been added, newly furnished with decks so that the rowers would be safe from the impact of projectiles. They filled these with archers and catapults. With 3 the fleet thus equipped the men embarked, roused by the pleas and tears of a whole crowd of older men, matrons, and girls urging them to rescue the city in its moment of crisis. Their spirits and confidence were as high as in the earlier battle, for by a common defect of our nature it 4 happens that we put more reliance in unseen and unknown things,[6] as occurred then. (The arrival of Lucius Nasidius had filled the city with a very great sense of hope and purpose.) When they got a suitable wind they left 5 the harbor and went to Nasidium at Tauroeis, a stronghold belonging to Marseilles. There they got their ships ready and again encouraged one another for battle and exchanged plans. The right wing was assigned to Marseilles, the left to Nasidius.

5. Brutus made for the same spot with an augmented fleet, for to the ships made on Caesar's orders at Arles he had added six captured from Marseilles.[7] In the preceding days he had repaired these and equipped them fully. Therefore after encouraging his men—"You have noth- 2 ing to worry about from beaten men whom you defeated when they were unscathed!"—he set out against the enemy ships full of good hope and spirit.

[7] See 1.36.4–5 for Brutus' original fleet of twelve ships.

3   Facile erat ex castris C. Treboni atque omnibus superioribus locis prospicere in urbem ut omnis iuventus quae[6]
in oppido remanserat omnesque superioris aetatis cum
liberis atque uxoribus [publicis custodiisque][7] aut muro ad
caelum manus tenderent aut templa deorum immortalium
adirent et ante simulacra proiecti victoriam ab dis ex-
4 poscerent. Neque erat quisquam omnium quin in eius diei
casu suarum omnium fortunarum eventum consistere
5 existimaret. Nam et honesti ex iuventute et cuiusque aetatis amplissimi nominatim evocati atque obsecrati naves
conscenderant, ut si quid adversi accidisset ne ad conandum quidem sibi quicquam reliqui fore viderent, si superavissent vel domesticis opibus vel externis auxiliis de salute
urbis confiderent.

      6. Commisso proelio Massiliensibus res nulla ad virtu-
tem defuit, sed memores eorum praeceptorum quae paulo
ante ab suis acceperant hoc animo decertabant ut nullum
aliud tempus ad conandum habituri viderentur et—quibus in pugna vitae periculum acciderat— non ita multo se
reliquorum civium fatum antecedere existimarent, quibus
2 urbe capta eadem esset belli fortuna patienda. Diduc-
tisque nostris paulatim navibus et artificio gubernatorum
⟨et⟩ mobilitati navium locus dabatur. Et si quando nostri
facultatem nacti ferreis manibus iniectis navem religave-

---

[6] *Nipperdey transposed* ⟨custodiis⟩ *to follow* quae *and
emended* publicis *to* supplices *below.*

[7] [publicis custodiisque] aut *Dübner*: custodiisque publicis
aut *Carter*: aut supplices (*sc.* manus) [c-] *Nipperdey*: supplices
sordidatique aut *Paul*

---

[8] Nipperdey's transposition adds "as guards" here.

From Trebonius' camp and every elevated location it 3
was easy to see into the city and how the whole fighting-
age generation that had stayed in town,[8] and all the older
men with their children and wives, were either stretching[9]
hands to heaven from the wall or visiting the gods' temples
and, prostrate before their likenesses, imploring them for
victory. Nor was there anyone who did not think that ev- 4
eryone's future fortunes were riding on that day's chances,
for the most highly regarded men of fighting age, as well 5
as the most eminent men of every age, had embarked after
being summoned individually and implored. So they realized that if things went badly they would have nothing left
to try, and were confident of the city's survival, either from
their own resources or with outside help, if they won.

6. In combat the men of Marseilles showed no lack
of courage. They remembered the injunctions received
shortly beforehand from their fellow citizens, and their
attitude as they fought was this: they did not seem likely
to have another opportunity to try, and they thought—
those who had risked their lives in battle—that they were
not anticipating by very much the fate of the rest, who
would have to suffer the same fortune of war if the city
was taken. Our ships gradually spread out, giving room to 2
the enemy pilots' skill and their ships' mobility. Whenever
our men found an opportunity and secured a ship by casting grappling hooks onto it, the enemy would come from

[9] For "were either stretching," the emendations mentioned in
the apparatus read, respectively, "and men posted as guards were
either stretching," "were either stretching suppliant," and "suppliant and in mourning garb were either stretching." Many other
emendations have been proposed for this difficult passage.

3 rant undique suis laborantibus succurrebant. Neque vero
coniuncti Albicis comminus pugnando deficiebant neque
multum cedebant virtute nostris. Simul ex minoribus navibus magna vis eminus missa telorum multa nostris de
improviso imprudentibus atque impeditis vulnera infere-
4 bant. Conspicataeque naves triremes duae navem D.
Bruti, quae ex insigni facile agnosci poterat, duabus ex
partibus sese in eam incitaverant. Sed tantum re provisa
Brutus celeritate navis enisus est ut parvo momento
5 antecederet. Illae adeo graviter inter se incitatae conflix-
erunt ut vehementissime utraque ex concursu laborarent,
6 altera vero praefracto rostro tota collabefieret. Qua re
animadversa quae proximae ei loco ex Bruti classe naves
erant in eas impeditas impetum faciunt celeriterque am-
bas deprimunt.

7. Sed Nasidianae naves nullo usui fuerunt celeriterque pugna excesserunt. Non enim has aut conspectus
patriae aut propinquorum praecepta ad extremum vitae
2 periculum adire cogebant. Itaque ex eo numero navium
nulla desiderata est. Ex Massiliensium classe V sunt depressae, IIII captae. Vna cum Nasidianis profugit, quae
3 omnes citeriorem Hispaniam petiverunt. At ex reliquis
una praemissa Massiliam huius nunti perferendi gratia
cum iam appropinquaret urbi omnis sese multitudo ad
cognoscendum effudit. Et re cognita tantus luctus excepit
4 ut urbs ab hostibus capta eodem vestigio videretur. Massilienses tamen nihilo setius ad defensionem urbis reliqua
apparare coeperunt.

8. Est animadversum ab legionariis qui dextram partem operis administrabant: ex crebris hostium eruptionibus magno sibi esse praesidio posse si pro castello ac re-

all directions to help the men in difficulties. The allied 3
Albici showed themselves adequate to close combat and
not much inferior to our men in prowess. At the same time
a large quantity of projectiles hurled from smaller vessels
some distance off unexpectedly caused many injuries to
our men, unwary and preoccupied as they were. Two tri- 4
remes, having spotted Decimus Brutus' ship, which was
easily recognizable from its flag, drove against it from two
sides. But Brutus, foreseeing the result, made such an
effort that his ship's speed put him a moment ahead. Driv- 5
ing in opposite directions they collided with such force
that both were in serious difficulties after the collision and
one lost its beak, capsizing completely. Noticing this, the 6
closest ships from Brutus' fleet attacked the entangled
triremes and quickly sank both.

7. As for Nasidius' ships, they were no use and quickly
left the battle, for they were not induced to put their lives
into the greatest danger by the sight of their fatherland or
the injunctions of their people. So none of these ships was 2
lost. Five from Marseilles' fleet were sunk, four captured.
One fled with those of Nasidius, which headed as a body
for Nearer Spain. One of the remaining ships was sent 3
ahead to bring the news to Marseilles. As it was approaching the city, the whole population poured out to hear.
When they heard the news, such grief took possession of
the city as to give the impression that it had been captured
by the enemy in that instant. Yet Marseilles began to pre- 4
pare what remained for the city's defense nonetheless.

8. The legionaries conducting operations on the right
realized that, in view of the enemy's frequent sorties, they
would be well protected if they built a masonry tower

ceptaculo turrim ex latere sub muro fecissent. Quam primo ad repentinos incursus humilem parvamque fece-
2 runt. Huc se referebant, hinc si qua maior oppresserat vis propugnabant, hinc ad repellendum et prosequendum hostem procurrebant. Patebat haec quoquo versus pedes
3 XXX, sed parietum crassitudo pedes V. Postea vero, ut est rerum omnium magister usus, hominum adhibita sollertia inventum est magno esse usui posse si haec esset in altitudinem turris elata. Id hac ratione perfectum est.

9. Ibi[8] turris altitudo perducta est ubi ‹tigna› contabulationis causa[9] in parietes instruxerunt, ita ut capita tignorum extrema parietum structura tegerentur ne quid emi-
2 neret ubi ignis hostium adhaeresceret. Hanc insuper contignationem quantum tectum plutei ac vinearum passum est latericulo adstruxerunt, supraque eum locum duo tigna transversa iniecerunt [ut] non longe ab extremis parietibus quibus suspenderent eam contignationem quae turri tegimento esset futura, supraque ea tigna derecto transversas trabes iniecerunt eaque axibus religaverunt.
3 Has trabes paulo longiores atque eminentiores quam extremi parietes erant effecerunt ut esset ubi tegimenta

---

[8] ibi] ubi *Oudendorp, who adopts Aldus' emendation below*
[9] ubi ‹tigna› contabulationis causa *Damon*: ut contabulationis causa ω: ad contabulationem, eam *Aldus*

---

[10] For Trebonius' twofold assault see 2.1.1–2.

[11] In the following chapters about this tower and the adjacent gallery (2.9–10), the text bristles with problems, and solutions are especially hard to identify, because both content and style are somewhat alien to Caesar's norm. As a result, the accounts of

at the foot of the wall as a stronghold and refuge.[10] At
first they made it low and small to counter sudden incur-
sions. This was the place to which they would retreat, and 2
from which they would resist if overwhelmed by a superior
force, running out to repel and pursue the enemy. The
tower was thirty feet long on each side, with walls five
feet thick. Later, however, experience being the universal 3
teacher, and with the application of human ingenuity, they
discovered that it would be very useful if this tower was
expanded upward. This is how it was done.[11]

9. The height of the tower was extended in the place
where they laid the beams on the walls to make the platform,[12] in such a way that the beam ends were covered by
the wall's outermost masonry, to prevent protrusions to
which the enemy's fire might adhere. On top of this plat- 2
form they built up as much brickwork as the wicker screen
overhead allowed, and at this level they laid two crosswise
beams not far from the ends of the walls; with these they
planned to hoist the platform that was going to be the
tower's roof. Above and at right angles to these beams they
laid joists and fastened the timbers together with planks.
They made these joists somewhat longer, extending be- 3
yond the edges of the walls, so that there would be a place

these engineering feats are unusually hard to follow. It is likely
that for these descriptions of siege works never seen by Caesar
himself—they were destroyed and replaced with different structures before his return to Marseilles (2.14.4, 2.15)—he relied
heavily on a report's wording.

[12] For "the height . . . platform," editors often follow Oudendorp and Aldus with "When the height of the tower reached the
level for a platform, they laid the beams onto the walls."

praependere possent ad defendendos ictus ac repellendos
cum intra eam contignationem parietes extruerentur,
4 eamque contabulationem summam lateribus lutoque con-
straverunt ne quid ignis hostium nocere posset, cento-
nesque insuper iniecerunt ne aut tela tormentis missa ta-
bulationem perfringerent aut saxa ex catapultis latericium
5 discuterent. Storias autem ex funibus ancorariis tres in
longitudinem parietum turris latas IIII pedes fecerunt
easque ex tribus partibus quae ad hostes vergebant emi-
nentibus trabibus circum turrim praependentes religaverunt, quod unum genus tegimenti aliis locis erant experti
6 nullo telo neque tormento traici posse. Vbi vero ea pars
turris quae erat perfecta tecta atque munita est ab omni
ictu hostium pluteos ad alia opera abduxerunt. Turris tectum per se ipsum pressionibus ex contignatione prima
7 suspendere ac tollere coeperunt. Vbi quantum storiarum
demissio patiebatur tantum elevarant, intra haec tegimenta abditi atque muniti parietes lateribus extruebant
rursusque alia pressione ad aedificandum sibi locum expe-
8 diebant. Vbi tempus alterius contabulationis videbatur
tigna item ut primo tecta extremis lateribus instruebant
exque ea contignatione rursus summam contabulationem
9 storiasque elevabant. Ita tuto ac sine ullo vulnere ac periculo VI tabulata extruxerunt. Fenestrasque quibus in locis
visum est ad tormenta mittenda in struendo reliquerunt.

10. Vbi ex ea turri quae circum essent opera tueri se
posse sunt confisi musculum pedes LX longum ex materia
bipedali quem a turri latericia ad hostium turrim mu-

---

[13] The figure sixty may be corrupt.

to hang screens to protect against and repel blows when
the walls were being built up under the platform's shelter.
They covered this platform with a layer of bricks and clay   4
to prevent damage by the enemy's fire. On top they piled
rag pallets to prevent artillery shot from smashing the
platform and rocks hurled by the catapults from shattering
the brickwork. They made three mats from anchor ropes,   5
as long as the tower walls and four feet wide, and fastened
them around the tower as a barrier on the three sides facing the enemy; the mats hung from the projecting joists.
They had learned elsewhere that this was the one sort of
protection that could not be pierced by any weapon or
catapult. When the completed portion of the tower had   6
been roofed and protected from every kind of enemy shot,
they took the overhead screens away for other operations.
They then began to hoist and raise the tower's roof as a
unit, using leverage from the first platform. When they   7
had lifted it as much as the fall of the mats allowed, concealed and secure within their protection they would build
walls of brick, and again make room for themselves to
build by another round of leverage. When it seemed to be   8
time for another platform, they would lay beams as before,
protected by the outermost bricks, and from this platform
they would again raise the topmost platform and mats. In   9
this way they built six stories safely and without injury or
danger. While building, they left openings for the use of
catapults where appropriate.

10. When they were sure that they could protect the
surrounding operations from this tower, they began to
make a gallery sixty feet long[13] from two-foot square timber; they planned to extend this from the brick tower to

rumque perducerent facere instituerunt. Cuius musculi
haec erat forma.

2   Duae primum trabes in solo aeque longae distantes
inter se pedes IIII collocantur inque his columellae pe-
3 dum in altitudinem V defiguntur. Has inter se capreolis
molli fastigio coniungunt ubi tigna quae musculi tegendi
causa ponant collocentur. Eo super tigna bipedalia inici-
4 unt eaque lamminis clavisque religant. Ad extremum
musculi tectum trabesque extremas quadratas regulas IIII
patentes digitos defigunt quae lateres qui superstruantur[10]
5 contineant. Ita fastigato atque ordinatim structo ⟨tecto⟩
ut trabes[11] erant in capreolis collocatae, in lateribus lutus,[12] musculus ut ab igni qui ex muro iaceretur tutus esset
6 contegitur. Super lateres coria inducuntur ne canalibus
aqua immissa lateres diluere posset. Coria autem ne rursus igni ac lapidibus corrumpantur centonibus contegun-
7 tur. Hoc opus omne tectum vineis ad ipsam turrim per-
ficiunt. Subitoque inopinantibus hostibus machinatione
navali phalangis subiectis ad turrim hostium admovent ut
aedificio iungatur.

11. Quo malo perterriti subito oppidani saxa quam
maxima possunt vectibus promovent praecipitataque
muro in musculum devolvunt. Ictum firmitas materiae
2 sustinet, et quicquid incidit fastigio musculi elabitur. Id

[10] superstruantur *Nipperdey*: super musculos struantur ω
[11] ⟨tecto⟩ *Oudendorp*
[12] in lateribus lutus *Damon*: in lateribus luto ω: [in] la- lutoque
Aldus: [in] la- [luto] *Apitz*: [in] latericulo *Paul*

---

[14] Literally, "four finger-widths square."

the enemy's tower and wall. The gallery's structure was like this:

First, two timbers of equal length were placed on the 2 ground four feet apart. In these they inserted posts five feet tall. They joined each post to its opposite with trusses 3 with a low pitch; on these they planned to place the beams to cover the gallery. On this structure they laid two-foot square beams and secured them with metal plates and spikes. At the edge of the gallery's roof and the ends of the 4 beams they fastened three-inch square[14] battens to hold in place the bricks to be laid on top. In this way, with the 5 roof peaked and constructed in layers—since beams had been placed on trusses, clay on bricks[15]—the gallery was covered so as to be safe from fire thrown from the wall. Hides were stretched over the bricks to prevent water 6 released from pipes from being able to wash away the brickwork. The hides were covered with rag pallets to prevent damage to these too from fire and stones. They 7 accomplished the whole project near their tower under the protection of screens. And suddenly, catching the enemy off guard, they used a naval maneuver—rollers under the gallery—and moved it up to the enemy's tower so as to abut its structure.

11. Terrified by this emergency the townspeople rolled forward the largest possible stones with crowbars and sent them flying off the wall onto the gallery. The strength of the timber withstood the impact, and anything that landed slid off because of the sloping roof. Seeing this, the enemy 2

[15] From "in this way" to "bricks," the text is very uncertain, but the variants do not make much difference to the sense.

ubi vident mutant consilium. Cupas taeda ac pice refertas incendunt easque de muro in musculum devolvunt. Involutae labuntur, delapsae ab lateribus longuriis furcisque ab

3 opere removentur. Interim sub musculo milites vectibus infima saxa turris hostium, quibus fundamenta continebantur, convellunt. Musculus ex turri latericia a nostris telis tormentisque defenditur. Hostes ex muro ac turribus submoventur. Non datur libera muri defendendi facultas.

4 Compluribus iam lapidibus ex illa quae suberat turri subductis repentina ruina pars eius turris concidit. Pars reliqua consequens procumbebat cum hostes urbis direptione perterriti inermes cum infulis se porta foras universi proripiunt. Ad legatos atque exercitum supplices manus tendunt.

12. Qua nova re oblata omnis administratio belli consistit, militesque aversi a proelio ad studium audiendi et

2 cognoscendi feruntur. Vbi hostes ad legatos exercitumque pervenerunt universi se ad pedes proiciunt. Orant ut ad-

3 ventus Caesaris expectetur: captam suam urbem videre, opera perfecta, turrim subrutam; itaque ab defensione desistere; nullam exoriri moram posse quominus, cum venisset, si imperata non facerent ad nutum, e vestigio

4 diriperentur. Docent: si omnino turris concidisset non posse milites contineri quin spe praedae in urbem irrumperent urbemque delerent. Haec atque eiusdem generis complura ut ab hominibus doctis magna cum misericordia fletuque pronuntiantur.

---

16 The fillets were ribbons signifying supplication and sacrifice typically worn by those petitioning a god.

changed their plan. They set on fire barrels filled with pinewood and pitch and rolled these off the wall onto the gallery. The tumbling barrels slid off and after sliding down were moved away from the sides by means of poles and pitchforks. Meanwhile beneath the gallery soldiers 3 with crowbars were extracting the lowest stones of the enemy tower, which formed its foundation. The gallery's defense was handled by our men from the brick tower with projectiles and catapults. The enemy was dislodged from their wall and towers; they were given no real chance to defend the wall. After a number of stones had been 4 removed from the adjacent tower, there was a sudden collapse and part of it gave way. The remainder consequently began to lean forward. The enemy, terrified by the prospect of a sacked city, rushed as one out through the gate, unarmed and wearing fillets.[16] They stretched out their hands for mercy to the officers and army.

12. With this new development all military operations ceased and the soldiers, once diverted from the fighting, became determined to listen and understand. The enemy, 2 reaching our officers and army, threw themselves as one before their feet. Their plea was this: "Wait until Caesar arrives. We see our city taken, your works complete, our 3 tower undermined. We are therefore abandoning our defense. Nothing can happen to delay an immediate sack if, after Caesar gets here, we do not do exactly what he orders." If the tower gave way altogether, they explained, it 4 would be impossible to keep the soldiers from breaking into the city in hopes of booty, and destroying it. These pleas and several more of the same sort—these were educated men, after all—were delivered with great pathos and lamentation.

13. Quibus rebus commoti legati milites ex opere deducunt, oppugnatione desistunt, operibus custodias relin-
2 quunt. Indutiarum quodam genere misericordia facto
adventus Caesaris expectatur. Nullum ex muro, nullum a
nostris mittitur telum. Vt re confecta omnes curam et dili-
3 gentiam remittunt. Caesar enim per litteras Trebonio
magnopere mandaverat ne per vim oppidum expugnari
pateretur, ne gravius permoti milites et defectionis odio et
contemptione sui et diutino labore omnes puberes inter-
4 ficerent. Quod se facturos minabantur aegreque tunc sunt
retenti quin oppidum irrumperent graviterque eam rem
tulerunt quod stetisse per Trebonium quominus oppido
potirentur videbatur.

14. At hostes sine fide tempus atque occasionem frau-
dis ac doli quaerunt. Interiectisque aliquot diebus nostris
languentibus atque animo remissis subito meridiano tempore cum alius discessisset alius ex diutino labore in ipsis
operibus quieti se dedisset, arma vero omnia reposita
contectaque essent, portis se foras erumpunt, secundo
2 magnoque vento ignem operibus inferunt. Hunc sic distulit ventus uti uno tempore agger plutei testudo turris
tormenta flammam conciperent et prius haec omnia
consumerentur quam quemadmodum accidisset animad-
3 verti posset. Nostri repentina fortuna permoti arma quae
possunt arripiunt. Alii ex castris sese incitant. Fit in hostes
impetus, sed eorum[13] [muro][14] sagittis tormentisque fu-
4 gientes persequi prohibentur. Illi sub murum se recipiunt

[13] sed eorum *Damon*: e- s- ω: [e-] sed *Vascosan*
[14] [muro] *Damon*: <ex> muro *Chacon*

142

13. Swayed by this, the officers withdrew the soldiers from their work, abandoned the assault, and left sentries at the siege works. After striking a sort of truce out of 2 compassion, they waited for Caesar's arrival. No weapons were thrown from the city wall, none by our men. As if the business was concluded, everyone relaxed his care and diligence, for Caesar had written to Trebonius with em- 3 phatic instructions not to allow the city to be taken by force. He wanted to prevent the soldiers, whose griev-ances were considerable—hostility because of Marseilles' defection, plus the disrespect for themselves, and their long-continued exertion—from killing all of the adult males. They were threatening to do just this, and it was 4 difficult to keep them from breaking into the town. They felt aggrieved, since Trebonius seemed to be the only rea-son they were not taking control of Marseilles.

14. The treacherous enemy, however, was seeking an opportune moment for a devious ruse. After a few days' interval our men were relaxed and inattentive, and sud-denly at midday, when some had left the siege works and others, after their long-continued exertions, were at ease in the works, and every weapon had been put away and secured, the enemy burst out through the gates. With a strong wind in their favor they set fire to the works. The 2 wind spread the blaze in such a way that the siege ramp, the screens, the "tortoise," the tower, and the catapults caught fire at the same time, and everything was con-sumed before anyone could see how it happened. Our 3 men, prompted by the unexpected calamity, seized what weapons they could; some rushed out of the camp. An attack was mounted, but the enemy's arrows and artillery fire prevented them from pursuing those in flight. The 4

ibique musculum turrimque latericiam libere incendunt.
Ita multorum mensum labor hostium perfidia et vi tem-
5 pestatis puncto temporis interiit. Temptaverunt hoc idem
Massilienses postero die. Eandem nacti tempestatem maiore cum fiducia ad alteram turrim aggeremque eruptione
6 pugnaverunt multumque ignem intulerunt. Sed ut superioris temporis contentionem nostri omnem remiserant
ita proximi diei casu admoniti omnia ad defensionem
paraverant. Itaque multis interfectis reliquos infecta re in
oppidum reppulerunt.

   15. Trebonius ea quae sunt amissa multo maiore militum studio administrare et reficere instituit. Nam ubi
tantos suos labores et apparatus male cecidisse viderunt
indutiisque per scelus violatis suam virtutem irrisui fore
perdoluerunt, quod unde agger omnino comportari posset
nihil erat reliquum omnibus arboribus longe lateque in
finibus Massiliensium excisis et convectis, aggerem novi
generis atque inauditum ex latericiis duobus muris senum
pedum crassitudine atque eorum murorum contignatione
facere instituerunt aequa fere latitudine atque ille conges-
2 ticius ex materia fuerat agger. Vbi aut spatium inter muros
aut imbecillitas materiae postulare videretur pilae inter-
ponuntur. Traversaria tigna iniciuntur quae firmamento
esse possint, et quicquid est contignatum cratibus conster-
3 nitur, lutoque crates integuntur. Sub tecto miles, dextra
ac sinistra muro tectus, adversus pluteo obiecto,[15] operi
4 quaecumque sunt usui sine periculo supportat. Celeriter

---

[15] pluteo obiecto *Damon*: plutei -to *ω*: plutei -tu *Aldus*

enemy retreated to the foot of the wall, and there they were free to set fire to the gallery and brick tower. The work of many months was thus annihilated in an instant as a result of enemy treachery and a violent windstorm. Marseilles tried the same thing the next day. With the same weather and more confidence they sallied out into combat beside the second tower and ramp. They set a great fire. But although our men had reduced their exertion from its earlier level, still, warned by the previous day's disaster they had made every preparation for defense. They therefore pushed the enemy back into the city with their task undone and many casualties.

15. Trebonius started to undertake the rebuilding of what had been lost, with greatly increased determination on the soldiers' part, for they saw that their immense efforts and preparations had turned out badly and resented the fact that their prowess would seem farcical after the criminal violation of the truce. Since nothing was left that could somehow be used to assemble a siege ramp—all of the trees far and wide in the territory of Marseilles had already been cut down and brought in—they started to make an unusual siege ramp of a new type from two brick walls six feet thick with a platform between them; it was about the same width as the ramp of solid fill had been. Whenever the gap between the walls or the weakness of the material seemed to demand it, they interspersed uprights. They laid crosswise beams that could serve as a base, and as the platform came into being a layer of wicker was added and the wicker was covered with clay. With this overhead, protected by walls on the right and left and in front by the interposition of a screen, the soldiers carried whatever was needed for the work without danger. The

145

res administratur. Diuturni laboris detrimentum sollertia et virtute militum brevi reconciliatur. Portae quibus locis videtur eruptionis causa in muro relinquuntur.

16. Quod ubi hostes viderunt ea quae diu longoque spatio refici non posse sperassent paucorum dierum opera et labore ita refecta ut nullus perfidiae neque eruptioni locus esset neque quicquam omnino relinqueretur qua aut telis militibus aut igni operibus noceri posset, eodemque exemplo sentiunt totam urbem, qua sit aditus ab terra, muro turribusque circumiri posse sic ut ipsi consistendi in suis munitionibus locus non esset cum paene inaedificata in muris ab exercitu nostro moenia viderentur ac telum manu coniceretur, suorumque tormentorum usum, quibus ipsi magna speravissent, spati propinquitate interire parique conditione ex muro ac turribus bellandi data se virtute nostris adaequare non posse intellegunt, ad easdem deditionis conditiones recurrunt.

17. M. Varro in ulteriore Hispania initio—cognitis iis rebus quae sunt in Italia gestae—diffidens Pompeianis rebus amicissime de Caesare loquebatur: praeoccupatum sese legatione ab Cn. Pompeio teneri obstrictum fide; necessitudinem quidem sibi nihilo minorem cum Caesare intercedere; neque se ignorare quod esset officium legati qui fiduciariam operam obtineret, quae vires suae, quae voluntas erga Caesarem totius provinciae. Haec omnibus ferebat sermonibus neque se in ullam partem movebat. Postea vero, cum Caesarem ad Massiliam detineri cognovit, copias Petrei cum exercitu Afrani esse coniunctas,

task was handled quickly: the wreck of their long struggle was soon made good by the soldiers' skill and valor. Sally ports were left at suitable locations along the wall.

16. The enemy saw that the works they had hoped could not be rebuilt for a long time and a considerable interval had been rebuilt with a few days' effort and exertion, with the result that there was no opportunity for a treacherous sortie and no way at all left of harming the soldiers with weapons or the works with fire. And they 2 perceived that the whole city, where approached by land, could be boxed in by a wall and towers in the same fashion, such that they would have no place to stand on their own defenses, since the fortifications built by our army seemed practically to abut their wall, and weapons were being thrown by hand. They also realized that their catapults, for 3 which they had had great hopes, lost their usefulness owing to the close quarters, and that they themselves could not match our men in prowess if the fighting was done on equal terms from walls and towers. So they resorted to surrender on the same terms.

17. In further Spain Marcus Varro lacked confidence in Pompey's cause at the outset, when he learned of events in Italy, and spoke in a very friendly fashion about Caesar. "Given the priority of my mission from Pompey, I am held 2 fast by obligations. Nevertheless, I have no less close a connection with Caesar. I am familiar with the duties of an officer who has a position of trust—and with my resources and my province's universal favor for Caesar." These were his words in every conversation, and he did 3 not move toward either side. Later, however, he learned 4 that Caesar was detained at Marseilles, that Petreius' forces and Afranius' army were united, that substantial

magna auxilia convenisse, magna esse in spe atque expectari, et consentire omnem citeriorem provinciam, quaeque postea acciderant de angustiis ad Ilerdam rei frumentariae accepit atque haec ad eum latius atque inflatius Afranius praescribebat, se quoque ad motus Fortunae movere coepit.

18. Dilectum habuit tota provincia. Legionibus completis duabus cohortes circiter XXX alarias addidit. Frumenti magnum numerum coegit quod Massiliensibus item quod Afranio Pompeioque[16] mitteret. Naves longas X Gaditanis ut facerent imperavit, complures praeterea 2 [in] Hispali faciendas curavit. Pecuniam omnem omniaque ornamenta ex fano Herculis in oppidum Gades contulit. Eo VI cohortes praesidi causa ex provincia misit. Gaiumque Gallonium equitem Romanum familiarem Domiti, qui eo procurandae hereditatis causa venerat missus a Domitio, oppido Gadibus praefecit. Arma omnia 3 privata ac publica in domum Galloni contulit. Ipse habuit graves in Caesarem contiones. Saepe ex tribunali praedicavit: adversa Caesarem proelia fecisse; magnum numerum ab eo militum ad Afranium perfugisse; haec se certis 4 nuntiis certis auctoribus comperisse. Quibus rebus perterritos cives Romanos eius provinciae sibi ad rem publicam administrandam sestertium CLXXX et argenti pondo XX 5 milia, tritici modium CXX milia polliceri coegit. Quas Caesari esse amicas civitates arbitrabatur his graviora onera iniungebat praesidiaque eo deducebat. Et iudicia in privatos reddebat qui verba atque orationem adversus rem

16 Pompeioque] Petrei- *ed. pr.*

reinforcements had arrived and more were hoped for and
expected, and that they had the unanimous support of
Nearer Spain. Subsequent events—Caesar's supply difficulties at Ilerda—came to his attention, and Afranius' letters informing him about these things were written with
undue generality and exaggeration. Then Varro's movements began to mirror those of Fortune.

18. He recruited troops throughout his province, bringing his two legions up to strength and supplementing them
with about thirty cohorts of allies. He collected a large
quantity of grain to send to Marseilles and also to Afranius
and Pompey. He ordered Cadiz to make ten warships and
arranged for the construction of several more in Hispalis.
He moved all of the money and treasures from the temple   2
of Hercules into the town of Cadiz; to guard the town he
sent six cohorts from the province. He also put Gaius Gallonius, a Roman of equestrian rank and a friend of Domitius, in charge of Cadiz; Gallonius was already there, having been sent by Domitius as his agent for an inheritance.
Varro moved all weapons, privately owned and public, into
Gallonius' house. He made speeches critical of Caesar,   3
often declaring from his official platform that battles had
turned out badly for Caesar, that a large number of soldiers had deserted him for Afranius: "I know this from
reliable reports, reliable authorities." The Roman citizens   4
in the province were thoroughly cowed by this; Varro
forced them to promise him eighteen million sesterces
and twenty thousand pounds of silver to use for public
business, and 120,000 measures of wheat. As for commu-   5
nities he thought friendly to Caesar, he imposed heavier
burdens on them and installed garrisons. He also issued
judgments against private individuals for having spoken or

publicam habuissent. Eorum bona in publicum addicebat. Provinciam omnem in sua et Pompei verba ius iurandum
6 adigebat. Cognitis iis rebus quae sunt gestae in citeriore Hispania, bellum parabat. Ratio autem haec erat belli ut se cum duabus legionibus Gades conferret, naves frumentumque omne ibi contineret. Provinciam enim omnem Caesaris rebus favere cognoverat. In insula frumento navibusque comparatis bellum duci non difficile existimabat.
7 Caesar etsi multis necessariisque rebus in Italiam revocabatur tamen constituerat nullam partem belli in Hispaniis relinquere quod magna esse Pompei beneficia et magnas clientelas in citeriore provincia sciebat. 19. Itaque duabus legionibus missis in ulteriorem Hispaniam cum Q. Cassio tribuno plebis, ipse cum DC equitibus magnis itineribus praegreditur edictumque praemittit: ad quam diem magistratus principesque omnium civitatum sibi
2 esse praesto Cordubae vellet. Quo edicto tota provincia pervulgato nulla fuit civitas quin ad id tempus partem senatus Cordubam mitteret, non civis Romanus paulo
3 notior quin ad diem conveniret. Simul ipse Cordubae conventus per se portas Varroni clausit, custodias vigiliasque in turribus muroque disposuit, cohortes duas, quae colonicae appellabantur, cum eo casu venissent, tuendi oppidi
4 causa apud se retinuit. Isdem diebus Carmonenses, quae est longe firmissima totius provinciae civitas, deductis tri-

---

17 "Colonials" refers to the origin of the cohorts' soldiers in a Roman colony such as Italica or Carteia.

given speeches against the public interest, confiscating their property. He forced the entire province to swear allegiance to himself and Pompey. After learning what had happened in Nearer Spain, he started preparing to fight. His plan of campaign was to move to Cadiz with two legions and to keep his ships and all of his food supplies there, for he was aware that his whole province favored Caesar's cause. He thought that it would not be difficult to prolong the war on an island with supplies and ships at hand.

Although matters both numerous and necessary were calling Caesar back to Italy, he had decided to leave no trace of war in Spain, since he knew that Pompey had done many favors and was patron to many in the nearer province. 19. So after ordering two legions to Further Spain with the plebeian tribune Quintus Cassius, he himself went ahead at speed with six hundred cavalry and sent on an edict indicating the day on which he wanted every community's magistrates and leading men to be ready for him in Corduba. When this edict was published throughout the province, there was no community that did not send part of its council to Corduba for the occasion, and no Roman citizen of any distinction who did not arrive on time. At the same time the association of Roman citizens at Corduba closed the gates to Varro, stationed sentries and lookouts in the towers and on the wall, and detained for the city's defense two cohorts, called "colonials," that had arrived by chance.[17] During the same period Carmo, which is by far the strongest city in the province and where

bus in arcem oppidi cohortibus a Varrone praesidio, per
se cohortes eiecit portasque praeclusit.

20. Hoc vero magis properare Varro ut cum legionibus
quam primum Gades contenderet, ne itinere aut traiectu
intercluderetur. Tanta ac tam secunda in Caesarem volun-
2 tas provinciae reperiebatur. Progresso ei paulo longius
litterae Gadibus redduntur: simul atque sit cognitum de
edicto Caesaris consensisse Gaditanos principes cum tribunis cohortium quae essent ibi in praesidio ut Gallonium
ex oppido expellerent, urbem insulamque Caesari ser-
3 varent; hoc inito consilio denuntiavisse Gallonio ut sua
sponte dum sine periculo liceret excederet Gadibus; si id
non fecisset sibi consilium capturos; hoc timore adductum
4 Gallonium Gadibus excessisse. His cognitis rebus altera ex
duabus legionibus, quae vernacula appellabatur, ex castris
Varronis adstante et inspectante ipso signa sustulit seseque
Hispalim recepit atque in foro et porticibus sine maleficio
5 consedit. Quod factum adeo eius conventus cives Romani
comprobaverunt ut domum ad se quisque hospitio cupi-
6 dissime reciperet. Quibus rebus perterritus Varro cum
itinere converso sese Italicam venturum praemisisset cer-
7 tior ab suis factus est praeclusas esse portas. Tum vero
omni interclusus itinere ad Caesarem mittit: paratum se
esse legionem cui iusserit tradere. Ille ad eum Sextum
8 Caesarem mittit atque huic tradi iubet. Tradita legione
Varro Cordubam ad Caesarem venit. Relatis ad eum publi-

three cohorts had been installed as a garrison in the citadel by Varro, expelled the cohorts on its own and closed the gates against them.

20. This increased Varro's haste to make for Cadiz as soon as possible with his legions, to avoid being cut off while marching or crossing; the province's attitude toward Caesar was found to be strongly favorable. After going a 2 little further, he received a letter from Cadiz. "As soon as they learned about Caesar's edict, the city leaders came to an agreement with the officers of the cohorts garrisoning Cadiz to expel Gallonius and hold the city and island for Caesar. After adopting this plan they announced to Gal- 3 lonius that he must leave Cadiz voluntarily while it was possible to do so without danger. If he didn't do so, they said, they were going to act for themselves. Gallonius, induced by this fear, left Cadiz." At this news one of Varro's 4 two legions, the one called "indigenous," removed its stan- dards from Varro's camp while he stood and watched; the legion went back to Hispalis and established itself in the forum porticoes without causing any trouble. Their action 5 was so well thought of by the town's association of Roman citizens that each member wanted above all to welcome them as guests into his own home. When Varro, thor- 6 oughly alarmed by this, changed his route and sent word that he would be coming to Italica, he was informed by supporters that the gates had been closed against him. Then, finally, cut off in every direction, he sent to Caesar: 7 "I am ready to surrender my legion to anyone you order." Caesar sent Sextus Caesar to him and ordered the legion to be surrendered to him. After the surrender Varro went 8 to Caesar at Corduba. Giving Caesar a faithful reckoning

cis cum fide rationibus quod penes eum est pecuniae tradit et quid ubique habeat frumenti ac navium ostendit.

21. Caesar contione habita Cordubae omnibus generatim gratias agit: civibus Romanis quod oppidum in sua potestate studuissent habere, Hispanis quod praesidia expulissent, Gaditanis quod conatus adversariorum infregissent seseque in libertatem vindicavissent, tribunis militum centurionibusque qui eo praesidi causa venerant

2 quod eorum consilia sua virtute confirmavissent. Pecunias quas erant in publicum Varroni cives Romani polliciti remittit. Bona restituit iis quos liberius locutos hanc poenam

3 tulisse cognoverat. Tributis quibusdam populis publicis privatisque praemiis reliquos in posterum bona spe complet. Biduumque Cordubae commoratus Gades proficiscitur. Pecunias monimentaque quae ex fano Herculis collata

4 erant in privatam domum referri in templum iubet. Provinciae Q. Cassium praeficit. Huic IIII legiones attribuit. Ipse iis navibus quas M. Varro quasque Gaditani iussu Varronis fecerant Tarraconem paucis diebus pervenit. Ibi totius fere citerioris provinciae legationes Caesaris adven-

5 tum expectabant. Eadem ratione privatim ac publice quibusdam civitatibus habitis honoribus Tarracone discedit pedibusque Narbonem atque inde Massiliam pervenit. Ibi legem de dictatore latam seseque dictatorem dictum a M. Lepido praetore cognoscit.

22. Massilienses omnibus defessi malis, rei frumentariae ad summam inopiam adducti, bis proelio navali su-

of public accounts, he surrendered the money in his possession and revealed what food supplies and ships he had anywhere.

21. Caesar held a public meeting at Corduba and thanked everyone by categories: Roman citizens, for their determination in keeping the city under their own control; Spaniards, for expelling garrisons; Cadiz, for thwarting enemy attempts and asserting its own independence; staff officers and centurions who were there on garrison duty, for putting heart in the city's plans by their own courage. He forgave the sums that Roman citizens had promised to 2 Varro for public purposes. He restored property to those who, he learned, had spoken too freely and been punished by confiscation. By allocating public and private rewards 3 to some communities he filled the rest with good hope for the future. After a two-day stay at Corduba, he set out for Cadiz. He ordered the money and dedications that had been moved from the temple of Hercules into a private house to be taken back into the temple. He put Quintus 4 Cassius in charge of the province, assigning him four legions. He himself reached Tarraco in a few days in the ships built by Marcus Varro and the people of Cadiz on Varro's orders. At Tarraco delegations from practically the whole of Nearer Spain were awaiting Caesar's arrival. Af- 5 ter conferring honors publicly and privately on certain communities in a similar fashion, he left Tarraco, traveling overland to Narbo and then Marseilles, where he learned of the passage of a law instituting a dictatorship, and that he had been proclaimed dictator by the praetor Marcus Lepidus.

22. The people of Marseilles were worn out by all of their problems. Reduced to an extreme shortage of provi-

perati, crebris eruptionibus fusi, gravi etiam pestilentia
conflictati ex diutina conclusione et mutatione victus—
panico enim vetere atque hordeo corrupto omnes alebantur, quod ad huiusmodi casus antiquitus paratum in publicum contulerant—deiecta turri, labefacta magna parte
muri, auxiliis provinciarum et exercituum desperatis—
quos in Caesaris potestatem venisse cognoverant—sese
2   dedere sine fraude constituunt. Sed paucis ante diebus L.
Domitius cognita Massiliensium voluntate navibus tribus
comparatis, ex quibus duas familiaribus suis attribuerat,
unam ipse conscenderat, nactus turbidam tempestatem
3   profectus est. Hunc conspicatae naves quae missu Bruti
consuetudine cotidiana ad portum excubabant sublatis
4   ancoris sequi coeperunt. Ex his unum ipsius navigium
contendit et fugere perseveravit auxilioque tempestatis ex
conspectu abiit, duo perterrita concursu nostrarum na-
5   vium sese in portum receperunt. Massilienses arma tormentaque ex oppido, ut est imperatum, proferunt, naves
ex portu navalibusque educunt, pecuniam ex publico tra-
6   dunt. Quibus rebus confectis Caesar magis eos pro nomine et vetustate quam pro meritis in se civitatis conservans duas ibi legiones praesidio relinquit, ceteras in
Italiam mittit. Ipse ad urbem proficiscitur.

    23. Isdem temporibus C. Curio in Africam profectus
ex Sicilia et iam ab initio copias P. Atti Vari despiciens duas
legiones ex IIII quas a Caesare acceperat D equites transportabat. Biduoque et noctibus tribus navigatione con-

sions, twice beaten in naval battles, routed in numerous
sorties, contending moreover with a troublesome sickness
in consequence of the long blockade and their spoiled
food—for they were eating old millet and rotting barley,
which had been acquired long ago and stockpiled for situations of this sort—with their tower in ruins and a large
portion of the wall weakened, despairing of reinforcements
from provinces and armies (which, they knew, had come
into Caesar's control), they decided to make an honest
surrender. But a few days beforehand Lucius Domitius,   2
recognizing their intention, procured three ships, gave
two of them to his friends, and embarked on one himself,
setting out when stormy weather gave him an opportunity.
He was spotted by the ships doing guard duty near the   3
harbor, sent regularly every day by Brutus. They hoisted
anchor and began a pursuit. One of Domitius' vessels, his 4
own, went straight ahead and persevered in its flight; it
disappeared with the storm's help. Two, thoroughly cowed
by the convergence of our ships, retreated to the harbor.
The people of Marseilles carried their weapons and cata-   5
pults out of the city, as had been ordered, brought the
ships from the port and dockyards, and surrendered the
money in their treasury. When these measures were com-   6
plete, Caesar let the city persist, more on account of its
fame and antiquity than for services to him. He left two
legions there as a garrison; the rest he sent to Italy. He
himself set out for Rome.

23. At this same period Gaius Curio was leaving Sicily
for Africa. To begin with, since he thought little of the
troops commanded by Publius Attius Varus, he transported two of the four legions he had received from Caesar, plus five hundred cavalry. After spending two days and

sumptis appellit ad eum locum qui appellatur Anquillaria.
2 Hic locus abest a Clipeis passuum XXII milia habetque
non incommodam aestate[17] stationem et duobus eminen-
3 tibus promunturiis continetur. Huius adventum L. Caesar
filius cum X longis navibus ad Clipea praestolans, quas
naves Vticae ex praedonum bello subductas P. Attius refi-
ciendas huius belli causa curaverat, veritusque navium
multitudinem ex alto refugerat appulsaque ad proximum
litus trireme constrata et in litore relicta pedibus Hadru-
4 metum perfugerat. Id oppidum C. Considius Longus
unius legionis praesidio tuebatur. Reliquae Caesaris naves
5 ⟨ex⟩ eius fuga[18] se Hadrumetum receperunt. Hunc secutus Marcius Rufus quaestor navibus XII quas praesidio
onerariis navibus Curio ex Sicilia eduxerat postquam in
litore relictam navem conspexit hanc remulco abstraxit.
Ipse ad C. Curionem cum classe redit.

24. Curio Marcium Vticam navibus praemittit. Ipse
eodem cum exercitu proficiscitur biduique iter progressus
2 ad flumen Bagradam pervenit. Ibi C. Caninium Rebilum
legatum cum legionibus reliquit. Ipse cum equitatu an-

[17] incommodam aestate ς: -a a- ω: -am [a-] *Chacon*
[18] ⟨ex⟩ eius fuga *Damon*: [eius] f- *Jurin*: ⟨visa⟩ eius f- *Paul²*.
Perhaps, e.g., eius f- ⟨desertae⟩?

---

[18] The precise location of Anquillaria is disputed; the distance
mentioned here is hard to reconcile with the time required to
march from Anquillaria to the Bagradas River (2.24.1). Scholars
have often emended one spot or the other.
[19] Chacon proposed excising the phrase "for summertime."
Since the surrender of Marseilles seems to have taken place in
October, while Curio arrived in North Africa at the beginning of

three nights on the voyage, he landed at a place called
Anquillaria. This place is twenty-two miles from Clipea.[18] 2
It has an anchorage suitable for summertime[19] and is enclosed between two lofty promontories. At Clipea the 3
younger Lucius Caesar[20] and ten warships had been lying
in wait for his arrival. These ships had been hauled out at
Utica after the pirate war; Publius Attius had arranged for
them to be repaired for the present war.[21] Worried about
the number of Curio's ships, Lucius Caesar had retreated
from the open sea. After beaching a decked trireme on the
nearest shore and abandoning it there, he had fled overland to Hadrumetum; the town was under the protection 4
of Gaius Considius Longus with a garrison of one legion.
The rest of Lucius Caesar's ships withdrew to Hadrumetum after he fled.[22] Marcius Rufus, a quaestor, followed 5
him with twelve ships that Curio had brought from Sicily
to protect the transports. Spotting the ship abandoned on
the shore, he towed it off. He himself returned to Curio
with his fleet.

24. Curio had Marcius sail ahead to Utica. He himself
headed there with his army and after a two-day advance
reached the Bagradas River. There he left his officer Gaius 2
Caninius Rebilus with the legions. He went ahead with the

August, the chronological overlap suggested by "at this same period" at 2.23.1 is loose.

[20] His like-named father had been Caesar's officer (1.8.2).

[21] The "pirate war" was Pompey's successful campaign in 67
to repress piracy in the Mediterranean.

[22] For "after he fled," Jurin and Paul proposed "because of his
flight" and "after observing his flight," respectively. One might
also repair this spot with "after being left forsaken by his flight."

tecedit ad Castra exploranda Cornelia quod is locus
3 peridoneus castris habebatur. Id autem est iugum derec-
tum eminens in mare, utraque ex parte praeruptum atque
asperum sed tamen paulo leniore fastigio ab ea parte quae
4 ad Vticam vergit. Abest derecto itinere ab Vtica paulo amplius passus mille. Sed hoc itinere est fons quo mare suc-
cedit longius, lateque is locus restagnat. Quem si qui vitare
voluerunt VI milium circuitu in oppidum perveniunt.[19]

25. Hoc explorato loco Curio castra Vari conspicit muro
oppidoque coniuncta ad portam quae appellatur Belica,
admodum munita natura loci, una ex parte ipso oppido
Vtica, altera [a] theatro, quod est ante oppidum—sub-
structionibus eius operis maximis, aditu ad castra difficili
2 et angusto.[20] Simul animadvertit multa undique portari
atque agi plenissimis viis, quae repentini tumultus timore
3 ex agris in urbem conferantur. Huc equitatum mittit ut
diriperet atque haberet loco praedae. Eodemque tempore
his rebus subsidio DC equites Numidae ex oppido pedi-
tesque CCCC mittuntur a Varo, quos auxili causa rex Iuba
4 paucis diebus ante Vticam miserat. (Huic et paternum
hospitium cum Pompeio et simultas cum Curione intercedebat, quod tribunus plebis legem promulgaverat qua lege
5 regnum Iubae publicaverat.) Concurrunt equites inter se,
neque vero primum impetum nostrorum Numidae ferre

---

[19] voluerunt . . . perveniunt *MU*: -erit . . . -it *S*: -erunt . . . -it
TV

[20] *Minimal repairs have been adopted, but the text of this
sentence remains problematic.*

---

[23] This distance seems too short; a number may have fallen
out of the text here.

cavalry to scout Castra Cornelia, since this location was
thought to be eminently suitable for a camp. It is a straight   3
ridge projecting into the sea, steep and rugged on both
sides but nevertheless with a slightly gentler slope on the
side facing Utica. By a straight-line route it is a little more   4
than a mile from Utica.[23] But in this direction there is a
spring, and the sea comes up rather close to it, and the
area is marshy for a wide stretch. Anyone who wants to
avoid it reaches Utica after a six-mile detour.

25. After scouting this site Curio viewed Varus' camp
adjacent to the city wall near the gate named for the god
Baal, a camp well fortified by the nature of its site, on one
side by Utica itself, on the other by the theater in front of
the city, the foundation of that building being very large
and the approach to the camp difficult and narrow. At the   2
same time he noticed that much property was being transported from every direction and moving along the utterly
packed roads; alarm at the sudden emergency caused its
removal from the country into the city. He sent in the   3
cavalry: they were to seize and keep it as booty. At the
same moment Varus sent six hundred Numidian cavalry
from the city to help the situation, plus four hundred infantry; King Juba had sent these troops to Utica a few days
earlier as reinforcements. (Juba was influenced by inher-   4
ited ties of hospitality with Pompey and a feud with Curio,
because as a plebeian tribune Curio had sponsored a law
making Juba's kingdom a Roman province.[24]) The cavalry   5
clashed, but the Numidians were not able to withstand the

---

[24] The law was passed in 50; the territory was ceded by Rome
to various client kings in the half-century after the victory over
Jugurtha in 105, most recently to Juba's father Hiempsal in 81.

potuerunt sed interfectis circiter CXX reliqui se in castra ad oppidum receperunt.

6 Interim adventu longarum navium Curio pronuntiare onerariis navibus iubet—quae stabant ad Vticam numero circiter CC—se in hostium habiturum loco qui non ex 7 vestigio ad Castra Cornelia naves traduxisset. Qua pronuntiatione facta temporis puncto sublatis ancoris omnes Vticam relinquunt et quo imperatum est transeunt. Quae res omnium rerum copia complevit exercitum.

26. His rebus gestis Curio se in castra ad Bagradam recipit atque universi exercitus conclamatione imperator appellatur. Posteroque die Vticam exercitum ducit et 2 prope oppidum castra ponit. Nondum opere castrorum perfecto equites ex statione nuntiant magna auxilia equitum peditumque ab rege missa Vticam venire. Eodemque tempore vis magna pulveris cernebatur, et vestigio tempo-3 ris primum agmen erat in conspectu. Novitate rei Curio permotus praemittit equites qui primum impetum sustineant ac morentur. Ipse celeriter ab opere deductis legio-4 nibus aciem instruit. Equitesque committunt proelium et priusquam plane legiones explicari et consistere possent tota auxilia regis impedita ac perturbata quod nullo ordine et sine timore iter fecerant in fugam [se] coniciunt. Equitatuque omni fere incolumi quod se per litora celeriter in oppidum recepit, magnum peditum numerum interficiunt.

27. Proxima nocte centuriones Marsi duo ex castris Curionis cum manipularibus suis XXII ad Attium Varum

---

[25] Acclamation by the label *imperator*, whose literal meaning is simply "commander," marked notable victories and was one of the prerequisites for a triumph. For its misuse see 3.31.1.

initial impact of our men. Instead, after about a hundred and twenty were killed, the rest withdrew into the camp next to the city.

Meanwhile Curio's warships arrived. He ordered an 6 announcement to the merchant vessels anchored at Utica, around two hundred in number, that he would consider anyone who did not immediately move his ship to Castra Cornelia to be an enemy. After this announcement all of 7 them instantly hoisted anchor, left Utica, and went where they were ordered. This development stocked the army with supplies of all kinds.

26. After these successes Curio went back to the camp at the Bagradas and was hailed as *imperator* by his entire army.[25] The next day he led his army to Utica and made camp near the city. Before the camp's fortifications were 2 complete the cavalry outposts announced that substantial infantry and cavalry reinforcements sent by Juba were coming to Utica. At the same time a large quantity of dust was spotted, and instantly the vanguard was in sight. Cu- 3 rio, disturbed by the unexpected development, sent the cavalry out to counter and delay the initial onslaught. He himself quickly took his legions from their work and drew up his line. The cavalry engaged. Before the legions could 4 be fully deployed into their positions, Curio's cavalry caused all of the king's forces to flee, encumbered as they were and flustered, since they had marched in complete disarray and unafraid. Although the king's cavalry was almost entirely unscathed, since it went quickly off to Utica along the shore, Curio's killed a large quantity of infantry.

27. The following night two Marsian centurions and twenty-two of their men deserted Curio's camp for Varus.

2 perfugiunt. Hi sive vere quam habuerant opinionem ad
eum perferunt sive etiam auribus Vari serviunt. Nam quae
volumus, et credimus libenter, et quae sentimus ipsi reliquos sentire speramus. Confirmant quidem certe totius
exercitus animos alienos esse a Curione, maximeque opus
esse in conspectu exercitum venire et colloquendi dare
3 facultatem. Qua opinione adductus Varus postero die
mane legiones ex castris educit. Facit idem Curio. Atque
una valle non magna interiecta suas uterque copias instruit.

28. Erat in exercitu Vari Sextus Quintilius Varus, quem
fuisse Corfini supra demonstratum est. Hic dimissus a
Caesare in Africam venerat. Legionesque eas traduxerat
Curio quas superioribus temporibus Corfinio receperat
Caesar, adeo ut paucis mutatis centurionibus idem ordines
2 manipulique constarent. Hanc nactus appellationis causam Quintilius circumire aciem Curionis atque obsecrare
milites coepit: ne primam sacramenti quod apud Domitium atque apud se quaestorem dixissent memoriam de-
ponerent, neu contra eos arma ferrent qui eadem essent
usi fortuna eademque in obsidione perpessi, neu pro iis
pugnarent a quibus <cum> contumelia perfugae appella-
3 rentur. Huc pauca ad spem largitionis addidit, quae ab sua
liberalitate si se atque Attium secuti essent expectare de-
4 berent. Hac habita oratione nullam in partem ab exercitu
Curionis fit significatio, atque ita suas uterque copias reducit.

29. At in castris Curionis magnus omnium[21] incessit

---

[21] omnium] -ibus *Jurin*: hostium *Herzog*: subito *Wölffel*

These made a report to Varus, either their true opinion or 2
one agreeable to Varus' ears. (What we desire we are glad
to believe, too, and we hope that others see things as we
do.) In fact they said with assurance that the whole army
was alienated from Curio, and that it would be very useful
for Varus' army to show itself and give an opportunity
for talks. Induced by this view of things Varus led his 3
troops out of camp the following day. Curio did the same,
and they drew up their forces on either side of a shallow
ravine.

28. Sextus Quintilius Varus, whose presence at Corfinium was mentioned above, was in Attius Varus' army;
he had come to Africa after his release by Caesar.[26] And
the legions that Curio had brought over were those that
Caesar had previously captured at Corfinium, so much so
that, although a few centurions had been changed, the
command structure and companies were the same as before. Having this rationale for addressing them, Quintilius 2
began to go from one spot to the next on Curio's line and
beseech the soldiers: "Do not discard your earliest memory of an oath, the one you swore in Domitius' presence
and mine when I was quaestor, or bear arms against men
who have suffered the same misfortunes as you and endured the same things under siege, or go into combat for
people by whom you are insulted as 'deserters.'" To this 3
he added a few words to raise hopes of largesse: "If you follow me and Attius, you will necessarily have expectations
from my generosity." After his speech there was no sign— 4
neither approval nor disapproval—from Curio's army, and
both men withdrew their troops.

29. However, in Curio's camp a vast fear attacked the

[26] For Varus at Corfinium, see 1.23.2.

timor animis. Is variis hominum sermonibus celeriter augetur. Vnusquisque enim opiniones fingebat et ad id quod
2 ab alio audierat sui aliquid timoris addebat. Hoc ubi uno
auctore ad plures permanaverat atque alius alii tradiderat
plures auctores eius rei videbantur.

3   †civile bellum
       genus hominum
       quod liceret libere facere et sequi quod vellet
       legiones hae quae paulo ante apud adversarios fuerant
       nam etiam Caesaris beneficium mutaverat
       consuetudo qua offerrentur
       municipia etiam diversis partibus coniuncta
       neque enim ex Marsis Paelignisque veniebant
       ut qui superiore nocte in contuberniis
       commilitesque nonnulli graviora
       sermones militum†

4   Dubia durius accipiebantur. Nonnulla etiam ab iis qui
diligentiores videri volebant fingebantur.

       30. Quibus de causis consilio convocato de summa re-
2 rum deliberare incipit. Erant sententiae quae conandum
omnibus modis castraque Vari oppugnanda censerent
quod huiusmodi militum [consiliis]²² otium maxime contrarium esse arbitrarentur. Postremo praestare dicebant

---

²² huiusmodi militum [consiliis] otium *Damon*: h- c- m- o-
Vossius: ⟨in⟩ h- m- c- o- *Clarke*: ⟨id⟩ h- m- c- [otium] *Madvig*

---

²⁷ For "fear attacked the general morale," Jurin, Herzog, and
Wölffel proposed "fear attacked everyone," "fear of the enemy
attacked morale," and "fear suddenly attacked morale," respectively.

²⁸ From "civil war" to "the talk of the soldiers," no continuous
text can be constituted. See the Introduction.

general morale.[27] This was quickly augmented in people's various conversations, for each man was inventing opinions and adding something of his own fear to whatever he had heard from another. When an opinion from one 2 source had made its way to several people, and each had transmitted it to others, there seemed to be a multiplicity of sources for it.

Civil war[28] . . . the sort of men . . . to do freely what one 3 could and pursue what he wanted . . . legions, those that had been on the enemy's side shortly beforehand . . . for even Caesar's favor had changed . . . the regularity with which they were offered . . . townships, even those aligned with different factions . . . for they weren't in origin from the Marsi or the Paeligni . . . just as those who the previous night in the tents . . . and some fellow soldiers more gravely . . . the talk of the soldiers.

Unknowns were interpreted for the worse, and some 4 things were even made up by people who wanted to seem particularly conscientious.

30 For these reasons Curio convened his council of war and initiated a discussion of the overall situation. Some opinions recommended that they should by all 2 means try and attack Varus' camp, since in their view inaction on the part of soldiers of this sort[29] was particularly inopportune. And to conclude: "It is preferable to

[29] For "inaction on the part of soldiers of this sort was particularly inopportune," Vossius, Clarke, and Madvig proposed "inaction on the part of soldiers was particularly inopportune for plans of this sort," "in the plans of soldiers of this sort, inaction was particularly inopportune," and "this was particularly inopportune for plans of this sort," respectively.

per virtutem in pugna belli fortunam experiri quam desertos et circumventos ab suis gravissimum supplicium pati.

3 Erant[23] qui censerent de tertia vigilia in Castra Cornelia
recedendum ut maiore spatio temporis interiecto militum
mentes sanarentur, simul si quid gravius accidisset magna
multitudine navium et tutius et facilius in Siciliam receptus daretur.

31. Curio utrumque improbans consilium quantum
alteri sententiae deesset animi tantum alteri superesse
dicebat: hos turpissimae fugae rationem habere, illos

2 etiam iniquo loco dimicandum putare. "Qua enim," inquit,
"fiducia et opere et natura loci munitissima castra ex-

3 pugnari posse confidimus? Aut vero quid proficimus si
accepto magno detrimento ab oppugnatione castrorum
discedimus? Quasi non et felicitas rerum gestarum exercitus benevolentiam imperatoribus et res adversae odia

4 concilient! Castrorum autem mutatio quid habet nisi turpem fugam et desperationem omnium[24] et alienationem
exercitus? Nam neque pudentes suspicari oportet sibi
parum credi neque improbos scire sese timeri, quod illis

5 licentiam timor augeat noster, his[25] studia deminuat. Quod
si iam," inquit, "haec explorata habeamus quae de exercitus alienatione dicuntur, quae quidem ego aut omnino
falsa aut certe minora opinione esse confido, quanto haec

---

[23] pati. Erant *Damon*: pati proiecerant *M and U in the margin*:
proiecerant *US*: perpeti erant *TV*

[24] omnium ω: o- ‹rerum› *Paul*

[25] his] his ‹suspicio› *Chacon*

---

[30] For "universal despair," Paul proposed "despair about everything."

experience the fortune of war courageously in combat than to be deserted and encircled by one's own men and then suffer the ultimate punishment." There were peo- 3 ple whose opinion was that they should retreat to Castra Cornelia in the middle of the night, so that the soldiers' morale had more time to recover and likewise so that if the situation got any worse their great multitude of ships would provide a safer and easier retreat to Sicily.

31. Curio disapproved of both ideas, saying that the one was as deficient in spirit as the other was excessive, that one group was planning an utterly shameful retreat while the other felt that they should fight even at a disadvantage. "What reason do we have to be confident that we 2 can storm a camp that is extremely well protected by fortifications and the nature of its position? On the other 3 hand, what do we gain if we suffer significant damage and abandon an attack on the camp? As if it is not the success of their exploits that wins an army's goodwill for commanders, while failures produce hatred! Further- 4 more, what does changing our camp's site signify except shameful retreat and universal despair[30] and disaffection in the army? For decent men should not suspect that our trust in them is insufficient, nor should reprobates know that we fear them, since our fear increases the insubordination of the latter and decreases[31] the determination of the former. Now if," he said, "we consider the asser- 5 tions about the army's disaffection to have been securely proven—things that I at least am confident are utterly false or surely less significant than people think—would it

[31] For "decreases," Chacon proposed "our suspicion decreases."

dissimulari et occultari quam per nos confirmari praestet!
6 An non uti corporis vulnera ita exercitus incommoda sunt
7 tegenda ne spem adversariis augeamus? At etiam ut media
nocte proficiscamur addunt quo maiorem, credo, licentiam habeant qui peccare conentur. Namque huiusmodi
res aut pudore aut metu tenentur, quibus rebus nox max-
8 ime adversaria est. Quare neque tanti sum animi ut sine
spe castra oppugnanda censeam neque tanti timoris uti
spe[26] deficiam, atque omnia prius experienda arbitror
magnaque ex parte iam me una vobiscum de re iudicium
facturum confido."

32. Dimisso consilio contionem advocat militum. Commemorat quo sit eorum usus studio ad Corfinium Caesar,
ut magnam partem Italiae beneficio atque auctoritate
2 eorum suam fecerit. "Vos enim vestrumque factum," inquit, "omnia deinceps municipia sunt secuta. Neque sine
causa et Caesar amicissime de vobis et illi gravissime iudi-
3 caverunt. Pompeius enim nullo proelio pulsus vestri facti
praeiudicio demotus Italia excessit. Caesar me, quem sibi
carissimum habuit, provinciam Siciliam atque Africam,
sine quibus urbem atque Italiam tueri non potest, vestrae
4 fidei commisit. At sunt qui vos hortentur ut a nobis descis-
catis. Quid enim est illis optatius quam uno tempore et nos
circumvenire et vos nefario scelere obstringere? Aut quid
irati gravius de vobis sentire[27] possunt quam ut eos proda-

---

[26] uti spe *Meusel*: ut ipse ω
[27] sentire] sancire *Paul*². *Perhaps* statuere?

---

32 For "what harsher feelings can angry men have," Paul and
I proposed "what harsher decision (or perhaps "ruling") can angry
men make."

not be much better to disguise and conceal them than to confirm them by our own actions? Should we not cover up 6 the army's troubles as we do wounds to the body, so as not to encourage the enemy? And yet on top of this they also 7 say that we should set out in the middle of the night—so that those who are going to try to misbehave have more license, I suppose! For this sort of behavior is kept in check either by decency or by fear, and nighttime is utterly antithetical to these. Therefore I am neither so brave as to 8 recommend that we make a hopeless attack on their camp, nor so timid as to give up hope. Furthermore, I think we should try everything before doing either, and I am quite confident that you and I will reach a decision together about this matter."

32. Curio dismissed his council and called a meeting of the soldiers. He reminded them of how Caesar used their support at Corfinium: he made a large part of Italy his own with their assistance and authorization. "You and your ac 2 tion," he said, "were followed by every town in turn, and there is every reason both for Caesar to take an extremely friendly view of you and for the enemy to feel extremely aggrieved, for Pompey was ousted without being beaten 3 in a single battle, leaving Italy thanks to the early verdict delivered by your action. Caesar entrusted me, whom he holds very dear, to your loyalty, as well as a province—Sicily and Africa—without which he cannot keep Rome and Italy safe. Granted, there are people who urge you to de- 4 fect. Well, what more can they desire than causing trouble for us while simultaneously involving you in an unspeakable crime? Or what harsher feeling can angry men have[32] about you than that you should betray those who

171

tis qui se vobis omnia debere iudicant, in eorum pot-
5 estatem veniatis qui se per vos perisse existimant? An vero
in Hispania res gestas Caesaris non audistis? duos pulsos
exercitus, duos superatos duces, duas receptas provincias;
haec acta diebus XL quibus in conspectum adversariorum
6 venerit Caesar. An qui incolumes resistere non potuerunt
perditi resistant? Vos autem incerta victoria Caesarem
secuti diiudicata iam belli fortuna victum sequamini—
7 cum vestri offici praemia percipere debeatis! Desertos
enim se ac proditos a vobis dicunt et prioris sacramenti
8 mentionem faciunt. Vosne vero L. Domitium, an vos Domitius deseruit? Nonne extremam pati fortunam paratos
proiecit ille, non sibi clam vobis salutem fuga petivit? Non
proditi per illum Caesaris beneficio estis conservati?
9 Sacramento quidem vos tenere qui potuit cum proiectis
fascibus et deposito imperio privatus et captus ipse in ali-
10 enam venisset potestatem? Relinquitur nova religio, ut eo
neglecto sacramento quo tenemini respiciatis illud quod
11 deditione ducis et capitis deminutione sublatum est. At,
credo, si Caesarem probatis iam[28] me offenditis. Qui de
meis in vos meritis praedicaturus non sum, quae sunt adhuc et mea voluntate et vestra expectatione leviora. Sed
tamen sui laboris milites semper eventu belli praemia
petiverunt, qui qualis sit futurus ne vos quidem dubitatis.
Diligentiam quidem nostram aut, quem ad finem adhuc

[28] iam] in *Estienne*

[33] For "critical," Estienne substituted "irritated because."

judge that they owe everything to you, and come into the
power of those who think that you brought about their
ruin? Have you really not heard about Caesar's exploits in 5
Spain? Two armies routed, two generals defeated, two
provinces recovered, all of it done forty days from when
Caesar came within sight of the enemy. Are those who 6
were unable to resist when they were sound going to resist
now that they are desperate? Are you who followed Caesar
when his victory was uncertain going to follow the defeated party now that the fortunes of war have been decided—when you ought to be receiving rewards for your
services? They say that they were abandoned and betrayed 7
by you, and refer to your former oath. But did you aban- 8
don Lucius Domitius, or did Domitius abandon you? Was
it not the case that he forsook men who were prepared to
endure the worst? Did he not seek safety for himself in
flight without your knowledge? After you were betrayed
by him, were you not saved by Caesar's favor? How could 9
he have used the oath to hold you, given that, after having thrown away the insignia of office and relinquished
command, as a private citizen and prisoner of war he has
himself come into the power of another? The result is a 10
strange sort of obligation: you are to neglect the oath that
currently binds you and respect one that has been invalidated by the general's surrender and loss of citizen status.
But if you approve of Caesar, you are currently critical[33] 11
of me, I suppose. I do not intend to boast about what I
have done for you, which is still less than I wish and you
expect. All the same, soldiers have always looked to the
outcome of a war when seeking rewards for their effort,
and not even you can be in any doubt about what sort of
outcome lies ahead. Why should I not mention my dili-

12 res processit, fortunam cur praeteream? An paenitet vos
quod salvum atque incolumem exercitum nulla omnino
nave desiderata traduxerim? Quod classem hostium primo
impetu adveniens profligaverim? Quod bis per biduum
equestri proelio superaverim? Quod ex portu sinuque
adversariorum CC naves oneratas adduxerim eoque illos
compulerim ut neque pedestri itinere neque navibus com-
13 meatu iuvari possint? Hac vos fortuna atque his ducibus
repudiatis ⟨an⟩ Corfiniensem ignominiam, an Italiae fugam, an[29] Hispaniarum deditionem—en[30] Africi belli
14 praeiudicia!—sequimini? Equidem me Caesaris militem
dici volui. Vos me imperatoris nomine appellavistis. Cuius
si vos paenitet vestrum vobis beneficium remitto. Mihi
meum restituite nomen ne ad contumeliam honorem dedisse videamini!"

33. Qua oratione permoti milites crebro etiam dicen-
tem interpellabant, ut magno cum dolore infidelitatis
suspicionem sustinere viderentur. Discedentem vero ex
contione universi cohortantur magno sit animo neu[31] du-
bitet proelium committere et suam fidem virtutemque
2 experiri. Quo facto commutata omnium et voluntate et
opinione, consensu suorum[32] constituit Curio cum primum sit data potestas proelio rem committere. Postero-

29 ⟨an⟩ Corfiniensem . . . an . . . an *Fabre*: co- . . . in . . . an [in
T] ω: Co- . . . [in] . . . [an] *Chacon*
30 en *Bücheler*: in ω: [in] *Chacon*
31 neu *M^{mr}*: ne ubi μ*S*: necubi *T*: nec ibi *V*
32 suorum *Estienne* (cf. 2.37.6): suo ω: summo *Hotoman*

34 For "can you be following?" Chacon proposed "follow!" He
also proposed deleting the word here rendered "in these you see,"

gence, or—as things have gone so far—my good luck? Are 12
you sorry that I brought the army across safe and sound
without losing a single ship? That I scattered the enemy
fleet at our first encounter upon arrival? That I was victorious twice in two days in cavalry battles? That I took two
hundred boats with their cargoes out of the enemy's harbor and control, and put the enemy under so much pressure that they cannot be supplied by land or sea? After 13
rejecting this good fortune and these leaders can you be
following[34] the lead of the humiliation at Corfinium, the
flight from Italy, the surrender of Spain? In these you see
the precedents for the war in Africa! For my part, I wanted 14
to be called Caesar's soldier; you addressed me with the
title *imperator*. If you now regret it, I renounce the favor.
Give me back the name I had! Otherwise people will think
that your honor to me was meant as an insult."

33. Provoked by this speech, the soldiers repeatedly
interrupted while Curio was still talking, making it apparent that they endured with great indignation the suspicion
of disloyalty. But as he was leaving the meeting they all
urged him to take heart and not hesitate to join battle[35]
and put their loyalty and courage to the test. As a result, 2
the general inclination and opinion shifted, so Curio had
the agreement of his side[36] when he decided to commit
the issue to battle as soon as an opportunity presented it-

which leaves "the precedents" in apposition to the preceding list
of setbacks.

[35] Editors often print the reading of T, which adds "anywhere
at all" after "battle."

[36] For "the agreement of his side," Hotoman substituted "the
utmost consensus."

que die productos eodem loco quo superioribus diebus
3 constiterat in acie collocat. Ne Varus quidem Attius dubi-
tat copias producere, sive sollicitandi milites sive aequo
loco dimicandi detur occasio, ne facultatem praetermittat.

34. Erat vallis inter duas acies, ut supra demonstratum
est, non ita magna at difficili et arduo ascensu. Hanc uterque si adversariorum copiae transire conarentur expecta-
2 bat quo aequiore loco proelium committeret. Simul ab
sinistro cornu P. Atti equitatus omnis et una levis armaturae interiecti complures, cum se in vallem demitterent,
3 cernebantur. Ad eos Curio equitatum et duas Marrucino-
rum cohortes mittit. Quorum primum impetum equites
hostium non tulerunt sed admissis equis ad suos refugerunt. Relicti ab his, qui una procurrerant levis armaturae
circumveniebantur atque interficiebantur ab nostris. Huc
tota Vari conversa acies suos fugere et concidi videbat.
4 Tum Rebilus, legatus Caesaris, quem Curio secum ex Sicilia duxerat quod magnum habere usum in re militari sciebat: "Perterritum," inquit, "hostem vides, Curio. Quid
5 dubitas uti temporis opportunitate?" Ille unum elocutus—
ut memoria tenerent milites ea quae pridie sibi confir-
massent—sequi sese iubet et praecurrit ante omnes.
Adeoque erat impedita vallis ut in ascensu nisi sublevati a
6 suis primi non facile eniterentur. Sed praeoccupatus animus Attianorum militum timore et fuga et caede suorum

---

[37] The phrase "at the same time" is puzzling and may indicate
that some text has been lost in the vicinity.

self. The next day he led his men to the position they had
held previously and placed them in battle formation. At- 3
tius Varus did not hesitate to lead his forces out, either, so
as not to pass up a chance, if he got the opportunity, of
either appealing to Curio's soldiers or fighting on favorable ground.

34. There was a ravine between the two lines, as was
indicated above. It was not particularly large but had a
difficult and steep ascent. Each side waited to see whether
the adversary's forces would attempt to cross it, hoping
to engage them on more favorable ground. At the same 2
time[37] on Publius Attius' left wing his entire cavalry was
visible with a number of light-armed troops in their midst
as they descended into the ravine. Curio sent his cavalry 3
against them, along with two cohorts of Marrucini. The
enemy cavalry did not withstand the initial impact; in fact
they fled to their own line at a gallop. Abandoned by these
troops, the light-armed soldiers who had advanced at a
run with them were surrounded and killed by our men.
Varus' entire line was facing this way and saw the flight and
slaughter of their men. Then Rebilus, an officer of Cae- 4
sar's, whom Curio had brought with him from Sicily because he knew that Rebilus had a lot of experience in
military matters, said: "You see that the enemy is thoroughly cowed, Curio. Why do you hesitate to use the opportunity of the moment?" Curio said just one thing 5
—"Remember the assurances you gave me yesterday!"—
then ordered the soldiers to follow him. He rushed on
ahead of everyone. The ravine was so difficult to negotiate
that the leaders in the ascent had a hard struggle unless
they were assisted from below by their own men. But the 6
morale of Attius' men was in the grip of fright and the

nihil de resistendo cogitabat, omnesque iam se ab equitatu circumveniri arbitrabantur. Itaque priusquam telum abici posset aut nostri propius accederent omnis Vari acies terga vertit seque in castra recepit.

35. Qua in fuga Fabius Paelignus quidam ex infimis ordinibus de exercitu Curionis primum[33] agmen fugientium consecutus magna voce Varum nomine appellans requirebat, uti unus esse ex eius militibus et monere ali-
2 quid velle ac dicere videretur. Vbi ille saepius appellatus aspexit ac restitit et quis esset aut quid vellet quaesivit, humerum apertum gladio appetit, paulumque afuit quin Varum interficeret. Quod ille periculum sublato ad eius conatum scuto vitavit. Fabius a proximis militibus circumventus interficitur.
3 Hac fugientium multitudine ac turba portae castrorum occupantur atque iter impeditur, pluresque in eo loco sine vulnere quam in proelio aut fuga intereunt, neque multum afuit quin etiam castris expellerentur. Ac nonnulli protinus
4 eodem cursu in oppidum contenderunt. Sed cum loci natura et munitio castrorum adiri ⟨prohibebat⟩[34] tum quod ad proelium egressi Curionis milites iis rebus indi-
5 gebant quae ad oppugnationem castrorum erant usui. Itaque Curio exercitum in castra reducit suis omnibus praeter Fabium incolumibus, ex numero adversariorum circiter DC interfectis ac mille vulneratis. Qui omnes discessu Curionis multique praeterea per simulationem

[33] primum] primus *Paul, as reported by Meusel*
[34] adiri ⟨prohibebat⟩ *Manutius*: adiri ω: aditu ⟨prohibebant⟩ *Bentley*

flight and slaughter of their men. There was no thought of resistance, and everyone believed that they were already being surrounded by the cavalry. So before a weapon could be thrown, or our men came closer, Varus' whole line turned back and withdrew into their camp.

35. During this retreat a certain Paelignian named Fabius, one of the lowest-ranking centurions in Curio's army, reaching the fugitives' front line,[38] began to look for Varus, calling him by name in a loud voice and giving the impression that he was one of Varus' soldiers and wanted to give him a warning or message. After his name was called repeatedly, Varus eyed him and stopped, asking who he was or what he wanted. Fabius then struck Varus' exposed shoulder with his sword and only missed killing him by a little, a danger that Varus escaped because he raised his shield against the attempt. Fabius was surrounded and killed by the closest soldiers.

The large crowd of fugitives filled the gateway of the camp and obstructed the road, and more men perished there unwounded than fell in the battle or retreat. They came quite close to being driven out of their camp, and some kept running straight on into the city. But the nature of the site and the camp's fortification prevented approach, as did the fact that Curio's soldiers, having marched out for a battle, had none of equipment used in assaulting a camp. Therefore Curio led his army back to camp with all of his men unscathed except Fabius, and about six hundred of the enemy dead and a thousand wounded. After Curio's departure all of the wounded men (and many, too,

[38] For "reaching the fugitives' front line," Paul proposed "the first to reach the line of fugitives."

vulnerum ex castris in oppidum propter timorem sese
6 recipiunt. Qua re animadversa Varus et terrore exercitus
cognito bucinatore in castris et paucis ad speciem taber-
naculis relictis de tertia vigilia silentio exercitum in oppidum reducit.

36. Postero die Curio obsidere Vticam valloque circummunire instituit. Erat in oppido multitudo insolens
belli diuturnitate oti, Vticenses pro quibusdam Caesaris in
se beneficiis illi amicissimi, conventus is qui ex variis generibus constaret, terror ex superioribus proeliis magnus.
2 Itaque de deditione omnes [in] palam loquebantur et cum
P. Attio agebant ne sua pertinacia omnium fortunas per-
3 turbari vellet. Haec cum agerentur nuntii praemissi ab
rege Iuba venerunt qui illum adesse cum magnis copiis
dicerent et de custodia ac defensione urbis hortarentur.
Quae res eorum perterritos animos confirmavit.

37. Nuntiabantur haec eadem Curioni sed aliquamdiu
fides fieri non poterat. Tantam habebat suarum rerum fi-
2 duciam, iamque Caesaris in Hispania res secundae in Africam nuntiis ac litteris perferebantur. Quibus omnibus
rebus sublatus nihil contra se regem nisurum existimabat.
3 Sed ubi certis auctoribus comperit minus V et XX milibus
longe ab Vtica eius copias abesse, relictis munitionibus
4 sese in Castra Cornelia recepit. Huc frumentum comportare, castra munire, materiam conferre coepit. Statimque
in Siciliam misit uti duae legiones reliquusque equitatus

pretending to be wounded) withdrew from the camp into the city because of their fear. Observing this and recogniz-   6 ing his army's terror, Varus left a trumpeter and a few tents in the camp for show and around midnight quietly took the rest of the army into the city.

36. The next day Curio began to blockade Utica and surround it with an earthwork. The city contained a mul- titude unaccustomed to war because of the long-standing peace, plus citizens of Utica, who were exceedingly friendly to Caesar because of certain favors to them, plus a com- munity of Romans, the sort of association that comprises various ranks—plus quantities of terror as a result of the past battles. Therefore everyone spoke openly about sur-   2 render and approached Publius Attius to discourage him from allowing everyone's future to be thrown into confu- sion because of his obstinacy. When this discussion was   3 still under way, messengers sent ahead by Juba arrived with word that he was nearby with a large force and an exhortation about the protection and defense of their city. These developments put heart into the terrified pop- ulation.

37. The same news reached Curio but was unable to gain credence for some time, so great was Curio's confi- dence in his situation. Caesar's successes in Spain, too,   2 were already being conveyed to Africa by messengers and letters. Elated by all of this Curio did not think that the king would exert himself against him. But when he learned   3 from reliable sources that the king's forces were less than twenty-five miles from Utica, he left his fortification and withdrew to Castra Cornelia. He began to convey grain to   4 this spot, to fortify a camp, and to collect timber. And he immediately sent word to Sicily that the two legions and

5 ad se mitteretur. Castra erant ad bellum ducendum aptissima natura loci et munitione et maris propinquitate et aquae et salis copia, cuius magna vis iam ex proximis erat

6 salinis eo congesta. Non materia multitudine arborum, non frumentum, cuius erant plenissimi agri, deficere poterat. Itaque omnium suorum consensu Curio reliquas copias expectare et bellum ducere parabat.

38. His constitutis rebus probatisque consiliis ex perfugis quibusdam oppidanis audit Iubam revocatum finitimo bello et controversiis Leptitanorum restitisse in regno; Saburram, eius praefectum, cum mediocribus copiis mis-

2 sum Vticae appropinquare. His auctoribus temere credens consilium commutat et proelio rem committere constituit. Multum ad hanc rem probandam adiuvat adulescentia, magnitudo animi, superioris temporis proven-

3 tus, fiducia rei bene gerendae. His rebus impulsus equitatum omnem prima nocte ad castra hostium mittit ad flumen Bagradam. Quibus praeerat Saburra, de quo ante erat auditum. Sed rex cum omnibus copiis insequebatur et VI milium passuum intervallo ab Saburra consederat.

4 Equites missi nocte iter conficiunt, imprudentes atque inopinantes hostes aggrediuntur. Numidae enim quadam barbara consuetudine nullis ordinibus passim consede-

5 rant. Hos oppressos somno et dispersos adorti magnum eorum numerum interficiunt. Multi perterriti profugiunt. Quo facto ad Curionem equites revertuntur captivosque ad eum reducunt.

39. Curio cum omnibus copiis quarta vigilia exierat

the remaining cavalry should be sent to him. His camp was 5
perfectly suited for prolonging a war, given the nature of
the site and its defenses and the sea's proximity and the
availability of water and salt, of which there was already a
great quantity heaped up from nearby saltworks. Timber 6
could not run short, owing to the multitude of trees, or
grain, of which the fields had a great abundance. With the
agreement of all of his men, therefore, he prepared to wait
for his remaining forces and prolong the war.

38. With these arrangements in place and his plans
approved, Curio heard from some townspeople deserting
Utica that Juba, recalled because of a border war and a
dispute with Leptis, had stayed behind in his kingdom.
Saburra, they said, a general of his, had been sent with a
modest force and was approaching Utica. Rashly believing 2
these informants, Curio changed his plan and decided to
commit the issue to battle. Many factors helped make
this plan appealing: youth, ambition, past outcomes, confidence in success. Urged on by such considerations, he 3
sent his entire cavalry at nightfall to the enemy camp at
the Bagradas River; Saburra, about whom he had heard
earlier, was in command there. But Saburra had behind
him the king and his entire force; Juba was encamped six
miles away. The cavalry Curio sent finished their journey 4
during the night; they attacked an enemy off guard and
unsuspecting, for the Numidians in their barbarian fashion had camped here and there in complete disarray. By 5
attacking while these were fast asleep and scattered, Curio's cavalry killed a large number of them; many fled in
terror. Thereafter the cavalry headed back to Curio with
prisoners in tow.

39. Curio had set out with his whole force before dawn,

cohortibus V castris praesidio relictis. Progressus milia
passuum VI equites convenit, rem gestam cognovit, ex
captivis quaerit quis castris ad Bagradam praesit. Re-
2 spondent Saburram. Reliqua studio itineris conficiendi
quaerere praetermittit. Proximaque respiciens signa "Vi-
detisne," inquit, "milites, captivorum orationem cum perfugis convenire? abesse regem, exiguas esse copias missas,
3 quae paucis equitibus pares esse non potuerint? Proinde
ad praedam, ad gloriam properate, ut iam de praemiis
4 vestris et de referenda gratia cogitare incipiamus." Erant
per se magna quae gesserant equites, praesertim cum
eorum exiguus numerus cum tanta multitudine Numida-
rum conferretur. Haec tamen ab ipsis inflatius commemo-
rabantur, ut de suis homines laudibus libenter praedicant.
5 Multa praeterea spolia praeferebantur, capti homines
equitesque[35] producebantur, ut quicquid intercederet
6 temporis hoc omne victoriam morari videretur. Ita spei
Curionis militum studia non deerant. Equites sequi iubet
sese iterque accelerat ut quam maxime ex fuga perterritos
adoriri posset. At illi itinere totius noctis confecti subsequi
non poterant atque alii alio loco resistebant. Ne haec quidem res Curionem ad spem[36] morabatur.

40. Iuba certior factus a Saburra de nocturno proelio
duo milia Hispanorum et Gallorum equitum, quos suae
custodiae causa circum se habere consuerat, et peditum
eam partem cui maxime confidebat Saburrae summittit.
Ipse cum reliquis copiis elephantisque LX lentius subse-

---

[35] equitesque] equique *Chacon*   [36] [ad spem] *Chacon*

---

[39] For "infantry and cavalry," Chacon proposed "men and
horses."   [40] Chacon proposed deleting "in his optimism."

leaving five cohorts on guard in the camp. After advancing six miles he met the cavalry, learned of their success, and asked the prisoners who was in charge of the camp at the Bagradas. "Saburra," they replied. In his hurry to complete the journey, he omitted the other questions. With his eyes on the nearest standards, he said "Do you see, soldiers, that the prisoners' words agree with the deserters? That the king is absent and has sent a weak force, one that was unable to measure up to a few cavalry? So make haste for booty and glory, in order that I can begin to think about your rewards and showing my gratitude." The cavalry's achievement was impressive in itself, especially when people compared their small number with the huge multitude of Numidians. But there was still exaggeration in their report, given that men are inclined to boast about their praiseworthy actions. In addition, many spoils of war were on display, and captured infantry and cavalry[39] were brought forward, so that every intervening moment seemed to delay victory. So the soldiers' enthusiasm matched Curio's optimism. He ordered the cavalry to follow him, and accelerated his march so as to be able to attack men when they were most thoroughly cowed after a rout. However, his cavalry, exhausted after a full night of riding, were unable to follow; they began to stay behind in bunches one after another. But not even this checked Curio in his optimism.[40]

40. Juba was informed by Saburra about the nighttime battle. He sent Saburra reinforcements: two thousand cavalry from Spain and Gaul, which he usually kept near him as a bodyguard, and those of his infantry that he trusted most. He himself followed more slowly with the rest of his

2 quitur. Suspicatus praemissis equitibus ipsum adfore Curionem Saburra copias equitum peditumque instruit atque his imperat ut simulatione timoris paulatim cedant ac
pedem referant; sese cum opus esset signum proeli daturum et quod rem postulare cognovisset imperaturum.
3 Curio ad superiorem spem addita praesentis temporis
opinione hostes fugere arbitratus copias ex locis superioribus in campum deducit.

41. Quibus ex locis cum longius esset progressus
confecto iam labore exercitu XVI milium spatio constitit.
2 Dat suis signum Saburra. Aciem constituit et circumire
ordines atque hortari incipit. Sed peditatu dumtaxat pro-
3 cul ad speciem utitur, equites in aciem immittit. Non deest
negotio Curio suosque hortatur ut spem omnem in virtute
reponant. Ne militibus quidem ut defessis neque equitibus ut paucis et labore confectis studium ad pugnandum
virtusque deerat, sed ii erant numero CC. Reliqui in iti-
4 nere substiterant. Hi quamcumque in partem impetum
fecerant hostes loco cedere cogebant, sed neque longius
fugientes prosequi ⟨neque⟩ vehementius equos incitare
5 poterant. At equitatus hostium ab utroque cornu circum-
6 ire aciem nostram et aversos proterere incipit. Cum cohortes ex acie procucurrissent Numidae integri celeritate
impetum nostrorum effugiebant, rursusque ad ordines
suos se recipientes circumibant et ab acie excludebant. Sic
neque in loco manere ordinesque servare neque procur-

troops and sixty elephants. Saburra, suspecting that Curio, 2
having sent cavalry ahead, was himself about to arrive,
deployed his cavalry and infantry forces. He ordered them
to yield ground gradually and retreat with a show of fear,
saying that he would give the signal for battle when the
time was right. His orders, he said, would be whatever
he saw the situation demanded. Curio's assessment of 3
the present situation—he thought the enemy was running
away—added to his original optimism, and he brought his
troops down from higher ground onto a level plain.

41. Curio advanced a good way from those heights.
With his army now exhausted from exertion, he halted
after sixteen miles. Saburra gave his men the signal. He 2
lined them up in formation and began to circulate among
the units, encouraging them. But he only used the infantry
at a distance and for show; he sent the cavalry against the
line. Curio was equal to the task and exhorted his men 3
to put their entire hope in courage. Neither the infantry, although weary, nor the cavalry, although few and exhausted from exertion, lacked the will for combat or the
courage, but the latter only numbered two hundred. The
rest had stayed behind on the march. Wherever our cav- 4
alry attacked, they forced the enemy to yield but were unable to pursue them in flight for any distance or spur their
horses to greater speed. The enemy cavalry, however, be- 5
gan to encircle our line on both flanks and ride the men
down from behind. When our cohorts advanced at a run 6
from the line, the Numidians would flee before their attack at full speed, and then circle around and cut our men
off from the line when they were going back to their formations. As a result it did not seem safe either to stay
in position and maintain their formations or to run for-

7 rere et casum subire tutum videbatur. Hostium copiae summissis ab rege auxiliis crebro augebantur. Nostros vires lassitudine deficiebant. Simul ii qui vulnera accepe- rant neque acie excedere neque in locum tutum referri poterant quod tota acies equitatu hostium circumdata te-
8 nebatur. Hi de sua salute desperantes, ut extremo vitae tempore homines facere consuerunt, aut suam mortem miserabantur aut parentes suos commendabant si quos ex eo periculo Fortuna servare potuisset. Plena erant omnia timoris et luctus.

42. Curio ubi perterritis omnibus neque cohortationes suas neque preces audiri intellegit unam ut in miseris re- bus spem reliquam salutis esse arbitratus proximos colles capere universos atque eo signa inferri iubet. Hos quoque
2 praeoccupat missus a Saburra equitatus. Tum vero ad summam desperationem nostri perveniunt et partim fu- gientes ab equitatu interficiuntur partim integri procum-
3 bunt. Hortatur Curionem Cn. Domitius praefectus equi- tum cum paucis equitibus circumsistens ut fuga salutem petat atque in castra contendat, et se ab eo non discessu-
4 rum pollicetur. At Curio numquam se amisso exercitu quem a Caesare fidei commissum acceperit in eius con- spectum reversurum confirmat atque ita proelians inter-
5 ficitur. Equites ex proelio perpauci se recipiunt. Sed ii quos ad novissimum agmen equorum reficiendorum causa substitisse demonstratum est fuga totius exercitus procul animadversa sese incolumes in castra conferunt. Milites ad unum omnes interficiuntur.

43. His rebus cognitis Marcius Rufus quaestor in ca- stris relictus a Curione cohortatur suos ne animo deficiant. Illi orant atque obsecrant ut in Siciliam navibus reporten-

ward and take one's chances. The enemy forces were fre- 7
quently supplemented by reinforcements sent by the king.
Our men's strength was beginning to fail from exhaustion. Moreover, the wounded could neither fall out nor be
transported to a safe location, because the entire line was
held surrounded by the enemy cavalry. As people gener- 8
ally do in their final moments, so these men, despairing of
safety, either bewailed their own deaths or commended
their relatives to anyone whom Fortune could save from
the present danger. Everything was full of fear and lamentation.

42. When Curio realized that with everyone terrified
neither his exhortations nor his entreaties were being
heard, thinking that despite his pitiable circumstances
there was one hope left, he ordered everyone to occupy
the closest hills and move the standards there. The cavalry
sent by Saburra seized these too ahead of him. Then in- 2
deed did our men reach the ultimate desperation; some
were killed in flight by the cavalry, some collapsed without
a wound. Gnaeus Domitius, a cavalry commander protect- 3
ing Curio with a few horsemen, urged him to seek safety
in flight and head for the camp, promising not to leave
him. But Curio declared that he would never return to 4
Caesar's sight after losing the army he had received in trust
from Caesar, and so died fighting. A very few cavalry came 5
back from the battle. But those who, as was explained, had
stopped in the rear in order to rest their horses, noticing
the rout of the whole army, got safely to the camp. The
infantry were killed to a man.

43. Learning of this, Marcius Rufus, the quaestor left
by Curio at the camp, urged his men not to lose heart.
They begged and pleaded to be ferried back to Sicily.

tur. Pollicetur magistrisque imperat navium ut primo ves-
2 pere omnes scaphas ad litus appulsas habeant. Sed tantus
fuit omnium terror ut alii adesse copias Iubae dicerent alii
cum legionibus instare Varum iamque se pulverem ve-
nientium cernere—quarum rerum nihil omnino acciderat—alii classem hostium celeriter advolaturam suspica-
rentur. Itaque perterritis omnibus sibi quisque consulebat.
3 Qui in classe erant proficisci properabant. Horum fuga
navium onerariarum magistros incitabat. Pauci lenunculi
4 ad officium imperiumque conveniebant. Sed tanta erat
completis litoribus contentio qui potissimum ex magno
numero conscenderent ut multitudine atque onere nonnulli deprimerentur, reliqui hoc timore propius adire tar-
darentur.

44. Quibus rebus accidit ut pauci milites patresque
familiae, qui aut gratia aut misericordia valerent aut ‹ad›[37]
naves adnare possent, recepti in Siciliam incolumes per-
venirent. Reliquae copiae missis ad Varum noctu legato-
2 rum numero centurionibus sese ei dediderunt. Quorum
cohortes militum postero die ante oppidum Iuba conspicatus, suam esse praedicans praedam magnam partem
eorum interfici iussit, paucos electos in regnum remisit,
cum Varus suam fidem ab eo laedi quereretur neque resis-
3 tere auderet. Ipse equo in oppidum vectus prosequenti-
bus compluribus senatoribus, quo in numero erat Ser.
Sulpicius et Licinius Damasippus, paucis diebus quae fieri
vellet Vticae constituit atque imperavit. Diebus aeque
post paucis se in regnum cum omnibus copiis recepit.

37 ‹ad› *Chacon*

He promised, and ordered the ship captains to have all of their longboats drawn up on shore at sunset. But so great 2 was the universal terror that some were saying that Juba's forces were at hand, others that Varus and his legions were imminent and that the dust cloud of their approach was already visible to them—not one of these things had happened—and others suspected that the enemy fleet was going to sail against them soon. Everyone was terrified, so each acted for himself. Those in the fleet set out in a hurry. 3 Their flight spurred on the transport captains. A few small vessels mustered as per their obligations and orders, but 4 such was the struggle on the packed beaches over who of the huge number was going to embark, that some boats were sunk by the weight of the crowd and the rest hesitated to come closer for fear of this.

44. The result of these developments was that a few soldiers and family men were taken on board and reached Sicily safely, if they prevailed by favor or compassion or managed to swim out to the ships. The rest of the troops sent a nighttime delegation of centurions to Varus and then surrendered to him. The units of these soldiers were 2 spotted by Juba the next day in front of Utica. Insisting that this was his booty, he ordered a large number of them to be killed and sent a few picked men to his kingdom, although Varus protested that his guarantee was being infringed by Juba; he did not dare resist. Juba himself rode 3 into Utica with several senators in his train, among them Servius Sulpicius and Licinius Damasippus. Within a short period he determined what he wished done at Utica and gave orders. After an equally short period he went back to his kingdom with his whole force.

LIBER III

1. Dictatore habente comitia Caesare consules creantur
Iulius Caesar et P. Servilius. Is enim erat annus quo per
2 leges ei consulem fieri liceret. His rebus confectis cum
fides tota Italia esset angustior neque creditae pecuniae
solverentur constituit ut arbitri darentur: per eos fierent
aestimationes possessionum et rerum, quanti quaeque
earum ante bellum fuisset, atque eae creditoribus trade-
3 rentur. Hoc et ad timorem novarum tabularum tollendum
minuendumque, qui fere bella et civiles dissensiones sequi consuevit, et ad debitorum tuendam existimationem
4 esse aptissimum existimavit. Item praetoribus tribunisque
plebis rogationes ad populum ferentibus nonnullos ambi-
tus Pompeia lege damnatos illis temporibus quibus in urbe
praesidia legionum[1] Pompeius habuerat—quae iudicia
aliis[2] audientibus iudicibus aliis sententiam ferentibus singulis diebus erant perfecta—in integrum restituit, qui se
illi initio civilis belli obtulerant si sua opera in bello uti

[1] legionum *is hard to credit and may be a gloss*
[2] aliis] a- <testes> *Chacon*

---

[1] In 52, when Pompey was sole consul in Rome.
[2] For the vague "at the hearing," Chacon proposed "hearing
the witnesses" on the basis of Asconius' commentary on Cicero's
pro Milone, a speech delivered at a trial that year (*Mil.* 34).

BOOK III

1. When Caesar held elections in his capacity as dictator, Julius Caesar and Publius Servilius were elected consuls, this being the year in which it was legally permissible for Caesar to be consul. After the elections were over, since 2 credit was rather tight throughout Italy and existing loans were not being repaid, he decided to provide arbitrators. These were to make assessments of real estate and goods, determining the prewar value of each item, and the possessions themselves were to be surrendered to creditors. He thought that this would be the most suitable measure 3 both for removing and reducing people's fear of a cancellation of debts (something that is apt to follow warfare and civil strife) and for preserving the borrowers' reputations. Furthermore, and using praetors and plebeian tribunes to 4 put the necessary legislation before the people, Caesar reinstated some men who had been convicted of bribery under the *lex Pompeia* in the period when Pompey had kept legionary garrisons[1] in Rome—in trials that were concluded in the space of a day, with one set of jurors at the hearing[2] and another giving the verdict. These men had offered themselves to him at the beginning of the civil war, in case he wanted to use their services in the war,

vellet, proinde aestimans ac si usus esset quoniam sui
5 fecissent potestatem. Statuerat enim prius hos iudicio
populi debere restitui quam suo beneficio videri receptos,
ne aut ingratus in referenda gratia aut arrogans in prae-
ripiendo populi beneficio videretur.

2. His rebus et feriis Latinis comitiisque omnibus per-
ficiendis XI dies tribuit dictaturaque se abdicat et ab urbe
2 proficiscitur Brundisiumque pervenit. Eo legiones XII
equitatum omnem venire iusserat. Sed tantum navium
repperit ut anguste XV milia³ legionariorum militum D
equites transportari possent. Hoc unum [inopia navium]
3 Caesari ad celeritatem conficiendi belli defuit. Atque eae
ipsae copiae hoc infrequentiores [copiae] imponuntur
quod multi [galli]⁴ tot bellis defecerant, longumque iter ex
Hispania magnum numerum deminuerat, et gravis au-
tumnus in Apulia circumque Brundisium ex saluberrimis
Galliae et Hispaniae regionibus omnem exercitum valetudine temptaverat.

3. Pompeius annuum spatium ad comparandas copias
nactus quod vacuum a bello atque ab hoste otiosum fuerat
magnam ex Asia Cycladibusque insulis Corcyra Athenis
Ponto Bithynia Syria Cilicia Phoenice Aegypto classem
coegerat, magnam omnibus locis aedificandam curaverat.
2 Magnam imperatam Asiae Syriae regibusque omnibus et
dinastis et tetrarchis et liberis Achaiae populis pecuniam

³ XV milia] *The number may be too small.*
⁴ [galli] *Klotz (see 3.87.2):* Galli<cis> *ed. pr.*

---

³ According to the manuscripts, it was Gallic troops that succumbed (or deserted). In the first edition the text was emended
to specify the Gallic campaigns as the occasion of the losses.

something that he rated as highly as if he had used them, since they had made themselves available. For he had 5 decided that they ought to be reinstated by a popular vote before it became clear that they had been restored by his favor, lest he give the impression of being either ungrateful in thanking them or highhanded in anticipating a favor granted by the people.

2. Caesar allocated eleven days to finishing this business, the Latin Festival, and all of the elections. He resigned from the dictatorship, left Rome, and went to Brundisium. He had ordered twelve legions and all of his 2 cavalry to go there. But he only found enough ships for transporting fifteen thousand tightly packed troops and five hundred cavalry. This one deficiency kept Caesar from bringing the war to a swift conclusion. And the force that 3 did embark was the scantier because many men had succumbed in the numerous wars,[3] and the long march from Spain had subtracted a large number, and an oppressive autumn in Apulia and around Brundisium, after the very healthy climate of Gaul and Spain, had afflicted his whole army with sickness.

3. Pompey, with a whole year[4] to obtain troops, a year clear of warfare and hostile engagements, had mustered a large fleet from Asia, the Cyclades, Corcyra, Athens, Pontus, Bithynia, Syria, Cilicia, Phoenicia, and Egypt; in all of these places he had also arranged for the construction of a large fleet. A large sum of money had been requisitioned 2 by him and collected from Asia, Syria, all of the kings,

[4] Pompey arrived in Greece in 49 (March), Caesar in 48 (January).

exegerat, magnam societates earum provinciarum quas
ipse obtinebat sibi numerare coegerat.

4. Legiones effecerat civium Romanorum VIIII: V ex
Italia, quas traduxerat, unam ex Cilicia veteranam, quam
factam ex duabus gemellam appellabat, unam ex Creta et
Macedonia ex veteranis militibus, qui dimissi a superioribus imperatoribus in his provinciis consederant, duas ex
2 Asia, quas Lentulus consul conscribendas curaverat. Praeterea magnum numerum ex Thessalia Boeotia Achaia Epi-
roque supplementi nomine in legiones distribuerat. His
3 Antonianos milites admiscuerat. Praeter has expectabat
cum Scipione ex Syria legiones duas. Sagittarios ⟨ex⟩
Creta Lacedaemone, ex Ponto atque Syria reliquisque
civitatibus tria milia numero habebat, funditorum cohortes sexcenarias duas, equitum VII milia. Ex quibus DC
Gallos Deiotarus adduxerat, D Ariobarzanes ex Cappadocia. Ad eundem numerum Cotus ex Thracia dederat et
4 Sadalam filium miserat. Ex Macedonia CC erant, quibus
Rhascypolis praeerat, excellenti virtute. D ex Gabinianis
Alexandria—Gallos Germanosque quos ibi A. Gabinius
praesidi causa apud regem Ptolomaeum reliquerat—
Pompeius filius cum classe adduxerat. DCCC ex servis

---

5 "Dynasts" and "tetrarchs" ruled small "kingdoms" on Rome's
eastern border; some are named in 3.4. See also 3.31.2.

6 The tax companies, headed by "publicans" (*publicani*), contracted with the Roman state to collect various taxes, a profitable
enterprise, particularly in the eastern provinces controlled by
Pompey. See also 3.31–32 and 3.103.

7 "Antonius' soldiers" are survivors of the Caesarian legions
defeated with C. Antonius in late 49; the episode is absent from
our text (see the Introduction). They now serve Pompey.

dynasts, and tetrarchs,[5] and the free peoples of Greece. Plus, a large sum was paid to him, under compulsion, by tax companies[6] in the provinces he controlled.

4. Pompey had brought up to strength nine legions of Roman citizens: five from Italy, which had crossed with him, a veteran legion from Cilicia, which he called "the twin" because it had been created from two, one from Crete and Macedonia, made from veteran soldiers who had settled in those provinces after being discharged by their former commanders, two from Asia, whose conscription the consul Lentulus had arranged. In addition, he had 2 distributed among the legions by way of supplement a large number of men from Thessaly, Boeotia, Achaia, and Epirus, and merged Antonius' soldiers into them.[7] Besides 3 these, he expected two legions with Scipio from Syria. He had archers from Crete and Lacedemon, from Pontus and Syria and other communities, about three thousand in number, two six-hundred-men cohorts of slingers, and seven thousand cavalry. Of these, Deiotarus had brought six hundred Galatians, Ariobarzanes five hundred from Cappadocia. Cotus of Thrace had supplied about the same number and sent his son Sadalas. There were two hundred 4 from Macedonia under the command of Rhascypolis, men of outstanding courage.[8] Pompey's son had brought, along with his fleet, five hundred ex-Gabinians from Alexandria, Gauls and Germans whom Aulus Gabinius had left as a garrison with King Ptolemy. From his slaves and his force

[8] The modifier "of outstanding courage" may instead apply to Rhascypolis, whose actions in a later war are reported by Dio at 47.25.2 and 47.48.2.

5   suis pastorumque suorum ⟨numero⟩ coegerat. CCC Tarcondarius Castor et Domnilaus ex Gallograecia dederant.
Horum alter una venerat, alter filium miserat. CC ex Syria
a Commageno Antiocho—cui magna Pompeius praemia
6   tribuit—missi erant, in his plerique hippotoxotae. Huc
Dardanos Bessos partim mercennarios partim imperio aut
gratia comparatos, item Macedones Thessalos ac reliquarum gentium et civitatum adiecerat atque eum quem
supra demonstravimus numerum expleverat.

    5. Frumenti vim maximam ex Thessalia Asia Aegypto
2   Creta Cyrenis reliquisque regionibus comparaverat. Hiemare Dyrrachi Apolloniae omnibusque oppidis maritimis
constituerat ut mare transire Caesarem prohiberet, eiusque rei causa omni ora maritima classem disposuerat.
3   Praeerat Aegyptiis navibus Pompeius filius, Asiaticis D.
Laelius et C. Triarius, Syriacis C. Cassius, Rhodiis C. Marcellus cum C. Coponio, Liburnicae atque Achaicae classi
4   Scribonius Libo et M. Octavius. Toti tamen officio mari-
timo M. Bibulus praepositus cuncta administrabat. Ad
hunc summa imperi respiciebat.

    6. Caesar ut Brundisium venit contionatus apud mi-
lites: quoniam prope ad finem laborum ac periculorum
esset perventum aequo animo mancipia atque impedimenta in Italia relinquerent, ipsi expediti naves conscenderent quo maior numerus militum posset imponi,
omniaque ex victoria et ex sua liberalitate sperarent.
Conclamantibus omnibus imperaret quod vellet, quod-

---

9 "Liburnians" were ships from Illyricum.

of herdsmen Pompey had assembled eight hundred. Tar- 5
condarius Castor and Domnilaus had supplied three hundred from Gallograecia; one of these men came himself,
the other sent his son. Two hundred had been sent from
Syria by Antiochus of Commagene—Pompey gave him
substantial rewards—the majority of them mounted archers. Plus, he had added Dardanians and Bessi, some of 6
them mercenaries, others procured by requisition or influence, likewise Macedonians and Thessalians and men
of other peoples and communities, filling out the above-
mentioned number.

5. Pompey had procured a very large quantity of provisions from Thessaly, Asia, Egypt, Crete, Cyrene, and the
other regions. He had decided to winter at Dyrrachium 2
and Apollonia and all the coastal towns in order to prevent
Caesar from crossing the Adriatic, and for this purpose he
had distributed his fleet all along the coast. The com- 3
mander of the ships from Egypt was his son Pompeius, of
the ships from Asia Minor, Decimus Laelius and Gaius
Triarius, of those from Syria, Gaius Cassius, of those from
Rhodes, Gaius Marcellus with Gaius Coponius, of the Liburnians[9] and the fleet from Achaia, Scribonius Libo and
Marcus Octavius. Marcus Bibulus had been placed in 4
overall charge of the maritime operation and was running
everything; supreme authority fell to him.

6. When Caesar reached Brundisium he addressed the
soldiers. "Since we have come nearly to the end of our
labors and dangers, leaving your slaves and baggage behind in Italy should not make you worried. Go onto the
ships unencumbered so that more men can be put on
board, and place all of your hopes on victory and my generosity." Everyone shouted that he should give whatever

199

cumque imperavisset se aequo animo esse facturos, II
2 Nonas Ianuarias naves solvit. Impositae, ut supra demon-
3 stratum est, legiones VII. Postridie terram attigit Cerauniorum saxa inter[5] et alia loca periculosa. Quietam nactus
stationem et portus omnes timens quod teneri ab adversariis arbitrabantur[6] ad eum locum qui appellabatur
Palaeste omnibus navibus ad unam incolumibus milites
exposuit.

7. Erat Orici Lucretius Vespillo, et Minucius Rufus
cum Asiaticis navibus XVIII quibus iussu D. Laeli prae-
2 erat, M. Bibulus cum navibus CX Corcyrae. Sed neque illi
sibi confisi ex portu prodire sunt ausi, cum Caesar omnino
XII naves longas praesidio duxisset, in quibus erant constratae IIII, neque Bibulus impeditis navibus dispersisque
remigibus satis mature occurrit, quod prius ad conti-
nentem visus est Caesar quam de eius adventu fama
omnino in eas regiones perferretur.

8. Expositis militibus naves eadem nocte Brundisium a
Caesare remittuntur ut reliquae legiones equitatusque
2 transportari possent. Huic officio praepositus erat Fufius
Calenus legatus qui celeritatem in transportandis legionibus adhiberet. Sed serius a terra provectae naves neque
3 usae nocturna aura in redeundo offenderunt. Bibulus
enim Corcyrae certior factus de adventu Caesaris, sperans
alicui se parti onustarum navium occurrere posse, inani-
bus occurrit. Et nactus circiter XXX in eas diligentiae[7]

---

[5] Cerauniorum saxa inter] inter Cerauniorum saxa *Hoffmann*
[6] quod . . . arbitrabantur] quos . . . arbitrabatur *ed. pr.*
[7] diligentiae] indiligentiae *Estienne*

---

[10] See 3.2.2 with its textual note.

orders he wanted, and that they would do whatever he ordered without worrying. He sailed on the 4th of January. As was indicated earlier, seven legions embarked.[10] 2 He reached land the next day between the Ceraunian 3 mountain cliffs and other dangerous locations. Finding a calm anchorage, and being leery of all the harbors because people thought they[11] were held by the enemy, he landed the soldiers from all of his ships at a place called Palaeste without losing a single ship.

7. Lucretius Vespillo was at Oricum along with Minucius Rufus and eighteen ships from Asia Minor that he commanded by order of Decimus Laelius; Marcus Bibulus was at Corcyra with 110 ships. But the former pair, 2 lacking self-confidence, did not dare venture out of the harbor, although Caesar had in his convoy twelve warships total for protection, four of them with decks. Nor did Bibulus confront him in time—his ships were tied up and his rowers dispersed—since Caesar was sighted offshore before even the rumor of his approach made it to that area.

8. Once the soldiers were on land, Caesar sent the ships back to Brundisium the same night so that the remaining legions and cavalry could be brought over. He put his of- 2 ficer Fufius Calenus in charge of this operation with instructions to act quickly in transporting the legions. But the ships set out rather late and did not make use of the evening breeze, so they ran into trouble on the return. For 3 Bibulus, learning at Corcyra of Caesar's approach and hoping to be able to encounter some of the loaded transports, encountered empty ones. After falling in with about thirty, he vented on them the rage prompted by his "dili-

[11] For "because people thought they," the first edition substituted "which he thought."

suae ac doloris iracundiam erupit omnesque incendit. Eodemque igne nautas dominosque navium interfecit, 4 magnitudine poenae reliquos terreri sperans. Hoc confecto negotio a Salonis[8] ad Orici portum[9] stationes litoraque omnia longe lateque classibus occupavit. Custodiisque diligentius dispositis ipse gravissima hieme in navibus excubans neque ullum laborem aut munus despiciens neque subsidium expectans si in Caesaris complexum[10] venire posset . . .

9. Discessu Liburnarum ex Illyrico M. Octavius cum iis quas habebat navibus Salonas pervenit. Ibi concitatis Dalmatis reliquisque barbaris Issam a Caesaris amicitia 2 avertit. Conventum Salonis cum neque pollicitationibus neque denuntiatione periculi permovere posset oppidum oppugnare instituit. Est autem oppidum et loci natura et 3 colle munitum,[11] sed celeriter cives Romani, ligneis effectis turribus, his sese munierunt. Et cum essent infirmi ad resistendum propter paucitatem hominum, crebris confecti vulneribus ad extremum auxilium descenderunt ser-

---

[8] Salonis *ed. pr.*: sasonis (*sc.* portu) ω

[9] orici ς, *Veith* (*see 3.15.1*): cor(i/y)c(i/y) ω: Curici *Mommsen*

[10] complexum] conspectum *Vascosan. Perhaps* classis (*sc.* Caesaris)?

[11] est . . . munitum] erat . . . <parum> m- *Jurin*: [e- . . . m-] *Meusel*

---

[12] For the sarcastic "diligence," Estienne substituted "negligence."

[13] Instead of emending to "from Salonae to the port of Oricum," Mommsen defended the manuscripts' "from the harbor of Sason Island to that of Curicum." This adds more than two hundred miles to the Pompeian blockade.

gence"[12] and vexation, burning them all. In the same conflagration he killed the crews and captains, hoping that the rest would be deterred by the enormity of the punishment. When this operation was complete, he had his various fleets take control of anchorages from Salonae to the port of Oricum[13] and every shoreline far and wide, and deployed his patrols more carefully. He himself, doing guard duty aboard ship in the depth of winter and thinking no hardship or task too small nor awaiting reinforcements if he could come into contact with Caesar . . .[14]

9. At the departure of the Liburnian ships from Illyricum[15] Marcus Octavius went to Salonae with the ships he had available. There he roused the Dalmatians and the other natives and deflected Issa from its allegiance to Caesar. Unable to influence the association of Roman citizens at Salonae either by promises or by heralding danger, he began to besiege the town. Salonae is fortified both by the nature of its site and by a hill, but the Roman citizens hastily built wooden siege towers and used these as their fortifications.[16] Being incapable—because of their small numbers—of standing firm in resistance, and overcome by numerous injuries, they came to the last resort, freeing all

4

2

3

[14] For the unparalleled expression "into contact with Caesar," Vascosan substituted "within eyesight of Caesar." Both "contact" and "eyesight" are necessarily metaphorical, since Caesar is on land and Bibulus is patrolling the Adriatic. The proposal to read "to grips with (Caesar's) fleet" fits the context more closely.

[15] Not mentioned heretofore.

[16] Given Salonae's actual topography (Wilkes, 221 n. 3), Jurin proposed adding "insufficiently" before "fortified," and Meusel excised "Salonae . . . hill."

vosque omnes puberes liberaverunt. Et praesectis om-
4 nium mulierum crinibus tormenta effecerunt. Quorum
cognita sententia Octavius quinis castris oppidum circum-
dedit atque uno tempore obsidione et oppugnationibus
5 eos premere coepit. Illi omnia perpeti parati maxime a re
frumentaria laborabant. Quare[12] missis ad Caesarem legatis auxilium ab eo petebant. Reliqua, ut poterant, incom-
6 moda per se sustinebant. Et longo interposito spatio cum
diuturnitas oppugnationis neglegentiores Octavianos effe-
cisset nacti occasionem meridiani temporis discessu eorum, pueris mulieribusque in muro dispositis ne quid
cotidianae consuetudinis desideraretur, ipsi manu facta
cum iis quos nuper maxime liberaverant in proxima Octavi
7 castra irruperunt. His expugnatis eodem impetu altera
sunt adorti, inde tertia et quarta et deinceps reliqua.
Omnibusque eos castris expulerunt et magno numero
interfecto reliquos atque ipsum Octavium in naves con-
8 fugere coegerunt. Hic fuit oppugnationis exitus. Iamque
hiems appropinquabat, et tantis detrimentis acceptis Octavius desperata oppugnatione oppidi Dyrrachium sese ad
Pompeium recepit.

10. Demonstravimus L. Vibullium Rufum, Pompei
praefectum, bis in potestatem pervenisse Caesaris atque
ab eo esse dimissum semel ad Corfinium iterum in Hispa-
2 nia. Hunc pro suis beneficiis Caesar idoneum iudicaverat

---

[12] quare missis *Brutus*: qui remissis *MUTV*: cui remis sis *S*: cui
rei missis *Nipperdey*

---

[17] For "therefore they sent a delegation," Nipperdey substituted "and they sent a delegation on this subject."

of the adult male slaves; they also cut off all the women's hair, making catapult ropes. Recognizing their decision 4 Octavius surrounded the town with five camps and began to apply pressure with a blockade and siege works simultaneously. Although prepared to endure everything, the 5 people of Salonae were in very great difficulties over provisioning. Therefore they sent a delegation[17] to Caesar requesting his help. The remaining hardships they withstood on their own, insofar as they could. After a considerable interval, when the protracted siege had made Octavius' men rather careless, they took advantage of midday, when the enemy fell back. Deploying children and women on the walls so that nothing of their daily routine would be noticeably absent, they joined forces with the men they had very recently set free and burst into the closest of Octavius' camps. After storming this they continued 7 straight on to the next, then the third and fourth, and finally the last. They ejected the enemy from every camp and killed a large number of them, then forced the rest and Octavius himself to take refuge on their ships. This put an end to the siege. For winter was approaching, and 8 after suffering such substantial losses Octavius despaired of the siege of Salonae and went back to Pompey at Dyrrachium.

10. I mentioned that Pompey's officer Lucius Vibullius Rufus came into Caesar's power twice and was released by him once at Corfinium and once in Spain.[18] In Caesar's 2 judgment the favors Vibullius had received from him

[18] For Corfinium, see 1.15.4. Vibullius' arrival in Spain is mentioned (1.38.1), but neither his second release nor his third capture is. See the Introduction.

quem cum mandatis ad Cn. Pompeium mitteret, eundemque apud Cn. Pompeium auctoritatem habere intellege-
3 bat. Erat autem haec summa mandatorum: debere utrumque pertinaciae finem facere et ab armis discedere neque
4 amplius fortunam periclitari; satis esse magna utrimque
incommoda accepta quae pro disciplina et praeceptis ha-
5 bere possent ut reliquos casus timerent, illum Italia expul-
sum amissa Sicilia et Sardinia duabusque Hispaniis et
cohortibus <in> Italia atque Hispania civium Romanorum
C atque XXX, <se> morte Curionis et detrimento Africani
exercitus et Antoni[13] militumque deditione ad Curictam;
6 proinde sibi ac rei publicae parcerent; quantum[14] in bello
Fortuna posset iam ipsi incommodis suis satis essent docu-
7 mento; hoc unum esse tempus de pace agendi dum sibi
uterque confideret et pares ambo viderentur; si vero alteri
paulum modo tribuisset Fortuna non esse usurum conditionibus pacis eum qui superior videretur, neque fore
aequa parte contentum qui se omnia habiturum con-
8 fideret; conditiones pacis, quoniam antea convenire non
potuissent, Romae ab senatu et a populo peti debere;

[13] et Antoni *Menge*: tanto [ton- *T^{ac}*] *ω*
[14] <quoniam> quantum *Klotz*

---

[19] Caesar's narrative of events at Curicta does not survive and
may never have been written, but other sources tell of a conflict
in the northern Adriatic between the Caesarians Dolabella and
C. Antonius against the Pompeians M. Octavius and Scribonius
Libo. The Caesarians were bested (App. *BC* 2.47.191), and Antonius was either captured by (Livy *Per.* 110; D.C. 41.40.2) or
surrendered to Libo (Flor. *Epit.* 2.13.31–32; Oros. 6.15.9). Ac-

made him a suitable person to send to Pompey with a message; he also knew that Vibullius had influence with Pompey. The gist of the message was this: "Both of us 3 ought to put an end to our obstinacy. We ought to set arms aside and not take any further chances. Both of us have 4 incurred substantial losses, enough that we can consider them an education and advice to be wary of misfortunes still to come: you have been driven out of Italy with the 5 loss of Sicily, Sardinia, both Spanish provinces, and citizen cohorts in Italy and Spain, 130 of them. For me, the death of Curio, the loss of the African army, and the capitulation of Antony and his soldiers at Curicta.[19] Accordingly, we 6 should spare ourselves and the state; of the power of fortune in war we ourselves with our setbacks should be[20] sufficient evidence. The moment for negotiating a peace 7 is when each party is confident in his position and the two seem to be equal. But if fortune ever grants a little more to either, the one who sees that he has the advantage will not adopt peace terms, nor will he be content with a fair share once confident of having everything. Peace terms 8 ought to be sought in Rome from the senate and people, since to date we have not been able to agree. Meanwhile 9

cording to Orosius, fifteen cohorts surrendered with him. Florus and Lucan (4.404–6) give the most precise location for the campaign, setting it on the island of Curicta; other sources speak of Illyricum or Dalmatia.

[20] For "we ourselves . . . should be," Klotz substituted "since . . . we ourselves . . . are."

9   interea et rei publicae[15] et ipsis parcere[16] oportere; si
uterque in contione statim iuravisset se triduo proximo
10 exercitum dimissurum, depositis armis auxiliisque quibus
nunc confiderent necessario populi senatusque iudicio
11 fore utrumque contentum; haec quo facilius Pompeio
probari possent omnes suas terrestres urbiumque copias
dimissurum . . .

11. Vibullius[17] his expositis [Corcyrae][18] non minus
necessarium esse existimavit de repentino adventu Caesaris Pompeium fieri certiorem uti ad id consilium capere
posset [antequam de mandatis agi inciperet][19] atque ideo
continuato nocte ac die itinere atque omnibus oppidis[20]
mutatis ad celeritatem iumentis ad Pompeium contendit
2   ut adesse Caesarem nuntiaret. Pompeius erat eo tempore
in Candavia iterque ex Macedonia in hiberna Apolloniam
Dyrrachiumque habebat. Sed re nova perturbatus maioribus itineribus Apolloniam petere coepit ne Caesar orae
3   maritimae civitates occuparet. At ille expositis militibus

---

[15] interea et rei publicae] in- e re publica esse *Hoffmann*: id
interesse reipublicae *Madvig*   [16] parcere *Damon*: placere ω
[17] Vibullius *Aldus*: bibu(l)lus ω
[18] [Corcyrae] *Nipperdey*
[19] [antequam . . . agi inciperet] *Damon*
[20] oppidis *Lipsius*: copiis ω

---

[21] For "meanwhile it is appropriate to spare the state and
ourselves. If . . . ," Hoffmann and Madvig proposed "meanwhile
it is in the public interest and ought to be pleasing to us, if . . . ,"
and "this (i.e., seeking peace terms at Rome) is beneficial to the
commonwealth and ought to be pleasing to us. If . . . ."
[22] The reference to "urban forces" is puzzling, but compare

it is appropriate to spare the state and ourselves.[21] If each immediately swears in an assembly that he will dismiss his army within the next three days, after putting down the weapons and resources that we currently rely on we will both, of necessity, be content with the verdict of the people and senate." In order to be able more easily to win Pompey's approval for these things, he said, he would dismiss all of his land-based and urban forces . . .[22]

11. Once the message was laid out [at Corcyra] Vibullius thought that it was equally necessary that Pompey be informed about Caesar's sudden arrival, so that he could make plans about it [before action began to be taken on the message],[23] and he therefore, without breaking his journey by night or day, and changing his teams at every town[24] for speed, hastened to Pompey to announce that Caesar was at hand. Pompey was in Candavia at the time, on his way from Macedonia to winter quarters in Apollonia and Dyrrachium. But perturbed by the unexpected development he began to make for Apollonia by forced marches in order to prevent Caesar from occupying the communities on the coast. Caesar, for his part, headed for Oricum

10

11

2

3

3.15.6. Some feel that the sentence is unlikely to be authentic; the gap marked in the text leaves room for a qualification to Caesar's otherwise implausible offer.

[23] Vibullius was not "at Corcyra"; the phrase was added to the text after his name was corrupted to that of a man who was there, Bibulus. The clause "before . . . proposals" can likewise be explained as originating in a marginal gloss based on 3.18.3; some editors prefer to emend its manifest problems of usage.

[24] Neither the word "town" nor any other of the many repairs proposed for the obviously corrupt text of the archetype here is particularly compelling.

eodem die Oricum proficiscitur. Quo cum venisset, L. Torquatus, qui iussu Pompei oppido praeerat praesidiumque ibi Parthinorum habebat, conatus portis clausis oppidum
4 defendere, cum Graecos murum ascendere atque arma capere iuberet, illi autem se contra imperium populi Romani pugnaturos negarent, oppidani autem etiam sua sponte Caesarem recipere conarentur, desperatis omnibus auxiliis portas aperuit et se atque oppidum Caesari dedidit incolumisque ab eo conservatus est.

12. Recepto Caesar Orico nulla interposita mora Apolloniam proficiscitur. Eius adventu audito L. Staberius, qui ibi praeerat, aquam comportare in arcem atque eam mu-
2 nire obsidesque ab Apolloniatibus exigere coepit. Illi vero daturos se negare neque portas consuli praeclusuros neque sibi iudicium sumpturos contra atque omnis Italia
3 praeiudicavisset.[21] Quorum cognita voluntate clam profugit Apollonia Staberius. Illi ad Caesarem legatos mittunt
4 oppidoque recipiunt. Hoc sequuntur Byllidenses Amantini et reliquae finitimae civitates totaque Epiros et legatis ad Caesarem missis quae imperaret facturos pollicentur.

13. At Pompeius cognitis his rebus quae erant Orici atque Apolloniae gestae Dyrrachio timens diurnis eo noc-
2 turnisque itineribus contendit. Simul [ac] Caesar appropinquare dicebatur.[22] Tantusque terror incidit eius exerci-

[21] praeiudicavisset *Paul* (*see 2.32.3*): p. R. iudicavisset ω (*with abbreviations or in full*) ω

[22] simul [ac] . . . dicebatur *Oudendorp*: [s- ac . . . d-] *Gruter*

the day he landed his soldiers. When he arrived, Lucius Torquatus, who was in command of the town by Pompey's order and had a garrison of Parthini there, closed the gates and attempted to defend the town. He ordered the Greeks 4 to mount the wall and take up arms. They, however, refused to fight against the legitimate authority of the Roman people. The townspeople, moreover, even tried to admit Caesar of their own accord. At that point, despairing of all help, Torquatus opened the gates and surrendered himself and the town to Caesar and was preserved unharmed by him.

12. After recovering Oricum, Caesar headed for Apollonia without delay. Hearing of his approach Lucius Staberius, who was in command there, began to collect water in the citadel, fortify the citadel, and demand hostages from the townspeople. But they said that they would not 2 give them, or close the gates against a consul, or make a decision for themselves contrary to the previous decision of all Italy. Recognizing their intention Staberius fled se- 3 cretly from Apollonia. They sent a delegation to Caesar and admitted him into Apollonia. This example was fol- 4 lowed by the people of Byllis, Amantia, and the other nearby cities and all of Epirus: they sent delegations to Caesar promising that they would do his bidding.

13. But Pompey, after learning about developments at Oricum and Apollonia, feared for Dyrrachium; he hastened there by day and night marches. Caesar was said to 2 be approaching at the same time.[25] And so great a fear of

[25] For "approaching at the same time," the archetype read "at the same time as Caesar was said to be approaching." Gruter excised the whole sentence as a gloss.

tus—quod properans noctem diei coniunxerat neque iter
intermiserat—ut paene omnes ex Epiro finitimisque regionibus signa relinquerent, complures arma proicerent,
3 ac fugae simile iter videretur. Sed cum prope Dyrrachium
Pompeius constitisset castraque metari iussisset perterrito
etiam tum exercitu princeps Labienus procedit iuratque
se eum non deserturum eundemque casum subiturum,
4 quemcumque ei Fortuna tribuisset. Hoc idem reliqui
iurant legati. Hos tribuni militum centurionesque sequun-
5 tur, atque idem omnis exercitus iurat. Caesar praeoccu-
pato itinere ad Dyrrachium finem properandi facit castraque ad flumen Apsum ponit in finibus Apolloniatium ut
[castellis vigiliisque][23] bene meritae civitates tutae essent
praesidio. Ibique reliquarum ex Italia legionum adventum
6 expectare et sub pellibus hiemare constituit. Hoc idem
Pompeius fecit et trans flumen Apsum positis castris eo
copias omnes auxiliaque conduxit.

14. Calenus legionibus equitibusque Brundisi in naves
impositis—ut erat praeceptum a Caesare—quam tum[24]
navium facultatem habebat, naves solvit paulumque a
portu progressus litteras a Caesare accipit quibus est certior factus portus litoraque omnia classibus adversariorum
2 teneri. Quo cognito se in portum recipit navesque omnes
revocat. Vna ex his, quae perseveravit neque imperio Ca-

[23] [castellis vigiliisque] *Kayser*
[24] quam tum *Faerno*: quantum ω

---

[26] The first part of this sentence is obscure, owing to the am-
biguity of the Latin. Some editors make Pompey the subject of
"joined" and "interrupted." The phrase "Caesar's army" imposes
an interpretation on the expression "his (or this) army."

Caesar's army ensued—because in his hurry he had joined night to day, not breaking his march[26]—that practically everyone from Epirus and the neighboring regions abandoned the standards, many discarded their weapons, and the Pompeian march resembled a retreat. When Pompey 3 had halted near Dyrrachium and ordered the camp to be laid out, and the army was still terrified, Labienus stepped forward first and swore that he would not desert Pompey and would undergo the same fate, whatever Fortune gave him. The remaining senior officers took the same oath; the 4 staff officers and centurions followed them, and the whole army took the same oath. Caesar, given that the route to 5 Dyrrachium was already held, stopped hurrying and made camp beside the Apsus River in the territory of Apollonia, so that[27] the cities that had served him well would be safe under guard. He decided to await the arrival of the remaining legions from Italy there, and to winter in tents. Pompey did the same: making camp across the Apsus 6 river, he collected there all of his troops and auxiliaries.

14. Calenus put the legions and cavalry on board the ships at Brundisium, as per Caesar's instructions, all the ships he had available, then weighed anchor. After going a little way out of the harbor, he received a letter from Caesar informing him that the harbors and the entire coastline were controlled by enemy fleets. Upon learning 2 this he returned to Brundisium and recalled all of the ships. One of them kept going and disobeyed Calenus'

[27] After "so that" the archetype had "with strongholds and lookouts," which Kayser excised as a gloss on "under guard." Some editors remove or emend the latter expression instead.

leni obtemperavit quod erat sine militibus privatoque consilio administrabatur, delata Oricum atque a Bibulo ex-
3 pugnata est. Qui de servis liberisque omnibus ad impuberes
supplicium sumit et ad unum interficit. Ita exiguo tempore
magnoque casu totius exercitus salus constitit.

15. Bibulus, ut supra demonstratum est, erat ⟨cum⟩
classe ad Oricum, et sicuti mari portibusque Caesarem
prohibebat ita ipse omni terra earum regionum prohibe-
2 batur. Praesidiis enim dispositis omnia litora a Caesare
tenebantur, neque lignandi atque aquandi neque naves ad
3 terram religandi potestas fiebat. Erat res in magna difficultate, summisque angustiis rerum necessariarum premebantur, adeo ut cogerentur sicuti reliquum commeatum ita ligna atque aquam Corcyra navibus onerariis
4 supportare. Atque etiam uno tempore accidit ut difficilio-
ribus usi tempestatibus ex pellibus quibus erant tectae
5 naves nocturnum excipere rorem cogerentur. Quas tamen
difficultates patienter atque aequo animo ferebant neque
sibi nudanda litora et relinquendos portus existimabant.
6 Sed cum essent in quibus demonstravi angustiis ac se Libo
cum Bibulo coniunxisset loquuntur ambo ex navibus cum
M. Acilio et Staio[25] Murco legatis, quorum alter oppidi
muris, alter praesidiis terrestribus praeerat: velle se de
maximis rebus cum Caesare loqui si sibi eius ⟨rei⟩ facultas
detur. Huc addunt pauca rei confirmandae causa ut de
7 compositione acturi viderentur. Interim postulant ut sint
8 indutiae, atque ab iis impetrant. Magnum enim quod adfe-

---

[25] Staio *Carter*: statio [-ilio *V*] ω

order; there were no soldiers on board and it was under private management. This ship got to Oricum and was captured by Bibulus. He punished them all, slave and free, 3 children included, executing every one. The safety of the entire army thus rested on a little time and a lot of luck.

15. Bibulus, as was indicated earlier, was with his fleet off Oricum. While preventing Caesar from using the sea and harbors, he was himself prevented from landing anywhere in the area, for by distributing detachments Caesar 2 controlled the entire shore, and Bibulus was given no chance either to collect firewood and water or to tie up ashore. His situation was very difficult, and his men were 3 afflicted by extreme shortages of necessities, to the extent that they were compelled to use cargo vessels from Corcyra to transport firewood and water as well as the rest of their provisions. Indeed at one point when the weather was 4 particularly bad it happened that they were forced to collect nighttime dew from the hides sheltering the decks. Nevertheless, they endured these difficulties patiently and 5 steadily, nor did they think they should leave the coastline unguarded or abandon the harbors. But when they were 6 in the aforementioned difficulties, and Libo had joined Bibulus, the two of them addressed Caesar's officers Marcus Acilius and Staius Murcus from shipboard. (One of these was in charge of the walls of Oricum, the other of the detachments on land.) They said that they would like to talk to Caesar about matters of the greatest importance, if they got the chance, adding a few things in support of their proposition to give the impression that they were going to discuss a settlement. They demanded a truce in 7 the meantime, and Caesar's officers granted it, for what 8 was being offered seemed significant, and they knew that

rebant videbatur, et Caesarem id summe sciebant cupere. Et profectum aliquid Vibulli mandatis existimabatur.

16. Caesar eo tempore cum legione una profectus ad recipiendas ulteriores civitates et rem frumentariam expediendam, qua anguste utebatur, erat ad Buthrotum, oppi-
2 dum <oppositum> Corcyrae. Ibi certior ab Acilio et Murco per litteras factus de postulatis Libonis et Bibuli legionem
3 relinquit, ipse Oricum revertitur. Eo cum venisset evocantur illi ad colloquium. Prodit Libo atque excusat Bibulum—quod is iracundia summa erat inimicitiasque habebat etiam privatas cum Caesare ex aedilitate et praetura conceptas: ob eam causam colloquium vitasse ne res maximae spei maximaeque utilitatis eius iracundia impediren-
4 tur; Pompei summam esse ac fuisse semper voluntatem ut componeretur atque ab armis discederetur; se[26] potestatem eius rei nullam habere propterea quod de consili sententia summam belli rerumque omnium Pompeio per-
5 miserint, sed postulatis Caesaris cognitis missuros ad Pompeium; atque illum reliqua per se acturum hortantibus ipsis; interea manerent indutiae dum ab illo rediri posset neve alter alteri noceret. Huc addit pauca de causa et de copiis auxiliisque suis.

17. Quibus rebus neque tum respondendum Caesar existimavit neque nunc ut memoriae prodatur satis causae

---

[26] Pompei . . . se *Bücheler*: p- . . . sed ω: [p-] <suam> . . . sed *Elberling*

---

[28] See 3.10–11.   [29] The years are 65 and 62, respectively.
[30] In place of Bücheler's emendation "Pompey's chief desire . . . We ourselves," many editors accept Elberling's "my (*or* our) chief desire . . . but I (*or* we)."

Caesar was extremely eager to get it. Plus, something seemed to have come of Vibullius' message.[28]

16. At the time, Caesar was at Buthrotum, a town across from Corcyra. He had gone there with one legion to recover the allegiance of the more distant communities and to expedite provisioning, since his provisions were scanty. While there he was informed about the demands 2 made by Libo and Bibulus by a letter from Acilius and Murcus. Leaving the legion there, he himself returned to Oricum. Upon arrival he summoned them to a meeting. 3 Libo came out and made excuses for Bibulus, because Bibulus was extremely irascible and in addition had a personal aversion to Caesar that went back to their aedileship and praetorship.[29] The reason Bibulus stayed away from the meeting, he said, was so that an extremely promising and beneficial development was not hindered by his irascibility. "Pompey's chief desire is and always has been to 4 settle matters and put arms aside. We ourselves[30] have no authority over the matter, since in accordance with the recommendation of the advisory council Pompey has been entrusted with the totality of the war and everything else. But Bibulus and I, after learning your demands, will send 5 to Pompey, and he will handle the rest himself with our encouragement. In the meantime the truce should continue until word can get back from Pompey, and neither side should harm the other." To this he added a few words about their cause and their troops and auxiliaries.

17. As for these points, Caesar did not think that they needed a response even then, nor do I now feel that there

2 putamus. Postulabat Caesar ut legatos sibi ad Pompeium
sine periculo mittere liceret idque ipsi fore reciperent aut
3 acceptos per se ad eum perducerent; quod ad indutias
pertineret, sic belli rationem esse divisam ut illi classe
naves auxiliaque sua impedirent, ipse ut aqua terraque eos
4 prohiberet, et si hoc sibi remitti vellent remitterent ipsi de
maritimis custodiis; si illud tenerent se quoque id reten-
turum; nihilo minus tamen agi posse de compositione, ut
haec non remitterentur, neque hanc rem illi[27] esse impe-
5 dimento. Libo neque legatos Caesaris recipere neque
periculum praestare eorum sed totam rem ad Pompeium
reicere, unum instare de indutiis vehementissimeque
6 contendere. Quem ubi Caesar intellexit praesentis periculi atque inopiae vitandae causa omnem orationem insti-
tuisse neque ullam spem aut conditionem pacis adferre,
ad reliquam cogitationem belli sese recepit.

18. Bibulus multos dies terra prohibitus et graviore
morbo ex frigore ac labore implicitus cum neque curari
posset neque susceptum officium deserere vellet vim
2 morbi sustinere non potuit. Eo mortuo ad neminem unum
summa imperi redit, sed separatim suam quisque classem
ad arbitrium suum administrabat.
3 Vibullius sedato tumultu quem repentinus adventus
Caesaris concitaverat, ubi primum rursus[28] adhibito Libone et L. Lucceio et Theophane, quibuscum communi-
care de maximis rebus Pompeius consuerat, de mandatis

27 illi *Madvig*: illis ω
28 ubi . . . rursus ω (*see 3.11.1*): ubi . . . e re visum est *Elberling*:
ibi . . . rursus *Vossius*

is sufficient reason for putting one on record. Caesar de- 2
manded an opportunity to send envoys to Pompey securely. "You and Bibulus should guarantee this, or yourselves assume responsibility for the envoys and escort
them to Pompey. As for the truce, our tactics are contrary, 3
such that you aim to block my ships and reinforcements
with your fleet, while I aim to keep you from getting water
and landing, and if you want me to suspend my blockade 4
you must suspend your naval patrols. But if you continue
your tactics I will continue mine, too. Still, a settlement
can be discussed even without suspensions, nor is the one
thing an impediment to the other." Libo neither took re- 5
sponsibility for Caesar's envoys nor promised them security, but referred the entire matter to Pompey; he insisted
on one thing and argued vehemently for it, a truce. When 6
Caesar realized that the motive for Libo's whole speech
was to escape his present predicament and the lack of
supplies, and that he offered no prospect of or proposal
for peace, he returned to thinking further about war.

18. Bibulus, prevented from landing for many days,
contracted an illness made worse by cold and hardship.
Since he was unable to receive treatment and unwilling to
abandon the task he had undertaken, he could not withstand the violence of his illness. After his death no one 2
individual held overall control, but independent commanders conducted naval operations at their own discretion.

Vibullius, when first he reopened negotiations on Cae- 3
sar's message—once the commotion that Caesar's unexpected arrival stirred up had been settled, and in the presence of Libo and Lucius Lucceius and Theophanes, with
whom Pompey was in the habit discussing his most impor-

219

4 Caesaris agere instituit—quem ingressum in sermonem
Pompeius interpellavit et loqui plura prohibuit. "Quid
mihi" inquit "aut vita aut civitate opus est quam beneficio
Caesaris habere videbor? cuius rei opinio tolli non poterit
cum in Italiam, ex qua profectus sum, reductus[29] existima-
5 bor bello perfecto."[30] Ab iis Caesar haec facta cognovit qui
sermoni interfuerunt. Conatus tamen nihilo minus est aliis
rationibus per colloquia de pace agere.

19. Vt inter bina castra Pompei atque Caesaris unum
flumen tantum intererat Apsus, crebraque inter se colloquia milites habebant, neque ullum interim telum per
2 pactiones loquentium traiciebatur, mittit P. Vatinium legatum ad ripam ipsam fluminis qui ea quae maxime ad pacem pertinere viderentur ageret et crebro magna voce
pronuntiaret: liceretne civibus ad cives de pace tuto[31] legatos mittere, quod etiam fugitivis ab saltu Pyrenaeo
praedonibusque licuisset, praesertim cum id agerent ne
3 cives cum civibus armis decertarent. Multa suppliciter
locutus, ut de sua atque omnium salute debebat, silen-
4 tioque ab utrisque militibus auditus—responsum est ab
altera parte: Aulum Varronem profiteri se altera die ad

29 reductus] . . . reductus *Kübler*
30 existimabor bello] existimabor. Bello *Orsini*
31 tuto *Vossius*: duo *UT*: duos *MSV*: suos *Brutus*

---

31 For "when first he reopened negotiations," Elberling and
Vossius proposed "when the time seemed right, opened negotiations" and "then re-opened negotiations," respectively; neither
emendation for this admittedly awkward sentence is persuasive.

32 For the lacuna proposed between *profectus sum* and *reductus*, Klotz suggested a supplement such as "(brought back) like a

tant affairs—after he embarked on his speech, Pompey   4
interrupted him and forbade him to say more.[31] "What use
is either life or citizenship to me if I am seen to have it by
Caesar's favor? And it will be impossible to eliminate this
view of things when people think that I have been brought
back to Italy, which was my starting point, after the conclusion of the war."[32] Caesar learned of these events from   5
those who took part in the discussion. He nevertheless
attempted in other ways to use talks to work for peace.

19. The two camps of Pompey and Caesar were separated by just one river, the Apsus, and the soldiers frequently held talks among themselves, and no weapons
were thrown for the duration by the speakers' agreement.
So Caesar sent his officer Publius Vatinius right up to the   2
riverbank to do the things that seemed most conducive to
peace and to repeat this message in a loud voice: "Are
citizens permitted to send a delegation to fellow citizens
in safety—something permitted even to deserters in the
wilderness of the Pyrenees, and to pirates[33]—especially
when their aim is to prevent armed conflict between fellow citizens?" Speaking at length and like a suppliant, as   3
he was right to do concerning his own and everyone's survival, he was heard in silence by soldiers on both sides. A   4
response came from the other side, that Aulus Varro

deserter." The thought could also be clarified by supplying "(starting point) for the war." Some editors follow Orsini in putting
"after the conclusion of the war" into the next sentence.

[33] Permitted, that is, by Pompey during his campaigns against
Sertorius and the pirates in the 70s and 60s.

colloquium venturum atque una visurum quem[32] ad modum tuto legati venire et quae vellent exponere possent,
5 certumque ei rei tempus constituitur. Quo cum esset
postero die ventum magna utrimque multitudo convenit
magnaque erat expectatio eius rei. Atque omnium animi
6 intenti esse ad pacem videbantur. Qua ex frequentia Titus
Labienus prodit. Summissa[33] oratione loqui de pace atque
7 altercari cum Vatinio incipit. Quorum mediam orationem
interrumpunt subito undique tela immissa, quae ille ob-
tectus armis militum vitavit. Vulnerantur tamen complures, in his Cornelius Balbus M. Plotius L. Tiburtius
8 centuriones militesque nonnulli. Tum Labienus: "Desi-
nite ergo de compositione loqui. Nam nobis nisi Caesaris
capite relato pax esse nulla potest."

20. Isdem temporibus M. Caelius Rufus praetor causa
debitorum suscepta initio magistratus tribunal suum iuxta
C. Treboni, praetoris urbani, sellam collocavit et si quis
appellavisset de aestimatione et de solutionibus quae per
arbitrum fierent—ut Caesar praesens constituerat—fore
2 auxilio pollicebatur. Sed fiebat aequitate decreti et huma-
nitate Treboni, qui ⟨pro⟩[34] temporibus clementer et moderate ius dicendum existimabat, ut reperiri non possent
3 a quibus initium appellandi nasceretur. Nam fortasse inopiam excusare et calamitatem aut propriam suam aut
temporum queri et difficultates auctionandi proponere

[32] visurum quem *Elberling*: vis utrumque ω
[33] summissa . . . atque] *Emendations have been proposed for
every word.*　　[34] ⟨pro⟩ *Damon*: ⟨his⟩ *ed. pr.*

[34] The generally accepted emendation "together with them
would see" does not fix every problem in this difficult sentence.

promised that he would come to a meeting on the following day and together with them would see how a delegation could come in safety and explain what they wanted.[34]
A specific time was fixed for this. When it reached this   5
time on the following day, a huge crowd gathered on both
sides and there was great anticipation about the matter;
indeed everyone seemed to be intent on peace. Titus La-   6
bienus stepped out of the crowd. In a low tone he began
to speak about peace and to quarrel with Vatinius. Their   7
ongoing talk was suddenly interrupted by a volley of weapons from all sides. Protected by his soldiers' shields, Labienus avoided them. But several men were wounded,
including Cornelius Balbus, Marcus Plotius, Lucius Tiburtius, plus some centurions and soldiers. Then Labi-   8
enus: "So stop talking about a settlement, for in our view
no peace is possible unless we get Caesar's head."

20. At this same period the praetor Marcus Caelius
Rufus took up the cause of debtors. At the beginning of
his year he established his official post close to the seat of
the urban praetor, Gaius Trebonius, and promised that he
would assist anyone appealing an assessment and the re-
payments arranged by an arbitrator according to the system Caesar set up when he was in Rome.[35] But it turned   2
out to be impossible to find anyone to initiate an appeal,
thanks to the equity of Caesar's decree and the decency of
Trebonius, who thought that in the circumstances judicial
rulings ought to be made with compassion and moderation. For even the average person, perhaps, will cite pov-   3
erty as an excuse, and blame a personal calamity or that of
the times, and put forward the difficulty of holding an

[35] See 3.1.2.

etiam mediocris est animi. Integras vero tenere posses-
siones, qui se debere fateantur, cuius animi aut cuius im-
4 pudentiae est? Itaque hoc qui postularet reperiebatur
nemo. Atque ipsis ad quorum commodum pertinebat
5 durior inventus est Caelius. Et ab hoc profectus initio, ne
frustra ingressus turpem causam videretur legem promulgavit ut sexenni die sine usuris creditae pecuniae solvan-
tur.

21. Cum resisteret Servilius consul reliquique magistratus et minus opinione sua efficeret ad hominum exci-
tanda studia sublata priore lege duas promulgavit, unam
qua mercedes habitationum annuas conductoribus dona-
2 vit, aliam tabularum novarum, impetuque multitudinis in
C. Trebonium facto et nonnullis vulneratis eum de tribu-
3 nali deturbavit. De quibus rebus Servilius consul ad senatum rettulit, senatusque Caelium ab re publica removen-
dum censuit. Hoc decreto eum consul senatu prohibuit et
4 contionari conantem de rostris deduxit. Ille ignominia et
dolore permotus palam se proficisci ad Caesarem simulavit. Clam, nuntiis ad Milonem missis, qui Clodio interfecto
eo nomine erat damnatus, atque eo in Italiam evocato
quod magnis muneribus datis gladiatoriae familiae reli-
quias habebat, sibi coniunxit eum atque[35] in Thurinum ad
5 sollicitandos pastores praemisit. Ipse cum Casilinum venisset unoque tempore signa eius militaria atque arma
Capuae essent comprensa et familia Neapoli visa[36] deque[37]

[35] eum atque *Apitz*: a- e- ω
[36] visa . . . appareret *Emendations have been proposed for
every word except* oppidi.   [37] deque *Damon*: qu(a)e ω

---

[36] From "and evidence" to "betrayal" the text is uncertain.

auction. But if a person who admits to owing money keeps his assets intact, what does that say about his character and his impudence? So no one was found to place a claim, and 4 Caelius was felt to be more obdurate than those whose interests were at stake. After this beginning, and so that 5 he would not seem to have embarked upon his disgraceful project in vain, he proposed a law making loans payable on their fifth anniversary without interest.

21. When the consul Servilius and the rest of the magistrates resisted, and he himself was achieving less than he expected by way of rousing people's enthusiasm, Caelius withdrew the first law and put forward two laws, one in which he remitted tenants' rent payments for a year, an- 2 other a cancellation of debts. After a crowd attacked Gaius Trebonius, and some people were injured, Caelius ejected Trebonius from his official seat. The consul Servilius re- 3 ferred these matters to the senate and the senate voted to remove Caelius from his public duties. With this decree in hand the consul barred Caelius from the senate and pulled him down off the rostra when he was trying to address a public meeting. Humiliated and hurt, Caelius pre- 4 tended in public that he was on his way to Caesar. In secret he sent messengers to Milo, who had been convicted of murder after the murder of Clodius, and summoned him to Italy, for Milo had the remnants of a band of gladiators from the large-scale shows he had given. Caelius joined Milo to his cause and sent him ahead to rouse the herdsmen. He himself went to Casilinum. At one and the same 5 moment military standards and weapons were seized at Capua and gladiators were seen at Naples and evidence emerged about the betrayal of the city.[36] With his plans

proditione oppidi appareret, patefactis consiliis exclusus
Capua et periculum veritus quod conventus arma ceperat
atque eum hostis loco habendum existimabat consilio des-
titit atque eo itinere sese avertit.

22. Interim Milo dimissis circum municipia litteris
‹se› ea quae faceret iussu atque imperio facere Pompei,
quae mandata ad se per Vibullium delata essent, quos ex
2 aere alieno laborare arbitrabatur sollicitabat. Apud quos
cum proficere nihil posset quibusdam solutis ergastulis
Compsam in agro Hirpino oppugnare coepit. Eo cum a Q.
Pedio praetore cum legione . . . lapide ictus ex muro per-
3 iit.[38] Et Caelius profectus, ut dictitabat, ad Caesarem pervenit Thurios. Vbi cum quosdam eius municipi sollicitaret
equitibusque Caesaris Gallis atque Hispanis, qui eo praesidi causa missi erant, pecuniam polliceretur ab his est
4 interfectus. Ita magnarum initia rerum, quae occupatione
magistratuum et temporum[39] sollicitam Italiam habebant,
celerem et facilem exitum habuerunt.

23. Libo profectus ab Orico cum classe cui praeerat
navium L Brundisium venit insulamque quae contra portum Brundisinum est occupavit quod praestare arbitrabatur unum locum—qua necessarius nostris erat egressus—
2 quam omnia litora ac portus custodia clausos tueri. Hic
repentino adventu naves onerarias quasdam nactus incendit et unam frumento onustam abduxit magnumque nostris terrorem iniecit. Et noctu militibus ac sagittariis in

[38] *Some text is missing either before or after* lapide.
[39] *After* temporum *Nitsche supplied* ‹difficultate›.

---

[37] This incomplete sentence cannot be certainly restored.
[38] Nitsche added "the difficulty of" before "the times."

laid bare, he was shut out of Capua. Fearing danger because the association of Roman citizens had taken up arms and thought him to be tantamount to a public enemy, he desisted from his plan and turned aside from the road to Capua.

22. Meanwhile Milo circulated a letter to various towns, saying that his actions were taken on Pompey's order and authority and that the message had been brought to him by Vibullius. He tried to rouse those whom he believed to be in difficulties with debt. Since he was unable to make 2 any progress with these, he opened the slave lockups and began to blockade Compsa in the territory of the Hirpini. There Milo perished, struck by a stone from the wall, after . . . by the praetor Quintus Pedius with a legion . . .[37] Caelius, having set out, as he said, for Caesar, reached 3 Thurii. There, while trying to rouse certain men from the town and promising money to some of Caesar's Gallic and Spanish cavalry who had been sent to garrison the place, he was killed by the cavalry. Thus the outbreak of major 4 developments, which kept Italy anxious with preoccupations about public office and the times,[38] had a swift and easy resolution.

23. Libo, setting out from Oricum with the fleet of fifty ships that was under his authority, came to Brundisium and occupied the island opposite Brundisium's harbor, thinking it preferable to contain one location with a guard and watch that one—the route by which our men would necessarily leave—not the whole coastline and every harbor. With his sudden arrival he captured and burned some 2 cargo vessels, towed one away laden with provisions, and inflicted great terror on our men. By night he landed some infantry and archers and drove off the island's cavalry gar-

terra expositis praesidium equitum deiecit. Et adeo loci opportunitate profecit uti ad Pompeium litteras mitteret: naves reliquas, si vellet, subduci et refici iuberet; sua classe auxilia sese Caesaris prohibiturum.

24. Erat eo tempore Antonius Brundisi. Virtute militum confisus scaphas navium magnarum circiter LX cratibus pluteisque contexit eoque milites delectos imposuit atque eas in litore pluribus locis separatim disposuit, navesque triremes duas quas Brundisi faciendas curaverat per causam exercendorum remigum ad fauces portus pro-
2 dire iussit. Has cum audacius progressas Libo vidisset sperans intercipi posse quadriremes V ad eas misit. Quae cum navibus nostris propinquassent nostri veterani in portum[40] refugiebant, illi studio incitati incautius sequeban-
3 tur. Iam ex omnibus partibus subito Antonianae scaphae signo dato se in hostes incitaverunt. Primoque impetu unam ex his quadriremem cum remigibus defensoribusque suis ceperunt, reliquas turpiter refugere coegerunt.
4 Ad hoc detrimentum accessit ut equitibus per oram maritimam ab Antonio dispositis aquari prohiberentur. Qua necessitate et ignominia permotus Libo discessit a Brundisio obsessionemque nostrorum omisit.

25. Multi iam menses erant, et hiems praecipitaverat, neque Brundisio naves legionesque ad Caesarem veniebant. Ac nonnullae eius rei praetermissae occasiones Caesari videbantur quod certi saepe flaverant venti, quibus

[40] veterani in portum] ut erat imperatum *Kübler*: ut convenerat ante i- p- *Castiglioni*

---

[39] For "our veterans retreated into the harbor," Kübler and

rison. He drew such profit from the position's advantages that he wrote to Pompey: "Order the rest of the ships to be hauled out and repaired, if you like; I will block Caesar's reinforcements with my fleet."

24. Antony was at Brundisium at the time. Confident of his soldiers' courage, he camouflaged about sixty of the warships' longboats with wicker screens, put picked men on board, and stationed them separately at various spots along the shore. He ordered two triremes that he had arranged to have built at Brundisium to advance to the harbor mouth on the pretext of training the rowers. Libo saw 2 them advance quite boldly. Hoping that they could be cut off, he sent five quadriremes against them. When these approached our ships, our veterans retreated into the harbor.[39] Spurred by enthusiasm, the enemy followed too recklessly. At that moment, and on his signal, Antony's 3 longboats drove against the enemy from all directions and in the initial attack captured one of their boats, a quadrireme with its rowers and marines, and forced the rest to make a shameful retreat. On top of the loss itself was the 4 fact that the enemy was prevented from getting water by cavalry that Antony had stationed all along the shore. Under duress and humiliated, Libo left Brundisium and abandoned his blockade of our men.

25. The months were adding up, and winter was far advanced, and the ships and legions from Brundisium had not reached Caesar. Indeed it seemed to Caesar that some occasions for crossing had been missed, since steady winds

Castiglioni suggested "retreated as had been ordered" and "retreated into the harbor as had been agreed beforehand," respectively.

2 necessario committendum existimabat. Quantoque eius amplius processerat temporis tanto erant alacriores ad custodias qui classibus praeerant maioremque fiduciam prohibendi habebant. Et crebris Pompei litteris castigabantur, quoniam primo venientem Caesarem non prohibuissent, ut reliquos eius exercitus impedirent. Duriusque cotidie tempus ad transportandum lenioribus ventis ex

3 pectabant. Quibus rebus permotus Caesar Brundisium ad suos severius scripsit: nacti idoneum ventum ne occasionem navigandi dimitterent sive ⟨. . . sive⟩ ad[41] litora Apolloniatium cursum dirigere atque eo naves eicere pos

4 sent. Haec a custodiis classium loca maxime vacabant quod se longius ⟨a⟩ portibus committere non auderent.

26. Illi adhibita audacia et virtute, administrantibus M. Antonio et Fufio Caleno, multum ipsis militibus hortantibus neque ullum periculum pro salute Caesaris recusantibus, nacti austrum naves solvunt atque altero die Apol

2 loniam Dyrrachiumque praetervehuntur. Qui cum essent ex continenti visi C. Coponius, qui Dyrrachi classi Rhodiae praeerat, naves ex portu educit. Et cum iam nostris remissiore vento appropinquasset idem auster increbuit

3 nostrisque praesidio fuit. Neque vero ille ob eam causam conatu desistebat, sed labore et perseverantia nautarum etiam vim tempestatis superari posse sperabat, praetervectosque Dyrrachium magna vi venti nihilo secius

[41] sive ⟨. . . sive⟩ ad *Damon*: si ad *Held. After* Apolloniatium *Hoffmann supplied* ⟨sive ad Labeatium⟩.

---

[40] For "for either ⟨. . .⟩ or," Held suggested "even for." Hoffmann pairs "the coast belonging to Apollonia" with "or that belonging to Labeate."

had often blown; on these, he kept thinking, they would be bound to place their trust. The more the time for the 2 crossing passed, the more attentive to patrolling the fleet commanders became and the more confidence they gained in deterrence. Plus, there were frequent scolding letters from Pompey urging them, since they had not stopped Caesar when he was first on his way, to block the rest of his forces. And they expected the weather to get more difficult for crossing every day, with lighter winds. Prompted by these considerations, Caesar wrote to his 3 men with some severity: "When you get a suitable wind, do not miss an opportunity for sailing, if you can set a course for either ⟨. . .⟩ or the coast belonging to Apollonia[40] and beach the ships there." These places were mostly 4 free of the fleets' patrols because they did not dare, he assumed, commit themselves too far from the harbors.

26. His men acted with daring and courage. With Mark Antony and Fufius Calenus directing operations, and the soldiers themselves urging them on and accepting any risk for Caesar's safety, they weighed anchor when they got a wind from the south. The following day they were being carried past Apollonia and Dyrrachium, and when they 2 were sighted from the mainland Gaius Coponius, who was in charge of the Rhodian fleet at Dyrrachium, led his ships out of the harbor. When he was already close to our ships in a rather light wind, that same south wind grew stronger and was a great help to our side. But this did not make 3 Coponius desist from his attempt; hoping, rather, that even the storm's violence could be overcome by the sailors' effort and perseverance, he kept up his pursuit as they were carried past Dyrrachium by the wind's great force.

4 sequebatur. Nostri usi Fortunae beneficio tamen impetum
classis timebant si forte ventus remisisset. Nacti portum
qui appellatur Nymphaeum, ultra Lissum milia passuum
tria, eo naves introduxerunt. (Qui portus ab africo tegeba-
tur, ab austro non erat tutus, leviusque tempestatis quam
5 classis periculum aestimaverunt.) Quo simul atque intro
est itum incredibili felicitate auster, qui per biduum flave-
rat, in africum se vertit.

27. Hic subitam commutationem fortunae videre licuit. Qui modo sibi timuerant hos tutissimus portus recipiebat, qui nostris navibus periculum intulerant de suo
2 timere cogebantur. Itaque tempore commutato tempestas
et nostros texit et naves Rhodias adflixit, ita ut ad unam
omnes constratae numero XVI eliderentur et naufragio
interirent, et ex magno remigum propugnatorumque numero pars ad scopulos allisa interficeretur, pars ab nostris
detraheretur. Quos omnes conservatos Caesar domum remisit.

28. Nostrae naves duae tardius cursu confecto in noctem coniectae, cum ignorarent quem locum reliquae ce-
2 pissent, contra Lissum in ancoris constiterunt. Has scaphis
minoribusque navigiis compluribus summissis Otacilius
Crassus, qui Lissi praeerat, expugnare parabat. Simul de
deditione eorum agebat et incolumitatem deditis pollice-
3 batur. Harum altera navis CCXX e legione tironum sus-
4 tulerat, altera ex veterana paulo minus CC. His cognosci
licuit quantum esset hominibus praesidi in animi firmitu-

Our men profited from Fortune's kindness but feared an 4
attack by the fleet in case the wind let up. Coming to a
harbor called Nymphaeum, three miles beyond Lissus,
they put in there. (This harbor was protected from a southwest wind but not safe from a south wind, and in their
reckoning there was less danger from the storm than from
the enemy fleet.) The moment they entered, with incred- 5
ible good fortune, the south wind, which had blown for
two days straight, turned into a southwest wind.

27. At this it was possible to see a sudden reversal of
fortune. Those who had recently been afraid for themselves were received into a perfectly safe harbor; those
who had been a danger to our ships were forced to be
afraid of their own danger. Thus with the change of cir- 2
cumstance the weather gave our men shelter and inflicted
such havoc on the Rhodian ships that every one of the
decked ships, sixteen in number, was lost to shipwreck,
and some of their large number of rowers and fighters
were dashed on the rocks and killed, others were rescued
by our men. Caesar spared all of these and sent them
home.

28. Two of our ships, having completed their journey
rather slowly, were delayed until dark. Since they did not
know what location the others had chosen, they anchored
off Lissus. Otacilius Crassus, who was in charge at Lissus, 2
sent up some longboats and small craft and prepared to
board them. At the same time he began negotiating for
their surrender, promising safety to those who surrendered. One of these ships carried two hundred and twenty 3
men from a newly recruited legion, the other a few less
than two hundred from a veteran legion. From these it was 4
possible to learn how much protection men derive from

dine. Tirones enim multitudine navium perterriti et salo nausiaque confecti iureiurando accepto—nihil his nocituros hostes—se Otacilio dediderunt. Qui omnes ad eum producti contra religionem iurisiurandi in eius conspectu
5 crudelissime interficiuntur. At veteranae legionis milites item conflictati et tempestatis et sentinae vitiis neque ex pristina virtute remittendum aliquid putaverunt. Sed tractandis conditionibus et simulatione deditionis extracto primo noctis tempore gubernatorem in terram navem ei-
6 cere cogunt. Ipsi idoneum locum nacti reliquam noctis partem ibi confecerunt. Et luce prima, missis ad eos ab Otacilio equitibus qui eam partem orae maritimae adservabant circiter CCCC quique eos armati ex praesidio secuti sunt, se defenderunt et nonnullis eorum interfectis incolumes se ad nostros receperunt.

29. Quo facto conventus civium Romanorum qui Lissum obtinebant, quod oppidum iis antea Caesar attribuerat muniendumque curaverat, Antonium recepit omnibusque rebus iuvit. Otacilius sibi timens ⟨ex⟩ oppido fugit et
2 ad Pompeium pervenit. Expositis omnibus copiis Antonius, quarum erat summa veteranarum trium legionum uniusque tironum et equitum DCCC, plerasque naves in Italiam remittit ad reliquos milites equitesque transpor-
3 tandos. Pontones, quod est genus navium Gallicarum, Lissi relinquit hoc consilio ut si forte Pompeius vacuam existimans Italiam eo traiecisset exercitum, quae opinio erat edita in vulgus, aliquam Caesar ad insequendum facultatem haberet. Nuntiosque ad eum celeriter mittit: quibus regionibus exercitum exposuisset et quid militum transvexisset.

sturdy morale. For the new recruits were thoroughly
cowed by the number of vessels and overcome by seasick-
ness. After receiving a sworn guarantee that the enemy
would not harm them, they surrendered to Otacilius. All
of them were brought before him and—a violation of the
sanctity of the oath—killed with extreme cruelty in his
sight. The veteran legions, however, although likewise suf- 5
fering from bad weather and bilge, felt that their courage
should be held to its former standard. Instead, after dragging out the first part of the night with negotiations and a
pretense of surrender, they forced their pilot to run the
ship aground; they found a suitable spot and spent the rest 6
of the night there. At first light, when Otacilius sent cavalry against them—around four hundred, who were
guarding that portion of the coast, followed by armed men
from the garrison—they defended themselves, killing
some of the enemy, and returned safely to our men.

29. After this development Antony was welcomed by
the association of Roman citizens in charge of Lissus, a
town that Caesar had earlier allocated to them while making arrangements for its defense. Antony was given every
sort of assistance. Otacilius, afraid for himself, fled from
the town and went to Pompey. Antony's troops were now 2
all disembarked; their total was three legions of veterans
and one of new recruits, plus eight hundred cavalry. He
sent most of the ships back to Italy to bring the rest of the
soldiers and cavalry. He left the pontoons, a variety of 3
Gallic ship, at Lissus with the intention that, if Pompey,
thinking Italy unguarded, happened to send his army
across—this idea had been aired to the general population—Caesar would have some means of following. He
then sent word quickly to Caesar about where he had set
his troops ashore and what forces he had brought across.

30. Haec eodem fere tempore Caesar atque Pompeius cognoscunt. Nam praetervectas Apolloniam Dyrrachiumque naves viderant ipsi—iter secundum eas terras[42] derexerant—sed quo essent eae delatae primis diebus igno-

2 rabant. Cognitaque re diversa sibi ambo consilia capiunt, Caesar ut quam primum se cum Antonio coniungeret, Pompeius ut venientibus in itinere se opponeret et si im-

3 prudentes ex insidiis adoriri posset. Eodemque die uterque eorum ex castris stativis a flumine Apso exercitum educunt, Pompeius clam et noctu, Caesar palam atque

4 interdiu. Sed Caesari circuitu maiore iter erat longius adverso flumine ut vado transire posset. Pompeius, quia expedito itinere flumen ei transeundum non erat, magnis

5 itineribus ad Antonium contendit. Atque ubi eum appropinquare cognovit idoneum locum nactus ibi copias collocavit suosque omnes castris continuit ignesque fieri pro-

6 hibuit quo occultior esset eius adventus. Haec ad Antonium statim per Graecos deferuntur. Ille missis ad Caesarem nuntiis unum diem sese castris tenuit. Altero die ad eum

7 pervenit Caesar. Cuius adventu cognito Pompeius ne duobus circumcluderetur exercitibus ex eo loco discedit omnibusque copiis ad Asparagium Dyrrachinorum pervenit atque ibi idoneo loco castra ponit.

31. His temporibus Scipio detrimentis quibusdam circa montem Amanum acceptis imperatorem se appella-

---

[42] secundum eas terras] -do austro *Paul. Perhaps* -dum eas oras?

---

[41] For "followed the coast in those regions," Paul proposed "sailed with a following south wind"; one might also emend to "directed their route along those shores."

30. Caesar and Pompey learned about these events almost simultaneously. (They themselves had seen the ships carried past Apollonia and Dyrrachium—the ships had followed the coast in those regions[41]—but in the first days thereafter did not know where they had ended up.) Seeing 2 the situation, they adopted contrasting plans, Caesar to join up with Antonius as soon as possible, Pompey to confront the newcomers en route, and in case he could attack them unawares from an ambush. They led the troops out 3 of their established camps and away from the Apsus on the same day, Pompey secretly and by night, Caesar openly and by day. But Caesar's route was the longer by a major 4 detour upstream, so that he could cross at a ford. Pompey hastened toward Antony by forced marches, since he did not have to cross the river on his unobstructed route. When he learned that Antony was getting close, he found 5 a suitable location and stationed his forces there. He kept all of his men in camp and forbade them to light fires, so that his arrival would be better concealed. These matters 6 were immediately reported to Antony by the Greeks. He sent messengers to Caesar and stayed in camp for one day; Caesar reached him the next. Upon learning of Caesar's 7 arrival Pompey left the area to avoid being surrounded by two armies. He went to Asparagium, a town belonging to Dyrrachium, and made camp there in a suitable location.

31. At this period Scipio had incurred some losses near the Amanus range and given himself the title *imperator*.[42]

[42] As governor of Syria (1.6.5). For *imperator*, see on 2.26.1.

2 verat. Quo facto civitatibus tyrannisque magnas imperave-
rat pecunias. Item a publicanis suae provinciae debitam
bienni pecuniam exegerat et ab isdem insequentis anni
mutuam praeceperat equitesque toti provinciae impera-
3 verat. Quibus coactis, finitimis hostibus Parthis post se
relictis, qui paulo ante M. Crassum imperatorem interfecerant et M. Bibulum in obsidione habuerant, legiones
4 equitesque ex Syria deduxerat. Summaque in sollicitudine
ac timore[43] Parthici belli [provincia] cum venisset,[44] ac
nonnullae militum voces cum audirentur—sese contra
hostem si ducerentur ituros, contra civem et consulem
arma non laturos—deductis Pergamum atque in locuple-
tissimas urbes in hiberna legionibus maximas largitiones
fecit. Et confirmandorum militum causa diripiendas his
civitates dedit.

32. Interim acerbissime imperatae pecuniae tota
provincia exigebantur. Multa praeterea generatim ad
2 avaritiam excogitabantur. In capita singula servorum ac
liberorum tributum imponebatur. Columnaria ostiaria
frumentum milites arma remiges tormenta vecturae imperabantur. Cuius modo rei nomen reperiri poterat hoc
3 satis esse ad cogendas pecunias videbatur. Non solum

---

[43] summaque in sollicitudine ac timore *MUST*: -amque in
-nem ac -rem V
[44] [provincia] . . . venisset (*sc.* Scipio) *Damon*: -a [-am *T*] . . .
v- ω: ⟨in⟩ provinciam . . . venisset *ed. pr.*

---

[43] For "although . . . situation," the first edition substituted
"although he had come into the province when it was in a state."
[44] Editors often print the reading of V: "although the province
had come into a state of extreme anxiety and fear."

Thereafter he had requisitioned great sums from com-   2
munities and rulers. Similarly, he had exacted from the tax
contactors in his province the amount they owed for a
two-year period, and had taken the amount for the following year in advance as a loan. Plus, he had requisitioned
cavalry from the entire province. After collecting these,   3
and leaving behind hostile Parthians on his borders—they
had killed the commander Marcus Crassus a short while
before and held Marcus Bibulus under siege—he had led
the legions and cavalry out of Syria. Although Scipio had   4
arrived in a situation[43] of extreme anxiety and fear[44] of a
Parthian war, and some soldiers were heard to say that
they would go if he led them against the enemy but would
not bear arms against a citizen and consul, he led the legions to Pergamum and some extremely wealthy cities for
their winter quarters and provided huge bounties. Moreover, in order to encourage the soldiers he allowed them
to pillage these cities.

32. Meanwhile the money requisitioned with extreme
harshness was being exacted throughout the province.[45] In
addition, many new categories were devised to serve people's greed. A poll tax was imposed on individuals enslaved   2
and free. "Column"- and "doorway"-taxes, provisions, soldiers, weapons, rowers, catapults, and conveyances were
requisitioned. If a name at least could be found for something, that seemed sufficient to collect funds.[46] Individuals   3

[45] In this paragraph it is unclear whether the province in question is Syria or Asia. See also note 49.

[46] The text is problematic, but the general point is clear.

urbibus sed paene vicis castellisque singulis ⟨singuli⟩ cum
imperio[45] praeficiebantur. Qui horum quid acerbissime
crudelissimeque fecerat is et vir et civis optimus habeba-
4 tur. Erat plena lictorum et imperiorum[46] provincia, dif-
ferta praefectis atque exactoribus, qui praeter imperatas
pecunias suo etiam privato compendio serviebant. Dictitabant enim se domo patriaque expulsos omnibus necessariis egere rebus, ut honesta praescriptione rem turpissi-
5 mam tegerent. Accedebant ad haec gravissimae usurae,
quod in bello plerumque accidere consuevit universis
imperatis pecuniis. Quibus in rebus prolationem diei do-
nationem esse dicebant. Itaque aes alienum provinciae eo
6 biennio multiplicatum est. Neque minus ob eam causam
civibus Romanis eius provinciae—sed in singulos conventus singulasque civitates—certae pecuniae imperabantur,
mutuasque illas ex senatus consulto exigi dictitabant. Publicani,[47] ut †in sorte†,[48] fecerant insequentis anni vectigal
promutuum.[49]

[45] ⟨singuli⟩ cum imperio *Oehler*: ⟨s-⟩ [cum i-] *Carter*

[46] et imperiorum *MUST*: -orumque *V*: et apparitorum *Forchhammer*　　　[47] publicani *Damon, with punctuation before* fecerant: -nis (*sc.* imperabatur) *ω. Unless you prefer with Glandorp
to supply* ⟨imperatum⟩ *before* insequentis *or with Nitsche to
emend* promutuum.

[48] in sorte [fo- *S*] *ω*: in Syria *Estienne*: in superiore (sc. *anno*)
Markland: ii sortem *Constans*

[49] promutuum [-mot- *S*] *ω*: prae⟨cipiebant⟩ mut- *Nitsche*

---

[47] Carter excised "with military authority" as being of dubious
historicity, but "practically" is an admission of exaggeration.

[48] For "authorities," Forchhammer proposed "magistrates' attendants."

with military authority[47] were put in charge not only of cities but practically of individual villages and outposts, and any of them who accomplished anything in a particularly harsh and cruel manner was considered an outstanding man and citizen. The province was full of lictors and 4 authorities,[48] bursting with officers and tax collectors. Beyond the requisitioned money, these men were attending to their private finances. (They used to say that, having been driven from home and country, they lacked every necessity, thus masking an utterly disgraceful matter with an honorable pretext.) On top of these things the interest 5 rate was utterly extortionate, as generally tends to happen in wartime when funds are requisitioned from everyone; in this business Scipio's agents would say that an extension was a gift. Thus within a two-year period the province's indebtedness increased severalfold. This was not taken as 6 a reason not to requisition specific sums from the province's Roman citizens, however, but the burden fell on individual civic associations and individual cities—while the Scipio's agents kept saying that these "loans" were being exacted in accordance with a decree of the senate. The tax contractors had made an advance loan of the following year's revenue, as †[49]

[49] For the daggered text, Estienne substituted "in Syria" (which would make the rest of the paragraph about Asia), while Markland suggested "in the previous (year)." Constans' emendation requires a more thorough overhaul, with *publicanis . . . promutuum* appended to the previous sentence: "(requisition) . . . from tax contractors, insofar as they had accrued capital, an advance loan . . . ."

33. Praeterea Ephesi a fano Dianae depositas antiquitus pecunias Scipio tolli iubebat. Certaque eius ⟨rei⟩ die constituta cum in fanum ventum[50] esset adhibitis compluribus ordinis senatori quos advocaverat Scipio, litterae ei redduntur a Pompeio: mare transisse cum legionibus Caesarem; properaret ad se cum exercitu venire omniaque
2 posteriora haberet.[51] His litteris acceptis quos advocaverat dimittit, ipse iter in Macedoniam parare incipit paucisque post diebus est profectus. Haec res Ephesiae pecuniae salutem attulit.

34. Caesar Antoni exercitu coniuncto deducta Orico legione quam tuendae orae maritimae causa posuerat temptandas sibi provincias longiusque procedendum exis-
2 timabat. Et cum ad eum ex Thessalia Aetoliaque legati venissent qui praesidio misso pollicerentur earum gentium civitates imperata facturas, L. Cassium Longinum cum legione tironum, quae appellabatur vicesima septima, atque equitibus CC in Thessaliam, item[52] C. Calvisium Sabinum cum cohortibus V paucisque equitibus in Aetoliam misit. Maxime eos, quod erant propinquae re-
3 giones, de re frumentaria ut providerent hortatus est. Cn. Domitium Calvinum cum legionibus duabus, undecima et duodecima, et equitibus D in Macedoniam proficisci ius-
4 sit. Cuius provinciae ab ea parte quae libera appellabatur

[50] ventum] -urus *Paul²*

[51] omniaque posteriora haberet *Paul, as reported by Meusel*: o- posteaqu(a)e h- *USTV*: o- quae h- *M*: omnibusque quae h- *ed. pr.*: omniaque posth- *Aldus*

[52] item *Constans*: ire ω: [i-] *Aldus*

---

[50] For "fixing . . . arrival," Paul proposed "When he had fixed

33. Furthermore, at Ephesus Scipio ordered long-standing deposits to be removed from the temple of Diana, fixing a date for it. Upon Scipio's arrival[50] in the temple accompanied by some men of senatorial rank whom he had summoned, a letter from Pompey was given to him: "Caesar has crossed the Adriatic with his legions. Make haste to come to me with your army and treat this as the highest priority."[51] Upon receiving this letter Scipio 2 dismissed the men he had summoned and began to make preparations for his own march to Macedonia, setting out within a few days. This development saved the money at Ephesus.

34. After the conjunction with Antony's army, Caesar withdrew the legion that he had stationed in Oricum to guard the coastline, thinking that he ought to rally the provinces and advance further. When delegations reached 2 him from Thessaly and Aetolia promising that their communities would do his bidding if he sent garrisons, he sent Lucius Cassius Longinus to Thessaly along with a legion of new recruits called the 27th and two hundred cavalry, and likewise Gaius Calvisius Sabinus to Aetolia with five cohorts and a small number of cavalry. His principal charge to them was to make provisioning arrangements, since those regions were close at hand. He ordered Gnaeus 3 Domitius Calvinus to set out for Macedonia with two legions, the 11th and 12th, and five hundred cavalry. Menedemus, the area's leading man, had been sent as a 4

a date on which he would arrive," which makes the coincidence of the letter's timing less striking.

[51] The text underlying "the highest priority" is uncertain, but the meaning is clear.

Menedemus, princeps earum regionum, missus legatus omnium suorum excellens studium profitebatur.

35. Ex his Calvisius primo adventu summa omnium Aetolorum receptus voluntate praesidiis adversariorum Calydone et Naupacto deiectis[53] omni Aetolia potitus est.
2 Cassius in Thessaliam cum legione pervenit. Hic cum essent factiones duae varia voluntate civitatum utebatur. Hegesaretos, veteris homo potentiae, Pompeianis rebus studebat. Petraeus, summae nobilitatis adulescens, suis ac suorum opibus Caesarem enixe iuvabat.

36. Eodemque tempore Domitius in Macedoniam venit. Et cum ad eum frequentes civitatum legationes convenire coepissent nuntiatum est adesse Scipionem cum legionibus magna opinione et fama omnium. Nam ple-
2 rumque in novitate ⟨rem⟩ fama antecedit. Hic nullo in loco Macedoniae moratus magno impetu tetendit ad Domitium. Et cum ab eo milia passuum XX afuisset subito se
3 ad Cassium Longinum in Thessaliam convertit. Hoc adeo celeriter fecit ⟨ut⟩ simul adesse et venire nuntiaretur. Et quo iter expeditius faceret M. Favonium ad flumen Haliacmonem, quod Macedoniam a Thessalia dividit, cum cohortibus VIII praesidio impedimentis legionum reliquit
4 castellumque ibi muniri iussit. Eodem tempore equitatus regis Coti ad castra Cassi advolavit, qui circum Thessaliam
5 esse consuerat. Tum timore perterritus Cassius cognito Scipionis adventu visisque equitibus, quos Scipionis esse arbitrabatur, ad montes se convertit, qui Thessaliam cin-

---

[53] deiectis *Chacon*: relic- ω

---

[52] The number seems high and has often been emended. If correct, it suggests that Scipio placed excessive value on the proceeds of his time in Syria and Asia (3.31–32).

representative from the part the province called "free Macedonia"; he promised that the enthusiasm of all of his compatriots was very high.

35. Of these, Calvisius was received upon arrival with the utmost goodwill of all Aetolians. He drove enemy garrisons out of Calydon and Naupactus and took control of the whole of Aetolia. Cassius arrived in Thessaly with his 2 legion, encountering different attitudes from place to place since there were two factions here. Hegesaretus, a man whose power was of long standing, favored the Pompeian cause. Petraeus, a younger man of the highest nobility, supported Caesar assiduously with resources belonging to himself and his associates.

36. Domitius came to Macedonia at the same time. Local delegations had begun to gather around him in large numbers, but then it was reported that Scipio was at hand with his legions, a man of impressive reputation and the subject of universal talk, for in novel situations rumor generally outstrips reality. Scipio did not linger anywhere in 2 Macedonia, but headed for Domitius with great urgency. Then, when he was twenty miles away from him, he suddenly changed direction toward Cassius Longinus in Thessaly, acting so quickly in this matter that his arrival 3 and his approach were reported simultaneously. (In order to expedite his march Scipio left Marcus Favonius at the Haliacmon River, which separates Macedonia from Thessaly, with eight cohorts to protect the legions' baggage,[52] and ordered a stronghold to be fortified there.) At the 4 same time the cavalry of King Cotus appeared unexpectedly near Cassius' camp; this force was often in the vicinity of Thessaly.[53] Cassius was terrified by the alarming 5

[53] Cotus' kingdom was in eastern Thrace, near the Bosporus.

gunt, atque ex his locis Ambraciam versus iter facere coe-
6 pit. At Scipionem properantem sequi litterae sunt conse-
cutae a M. Favonio: Domitium cum legionibus adesse
neque se praesidium ubi constitutus esset sine auxilio
7 Scipionis tenere posse. Quibus litteris acceptis consilium
Scipio iterque commutat. Cassium sequi desistit, Favonio
8 auxilium ferre contendit. Itaque die ac nocte continuato
itinere ad eum pervenit tam opportuno tempore ut simul
Domitiani exercitus pulvis cerneretur et primi antecur-
sores Scipionis viderentur. Ita Cassio industria Domiti,
Favonio Scipionis celeritas salutem attulit.

37. Scipio biduum castris stativis moratus ad flumen
quod inter eum et Domiti castra fluebat, Haliacmonem,
tertio die prima luce exercitum vado traducit. Et castris
positis postero die mane copias ante frontem castrorum
2 instruit. Domitius tum quoque sibi dubitandum non puta-
vit quin productis legionibus proelio decertaret. Sed cum
esset inter bina castra campus circiter milium passuum VI
Domitius castris Scipionis aciem suam subiecit. Ille a vallo
3 non discedere perseveravit. At tamen aegre retentis Do-
mitianis militibus est factum ne proelio contenderetur, et
maxime quod rivus difficilibus ripis subiectus castris Sci-
4 pionis progressus nostrorum impediebat. Quorum studium alacritatemque pugnandi cum cognovisset Scipio,
suspicatus fore ut postero die aut invitus dimicare cogeretur aut magna cum infamia castris se contineret, qui

---

54 The number six is often reduced by emendation.

development. Aware of Scipio's approach, and seeing cavalry that he thought belonged to Scipio, he headed for the mountains that encircle Thessaly and began to march out of this region in the direction of Ambracia. Scipio hurried 6 in pursuit, but a letter arrived from Marcus Favonius: "Domitius is at hand with his legions, and without your help I cannot keep a garrison where I have been stationed." On receipt of the letter Scipio changed his plan 7 and his route. He stopped pursuing Cassius and hurried to help Favonius. As a result, after marching continuously 8 day and night, he arrived at such an opportune moment that the dust of Domitius' army and the first of Scipio's advance troops came into view simultaneously. Thus Cassius was saved by Domitius' effort, Favonius by Scipio's speed.

37. Scipio lingered for two days in the established camp beside the river that flowed between him and Domitius' camp, the Haliacmon. At dawn on the third day he led his army across at a ford. He made camp and early the next day drew up his forces in front of his camp. Domitius felt 2 even then that he should not hesitate to bring out his legions and decide matters with a fight. Moreover, although there was level ground between the two camps for about six miles,[54] Domitius positioned his line close to Scipio's camp, while Scipio persisted in his refusal to move away from the rampart. Domitius' soldiers were held back with 3 difficulty, but in the end there was no engagement, mostly because a river close to Scipio's camp had banks that were hard to negotiate and slowed our men's advance. Recog- 4 nizing their determination and eagerness for battle, Scipio suspected that the next day he would be forced to fight against his will or else stay in camp getting thoroughly

magna expectatione venisset temere progressus turpem
habuit exitum. Et noctu neque conclamatis quidem vasis
flumen transiit atque in eandem partem ex qua venerat
rediit ibique prope flumen edito natura loco castra posuit.
5 Paucis diebus interpositis noctu insidias equitum collocavit quo in loco superioribus fere diebus nostri pabulari
consuerant, et cum cotidiana consuetudine Q. Varus,
praefectus equitum Domiti, venisset, subito illi ex insidiis
6 consurrexerunt. Sed nostri fortiter impetum eorum tulerunt, celeriterque ad suos quisque ordines rediit, atque
7 ultro universi in hostes impetum fecerunt. Ex his circiter
LXXX interfectis, reliquis in fugam coniectis, duobus
amissis in castra se receperunt.

38. His rebus gestis Domitius sperans Scipionem ad
pugnam elici posse simulavit sese angustiis rei frumentariae adductum castra movere. Vasisque militari more
conclamatis progressus milia passuum tria loco idoneo et
2 occulto omnem exercitum equitatumque collocavit. Scipio ad sequendum paratus equitatus magnam partem ad
3 explorandum iter Domiti et cognoscendum praemisit. Qui
cum essent progressi primaeque turmae insidias intra-
vissent, ex fremitu equorum illata suspicione ad suos se
recipere coeperunt, quique hos sequebantur celerem eo-
4 rum receptum conspicati restiterunt. Nostri cognitis [ho-
stium][54] insidiis, ne frustra reliquos expectarent, duas

[54] [hostium] *Apitz*: -i *Vossius*: < per exploratores > -ium *Kübler*:
suis *Dübner*

vilified. The man of whom great things were expected when he arrived had advanced rashly; the outcome was ignominious. He crossed the river by night without even giving the signal to pack up. Returning to his starting point he made camp there beside the river on a natural rise. During the night a few days later he laid a cavalry ambush 5 where our men had recently been accustomed to forage, and when Quintus Varus, Domitius' cavalry commander, arrived following the regular routine, the enemy suddenly burst out of their ambush. Our men, however, bravely 6 withstood their attack. Each man returned quickly to his formation, and as one they made a spontaneous attack on the enemy. After killing about eighty of them and putting 7 the rest to flight ours returned to camp with a loss of two.

38. Following these developments Domitius hoped that Scipio could be enticed to fight. He pretended that supply difficulties had induced him strike camp. After giving the regulation order to pack up, he advanced three miles and stationed the whole army, cavalry included, in a suitable and hidden location. Scipio was prepared to fol- 2 low him, and sent ahead a large portion of his cavalry to scout out and reconnoiter Domitius' route. When these 3 had advanced and the first squadrons had entered the ambush, the sound of horses made them suspicious and they began to return to their own lines, while those behind them noticed the rapid retreat and halted. Our men, after 4 the ambush was recognized,[55] and so as not to wait in vain for the rest of the enemy, falling in with two squadrons . . .

[55] In "after the ambush was recognized," an unwanted possessive "of the enemy" has been excised. Other repairs are possible.

nacti turmas . . .[55] exceperunt. In his fuit[56] M. Opimius praefectus equitum. Reliquos[57] omnes earum turmarum aut interfecerunt aut captos ad Domitium deduxerunt.

39. Deductis orae maritimae praesidiis Caesar, ut supra demonstratum est, tres cohortes Orici oppidi tuendi causa reliquit isdemque custodiam navium longarum tradidit quas ex Italia traduxerat. Huic officio oppidoque Caninia-
2 nus legatus praeerat. Is naves nostras interiorem in portum post oppidum reduxit et ad terram deligavit faucibusque portus navem onerariam submersam obiecit et huic alteram coniunxit. Super quas turrim effectam ad ipsum introitum portus opposuit et militibus complevit tuendamque ad omnes repentinos casus tradidit.

40. Quibus cognitis rebus Cn. Pompeius filius, qui classi Aegyptiae praeerat, ad Oricum venit submersamque navem remulco multisque contendens funibus adduxit. Atque alteram navem, quae erat ad custodiam ab Acilio posita, pluribus aggressus navibus, in quibus ad libram fecerat turres, [ut] ex superiore pugnans loco integrosque semper defatigatis summittens, et reliquis partibus simul ex terra scalis et classe moenia oppidi temptans uti adversariorum manus diduceret, labore et multitudine telorum nostros vicit. Deiectisque defensoribus, qui omnes scaphis
2 excepti refugerant, eam navem expugnavit. Eodemque tempore ex altera parte molem tenuit naturalem obiec-

---

[55] turmas . . . exceperunt *Damon*: turmas exceperunt . . . *Freudenberg*   [56] in his fuit] unus fugit *Roscher*
[57] [reliquos] *Dederich*

---

[56] A textual gap and related problems here occlude the fate of Marcus Opimius.

captured.[56] Among these was[57] Marcus Opimius, a cavalry commander. All of the remaining men of those squadrons our men either killed or captured and took to Domitius.

39. When Caesar removed his garrisons from the coastline, as was indicated earlier,[58] he left three cohorts at Oricum to defend the town, having also given them oversight of the warships that he had brought over from Italy. His officer Caninianus was in charge of the task and the town.[59] He brought our ships into the inner harbor behind 2 the town and moored them. At the mouth of the harbor he sank a transport ship as an obstacle, fastening another to it. He positioned a tower built on top of them next to the harbor entrance and filled it with soldiers who were to defend it against every eventuality.

40. Learning of this, Pompey's son Gnaeus, who was in charge of the Egyptian fleet, came to Oricum and towed away the sunken ship, pulling hard with numerous cables. He attacked the other ship, which had been put there by Acilius to guard the place, using several ships on which he had built towers of equal height. By fighting from a higher position, constantly sending fresh troops to support tired ones, and testing the town walls elsewhere by land with ladders and simultaneously with the fleet so as to divide his opponents' forces, he overcame our men with effort and a multitude of projectiles. After dislodging the defenders, who had all fled after being taken on board longboats, he boarded that ship. At the same time Gnaeus took 2 possession of a jetty on the other side, a natural barrier

---

[57] For "among these was," Roscher proposed "One man got away."   [58] At 3.34.1.

[59] His full name was Marcus Acilius Caninianus (3.40.1).

tam, quae paene insulam oppidum effecerat. IIII biremes
subiectis scutulis impulsas vectibus in interiorem portum
3   traduxit. Ita ex utraque parte naves longas aggressus, quae
erant deligatae ad terram atque inanes, IIII ex his abduxit,
4   reliquas incendit. Hoc confecto negotio D. Laelium ab
Asiatica classe abductum reliquit, qui commeatus Byllide
5   atque Amantia importari in oppidum prohibebat. Ipse Lissum profectus naves onerarias XXX a M. Antonio relictas
intra portum aggressus omnes incendit. Lissum expugnare
conatus, defendentibus civibus Romanis qui eius conventus erant militibusque quos praesidi causa miserat Caesar,
triduum moratus paucis in oppugnatione amissis re infecta
inde discessit.

    41. Caesar postquam Pompeium ad Asparagium esse
cognovit eodem cum exercitu profectus expugnato in itinere oppido Parthinorum, in quo Pompeius praesidium
habebat, tertio die [Macedoniam] ad Pompeium pervenit
iuxtaque eum castra posuit. Et postridie eductis omnibus
copiis acie instructa decernendi potestatem Pompeio fe-
2   cit. Vbi illum suis locis se tenere animadvertit reducto in
castra exercitu aliud sibi consilium capiendum existimavit.
3   Itaque postero die omnibus copiis magno circuitu difficili
angustoque itinere Dyrrachium profectus est sperans
Pompeium aut Dyrrachium compelli aut ab eo intercludi
posse, quod omnem commeatum totiusque belli appara-
4   tum eo contulisset. Vt accidit. Pompeius enim primo igno-

---

[60] See 3.30.7.

that had made the town a peninsula. He moved four biremes across it into the inner harbor, using rollers underneath and poles for propulsion. Attacking our warships   3
thus from both sides (they were moored and empty) he
towed away four of them and burned the rest. After fin-   4
ishing this task Gnaeus took Decimus Laelius from the
Asiatic fleet and left him there; Laelius began to prevent
the importation of supplies from Byllis and Amantia into
Oricum. Moving on to Lissus, Gnaeus attacked thirty   5
transport vessels that Antony had left inside the harbor,
burning them all. He tried to take Lissus by storm. When
a defense was mounted by Roman citizens belonging to its
community association and soldiers sent by Caesar to garrison the town, Gnaeus lingered for three days, lost a few
men in the attack, and left the place without accomplishing his purpose.

41. When Caesar learned that Pompey was at Asparagium,[60] he headed there himself with his army. On the way,
he stormed a town of the Parthini in which Pompey had a
garrison. He reached Pompey on the third day and made
camp beside him. The next day he led out all of his forces,
drew up his line, and gave Pompey a chance to decide
matters militarily. When he noticed that Pompey was   2
holding his position, he led his army back to camp, thinking that he would have to adopt a different plan. Therefore   3
the next day he set out for Dyrrachium with all of his
forces, taking a difficult and narrow route involving a substantial detour. His hope was that Pompey could either be
forced to go to Dyrrachium or cut off from it, given that
Pompey had conveyed there all of his supplies and his
whole stock of military equipment. And so it happened.
For Pompey was unaware of Caesar's plan at first, since he   4

rans eius consilium quod diverso ab ea regione itinere profectum videbat angustiis rei frumentariae compulsum discessisse existimabat. Postea per exploratores certior factus postero die castra movit breviore itinere se occur-
5 rere ei posse sperans. Quod fore suspicatus Caesar militesque adhortatus ut aequo animo laborem ferrent parva parte noctis itinere intermisso mane Dyrrachium venit cum primum agmen Pompei procul cerneretur atque ibi castra posuit.

42. Pompeius interclusus Dyrrachio ubi propositum tenere non potuit secundo usus consilio edito loco, qui appellatur Petra aditumque habet navibus mediocrem atque eas a quibusdam protegit ventis, castra communit.
2 Eo partem navium longarum convenire, frumentum commeatumque ab Asia atque omnibus regionibus quas tene-
3 bat comportari imperat. Caesar longius bellum ductum iri existimans et de Italicis commeatibus desperans quod tanta diligentia omnia litora a Pompeianis tenebantur classesque ipsius quas hieme in Sicilia Gallia Italia fecerat morabantur, in Epirum rei frumentariae causa Q. Tillium et L. Canuleium legatos[58] misit. Quodque hae regiones aberant longius locis certis horrea constituit vecturasque
4 frumenti finitimis civitatibus discripsit. Item Lisso Parthinisque et omnibus castellis quod esset frumenti conquiri
5 iussit. Id erat perexiguum cum ipsius agri natura, quod sunt loca aspera ac montuosa ac plerumque frumento utuntur importato, tum quod Pompeius haec providebat et superioribus diebus praedae loco Parthinos habuerat

[58] legatos *V*: -tum *MUST*

saw him taking a path going in a direction away from that area, and thought that he had been forced to leave by supply difficulties; later he received information from his scouts. He struck camp the next day, hoping that his shorter route would allow him to confront Caesar. Suspecting that this would happen, Caesar urged his soldiers to endure hardship steadily, and despite a halt lasting a small part of the night reached Dyrrachium early in the morning as the front of Pompey's column came into view in the distance. He made camp there.

42. Pompey was cut off from Dyrrachium. Unable to achieve his purpose, he adopted a second plan, fortifying a camp on a height called Petra; this is reasonably accessible to ships and protects them from some winds. He ordered some of his warships to muster there, and provisions and supplies to be transported from Asia and all of the regions he controlled. Caesar thought that the war was going to be drawn out, and had given up hope of convoys from Italy, since every coastline was controlled so diligently by the Pompeians and his own fleets were slow in coming. (He had had them built during the winter in Sicily, Gaul, and Italy.) So he sent his officers Quintus Tillius and Lucius Canuleius to Epirus to arrange for provisions, and because those regions were quite far away he established grain depots in specific locations and assigned to nearby communities the responsibility for transport. He also ordered a search for whatever grain there was in Lissus, among the Parthini, and in all of the outposts. The quantities were extremely meager both because of the nature of the terrain, since these places are rugged and hilly and generally need imported grain, and because Pompey had taken precautions: treating the Parthini as

frumentumque omne conquisitum spoliatis effossisque
eorum domibus per equites in Petram comportarat.

43. Quibus rebus cognitis Caesar consilium capit ex
loci natura. Erant enim circum castra Pompei permulti
editi atque asperi colles. Hos primum praesidiis tenuit
2 castellaque ibi communiit. Inde ut loci cuiusque natura
ferebat ex castello in castellum perducta munitione cir-
3 cumvallare Pompeium instituit, haec expectans[59]—quod
angusta re frumentaria utebatur quodque Pompeius multitudine equitum valebat—quo minore periculo undique
frumentum commeatumque exercitui supportare posset,
simul uti pabulatione Pompeium prohiberet equitatumque eius ad rem gerendam inutilem efficeret, tertio ut
auctoritatem, qua ille maxime apud exteras nationes niti
videbatur, minueret, cum fama per orbem terrarum per-
crebuisset: illum a Caesare obsideri neque audere proelio
dimicare.

44. Pompeius neque a mari Dyrrachioque discedere
volebat, quod omnem apparatum belli—tela arma tormenta—ibi collocaverat frumentumque exercitui navibus
supportabat, neque munitiones Caesaris prohibere poterat nisi proelio decertare vellet. Quod eo tempore statue-
2 rat non esse faciendum. Relinquebatur ut extremam rationem belli sequens quam plurimos colles occuparet et
quam latissimas regiones praesidiis teneret Caesarisque
3 copias quam maxime posset distineret. Idque accidit. Castellis enim XXIIII effectis XV milia passuum circuitu

---

[59] expectans ω: sp- *Vascosan*

---

[61] For "expectations," Vascosan substituted "objectives," which
entails the removal of "would" later in the sentence.

war booty, he sought out all of their grain and had his cavalry transport it to Petra, ransacking their houses and leaving them dug up.

43. After learning of these matters Caesar adopted a plan suited to the terrain. (Around Pompey's camp there were numerous high and rugged hills.) To begin with, he used garrisons to hold them and built fortified outposts there. Then he began to wall Pompey in with a fortification 2 running from outpost to outpost insofar as the terrain allowed. His expectations[61]—given that his provisions were 3 scanty and Pompey had a numerical superiority in cavalry—were these: that he would be able to transport grain and other supplies to his army with less danger and from every direction; also that he would prevent Pompey from foraging, and render his cavalry useless for action; and thirdly that he would undermine Pompey's apparent authority, especially with foreign nations, when the story spread worldwide that Pompey was besieged by Caesar and did not dare fight a battle.

44. Pompey was unwilling to distance himself from the sea and Dyrrachium, because he had deposited all of his military equipment—projectiles, arms, catapults—in Dyrrachium and was using ships to provision his army. But he was also unable to block Caesar's fortifications unless he was willing decide matters with a battle, which he had decided should not be done at that time. It remained to 2 pursue the final military option: occupy as many hills as possible, hold as much territory as he could with garrisons, and extend Caesar's forces as much as possible. And this is what occurred. Pompey built twenty-four outposts and 3 enclosed within a fifteen-mile circuit a space that he used

amplexus hoc spatio pabulabatur, multaque erant intra
eum locum manu sata quibus interim iumenta pasceret.

4 Atque ut nostri perpetuas munitiones addebant perductas[60] ex castellis in proxima castella—ne quo loco erumperent Pompeiani ac nostros post tergum adorirentur timebant[61]—ita illi interiore spatio perpetuas munitiones
efficiebant ne quem locum nostri intrare atque ipsos a
5 tergo circumvenire possent. Sed illi operibus vincebant
quod et numero militum praestabant et interiore spatio
6 minorem circuitum habebant. Quaecumque erant loca
Caesari capienda—etsi prohibere Pompeius totis copiis et
dimicare non constituerat tamen suis locis sagittarios funditores mittebat, quorum magnum habebat numerum,
7 multique ex nostris vulnerabantur magnusque incesserat
timor sagittarum, atque omnes fere milites aut ex coactis
aut ex centonibus aut ex coriis tunicas aut tegimenta fecerant quibus tela vitarent.

45. In occupandis praesidiis magna vi uterque niteba-
tur, Caesar ut quam angustissime Pompeium contineret,
Pompeius ut quam plurimos colles quam maximo circuitu
2 occuparet. Crebraque ob eam causam proelia fiebant. In
his cum legio Caesaris nona praesidium quoddam occupavisset et munire coepisset huic loco propinquum et contrarium collem Pompeius occupavit nostrosque opere
3 prohibere coepit. Et cum una ex parte prope aequum
aditum haberet primum sagittariis funditoribusque circu-
miectis postea levis armaturae magna multitudine missa
tormentisque prolatis munitiones impediebat, neque erat

---

[60] addebant perductas *Weber*: videbant perductas *ω*
[61] *From* nostri . . . timebant *the text is very uncertain*.

for foraging; within this area there were many crops with which he could feed his pack animals meanwhile. Just as 4 our men were adding continuous fortifications running from outpost to adjacent outpost—they worried that the Pompeians would make a sortie somewhere and attack our men on the rear—so the enemy were producing continuous fortifications inside them so that our men would not be able to enter somewhere and surround them from behind.[62] But the Pompeians were beginning to prevail in 5 the works, since they were superior in manpower and had a shorter circuit, being on the inside. Whatever positions 6 Caesar had to occupy, Pompey, although he had decided not to use his whole force to prevent him or to engage, nevertheless sent out archers and slingers, of whom he had a great many, and many of our men were taking wounds, 7 plus there was a great fear of arrows. Indeed almost all of the soldiers had made shirts or cloaks of felt or patchwork or hides in order to escape the projectiles.

45. Each side exerted itself with great vigor in occupying positions, Caesar in order to confine Pompey within the narrowest limits, Pompey in order to occupy as many hills as possible in the widest circuit. Frequent clashes occurred because of this. In one of them, after Caesar's 2 ninth legion occupied a certain position and began to fortify it, Pompey occupied a hill adjacent to and facing this position and began to hinder our men in their work. From 3 one direction he had a nearly level approach and repeatedly blocked the fortifications, first by surrounding the position with archers and slingers, then by sending a large mass of light-armed troops and bringing forward cata-

[62] The text of this sentence is uncertain, but its point is clear.

4 facile nostris uno tempore propugnare et munire. Caesar
cum suos ex omnibus partibus vulnerari videret recipere
5 se iussit et loco excedere. Erat per declive receptus. Illi
autem hoc acrius instabant neque regredi nostros patiebantur, quod timore adducti locum relinquere videbantur.
6 Dicitur eo tempore glorians apud suos Pompeius dixisse:
non recusare se quin nullius usus imperator existimaretur
si sine maximo detrimento legiones Caesaris sese rece-
pissent inde quo temere essent progressae.

46. Caesar receptui suorum timens crates ad extremum
tumulum contra hostem proferri et adversas locari, intra
has mediocri latitudine fossam tectis militibus[62] obduci
iussit locumque in omnes partes quam maxime impediri.
2 Ipse idoneis locis funditores instruxit ut praesidio nostris
se recipientibus essent. His rebus completis legionem
3 reduci iussit. Pompeiani hoc insolentius atque audacius
nostros premere et instare coeperunt cratesque pro muni-
4 tione obiectas propulerunt ut fossas transcenderent. Quod
cum animadvertisset Caesar, veritus ne non reducti sed
deiecti viderentur maiusque detrimentum caperetur, a
medio fere spatio suos per Antonium, qui ei legioni praeerat, cohortatus tuba signum dari atque in hostes impetum
5 fieri iussit. Milites legionis nonae subito conspirati pila

---

[62] tectis militibus ω. *Perhaps* tectis longuriis?

---

[63] The plural is suspect.
[64] For "under their protection soldiers dig a trench of moderate width," it might be better to read "downhill of these a trench
of moderate width with hidden stakes be dug," in order to set up
"the concealed stakes" at 3.46.5. Vielhaber proposed excising the
latter phrase.

pults, and it was not easy for our men to resist and fortify at the same time. When Caesar saw that his men were 4 taking wounds from every direction, he ordered them to withdraw and leave their position; the retreat was downhill. The enemy, however, began applying more intense 5 pressure and refusing to allow our men to retreat, since it looked like fear had induced them to abandon their position. On that occasion Pompey is said to spoken boastfully 6 to his friends: "I don't object to your thinking me a useless commander if Caesar's legions[63] manage to withdraw without huge damage from the position to which they have rashly advanced."

46. Fearing for his men's retreat Caesar ordered brushwood bundles to be brought forward against the enemy to the top of the hill and placed frontally. Under their protection the soldiers were to dig a trench of moderate width as a barrier[64] and the place was to be rendered as impassible as possible in every direction. He himself stationed 2 slingers in suitable positions to protect our men as they withdrew. When these arrangements were complete he ordered the legion to be led back. At this the Pompeians 3 began to press and close in on our men more insolently and boldly, pushing the defensive obstacle of brushwood bundles out of their way so that they could cross the trench segments. When Caesar noticed this he worried that it 4 would look like a rout of his men rather than a retreat, and that they would take more damage. So at about the halfway point, after rallying them with Antony's help (he was in command of the legion), he ordered the signal to be sounded and an attack made on the enemy. The soldiers 5 of the ninth legion immediately pulled together and

coniecerunt et ex inferiore loco adversus clivum incitati cursu praecipites Pompeianos egerunt et terga vertere coegerunt. Quibus ad recipiendum crates derectae[63] longuriique obtecti[64] et institutae fossae magno impedimento

6 fuerunt. Nostri vero, qui satis habebant sine detrimento discedere, compluribus interfectis, V omnino suorum amissis quietissime receperunt pauloque citra eum locum aliis comprehensis collibus munitiones perfecerunt.

47. Erat nova et inusitata belli ratio cum tot castello-rum numero tantoque spatio et tantis munitionibus et toto

2 obsidionis genere tum etiam reliquis rebus. Nam quicum-que alterum obsidere conati sunt perculsos atque infirmos hostes adorti aut proelio superatos aut aliqua offensione permotos continuerunt cum ipsi numero equitum mili-tumque praestarent. Causa autem obsidionis haec fere

3 esse consuevit ut frumento hostes prohiberent. At tum integras atque incolumes copias Caesar inferiore militum numero continebat cum illi omnium rerum copia abun-darent. Cotidie enim magnus undique navium numerus conveniebat quae commeatum supportarent, neque ullus flare ventus poterat quin aliqua ex parte secundum cur-

4 sum haberent. Ipse autem consumptis omnibus longe la-
5 teque frumentis summis erat in angustiis. Sed tamen haec singulari patientia milites ferebant. Recordabantur enim eadem se superiore anno in Hispania perpessos labore et patientia maximum bellum confecisse, meminerant ad

---

63 derectae ω: deiectae *Vielhaber*
64 [longuriique obtecti] *Vielhaber*

---

65 For "lines of," Vielhaber proposed "displaced."

hurled their spears. With a running charge from below uphill, they drove the Pompeians headlong and forced them to turn back. In their retreat the enemy found the lines of brushwood bundles,[65] the concealed stakes, and the unfinished trench segments to be a significant obstacle. Our men, however, who considered it enough to get away without damage, withdrew unprotestingly after killing several of the enemy, having lost altogether five of their own. After taking some other hills a little further out, they finished the fortifications. 6

47. It was a new and untried strategy, considering not only the number of outposts, the size of the area, the length of the fortifications, and the general type of blockade, but other things as well. For all others who have tried to blockade someone have attacked and confined enemies that have been demoralized and weak, or defeated in battle, or cowed by some reverse, while they themselves have had numerical superiority in cavalry and infantry. Moreover, the purpose of a blockade is generally to keep the enemy from getting provisions. But on that occasion Caesar was trying to contain a force that was whole and unscathed with a smaller number of soldiers. Plus, the enemy had an abundant stock of everything, for a great number of ships converged every day bringing supplies from every direction, and every wind that blew made for good sailing from some direction. He himself, however, was in great difficulties, since all of the grain crops far and wide had been consumed. But the soldiers nevertheless tolerated their sufferings with remarkable patience. (They reminded themselves that they had suffered the same things the previous year in Spain, and that with effort and patience they had brought a very important war to conclu- 2

3

4

5

Alesiam magnam se inopiam perpessos, multo etiam maiorem ad Avaricum, maximarum se gentium victores dis-
6 cessisse. Non illis hordeum cum daretur, non legumina
recusabant. Pecus vero, cuius rei summa erat ex Epiro
copia, magno in honore habebant. 48. Est etiam genus
radicis inventum ab iis qui fuerant †valeribus†[65] quod
appellatur chara, quod admixtum lacte multum inopiam
2 levabat. [Id ad similitudinem panis efficiebant.][66] Eius
erat magna copia. Ex hoc effectos panes, cum in colloquiis
Pompeiani famem nostris obiectarent, vulgo in eos iaciebant ut spem eorum minuerent.

49. Iamque frumenta maturescere incipiebant atque
ipsa spes inopiam sustentabat quod celeriter se habituros
copiam confidebant. Crebraeque voces militum in vigiliis
colloquiisque audiebantur: prius se cortice ex arboribus
2 victuros quam Pompeium e manibus dimissuros. Libenter
etiam ex perfugis cognoscebant equos eorum tolerari,[67]
reliqua vero iumenta interisse; uti autem ipsos valetudine
non bona, cum angustiis loci et odore taetro ex multitudine cadaverum et cotidianis laboribus insuetos operum,
3 tum aquae summa inopia adfectos. Omnia enim flumina
atque omnes rivos qui ad mare pertinebant Caesar aut
averterat aut magnis operibus obstruxerat, atque ut erant

---

[65] fuerant in vallibus *Nipperdey*: f- in Balearibus *Herzog*: f- in
operibus *Kindscher*: f- ab alebribus *Holder*: vivebant oleribus
Madvig
[66] [Id . . . efficiebant.] *Vielhaber*
[67] ‹vix› tolerari *Manutius*

---

[66] Spain: 1.48–52. Alesia and Avaricum: *BG* 7.68–90 and 17.
[67] No emendation so far proposed is persuasive.

sion. They remembered that after suffering great scarcity at Alesia, and even more at Avaricum, they had left the field as conquerors of supremely great peoples.[66]) When given barley they did not object, nor beans. As for herd animals, of which there was a large supply in Epirus, they valued them highly. 48. There was also a kind of root vegetable, found by those who had been . . .[67] This was called "chara," and mixed with milk it did much to alleviate the scarcity; the supply was abundant. They made loaves from it, and when the Pompeians, in crosstalk, referred mockingly to their hunger, our men generally threw these at them to lessen their hopes.

49. In addition, the grain crops were already beginning to ripen, and hope itself parried the scarcity, since the men were confident that they would soon have plenty. There was a saying among the soldiers on watch and in crosstalk: "We will eat the bark from the trees before we let Pompey out of our grasp." They were also pleased to learn from deserters that, while the enemy's horses were being kept alive,[68] the rest of their pack animals had perished, and the men themselves were not in good health, suffering both from the limited space and the foul odor of numerous corpses and their daily labors—they were unaccustomed to working—and from an extreme shortage of water, for Caesar had either diverted or obstructed with large earthworks all of the rivers and streams that ran to the sea. Indeed, insofar as the area was hilly and the ravines' nar-

6

2

2

3

[68] Madvig proposed adding "barely" before "being kept alive."

loca montuosa et ut specus angustiae[68] vallium, has subli-
cis in terram demissis praesaepserat terramque aggesserat
4 ut aquam continerent. Ita illi necessario loca sequi de-
missa ac palustria et puteos fodere cogebantur atque hunc
laborem ad cotidiana opera addebant. Qui tamen fontes a
quibusdam praesidiis aberant longius et celeriter aestibus
5 exarescebant. At Caesaris exercitus optima valetudine
summaque aquae copia utebatur. Tum commeatus omni
genere praeter frumentum abundabat. Quibus cotidie
melius succedere[69] tempus maioremque spem maturitate
frumentorum proponi videbant.

50. In novo genere belli novae ab utrisque bellandi
rationes reperiebantur. Illi cum animadvertissent ex igni-
bus noctu cohortes nostras ad munitiones excubare, silentio aggressi universas[70] inter multitudinem sagittas con-
2 iciebant et se confestim ad suos recipiebant. Quibus rebus
nostri usu docti haec reperiebant remedia, ut alio loco
ignes facerent . . .

51. Interim certior factus P. Sulla, quem discedens castris praefecerat Caesar, auxilio cohorti venit cum legioni-

[68] ut specus angustiae *Menge*: ad s- a- ω: instar specuum a-
Freudenberg: asperae a- *Wölffel*: fauces angustae *Schiller*

[69] succedere *ed. pr.*: subte(r)rere ω: se terere *Madvig. Perhaps*
sibi cedere?

[70] universas ω: universi *Nipperdey*: ignes versus *Jurin*

[69] For Menge's emendation "narrows were like a water conduit," others propose "narrows functioned as water conduits,"
"narrows were steep," and "outlets were narrow."

[70] For the first edition's emendation "the time was going by
better," Madvig proposed "they were passing the time." Another
possibility is "the occasion was turning out better for them."

rows were like a water conduit,[69] he had barricaded the ravines with poles sunk into the ground, heaping up earth in order to hold back the water. The enemy was thus nec- 4 essarily compelled to have recourse to low-lying and marshy areas and to dig wells, and this effort was an addition to their daily labors. Even so, their sources were at a considerable distance from some of the guard posts and dried up quickly in the heat. But Caesar's army had excel- 5 lent health and a very large supply of water at its disposal. For the moment, it had an abundance of every kind of provisions except grain, and the men saw that thanks to these the time was going by better[70] each day, and that a greater hope lay ahead in the ripeness of the grain crops.

50. This being a new type of warfare, new combat methods were devised by each side. The enemy, when they noticed from the fires at night that our cohorts were doing guard duty beside the fortifications, would approach noiselessly and shoot a volley of arrows[71] into their midst, then return immediately to their own lines. Learning from 2 experience, our men devised the following remedies for this: they would build their fires in one place . . .[72]

51. Meanwhile, Publius Sulla, whom Caesar put in charge of the camp when he left, upon being informed of this came to the cohort's aid with two legions; at Sulla's

[71] For "shoot a volley of arrows," Nipperdey and Jurin proposed "shoot their arrows as one" and "shoot their arrows in the direction of the fires," respectively.

[72] Some text has been lost here, perhaps as much as a page. In the following paragraphs, there are references to events that must have been reported in this lacuna.

bus duabus. Cuius adventu facile sunt repulsi Pompeiani.

2 Neque vero conspectum aut impetum nostrorum tulerunt, primisque deiectis reliqui se verterunt et loco cesse-

3 runt. Sed insequentes nostros, ne longius prosequerentur, Sulla revocavit. At plerique existimant: si acrius insequi voluisset, bellum eo die potuisse finiri. Cuius consilium

4 reprehendendum non videtur. Aliae enim sunt legati partes atque imperatoris. Alter omnia agere ad praescriptum,

5 alter libere ad summam rerum consulere debet. Sulla a Caesare ⟨in⟩ castris relictus liberatis suis hoc fuit contentus neque proelio decertare voluit—quae res tamen fortasse aliquem reciperet casum—ne imperatorias sibi

6 partes sumpsisse videretur. Pompeianis magnam res ad receptum difficultatem adferebat. Nam ex iniquo progressi loco in summo constiterant. Si per declive sese reciperent nostros ex superiore insequentes loco verebantur. Neque multum ad solis occasum temporis supererat. Spe enim conficiendi negoti prope in noctem rem deduxerant.

7 Ita necessario atque ex tempore capto consilio Pompeius tumulum quendam occupavit qui tantum aberat a nostro castello ut telum tormentumve missum adigi non posset. Hoc consedit loco atque eum communivit omnesque ibi copias continuit.

52. Eodem tempore duobus praeterea locis pugnatum est. Nam plura castella Pompeius pariter distinendae manus causa temptaverat ne ex proximis praesidiis succurri

2 posset. Vno loco Volcacius Tullus impetum legionis sustinuit cohortibus tribus atque eam loco depulit, altero Ger-

arrival the Pompeians were easily driven back. In fact, 2
they did not endure the sight or the onset of our men, but
after the firstcomers were dislodged the rest turned
around and abandoned their position. But Sulla recalled 3
our men from the pursuit to prevent them from advancing
too far. (Most people think that if he had been willing to
pursue more aggressively the war could have been finished that day. But his decision does not seem to deserve
criticism, for officers and commanders have different 4
roles. The one ought to do everything as instructed, the
other to act freely in view of the overall situation. Sulla had 5
been left by Caesar in camp, and once his men had been
extricated he was content with this and unwilling to decide
matters with a battle—which might have a disastrous outcome—lest people think he had assumed the commander's role.) His action gave the Pompeians great difficulty 6
in their retreat, for they had advanced from a position of
disadvantage and halted on the summit, and were worried
about our men pursuing from above if they retreated
downhill. Nor was there much time left before sunset, for
they had prolonged the action practically until dark in the
hope of finishing the operation. So Pompey, improvising, 7
was forced to occupy a certain hill far enough away from
our camp to be out of reach of projectiles discharged by
hand or catapult. He established himself there, fortified
the position, and kept his whole force inside it.

52. There were battles in two other places at this same
time, for Pompey had made similar attacks on several outposts to spread the enemy forces, aiming to prevent the
possibility of assistance coming from the closest garrisons.
In one place Volcacius Tullus and three cohorts withstood 2
the attack of a legion and drove it off, in another some

mani munitiones nostras egressi compluribus interfectis
sese ad suos incolumes receperunt.

53. Ita uno die VI proeliis factis—tribus ad Dyrrachium, tribus ad munitiones—cum horum omnium ratio
haberetur ad duo milia numero ex Pompeianis cecidisse
reperiebamus, evocatos centurionesque complures. In eo
fuit numero Valerius Flaccus L. filius eius qui praetor
2 Asiam obtinuerat. Signaque sunt militaria VI relata. Nostri
3 non amplius XX omnibus sunt proeliis desiderati. Sed in
castello nemo fuit omnino militum quin vulneraretur,
4 IIIIque ex una[71] cohorte centuriones oculos amiserunt. Et
cum laboris sui periculique testimonium adferre vellent
milia sagittarum circiter XXX in castellum coniecta Caesari renumeraverunt. Scutoque ad eum relato Scaevae
5 centurionis inventa sunt in eo foramina CCXXX.[72] Quem
Caesar, ut erat de se meritus et de re publica, donatum
milibus †CC atque†[73] ab octavis ordinibus ad primipilum
se traducere pronuntiavit. Eius enim ope castellum magna
ex parte conservatum esse constabat. Cohortemque postea
duplici stipendio frumento vestiariis[74] militaribusque do-
nis amplissime donavit.

54. Pompeius noctu magnis additis munitionibus reliquis diebus turres extruxit et in altitudinem pedum XV

71 una] VIII[a] *Paul*

72 CCXXX *MU*: CCXX *STV*: CXX *in V. Max. 3.2.23, Suet.* Jul.
68.4, Flor. Epit. *2.13.40, App.* BC *2.60.249,* ἑκατὸν καὶ τριάκο-
ντα *in Plut.* Caes. *16.3*

73 *The text cannot be restored with any certainty here.*

74 vestiariis *Nicasius*: vespe(t/c)iariis ω: veste cibariis *Cujas*

73 Only three are reported in the text as we have it.

Germans went outside the fortifications, killed a few of the enemy, and withdrew unscathed to their own lines.

53. Thus in one day there were six battles: three at Dyrrachium, three beside the fortifications.[73] When a tally was made of all of them, we found that around two thousand of the Pompeians had fallen, a few of them reenlisted men and centurions. In this group was Valerius Flaccus, the son of the Lucius Flaccus who had been a praetorian governor of Asia. In addition, six military standards were captured. No more than twenty of our men were lost in all 2 of the battles. But in the outpost every single man had 3 taken a wound, and four centurions from that one cohort[74] had lost an eye. When the men wanted to provide evi- 4 dence of their dangerous struggle, they counted out for Caesar about thirty thousand arrows that had been shot into their outpost. The shield of the centurion Scaeva, when brought to him, was found to have been pierced 230 times.[75] In view of his services to himself and the re- 5 public, Caesar announced that Scaeva had been given a reward of . . .[76] and that he was promoting him from the eighth rank to chief centurion, for everyone agreed that the outpost was saved mostly by his help. Caesar later rewarded his cohort very generously with double pay, food and clothing allowances,[77] and military decorations.

54. Pompey added largely to his fortifications during the night. On subsequent days he built towers, and after

[74] For "from that one cohort," Paul proposed "from the eighth cohort," to explain "from the eighth rank" below.
[75] The number is suspect.   [76] The details are lost in a textual corruption.   [77] For "food and clothing allowances," Cujas proposed "grain, clothing, rations."

2 effectis operibus vineis eam partem castrorum obtexit. Et
V intermissis diebus alteram noctem subnubilam nactus
obstructis omnibus castrorum portis et ad impediendum
obiectis tertia inita vigilia silentio exercitum eduxit et se in
antiquas munitiones recepit.

55. Aetolia Acarnania Amphilochis per Cassium Longinum et Calvisium Sabinum, ut demonstravimus, recep-
tis temptandam sibi Achaiam ac paulo longius progredien-
2 dum existimabat Caesar. Itaque eo Q. Calenum misit
3 eique Sabinum et Cassium cum cohortibus adiungit. Quorum cognito adventu Rutilius Lupus, qui Achaiam missus
a Pompeio obtinebat, Isthmum praemunire instituit ut
4 Achaia Fufium prohiberet. Calenus Delphos Thebas et
Orchomenum voluntate ipsarum civitatum recepit, nonnullas urbes per vim expugnavit. Reliquas civitates circummissis legationibus amicitia Caesari conciliare studebat. In his rebus fere erat Fufius occupatus.

56. Omnibus deinceps diebus Caesar exercitum in
aciem aequum in locum produxit si Pompeius proelio
decertare vellet, ut paene castris Pompei legiones subiceret. Tantumque a vallo eius prima acies aberat uti ne
2 telo tormentove adigi posset. Pompeius autem ut famam
opinionemque hominum teneret sic pro castris exercitum
constituebat ut tertia acies vallum contingeret, omnis quidem instructus exercitus telis ex vallo abiectis protegi posset.

57. Haec cum in Achaia atque apud Dyrrachium ge-

---

[78] If the number of cohorts was specified in the original, it has
been lost; Plutarch mentions fifteen (*Caes.* 43.1). The commander of the expedition was Quintus Fufius Calenus; his three
names are distributed oddly in this paragraph.

his works reached a height of fifteen feet he protected that
part of his camp with screens. He let five days elapse, then   2
got another overcast night. After building and heaping
obstructions at all of the camp's gates to make them impassable, he led his army out in silence at midnight and
returned to his former fortifications.

55. After recovering Aetolia, Acarnania, and the people
of Amphilochia thanks to Cassius Longinus and Calvisius
Sabinus, as I indicated, Caesar began to think that he
ought to try Achaea and make a little further progress. So   2
he sent Quintus Calenus there in tandem with Sabinus
and Cassius and their cohorts.[78] Upon learning of their   3
approach Rutilius Lupus, who had been sent by Pompey
and controlled Achaea, began to seal off the Isthmus in
order to keep Fufius out of Achaea. Calenus recovered   4
Delphi, Thebes, and Orchomenus by the communities'
own wishes; some cities he took by storm. He sent delegations around the remaining communities, eager to bring
them over to Caesar in friendship. By and large this is what
Fufius spent his time on.

56. Every day thereafter Caesar led his army out onto
level ground for battle, in case Pompey wanted to decide
matters by a fight, positioning his legions practically adjacent to Pompey's camp. Indeed the distance from Pompey's rampart to Caesar's front line was just enough that
projectiles thrown or shot could not reach it. Pompey,   2
however, wanting to retain his general renown and reputation, placed his army in front of the camp with the third
line touching the rampart and his whole force drawn up
in such a way that weapons cast from the rampart could
cover it.

57. With these operations under way in Achaea and

rerentur Scipionemque in Macedoniam venisse constaret
non oblitus pristini instituti Caesar mittit ad eum A. Clodium, suum atque illius familiarem, quem ab illo traditum
initio et commendatum in suorum necessariorum numero
2 habere instituerat. Huic dat litteras mandataque ad eum,
quorum haec erat summa: sese omnia de pace expertum
nihil adhuc[75] arbitrari vitio factum eorum quos esse auctores eius rei voluisset quod sua mandata perferre non
3 opportuno tempore ad Pompeium vererentur; Scipionem
ea esse auctoritate ut non solum libere quae probasset
exponere sed etiam ex magna parte compellare atque er-
rantem regere posset; praeesse autem suo nomine exercitui, ut praeter auctoritatem vires quoque ad coercen-
4 dum haberet; quod si fecisset, quietem Italiae, pacem
provinciarum, salutem imperi uni omnes acceptam rela-
5 turos. Haec ad eum mandata Clodius refert. Ac primis
diebus, ut videbatur, libenter auditus, reliquis ad colloquium non admittitur castigato Scipione a Favonio, ut
postea confecto bello reperiebamus. Infectaque re sese ad
Caesarem recepit.

58. Caesar quo facilius equitatum Pompeianum ad
Dyrrachium contineret et pabulatione prohiberet aditus
duos, quos esse angustos demonstravimus, magnis operi-
2 bus praemunivit castellaque his locis posuit. Pompeius ubi
nihil profici equitatu cognovit paucis intermissis diebus
3 rursus eum navibus ad se intra munitiones recepit. Erat

---

[75] *After* adhuc *Meusel supplied* ‹effecisse; hoc›.

---

[79] The narrative was presumably in the lacuna (note 72).

near Dyrrachium and the reports consistent that Scipio had reached Macedonia, Caesar, still having his original initiative in mind, sent Aulus Clodius to him. Clodius had connections to each of them; Caesar began to consider him as one of his own friends after Scipio first sent him along with a recommendation. Caesar gave Clodius a let- 2 ter and a message to Scipio, of which these were the key points: "In my opinion, given that I have tried for peace by every possible means, it is the fault of the men whom I wanted to be its prime movers that nothing has been done, since they were afraid to present my message to Pompey at an inopportune time. You, Scipio, have the 3 authority not only to explain freely whatever plan you approve, but also to be able to confront and correct missteps. You command an army in your own name, so that beyond authority you have the power to apply coercion. And if you 4 do so, everyone will credit you with having brought about calm for Italy, peace for the provinces, and salvation for the empire." Clodius took this message to Scipio. At first 5 he was heard willingly, or so it seemed, but thereafter he was not admitted to discussions, once Scipio had received a scolding from Favonius. (So I learned later, after the end of the war.) Clodius returned to Caesar without accomplishing his business.

58. In order to make it easier to confine Pompey's cavalry at Dyrrachium and prevent it from foraging, Caesar sealed off the two approaches (which were narrow, as I indicated[79]) with substantial earthworks, establishing strongholds there. When Pompey realized that his cavalry 2 was accomplishing nothing, he let a few days elapse, then brought them back by sea to where he was, inside the original fortifications. Fodder was extremely scarce, so 3

summa inopia pabuli, adeo ut foliis ex arboribus strictis et teneris harundinum radicibus contusis equos alerent. Frumenta enim quae fuerant intra munitiones sata con-

4 sumpserant. Cogebantur Corcyra atque Acarnania longo interiecto navigationis spatio pabulum supportare quodque erat eius rei minor copia hordeo adaugere, atque his

5 rationibus equitatum tolerare. Sed postquam non modo hordeum pabulumque omnibus locis herbaeque desectae sed etiam frons ex arboribus deficiebat, corruptis equis macie conandum sibi aliquid Pompeius de eruptione existimavit.

59. Erant apud Caesarem ex equitum numero Allobroges duo fratres, Roucillus et Egus, Adbucilli filii qui principatum in civitate multis annis obtinuerat, singulari virtute homines, quorum opera Caesar omnibus Gallicis

2 bellis optima fortissimaque erat usus. His domi ob has causas amplissimos magistratus mandaverat atque eos extra ordinem in senatum legendos curaverat agrosque in Gallia ex hostibus captos praemiaque rei pecuniariae[76]

3 magna tribuerat locupletesque ex egentibus fecerat. Hi propter virtutem non solum apud Caesarem in honore erant sed etiam apud exercitum cari habebantur. Sed freti amicitia Caesaris et stulta ac barbara arrogantia elati despiciebant suos stipendiumque equitum fraudabant et

4 praedam omnem domum avertebant. Quibus illi rebus permoti universi Caesarem adierunt palamque de eorum iniuriis sunt questi et ad cetera addiderunt: falsum ab iis equitum numerum deferri quorum stipendium averterent.

60. Caesar neque tempus illud animadversionis esse

[76] pecuniariae] pecuariae *"consisting of livestock"* Paul

much so that they were feeding the horses with leaves stripped from trees and a mash made of the soft roots of reeds. (They had consumed the grain crops inside the fortifications.) They were compelled to supply fodder from 4 Corcyra and Acarnania, a long way away by boat, and, because there was too little of it, to supplement it with barley; with these measures they sustained the cavalry. But after not only barley and fodder and hay but also the 5 trees' foliage began to run short everywhere, and the horses were thin and wasted, Pompey thought that he ought to try to break out somehow.

59. Among the cavalry with Caesar were two Allobrogian brothers, Roucillius and Egus, sons of Adbucillus, who had been his community's leader for many years. They were men of remarkable prowess, and their service to Caesar in all of his Gallic campaigns had been excellent and valiant. For these reasons he had entrusted them with 2 the most important magistracies at home, arranged for them to be specially adlected into their senate, granted them captured territory in Gaul and substantial monetary prizes, and brought them from poverty to wealth. On ac- 3 count of their prowess they were not only valued by Caesar but also popular with the army. But, relying on Caesar's friendship and carried away by a foolish native pride, they treated their men with contempt, cheating the cavalry of its pay and diverting all of the booty to themselves. Dis- 4 mayed by these developments, the whole force approached Caesar, complaining openly about the injuries done by these men. A further complaint was that they were falsifying the cavalry numbers and pocketing the pay.

60. Caesar thought that this was not the moment for a

existimans et multa virtuti eorum concedens rem totam distulit. Illos secreto castigavit quod quaestui equites haberent monuitque ut ex sua amicitia omnia expectarent et
2 ex praeteritis suis officiis reliqua sperarent. Magnam tamen haec res illis offensionem et contemptionem ad omnes attulit. Idque ita esse cum ex aliorum obiectationibus tum etiam ex domestico iudicio atque animi conscientia
3 intellegebant. Quo pudore adducti—et fortasse non se liberari sed in aliud tempus reservari arbitrati—discedere ab nobis et novam temptare fortunam novasque amicitias
4 experiri constituerunt. Et cum paucis collocuti clientibus suis, quibus tantum facinus committere audebant, primum conati sunt praefectum equitum C. Volusenum interficere, ut postea bello confecto cognitum est, ut cum
5 munere aliquo perfugisse ad Pompeium viderentur. Postquam id facinus difficilius[77] visum est neque facultas perficiendi dabatur, quam maximas potuerunt pecunias mutuati proinde ac ‹si› suis satis facere et fraudata restituere vellent, multis coemptis equis ad Pompeium transierunt cum iis quos sui consili participes habebant.

61. Quos Pompeius quod erant honesto loco nati et instructi liberaliter magnoque comitatu et multis iumentis venerant virique fortes habebantur et in honore apud Caesarem fuerant—quodque novum et praeter consuetudinem acciderat—omnia sua praesidia circumduxit atque
2 ostentavit. Nam ante id tempus nemo aut miles aut eques a Caesare ad Pompeium transierat, cum paene cotidie a

---

[77] facinus difficilius *Clarke*: f- μ: facilius *T*: difficilius SV^c (V^{ac} *is illegible*)

punishment and made great allowances for their valor; he postponed the whole business, rebuking them in private for having taken financial advantage of the cavalry. He advised them to place all of their hopes in his friendship and to expect future benefits in line with past ones. Still, their behavior brought them great dislike and universal contempt, and they perceived that this was so both from other men's reproaches and from their own judgment and conscience. Induced by this shame—and thinking, perhaps, that they were being not acquitted but deferred—they decided to abandon us, try fortune anew, and test new friendships. After conferring with a few of their dependents, men with whom they dared share a deed of this enormity, they first attempted to kill the cavalry commander Gaius Volusenus (as was discovered later, after the conclusion of the war) so that people would think they had deserted to Pompey with some service to show. After the deed was found to be rather difficult, and no opportunity for carrying it out presented itself, they borrowed as much money as they could under the pretense of wanting to satisfy the claims of their men and restore the misappropriated funds, then bought a large number of horses and went over to Pompey accompanied by those with whom they had shared their plan.

61. Pompey made the rounds of his garrisons with them and showed them off, for their birth was respectable and their gear sumptuous, they had arrived with a large company and many animals, were reputed to be brave men, and had had Caesar's respect—plus, the event was an unusual novelty. (Before that point no one from the infantry or cavalry had crossed over from Caesar to Pompey, although there were practically daily desertions from

279

Pompeio ad Caesarem perfugerent, vulgo vero universi in Epiro atque Aetolia conscripti milites earumque regionum omnium quae a Caesare tenebantur. Sed hi cognitis omnibus rebus, seu quid in munitionibus perfectum non erat seu quid a peritioribus rei militaris desiderari videbatur, temporibusque rerum et spatiis locorum in custodiarum varia diligentia animadversis prout cuiusque eorum qui negotiis praeerant aut natura aut studium ferebat, haec ad Pompeium omnia detulerant.

62. Quibus ille cognitis eruptionisque iam ante capto consilio, ut demonstratum est, tegimenta galeis milites ex viminibus facere atque aggerem iubet comportare. His paratis rebus magnum numerum levis armaturae et sagittariorum aggeremque omnem noctu in scaphas et naves actuarias imponit. Et de media nocte cohortes LX ex maximis castris praesidiisque deductas ad eam partem munitionum ducit quae pertinebant ad mare longissimeque a maximis castris Caesaris aberant. Eodem naves quas demonstravimus aggere et levis armaturae militibus completas quasque ad Dyrrachium naves longas habebat mittit et quid a quoque fieri velit praecipit. Ad eas munitiones Caesar Lentulum Marcellinum quaestorem cum legione nona positum habebat. Huic, quod valetudine minus commoda utebatur, Fulvium Postumum adiutorem summiserat.

63. Erat eo loco fossa pedum XV et vallus contra hostem in altitudinem pedum X, tantundemque eius valli agger in latitudinem patebat. Ab eo intermisso spatio pedum DC alter conversus in contrariam partem erat vallus humiliore paulo munitione. Hoc enim superioribus diebus timens Caesar, ne navibus nostri circumvenirentur, dupli-

Pompey to Caesar, indeed mass desertions were common
among the soldiers enlisted in Epirus and Aetolia and all
the regions then held by Caesar.) Moreover, they knew 3
whatever was unfinished in the fortifications or seemed
inadequate to military experts, and had taken notice of the
timing of events and the distances between places in view
of the sentries' diligence, which varied according to the
nature or determination of the men in charge of operations, and had told Pompey everything.

62. After learning all of this Pompey, who had a break-
out plan already in hand, as was mentioned, ordered his
men to make wicker coverings for their helmets and to
assemble rubble. When these things were ready, and night 2
had fallen, he put a large number of light-armed soldiers
and archers and all of the rubble into longboats and fast
vessels. In the middle of the night he took sixty cohorts
from his main camp and garrisons and led them to the
section of fortifications where they reached the sea and
were as far as possible from Caesar's main camp. To the 3
same place he sent the ships that, as I indicated, were full
of rubble and men from light-armed units, as well as the
warships he had at Dyrrachium, and gave instructions
about what he wanted each to do. Caesar had stationed his 4
quaestor Lentulus Marcellinus at these fortifications with
the ninth legion, and since Lentulus was in rather poor
health he had sent Fulvius Postumus as an assistant.

63. At this location there was a fifteen-foot trench and
a rampart facing the enemy ten feet high, and the rampart's earthwork was equally wide. Six hundred feet away
there was a second rampart facing the other direction with
a slightly lower fortification. (During the preceding days 2
Caesar, worried that our men would be outflanked by

cem eo loco fecerat vallum ut si ancipiti proelio dimicare-
3 tur posset resisti. Sed operum magnitudo et continens
omnium dierum labor, quod milia passuum in circuitu
XVII [munitiones] erat[78] complexus, perficiendi spatium
4 non dabat. Itaque contra mare transversum vallum qui has
5 duas munitiones contingeret nondum perfecerat. Quae
res nota erat Pompeio, delata per Allobrogas perfugas,
6 magnumque nostris attulit incommodum. Nam ut ad mare
nostrae[79] cohortes nonae legionis excubuerant accessere
subito prima luce Pompeiani [exercitus adventus extitit].[80]
Simul navibus circumvecti milites in exteriorem vallum
tela iaciebant fossaeque aggere complebantur, et legionarii interioris munitionis defensores scalis admotis tormentis cuiusque generis telisque terrebant. Magnaque multitudo sagittariorum ab utraque parte circumfundebatur.
7 Multum autem ab ictu lapidum, quod unum nostris erat
telum, viminea tegimenta galeis imposita defendebant.
8 Itaque cum omnibus rebus nostri premerentur atque
aegre resisterent animadversum est vitium munitionis
quod supra demonstratum est, atque inter duos vallos, qua
perfectum opus non erat, per mare[81] navibus expositi in
aversos nostros impetum fecerunt atque ex utraque munitione deiectos terga vertere coegerunt.

[78] [munitiones] erat *Chacon*: -es e- *STV*: -es erant *MU*: -e erat
Clarke

[79] nostrae] II *Dederich*

[80] [exercitus adventus extitit] *Nipperdey, who also excised*
nonae legionis *above. Other repairs have been proposed.*

[81] per mare] Pompeiani *Paul*: [p- m-] *Nicasius*

---

[80] The number is suspect.

ships, had constructed this double rampart so that resistance would be possible if there was a fight on two sides at once. But with the scale of the works and the continuous 3 daily toil—given that his enclosure was seventeen miles[80] around—there was not time to finish.) So he had not yet 4 finished the transverse wall facing the sea, which was to extend from one fortification to the other. This fact was 5 known to Pompey, having been reported by the Allobrogian deserters, and it caused great harm to our men. For 6 the Pompeians arrived unexpectedly at first light where our cohorts[81] of the ninth legion had been doing guard duty by the sea. At one and the same moment the soldiers conveyed by boat were hurling weapons onto the outer rampart, the trenches were being filled with rubble, and legionaries were terrorizing the defenders of the inner fortification by bringing up ladders, catapults of every sort, and weapons. Plus, a great mass of archers was spreading around them from both sides. Furthermore, the wicker 7 coverings on the enemy helmets provided significant protection from the impact of stones, which were the only weapons our men had. Thus our men were under every 8 sort of pressure and were having trouble resisting when the above-mentioned flaw in the fortification was observed. The men conveyed by sea[82] were put ashore from the ships between the two ramparts, where the work was unfinished. They attacked our men from behind and after driving them away from both fortifications forced them to turn and run.

[81] For "our cohorts," Dederich proposed "two cohorts." Klotz excised "of the ninth legion" instead.   [82] For "by sea," Paul proposed "Pompeians," Nicasius excision.

64. Hoc tumultu nuntiato Marcellinus cohortes subsidio nostris laborantibus submittit ex castris. Quae fugientes conspicatae neque illos suo adventu confirmare
2 potuerunt neque ipsae hostium impetum tulerunt. Itaque quodcumque addebatur subsidio id corruptum[82] timore fugientium terrorem et periculum augebat. Hominum
3 enim multitudine receptus impediebatur. In eo proelio cum gravi vulnere esset adfectus aquilifer et a viribus deficeretur conspicatus equites nostros "Hanc ego" inquit "et vivus multos per annos magna diligentia defendi et nunc moriens eadem fide Caesari restituo. Nolite, obsecro, committere—quod ante in exercitu Caesaris non accidit—ut rei militaris dedecus admittatur, incolumemque
4 ad eum deferte." Hoc casu aquila conservatur omnibus primae cohortis centurionibus interfectis praeter principem priorem.

65. Iamque Pompeiani magna caede nostrorum castris Marcellini appropinquabant non mediocri terrore illato reliquis cohortibus, et M. Antonius, qui proximum locum praesidiorum tenebat, ea re nuntiata cum cohortibus XII descendens ex loco superiore cernebatur. Cuius adventus Pompeianos compressit nostrosque firmavit, ut se ex
2 maximo timore colligerent. Neque multo post Caesar— significatione per castella fumo facta, ut erat superioris temporis consuetudo—deductis quibusdam cohortibus ex
3 praesidiis eodem venit. Qui cognito detrimento, cum animadvertisset Pompeium extra munitiones egressum castra

---

[82] corruptum] correptum *Madvig*

---

[83] For "rendered useless," Madvig proposed "seized."

64. At news of this emergency Marcellinus sent cohorts from the camp to the support of our struggling men. The cohorts, seeing people running away, failed to steady the latter with their arrival and themselves gave way before the enemy's attack. Thus whatever was added by way of support was rendered useless[83] by the fugitives' fear and then increased the terror and danger, for the mass of men was an impediment to retreat. In this battle an eagle bearer, gravely wounded and with his strength failing, caught sight of our cavalry and said: "I have defended this eagle with great diligence through the many years of my life. Now that I am dying, loyal as ever I restore it to Caesar. My fellow soldiers, do not, I beg you, make us guilty of a military disgrace—something that has not happened before now in Caesar's army—but take it back safe to him." By this chance the eagle was saved, even though every centurion of the first cohort was killed except the second in command.

65. The Pompeians were already approaching Marcellinus' camp, after slaughtering large numbers of our men and inflicting no small amount of terror on the remaining cohorts, when Antony came into view. (He held the nearest of the garrisons and made his way down from a higher position with twelve cohorts when the situation was reported to him.) His arrival checked the Pompeians and put confidence into our men, so that they pulled themselves together after their utter panic. Soon thereafter Caesar arrived at the head of some garrison cohorts; the signal had been sent from outpost to outpost by smoke, as had been regular practice earlier. Caesar, perceiving the damage and noticing that Pompey had gone outside of his fortifications and ⟨was fortifying⟩ a camp alongside the

secundum mare ⟨munire⟩ ut libere pabulari posset nec
minus aditum navibus haberet, commutata ratione belli
quoniam propositum non tenuerat iuxta Pompeium munire iussit.

66. Qua perfecta munitione animadversum est ab spe-
culatoribus Caesaris cohortes quasdam, quod instar legionis videretur, esse post silvam et in vetera castra duci.
2 Castrorum hic situs erat. Superioribus diebus nona Caesaris legio, cum se obiecisset Pompeianis copiis atque
opere, ut demonstravimus, circummuniret, castra eo loco
3 posuit. Haec silvam quandam contingebant neque longius
4 a mari passibus CCC aberant. Post mutato consilio quibusdam de causis Caesar paulo ultra eum locum castra
transtulit. Paucisque intermissis diebus eadem haec Pompeius occupaverat. Et quod eo loco plures erat legiones
habiturus relicto interiore vallo maiorem adiecerat muni-
5 tionem. Ita minora castra inclusa maioribus castelli atque
6 arcis locum obtinebant. Item ab angulo castrorum sinistro
munitionem ad flumen perduxerat circiter passuum
CCCC quo liberius ac sine periculo milites aquarentur.
7 Sed is quoque mutato consilio quibusdam de causis, quas
commemorari necesse non est, eo loco excesserat. Ita
complures dies manserant[83] castra. Munitiones quidem
omnes integrae erant.

67. Eo signa legionis illata speculatores Caesari renun-
tiarunt. Hoc idem visum ex superioribus quibusdam castellis confirmaverunt. Is locus aberat ⟨a⟩ novis Pompei

[83] ⟨vacua⟩ manserant *Chacon*

sea in order to be able to get fodder freely as well as to have access to his ships, changed his plan of campaign—since he had not obtained his objective—and ordered his men to fortify alongside Pompey.

66. After the fortification was complete, Caesar's scouts noticed that some enemy cohorts amounting, it seemed, to a full legion, were behind a wood and were being taken back to an old camp. The situation at the camp was as fol- 2 lows. Some days earlier Caesar's ninth legion had made camp there after their confrontation with the Pompeian forces while encircling them with an earthwork, as I indicated.[84] The camp abutted a wooded area and was no more 3 than three hundred paces from the sea. Afterwards Caesar 4 changed his mind for a variety of reasons and moved his camp some way past this site. After a few days' interval Pompey occupied the camp. Since he was planning to keep more legions there, he extended its fortification but left the inner rampart alone. Thus the smaller camp en- 5 closed within the larger functioned as a stronghold and citadel. He also built a fortification running about four 6 hundred paces from the left-hand corner of the camp to a river, so that his soldiers could get water more freely and without danger. But he too changed his mind for a variety 7 of reasons that do not need mention, and left the place. The camp had remained in this state[85] for several days; all of its fortifications were intact.

67. The scouts reported to Caesar that a legion's standards had been taken to this location. As confirmation they said that the same thing had been seen from some of the

---

[84] See 3.45–46.   [85] For "remained in this state," Chacon proposed "thus remained empty."

2 castris circiter passus D. Hanc legionem sperans Caesar
se opprimere posse et cupiens eius diei detrimentum
sarcire reliquit in opere cohortes duas quae speciem mu-
3 nitionis praeberent, ipse diverso itinere quam potuit oc-
cultissime reliquas cohortes numero XXXIII, in quibus
erat legio nona multis amissis centurionibus deminutoque
militum numero, ad legionem Pompei castraque minora
4 duplici acie eduxit. Neque eum prima opinio fefellit. Nam
et pervenit priusquam Pompeius sentire posset et tametsi
erant munitiones castrorum magnae tamen sinistro cornu,
ubi erat ipse, celeriter aggressus Pompeianos ex vallo de-
5 turbavit. Erat obiectus portis ericius. Hic paulisper est
pugnatum cum irrumpere nostri conarentur, illi castra
defenderent fortissime T. Puleione, cuius opera proditum
exercitum C. Antoni demonstravimus, e[84] loco pro-
6 pugnante. Sed tamen nostri virtute vicerunt. Excisoque
ericio, primo in maiora castra post etiam in castellum,
quod erat inclusum maioribus castris, irruperunt quod eo
pulsa legio sese receperat. Nonnullos ibi repugnantes interfecerunt.

68. Sed Fortuna, quae plurimum potest cum in reliquis
rebus tum praecipue in bello, parvis momentis magnas
2 rerum commutationes efficit, ut tum accidit. Munitionem
quam pertinere a castris ad flumen supra demonstravimus
dextri Caesaris cornu cohortes ignorantia loci sunt secutae

[84] e *MUST*: eo V

---

[86] The name suggests that spikes were the principal feature
of this rarely mentioned defensive structure.

higher outposts. The place was about five hundred paces
from Pompey's new camp. Hoping that he could crush this 2
legion, and wanting to repair the day's damage, Caesar left
two cohorts at the works to give the appearance of fortification; he himself, taking a different route in the greatest 3
possible secrecy, led out the rest of his cohorts, thirty-
three in number, among them the ninth legion, despite the
loss of many of its centurions and the overall reduction to
its manpower. They headed for Pompey's legion and his
secondary camp in two lines. Caesar's initial expectation 4
was not wrong, for he both arrived before Pompey could
get word and dislodged the Pompeians from the rampart
with a swift attack on the left wing, where he himself was,
despite the fact that the camp's fortifications were extensive. The entrance was blocked by a "hedgehog."[86] There 5
was a brief fight here while our men were trying to break
in and the enemy were defending the camp, with a very
valiant sally[87] by Titus Puleio, whose responsibility for the
betrayal of Gaius Antonius' army I indicated. But their 6
courage made our men victorious nevertheless. After cutting away the "hedgehog" they burst into the larger camp
first and then into the stronghold it enclosed, since the
legion had taken refuge there after being routed. There
they killed some who fought back.

68. But Fortune has vast power both in other activities
and particularly in warfare, causing huge reversals by tilt-
ing her balance slightly, as happened then. Unfamiliar 2
with the location, the cohorts on Caesar's right wing followed the fortification whose line, as I indicated earlier,

---

[87] Editors often adopt the reading of V, which yields "valiant
defense at that location" in place of "valiant sally."

cum portam quaererent castrorumque eam munitionem
3 esse arbitrarentur. Quod cum esset animadversa[85] coniuncta esse flumini, prorutis munitionibus defendente
nullo transcenderunt, omnisque noster equitatus eas cohortes est secutus.

69. Interim Pompeius hac satis longa interiecta mora
et re nuntiata V legiones ab opere deductas subsidio suis
duxit. Eodemque tempore equitatus eius nostris equitibus
appropinquabat et acies instructa a nostris qui castra occu-
2 paverant cernebatur. Omniaque sunt subito mutata. Pompeiana legio celeris spe subsidi confirmata ab decimana
porta resistere conatur atque ultro in nostros impetum
faciebat. Equitatus Caesaris quod angusto itinere per ag-
geres ascendebat receptui suo timens initium fugae facie-
3 bat. Dextrum cornu, quod erat a sinistro seclusum, terrore
equitum animadverso, ne intra munitionem opprimeretur
ea parte quam proruerat sese recipiebat. Ac plerique ex
his ne in angustias inciderent X pedum munitione se in
fossas praecipitant. Primisque oppressis reliqui per horum
4 corpora salutem sibi atque exitum pariebant. Sinistro
cornu milites cum ex vallo Pompeium adesse et suos fugere cernerent, veriti ne angustiis intercluderentur cum
extra et intus hostem haberent, eodem quo venerant re-
ceptu sibi consulebant. Omniaque erant tumultus timoris
fugae plena, adeo ut cum Caesar signa fugientium manu
prenderet et consistere iuberet alii [dimissis equis][86] eun-

85 animadversa *Damon*: -sum ω
86 [dimissis equis] *Nipperdey*: admissis e- *Faerno*: d- armis
Bähr: ⟨non⟩ d- signis *Koch*: nihilo sequius *Haupt*

extended from the camp to the river; they were looking for the entrance and thought this was the fortification of the camp itself. But when its connection to the river was noticed, they knocked down the undefended fortifications and went through. And our entire cavalry followed these cohorts.

69. Meanwhile Pompey, after a considerable delay, got word. Taking five legions from the works he led them to the relief of his men. At one and the same moment his cavalry approached ours and his legionary line was spotted by those of our men who were in possession of the camp. The reversal was sudden and complete. The Pompeian legion took heart in the hope of quick relief and attempted resistance from the camp's rear gate, initiating an attack on our men. Caesar's cavalry, coming up through the earthworks on a narrow path and fearing for its retreat, caused the beginning of the flight. The right wing, which was cut off from the left, noticed the cavalry panicking. To avoid being crushed inside the fortifications, it began to withdraw where it had knocked them down, and most of the men flung themselves from the ten-foot high wall into the trenches to avoid entering that narrow passage. The first were crushed but the rest saved themselves and got away over their bodies. On the left wing the soldiers perceived from the wall that Pompey was at hand and their own men were in flight. Afraid that they would be cut off in a narrow space, given that they had the enemy both inside and outside the camp, they took thought for themselves by retreating the same way they had come. Everything was full of confusion, fear, and flight, to such an extent that when Caesar tried to grab the standards of the fleeing men and ordered them to stop, some took refuge

dem cursum confugerent,[87] alii ex metu etiam signa dimitterent, neque quisquam omnino consisteret.

70. His tantis malis haec subsidia succurrebant quo
minus omnis deleretur exercitus, quod Pompeius insidias
timens—credo quod haec praeter spem acciderant eius
qui paulo ante ex castris fugientes suos conspexerat—
munitionibus appropinquare aliquamdiu non audebat
equitesque eius angustiis [portis][88] atque iis a Caesaris
2 militibus occupatis ad insequendum tardabantur. Ita par-
vae res magnum in utramque partem momentum habuerunt. Munitiones enim a castris ad flumen perductae
expugnatis iam castris Pompei prope iam expeditam Caesaris victoriam interpellaverunt. Eadem res celeritate in-
sequentium tardata nostris salutem attulit.

71. Duobus his unius diei proeliis Caesar desideravit
milites DCCCCLX et notos equites Romanos [Flegma-
tem] Tuticanum Gallum senatoris filium, C. Flegmatem
Placentia, A. Granium Puteolis, M. Sacrativirum Capua,
2 tribunos militum [L], et centuriones XXXII. Sed horum
omnium pars magna in fossis munitionibusque et fluminis
ripis oppressa suorum in terrore ac fuga sine ullo vulnere
3 interiit. Signaque sunt militaria amissa XXXII. Pompeius
eo proelio imperator est appellatus. Hoc nomen obtinuit
atque ita se postea salutari passus neque[89] in litteris

----

[87] eundem . . . confugerent] *Many emendations have been
proposed for this stretch of text.*

[88] angustiis [portis] *Nipperdey*: angustis portis ω

[89] neque *Nipperdey*: sed ω

----

[88] Before "fled running," the manuscripts read "after letting
their horses go," which Nipperdey excised because the cavalry is

in running[88] as before, others in their fear even let go of the standards, and no one at all stopped.

70. The situation was extremely bad, but the following factors helped prevent the complete destruction of the army. Pompey, fearing an ambush, did not dare approach the fortifications for quite some time—in my view, because things had turned out contrary to the expectation of a man who had seen his men running away from their camp shortly before—and his cavalry was slowed down in its pursuit by the narrow space, particularly since it was held by our men. Trivial things thus tilted the balance strongly in both directions. For the fortifications built from the camp to the river interrupted a victory that Caesar had all but in hand after capturing Pompey's camp, and the same thing saved our men by slowing the pace of their pursuers.

71. In the two battles of this one day Caesar lost nine hundred and sixty soldiers, plus eminent men of equestrian status, Tuticanus Gallus, a senator's son, Gaius Flegmas of Placentia, Aulus Granius of Puteoli, Marcus Sacrativir of Capua, who were military tribunes, and thirty-two centurions. A considerable portion of the total perished without a wound in the trenches and fortifications and on the banks of the river, overwhelmed by the terror and flight of their own side. Thirty-two military standards were also lost. Pompey was hailed as *imperator* in that battle. He kept this title and, while allowing himself to be addressed thus afterward, was not in the habit of writing it

elsewhere (3.68.3). Other repairs include "after spurring on their horses," "after letting go of their weapons," "without letting go of the standards," and "nevertheless."

[quas]⁹⁰ scribere est solitus neque in fascibus insignia lau-
4 reae praetulit. At Labienus, cum ab eo impetravisset ut
sibi captivos tradi iuberet, omnes reductos—ostentationis,
ut videbatur causa quo maior perfugae fides haberetur—
commilitones appellans et magna verborum contumelia
interrogans solerentne veterani milites fugere, in omnium
conspectu interfecit.

72. His rebus tantum fiduciae ac spiritus Pompeianis
accessit ut non de ratione belli cogitarent sed vicisse iam
2 sibi viderentur. Non illi paucitatem nostrorum militum,
non iniquitatem loci atque angustias praeoccupatis nostris
et ancipitem terrorem intra extraque munitiones, non abs-
cisum in duas partes exercitum, cum altera alteri auxilium
3 ferre non posset, causae fuisse cogitabant. Non ad haec
addebant: non ex concursu aciei⁹¹ facto, non proelio dimi-
catum; sibique ipsos multitudine atque angustiis maius
4 attulisse detrimentum quam ab hoste accepissent. Non
denique communes belli casus recordabantur: quam par-
vulae saepe causae vel falsae suspicionis vel terroris repentini vel obiectae religionis magna detrimenta intulissent;
quotiens vel ducis vitio vel culpa tribuni in exercitu esset
offensum. Sed proinde ac si virtute vicissent neque ulla
commutatio rerum posset accidere per orbem terrarum
fama ac litteris victoriam eius diei concelebrabant.

73. Caesar a superioribus consiliis depulsus omnem
2 sibi commutandam belli rationem existimavit. Itaque uno

⁹⁰ [quas] *Peskett. The sense is clear from D.C. 41.52.1.*
⁹¹ aciei *Chacon*: agri ω: acri *ed. pr.*

---

⁸⁹ For "formations came together and did battle," editors often adopt the Livian "battle was joined after a fierce clash."

in his letters, nor did he display the laurel insignia on his fasces. Labienus, however, got Pompey to order the pris- 4 oners of war to be handed over to him. He collected them all and—apparently making a demonstration in order to give greater credibility to a deserter's loyalty, calling them his "fellow soldiers" and asking, among many other insults, whether veterans were in the habit of running away— killed them in full view.

72. These developments added so much confidence and morale to the Pompeians that they stopped thinking about strategy and felt that they had already won. They 2 did not think about contributory factors: the small number of our men, the disadvantages of the site, the confined space with the enemy in control of the camp, the twofold terror inside and outside of the fortifications, nor about the fact that the army was cut in two, so that one part could not help the other. Nor did they add that it was not a fight 3 in which formations came together and did battle,[89] or that the damage his men did to themselves with the crowding and the narrow space was greater than the damage taken from the enemy. Finally, they did not remember the nor- 4 mal chances of war: how small factors such as a false suspicion or a sudden alarm or a religious scruple have caused huge losses, how often an army has run into trouble owing to its commander's fault or an officer's mistake. But just as if courage had made them victorious, and no reversal was possible, they used word of mouth and letters to broadcast the day's victory worldwide.

73. Turned back from his earlier objectives, Caesar thought his whole strategy should be changed. So he si- 2

tempore praesidiis omnibus deductis et oppugnatione
dimissa coactoque in unum locum exercitu contionem
apud milites habuit. Hortatusque est ne ea quae acci-
dissent graviter ferrent neve his rebus terrerentur multisque secundis proeliis unum adversum et id mediocre
3   opponerent; habendam Fortunae gratiam quod Italiam
sine aliquo vulnere cepissent, quod duas Hispanias, belli-
cosissimorum hominum ⟨provincias, superatis⟩[92] peritis-
simis atque exercitatissimis ducibus pacavissent, quod
finitimas frumentariasque provincias in potestatem rede-
gissent; denique recordari debere qua felicitate inter
medias hostium classes oppletis non solum portibus sed
4   etiam litoribus omnes incolumes essent transportati; si
non omnia caderent secunda Fortunam esse industria
sublevandam; quod esset acceptum detrimenti, cuiusvis
5   potius quam suae culpae debere tribui; locum se notum[93]
ad dimicandum dedisse, potitum se esse hostium castris,
expulisse ac superasse pugnantes; sed sive ipsorum pertur-
batio sive error aliquis sive etiam Fortuna partam iam
praesentemque victoriam interpellavisset dandam omnibus operam ut acceptum incommodum virtute sarciretur;
6   quod si esset factum ⟨futurum⟩[94] ut detrimentum in bo-
num verteret, uti ad Gergoviam accidisset, atque ei qui
ante dimicare timuissent ultro se proelio offerrent.

74. Hac habita contione nonnullos signiferos ignominia
2   notavit ac loco movit. Exercitui quidem omni tantus inces-

---

[92] ⟨provincias, superatis⟩ *Damon. Other repairs are possible.*
[93] se notum *Damon* (*see 3.66.2*): secum μST: se eis V: se aequum *Vittori*
[94] ⟨futurum⟩ *Meusel*

multaneously withdrew all of the garrisons and abandoned the blockade. He gathered the army together and addressed his soldiers, urging them not to be troubled by what had happened, or frightened by it, but rather to compare their many successes with this single reverse, not a serious one, either. "You should be grateful to Fortune: 3 you took Italy without any bloodshed, pacified the two Spains—⟨provinces⟩ containing extremely warlike peoples—⟨after overcoming⟩ Pompey's most skillful and experienced leaders, and you brought nearby grain-producing provinces back under control. Finally, you must remember how much good luck you all enjoyed in being transported safely through the midst of enemy fleets, when not only ports but also the coastline was held against us. If not everything has turned out well, we should help 4 Fortune with our own exertions. As for the damage incurred, no one deserves the blame less than me. I gave you 5 a familiar[90] position for the fight, gained control of the enemy camp, drove the enemy off, and defeated them in battle. Whatever interrupted a victory that was already won and in our grasp, whether it was confusion on your part or some mistake or even Fortune herself, we must all ensure that courage provides a repair for the setback we have suffered. If this is done, the damage will turn into 6 advantage, as happened at Gergovia, and those who before now were afraid to fight will offer themselves for battle of their own accord."

74. After delivering this speech he reprimanded and demoted some standard bearers. Throughout the army 2

[90] For Caesar's defensive "familiar," Vittori proposed "favorable." Neither matches the narrative of the debacle (1.66–69).

sit ex incommodo dolor tantumque studium infamiae sar-
ciendae ut nemo aut tribuni aut centurionis imperium
desideraret et sibi quisque etiam poenae loco graviores
imponeret labores, simulque omnes arderent cupiditate
pugnandi, cum superioris etiam ordinis nonnulli ratione
permoti manendum eo loco et rem proelio committendam
3 existimarent. Contra ea Caesar neque satis militibus perterritis confidebat spatiumque interponendum ad recre-
andos animos putabat.

Relictis munitionibus magnopere rei frumentariae timebat. 75. Itaque nulla interposita mora sauciorum modo
et aegrorum habita ratione ⟨impedimenta⟩ omnia silentio
prima nocte ex castris Apolloniam praemisit. Haec con-
quiescere ante iter confectum vetuit. Iis una legio missa
2 praesidio est. His explicitis rebus duas in castris legiones
retinuit, reliquas de quarta vigilia compluribus portis
eductas eodem itinere praemisit. Parvoque spatio intermisso, ut et militare institutum servaretur et quam suetissima[95] eius profectio cognosceretur conclamari iussit
statimque egressus et novissimum agmen consecutus ce-
3 leriter ex conspectu castrorum discessit. Neque vero Pompeius cognito consilio eius moram ullam ad insequendum
intulit sed eadem[96] spectans si itinere impedito[97] perterritos deprendere posset exercitum e castris eduxit equita-

---

[95] quam suetissima *Fabre*: q- -me ω: q- serissime *Scaliger.*
Perhaps consuetudine?   [96] eadem] eodem *Hoffmann*
[97] impedito ς (*see 3.77.2*): impeditos [-iment- *S*] ω

---

[91] For "seem as ordinary as possible," Scaliger substituted
"recognized as late as possible." One might also substitute "appear customary."

remorse over the setback took hold, and the men were so determined to repair the disgrace that no one needed the orders of a centurion or officer; every man punished himself with fatigues. Everyone was likewise ablaze with desire for combat, and some higher ranking men, inspired by Caesar's argument, thought they should stay there and decide matters in battle. Caesar, by contrast, did not have 3 enough confidence in the terrified soldiers and felt that he had to allow some time for reviving morale.

Now that he had abandoned the siege works he was very anxious about provisions. 75. Therefore he did not delay except to attend to the men who were wounded and sick. At nightfall he sent his whole baggage train in silence out of the camp and on to Apollonia with orders not to rest before finishing the march; one legion was sent as protection. After completing these arrangements, and holding 2 two legions in camp, he had the rest move out before dawn by various gates; he sent them on by the same route. A short time later he had the signal for packing up sounded, so as to keep to military custom and make his departure seem as ordinary as possible.[91] Then he left immediately and caught up with the rearguard, disappearing quickly from view of the camp. And Pompey, once he realized 3 Caesar's intention, did not delay pursuit. Expecting the same results if he could catch terrified men marching under encumbrances,[92] he moved his army out of camp. He

---

[92] For Pompey's reasoning, see 3.30.2. For "expecting the same results," Hoffmann suggested "with the same expectations (as Caesar's)."

tumque praemisit ad novissimum agmen demorandum,
neque consequi potuit quod multum expedito itinere
4 antecesserat Caesar. Sed cum ventum esset ad flumen
Genusum, quod ripis erat impeditis, consecutus equitatus
5 novissimos proelio detinebat. Huic suos Caesar equites
opposuit expeditosque antesignanos admiscuit CCCC.
Qui tantum profecerunt ut equestri proelio commisso pellerent omnes compluresque interficerent ipsique incolumes se ad agmen reciperent.

76. Confecto iusto itinere eius diei, quod proposuerat
Caesar, traductoque exercitu flumen Genusum veteribus
suis in castris contra Asparagium consedit militesque omnes intra vallum castrorum continuit equitatumque per
causam pabulandi emissum confestim decimana porta in
2 castra se recipere iussit. Simili ratione Pompeius confecto
eius diei itinere in suis veteribus castris ad Asparagium
3 consedit. Eius milites quod ab opere integris munitionibus vacabant alii lignandi pabulandique causa longius
progrediebantur, alii, quod subito consilium profectionis
ceperant magna parte impedimentorum et sarcinarum
relicta, ad haec repetenda invitati propinquitate superiorum castrorum depositis in contubernio armis vallum re-
4 linquebant. Quibus ad sequendum impeditis Caesar, quod
fore providerat, meridiano fere tempore signo profectionis dato exercitum educit. Duplicatoque eius diei itinere
VIII milia passuum ex eo loco procedit. Quod facere Pompeius discessu militum non potuit.

77. Postero die Caesar similiter praemissis prima nocte
impedimentis de quarta vigilia ipse egreditur ut si qua
esset imposita dimicandi necessitas subitum casum expe-

---

93 See 3.41.

sent the cavalry ahead to delay the rearguard, but it was unable to do so because Caesar had marched without encumbrances and was far ahead. At the Genusus River, 4 however, whose banks were hard to negotiate, the cavalry caught up with the rearguard and attacked, holding them up. Caesar deployed his own cavalry in response, mixing 5 in four hundred unencumbered elite troops; these were so effective that in a cavalry engagement they routed the enemy, killed several, and returned to the column unscathed.

76. After finishing the regular march that he had announced for that day, and taking his army across the Genusus, Caesar halted in his old camp facing Asparagium.[93] He kept all of his soldiers inside the rampart; the cavalry, sent out under the pretense of foraging, was ordered to return quickly to camp through the rear gate. Pompey 2 likewise halted in his old camp near Asparagium when he had finished the day's march. His soldiers had a respite 3 from work since the fortifications were intact; some went a distance to gather wood and fodder, others—since the decision to move out had been taken suddenly and most of their baggage and packs had been left behind, and tempted to collect them by the proximity of the previous camp—stowed their weapons in the tents and began leaving the rampart. When they were hindered from pursuit 4 (which Caesar had foreseen), he gave the signal for departure around midday and moved his army out. Doubling his day's march he advanced eight miles from that spot, which Pompey was unable to do because of the dispersal of his men.

77. The next day Caesar similarly sent the baggage ahead at nightfall and himself left before dawn so that if any need to fight arose he could meet the emergency with

2 dito exercitu subiret. Hoc idem reliquis fecit diebus. Quibus rebus perfectum est ut altissimis fluminibus atque impeditissimis itineribus nullum acciperet incommodum.

3 Pompeius enim, primi diei mora illata et reliquorum dierum frustra labore suscepto cum se magnis itineribus extenderet et praegressos consequi cuperet, quarta die finem sequendi fecit atque aliud sibi consilium capiendum existimavit.

78. Caesari ad saucios deponendos stipendium exercitui dandum socios confirmandos praesidium urbibus

2 relinquendum necesse erat adire Apolloniam. Sed his rebus tantum temporis tribuit quantum erat properanti necesse. Timens Domitio ne adventu Pompei praeoccuparetur ad eum omni celeritate et studio incitatus ferebatur.

3 Totius autem rei consilium his rationibus explicabat: ut, si Pompeius eodem contenderet, abductum illum a mari atque ab iis copiis quas Dyrrachi comparaverat—frumento ac commeatu—abstractum pari conditione belli secum decertare cogeret; si in Italiam transiret, coniuncto exercitu cum Domitio per Illyricum Italiae subsidio proficisceretur; si Apolloniam Oricumque oppugnare et se omni maritima ora excludere conaretur, obsesso Scipione ne-

4 cessario illum suis auxilium ferre cogeret. Itaque praemissis nuntiis ad Cn. Domitium Caesar scripsit et quid fieri vellet ostendit. Praesidioque Apolloniae cohortium IIII, Lissi una, tribus Orici relictis, quique erant ex vulneribus aegri depositis, per Epirum atque Athamaniam iter facere

5 coepit. Pompeius quoque de Caesaris consilio coniectura iudicans ad Scipionem properandum sibi existimabat: si Caesar iter illo haberet, ut subsidium Scipioni ferret; si ab ora maritima Oricoque discedere nollet quod legiones

an unencumbered army; he did the same on subsequent days. These tactics meant that he suffered no setback at 2 rivers that were extremely deep and on roads that were hard to negotiate, for Pompey, after the first day's delay 3 and the wasted effort of subsequent days as he exerted himself with forced marches and hoped to catch the men ahead, stopped his pursuit on the fourth day, thinking that he had to devise a new plan.

78. Caesar had go to Apollonia to settle the wounded, pay the army, encourage the allies, and garrison various cities. But the time he spent on these matters was limited 2 by his need for haste. Fearing that Pompey's arrival might take Domitius by surprise, he moved in Domitius' direction with all speed; determination spurred him on. He laid 3 out his overall plan reasoning as follows: "If Pompey heads for the same place, I will force him to decide matters between us with a battle on equal terms, away from the sea and separated from all of the resources—provisions and supplies—available to him at Dyrrachium. If he crosses to Italy, I will join forces with Domitius and set out to relieve Italy via Illyricum. If he tries to attack Apollonia and Oricum and cut me off from the whole coastline, I will lay siege to Scipio and force Pompey by necessity to assist his own side." So he sent written word to Gnaeus Domitius, 4 showing what he wanted done. He garrisoned Apollonia with four cohorts, Lissus with one, and Oricum with three, settled those who were ill from their wounds, and began his march through Epirus and Athamania. Pompey, too, 5 was making decisions based on conjecture about Caesar's plans. He thought he ought to hurry toward Scipio, intending, if Caesar went there, to assist Scipio. If Caesar was unwilling to leave the coast and Oricum, in the expec-

equitatumque ex Italia expectaret, ipse ut omnibus copiis Domitium aggrederetur.

79. His de causis uterque eorum celeritati studebat, et suis ut esset auxilio ⟨et⟩ ad opprimendos adversarios ne
2 occasioni temporis deesset. Sed Caesarem Apollonia a derecto itinere averterat. Pompeius per Candaviam iter in
3 Macedoniam expeditum habebat. Accessit etiam ex improviso aliud incommodum, quod Domitius, ⟨cum⟩[98] dies complures castris Scipionis castra collata habuisset, rei frumentariae causa ab eo discesserat et Heracliam Senticam,[99] quae est subiecta Candaviae, iter fecerat, ut ipsa
4 Fortuna illum obicere Pompeio videretur. (Haec ad id tempus Caesar ignorabat.) Simul a Pompeio litteris per omnes provincias civitatesque dimissis proelio ad Dyrrachium facto latius inflatiusque multo quam res erat gesta fama percrebuerat: pulsum fugere Caesarem paene omnibus copiis amissis. Haec itinera infesta reddiderat, haec
5 civitates nonnullas ab eius amicitia avertebat. Quibus accidit rebus ut pluribus dimissi itineribus a Caesare ad Domitium et a Domitio ad Caesarem nulla ratione iter conficere
6 possent. Sed Allobroges, Roucilli atque Egi familiares, quos perfugisse ad Pompeium demonstravimus, conspicati ⟨in⟩ itinere exploratores Domiti, seu pristina sua consuetudine quod una in Gallia bella gesserant seu gloria elati cuncta ut erant acta exposuerunt et Caesaris profec-
7 tionem, adventum Pompei docuerunt. A quibus Domitius

[98] ⟨cum⟩ *Paul*   [99] [Senticam] *Cellarius*

[94] There are several towns named Heraclia. Heraclia Sentica is not in fact adjacent to Candavia, hence Cellarius' excision, but the error may be Caesar's (for Heraclia Lyncestis).

tation of legions and cavalry from Italy, he himself would attack Domitius with all of his forces.

79. For these reasons each of them was determined to make haste, in order to relieve his own side and avoid wasting an opportunity to crush his adversaries. But Apollonia had been a detour for Caesar, while Pompey's march through Candavia to Macedonia was unencumbered. An additional and unexpected setback occurred in that Domitius, although for several days he had been keeping his camp in contact with Scipio's, had parted ways for the sake of his food supply and marched to Heraclia Sentica, which is near Candavia,[94] so that Fortune seemed to be putting him in Pompey's way. (Caesar was unaware of this at the time.) At the same time, because of the letters distributed by Pompey to every province and city after the battle at Dyrrachium, a report had spread whose terms were overly general and exaggerated beyond the event itself: Caesar had been routed and was now in flight after losing almost all of his forces. This rendered the roads unsafe and deflected some cities from their allegiance to Caesar. As a result, messengers sent by Caesar to Domitius and Domitius to him on various routes could find no way to complete their journeys. Some Allobroges, however, connections of Roucillus and Egus, whose desertion to Pompey I mentioned, caught sight of Domitius' scouts on the march, told them everything as it had happened, and informed them about Caesar's march and Pompey's approach, either from past habit (they had fought on the same side in Gaul) or carried away with self-importance. With their information

certior factus vix IIII horarum spatio antecedens hostium
beneficio periculum vitavit et ad Aeginium, quod est
obiectum oppositumque Thessaliae, Caesari venienti occurrit.

80. Coniuncto exercitu Caesar Gomphos pervenit,
quod est oppidum primum Thessaliae venientibus ab
Epiro. Quae gens paucis ante mensibus ultro ad Caesarem
legatos miserat ut suis omnibus facultatibus uteretur,
2 praesidiumque ab eo militum petierat. Sed eo fama iam
praecurrerat quam supra docuimus de proelio Dyrra-
3 chino, quod multis auxerant partibus. Itaque Androsthenes, praetor Thessaliae, cum se victoriae Pompei comi-
tem esse mallet quam socium Caesaris in rebus adversis,
omnem ex agris multitudinem servorum ac liberorum in
oppidum cogit portasque praecludit et ad Scipionem
Pompeiumque nuntios mittit ut sibi subsidio veniant: se
confidere munitionibus oppidi si celeriter succurratur;
4 longinquam oppugnationem sustinere non posse. Scipio
discessu exercituum a Dyrrachio cognito Larisam legiones
adduxerat. Pompeius nondum Thessaliae appropinquabat.

5 Caesar castris munitis scalas musculosque ad repenti-
6 nam oppugnationem fieri et crates parari iussit. Quibus
rebus effectis cohortatus milites docuit quantum usum
haberet ad sublevandam omnium rerum inopiam potiri
oppido pleno atque opulento, simul reliquis civitatibus
huius urbis exemplo inferre terrorem et id fieri celeriter,
7 priusquam auxilia concurrerent. Itaque usus singulari
militum studio, eodem quo venerat die post horam nonam
oppidum altissimis moenibus oppugnare aggressus ante

---

95 At Larisa Scipio was about forty-five miles from Gomphi.

and a lead of barely four hours Domitius avoided danger
thanks to the enemy and met Caesar on his way near Aeginium, which borders Thessaly and faces it.

80. With his forces united, Caesar went to Gomphi,
which is the first town in Thessaly for those coming from
Epirus. This community had spontaneously sent a delegation to Caesar a few months earlier, inviting him to make
use of all of their resources; they had asked him for a garrison of soldiers. But the aforementioned report about the   2
Dyrrachium battle had already outstripped him, and they
had augmented it considerably. So Androsthenes, the top   3
man in Thessaly, preferring to be a companion to Pompey's victory than Caesar's ally in adversity, drove the
whole population of slaves and free men from the countryside into the town, shut the gates, and sent messengers
to Scipio and Pompey with a request for help: "I have
confidence in the town's defenses if help comes quickly.
We cannot withstand a long siege." Scipio, upon learning   4
of the armies' departure from Dyrrachium, had led his
legions to Larisa; Pompey was not yet near Thessaly.[95]

After fortifying his camp Caesar ordered ladders and   5
galleries built and brushwood bundles readied for an immediate assault. When these were finished he rallied his   6
troops, explaining how useful it would be for relieving the
general scarcity to take control of a town that was well
stocked and wealthy, and at the same time to strike terror
into other cities with the example of this one, and to do so
quickly, before reinforcements could arrive. Taking ad   7
vantage of the soldiers' remarkable determination, he began the attack in the middle of the afternoon the day he
arrived The town had exceptionally high fortifications,

solis occasum expugnavit et ad diripiendum militibus concessit statimque ab oppido castra movit et Metropolim venit sic ut nuntios expugnati oppidi famamque antecederet.

81. Metropolitae primum eodem usi consilio isdem permoti rumoribus portas clauserunt murosque armatis compleverunt. Sed postea casu civitatis Gomphensis cognito ex captivis quos Caesar ad murum producendos
2 curaverat portas aperuerunt. Quibus diligentissime conservatis collata fortuna Metropolitum cum casu Gomphensium nulla Thessaliae fuit civitas praeter Larisaeos, qui magnis exercitibus Scipionis tenebantur, quin Caesari
3 parerent atque imperata facerent. Ille idoneum locum ‹frumentaque›[100] in agris nactus, quae prope iam matura erant, ibi adventum expectare Pompei eoque omnem belli rationem conferre constituit.

82. Pompeius paucis post diebus in Thessaliam pervenit contionatusque apud cunctum exercitum suis agit gratias, Scipionis milites cohortatur ut parta iam victoria praedae ac praemiorum velint esse participes. Receptisque omnibus in una castra legionibus suum cum Scipione honorem partitur classicumque apud eum cani et
2 alterum illi iubet praetorium tendi. Auctis copiis Pompei duobusque magnis exercitibus coniunctis pristina omnium confirmatur opinio et spes victoriae augetur, adeo ut quicquid intercederet temporis id morari reditum in Italiam videretur, et si quando quid Pompeius tardius aut consideratius faceret unius esse negotium diei sed illum delectari imperio et consulares praetoriosque servorum habere

___

[100] ‹frumentaque› *Damon* (*see 3.84.1*). *Other repairs yield the same basic sense.*

but he stormed it before sunset and turned it over to his soldiers for plundering. He immediately moved his camp away from Gomphi and went to Metropolis, so that he arrived before messengers and news about the fallen town.

81. The townsfolk, adopting the same plan initially and prompted by the same rumors, closed their gates and had armed men occupy the walls. But later, when they learned about Gomphi's disaster from prisoners brought forward to the wall on Caesar's instructions, they opened the gates. Great care was taken to keep them safe, and after compar- 2 ing the fortune of Metropolis with Gomphi's disaster every single city in Thessaly (except Larisa, which was in the grip of large armies under Scipio) became obedient to Caesar and did what he ordered. For his part, having found a 3 suitable location and grain in the fields, nearly ripe al- ready, Caesar decided to await Pompey's arrival there and base his whole strategy on that location.

82. Pompey arrived in Thessaly a few days later. In an address to the whole army he thanked his men and en- couraged Scipio's soldiers: since victory was already in hand, they should agree to share the booty and rewards. He put all of the legions into a single camp and gave Scipio a half-share of the command; by Pompey's order bugle calls were given in Scipio's area and a second headquarters was erected for him. With Pompey's forces thus strength- 2 ened and the conjunction of two large armies everyone's original expectation was validated and their hope of vic- tory became so strong that the intervening time seemed to be a postponement of their return to Italy, and when- ever Pompey acted somewhat slowly or warily, people said that it was a one-day job but he was enjoying his power

3   numero dicerent. Iamque inter se palam de praemiis[101] ac
de sacerdotiis contendebant in annosque consulatum defi-
niebant, alii domos bonaque eorum qui in castris erant
4   Caesaris petebant. Magnaque inter eos in consilio fuit
controversia oporteretne Lucili Hirri, quod is a Pompeio
ad Parthos missus esset, proximis comitiis praetoriis absentis rationem haberi, cum eius necessarii fidem implo-
rarent Pompei—praestaret quod proficiscenti recepisset
ne per eius auctoritatem deceptus videretur—reliqui in
labore pari ac periculo ne unus omnes antecederet recusarent.

83. Iam de sacerdotio Caesaris Domitius Scipio Spin-
therque Lentulus cotidianis contentionibus ad gravissimas
verborum contumelias palam descenderunt, cum Lentulus aetatis honorem ostentaret, Domitius urbanam gratiam dignitatemque iactaret, Scipio adfinitate Pompei
2   confideret. Postulavit etiam L. Afranium proditionis exercitus Acutius Rufus apud Pompeium, quod ⟨bellum
3   male⟩[102] gestum in Hispania diceret. Et L. Domitius in
consilio dixit: placere sibi bello confecto ternas tabellas
dari ad iudicandum iis qui ordinis essent senatori belloque
una cum ipsis interfuissent; sententiasque de singulis
ferrent qui Romae remansissent quique intra praesidia

---

[101] praemiis] provinciis *Kraffert*: praeturis *Markland*: imperiis *Paul. Novák excised* de sacerdotiis *instead.*

[102] quod ⟨bellum male⟩ . . . diceret *Koch. Frese defends the
transmitted text, Gruter excises it.*

---

96 Scholars have proposed replacing the vague "rewards" with
"provinces," "praetorships," or "commands," or else excising the
specific "priesthoods."

and treating former consuls and praetors as his slaves. They were already squabbling openly about rewards[96] and 3 priesthoods, and were determining future years' consulships; some were demanding the houses and property of men who were in Caesar's camp. There was also a long 4 argument in council about whether or not it was right for Lucilius Hirrus to be a candidate in absentia at the next praetorian elections, since he had been sent by Pompey to the Parthians. His friends implored Pompey to keep his word—"Stand by the terms you offered when he was leaving, lest people think he was deceived by your guarantee"—and the rest said that no one should outstrip everyone when their hardship and danger had been the same.

83. By now in their daily squabbles on the subject of Caesar's priesthood Domitius, Scipio, and Lentulus had sunk to open and extremely offensive insults, with Lentulus flaunting the prestige of his age, Domitius boasting about his influence and standing in Rome, and Scipio trusting in his relationship with Pompey. Acutius Rufus 2 even brought a charge of betraying the army against Lucius Afranius, with Pompey as judge, the grounds being Rufus' statement that the war in Spain was conducted badly.[97] Lucius Domitius said in council: "In my opinion, 3 once the war is over, three tablets should be provided for the verdicts of those who are of senatorial standing and have taken part with us in the fighting, and we should record a vote on every man who stayed in Rome or who was under Pompey's protection but did not contribute to the

97 For "the war . . . was conducted badly," the transmitted text reads "which (i.e., the betrayal) . . . was perpetrated." Gruter excised the clause.

Pompei fuissent neque operam in re militari praesti-
tissent; unam fore tabellam iis ⟨qui⟩[103] liberandos omni
periculo censerent; alteram, qui capitis damnarent; ter-
4 tiam, qui pecunia multarent. Postremo omnes aut de honoribus suis aut de praemiis pecuniae aut de persequendis
inimicitiis agebant, neque quibus rationibus superare possent sed quemadmodum uti victoria deberent cogitabant.

84. Re frumentaria praeparata confirmatisque militibus et satis longo spatio temporis a Dyrrachinis proeliis
intermisso quo satis perspectum habere ⟨Caesar ani-
mum⟩[104] militum videretur, temptandum existimavit
quidnam Pompeius propositi aut voluntatis ad dimican-
2 dum haberet. Itaque ex castris exercitum eduxit aciemque
instruxit primum suis locis pauloque a castris Pompei longius, continentibus vero diebus ut progrederetur a castris
suis collibusque Pompeianis aciem subiceret. Quae res in
3 dies confirmatiorem eius exercitum efficiebat. Superius
tamen institutum in equitibus quod demonstravimus ser-
vabat, ut quoniam numero multis partibus esset inferior
adulescentes atque expeditos ex antesignanis—electos
milites ad pernicitatem—armis[105] inter equites proeliari
iuberet, qui cotidiana consuetudine usum quoque eius
4 generis proeliorum perciperent. His erat rebus effectum

[103] iis ⟨qui⟩ *Damon*: in *MUS^c*: qui *M^{mr}TV*: qua *Oudendorp here and for* qui *in the next two clauses*

[104] ⟨Caesar animum⟩ *Bücheler*

[105] electos milites ad pernicitatem armis] *The text is very uncertain here.*

<hr>

[98] The voting mechanism is not clear. With the transmitted
text, minimally emended, it involves lists of those who support

military effort: one tablet for those who decide that they should be completely exonerated, another for those who sentence them to death, and a third for those who impose a monetary penalty."[98] In short, everyone was concerned 4 with offices for themselves or financial rewards or getting back at their enemies, not thinking about what strategies would enable them to win but about how they ought to put their victory to use.

84. After having arranged his provisioning and put heart into his soldiers Caesar thought that he should find out what Pompey's intention or desire for a fight was, now that enough time had elapsed since the Dyrrachium battles for him to feel that he had sufficiently observed the soldiers' morale. So he led the army out and drew up his 2 line, at first in a spot he controlled, some distance from Pompey's camp, but on the following days advancing further from his own camp and setting his line at the foot of the hills controlled by Pompey. This made his army more confident every day. He maintained the previous arrange- 3 ment among the cavalry that I mentioned: since he was numerically inferior by a wide margin, he ordered young and unencumbered men from the frontline fighters—soldiers chosen for speed—to do battle in the midst of the cavalry, men who by daily practice were gaining experience of this type of battle, too.[99] The result of these mea- 4

each of the three verdicts for each defendant. This interpretation takes the two distributives (*ternas . . . singulis*) together. With Oudendorp's emendation, each senator uses three tablets for his votes, presumably by listing the defendants thereon.

[99] See 3.75.5.

ut equitum mille etiam apertioribus locis VII milium Pompeianorum impetum, cum adesset usus, sustinere auderent neque magnopere eorum multitudine terrerentur.
5 Namque etiam per eos dies proelium secundum equestre fecit atque Egum[106] Allobrogem, ex duobus quos perfugisse ad Pompeium supra docuimus, cum quibusdam interfecit.

85. Pompeius, qui castra in colle habebat, ad infimas radices montis aciem instruebat, semper ut videbatur ex-
2 pectans si iniquis locis Caesar se subiceret. <Ille>[107] nulla ratione ad pugnam elici posse Pompeium existimans hanc sibi commodissimam belli rationem iudicavit, uti castra ex eo loco moveret semperque esset in itineribus, haec spectans, ut movendis castris pluribusque adeundis locis commodiore frumentaria re uteretur simulque in itinere ut aliquam occasionem dimicandi nancisceretur et insolitum ad laborem Pompei exercitum cotidianis itineribus defati-
3 garet. His constitutis rebus signo iam profectionis dato tabernaculisque detensis animadversum est paulo ante extra cotidianam consuetudinem longius a vallo esse aciem Pompei progressam, ut non iniquo loco posse dimi-
4 cari videretur. Tum Caesar apud suos cum iam esset agmen in portis "Differendum est" inquit "iter in praesentia nobis et de proelio cogitandum, sicut semper depoposcimus. Animo sumus[108] ad dimicandum parati. Non facile occasionem postea reperiemus." Confestimque expeditas copias educit.

[106] egum *V*: uncum *MUT*: unum *S*   [107] <Ille> *Meusel*
[108] sumus *MUTV*: suus (*or* sivis) *S*: simus *Manutius*

[100] For "we are," Manutius substituted "let us be."

sures was that his one thousand cavalrymen, with experi- ence behind them, dared to withstand the attack of Pompey's seven thousand, even on relatively open terrain, and were not much dismayed by their numbers. (He even 5 fought a successful cavalry battle during that period, and killed an Allobrogian, Egus, from the two whose desertion to Pompey I mentioned earlier, along with some others.)

85. Pompey, whose camp was on a rise, would draw up his line on the hill's lowest slopes, perpetually waiting, it seemed, to see whether Caesar would move into a disad- vantageous position. Caesar, thinking that there was no 2 way Pompey could be drawn out to do battle, decided that the most convenient strategy was to move his camp from that location and stay perpetually on the march. He had these things in view: if he moved his camp and went to various places, provisioning would be more convenient; also, on the march he might get an opportunity to fight; and with daily marches he would exhaust Pompey's army, which was not accustomed to hardship. He had decided 3 accordingly and given the order for departure, and the tents had been taken down, when people noticed that shortly beforehand, and in a departure from its daily prac- tice, Pompey's line had advanced some distance from the rampart, so that it seemed possible to fight on ground that was not disadvantageous. At that point Caesar said to his 4 men, when his column was already at the gate: "We must postpone our march for now and think about battle—our perpetual request! We are[100] mentally ready to fight; here- after it will not be easy to find an occasion." He quickly led out unencumbered troops.

86. Pompeius quoque, ut postea cognitum est, suorum omnium hortatu statuerat proelio decertare. Namque etiam in consilio superioribus diebus dixerat: priusquam concurrerent acies fore uti exercitus Caesaris pelleretur.
2 Id cum essent plerique admirati "Scio me" inquit "paene incredibilem rem polliceri. Sed rationem consili mei acci-
3 pite quo firmiore animo ⟨ad⟩[109] proelium prodeatis. Persuasi equitibus nostris, idque mihi facturos confirmaverunt, ut cum propius sit accessum, dextrum Caesaris cornu ab latere aperto aggrederentur et circumventa ab tergo acie prius perturbatum exercitum pellerent quam a
4 nobis telum in hostem iaceretur. Ita sine periculo legionum et paene sine vulnere bellum conficiemus. Id autem
5 difficile non est cum tantum equitatu valeamus." Simul denuntiavit ut essent animo parati in posterum et quoniam fieret dimicandi potestas, ut saepe cogitavissent,[110] ne suam neu reliquorum opinionem fallerent.

87. Hunc Labienus excepit et cum Caesaris copias despiceret, Pompei consilium summis laudibus efferret "Noli" inquit "existimare, Pompei, hunc esse exercitum
2 qui Galliam Germaniamque devicerit. Omnibus interfui proeliis neque temere incognitam rem pronuntio. Perexigua pars illius exercitus superest. Magna pars deperiit, quod accidere tot proeliis fuit necesse, multos autumni pestilentia in Italia consumpsit, multi domum discesse-
3 runt, multi sunt relicti in continenti. An non exaudistis ex iis qui per causam valetudinis remanserunt cohortes esse

---

[109] ⟨ad⟩ *Meusel*   [110] cogitavissent] flagitavissent *Markland*

---

[101] For "thought about," Markland proposed "demanded." Other emendations have been proposed.

86. Pompey, too, as people learned later, had decided to settle matters with a battle, on the urging of everyone on his side. For in council recently he had even said that Caesar's army would be routed before the lines met. When 2 most present expressed surprise he said: "I know that I am making a nearly incredible promise. But here is the thinking behind my plan, so that you can approach the battle with sturdier morale. I have persuaded our cavalry—and 3 they have assured me that they will do this—to attack Caesar's right wing on its open flank when the approach is complete. Once they have encircled Caesar's line from the back, they are going to rout the army in disarray before our men throw a weapon at the enemy. We will thus finish 4 the war with no danger to the legions and practically without a wound. It is not a difficult matter, given how strong we are in cavalry." He also announced that they should be 5 mentally ready for the next day. "Since there will be an opportunity for fighting, something you have thought about[101] often, do not disprove the opinion that I and everyone else has of you."

87. Labienus went next, expressing scorn for Caesar's troops and praising Pompey's plan with the utmost enthusiasm: "Do not suppose, Pompey, that this is the army that conquered Gaul and Germany. I took part in all of the 2 battles; I am not speaking at random about something unfamiliar to me. The surviving portion of that army is exceedingly small. Most of it has perished, as was bound to happen in so many battles. Disease took many in the fall in Italy, many went home, many were left behind in Italy. Have you not heard that they formed cohorts in Brundi- 3 sium from those who stayed behind because of ill-health?

4 Brundisi factas? Hae copiae quas videtis ex dilectibus
horum annorum in citeriore Gallia sunt refectae, et plerique sunt ex colonis[111] Transpadanis. Ac tamen quod fuit
5 roboris duobus proeliis Dyrrachinis interiit." Haec cum
dixisset iuravit se nisi victorem in castra non reversurum
6 reliquosque ut idem facerent hortatus est. Hoc laudans
Pompeius idem iuravit. Nec vero ex reliquis fuit quisquam
7 qui iurare dubitaret. Haec cum facta sunt in consilio
magna spe et laetitia omnium discessum est. Ac iam animo
victoriam praecipiebant, quod de re tanta et a tam perito
imperatore nihil frustra confirmari videbatur.

88. Caesar cum Pompei castris appropinquasset ad
2 hunc modum aciem eius instructam animadvertit. Erant
in sinistro cornu legiones duae traditae a Caesare initio
dissensionis ex senatus consulto, quarum una prima, altera
3 tertia appellabatur. In eo loco ipse erat Pompeius. Mediam aciem Scipio cum legionibus Syriacis tenebat. Cili-
ciensis legio coniuncta cum cohortibus Hispanis, quas
traductas ab Afranio docuimus, in dextro cornu erant col-
4 locatae. Has firmissimas se habere Pompeius existimabat.
Reliquas inter aciem mediam cornuaque interiecerat nu-
5 meroque cohortes CX expleverat. Haec erant milia XLV,
evocatorum circiter duo quae ⟨se⟩[112] ex beneficiariis superiorum exercituum ad eum converterant,[113] quae tota
acie disperserat. Reliquas cohortes VII castris propinquis-

---

[111] ex colonis *MUST*: coloniis *V*   [112] ⟨se⟩ *Damon*
[113] converterant] convenerant *S*

---

[102] For "settlers," some editors print a lightly emended version of V's text, "colonies."   [103] This has not in fact been
explained. For the "loose ends" in the *BC*, see the Introduction.

The forces that you see were reconstituted by recruitment 4
in those years in Nearer Gaul, and most of the men come
from Transpadane settlers.[102] Even so, whatever was reliable fell in the two battles at Dyrrachium." After speaking 5
thus, he took an oath that he would not return to camp
except as a victor, and he urged the rest to do the same.
Pompey applauded and took the same oath. And not one 6
of the rest hesitated to take the oath. After these events in 7
council, they broke up in high hope and general rejoicing.
Indeed they already felt that victory was theirs, since on
so important a matter it seemed impossible that the assurances given by so experienced a commander were empty.

88. When Caesar drew near Pompey's camp, he observed that his line was drawn up as follows. On the left 2
wing were the two legions handed over by Caesar at the
beginning of the conflict in accordance with the senate's
decree. One of these was called the "First," the other the
"Third." Pompey was in this area. Scipio held the middle 3
of the line with legions from Syria. A legion from Cilicia
together with cohorts from Spain—brought over, as I explained, by Afranius[103]—had been positioned on the right
wing. Pompey thought that these were his strongest units. 4
He had placed the rest between the middle of the line and
the wings, to a total of a hundred and ten cohorts. These 5
amounted to forty-five thousand men, and there were
about two thousand reenlisted men who had made their
way to him,[104] special-assignment soldiers from his former
armies.[105] His last seven cohorts he had stationed to guard

[104] For the lightly emended "had made their way to him,"
many editors adopt the text of S, "had joined him."

[105] For the category (*beneficiarius*), compare 1.75.2.

6 que castellis praesidio disposuerat. Dextrum cornu eius
rivus quidam impeditis ripis muniebat. Quam ob causam
cunctum equitatum sagittarios funditoresque omnes sinistro cornu obiecerat.[114]

89. Caesar superius institutum servans decimam legionem in dextro cornu nonam in sinistro collocaverat,
tametsi erat Dyrrachinis proeliis vehementer attenuata.
Et huic sic adiunxit octavam ut paene unam ex duabus
2 efficeret atque alteram alteri praesidio esse iusserat. Cohortes in acie LXXX constitutas habebat, quae summa erat
milium XXII. Cohortes duas castris praesidio reliquerat.
3 Sinistro cornu Antonium, dextro P. Sullam, media acie Cn.
Domitium praeposuerat. Ipse contra Pompeium constitit.
4 Simul iis rebus animadversis quas demonstravimus, timens ne a multitudine equitum dextrum cornu circumve-
niretur, celeriter ex tertia acie singulas[115] cohortes detraxit
atque ex his quartam instituit equitatuique opposuit et
quid fieri vellet ostendit monuitque eius diei victoriam in
5 earum cohortium virtute constare. Simul tertiae aciei
[totique exercitui][116] imperavit ne iniussu suo concurreret:
se cum id fieri vellet vexillo signum daturum.

90. Exercitum cum militari more ad pugnam cohorta-
retur suaque in eum perpetui temporis officia praedicaret
in primis commemoravit: testibus se militibus uti posse

---

114 obiecerat] adiecerat *Meusel*
115 ex tertia (*or* terna) acie singulas] extrema acie sex *Latino
Latini*: sex tertiae aciei singulas *Markland*
116 [totique exercitui] *Novák*

---

106 For "facing the enemy on," Meusel substituted "beside."
107 The numbers in this paragraph are disputed.

the camp and nearby outposts. His right wing was pro-   6
tected by a river with banks that were hard to negotiate.
For this reason he had set his whole cavalry and all of his
archers and slingers facing the enemy on[106] his left wing.

89. Caesar, keeping to previous arrangements, had
placed the tenth legion on his right wing, the ninth on the
left, despite the fact that it was seriously shorthanded after
the battles at Dyrrachium. He linked the eighth to it in
such a way that he made the two practically one. He had
also ordered each to protect the other. He had drawn up   2
eighty cohorts in his line, a total of twenty-two thousand
men. He had left two[107] cohorts to guard the camp. On the   3
left wing he had put Antony in command, on the right
Publius Sulla, and in the middle of the line Gnaeus Domitius. He himself stood opposite Pompey. In addition, hav-   4
ing observed the arrangements I mentioned and worrying
that his right wing might be encircled by the mass of cavalry, he quickly withdrew individual cohorts from his third
line.[108] From these he created a fourth line facing the
cavalry and showed what he wanted done, with a warning
that the day's victory rested on the courage of those cohorts. He also ordered the third line not to engage without   5
his orders: "I will signal with a flag when I want it done."

90. While giving the customary combat exhortation,
and citing his continual services to the army, Caesar emphasized these points: "You soldiers can attest to the fact

[108] For "individual cohorts from his third line," where the
manuscripts are divided between *tertia* and *terna*, Latino Latini
proposed "six cohorts from his last line" (Plut. *Caes*. 44.3, and
other ancient sources), Markland "six cohorts one by one from the
third line" (cf. *BG* 7.47.7).

quanto studio pacem petisset, quae per Vatinium in colloquiis, quae per Aulum Clodium cum Scipione egisset, quibus modis ad Oricum cum Libone de mittendis legatis
2 contendisset; neque se umquam abuti militum sanguine
neque rem publicam alterutro exercitu privare voluisse.
3 Hac habita oratione exposcentibus militibus et studio
pugnae ardentibus tuba signum dedit.

91. Erat Crastinus evocatus in exercitu Caesaris, qui
superiore anno apud eum primum pilum in legione de-
2 cima duxerat, vir singulari virtute. Hic signo dato "Sequimini me," inquit "manipulares mei qui fuistis, et vestro
imperatori quam constituistis[117] operam date. Vnum hoc
proelium superest. Quo confecto et ille suam dignitatem
3 et nos nostram libertatem recuperabimus." Simul respiciens Caesarem "Faciam" inquit "hodie, imperator, ut aut
4 vivo mihi aut mortuo gratias agas." Haec cum dixisset primus ex dextro cornu procucurrit atque eum electi milites
circiter CXX voluntarii [eiusdem centuriae][118] sunt prose-
cuti.

92. Inter duas acies tantum erat relictum spati ut satis
2 esset ad concursum utriusque exercitus. Sed Pompeius
suis praedixerat ut Caesaris impetum exciperent neve se
loco moverent, aciemque eius distrahi paterentur. Idque
admonitu C. Triari fecisse dicebatur, ut primus excursus
visque militum infringeretur aciesque distenderetur, atque in suis ordinibus dispositi dispersos adorirentur.

---

[117] quam constituistis *MUST*: quem c- V: quam institu- *Paul*
[118] [eiusdem centuriae] *Fröhlich*

---

[109] Vatinius: 3.19; Clodius: 3.57; Libo: 3.16–17.

that I sought peace with great determination. You know what I accomplished through Vatinius in talks and through Aulus Clodius with Scipio, and how I exerted myself at Oricum with Libo over sending delegations.[109] I never 2 waste soldiers' blood, and I did not want to deprive the state of one of its two armies." After this speech, when the 3 soldiers were clamoring and blazing with enthusiasm for battle, he let the signal sound.

91. There was a reenlisted man, Crastinus, in Caesar's army, who had been his chief centurion in the tenth legion the year before, a man of remarkable courage. After the 2 signal was given, Crastinus said "Follow me, you who were men of my unit, and give your commander the effort you have resolved on.[110] This one battle remains. Once it is over, he will have his dignity again and we our liberty." At 3 the same time, looking at Caesar, he said, "My actions today, general, will make you thank me either alive or dead." After saying this he was the first to run forward 4 from the right wing, and about a hundred and twenty picked soldiers, volunteers, followed him.

92. Between the two lines just enough space had been left for a charge by each army. But Pompey had instructed 2 his men to absorb Caesar's charge; they were not to move from their position, but to allow his line to break itself up. People say that he did this on the advice of Gaius Triarius, so that the soldiers' first powerful charge would be rendered ineffective and Caesar's line distended, and that his own men in proper formation could attack a scattered

[110] For "the effort you have resolved on," the manuscript V has "whom you have put in power," and Paul proposed "the effort you initiated."

3 Leviusque casura pila sperabat in loco retentis militibus
quam si ipsi immissis telis occurrissent, simul fore ut du-
plicato cursu Caesaris milites exanimarentur quod[119] et
4 lassitudine conficerentur. Quod nobis quidem nulla ratione factum a Pompeio videtur propterea quod est quae-
dam animi incitatio atque alacritas naturaliter innata om-
5 nibus quae studio pugnae incenditur. Hanc non reprimere
sed augere imperatores debent. Neque frustra antiquitus
institutum est ut signa undique concinerent clamoremque
universi tollerent, Quibus rebus et hostes terreri et suos
incitari existimaverunt.

93. Sed nostri milites dato signo cum infestis pilis procucurrissent atque animadvertissent non concurri a Pompeianis, usu periti ac superioribus pugnis exercitati sua
sponte cursum represserunt et ad medium fere spatium
constiterunt ne consumptis viribus appropinquarent. Parvoque intermisso temporis spatio ac rursus renovato cursu
pila miserunt celeriterque, ut erat praeceptum a Caesare,
2 gladios strinxerunt. Neque vero Pompeiani huic rei defue-
runt. Nam et tela missa exceperunt et impetum legionum
tulerunt et ordines conservaverunt pilisque missis ad gla-
3 dios redierunt. Eodem tempore equites ab sinistro Pompei cornu, ut erat imperatum, universi procucurrerunt
4 omnisque multitudo sagittariorum se profudit. Quorum
impetum noster equitatus non tulit sed paulum loco motus
cessit. Equitesque Pompei hoc acrius instare et se turma-
tim explicare aciemque nostram a latere aperto circumire

119 quod *omitted by* S

---

111 For "because they would also," editors often print the
reading of S, "and they would be."

enemy. Pompey also hoped that the spears would fall more 3
lightly on soldiers held in place than if they themselves ran
into projectiles coming at them, likewise that Caesar's soldiers would be disheartened by the double run because
they would also[111] be undone by exhaustion. But to me at 4
least this action seems to have been taken by Pompey for
no valid reason, because there is a certain stirring of the
spirit and an eagerness naturally inborn in all men that is
kindled by enthusiasm for combat. Commanders should 5
not repress this but augment it. Nor is it a pointless ancient
institution that battle signals sound from all sides and every man raises a shout. By these things, they thought, the
enemies are terrified and one's own men incited.

93. Our soldiers ran forward at the signal with spears
poised to throw, then noticed that the Pompeians were not
running toward them. Taught by experience and trained
in earlier battles they stopped their run of their own accord and halted about half way so that they would not
approach drained of strength. After a short interval they
started running again, then hurled their spears and
promptly, on Caesar's instructions, drew their swords. Nor 2
did Pompey's men fall short, for they absorbed the salvo
of projectiles and withstood the legions' impact and kept
their formations intact, and after throwing their own
spears they went for their swords. At this moment the 3
cavalry on Pompey's left wing charged as one, as ordered,
and the entire mass of archers streamed forward. Our cav- 4
alry failed to withstand the impact, and after being pushed
out of position they gave a little ground. At this, Pompey's
cavalry began to apply more intense pressure and, deploying by squadrons, to encircle our line on its unprotected

5 coeperunt. Quod ubi Caesar animadvertit quartae aciei,
  quam instituerat ex cohortium numero,[120] dedit signum.
6 Illae celeriter procucurrerunt infestisque signis tanta vi in
  Pompei equites impetum fecerunt ut eorum nemo consisteret omnesque conversi non solum loco excederent sed
7 protinus incitati fuga montes altissimos peterent. Quibus
  submotis omnes sagittarii funditoresque destituti iner-
8 mes[121] sine praesidio interfecti sunt. Eodem impetu cohortes sinistrum cornu pugnantibus etiam tum ac resisten-
  tibus in acie Pompeianis circumierunt eosque a tergo sunt
  adorti.

94. Eodem tempore tertiam aciem Caesar, quae quieta
fuerat et se ad id tempus loco tenuerat, procurrere iussit.
2 Ita cum recentes atque integri defessis successissent, alii
  autem a tergo adorirentur, sustinere Pompeiani non po-
3 tuerunt atque universi terga verterunt. Neque vero Caesarem fefellit quin ab iis cohortibus quae contra equitatum
  in quarta acie collocatae essent initium victoriae oriretur,
4 ut ipse in cohortandis militibus pronuntiaverat. Ab his
  enim primum equitatus est pulsus, ab isdem factae caedes
  sagittariorum ac funditorum, ab isdem acies Pompeiana a
  sinistra parte [erat] circumita atque initium fugae factum.
5 Sed Pompeius ut equitatum suum pulsum vidit atque eam
  partem cui maxime confidebat perterritam animadvertit,
  aliis diffisus acie excessit protinusque se in castra equo
  contulit et iis centurionibus quos in statione ad praetoriam

---

120 ex cohortium numero] sex c- n- *Orsini*: sex c- [n-] *Faerno*
121 [inermes] *Paul*

---

112 For "with some of his cohorts," Orsini and Faerno proposed "of a total of six cohorts" and "of six cohorts," respectively.

flank. When Caesar noticed this, he gave the signal to the 5
fourth line, which he had set up with some of his cohorts.[112] They rushed forward promptly, and in attacking 6
made so powerful an impact on Pompey's cavalry that
none of them stood fast; the Pompeians all turned around
and not only left their position but straightaway and in a
hurried retreat headed for the highest hills. Once these 7
were out of the way, the archers and slingers were left
defenseless,[113] without a guard; they were all killed. In the 8
same movement our cohorts outflanked the left wing,
where the Pompeians in the line were still fighting and
resisting, and attacked them from behind.

94. At this point Caesar ordered the third line to
charge; it had not seen action and had held its position
until now. Therefore, since fresh, sound troops were re- 2
lieving tired ones, and others were attacking from behind,
the Pompeians all turned and ran, finding resistance impossible. Nor was Caesar wrong in thinking that the first 3
stage of victory would come from the cohorts stationed in
the fourth line facing the cavalry, as he himself had predicted in exhorting the men. It was by these that the Pom- 4
peian cavalry was routed, first, and these same units
slaughtered the archers and slingers, and likewise outflanked Pompey's line on the left and started the flight. As 5
for Pompey, when he saw his cavalry routed and realized
that the unit he trusted most was terrified, having no confidence in the rest he left the line and rode immediately
to his camp. To the centurions stationed at the main gate

---

[113] I have rendered the surprising adjective "unarmed" meta-
phorically; Paul excised it.

portam posuerat clare ut milites exaudirent "Tuemini"
inquit "castra et defendite diligenter si quid durius acci-
derit. Ego reliquas portas circumeo et castrorum praesidia
6 confirmo." Haec cum dixisset se in praetorium contulit
summae rei diffidens et tamen eventum expectans.

95. Caesar Pompeianis ex fuga intra vallum compulsis
nullum spatium perterritis dare oportere existimans milites cohortatus est ut beneficio Fortunae uterentur cas-
2 traque oppugnarent. Qui etsi magno aestu fatigati—nam
ad meridiem res erat perducta—tamen ad omnem labo-
3 rem animo parati imperio paruerunt. Castra a cohortibus
quae ibi praesidio erant relictae industrie defendebantur,
4 multo etiam acrius a Thracibus barbarisque auxiliis. Nam
qui acie refugerant milites et animo perterriti et lassitudine confecti missis plerique armis signisque militaribus
magis de reliqua fuga quam de castrorum defensione cogi-
5 tabant. Neque vero diutius qui in vallo constiterant multitudinem telorum sustinere potuerunt sed confecti vulneribus locum reliquerunt protinusque omnes ducibus usi
centurionibus tribunisque militum in altissimos montes
qui ad castra pertinebant confugerunt.

96. In castris Pompei videre licuit trichilas structas,
magnum argenti pondus expositum, recentibus caespiti-
bus tabernacula constrata, Luci etiam Lentuli et nonnul-
lorum tabernacula protecta edera, multaque praeterea
quae nimiam luxuriem et victoriae fiduciam designarent,
ut facile existimari posset nihil eos de eventu eius diei ti-
2 muisse qui non necessarias conquirerent voluptates. At hi

he said loudly, so that the soldiers could hear: "Watch over
the camp and defend it diligently if the situation gets any
worse. I am going round the other gates and strengthening
the units guarding the camp." After saying this he went to   6
headquarters, skeptical of success but nevertheless awaiting the outcome.

95. Once the fleeing Pompeians had been driven behind the protection of their rampart, Caesar exhorted his
troops, thinking that they should give no respite to terrified men: "Use the gift of Fortune! Attack the camp!"
Although the intense heat had made them weary—the   2
business had dragged on until midday—they nevertheless
obeyed his command, mentally ready for any effort. The   3
camp was energetically defended by the cohorts that had
been left behind to guard it, but even more vehemently
by the Thracian and native auxiliaries. (The soldiers who   4
had fled from the line, mentally terrified and overcome by
weariness, had mostly abandoned their weapons and their
units' standards, and were thinking more about onward
flight than about the camp's defense.) But those who had   5
made a stand on the rampart were not long able to withstand the huge number of projectiles; overcome by their
wounds they abandoned the position. Immediately thereafter they all followed the lead of centurions and staff officers in taking refuge in the highest hills near the camp.

96. In Pompey's camp one could see the gazebos that
had been built, the large quantity of silverware set out, the
tents floored with freshly cut turf—those of Lucius Lentulus and others even bowered with ivy—and many things
besides that indicated undue extravagance and confidence
in victory. People readily supposed, therefore, that men
who went after unnecessary pleasures had not been at all

miserrimo ac patientissimo exercitu Caesaris luxuriem obiciebant, cui semper omnia ad necessarium usum defuissent.

3 Pompeius iam cum intra vallum nostri versarentur equum nactus detractis insignibus imperatoris decimana porta se ex castris eiecit protinusque equo citato Larisam

4 contendit. Neque ibi constitit sed eadem celeritate paucos suos ex fuga nactus nocturno itinere non intermisso comitatu equitum XXX ad mare pervenit navemque frumentariam conscendit, saepe, ut dicebatur, querens tantum se opinionem fefellisse ut a quo genere hominum victoriam sperasset ab eo initio fugae facto paene proditus videretur.

97. Caesar castris potitus a militibus contendit ne in praeda occupati reliqui negoti gerendi facultatem dimit-

2 terent. Qua re impetrata montem opere circummunire instituit. Pompeiani quod is mons erat sine aqua diffisi ei loco relicto monte universi iugis eius Larisam versus reci-

3 pere coeperunt. Qua spe[122] animadversa Caesar copias suas divisit partemque legionum in castris Pompei remanere iussit, partem in sua castra remisit, IIII secum legiones duxit commodioreque itinere Pompeianis occurrere coepit. Et progressus milia passuum VI aciem in-

4 struxit. Qua re animadversa Pompeiani in quodam monte constiterunt. Hunc montem flumen subluebat. Caesar milites cohortatus [est], etsi totius diei continenti labore

---

122 spe] re *ed. pr.*

---

114 For "what they were hoping," the first edition substituted "what they were doing."

worried about the day's outcome. And yet the Pompeians 2
used to reproach the extravagance of Caesar's utterly pitiable and long-suffering army, which was constantly short
of every necessity.

When our men were circulating inside his defenses, 3
Pompey got a horse, removed his general's insignia, and
left the camp by the rear gate; his immediate destination,
at a gallop, was Larisa. Not halting there but continuing 4
at the same pace after meeting a few of his men who had
escaped, and without breaking his journey during the
night, he reached the sea with an escort of thirty cavalry
and boarded a grain ship, complaining frequently, so people said, that his expectation had proven him so wrong:
given that the rout had begun with the category of men on
whom his hopes of victory rested, it would almost look like
he was the victim of treachery.

97. After taking control of Pompey's camp Caesar
pleaded with the soldiers not to spend time on plunder
and throw away the chance of finishing their work. Suc- 2
cessful in this, he began to encircle the hill with fortifications. The Pompeians, having no confidence in their position because the hill was waterless, abandoned that hill
and began to withdraw en masse along the ridges toward
Larisa. Caesar realized what they were hoping[114] and di- 3
vided his forces: he ordered some legions to remain in
Pompey's camp, sent some back to his own camp, and took
four with him as he started along an easier route toward
confrontation with the Pompeians. After advancing six
miles he drew up his line. Seeing this the Pompeians 4
halted on a hill with a river at its base. After exhorting his
soldiers, and despite the fact that they were exhausted by
a full day's continual exertions and night was already com-

erant confecti noxque iam suberat, tamen munitione flumen a monte seclusit ne noctu aquari Pompeiani possent.
5 Quo perfecto opere illi de deditione missis legatis agere coeperunt. Pauci ordinis senatorii, qui se cum iis coniunxerant, nocte fuga salutem petiverunt.

98. Caesar prima luce omnes eos qui in monte consederant ex superioribus locis in planitiem descendere atque
2 arma proicere iussit. Quod ubi sine recusatione fecerunt passisque palmis proiecti ad terram flentes ab eo salutem petiverunt consolatus consurgere iussit. Et pauca apud eos de lenitate sua locutus quo minore essent timore omnes conservavit militibusque suis commendavit ne qui eorum
3 violaretur neu quid sui desiderarent. Hac adhibita diligentia ex castris sibi legiones alias occurrere et eas quas secum duxerat invicem requiescere atque in castra reverti iussit. Eodemque die Larisam pervenit.

99. In eo proelio non amplius CC milites desideravit.
2 Sed centuriones, fortes viros, circiter XXX amisit. Interfectus est etiam fortissime pugnans Crastinus, cuius mentionem supra fecimus, gladio in os adversum coniecto.
3 Neque id fuit falsum quod ille in pugnam proficiscens dixerat. Sic enim Caesar existimabat eo proelio excellentissimam virtutem Crastini fuisse optimeque eum de se
4 meritum iudicabat. Ex Pompeiano exercitu circiter milia XV cecidisse videbantur. Sed in deditionem venerunt amplius milia XXIIII. Namque etiam cohortes quae praesidio in castellis fuerant sese Sullae dediderunt. Multi praeterea in finitimas civitates refugerunt. Signaque militaria ex

ing on, Caesar succeeded in cutting off the hill from the
river by means of a fortification, so that the Pompeians
would be unable to obtain water by night. When the earth-   5
work was complete, the enemy sent a delegation and began negotiations for surrender. A few men of the senatorial order who had joined them sought safety in flight that
night.

98. At dawn Caesar ordered all those who had halted
on the hill to descend from the high ground into the plain
and throw down their weapons. They did so without pro-   2
test. With outstretched hands, prostrate and weeping,
they sought safety from him. He comforted them and ordered them to stand. Speaking briefly to them about his
clemency, to lessen their fear, he spared them all and commended them to his soldiers: "None of them is to be
harmed or deprived of any possessions." After attending   3
to this he ordered other legions to come from camp and
meet him, and those that he had brought with him to have
their turn at resting and return to camp. He went to Larisa
the same day.

99. In that battle Caesar lost no more than two hundred
soldiers. But his losses included around thirty centurions,
brave men. Crastinus, too, whom I mentioned earlier, was   2
killed fighting with exemplary bravery, taking a sword to
the face. Nor was he wrong in what he said as he went into   3
combat. For Caesar thought that Crastinus' courage in
that battle was simply unmatched, and felt that Crastinus
had earned his best thanks. Of the Pompeian army it ap-   4
peared that around fifteen thousand had fallen. But more
than twenty-four thousand surrendered, for even the cohorts that had been in the outposts surrendered to Sulla.
Many, too, fled to nearby cities. After the battle 180 mili-

proelio ad Caesarem sunt relata CLXXX et aquilae VIIII.
5 L. Domitius ex castris in montem refugiens, cum vires
eum lassitudine defecissent, ab equitibus est interfectus.

100. Eodem tempore D. Laelius cum classe ad Brundisium venit eademque ratione qua factum a Libone antea
demonstravimus insulam obiectam portui Brundisino te-
2 nuit. Similiter Vatinius, qui Brundisio praeerat, tectis in-
structisque scaphis elicuit naves Laelianas atque ex his
longius productam unam quinqueremem et minores duas
in angustiis portus cepit. Itemque per equites dispositos
3 aqua prohibere classiarios instituit. Sed Laelius tempore
anni commodiore usus ad navigandum onerariis navibus
Corcyra Dyrrachioque aquam suis supportabat neque a
proposito deterrebatur neque ante proelium in Thessalia
factum cognitum aut ignominia amissarum navium aut
necessariarum rerum inopia ex portu insulaque expelli
potuit.

101. Isdem fere temporibus C. Cassius cum classe
Syrorum et Phoenicum et Cilicum in Siciliam venit. Et
cum esset Caesaris classis divisa in duas partes—dimidiae
parti praeesset P. Sulpicius praetor ‹ad› Vibonem, ad fretum dimidiae M. Pomponius ad Messanam—prius Cassius ad Messanam navibus advolavit quam Pomponius de
2 eius adventu cognosceret, perturbatumque eum nactus
nullis custodiis neque ordinibus certis, magno vento et
secundo completas onerarias naves taeda et pice et stuppa
reliquisque rebus quae sunt ad incendia in Pomponianam
classem immisit atque omnes naves incendit XXXV, e qui-
3 bus erant XX constratae. Tantusque eo facto timor incessit
ut cum esset legio praesidio Messanae vix oppidum defen-

---

[115] See 3.23–24.

tary standards were brought to Caesar, and nine eagles. Lucius Domitius, who fled the camp for high ground, was 5 killed by the cavalry when, in his exhaustion, strength failed him.

100. In this same period Decimus Laelius went to Brundisium with his fleet and seized the harbor's barrier island just as Libo did, as I indicated earlier.[115] Vatinius, 2 who was in command at Brundisium, likewise used small craft supplied with decks and tackle to lure out Laelius' ships, capturing one quinquereme that advanced too far and two smaller boats in the harbor mouth. He too began to prevent the crews from getting water by deploying cavalry. But Laelius, with a better season for sailing, supplied 3 water to his men using cargo ships from Corcyra and Dyrrachium. He was not deterred from his operation, nor could he be expelled from the harbor and island by either the humiliation of losing ships or the shortage of necessities—until he learned about the battle in Thessaly.

101. At about the same time Gaius Cassius went to Sicily with his fleet of Syrians, Phoenicians, and Cilicians. Caesar's fleet was divided into two parts: the praetor Publius Sulpicius was in command of half of it, at Vibo, and at the Strait Marcus Pomponius was in command of half, at Messana. Cassius therefore descended on Messana with his ships before Pomponius could learn of his arrival. He 2 caught him in disarray, without reliable patrols or formations. With a strong wind in his favor Cassius filled cargo ships with pine, pitch, tow, and other combustibles and sent them against Pomponius' fleet, burning all thirty-five, twenty of them decked vessels. This caused so much alarm 3 that Messana, despite its legionary garrison, was barely

335

deretur. Et nisi eo ipso tempore quidam nuntii de Caesaris victoria per dispositos equites essent allati existimabant

4 plerique futurum fuisse uti amitteretur. Sed opportunissime nuntiis allatis oppidum fuit defensum Cassiusque ad Sulpicianam inde classem profectus est Vibonem. Applicatisque nostris ad terram navibus propter eundem timorem [pari atque antea ratione egerunt][123] Cassius secundum nactus ventum onerarias naves [circiter XL][124] praeparatas ad incendium immisit. Et flamma ab utroque

5 cornu comprensa naves sunt combustae V. Cumque ignis magnitudine venti latius serperet milites qui ex veteribus legionibus erant relicti praesidio navibus ex numero ae-

6 grorum ignominiam non tulerunt sed sua sponte naves conscenderunt et a terra solverunt impetuque facto in Cassianam classem quinqueremes duas, in quarum altera erat Cassius, ceperunt. Sed Cassius exceptus scapha refu-

7 giit. Praeterea duae sunt depressae triremes. Neque multo post de proelio facto in Thessalia cognitum est, ut ipsis Pompeianis fides fieret. Nam ante id tempus fingi a legatis amicisque Caesaris arbitrabantur. Quibus rebus cognitis ex his locis Cassius cum classe discessit.

102. Caesar omnibus rebus relictis persequendum sibi Pompeium existimavit quascumque in partes se ex fuga recepisset, ne rursus copias comparare alias et bellum renovare posset. Et quantumcumque itineris equitatu efficere poterat cotidie progrediebatur legionemque unam

2 minoribus itineribus subsequi iussit. Erat edictum Pompei nomine Amphipoli propositum uti omnes eius provin-

[123] [pari . . . egerunt] *Damon*
[124] *Forchhammer excised* circiter XL, *Nipperdey moved it to* *before* propter.

defended. Most people think that, if the news about Caesar's victory had not arrived right then, relayed by the
cavalry, the city would have been lost. But since the news   4
did arrive in a most timely fashion, the city's defense held
and Cassius set out from there for Sulpicius' fleet at Vibo.
After our ships were beached because of the same fear,[116]
Cassius, getting a favorable wind, sent against them cargo
ships equipped for conflagration. The flames took hold at
both ends of the line and five ships were burned. Although   5
the strength of the wind was extending the fire's spread,
the soldiers from veteran legions who had been left to
guard the ships—they were on sick leave—refused to be
humiliated, boarding and launching some ships of their   6
own accord. They attacked Cassius' fleet and captured two
quinqueremes. Cassius was aboard one of them but fled
in a longboat. Two further triremes were sunk. Soon there-   7
after people learned about the battle fought in Thessaly,
to the point that even Pompeians believed it. (Before this
they thought it was an invention by Caesar's officers and
friends.) When he understood the situation, Cassius left
the area with his fleet.

102. Caesar thought that he should leave all else aside
and pursue Pompey wherever he went after his escape, to
make it impossible for him to procure other troops and
renew the war. He covered as much ground as he could
each day with the cavalry, and ordered one legion to follow
by shorter stages. An edict in Pompey's name was pub-   2
lished at Amphipolis ordering an assembly of all of the

116 After "because of this same fear," the manuscripts read
"acted in the same way as before," which lacks a subject. Various
excisions have been proposed to repair this spot.

ciae iuniores—Graeci civesque Romani—iurandi causa
3 convenirent. Sed utrum avertendae suspicionis causa
Pompeius proposuisset ut quam diutissime longioris fugae
consilium occultaret, an novis dilectibus, si nemo preme-
ret, Macedoniam tenere conaretur existimari non poterat.
4 Ipse ad ancoram una nocte constitit. Et vocatis ad se Amphipoli hospitibus et pecunia ad necessarios sumptus cor-
rogata cognitoque Caesaris adventu ex eo loco discessit et
5 Mytilenas paucis diebus venit. Biduum tempestate reten-
tus navibusque aliis additis actuariis in Ciliciam atque inde
6 Cyprum pervenit. Ibi cognoscit consensu omnium Antio-
chensium civiumque Romanorum qui illic negotiarentur
arcem captam[125] esse excludendi sui causa nuntiosque
dimissos ad eos qui se ex fuga in finitimas ⟨civitates⟩ rece-
pisse dicerentur: ne Antiochiam adirent; id si fecissent
7 magno eorum capitis periculo futurum. Idem hoc L. Lentulo, qui superiore anno consul fuerat, et P. Lentulo
consulari ac nonnullis aliis acciderat Rhodi, qui cum ex
fuga Pompeium sequerentur atque in insulam venissent
oppido ac portu recepti non erant missisque ad eos nuntiis—ex his locis discederent—contra voluntatem suam
8 naves solverunt. Iamque de Caesaris adventu fama ad civitates perferebatur.

103. Quibus cognitis rebus Pompeius deposito adeun-
dae Syriae consilio pecunia societatibus[126] sublata et a

---

[125] arcem captam *Oudendorp*: arcem aram captam *M and U
in the margin*: aram captam *UTV*: aram capta *S*: arma capta
Forchhammer

[126] societatibus *Holder*: societatis ω

province's fighting-age men—Greeks and Roman citizens—to take the military oath. It was impossible to know 3
whether Pompey published it to avert suspicion, so that he could conceal his plan of onward flight for as long as possible, or in an attempt to hold Macedonia with new recruits, if no one applied pressure. Pompey spent one night 4
at anchor, summoning his connections at Amphipolis and collecting money for necessary expenses. Learning of Caesar's approach he left that location and within a few days came to Mytilene. After being delayed two days by 5
weather and acquiring some additional fast vessels he went on to Cilicia and thence to Cyprus. There he learned 6
that the people of Antioch and all of the Roman citizens in business there had by common consent seized the citadel[117] in order to keep him out, and had sent word to the Pompeians who, people said, had gone to nearby communities after their escape: "Do not come to Antioch. If you do, your lives will be in great danger." The same thing 7
had happened to Lucius Lentulus, the previous year's consul, at Rhodes, and to the ex-consul Publius Lentulus, and some others. These men were following Pompey after their escape, and when they reached Rhodes they were not received into the city or harbor. After messengers were sent to tell them to leave the area, they reluctantly set sail. Communities were already getting word of Caesar's approach. 8

103. Pompey, when he understood the situation, dropped the plan of approaching Syria. He raised money

[117] For "seized the citadel," some editors print an emendation based on the text of S, meaning "taken up arms."

quibusdam privatis sumpta et aeris magno pondere ad militarem usum in naves imposito duobusque milibus hominum armatis—partim quos ex familiis societatum delegerat, partim a negotiatoribus coegerat, quosque ex suis quisque ad hanc rem idoneos existimabat—Pelusium

2 pervenit.[127] Ibi casu rex erat Ptolomaeus, puer aetate, magnis copiis cum sorore Cleopatra bellum gerens, quam paucis ante mensibus per suos propinquos atque amicos regno expulerat. Castraque Cleopatrae non longo spatio

3 ab eius castris distabant. Ad eum Pompeius misit ut pro hospitio atque amicitia patris Alexandria reciperetur at-

4 que illius opibus in calamitate tegeretur. Sed qui ab eo missi erant confecto legationis officio liberius cum militibus regis colloqui coeperunt eosque hortari ut suum ‹quisque›[128] officium Pompeio praestaret neve eius fortu-

5 nam despiceret. In hoc erant numero complures Pompei milites, quos ex eius exercitu acceptos in Syria Gabinius Alexandriam traduxerat belloque confecto apud Ptolomaeum, patrem pueri, reliquerat.

104. His tum cognitis rebus amici regis, qui propter aetatem eius in procuratione erant regni, sive timore adducti, ut postea praedicabant, sollicitato exercitu regio ne Pompeius Alexandriam Aegyptumque occuparet sive despecta eius fortuna, ut plerumque in calamitate ex amicis

---

[127] *No satisfactory repair for this unwieldy sentence has yet been proposed.*

[128] ‹quisque› *Damon. Other editors make the verbs plural.*

---

[118] That is, Roman tax-farming companies; see the note on 3.3.2.

from companies[118] and took it from certain private individuals and loaded a great weight of bronze for military
purposes on his ships, plus two thousand armed men,
partly those he had chosen from the companies' work-
forces, partly collected from traders, and those that anybody thought suitable for this affair from his own people.
He then went to Pelusium. By chance King Ptolemy was   2
there, a boy in years but deploying large forces in the war
with his sister Cleopatra, whom he had expelled from the
kingdom a few months earlier with the help of his relatives
and favorites.[119] Cleopatra's camp was not far from his.
Pompey sent word to him: "My reception in Alexandria   3
should match the welcome and friendship given by your
father, and in this calamity your resources should provide
protection." Those who had been sent by Pompey, how-   4
ever, began to speak quite freely with the king's soldiers
once their mission's business was finished, and to urge
them that each do his duty by Pompey and not despise his
misfortune. Among the latter were many of Pompey's sol-   5
diers, whom Gabinius had received from Pompey's army
in Syria, taken to Alexandria, and left there with Ptolemy,
the boy's father, when the war was over.[120]

104. This came to the attention of the king's favorites,
who were managing the kingdom because of his age. Perhaps they were motivated by the worry, as they later declared, that Pompey would make an appeal to the royal
army and occupy Alexandria and Egypt. Or perhaps his
misfortune made them contemptuous; it often happens
that in a calamity enemies emerge from among one's

[119] "Favorites" (*amici*) were courtiers in Hellenistic courts.
[120] Gabinius restored the elder Ptolemy to his throne in 55.

inimici existunt, iis qui erant ab eo missi palam liberaliter
2 responderunt eumque ad regem venire iusserunt. Ipsi
clam consilio inito Achillam, praefectum regium, [sin-
gium] singulari hominem audacia, et L. Septimium, tribu-
3 num militum, ad interficiendum Pompeium miserunt. Ab
his liberaliter ipse appellatus et quadam notitia Septimi
productus, quod bello praedonum apud eum ordinem
duxerat, naviculam parvulam conscendit cum paucis suis.
Ibi ab Achilla et Septimio interficitur. Item L. Lentulus
comprenditur ab rege et in custodia necatur.

105. Caesar cum in Asiam venisset reperiebat T. Am-
pium conatum esse pecunias tollere Epheso ex fano
Dianae eiusque rei causa senatores omnes ex provincia
evocavisse ut his testibus in summam pecuniae uteretur,
2 sed interpellatum adventu Caesaris profugisse. Ita duobus
temporibus Ephesiae pecuniae Caesar auxilium tulit.
3 Item[129] constabat Elide in templo Minervae—repetitis atque enumeratis diebus—quo die proelium secundum
Caesar fecisset simulacrum Victoriae, quod ante ipsam
Minervam collocatum esset et ante ad simulacrum Minervae spectavisset, ad valvas se templi limenque convertisse.
4 Eodemque die Antiochiae in Syria bis tantus exercitus
clamor et signorum sonus exauditus est ut in muris armata
5 civitas discurreret. Hoc idem Ptolomaide accidit. Perga-
mique in occultis ac reconditis templi, quo praeter sacer-
dotes adire fas non est, quae Graeci ἄδυτα appellant,

---

[129] . . . item *Glandorp*

---

[121] For the other, see 3.33.2.
[122] Glandorp hypothesized a lacuna before "likewise," the
point of which is unclear.   [123] Literally, "no-go" areas.

friends. They gave an outwardly kind response to Pompey's emissaries, ordering him to approach the king. In 2 secret they formed a plot and sent men to kill Pompey: Achillas, the king's general, a man of remarkable nerve, and Lucius Septimius, a staff officer. Addressed kindly by 3 them, and drawn forward by a degree of familiarity with Septimius, since the latter held the rank of centurion under him during the war against the pirates, Pompey boarded the tiny little vessel with a few of his friends. There he was killed by Achillas and Septimius. Ptolemy laid hands on Lucius Lentulus, too; he was killed in prison.

105. When Caesar reached Asia he found that Titus Ampius had attempted to remove funds from the Diana temple at Ephesus; to that end, Caesar learned, Ampius had summoned all of the province's senators, intending to use them as witnesses to the sum, but was interrupted by Caesar's arrival and fled before him. That made two times 2 that Caesar proved helpful to the money at Ephesus.[121] People likewise[122] agreed, after thinking back and count- 3 ing the days, that on the day when Caesar fought his victorious battle, the statue of Victory in the Minerva temple at Elis—it stood in front of Minerva herself and until then faced Minerva's statue—turned toward the doorway and threshold of the temple. On the same day at Antioch in 4 Syria the shouts of an army and horn calls were heard twice, so loud that the populace armed itself and rushed to positions on the walls. The same thing happened at Ptolemais. At Pergamum, moreover, there was a drum- 5 ming in the unseen inner parts of the temple, access to which is permitted only to priests; the Greeks call these ἄδυτα.[123] Likewise at Tralles in the temple of Victory, 6

6 tympana sonuerunt. Item Trallibus in templo Victoriae, ubi Caesaris statuam consecraverant, palma per eos dies integra[130] inter coagmenta lapidum ex pavimento extitisse ostendebatur.

106. Caesar paucos dies in Asia moratus cum audisset Pompeium Cypri visum, coniectans eum in Aegyptum iter habere propter necessitudines regni reliquasque eius loci opportunitates, cum legione una quam se ex Thessalia sequi iusserat et altera quam ex Achaia a Q. Fufio legato evocaverat equitibusque DCCC et navibus longis Rhodiis

2 X et Asiaticis paucis Alexandriam pervenit. In his erant legionibus hominum milia tria CC. Reliqui vulneribus ex proeliis et labore ac magnitudine itineris confecti conse-

3 qui non potuerant. Sed Caesar confisus fama rerum gestarum infirmis auxiliis proficisci non dubitaverat atque[131]

4 omnem sibi locum tutum fore existimabat.[132] Alexandriae de Pompei morte cognoscit. Atque ibi primum e nave egrediens clamorem militum audit, quos rex in oppido praesidi causa reliquerat, et concursum ad se fieri videt quod fasces anteferrentur. In hoc omnis multitudo maies-

5 tatem regiam minui praedicabat. Hoc sedato tumultu crebrae continuis diebus ex concursu multitudinis concitationes fiebant, compluresque milites huius urbis[133] omnibus partibus interficiebantur.

[130] integra *Oudendorp*: in tecto [per V] ω: sub tecto *Kübler*: [in t-] *Apitz*   [131] atque] aeque *Nipperdey*, [a-] *ed. pr.*, *both of them reading* existimans *below.*
[132] existimabat *MU*: existimans *STV*
[133] huius urbis] eius [urbis] *Paul*: in viis urbis *Madvig*

---

[124] In place of "between undamaged . . . joints," Kübler substituted "inside, between . . . joints." Apitz excised the phrase.

where they had consecrated a statue of Caesar, a palm tree was shown to have emerged from the pavement around that time, between undamaged masonry joints.[124]

106. Caesar, after few days' stay in Asia, heard that Pompey had been seen at Cyprus. He guessed that Pompey was heading for Egypt on account of his ties to that kingdom and the location's other advantages. Taking the one legion that he had ordered to follow him from Thessaly and another that he had summoned from his legate Quintus Fufius in Achaea, plus eight hundred cavalry, ten Rhodian warships, and a few others from Asia, he went to Alexandria. There were only 3,200 men in these legions; 2 the rest, rendered unfit by wounds from the battles and the hardship and length of the journey, had not been able to reach him. Counting on the fame of his achievements 3 Caesar had not hesitated to set out with poor support, and thought he would be safe everywhere.[125] At Alexandria he 4 learned about Pompey's death. Upon disembarking he heard shouts from the soldiers whom the king had left on guard in the city, and saw people converging on him, apparently because he had the fasces ahead of him. The whole crowd was shouting that this amounted to a slight on the king's majesty. This riot was calmed, but there were 5 frequent disturbances every day thereafter as crowds gathered, and several soldiers were killed in every district of the city.[126]

[125] For "and thought he would be safe," Nipperdey substituted "thinking he would be equally safe," and the first edition excised the disputed word.

[126] For "soldiers . . . of the city," Paul and Madvig proposed "of his soldiers" and "soldiers . . . on the city streets," respectively.

107. Quibus rebus animadversis legiones sibi alias ex Asia adduci iussit, quas ex Pompeianis militibus confecerat. Ipse enim necessario etesiis tenebatur, qui navigantibus Alexandria fiunt adversissimi venti. Interim controversias regum ad populum Romanum et ad se, quod esset consul, pertinere existimans, atque eo magis officio suo convenire quod superiore consulatu cum patre Ptolomaeo et lege et senatus consulto societas erat facta, ostendit sibi placere regem Ptolomaeum atque eius sororem Cleopatram exercitus quos haberent dimittere et de controversiis iure apud se potius quam inter se armis disceptare.

108. Erat in procuratione regni propter aetatem pueri nutricius eius, eunuchus nomine Pothinus. Is primum inter suos queri atque indignari coepit regem ad causam dicendam evocari. Deinde adiutores quosdam consili sui[134] nactus ex regis amicis exercitum a Pelusio clam Alexandriam evocavit atque eundem Achillam, cuius supra meminimus, omnibus copiis praefecit. Hunc incitatum suis et regis inflatum pollicitationibus[135] quae fieri vellet litteris nuntiisque edocuit. In testamento Ptolomaei patris heredes erant scripti ex duobus filiis maior et ex duabus ea quae aetate antecedebat. Haec uti fierent, per omnes deos perque foedera quae Romae fecisset eodem testamento Ptolomaeus populum Romanum obtestabatur. Tabulae testamenti unae per legatos eius Romam erant

---

[134] consili sui *Estienne*: conscios sui *MU*: conscii [-sciis *S*] suis *STV*: conscios ⟨consili⟩ sui *Apitz*

[135] *Many small repairs have been suggested for the first part of this sentence.*

---

[127] In 59.

107. When Caesar understood the situation, he ordered other legions to be brought to him from Asia, those that he had formed from Pompey's soldiers. He himself was perforce pinned down by the etesian winds, which are extremely unfavorable for anyone sailing from Alexandria. Meanwhile, thinking that the quarrel between the rulers 2 pertained to the Roman people and to himself, since he was consul, and that it was a matter of particular obligation for him because the alliance with the elder Ptolemy had been made by law and senatorial decree during his earlier consulship,[127] Caesar made his view clear: King Ptolemy and his sister Cleopatra should dismiss their armies and debate the points at issue on legal grounds before him rather than in arms against one another.

108. Because of the boy's age, the man who was managing the kingdom was his guardian, a eunuch named Pothinus, who began to complain and object that the king was being summoned to plead his case—at first among his own friends. Then, when he found among the king's favorites 2 some helpers for his plan,[128] he secretly summoned the army from Pelusium to Alexandria and put Achillas, whom I mentioned earlier, in charge of all his forces. Achillas was 3 spurred on by Pothinus' promises and exalted by those of the king; in a letter and messages Pothinus explained what he wanted done. In his will the elder Ptolemy had written 4 down as heirs the elder of his two sons and of his two daughters the one who had seniority. He implored the 5 Roman people in this same will to ensure that the succession happened, invoking all the gods and the treaties he had made at Rome. One copy of the will was brought to 6

[128] The precise wording is uncertain, but the sense is clear.

allatae ut in aerario ponerentur. *Quae cum* propter publicas occupationes poni non potuissent apud *Pompeium* sunt depositae. Alterae eodem exemplo relictae *atque* obsignatae Alexandriae proferebantur.

109. De his rebus cum ageretur apud Caesarem isque maxime vellet pro communi amico atque arbitro controversias regum componere, subito exercitus regius equi-
2 tatusque omnis venire Alexandriam nuntiatur. Caesaris copiae nequaquam erant tantae ut iis extra oppidum si esset dimicandum confideret. Relinquebatur ut se suis locis oppido teneret consiliumque Achillae cognosceret.
3 Milites tamen omnes in armis esse iussit regemque hortatus est ut ex suis necessariis quos haberet maximae auctoritatis legatos ad Achillam mitteret et quid esset suae vo-
4 luntatis ostenderet. A quo missi Dioscorides et Serapion, qui ambo legati Romae fuerant magnamque apud patrem Ptolomaeum auctoritatem habuerant, ad Achillam perve-
5 nerunt. Quos ille cum in conspectum eius venissent, priusquam adiret[136] aut cuius rei causa missi essent cognosceret, corripi atque interfici iussit. Quorum alter accepto vulnere †occupatus†[137] per suos pro occiso sublatus, alter
6 interfectus est. Quo facto regem ut in sua potestate haberet Caesar efficit, magnam regium nomen apud suos auctoritatem habere existimans et ut potius privato paucorum et latronum quam regio consilio susceptum bellum videretur.

[136] adiret *MUTV*: audiret *S*
[137] occupatus] occipitis *Jurin*: ⟨pallore⟩ occupatus *Schnelle*: occubans *Cornelissen*: [o-] *Madvig. Perhaps* occultatus?

---

[129] Numerous repairs have been proposed for the unintelli-

348

Rome by envoys to be deposited in the treasury. Since owing to political preoccupations it was impossible to make the deposit, it was left with Pompey. A second copy with the same text, left sealed at Alexandria, was brought out.

109. While these matters were being discussed before Caesar, who as a friend to both parties and an arbiter wanted above all to settle the rulers' dispute, news suddenly arrived that the king's army and his entire cavalry were on the way to Alexandria. Caesar's forces were too 2 few for him to trust if they had to fight outside the city. His only option was to stay where he was inside the city and find out Achillas' plan. He nevertheless ordered everyone to arm themselves and urged the king to send the most influential of his entourage as a delegation to Achillas and communicate his wishes. The king's emissaries were 4 Dioscorides and Serapion, who had both been ambassadors to Rome and were extremely influential with the elder Ptolemy. They reached Achillas, but when he caught 5 sight of them, before making contact or learning why they had been sent, he ordered them to be seized and killed. One of them, after taking a wound . . .[129] was carried off through the midst his men as if dead, the other was killed. Thereafter Caesar ensured that he had the king in his 6 power, thinking that the king's name had great authority with his subjects and so that people would see that the war was undertaken not on the king's initiative but on the independent initiative of a few troublemakers.

gible word that follows "after taking a wound," among them "turning pale," "collapsing," and excision. Another possibility is "hidden," which makes better sense of *per suos*.

110. Erant cum Achilla eae copiae ut neque numero neque genere hominum neque usu rei militaris contemnen-
2 dae viderentur. Milia enim XX in armis habebat. Haec constabant ex Gabinianis militibus, qui iam in consuetudinem Alexandrinae vitae ac licentiae venerant et nomen disciplinamque populi Romani dedidicerant uxoresque
3 duxerant, ex quibus plerique liberos habebant. Huc accedebant collecti ex praedonibus latronibusque Syriae Ciliciaeque provinciae finitimarumque regionum. Multi prae
4 terea capitis damnati exulesque convenerant. Fugitivis omnibus nostris certus erat Alexandriae receptus certaque vitae conditio ut dato nomine militum esset numero. Quorum si quis a domino prehenderetur, consensu militum eripiebatur, qui vim suorum, quod in simili culpa versa
5 bantur, ipsi pro suo periculo defendebant. Hi regum amicos ad mortem deposcere, hi bona locupletum diripere, stipendia augendi causa regis domum obsidere, regno expellere alios, ⟨alios⟩ arcessere vetere quodam Alexandrini exercitus instituto consuerant. Erant praeterea equi
6 tum milia duo. Inveteraverant hi omnes compluribus Alexandriae bellis, Ptolomaeum patrem in regnum reduxerant, Bibuli filios duos interfecerant, bella cum Aegyptiis gesserant. Hunc usum rei militaris habebant.

111. His copiis fidens Achillas paucitatemque militum Caesaris despiciens occupabat Alexandriam praeter eam oppidi partem quam Caesar cum militibus tenebat, primo impetu domum eius irrumpere conatus, sed Caesar dispo
2 sitis per vias cohortibus impetum eius sustinuit. Eodemque

---

[130] Ptolemy was restored in 55, Bibulus' sons killed in 51.

110. The forces with Achillas had to be taken seriously, Caesar felt, given their number, identity, and military experience. For Achillas had twenty thousand under arms, 2 originally Gabinius' men, who had become accustomed to the dissolute lifestyle of Alexandria, forgotten the name and discipline of the Roman people, and taken wives; most of them had children. In addition, there was a collection 3 of former pirates and troublemakers belonging to Syria and the province of Cilicia and nearby regions. They had also been joined by a large number of exiles under a death sentence. All of our runaway slaves were guaranteed a 4 welcome and livelihood in Alexandria, provided that each signed up and was enrolled as a soldier. If a master laid hands on any of them, concerted action on the part of the soldiers pulled him away; they protected their companions against violence as if the danger was personal, since they all had the same illegal status. These men made a habit of 5 demanding the execution of the rulers' favorites, confiscating property from the wealthy, blockading the palace to get a pay raise, deposing some rulers and issuing invitations to others—all in accordance with a long-established custom of Alexandria's army. There were also two thousand cavalry. These men were all veterans of several wars 6 in Alexandria: they had restored the elder Ptolemy to his kingdom, killed Bibulus' two sons, fought the Egyptians.[130] Such was their military experience.

111. Confident in these troops and contemptuous of Caesar's small force Achillas occupied Alexandria, except for the part of the city that Caesar controlled with his soldiers. In the initial assault he tried to break into Caesar's quarters, but Caesar had deployed his cohorts in the streets and withstood the attack. There was fighting at the 2

tempore pugnatum est ad portum, ac longe maximam ea
3 res attulit dimicationem. Simul enim diductis copiis pluribus viis pugnabatur, et magna multitudine naves longas
occupare hostes conabantur. (Quarum erant L auxilio mis-
sae ad Pompeium, proelioque in Thessalia facto domum
redierant, quadriremes[138] omnes et quinqueremes aptae
instructaeque omnibus rebus ad navigandum. Praeter has,
XXII quae praesidi causa Alexandriae esse consuerant,
4 constratae omnes.) Quas si occupavissent classe Caesaris
5 erepta portum ac mare totum in sua potestate haberent
commeatu auxiliisque Caesarem prohiberent. Itaque
tanta est contentione actum quanta agi debuit cum illi
celerem in ea re victoriam, hi salutem suam consistere
6 viderent. Sed rem obtinuit Caesar. Omnesque eas naves
et reliquas quae erant in navalibus incendit quod tam late
tueri parva manu non poterat, confestimque ad Pharum
navibus milites exposuit.

112. Pharus est in insula turris magna altitudine miri-
2 ficis operibus extructa, quae nomen ab insula cepit. Haec
insula obiecta Alexandriae portum efficit. Sed a superioribus regibus in longitudinem passuum DCCCC in mare
iactis molibus angusto itinere et[139] ponte cum oppido con-
3 iungitur. In hac sunt insula domicilia Aegyptiorum et vicus
oppidi magnitudine. Quaeque ubique naves imprudentia
aut tempestate paulum suo cursu decesserunt has more
4 praedonum diripere consuerunt. Iis autem invitis a quibus

---

138 quadriremes (*i.e.,* IIIIdriremes) *Paul*: illae triremes ω
139 et] ut *Kraffert*

---

131 For "and a bridge," Kraffert proposed "like a bridge," since
there were two strategically important bridges on the Heptasta-
dion (*BAlex* 19.1-2).

harbor at the same time, and this affair turned into the biggest battle by far, for there was fighting in various 3 streets where troops had been deployed, and the enemy was simultaneously making an attempt with large numbers to seize the warships. (There were fifty of these that had been sent in support of Pompey and returned home after the battle in Thessaly, all quadriremes and quinqueremes, ready and completely fitted out for sailing, and beyond these, twenty-two that regularly guarded Alexandria, all of them decked ships.) If they seized these, taking away Cae- 4 sar's fleet, they were going to have the harbor and the sea as a whole in their power and prevent Caesar from getting supplies and reinforcements. So the struggle was consis- 5 tent with the stakes, since one side saw that a swift victory was at issue in this action, the other that their lives were. But Caesar met his objective. He also burned all of the 6 enemy ships, plus the others in the boatyards, because he could not guard so much territory with his small corps, and immediately landed troops near the lighthouse.

112. The lighthouse is a tower on Pharus Island, very tall and of marvelous construction; it takes its name from the island. This barrier island at Alexandria makes a har- 2 bor. But previous rulers joined it to the city with a narrow causeway and a bridge[131] by extending jetties into the sea for a stretch of nine hundred paces.[132] The island con- 3 tained some Egyptian residences and a settlement the size of a town. Whenever ships deviated slightly from their course, in ignorance or bad weather, they would as a rule be plundered by the inhabitants, pirate fashion. (Because 4

[132] Named for its length: "seven stades" in Greek units.

Pharus tenetur non potest esse propter angustias navibus
5 introitus in portum. Hoc tum veritus Caesar hostibus in
pugna occupatis militibusque expositis Pharum prehendit
6 atque ibi praesidium posuit. Quibus est rebus effectum uti
tuto frumentum auxiliaque navibus ad eum supportari
possent. Dimisit enim circum omnes propinquas provin-
7 cias atque inde auxilia evocavit. Reliquis oppidi partibus
sic est pugnatum ut aequo proelio discederetur et neutri
pellerentur. Id efficiebant angustiae loci. Paucisque utrimque interfectis Caesar loca maxime necessaria complexus
8 noctu praemuniit. In eo tractu oppidi pars erat regiae ex-
igua, in quam ipse habitandi causa initio erat inductus, et
theatrum coniunctum domui, quod arcis tenebat locum
9 aditusque habebat ad portum et ad reliqua[140] navalia. Has
munitiones insequentibus auxit diebus ut pro muro obiec-
10 tas haberet neu dimicare invitus cogeretur. Interim filia
minor Ptolomaei regis vacuam possessionem regni sperans ad Achillam sese ex regia traiecit unaque bellum ad-
11 ministrare coepit. Sed celeriter est inter eos de principatu
controversia orta, quae res apud milites largitiones auxit.
Magnis enim iacturis sibi quisque eorum animos concilia-
12 bat. Haec dum apud hostes geruntur Pothinus [nutricius
pueri et procurator regni, in parte Caesaris,][141] cum ad
Achillam nuntios mitteret hortareturque ne negotio de-
sisteret neve animo deficeret, indicatis deprehensisque
internuntiis a Caesare est interfectus. [Haec initia belli
Alexandrini fuerunt.][142]

140 reliqua] regia *Morus*
141 [nutricius . . . Caesaris] *Kraner*
142 [haec . . . fuerunt] *Forchhammer*

of the narrow channel it is impossible to enter the harbor
against the will of anyone who holds the lighthouse.) Wor- 5
ried about this, and while the enemy was occupied in fighting, Caesar landed soldiers and seized the lighthouse, then
established a garrison there. The result of this operation 6
was that provisions and reinforcements could be shipped
to him safely. For he sent word around all the nearby
provinces, summoning reinforcements from them. In the 7
rest of the city the fighting was such that the two sides
separated after an indecisive engagement and neither was
routed. This was the result of the site's narrow dimensions.
After a few casualties on both sides, Caesar took control
of crucial positions and sealed them off during the night.
A small section of the palace was in this area of the city; 8
Caesar had been installed in residence here at the outset.
There was also a theater adjacent to the residence, which
functioned as a stronghold and gave access to the harbor
and the other[133] boatyards. He extended his fortifications 9
on the following days so that he would have a wall-like
barrier and would not be forced to fight against his will.
Meanwhile King Ptolemy's younger daughter left the pal- 10
ace and went over to Achillas and began to direct the war
together with him, hoping to seize a vacant throne. But a 11
dispute over leadership arose between them right away,
and this increased the largesse to the soldiers, for each was
spending a lot in trying to win their loyalty. While this was 12
going on in the enemy camp, Pothinus was sending messages to Achillas and exhorting him not to abandon his task
or lose heart. His go-betweens were named and caught,
and he was put to death by Caesar.

[133] For "other," Morus substituted "royal" (*BAlex* 13.1).

INDEX

Place-names marked with an asterisk (*) are included on the maps. Cities are in Italy unless otherwise identified. Individuals are given their entry number in Brill's New Pauly (NP), where available.

All dates are BC.

The following abbreviations are employed: aed. = aedile, cens. = censor, cos. = consul, cos. suff. = suffect consul, mod. = modern place-name, pr. = praetor, qu. = quaestor, tr. pl. = tribune of the plebs.

Acarnania* (district on the Adriatic coast of central Greece), 3.55.1, 3.58.4

Achaia/-icus* (southern Greece), 3.3.2, 3.4.2, 3.5.2, 3.55.1, 3.55.3, 3.57.1, 3.106.1

Achillas (commander of Ptolemy's army in Alexandria), 3.104.2–3, 3.108.2, 3.109.2–4, 3.110.1, 3.111.1, 3.112.10, 3.112.12

Acilius Caninianus, M. (NP I.9; Caesarian legate, later governor of Sicily; pr. possibly 47), 3.15.6, 3.16.2, 3.39.1, 3.40.1

Acutius Rufus (NP 2; Pompeian), 3.83.2

Adbucillus (Allobrogian leader), 3.59.1

Aeginium* (a town in Macedonia; mod. Kalambaka), 3.79.7

Aegyptus/-tius* (Egypt, an independent kingdom), 3.3.1, 3.5.1, 3.5.3, 3.40.1, 3.112.3

Aelius Tubero, L. (NP I.14; Pompeian, titular governor of the province of Africa in 49, pardoned by Caesar after Pharsalus), 1.30.2, 1.31.2–3

Aemilius Lepidus, M. (NP I.12; Caesarian governor of Spain to 47, magister equitum to 44, later triumvir with Antony and Octavian; pr. 49, cos. 46), 2.21.5

Aetolia* (district of central Greece northwest of the Corinthian Gulf), 3.34.2, 3.35.1, 3.55.1, 3.61.2

Afranius, L. (NP 1; Pompeian commander in Spain, pardoned by Caesar after Ilerda,

INDEX

fought at Pharsalus, died in the aftermath of Thapsus; *cos*. 60), 1.37.1, 1.37.3, 1.38.1–4, 1.39.1, 1.40.4, 1.41.2–3, 1.41.5, 1.42.2, 1.43.1, 1.43.4, 1.48.5, 1.49.1, 1.51.1, 1.51.4, 1.53.1–2, 1.60.5, 1.61.2, 1.63.3, 1.65.1, 1.67.1, 1.70.1, 1.70.3, 1.71.4, 1.72.5, 1.73.4, 1.74.3, 1.75.1, 1.76.3, 1.84.3, 1.87.3, 2.17.4, 2.18.1, 2.18.3, 3.83.2, 3.88.3; Afranianus, 1.43.5, 1.46.5, 1.47.2, 1.54.1, 1.69.1, 1.70.2, 1.71.3, 1.78.1, 1.83.1; Afrani *filius*, 1.74.6, 1.84.2

Africa/-cus* (Roman province in North Africa), 1.30.2–3, 1.31.2, 2.23.1, 2.28.1, 2.32.3, 2.32.13, 2.37.2, 3.10.5; africus *ventus* (southwest wind), 3.26.4–5

Ahenobarbus. *See* Domitius

Alba* (town on the *via Valeria* between Rome and the Adriatic; mod. Albe), 1.15.7, 1.24.3

Albici (Gallic tribe), 1.34.3, 1.56.2, 1.57.3, 1.58.4, 2.2.6, 2.6.3

Alesia (site of a Caesarian victory in Gaul in 52), 3.47.5

Alexandria/-inus* (capital of Egypt), 3.4.4, 3.103.3, 3.103.5, 3.104.1, 3.106.1, 3.106.4, 3.107.1, 3.108.2, 3.108.6, 3.109.1, 3.110.2, 3.110.4–5, 3.110.6, 3.111.1, 3.112.12

Allobrox (member of the Gallic tribe the Allobroges), 3.59.1, 3.63.5, 3.79.6, 3.84.5

Amantia/-ini* (a town in the mountains of Epirus; near mod. Plloca, Albania), 3.12.4, 3.40.4

Amanus *mons** (mountain range between Cilicia and Syria; mod. Nur Dağlari), 3.31.1

Ambracia* (town in Epirus; mod. Arta, Albania), 3.36.5

Amphilochia/-chi* (region on the Adriatic coast of central Greece, south of Epirus), 3.55.1

Amphipolis* (town near the mouth of the Strymon River), 3.102.2, 3.102.4

Ampius Balbus, T. (NP 2; Pompeian legate in Asia; *pr.* 59), 3.105.1

Anas* (mod. Guadiana River), 1.38.1

Ancona* (town in Picenum on the Adriatic coast of Italy), 1.11.4

Androsthenes (Thessalian leader), 3.80.3

Annius Milo, T. (NP 67; Pompeian; *pr.* 55), 3.21.4, 3.22.1

Anquillaria (coastal town near Utica), 2.23.1

Antiochia/-chenses* (capital of Roman province of Syria), 3.102.6, 3.105.4

Antiochus Commagenus (ruler of Commagene), 3.4.5

Antonius, C. (NP I.3; Caesarian

legate, brother of M. Antonius), 3.10.5, 3.67.5; Antonianus, 3.4.2

Antonius, M. (NP I.9; Caesarian legate in Gaul and Greece, later triumvir; *tr. pl.* 49, *cos.* 44), 1.2.7, 1.11.4, 1.18.2–3, 3.24.1, 3.24.4, 3.26.1, 3.29.1–2, 3.30.2, 3.30.4, 3.30.6, 3.34.1, 3.40.5, 3.46.4, 3.65.1, 3.89.3; Antonianus, 3.24.3

Apollonia/-ates* (port town in southern Illyricum; near mod. Fier, Albania), 3.5.2, 3.11.2, 3.12.1, 3.12.4, 3.13.1, 3.13.5, 3.25.3, 3.26.1, 3.30.1, 3.75.1, 3.78.1, 3.78.3–4, 3.79.2

Appuleius Saturninus, L. (NP I.11; revolutionary tribune, associate of Marius; *tr. pl.* 103, 100), 1.7.6

Apsus* (mod. Seman River), 3.13.5–6, 3.19.1, 3.30.3

Apulia* (district on the southern Adriatic coast of Italy; mod. Puglia), 1.14.3, 1.17.1, 1.23.5, 3.2.3

Aquitani (Gallic tribe), 1.39.2

Arecomici. *See* Volcae

Arelate* (mod. Arles, France), 1.36.4, 2.5.1

Ariminum* (mod. Rimini), 1.8.1, 1.10.3, 1.11.1, 1.11.4, 1.12.1

Ariobarzanes (ruler of Cappadocia), 3.4.3

Arretium* (mod. Arezzo), 1.11.4

Asculum Picenum* (town on the *via Salaria*; mod. Ascoli Piceno), 1.15.3

Asia/-aticus* (Roman province in western Asia Minor), 1.4.5, 3.3.1–2, 3.4.1, 3.5.1, 3.5.3, 3.7.1, 3.40.4, 3.42.2, 3.53.1, 3.105.1, 3.106.1, 3.107.1

Asparagium* (town on the Genusus River in Illyricum), 3.30.7, 3.41.1, 3.76.1–2

Athamania* (district of Epirus), 3.78.4

Athenae* (mod. Athens), 3.3.1

Attius Paelignus, C. (NP I.3; Pompeian), 1.18.1, 1.18.3–4

Attius Varus, P. (NP I.5; Pompeian, governor of Africa in 53, fought Caesar in Africa after Pharsalus, fell at Munda; *pr.* before 53), 1.12.3, 1.13.1–2, 1.13.4, 1.31.2, 2.23.1, 2.23.3, 2.25.1, 2.25.3, 2.27.1–3, 2.28.1, 2.28.3, 2.30.2, 2.33.3, 2.34.2–3, 2.34.6, 2.35.1–2, 2.35.6, 2.36.2, 2.43.2, 2.44.1–2; Attianus, 1.13.5, 2.34.6

Attius Varus, Q. (NP I.6; Caesarian cavalry officer), 3.37.5

Avaricum* (site of a Caesarian victory in Gaul; mod. Bourges, France), 3.47.5

Aurelius Cotta, L. (NP I.9; neutral, later Caesarian; *pr.* 70), 1.6.5

Aurelius Cotta, M. (NP I.12; Pompeian; *pr.* about 54), 1.30.2–3

Ausetani (Spanish tribe), 1.60.2
Auster *ventus* (south wind),
  3.26.2, 3.26.5
Auximum/-imates* (town in Picenum; mod. Osimo), 1.12.3,
  1.13.1, 1.13.5, 1.15.1, 1.31.2

Bagradas* (river debouching at
  Utica; mod. Ksar Baghai),
  2.24.1, 2.26.1, 2.38.3, 2.39.1
Balbus. *See* Cornelius
Belica *porta* (gate of Baal),
  2.25.1
Bessi (Thracian tribe), 3.4.6
Bibulus. *See* Calpurnius
Bithynia* (Roman province in
  northwest Asia Minor), 3.3.1
Boeotia* (district of central
  Greece), 3.4.2
Britannia* (Britain), 1.54.1
Brundisium/-sinus* (mod.
  Brindisi), 1.24.1, 1.24.5,
  1.25.1–4, 1.26.1, 1.27.1,
  1.28.1, 1.28.4, 1.30.1, 3.2.1,
  3.2.3, 3.6.1, 3.8.1, 3.14.1,
  3.23.1, 3.24.1, 3.24.4, 3.25.1,
  3.25.3, 3.87.3, 3.100.1–2
Bruttii (southern Italian tribe),
  1.30.4
Brutus. *See* Junius
Buthrotum* (mod. Butrint, Al-
  bania), 3.16.1
Byllis/-idenses* (town on the
  Aous River in Epirus; near
  mod. Hekal, Albania), 3.12.4,
  3.40.4

Caecilius, T. (Pompeian), 1.46.5
Caecilius Metellus, L. (NP I.14;
  Pompeian; *tr. pl.* 49), 1.33.3

Caecilius Metellus Piso Scipio,
  Q. (NP I.32; Pompey's father-
  in-law, defeated by Caesar at
  Thapsus in 46, died in the aftermath; *cos.* 52), 1.1.4, 1.2.1,
  1.2.6, 1.4.1, 1.4.3, 1.6.1, 1.6.5,
  3.4.3, 3.31.1, 3.33.1, 3.36.1,
  3.36.5–8, 3.37.1–4, 3.38.1–2,
  3.57.1, 3.57.3, 3.57.5, 3.78.3,
  3.78.5, 3.79.3, 3.80.3–4,
  3.81.2, 3.82.1, 3.83.1, 3.88.3,
  3.90.1
Caecilius Rufus, L. (NP I.34;
  Pompeian; *pr.* 57), 1.23.2
Caelius Rufus, M. (NP I.4; renegade Caesarian; *pr.* 48),
  1.2.3, 3.20.1, 3.20.4, 3.21.3,
  3.22.3
Caesar. *See* Julius
Calagurritani* (residents of
  Calagurris; mod. Calahorra,
  Spain), 1.60.1
Calenus. *See* Fufius
Calidius, M. (NP 2; Caesarian
  legate in 48 and 47; *pr.* 57),
  1.2.3, 1.2.5
Calpurnius Bibulus, M. (NP I.5;
  commander-in-chief of Pompey's Adriatic fleet; *cos.* 59),
  3.5.4, 3.7.1–2, 3.8.3, 3.14.2,
  3.15.1, 3.15.6, 3.16.2–3,
  3.18.1, 3.31.3; Bibuli *filii*,
  3.110.6
Calpurnius Piso Caesoninus, L.
  (NP I.19; Caesar's father-in-
  law; *cos.* 58), 1.3.6
Calvinus. *See* Domitius
Calvisius Sabinus, C. (NP 6;
  Caesarian legate in Aetolia,
  later governor of Africa; *cos.*

suff. 39), 3.34.2, 3.35.1,
3.55.1–2

Calydon* (town in Aetolia; near
mod. Evinochori, Greece),
3.35.1

Camerinum* (mod. Camerino),
1.15.5

Campania* (central Italian district), 1.14.5

Candavia* (district of Illyricum), 3.11.2, 3.79.2–3

Caninianus. *See* Acilius

Caninius Rebilus, C. (NP 5;
Caesarian legate and advisor
to Curio; governor of Africa
in 46; fought for Caesar at
Thapsus and in the Spanish
campaign of 45; *cos. suff.* 45),
1.26.3, 1.26.5, 2.24.2, 2.34.4

Cantabri (Spanish tribe),
1.38.3

Canuleius, L. (Caesarian legate), 3.42.3

Canusium* (mod. Canosa),
1.24.1

Capitolium (Rome's Capitoline
Hill), 1.6.7

Cappadocia* (kingdom in central Asia Minor), 3.4.3

Capua* (town in Campania),
1.10.1, 1.14.4, 3.21.5, 3.71.1

Caralitani* (residents of Caralis;
mod. Cagliari), 1.30.3

Carmonenses* (residents of
Carmo; mod. Carmona,
Spain), 2.19.4

Casilinum* (town on the *via
Appia* in Campania; near
mod. Capua), 3.21.5

Cassius Longinus, C. (NP I.10;

Pompeian, pardoned by Caesar in 47, instigator of Caesar's assassination in 44, died
at Philippi in 42; *tr. pl.* 49),
3.5.3, 3.101.1, 3.101.4,
3.101.6–7

Cassius Longinus, L. (NP I.14;
Caesarian legate, brother of
I.10; *tr. pl.* 44), 3.34.2, 3.35.2,
3.36.2, 3.36.4–5, 3.36.7–8,
3.55.1–2

Cassius Longinus, Q. (NP I.16;
Caesarian, governor of Spain
49–47, probably brother of
I.10; died in Spain in 47; *tr.
pl.* 49), 1.2.7, 2.19.1, 2.21.4

Castor. *See* Tarcondarius

Castra Cornelia* (coastal ridge
near Utica, remembered as
the location of Scipio's camp
in the second Punic War;
near mod. Kelaat el Anda-
luus, Tunisia), 2.24.2, 2.25.6,
2.30.3, 2.37.3

Castulonensis *saltus* (mountainous area in southern Spain,
perhaps the mod. Despe-
ñaperros gorge), 1.38.1

Cato. *See* Porcius

Celtiberia* (district in central
Spain), 1.38.3, 1.61.2

Ceraunia* (mountainous promontory on coast of Epirus;
mod. Karaburun, Albania),
3.6.3

Cilicia/-ces* (province in eastern Asia Minor between the
Taurus range and the sea),
3.3.1, 3.4.1, 3.88.3, 3.101.1,
3.102.5, 3.110.3

Cinga* (mod. Cinca River), 1.48.3

Cingulum* (mod. Cingoli), 1.15.2

Claudius Marcellus, C. (NP I.9; Pompeian; *cos.* 49), 1.6.4, 1.14.2, 3.5.3

Claudius Marcellus, M. (NP I.15; Pompeian, pardoned by Caesar in 46; *cos.* 51), 1.2.2, 1.2.5

Cleopatra (NP II.12; last Ptolemaic queen of Egypt), 3.103.2, 3.107.2

Clipea* (mod. Kélibia, Tunisia), 2.23.2–3

Clodius, A. (Caesarian), 3.57.1, 3.57.5, 3.90.1

Clodius, P. (NP I.4; *tr. pl.* 58), 3.21.4

Commagenus. *See* Antiochus

Compsa* (mod. Conza della Campania), 3.22.2

Considius Longus, C. (NP I.3; Pompeian legate in Africa, killed in the aftermath of Thapsus; *pr.* before 54), 2.23.4

Coponius, C. (NP 1; Pompeian fleet commander), 3.5.3, 3.26.2

Corcyra* (mod. Corfu or Kérkyra, Greece), 3.3.1, 3.7.1, 3.8.3, 3.15.3, 3.16.1, 3.58.4, 3.100.3

Corduba* (mod. Córdoba, Spain), 2.19.1–3, 2.20.8, 2.21.1, 2.21.3

Corfinium/-nienses* (strategi-cally important town in the Abruzzo region; mod. Corfinio), 1.15.6, 1.16.1, 1.18.1, 1.19.4, 1.20.1, 1.21.6, 1.23.4–5, 1.24.1, 1.25.1, 1.34.1, 2.28.1, 2.32.1, 2.32.13, 3.10.1

Cornelius Balbus, L. (Caesarian centurion, nephew of a leading Caesarian adherent of the same name), 3.19.7

Cornelius Lentulus Crus, L. (NP I.50; Pompeian, murdered by Ptolemy in Egypt in 48; *cos.* 49), 1.2.2, 1.2.4–5, 1.4.2, 1.5.4, 1.14.1, 1.14.4, 3.4.1, 3.96.1, 3.102.7, 3.104.3

Cornelius Lentulus Marcellinus, P. (Caesarian legate at Dyrrachium), 3.62.4, 3.64.1, 3.65.1

Cornelius Lentulus Spinther, P. (NP I.54; Pompeian, pardoned by Caesar at Corfinium, fought at Pharsalus; *cos.* 57), 1.15.3, 1.16.1, 1.21.6, 1.22.1, 1.22.6, 1.23.2, 3.83.1, 3.102.7

Cornelius Sulla, L. (NP I.90; the dictator), 1.4.2, 1.5.1, 1.7.3

Cornelius Sulla, P. (NP I.89; Caesarian legate, expelled from the senate in 65), 3.51.1, 3.51.3, 3.51.5, 3.89.3, 3.99.4

Cornelius Sulla Faustus, L. (NP I.87; Pompeian, son of the dictator, son-in-law of Pompey, fought at Pharsalus, died in the aftermath of Thapsus; *qu.* 54), 1.6.3–4

Cosanum* (the district of Cosa in Etruria; near mod. Ansedonia), 1.34.2

Cotta. *See* Aurelius

Cotus (king of Thrace and supporter of Pompey), 3.4.3, 3.36.4

Crassus. *See* Licinius; Otacilius

Crastinus (Caesarian), 3.91.1, 3.99.2–3

Cremona* (town in the Po valley near Mantua), 1.24.4

Creta* (mod. Crete, Greece), 3.4.1, 3.4.3, 3.5.1

Curicta* (mod. Krk, Croatia), 3.10.5

Curio. *See* Scribonius

Curius. *See* Vibius

Cyclades *insulae** (a cluster of islands in the southern Aegean), 3.3.1

Cyprus* (mod. Cyprus), 3.102.5, 3.106.1

Cyrenae* (district of northern Africa; together with Crete, a Roman province; now Libya), 3.5.1

Dalmatae (Dalmatian tribe), 3.9.1

Damasippus. *See* Licinius

Dardani (Illyrian tribe), 3.4.6

Decidius Saxa, L. (NP 1; Caesarian; *tr. pl.* 44), 1.66.3

Deiotarus (ruler of Galatia, supporter of Pompey, pardoned by Caesar in 45), 3.4.3

Delphi* (mod. Delphi), 3.55.4

Dianae *templum* (temple of Diana in Ephesus), 3.33.1, 3.105.1

Dioscorides (emissary of the Ptolemies), 3.109.4

Domitius, Cn. (Caesarian), 2.42.3

Domitius Ahenobarbus, L. (NP I.8; Pompeian, appointed to replace Caesar in Gaul, fought at Corfinium and Massilia, died in the aftermath of Pharsalus; *cos.* 54), 1.6.5, 1.15.6–7, 1.16.2, 1.17.1, 1.19.1, 1.19.3–4, 1.20.1–2, 1.20.4–5, 1.21.6, 1.23.2, 1.23.4, 1.34.2, 1.36.1, 1.56.1, 1.56.3, 1.57.4, 2.3.1, 2.3.3, 2.18.2, 2.22.2, 2.28.2, 2.32.8, 3.83.1, 3.99.5; Domitianus, 1.16.3, 1.22.2, 1.23.5, 1.25.1; Domiti *filius*, 1.23.2

Domitius Calvinus, Cn. (NP I.10; Caesarian legate in Macedonia and later Asia Minor; *cos.* 53, 40), 3.34.3, 3.36.1–2, 3.36.6, 3.36.8, 3.37.1–2, 3.37.5, 3.38.1–2, 3.38.4, 3.78.2–5, 3.79.3, 3.79.5–7, 3.89.3; Domitianus, 3.36.8, 3.37.3

Domnilaus (ruler in Galatia, supporter of Pompey), 3.4.5

Dyrrachium/-inus* (mod. Durrës, Albania), 1.25.2, 1.27.1, 3.5.2, 3.9.8, 3.11.2, 3.13.1, 3.13.3, 3.13.5, 3.26.2–3, 3.30.1, 3.30.7, 3.41.3, 3.41.5,

3.42.1, 3.44.1, 3.53.1, 3.57.1,
3.58.1, 3.62.3, 3.78.3, 3.79.4,
3.80.2, 3.80.4, 3.84.1, 3.89.1

Egus (Allobrogian cavalry officer, originally Caesarian),
3.59.1, 3.79.6, 3.84.5

Elis* (district of the northwestern Peloponnese), 3.105.3

Ephesus/-esius* (capital of the
Roman province of Asia;
mod. Selçuk), 3.33.1–2,
3.105.1–2

Epirus* (district of northwestern Greece), 3.4.2, 3.12.4,
3.13.2, 3.42.3, 3.47.6, 3.61.2,
3.78.4, 3.80.1

Fabius, C. (NP I.4; Caesarian
legate), 1.37.1, 1.37.3, 1.40.1,
1.40.7, 1.48.2; Fabianus,
1.40.3–4

Fabius Paelignus (Caesarian),
2.35.1–2, 2.35.5

Fanum* (town on the Adriatic
coast of Italy; mod. Fano),
1.11.4

Favonius, M. (NP 1; Pompeian,
legate of Scipio, adherent of
Cato, pardoned by Caesar,
died at Philippi; pr. 49),
3.36.3, 3.36.6–8, 3.57.5

Faustus. See Cornelius

Firmum* (town in Picenum;
mod. Fermo), 1.16.1

Flaccus. See Valerius

Flegmas, C. (Caesarian), 3.71.1

Fortuna, 1.40.7, 1.52.3, 2.17.4,

2.41.8, 3.10.6–7, 3.13.3,
3.26.4, 3.68.1, 3.73.3–5,
3.79.3, 3.95.1

Frentani (Italian tribe on the
Adriatic coast), 1.23.5

Fretum Siculum* (the strait of
Messina), 1.29.2, 2.3.1,
3.101.1

Fufius Calenus, Q. (NP I.4;
Caesarian legate, later provincial governor, friend of
Antony, opponent of Cicero;
cos. suff. 47), 1.87.4, 3.8.2,
3.14.1–2, 3.26.1, 3.55.2–4,
3.106.1

Fulginius, Q. (Caesarian centurion), 1.46.4

Fulvius Postumus (Caesarian
officer), 3.62.4

Gabinius, A. (NP I.2; Caesarian
legate after returning from
exile in 49, died 47; formerly
governor of Syria, he restored
Ptolemy Auletes to throne in
Egypt and was convicted of
bribery; cos. 58), 3.4.4,
3.103.5; Gabinianus, 3.4.4,
3.110.2

Gades/-ditani* (mod. Cadiz,
Spain), 2.18.1–2, 2.18.6,
2.20.1–3, 2.21.1, 2.21.3–4

Gallia/-i/-icus* (Caesar's
province[s] 58–50), 1.6.5,
1.7.7, 1.10.3, 1.18.5, 1.22.5,
1.29.2–3, 1.33.4, 1.39.2,
1.48.4, 1.51.1, 1.51.4, 2.1.2,
2.40.1, 3.2.3, 3.4.3–4, 3.22.3,

3.29.3, 3.42.3, 3.59.1–2, 3.79.6, 3.87.1, 3.87.4

Gallograecia* (region of central Anatolia, also known as Galatia), 3.4.5

Gallonius, C. (Pompeian), 2.18.2, 2.20.2–3

Gallus. *See* Tuticanus

Genusus* (mod. Shkumbin River), 3.75.3, 3.76.1

Gergovia* (site of a Caesarian defeat in Gaul; mod. Gergovie), 3.73.6

Germania/-i* (region across the Rhine from Gaul), 1.7.7, 1.83.5, 3.4.4, 3.52.2, 3.87.1

Gomphi/-phensis* (near mod. Gomfoi, Greece), 3.80.1, 3.81.1–2

Gracchi. *See* Sempronius

Graecia/-i* (mod. Greece), 1.25.3, 3.11.4, 3.30.6, 3.102.2, 3.105.5

Granius, A. (Caesarian), 3.71.1

Hadriaticum *mare** (mod. Adriatic), 1.25.3

Hadrumetum* (mod. Sousse, Tunisia), 2.23.3–4

Haliacmon* (river in Macedonia), 3.36.3, 3.37.1

Hegesaretos (Thessalian supporter of Pompey), 3.35.2

Helvii (Gallic tribe), 1.35.4

Heraclia Sentica (see note), 3.79.3

Herculis *fanum* (temple in Gades), 2.18.2, 2.21.3

Hiberus* (mod. Ebro River), 1.60.2, 1.61.5, 1.62.3, 1.63.2, 1.65.4, 1.68.1, 1.68.3, 1.69.4, 1.72.5, 1.73.1

Hirpinus *ager** (region of central Italy crossed by major roads), 3.22.2

Hirrus. *See* Lucilius

Hispalis* (mod. Seville, Spain), 2.18.1, 2.20.4

Hispania/-i* (the name of two Roman provinces distinguished as Nearer and Further Spain), 1.10.3, 1.22.4, 1.29.3, 1.30.1, 1.34.1, 1.37.1, 1.38.1–2, 1.39.1–3, 1.48.7, 1.74.5, 1.85.6–7, 1.86.3, 1.87.5, 2.1.1–2, 2.7.2, 2.17.1, 2.18.6–7, 2.19.1, 2.21.1, 2.32.5, 2.32.13, 2.37.2, 3.2.3, 3.10.1, 3.10.5, 3.47.5, 3.73.3, 3.83.2

Iacetani (Spanish tribe on the east coast north of the Ebro), 1.60.2

Igilium* (mod. Giglio), 1.34.2

Iguvium/-ini* (mod. Gubbio), 1.12.1, 1.12.3

Ilerda* (mod. Lérida, Spain), 1.38.4, 1.41.2, 1.43.1, 1.45.1, 1.48.5, 1.49.2, 1.56.1, 1.59.1, 1.63.1, 1.69.1, 1.73.2, 1.78.1–2, 2.17.4

Illurgavonensis (Spanish tribe), 1.60.2, 1.60.4

Illyricum* (Roman province in the Balkans, part of Caesar's

command 58–50), 3.9.1,
3.78.3
Issa* (mod. Vis, Croatia), 3.9.1
Isthmus* (Isthmus of Corinth),
3.55.3
Italia* (mod. Italy), 1.2.2, 1.6.3,
1.6.8, 1.9.1, 1.9.4–5, 1.25.3–4,
1.27.2, 1.29.3, 1.30.3, 1.35.1,
1.48.4, 1.53.2, 2.17.1, 2.18.7,
2.22.6, 2.32.1, 2.32.3, 2.32.13,
3.1.2, 3.4.1, 3.6.1, 3.10.5,
3.12.2, 3.13.5, 3.18.4, 3.21.4,
3.22.4, 3.29.2–3, 3.39.1,
3.42.3, 3.57.4, 3.73.3, 3.78.3,
3.78.5, 3.82.2, 3.87.2
Italica* (near mod. Santiponce,
Spain), 2.20.6

Januarius (January), 1.5.4, 3.6.1
Juba (king of Numidia and supporter of Pompey, committed
suicide after Thapsus), 1.6.3,
2.25.3–4, 2.36.3, 2.38.1,
2.40.1, 2.43.2, 2.44.2
Julius Caesar, C. *passim*
Julius Caesar, C. *adulescens*
(NP I.7; Pompeian, served
with Cato in Africa, later pardoned), 1.8.2, 1.10.1,
2.23.3–4
Julius Caesar, L. (NP I.6; Caesarian legate in Gaul, possibly
Pompeian in civil war, proscribed in 43, later pardoned;
cos. 64), 1.8.2
Julius Caesar, Sex. (NP I.10;
Caesarian in Spain in 49,
later governor of Syria, over-

thrown and murdered in 46;
qu. 48), 2.20.7
Junius Brutus, D. (NP I.12;
Caesarian naval commander
in Gaul and at Marseilles,
later governor of Gaul and
Cisalpine Gaul, one of Caesar's assassins, died resisting
Antony in 43; *pr.* 45), 1.36.5,
1.56.4, 1.57.1, 2.3.3, 2.5.1,
2.6.4, 2.6.6, 2.22.3

Labienus, T. (NP 3; Caesarian
legate 58 –50; Pompeian in
the civil war, fought Caesar at
Pharsalus and in Africa, died
at Munda; *pr.* possibly 59),
1.15.2, 3.13.3, 3.19.6, 3.19.8,
3.71.4, 3.87.1
Lacedaemon* (district of the
Peloponnese), 3.4.3
Laelius, D. (NP I.4; Pompeian
fleet commander in 49, Caesarian after Pharsalus; *tr. pl.*
54), 3.5.3, 3.7.1, 3.40.4,
3.100.1–3
Larinates (tribe on Adriatic
coast of Italy), 1.23.5
Larisa/-saei* (principal town of
Thessaly; mod. Larissa,
Greece), 3.80.4, 3.81.2,
3.96.3, 3.97.2, 3.98.3
Latinae *feriae* (annual festival,
usually held before the campaigning season), 3.2.1
Lentulus. *See* Cornelius
Lepidus. *See* Aemilius
Leptitani* (inhabitants of Lep-

INDEX

tis; mod. Al Khums, Libya), 2.38.1

Libo. *See* Scribonius

Liburnus/–nicus (pertaining to Liburnia in Illyricum), 3.5.3, 3.9.1

Licinius Crassus, M. (NP I.11; triumvir, died in Parthia 53; *cos.* 70, 55), 3.31.3

Licinius Damasippus (Pompeian), 2.44.3

Lissus* (near mod. Lezhë, Albania), 3.26.4, 3.28.1–2, 3.29.1, 3.29.3, 3.40.5, 3.42.4, 3.78.4

Longinus. *See* Cassius

Lucani (inhabitants of Lucania in southern Italy), 1.30.4

Lucceius, L. (Pompeian), 3.18.3

Luceria* (mod. Lucera), 1.24.1

Lucilius Hirrus, L. (NP I.5; Pompeian emissary to Parthia, later Caesarian, proscribed in 43 but escaped to join Sextus Pompey; *tr. pl.* 53), 1.15.5, 3.82.4

Lucretius, Q. (possibly identical with the following), 1.18.1, 1.18.3

Lucretius Vespillo, Q. (NP II.5; Pompeian, proscribed in 43, later pardoned; *cos.* 19), 3.7.1

Lupus. *See* Rutilius

Lusitania/-i* (part of Roman province of Further Spain; roughly mod. Portugal), 1.44.2, 1.48.7

Macedonia/-nes* (Roman province of Greece, north and east of Epirus), 3.4.1, 3.4.4, 3.4.6, 3.11.2, 3.33.2, 3.34.3–4, 3.36.1–3, 3.57.1, 3.79.2, 3.102.3

Magius, N. (NP I.6; Pompeian), 1.24.4, 1.26.2

Manlius Torquatus, L. (NP I.18; Pompeian, died in the aftermath of Thapsus, interlocutor in Cicero's *De Finibus*; Caesar is silent about successes at Dyrrachium credited to T. by other sources; *pr.* 49), 1.24.3, 3.11.3

Marcellinus. *See* Cornelius

Marcellus. *See* Claudius

Marcius Philippus, L. (NP I.14; nonpartisan, stepfather of Octavian; *cos.* 56), 1.6.5

Marcius Philippus, L. (NP I.15; Caesarian; *tr. pl.* 49, *pr.* 44, *cos. suff.* 38), 1.6.4

Marcius Rufus (NP I.23; Caesarian; *qu.* 49), 2.23.5, 2.24.1, 2.43.1

Marrucini (Italian tribe on the Adriatic coast), 1.23.5, 2.34.3

Marsi (Italian tribe in central Italy, active in the Social War, which is sometimes called the *bellum Marsicum*), 1.15.7, 1.20.3, 2.27.1, 2.29.3

Massilia/-lienses* (mod. Marseilles, France), 1.34.2–4, 1.35.1, 1.36.1, 1.36.4–5, 1.56.1, 1.56.4, 1.57.2, 1.57.4,

1.58.1, 1.58.5, 2.1.1, 2.1.3, 2.3.1, 2.3.3, 2.4.1, 2.4.5, 2.5.1, 2.6.1, 2.7.2–4, 2.14.5, 2.15.1, 2.17.4, 2.18.1, 2.21.5, 2.22.1–2, 2.22.5

Mauretania* (kingdom in northwest Africa), 1.6.3, 1.39.3, 1.60.5

Menedemus (leading man of Macedonia), 3.34.3

Messana* (mod. Messina), 2.3.2, 3.101.1, 3.101.3

Metellus. See Caecilius

Metropolis/-itae* (city in Thessaly; near mod. Mitropoli, Greece), 3.80.7, 3.81.1–2

Milo. See Annius

Minerva (Roman goddess), 3.105.3

Minucius Rufus (NP I.9; Pompeian), 3.7.1

Minucius Thermus (NP I.18; Pompeian; pr. 58), 1.12.1–2

Munatius Plancus, L. (NP I.4; Caesarian legate in Gaul, Spain, and Africa, later governor of Gaul; pr. 45, cos. 42), 1.40.5

Murcus. See Staius

Mytilenae* (principal town on Lesbos), 3.102.4

Narbo* (mod. Narbonne, France), 1.37.1, 2.21.5

Nasidius, L. (NP 1; Pompeian fleet commander, died in the aftermath of Thapsus; 2.3.1, 2.4.4–5; Nasidianus, 2.7.1–2

Naupactus* (strategically important port city on Corinthian Gulf; mod. Nafpaktos, Greece), 3.35.1

Neapolis* (mod. Naples), 3.21.5

Noricus rex (king of Noricum, the eastern Alpine region, later a Roman province), 1.18.5

Numidia/-dae* (kingdom in Africa ruled by Juba), 2.25.3, 2.25.5, 2.38.4, 2.39.4, 2.41.6

Nymphaeum* (mod. Shëngjin, Albania), 3.26.4

Oceanus* (mod. Atlantic), 1.38.3

Octavius, M. (NP I.12; Pompeian fleet commander, later fought Caesar in Africa), 3.5.3, 3.9.1, 3.9.4, 3.9.6–8; Octavianus, 3.9.6

Opimius, M. (Pompeian), 3.38.4

Orchomenus* (city in Boeotia), 3.55.4

Oricum* (port city in Epirus; near mod. Vlorë, Albania), 3.7.1, 3.8.4, 3.11.3, 3.12.1, 3.13.1, 3.14.2, 3.15.1, 3.16.2, 3.23.1, 3.34.1, 3.39.1, 3.40.1, 3.78.3–5, 3.90.1

Oscenses* (inhabitants of Osca, in northeastern Spain; mod. Huesca), 1.60.1

Otacilius Crassus (NP I.1; Pompeian), 3.28.2, 3.28.4, 3.28.6, 3.29.1

Otogesa (Spanish town on the Ebro, its precise modern

identity is uncertain), 1.61.5, 1.68.1, 1.70.4

Paeligni (central Italian tribe near Corfinium, active in Social War), 1.15.7, 2.29.3
Paelignus. *See* Attius; Fabius
Palaeste* (mod. Palasë, Albania), 3.6.3
Parthi/-icus* (Rome's principal rival in the East), 1.9.4, 3.31.3–4, 3.82.4
Parthini (Illyrian tribe based near Dyrrachium), 3.11.3, 3.41.1, 3.42.4–5
Pedius, Q. (NP 1; Caesarian legate in Gaul, son of Caesar's sister; *cos. suff.* 43), 3.22.2
Pelusium* (strategically important city in eastern part of Nile delta; mod. Tall al-Faramā), 3.103.1, 3.108.2
Pergamum* (important city in Asia Minor; mod. Bergama, Turkey), 3.31.4, 3.105.5
Petra (rocky promontory near Dyrrachium), 3.42.1, 3.42.5
Petraeus (Thessalian adherent of Caesar), 3.35.2
Petreius, M. (NP 1; Pompeian legate in Spain, fought Caesar in Africa, committed suicide after Thapsus; *pr.* around 64), 1.38.1–4, 1.39.1, 1.40.4, 1.42.2, 1.43.1, 1.53.1, 1.61.2, 1.63.3, 1.65.1, 1.66.3, 1.67.1, 1.72.5, 1.73.4, 1.74.3, 1.75.2, 1.76.1, 1.87.3, 2.17.4, 2.18.1
Pharus (barrier island at Alex-

andria, also the lighthouse on the island), 3.111.6, 3.112.1, 3.112.4–5
Philippus. *See* Marcius
Phoenice/-ices* (coastal region in the Roman province of Syria), 3.3.1, 3.101.1
Picenum/-us* (Pompey's home region on Italy's northern Adriatic coast, active in the Social War), 1.12.3, 1.15.1, 1.15.4, 1.29.2
Pisaurum* (mod. Foglia), 1.11.4, 1.12.1
Piso. *See* Calpurnius
Placentia* (mod. Piacenza), 3.71.1
Plancus. *See* Munatius
Plotius, M. (Caesarian), 3.19.7
Pompeius Magnus, Cn. (NP I.3; *cos.* 70, 55, 52), 1.1.4, 1.2.1, 1.2.3, 1.2.6, 1.3.1–2, 1.3.4, 1.4.3–4, 1.6.1, 1.6.3, 1.7.1, 1.7.4, 1.8.2–4, 1.9.1, 1.9.5, 1.10.1, 1.10.3–4, 1.13.4, 1.14.1–2, 1.15.4, 1.17.1, 1.18.6, 1.19.1, 1.19.4, 1.23.4, 1.24.1, 1.24.4–5, 1.25.2, 1.26.1–3, 1.26.5, 1.27.2, 1.28.1–3, 1.29.1, 1.29.3, 1.30.1, 1.30.5, 1.32.3, 1.32.8, 1.33.2, 1.34.1, 1.34.3, 1.35.4, 1.38.1, 1.39.3, 1.53.2, 1.60.5, 1.61.3, 1.76.1, 1.84.3, 2.3.1, 2.17.2, 2.18.5, 2.18.7, 2.25.4, 2.32.3, Book 3 *passim*; Pompeianus, 1.15.5, 1.28.1, 1.40.2, 2.17.1, 3.35.2, 3.42.3, 3.44.4, 3.46.3, 3.46.6, 3.51.1,

3.51.6, 3.53.1, 3.58.1, 3.63.6, 3.65.1, 3.66.2, 3.67.4, 3.69.2, 3.72.1, 3.84.2, 3.84.4, 3.93.1–2, 3.93.8, 3.94.2, 3.94.4, 3.95.1, 3.97.2–4, 3.99.4, 3.101.7; *Pompeia lex* (law on electoral corruption passed by Pompey in 52), 3.1.4

Pompeius Magnus, Cn. *filius* (NP I.4; Pompeian fleet commander, led the opposition to Caesar in Spain in 45, died at Munda), 3.4.4, 3.5.3, 3.40.1

Pomponius, M. (Caesarian fleet commander), 3.101.1; Pomponianus, 3.101.2

Pontus* (region on the south coast of the Black Sea, kingdom of Mithridates, later part of Roman province of Bithynia), 3.3.1, 3.4.3

Porcius Cato, M. (NP I.7; long-standing political opponent of Caesar, Pompeian in the civil war, committed suicide after Thapsus; *pr.* 54, defeated in consular elections for 51), 1.4.1, 1.30.2, 1.30.4, 1.32.3

Postumus. *See* Fulvius

Pothinus (regent for Ptolemy XIII in Egypt), 3.108.1, 3.112.12

Ptolomaeus Auletes (NP 18; king of Egypt, restored to throne by Gabinius in 55, died 51), 3.4.4, 3.103.5, 3.107.2, 3.108.4–5, 3.109.4, 3.110.6, 3.112.10

Ptolomaeus XIII (NP 20; joint ruler of Egypt with Cleopa-tra, fought Caesar in Alexandria, died 47), 3.103.2, 3.103.5, 3.107.2

Ptolomais* (one of several towns of this name, probably the town in Roman Syria; mod. Acre in Israel), 3.105.5

Puleio, T. (Caesarian, renegade?), 3.67.5

Pupius, L. (Pompeian veteran), 1.13.4–5

Puteoli* (mod. Pozzuoli), 3.71.1

Pyrenaeus *saltus* (a pass through the Pyrenees, possibly Col de la Perche), 1.37.1, 3.19.2

Quintilius Varus, Sex. (NP I.3; Pompeian, pardoned by Caesar at Corfinium, fought Curio in Africa; *qu.* 49), 1.23.2, 2.28.1–2

Ravenna* (a town in Cisalpine Gaul; mod. Ravenna), 1.5.5

Rebilus. *See* Caninius

Rhascypolis (Macedonian cavalry commander, adherent of Pompey), 3.4.4

Rhodanus* (the Rhone), 2.1.2

Rhodus/-dius* (mod. Rhodes, Greece), 3.5.3, 3.26.2, 3.27.2, 3.102.7, 3.106.1

Roma/-manus* (mod. Rome), 1.7.5, 1.9.2, 1.9.5, 1.14.1, 1.17.2, 1.22.5, 1.23.1–2, 1.30.4, 1.33.2, 1.35.3, 1.53.1–2, 1.77.2, 2.18.2, 2.18.4, 2.19.2, 2.20.5, 2.21.1–2, 3.4.1, 3.9.3, 3.10.5, 3.10.8, 3.11.4,

3.29.1, 3.32.6, 3.40.5, 3.71.1,
3.83.3, 3.102.2, 3.102.6,
3.107.2, 3.108.5–6, 3.109.4,
3.110.2

Roscius, L. (NP I.3; Caesarian
legate in Gaul; *pr.* 49), 1.3.6,
1.8.4, 1.10.1

Roucillus (Allobrogian cavalry
officer, originally Caesarian),
3.59.1, 3.79.6

Rubrius, L. (Pompeian senator),
1.23.2

Rufus. *See* Acutius; Caecilius;
Caelius; Marcius; Minucius;
Sulpicius; Vibullius

Ruteni (tribe in central Gaul),
1.51.1

Rutilius Lupus, P. (NP I.2;
Pompeian; *pr.* 49), 1.24.3,
3.55.3

Sabinus. *See* Calvisius

Saburra (Numidian general),
2.38.1, 2.38.3, 2.39.1, 2.40.1–
2, 2.41.2, 2.42.1

Sacrativir, M. (Caesarian military tribune), 3.71.1

Sadalas (Thracian prince), 3.4.3

Salonae* (harbor town on Adriatic coast of Illyricum; near
mod. Solin, Croatia), 3.9.1–2

Sardinia* (mod. Sardegna, Italy), 1.30.2–3, 1.31.1, 3.10.5

Saturninus. *See* Appuleius

Saxa. *See* Decidius

Scaeva (Caesarian), 3.53.4

Scipio. *See* Caecilius

Scribonius Curio, C. (NP I.4;
Caesarian tribune, formerly
an opponent of the First Triumvirate and supporter of
Clodius, died as Caesar's legate in Africa in 49; *tr. pl.* 50),
1.12.1, 1.12.3, 1.18.5, 1.30.2,
1.30.5, 1.31.1, 2.3.2, 2.23.1,
2.23.5, 2.24.1, 2.25.1, 2.25.4,
2.25.6, 2.26.1, 2.26.3, 2.27.1–
3, 2.28.1–2, 2.28.4, 2.20.1,
2.31.1, 2.33.2, 2.34.3–5,
2.35.1, 2.36.1, 2.37.1, 2.37.6,
2.38.5, 2.39.1, 2.39.5–6,
2.40.2–3, 2.41.3, 2.42.1,
2.42.3–4, 2.43.1, 3.10.5

Scribonius Libo, L. (NP I.7;
Pompeian commander, re-
turned to Rome after Pharsalus, supported Sex. Pompeius,
was proscribed in 43, later
supported Antony; *cos.* 34),
1.26.3–5, 3.5.3, 3.15.6,
3.16.2–3, 3.17.5, 3.18.3,
3.23.1, 3.24.2, 3.24.4, 3.90.1,
3.100.1

SCU (the senate's final decree,
declaring a state of emergency, passed on January 7,
49, and at earlier crises: 121
[C. Gracchus], 100 [Saturni-
nus], 77 [Lepidus], 63 [Cati-
line], 52 [after murder of
Clodius]), 1.5.3–4, 1.75

Sempronii Gracchi (revolutionary tribunes of the late 2nd
c.), 1.7.6

Sentica. *See* Heraclia

Septimius, L. (former Pompeian centurion), 3.104.2–3

Serapion (courtier in Alexandria), 3.109.4

Sertorius, Q. (Marian officer,

opponent of Sulla, in the early 70s he organized and led Spanish troops against Roman troops, including some led by Pompey, died 73; *pr.* 85?), 1.61.3

Servilius Vatia Isauricus, P. (NP I.24; Caesarian, later governor of Asia; *cos.* 48, 41), 3.1.1, 3.21.1, 3.21.3

Sicilia* (Roman province; mod. Sicily), 1.25.1, 1.30.2, 1.30.4, 1.31.1, 2.3.1, 2.23.1, 2.23.5, 2.30.3, 2.32.3, 2.34.4, 2.37.4, 2.43.1, 2.44.1, 3.10.5, 3.42.3, 3.101.1

Sicoris* (mod. Segre River), 1.40.1, 1.48.3, 1.61.1, 1.61.6, 1.62.3, 1.63.1, 1.83.4

Spinther. *See* Cornelius

Staberius, L. (Pompeian), 3.12.1, 3.12.3

Staius (NP I; Caesarian legate in Greece and Africa, later sided with Caesar's assassins and Sex. Pompeius, died ca. 40; *pr.* 45?), 3.15.6, 3.16.2

Sulla. *See* Cornelius

Sulmonenses* (inhabitants of Sulmo; mod. Sulmona), 1.18.1–2

Sulpicius, Ser. (Pompeian, probably son of NP 1.23), 2.44.3

Sulpicius Rufus, P. (NP I.20; Caesarian legate in Gaul, later fleet commander; *pr.* 48, *cens.* 42), 1.74.6, 3.101.1; Sulpicianus, 3.101.4

Syria/-i/-iacus* (Roman province of Syria), 1.4.5, 1.6.5, 3.3.1–2, 3.4.3, 3.4.5, 3.5.3, 3.31.3, 3.32.6, 3.88.3, 3.101.1, 3.103.1, 3.103.5, 3.105.4, 3.110.3

Tarcondarius Castor (ruler of a kingdom in central Asia Minor, son-in-law of Deiotarus, Pompeian adherent), 3.4.5

Tarracina (coastal town in Latium; mod. Terracina), 1.24.3

Tarraco/-onenses* (port city on the Mediterranean; mod. Tarragona, Spain), 1.60.2, 1.73.2, 1.78.3, 2.21.4–5

Tauroeis (outpost of Marseilles; mod. Le Brusc-Six-Fours, France), 2.4.5

Terentius Varro, M. (NP I.15; long-standing associate of Pompey, Pompeian legate in Spain, pardoned by Caesar after Pharsalus, polymath author, correspondent of Cicero, proscribed in 43 but survived, died 27; *pr.* 68), 1.38.1–2, 2.17.1, 2.19.3–4, 2.20.1, 2.20.4, 2.20.6, 2.20.8, 2.21.2, 2.21.4

Terentius Varro Murena, A. (NP I.18; Pompeian; possibly *aed.* 44), 3.19.4

Thebae* (principal city in Boeotia; mod. Thiva, Greece), 3.55.4

Theophanes (NP 1; originally from Mytilene, later a Roman citizen, Pompey's confidant and historian), 3.18.3

Thermus. *See* Minucius

INDEX

Thessalia/-i* (large region in northeastern Greece, surrounded by mountains), 3.4.2, 3.4.6, 3.5.1, 3.34.2, 3.35.2, 3.36.2–5, 3.79.7, 3.80.1, 3.80.3–4, 3.81.2, 3.82.1, 3.100.3, 3.101.7, 3.106.1, 3.111.3

Thracia/-ces* (independent kingdom extending along the north coast of the Aegean to the Black Sea), 3.4.3, 3.95.3

Thurii/-rinus* (city in Magna Graecia on the Ionic Gulf; near mod. Sibari; one of Spartacus' conquests), 3.21.4, 3.22.3

Tiburtius, L. (Caesarian), 3.19.7

Tillius, Q. (Caesarian legate, later one of Caesar's assassins, probably died at Philippi; *pr.* 45?), 3.42.3

Torquatus. *See* Manlius

Tralles* (town in the Roman province of Asia, in the valley of the Maeander River; near mod. Aydin, Turkey), 3.105.6

Transpadanus (peninsular Italy between the Po and the Alps, in the province of Cisalpine Gaul), 3.87.4

Trebonius, C. (NP I.1; Caesarian legate in Gaul, later one of Caesar's assassins, governor of Asia, died fighting Caesarian forces in 43; pr. 48, *cos. suff.* 45), 1.36.5, 2.1.1, 2.1.4, 2.5.3, 2.13.3–4, 2.15.1, 3.20.1–2, 3.21.2

Triarius. *See* Valerius

Tubero. *See* Aelius

Tullus. *See* Volcacius

Tuticanus Gallus (Caesarian), 3.71.1

Utica/-censes* (port town and capital of the Roman province of Africa; near mod. Henchir-bou-Chateur, Tunisia; site of Cato's suicide), 1.31.3, 2.23.3, 2.24.1, 2.24.3–4, 2.25.1, 2.25.3, 2.25.6–7, 2.26.1–2, 2.27.2, 2.36.1, 2.38.1, 2.44.3

Valerius, Q. (NP I.41; Caesarian legate; *pr.* 57), 1.30.2, 1.31.1

Valerius Flaccus, L. *et filius* (NP I.24 and 16, the latter a Pompeian, the former *pr.* 63), 3.53.1

Valerius Triarius, C. (NP I.53; Pompeian fleet commander, interlocutor in Cicero's *De Finibus*), 3.5.3, 3.92.2

Varro. *See* Terentius

Varus. *See* Attius; Quintilius

Varus* (the Var River, in France), 1.86.3, 1.87.1, 1.87.5

Vatinius, P. (NP I.2; long-standing Caesarian, legate in Gaul and the Adriatic, later governor of Illyricum, triumphed in 42; *pr.* 55, *cos.* 47), 3.19.2, 3.19.6, 3.90.1, 3.100.2

Vespillo. *See* Lucretius

Vettones (tribe in central Spain), 1.38.1–2, 1.38.4

373

Vibius Curius (NP I.1; Caesarian), 1.24.3

Vibo* (port city in Magna Graecia; mod. Vibo Valentia), 3.101.1, 3.101.4

Vibullius Rufus, L. (NP I.1; Pompeian officer, twice pardoned by Caesar), 1.15.4, 1.34.1, 1.38.1, 3.10.1, 3.11.1, 3.15.8, 3.18.3, 3.22.1

Victoriae *simulacrum* (statue of Victory in the temple of Minerva at Elis), 3.105.3

Victoriae *templum* (temple of Victory at Tralles), 3.105.6

Volcacius Tullus, C. (Caesarian), 3.52.2

Volcae Arecomici (Gallic tribe in southern France; the Roman road to Spain ran through their territory), 1.35.4

Volusenus, C. (NP 1; Caesarian cavalry prefect Gaul and Greece), 3.60.4

MAPS

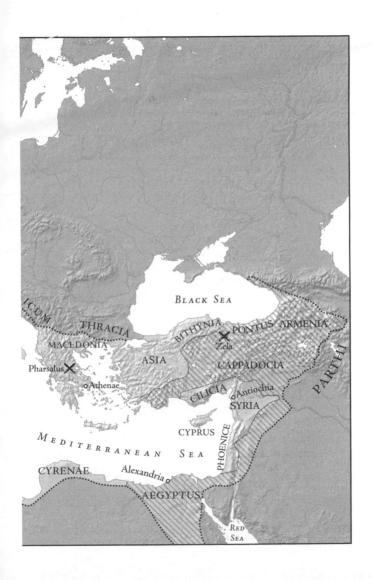

The Roman Empire - West

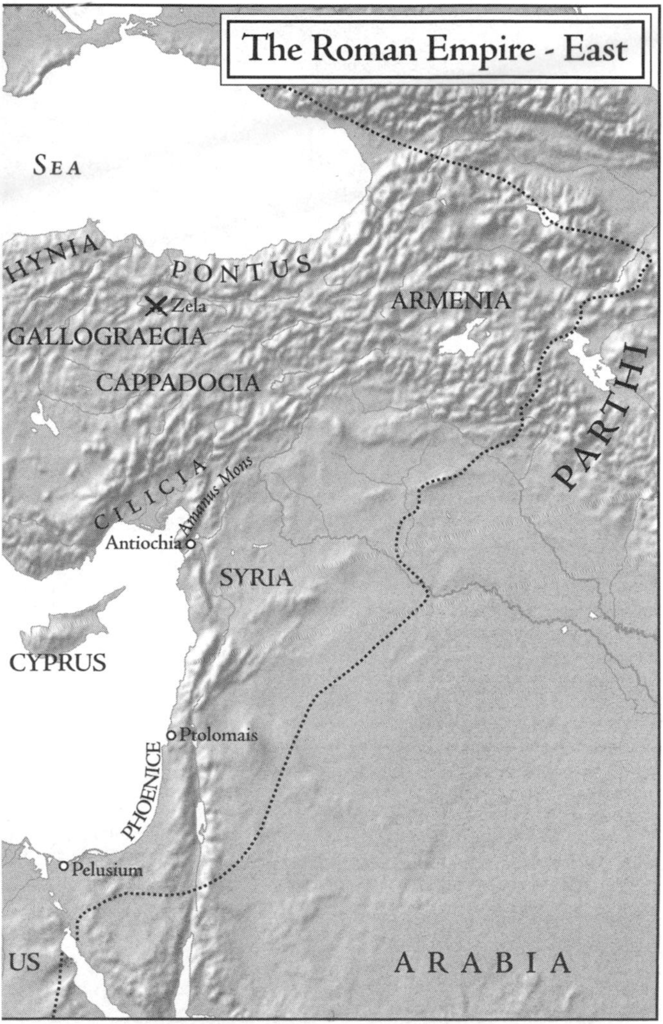

The Roman Empire - East

Sea

HYNIA

PONTUS

✕ Zela

ARMENIA

GALLOGRAECIA

CAPPADOCIA

PARTHI

CILICIA

Amanus Mons

Antiochia ○

SYRIA

CYPRUS

PHOENICE

○ Ptolomais

○ Pelusium

US

ARABIA

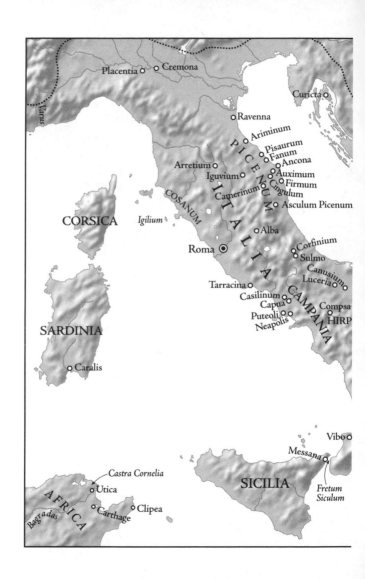

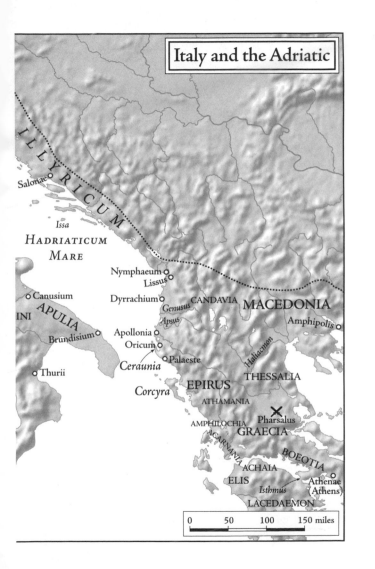

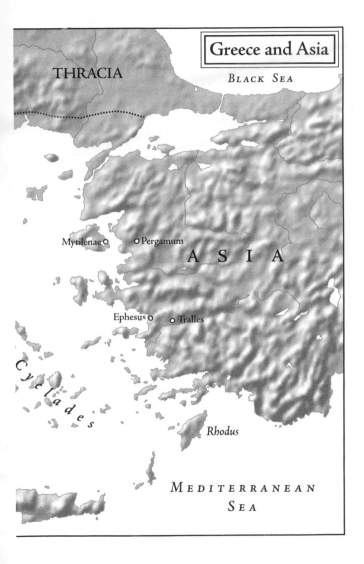

Greece and Asia

THRACIA

BLACK SEA

Mytilenae o   o Pergamum

A S I A

Ephesus o   o Tralles

Cyclades

Rhodus

MEDITERRANEAN
SEA